Estate Planning and Taxation

2003 - 2004 EDITION

by **JOHN C. BOST,** J.D., M.S.(Tax)

Professor of Finance
San Diego State University

KENDALL/HUNT PUBLISHING COMPANY
4050 Westmark Drive   Dubuque, Iowa 52002

This text, and its associated supplemental material, is designed to provide accurate and authoritative information regarding estate planning and taxation. In publishing this book, neither the author nor the publisher is engaged in rendering legal, estate, financial, or tax planning advice, or any other professional services. If legal advice or other expert assistance is required, the services of a competent professional should be sought.

Formerly entitled *Introduction to Estate Planning*.

Copyright © 1987, 1989 by Richard D. Irwin, Inc.

Copyright © 1992, 1993, 1994, 1995, 1996, 1997, 1998, 1999, 2000, 2001, 2003 by Kendall/Hunt Publishing Company

ISBN 0-7575-0035-8

Printed in the United States of America
10 9 8 7 6 5 4 3 2

CONTENTS

Illustrations Table   ix

Preface   xi

Dedication and Acknowledgments   xiii

ETAX 2002 Program Information   xv

Part 1 Overview and Conceptual Background   1

1 Introduction to Estate Planning   3

What Is Estate Planning? Developing an Estate Plan. *Establishing the Client-Planner Relationship. Acquiring Client Facts and Goals. Analyzing and Evaluating the Client's Financial Status. Developing and Presenting Recommendations and/or Alternatives. Implementing the Plan. Monitoring the Financial Planning Recommendations.* The Estate Planning Team. *Attorney. Accountant. Life Underwriter. Trust Officer. Financial Planner.* The Need to Encourage Planning. Organization of the Book. Appendix 1A: Sample Client Fact Finding Questionnaire.

2 Basic Estate Planning Concepts   27

Overview. Concepts Dealing with Estates. Concepts Dealing with Transfers of Property. *Transfers of Legal, Beneficial, or Legal and Beneficial Interests. Complete Versus Incomplete Transfers; Property in General Versus a Specific Property Interest. Sale Versus Gift. Inter Vivos Transfer Versus Transfer at Death. Fair Market Value of Transfer.* Beneficiaries. Wills, Trusts, and Probate. *Disclaimers.* Life Insurance. Taxation. Property Interests. *Classification of Property by Physical Characteristics. Basic Interests in Property. Concurrent Ownership. Legal Versus Beneficial Interests: Introduction to the Trust. Power of Appointment. Present Versus Future Interests and Vested Versus Contingent Interests. Mathematics of Remainders, Reversions and Income Interests.* Overview of Goals of Estate Planning. Important Concepts and Terms Covered in This Chapter.

Part 2 Constraints in Planning   79

3 Estate Planning Documents   81
Overview. Joint Tenancy Arrangements. Property Transfer by Contract. *Life Insurance. Pension and Profit Sharing Plans.* Wills and Trusts. The Will. *Who May Execute a Will. Statutory Requirements for Wills. No Contest Clause. The Simple Will.* The Trust. *Living Trust Instrument.* The Testamentary Trust. The Rule Against Perpetuities.

4 The Transfer of Wealth   125
Overview. Rationale for Probate Distribution. Nonprobate Versus Probate Assets. Intestate Succession Laws. *Degrees of Consanguinity. Per Stirpes Versus Per Capita. Intestacy in UPC States. Intestacy in Non-UPC States. Advancements.* Legal Rights of Omitted and Adopted Children. *After-born, Omitted Children. Omitted Children. Adopted Children.* Legal Rights of Omitted, Divorced, and Disinherited Spouses. *Omitted Spouse. Effect of Divorce. Protection Against Disinheritance of Spouse.* Principles of Probate Administration. *Substantial Formal Supervision: The Non-UPC Model. Estate Administration in UPC States: A Study in Flexibility.* Appendix 4A: Summary Probate Proceedings in California: One Non-UPC State's Alternatives to Formal Probate. *Affidavit of Right. Summary Distribution to Surviving Spouse. Property Held as Community or Quasi-community Property. Summary Distribution Petition.*

5 The Federal Unified Transfer Tax   179
Overview. Brief History. Unified Transfer Tax Framework. Unified Rate Schedule. Unified Credit. Unlimited Marital Deduction. Unlimited Charitable Deduction. The Annual Exclusion for Lifetime Gifts. Cumulative Taxation of Wealth Transfers. The Credits. *Credit for State Death Taxes.* Federal Generation-skipping Transfer Tax. Imperfect Unification.

6 The Federal Estate Tax   229
Overview. One: The Gross Estate. *Basic Interests Owned at Death: §2033. Dower and Curtesy Interests: §2034. Survivorship Annuities: §2039. Joint Tenancy and Tenancy by the Entirety: §2040. Power of Appointment: §2041. Insurance on Decedent's Life: §2042.* Transfers with Retained Interest or Control. *Transfer with Retained Life Estate: §2036. Transfers Taking Effect at Death: §2037. Revocable Transfers: §2038. Gift Taxes on Any Transfer within Three Years of Death: §2035(b). Certain Transfers within Three Years of Death: §2035(a). Part-Sale, Part-Gift Transfers: §2043.* Two: Estate Tax Deductions. *Marital Deduction: §2056. Charitable*

Deduction: §2055. Three: Estate Tax Credits. *Credit/Offset for Gift Taxes Paid or Payable.* The Prior Transfer Credit: § 2013. *An Extended PTC Example. Credit for Foreign Death Taxes. Adjustment to the Unified Credit for Certain Pre-1977 Gifts*

7   The Federal Gift Tax and Basis Rules   299
Overview. Federal Gift Tax. *Requirements for a Valid Gift: Influence of Local and Federal Law. Who Is Subject to Gift Tax? Aspects of Taxable Gifts. Filing and Payment Requirements. Deductible Gifts. Gift Tax Annual Exclusion and the Present Interest Requirement. The Kiddie Tax. Gift Splitting. Powers of Appointment. Life Insurance. Gifts into Joint Tenancy. Disclaimers. Miscellaneous Gift Tax Applications.* Basis Rules. *Basis Afer Estate Tax Repeal. Reporting Requirements After Repeal.*

8   Fiduciary Income Taxation   347
Overview. Fiduciary Accounting. *Goals of Fiduciary Accounting. Allocation Between Corpus and Income. Effect of Fiduciary Accounting Income on Taxable Income.* Fiduciary Income Taxation. *Subchapter J: An Overview of Fiduciary Taxation. Fiduciary Taxable Income: § 641(b). Tax Accounting Method. Selecting a Fiduciary Income Tax Year. An Overview of the Computations. Taxable Income of a Fiduciary Entity. Deductions Allowed in Computing Taxable Income.* The Effect of Transfers and Distributions. *General Rule for Property Transfers. Transfers Subject to §663(a). Transfers Subject to a §643(e)(3) Election. Transfers to Satisfy a Pecuniary Bequest. Transfers of Passive Activities.* Income Distribution Deduction and the Taxation of Beneficiaries. *Key Definitions. Computation of DNI and the Income Distribution Deduction. Taxation of Beneficiaries. Tiers, Tiers, So Many Tiers. Income in Respect of a Decedent. Estate Tax Deduction. Throwback Rules.* Conclusion.

Part 3 The Techniques of Planning   401

9   The Goals of Estate Planning   403
Overview and Caution. Nonfinancial Goals. *Caring for Future Dependents. Accomplishing Fair and Proper Distribution of Property. Maintaining Privacy in the Transfer Process. Prompt Property Transfer. Maintaining Control Over Assets.* Financial Goals. *Non-tax Financial Goals. Tax Related Financial Goals.*

10 The Decision to Avoid Probate   419
Overview. The Benefits and Drawbacks of Probate. *The Benefits of Probate. The Drawbacks of Probate.* The Joint Tenancy Alternative. *Advantages of Joint Tenancy. Disadvantages of Joint Tenancy.* The Living Trust Alternative. *Advantages of the Living Trust. Disadvantages of the Living Trust.* Quantitative Model for Comparison of Costs

of Probate Versus Living Trust. Which Alternative Is Best?

11 Common Estate Plans: Using Bypass and Marital Deduction Trusts   455
Overview. Abbreviations, Simplifications, and Assumptions. The Marital Deduction: Then and Now. *A Blip in the Law.* The Terminable Interest Rule. *The Elements of the Terminable Interest Rule. Why Have a Terminable Interest Rule?* Terminable Interest Rule Exceptions. *Qualified Terminable Interest Property (QTIP): §2056(b)(7). General Power of Appointment Exception: §2056 (b)(5). Pensions for the Benefit of S2: §2056(b)(7)(C). Charitable Remainder Trusts with a Life Estate for S2: §2056(b)(8).* The Basic Estate Planning Patterns. *Planning Option 1: Simple 100 Percent Marital Deduction. Advantages of the 100 Percent Marital Deduction. Disadvantages of the 100 Percent Marital Deduction.* Bypass Planning. Multiple Trusts in Estate Planning: Basic Patterns. Planning Option 2: The AB Trust. *The Character of Trust A. The Character of Trust B. AB Trust Plan's Benefits.* Planning Option 3: The ABC Trust. *The Character of Trust A. The Character of Trust B. The Character of Trust C. The Appropriate QTIP Election. Step by Step: Determining and Using the QTIP Fraction. Extended Example. Step by Step: Applied to the ABC Trust Plan.* Optimal Allocation: The Partial QTIP Election. *Partial QTIP Election Examples. Equalizing Estates. Allocating Assets to the Trusts.*

12 Advanced Bypass and Marital Deduction Planning   513
Overview. Variations on a Theme. The AsuperB Trust Plan. The AB with Disclaimer into C Trust Plan. The A With Disclaimer into B Trust Plan. Planning in the Era of Uncertainty. Noncitizen Surviving Spouses: The QDOT Trust. Estate Plans Seldom Seen. Estate Trust. The Traditional AB Trust. The Estate Equalization AB Trust. General Comments on Estate Planning Using Trusts. The Prior Transfer Credit and Bypass Trusts. The Prior Transfer Credit and the QTIP Election. The Generation Skipping Transfer Tax. *Purpose of the GST tax. Overview of the GST Tax. Calculating the GST Tax. Applicable Rate. Timing the Exemption Allocation. Special Rules Pertaining to Generations and the GST Tax. Planning Considerations: Efficient Utilization of the Exemption. Credit for Certain State Taxes. Certain Transfers Excluded from the GST Tax. Grandfathering in Some Grand Old Trusts. The Need for GST Tax Planning.*

13 Gift Planning Fundamentals   575
Overview. Non-tax Motives For Making Gifts. Tax Considerations in Making Gifts. *Tax Advantages of Gifting. Tax Disadvantages of Gifting.* Types of Assets to Give. *Basis Considerations. Postgift Appreciation. Administration Problems. Other Asset Choice Considerations.* Gifts to One's Spouse: Techniques and Considerations. *Inter-spousal Gifts to Reduce Death Taxes. Inter-spousal Gifts to Reduce Income Taxes.* Gifts

to Minors: Techniques and Considerations. *Custodial Gifts. Gifts to Trusts That Benefit Minors. Paying for College.*

14 Planning Lifetime Transfers   611
Overview. Intrafamily Transfers for Consideration. *Intrafamily Loan. Ordinary Sale. Bargain Sale. Installment Sale. Private Annuity.* Incomplete Intrafamily Transfers. *Intentionally Defective Irrevocable Trust. Gift-Leaseback. Trusts and the Anti-Freeze Rules: §2701-§2704. The Impact of EGTRRA on Transfers with a Retained interest. Retained Interests Before the Ice Age. Grantor Retained Interest Trust. GRIT Planning.* Planning for Charitable Transfers. *Tax Consequences of Charitable Transfers. Outright Gifts to Charity. Gifts of Split Interests.* Conclusion. Appendix 14A: *Defective Incomplete Transfers.* Overview. Interest-Free Loans. *Gift Tax Consequences. Income Tax Consequences. Estate Tax Consequences.* Short-Term Trust. *Gift Tax Consequences. Income Tax Consequences. Estate Tax Consequences to the Grantor.* Spousal Remainder Trust. Sale of a Remainder Interest and Joint Purchase. The Family Estate Trust: A Trap for the Unwary.

15 Liquidity Planning   667
Overview. Summary of Cash Needs at Death. Sale of Assets During Lifetime. Life Insurance. *Types of Insurance. Taxation of Life Insurance. Life Insurance Planning.* Flower Bonds. Liquidity Planning Devices Unique to Business Owners. *Sale of the Business.* Estate Tax Extension and Deferral: §§6161 and 6163. *Installment Payment of the Estate Tax: §6166. Stock Redemption: §303. Special Use Valuation: §2032A. Family-owned Business Interest Deduction: §2057. Qualified Conservation Easement: §2031(c).* Valuation Discounts and Control Premiums. *Minority Interest Discount for Business Interests. Lack of Marketability Discount for Business Interests. Fractional Interest Discount for Real Property. Other Valuation Discounts.* Family Limited Partnerships. The Limited Liability Company.

16 Planning for Closely Held Business Interests   725
Overview. Valuing The Business. Planning in General for Closely Held Business Interests. *Withdrawal from the Firm: Minimizing Decline in Income and Value. Transferring a Business Interest. The Need for Early Planning. Business* Buyout Agreements. *Types of Agreements: Cross Purchase, Entity-Redemption, or Mixed. Taxation of Buyout Agreements. Funding.* Freezing the Value of the Business Interest. Overview. *Corporate Recapitalization. Partnership Capital Freeze.*

17 Miscellaneous Lifetime Planning   763
Overview. Planning for the Care of Family Members. *Planning for the Care of Minor Children. Selection of Executor and Executor's Powers. Allocation of Death*

Taxes. Survival Clauses. Selection of Trustee and Trustee's Powers. Timing Trust Distributions. Restrictions against Assignment. Trust Taxation: A Summary. Planning for Nontraditional Relationships. *Greater Need to Avoid Intestacy. Less Shelter from Estate Tax May Dictate Larger Bypass. Greater Need for Life Insurance at First Death. Lifetime Gifting More Important. Joint Tenancies in Community Property States May Be More Attractive.* Planning for Incapacity. *Property Management for an Incapacitated Person. Personal Care for the Incapacitated Person.*

18 Postmortem Tax Planning   **811**
Overview. Tax Returns after Death. *Transfer Taxes. Income Taxes.* Planning Devices to Reduce Income Taxes. *Expense Elections Available to the Executor. Selection of Estate Taxable Year. Distribution Planning.* Planning Devices to Reduce Death Taxes. *Alternate Valuation Date Election. Effective Disclaimers. QTIP Election Planning. Additional Postmortem Death Tax-Saving Devices.*

Appendix A   Tax and Valuation Tables   **833**
Appendix B   Teaching Aids CD ROM Contents   **849**
Glossary   **899**
Index   **927**

ILLUSTRATIONS TABLE

Figure 1-1	The Estate Planning Process	4
Appendix 1A	Sample Client Fact-Finding Questionnaire	21
Figure 2-1	The Parties to a Trust	50
Figure 2-2	The Parties to a Power of Appointment	54
Exhibit 3-1	Simple Will	90
Exhibit 3-2	Living Trust Instrument	101
Exhibit 3-3	Testamentary Trust (Trust-Will)	108
Figure 4-1	A Decedent's Property Interests	129
Figure 4-2	Degrees of Consanguinity	131
Figure 4-3	Distribution by Per Stirpes and Per Capita	133
Exhibit 4-1	Intestate Succession under the Uniform Probate Code	138
Exhibit 4-2	Newspaper Notice of Petition to Administer Estate	155
Table 4-1	California Statutory Probate Fees	158
Table 5-1	Federal Gift Tax (Form 709) Basic Model - No Prior Gifts	185
Table 5-2	Federal Gift Tax (Form 709) Overview Model - Prior Gifts	187
Table 5-3	Federal Estate Tax (Form 706) Basic Model - No Prior Gifts	189
Table 5-4	Federal Estate Tax (Form 706) Overview Model	190
Table 5-5	Federal Unified Transfer-Tax Rates Since 1/1/77	194
Table 5-6	Unified Credits (UCr), Applicable Exclusion Amount (AEA), and the End of the Bubble by Year Since 1977	199
Table 5-7A	Federal Credit for State Death Taxes 1977-2001	207
Table 5-7B	Federal Credit for State Death Taxes 2002-2005	208
Table 6-1	Federal Estate Tax (Form 706) Comprehensive Outline	230
Rules Box	The Connection Between Gifts & Donor's Estate	264
Table 8-1	Federal Income Tax Rates: Estates and Trusts	355

Figure 9-1	Maximum Marginal Federal Income Tax Rates, 1952 - Present	410
Table 10-1	Present Value of Costs of Probate	447
Table 10-2	Present Value of Costs of Living Trust	447
Table 14-1	Comparative Advantages of Lifetime Transfers	649
Table 17-1	Summary of Trust Taxation	782
Exhibit 17-1	Durable Power of Attorney (for property)	788

Appendix A	Tax and Valuation Tables	833
TABLE 1	Federal Unified Transfer-Tax Rates - Since 1/1/77	834
TABLE 2	Federal Unified Credits, Applicable Exclusion Amounts, and the End of the Bubble by Year Since 1977	836
TABLE 3A	Credit for State Death Taxes 1977-2001	837
TABLE 3B	Credit for State Death Taxes 2002-2005	838
TABLE 4	Federal Gift Tax Rates prior to January 1, 1977	839
TABLE 5	Federal Estate Rates prior to January 1, 1977	840
TABLE 6	Federal Income Tax Rates: Estates and Trusts - 2003	841
TABLE 7	Estate Planning Indexed Values	841
TABLE K	Adjustment Factors for Annuities Payable at the End of Each Interval	842
TABLE B	Term Certain (6% and 8%)	843
TABLE B	Term Certain (10% and 12%)	844
TABLE S	Single Life (6% and 8%)	845
TABLE S	Single Life (10% and 12%)	846
TABLE 90CM - Mortality Table		847
TABLE §7520 Monthly Rates -The Factors for Valuing Split Interest (e.g., Life Estates and Remainders)		848
Appendix B	Teaching Aids CD ROM Contents	849

PREFACE

Estate Planning and Taxation is a textbook designed to be used in an academic program. Its concepts are introduced logically rather than encyclopedically; and as the reader's knowledge grows, more advanced principles are covered.

Estate Planning and Taxation is for the professional or student pursuing a career in financial services, taxation, or law in which estate planning and estate and gift taxation is but one of several principal areas of practice. Applicable careers include law, tax accounting, financial planning, insurance sales, paralegal work, banking, trust management, investment brokerage and management, and real estate. Since much of the subject matter is Internal Revenue Code driven, the textbook draws heavily on primary sources of the law, both Code and cases. The textbook is adaptable to law school courses in estate planning and taxation, giving the law student a strongly quantitative slant that is sometimes overlooked in traditional law books, even those dealing with taxes.

The book is divided into three parts. The first two present the basic language and constraints found in estate planning, including the underlying tax and nontax laws that serve as the basis for planning. The third, and largest, part surveys the major estate planning strategies used currently by practitioners. Tax analysis is emphasized. This sequential approach aids learning because estate planning techniques presuppose a familiarity with many fundamental legal concepts, including tax principles.

The organization of *Estate Planning and Taxation* seeks to present a concise, integrated overview, highlighting the essence of concepts without confusing the reader with every technical qualification and reference, a problem which has impaired the readability of many books in the field. For example, the text expects the student to learn only those case names and Code section numbers that have attained the status of common industry jargon (chapter endnotes cite many others). Nonetheless, the book's content is comprehensive. For example, with its quantitative orientation, it demonstrates numerically, wherever possible, the consequences of planning, and of the failure to plan, on family wealth.

Many pedagogical devices are used to aid comprehension. Numerous examples are included in each chapter to clarify concepts. Each chapter contains end-of-chapter questions and problems, many with solutions. Appendixes include a glossary, sample tax returns, tax and valuation tables, as well as those sections of the Internal Revenue Code most relevant to estate planning. A manual containing a test bank is available to instructors who adopt the book.

Estate Planning and Taxation can be used in a two-hour or three-hour quarter or semester introductory college undergraduate course, graduate, or law school course. It can be read in conjunction with a correspondence, certificate-type course offered to the financial services industry; and it can be read independently by anyone seeking a moderately technical overview, including the practitioner in accounting or financial services, the law student, the attorney in general practice, and the very determined lay reader.

DEDICATION AND ACKNOWLEDGMENTS

DEDICATION This edition is dedicated to the teachers and students who have made suggestions that have helped improvement of this textbook. Your continued support and advice is sincerely appreciated.

RECOGNITION FOR WORK ON THIS EDITION Credit for improving this textbook must be given to steadfast friends and colleagues. Matthew Balderston, San Diego State University graduate student in the Masters in Tax and Financial Services program, deserves special mention for his work on the material for the CD supplement.

RECOGNITION FOR PAST CONTRIBUTIONS My thanks to the many individuals whose previous contributions continue to be reflected in this textbook: Michael Ahearn, Martin Anderson, Robert Barnhill, Karen Booth, J. Buckhold, Daniel J. Burnside, Paul M. Cheverton, Neil Cohen, Larry Cox, Jeffrey Dennis-Strathmeyer, D. J. Devin, Mark Dorfman, W. W. Dotterweich, Jon Gallo, Randy Gardner, William S. Gray, Keith Fevurly, Mark Greene, Benjamin Henszey, Carole Hill, Joseph W. Janick, Jerry Kasner, Fred Keydel, James K. Leese, Russell H. May, Shekhar Misra, Karen Molloy, Burton Nissing, Gregg Parish, Mary Reese, Phelder St. Germain, Janice Samuells, John Schooling, Jack Stephens, and Richard Wellman.

SPECIAL THANKS To past, present, and future students of estate planning for whom this text was created and for whom it continues; to the late Professor Chris J. Prestopino (1943 - 1994), who initiated this textbook; and to my wife, Jennifer, and our two daughters, Heather and Laura, my personal reason for learning about estate planning.

Thank you readers of earlier editions for your suggestions. I welcome and encourage comments from students, instructors, and professionals who use this textbook. Through a continuing dialog we can make this book even better in the future. I take full responsibility for any errors that remain.

John C. Bost
email: john.bost@sdsu.edu

Please visit Sushibrain.com for updates and corrections. If you find an error or a questionable statement, check the "Corrections Table" for this edition (2003-2004) at the website to see whether the matter has already been covered, and if not, please contact me by email.

ETAX Program Information

On the CD ROM that comes with this textbook is a spread sheet program, ETAX 2002.XLS, for use with EXCEL (Microsoft). Any revised or update of this program will be available for downloading from my website at <Sushibrain.com>. ETAX 2002 is an estate and gift tax spreadsheet program designed for educational use only. However, it will do basic estate tax, state death tax credit, and cumulative gift tax calculations. It will not add to the gross estate the gift taxes paid on gifts made within three years of death (IRC § 2035(b)); it does not calculate the tax for pre-1977 transfers; and it will not calculate the prior transfer credit (IRC § 2013).

Once you bring the file into EXCEL, save it to your hard drive. Only certain cells will allow data entry:

- Estates: the **year of death**, the **gross estate**, and **deductions** (you will have to do your own total for marital, charitable, debts and expenses).
- Gifts: the **year of the current gifts**, the **year of prior gifts**, the **current year's gifts** (you must subtract the annual exclusions), and **prior year's gifts** (i.e., the taxable amount after subtracting the annual exclusions).
- After entering the data, hit calculate. Your spreadsheet setup should be set for at least five iterations, ten if you want to try to do inter-related calculations such as net gifts. To determine whether you have the iterations set high enough, enter figures high enough to generate a tax at the cells for prior gifts, current gifts, and the gross estate and see whether the resulting tax amounts change after you hit calculate a second time. If they do, notice how many times you must hit calculate before they do not change and set the iterations accordingly.

PART 1

Overview and Conceptual Background

CHAPTER 1

Introduction to Estate Planning

WHAT IS ESTATE PLANNING?

Estate planning is an essential part of financial planning. Financial planning helps people plan for and meet their needs and wants during their lives. Education planning helps them educate their children. Insurance planning helps provide security against events such as disabilities or accidents. Retirement planning helps create a secure and pleasant retirement. Estate planning's focus is the time and situations surrounding the end of life. People do not live forever; sooner or later, death will bring about a fundamental transition. Estate planning seeks to maximize end-of-life well being for the client and the client's survivors. One definition of **estate planning is "personal and financial planning for end-of-life transitions involving the transfer of personal responsibilities and financial assets and liabilities."**

Figure 1 - 1 The Estate Planning Process

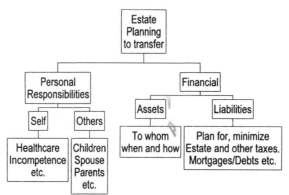

There are two main threads in estate planning, the personal and the financial. Planning for their transfer as part of the end-of-life transition is an essential element of both. Planning for the transfer of personal responsibilities for self includes such issues as healthcare, incompetence, management of property and personal care. Personal responsibilities for others include children and other dependants. Planning for the transfer of financial assets and liabilities includes ensuring assets are efficiently transferred to the chosen recipients and that liabilities are efficiently met. A major part of efficiency is minimizing the amount the government takes as taxes. Because all elements of estate planning are so closely intertwined, it is difficult to separate them. This text is used by students of financial planning so its main focus will be on financial issues and future wealth transfers. As estate size increases, the importance of taxes as a financial issue increases. Therefore, a major focus of this text is taxes and strategies and tactics for minimizing them.

Planning for future wealth transfers usually requires the preparation of contracts, such as life insurance policies and other documents including wills, trusts, deeds, and powers of attorney. These documents set forth in writing a blueprint for the future management of the individual's financial affairs.

Successful estate planning requires an understanding of many areas of law including the law of property, wills, trusts, future interests, estate administration, intestacy, insurance, income taxation, gift taxation, and estate taxation.

How can knowledge of such an extensive subject benefit you, the reader? As a knowledgeable planner, you can help clients avoid the adverse consequences of inadequate or faulty estate planning. Here are some common situations that arise without proper planning.

EXAMPLE 1 - 1. Joanne died last week, survived by her husband and their two young daughters. Because Joanne did not write a will, the intestate laws of her state require that two-thirds of her $300,000 estate *pass to her daughters*, who will each, upon turning 18, receive the property outright from their guardian-father. The other one-third passes to Joanne's husband. He is shocked that he is not inheriting it all and that as guardian of the daughters' estates he must file annual accountings with the court. In addition to the problem of inefficient distribution, larger estates may owe both state and federal taxes—taxes that could have been minimized by estate planning.

EXAMPLE 1 - 2. Marge and Henry, parents of five-year-old twins, died suddenly without an estate plan. The probate court appointed Marge's sister Julie as *guardian* for the twins. Marge and Henry had been quite critical of how Julie and her husband were raising their own children, but they had not expressed their concerns to anyone else and the court simply followed statutory guidelines in selecting Marge's sister for the job.

EXAMPLE 1 - 3. Maggie was 80 when she died leaving an estate with a net value of $300,000. Six weeks prior to her death, she gave ABC common stock worth $90,000 to her son, Charlie. Maggie's $14,000 basis in the stock became Charlie's basis. Now, if he sells it he will recognize considerable capital gains. Had Maggie kept the stock until her death, giving it to Charlie at that time, he could have sold it at little or no income tax cost, because his basis would have been the stock's value as of her date of death.

EXAMPLE 1 - 4. Shortly before Christine died at the age of 75, her family lawyer drafted a *simple will*, leaving her wealth (estimated to be $1,500,000) to her husband, Evan. He is quite ill and, since his own estate is worth about the same as Christine's, he realizes that, as owner of all the family wealth, estate taxes may be due shortly when he dies. Most of the tax could have been avoided if Christine's estate plan had just incorporated the sophisticated estate planning device known as a *bypass trust*.

EXAMPLE 1 - 5. Suppose that instead of receiving the property by will (as in the preceding example), Evan received it as surviving *joint tenant*. Evan's estate would be faced with the same estate tax problem at his death.

EXAMPLE 1- 6. Leslie is the elderly founder of a highly successful real estate sales company. Unfortunately, she has not done any estate planning and is now very ill. Her children are struggling with several problems, including how to generate sufficient *liquidity* to pay the estate taxes and whether to sell the business. Because only a person with a real estate license (which none of the children have) can operate a real estate office, they fear that the business will sell for much less after Leslie dies compared to its value now. Indeed, it could have sold for even more money several years ago when Leslie would have been active in seeking buyers and working with them on a transition.

EXAMPLE 1 - 7. Elmer, a wealthy man, had a severe stroke three months ago. Unable to communicate, he is hooked up to machines that keep him alive. The doctors say his prognosis is very poor. His family realizes that they should have encouraged Elmer to consult an estate planner years ago while he was still able to express his desires. Documents could have been drafted that would have nominated a person or persons to manage his wealth during his incapacity and would have directed the eventual distribution of his wealth after his death. Other documents would have articulated the appropriate level of medical intervention. Whether the decisions of the doctors and the family concerning his care or the pattern of distribution mandated by the laws of intestate succession really match his desires will never be known. In addition, if the family cannot reach agreement on medical treatment, a costly court battle could ensue.

EXAMPLE 1 - 8. Several years before he died, Marty executed a revocable living trust leaving all his property to several close friends rather than to the few relatives who had been rather cool to him for years. The trust was completed by filling in the blanks of a form photocopied from the pages of a popular "how to" book. Thinking that the trust took care of his estate, Marty tore up his will (the one that left everything to the same set of friends as specified in the trust). He failed to transfer his assets into the trust and he did not make a new will. A careful reading of the how-to book would have called to his attention the need to fund the trust by transferring assets to the trustee of the trust and the importance of something called a *pour-over will*. Marty did not realize that his self-made estate plan was ineffective in avoiding probate. Worse yet, it did not control who received his estate. Because he did not transfer his property to the trustee of the trust and because he died without a will, Marty's estate will be distributed to his relatives in a manner specified in his state's intestate succession laws.

EXAMPLE 1 - 9. At his death, Coldwell owned real estate in six states, including his state of residence. His simple will left his estate to his three children. In addition to the *probate* in his state of domicile, there were five ancillary probates, forcing Coldwell's family to pay court filing fees and hire probate attorneys in all six states. Had Coldwell's estate plan used a *living trust*, these probates (and their associated expenses) would have been avoided.

EXAMPLE 1 - 10. Many years before her death Lola bought Sammy's $30,000 life insurance policy for $5,000. They jointly notified the insurance company to change the beneficiary to Lola and send all further premium notices to her address, but they did not request a change of ownership. Since Lola had worked in real estate, she insisted they complete a form called a "Bill of Sale" that she purchased at a stationery store, setting forth the details of the sale, including the identification of policy, and that Sammy sign it before a notary. She recorded this document at the county recorder's office. Eventually Lola had paid sufficient premiums to pay the policy completely. After Lola went into a nursing home, Sammy used a change of beneficiary form supplied by the insurance company to change the beneficiary back to his daughter. After Lola died, her son discovered the Bill of Sale and contacted the insurance company only to learn that Sammy had died two years earlier and they had paid the proceeds to Sammy's daughter. Because the company had never been notified of the change in ownership, they correctly followed Sammy's change of beneficiary designation. His daughter might have been liable, but she lived in another state and claimed to have spent almost all the money. Lola's son concluded that the amount he would have to pay lawyers and the uncertainty of collecting made it unrealistic to pursue his claim. If Lola had just had Sammy signed an irrevocable assignment of the policy to her and sent it to the insurance company, he would have been unable to change the beneficiary designation.

Problems like these occur because people tend to avoid estate planning or attempt "do-it-yourself" solutions that do not work in the manner desired. Lay people have many misconceptions about estate planning because it is a technical subject and the laws vary from state to state. Many people choose to ignore their estate planning needs because estate planning forces them to discuss matters related to their own death. Overcoming inertia often requires the thoughtful, caring encouragement of loved ones and the sensitive approach of the estate planner.

DEVELOPING AN ESTATE PLAN

Developing an estate plan should result in a set of recommendations and related documents that skillfully allow for the best use, conservation, and transfer of the client's wealth. In 1996, the Certified Financial Planner Board of Standards, Inc., (the Board or the CFP Board) identified the following steps in the financial planning process: (1) establishing and defining the client-planner relationship; (2) gathering client data, including goals; (3) analyzing and evaluating the client's financial status (an income statement and net-worth balance sheet); (4) developing and presenting financial planning recommendations and/or alternatives; (5) implementing the financial planning recommendations; and (6) monitoring the financial planning recommendations.

Establishing the Client-Planner Relationship

The planner must take the lead in explaining to the client the financial planning process. Some of the issues and concepts will already be familiar to the client, e.g., the purpose of a will, but other matters such as estate taxation or the use of trusts may be quite foreign. The role of the estate planner should be made clear and should be set forth in an engagement letter that spells out the services to be performed. The cooperation of the client is important to building a successful plan. So the planner must make the client aware of his or her responsibilities, including gathering information, working with the planner to implement the plan, and keeping the planner informed of changes that might require its modification.

Acquiring Client Facts and Goals

To make meaningful recommendations, the planner must acquire sufficient information about the client and the client's family. Essential information must be collected to give the planner a fairly complete picture of the client's family, his or her financial situation, and what the client expects to achieve by implementing an estate plan.

The importance of family. The estate planning opportunities for a wealthy married couple seeking to transfer an estate to the next generation are greater than those available for a single wealthy parent. Likewise, the estate planning needs of a young couple with minor children will be quite different from a couple whose children are grown. Family members may also be suitable choices for fiduciary positions such as executor, guardian, and trustee. The planner needs to be aware of special concerns, e.g., a child with special health needs or a child who is having drug addiction problems. In these situations, special trust planning that provides for long-term asset management may be appropriate.

The client's financial situation and objectives. To understand the client's financial situation, the planner will require several types of statements. First, he or she will need a current *balance sheet*, showing the fair market value of all assets and liabilities. Information on each asset should include the manner in which title is held, the date of acquisition, and current adjusted tax basis.

> EXAMPLE 1 - 11. Relying on Marlene's representation that all her property was in her name alone, an inexperienced planner failed to *examine a copy of the deed*, and prepared a will that left all her property to her husband. After she died, it was discovered that the most valuable parcel of real estate (acquired by Marlene long before the couple had married) was held in joint tenancy with Marlene's niece. Of course, the niece became the sole owner.

For liabilities, the client should list the lender and the loan terms (maturity, a payment schedule, interest rate, collateral, etc.). In addition to a description of assets and liabilities, the planner will need a *cash flow statement*, describing sources of income and major categories of expenses.

The planner will also need other facts, such as information about the client's expectation of receiving significant gifts or inheritances, and the names of the client's other advisers, including accountants, lawyers, investment brokers, life underwriters, real estate agents, physicians, and religious advisers. Further, the planner will need a description of the client's and the spouse's financial objectives, a self-appraisal of their ability to manage their finances, and the location of any estate planning documents such as wills.

The process of gathering client data, organizing it and putting it in written form is extremely important even though it can be tedious. Often clients use the planner's summary document as a convenient reference. Gathering information can alert a client to important issues so they can be considered calmly and preemptively rather than in the stress of damage control. For example, when gathering documents, a client may realize an insurance policy is misplaced and be able to make a simple call to replace it.

The client's objectives. The planner also needs an understanding of the client's objectives, especially with regard to dispositive preferences (i.e., the plan as to who gets what) for the spouse, the children, and charities; and whether significant transfers are likely to be made during the person's life or only at his or her death.

Many planners develop questionnaires to help them acquire information as efficiently as possible and checklists to help them avoid overlooking important issues. A sample questionnaire is included in Appendix 1A at the end of this chapter.

The planner should routinely examine existing documents, such as the will and evidence of title to property. Too often, client questionnaire information is inaccurate. Double checking as much information as possible can help avoid mistakes that would be damaging to the client or embarrassing to the planner.

Analyzing and Evaluating the Client's Financial Status

After acquiring the necessary facts, the planner will review the facts and prepare a plan making preliminary recommendations and, where appropriate, alternatives. The most common recommendations fall into two areas: financial planning for property transfers and personal planning for the client's incapacity and death.

Developing and Presenting Recommendations and/or Alternatives

Financial planning for property transfers. The major purpose of the plan is to efficiently distribute the client's wealth to the proper persons, in the proper amount, and at the proper time. To do this, the planner must keep in mind the following considerations that relate to more specific estate planning goals:

- Deciding whether to use a trust or some other means to *avoid probate* as a means of transferring property at the death of the client
- Examining alternatives to reduce and possibly eliminate *transfer taxes* at the death of the client and the client's spouse
- Considering *lifetime transfers*, partly to reduce transfer costs and partly to shift taxable income to a person with a lower tax bracket
- Arranging to provide the needed *liquidity* at the client's disability or death
- Devising a strategy to unwind the client's *business affairs* in a manner that maintains the greatest income and value for the survivors

Personal planning for incapacity and death. Personal planning for a client's incapacity tends to focus on arranging for someone to care for the client and the client's property if the client becomes incapacitated. It may also include making funeral or cremation arrangements, and assuring that at the time of death certain religious formalities will be faithfully followed. Personal planning also includes the important task of arranging for someone to care for the client's children if both parents become incapacitated (or die) before the children reach adulthood.

Because this text is primarily devoted to these and other objectives and techniques, further explanation will be provided in subsequent chapters.

Implementing the Plan

After the specifics of a plan are agreed upon, the planner and client should implement it. Transfer documents are drafted by an attorney and executed by the client. An insurance agent may be needed to secure the appropriate insurance contracts. If a trust is included in the plan and the client wants a bank trust department named as either initial trustee or as a successor trustee, one of the bank trust officers should be contacted for authorization and advice before the trust document is completed. The trust officer may want the bank's legal department to review the document to make sure that its terms are ones they are willing to carry out. The client should feel comfortable with the bank trust department's personnel, including their investment philosophy and how they interact with trust beneficiaries.

A person "executes" a document by taking all of the steps necessary to render it valid. For example, execution of a will normally requires, among other things, that the client sign the will in the presence of witnesses who, by their own signatures, attest to the authenticity of the client's signature. Other documents have other technical requirements such as a simple signature or a notarized signature.

Monitoring the Financial Planning Recommendations

Depending on the scope of the engagement, part of the estate planning process may include monitoring the estate plan over a long period of time. Laws change, and the client's personal situation and objectives may change. By keeping current, the planner can periodically suggest appropriate revisions to the plan. Events that are likely to require plan revision include marriage, divorce, birth of a child, new legislation, and new court decisions.

For example in 1981, Congress passed the Economic Recovery Tax Act (ERTA) which made many significant changes to the federal transfer taxation laws. One major change involved the taxation of property passing at death to a surviving spouse. Prior to the change, wills and trusts of wealthy individuals were likely to contain a provision that had the effect of passing to the surviving spouse only half of the decedent's estate, because that was the maximum amount that qualified for the marital deduction.

However, for transfers that occurred after 1981, the maximum marital deduction increased to cover the person's *entire* estate so long as it was left to the surviving spouse. Concerned that many clients whose estate plans were drafted with the old maximum in mind might not want to leave their entire estate to their spouses, Congress included a transition rule that had the effect of limiting, for most estates, the transfer to the surviving spouse of half of the decedent's estate if the plan used words like, "I leave to my spouse the maximum amount that qualifies for the marital deduction." The transition rule required the phrase be interpreted as though it said, "I leave to my spouse the maximum amount that qualifies for the marital deduction *based upon the law in effect at the time this document was executed*." Thus, people who wanted the new 100% marital deduction had to change their wills to get it even though the language they originally used should have had that effect.

The 100% marital deduction became available to those who revised their plans after the law changed, and the estate plans for those people living (dying) in states that passed legislation that said "maximum marital deduction" are to be interpreted to mean the maximum under the new federal law. Thus, most transfer documents had to be revised to take advantage of the more beneficial tax provisions. Many planners contacted their clients to encourage them to update their plans in light of the new law. Chapter 18 has a discussion of the use of disclaimers and other postmortem tax planning techniques to remedy some of the problems that may occur for wealthy clients who die without revising their pre-ERTA estate plans.

THE ESTATE PLANNING TEAM

Generally, estate planning is not conducted by just one professional. The job requires the diverse knowledge and skills of a number of practitioners, including attorneys, accountants, life underwriters, trust officers, and financial planners. These professionals are referred to as the *estate planning team*. Next, we describe the unique contribution each team member makes to the overall planning process.

Attorney

In most states, only an attorney may legally accept payment for rendering legal advice and drafting legal documents. This makes the attorney an indispensable team member in the estate planning process. If the documents are to correctly express the client's estate plan, their preparation requires an attorney with the ability to make precise legal distinctions. The working years for these documents may be measured in decades, operating long after the client is deceased, and they are likely to be viewed as the final authority concerning the client's estate planning objectives. Thus, by putting an estate plan in print, the attorney puts his or her professional skill to the test. Eventually, the results (good or bad) will be there for all to see.

Most attorneys accept the responsibility of coordinating the actions of the other members of the estate planning team. This is especially true if the attorney specializes in estate planning and taxation.

The attorney's role might not end at the client's death. He or she may be hired to advise the personal representative of the deceased client's estate. The attorney is likely to aid in the transfer of the client's assets to surviving beneficiaries or in the allocation of assets to various trusts. In addition, the attorney may engage in postmortem tax planning, a job which, as we will see in Chapter 18, entails choosing certain tax options available after the client's death and the preparation of various estate tax returns.

Accountant

By preparing the client's financial statements and yearly tax returns, the accountant is likely to be the professional having the earliest and most frequent contact with the client. Typically, these forms are so financially revealing to accountants that financial planners have described them as the client's "annual financial report."

The accountant is often able to spot specific financial problems requiring attention, especially with regard to the client's business interests. Perhaps the accountant's most important service to the client, insofar as estate planning is concerned, is in encouraging the client to begin the estate planning process. Once the process begins, the accountant may be hired to prepare the client's financial balance sheet, income statement, and cash flow statements. After the client's death, the accountant will probably be called upon to complete the required income tax returns and, if necessary, the estate tax returns.

Life Underwriter

The life underwriter's crucial role is to help the client select appropriate insurance to meet the liquidity needs that arise in the event of the client's disability or death. The efficient use of life insurance requires an understanding of estate planning to minimize transfer costs and assure an adequate level of financial support for the client's surviving beneficiaries.

Given life insurance's natural connection to wealth transfer planning, the life underwriter may be the first professional to recommend estate planning to the client. He or she may therefore be in a position to select the other members of the client's estate planning team.

Trust Officer

A skilled professional executor and trustee, the trust officer performs fiduciary services for clients and estates. A *fiduciary* is a person having a legal duty to act for the benefit of another. The word fiduciary is derived from the Latin word for "trust." A fiduciary is any person in a position of trust, loyalty, and confidence, who has the legal duty to act for the benefit of another person, putting that other person's interests above his or her own. Besides trustees, fiduciaries include executors, administrators of estates, guardians, and agents (see Chapter 2 for a further discussion).

If selected to serve as the *executor* of the client's estate, the trust officer manages assets that are transferred through the probate process. Similarly, if selected to serve as *trustee* of a trust created by the client, the trust officer manages assets placed in the trust. Thus, the trust officer can be particularly helpful in the planning stage on the long-term management of assets. It is wise in the planning stages to determine what parameters have been set by various trust departments with regard to the trusts or estates each is willing to handle. Some bank trust departments will not accept a fiduciary position for estates below a certain size, such as those below $500,000. They may also be reluctant to serve as trustee if too much supervision of a beneficiary is expected or if the trust is expected to retain assets that are difficult to manage.

> EXAMPLE 1 - 12. Martha's trust named her local bank's trust department to serve as successor trustee of her living trust. After her death, the trust is to provide income during the life of her son, Curtis, and after his death, it is to be distributed to his issue (children, grandchildren, etc.) if any. Otherwise, it will be distributed to Martha's brother William, or William's issue. Because Curtis had a long history of substance abuse, the trust had a clause that required the trustee to withhold distribution of income if Curtis failed to stay free of drugs and alcohol. It also allowed the trustee to distribute *trust corpus* (trust principal) if the trustee thought it would contribute to Curtis's well-being. When Martha died, Curtis was 50, unemployed, and childless. Since the bank's trust officers had not been consulted when the trust was drafted, the bank refused to serve as trustee. It considered the responsibility of deciding when and whether to distribute income and corpus to Curtis to be too great a burden. *** *Query 1. What risk would the bank take if it accepted the job of trustee?*

Financial Planner

The financial planner is the newest member of the estate planning team. The financial planner is the professional skilled in integrating the various parts of a client's financial plan, e.g., making recommendations concerning insurance, investments, retirement planning, income tax planning, and estate planning. He or she may be best suited to serve as the team captain, coordinating the work of the others. The financial planner does not, however, draft the legal documents. As stated earlier, in most states only an attorney is legally permitted to accept payment for creating the documents. As the profession matures, it is expected that the financial planner's role will increase.

THE NEED TO ENCOURAGE PLANNING

Many individuals need estate planning but fail to seek it. They simply ignore issues involving their own death, refusing to accept the fact that death can occur quite unexpectedly, and that all of us must die someday. Others are so busy pursuing their careers that they do not make time for planning. Still others lead lives that seem too unsettled to undertake long-range planning. Finally, some fear the family conflicts and expenses that are likely to arise at their death—without considering that good planning is likely to minimize the potential problems, even if not all problems can be resolved.

For these reasons, members of the estate planning team should actively encourage individuals to create an estate plan. As mentioned earlier, good planning will help dispose of assets fairly, minimize taxes and expenses at death, provide for the care of disabled family members, generate sufficient liquidity, provide for continued income for dependent survivors, and arrange for efficient business succession.

ORGANIZATION OF THE BOOK

This book is divided into three parts. Part 1 (this chapter and the next) introduces the major estate planning concepts used throughout the text. It describes the basic concepts of estate planning and defines many estate planning terms.

Part 2 (Chapters Three through Eight) provides the more detailed background knowledge required to understand the techniques of estate planning. It introduces the constraints in planning. In these chapters we cover the principles of transfer taxation (gift and estate) and property law. These are subjects of great importance to estate planning.

Part 3 utilizes the material in Parts 1 and 2 to survey the actual techniques used in planning. The probate process is discussed as are alternatives to probate. We consider the various methods used to defer, reduce, or completely eliminate a wealthy person's estate taxes. A wealth of other matters are covered, such as: planning for lifetime transfers to members of the family, friends, and charities; assuring that the estate has adequate liquidity to meet its needs; the special planning needed for owners of closely-held businesses; miscellaneous techniques such as providing for the care of minor children, selecting a trustee, and planning for the a person's incapacity; and, finally, postmortem planning for those issues that must be dealt with immediately after a person dies.

QUERY ANSWERED:

1. The bank's risk is that, if it doesn't monitor Curtis properly and wrongly makes distributions while he is having drug problems, it might be sued by Curtis for allowing his condition to worsen, it might be sued by someone

injured by Curtis, or it might be sued by the remaindermen whose remainder interests are diminished. Although the likely success of such suits may be low, and the cost of defending the suits will probably be chargeable to the trust, most trust departments would rather not assume responsibility for a trust whose terms invite a lawsuit.

QUESTIONS AND PROBLEMS

1. At a dinner party, one of your clients asks you what estate planning entails. Define estate planning for her, and name the areas of the law embraced by it.

2. Write an essay that addresses the issue of why many people avoid doing even the simplest estate planning, e.g., not even having wills or durable powers for healthcare.

3. A man comes into your office to inquire about your services. You find out that he owns a closely-held business and has a wife and two young children. He has not yet done any estate planning. Explain briefly how failure to plan could lead to adverse consequences.

4. Visit Pennsylvania attorney Robert Clofine's webpage (estateattorney.com). Find and describe at least one item that appears there that has relevance to estate planning–hopefully one with information that was new to you.

5. Fill in the questionnaire in Appendix 1A with information about yourself. Which items are likely to be the most difficult to complete? Why?

6. Interview by telephone or in person a trust officer to find out the type of services offered, a fee schedule, and whether his or her organization has minimum trust values below which it will not serve as trustee.

7. Outline the steps required to develop an estate plan.

8. Assuming an estate planner is competent and makes recommendations appropriate for his or her client, what action or lack of action is (are) most likely to eventually cause a conflict between the planner and the client?

9. Explain the unique contribution made by each member of the estate planning team.

10. Should state law be changed to allow competent financial planners to draft estate planning documents such as wills and trusts without a law degree? Before taking a position one way or the other, state the merits and demerits of doing this. If it were to be done (not that you would support it), what safeguards should be put into place?

ANSWERS TO QUESTIONS AND PROBLEMS *(odd numbered only)*

1. Estate planning is the study of the principles of planning for the use, conservation, and efficient transfer of an individual's wealth. It embraces the law of property, wills, trusts, future interests, estate administration, intestacy, insurance, income taxation, gift taxation, and death taxation.

3. Examples of how failure to plan could lead to adverse consequences include the following:

    a. Premature death of husband and wife in a common accident resulting in the court appointing an undesirable parental guardian for the children.

    b. Inability to sell the business after the premature death of the owner.

        Please refer to examples 1-1 through 1-10 for common illustrations of the failure to plan.

5. Clients may have difficulty completing the portions of the questionnaire that inquire about how title to property is held, ask for the fair market value of assets, or request information concerning employee benefit plans. Individuals with minor children may find it difficult to choose personal guardians.

7. Steps required in developing an estate plan: The following is taken from the CFP Board of Standard's definition of the financial planning process adopted 9/14/96:

    i.   Establishing and defining the client-planner relationship
    ii. Gathering client data including goals
    iii. Analyzing and evaluating the client's financial status
    iv. Developing and presenting financial planning recommendations and/or alternatives
    v.   Implementing the financial planning recommendations
    vi. Monitoring the financial planning recommendations

9. The unique contribution made by each member of the estate planning team includes:
   a. Attorney: drafting legal documents
   b. Accountant: preparing the client's financial statements and tax returns often gives him or her the greatest and earliest financial contact with the client
   c. Life Underwriter: providing insurance contracts to meet liquidity needs at the client's death
   d. Trust Officer: providing fiduciary services as experienced trustee and/or executor
   e. Financial Planner: potentially capable of creating a complete financial plan, one including recommendations concerning insurance, investments, retirement planning, income tax planning and estate planning

Sample Client Fact-Finding Questionnaire

Susan R. Goodall
5556 Long Street, Suite 245
Anytown, ST 54321
888/555-3456

DATA SHEET FOR ESTATE PLAN
Married Persons
(With Minor Children)

Please print or type the following information. If you need more space, use the reverse side (include the question number). If you are not certain about an answer, put a question mark. If you have questions, write them down at the end of this data sheet. *It is more important that you return this in a timely fashion than that it is complete.*

1. Husband's (H) full name _____
   Name used on real estate documents _____
   Other or former names _____
   Wife's (W) full name _____
   Name used on real estate documents _____
   Other or former names _____
   Citizenship: Husband _____ Wife _____

2. a. Residents of _____ County.
   b. Address _____

   _____

   c. Home phone # _____   Business # _____

3. Date of Birth: (H) _____   (W) _____
   Place of Birth: (H) _____   (W) _____
   Date of Marriage: _____ Place: _____
   Approximate dates moved to California   (H) _____ (W) _____
   Social Security #: (H) _____   (W) _____
   Occupation: (H) _____
   (W) _____

4. FAMILY:
   a. Children of this marriage:

Name	Birth date	Residence (If still living with you, put "Home")

   b. Are there children by prior marriages? Yes/no. Whose child? Please give full information below:

Name	Birth date	Residence (If still living with you, put "Home")

   c. If there are deceased children who left issue, please give information below:

   _____

   _____

d. Living parents (names/addresses):
(H) _____
_____
(W) _____
_____

e. Brothers and Sisters (names/addresses):
(H) _____
_____
(W) _____
_____

f. Should you or your children adopt a child (or children) should they inherit on the same basis as natural children and/or grandchildren? _____

5. Friends to whom you intend to leave bequests (names/addresses):
a. _____
b. _____

6. Estate information (to nearest $10,000)
a. The <u>net</u> value of our assets is approximately $_____
b. Our three major assets and their approximate <u>net</u> values are:

(1) _____ (value $_____)
(2) _____ (value $_____)
(3) _____ (value $_____)

7. How is title to your property actually held? Bring title documents with you when you come to see me.

8. Give the following information about your life insurance:

Whose Life? H or W	Company/ Policy No.	Owner H/W/Both	Beneficiary & 1st Alternate	Amount
____	_____	_____	_____	_____
____	_____	_____	_____	_____

9. Have you entered into a community property agreement? Yes/no
   Have you entered into a prenuptial or postnuptial agreement? Yes/no

10. Distribution. Put your thoughts in general terms at part (b). We will discuss details at the time of interview.

    a. Specific gifts (show gift, i.e., heirlooms, money, etc. and the beneficiaries' names and addresses).
       1. _____
          _____
       2. _____
          _____
       3. _____
          _____
       4. _____
          _____

       For specific gifts, indicate which alternative:
          1st alternative: Property left free and clear _____
          2nd alternative: Property left with encumbrances _____

    b. Residue (1st) _____
       _____
       (2nd) (if people in 1 predecease me) _____
       _____
       (3rd) (if people in 1 & 2 predecease me) _____
       _____

11. Please circle the answer to the following questions. (If yes, give details and, if appropriate, approximate values on the reverse side. If a document is involved, attach a photocopy.)

    a. In any year, have you made gifts to anyone of more than $3,000 prior to 1982 or $10,000 after 1981? (H)Yes/no (W) Yes/no

    b. Does either of you expect to inherit or receive gifts totaling in excess of $100,000 from your parents and/or from others? (H) Yes/no (W) Yes/no

   c. Do you have powers of appointment? (H) Yes/no (W) Yes/no

   d. Do you have Wills already drawn? (H) Yes/no (W) Yes/no

12. If a trust is contemplated: Proposed Trustee (give the relationship, name, and address if not already listed):
   1st choice: _____
   2nd choice: _____
   3rd choice: _____

13. If there are minor children: Proposed Guardian (relationship/name/address if not already listed):

   1st choice: _____
   2nd choice: _____
   3rd choice: _____

14. Proposed executor (relationship/name/address if not already listed):

   (H) 1st choice: _____
        2nd choice: _____
        3rd choice: _____

   (W)1st choice: _____
        2nd choice: _____
        3rd choice: _____

15. Are specific burial instructions available to the executor? If yes, explain:
   (H) _____
   (W) _____

16. Do you have a safe deposit box? Yes/no
   a. Where? _____
   b. Who has access? H _____ W _____ Other _____

17. Where shall the original of the will be kept? (check one)
    a. Client's (your) safe deposit box _____
    b. Other place _____ Where? _____

18. How many photocopies of each will do you want, i.e., in addition to the original? H _____ W _____ (Giving a copy to your executor is optional.)

19. Questions to ask your attorney:

    a. _____

    b. _____

    c. _____

    d. _____

    e. _____

    f. _____

    g. _____

    h. _____

CHAPTER 2

Basic Estate Planning Concepts

OVERVIEW

This chapter introduces many basic concepts regularly employed in estate planning. Because they will be referred to throughout the text, the reader is advised to know them well. Some of these concepts are so straightforward that mere use of them in a sentence will make their meaning clear. More involved terms are defined and illustrated. These terms, along with others introduced in later chapters, are included in the Glossary at the end of this book.

CONCEPTS DEALING WITH ESTATES

An *estate* is a quantity of wealth or property. *Property* represents something over which the owner may lawfully exercise the right to use, control, or dispose. More simply, property is anything that can be owned.

Ordinarily, for a person or a family, an estate represents the total amount of property owned. However, the word *estate* is used in several other contexts in estate planning to mean some other amount. First, in certain situations, estate means the *net* value of property owned, calculated by subtracting the amount of the estate owner's liabilities from the value of all property owned. Second, estate can be limited to the *probate estate*, which constitutes all property that passes to others by means of the probate process after the death of the owner. Third, estate may mean the *gross estate* or the *taxable estate*, two concepts used only in connection with taxation at death. As we will see later, the probate estate and the tax-related estate may be very different in size and composition. The net estate and the probate estate are generally less than all property owned; the net estate is less because liabilities are subtracted, and the probate estate is less because many things owned, such as those held in joint tenancy and life insurance, pass outside the probate process. The gross estate will equal or exceed the value of all property owned because it includes all things owned and may also include things that are not owned, such as gift taxes paid on gifts made within three years of the donor's death. In Chapter 6 we will cover the concepts of the gross estate and the taxable estate in detail.

CONCEPTS DEALING WITH TRANSFERS OF PROPERTY

One of the primary areas of emphasis in estate planning is the transfer of property. This section will cover the terminology used in this area.

Transfers of Legal, Beneficial, or Legal and Beneficial Interests

A *transfer* or *assignment* of property refers to any type of passing of property in which the *transferor* gives up an *interest* to the *transferee*. The interest transferred can be purely legal, purely beneficial, or both legal and beneficial. *Legal interest* refers to a situation where title passes. For example, an independent trustee of a trust takes title to all trust assets in order to manage the trust property, but cannot use it in a manner inconsistent with the trust agreement. A mother who takes title as custodian of a bank account established for her child's benefit under the Uniform Transfers to Minors Act[1] has legal title, but the beneficial interest is owned by the child.

On the other hand, a purely *beneficial interest* occurs when a transferee receives something that carries an economic benefit, but not title. Examples of beneficial interest in property include the temporary or permanent right to possess, consume, pledge, or otherwise benefit from property. If a friend lends you her car while your car is in the shop, you have a beneficial interest in the car without having title. As we will see, a trust beneficiary's rights are purely beneficial.

Finally, an interest given up by the transferor can be both legal and beneficial, such as where the transferee receives both title and the beneficial interest. An *outright transfer* occurs when one receives both legal and beneficial interests, without restrictions or conditions, as typically happens when one person gives another a birthday present.

Complete Versus Incomplete Transfers; Property in General Versus a Specific Property Interest

Complete versus incomplete transfers: overview. A transfer of property is said to be *complete* and *irrevocable* when it is no longer rescindable or amendable (i.e., when the transferor has totally relinquished all dominion and control over that property). For example, after purchasing this book, at the expiration of the returns period, you have made a completed transfer of money. On the other hand, a transfer is said to be *incomplete* and *revocable* while it is still rescindable or amendable (i.e., made without total relinquishment of dominion and control over that property).

Property in general versus an interest in property. To fully distinguish between complete and incomplete transfers, one must grasp the difference between property in general and a specific interest in property. *Property in general*, such as 100 shares of ABC stock, means the entire asset, whether physical or intangible, including all rights and interests that go with ownership. In contrast, an *interest in property* means one or more rights to property, such as the right to the first five years of dividends from the 100 shares of ABC stock.

In estate planning, more than one interest in a piece of property may be transferred in a way that highlights the divisibility of the interests associated with property ownership.

> EXAMPLE 2 - 1. Tom transfers 100 shares of stock in trust to Terry. The trust terms give Alan the right to all income for five years, followed by Barbara having the right to receive income for ten years, and finally, after 15 years, the trust is to terminate with the trust assets distributed to Carl. Each person has received an "interest" in the stock. Terry's interest is a legal one (title), Alan and Barbara each have a beneficial one, and Carl's interest is both beneficial and legal. We'll take a more detailed look at trusts later in the chapter.

Complete, incomplete, and partially complete transfers. A transfer of each specific interest in property is either complete or incomplete, while the transfer of more than one interest can be either *totally complete, partially complete, or totally incomplete.*

> EXAMPLE 2 - 2. Continuing with the same facts as above, if Tom retained the right to revoke or amend the entire trust, his transfers of property into trust would be incomplete. On the other hand, if Tom retained the right to revoke or amend only Alan's interest, the transfer of Alan's interest would be incomplete, the transfer of Barbara and Carl's interests would be complete, and Tom's overall transfer of the stock would be said to be partially complete. Finally, if Tom retained no rights whatsoever over the stock, the transfers of interest to Alan, Barbara, and Carl would all be complete.

When we study gift taxes, it will become clear that this issue of whether a transfer is complete or incomplete is important because gift tax law treats completed transfers, even of just a partial interest, as gifts subject to gift taxation.

Sale Versus Gift

Most commonly, completed transfers of property interests are undertaken by sale, by gift, or by a combination of both sale and gift. A *sale* is a transfer of property under which each transferor exchanges *consideration* regarded as equivalent in value. By contrast, a gift is a transfer of property for which the transferor takes back little or nothing of economic value in exchange. The most common methods of making gift transfers are *outright* and *in trust.*

A bargain sale. A bargain sale occurs when a person (the transferor) knowingly transfers property in exchange for property with an economic value less than the property he or she is giving up. A bargain sale involves a transfer that is a part sale and part gift. The notion of the bargain sale requires us to define a gift somewhat more broadly than in the last paragraph. Usually a gift is something given with nothing in return; however, a bargain sale is obviously a gift, even though property is received in exchange. Federal tax law treats the actual amount of the gift as the difference between the respective values of the consideration exchanged. Thus, a transfer during the life of the transferor will be either a gift or a sale, with a gift defined to include a *bargain sale* (i.e., an exchange of considerations of unequal value, where the parties know and intend them to be unequal).

Inter Vivos Transfer Versus Transfer at Death

A transfer of property can be *inter vivos*, meaning that it is made while the transferor is alive, or it can be made at death. Inter vivos is Latin for "among the living." Transfers at death may be made pursuant to a valid document, also called an *instrument*, prepared by the owner before death (e.g., will, trust, title by joint tenancy, or insurance beneficiary designation), or pursuant to state law (intestate succession) in the event that no such document exists.

Fair Market Value of Transfer

The value of a transfer is measured by its fair market value at the time of the transfer. Determining fair market value is the subject of several sections in the text. A generally accepted definition of *fair market value* is "the price at which the property would change hands between a willing buyer and a willing seller, neither being under any compulsion to buy or sell, and both having reasonable knowledge of the relevant facts." The IRS uses this definition in the regulations for valuing gifts and estates.[2]

BENEFICIARIES

A *beneficiary* or *donee* is a person who receives a gift of a beneficial interest in property from a transferor. The transferor is called a *donor*. Although, in the most general sense, donee and beneficiary are synonymous, in certain contexts one or the other term is more commonly used. For example, the recipient of an outright *inter vivos* gift from the donor is usually called a donee. On the other hand, the recipient of a bequest by a will or an interest in a trust is usually called a beneficiary. Occasionally, the term *donee* is used to describe one who has received something without also receiving any beneficial interest, such as where one is given a limited power of appointment, an estate planning tool discussed later.

WILLS, TRUSTS, AND PROBATE

In estate planning, a *decedent* is a person who has died. When a person dies, property owned by the decedent must be transferred. Each state takes special interest in ensuring that all property owned by the decedent is transferred to the proper parties. State law recognizes certain documents prepared by the decedent (wills, trusts, joint tenancy arrangements, life insurance policies, etc.) as legally binding guides for the proper disposition of the decedent's property. A *will* is a written document that expresses a person's desired distribution of his or her property at death. The person making a will is called the *testator*. The will is said to make *testamentary* transfers, and the actual process by which transfer is accomplished is the probate process. At the death of a person, his or her will controls the transfer of property only if there is no guide to the transfer that is recognized as superior. Thus, the will controls property in the decedent's name alone or held with another as a tenant in common, but not property held in trust or in joint tenancy. Property held in trust will be transferred according to the terms of the trust, not according to the terms of the settlor's will. Any attempt to transfer joint tenancy property by a decedent co-owner's will must fail since the right of survivorship prevails over provisions in a will.

A trust is a fiduciary relationship in which one person (the *trustee*) is the holder of the title to property (the *trust estate* or the *trust corpus*), subject to an equitable obligation to keep or use the property for the benefit of another (the *beneficiary*). The *trust instrument* is the written agreement between the *settlor* (the person creating and funding the trust) and the *trustee* that sets forth for whose benefit the trust is created, how the trust estate is to be managed, its duration, and to whom the corpus must be given when the trust terminates. Trusts are described in greater detail later in the chapter.

Intestate, testate, and partially intestate. If a valid will is found, the decedent is said to have died *testate*. If the will does not dispose of all the decedent's property, the decedent is said to have died *partially intestate*. If no will is found, the decedent is said to have died *intestate*. However, if all property is disposed of by alternative means (e.g., trusts, joint tenancy), a will may not be necessary, and the absence of a will would not cause any problems as there would be no property without some mechanism of transfer.

In some cases, the moment that death occurs has significance because it determines the rights of beneficiaries, and, quite obviously, it is extremely important if the dying person has authorized organ donations. The Uniform Determination of Death Act addresses this issue by defining death as follows:

> § 1. [Determination of Death]. An individual who has sustained either (1) irreversible cessation of circulatory and respiratory functions, or (2) irreversible cessation of all functions of the entire brain, including the brain stem, is dead. A determination of death must be made in accordance with accepted medical standards.[3]

Probate and the personal representative. *Probate* is the legal process of administering the estate of a decedent. The probate estate consists of all property belonging to the decedent for which there is no other mechanism of transfer. Thus, the probate estate is that property whose disposition is guided by either the decedent's will or the state laws of intestate succession. Generally, *probate assets* fall into one of three groups: property owned by the decedent as an individual, interests of the decedent held with others as tenants-in-common, and, in some community property states, the decedent's one-half interest in community property. Some community property states, such as California, no longer require a probate for property going to the surviving spouse whether that property is the decedent's half of the community property or is the decedent's separate property. *Non-probate assets* include property held in trusts or in joint tenancy, the proceeds of most insurance policies on the life of the decedent (unless payable to the decedent's estate), and most retirement plan assets. Many of these terms will be described later in the chapter.

In probate administration, the judge of the probate court determines the validity of the will, if any, and (after a period of administration) authorizes distribution of the probate estate to creditors and beneficiaries. The court appoints a *personal representative* to act as fiduciary to represent and manage the probate estate. If the court appoints the person nominated in the will to be personal representative that person is called the *executor*. In some states, a female personal representative is called an *executrix*, however the trend is to use the term executor regardless of gender. An *administrator* is a person appointed by the court to represent the estate of a person who died intestate. At times courts appoint someone other than the person(s) nominated in the will. The person nominated may have predeceased the testator, may be incapacitated, or perhaps is unfit (e.g., is serving time in prison for bank robbery). If the decedent died with a valid will, but the court appoints someone other than the person nominated in it, the personal representative is called an *administrator with will annexed*.

The word "fiduciary" is derived from the Latin word for "trust." A *fiduciary* is a person in a position of trust, loyalty, and confidence, who has the legal duty to act for the benefit of another, putting that person's interests above his or her own. Besides personal representatives, fiduciaries include trustees, guardians, and agents.

Recipients of probate property. Beneficiaries of a decedent's probate property are called heirs, devisees, or legatees. An *heir* is a person who inherits property from a decedent whether by will, intestate succession, or any other mechanism of transfer such as through a trust or by joint tenancy. *Heir at law* refers to the person (or persons) who have a right to an intestate decedent's property. This is usually accomplished by defining them as included in the issue of the adoptive parent. Degrees of blood relationship, which are important in determining heirs at law, will be covered in Chapter 4. A *devisee* is a beneficiary, under a will, of a gift of real property. A devisee is said to receive a *devise*. A *legatee* is a beneficiary, under a will, of a gift of personal property. A legatee is said to receive a *legacy* or a *bequest*. The trend in modern usage is to use the term bequest for any testamentary gift, whether of real or personal property. The Uniform Probate Code, discussed in the next chapter, uses the term "devise" both as a noun and a verb, to mean a bequest or the act of making a bequest (whether of real or personal property) in connection with transfers by will.

Issue refers to a person's offspring or progeny, including children, grandchildren, great-grandchildren, and the like. A *descendant* is one who is descended from a specific ancestor. Thus, the terms issue and descendants are used interchangeably. Most state succession statutes treat adopted children as though naturally born to their adoptive parents.

Types of bequests. Bequests are categorized as specific, pecuniary, general, residuary, and/or class gifts. A *specific bequest* is a gift of a particular item of property capable of being identified and distinguished from all other property in the testator's estate, e.g., "I leave all my household furnishings to Sally Ann," and "I leave my high school ring to my brother Bill." If the property subject to a specific bequest is sold, given away, or lost before the testator's death, under the common law doctrine of *ademption* (from the Latin *ademptio* - a taking away) the bequest fails, meaning the person does not receive anything to replace the missing property. Although most states follow the common law doctrine, some states' statutes have exceptions that do not result in ademption in certain circumstances, e.g., an asset was acquired by the decedent in a manner that made it clear it was intended to replace specific devised real or tangible property.[4] A *general bequest* is a gift that can be satisfied out of the general assets of the estate, e.g., the bequest "I leave 10 percent of my estate to my brother Henry."

At common law the term *legacy* meant a testamentary gift of money; however, it has come to mean any bequest. *Pecuniary bequest* is the term used to describe a bequest expressed as a specific dollar amount. It is called a pecuniary bequest even though the executor has the option of satisfying it with cash or with assets worth the specified dollar amount. Since the bequest could be paid from any account, or be satisfied by the transfer of any asset not specifically bequeathed, a pecuniary bequest is a type of general bequest. Pecuniary bequests are commonly found in complex estate plans aimed at minimizing death taxes. The bequest is likely to be expressed in terms of a formula, such as "I leave to my spouse the least amount needed to reduce my death taxes to zero." A pecuniary bequest is distinguished from a *fractional share bequest*, which uses fractions (or percentages) in defining the interests of beneficiaries to certain property or to a portion of the estate (e.g., "I leave 65 percent of the residue of my estate to my sister Gladys, and the other 35 percent to my brother Marco.")

What remains of the estate after all the foregoing bequests are taken into account is called the *residue* of the estate. A *residuary bequest* is a gift of that part of the testator's estate not otherwise disposed of by the will, e.g., "I leave the rest of my estate to Robert Moon." Generally, debts are paid out of the residue and not charged against the specific bequests.

A *class gift* is a gift to a group of individuals that may not be completely defined at the time the gift is made (e.g., "I leave the residue of my estate to my grandchildren living at the time of my death.")

Occasionally, a testator dies leaving insufficient assets to satisfy all bequests and pay all creditors. Under the procedure called *abatement*, bequests are eliminated or reduced so that all debts (and administration expenses) are paid in full, or else the estate is exhausted. In those states that follow the Uniform Probate Code (UPC), shares of the beneficiaries abate in the following order: (1) probate property not disposed of in the will, if there are no residuary bequests, (2) residuary bequests, (3) general bequests, and (4) specific bequests. Some state statutes abate gifts to a spouse, or to issue, only after abatement of gifts to persons not related to the decedent.

EXAMPLE 2 - 3. Lawrence died in a UPC state. Lawrence's will leaves his car to his son, Sam, $20,000 cash to his sister, Vira, and the residue of his estate to his wife, Mary Ellen. Assume that at his death Lawrence owned only the car and $25,000 in cash, and he owed $6,000 in debts. Most states (perhaps all) would require the $6,000 debt be paid, leaving just $19,000 in cash. The UPC abatement would result in Vira getting the $19,000 balance, the car would go to Sam, and Mary Ellen would receive nothing.

Disclaimers

Most people would welcome a large bequest, especially if it came from a distant relative. After all, such gifts may make for financial security. Yet there are times when it makes sense for a beneficiary to refuse a gift or bequest. A *disclaimer* is an unqualified refusal to accept a gift or bequest. Disclaiming may be preferable when it avoids, reduces, or delays transfer taxes. Usually, a person will disclaim property only if it will then pass to a person the disclaimant wants to have it.

To be *tax-effective,* the disclaimer must meet the requirements of both state property law and federal tax law. Under property law, a disclaimant is treated as having *predeceased* the decedent-donor. Consequently, the disclaimed property will pass under one of two possible sets of legal guidelines. Either it will pass to the "alternate taker" in accordance with the terms of the decedent's transfer document (which is usually a will or trust) or, if no such document exists or if the document does not name an alternate taker, the property will pass under laws of intestacy.

EXAMPLE 2 - 4. Bachelor Barry died recently, and his will left an estate valued at $500,000 to his brother Mike, if living, otherwise to Mike's issue. Mike, age 87, wealthy and in poor health, has three living children. If he immediately disclaims the inheritance, it will pass under the will to his children. The transfer will not be treated as a gift from Mike, but rather as though it passed to them directly from Barry.

EXAMPLE 2 - 5. Changing the facts in the previous example a bit, assume Barry's will stated that if Mike predeceased Barry, then the bequest would go to Barry's long time friend Charlie. If Mike disclaims, Barry's estate will pass to Charlie rather than to Mike's children. Of course, Mike could assign his interest in the estate to his children, but that would be a gift from him to them.

A disclaimer is considered to be tax-effective if it complies with the requirements in IRC § 2518 so the transfer is not treated as a gift by the disclaimant. When we take up estate and gift taxes, we will cover in detail the requirements for a tax-effective disclaimer, and we will illustrate ways in which disclaimers are used to improve estate plans.

LIFE INSURANCE

A *life insurance* policy is a contract in which the insurance company, in exchange for the payment of premiums, agrees to pay a cash lump-sum amount (called the *face value* or *policy proceeds*) to a person designated in the policy to receive it (the *beneficiary*) on the death of the subject of the insurance (the *insured*). Usually, the policy names alternate beneficiaries who will receive the proceeds if the named beneficiary dies. One other important party in the life insurance contract is the *owner*, who has title to the policy, and who generally possesses both legal and beneficial interests in the policy. As beneficial owner, the policy owner has the right to benefit from the policy. Beneficial rights usually include the right to receive policy dividends, the right to designate and to change the beneficiary, and the right to surrender the policy. These rights can have economic value, even before the death of the insured. Whether a life insurance policy has economic value prior to the insured's death depends on the type of policy. If the owner holds title to the policy as the trustee of an irrevocable life insurance trust, then the owner will have legal title but will most likely not have a beneficial interest. Irrevocable life insurance trusts are used to keep life insurance proceeds out of the estate of the insured. Such trusts are discussed in detail later.

Most *term life insurance* policies have minimal cash value prior to the death of the insured because the premium charged, which increases over time along with the increasing risk of death, simply buys pure protection. If the insured dies during the policy term, the company will pay the face value; otherwise, it will pay nothing. Some multi-year term policies (called *level term*) have a constant premium for a stated period (e.g., five or ten years). This requires a cash build-up during the early years of the period which is used to pay the higher mortality risk in the later years.

In contrast to a term policy, a *cash value* policy accumulates economic value because the insurer charges a constant premium that is considerably higher than mortality costs require during the earlier years. Part of this overpayment accumulates as a *cash surrender value*, which, prior to the death of the insured, can be used by the owner in one of two ways: (1) at any time the owner can surrender the policy and receive this value in cash, or (2) the owner can request a policy loan and borrow up to the amount of this value.

Life insurance makes a significant contribution to estate planning because a policy can have value prior to the insured's death, can pay cash to the beneficiaries on the insured's death, and can be structured to avoid estate tax. It is said to be the only asset that can create an *instant* estate of substantial magnitude for a person of otherwise modest wealth. For a family that includes dependent children, this may be an important means of assuring the financial well-being of the surviving family members if a parent dies. For the wealthy family, life insurance may provide needed cash to pay the death taxes. A discussion of the types of life insurance and irrevocable life insurance trusts is found in Chapter 15. To use life insurance properly, the planner must be aware of the impact of taxes, a subject explained in detail in Chapters 5 through 8.

TAXATION

In estate planning, the two principal types of taxing authorities are the individual states and the federal government. The four major types of taxes are gift tax, death tax, generation-skipping transfer tax, and income tax.

A *gift tax* is a tax on a lifetime gift; that is, a lifetime transfer of property for less than full consideration.

A *death tax* is essentially a tax levied on certain property owned or transferred by the decedent at death. There are two basic types of death tax statutes, which, depending on the format, are referred to as either an estate tax or an inheritance tax. An *estate tax* is a tax on the decedent's right to transfer property, while an *inheritance tax* is a tax on the right of a beneficiary to receive property from a decedent. Either way, their net effect is essentially the same: they are both considered death taxes, and the tax is usually paid by the executor out of the decedent's estate before the property is transferred to the heirs. With an inheritance tax, the amount of death tax paid on any given size inheritance is likely to be greater for remote relatives as compared to close relatives, and greatest for non-relatives. For example, amounts going to a surviving spouse might not be taxed at all, and bequests to a child might have a high exemption amount and/or a lower tax rate than property going to a non-relative. The federal death tax is referred to as the federal estate tax. The characteristic of an estate tax is that, for any given net estate (i.e., after debts and expenses), the tax will be the same regardless of who receives it. For example in the year 2003, the federal tax on a $5 million bequest, after applying a $195,800 federal state death tax credit, would be $1,709,200 whether the estate went to the decedent's children or went entirely to non-relatives.

However, the federal estate tax is not a pure estate tax because it has two deductions based on the status of the beneficiary. A complete marital deduction is allowed for all property going to a surviving spouse (for a non-USA citizen spouse a special trust might be required, but we'll save that discussion until later), and a complete charitable deduction is allowed for property going to qualified charities. Since these are complete (100%) deductions, subtracted from the gross estate before arriving at the taxable estate, and they are the only two deductions based on the character of the beneficiary, little is lost in our thinking of the federal death tax as an estate tax.

At the state level, most states impose an estate tax and others have an inheritance tax. The trend is to impose an estate tax that results in no additional cost to the estate because, although it is paid to the state, the state death tax statute sets the death taxes as equal to the state's allowable share of the federal state death tax credit. Because of the federal credit for state death taxes, this so-called "*pick-up tax*" reduces the federal death tax by an equivalent amount (i.e., a dollar-for-dollar credit), thus there is no increase in the combined taxes. The calculation for the "pick-up tax" is explained in Chapter 5. Thirty-three states (including California, Florida, Nevada, and New York) use the "pick-up tax."*** *Query 1. Based on the above discussion, what is the death tax collected by the state of Florida if one of its citizens dies in 2003 leaving a taxable estate of $5 million?*

A *generation-skipping transfer tax* is a tax on certain property transferred to someone who is more than one generation younger than the donor - a "skip person." Thus, the surviving spouse and the children of a decedent are not skip persons, but grandchildren and great-grandchildren are. Without this tax, wealth could skip several generations and escape one or more levels of transfer tax. For example, without the GSTT, a gift or estate transfer of a $10 million parcel of land to a grandchild would be subject once to a gift tax or death tax, but it would not be taxed twice. It would be taxed twice if it went through the natural succession, i.e., once when the property passes from the client to the child, and again when it passes from the child to the grandchild. Chapter 12 covers the GSTT in more detail. It is enough to say here that the federal generation-skipping transfer tax has a $1 million exemption per transferor, making careful planning in this area necessary only for clients with fairly substantial estates. Indeed, recent legislation dramatically increases the exemption during the period 2004-2009 and eliminates the GSTT entirely in 2010.[5]

An *income tax* is essentially a tax levied on income earned by a taxpayer during a given year. Income tax laws usually distinguish five different taxpayers or entities that must report income by filing income tax returns: individuals, partnerships, corporations, estates, and trusts. Principles of taxation can differ substantially for each. For instance, partnerships generally do not pay income taxes because the partnership is treated as a *passthrough* entity, income and deductions are passed through to be reported by the individual partners. Each taxpayer, including partnerships, must submit an annual income tax return that reports certain items including income, deductions, credits, and the tax due (calculated by using tax tables applicable to that entity). Married individuals may file a joint income tax return in which they report their combined income, deductions, and other information on one return. This textbook will not try to cover income taxes in detail as it is beyond the scope of this course; however, a good introduction to the income taxation of trusts and estates is found in Chapter 8.

PROPERTY INTERESTS

Estate planning seeks to preserve and efficiently transfer an individual's wealth. Wealth is generally thought of as the property a person owns. This section will describe some of the ways in which property can be owned. Essentially, ownership can be classified in the following six ways:

- The physical characteristics of property (e.g., real versus personal)
- The extent of ownership interest in property (e.g., fee simple or a life estate)
- The type of co-ownership (e.g., joint tenancy versus tenants in common)
- A legal versus a beneficial interest (e.g., property held in the name of the trustee versus a trust beneficial interest)
- A present versus a future interest (e.g., an income interest in a trust versus a remainder interest)
- A vested versus a contingent interest (e.g., outright ownership of land versus a contingent remainder interest, where the remainderman must outlive the income beneficiary or the trust property reverts back to the trustor's estate)

Classification of Property by Physical Characteristics

Property is classified as real or personal. *Real* property includes ownership interests in land and any improvements, such as buildings, fences, trees, and the like, that are attached to the land. Curiously, an interest for years (a leasehold) in real estate is considered personal property. Accordingly, a good functional definition of *personal property* is all property except interests in land and its improvements.

Property is further divided into tangible and intangible property. Something is tangible if it can be perceived by the senses as having a physical existence. *Tangible personal property* is personal property whose utility comes primarily from its physical characteristics rather than the legal rights conferred on the owner or possessor of the property. Conversely, *intangible personal property* derives its value from the legal rights it represents. Thus a newspaper is tangible personal property because its value is based on the news printed therein. Initially, one might pay 35 cents to read it. A few days later, the value may drop to almost nothing, being useful only to wrap dead fish or as recycled newspaper. Yet, a very old paper with an article of historical significance on the front page may be worth a lot to collectors of old newspapers. On the other hand, a stock certificate is valuable to the owner of the certificate if the company is a going business, not because of the physical characteristics of the paper it is printed on, but because of the rights it represents, such as the right to vote for the board of directors, the right to dividends when they are declared, and certain liquidation rights. If the company has gone out of business, then the stock certificate has become tangible personal property. The certificate may be worth only the value of the paper it is printed on, or, if it is old or unusual for some reason, it may be of some value as a collector's item.

Intangible personal property includes a *chose in action*, which is a claim for money or property that could be recovered from another in a lawsuit, if such is necessary. A chose in action, pronounced "shows," represents the right to money or property that is owed to the holder of the chose. That right can be transferred, sold, or assigned to another, who can then act on it in his or her own name. The person holding the chose as a result of a transfer is entitled to keep any recovery.

EXAMPLE 2 - 6. Betty borrows $9,000 from Lenny, agreeing to pay it back by December 31 of this year. Lenny signs a piece of paper assigning to his daughter, Christine, his right to collect the debt. Since the debt could be collected by a lawsuit if necessary, it is considered to be a chose in action, and the assignment to Christine gives her the right to collect it.

Basic Interests in Property

The three basic interests in property are fee simple, life estate, and estate for years.

Fee simple. A *fee simple* interest, often called a *fee* or a *fee simple absolute*, represents the greatest interest that a person can have over *real* property and corresponds to our usual notion of full ownership. Common rights include the right to possess, use, pledge, or transfer the property. If you own a house, even if it is subject to a mortgage, you probably have it in fee.

Life estate. A *life estate* interest in property, like a fee simple, is a powerful form of ownership, but is different in that the interest ceases on someone's death. Ordinarily, the *measuring life* is that of the owner of the interest. However, it could be any other person.

EXAMPLE 2 - 7. Doctor Bud assigns his interest in a house to Gladis, his widowed mother, for her to use and enjoy until her death. Gladis has received a life estate in the house. Her own life is the measuring life.

A life estate for the life of someone other than the owner of the interest is called an estate *for the life of another*. These are rarely used.

EXAMPLE 2 - 8. Facts are similar to the previous example, except that Gladis's interest will cease on the death of Bud. Gladis still has a life estate in the house but now Bud's life, rather than her life, is the measuring life. She has an estate for the life of another.

Ordinarily, the owner of a life estate enjoys, for the length of a measuring life, complete ownership, nearly equivalent to a fee, except that it will end on the life tenant's death. However, life estates are sometimes created so that the recipient enjoys only a partial present interest in the property.

EXAMPLE 2 - 9. Aunt Jane, owner of dividend-paying common stock, gives to her niece Barbie the right to receive the dividends for as long as Barbie lives. Barbie has received a life estate in the income of the stock. Under the customary arrangements, Barbie does not have many rights in the stock itself. For example, she does not have the right to possess or sell the stock, or to use it as collateral against a loan. The stock will be held by someone else, either the original owner, or more commonly, a trustee under a trust arrangement.

Trusts are used extensively in estate planning and will be discussed in every chapter of this book. An introduction to trusts follows this discussion of property.

Interest for years. Often, a person transfers possession and/or enjoyment of property to another for a fixed period. This is called an *estate for years*—even if the fixed period is something other than a certain number of years.

EXAMPLE 2 - 10. Professor Jackson rents his cottage to Dr. Johnson, a visiting professor, for the spring semester. Dr. Johnson has an estate "for years" even though the semester is only four months long.

EXAMPLE 2 - 11. Mary is presently enjoying a life estate, for her life, in the income from certain common stock. Today Mary transfers to Mark her interest for the next two years. If Mary does not survive the full two years, Mark's interest will be cut off on Mary's death. Mary cannot transfer any greater interest than she actually owns, and Mark's interest is limited to that which Mary can legally give; thus, Mark has an income interest in the stock, ending at the earlier of two years or Mary's death.

A common example of an interest for years is a *leasehold*, which entitles the lessee to possess and use the property (e.g., a house or computer) for a specified time, usually in exchange for a fixed series of payments. Leasehold interests can amount to a valuable part of a lessee's wealth if the fixed payments are below current market rates, and if the lessee is permitted to "sublet" the property.

EXAMPLE 2 - 12. Five years ago, Freda acquired a 15-year leasehold interest in a commercial building and is obligated to pay $15,000 per year for the entire period. If the rent for comparable buildings is $25,000 per year for the next ten years, and assuming a discount rate of 8%, the value of Freda's leasehold is the present value of $10,000 for ten years, discounted at 8%, or $67,101 [see Table B, annuity factor of 6.7101]. Freda could possibly sell her interest for that amount.

Concurrent Ownership

Property may be owned individually, in which case one person owns and uses it, or it may be owned concurrently, by two or more persons. Where there is *concurrent ownership*, title may be taken as joint tenancy, tenants by the entirety, tenants in common, or as community property.

A common characteristic of all types of concurrent ownership is the *undivided* right to use the entire property, not just a physically identifiable portion. In addition, the co-owners usually each have the right, in the event of a dispute, to have the property physically divided (partitioned), at which time concurrent ownership ends. If the nature of the property is such that it cannot be partitioned, a court may order it sold and the proceeds divided among the owners according to their respective shares.

Joint tenancy interests. The defining characteristic of property held in joint tenancy is that, on the death of one co-owner, the decedent's interest automatically passes to the surviving owner(s). The owners are said to hold title in *joint tenancy*, or it may be said that they are *joint tenants*. Property law, developed as part of our common law, requires that the interests all be equal, and the owners' respective shares should not be stated as part of the title, thus, "Jim, John, and Jose, as joint tenants," not "Jim, John, and Jose, as joint tenants each owning a one-third share." Because tenants in common can own unequal shares, the share of each is usually expressed in the title; therefore the second statement, with the shares defined as "one-third," might result in a claim by the heirs of a deceased co-owner that tenants in common was actually intended and that the one-third interest belongs to them and not to the surviving co-owners.

Under joint tenancy, ownership passes to the surviving cotenant automatically at a cotenant's death by *operation of law*, meaning that the law recognizes the transfer as immediate on the cotenant's death without any action required by the survivors. However some authorities, such as banks, will require document revision in order to transact further business. A title company will want proof of the death of a joint tenant before it will issue title insurance should the survivors try to transfer title to someone else.

EXAMPLE 2 - 13. John and Mary own a house as joint tenants. At John's death, Mary automatically becomes the sole owner of the house. However, as a practical matter, she might have to record an affidavit establishing the death of a joint tenant, with a certified death certificate attached, in order to clear the title.

The automatic right of survivorship inherent in joint tenancy prevails over other means of transfers at death, including the will and the trust instrument.

EXAMPLE 2 - 14. Continuing the prior example, if, John had executed a will that left his one-half interest in the house to his son, Mary would still receive it by right of survivorship. The joint tenancy designation supersedes the will.

However, in certain jurisdictions, agreements can be executed between joint owners to nullify a joint tenancy designation.

EXAMPLE 2 - 15. Continuing prior examples, if John and Mary were to execute a written *agreement* stating their intention that the house, presently held in joint tenancy, is in fact to be held by them as community property or as tenants in common (see description below), many jurisdictions will honor the agreement, and the house would not pass to Mary by automatic right of survivorship.

Joint tenancy interests in real estate are created by a written document called a deed. In most states, one cotenant can unilaterally "sever" the joint tenancy without the knowledge or consent of the other tenant(s).

EXAMPLE 2 - 16. Oscar, Ray, Sam, and Clark own Green Acre Ranch as joint tenants. Without telling the other three, Sam deeds his interest to his friend Ed. Sam has broken the joint tenancy insofar as his interest is concerned. Ed owns a one-fourth interest as a tenant in common with the other three holding title to three-fourths as joint tenants. If Ray then dies, Oscar and Clark will own the three-fourths as joint tenants, and Ed will continue to own one-fourth. If Ed dies, his share will go to his heirs, not to the other co-owners.

Joint tenancies are commonly created among family members, as they are the most likely to appreciate the simplicity of this means of transfer and are least likely to be concerned that the ultimate owner of the property may be determined by whom among them lives the longest.

Interests by the entirety. An *interest by the entirety* is like a joint tenancy in that it carries that key characteristic of joint tenancy, the right of survivorship; however, an interest by the entirety can be created only between husband and wife. Unlike joint tenancy, neither spouse may transfer or encumber the property without the consent of the other. Tenants by the entirety is a common law concept, generally not recognized in the community property states. In addition, a few of the common law states no longer recognize this form of ownership and will treat an attempt to create it as merely joint tenancy. Where it is recognized, since it is available only to married couples, a divorce will cause a tenants by the entirety title to automatically transmute into a tenants in common form of title.

Tenants in common. Like joint tenancy, *tenants in common* interests are held by two or more persons, each having an undivided right to possess property. Unlike joint interests, however, interests in common may be owned in unequal percentages, and when one owner dies the remaining owners do not automatically succeed in ownership. Instead, the decedent's interest passes through his or her estate, by will or by the laws of intestate succession. The interest can also be transferred to the trustee of a trust and pass according to the provisions of the trust.

> EXAMPLE 2 - 17. Jack owns a 16 percent real estate interest in common with two other individuals who, combined, own the other 84 percent. Jack's will leaves his entire estate to his wife, Deanna. On Jack's death, his will determines who will get his interest. Therefore, the 16 percent interest will pass by the probate process to his wife, Deanna, not to the other cotenants.

Interests in common are the title of choice for non-related parties since this form of title, in contrast to joint tenancy interests, creates a means of enjoying common ownership without any of the co-owners losing the right of disposition at death.

Community property interests. In the eight states recognizing it, *community property* is that property acquired by the efforts of either spouse during their marriage while living in a community property state, and other property which by the agreement of the spouses is converted from separate property into community property. *Separate property* is all other property owned by the spouses (e.g., acquired by only one of the spouses by gift, devise, bequest or inheritance, or by a spouse domiciled in a common law state, or acquired by either spouse prior to their marriage). The traditional community property states are Arizona, California, Idaho, Louisiana, Nevada, New Mexico, Texas, and Washington. In addition, Wisconsin has adopted the Uniform Marital Property Act (UMPA)[6], which creates a presumption that property owned by the spouses is property of the marriage, and, as such, it does not belong to just one spouse. This presumption holds even if title to property is in one spouse's name alone. The "marriage property" presumption can be overcome by evidence that sufficiently establishes otherwise, e.g., evidence that it was owned prior to the marriage or acquired by inheritance.

When it comes to classifying income, most of the community property states follow what is referred to as the California rule, which is that income from community property is community property, as is anything bought with that income, and income from separate property is separate property, as is anything bought with that income. Three community property states, Texas, Idaho, and Louisiana, follow what is called the Texas rule and treat income earned from separate property during the marriage as community property. Likewise, Wisconsin law provides, with some exceptions, that "income earned or accrued by a spouse or attributable to property of a spouse during marriage and after the determination date is marital property."[7] The "determination date" is the later of the couple's marriage, their domicile in Wisconsin, or the enactment of Wisconsin's Marriage Property Act. Even Texas-rule states treat the gain on separate property that is sold as separate property, and, of course, anything bought with the proceeds of the sale is separate property.

Community property is owned equally by both spouses. Generally, both spouses must consent to a gift of community property. Community property states allow couples to convert community property to separate property, and vice versa, although some states require a written agreement wherein the spouse whose interest is reduced acknowledges the fact that something has been lost. Separate property is considered entirely owned by the acquiring spouse. In states without community property provisions, of course, all property is separate property. In those states, it would simply be referred to as "the property owned by" Sam, Wanda, or whomever.

> EXAMPLE 2 - 18. Pat and Mary live in New Mexico, a community property state. When they married two years ago, Pat owned a sports car that Mary now uses. Last year Mary's father gave her 100 shares of XYZ stock, which pays a quarterly dividend. Mary used the last dividend check to buy a bicycle. Pat bought a rowboat from money saved from his July paycheck. The stock and bicycle are Mary's separate property. The car is Pat's separate property. All the other assets, including both salaries and the rowboat, are community property. ***Query 2-2. If Louisiana was their home, what difference would it make insofar as property ownership goes?*

Community property laws represent the attempt by certain state governments to impose greater fairness in property ownership by married couples. Under old English common law, the husband owned all property that either husband or wife acquired during their marriage. Even after most states recognized the right of married women to own property, during pre-World War II America, the husband typically earned most of the outside income while the wife performed the non income-producing household chores; therefore, husbands usually acquired title to almost all the family wealth. At early common law, a wife was entitled to own none of this property until her husband's death, at which time she received a life estate in one-third of her husband's real property. Called a "dower" interest, it has been modified by most common law states; however, it seldom gives the non-working spouse the advantages inherent in the law of community property, which automatically gives both spouses an immediate equal share in all the property acquired by their efforts during the course of their marriage.

Arizona, California, Idaho, Washington, and Wisconsin have a concept called *quasi-community property*, which is defined as that property, acquired by a resident while domiciled in a non-community property state, which would have been community property had the resident been domiciled in a community property state at the time of acquisition. For example, if a married couple moves to California owning common stock acquired with salary earned during the marriage while they were residents of New York, the stock is quasi-community property. Essentially, quasi-community property is treated as separate property of the acquiring spouse until divorce or death. If the parties divorce, the property is divided in a manner similar to community property. Treatment at death depends on which spouse dies first. If the acquiring spouse dies first, the surviving spouse is entitled to one-half of the property. On the other hand, the other spouse's interest in the property ceases, if he or she dies first.

Joint tenancy (JT) and community property (CP) have several major similarities and differences that are summarized in the outline below:

1. Major Similarities:
   a. Both involve ownership by more than one person.
   b. The owners have equal ownership rights and equal rights to use the entire property. Their interests are undivided.
   c. Any owner may demand a division of the property into separate, equal shares.
2. Major Differences:
   a. CP exists only between spouses. JT can exist between any two or more persons.
   b. CP rights arise automatically, by operation of law under state statute, even if title or possession is taken by just one of the spouses. Hence, CP is created immediately on acquisition of the property. JT rights

are usually created by an agreement of the parties (e.g., they ask that stock be issued in their names as joint tenants) and are not governmentally imposed.

c. JT includes automatic right of succession to ownership (right of survivorship) by surviving joint owners. This right takes priority over any will. In contrast, CP includes no automatic succession to ownership of the decedent's share by the surviving spouse. Therefore, at death, a spouse can transfer his or her share of CP, by will, to someone other than the spouse. However, intestacy will ordinarily result in succession by the surviving spouse under most state laws of intestate succession.

d. Property held in JT will not be subject to the probate process. In contrast, the decedent's share of CP may be subject to probate. Some CP states no longer require a probate if the property is left to the surviving spouse or if, because of intestacy, the surviving spouse will receive the property by the laws of intestate succession.

It is important to make two observations regarding item 2c: First, some states, such as New York, recognize an agreement between the spouses declaring that specified property is held in joint tenancy "for convenience only;" and second, Arizona, Idaho, Nevada, and Washington have enacted statutes that allow the designation "community property with right of survivorship." This results in the property being treated like joint tenancy. The decedent spouse's will does not control disposition, and the property transfers to the surviving spouse by operation of law, meaning there is no need for probate.

Legal Versus Beneficial Interests: Introduction to the Trust

Usually, the owner of property has all the rights to possess and enjoy it; however, these interests can be divided so one party has just the "bare legal title" and is responsible for preserving and managing property for the benefit of another, and the other is entitled to enjoy the property in specified ways. The former holds the *legal interest* while the latter holds a *beneficial interest*, also called an *equitable interest*, in the property. Trusts are the most common legal arrangement to employ this division.

There are three major parties to the trust: trustor, trustee, and beneficiary. The *trustor*, also called *grantor*, *creator*, or *settlor*, is the person who creates the trust, and whose property is used to *fund* the trust. The property held in a trust is called the *principal*, but also the *corpus,* the *res* (Latin for things), or the *trust estate*. The *trustee* is the person, persons, or entity (e.g., bank trust department) who takes legal title to the trust property and manages the trust estate. Usually the trust instrument names an initial trustee and several alternates. The trust *beneficiary* is the person or persons who are named to enjoy beneficial interest in the trust. Placing property in a trust is called *funding* the trust. Funding is accomplished by transferring title of the property into the name of the trustee. Figure 2-1 illustrates the relationship between the parties to the trust.

A trust can be *living* or *inter vivos*, meaning it is funded during the life of the trustor, or it can be *testamentary*, to take effect at the trustor's death with the funding mechanism being the probate process. A testamentary trust is one created by the trustor's will. An example of the provisions of a testamentary trust can be found in Chapter 3, Exhibit 3-3.

EXAMPLE 2 - 19. On November 23, 1996, trustor Harold Stuart transferred 1,000 shares of ABC stock in trust to Uncle Jay as trustee, with the income payable to Harold's son, Chet, for 11 years, after which the corpus of the trust reverts to Harold. Jay receives only legal title which would probably read, "Jay Stuart, as trustee of the Chet Stuart Trust, dated 11/23/96." Jay is responsible for managing the property during the term of the trust. He can sell the stock and buy other investments in his name, as trustee, but he may not use trust assets for his own benefit, and he is required to distribute all income to Chet, the income beneficiary. Chet has a beneficial interest, that is, an estate for years in the income of the trust.

FIGURE 2 - 1   The Parties to a Trust

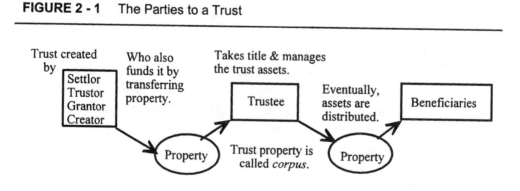

Reasons for creating trusts. Clients may wish to include trusts in their estate plans for five principal reasons: to provide for multiple beneficiaries, to manage their property if they become incapacitated, to protect beneficiaries from themselves and others, to avoid probate, and to avoid or reduce transfer taxes. Since these factors are discussed in detail in numerous sections of the text, the following commentary will be brief.

First, clients may wish to *leave their property to more than one person*, either at the same time or successively, over a period of time, and may need an arrangement that will fairly protect each beneficiary's individual property rights.

> EXAMPLE 2 - 20. After his death, Constantine wants to let his second wife enjoy the use of his property for the rest of her life. After her death, Constantine wants the income from his property to be payable to the children of his first marriage until they reach age 30, at which time he wants them to receive the principal outright. By executing a trust, Constantine can appoint a responsible trustee (even his second wife, if both of them are comfortable with the arrangement) to manage the property for what may turn out to be a very long time.

A transfer into a trust is sometimes called a *split interest* transfer, because it divides rights to the corpus into two or more interests, usually an income interest for a specified period of years or for the beneficiary's life, and a "remainder" interest in the principal. Remainder interests will be described shortly and income versus principal interests will be covered a little later.

Second, clients may create trusts to *manage their property if they become incapacitated*. If, due to injury or old age, a person becomes unable to manage his or her property, who will do so? On petition, a court will appoint someone to manage the estate of a disabled person. Depending on the jurisdiction, the court-appointed caretaker is called a *conservator* (i.e., one charged with "conserving" the disabled person's assets) or a *guardian* (i.e., one "guarding" the person's interests). Some states use the term guardian only for minors and use the term conservator for adults (the person being cared for is called the *conservatee*). Other states use guardian whether the person cared for is a minor or an adult. In either case, the person caring for the estate must make annual reports to the court and, depending on the circumstances, may have to get court approval for certain expenditures or to sell certain assets.

> EXAMPLE 2 - 21. Several years ago, Linda Smith created a *revocable living trust*, changing the title of all her property to read "Linda Smith, trustee of the Linda Smith Revocable Living Trust, dated March 19, 1998." The terms of the trust provide that if Linda becomes incapacitated during her lifetime, her brother Tom will become successor trustee. Linda has taken steps to avoid expensive court procedures to determine who should be appointed guardian or conservator of her

property if she becomes incapacitated before death. The trust has the added benefit of allowing Linda's estate to avoid probate when she dies.

Third, clients may wish to create trusts to *protect beneficiaries from themselves and others*.[8] As we will see in the next chapter, trust documents typically contain provisions restricting use of the property by beneficiaries. For example, trust instruments often provide that the trustee's discretion will determine the amount and timing of distributions to beneficiaries. In addition, they often prohibit any beneficiary from pledging his or her interest in the trust property as collateral for a loan. Many other restrictions can be included.

Fourth, a trust that is funded during the trustor's lifetime allows the property that is placed in the trust to *avoid the probate process*. Trusts funded while the trustor is alive are called *living trusts*. Trusts can also be funded through the probate process, either by means of a *pour-over will* (a will that has a previously established trust as its primary beneficiary) or by means of a *testamentary trust* (a trust is incorporated within the body of the will). The probate process, and various means of avoiding probate, are discussed in more detail in Chapter 10.

Fifth, clients may wish to use trusts to *avoid or reduce taxes*. On the inside front cover of the textbook is a table that shows the amount that can be passed tax-free (meaning without the payment of gift or estate taxes). Note that for the year 2002 the applicable exclusion amount (i.e., the tax-free amount) is $1,000,000. In general, the applicable exclusion amount has little relevance when property is transferred from one spouse to the other because there is a 100% marital deduction, but it is very important when property passes to other family members, e.g., to the children. A fair amount of estate planning revolves around using the two applicable exclusion amounts, one for each parent, while keeping the couple's combined estate intact for as long as either of them is alive. This is usually accomplished by holding in trust, for the benefit of the surviving spouse, the estate of the first spouse to die, with the children named as the remaindermen. By doing this, the trust estate is not merged with the surviving spouse's estate, and both spouses' applicable exclusion amounts are used. This text will have a great deal to say about tax planning using trusts after examining the taxation of gifts, estates, trusts, and beneficiaries in Chapters 5 through 7.

Power of Appointment

In arranging property transfers into trust or otherwise, clients can add considerable flexibility to their estate plans by granting a power of appointment. A *power of appointment* is a power to name someone to receive a beneficial interest in property. The grantor of the power is called the *donor*. The person receiving the power is called the *holder* or *donee*. The parties to whom the holder may appoint (i.e., give) property by *exercising* the power are called the *permissible appointees*, and the parties whom the holder actually appoints are called the *appointees*. In addition, the persons who receive the property if the holder permits the power to *lapse* (i.e., does not exercise the power within the permitted period) are called the *takers in default*. In some cases, the holder of a power of appointment can *release* the power by formally relinquishing the right to exercise the power.

Depending on how it is written, a power of appointment can be exercisable either during the lifetime of the holder or at his or her death, or both during lifetime and at death. If exercisable during lifetime it is exercisable either sometime during the holder's entire lifetime, or only for a stated period. A *testamentary* power is only exercisable at the holder's death, usually by a provision in the holder's will. The broadest powers allow the holder to exercise both during lifetime and at death.

> EXAMPLE 2 - 22. Assume that Dona grants Harold a power of appointment over her 100 shares of ABC stock, permitting Harold to appoint the stock to Anna, Bobby, or Carol, and designating Terry as the taker in default should Harold fail to appoint the stock within 90 days. Shortly thereafter, Harold appoints Bobby to receive the stock. Dona was the donor, Harold was the holder (of the power), Anna, Bobby, and Carol were the permissible appointees, and Bobby was the actual appointee (of the stock). Terry, the taker in default, didn't get to "take" because the holder did not permit the power to lapse.

Powers of appointment are most often established within the framework of a trust. Figure 2-2 illustrates the relationship between the parties involved in the power of appointment.

FIGURE 2 - 2   The Parties to a Power of Appointment

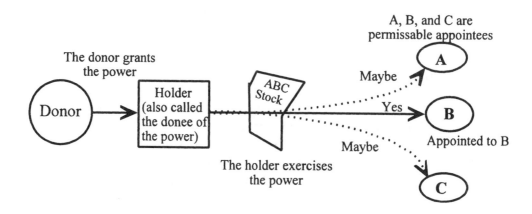

Comparing the relationship between the parties to a power of appointment with the parties to a trust, the donor of the power is usually the trustor. The holder is commonly the trustee but may also be one or more beneficiaries or a trusted friend of the trustor. The permissible appointees are usually the trust's beneficiaries. Trustee powers of appointment may be over trust income, principal, or both income and principal. Trustees may also be granted the power to *distribute income* among a group of beneficiaries, which is referred to as "sprinkling the income" of the trust. Where the trustee has this discretion, the trust is referred to as a "sprinkling trust." Almost humorously (we estate planners are always looking for a good laugh), the term "spray" is sometimes used to describe a trust clause that gives the trustee discretion to *distribute principal* in different amounts among permissible beneficiaries. Trust powers of appointment are extremely important estate planning tools and will be discussed frequently in this book.

In the chapter on estate taxes, we will see that death taxes play an important role in the use of powers of appointment—so much so that we commonly classify two types of powers using Internal Revenue Code classifications. Under the Code, a power of appointment is either a *general* power of appointment or a *non-general* power of appointment, also called a *limited* or *special* power of appointment. We'll define these terms in greater detail when we start working on estate taxes, noting how the wording of a power can cause property to be included in the holder's estate, subjecting it to tax. The next example shows a common use of a power of appointment.

> EXAMPLE 2 - 23. Charles, a single parent, died recently, and his will placed some of his property in trust for the benefit of his children. A bank is named trustee and is given a non-general power of appointment over the corpus. The bank has, among other things, discretion to distribute corpus to the children in accordance with their needs "for their proper support, health, and education." This year, the trustee has distributed $6,000 to one son and $4,000 to a daughter to pay their college tuition.

Powers of appointment can add great flexibility to a person's estate plan by enabling someone to direct trust dispositions after taking into account changes in circumstances that occur long after the person's death. According to common law, property subject to a power of appointment is not considered legally owned by the holder, rather, the holder is treated as merely a proxy for the donor. However, when it comes to federal estate and gift tax law, some powers cause the holder to be treated as if he or she owned the property, at least to the extent that the holder has control over the property. We take up the matter of general and limited powers later in the text.

Present Versus Future Interests and Vested Versus Contingent Interests

A beneficial interest in property may be classified as a present interest or a future interest, depending on whether the owner has the immediate right to possess or enjoy the property. We will see later that this distinction is of great importance in connection with the $10,000 annual gift tax exclusion.

An owner of a *present interest* has an immediate right to possess or enjoy the property while an owner of a *future interest* does not, because the latter's right to possess or enjoy the property is delayed, either by a specific period of time or until the happening of a future event. The most common types of future interests are reversions and remainders. A *reversion* is a future interest in property that is retained by the transferor after the transferor transfers to another some interest in the property. The reversion will become a present interest of the transferor, or the transferor's estate, at the termination of all interests that were transferred, i.e., at some point in time the donor will get the property back.

EXAMPLE 2 - 24. Jerry transfers property, in trust, to Eve for her life. The trust document was silent as to what should happen to the property after Eve's death. By not designating a remainderman, Jerry has retained a reversion, also called a reversionary interest. The trust property will belong to Jerry, if he is still alive when Eve dies, otherwise, it will belong to his estate (the interest will pass according to his estate plan).

Technically, a *remainder* is the right to use, possess, and enjoy property after all prior owners' interests end, and all interests must have been created at the same time by a single document. It is a type of future interest held by someone other than the transferor and it will become a present interest when all other interests have ended. The preceding definition of remainder is unnecessarily technical for our purposes, because most remainders in estate planning are quite simple. In estate planning, remainders usually arise in the context of trusts, where the remainderman is entitled to the remaining trust assets at the termination of the trust. In many, if not most, trust situations, the remaindermen are the settlors' children or grandchildren, who will receive the remainder at the death of both settlors (usually a married couple) who are likely to have retained joint life estates in a revocable trust. In some of these estate plans, the trust changes at the death of one spouse into several trusts, including one or more irrevocable trusts. Where multiple trusts are formed at the death of one spouse, the survivor usually has a life estate in all the trusts, even any that are irrevocable, and the children wait as remaindermen until the surviving spouse dies.

EXAMPLE 2 - 25. George irrevocably transfers property to Sally for her life, then to John or his estate. John's future interest in the property is a remainder. It is not a reversion because it does not return to George.

A *vested remainder* is a remainder that is non-forfeitable; it is a remainder whose possession and enjoyment are delayed *only by time*, and is not dependent on the happening (or not happening) of any future event.

EXAMPLE 2 - 26. With regard to the transfer by George in the previous example, John's remainder is vested. Nothing prevents him or his estate from receiving possession, except the passage of time. Morbidly but accurately speaking, eventually Sally will die.

A *contingent remainder* is a remainder that is not vested; that is, it is a remainder whose possession and enjoyment are dependent on the happening of a future event, not on just the passage of time.

EXAMPLE 2 - 27. Catherine transfers property to Flo for her life, then outright in fee simple to Jason, if alive, otherwise to Chris, if alive, and if not, then it reverts to Catherine. Jason and Chris each have a contingent remainder interest in the property and Catherine has a contingent reversionary interest. If Jason outlives Flo, the property is his; Chris is next in line if Jason doesn't make it. Finally, Catherine, or her estate, will get the property back if neither Jason nor Chris lives.

Totten Trusts. The *Totten trust* is not really a trust at all, but rather is a bank account that is payable to another on the death of the account owner. It got its names from a case in which the court decided in favor of the designated other person, over the claim of the decedent's executor. This mechanism of transferring a bank account at the death of the owner is recognized in most, but not all, states. Title is likely to read, "Jane Smith, in trust for Michael Smith," or "Jane Smith, payable on her death to Michael Smith." In either case, Michael's interest does not vest until Jane dies. Indeed, in spite of the use of the words, "in trust for," there is no trustee and neither Jane nor the financial institution has a fiduciary responsibility to Michael. Jane may withdraw all the funds or she may change title without Michael ever knowing that the account existed. Once Jane dies, Michael would be able to claim the account by presenting a certified death certificate.

A few more examples, presented in the context of common transfer devices, should help to clarify the distinctions discussed above.

EXAMPLE 2 - 28. When Gary died, his will created a trust funded with his entire estate. The terms of the trust give income to his wife, Joan, for her life. At Joan's death, the trust terminates and the property passes outright in fee to Gary's son Max, if still alive, otherwise to the Salvation Army. At Gary's death, Joan received a present interest called a life estate in the income, and Max and the Salvation Army each received a future interest, called a contingent remainder. Max and the Salvation Army share something in common; only one of the interests can ever become a present interest since an event will occur which will defeat one or the other interest. Max's interest will cease if he predeceases Joan. The Salvation Army's interest will cease if Max survives Joan. Therefore, both have contingent remainder interests because possession is dependent on the happening of a future event, not on just the mere passage of time.

EXAMPLE 2 - 29. Sam left property in trust, giving his wife, June, income for life with the remainder going to Sam's son, Kurt, or Kurt's estate. Kurt has a vested remainder in the property. Although initially a future interest, it is certain that it will become a present interest someday; it cannot be defeated. Only the passage of time keeps Kurt's interest from being a present interest. Of course, Kurt may not be alive to enjoy the property, but the beneficiaries of his estate will.

We have seen that the transfer of property in trust results in a division into two interests, with the trustee receiving the legal interest and the beneficiaries receiving the beneficial interests. In addition, transfers into trust typically result in a second type of division of interests when the beneficial interests are split among two or more beneficiaries. Ordinarily, one group of beneficiaries, called the *income beneficiaries,* receives a life estate or estate for years in the trust income, while the other group, called the *remaindermen*, receives the remainder at the termination of the income interests. The many reasons for splitting beneficial interests into a life estate, or into an estate for years and a remainder, will be explained in later chapters. At present, the reader should simply be aware of the interest-splitting nature of the trust. You should recognize that, at the time of the transfer into the trust, the life estate and estate for years are usually, but not always, present vested interests; the remainder is a future interest, either vested or contingent.

Mathematics of Remainders, Reversions, and Income Interests

The previous section described the nature of remainders, reversions, life estates, and interests for years. These concepts are important to understanding later chapters, because many common estate planning techniques require their creation.

Up to now, the description of these interests has been qualitative rather than quantitative. Estate planning is inherently "numbers oriented" for two principal reasons. First, estate planning decisions often have a sizable impact on *family wealth*, and clients want to discuss that effect with the planner. Second, property transfer decisions often have *tax consequences* that must be projected and evaluated.

Thus, it is important to understand the quantitative nature of remainders, reversions, life estates, and interests for years. This section demonstrates how they are calculated.

Overview of IRS valuation tables. The calculations can be most easily performed with the help of tables published by the Internal Revenue Service. The Service's complete "Alpha" volume runs 800 pages and costs about $32.[9] It includes six different tables and lists tens of thousands of values, most of which are derived from discount rates ranging from 2.2 percent to 26 percent, at two-tenths of one percentage point intervals. This conforms precisely with Internal Revenue Code valuation rules, often requiring the use of a current monthly discount rate that is equal to 120 percent of what is called the "applicable federal mid-term rate" (AFMR), which, in turn, is derived from the average market yield on U.S. Treasury obligations with maturities of three to nine years.[10] The rate, often referred to as the §7520 rate, has been rounded to the nearest two tenths of a percentage. Since these rates are published monthly by the Treasury Department, you do not have to figure out the rate. If a rate is given in an example or in problems at the end of the chapters, use that rate to determine the appropriate table to use (do not multiply it by 120% as that has already been done).

For obvious practical reasons, this text cannot include all pages from the IRS volume but reproduces many of the most useful ones. Appendix A includes part of IRS Tables "S," "B," "K," and " 90CM," the four most commonly used tables in estate planning. Table S and Table B are abridged to list a sampling of present value factors for discount rates of 6, 8, 10, and 12%. Table K gives adjustment factors where annuity payments are made other than annually. Tables S and B assume an annual payment, with the first payment at the end of the first year. We will be using the actuarial factors in examples and problems as they are especially helpful in the *planning* stage, when estimates are useful in calculating the values of life estates, remainders, and the like. Table 90CM is a one-page mortality table, useful for valuing interests that are contingent on survival.

The following series of examples will illustrate the use of these four tables for the valuation of four basic property interests: remainders, reversions, annuities for life, and annuities for a *term certain*. The discussion makes it clear that the choice of table for a particular problem depends in part on whether the interest to be valued is predicated on the fact that someone will be paid either all income or a fixed annuity (1) for a fixed number of years, or (2) for life. All examples will assume, unless otherwise stated, that the appropriate rate is 10%, payments are annual, and that the first payment is at the end of the first year.

Valuations predicated on income for term certain: IRS Table B. Each of the first four examples show the value of an income interest that is for a *fixed period of time*, also called a *term certain*.

Valuation of income for term certain. We use IRS Table B to determine the value of a beneficiary's income interest for a term certain. The term is usually given as a certain number of years.

EXAMPLE 2 - 30. Today Dana creates an irrevocable trust, transferring $200,000 in property to the trustee. The trustee is required to distribute annually all income earned from the property to Harry (or his heirs) for a period of ten years. Then, the trust terminates, and all trust principal will be distributed to Stephen (or his heirs). The current value of Harry's ten-year annuity for a term certain is calculated using Table B (10%) as follows: the income interest factor for 10 years is 0.614457, thus the current value of Harry's income interest is $122,891 [$200,000 * 0.614457].

Valuation of a vested remainder after income for a term certain. Similarly, IRS Table B allows us to determine what portion of the property's total value should be allocated to a beneficiary's vested remainder interest that follows someone else's income interest for a definite period of time (i.e., after the "term certain").

EXAMPLE 2 - 31. Continuing as in the previous example, the current value of Stephen's vested remainder interest can be calculated starting with the same table. The remainder factor found in Table B (10%) corresponding to 10 years is 0.385543. Thus, the present value of his vested remainder interest is $77,109 [$200,000 * 0.385543].

In the previous two examples, since Harry and Stephen's interests represent the only two interests in the trust assets, it is logical that the sum of their initial values should total $200,000, the initial value of the trust principal. And for the same reason, it is also logical that the sum of the two table values should add up to one. Consequently, each table value can be determined in a slightly different way. If one value is known, the other can be determined by simply subtracting the known value from 1.0. Thus, the table value for Stephen's interest, 0.385543, could have been calculated by subtracting the table value for Harry's interest, 0.614457, from the number 1.0; or, the remainder value could have been determined by subtracting the value of the income interest from the value of the whole trust (e.g., $200,000 - $122,891 = $77,109).

Valuation of a reversion. In determining the value of a reversionary interest, one takes the same steps as if it were a remainder interest.

> EXAMPLE 2 - 32. Revising the terms of the trust in the above ongoing example, assume that, at the end of 10 years, the trust will terminate and trust principal will be distributed back to the trustor, Dana (or her heirs). The initial value of Dana's *reversion*, $77,109, is exactly equal to the value of Stephen's remainder.

Valuation of a remainder (after term certain) contingent on survival. A remainder after a term certain that is contingent on the remainderman's survival of the term is calculated by multiplying the value of the vested remainder by the probability of the remainderman being alive at the end of the trust. IRS Mortality Table, 90CM, reprinted in Appendix A, shows the number of people expected to be living at each age based on statistics for the 1990 census. For example, out of 100,000 people born alive (age 0 = birth), only 95,373 of them are expected to be alive at age 40. Calculating the probability of a person age X surviving to age Y is determined by dividing the number of people alive at age Y by the number alive at age X. Thus, the probability of a newborn reaching age of 40 is 0.95373 [95,373 ÷ 100,000].

> EXAMPLE 2 - 33. Revising the facts again in this ongoing example, assume that Stephen is currently age 40, that his remainder is contingent on his surviving the ten-year period, and that if he fails to survive, the trust principal will pass to someone else. Using Table 90CM, the probability of Stephen surviving to age 50 is calculated by dividing 92,370 (the number alive at age 50) by 95,373 (the number alive at age 40), resulting in the quotient 0.96851. Thus, the value of Stephen's *contingent remainder* is $74,681 [0.96851 * $77,109].

Valuation of an annuity for a term certain. Now, consider a new example in which the annual annuity payment for a term certain is known.

> EXAMPLE 2 - 34. A trust provides for an annual distribution to Brett of $4,000 per year for 15 years, with the first payment to be made exactly one year after the trust is established. The current value of Brett's 15-year annuity interest is calculated in the following manner: Using IRS Table B (10%), the annuity value corresponding to 15 years is 7.6061. Thus, the current value of Brett's annuity interest is $30,424 [$4,000 x 7.6061]. The values in the annuity column are simply the present value factors for an annuity of $1 for a set period of time.

All the calculations in the above examples involve either an income interest or an annuity for a fixed number of years. The next section deals with examples involving a different inherent property interest: an income interest or an annuity for life.

Valuations predicated on an income interest for life: IRS Table S. Each of the next three examples demonstrates the calculation of the value of an income interest that is for someone's lifetime. For these calculations, we must use IRS Table S for the appropriate interest rate (see Appendix A).

Valuation of a life estate. IRS Table S indicates what portion of a property's total value is reflected in the value of a beneficiary's income or annuity interest for life. The regulations do not allow the use of Table S where the person with the measuring life (e.g., the person with a life estate) is terminally ill at the time the interest is being valued. The regulations define terminal illness as "an incurable illness or other deteriorating physical condition . . . if there is at least a 50 percent probability that the individual will die within one year." However, if the person actually lives 18 months or longer, there is a presumption that the person was not terminally ill, unless the contrary is established by clear and convincing evidence.[11] In the examples that follow, unless stated to the contrary, we will assume that the person was not terminally ill, and that Table S can be used to value the interests.

EXAMPLE 2 - 35. This year Martha creates a trust and funds it with assets that have a value of $100,000. The trust provides Charles, age 50, with a life estate. At Charles's death, distribution of the remainder is to be made to Samuel (or his heirs). Using IRS Table S (10%), the current value of Charles's life estate is calculated as follows: the "life estate" factor corresponding to age 50 is 0.87963. Thus, the current value of Charles's life estate interest is $87,963 [$100,000 x 0.87963].

Valuation of vested remainder after life estate. Similarly, IRS Table S indicates what portion of a trust's total value should be allocated to a beneficiary's vested remainder after the termination of an annuity for life.

EXAMPLE 2 - 36. Continuing the previous example, the current value of Samuel's remainder interest is determined from the same table. For 10%, the "remainder" value corresponding to age 50 is 0.12037. Thus the current value of Samuel's vested remainder interest is $12,037 [$100,000 x 0.12037].

Similar to the earlier discussion, since Charles's and Samuel's interests represent the only two interests in the trust assets, it is logical that the sum of their current values should total $100,000, the current total value of the trust principal. And again, for the same reason, the sum of the two table values adds up to one. Finally, we can determine each of the table values by subtracting the known table value from 1.0.

Valuation of reversion after life estate. As with reversions after an income interest or an annuity interest for a term certain, reversions after a life estate are calculated in exactly the same manner as remainders.

Valuation of annuity for life. Now consider a different example in which the annuity payment is fixed as a specific dollar amount.

EXAMPLE 2 - 37. Muhammad, age 40, is the beneficiary of a testamentary trust which is required to pay him $10,000 per year for life, with the first payment to be made in exactly one year. Again, using IRS Table S (10%), the "annuity" value corresponding to age 40 is 9.3589.[12] Thus, the current value of this life estate is $93,589 [$10,000 * 9.3589]. If the payments were to be made monthly (instead of annually) with the first payment at the end of the first month, we would use Table K as well. The factor from Table K for a monthly payment, 10% rate, is 1.0450, hence the value would be $97,801 [$93,589 * 1.0450].

These IRS tables will be used to value property interests in several sections of the text, covering such estate planning techniques as annual exclusion gifts (Chapter 7), a minor's income trusts (Chapter 13), private annuities (Chapter 14), and charitable remainder trusts (Chapter 14).

OVERVIEW OF GOALS IN ESTATE PLANNING

Finally, let's summarize the major goals of estate planning. These goals, outlined below, are described in detail in Chapter 9 as an overview of the specific techniques detailed in Chapters 10 through 18.

1. Nonfinancial Goals
   a. Caring for future dependents
   b. Accomplishing fair and proper distribution of property.
   c. Attaining privacy in the property transfer process
   d. Attaining speed in the property transfer process
   e. Maintaining control over assets
2. Financial Goals
   a. Non-tax financial goals
      i. Minimizing non-tax estate transfer costs.
      ii. Maintaining a satisfactory standard of living.
      iii. Ensuring proper disposition by careful drafting.
      iv. Preserving business value.
      v. Attaining lifetime and postmortem flexibility.
      vi. Maximizing benefits for the surviving spouse.
   b. Tax-saving goals
      i. Income tax-saving goals
         (1) Obtaining a stepped-up basis.
         (2) Shifting income to a lower bracket taxpayer.
         (3) Deferring recognition of income.
      ii. Transfer tax-saving goals and planning
         (1) Reducing the estate tax value.
         (2) Freezing the estate tax value.
         (3) Leveraging the use of exclusions, exemptions, and credits.
         (4) Delaying payment of the transfer tax.
         (5) Minimizing the generation-skipping transfer tax.

The next chapter will apply many of the concepts introduced in this chapter to describe the provisions of the major documents used in the property transfer process.

IMPORTANT CONCEPTS AND TERMS COVERED IN THIS CHAPTER

Estate
Property
Probate estate
Gross estate
Taxable estate
Transfer
Assignment
Transferor and Transferee
Legal interest
Beneficial interest
Transfer
Outright gift
Complete (transfer)
Irrevocable (transfer)
Incomplete (transfer)
Revocable (transfer)
Interest in property
Partially complete (transfer)
Sale
Consideration
Gift
Bargain sale
Inter vivos
Instrument
Beneficiary
Donee
Donor
Decedent
Will
Testamentary
Executed
Testator
Trust
Intestate
Testate
Partially intestate
Probate
Personal representative
Fiduciary
Executor

Administrator
Heir
Devisee
Legatee
Legacy
Issue
Descendant
Specific bequest
Ademption
General bequest
Pecuniary bequest
Residuary bequest
Residue
Class gift
Abatement
Disclaimer
Life insurance
Insured
Term life insurance
Level term life insurance
Cash surrender value
Cash value life insurance
Unified transfer tax
Gift tax
Death tax
Inheritance tax
Estate tax
Generation-skipping
   transfer tax
Fee simple
Life estate
Measuring life
Interest for years
Leasehold
Real property
Personal property
Tangible personal property
Intangible personal property
Chose in action
Concurrent ownership

Joint interest
Joint tenancy
Interest by the entirety
Tenants in common
Community property
Separate property
Trust
Trustor, grantor, creator
   or settlor
Trust principal or corpus
Trustee
Trust beneficiary
Living trust
Testamentary trust
   or trust-will
Totten trust
Power of appointment
Donor or creator (of a power)
Holder or donee (of a power)
Permissible appointee
Appointee
Exercise (a power)
Release (a power)
Lapse (of a power)
Taker in default
Present interest
Future interest
Reversion
Remainder
Vested remainder
Contingent remainder
Income beneficiary
Remainderman

QUERIES ANSWERED:

1. Since Florida is a "pick-up tax" state, its death taxes equal the federal state death tax credit of $195,800. Thus, for a $5 million taxable estate, the total taxes in Florida would be $1,905,000 [$195,800 + $1,709,200].

2. The bicycle would be community property because, like Texas and Idaho, Louisiana treats income from separate property as community property.

QUESTIONS AND PROBLEMS

1. Describe four different meanings of the concept "estate."

2. (a) Contrast a legal interest from a beneficial interest. (b) Why might a person want to transfer such interests in the same property to different individuals, rather than outright to one person?

3. Kasner "sells" a $10,000 car to his son for $4,000. Technically speaking, is this a sale or a gift? Why?

4. (a) What is probate? (b) What types of assets are subject to probate administration? (c) What types of assets are not subject to probate? (d) Does having a will avoid probate?

5. Contrast the insured, the owner, and the beneficiary of a life insurance policy.

6. At the moment of Lou's death, a life insurance policy was in force in the amount of $250,000, which had a cash surrender value of $60,000. Lou had the power under the policy to change the beneficiary. After Lou's death, his wife, Mary, received a check from the insurance company.

   a. Identify by name the: (1) Insured, (2) Beneficiary, and (3) Owner.
   b. Did Lou's wife receive $60,000, $190,000, $250,000, or $310,000? Why?
   c. What is the likely purpose of a policy such as this one?

7. Contact an insurance agent to obtain premium information for a $100,000 policy given the following information:

	Insured (one-year term policy)	age	policy	annual premium
a	Male, average health	20	1 year term	
b	same: three-pack smoker	20	1 year term	
c	Female, average health	20	1 year term	
d	same: three-pack smoker	20	1 year term	
e	Male, average health	40	1 year term	
f	same: three-pack smoker	40	1 year term	
g	Female, average health	40	1 year term	
h	same: three-pack smoker	40	1 year term	
i	Male, average health	60	1 year term	
j	same: three-pack smoker	60	1 year term	
k	Female, average health	60	1 year term	
l	same: three-pack smoker	60	1 year term	

	Insured (whole life/cash value)	age	policy	annual premium
a	Male, average health	20	WL	
b	same: three-pack smoker	20	WL	
c	Female, average health	20	WL	
d	same: three-pack smoker	20	WL	
e	Male, average health	40	WL	
f	same: three-pack smoker	40	WL	
g	Female, average health	40	WL	
h	same: three-pack smoker	40	WL	
i	Male, average health	60	WL	
j	same: three-pack smoker	60	WL	
k	Female, average health	60	WL	
l	same: three-pack smoker	60	WL	

8. (a) Why is a fee simple interest greater than a life estate or an interest for years? (b) Can you think of any way in which all three interests can be considered nearly equal?

9. Compare and contrast joint tenancy with tenants in common.

10. Beth tells you she has a property interest having all the following characteristics: concurrent ownership with two of her friends, automatic right of succession to ownership, and all three owners are allowed to own unequal percentages. Why must she be mistaken? Explain.

11. Define community property and separate property.

12. Compare community property with joint tenancy.

13. Cindy and Dennis are residents of a community property state. Consider these transactions year by year:

1999 - They married. They each owned a car and some furnishings. Cindy was finishing college.
2000 - Dennis was working full-time. Cindy had a baby girl and works full time as a homemaker. Dennis's dad gave him 10,000 shares of IBM stock in honor of the addition to the family.
2001 - Cindy inherited a duplex from her mother. It was worth $100,000. The executor quit claimed the property to her in her name alone. She collects the rent and places it in a joint tenancy account with Dennis. Although occasionally she cashes a rent check and buys an antique. They used a savings account that had as its source Dennis's salary as down-payment on a house. He had been putting money in it for seven years.
2002 - Dennis used income from the dividends on his IBM stock to purchase 300 shares of Exxon stock, taking title in his own name.
2003 - They filed for divorce.
Characterize their property in the order first mentioned and state how it should be split. Where it would make a difference whether the state of domicile was California or Texas, explain why.

14. Briefly answer this question:"Why do estate planners recommend trusts?"

15. Use the internet [http://www.ca-probate.com/wills.htm]to find copies of the wills of some famous people. (a) Review the copy of David Packard's will. He was a co-founder of Hewlett-Packard. Who or what will receive the residue of his estate? What is the estimated worth of his estate? (b) Review several other wills, notice the pattern. Find something of interest in one of the wills to share with the class.

16. If you are the holder of a power of appointment, how might you be assisting in the donor's estate plan?

17. Contrast a present interest with a future interest.

18. (a) If Cheryl named Paul today to be the remainder beneficiary of her probate avoiding trust, is Paul's interest most likely a present or future interest? (b) If future, is it most likely to be a vested or contingent one? (c) If contingent, when will it vest, if ever? Explain each answer carefully.

19. When he was 65, Edward transferred his home worth $300,000 to an irrevocable trust. By the terms of the trust, Edward has the right to remain in the house for a period of four years. At the end of that period, the trust will terminate and the house will be distributed to his son, Kevin, age 44 (or to Kevin's estate). (a) At a rate of 8%, calculate the current value of Kevin's remainder interest. (Note: this would be a vested gift to Kevin). (b) Recalculate Kevin's remainder interest if it was contingent on Edward surviving the four-year income period (i.e., he kept a contingent reversion).

20. On her 75th birthday, Gertrude transfers her home worth $700,000 to an irrevocable trust. The trust terms provide that Gertrude has the right to remain in the house for a period of 10 years. At the end of that period, the trust will terminate and the house will be distributed to her issue. (a) At a rate of 8%, calculate the current value of the remainder interest. (Note: this would be a vested gift to the issue). (b) Recalculate the remainder interest if it was contingent on Gertrude surviving the income period.

21. Roberta created an irrevocable trust using investment assets worth $700,000. Her friend Mo, age 65, will receive all the income, payable annually for his lifetime. At his death, all principal will pass outright to Roberta's niece Sherrie (or to her estate). (a) At a rate of 6%, calculate the current value of Mo's and Sherrie's property interests. (b) Also, calculate the values at 12%. (c) Comment on the influence of a higher discount rate.

22. Melissa created an irrevocable trust using investment assets worth $300,000. The rate for calculating split gifts was 6%. Melissa's friend Murray, age 50, will receive all the income, payable annually for his lifetime. At his death, all principal will pass outright to another friend, Marci, age 30, or to Marci's estate. (a) calculate the current value of Murray's and Marci's property interests. (b) Calculate the values if Murray was 60 and Marci was 80 when Melissa established the trust. (c) Comment on the influence of the parties' ages on the values.

23. Keri, age 30, is the beneficiary of an annuity that will pay her $300 per week for life. (a) At 6%, calculate the current value of this life income interest. (Remember to adjust for the weekly payment.) (b) At 12%?

24. Dako, age 80, is beneficiary of a trust which will pay him $2,000 per month for life. (Remember to adjust for the monthly payment.) (a) At 8%, calculate the current value of this life income interest. (b) At 10%?

25. What happens if George places property in an irrevocable trust with terms that give his brother James a life estate, but are silent as to what should happen to the trust property when James dies?

26. Discussion Case: Stanley Pigeon was found dead in his luxury New York condominium apartment. All indications are that he died of natural causes. An envelope was found in his desk with a note reading, "open after my death, Stanley Pigeon." A note inside read as follows:

> *If you are reading this, I must be dead. If there is anything left after paying my debts, I want my friend Lee to have all my tangible personal property, including my XYZ stock held at Bixby Brokerage. I give my real estate in New Jersey to my friend Fred. I give $10,000 from my First National Bank account to my card buddies, Marcia, Pam, and Phil. I want my son Mark to have $5,000 as that should be enough for him. There aren't any other kids, so don't look for them. Anything else that I own should be given to my friend Susan. She can handle getting my stuff to the right people.*
>
> *Signed on 6/30/03 by Stanley Pigeon*

As it turns out, Macia predeceased Stanley. There were hardly any debts. The Bixby Brokerage account was held in joint tenancy with Julie, Stanley's mother. Although not very well-off financially, Julie does not want the Bixby account or anything else from the estate other than some photo albums. It appears true that there are no children other than Mark, and he has no issue. State law for transferring property where there is no will, or where the will fails to cover all the estate, typically gives all the estate in this order: first to a surviving spouse, next, if no spouse, to issue, and if there are no issue, then to the decedent's parent(s). The only relatives are Stanley's mother and his son.

At this point in your study of estate planning you are not expected to know the answers to all the questions raised here. The goal is to get you to think about the issues and suggest possible, reasonable solutions. (a) What is likely to happen to the XYZ stock? Is there a problem with it being referred to as tangible personal property? How should it have been categorized? (b) What is the term for the part of the estate left to Marcia? Given that she predeceased Stanley, what happens to this part, i.e., who is likely to get it? (c) Given Marcia's death, if the court appoints Fred to represent the estate, what is the correct term for his position? What are the proceedings that will eventually sort out this estate called? (d) What is the term for a bequest stated in a specific monetary amount? Is it clear whether Marcia, Pam, and Phil were left $10,000 each or was the intent for Marcia, Pam, and Phil to split $10,000 three ways? How should a court resolve this? Would statements that Stanley made around the card table be relevant evidence, e.g., "you can all go on a real nice cruise in my memory after I'm gone"? Does it matter whether there is $40,000 in the account or just $12,000? If the court concludes the intent was to give just $10,000 shared by the card players, should Pam and Phil each get $5,000 or $3,333? What should Stanley have written to make it clear one way or another? (e) If the law is as stated above, who would get Marcia's share of the estate? Might the statement about Mark just getting $5,000 be considered a disinheritance clause as to anything above that amount? If that was Stanley's intent, how could he have made it clearer? (f) If Julie does not want the Bixby account and would like Lee to have the XYZ stock what should she do? If the court has ruled that Mark is disinherited insofar as anything other than the $5,000, what will happen to the property that Julie refuses to accept? Would it be better for Julie to take the property and then give it away?

ANSWERS TO QUESTIONS AND PROBLEMS *(odd numbered only)*

1. Four different meanings of *estate*:

   a. Estate: A quantity of wealth or property
   b. Net Estate: Property owned reduced by the estate owner's liabilities
   c. Probate Estate: Property passing through the probate process
   d. Gross Estate and Taxable Estate: Property subject to death taxation

3. Kasner has undertaken a *bargain sale*, which is a hybrid of gift and sale but is commonly classified as a gift. While a sale is a transfer in exchange for full consideration, a gift (and a bargain sale) is a transfer for *less than* full and adequate consideration.

5. *Insured:* the subject of the insurance; that is, the one whose death triggers payment of the proceeds.
   Owner: usually the possessor of both legal and beneficial interests in the policy. Commonly held "incidents" of ownership include the right to dividends, to surrender the policy, to pledge the policy, and to change the beneficiary.
   Beneficiary: the person who is named to receive the proceeds.

7. Insurance Table: compare various ages & premiums; smoker/non-smoker premiums; and term/whole life premiums.

9. Joint tenancy (JT) and tenancy in common (TIC) contrasted:

   Differences:
   a. JT: equal ownership; TIC: can be unequal.
   b. JT: automatic survivorship; TIC: no automatic survivorship.

   Similarities:
   a. both held by two or more persons.
   b. both involve an undivided right to possess the property.

11. *Community property* is any property acquired by the efforts of either spouse during the marriage while domiciled in a community property state. It also includes any property which by agreement of the couple they convert from separate into community. Some states require said conversion to be in writing. Excluded is property acquired by gift, devise, bequest or inheritance and the income from separate property. Texas, Idaho, and Louisiana treat income from separate property as community property.
Separate property is defined as any property that is not community property, i.e., all property acquired by a person not during marriage, or during marriage in a common law state, and property acquired during a marriage by gift, devise, bequest or inheritance, or often, income earned on property so acquired.

13. Dennis and Cindy's Property: Each would own his or her own car as separate property, assuming it was fully paid for when they married, if not, then it might have some community property character to the extent salary was used to make the payments. The IBM shares, as inherited property, are Dennis's separate property. Likewise, the inherited duplex belongs to Cindy. The California rule for income is that it keeps the character of the property that produces it, hence rent from the duplex would be Cindy's separate property and the IBM dividends would be Dennis's separate property as would anything purchased with them (i.e., the antiques belong to Cindy and the Exxon stock belongs to Dennis). The Texas rule is that income during marriage is community property regardless of source, hence the antiques and Exxon would be community property and be split equally. The joint bank account is equally owned (Cindy transmuted her separate property rent into jointly owned property), and joint tenancy property is equally owned. However, in a divorce situation, the court might consider its source and award it to Cindy. The house came from a mixed source: part of the money was there from Dennis's earnings before the marriage and that portion has a separate property character; after marriage, the salary had a community character. Any paying down of the mortgage from his salary would create equity that was community. Some states allow a tracing of the consideration that went into paying for the house and would find it to be partially the separate property of Dennis and partially their community property.

15. Internet: (a) A charitable foundation named after Mr. Packard and his wife: the David and Lucile Packard Foundation. Header above the will estimates the value of the estate to be $7 billion. (b) Obviously what different people find interesting will vary.

17. The owner of a present interest has an immediate right to possess or enjoy the property, while the owner of a future interest does not, because possession or enjoyment is delayed, solely in time, or until the happening of a future event.

19. Edward: Note that Kevin's age is not relevant to the calculations. (a) Using Table B, 8%, four years: $300,000 * .735030 = $220,509. (b) contingent: $220,509 * 73186/79519 = $202,947.

21. Roberta: (a) Table S, 6%, life estate for 65-year-old. $700,000 * .58291 = $408,037 as Mo's interest. Sherrie's interest is $700,000 * $.41709 = $291,963. This is of course the same as $700,000 - $408,037. (b) Same, except using 12%: $700,000 * .77305 = $541,135 for Mo & $158,865 for Sherrie. (c) As the discount rate increases, the value of the remainder interest drops and the value of the life estate rises. Since the rate is the assumed rate of return, the higher it is, the greater the value of the income interest with a corresponding decrease in the value of the remainder interest. For a term certain, the remainder value is determined by the fraction one, as the numerator, and a denominator of the quantity one plus the discount rate, raised to the power of the number of years, e.g., with a six percent rate, the remainder value at the end of ten years is $1/(1.06)^{10}$ which equals 0.558395, whereas with a 12% rate the value of a remainder after ten years, expressed as $1/(1.12)^{10}$, giving us a factor of 0.321973 for the remainder interest.

23. Keri: (a) Table S, 6%, age 30, weekly annuity: $300 * 52 * 15.078 * 1.0291 = $242,062. (b) same @ 12%: $300 * 52 * 8.1274 * 1.0577 = $134,103.

25. One rule of gift law is that when a transfer is made, what is not given away must have been kept, hence George must have kept a reversionary interest

ENDNOTES

1. Completed by the Uniform Law Commissioners in 1983 and amended in 1986. As of November 2002, the Uniform Transfer to Minors Act had been adopted by all states except South Carolina and Vermont. However, the Vermont legislature is considering adoption. See *http://www.nccusl.org/index.htm.*

2. IRS Reg. 20.2031-1(b).

3. The National Conference of Commissioners on Uniform State Laws, Uniform Determination of Death Act, Approved and Recommended for Enactment in All the States (1980). As of 2002, adopted in 40 states and the District of Columbia, Puerto Rico, and the Virgin Islands. See *http://www.nccusl.org/index.htm.*

4. For the Uniform Probate Code's six exceptions. See UPC § 2-606.

5. See the discussion in Chapter 12.

6. UMPA, completed by the Uniform Law Commissioners in 1983, has been adopted, as of 2000, only by Wisconsin. See *http://www.nccusl.org/ index.htm.*

7. Wisconsin Statutes, § 766.31 (4). See *http://www.legis.state.wi.us/rsb/ Statutes.html,* click on the link to Chapter 766, *"Property rights of married persons; marital property."*

8. Somewhat humorously, Edward Schlesinger has described the trust as capable of protecting assets from "inability, disability, creditors, and predators."

9. The Alpha volume, Publication 1457, can be purchased from the U.S. Government Printing Office. These tables are also available in the form of easy-to-use computer software. For example, *Tiger Tables,* available from Lawrence P. Katzenstein at (314) 231-2800, computes all Alpha values plus many other factors, including unitrust remainder factors for from one to ten lives, probabilities of survival, annuity adjustment factors for annuities due, the value of an income beneficiary's interest in a trust with a 5 and 5 power, and commutation tables.

10. See IRC § 7520 (see App. A) and § 1274(d)(1). Current AFMR rates are released regularly by popular income tax report publishers, such as Prentice Hall and Commerce Clearing House (CCH). CCH reports the monthly changes in the "New Developments" volume of the *Standard Federal Tax Reports.* In that volume, see "New Matters....Cumulative index to 200_ developments," under IRC § 7872, under "Applicable Federal Rates Established for (Month),

200_ Rulings" section. CCH also reports these rates in the "Cumulative Index" of its *Federal Estate and Gift Tax Reports*, again under Code §7872. Look for "Applicable Federal Rates..." Monthly news releases are usually issued by the IRS one to two weeks prior to the beginning of the current month and are published in the report of the first week of that month. The AFMR rates also appear under the heading "Credit Markets" in Section C of the *Wall Street Journal* between the 17th and the 22nd of each month.

11.   IRC §§ 1.7520-3(b)(3); 20.7520-3(b)(3)(i); 25.7520-3(b)(3).

12.   Students of finance may notice that traditional financial mathematics can *not* derive this number. It is based not only on the time value of money, but also on life expectancy.

Constraints in Planning

CHAPTER 3

Estate Planning Documents

OVERVIEW

Estate planning seeks to facilitate the transfer of the client's wealth as efficiently as possible. Efficiency in estate transfer usually requires the preparation of one or more formal documents that will be accepted by the authorities who ultimately authorize and make the transfers. For example, the proper preparation and execution of a will are essential to the efficient disposal of any probate property. The will must be drafted clearly to ensure that the testator's desires are correctly expressed, and it must be signed and witnessed according to law so the probate judge will accept it as the guide for the title transfer process.

This chapter, the first of two introducing the principles of property transfer, explores the documents commonly used in the process of transferring wealth. Specifically, it examines the creation of four common property transfer mechanisms: joint tenancy, contract, the will, and the trust. The next chapter examines the actual process of property transfer whether guided by these documents or by the law of intestate succession.

Generally, property transfers are regulated by state, not federal, law. State laws in this area vary, but there are definite patterns we can discuss. For instance, more than half the states have adopted all or a significant part of the Uniform Probate Code (UPC) and, therefore, have many property distribution laws in common. The UPC was introduced in 1966, partly in answer to the criticisms that probate procedures in the United States were too costly, too time-consuming, and too complicated. Idaho was the first state to adopt it in 1972. To read Idaho's version of the UPC and to see which other states have adopted it, visit the web site maintained by University of Pennsylvania Law School, *http://www. law.upenn.edu/bll/ulc/ulc_frame.htm.*[1] In presenting the material in this and the next chapter, we will often refer to the laws of those states that have adopted the UPC, especially in three major areas: will execution, intestate succession, and probate administration.

JOINT TENANCY ARRANGEMENTS

The acquisition of title in joint tenancy is ordinarily a simple matter, requiring the completion of one or two preprinted forms. Transfers can be done with or without the aid of an attorney. Deeds to transfer real property into joint .tenancy are usually drafted by an attorney, although in some states the job may be done by a real estate agent, by the title company, or by an escrow agent. Similarly, when two or more people open an account such as a stock brokerage account or bank account, the professionals involved generally will ask whether title will be in joint tenancy or tenancy in common.

Later in the text the reader will learn several significant disadvantages to taking title in joint tenancy. Deciding whether joint tenancy is appropriate is not always clear; however, our focus at this point is on how title in joint tenancy is taken, not whether it should be taken.

PROPERTY TRANSFER BY CONTRACT

A significant part of a person's estate plan may be transferred pursuant to a contract. Examples of property that is transferred after the death of the owner (or the insured) are life insurance, pension and profit sharing plans, and individual retirement accounts (IRAs).

Life Insurance

Wealth derived from life insurance comes in two forms: the policy itself and the policy death proceeds. The policy may be transferred while the insured is alive.

After the insured's death, the proceeds are paid by the insurance company to the designated beneficiaries.

During the policy application process, the applicant designates the beneficiary who will receive the proceeds at the insured's death. Once the policy is issued, up until the death of the insured, the policy owner can easily change the beneficiary designation by giving the company written notice using its beneficiary designation form. Very rarely, there is an irrevocable beneficiary designation, i.e., the designation cannot be changed without the consent of the beneficiary or someone besides the owner. Such irrevocable designations may be the result of a divorce settlement or as a condition of a personal loan. Once certain conditions are met, the owner-insured may be free to change beneficiaries, e.g., once the children are grown or the loan is repaid.

Arranging the transfer of title to a life insurance policy itself from one owner to another is simple. All that is required is the completion of a short assignment form that can be obtained from the insurance company.

Pension and Profit Sharing Plans

Pension and profit sharing plans are contracts between the employee-client and the employer. Ordinarily, the employer requests that the employee fill out a written form designating the beneficiary, the party who will be entitled to any benefits paid after the employee's death. Thus, the actual process of beneficiary designation for most retirement plans is simple and straightforward.

WILLS AND TRUSTS

In contrast with the above transfer arrangements, the document preparation process for the will and the trust are not simple, for two reasons. First, unlike joint tenancy and written contracts, the will and the trust are capable of disposing of nearly all the client's estate, as well as providing for the care of the client's minor children. Thus, the will and the trust will inevitably be more complicated. Second, unlike insurance and retirement contracts, which are drafted by the insurer or the employer, wills and trusts are semi-custom, drafted to fit each client's unique circumstances. The responsibility for choosing the terms for the lawyer to draft into the will and trust falls to each individual.

The following material presents an overview of will and trust construction. Major topics include the legal requirements for a valid will, common will provisions, essential characteristics of trusts, and common provisions of the living trust and the testamentary trust.

THE WILL

Many people die leaving no formal directions as to the disposal of their property, who should manage their estate, or who should care for their minor children. In such cases, the state seeks to make these decisions equitably and sensibly, applying statutory rules to the surviving family situation. However, state law may conflict with the wishes of a decedent, whether unstated or even as recollected by the survivors. Compared to a properly planned estate, intestacy can result in unsuitable property disposition and higher taxes. Individuals can avoid an undesirable outcome by expressing, while still alive, their desires in a legally binding document that serves as a set of directions to be followed by those who survive. The will is the most common formal document for this purpose.

A will is a legally enforceable document that expresses the testator's directions for disposing of his or her probate property at death. In some states, wills can be oral, but laws usually greatly restrict the scope of their ability to dispose of wealth, generally limiting the application of oral wills to personal property worth less than a modest amount, such as $2,000. In addition, the testator, on execution, is often required to be a member of the armed forces or in peril of death. Practically speaking, wills prepared in the estate planning process are written.

Who May Execute a Will

In most states, any individual 18 or older who is of sound mind may dispose of his or her property by will. The implications of this are twofold. First, individuals under age 18 cannot transfer property by will unless they are emancipated minors. A minor is emancipated if a court, after a petition and hearing, determines that the child should be free from parental control and given the status of an adult for contractual and other legal matters. In most states, a person under age 18 is considered an adult if he or she is married. Thus, in most instances, a deceased minor's property will pass according to the laws of intestate succession, which will usually result in the property passing to the child's parents or if the parents are also deceased, then to siblings. Second, a will can be denied probate if it can be established that the testator, at date of execution of the will, lacked testamentary capacity, was subject to undue influence or fraud, or acted mistakenly. These four concepts are discussed next.

Testamentary capacity. *Testamentary capacity* concerns the testator's mental ability to execute a legally enforceable will. A testator has testamentary capacity if he or she possesses each of the following three attributes:

1. Sufficient mental capacity to understand the nature of the act being undertaken (executing a will).
2. Sufficient mental capacity to understand and recollect the general nature of his or her property.
3. Sufficient mental capacity to remember and understand his or her relationship to the persons who have natural claims on his or her bounty and whose interests are affected by the provisions of the will.

Essentially, in addition to being an adult, testators must know that they are executing a will, they must be aware of what they own, and they must be cognizant of family and friends. On its face, this test seems quite severe; strictly construed, it might prevent many older testators from executing a valid will. However, mere age and physical disability do not negate testamentary capacity. Probate courts have admitted to probate wills executed by individuals who were forgetful, absent-minded, alcoholic, or behaving peculiarly—even persons declared mentally incompetent, insane, under conservatorship, or who committed suicide shortly after executing a will. Indeed, the threshold is lower than that for contractual capacity, which may be as it should, given that the formation of a contract requires the ability to negotiate with another person, whereas executing a will does not. Nonetheless, failure to meet one or more of these three requirements will result in a finding of insufficient testamentary capacity. Examples of sufficient evidence of incompetence include senility, ongoing hallucinations, irrational beliefs, irrational behavior, and totally groundless beliefs about the testator's spouse, children, or other family members. Generally, the outcome hinges on whether, at the time the will was executed, the three-prong test was met. Appellate courts are reluctant to "set aside" a will. They have reversed many cases where the jurors found that the testator lacked testamentary capacity, especially those cases where the testator disinherited immediate family members in favor of newly found friends. As a consequence, affirmed findings of testamentary incapacity are very rare.

Anticipating the possibility of a will contest based on lack of testamentary capacity, some attorneys videotape the will execution of a testator who may have questionable capacity, believing that the taping will make capacity more credible. Others believe that videotaping can enhance the success of a contest, reasoning that testators may look terrible on the screen (especially if they are shown lying in a hospital bed), and that the taping constitutes evidence that even the will drafting attorney lacked confidence in the testator's capacity.

Undue influence. A will executed by a testator who was subject to undue influence by someone who stands to benefit, directly or indirectly, may also be denied probate. Undue influence is influence by a confidante that has the effect of overcoming the testator's free will. Examples include improper persuasion and psychological domination, as when "Snake Oil Sam," the smooth-talking newcomer, makes a romantic play for the 92-year-old widow, "encouraging" her to disinherit her children and leave her entire estate to him.

Winning an undue influence case can be difficult. These cases often involve a person with a weak, unsound, or impaired mind. Indeed, the family may not be aware of a new, less favorable will until after the testator is dead. An element of fraud or deceit is a common thread in these cases. Juries tend to side with family members against outsiders whom they see as meddling non-relatives. Thus, a jury is likely to "rewrite" a will in keeping with what the jurors think is fair to the family. But, unless the evidence of undue influence is clearly in the record, this type of verdict is likely to be reversed on appeal.

Fraud. *Fraud* involves deception through false information. Some courts distinguish two types of fraud based on the action of the deceiver. *Fraud in the inducement* is where the testator is persuaded by lies of the wrongdoer to change his or her estate plan. For example, fraud exists if a niece tells her great-uncle she is penniless when, in fact, she is wealthy, or a daughter incorrectly tells her mother that her sister instigated a conservatorship proceeding, when actually they acted together. The other type is called *fraud in the execution*, where the person is deceived into signing a document not knowing that it is a will. An example would be obtaining a person's autograph on a blank sheet of paper, then, with the help of accomplices, placing will language above it and witness signatures below to create what appears to be a genuine will.

Mistake. Very rarely, a will can be successfully contested on the basis of a mistake. Examples include: (a) the testator leaves her estate to only one son, mistakenly believing that the other is wealthy; (b) the testator mistakenly leaves out an intended clause; or (c) the will mistakenly includes an unintended clause.

Ordinarily, a finding of lack of testamentary capacity will invalidate the entire will, while a finding of undue influence, fraud, or mistake might invalidate only those provisions that relate to the specific problem.

Statutory Requirements for Wills

Most states, including those that have adopted the Uniform Probate Code, recognize at least two types of wills, the *witnessed will* and the *holographic will*.

Witnessed will. Although state laws vary, a witnessed or *attested will* must meet the following three requirements:

1. It must be in writing (handwritten, typed, etc.).
2. The testator must sign the will in the presence of two witnesses (three in a few states).
3. The two witnesses must sign their names to the will, understanding that the instrument they sign is the testator's will. The main purpose of requiring witnesses is to prevent forgery and coercion of the testator.

Beneficiaries should not be witnesses to a will because that could imperil their right to receive some or all their bequest. In many states, a bequest to a witness is void, unless the witness is an heir. And in that case, the witness can take no more than his or her intestate share. In some other states, a beneficiary can witness the will, but if someone raises an undue influence challenge, the "interested witness" may take more than the intestate share only if he or she is able to rebut a statutory presumption that the bequest was procured by duress, menace, fraud, or undue influence. Inability to rebut this presumption might not totally invalidate the will, but it will probably invalidate some or all the bequest to that witness.

Holographic will. If a written will does not meet all the requirements for a witnessed will, in most states, including those adopting the UPC, it can still be admitted to probate if it meets the requirements for a holographic will. Typical state requirements for a holographic will are:

1. Signature is in the testator's handwriting.
2. All the "material provisions" of the will are in the testator's handwriting.

In the past, courts often refused to admit to probate holographic documents unless it was clear from reading just the handwritten portions that the document was the decedent's will. In determining what parts of the will must be in the testator's handwriting, some still follow the old rule, but many states now allow a preprinted will form to be treated as a holographic will so long as both the material provisions and the signature are in the decedent's own handwriting.[2] The material provisions are the dispositive ones (who gets what), the identity of the executor, the nomination of guardians, and the like.

Recently, the Uniform Probate Code added a section that allows a court to accept as testamentary documents instruments that do not meet the formal execution requirements of a witnessed will or the handwriting requirements of a holographic will. However, the proponent of the imperfectly executed will must establish by "clear and convincing evidence" that the writing being offered was intended by the decedent to be his or her will (or a codicil).[3] Clear and convincing evidence is a higher standard of proof than the usual civil case burden known as a preponderance of the evidence.

Contrasting witnessed and holographic wills. There are two major differences between the two sets of formal requirements: first, the witnessed will requires the performance of certain activities by two witnesses. In contrast, the holographic will may, but need not, be witnessed. Second, the holographic will requires that all material provisions of the will be in the testator's handwriting. In contrast, the witnessed will requires that only the testator and the witnesses' signatures be in the person's own hand, and even this may be unnecessary when a proper authorization is arranged. A testator can execute a will by directing another person to sign for him or her in the presence of the witnesses.[4] In this case, it may be a good idea to videotape the signing ceremony.

No Contest Clause

In the last few pages, we have described several technical requirements for a valid will including testamentary capacity, absence of undue influence, fraud, mistake, and certain specific execution requirements such as signatures by witnesses and the testator. Anticipating that dissatisfied persons may claim that one or more violations of these requirements have occurred, as a pretext for obtaining more of the estate, testators may insert in their will a "no contest" clause such as the one that follows:

> *I have purposely made no provisions herein for any other person or persons, other than as set forth in this will, and if any person contests this will, I revoke any share or interest given such person, and said share or interest shall be disposed of as though said person predeceased me without leaving issue.*

This usually, but not always, discourages will contests for several reasons. First, it will discourage only beneficiaries named in the will, not disinherited persons who stand to lose nothing by contesting. Second, beneficiaries may still wish to contest if they expect to gain considerably more than they will lose. Finally, in states that have adopted the UPC, such clauses are unenforceable if the contestant had probable cause for instituting the proceedings.[5] Perhaps most testators would desire this result anyway.

What situations tend to invite will contests? The most common are where the testator chooses to disinherit family members in favor of a friend, a charity, a spouse married shortly before death, or where a testator treats children unequally. If the testator is very old or is ailing physically or mentally, a contest is even more likely.

Will contests are infrequent, and successful contests are very uncommon. One study showed that fewer than three percent of wills offered for probate were challenged, and more than two-thirds of those challenges were unsuccessful. However, will contests may become more common for several reasons. As the general population continues to age, more elderly people of means will acquire "friends" who offer to assist them in their finances and work their way into the person's estate plan. A high divorce rate has increased the number of children of former marriages, a group that is less likely to get along with the surviving spouse of a later marriage. When any of these situations or factors apply to a particular client, attorneys should take special precautions in drafting and executing the will.

The Simple Will

Wills can be quite lengthy and complex, but this section focuses on a relatively simple will. A *simple will*, as it is generally called, is a will prepared for a family having a small, or even a modest estate, where death taxes are not a significant concern. We will cover estate taxes in Chapter 5; and you will see that we are in a period of transition. The amount that can pass tax-free (assuming the decedent has not made significant lifetime gifts) is increasing, growing from the pre-1998 figure of $600,000 to $3,500,000 in 2009. Complete repeal of the estate tax takes place in 2010. However a "sunset" provision repeals the repeal as of 2011. There is considerable agreement that Congress will not allow this provision to take effect, so the shape of post-2010 tax law is uncertain. The estate tax repeal may be made permanent or the tax-free amount may be set at a high level and indexed for inflation.

The simple will usually includes all the following: nominating an executor and, if there are minor children, a guardian; a waiver of the probate bond; and, in most cases, giving the testator's property to the spouse, if alive, otherwise to the children by right of representation.

Exhibit 3-1 presents a simple will that demonstrates the essential nature of this probate property transfer document. The reader is encouraged to study it carefully so that the analysis that follows is more readily understood.

EXHIBIT 3 - 1 Simple Will

WILL

OF

WILLARD THOMAS SMITH

I, Willard Thomas Smith, a resident of Mytown, Anystate, declare this to be my will. I revoke all prior Wills and Codicils.

EXHIBIT 3 - 1 Simple Will *continued*

First: Family and Guardian I am married to Sue L. Smith, referred to in this will as "my wife." I have three children, all from this marriage, whose names and birthdays are:

Kristi M. Smith	June 27, 1987
Heather L. Smith	April 19, 1989
Todd R. Smith	May 11, 1991

Reference to "my children" or to "my child," shall include children born later and children adopted by me. I have no deceased children.

If my wife does not survive me, and it is necessary to appoint a guardian, I appoint Curtis J. Quint guardian of the person and estate of each such minor child. If for any reason Curtis J. Quint does not act as guardian, I appoint Maria S. Cruise as guardian of the person and estate of each such minor child.

Second: Executor The executor shall serve as follows:

A. *Designation* I appoint my wife as my executor. If for any reason she does not so act, I appoint James A. Reliable to be my executor. If for any reason neither my wife nor James A. Reliable acts as executor, I appoint Third National Bank of Mytown to be my executor.

B. *Bond waiver* No bond, surety, or other security shall be required of my executor.

Third: Disposition of Property I make the following gifts of property:

A. *Tangible personal property* If my wife survives me by 30 days, I give her all my interest in our tangible personal property. If my wife does not survive me by 30 days, I give my tangible personal property to my issue, by right of representation, provided they survive me for that period. My executor shall consider their personal preferences in making the division. My executor has my permission to sell any of that property and distribute the proceeds to equalize the shares. My executor shall be discharged for all tangible personal property so given to any minor child if the child, or adult having the child's custody, gives a written receipt to my executor.

B. *Residue* If my wife survives me by 120 days, I give her the residue of my estate. If my wife does not survive me by 120 days, I give the residue to my issue, by right of representation, provided they survive me for that period. If neither my wife nor any of my descendants survives me by 120 days, I give the residue of my estate according to Anystate's laws of descent and distribution, one half as if I had died with no will on the last day of that 120-day period, and one half as if it were my wife's estate and she had died with no will on that last day.

C. *Taxes from residue* All death taxes imposed because of my death, as well as interest and penalties on those taxes, whether on property passing under this will or otherwise, shall be paid by my executor from the residue of my estate.

EXHIBIT 3 - 1 Simple Will *continued*

Fourth: Powers of Executor My executor shall have unrestricted powers, without court order, to settle my estate as this will provides. In addition, my executor shall have the following powers:

1. To make interim distributions of principal and income to those entitled to it.
2. To sell, exchange, mortgage, pledge, lease or assign any property belonging to my estate.
3. To continue operation of any business belonging to my estate.
4. To invest and reinvest any surplus money.

I have signed my name to this instrument on March 19, 2002, at Mytown, Anystate.

Willard Thomas Smith
_____
Willard Thomas Smith

Statement of Witnesses We, the undersigned the witnesses, on March 19, 2002, sign our names to this instrument, being first duly sworn, and do hereby declare to the undersigned authority that the testator signs and executes this instrument as his last will and that he signs it willingly (or willingly directs another to sign for him), and that each of us, in the presence and hearing of the testator, hereby signs this will as witness to the testator's signing, and that to the best of our knowledge the testator is eighteen years of age or older, of sound mind, and under no constraint or undue influence.

_____*John Meeks*_____   _____*Jennifer Jarrett*_____
1341 Park St., Little Town, Anystate   42 Short Rd., Little Town, Anystate

---

Analysis of the simple will. Let's analyze the major provisions of this will, section by section.

Will of Willard Thomas Smith. In this introductory paragraph, the testator "declares" the document to be his will, satisfying the legal requirement that there be evidence of testamentary intent.

A *codicil* is a separate written document that amends or revokes a will. It is executed if the testator wishes to make changes or additions to his or her will. It must meet all the legal requirements of a will, including subscription by witnesses, although in states that recognize holographic wills, a holographic codicil even to a witnessed will is acceptable if the codicil meets that state's requirements for a holographic will.

One of the more common methods of revoking a prior will is by executing a later will that declares such revocation, as is done in the Smith will. Revocation by "cancellation" with a "subsequent instrument," as it is termed, can also be undertaken in any other signed, witnessed statement. A will can also be revoked by a physical act, such as burning, tearing, canceling, or otherwise destroying it, when such is done by the testator with an intent to revoke.[6]

Revoking all prior wills and codicils eliminates the danger that provisions in prior wills that are inconsistent with the present will may cause confusion. Without a revocation clause, needless litigation might arise over whether the provisions in two or more wills are inconsistent. For example, in one state supreme court case, a decedent-testator had written two "last" wills within three weeks. The first simply left "a tract of land" to a friend. The second contained no revocation clause and left "all my effects" to siblings Y and Z. The court permitted a trial to determine whether the first will should be construed along with the second, reasoning that they were not necessarily inconsistent because the testator could have used the word "effects" to mean only personal property.[7] If the testator's intent was to leave everything to Y and Z, inclusion of a revocation clause would have assured this result. If the intent was to preserve the gift of the land to the friend, then that should have been clearly stated in the second will.

First: Family and guardian. Naming all members of the immediate family assists the personal representative in finding relatives and locating assets.

Including *after born children* in the will prevents a child born after the execution of the will from inheriting under the laws of intestate succession, a consequence which would probably conflict with the testator's intent.

A child who is still a minor when both parents are dead will have a *guardian* of the person and of the estate appointed by the probate court. A guardian of the person is responsible for the minor child's care, custody, control, and education, while a guardian of the child's estate is responsible for managing the minor child's property. A testator's nomination carries great weight and is usually followed; however, the probate judge does have the power to appoint someone else if there is good cause for not following the nomination. Nominating an alternate guardian increases the likelihood that the testator's preferences will be followed.

Second: Executor. Similar to the nomination of a guardian, the nomination of an executor and an alternate executor is helpful to the probate court in its selection process. The court will follow the recommendation of the testator unless there is good cause to do otherwise.

Unless the bond is waived in the will, the executor is required to post a *fiduciary bond*. A bonding company, for a fee, insures the estate assets against losses caused by the personal representative's breach of fiduciary obligations, whether the breach is the result of negligence or willful misconduct. The will can waive the bond requirement. The testator may consider a bond unnecessary because it results in additional expense to the estate, and/or because the executor is a highly trusted member of the testator's family, such as the surviving spouse, and/or is also one of the major beneficiaries of the estate. Ordinarily, the bond amount will be set by the court to be equal to the total value of the personal probate property plus one year's estimated income from all the probate property. The idea here is that the personal representative could run off with everything but the real property.

Third: Disposition of property. This simple will essentially leaves all property to the testator's spouse, if surviving, otherwise to the children. The contingent interest of the children is sometimes referred to as a "gift-over" to the children. The will distinguishes the tangible personal property from the residue, which consists of all other probate assets. Thus, the spouse must survive by 30 days to take tangible personal property and 120 days to take the residue. If the spouse does not survive the requisite time period, the property passes to the children who do so survive.

Inclusion of a survival requirement, such as 30 days or 120 days, reduces the likelihood that the death of both spouses in a common accident will result in subjecting some of the family property to two successive probates. This *survival clause*, as it is called, helps in situations not covered by the Uniform Simultaneous Death Act (USDA).

Enacted by every state, the USDA provides that when transfer of title to property depends on the order of deaths, and when no sufficient evidence exists that two people died other than simultaneously, the property of each is disposed of as if each had survived the other. Thus, in the case of a childless married couple, the husband's estate would pass to his blood relatives and the wife's estate would pass to her blood relatives. This statute is of limited value, however, because it does not avoid double probate when the order of deaths can in fact be established. In some states, if it can be established that one spouse survived the other, even only by seconds, then the USDA will not apply and, absent a survival clause, there will be a double probate of the property owned by the first spouse to die. Perhaps worse, all the property may ultimately pass to that spouse's in-laws, rather than the surviving relatives. Some states, including California, have legislated safeguards against inheritance by in-laws by requiring that the portion of the decedent's estate attributable to the predeceased spouse pass, in some circumstances, to the predeceased spouse's children, parents, or other kin.[8] The Uniform Probate Code requires a beneficiary of an estate to outlive the decedent by 120 hours or be deemed to have predeceased the decedent. This rule is not applied if it would cause the decedent's property to escheat (revert) to the state.

With regard to insurance on the life of a decedent, the USDA states that, in the event of an apparent simultaneous death of the insured and the beneficiary, the policy proceeds are to be distributed as if the insured survived the beneficiary. Thus, the proceeds will be paid to the contingent beneficiary, and if none, then to the owner's probate estate.

Section B of Article Three, covering the "residue," is called the *residuary clause*. Failure to include it in a will can result in partial intestacy. In a recent case, the attorney who had drafted the decedent's will admitted that he mistakenly omitted the residuary clause, but his notes showed that the decedent wanted the residue to go to a specific friend. The court would not allow admission of this evidence, ruling that extrinsic evidence is admissible to explain poorly drafted parts of a will, but cannot be used to put in parts that are missing.[9]

Disposing of estate property by differentiating the tangible personal property from the residue can speed up probate distribution and can often save income taxes. In the chapter on fiduciary income taxes, the concept of distributable net income, or DNI, is discussed. A *specific bequest* of property, such as when the testator specifies a bequest of the tangible personal property, prevents the distribution from being labeled DNI. This generates less taxable income to the distributees (often the spouse and/or children), and correspondingly more taxable income to the estate, which is (hopefully) in a lower rate bracket.

Instead of "tangible personal property," some wills ill-advisedly use the term "personal effects," which really means "tangible personal property, worn or carried about the person or having some intimate relation with the person." Since automobiles and some other property are not considered "personal effects," the broader term *tangible personal property* is preferred. Early distribution of this property also allows the executor to avoid the cost and trouble of storing it.

Distribution by *right of representation*, or *per stirpes* as it is also called, is a method of allocating a bequest of the decedent's property such that it follows the natural line of descent (e.g., the children of a predeceased child share that child's portion of the estate.)

The laws of intestate succession, also known as "laws of descent and distribution," vary somewhat from state to state. They spell out the priority of succession rights of the decedent's spouse and kin in the event of intestacy. In the event that his wife and all his descendants fail to survive him by 120 days, the testator has generously chosen to divide his property in halves, with one half going by intestate succession to his relatives and the other half going by intestate succession to his wife's relatives.

Fourth: Powers of executor. Granting explicit powers to the executor can eliminate the need to secure permission of the probate court to undertake certain administrative actions. Ordinarily, testators would like their executors to act without undue delay.

Signature clause and the statement of witnesses. Every state imposes formal requirements regarding the signing of the will by the testator and the role of the witnesses. The paragraph above the witnesses' signatures increases the likelihood of compliance with these formal requirements by explicitly stating them and having the witnesses, by their signatures, acknowledge that such were carried out. The last sentence above the signatures of the witnesses offers some additional evidence of the testator's capacity to execute a will. The Statement of Witnesses is also referred to as the *attestation clause*. When a will is signed and witnessed in the proper manner, such that it is a valid will, it is said to be executed.

Other aspects of the simple will. Simple wills are most commonly drafted by attorneys for clients with modest estates where death taxes are not a concern. For a married couple, a simple will is usually prepared for each spouse. In most cases, the dispositive clauses are almost identical. Thus, the husband's will leaves all to his wife, if she survives, otherwise to their children. And the wife's will leaves all to her husband, if he survives, otherwise to their children. Such simple wills are commonly called *reciprocal wills*, *mirror wills*, or *mutual wills*.

Occasionally, clients will want *contractual wills*, ones that cannot be revised once one of the parties (usually a spouse) dies. Sometimes these are done in the form of a single will for two people, called a *joint will,* although a joint will need not be contractual. Contractual wills are rare because most clients want the flexibility of being able to change an estate plan after one spouse dies. Joint wills should be avoided unless the clients really want a contractual will, because even if the clients did not intend the joint will to be irrevocable once one of the testators dies, a court may rule that this was the intent because there can be little other reason to create one will for two people.

Wills that are more complex are less likely to be reciprocal in content. Typically, they are prepared by attorneys specializing in estate planning to reflect the inherently different preferences and different financial and tax circumstances of the spouses. This text will highlight many of these differences in later chapters.

Where should the original copy of the will be kept? The client's safe deposit box makes good sense in those states (e.g., California) that do not seal boxes at the owner's death. In states where safe deposit boxes are sealed at the owner's death, access to the will is delayed until a state official can join the prospective executor in inventorying the contents of the box so as to ensure that the executor accounts for any jewelry, bearer bonds, and the like that might be there. Some attorneys recommend their own safe. Some people might view this as self-serving, since the executor will have to come to the attorney's office to take charge of the will, thus giving the attorney a good chance of serving as the probate attorney. However, since the testator selected that attorney to draft the estate plan, it would seem reasonable to select that attorney to handle the probate. Some attorneys simply recommend a secure, handy place in the client's home.

THE TRUST

The principal parties to a trust are the trustor, the trustee, and the beneficiary. As a legal arrangement, a trust is created by the trustor and divides and transfers interests in property between two or more people. Any interests or control over the trust not given to the beneficiaries are either retained by the trustor, granted to the trustee, or held by both.

A trust can take effect during the lifetime of the trustor, or it can take effect at the trustor's death. The former is called a *living* (or *inter vivos*) *trust*, while the latter is called a *testamentary trust* - a complex will that is also called a "trust-will." The testamentary trust document is covered later in the chapter.

At any given moment, a trust is either revocable and amendable, in which case the trustor is capable of voiding (canceling) or amending it, or it is irrevocable, that is, not voidable or amendable. A living trust usually contains specific language stating whether it is revocable or irrevocable. A revocable living trust usually, but not always, becomes irrevocable at the death of the trustor(s). Like the contents of most wills, the provisions of a testamentary trust can be amended or revoked before the testator's death by codicil, revocation, or destruction of the document. At the testator's death, a testamentary trust takes effect and becomes irrevocable since the only person capable of amending or revoking it, the testator, is, of course, permanently unavailable.

A trust usually contains two different legal types of property, principal and income. The *principal* of a trust is its invested wealth. Its size will fluctuate with changes in the market value, by additions (income or additional property), by charges (expenses or losses), and by distributions from it. In contrast with trust principal, the *income* of a trust is the return in money or property derived from use of the trust principal. Examples of income include cash dividends, rent, and interest. Trust income also has charges against it, most of which reflect expenses incurred in managing the trust property (e.g., insurance premiums and some portion of the trustee's fee). Any trust income not distributed to beneficiaries is said to be accumulated in the trust and is generally accounted for as retained income, not principal, unless the trust agreement requires that accumulated income be added to principal.

The accounting distinction between principal and income is particularly important, because most trusts contain provisions that bestow rights to principal and income to different beneficiaries. In the chapter on fiduciary income taxes, we will see that the distinction between principal and income will influence trust income taxation.

The beneficiaries of an irrevocable trust are usually either *income beneficiaries* (i.e., those having an interest in the income) or *principal beneficiaries* (for example, a remainderman who stands to receive principal outright when the trust terminates). These two types of beneficiaries may have conflicting or "adverse" interests, because the increased distributions to one will generally decrease the distributions to the other. For example, high-yield/low-growth stock would tend to benefit the income beneficiaries more than the remaindermen whereas low-yield/high-growth stock would favor the remaindermen more than the income beneficiaries.

The following material describes a living trust and a testamentary trust. Keep in mind that individual trusts vary greatly, so it is a stretch to call any trust used as an example here typical. These examples are merely to illustrate the basic form of each document. There are other ways of classifying trusts, especially in connection with tax planning. The chapters in Part 3 introduce several tax-saving trusts, including the bypass trust, the Crummey trust, and the QTIP trust.

Living Trust Instrument

A living trust is created by a document of agreement between the trustor (or settlor) and the trustee. Before we examine the actual instrument, let's compare and contrast the characteristics of a living trust with a will.

Similarities. The will and the living trust instrument are similar in three important ways. First, both serve as the guide to the disposition of property at death. Second, both have a fiduciary (the executor or the trustee) who is responsible for managing property for a period of time until the transfers can be completed. Third, both instruments are generally amendable and revocable, at least until the person creating the instrument dies. The will can nearly always be amended by a codicil, or revoked by its destruction or by execution of a later will that explicitly revokes earlier ones. One exception, of course, is the *contractual will*, which becomes irrevocable after the death or incapacity of the first co-testator. The living trust is either revocable or irrevocable. In most states, a trust must state that it is revocable, otherwise it becomes irrevocable upon execution. In the other states, the opposite rule is in effect, such that a trust is revocable unless stated to be irrevocable.

Differences. The will and the living trust instrument are different in three important ways. First, they dispose of a totally different set of property. A living trust instrument disposes of property owned by the trustee in trust for the trustor (decedent), while a will disposes of probate property owned by the decedent at death. Thus, with regard to property transfers, the living trust instrument and the will are mutually exclusive; property owned by the trustee is not probate property, while probate property is owned by the decedent, not the trustee. Of course, the decedent's will can transfer property, by way of the probate process, to the trustee of his or her living trust, or even to the trustee of a trust he or she did not create, such as one created by one's spouse. A will that transfers property to a trustee is called a *pour-over will,* because it scoops up property and "pours" it into an existing trust.

Second, with regard to choosing a fiduciary, a living trust instrument *appoints* a trustee whereas a will *nominates* an executor. A testamentary trust must nominate both an executor and a trustee. Since the trustor of a living trust is alive when the trustee is appointed, the trustor has control over the appointment. The trust instrument is a legal contract between the trustor and the trustee. On the other hand, the probate judge appoints the executor of a will after the testator's death. The judge may appoint someone other than the nominated executor for any number of reasons, including the nominee's inability to serve due to death, disability, or incompetence.

Third, while the formal execution requirements for writing a will are quite strict, the requirements for properly executing a trust instrument are simple to meet. In most cases, the trust document is simply dated and signed by the trustor and the trustee. Witnesses are not required. However some attorneys have the trustor's signature notarized to assure others of its validity, especially those who might have to rely on the document at a time when the trustor is incapacitated or deceased. Although the formalities surrounding the execution of a trust document are simpler than those for a will, the mental capacity necessary is set at a higher standard. The settlor must have contractual capacity. Given the nature of the trust document, this would be, in addition to testamentary capacity, the ability to understand and enter into a bilateral contractual agreement. In most states, one contesting a settlor's (or a testator's) capacity has the burden of proving the lack of capacity by "clear and convincing" evidence. This is a more difficult (i.e., higher) standard than the typical "preponderance" of evidence burden generally placed on the plaintiff in a civil case.

Exhibit 3-2 presents a fairly simple living trust. It is not designed to break into several irrevocable trusts at the trustor's death as some do in order to save estate taxes. We will discuss those later.

EXHIBIT 3 - 2 Living Trust Instrument

JOHN C. JONES
Revocable Living Trust

Dated March 19, 2002

TRUST AGREEMENT made March 19, 2002, between John C. Jones, as trustor, resident of Common County, Anystate, and John C. Jones, resident of Common County, Anystate, as trustee.

1. Trust property. The trustor has set aside and holds in trust the property described on Schedule One, attached to this instrument. The trustee agrees to hold such property and any later accepted property, in trust, under the terms and conditions provided herein.

2. Successor trustee. If John C. Jones for any reason ceases to act as trustee, his wife, Sarah E. Jones, shall serve as trustee. If Sarah E. Jones is unable or for any reason ceases to act as trustee, then First National Bank of Anytown shall serve as trustee.

3. Power to amend or revoke. The trustor reserves the right at any time to amend or revoke this trust, in whole or in part, by an instrument in writing signed by him and delivered during his lifetime to the trustee.

4. Operation of trust during trustor's lifetime. During the trustor's lifetime, the trustee shall administer and distribute the trust as follows:

a. Trust income. The trustee shall pay the net income to the trustor at convenient intervals but at least quarter-annually.

b. Trust principal. The trustee shall pay to the trustor from time to time such amounts of the principal of this trust as the trustor shall direct in writing or as the trustee deems advisable for the trustor's support and comfort.

5. Operation of trust after trustor's death. On the death of the trustor, the trust estate shall be held, administered, and distributed as follows:

a. Wife survives by four months. If the trustor's wife survives trustor by four months, the trustee shall distribute the entire trust estate to the trustee of her revocable trust, dated the same date as this trust, to be held and administered according to its terms. If said trust is no longer in existence, then distribution shall be to trustor's wife, free of trust.

b. Wife does not survive by four months. If the trustor's wife does not survive the trustor by four months and if no then-living child of the trustor is under age twenty-one, then the trustee shall divide the trust into as many equal shares as there are children of the trustor's then living and children of the trustor's then deceased with descendants then living. Each share set aside for a child then deceased with descendants then living shall be further divided into shares for such descendants, by right of representation. The trust estate shall be held, administered, and distributed in the manner described in subsections 5(b)(2)(a) and (b), below.

EXHIBIT 3 - 2 Living Trust Instrument *continued*

If neither the trustor's wife nor any of the trustor's descendants survive the trustor by four months, the trustee shall distribute the entire trust estate according to Anystate's laws of descent and distribution, one half as if the trustor had died with no will on the last day of the four-month period and one half as if it were the trustor's wife's estate and she had died with no will on the last day. If the trustor's wife does not survive the trustor by four months and if any then-living child of the trustor is under age twenty-one, then the trust estate shall be held, administered, and distributed as follows:

(1) *Any child under age twenty-one.* So long as any of the trustor's children are living who are under twenty-one, the trustee shall pay to or apply for the benefit of all the trustor's children as much of the net income and principal as the trustee in the trustee's discretion deems necessary for their proper support, health, and education, after taking into consideration, to the extent that the trustee considers advisable, the value of the trust assets, the relative needs, both present and future, of each of the beneficiaries, and their other income and resources made known to the trustee and reasonably available to meet beneficiary needs. The trustee may make distributions under this provision that benefit one or more beneficiaries to the exclusion of others. Any net income not distributed shall be accumulated and added to principal.

(2) *Youngest child reaches age twenty-one.* When the youngest of the trustor's then-living children reaches age twenty-one, the trustee shall divide the trust into as many equal shares as there are children of the trustor's then living and deceased children who left issue. Each share set aside for the issue of a deceased child shall be further divided into shares, by right of representation, for such descendants. Each such share shall be distributed, or retained in trust, as hereafter provided.

(*a*) Each share set aside for a descendant shall be distributed to that descendant free of trust when he or she reaches age twenty-one.

(*b*) Each share set aside for a descendant who has not then reached age twenty-one shall be retained in trust. The trustee shall pay to or for the benefit of that descendant as much of the income and principal of the trust as the trustee, in the trustee's discretion, considers appropriate for that descendant's support, health, and education. When that descendant reaches age twenty-one, the descendant's share shall be distributed to that descendant, free of trust. If that descendant dies before receiving distribution of that descendant's entire share, the undistributed balance of that descendant's share shall be distributed, free of trust, to that descendant's then-living descendants, by right of representation, or if there are none, to the trustor's then-living descendants, by right of representation. The share of a descendant for whom there exists a trust created by this instrument, shall augment that descendant's trust.

6. Restriction against assignment, etc. No interest in the principal or income of this trust shall be anticipated, assigned, encumbered, or subject to any creditor's claim or to legal process before its actual receipt by the beneficiary.

EXHIBIT 3 - 2 Living Trust Instrument *continued*

---

7. Perpetuities saving. Any trust created by this will that has not terminated sooner shall terminate twenty-one years after the death of the last survivor of the class composed of my wife and those of my descendants living at my death.

8. Powers of trustee. To carry out the purposes of this trust, the trustee is vested with the following powers with respect to the trust estate and any part of it, in addition to those powers now or hereafter conferred by law:

a. To continue to hold any property, including shares of the trustee's own stock, and to operate at the risk of the trust estate any business that the trustee receives or acquires under the trust as long as the trustee deems advisable.

b. To manage, control, grant options on, sell (for cash or on deferred payments), convey, exchange, partition, divide, improve, and repair trust property.

c. To lease trust property for terms within or beyond the term of the trust and for any purpose, including exploration for and removal of gas, oil, and other minerals and to enter into community oil leases, pooling, and unitization agreements.

d. To borrow money and to encumber or hypothecate trust property by mortgage, deed of trust, pledge, or otherwise.

e. To invest and reinvest the trust estate in every kind of property, real, personal, or mixed, and every kind of investment, specifically including, but not by way of limitation, corporate obligations of every kind, stocks (preferred or common), shares of investment trusts, investment companies and mutual funds, and mortgage participations, which persons of prudence, discretion, and intelligence acquire for their own account, and any common trust fund administered by the trustee.

f. In any case in which the trustee is required, pursuant to the provisions of the trust, to divide any trust property into parts or shares for the purpose of distribution, or otherwise, the trustee is authorized, in the trustee's absolute discretion, to make the division and distribution partly in kind and partly in money, and for this purpose to make such sales of the trust property as the trustee may deem necessary on such terms and conditions as the trustee shall see fit.

IN WITNESS THEREOF this instrument has been executed as of the date set forth on the first page of this instrument.

John C. Jones
John C. Jones, Trustor

John C. Jones
John C. Jones, Trustee

[Notarization of the signatures would appear here]

Analysis of the living trust instrument. Let's examine the major provisions of this living trust instrument section by section.

Trust agreement. A trust is, in effect, a contract or agreement between two parties, the trustor and the trustee. Both sides agree to perform certain tasks: among other things, the trustor agrees to deliver property described in Schedule One (not shown) to the trustee, and the trustee agrees to hold, administer, and distribute the trust property in keeping with the terms of the trust.

In this living trust instrument, the trustor names himself to be initial trustee and names alternate successor trustees to take over when he resigns, becomes incapable of performing because of incapacity, or death. In other words, he might want to travel without worrying about managing the trust property or he might become too ill to manage it.

1. Trust property. The instrument specifies that additional assets may be put in trust in the future, even after the trustor's death. For example, a trustor's will can be directed to "pour over" probate property into a trust.

2. Successor trustee. Since the trust instrument states the trustee's name in the opening paragraph, this section needs only name successor trustees. It is usual to name one or more of the remaindermen, if they are adults, as successors, since the remaindermen have a vested interest in managing and transferring the property efficiently. Sometimes the children are named as successor trustees, with the requirement that they have reached a certain age (e.g., twenty-five), in order to serve. Naming a bank, or other corporate entity, as a successor trustee virtually ensures that an experienced trustee will be available to serve for the duration of the trust. Some corporate fiduciaries will not assume the position of trustee unless the corpus is some minimum value. Where a corporate trustee is being considered, a meeting with the trust officers should be arranged to decrease the likelihood that the position will be refused later.

3. Power to amend or revoke. This trust can be amended or revoked by a written document signed by the trustor and delivered to the trustee. An amendment is similar to a codicil to a will but without the strict formal execution requirements.

4. Operation of trust during trustor's lifetime. During the trustor's lifetime, the trustee is required to pay to the trustor all income at least quarterly and any principal as requested. The reader will notice the wording assumes the trustor and the trustee are different parties. However, as mentioned above, most living trusts name the trustor as the initial trustee. Nevertheless, this paragraph is used in anticipation that, at some point, a successor trustee will take over the management of the trust.

5. Operation of trust after trustor's death. This section is substantially longer than the Disposition of Property section in the simple will. It provides for several alternative outcomes depending on who survives. First, the trust terminates if the trustor's spouse survives the trustor by four months, with the result that all trust property will pass to her revocable trust or, if it is no longer in existence, then outright to her.

Second, if the trustor's spouse does not survive by four months and all the trustor's children are over age twenty-one, the trust will terminate and distribute all assets free of trust to the children. However, if one or more of the trustor's living children are younger than twenty-one, the trust continues as one trust. The trustee is instructed to collectively use trust principal and income to provide for all the children's support, education, and other reasonable needs. Thus, the trustee has a limited power of appointment over the entire trust income and principal, with all living descendants named as permissible appointees. Then, when the youngest child reaches twenty-one, the trust is divided into equal shares, one for each child then living, and one for each deceased child for whom there are living descendants. The trust directs distribution to the younger generations by right of representation, also called "traditional per stirpes," a concept more fully explained in a later chapter. Each share is then distributed outright to each descendant when he or she reaches age twenty-one. Thus, at the time the corpus is split, each child and any other descendant beneficiary who is at least age twenty-one will receive his or her share.

Third, if the trustor's spouse fails to survive the trustor by four months and no living child is under age twenty-one, the trust may or may not terminate, depending on whether there are underage descendants of deceased children. In any event, however, the trust estate is immediately divided into shares, and each child immediately receives his or her share. The balance of the trust corpus (held for these underage descendants of deceased children) will be administered in a manner (described below) quite similar to the way it is administered for a living child under age twenty-one. As each of these descendants reaches age twenty-one, he or she will receive an outright distribution of his or her share. Accordingly, the trust will terminate when the youngest living descendant of deceased children reaches age twenty-one.

Finally, if the trustor is survived by neither a spouse nor descendants, the trust terminates and the trust property passes by intestate succession, with one half to the trustor's relatives and the other half to the trustor's spouse's relatives. The laws of intestate succession are covered in the next chapter.

The above disposition, using a trustee, has much to recommend it over the will's provisions making outright gifts to the minor children, which requires a court-appointed guardian.

6. Restriction against assignment. This is an example of a *spendthrift clause.* Without it, the laws of many states would allow trust beneficiaries to transfer and encumber their interests in the trust property, and would enable the beneficiaries' creditors to seize trust assets to satisfy their claims. For example, beneficiaries may not borrow money secured by their share of trust property, sell a future interest in it, or devise it. A spendthrift clause restricts such transfers. However, it only protects trust property while held by the trustee, not after it has been transferred outright to a beneficiary.

7. Perpetuities saving. This clause is included to prevent a contingent gift from being ruled invalid because it violates a law found in almost all states that requires interests to vest within some reasonable time after the transfer. This law is called the rule against perpetuities.

8. Powers of trustee. Since a trustee is likely to manage trust property for a considerably longer period than an executor is likely to manage an estate, the powers granted to the trustee are usually stated in more detail than those granted in a will to an executor. In addition to these powers, both the executor and trustee automatically have other implicit powers derived from statutory law and from case law, unless the document specifically prohibits such powers. For example, trustees have the power to defend against claims brought against the trust property, whether that power is specifically granted in the document.

This living trust is uncomplicated primarily because it does not attempt to save estate taxes. If the other spouse survives the trustor spouse by four months, all corpus will pass to the surviving spouse's revocable trust or outright to her. Like the simple will, it is created for families with modest estates, for whom death tax planning is not a significant concern. We will introduce a more complicated tax-saving living trust in the two chapters that deal with estate plans for the wealthy, where estate taxes are a concern.

THE TESTAMENTARY TRUST

The testamentary trust, or trust-will, is the third principal document of property disposition commonly prepared by attorneys in the estate planning process. In essence, a testamentary trust is actually one type of will; it serves as the guiding document for the distribution of the testator-trustor's probate property at death. In addition, it disposes of some, or all, of the probate property to the trustee of a trust that is newly created according to trust terms that are set forth as part of the will. This trust takes effect after the testator's death at the end of the probate process. The actual creation of the trust, and the funding mechanism, is the order for distribution. The order names (appoints) the trustee, sets forth all the terms of the trust (generally quoting verbatim from the testamentary trust document), and orders the executor to distribute the estate to the trustee. The trustee uses the order as the governing document when dealing with third parties, such as banks, brokers, and title companies, rather than the original trust-will. Recording a certified copy of the order in those counties where real property is located serves to transfer the property from the estate to the trustee.

As a will, the testamentary trust must conform to all legal requirements for the execution of a will. It therefore contains all essential provisions found in any will, such as nomination of a guardian of the person and estate of the testator's minor children, nomination of executors, and a section for the attestation by witnesses. It may also have provisions that make outright gifts of certain property (e.g., the tangible personal property may be given to the spouse or children free of trust).

In addition to containing all provisions customarily found in other wills, the testamentary trust, like the living trust, must include other unique clauses that relate to the trust itself. Thus, it will include provisions for distributing probate property into the trust, for naming one or more trustees, for stating who will be the trust beneficiaries, for specifying how much income and principal they will receive and when they will receive it, and for describing the trustee's duties and powers in connection with managing the trust property. Of course, all but the first clause just mentioned are also included in a living trust.

It should be noted that being a will, the testamentary trust is not an "agreement" between testator and future trustee. In fact, the potential trustee may not even be aware that he or she will one day be asked to perform this task, and may not even be born when the testamentary trust was signed. Before the court order of distribution, the nominated trustee will have to file with the court a consent to serve as trustee. Exhibit 3-3 presents a relatively uncomplicated testamentary trust.

EXHIBIT 3 - 3 Testamentary Trust (Trust-Will)

WILL OF

WILLARD THOMAS SMITH

I, Willard Thomas Smith, a resident of Mytown, Anystate, declare this to be my will. I revoke all prior Wills and Codicils.

First: Family and Guardian I am married to Sue L. Smith, referred to in this will as "my wife." I have three children, all from this marriage, whose names and birthdays are:

Kristi M. Smith	June 27, 1987
Heather L. Smith	April 19, 1989
Todd R. Smith	May 11, 1991

Reference to "my children" or to "my child," shall include children born later and children adopted by me. I have no deceased children.

If my wife does not survive me, and it is necessary to appoint a guardian, I nominate Curtis J. Quint guardian of the person and estate of each such minor child. If for any reason Curtis J. Quint does not act as guardian, I nominate Maria S. Cruise as guardian of the person and estate.

Second: Selection of Fiduciaries I nominate the following fiduciaries:

A. *Designation of Executor* I nominate my wife as my executor. If for any reason she does not so act, I nominate James A. Reliable to be my executor. If for any reason neither my wife nor James A. Reliable acts as executor, I nominate Third National Bank of Mytown to be my executor.

B. *Designation of trustee* I nominate such of my children as are over age twenty-five as co-trustees. If my children are unable to serve as trustees, then I nominate James A. Reliable as the trustee of all trusts provided for under this will. If for any reason neither my children nor James A. Reliable are available to serve as trustee, I nominate Third National Bank of Mytown as trustee.

EXHIBIT 3 - 3 Testamentary Trust (Trust-Will) *continued*

C. *Bond waiver* No bond, surety, or other security shall be required of my executor or of my trustee.

Third: Disposition of Property I make the following provisions for my probate property:

A. *Tangible personal property* If my wife survives me by 30 days, I give her all my interest in any tangible personal property. If my wife does not survive me by 30 days, I give my tangible personal property in equal shares to those of my children who survive me by 30 days. My executor shall consider their personal preferences in making that division. If my children are still minors, my executor has my permission to sell any of that property and distribute the proceeds to equalize the shares. My executor shall be discharged for all tangible personal property so given to any minor child if the child or adult having the child's custody gives a written receipt to my executor.

B. *Residue* If my wife survives me by four months, I give her the residue of my estate. If my wife does not survive me by four months and all my living children are then over age twenty-one, I give the residue in equal shares: one to each child who survived me by four months, and one share for each deceased child whose issue is then living. If any issue of a deceased child entitled to a share is under age twenty-one, his or her share shall be administered as set forth at subparagraph two of this Third Article.

If my wife does not survive me and if any child of mine is under age twenty-one, then the residue of my estate shall not vest in the children as provided above; rather, such property shall be distributed in trust to the trustee named above, to be held, administered, and distributed as follows:

1. *Any child under age twenty-one* So long as a child is under age twenty-one, the trustee shall pay to or apply for the benefit of my children, as much of the net income and principal as the trustee in the trustee's discretion deems appropriate for their proper support, health, and education, after taking into consideration, to the extent that the trustee considers it advisable, the value of the trust assets, the relative needs, both present and future, of each of the beneficiaries, and their other income and resources made known to the trustee and reasonably available to meet beneficiary needs. The trustee may make distributions under this provision that benefit one or more beneficiaries to the exclusion of others. Any net income not distributed shall be accumulated and added to principal.

2. *Youngest child reaches age twenty-one* When the youngest child reaches age twenty-one, the trustee shall divide the trust into as many equal shares as there are children of mine then living and children of mine then deceased with descendants then

---

EXHIBIT 3 - 3 Testamentary Trust (Trust-Will) *continued*

---

living. Each share set aside for a child of mine then deceased with descendants then living shall be further divided into shares for such descendants, by right of representation. Each such share shall be distributed, or retained in trust, as hereafter provided.

      a.   Each share set aside for a child, or for the descendant of a deceased child who has reached age twenty-one, shall be distributed free of trust.

      b.   Each share set aside for a descendant who has not reached age twenty-one shall be retained in trust. The trustee shall pay to, or for the benefit of, that descendant as much of the income and principal of the trust as the trustee, in the trustee's discretion, considers appropriate for that descendant's support, health, and education. When the descendant reaches age twenty-one, that descendant's entire share shall be distributed to that descendant, free of trust. If that descendant dies before receiving distribution of that descendant's entire share, the undistributed balance of that descendant's entire share shall be distributed to that descendant's then-living descendants, by right of representation, or if there are none, to my then-living issue, by right of representation. In the latter event, the share of a descendant for whom there exists a trust created by this instrument shall augment that descendant's trust.

      C. *Taxes from residue* All death taxes imposed because of my death and interest and penalties on those taxes, whether on property passing under this will or otherwise, shall be paid by my executor from the residue of my estate.

      D. *Restriction against assignment, etc.* No interest in the principal or income of this trust shall be anticipated, assigned, encumbered, or subject to any creditor's claim or to legal process before its actual receipt by the beneficiary.

      E. *If all beneficiaries die before full distribution* If neither my wife nor any of my descendants survives me by four months, I give the residue of my estate according to Anystate's laws of descent and distribution, one half as if I had died with no will on the last day of that four-month period, and one half as if it were my wife's estate and she had died with no will on that last day.

      F. *Perpetuities saving* Any trust created by this will that has not terminated sooner, shall terminate twenty-one years after the death of the last survivor of the class composed of my wife and those of my issue living at my death.

Fourth: Powers of Executor My executor shall have unrestricted powers, without court order, to settle my estate as this will provides. In addition, my executor shall have all powers my executor thinks necessary or desirable to administer my estate, including the following:

EXHIBIT 3 - 3 Testamentary Trust (Trust-Will) *continued*

A. To make distributions of principal and income on an interim basis to those entitled to it.

B. To sell, exchange, mortgage, pledge, lease, or assign any property belonging to my estate.

C. To continue operation of any business belonging to my estate.

D. To invest and reinvest any surplus money.

Fifth: Powers of Trustee To carry out the purposes of any trust created under Article Three, and subject to any limitations stated elsewhere in this will, the trustee is vested with the following powers with respect to the trust estate and any part of it, in addition to those powers now or hereafter conferred by law:

A. To continue to hold any property, including shares of the trustee's own stock, and to operate at the risk of the trust estate any business that the trustee receives or acquires under the trust as long as the trustee deems advisable.

B. To manage, control, grant options on, sell (for cash or on deferred payments), convey, exchange, partition, divide, improve, and repair trust property.

C. To lease trust property for terms within or beyond the term of the trust and for any purpose, including exploration for and removal of gas, oil, and other minerals and to enter into community oil leases, pooling, and unitization agreements.

D. To borrow money and to encumber or hypothecate trust property by mortgage, deed of trust, pledge, or otherwise.

E. To invest and reinvest the trust estate in every kind of property, real, personal, or mixed, and every kind of investment, specifically including, but not by way of limitation, corporate obligations of every kind, stocks (preferred or common), shares of investment trusts, investment companies and mutual funds, and mortgage participations, which persons of prudence, discretion, and intelligence acquire for their own account, and any common trust fund administered by the trustee.

F. In any case in which the trustee is required, pursuant to the provisions of the trust, to divide any trust property into parts or shares for the purpose of distribution, or otherwise, the trustee is authorized, in the trustee's absolute discretion, to make the division and distribution in kind, including undivided interests in any property, or partly in kind and partly in money, and for this purpose to make such sales of the trust property as the trustee may deem necessary on such terms and conditions as the trustee shall see fit.

EXHIBIT 3 - 3 Testamentary Trust (Trust-Will) *continued*

I have signed my name to this instrument on March 19, 2002, at Mytown, Anystate.

Willard Thomas Smith

Statement of Witnesses We, the undersigned witnesses, on March 19, 2002, sign our names to this instrument, being first duly sworn, and do hereby declare to the undersigned authority that the testator signs and executes this instrument as his last will and that he signs it willingly (or willingly directs another to sign for him), and that each of us, in the presence and hearing of the testator, hereby signs this will as witness to the testator's signing, and that to the best of our knowledge the testator is eighteen years of age or older, of sound mind, and under no constraint or undue influence.

John Meeks	*Jennifer Jarrett*
1341 Park St., Little Town, Anystate	42 Short Rd., Little Town, Anystate

---

Notice that, unlike the living trust shown in Exhibit 3-2, this particular testamentary trust creates only a *contingent trust* (i.e., a trust that comes into existence only if a certain combination of events happens, specifically, if the testator's wife fails to survive him and one or more beneficiaries is under age twenty-one). Not all testamentary trusts are contingent. For example, a testamentary trust could provide that a trust be created that gives the surviving spouse a life estate, followed by a life estate for the children, with the remainder going to the grandchildren.

The Rule Against Perpetuities

The rule against perpetuities (the rule) originated in English common law. The rule acts to prevent a transferor from controlling the disposition of property for an unreasonably long period after making the transfer. The rule is generally stated as follows:

No interest is good unless it must vest, if at all, not later than twenty-one years after some life in being at the creation of the interest.

Thus, the rule has the effect of invalidating a future contingent interest which might not vest within twenty-one years after the death of certain people alive (the measuring lives) at the time the document creating the interest became irrevocable.[10] The statutes of all states except Alaska, Idaho, Wisconsin, North Dakota, and South Dakota contain some variation of this rule. Charitable trusts are exempt from the rule, making them potentially infinite in duration.

In estate planning, an interest in property can take effect during the transferor's lifetime, or it can take effect at the transferor's death. A transfer into an irrevocable living trust is an example of the creation of a property interest that will take effect during the transferor's lifetime, whereas a transfer into the typical revocable living trust and a transfer by will are examples of transfers that create interests that do not take effect until the transferor's death.

Thus, to satisfy the requirements of the rule, the interest must vest, if at all, within twenty-one years after the death of someone alive at the moment of transfer into an irrevocable trust, or at the moment of the transferor's death, for interests created by will or by revocable living trust.

The rule is satisfied if an interest vests (or fails) immediately on its transfer. Thus, a statement in a will giving a bequest "to John, for his life, then to Mary or her estate," creates vested interests for both John and Mary at the testator's death. Nothing (except, in Mary's case, the passage of time) will prevent them from receiving possession of the property. Of course, if John dies before the testator, his interest (a life estate) will immediately fail. Therefore, the rule need only be used to determine the validity of contingent future interests; that is, interests that are not vested when created.

The requirement that the interest must vest "if at all" means that a contingent future interest will not violate the rule merely because it failed to vest due to the happening of a contingency that did not work in favor of a named party. Thus, the transfer "to Jane if she survives Margo" gives Jane a contingent future interest that must vest or fail to vest within the permitted time. Failure to vest will not violate the rule, so long as that failure (or non-failure) must occur within the required period. Thus, Jane will or will not survive Margo, an outcome that will be determined as soon as one of them dies. If one cannot be sure that one or the other of these outcomes will definitely happen during the period, then the interest violates the rule.

To qualify under the rule, an interest must vest or fail to vest "not later than twenty-one years after some life in being at the creation of the interest." The "life in being" concept is difficult to explain precisely. For our purposes, however, we can say that the persons permitted to be "lives in being" are usually those mentioned or identified in the transfer document itself. Thus, for the transfer "to Carrie for her life, then to Carrie's living children," Carrie would be the sole measuring life. She is alive at the creation of the children's interest, and the length of her life span will determine the devolution of the property. Taking a second example, the provision that a trust will terminate "twenty-one years after the death of the last survivor of the class composed of my wife and those of my issue living at my death" identifies the measuring lives as all the people in the class. This "perpetuities saving clause," included in the testamentary trust in Exhibit 3-3, is a clause that can further protect an interest from vesting too remotely.

The requirement of vesting within "twenty-one years" after the death of a life in being was originally included to enable the transferor to control the disposition of property for his or her life, for the lives of the children, and for the period of the grandchildren's minority, but no longer. For those individuals, all interests created which are contingent solely on parent survival will usually vest within the required period. The children's interest will vest by the time of the death of the transferor, and the grandchildren's interest will vest within twenty-one years of the death of the last surviving child. Thus, their interests will vest within the required period. On the other hand, a great-grandchild's interest will typically (but not always) vest after the twenty-one year period, and thus will usually fail.

A violation of the rule will cause that particular interest to be void. The interest will then revert to the transferor or the transferor's successors.

Let us consider some examples. In each case, assume that the transferor has died, leaving a will containing the disposition clause shown as the initial quote.

EXAMPLE 3 - 1. Ted's will stated, "To my wife, Mary, for her life, then to Bill or his estate." Both Mary's and Bill's interests vested immediately when the will took effect (at Ted's death) because at that point, nothing except the passage of time could delay their possession or enjoyment. Therefore, neither interest is contingent, that is, dependent on the happening of a future event, other than the passage of time.

Applying the rule, their interests "must vest...not later than...." Thus, both interests are valid under the rule.

EXAMPLE 3 - 2. Continuing with the prior example, assume the following is also included in Ted's will: "...then to my great, great, great-grandchildren..." Assuming that Ted is survived only by children and grandchildren, it is possible that the great, great, great-grandchildren's contingent interest will vest more than twenty-one years after the death of all children and grandchildren, who are the only apparent lives in being at Ted's death. Thus, their interests are void.

EXAMPLE 3 - 3. Theresa's will stated, "To my husband, Bert, for his life, then to my son James, if still living, otherwise to Ron or his estate." Bert's vested interest is valid under the rule for the same reason that Mary's was in the preceding example. Both James and Ron have contingent interests in the property. Thus, we must ask whether they must vest within the specified time. Both James's and Ron's interests will vest, if at all (either one or the other will never vest, depending on whether James survives Bert), within "twenty-one years after some life in being". Bert is "a life in being" at the time of Theresa's death, and both interests will vest or will fail to vest at his death well within the time limit of the rule. Therefore, both James's and Ron's interests are valid under the rule.

EXAMPLE 3 - 4. Tom's will stated, "To my wife Sarah, for her life, then to my son Greg, for his life, then equally to Greg's living children when the youngest child reaches age 25." Are Greg's children's interests valid under the rule? Sarah, Greg, and any children alive when the trust became irrevocable at Tom's death are "lives in being" at the creation of the interest. But more children could be born to Greg, and they would not be lives in being at the time the trust became irrevocable, yet they would (by the terms of the trust) each have an interest that could vest, more than twenty-one years after the deaths of Sarah, Greg, and any of the children that were born when the trust became irrevocable. Therefore, the grandchildren's interests are void, and Tom or his successors would receive a reversionary interest that follows the death of Greg. Since Tom's only living issue is Greg, violation of the rule probably means that Greg would have the interests in fee. Note that had the trust called for the interests to vest when Greg's oldest living child reaches age twenty-one, then all the children's interests would vest within a life in being plus twenty-one years, even if none of the children were born when the trust became irrevocable, since all children would be born within Greg's lifetime.

Here are two general rules of thumb when applying the rule to transfers of interests to surviving issue:

1. Transferors usually can create valid contingent interests for their grandchildren, as long as the interests must vest by the time their grandchildren reach age twenty-one. The law tacks on the period of

gestation to the twenty-one years; hence a grandchild born after the father's death can have his or interest vest at age twenty-one without violating the rule.

2. Transferors usually can create valid interests for their great-grandchildren only if they outlive their children or specify the measuring lives as persons alive at the transferor's death, e.g., "all interests shall vest no later than twenty-one years after the death of the last survivor of settlor's issue who was alive when this trust became irrevocable."

Today, not all dispositions in violation of the rule are invalid. Two types of safeguards designed to overcome the rule are available to transferors. First, most states have enacted statutes that limit application of the rule, or even invalidate it entirely. For example, many states have enacted a "wait and see" statute which, in effect, finds an interest void only if the interest turns out in fact not to vest within the required period. In addition, some states have a type of wait-and-see statute stating that any interest which actually vests within a certain period of time (e.g., 60 years) after its creation cannot be declared void, even if it violates the rule. In 1986 the National Conference of Commissioners on Uniform State Laws approved the Uniform Statutory Rule Against Perpetuities, recommending that all states enact it. It includes a wait-and-see period of 90 years after creation.

Another statutory safeguard is the application of the "*cy pres*" rule to enable the courts to correct violations of the rule, if at all possible, so that the transferor's intentions can be respected. *Cy pres*, French for "as near as possible," is a principle used primarily in the context of charitable bequests, to permit the substitution of one beneficiary for another when the original charitable purpose is impossible, illegal, or impractical to carry out. For example, over a century ago, one testator left property in trust to fight for the cause of abolition. After the 13th Amendment freed the slaves, a court applied *cy pres* to permit the trust to continue by assisting freed slaves.

The second type of safeguard is to protect against a perpetuities violation and involves the lawyer's insertion in the document of the earlier mentioned perpetuities saving clause, similar to the one in the testamentary trust in Exhibit 3-3. Such a provision, however, may act to prevent the client from making an otherwise valid transfer, perhaps simply because the attorney chose not to test the interest against the rule. In fact, none of the above safeguards is as effective as the thoughtful analysis and planning of an expert.

Yet, one must have some sympathy for the lawyers who use the clause. The rule often requires complex analysis to test a given interest, and it can even puzzle experts. One state supreme court held that, given the complexity of the rule, an attorney who created a will that violated the rule was not liable because he had used the ordinary skill commonly exercised by lawyers.[11] It is doubtful that a similar case would be decided the same way today.

The purpose of this discussion has been to present an overview of the rule against perpetuities. All members of the estate planning team should have at least a general understanding of the rule, primarily because it constitutes a constraint on how far into the future one can maintain control.

This chapter has introduced the documents used in the transfer of an estate, with particular emphasis on the simple will, the living trust, and the testamentary trust. The next chapter focuses on the actual process of transfer of the property disposed of by these documents, with particular emphasis on the probate process and its handling of intestate succession. Later chapters will again discuss trusts in connection with saving estate taxes, with special emphasis on what are called bypass trusts and marital deduction trusts.

QUESTIONS AND PROBLEMS

1. (a) Which of the following types of property can be held in joint tenancy: real estate, stocks, vehicles, bank accounts, and/or tangible personal property? (b) What is the main advantage to this form of title?

2. Does the right to choose or change the beneficiary designation reside with the insured? Explain.

3. Is the insured the only one allowed to own life insurance on his or her life? If not, how does one go about changing ownership to a life insurance policy?

4. (a) Name the major documents used in the estate planning process to transfer wealth. (b) Do they all require the same effort in their preparation? Why or why not?

5. Describe the five major reasons why a will might not be admitted to probate.

6. Name and describe the two different types of wills recognized by many states.

7. Can a valid will meet the typical statutory requirements for both the witnessed will and the holographic will? Why or why not?

8. (a) What is a simple will? (b) List its major sections.

9. (a) What is a codicil? (b) Why is it mentioned in the typical will?

10. (a) Why does the will nominate two types of guardians? (b) Must the probate judge follow the testator's nominations?

11. Why might it be a mistake to waive (as part of one's will) the requirement of an executor's bond? When does waiving one make the most sense?

12. What is the purpose of a clause directing that all death taxes be paid from the residue?

13. Why does the disposition section in a will contain a survival clause?

14. Describe the contents of the "Statement of Witnesses" section of a will.

15. (a) Distinguish between a living trust and a testamentary trust. (b) Are all testamentary trusts established in wills?

16. (a) Of the three documents highlighted in this chapter, how many are wills? (b) How many create trusts?

17. Contrast the living trust in Exhibit 3-2 with the testamentary trust in Exhibit 3-3 in terms of: (a) When the trust takes effect. (b) Who is the appointed or nominated trustee. (c) Whether the trust principal is subject to probate administration at the trustor's death. (d) Who are the income beneficiaries. (e) Who are the remaindermen.

18. (a) Describe, in general, how the living trust included in Exhibit 3-2 disposes of income and principal. (b) Which parties stand to receive a contingent future interest? (c) When, if ever, will each future interest become vested?

19. List the sections of a testamentary trust that are common to all witnessed wills and the sections that are found only in testamentary trusts.

20. Finnegan, a widower, died last week. He is survived by the following family members (current ages in parentheses): Two children, Joe (30) and Gary (17). Joe has four children, Jackie (5), John (3), Carol (2), and Bob (1). Finnegan is also survived by three other grandchildren: Floyd (4) and Fred (3), the sons of Finnegan's deceased daughter Kerri, and Kitty (9), the daughter of Finnegan's deceased daughter Shirley. Kerri's and Shirley's husbands, Kurt (29), and Rolf (31), are still alive. Joe has come to your office requesting some information. Assuming that Finnegan's large estate will be distributed in accordance with the testamentary trust contained in Exhibit 3-3, answer the following: (a) Who will receive the property (i.e., principal), and (b) assuming no more family members die at a young age, when will they receive it?

21. What is the purpose of the rule against perpetuities?

22. Helen's will leaves one half of her wealth outright to Vinnie and the other half in trust for Johnny, with all income payable annually to Johnny and, at the earlier of Johnny's death or his reaching age twenty-one, corpus to Johnny or his estate. Does this will violate the rule? Why or why not?

23. Holly's will leaves her property in trust, with income to her living children for life, then income to her then-living grandchildren for their lives, and then remainder over to her then living great-grandchildren. Who will get Holly's property?

24. Generally, how do drafters of trust documents avoid violation of the rule today?

ANSWERS TO QUESTIONS AND PROBLEMS *(odd numbered only)*

1. (a) All the property listed can be held in joint tenancy, indeed it is hard to think of any that cannot be. It might be harder to establish that form of ownership for tangible personal property unless one has some type of title certificate (e.g., car registration would make it clear how title is held). Nevertheless, three friends could buy a kayak together and agree that they will own it equally, if one dies the survivors will own it, etc., and the owners would joint tenants. (b) Advantage? The good old right of survivorship. The simplicity of transfer of title if one co-owner dies.

3. No, it is very common to have someone else own the policy, i.e., the spouse of the insured (less common today with the 100% marital deduction than it was prior to 1982), the children of the insured, or the trustee of an irrevocable life insurance trust. To change ownership, the owner uses a form supplied by the insurance company that will accomplish this; it is likely to be titled "Assignment of Policy" or "Change of Ownership." This needs to be distinguished from merely changing beneficiary designation, since in changing beneficiary designations the owner does not part with ownership or control, whereas changing ownership obviously results in parting with all benefits, title, and control.

5. Five major reasons why a will may not be admitted to probate:

   (a) Lack of testamentary capacity; that is, failure to be aware: (1) that they are executing a will; (2) of what they own; (3) of their heirs
   (b) Undue influence, or over-persuasion
   (c) Fraud
   (d) Mistake
   (e) Format (formality) problems, e.g., one witness where the state of domicile requires two

7. In many states, a valid will can theoretically meet the typical requirements for both the witnessed will and the holographic will because the formal requirements are not usually mutually exclusive. Such a will would usually have to be written, with all material provisions written in the testator's hand, and signed in the presence of two witnesses.

9. (a) A codicil is a separate written document that amends or revokes a prior will.
   (b) It is mentioned in the revocation clause to prevent needless litigation over the construction of two or more wills.

11. Not waiving the bond can protect the estate from breaches of trust by the executor. This may be important when the testator nominates or anticipates that the probate judge may appoint a non-professional, who is not related to the decedent, to be executor.

13. A survival clause avoids the risk of (1) double probate, and (2) unintended disposition to in-laws, etc., when one spouse survives the other a short period.

15. (a) A living trust takes effect during the trustor's lifetime, while a testamentary trust takes effect after the testator's death. The latter is funded through the probate process.
   (b) Yes, by definition all testamentary trusts are established in wills.

17.		**3-2 living trust**	**3-3 testamentary trust**
a.	takes effect?	on execution and funding	upon probate order
b.	nominated trustees?	John C. Jones (trustor and trustee)	children over age 25, if none, then James A. Reliable.
c.	probated?	no, probate avoidance	yes, the funding mechanism is the probate process
d.	income beneficiaries?	initially the trustor, John C. Jones, then children, if wife does not survive the four-month survivorship period	none, if wife survives, otherwise the children until they reach the ages set for termination of the trust

e. remaindermen? wife, if she survives the four-month survivorship period, otherwise the children. the children, but only if the trust is funded. This happens if wife does not survive the four-month survivorship period.

19. Sections common to all witnessed wills: (1) Declaration and Revocation, (2) Family and Guardian, (3) Executor, (4) Disposition of Property, (5) Powers of Executor, (6) Statement of Witnesses.

Sections found only in trust wills: (1) Designation of Trustee, (2) Powers of Trustee.

21. The purpose of the rule is to prevent a transferor of property from controlling the disposition of property for an unreasonably long period after making the transfer.

23. Both Holly, her children, and any grandchild alive when she dies are lives in being insofar as this trust is concerned. The income interests of the children and the grandchildren vest within the rule's outer limits but the remainder to the great-grandchildren violates the rule. The great-grandchildren's interests fail because there is a chance that a child could give birth to a child (Holly's grandchild) after Holly died. That grandchild would not be a life in being, hence any child born to that grandchild (i.e., the child would be Holly's great-grandchild) would have, according to the trust, an interest that was not within the outer limits of the rule. Due to the violation of the rule, the remote interests of the great-grandchildren are cut off and the grandchildren would end up with remainder interests instead of just income interests. Note that the common law rule does not take a wait and see approach, e.g., it does not allow us to wait and see whether any grandchildren are born after Holly dies.

ENDNOTES

1.   According to the National Conference of Commissioners on Uniform State Laws, (see Legislative Status & Information on Uniform Acts at *http://www.nccusl.org*), the following states have adopted all or part of the UPC: Alaska, Arizona, Colorado, Hawaii, Idaho, Maine, Massachusetts, Michigan, Minnesota, Missouri, Montana, Nebraska, New Jersey, New Mexico, North Dakota, Pennsylvania, South Carolina, South Dakota, Utah, Vermont, and Wisconsin. Numerous other states have borrowed heavily from the UPC.

2.   See California Probate Code § 6111(c) @ *http://www.leginfo.ca.gov/calaw.html*.

3.   See UPC § 2-503 (e.g., see South Dakota's Title 29A-2-503 at http://legis.state.sd.us/statutes/index.cfm.

4.   UPC § 2-504, see South Dakota's UPC at http://legis.state.sd.us/statutes/index.cfm

5.   UPC § 2-517 see South Dakota's UPC at http://legis.state.sd.us/statutes/index.cfm.

6.   UPC § 2-507 see South Dakota's UPC at http://legis.state.sd.us/statutes/index.cfm.

7.   *Wolfe's Will*, 185 NC 563 (1923).

8.   Cal. Probate Code § 6402.5 @ *http://www.leginfo.ca.gov/calaw.html*.

9.   *Knupp v. District of Columbia*, 578 A. 2d 702 (D.C. Ct. App., 1990).

10.   For an interesting discussion of the rule against perpetuities, see *http://www.wwlia.org/ruleperp.htm*

11.   *Lucas v. Hamm*, 56 Cal. 2d 583 (1961).

CHAPTER 4

The Transfer of Wealth

OVERVIEW

This chapter considers the actual processes by which property is transferred, emphasizing transfers taking effect at death. We will consider both probate and nonprobate transfers and the law of intestate succession that serves as a guide where no other legally recognized guidance exists.

RATIONALE FOR PROBATE DISTRIBUTION

When a person dies, steps must be taken to transfer ownership of his or her property interests to the proper beneficiaries. Each of the 50 states and the District of Columbia has enacted a probate code that establishes the rules for transferring a decedent's property. These codes serve a dual purpose; they attempt to protect both creditors of the decedent's estate and assure that the appropriate beneficiaries eventually end up with the property after debts and expenses are paid. Where a will exists, the codes seek to assure that the nominated executor is appointed unless there is good cause for appointing someone else. The notice provisions seek to assure that the creditors have a chance to file their claims and that potential beneficiaries, including heirs that have been disinherited, are aware of the proceedings so that the interested parties can raise an issue if the will being offered for probate is not the last will or if there is some irregularity concerning the will being offered. The code sets forth the contents of the petition that starts the probate process and specifies the steps that the administrator must take from start to final distribution. Of course, if there is no will, the probate procedures are still very much the same. The main difference is that the intestate succession laws serve as the guide rather than the will. Will or no will, most of the steps are the same. The notices, the marshaling of assets, the filing of an inventory, reports to the court, filing an accounting, and obtaining an order for distribution all have to be done.

NONPROBATE VERSUS PROBATE ASSETS

In a sense, the probate process stands last in line. Only that property for which there is no other mechanism of transfer is swept into the probate process. As discussed in the last chapter, the other mechanisms include certain title, contract, and trust arrangements. About all that is left, after the nonprobate mechanisms are taken into account, is property held in the decedent's name alone, or held with others as tenants in common or with a spouse as community property. Even community property may avoid probate if it is left to the surviving spouse.

Like probate, the nonprobate mechanisms for transfer are sanctioned by law. However, they are subject to much less state supervision. With title held as *tenancy by the entirety* or *joint tenancy,* the right of survivorship results in the automatic transfer of ownership to the surviving co-tenants, with the right previously held by the decedent-owner ceasing immediately on death. This automatic transfer is said to be a transfer by *operation of law*. Although title may pass automatically, as a practical matter, additional steps may be necessary to clear title to joint tenancy property. The decedent's name will need to be removed from the actual documents. Fortunately, this is usually processed quickly by the authorities (banks, motor vehicle bureau, etc.) when a surviving cotenant appears before them with a certified copy of the death certificate. For real estate, to satisfy title companies, the survivors will have to record, in each county where the jointly held land is located, a notarized "affidavit of death of joint tenant" verifying that the person identified in the attached certified death certificate was the co-owner of the parcels identified in the affidavit.

Property that, at the decedent's death, is held in a revocable or irrevocable *living trust* is not held in the decedent's name, but rather the legal title is in the name of the trustee. Since probate administration is concerned with transfer of property held in the decedent's name (individually or concurrently), property held by a trustee is not subject to probate administration. If, in accordance with the underlying trust document, the trustor's death triggers a transfer out of trust to the remainderman, the transfer process is uncomplicated. The trustee simply makes the distribution by deed or assignment, depending on the nature of the assets.

Where the decedent settlor (trustor) was serving as trustee at the time of his or her death, most state laws allow the successor trustee to immediately take over the administration of the estate. Hence no probate administration is required. The successor will have to establish for the benefit of those involved with the transfer process (e.g., brokerage houses, title companies, etc.) that the settlor is dead, by producing a certified death certificate, and that he or she is the successor trustee, by some reliable means such as an official photo identification (e.g., the successor trustee's driver's license). A reliable copy of the trust or a short form of the trust may have to be shown also.

Property owned by the decedent to be transferred at death *into*, rather than out of, a trust will be subject to probate administration. In such instances, the probate process is the funding mechanism for the trust. This will occur for all testamentary trusts because no separate trust exists prior to the death of the testator. Near the conclusion of the probate, the court order for distribution to the trustee has a dual purpose: (1) it serves as the trust funding mechanism, and (2) it serves as the trust document since the terms of the trust, taken from the will, are repeated as part of the order. Where real property is transferred pursuant to a probate order for distribution, whether to the trustee of a testamentary trust or to someone else, no deed is necessary. Rather, the executor records a certified copy of the order in the county where the real property is located. Generally, when a living trust is used, a probate is unnecessary. Nevertheless, the trustor will have created a pour-over will, so called because it scoops up assets left out of the trust and "pours" them into it. This "pouring" is done through the probate process, which concludes with an order for distribution to the trustee of the living trust. Of course, with the living trust, the order does not include the language of the trust because it is already in existence as a separate document.

Property disposed of by contract, including *life insurance proceeds* on the life of the decedent and *retirement benefits*, is not subject to probate administration because title to such assets is not held by the decedent. Instead, title is held by the insurance company or the pension fund, respectively, and each has agreed to transfer title directly to the named beneficiary at the death of the decedent. The insurance company or pension fund pays the named beneficiary in accordance with the payout option selected by the decedent or by the beneficiary. Note that the law sanctions the transfer by contract of only certain kinds of assets, mainly those that are closely connected to death (insurance) or retirement (pensions and the like).

Because the law does not sanction a general contract (as opposed to a trust agreement) as a testamentary transfer device, a person attempting to contract with a friend for the transfer of all his or her property after death would be unlikely to receive the cooperation of those entities holding the decedent's personal property (e.g., banks, brokerage firms, etc.) or the blessing of title companies for transferring the decedent's real estate. In addition to not avoiding probate, because the contract would not be executed with the formalities required of a will, it probably would not serve as a guide in the probate process either.[1]

In contrast with title held in joint tenancy, title held by a decedent either as an *individual*, as a *tenant in common*, or as *community property* does not in itself create a mechanism (or guide) for title transfer. As a result, the states have established the probate process to transfer title, using either the decedent's will or the laws of intestate succession as the guide.

Although it is difficult to gather accurate statistics, it is generally estimated that about half of all adults die without a will. In such circumstances, the state's intestate succession laws will determine proper distribution of property for which there is no other guide for transfer. The mechanism for the intestate distribution is the probate process. In fact, probating an intestate decedent's estate might be even more important than for a testate decedent, to ensure correct identification of heirs as well as to ensure distribution to them.

Figure 4-1 diagrams the probate and nonprobate interests of a decedent at the moment of death. The left side contains probate assets, including the decedent's

---

FIGURE 4 - 1 A Decedent's Property Interests

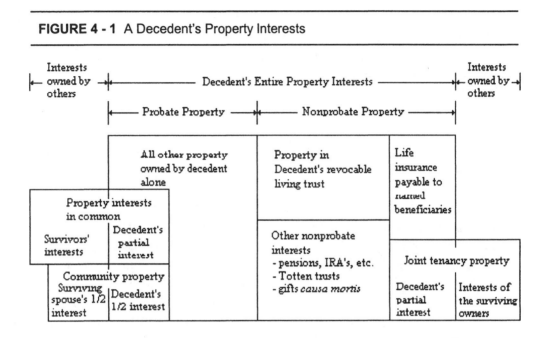

one-half interest in community property, the decedent's interests in probate held in common with others, and the catchall--all other probate property owned individually by the decedent. This would include the value of life insurance *on the life of another* owned by the decedent. Of course, where there is co-ownership, the portion of the interest held *by others,* whether as tenants in common, joint tenants, or as community property, is not part of the decedent's probate or nonprobate estate. One should also note that some community property states, such as California, no longer require a probate for property going to a surviving spouse, whether going to her (or him) by virtue of the decedent's will or by intestate succession. Those states may require the surviving spouse to file a simple request for confirmation by the court of the survivor's right to take the property, followed by notice to interested parties, then a hearing, and, finally, a court order granting the confirmation.

The right side contains the nonprobate property, including interests in living trusts that are revocable by the decedent, property held in joint tenancy or as tenants by the entirety, life insurance policies on the decedent's life other than those payable to the decedent's estate, and certain other nonprobate interests. Life insurance proceeds payable to the decedent's (probate) estate must, by definition, be a probate asset, since the probate estate will collect the proceeds and hold them pending an order for distribution. Policies issued since World War II are not likely to be paid into the insured's probate estate. In addition to having several layers of alternate beneficiaries, the policy will probably have a provision very similar to intestate succession designating the order of beneficiaries in the event that the named beneficiaries predecease the insured and only as a last resort have the proceeds payable to the decedent's estate.

The logic of Figure 4-1 suggests a relatively straightforward *procedure* to determine which of a decedent's assets will be subject to probate administration. First, list all the decedent's property interests held immediately prior to death, including all insurance policies. Then delete from the list all assets for which there is a nonprobate mechanism of transfer, such as property in living trusts, joint tenancy property, and interests payable to a designated beneficiary, such as life insurance, pensions, and finally miscellaneous nonprobate interests such as Totten trusts. What is left should be the decedent's probate estate, mostly property in the decedent's name alone (including insurance on another's life) or held with others as tenants-in-common, and for states that still require probate for community property even when it goes to the surviving spouse, the decedent's half of the community property.

So far, we have seen how the decedent's probate property is determined. The next logical step is to decide who will receive this property. For this, one first looks to the will. If there is no will, the state laws of intestate succession are applied. Details of these succession laws are covered next.

INTESTATE SUCCESSION LAWS

We have seen that a person who dies without a will is said to die intestate and that any probate property will then pass under the state's laws of intestate succession. Further, a person receiving property under these laws is called an heir and is said to inherit the property.

In determining who should inherit, the members of the various state legislatures have used their knowledge of human nature (and a little intuition) to design estate plans for persons dying intestate. Thus, they usually give priority to the decedent's spouse, next to the decedent's issue, and, if there is neither spouse nor issue, then to the decedent's other blood relatives, with priority given to the closest relatives. We will review the Uniform Probate Code's version of intestate succession after we cover degrees of consanguinity (kinship) and several alternative patterns for allocating property among a decedent's relatives. These concepts are relevant to both intestate and testate property distribution. They are important to understand although they are quite technical because they can make major differences in how money and property are distributed.

Degrees of Consanguinity

Degrees of consanguinity refers to the level of closeness in the blood relationship between a decedent and the decedent's various relatives. As we have said, and as Figure 4-2 depicts, descendants (issue) of the decedent include children, grand-

FIGURE 4 - 2 Degrees of Consanguinity

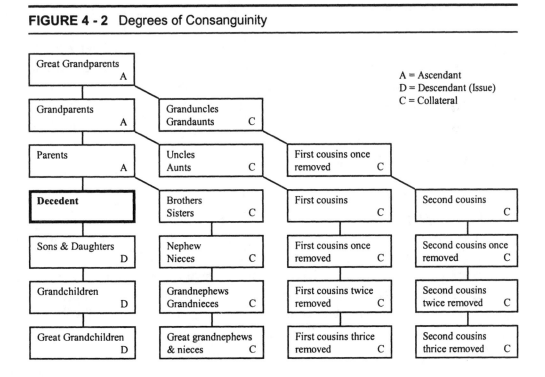

children, great-grandchildren, and so on. Ascendants (ancestors) include parents, grandparents, great-grandparents, and the like. Descendants and ascendants of a person are said to be in the person's *lineal*, or vertical line. The other relationships shown are *collateral*, meaning that they share with the person a common ancestor, but they are neither ascendants nor descendants of the person and thus are not in the person's lineal or vertical line. For example, a nephew of a person is not his or her issue, but shares a common ascendant with the person, namely the person's parent. Since a relative's share of a person's intestate estate is determined by the closeness of the relationship, the decedent is shown at the "center" of the lineal column of Figure 4-2.

The most common method of measuring a relative's degree of consanguinity to the decedent is to count the "steps" along degree lines, the lines shown linking the boxes. Degree lines run only between child and parent and parent and child. To find degree of closeness or consanguinity we first count ascendant lines to the common ancestor, then collateral. For example, the decedent's brother is two steps from the decedent. We count one ascendant step to the common ancestor parent and then one collateral step to the brother. The decedent's uncle is three steps from the decedent because we first count two ascendant steps upward to the common ancestor and then one collateral step to the uncle. Figure 4-2 can be helpful in determining relative closeness to the decedent of distant surviving relatives, especially in those states that have not adopted the more restrictive succession rules of the Uniform Probate Code. Generally, only persons of the same degree of closeness share an intestate decedent's estate.

Per Stirpes Versus Per Capita

If an intestate decedent's only heirs are one living son and two grandchildren who are the daughters of the decedent's predeceased daughter, how much will each one inherit? Will they each inherit one-third of the estate, or will the son be entitled to a larger proportion because he is a closer descendant? The technical terms used to answer questions like these are per capita and per stirpes. Per capita is Latin for "by the head" and per stirpes is Latin for "by the roots." A *per capita* distribution requires that all descendants receive an equal share of the property, or "share and share alike." On the other hand, a traditional *per stirpes* distribution, also known by the more descriptive term *by right of representation,* gives larger distributions to descendants of a closer degree of consanguinity to the decedent. As if this were not complicated enough, the 1990 revision of the Probate Code uses a hybrid of per stirpes called *"per capita at each generation per stirpes."* This form is the most complicated to understand but the most important because it is the most common. The examples below illustrate:

Consider the following family tree illustrated in Figure 4-3. Cross-marks in the diagram indicate descendants who have predeceased the decedent.

FIGURE 4 - 3   Example Illustrating Distribution by Per Capita and Per Stirpes

---

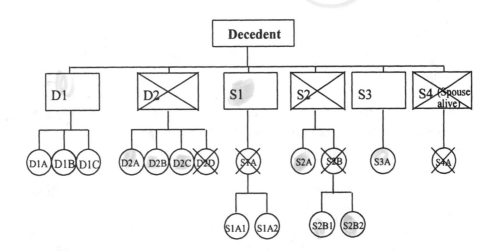

The decedent had the following descendants: Two daughters, D1 and D2, and four sons, S1, S2, S3 and S4. Only D1, S1, and S3 survived the decedent. D1 has three children, D1A, D1B and D1C, all alive. D2 is survived by three children, D2A, D2B, D2C, all alive, but the fourth child, D2D, predeceased the decedent, leaving no issue. S1 had only one child, S1A, who is deceased, but is survived by two children, S1A1 and S1A2. S2 had two children, S2A and S2B. S2A is alive. S2B is deceased, but is survived by two children, S2B1 and S2B2. S3 and his son S3A both survived the decedent. S4 and his child, S4A, predeceased the decedent. S4 left a spouse but no descendants.

All three rules of distribution, described next, share one basic characteristic: the same people receive a share of the estate. Only the various portions change depending on which rule is applicable. Under all three rules, as one goes down each line of descent, only the surviving members of the *closest generation level* receive a share. In other words, if an ancestor is alive then those in line below do not receive a share.

Thus, in our illustration, only the following nine descendants will receive property under any of the three rules: D1, D2A, D2B, D2C, S1, S2A, S2B1, S2B2, and S3. Why do the others receive nothing? Either because they did not survive the decedent (D2, D2D, S2, S2B, S4, and S4A), or because one of their ancestors (who were descendants of the decedent) survived the decedent (applies to D1A, D1B, D1C, S1A1, S1A2, and S3A).

It also follows that no property will be allocated to any family line if all descendants in that line have predeceased the decedent. For example, S4's blood line (S4A) and S4's spouse, receive nothing.

The three distribution rules differ, however, with regard to *how much* property each descendant will receive. The discussion below will analyze each rule separately. It is complicated but short, so read it very carefully. Once you "get it" it will not be hard to remember or apply any of the three rules.

Per capita. A per capita distribution simply requires that all eligible descendants receive an *equal amount* of the property. Thus, in the example, D1, D2A, D2B, D2C, S1, S2A, S2B1, S2B2, and S3 would each receive a one-ninth share.

Per stirpes: two forms. Historically, two different forms of per stirpes have evolved, traditional per stirpes and per capita at each generation per stirpes. *Traditional per stirpes,* also referred to as by *right of representation,* has been used for hundreds of years. Under it, surviving descendants of predeceased children may take unequally depending on how many in their family survive. *Per capita at each generation per stirpes,* which treats all members of each generation equally, has become more common since it replaced traditional per stirpes in the 1990 revision of the Uniform Probate Code.[2] Compared to per capita, either form of per stirpes distribution gives a larger distribution to closer descendants than to those who are further removed.

Determining distributions under either form of per stirpes requires a two-step process. The first step is the same in both forms; the second step differs.

Traditional per stirpes. First, the property is divided into shares, one share for each surviving child and one share for each of the decedent's predeceased children having living issue. Each surviving child gets his or her share directly. Second, the share for each predeceased child with living issue is divided equally among the issue - one share for each living child and one share for each predeceased child with living issue. Step two is just like step one but at the next generation. The process repeats until all the shares are taken. A share only goes to the next generation if the previous generation is not alive to take it. The next living generation is said to "represent" its parent.

- In our example, each living child, D1, S1 and S3, will receive a one-fifth share and their descendants receive nothing.
- D2 is a predeceased child with three living children and none who died with issue. Those three children will each take one-third of their mother's 1/5 share or 1/15.
- S2 is a predeceased child with one living child and one predeceased child with living issue. Thus, S2's share is divided in two; one share goes to his living son, S2A who gets ½ of his father's 1/5 share or 1/10.
- S2B is a predeceased child with living issue. His share is divided among his issue. Thus, his ½ of his father's 1/5 share is divided between his two children who each takes 1/20.

Summarizing, a traditional per stirpes distribution of the decedent's estate will be divided as follows:

D1, S1 and S3	1/5 each;
D2A, D2B, and D2C	1/15 each (i.e., 1/5 x 1/3);
S2A	1/10 (i.e., 1/5 x 1/2); and
S2B1 and S2B2	1/20 each (i.e., 1/5 x 1/2 x 1/2).

Per capita at each generation per stirpes. Per capita at each generation per stirpes distributes the property that goes to the decedent's three living children the same as per stirpes. The difference is in the property that goes to the descendants of the decedent's deceased children - grandchildren and great-grandchildren. The shares of those entitled to receive a portion of the estate at each generational level are combined and then divided equally.

First, the property is divided into shares, one share for each surviving child and one share for each of the decedent's predeceased children having living issue. Each surviving child gets his or her share directly. Second, all the shares for the predeceased children having living issue are combined and divided equally among all number of living issue plus those who have died leaving issue at that generation. The living children take their share directly. The share for predeceased children goes to the next generation. The process repeats until all the shares are taken. A share only goes to the next generation if the previous generation is not alive to take it.

- Thus, in the illustration, similar to traditional per stirpes, each living child, D1, S1, and S3 would receive a one-fifth share and their descendants receive nothing.
- D2 and S2 died leaving issue. Their shares are combined and go to their combined descendants.
- D2 has three living children and none who have died leaving living issue. S2 has one living child, S2A, and one predeceased child with living issue, S2B. The total combined number is 5. Thus, the four living children of D2 and S2 each get 1/5 of the combined 2/5, or 2/25. If they had descendants, their descendants would receive nothing.
- The 2/25 share for S2B, a predeceased child with living issue is divided at the next generation. Since there is only one share to divide, and there are only two living issue to share it, each takes half their predeceased parent's share, or 1/25.

Summarizing, a per capita at each generation per stirpes distribution of the decedent's estate will be as follows:

D1, S1 and S3:	1/5 each;	
D2A, D2B, D2C and S2A:	2/25 each;	(2/5 x 1/5)
S2B1 and S2B2:	1/25 each.	(1/2 x 2/25).

Notice that each eligible grandchild inherits the *same amount* (2/25s), rather than different amounts as in the case of traditional per stirpes. Whew!

Comparison of the three rules. One advantage of per capita at each generation per stirpes is that it gives equal shares to those who are equally related. One advantage of traditional per stirpes is that it passes the same share that the descendants would receive had their ancestors survived, and then died bequeathing the property to the next generation. One advantage of the per capita rule is that it treats everyone equally. This issue is important in planning because clients may strongly prefer one of these types of distribution over the others, and their will or trust document should reflect that preference.

Many people would prefer the per capita at each generation per stirpes method if it were explained to them so they could understand it. In contrast, most *attorneys* use estate planning books and estate plan drafting programs that use traditional per stirpes as the default rule. Most state intestate succession laws, including those that have adopted the UPC, use one of the forms of per stirpes.

All three distribution rules are similar in that they dispose of an intestate estate to the same descendants. For each, all descendants who are more remotely related to the decedent will not inherit if an ascendant in a generation closer to the decedent is alive. Preventing inheritance by more remote descendants has the advantage of reducing the number of heirs, thereby making inheritable property more marketable and minimizing the likelihood of inheritance by minors and the need for court-appointed guardians.

Finally, answering the question posed at the beginning of this section, under either form of per stirpes, the son would inherit one half and the granddaughters would each inherit one quarter of the estate. Under per capita distribution, each would inherit one-third.

Intestacy in UPC States

We are now ready to look at the rules of intestate succession used in states that have adopted the Uniform Probate Code. Note that the UPC uses the term descendant rather than issue, reflecting a modern trend to avoid a biological connotation and extend inheritance rights to adopted children.

The Code's principal intestate sections, revised in 1990, are reproduced in Exhibit 4-1. In general, § 2-101 prefaces the next four sections, which specify actual succession. The intestate share of the surviving spouse is determined by referring to § 2-102 for common law states, or to § 2-102A for community property states. The intestate share of heirs, other than the surviving spouse, is determined by referring to § 2-103. Section 2-104 covers survival situations. Finally, if there are no "takers" under the above sections, § 2-105 requires a procedure called "escheat" whereby the property ends up going to the state of domicile. A more specific analysis follows the Code.

EXHIBIT 4 - 1 Intestate Succession under the Uniform Probate Code

---

2-101 Intestate Estate

(a) Any part of a decedent's estate not effectively disposed of by will passes by intestate succession to the decedent's heirs as prescribed in this Code, except as modified by the decedent's will.

(b) A decedent, by will, may expressly exclude or limit the right of an individual or class to succeed to property of the decedent passing by intestate succession. If that individual or a member of that class survives the decedent, the share of the decedent's intestate estate to which that individual or class would have succeeded, passes as if that individual or each member of that class had disclaimed his (or her) intestate share.

2-102 Share of Spouse (Common Law States)

The intestate share of a decedent's surviving spouse is:
(1) the entire intestate estate if:
    (i) no descendant or parent of the decedent survives the decedent; or
    (ii) all of the decedent's surviving descendants are also descendants of the surviving spouse and there is no other descendant of the surviving spouse who survives the decedent;
(2) the first ($200,000), plus three fourths of any balance of the intestate estate, if no descendant of the decedent survives the decedent, but a parent of the decedent survives the decedent;
(3) the first ($150,000), plus one-half of any balance of the intestate estate, if all of the decedent's surviving descendants are also descendants of the surviving spouse, and the surviving spouse has one or more surviving descendants who are not descendants of the decedent;
(4) the first ($100,000), plus one-half of any balance of the intestate estate, if one or more of the decedent's surviving descendants are not descendants of the surviving spouse.

2-102A Share of the Spouse (Community Property States)

(a) The intestate share of a surviving spouse in separate property is:
    (1) the entire intestate estate if:
        (i) no descendant or parent of the decedent survives the decedent; or
        (ii) all of the decedent's surviving descendants are also descendants of the surviving spouse and there is no other descendant of the surviving spouse who survives the decedent;
    (2) the first ($200,000), plus three fourths of any balance of the intestate

EXHIBIT 4 - 1 Intestate Succession under the UPC *(continued)*

estate, if no descendant of the decedent survives the decedent, but a parent of the decedent survives the decedent;

(3) the first ($150,000), plus one-half of any balance of the intestate estate, if all of the decedent's surviving descendants are also descendants of the surviving spouse and the surviving spouse has one or more surviving descendants who are not descendants of the decedent;

(4) the first ($100,000), plus one-half of any balance of the intestate estate, if one or more of the decedent's surviving descendants are not descendants of the surviving spouse.

(b) The one-half of community property belonging to the decedent passes to the surviving spouse as the intestate share.

2-103 Shares of Heirs Other than Surviving Spouse

Any part of the intestate estate not passing to the decedent's surviving spouse under Section 2-102, or the entire intestate estate if there is no surviving spouse, passes in the following order to the individuals designated below who survive the decedent:

(1) to the decedent's descendants by representation;

(2) if there is no surviving descendant, to the decedent's parents equally if both survive, or to the surviving parent;

(3) if there is no surviving descendant or parent, to the descendant of the decedent's parents or either of them by representation;

(4) if there is no surviving descendant, parent, or descendant of a parent, but the decedent is survived by one or more grandparents or descendants of grandparents, half of the estate passes to the decedent's paternal grandparents equally if both survive, or to the surviving paternal grandparent, or to the descendants of the paternal grandparents or either of them if both are deceased, the descendants taking by representation; and the other half passes to the decedent's maternal relatives in the same manner; but if there be no surviving grandparent or descendant of a grandparent on either the paternal or the maternal side, the entire estate passes to the decedent's relatives on the other side in the same manner as the half.

EXHIBIT 4 - 1 Intestate Succession under the UPC *(continued)*

2-104 Requirement that Heir Survive Decedent for 120 Hours

An individual who fails to survive the decedent by 120 hours is deemed to have predeceased the decedent for purposes of intestate succession.

2-105 No Taker

If there is no taker under the provisions of this Article, the intestate estate passes to the state.

Intestate share to surviving spouse. In *common law states*, under § 2-102, the surviving spouse is entitled to all the decedent's intestate estate if the decedent leaves no parent or descendant, or if the decedent does leave descendants, but neither the decedent nor the surviving spouse have other descendants (e.g., child of a former marriage). Alternatively, the spouse takes the first $100,000 to $200,000, plus a fraction of the rest ranging from one-half to three-fourths, depending on whether parents or descendants of the decedent and/or spouse survive. An example of § 2-102(3) is where the decedent and surviving spouse leave a child and the surviving spouse has a child from a former marriage. An example of § 2-102(4) is where the decedent leaves a child from a former marriage.

Under § 2-102A, the surviving spouse's intestate share in *community property states* is identical to that for common law states, except for an additional provision for the distribution of the community property. Thus, that spouse takes the same share of the decedent's separate property as he or she would take in a common law state. In addition, the surviving spouse is entitled to the decedent's entire half of the community property.

Intestate share to others. According to § 2-103, other relatives of the decedent are divided into a hierarchical list of classes, corresponding to the degree of blood relationship to the decedent. Thus, to determine which class is entitled to succession of an intestate decedent's property, one would move down the list, stopping at the first class containing at least one living member. Distribution would be made only to members within that class. A summary of this prioritized list follows:

1. Surviving descendants, per stirpes
2. Parents
3. Descendants of parents, per stirpes
4. Paternal and maternal grandparents and their descendants, one-half to each side, per stirpes

UPC § 2-106, not quoted above, requires a "per capita at each generation" form of per stirpes whenever descendants inherit by right of representation.

Under § 2-104, any heir must survive the decedent by 120 hours to take by intestate succession. This state-imposed survival requirement has the effect of avoiding double probate in some common accident situations.

Finally, under § 2-105, if none of the above relatives survive, then the decedent's intestate property passes to the state, under the doctrine of *escheat*. In English feudal law, escheat meant that the feudal lord received a reversion in the property, either because the tenant died without issue or because the tenant committed a felony. In American law, escheat has come to mean a reversion of the decedent's property to the state because no individual is "competent" to inherit. In most states, including California, there will be no escheat unless the decedent is not survived by *any* kin, no matter how remote the relationship. The UPC, on the other hand, limits inheritance to the closer relatives, under the arguable premise that more remote "laughing heirs" would be receiving a windfall not ever intended by the decedent. One wonders whether the typical decedent really would have preferred leaving property to the state or a favorite charity, rather than to some distant relatives. "Heir hunting" firms exist to locate beneficiaries who cannot be found by the estate's personal representative. They routinely pull probate court files to see whether a missing heir is mentioned in the proceedings. If so, the firm will try to locate the missing heir and give the person the information necessary to claim the inheritance, but only if the heir agrees to pay a fee. The fee is usually a percentage (e.g., 25 to 33%) of the value of the inherited property.

The examples listed next illustrate the principles of intestate succession. In each case, assume that D is a decedent who died a resident of a common law UPC state, and owned $300,000 in property. Relevant UPC sections are given in brackets.

EXAMPLE 4 - 1. D is survived only by spouse and a cousin. His spouse will inherit all. [§ 2-102(1)(I)].

EXAMPLE 4 - 2. D is survived by spouse and their five children, one of whom has a daughter. The spouse will inherit all. [§ 2-102(1)(ii)].

EXAMPLE 4 - 3. Facts similar to Example 4-2, above, except that spouse also has a child of a former marriage. The spouse inherits $150,000 plus one-half of the rest, or a total of $225,000. Each of the five children inherits an equal share of the rest, i.e., $15,000. D's granddaughter inherits nothing. [§ 2-102(3) and § 2-103(1)].

EXAMPLE 4 - 4. Facts similar to Example 4-2, above, except that decedent also has a child of a former marriage. The spouse inherits $100,000, plus one-half of the rest, or a total of $200,000. Each of the children inherits an equal share of the rest, i.e., $16,667 ($100,000 ÷ 6). D's granddaughter inherits nothing. [§ 2-102(4) and § 2-103(1)].

EXAMPLE 4 - 5. Facts similar to Example 4-2, above, except that spouse survived decedent by only five hours. The spouse will not inherit. Each of the five children will inherit one-fifth of the total, i.e., $60,000. D's granddaughter still inherits nothing. [§ 2-104 and § 2-103(1)].

EXAMPLE 4 - 6. D is survived by parents and two children. The children take all. [§ 2-103(1)].

EXAMPLE 4 - 7. D is survived by spouse, a parent, and a sister. The spouse inherits $275,000 and the parent inherits $25,000. The sister receives nothing. [§ 2-102(2) and § 2- 103(2)].

EXAMPLE 4 - 8. D is survived by a sister and two nephews, the sons of D's deceased brother. Based on the required per stirpes distribution, sister inherits $150,000 and each of the nephews takes $75,000. [§ 2-103(3)].

EXAMPLE 4 - 9. D's closest surviving relative is a second cousin. All property will escheat to the state. [§ 2-105].

If the decedent had been a resident of a community property state, each of the above dispositions of the decedent's individually owned property would still be correct. In addition, the decedent's half of the community property would pass to the surviving spouse, with the result that the surviving spouse would receive all of the community property.

Intestacy in Non-UPC States

The intestate succession laws in non-UPC states vary considerably, but all have a common thread; a spouse takes priority, followed by issue, and, if none, the more remote heirs' interests are determined by degrees of consanguinity. For example, if an intestate decedent is survived by children but no spouse, the children usually take all. If the decedent leaves a spouse and children, the spouse and the children will usually share the property, with the spouse receiving one-third to one-half of the estate and the children the rest. If the decedent is survived by a spouse but no children, the spouse usually receives all. If, in addition to the spouse, the decedent's parents are still alive, then in some states the spouse gets all, and in others, the spouse shares a portion with the parents. Since state's intestate succession laws do vary, the reader is urged to make an independent investigation of the succession laws in his or her own state. One source is through the Washburn University School of Law's website (*http://www.washlaw.edu/ uslaw/statelaw.html*).

Advancements

An *advancement* is a lifetime gift that the donor wants to have treated as an advanced distribution from the donor's estate to be taken into account when the donor dies. Nearly all states have statutes spelling out what is needed to prove that such was the donor's intent. Most states, including those adopting the UPC, require that the donor's intent be in writing or that the donee acknowledge that the gift was understood to be an advancement. If the recipient of the property fails to survive the decedent, the property is not taken into account in computing the intestate share to be received by the recipient's issue, unless the declaration or acknowledgment provides otherwise. Where advancement occurs, the value of the gift when given is added to the net value of the decedent's estate before determining intestate shares. The donee's share is then reduced by the value of the gift. If the donee's intestate share is less than the value of the gift, the donee does not have to return the excess, but will not otherwise share in the estate. The other heirs' shares are redetermined excluding the donee and the gift to the donee.

> EXAMPLE 4 - 10. Sherry died intestate, survived by her three children, Marie, Dean, and Barbara. Her estate was valued at $120,000. Two years before she died, Sherry gave Marie XYZ stock valued at $30,000. With the gift was a typed letter from Sherry saying that she knew Marie needed the income from the stock and she should not have to wait until Sherry died to get it, but Marie should understand that

it would be taken into account when her estate was divided up. Even though the letter would not qualify as a will (it was neither holographic nor witnessed), the gift will be treated as an advancement. The children will inherit the following amounts: $20,000 to Marie and $50,000 each to Dean and Barbara, and the date-of-death value of the stock is immaterial. If Sherry's gift had not been an advancement, each of the children would inherit $40,000. In either outcome, Marie will keep the $30,000 gift.

EXAMPLE 4 - 11. Same as before, except Sherry's estate was valued at $45,000, not including the gift to Marie. When the gift is added back, each child's share is $25,000. This is less than what Marie has already received. Therefore she receives nothing, the gift is ignored, and the $45,000 is split equally by Dean and Barbara.

The advancement rules apply only to intestate succession, on the assumption that a testator wishing to reduce a beneficiary's share would do so in the will itself or by codicil. A handwritten statement evidencing an advancement may be treated as a holographic codicil in those states that recognize holographic wills.

LEGAL RIGHTS OF OMITTED AND ADOPTED CHILDREN

After-born, Omitted Children

Occasionally, a parent dies leaving a will that was executed prior to the birth of a child. Will that after-born child receive anything? In most states, including UPC states,[3] an after-born child is entitled to take the share he or she would have received had the decedent died without a will, unless any one of the following is true: (a) the omission was intentional; (b) the will left substantially all of the estate to the other parent; or (c) the testator made some other provision for "after-born" children."

The child's intestate portion can be the entire estate where the child has no brothers or sisters and the decedent-parent was unmarried, or it might be nothing, as in community property states where the surviving spouse inherits all the community property. In a community property state, the omitted child might have a claim to a share of the decedent's separate property.

Omitted Children

An omitted child is defined as any living child (or living issue of any deceased child) who was not provided for in his or her deceased parent's will. This may occur because the child was born after the will was executed and the parent's will did not have a clause providing for later born children, or the child may have been alive at the time the will was executed but the parent chose, for whatever reason, not to mention the child. While some states still permit an omitted child who was born at the time the will was executed to take an intestate share, others, including UPC states, do not. An omitted spouse, an omitted child, and the omitted issue of an omitted deceased child, are referred to as *pretermitted* heirs.

The most common planning strategy to avoid an excessive inheritance by after-born children is to treat them similar to other children by using class gift terminology. For example, by using the terms "descendants" or "issue" in the will or trust to designate the persons who will inherit, rather than specifically naming children, pretermitted child situations are avoided. Thus, property left to someone other than the children will avoid being reduced by an omitted heir's claim.

Adopted Children

Most states (perhaps all), including those that have incorporated the UPC,[4] treat *adopted children* the same as birth children of their *adoptive parents* for intestate succession purposes. So, an adopted child will inherit from the adoptive parents (and their blood relatives), and the adoptive parents (and their blood relatives) will inherit from the adopted child. Conversely, most states give the *biological parents* of a child adopted by another no rights to inherit by intestate succession from their biological child. Similarly, adopted children usually have no succession right to the interests of their biological parents. Called the "fresh start" policy, this rule, breaking inheritance rights between adopted children and their biological parents, reflects public policy belief that implementing a complete substitution of the adoptive family for the biological family is in the child's best interest. Of course any of the parties can change the results by doing an estate plan that does not follow the intestate pattern, hence the biological parent who has established a relationship with her adopted child can leave that child property if she so chooses. If she does not so choose, and fails to mention the child, the child is not considered a pretermitted heir.

> EXAMPLE 4 - 12. Sam and Sue placed their infant child, Gloria, up for adoption. She was adopted by Kevin and Kay. If Sam later dies intestate, in most states Gloria would not inherit any of Sam's property. If Kay then dies intestate, Gloria would inherit equally with Kay's biological children. If Gloria subsequently dies intestate, Kevin and Kay's issue could inherit, but neither Sue, her issue, nor Sam's issue would. Of course, any of these individuals may receive property if they are named in a given decedent's will.

The fresh start rule does not usually apply in the case of a "stepparent adoption," where an adult child is adopted by a stepparent, usually after divorce or after death of a biological parent. An exception is made, allowing inheritance by these adopted children from both their biological parents and their stepparents, reflecting public policy belief that such children will be better off maintaining contact with their biological relatives.

> EXAMPLE 4 - 13. Mike was six years old when his biological parents, Edith and Frank, divorced. Edith subsequently married Archie, who adopted Mike. In most states, Mike will inherit from both Edith and Frank and from Archie.

Omitted heir situations have a peculiar consequence. They result in the limited application of the intestacy laws to a decedent who actually died testate (i.e., with a valid will). Another example of the need for intestacy proceedings when a valid will exists is the situation called *partial intestacy*, in which a will does not dispose of all the decedent's probate property, as when it fails to contain a residuary clause. The latter is more likely to occur when a layperson does a holographic will than when an attorney drafts the will.

LEGAL RIGHTS OF OMITTED, DIVORCED, AND DISINHERITED SPOUSES

Omitted Spouse

A spouse is most likely to be omitted when the testator married *after* executing a will. The omitted or pretermitted spouse is generally treated in the same manner as an omitted child. In most states, the spouse takes an intestate share unless the omission was intentional or unless provision was made elsewhere for the spouse. And, as in the case of omitted children alive at the execution of the will, an omitted spouse whom the testator married *before* executing the will may or may not take an intestate share, depending on the applicable state law. In UPC states, that spouse would not take an intestate share.

> EXAMPLE 4 - 14. Prior to Claude and Betty's engagement, Claude prepared his only will. Claude died in a skiing accident on their honeymoon. In most states, since Claude's premarital will *does not provide* for Betty and the omission appears unintentional, the will can be admitted to probate but Betty will receive her intestate share of Claude's property. If, on the other hand, the will *has provided* for Betty,

in some states she will receive just the amount devised to her, which could be more or less than her intestate share. In states that allow a surviving spouse to elect to claim a dower interest in lieu of the amount left by will, Betty could choose to take the dower share instead of what the will has provided for her.

Effect of Divorce

In most states, bequests to a spouse contained in a will executed prior to a divorce are automatically revoked by the *dissolution of marriage*, and, for purposes of the will, the surviving ex-spouse is treated as having predeceased the testator. Thus, in most situations, the property will pass to an alternate beneficiary, probably the decedent's issue, if any. Interestingly, a divorce would not invalidate a bequest to relatives or friends of the ex-spouse.

In contrast to wills, a divorce in itself may not invalidate an existing provision designating the ex-spouse as a beneficiary in life insurance policies and retirement contracts.

Protection Against Disinheritance of Spouse

Can one spouse totally "disinherit" the other? Most states have laws designed to prevent this. States handle the potential problem of a penniless widow (or widower) by enforcing one or more of the following concepts: community property, dower and curtesy, the spousal right of election, family allowance, and homestead property.

Community property. As we have seen, *community property states* protect spouses by attributing to each spouse ownership of one-half of all property acquired by his/her efforts during the marriage while domiciled in a community property state. One would expect spouses to have nearly equal estates if they have been married most of their working years and they lived those years in community property states. Of course, a significant inheritance by one of the spouses will result in unequal wealth unless that spouse decides to convert the inherited property into community property. Recently married spouses or spouses that marry late in life, especially after retirement, may own little or no community property. The laws of the community property states do not require the decedent to leave the survivor any of the decedent's half of the community property or any of his or her separate property. Nevertheless, some protection is available under the Retirement Equity Act of 1984, which provides that after a person is married for one year to an employee who is a participant in a retirement plan, the only payment option is a joint annuity unless the nonparticipant spouse consents in writing to some other option.

Dower and curtesy. Originating in English common law, a *dower* represented a surviving wife's life estate interest in a portion of the real property owned by her deceased husband. A *curtesy* represented a surviving husband's life estate in a portion of the real property owned by his deceased wife. These interests have all but disappeared from our legal landscape.

Spousal right of election. All common law states, except Georgia, have enacted legislation replacing dower and curtesy with a spousal right of election, which essentially gives a surviving spouse a choice. Either the spouse can "take under the will," that is, accept the provisions of the deceased spouse's will, if any, or the spouse can "take against the will," that is, elect instead to receive a statutorily specified "elective share." In most states, the "elective share" is equal to that share the spouse would have inherited had the decedent died intestate.

The elective share statutes are not foolproof for at least two reasons. First, a person may be encouraged by a wealthy fiancé to execute a premarital or post-marital agreement *waiving*, or greatly reducing, elective share rights. Such agreements are recognized in most states, provided that they are entered into freely, that they fully disclose both spouses' finances without misrepresentation, and that they clearly spell out those elective rights to be waived. Second, lifetime giving strategies, either outright or in trust, may be successful in circumventing forced share litigation. While the courts in many states have tried to overcome these transfers, success has been spotty.

The elective share provisions of the Uniform Probate Code were revised in 1990 in an attempt to overcome these deficiencies by being more equitable and less arbitrary than elective share statutes predicated solely on intestacy. They allow the surviving spouse a sliding scale elective share. The share is equal to a percentage of the "augmented estate." The augmented estate includes the probate estate plus the decedent's interest in property characterized by right of survivorship (joint tenancy, etc.) held with a non spouse, proceeds on certain life insurance on the decedent's life payable to a non spouse, and many transfers of property by the decedent during the two-year period preceding death if the decedent retained certain interests in the property transferred (such as assets transferred to a revocable trust). The new provisions allow shares ranging from

3 percent, if the spouses were married less than one year, to 50 percent for marriages of 15 years or more, with a minimum share of $50,000. These provisions tend to reduce the significance of the manner in which the decedent held title on the share the pretermitted surviving spouse is allowed to claim.

Family allowance. All states give the probate court legal authority to grant a family allowance to support the decedent's spouse and minor children during the period of estate administration. This special award is needed because the court will ordinarily delay property distributions until it can determine that all debts can be paid. The family allowance takes precedence over claims by taxing authorities and unsecured creditors. Even a disinherited spouse or a dependent child might be given a family allowance. The size of the family allowance, which is usually paid in installments, will vary depending on the survivors' needs and the size of the estate.

Homestead and other exempt property. Finally, most states protect surviving family members from losing certain property to the decedent's unsecured creditors or by the terms of the decedent's will. The *homestead*, as it is called, usually includes the family home and adjacent property, subject to maximum acreage limitations. Some state statutes may also exempt other property, such as household furnishings, a vehicle, wearing apparel, and the like. Depending on the state, such assets are offered the following protection: exemption from forced sale while the surviving spouse and the decedent's descendants are minors, restriction from inter vivos alienation, testamentary disposition and intestate descent, and exemption from certain taxation. These statutes vary greatly from state to state. The UPC also grants a monetary homestead allowance of $15,000 for the spouse and $15,000 divided among all dependent minor children.[5]

Thus, most states have laws that prevent the death of one spouse from impoverishing the surviving spouse. Surviving children are, however, generally not afforded the same protection. In some other countries, such as France and Switzerland, most of a parent's estate must be left to the spouse and children. It may seem unfair that children in the United States are not similarly protected, since spouses have the ability to protect themselves when they marry but children have no choice when they enter the parent-child relationship. In addition, young children generally cannot support themselves. However, our society's refusal to protect children likely stems from a policy interest in discouraging expensive guardianships on the assumption that the protected spouse will support the minor children. Nonetheless, this is not an ideal solution in a world filled with second and third marriages, where the surviving spouse and the decedent's children may not be related.

Next, we direct our study to the final major subject in this chapter: probate administration process.

PRINCIPLES OF PROBATE ADMINISTRATION

The principles underlying probate administration of an American decedent's estate originated in England, where public officials and the Church of England took control of a decedent's property, or at least supervised those individuals taking control, and then distributed it to the heirs and devisees. The word *probate* stems from the Latin word *to prove*, meaning to certify the validity of a will. When a will is "approved," it is admitted to probate. Today, the term probate is seldom used in the restrictive sense of proving the validity of a will. In modern usage, probate refers to the entire court-related process of the administration of a decedent's estate, including those estates of people who die intestate, and thus have no will to prove.

Probate has been said to have three main *purposes*. First, it *protects creditors* by mandating that valid debts of the decedent be paid. Second, it implements the dispositive wishes of the testator by *supervising the distribution* of estate assets to beneficiaries. And third, probate serves to *transfer clear title* to those who receive the property.

Presenting a comprehensive overview of the principles of probate administration in the United States requires generalization since each state has its own set of laws. There are, however, many similarities. Nearly all *formal probate* procedures have the following four attributes:

1. Appointment of the estate's personal representative by the *court*.
2. Presentation of at least two *petitions* and at least two court *hearings*, for which written *notice* has been given to all interested parties. (Interested parties are those who could be affected by the probate process, including beneficiaries, creditors, and fiduciaries nominated in the will.) Notice to creditors is usually done through newspaper publication.
3. Issuance, by the court, of signed *orders* as a precondition to the performance by the personal representative of certain major steps, such

as the sale of real property, payment of attorney's fees, and distribution of probate property.

4. Review and approval, by the court, of one or more financial *accountings* and *reports* on significant matters of concern to the interested parties.

These requirements reflect the strong interest each state has in protecting creditors and beneficiaries.

In addition to providing these elaborate procedures, about half the states offer the option of *less formal* settlement procedures. These states have adopted all or most of the provisions of the Uniform Probate Code. Flexibility under the UPC enables the estate's interested parties to choose whether to be extensively supervised by the court in the usual manner, to be supervised only with regard to certain specific acts, or to be almost totally unsupervised. While the states that do not allow for less formal administration might still allow for some degree of informality, most of their estates must follow the traditional formal procedures.

This section will examine the traditional approach and the flexible approach to estate administration, partly to show that their underlying philosophies are very different, and partly to give the reader an indication of the current trend in probate reform. Actually, this reform has influenced all states to some degree, including those offering much less flexibility. The traditionalist states are deregulating, but in a more fragmentary manner, as we shall see.

Substantial Formal Supervision: The Non-UPC Model

California is a non-UPC state. Below is a summary of its *formal probate* procedures to illustrate the major requirements of a formal probate. Most states have similar procedures but details will vary from state to state. In UPC states, the executor has the option of using the formal or informal method, unless the probate court registrar (clerk of the court) determines that there is a reason the probate should be formal.[6] Sections of the California Probate Code are cited parenthetically and are at *http://www.leginfo.ca.gov/calaw.html.*

The formal probate process. After a person has died, the executor is expected to start the formal probate process as soon as is reasonably possible.

Petition for probate. The person nominated as executor is required to file a petition for probate within 30 days of gaining knowledge of the testator's will and of his or her nomination. (§ 8001) The original will should also be filed with the clerk of the superior court in the county where the decedent resided. California law recognizes a tort cause of action that can be brought against a person for fraudulently destroying, concealing, or "spoiling" a will.

In addition, any person "interested" in the estate may make a similar petition (§ 8000). Where there is no will, hence no executor, the interested person is likely to be a close relative. Rarely is more than one petition filed. On filing the petition, the court clerk must schedule a hearing on the petition within 45 days (§ 8003). Ordinarily, the person nominated in the will to be executor files the petition, requesting (1) probate of the will, (2) letters testamentary, and (3) authorization to administer under the Independent Administration of Estates Act. Each request will be described briefly.

1. *Probate of the will:* If, after the hearing, the will is "admitted to probate," that will is thereby considered to be the only valid will and, except in the most unusual circumstances, it will serve as the blueprint for distribution.

2. *Letters testamentary* or *letters of administration:* Also known as "letters," this document, usually just one page long, contains the court's formal identification of the person selected by the court as representative of the decedent's estate. A court-certified copy of the letters empowers the personal representative to deal with third parties on behalf of the estate. They are called "letters testamentary" if the person selected was nominated in the decedent's will, and "letters of administration" where the selected personal representative was not named in the will. Where there is no will, the personal representative is referred to as simply the administrator. The administrator is called an *administrator with will annexed* if there is a will admitted to probate but either no executor was named in the will (probably a homemade will done without attorney involvement) or neither the named executor nor the alternate executors were appointed by the court (perhaps they were unsuitable or unavailable).

3. *Authorization to administer under Independent Administration of Estates Act*: The California Probate Code allows a somewhat simplified formal probate administration. Essentially, it eliminates the requirement of obtaining court approval for many of the common transactions undertaken by the personal representative. However, some actions are not exempt and require either express court approval or written notice to all beneficiaries of a proposed course of action, giving them a period of 15 days in which to lodge an objection before the action is taken (§§ 10400-10600).

In addition to making these requests, the petition also makes several representations, including facts about the bond, the heirs, and the beneficiaries. A *probate bond* (also called a *fiduciary bond*) is required unless the will waives it or unless all potential beneficiaries agree to waive it (§ 8481). The bond protects the estate from a financial loss in the event of wrongful conduct by the personal representative. If the personal representative misappropriates estate property or loses it due to negligence, the bonding company must make the estate whole and then has the right to pursue the personal representative. This right of the bonding company to seek to recover from the personal representative any money it had to pay the estate is called a *right of subrogation*. Ordinarily, the bond amount will be equal to the total value of the personal probate property plus one-year's estimated income from all of the probate property, but not real property because it is less vulnerable to misappropriation (§ 8482). The bond premium, typically one-half to one percent of the amount of the bond, is charged to the estate. The petition for probate must state either that the will waived the bond, that the beneficiaries all request the waiver of the bond (in which case the waivers should be filed with the petition), or that the requirements for a bond will be met. Where a bond is required, evidence that it has been issued is required before the court will issue letters. As a second representation, the petition for probate is required to identify all beneficiaries named in the will and any heirs at law even though not named as beneficiaries.

Two other forms are ordinarily filed with the court clerk at the time of filing the petition for probate. First, a *Proof of Subscribing Witness* is submitted, in which at least one witness to the will declares that he or she signed the original document, that the decedent appeared to be of sound mind and over age 18 at the time of the signing, and that the witness knows of no evidence that the will was signed under duress, menace, fraud or undue influence. If a witness cannot be found, or if all witnesses have died, proof can be offered by handwriting analysis. To make this task unnecessary, in the spirit of probate simplification, most states now recognize what is called a *self-proved* will, also called a *self-executing* will. This is a will containing a formal affidavit as part of the original attestation portion of the will, wherein the witnesses state that all formalities were followed. This statement will stand unless an interested party challenges the validity of the will. At a minimum, this generally eliminates the need to locate witnesses to attest to the will's validity many years after the execution of the will. In some states, the affidavit creates a presumption that all formalities were correctly followed, thus putting the burden on any challenger to prove that such was not the case. The "Statement of Witnesses" clauses in the sample wills set forth in Exhibits 3-1 and 3-3 are self-proving.

The second form ordinarily filed along with the probate petition is the *Notice of Petition to Administer Estate* and contains the same information as the announcement notice that must be published (three times prior to the hearing) in a newspaper of general circulation in the city (or county) in which the decedent resided. Exhibit 4-2 shows an example of the information that might be found in a published notice.

The notices, both filed and published, are intended to announce the following to interested parties and to the public:

1. That a petition for probate has been filed.
2. That a hearing will be held.
3. That interested parties may attend the hearing to object to the granting of the petition.
4. That creditors must file claims against the estate within four months after the issuance of letters.
5. That anyone may examine the probate file.
6. That the petitioner is requesting authority to administer the estate under the Independent Administration of Estates Act.

Copies of the filed notice must be mailed to all heirs and potential beneficiaries at least 15 days prior to the date of the hearing (§ 8110).

The hearing. The initial "hearing" for any particular probate estate may last less than a minute. The judge gives anyone in the courtroom the opportunity to object. Objections are rarely raised. Grounds for objection include the allegation that a more recently executed will exists or that even though the will in question is the only one or the most recent one, it should not be admitted to probate because it was not properly executed due to the testator's lack of capacity, undue influence, fraud, or mistake. If there are objections, the judge will set the matter for further proceedings to settle the dispute, which, if not immediately resolved,

---

EXHIBIT 4-2 Replica of a Newspaper Notice of Petition to Administer Estate

---

NOTICE OF PETITION TO ADMINISTER ESTATE OF
JOHN PAUL JONES, a.k.a. J. P. JONES
CASE NUMBER: P781431

To all heirs, beneficiaries, creditors, contingent creditors, and persons who may otherwise be interested in the will or estate, or both, of JOHN PAUL JONES, a.k.a. J. P. JONES.
A PETITION has been filed by Mary Jones in the Superior Court of Anystate, County of Anycounty.
THE PETITION requests that Mary Jones be appointed as personal representative to administer the estate of the decedent.
THE PETITION requests the decedent's WILL and codicils, if any, be admitted to probate. The will and any codicils are available for examination in the file kept by the court.
A HEARING on the petition will be held on 03-19-01 at 8:30 a.m. in Department 1 located at Superior Court of Anystate, County of Anycounty, 25 County Center Drive, Anycity, Anystate 99999.
IF YOU OBJECT to the granting of the petition, you should appear at the hearing and state your objections or file written objections with the court before the hearing. Your appearance may be in person or by your attorney.
IF YOU ARE A CREDITOR or a contingent creditor of the deceased, you must file your claim with the court and mail a copy to the personal representative appointed by the court within four months from the date of first issuance of letters as provided in Section 9100 of the Anystate Probate Code. The time for filing claims will not expire before four months from the hearing date noticed above.
YOU MAY EXAMINE the file kept by the court. If you are a person interested in the estate, you may file with the court a formal Request for Special Notice of the filing of an inventory and appraisal of estate assets or of any petition or account as provided in Section 1250 of the Anystate Probate Code. A Request for Special Notice form is available from the court clerk.
Attorney for petitioner: Gordon C. Brown, BROWN & BROWN,
P.O. Box 0000, Anycity, Anystate, 99999-1111.
PUBLISHED: February 19, 22, and 26, 2002.

---

can turn into a *will contest*. If the petition for probate is granted, the judge signs an *Order for Probate* that states the court's findings, specifically:

1. All notices have been filed.
2. The decedent died on the specified date.
3. The will in question should be admitted to probate.

4. The petitioner is the appropriate person to serve as the estate's personal representative, either as executor or as administrator with will annexed.

Then, the Order usually requires that:

1. The will is admitted to probate.
2. The named personal representative is appointed.
3. A bond is (or is not) required.
4. The personal representative is (or is not) given authority to administer the estate under the Independent Administration of Estates Act.
5. Letters are issued (on the posting of the bond, if such is required).

Upon issuance of the Order for Probate, the personal representative secures his or her certified letters from the probate clerk, thus completing the first stage of the formal dealings between the personal representative and the court.

After the hearing. Next, usually in conjunction with the estate's attorney, the personal representative undertakes the marshaling of estate assets and expected claims. Within three months of appointment, the personal representative must file with the probate court a formal document called *Inventory and Appraisement*. This form lists all probate assets showing their fair market value. The personal representative is permitted to determine the value of cash items (e.g., bank deposits, etc.). Other assets must be valued by an appraiser who, depending on state law, may be selected by the court from a list of court-approved independent appraisers. Finding a qualified appraiser may also be one of the duties of the personal representative.

The Inventory and Appraisement performs several important functions. First, it lists those assets for which the personal representative is responsible. Second, as a public document available for public inspection at the courthouse, it describes the contents of the probate estate to all interested parties, including potential heirs, legatees, devisees, and creditors. Third, it provides information to the court to determine, among other things, the proper fiduciary bond amount, the amount of the family allowance, and, if property is sold, the minimum bid that the court will approve. Finally, it may influence the taxing authorities with regard to valuation of assets included on the estate tax returns.

During the *creditors' claim period*, which in most states lasts for four months after the date the letters are issued, each creditor is expected to file with the court or personal representative a document called a *creditor's claim form*. Failure to file within the claim period will bar later collection, unless an exception is allowed (§ 9100). Exceptions include:

1. Creditors who did not have actual knowledge of the proceedings (§ 9103).
2. Taxes owed (taxing authorities are not subject to the creditor's period (§ 9201)).

Availability of a shortened creditor's period is said to be a major advantage of the probate process compared to other mechanisms for the transfer of a decedent's estate, at least for estates that anticipate potential problems with creditors.

During estate administration, the personal representative is responsible for handling the financial affairs of the estate, such as:

1. Paying bills (rent, utilities, property insurance premiums)
2. Accumulating liquid assets so that large bills can eventually be paid (e.g., taxes and legal fees)
3. Protecting estate assets from exposure to loss by insuring and safeguarding them

Distribution of estate assets. The net estate will be distributed to the beneficiaries only after all matured debts and taxes, except the federal estate tax, have been paid. However, a partial distribution to beneficiaries may be made on court approval of a *Petition for Preliminary Distribution*. Ordinarily, this petition is filed only after the end of the creditor's period. Further, the court must be satisfied that the distribution can be made "without loss to creditors or injury to the estate or any interested person." No more than 50 percent of the estate can be distributed in a preliminary distribution (§§ 11620-24).

"Final Distribution" is made upon approval of a petition at a hearing, after the court determines that all current debts and taxes have been paid (§ 11640). At the same time, the judge normally approves a final estate accounting, attorney's fees, and executor's commissions (§§ 12200-252). The accounting may be avoided by waiver of all the beneficiaries (§ 933). After distribution and the payment of fees, the executor requests and receives a final discharge (§§ 12200-252).

The entire formal probate administration procedure takes from eight to 24 months in most cases.

Attorneys' fees for California probate administration work are determined by statute, in the absence of a different agreement by the parties. Statutory probate fees are summarized in Table 4-1.

TABLE 4-1 California Statutory Probate Fees

Probate Estate		Rate	Cumulative: Estate/Fee	
First	$15,000	4.0%	$15,000	$600
Next	$85,000	3.0%	$100,000	$3,150
Next	$900,000	2.0%	$1,000,000	$21,150
Next	$9,000,000	1.0%	$10,000,000	$111,150
Next	$15,000,000	0.5%	$25,000,000	$186,150
Over	$25,000,000	Reasonable amount set by the court		

California Probate Code § 10810.

These fees are based on the *gross* probate estate, not net of liabilities, plus gains from the sale of assets, plus income, and less losses from the sale of assets. Gains and losses are based on the date-of-death appraised values. California executors are entitled to the same amount (§ 10800) as shown above for attorneys. California is one of the states that has statutory fees. In most states, probate administration fees must simply be "reasonable" and specific amounts or percentages are not mandated. In other states, probate fees must be "reasonable," but not in excess of a certain percentage (e.g., Iowa sets an upper limit of 2 percent times the value of the probate estate).

EXAMPLE 4 - 15. California attorney Spector works with executor Gregory to probate a $500,000 estate. Included in the estate is a house worth $200,000 that has a $150,000 mortgage. Both the attorney and the executor receive a fee of $11,150 based on the gross (not the net) value of the estate. [4% * $15,000 + 3% * $85,000 + 2% * $400,000]. Additional fees will be allowed for "extraordinary services" such as sale of real property, estate litigation, and preparation of tax returns. Note that the combined charge is 4.46% of the gross value of the probate estate.

Sometimes attorneys are asked by survivors to act as both estate attorney and executor. Whether they will receive a full double fee will depend on several factors, including state law and the attitude of the specific probate judge. Some states, including California and New York, have made this "double dipping" illegal in the absence of prior court approval. In other states, probate judges frequently reduce the fee in such situations. A possible solution is for persons to negotiate probate fees with the estate planning attorney while they still can, so the chore does not fall on the shoulders of grieving survivors. The probate court would probably nullify an agreement that called for fees in excess of the court's own guidelines or in excess of the fees set by statute.

Summarizing the essential components of formal supervision: Formal probate in most non-UPC states requires at least four document filings (petition for probate, a certification establishing that notice of death has been published, an inventory and appraisement, and a petition for authority to make a final distribution), requires at least two formal court hearings (one for the admission of the will to probate and to appoint the personal representative, and another to approve the final accounting and the request for authority to distribute the estate), one newspaper publication of notice, and at least one accounting (unless it is waived by all estate beneficiaries). Many states have acted to simplify probate administration, a major example of which is outlined next.

We now turn to the second major type of state probate supervision, the flexible approach under the Uniform Probate Code. A discussion of one non-UPC state's less comprehensive attempt at simplifying probate procedures can be found in Appendix 4A at the end of this chapter.

Estate Administration in UPC States: A Study in Flexibility

Personal representatives in non-UPC states usually must use formal probate, although summary probate procedures may be available for smaller estates and for property passing outright to the surviving spouse.

In contrast, probate procedures in a UPC state are much more flexible, allowing interested parties to select the degree of supervision they desire. The basic choices are three: complete court-supervised administration; totally unsupervised (informal) administration; or a combination of unsupervised and supervised administration. The UPC also provides a simple summary procedure for estates worth less than $5,000. It is similar to California's affidavit-of-right procedure, described in Appendix 4A. In most states, modest estates can be settled without any administration.

Complete court-supervised administration. Some complex or unusual estates in UPC states may be subject to supervised administration. UPC supervised administration is a bit less regulated than a non-UPC supervision such as California's formal continuing court supervision probate. The personal representative is given greater freedom to act independently. Usually, there is no court involvement between the time letters are issued and the time the personal representative petitions the court for closing of the estate. Most personal representatives of estates in UPC jurisdictions choose not to be subject to supervised administration. Occasionally, an interested party will have reason to lack trust and request it because he or she wants notice of what the personal representative is doing. In contrast, probate administration in non-UPC states, as we have seen, requires court approval of all major transactions.

Informal and formal administration. In UPC jurisdictions one of two types of procedures is followed: informal or formal administration.

Informal administration procedures usually require no court appearances and very little notice. The application for informal appointment is the simplest way for a personal representative to be appointed. The prospective personal representative files an application with a court registrar, whose role is administrative rather than judicial. Once appointed, the personal representative has the powers needed to perform the job, including the power to deal with creditors and distributees. The personal representative is required to give notice of the appointment to all heirs and devisees by ordinary mail within 30 days of appointment. Within three months, the personal representative must prepare an inventory of the estate and mail it to all parties requesting it. The entire inventory can be valued by the personal representative unless an interested party objects.

Even with informal administration, the personal representative must give formal newspaper notice, similar to the procedure for a formal probate, in order to limit the creditor's claim period to four months from date of first publication. Without published notice to creditors, the limitations period usually runs to three years after the date of the decedent's death.

Six months after appointment, the personal representative can apply to the registrar to close the estate. After another six months, assuming no one has lodged an objection, the personal representative is discharged from all liability except due to fraud or other major offenses. Unless the newspaper notice was given, distributees of estate property will continue to be liable for estate debts until the later of three years after date of the decedent's death or one year after the date of the distribution.

Formal administration procedures under the UPC include the petition for *formal testacy* (proving the will), petition for formal appointment of the personal representative, and petition for formal closing. Each is undertaken in a manner similar to that for supervised administration and requires giving proper notice to interested parties, filing a petition with the court, and appearing at a court hearing.

During informal proceedings, a dissatisfied interested party can petition the court for a formal resolution of a controversy, whereupon the matter will be taken up "in" court. Once the dispute is settled, administration can resume in informal proceedings "out" of court. The UPC's unique method of settling disputes has been described as an "in and out" method.

In addition to the right to petition the court, interested parties have other protective remedies, including the right to request that the personal representative obtain a bond even though it was waived in the will, the right to request a restraining order to keep the personal representative from doing some specific act (such as selling a family heirloom), and the right to demand notice by receiving a copy of any filings or orders in connection with the estate. With the exception of the right to notice, the requests are subject to the court's discretion.

We can now see the relationship between informal and formal proceedings under the UPC. At each significant step in the probate process, the interested parties can elect a different degree of supervision. For example, the probate process may begin with an application for informal supervision of the personal representative. Then a controversy may arise that requires court resolution. Finally, the personal representative may feel compelled to file a formal petition for closing. Only rarely will an interested party petition for completely supervised administration. Generally, it is the desire of all beneficiaries to minimize judicial supervision, because supervision tends to delay distribution.

The movement toward reduced court involvement in estate administration has spread to many non-UPC states, due in part to the influence of the UPC. As illustrated in Appendix 4A, traditional states have moved to reduce court supervision by adopting summary procedures, set-asides, and procedures to reduce the personal representative's court reporting requirements. The overall effect of all state deregulation has been to reduce court congestion considerably.

The next chapter will require a change of focus, from the qualitative to the quantitative. It will be the first of four to introduce the principles of taxation.

QUESTIONS AND PROBLEMS (To find state probate codes, see question 3.)

1. True or false: A decedent's intestate property does not go through the probate administration process. Explain.

2. What goals do states seek to accomplish through their respective probate codes?

3. Describe your state's laws covering inheritance by intestate succession. They are usually found in a chapter of that state's probate or estates and trusts code. The names for these codes vary, for instance: *Decedent's Estates, Guardianships, Protective Proceedings and Trusts* (Arizona); *Estates, Powers & Trusts* (New York); or *Probate Code* (California). (See http://www.statelocalgov.net/)

   If your state is unavailable, describe the UPC rules using South Dakota's *Uniform Probate Code*; go to *http://legis.state.sd.us/statutes/index.cfm/* and click on "South Dakota Codified Laws," and work your way to *Title 29A.*

4. Use South Dakota's law (see question three for the web address) to answer the following:(a) if a person dies intestate, all other things being equal, what is the priority as to whom the court will choose as administrator? (b) Use California law to decide this issue: Laura died, leaving a valid holographic will that failed to name an executor. The estate is worth approximately $400,000. The will leaves $25,000 to Laura's only daughter, Janet, and the residue is left 40% to grandson Kirk, who is sixteen, and 60% to her nephew Brian. Both Brian and Janet filed petitions to administer the estate. No one contests the validity of the will, nor does anyone claim that there was undue influence. Who is likely to prevail? Explain.

5. Consider the relationships between an individual (i.e., anyone) and various relatives. For each of the following state whether the person is an ascendant,

a descendant, a collateral relative, or none of the above; and give the degrees of consanguinity: (a) great-grandfather; (b) husband; (c) first cousin twice removed; (d) grandchild; and (e) nephew.

6. State who is "closer" to a person (i.e., any individual) and state for each relationship the degrees of consanguinity, her: a. son or brother, b. grandchild or aunt, c. grandparent or sister.

7. Describe one characteristic that is common to all three rules of distribution discussed in this chapter.

8. Widow Anna died testate. She had three sons and one daughter. Her second son died ten years before her, but his two children have survived. Her daughter died three years ago and left one child. Describe how Anna's property will be distributed to her descendants if her will says to my issue by (1) per capita distribution, (2) traditional per stirpes, and (3) per capita at each generation per stirpes.

9. Bachelor Harry has an interest in a house, some furniture, a car, some common stock, and a life insurance policy on his life. The *car* is in joint tenancy with his mother. The *house* is in trust, and the trust instrument says "for Harry's use for life, then to cousin Joe." The life insurance policy names his cousin, Joe, as the beneficiary. Harry owns the *furniture* and the *policy* as an individual. With regard to the *stock*, Harry is an equal tenant in common with Sam. Harry's will says "I leave my car, my stock, my life insurance proceeds and my house to Betty." It has no other dispositive provisions.
   a. Assuming that Mother and Joe are Harry's only living relatives and that Betty is a close friend, who will receive what if Harry dies?
   b. What will be included in Harry's probate estate? His non-probate estate? His testate estate? His intestate estate?
   c. Who will be an heir? A legatee? A devisee?
   d. In your state (or under the UPC, if state law is unavailable), will your answers to the above questions change if Harry was also survived by a son? Why or why not?

10. Bob died leaving no will. At the time of his death, Bob owned his home in joint tenancy with a close friend, John. He was also the sole owner of a car, a racing horse, and a $50,000 savings account. Bob is survived by his mother, an uncle and two cousins. Assuming UPC state law, who is entitled to Bob's property?

11. When he executed his will, Frank and Joan had two young children, Mattie and Ned. Frank's will left half his property to his wife Joan and half to their daughter Mattie. A year after the will was signed, Pam was born into the family. Today, Frank cannot for the life of him figure out why he left half his estate to his little daughter, none to his son, and just half to his wife. Frank says he wants to leave all his property (worth $180,000) to Joan when he dies, and if she predeceases him, then to his issue by right of representation. (a) From an estate planning standpoint, what is the first thing he should do? The second and third things? (b) How would his estate be shared if he died now without changing his will? Apply your state law or, if unavailable, South Dakota's UPC.

12. When George was an enlisted man in the Army, he went to the base legal officer and signed a simple will leaving everything to Lucy, his mother. George, now a civil engineer, recently married Karla. George would like his wife to receive most of his estate (estimated worth of $500,000–not counting a pension death benefit equal to 40% of his salary that would be paid monthly to Karla). Since he has been helping his mother out financially over the years, he would like his mother to receive about $300 per month for her lifetime. (a) From an estate planning stand point, what is the first thing he should do? (b) How can he accomplish the goal of helping his mother? What more do you need to know about this goal? (c) How would his estate be shared if he died now without changing his will? Apply your state law or, if unavailable, the UPC.

13. Explain how to determine whether the property is subject to probate administration.

14. Matthew, a wealthy man, died when his private plane crashed. Janet has been named executor of his estate. Based on the laws of your state, or the UPC,

what are the major steps that Janet should undertake from the time she learns of Matthew's death through to the close of the probate?

15. Find, cutout or photocopy (especially if it is not your newspaper), and bring to class a newspaper published "notice" of petition to administer an estate. [You might call a law office to find which local papers are most likely to publish these notices.] What is its purpose?

16. Attend a probate hearing. Give the date of attendance, a brief summary of what you observed, and the types of matters considered by the court.

17. It is generally said that formal probate in a non-UPC state places a greater burden on the executor than would be the case in a UPC state. Give a couple of examples of differences between the two types of codes that support that proposition.

18. (a) What is the purpose of the "inventory and appraisement?" (b) What is the purpose of the creditor's claim? Who files it?

19. (a) What is meant by "the personal representative of the estate?" In situations where the representative is referred to as "administrator," does that mean the decedent died intestate? Explain. (b) Ordinarily, what must the personal representative accomplish before a judge will permit final distribution under supervised probate?

20. Describe what is meant by "letters" in the probate process. What kinds of letters are there? How long is this document likely to be?

21. a. To what extent do the laws of intestate succession seem inefficient for parents of minor children?
    b. To what extent does a will leaving everything outright to the surviving parent solve the problem? To what extent do you think such a will fails to solve it?
    c. What might be a better solution?

22. (a) In considering the rights of children who are not left any part of their parent's estate, why do some states allow claims by omitted after-born children (i.e., born after the will was executed) but not by omitted children who were already born when the will was executed? (b) What is the logic behind limiting omitted children born after the will was executed to a share no greater than that of their siblings born when the will was executed?

23. Charlie died intestate. His estate is valued at $400,000. He is survived by his four children: Matt, Chris, Joe and Doug. Five years before Charlie died, he gave stock to Joe valued at $60,000. If this gift is considered an advancement, how much would each of his children receive? If this gift is not considered an advancement, how much would each child receive? What determines whether it was an advancement?

24. Ralph has two children, Betty and Bill. Bill wants to start a company and asks Ralph to give him an advancement of $100,000. Ralph's intent that the gift is an advancement is recorded in writing. What will each child receive if: (a) Ralph died intestate with an estate of $500,000? (b) Ralph died intestate with an estate of $150,000? (c) Ralph died with a valid will that left his estate to his issue by right of representation?

25. (a) Using the California Statutory Probate Fee table, determine the attorney's and executor's fees in the following: The decedent had these probate assets: A house worth $250,000 that had a $200,000 mortgage; a car worth $15,000 with a $10,000 lien for a car loan, a brokerage account (stocks and bonds) worth $100,000, and miscellaneous household furniture valued at $25,000. There was credit card debt of $6,000 and total accounting fees of $1,000 for preparing the decedent's last 1040 and the estate 1041. (b) What percentage are the total attorney and executor fees as compared to the gross value of the probate estate? Of the net value of the probable estate?

26. One day, Mark learned that his biological mother, Nancy, died in a plane crash. He also learned she was very wealthy and did not mention him in her will. He went to court claiming he was her child and had records and DNA evidence to prove it. He seeks to receive his share of the $1.2 million estate. Besides Mark, Nancy left one daughter with no children and two

grandchildren from a predeceased son. (a) How much of the estate will Mark receive, assuming that Mark was adopted by the Smith family at his birth? (b) How much would Mark receive if he was never adopted, but had grown up in foster homes?

27. Denise died recently. Determine what portion, if any, of each item described below is a probate asset.
    a. An automobile, held jointly with Jake.
    b. A money fund account, owned by Denise as an individual.
    c. A life insurance policy (L1) on Denise's life, owned by Denise. Herb is beneficiary.
    d. A life insurance policy (L2) on Denise's life, owned by her. James, the sole beneficiary, died three years ago.
    e. A life insurance policy (L3) on Herb's life, owned by Denise, who is also beneficiary.
    f. Common stock, owned by the trustee of a living trust. At the moment of her death, Denise was trustor, trustee, and one of the beneficiaries. Herb was the remainderman.
    g. Commercial real estate owned in common by Denise (40%) and Herb (60%).
    h. Defined benefit pension plan. Denise was participant, and Bob is named surviving beneficiary.
    i. Residence, owned by Denise and Herb as community property.

28. John died intestate, survived by his mother Jan, his wife Alice, and their young child Jenny. His estate consists of the following assets: 1. A home placed in joint tenancy with Jan before he married Alice. 2. Corporate bonds held as community property with Alice. 3. Shares of common XYZ stock held as separate property. 4. A life insurance policy with his friend Carl as the beneficiary. 5. A store owned as tenants in common with Paul, his business associate. 6. A car and a checking account, both in join tenancy with Alice. 7. A transfer-on-death savings account naming Jenny as transferee.(a) Which assets are probate estate assets and which ones are nonprobate assets? (b) Who would receive each asset described above? (c) How should the savings account (item 7) be handled?

SUMMARY PROBATE PROCEEDINGS IN CALIFORNIA: ONE NON-UPC STATE'S ALTERNATIVES TO FORMAL PROBATE

As we have seen, formal probate typically requires at least four document filings, two formal court hearings, one newspaper publication of notice, and at least one and possibly two accountings. Although these procedures were designed to protect estate assets and ensure their proper distribution, many are considered unnecessary in simple estate situations. Over the years, both UPC and non-UPC states have simplified probate procedures for less complicated estates.

This Appendix will summarize the progress of probate simplification in California, a state that has not adopted the UPC. Presently, California has two major types of "summary probate," neither of which requires newspaper notice and both of which require not more than one petition and hearing. The two types, discussed next, are the affidavit of right and the summary distribution to the surviving spouse. As you read this, keep in mind that many UPC states have procedures similar to these.

Affidavit of Right

The affidavit of right is a procedure that permits the settlement of a decedent's affairs more rapidly than formal probate. It is available if the gross estate (real and personal property) does not exceed $100,000 in value after excluding all property for which there is some other (non-probate) mechanism of transfer. Property in trust, joint tenancy property, life insurance going to named beneficiaries, and Totten trust accounts do not count as part of the $100,000. Also not counted toward the $100,000 limit are motor vehicles and mobile homes, $5,000 in salary, and any property subject to a summary distribution to the surviving spouse (a proceeding described below). The affidavit of right method of transferring property without any court involvement only applies to a decedent's right to money, tangible personal property, or evidences of a debt, obligation, interest, right, security, or chose in action. The procedure differs slightly if real estate is involved and does require minimal court involvement.

For non-real estate assets, an affidavit signed by the "successor of the decedent" is presented to the person or institution holding the property. That party is then required to turn ownership of the property over to the person with the claim. The successor of the decedent is the person with the most legitimate claim to the property. He or she may be an executor named in the decedent's will, the trustee (if there is a pour-over will), or in the case of intestacy, a guardian (on behalf of a minor), or one of the heirs claiming on his or her own behalf. Forty days must have lapsed since the decedent's death, and the affidavit must state that no probate has started and that the total property being claimed by this method does not exceed $100,000. It must also state the basis for the person's claim that he or she has the right to the possession of the property. A certified copy of the decedent's death certificate is attached to the affidavit. The recipient of the property is liable for any liens or taxes that are associated with the asset. Of course, if the property is being collected by an executor or trustee, he or she must then make transfers in keeping with the controlling document, i.e., the will or the trust. (§§ 13100-13116)

The affidavit of right for *real property* can be used to claim real estate that belonged to the decedent, but only for property up to $20,000 in value. The claimant must wait six months after the decedent's death before presenting an affidavit similar to the one discussed for personal property. This one must be presented first to the superior court, together with a petition requesting certification. The claimant's signature must be notarized. In addition to the death certificate, an inventory of all the decedent's real property must be included in the petition and an appraisal of the property must be attached. If the testator had a guardian or conservator at the time of his or her death, that person must be given notice of the petition. If the paperwork appears to be in order, the court clerk will issue a certified copy of the affidavit, which the claimant must then record (without all the attachments) in the office of the county recorder for the county where the property is located. The recorded affidavit serves as a quitclaim deed from the decedent to the persons designated in the certified affidavit as the successors of the decedent (§§ 13200-13210). Note that this is done without a court hearing.

Summary Distribution to Surviving Spouse

Married spouses in California frequently own separate and community property that, at death, passes outright to the surviving spouse, either because the spouse was named in the will or by the laws of intestate succession. In two important ways, California probate law has simplified the administration requirements of such property.

Property Held as Community or Quasi-Community Property

Similar to the affidavit of right discussed above, the surviving spouse who succeeds to the decedent spouse's community property or quasi-community property, either by will or by intestate succession, can claim it by affidavit. Quasi-community property is that property that would have been community property except for the fact that it was acquired while the couple was living in a non-community property state. There is a 40-day waiting period, but the spouse does not have to seek court certification of the affidavit even if real property is involved. If real estate is involved, the affidavit must be notarized so that it can be recorded in the county where the real estate is located. Unlike the affidavit of right discussed above, there is no upper dollar limit. A person other than the surviving spouse can stop the transfer of title by recording, with the county recorder, a notice of the existence of a competing claim. Generally, such a claim is based on the existence of a will leaving an interest in the property to the person giving notice (§§ 13500-13545).

Summary Distribution Petition

Second, the surviving spouse can elect what is called summary distribution, which is one that follows a court hearing for the purpose of obtaining written confirmation by the court that such property has in fact passed to him or her. This may be helpful to clear title. At the hearing, if there is no objection, the judge confirms that the property is, in fact, either community or separate property, and that it should, in fact, pass to the surviving spouse. The judge signs an order confirming these findings. A summary distribution petition may be filed regardless of the amount or type of other property owned by the decedent at death. Formal probate may be required for other assets. Further, an affidavit of right and a summary distribution petition may both be used in the same estate for different property, provided that all the requirements are met. Thus the spouse may claim bank accounts by use of a simple affidavit and the summary court proceeding to confirm his or her rights in real estate or in a business (§§ 13500-13660).

Attorney fees for handling a summary distribution for the surviving spouse are not set by statute. In practice, these fees are substantially less than those for formal probate. one-third of the statutory fee is an amount commonly charged and many attorneys will do this for an hourly fee that is substantially less for large estates. Even less is charged for helping with the affidavits needed for a spousal set-aside without a petition for summary distribution.

ANSWERS TO QUESTIONS AND PROBLEMS *(odd numbered only)*

1. False. To be intestate is to die leaving probate property that is not disposed of by a valid will. Thus, by definition, intestate property is probate property. Logically, one could argue that intestate property needs probating even more than property disposed of by will, since a legal process is needed to help determine who is to receive the property, as well as to ensure that the intended beneficiaries *will actually receive* it.

3. Under the UPC, as in non-UPC states, succession is determined by first recognizing the interest of a surviving spouse and next by the degree of kinship. Thus, generally, the surviving spouse takes all if there is no surviving issue or parent of the decedent. If there is surviving issue or parent, the spouse will probably share the estate with them. And if there is no surviving spouse, issue, parent, issue of parent, grandparent, or issue of grandparents, then the property escheats to the state.

5. (a) great-grandfather: ascendant (3); (b) husband: none of the above; (c) first cousin twice removed: collateral (6); (d) grandchild: descendant (2); and (e) nephew: collateral (3) .

7. Under all three rules (per capita, traditional per stirpes, and per capita at each generation per stirpes), the intestate estate is passed to the same descendants. Notice that one inherits only if those above him or her (that is those in closer relationship) in the line of descent are deceased. Although the same people inherit, the difference in the three rules is found in the amounts allocated to the various descendants.

9. a. Based on the procedure described in the text, first the <u>nonprobate assets</u> should be considered. Disposal instruments for them supersede the will. Accordingly, the <u>life insurance proceeds</u> will go to Joe, as named beneficiary. The <u>house</u> will pass to Joe, under the terms of the trust. The <u>car</u> will go to Mom, by right of survivorship under joint tenancy. The remaining assets (interest in the common stock, furniture) are <u>probate assets</u>. The <u>stock</u> will pass to Betty, under the will. And finally, the <u>furniture</u> will pass by intestacy to Mom, Harry's closest surviving relative.

b. In Harry's probate estate: furniture and stock. In Harry's nonprobate estate: house, car, and life insurance proceeds. In Harry's testate estate: stock. In Harry's intestate estate: furniture.

c. Mother is the only heir. An heir is a beneficiary who would receive property that passes by intestacy. Betty is the only legatee. A legatee is a beneficiary, under a will, of a gift of personal property. Technically, no one is a devisee; that is, a recipient, by will, of real property.

d. If Harry is also survived by a son, in most states, including those adopting the UPC, *descendants will inherit before parents*. Thus, the son, rather than his mother, will likely inherit the furniture. Also, in some states, the son would receive the stock, under the rule that an omitted child takes an intestate share of the entire probate estate.

11. (a) Frank should immediately revoke his present will. In most states, intestate succession would give everything to his wife, Joan. He might also want to do a holographic will naming Joan as the executor and leaving her his estate, with their issue as alternate beneficiaries. He should also name guardians for the children. Finally, he should have an attorney draft a will and/or trust to provide for long-term management in the event that both he and his wife die while the children are young. (b) Ned, possibly, and Pam, definitely, are pretermitted heirs. State laws vary but Pam would have a claim for an intestate share of the estate and, given that Mattie was given a significant share of the estate, Pam would probable receive a portion of the estate. In those states that allow claims only by after-born children, Ned would not have a claim. If Ned was mentioned in the will, but left nothing, it is unlikely that he would have a claim under any state's omitted heir statute.

13. Determining whether the property is subject to probate administration is a relatively straightforward procedure. First, list all the decedent's property interests held immediately prior to death, including all insurance policies. Then delete from the list all assets for which there is a nonprobate mechanism of transfer, such as property in living trusts, joint tenancy property, and interests payable to a designated beneficiary, such as life insurance, pensions, and finally miscellaneous nonprobate interests such as

Totten trusts. What is left should be the decedent's property interests subject to probate administration, mostly property in the decedent's name alone or held with others as tenants-in-common, and for states that still require probate for community property even when it goes to the surviving spouse, the decedent's half of the community property.

15. The notice of death and petition to probate an estate should be available in the legal notices section of most local newspapers. However, some newspapers are more popular than others because of cost. Smaller circulation newspapers that meet the minimum subscription requirements for state or local law regarding legal notices may have more notices published in them than do better-known newspapers with wider circulation.

17. In a UPC state the executor is generally allowed to sell property, even real estate, without getting court authority for each sale, whereas, in non-UPC states the executor may have to get authority for each sale and may even have to bring the terms of the contract of sale to the attention of the court for final approval. Indeed, for certain types of sales, e.g., real estate, the law might require a hearing where other prospective buyers have an opportunity to over-bid the initial buyer (the one whose contract is brought before the court). Obviously, in the latter case the executor's acceptance of an offer to purchase must be conditioned on the court's giving its approval and on no one over bidding the original purchaser at the hearing.

The executor in a UPC state can make limited distributions and pay debts without seeking prior court approval, and then report these transactions at the time of his or her final report. In a formal non-UPC probate, the executor is expected to get court authorization before doing these things.

19. (a) The personal representative of the estate is the person appointed by the probate court to act on behalf of the decedent's estate. He or she is given (pays a couple of bucks, actually) "letters" from the court (certified by the clerk of the court) that verified the person's appointment. This allows the person to represent the estate in the sense of being able to collect assets and pay the debts of the decedent. If the term administrator is used, it means that the person appointed was not named as the representative in the decedent's

will. If someone named in the will serves, he or she is called the executor. Someone other than an executor serving may be due to the person dying intestate (hence no will to nominate anyone), or all the persons nominated in the will are unable or unwilling to serve, or the will fails to nominate anyone. If there is a will admitted to probate but someone other than an executor is serving, then the person is called "the administrator with will annexed." (b) Before final distribution is allowed, the personal representative must give a full report and an accounting that shows that all approved debts have been paid and that the estate is ready for final settlement. Generally, that is also the time to request authority to pay the fees of the representative and the attorney.

21. a. Parents of minor children may find the UPC intestacy laws undesirable because guardians of the children's estates must be appointed. This will occur under the UPC only if one or both of the parents have children by a former marriage (actually, if there are children not of the marriage). In many non-UPC states, children will inherit even if there are no children from a prior marriage.

b. A will leaving everything outright to the surviving spouse may prevent guardianship proceedings, but its assumption that the surviving spouse will take care of all children may not be correct if the spouse is not the parent of the decedent's children or if the survivor has children by a prior marriage. Further, the spouse could remarry, diverting assets intended for the children. Finally, the surviving spouse could die before the children reached adulthood, thus creating the need for guardianships.

c. A better alternative would be providing for a trust for the benefit of the children. Trustees are subject to less court supervision and can use discretion in sprinkling trust income unequally according to the children's needs. Guardians are required to treat each child equally. Finally, trustees are usually granted broad powers and great autonomy in managing trust assets, making a trust more efficient than a guardianship.

23. If the $60,000 gift was considered to be an advancement, Joe would receive $55,000 ($460,000/4 = $115,000, less the $60,000 already received). His siblings would each receive $115,000. If the $60,000 gift was not considered an advancement, each child (including Joe) would receive $100,000.

25. (a) The fees are based on the value of the gross probate estate ($390,000), not the net value. The fees are $8,950 for the executor and the same for the attorney for a total of $17,900. (b) This is 4.6% of the gross probate estate. The net value of the estate is $155,100 ($390,000 - $200,000 -$10,000 - $6,000 - $1,000 - $17,900) and the percentage is 11.5%.

27. The estate of Denise. Generally probate assets include: (i) property owned by the decedent as an individual; (ii) decedent's share of interests held in common with others; (iii) in some states, the decedent's one-half community property interests.

    a. Automobile, held jointly with Jake: Nonprobate asset. Will pass to Jake by right of survivorship, i.e., by operation of law.

    b. Money fund account, owned by Denise as an individual: Probate asset.

    c. Life insurance policy (L1) on Denise's life, owned by Denise. Herb is beneficiary: Non-probate asset.

    d. Life insurance policy (L2) on Denise's life, owned by her. James, the sole beneficiary, died three years ago: Probate asset, if the proceeds are paid to (policy owner) Denise's estate, by default. However, if the policy has alternative dispositions (e.g., first to a spouse, next to issue, then to parents, etc., and only lastly to the insured's estate) then those will be followed and this will not become a probate asset.

    e. Life insurance policy (L3) on Herb's life, owned by Denise, who is also beneficiary: Probate asset, policy is owned by Denise as an individual.

    f. Common stock, owned by trustee of a living trust. Denise is trustor, trustee, and one of the beneficiaries: Nonprobate asset. Not owned by Denise, as an individual.

    g. Commercial real estate owned in common by Denise (40%) and Herb (60%): Denise's 40% interest is probate asset.

    h. Defined benefit pension plan. Denise is participant, and Bob is named surviving beneficiary: Non-probate asset.

    i. Residence, owned by Denise and Herb as community property: Denise's one-half community interest is probate asset in some states and, provided her husband will receive the property, whether by will or by intestate succession, the property is set-aside to the surviving spouse without the need for a probate.

ENDNOTES

1. But see UPC § 2-503, whereby, in certain circumstances, a document may be accepted by the probate court as a will even though it does not meet the formal execution requirements. Where the UPC is cited, see South Dakota's UPC at http://legis.state.sd.us/statutes/index.cfm.

2. UPC § 2-106.

3. UPC § 2-302.

4. UPC § 2-114(b).

5. UPC § 2-402.

6. UPC § 3-305

CHAPTER 5

The Federal Unified Transfer Tax

OVERVIEW

This chapter is the first of three covering the taxation of wealth transfers. Since wealth is transferred during life and at death, we examine the tax imposed on both types of transfers, i.e., gifts and estates. Given the dramatic change in the law with the passage of the Economic Growth and Tax Relief Reconciliation Act of 2001, signed by President Bush on June 7, 2001, we will cover the changes that will lead to full repeal of the estate tax in 2010. Individuals may be able to save taxes by transferring wealth to grandchildren or great-grandchildren. However, such transfers may be subject to another transfer tax, the generation-skipping transfer (GST) tax, which will be covered very briefly in this chapter and in more detail in Chapter 12. It is important to understand that these taxes are excise taxes, not property taxes. An *excise tax* is a tax on a transaction. In this case it is levied on the transfer of wealth, with the tax based on the net value of property transferred. We begin with the basics of gift tax and estate tax law. Keep in mind that these two taxes are really part of a unified transfer tax system.

BRIEF HISTORY

There have been four federal estate taxes over the years or at least some form of extraction of revenue related to transfers at death. All were implemented to provide revenue to finance military action or recovery from military action. The first three did not last very long. The fourth almost made it for a full century.

The first tax related to decedents' estates was not really an estate tax; it merely required executors to purchase federal stamps for wills and estates. It was enacted in 1797 to help pay for naval rearmament following the Revolutionary War, and it was terminated four years later. An inheritance tax with rates from .75% to 5% was enacted in 1862 to help pay the Union Army during the Civil War. In 1864 the top rate was raised to 6% and the tax was abolished in1870. To help finance the Spanish-American War, an estate tax with a top rate of 15% on estates of more than $1 million was enacted in 1898 and abolished in 1902.

The fourth estate tax is our present one. Enacted in 1916 to help finance the U.S. effort in World War I, it had a top rate of 10% for estates over $5 million. In 1917 this was raised to 25% for estates over $10 million, which of course at the time would have been considered an extremely large estate. However, there was no marital deduction, so the tax was applied even if the entire estate went to a surviving spouse. As a tax on transfers at death only, it was relatively easy to circumvent through the use of gifts. In 1924, Congress plugged this loophole by enacting a gift tax. The gift tax was repealed in 1926 and reenacted in 1932. After the war, Congress retained the estate tax but dropped the top rate to 20% in 1926. During the Depression the top rate soared to 60% in 1934 and to 70% in 1935. During the World War II period, the top rate went even higher–to 77% for taxable estates greater than $10 million.

Since its revenue yield is negligible–generally less than one percent of all federal taxes–the estate tax is thought to be justified, if at all, as a method of redistributing wealth, that is to break up very large estates, thus decreasing the tendency for wealth to be concentrated in the hands of a very small portion of the population.

Prior to the gift tax and estate tax being unified in 1977, there were a number of imperfections in the system that could be exploited to reduce taxes on the transfer of wealth. Because the gift tax rates were only 75% of the estate tax rates, giving large gifts reduced taxes for the very wealthy. For any given size taxable estate, the fact that the decedent had made prior taxable gifts did not increase the decedent's estate tax. Estates of decedents who had made taxable gifts still started at the lowest marginal rates and had the same estate tax exemption as estates of persons who had not made taxable gifts. They were said to "take two trips up the rate ladder" since the gift tax and the estate tax are both progressive. Before the 1977 unification of the estate and gift taxes, there was an annual exclusion of $3,000 per donee, a $30,000 lifetime gift exemption for each donor, and a $60,000 estate exemption, which was undiminished by the decedent's use of the gift exemption. The annual exclusion (now an "indexed" $10,000 per year) is the amount that is deducted or excluded from taxable gifts. Since it is a per donee deduction, there is no limit to the number of annual exclusions a donor can claim in a calendar year. Furthermore, the exclusion is available even if the donees are not related to the donor.[1] On January 1, 1982, the annual exclusion increased from $3,000 per donee per year to $10,000 per donee per year. Learning to calculate the taxes on pre-1977 transfers is not necessary, although the following examples demonstrate the dramatic change brought about by unification of the two taxes:

EXAMPLE 5 - 1. In 1970, Adele made a gift worth $1,000,000 to her friend Lance. She used her $30,000 lifetime exemption and the $3,000 annual exclusion to bring the taxable gift down to $967,000. Adele paid gift tax of $235,118.

EXAMPLE 5 - 2. When Adele died in 1975, her net estate was left in equal shares to five friends. The gross estate was worth $1,150,000. There were debts and expenses of $150,000 which, combined with the $60,000 estate exemption, resulted in a taxable estate of $940,000. Adele's estate paid estate tax of $303,500. Even though Adele had made the earlier gift to Lance, it did not affect the amount of the estate tax. Note that for estates there is no per-beneficiary exclusion comparable to the gift tax annual exclusion.

EXAMPLE 5 - 3. Brian died in 1975 with an estate identical to Adele's. It too was left to five friends. The gross estate was worth $1,150,000. There were debts and expenses of $150,000, which combined with the $60,000 estate exemption, resulted in a taxable estate of $940,000. Brian's estate paid estate tax of $303,500. The tax on Brian's estate was exactly the same as Adele's, even though Adele had made a huge taxable gift during her lifetime and Brian had not made any taxable gifts.

With the passage of the Tax Reform Act of 1976, a single "unified" rate schedule was adopted, taxing lifetime gifts and transfers at death at the same rate. With the implementation of the "unified" system, the transfer of the estate at death is treated almost as though it were just another gift. Adjusted taxable gifts (i.e., the value of gifts reduced by annual exclusions) serve to boost the donor's taxable estate into its appropriate marginal rate. Furthermore, the donor's post-1976 taxable gifts reduce the amount of unified credit available to shelter transfers at death. Before we get into the details of the calculations, compare the tax results in the following examples that repeat the facts of the three prior situations in the current estate tax era. The next examples will use transfers between 1987 and 1997, a period when the rates, the unified credit, and the annual exclusion remained constant. The annual exclusion was increased from $3,000 to $10,000 for gifts after 1981, and indexed for inflation starting in 1999.

EXAMPLE 5 - 4. In 1990, Catherine made a gift worth $1,000,000 to her friend Nathan. She used the $10,000 annual exclusion to bring the taxable gift down to $990,000. Catherine paid gift tax of $149,100. Note that there is no donor lifetime exemption after 1976.

EXAMPLE 5 - 5. When Catherine died in 1995, her net estate was left in equal shares to five friends. The gross estate was worth $1,150,000. There were debts and expenses of $150,000, which resulted in a taxable estate of $1,000,000. Note, there is no estate exemption for decedents dying after 1976. Because of her earlier gift, $990,000 is added back to Catherine's estate to determine the marginal rate, and her unified credit has already been used up against the taxable gift. Catherine's estate paid estate taxes of $434,400. Compare Catherine's estate tax amount to that of Edward's estate in the example that follows.

EXAMPLE 5 - 6. Edward died in 1995 with an estate identical to Catherine's, except that Edward had never made any post-1976 taxable gifts. He also left his estate to five friends. The gross estate was worth $1,150,000. There were debts and expenses of $150,000, which resulted in a taxable estate of $1,000,000. Edward's estate paid estate tax of $153,000. Catherine's estate tax was $434,400, which is $281,400 more than Edward's estate tax, because her estate was taxed at a higher marginal rate and her unified credit was used up on the 1990 gift to Nathan. Also note that Edward's estate tax on his taxable estate of $1,000,000 was $3,900 more than the gift tax on Catherine's $1,000,000 gift. *** *Query 5 - 1. How do you account for the $3,900 difference? What is the transfer tax marginal rate just below $1,000,000?*

EXAMPLE 5 - 7. Suppose Catherine had not made the 1990 gift and that her estate was worth $2,150,000 when she died in 1995. Assume that debts and expenses stayed at $150,000, resulting in a taxable estate of $2,000,000. The estate tax would be $588,000. Compare this to the total paid when there was a gift of $1,000,000, followed by the donor's taxable estate of $1,000,000. There is a $4,500 difference in having it all taxed at death. *** *Query 5 - 2. How do you account for the difference? What is the marginal rate just below $2,000,000?*

Recent legislation repealing the estate tax. The passage of the Economic Growth and Tax Relief Reconciliation Act of 2001 (EGTRRA) made numerous changes to the transfer tax law; indeed it repeals the estate tax altogether, at least for the year 2010. For transfer taxes (i.e., gifts and estates) the top marginal rate (55% in 2001) drops to 50% in 2002 and then declines gradually over the next several years until it reaches 45% in 2007. The top rate remains at 45% until the estate tax is repealed in 2010. The amount that can pass free of transfer taxes is called the applicable exclusion amount (AEA). This "tax-free" amount was called the unified credit equivalent, or the credit shelter amount, prior to the 1997 Tax Relief Act using the term *applicable exclusion amount* as a proxy for the unified credit shelter amount.

EGTRRA dramatically increases the AEA over the remaining life of the estate tax. In 2001, the AEA was $675,000 and was slated to slowly rise to $1,000,000 by 2006. With EGTRRA, it jumps to $1,000,000 in 2002. For estates, it rises in several steps to reach $2,000,000 in 2006, remains at that level through 2008, then jumps again to $3,500,000 for deaths in 2009. The gift tax AEA remains constant at $1,000,000, even as the estate tax AEA increases, and remains at that level after the estate tax is repealed. For gifts in 2010 and beyond, the gift tax maximum marginal rate drops to 35%.

There is one major caveat to our discussion of EGTRRA's repeal of the estate tax and decrease in the gift tax top marginal rates. The very last section of the Act provides that

> *All provisions of, and amendments made by, this Act shall not apply—*
>   *(1) to taxable, plan, or limitation years beginning after December 31, 2010, or*
>   *(2) in the case of title V, to estates of decedents dying, gifts made, or generation-skipping transfers, after December 31, 2010.*[2]

This means that, unless another bill is passed by Congress and signed by the President, as of January 1, 2011, it will be as if EGTRRA never happened; the estate tax will return, the AEA for estates will fall back to $1,000,000 (the level it would have reached by 2006 under the pre-EGTRRA law), and a top marginal rate of 55%, a surcharge of 5% on taxable transfers over $10,000,000, and the GST tax will all reappear. The ETAX2002 spreadsheet program (see page xviii at the beginning of the book) was written with the presumption that prior to 2011, a law will pass making the EGTRRA changes permanent, at least as permanent as such things tend to be.

There is a fair probability that the economic slowdown, coupled with the EGTRRA tax cuts, and likely spending increases (whether for social security, defense, or education) will cause budget deficits to loom large. If that happens, Congress, instead of letting EGTRRA lapse altogether, might hold the AEA at $3,500,000 (i.e., the 2009 amount) and index it for inflation. A change such as that, combined with planning techniques, would eliminate the transfer tax for all but the wealthiest estates, perhaps only the top one-tenth of one percent (as compared to taxing the top one or two percent in 2001). To make such legislation palatable, Congress might allow closely held businesses to pass tax-free to family members, perhaps with a carryover basis and/or with a recapture provision covering the estate tax saved if the business passes out of family control by sale or gift within a set period of time. It will be interesting to see what happens.

In spite of unification, there are advantages to using gifts (large and small) as part of a wealthy person's estate plan. We shall explore later how gifts save transfer taxes by utilizing the annual exclusion, by removing the gift tax from the transfer tax base, and by keeping future appreciation out of the transfer tax base.

UNIFIED TRANSFER TAX FRAMEWORK

The basic model of the present system is to tax wealth transfers cumulatively, while allowing the donors of gifts and estates modest in size to escape transfer taxes through a combination of annual exclusions (for gifts only) and the unified credit (applicable to both gifts and estates), which corresponds to the AEA discussed earlier. Increases to the unified credit and decreases to the top marginal rates were being phased in even before EGTRRA. Before we go into details on the phase in, peek ahead to Table 5-5, which shows the present marginal rates and Table 5-6, which shows the changing unified credit from 1977 (the start of unified transfer taxes) through 2010, when the repeal of the estate tax is slated to take effect. The latter table also shows the AEA, meaning the amount that passes tax-free because it is covered by the available unified credit. Fear not! It is a little complicated at first, but we will take this transfer tax business step-by-step, assuring you of mastery. Many of the examples exploring the fundamentals of the transfer tax system will use years between 1987 and 1997, inclusive, because the rates, the unified credit, and the annual exclusion were all unchanged during that period, making it easier to follow along with the calculations. We start with simple gifts, ones where the donor made no prior taxable gifts, then move to examples where the donor has made prior gifts. Next we go to a simple taxable estate, one where the donor made no prior post-1976 taxable gifts. Finally, we look at an estate where the decedent had made post-1976 taxable gifts.

A copy of the Federal Gift Tax Return, Form 709, is included on the "Teaching Aids" CD ROM that came with this book (see file "Form 709 Gift Tax.pdf"). The return illustrates the gift tax scheme. The *donor* is responsible for filing the return and paying the tax. The return is due on April 15 of the year following the taxable gifts. An extension to file the donor's income tax return acts as an automatic extension (to the same due date) of the donor's gift tax return. If the donor fails to pay the gift tax, the donee is secondarily liable for payment of the tax (up to the value of his or her gift).

Gift taxes for the first-time donor. The steps for calculating the gift tax for a donor who has made no prior taxable gifts are summarized as follows: determine the fair market value (FMV) of the property as of the date of the gift; from the FMV subtract the annual exclusions (an indexed $10,000 each calendar year for each donee), the marital deduction, and any attached mortgages or liens; on this net amount (the taxable gift) use the transfer tax rate table to calculate the tentative tax; and, finally, subtract the unified credit for the year of the gift from the tentative tax to determine the gift tax that must be paid.

TABLE 5 - 1   Federal Gift Tax (Form 709) Basic Model - No Prior Gifts

---

Total current year's gross gifts	$xxx,xxx
Less: Annual exclusion(s) and deductions	(xxx,xxx)
Equals: Total taxable gifts	$xxx,xxx
Calculate: Tentative tax on total taxable gifts	$xxx,xxx
Less: unified credit (not to exceed tentative tax)	(xxx,xxx)
Equals: Current gift tax	$xx,xxx

EXAMPLE 5 - 8. In 1989, Deborah made a gift of GnuCo stock worth $430,000 to her sister, Ophelia. Deborah had never made a taxable gift before. The tentative tax on a $420,000 taxable gift (remember the annual exclusion) is $128,600. When $128,600 of Deborah's unified credit was applied (unified credit up to $192,800 was available in 1989), no gift taxes were due.

EXAMPLE 5 - 9. In 1993, Edward made a gift of 1,000 shares of PlehCo stock worth $850,000 to his sister, Gloria. Edward had never made a taxable gift before. The tentative tax on an $840,000 gift is $283,400 which, when reduced by the $192,800 unified credit, resulted in Edward paying gift taxes of $90,600.

EXAMPLE 5 - 10. In 1993, Francis made gifts of 1,000 shares of RenCo stock worth $850,000. His brother, Peter, received 500 shares and his sister, Patricia, received the other 500 shares. The tentative tax on taxable gifts of $830,000 (this time there are two annual exclusions) is $279,500 and the gift tax, after the $192,800 unified credit, is $86,700.

*** *Query 5 - 3. Given the following information, what gift tax did Martha pay? In 1990, Martha gave Quin an apartment building worth $750,000. It was free and clear of debt and liens. Martha was new to making large gifts.*

Gift taxes for the experienced donor. Where there have been prior gifts, the steps for calculating the gift tax for new gifts are as follows: the FMV's for all current period (during calendar year) gifts are determined; the annual exclusions and deductions (marital, charitable, and mortgages or liens attached to the property transferred) are subtracted from the current year's FMV (the gross gifts amount) to arrive at current taxable gifts; the current taxable gifts are added to the taxable gifts for prior years to determine the total taxable gifts; then, using the tax rate table, a tentative tax is calculated for both the prior years' cumulative taxable gifts and the total taxable gifts; from the tentative tax on the total taxable gifts, the tentative tax on prior taxable gifts is subtracted to arrive at the tentative tax on current period taxable gifts; the unused unified credit is determined by subtracting the unified credit used for prior years' post-76 taxable gifts from the total unified credit allowable for the current year; and, finally, the unused unified credit (the credit still available) is subtracted from the tentative tax for current gifts to determine the gift tax that must be paid. Note that if the total value of gifts during the year to a particular donee are less than the annual exclusion amount, then those gifts do not need to be reported on the gift tax return (i.e., they will not appear on Form 709). In working problems, students must be careful not to take a full annual exclusion unless the value of the gift exceeds the annual exclusion amount. The best advice is to just ignore those outright gifts to one person where the cumulative value for the year is less than the annual exclusion amount. Of course the preceding advice assumes that the gift is one of a present interest (e.g., an outright gift of property), since there is no annual exclusion available for gifts of a future interest.

TABLE 5 - 2 Federal Gift Tax (Form 709) Overview Model - **With** Prior Gifts

---

Total current year's gross gifts	$xxx,xxx
Less: Annual exclusion(s) and deductions	(xx,xxx)
Equals: Current taxable gifts	$xxx,xxx
Plus: Total prior taxable gifts	xx,xxx
Equals: Total (current and prior) taxable gifts	$xxx,xxx

Calculate: Tentative tax on total taxable gifts	$xxx,xxx
Less: Tentative tax on total prior taxable gifts	(xx,xxx)
Leaves: Tentative tax on current taxable gifts	$xxx,xxx
Less: Unused unified credit (not to exceed tentative tax)	(xx,xxx)
Equals: Current gift tax	$xxx,xxx

For each example below, refer back to the earlier examples to see how they boost the later transfers into higher marginal rates. Note that it is the taxable amount (not the gross amount) that does the boosting and that we take into account that the earlier taxable gifts used up some (or all) of the unified credit.

EXAMPLE 5 - 11. In 1991, Deborah (see EXAMPLE 5-8) gave additional GnuCo stock worth $730,000 to her friend, Gerry. The gift tax was calculated as follows:

Total current year's gross gifts	$730,000	
- Annual exclusions	($10,000)	
= Current taxable gifts		$720,000
+ Total prior taxable gifts		$420,000
= Total taxable gifts		$1,140,000
Tentative tax on total taxable gifts		$403,200
- Tentative tax on prior taxable gifts		($128,600)
= Tentative tax on current taxable gifts		$274,600
- Unused unified credit [$192,800 - $128,600]		($64,200)
Equals: Current gift tax		$210,400

Note that it was not necessary to recalculate the tentative tax on the prior taxable gifts since that figure was already available. We have this luxury of just picking up the tentative tax on the prior gifts from the earlier calculation only if the highest marginal rates applicable to the prior gift are the same as would have been applied had the gift been made in the present year. As the top marginal rate decreases over the years, if prior years taxable gifts exceed $2 million, it will be necessary to recalculate the tentative tax on those prior years gifts in order to arrive at the correct tentative tax for the current year's taxable gifts. This recalculation will also be necessary for an estate if the decedent made gifts that reached marginal rates higher than those in effect when the donor died.

EXAMPLE 5 - 12. In 1992, Deborah gave gold bars worth $650,000 to George, her favorite former teacher, and bonds worth $380,000 to her friend, Samantha. The gift tax was calculated as follows:

Total current taxable gifts	$1,030,000	
- Annual exclusions	($20,000)	
= Current taxable gifts		$1,010,000
+ Prior period gifts		$1,140,000
= Total taxable gifts		$2,150,000
Tentative tax on total taxable gifts		$854,300
- Tentative tax on prior taxable gifts		($403,200)
= Tentative tax on current taxable gifts		$451,100
- Unused unified credit [$192,800 - $192,800]		$0
Equals: Current gift tax		$451,100

Again, note that neither the prior taxable gifts nor the tentative tax on prior taxable gifts had to be calculated, since both figures were already available. The prior taxable gifts were the total gifts from the last taxable period reduced by the allowable annual exclusions. The tentative tax was calculated as one of the steps in determining the gift tax for the earlier period.

*** *Query 5 - 4. On the gifts described next, taking into account Martha's earlier gift, what gift tax did she have to pay? In 1993, Martha gave three more gifts: a new car costing $36,000 to Jake; cash in the amount of $43,000 to Marilyn; and PontoCo common stock worth $88,000 to Eddie.*

Estate taxes for the stingy decedent. Sorry, did not mean stingy, frugal is better. The steps for calculating the estate tax for a decedent who never made any post-76 taxable gifts are summarized as follows: From the decedent's gross estate (generally, all that the person owned at death), subtract the marital deduction and any debts, mortgages, liens, and the expenses of the decedent's estate (i.e., executor's fees, appraiser's fees, and attorney's fees) to arrive at the *taxable estate*. The transfer tax rate table is used to calculate a tentative tax on the taxable estate. Finally, the death taxes that must be paid are determined by subtracting the unified credit from the tentative tax.

TABLE 5 - 3 Federal Estate Tax (Form 706) Basic Model - **No** Prior Gifts

Gross estate	$xxx,xxx
Less: Total deductions	(xx,xxx)
Leaves: Taxable estate	$xxx,xxx
Calculate: Tentative estate tax	$x,xxx,xxx
Less: Unified credit	(xxx,xxx)
Total Death taxes (most states)	$xxx,xxx
Less: State death tax credit	(xxx,xxx)
Less: Other credits	(xx,xxx)
Equals: federal estate tax	$xxx,xxx

EXAMPLE 5 - 13. When he died in early 1997, Gregg left his entire estate to his three children. The gross estate was valued at $5,840,000. Total debts were $315,000 and expenses of administration were $55,000. He had made no post-1976 taxable gifts. His estate tax is as follows:

Gross Estate	$5,840,000
- Debts & expenses	($370,000)
= Taxable estate = Estate tax base	$5,470,000
Tentative tax on estate tax base	$2,649,300
- Unified credit	($192,800)
= Total Death taxes (for most estates)	$2,456,500

*** *Query 5 - 5. Given the following information, what death tax did Georgine's estate pay? Georgine died in 1996, leaving her $800,000 estate to her children by right of representation. Debts totaled $150,000 and expenses were $50,000. Calculate her estate's death tax.*

*** *Query 5 - 6. Given this information, what death tax did Harold's estate pay? Harold died in 1996, leaving his $980,000 estate to his brother. Debts totaled $65,000 and expenses were $20,000. Calculate his estate's death tax.*

Estate taxes for the generous decedent. Here, we put it all together. The estate taxes for an estate with prior post-76 gifts are calculated taking those gifts into account. These gifts are referred to as *adjusted taxable gifts.* They are adjusted in the sense that the gross value has been reduced by the annual exclusion and that all gifts that qualified for the marital or charitable deduction are excluded. The sole purpose of the adjusted taxable gifts coming into the estate tax equation is to move the decedent's taxable estate up into the appropriate marginal rates. The rates are appropriate in the sense that we now have a unified transfer tax system and the earlier gifts have already occupied the lower marginal rates. The steps are as follows: Similar to what was done for gifts, start with the gross estate (typically, the FMV of all that the decedent owned at the date of death); subtract debts, expenses, gifts to charities, and other deductions to arrive at the taxable estate; add the adjusted taxable gifts to determine the total estate tax base; use the tax rate table to determine the tentative tax on the total tax base; from the tentative tax, subtract the gift taxes payable on post-76 gifts (for most estates, the gift taxes payable will be the same as the total gift taxes paid on the post-76 gifts but keep in mind the decreasing marginal rate problem); subtract the unified credit to arrive at total death taxes (true for those estates that pay only a "pickup" tax, discussed later); and, finally, from the total death taxes subtract the state death tax credit (discussed shortly) to arrive at the federal estate tax.

TABLE 5 - 4 Federal Estate Tax (Form 706) Overview Model - **With** Prior Gifts

Gross estate	$xxx,xxx
Less: Total deductions	(xxx,xxx)
Leaves: Taxable estate	xxx,xxx
Plus: Adjusted taxable gifts (post-76)	xx,xxx
Equals: Estate tax base	$xxx,xxx

Calculate: Tentative estate tax	$xxx,xxx
Less: Gift taxes payable on post-76 taxable gifts	(xxx,xxx)
Less: Unified credit	(xxx,xxx)
Less: State death tax credit	(xxx,xxx)
Less: Other credits	(xx,xxx)
Equals: Federal estate tax	$xxx,xxx

Please note that the gift taxes payable credit is not the tentative tax on those earlier gifts, but rather is the dollar amount after application of the unified credit. Because this credit is designed to compensate for adding the adjusted taxable gifts to the estate tax base and because it is calculated using the gift taxes payable (i.e., the amount by which the tentative tax using date-of-death tax rates exceeds the date-of-gift unified credit) rather than the tentative tax, we must use the full unified credit for the year of death to arrive at the death taxes.

The state death tax credit does not reduce the total estate taxes. It merely divides the total death taxes between the federal and state governments. Every taxable estate large enough to pay federal estate taxes will use the unified credit and the state death tax credit. The former will apply to every estate to keep the smaller ones (or cumulative transfers, if you will) from being taxed, and the latter is used because every state in the nation collects death taxes that at least equal the federal state death tax credit.

The United States Estate (and Generation-Skipping Transfer) Tax Return, Form 706, is included on the "Teaching Aids" CD ROM (see file "Form 706 Estate Tax.pdf"). The return is commonly referred to as the 706. The due date for the 706 is nine months after the date of death. Hence, the 706 for the estate of a wealthy person who died on May 15th is due February 15th of the following year unless that falls on a holiday or weekend, in which case the return is due on the next business day. We will cover extensions later.

In the example that follows, you need to refer back to the example where Deborah made gifts in 1989, 1991, and 1992 to see how those prior gifts affect her estate taxes. You may wish to tag those pages to allow you to flip back and forth as you tackle this problem.

EXAMPLE 5 - 14. Deborah died on March 10, 1997, and left her estate to her four children. Her estate was worth $5,840,000, debts were $315,000, and expenses totaled $55,000. Her estate taxes were due December 10, 1997 (nine months to the day following her death).Taking into account the gifts she made in 1989, 1991, and 1992, her estate tax is as follows:

Gross Estate	$5,840,000
- Debts & expenses	($370,000)
- Marital & charitable deductions	$0
= Taxable estate	$5,470,000
+ Adjusted taxable gifts (post-76)	$2,150,000
= Estate tax base	$7,620,000

Tentative tax on estate tax base	$3,831,800
- Gift tax payable on post-76 taxable gifts	($661,500)
- Unified credit	($192,800)
= Total Death taxes (for most estates)	$2,977,500
- State death tax credit (we're jumping ahead)	($447,200)
- Other credits	$0
= Federal Estate Tax	$2,530,300

Note that to calculate the gift tax payable credit one must add up all the taxes paid, NOT the tentative tax on those prior gifts. The gift taxes paid (payable) is the amount in excess of the available unified credit. Because the entire prior adjusted taxable gifts (post-1976) are included in the tax base, the full unified credit is used in the calculation. *** *Query 5 - 7. Given the following information and taking into account her earlier gifts, what death tax did Martha's estate pay? Martha died in 1996, leaving her $2,550,000 estate to her children. There were debts of $240,000 and expenses of $60,000.*

UNIFIED RATE SCHEDULE

As a result of the Economic Recovery Tax Act of 1981 (ERTA), revised by the Tax Reform Act of 1984 and the Revenue Act of 1987, rates on taxable transfers in excess of $3 million have decreased periodically. With the addition of EGTRRA, top rates will continue downward through the phase-out of the estate tax in 2010. Table 5-5 on pages 196 -7 shows the federal unified transfer tax rate schedule. It is *unified* in the sense that the same rate schedule is used to calculate the tentative tax on taxable gifts and on taxable estates. The phase-in of the decreasing top marginal rates shown in Table 5-5 is repeated as Table 1 in Appendix A at the end of the book. The table is divided into 13 parts representing the various periods of decreasing maximum marginal rates from 1977 through the phase-out in 2010. The first part shows the rates for *all* transfer years after 1976 for taxable amounts up to $2 million. The next four parts constitute transition rates that apply to taxable transfers on amounts over $2 million during 1977 - 81, 1982, 1983, and 1984 - 86, a period during which the top rate moved down from a high of 70% to a high of 55%. The next two periods, 1987 - 97 and 1998 - 2001, had the same marginal rates as the immediate prior period but a 5% surcharge was added for taxable transfers over $10 million. The next five parts show that the top rate dropped to 50% in 2002 and then decreases by one percentage point each of the next four years before settling at 45% for the last three years of the estate tax. Finally, in 2010 the estate tax is gone and only the gift tax remains with a top marginal rate of 35% for taxable transfers above $500,000. A few examples will demonstrate the application of the unified rates. The facts in these examples are intended to be sufficiently general to apply to both lifetime gifts and transfers at death.

> EXAMPLE 5 - 15. The tentative tax on a $600,000 taxable transfer is $192,800. This represents the sum of $155,800 plus $37,000, which is 37% of $100,000, the excess of $600,000 over $500,000. Since the same rate table applies to all years for amounts up to $2 million, $192,800 would be the tentative tax on the amount $600,000 for all years after 1976. Of course, for the years 1987 through 1997 the unified credit was $192,800, hence it covered taxable transfers up to $600,000.

> EXAMPLE 5 - 16. The tentative tax on the taxable amount $3,250,000 in any year prior to 1984 is $1,433,300. This represents the sum of $1,290,800 plus $142,500, which is 57% of $250,000, the excess of $3,250,000 over $3,000,000. Because of the decrease in the top marginal rate, the same transfer after 1983 results in taxes of $1,428,300 (i.e., $1,290,800 plus 55% times $250,000).

The Revenue Act of 1987 phased out the tax benefits of the lower rates and the unified credit (described below) for taxable transfers made after December 31, 1987, that exceed $10 million. The Tax Payer Relief Act of 1997 changed the language of IRC § 2001(c)(2) such that the 5% recapture for transfers after 1997 "recaptures" the taxes saved by the lower rates but does not recapture the benefit of the unified credit. This recapture is implemented by imposing an additional 5% tax on taxable transfers above $10 million, with the surcharge ending when the benefits of the lower rates (for years 1988 - 1997, both the lower rates and the unified credit) have been recaptured. The range over which the rate jumps from 55% to 60% before dropping back to 55% is referred to as the "bubble." When the unified credit was $192,800 (years 1987 - 1997), the surcharge applied to taxable transfers between $10,000,000 and $21,040,000 (the surcharge went into effect in 1988).[3] Because the law for the period 1998 - 2001 recaptures just the benefit of the graduated marginal rates (i.e., those rates below 55% for taxable transfers of less than $3,000,000), the recapture is complete at taxable transfers totaling $17,184,000, at which point the marginal rate drops back to 55%. EGTRRA eliminated the surcharge for transfers after December 31, 2001.

TABLE 5 - 5 Federal Unified Transfer-Tax Rates - Since 1/1/77

If the Amount is:		Tentative Tax:		
Over	But Not Over	Base Amount +	Percent	On Excess Over
For years (1976-2009) the marginal rates are the same for taxable transfers up to $2,000,000.				
$0	$10,000	$0	18%	$0
$10,000	$20,000	$1,800	20%	$10,000
$20,000	$40,000	$3,800	22%	$20,000
$40,000	$60,000	$8,200	24%	$40,000
$60,000	$80,000	$13,000	26%	$60,000
$80,000	$100,000	$18,200	28%	$80,000
$100,000	$150,000	$23,800	30%	$100,000
$150,000	$250,000	$38,800	32%	$150,000
$250,000	$500,000	$70,800	34%	$250,000
$500,000	$750,000	$155,800	37%	$500,000
$750,000	$1,000,000	$248,300	39%	$750,000
$1,000,000	$1,250,000	$345,800	41%	$1,000,000
$1,250,000	$1,500,000	$448,300	43%	$1,250,000
$1,500,000	$2,000,000	$555,800	45%	$1,500,000
Top Rates: 1977 through 1981				
$2,000,000	$2,500,000	$780,800	49%	$2,000,000
$2,500,000	$3,000,000	$1,025,800	53%	$2,500,000
$3,000,000	$3,500,000	$1,290,800	57%	$3,000,000
$3,500,000	$4,000,000	$1,575,800	61%	$3,500,000
$4,000,000	$4,500,000	$1,880,800	65%	$4,000,000
$4,500,000	$5,000,000	$2,205,800	69%	$4,500,000
$5,000,000		$2,550,800	70%	$5,000,000
Top Rates: 1982				
$2,000,000	$2,500,000	$780,800	49%	$2,000,000
$2,500,000	$3,000,000	$1,025,800	53%	$2,500,000
$3,000,000	$3,500,000	$1,290,800	57%	$3,000,000
$3,500,000	$4,000,000	$1,575,800	61%	$3,500,000
$4,000,000		$1,880,800	65%	$4,000,000
Top Rates: 1983				
$2,000,000	$2,500,000	$780,800	49%	$2,000,000
$2,500,000	$3,000,000	$1,025,800	53%	$2,500,000
$3,000,000	$3,500,000	$1,290,800	57%	$3,000,000
$3,500,000		$1,575,800	60%	$3,500,000
Top Rates: 1984 - 1986				
$2,000,000	$2,500,000	$780,800	49%	$2,000,000
$2,500,000	$3,000,000	$1,025,800	53%	$2,500,000
$3,000,000		$1,290,800	55%	$3,000,000

(Rate Table 5-5 Continued)

Top Rates: 1987 - 1997

$2,000,000	$2,500,000	$780,800		49%	$2,000,000
$2,500,000	$3,000,000	$1,025,800		53%	$2,500,000
$3,000,000	$10,000,000	$1,290,800		55%	$3,000,000
$10,000,000	$21,040,000	$5,140,800	**	60%	$10,000,000
$21,040,000		$11,764,800		55%	$21,040,000

Top Rates: 1998 - 2001

$2,000,000	$2,500,000	$780,800		49%	$2,000,000
$2,500,000	$3,000,000	$1,025,800		53%	$2,500,000
$3,000,000	$10,000,000	$1,290,800		55%	$3,000,000
$10,000,000	$17,184,000	$5,140,800	**	60%	$10,000,000
$17,184,000		$9,451,200		55%	

Top Rates: 2002

$2,000,000	$2,500,000	$780,800	49%	$2,000,000
$2,500,000		$1,025,800	50%	$2,500,000

Top Rate: 2003

$2,000,000	$780,800	49%	$2,000,000

Top Rate: 2004

$2,000,000	$780,800	48%	$2,000,000

Top Rate: 2005

$2,000,000	$780,800	47%	$2,000,000

Top Rate: 2006

$2,000,000	$780,800	46%	$2,000,000

Top Rate: 2007-2009

$2,000,000	$780,800	45%	$2,000,000

2010 and beyond

Repealed for Estates. The maximum rate for gifts is 35% starting at $500,000.

** From 1988 - 1997, transfers between $10,000,000 and $21,040,000 were subject to a 5% surcharge, imposed until the benefit of the unified credit and of lower marginal rates was taken back. Transfers taking place 1998-2001 have the 5% surcharge applied to transfers between $10,000,000 and $17,184,000 (taking back the benefit of the lower rates, but not the benefit of the unified credit). The surcharge is eliminated for transfers after 2001.

The federal unified transfer tax rates have been quite progressive with marginal rates ranging from 18% to as high as 77% for pre-1976 taxable estates in excess of $10 million. EGTRRA lowered the top marginal rate to 50% in 2002 (lowering it one percent each year until it reaches 45% in 2007). The *marginal rate* is the rate levied on the next taxable dollar. The *average rate*, on the other hand, is obtained by dividing the tax by the total taxable amount. The following two examples demonstrate the manner in which the surcharge was used to take back the benefit of the unified credit (1988 - 1997) and of the lower marginal rates (1988-2001) prior to its repeal effective for transfers after 2001).

> EXAMPLE 5 - 17. The *tentative tax* on a taxable transfer of $21,040,000 in any year between 1988 and 1997 is $11,764,800. This amount represents the sum of a) $5,140,800 [the tentative tax on $10,000,000] and b) $6,624,000 [which is 60% of $11,040,000, the excess of $21,040,000 over $10,000,000]. The tentative tax less the unified credit [$11,764,800 - $192,800] results in total taxes of $11,572,000, i.e., exactly 55% of $21,040,000.

> EXAMPLE 5 - 18. The *tentative tax* on a taxable transfer of $3,000,000 (in any year prior to 2002) is $1,290,800, whereas the tax on that amount at a flat 55% is $1,650,000. The $359,200 difference is the amount saved by the graduated rates. Since the surcharge is 5%, the taxable transfer that must be subject to the surcharge in order to completely recapture the savings is $359,200 ÷ 0.05 = $7,184,000; which when added to $10,000,000 equals $17,184,000 which is the end of the bubble for the years 1998-2001.

UNIFIED CREDIT

In tax law, a *credit* is a dollar-for-dollar reduction in the *tentative tax*. A *deduction* is a dollar-for-dollar reduction from the gross amount to arrive at the amount taxable. A deduction provides only a fractional reduction in the amount of tax. The fraction is determined by the top marginal tax rates applicable to the particular transfer. The most important transfer tax credit of the five we will study is the unified credit. It will be covered next and the state death tax credit a little later in this chapter. The unified credit is the most important in that it comes into play every time there is a taxable transfer, whether by gift or estate. The other credits only apply to the estate tax. We will cover the state death tax in this chapter because it applies to all estates that exceed the applicable exclusion amount. The other three credits are the gift tax payable credit (introduced already in this chapter), the prior transfer credit, and the credit for foreign death taxes. These other credits are less likely to be encountered and will be covered at the end of the next chapter.

Prior to 1977 (the first year of the unified credit), a donor was allowed a lifetime exemption (deduction) of $30,000 for gifts in excess of the $3,000 per donee annual exclusions; and an estate exemption (deduction) of $60,000 when the person died. These had the effect of eliminating taxation on modest lifetime gifts and small estates. These were called the $30,000 gift exemption and the $60,000 estate exemption. Using the gift exemption did not reduce the estate exemption. Thus, an estate with a net value of less than $60,000 was tax-free, regardless of the amount of lifetime taxable gifts by the decedent. The Tax Reform Act of 1976 (TRA 76) eliminated the two exemptions and substituted a single *unified credit* applicable to both taxable gifts and taxable estates after 1976. With the new law, the unified credit available at the death of a donor is decreased to the extent that the donor's lifetime gifts used it up.

The unified credit has increased over the years, as shown in Table 5-6. After a decade of increases, the period from 1987 through 1997 saw the unified credit remain steady at $192,800. During that period, the credit sheltered $600,000 in net value transferred from gift and estate taxes. With the Tax Payer Relief Act of 1997, the amount that could pass tax-free increased, almost yearly, and was scheduled to reach $1,000,000 in the year 2006; however EGTRRA accelerated and expanded the increase. As the table shows, the estate tax unified credit covers the tentative tax on taxable transfers of $1,000,000 starting in 2002. It eventually shelters taxable estates of $3.5 million in 2009 just before the estate tax is phased out in 2010. As discussed earlier in this chapter, we use AEA as an abbreviation for the taxable amount that can be transferred free of taxes. What really happens is that the transfer generates a tentative tax that is just covered by the unified transfer tax credit.

Table 5-6 shows the unified credit, the applicable exclusion amount, and the "end of the bubble" since 1977 for both estates and gifts. The *applicable exclusion amount* is the taxable transfer that produces a tentative tax completely sheltered (offset) by that year's unified credit. The last column shows the end of the 60% marginal rate range (the bubble), i.e., the point at which the marginal rate finally drops back to 55% for the years 1988-2001. As stated earlier, the 5% surcharge only applies to taxable transfers above the $10,000,000 level made during 1988-2001. As previously stated, the unified credit for gifts and estates is the same until 2004, at which point the estate tax AEA increases to $1,500,000 (and continues to increase periodically) but the gift tax AEA remains at $1,000,000.

It is unfortunate that Congress put the term *applicable exclusion amount* in the Code to describe tax-free amount. Better terms would have been either the *credit shelter amount* or the *unified credit equivalent*.[4] The 1999 unified credit in the amount of $211,300 shelters $650,000 in taxable transfers from the estate (or the gift) tax, because the tentative tax on that size transfer is exactly $211,300. In 2002, the AEA (i.e., the sheltered amount) rises to $1,000,000 because the tentative tax on that amount is $345,800, exactly matching the unified credit for that year. In doing the calculations, we do not "exclude" the applicable exclusion amount; instead, we determine a tentative tax on the taxable transfer and then apply the appropriate unified credit. Oh well, we will fall in line and refer to this tax-free amount as the applicable exclusion amount, but please never subtract it when calculating the transfer tax.

EXAMPLE 5 - 19. After the unified credit is subtracted, the *net tax* on the amount $600,000 in 1983 is $113,500, which is the tentative tax of $192,800, reduced by the 1983 unified credit of $79,300.

EXAMPLE 5 - 20. Facts as in the prior example, except the applicable year is any year between 1987 and 1997. After the unified credit is subtracted, the net tax on $600,000 is zero, which is the tentative tax of $192,800, reduced by the unified credit of $192,800. Thus, for those years, the first $600,000 in taxable transfers was totally sheltered by the unified credit.

EXAMPLE 5 - 21. A $2,500,000 taxable gift (gross gift less the annual exclusion) is made in 2002. The tentative tax is $1,025,800. The unified credit of $345,800 reduces the tentative tax to $680,000. Note that the applicable exclusion amount did not enter into the calculation of the gift tax in this example, nor in any of the prior examples.

TABLE 5 – 6 Unified Credits (UCr), Applicable Exclusion Amounts (AEA), and the End of the Bubble by Year Since 1977

Year	UCr Estates	AEA Estates	End of Bubble	UCr Gifts	AEA Gifts
1977	$30,000	$120,667		$30,000	$120,667
1978	$34,000	$134,000		$34,000	$134,000
1979	$38,000	$147,333		$38,000	$147,333
1980	$42,500	$161,563		$42,500	$161,563
1981	$47,000	$175,625		$47,000	$175,625
1982	$62,800	$225,000	*The 5%*	$62,800	$225,000
1983	$79,300	$275,000	*surcharge*	$79,300	$275,000
1984	$96,300	$325,000	*started in*	$96,300	$325,000
1985	$121,800	$400,000	*1988*	$121,800	$400,000
1986	$155,800	$500,000		$155,800	$500,000
1987	$192,800	$600,000		$192,800	$600,000
1988	$192,800	$600,000	$21,040,000	$192,800	$600,000
1989	$192,800	$600,000	$21,040,000	$192,800	$600,000
1990	$192,800	$600,000	$21,040,000	$192,800	$600,000
1991	$192,800	$600,000	$21,040,000	$192,800	$600,000
1992	$192,800	$600,000	$21,040,000	$192,800	$600,000
1993	$192,800	$600,000	$21,040,000	$192,800	$600,000
1994	$192,800	$600,000	$21,040,000	$192,800	$600,000
1995	$192,800	$600,000	$21,040,000	$192,800	$600,000
1996	$192,800	$600,000	$21,040,000	$192,800	$600,000
1997	$192,800	$600,000	$21,040,000	$192,800	$600,000
1998	$202,050	$625,000	$17,184,000	$202,050	$625,000
1999	$211,300	$650,000	$17,184,000	$211,300	$650,000
2000	$220,550	$675,000	$17,184,000	$220,550	$675,000
2001	$220,550	$675,000	$17,184,000	$220,550	$675,000
2002	$345,800	$1,000,000		$345,800	$1,000,000
2003	$345,800	$1,000,000	*and it*	$345,800	$1,000,000
2004	$555,800	$1,500,000	*ended in*	$345,800	$1,000,000
2005	$555,800	$1,500,000	*2002*	$345,800	$1,000,000
2006	$780,800	$2,000,000		$345,800	$1,000,000
2007	$780,800	$2,000,000		$345,800	$1,000,000
2008	$780,800	$2,000,000		$345,800	$1,000,000
2009	$1,455,800	$3,500,000		$345,800	$1,000,000
after 2009	Estate tax repealed. Gift tax at top individual income tax rate.			$330,800	$1,000,000

Warning: Do NOT deduct the applicable exclusion amount. You must subtract the unified credit from the tentative tax for all of these transfer tax calculations. The only appropriate use of the term applicable exclusion amount is in giving general advice to clients, such as "in 2003, the tax-free applicable exclusion amount is $1,000,000." However, less confusion would result by just saying, "the amount that can pass tax-free is $1,000,000."

In many situations, the allowable unified credit will be less than the amount in Table 5 - 6. The actual amount of the allowable unified credit is the *lesser of either* the unused unified credit in the year of the transfer *or* the amount of the tentative tax. For example, the allowable unified credit for a $250,000 gift made in 2003 (assuming no prior taxable gifts) is $70,800, i.e., the lesser of $345,800, the unified credit available in 2003, and $70,800, the tentative tax on $250,000.

UNLIMITED MARITAL DEDUCTION

Since 1982, virtually all transfers to a *spouse*, whether made during lifetime or at death, have been tax-free; the amount of the transfer is treated as a "marital" deduction from the total gross estate or gross gifts. A brief history of the gift tax and estate tax marital deductions is described next.

The *gift tax marital deduction* was first enacted in 1948 to equalize tax treatment for married taxpayers in common law and community property states. It allowed a deduction for up to 50% of the value of noncommunity property gifts made to a spouse. TRA 76 changed this limit to 100% of the first $100,000, no deduction for the next $100,000, and 50% for all amounts exceeding $200,000.

The *estate tax marital deduction* was also first enacted in 1948, also to equalize tax treatment across the states. Its amount was limited to one half of the adjusted gross estate. TRA 76 changed this limit to the greater of $250,000 or one half of the adjusted gross estate, subject to further adjustments for any gift tax marital deduction taken and for property held as community property. The *adjusted gross estate* was defined essentially as the decedent's separate property, reduced by deductions for funeral and administration expenses, claims against the estate, and losses during administration.

The *present* 100% "unlimited" gift and estate tax marital deductions became effective in 1982.[5] In 1989 the marital deduction was eliminated for transfers to non-U.S. citizen spouses (taking place after November 10, 1988) unless certain arrangements are made, such as placing the transferred property in special trusts called qualified domestic trusts (QDOT's) or the surviving spouse becomes a citizen before the estate tax return is filed (even if filed late).[6] We will cover transfers to non-citizen spouses in more detail later in the book, but for now we will focus on the basics.

> EXAMPLE 5 - 22. Last year, Wilder gave property worth $10 million to his wife, Simba, a U.S. citizen. Although Wilder's "gross gift" was $10 million, his taxable gift is reduced to zero by the unlimited marital deduction. Thus, there is no tentative tax.

> EXAMPLE 5 - 23. Based on the facts in the prior example, assume instead that Wilder died last year leaving his entire $10 million estate to his wife. His taxable estate and tentative tax are zero, as a result of subtracting the $10 million marital deduction from the $10 million gross estate.

> EXAMPLE 5 - 24. On Henry's death in 2004 his will provided that his entire estate worth a net of $10 million goes outright to his wife, Kioko. Although she has lived in the U.S. for over 40 years, Kioko kept her Japanese citizenship and did not become a citizen of the United States. If she does not arrange to have the portion above the AEA placed in a QDOT, the estate will have to pay estate taxes of $4,065,000. Note that Henry's estate has an AEA of $1,500,000; it is only the marital deduction that is lost. So, to avoid the estate tax, Kioko must place assets worth at least $8,500,000 in a QDOT or she must become a U.S. citizen before the estate tax return is filed.

The current unlimited marital deduction will be examined in greater detail in the chapters that follow. Wealth transfer taxes incorporate other significant deductions, but their examination will also be deferred.

UNLIMITED CHARITABLE DEDUCTION

When determining transfer taxes, there is a 100% deduction for gifts or bequests made to qualified charities. Contrast this with income tax law, which limits the amount that can be deducted based on the type of gift, the nature of the charity (e.g., private foundation versus public charity), and the donor's adjusted gross income. We will reserve for a later discussion the complexities that arise when charitable gifts are made using trust arrangements that benefit both family members and charities.

THE ANNUAL EXCLUSION FOR LIFETIME GIFTS

Any donor can give to anyone (i.e., to any donee) gifts with a value up to $10,000 during any calendar year without reporting it and, of course, without it reducing the donor's unified credit or available AEA. This exclusion from the transfer tax is called the gift tax *annual exclusion*. The $10,000 amount has been indexed for inflation starting for years after 1998, with 1997 being the base year. It will change slowly (every three or four years, if inflation stays low), since the indexed amount is to be rounded down to the next lower multiple of $1,000.[7] The first increase took it to $11,000 the year 2002. It is likely to change again in 2004.

> EXAMPLE 5 - 25. In 1999, Warren gave $30,000 cash to his son, Bob, and a boat valued at $15,000 to his fishing buddy, Bill. Assuming no other deductions, and that Warren made no other gifts that year, he would file only one gift tax return, and his current taxable gifts for 1999 would equal $25,000. The first portion of Warren's gift tax return would look as follows:
>
> | | |
> |---|---|
> | Total current year's gross gifts | $45,000 |
> | Less: Annual exclusions and deductions | ($20,000) |
> | Equals: Current taxable gifts | $25,000 |

> EXAMPLE 5 - 26. In 1999, Mary gave an apartment building worth $275,000 to her three children as tenants in common. She also gave her brother Frank a used car worth $6,500. She would report gross gifts of $275,000 and taxable gifts, after taking the three annual exclusions, of $245,000. The gift to Frank should not be reported since it is under the annual exclusion amount.

Prior to 1982, the annual exclusion amount was $3,000 and the maximum marital deduction was 50% of the net value of the gift. In 1982, the marital deduction increased to 100% and the annual exclusion increased to $10,000. To qualify for the annual exclusion, the gift must be one of a *present interest*, meaning that the donee has immediate access to the gift for use and enjoyment.[8] Thus, a gift to an irrevocable trust giving one person a life estate and another the remainder creates two gifts, only one of which qualifies for the annual exclusion. The value of the life estate qualifies for the annual exclusion because it is a gift of a present interest, but the remainder does not qualify because it is a gift of a future interest.

When Congress eliminated the marital deduction for transfers to non-U.S. citizen spouses it created a special $100,000 annual exclusion for gifts between spouses where the donee is a non-citizen.

EXAMPLE 5 - 27. In 2003, Marcus gave stock worth $175,000 to his wife Lorena. He is a citizen of the United States, but, while Lorena is a legal resident, she has kept her Mexican citizenship. Marcus must file a gift tax return, but is allowed to claim a $112,000 annual exclusion (the indexed amount for 2003), hence the taxable gift is $63,000.

CUMULATIVE TAXATION OF WEALTH TRANSFERS

In wealth transfer taxation, succeeding transfers are unified, in part because they are taxed cumulatively. Under the *cumulative gift doctrine*, all past and present gifts are accumulated; that is, prior taxable gifts are added to current taxable transfers (whether lifetime gifts or the donor's estate at death) to determine the transfer tax base. There is one purpose, and only one purpose, to having adjusted taxable gifts as part of the estate tax calculation, and that is to boost the decedent's estate into higher marginal rates. These are the appropriate marginal rates when the net estate is viewed as just another in a series of transfers.

As we have seen, TRA 76 created the *unified transfer tax*, combining gift and estate taxation into a single tax structure having one rate schedule. However, TRA 76 did not achieve complete unification; for instance, the annual exclusion is available only for lifetime gifts. Unification did not produce a tax system that makes planners indifferent as to the timing of transfers; that is, whether one would recommend gifts over holding property until death, or vice versa, depends on the circumstances. For example, lifetime gifts use up less unified credit because of the annual exclusion, but appreciated property transferred at death receives a step-up in basis.

To recapitulate, let us review the points demonstrated in the earlier examples before we go on to cover the state death tax credits.

First, in calculating the gift tax, one includes in the item called "total prior taxable gifts" all taxable gifts made *since 1932*, the year of enactment of the gift tax. On the other hand, as we have said, in calculating the federal estate tax base, one includes in the item called "adjusted taxable gifts" only the taxable gifts made since January 1, 1977, i.e., since unification.

Second, in the *gift tax* model, the "unused unified credit" is the amount of the current unified credit reduced by the unified credit amount already used up to offset tentative gift taxes on gifts in prior years. It is based on the premise that once the amount of the (lifetime) unified credit is used up, each additional dollar of taxable gift is fully taxable. By way of contrast, in the *estate tax* model, the entire unified credit is subtracted from the tentative tax, because the "gift tax payable" credit for prior gift taxes is limited to the amount of gift taxes that would have been paid on the post-1976 gifts using the rates in effect at the date of death. This means that the gift taxes payable credit might be less than what was actually paid. This occurs where there were pre-1977 taxable gifts that pushed the post-1976 taxable gifts into higher marginal rates, or where very large post-1976 gifts were given at a time when the top marginal rates were higher than those in effect when the donor died.

For most estates with previous taxable gifts, the gift tax payable credit will equal the gift tax paid because only rarely do donors make taxable gifts large enough to result in an actual tax payment. And the recalculation issue will arise only if the donor made very large gifts both before and after January 1, 1977, or made extremely large gifts that went into marginal rates which were higher than those applied to the donor's estate. Assuming that all taxable gifts by the decedent were post-1976, whether the executor will have to do the recalculation rather than just using the gift taxes paid depends on several things: when the gift(s) were given; the taxable amount; and when the donor died.

For a death in 2001, recalculation is required if the decedent made taxable gifts in excess of $3,000,000 between 1977 and 1984 inclusive or in excess of $3,500,000 between 1977 and 1983, if the gift pushes the taxable estate above $10,000,000 and into the bubble, i.e., a top rate of 60%. For any death after 2001, any post-1976 taxable gift over $2,000,000 will require a recalculation for estate tax purposes. In the examples that follow, to simplify, we will assume all of the gifts occurred in the same year, but the result would be the same even if spread over several years, with the year given in the example being the last year of the cumulative gift giving. In each example, to determine the gift tax payable credit, one must use the unified credit in effect when the gift was made but the rate schedule in effect when the donor died.

> EXAMPLE 5 - 28. Donor made taxable gifts of $3,500,000 in 1985 and paid gift taxes of $1,444,000. When Donor died in 2001 her taxable estate was $5,000,000. Since the top rate (i.e., 55%) is the same for transfers in 1985 and in 2001, the gift tax payable and gift taxes paid are the same (i.e., $1,444,000).

> EXAMPLE 5 - 29. Donor made taxable gifts of $3,500,000 in 1983 and paid gift taxes of $1,496,500. When Donor died in 2001 her taxable estate was $5,000,000. Since the top rate in 1983 is higher (i.e., this gift goes into the 57% marginal rate)

than the top tax rate in 2001, the gift tax payable (i.e., recalculated using the date-of- death rates) is higher than the gift taxes paid, and the credit is only $1,486,500.

EXAMPLE 5 - 30. Donor made taxable gifts of $5,000,000 in 1999 and paid gift taxes of $2,179,500. When Donor died in 2004 his taxable estate was $20,000,000. Since the rate applied to the gift in 1999 is higher (i.e., the gift goes through marginal rates of 49%, 53%, and 55%) than the tax rate in effect in 2004 (i.e., a maximum of 48%), the gift tax payable is recalculated using date-of-death rates resulting in a credit that is lower than the $2,009,500 gift taxes actually paid.

Third, the tax on very large estates has decreased over the years. This is because the top marginal rates have decreased and the unified credit has increased. The top marginal rate drops from 70% for estates above $5 million in 1977 to 45% for estates above $2 million in 2007. The unified credit has increased over the years. The only period it remained steady was from 1987 through 1997 when a unified credit of $192,800 covered a taxable transfer of $1 million. The Tax Payer Relief Act of 1997 started it rising, and EGTRRA accelerated the increase through the year 2009 when it is supposed to reach $1,455,800 which translates into an applicable exclusion amount of $3.5 million. EGTRRA clouded the picture with its sunset provision that, after the elimination of the estate tax for the year 2010, restores both the estate and the gift tax to what it would have been had EGTRRA not become law, e.g., a $1 million applicable exclusion amount and a 55% maximum rate.

Fourth, gifts are valued as of the day given and estates are valued as of the day of the decedent's death. However, estates are allowed to elect an alternate valuation date of six months after the date of death, if certain criteria are met. An estate is allowed to make this *alternative valuation election* only if doing so will decrease (1) the gross estate and (2) the estate tax. It must also decrease the GST tax, if said tax is applicable. If the election is made, any property still held by the estate for the full six months is valued as of the six-month date, rather than the date of death; whereas, assets sold, distributed, or otherwise disposed of during the six-month period are valued as of the date each was transferred.[9] Where alternate valuation is elected, the alternate values determine the new basis, except as in the case when it is not elected, items that are income in respect to a decedent (IRD) do not get a step-up in basis. IRD includes those items that would have been income to the decedent had he lived, e.g., pension funds, IRA accounts, gain still to be recognized on an installment sell. The example that follows demonstrates the application of the alternative valuation election.

EXAMPLE 5 - 31. Wanda died on June 10, 2003, leaving property to her children. Art, her executor, has determined that the estate qualifies for the alternate valuation. Some of the assets included in her estate and their values at different times following her death were as follows:

Items:	FMV on 6/10/03	12/10/03	comments:
Home	$200,000	**$210,000**	Distributed 4/20/04, value $215,000.
HighTeck, Inc.	$40,000	**$15,000**	Distributed 4/20/04, value $12,000.
Old Blue, Inc.	$25,000	**$27,000**	Sold on 1/15/04 for $28,000.
BioDice, Inc.	$50,000	$30,000	Sold on 8/12/03 for **$35,000.**
Bond	$10,000	**$10,500**	Distributed 4/20/04, value $10,200.
Utility Inc.	$112,000	$120,000	Distributed 10/31/03, value **$115,000.**

Those items held the six-month period take as their estate tax value the value at the end of that period, hence: the home, High Teck, Inc., Old Blue, and the bond are scheduled on the return at their value on 12/10/03. Within the six-month period BioDice, Inc., was sold and Utility, Inc., was distributed so they take the sale price and distribution value, respectively. Scheduled values (i.e., what will be used on the estate tax return to determine the tax) are shown in bold. Note that, if alternate value is elected, the date-of-death value is not used (unless one sold or distributed the property on that date, an unlikely event) even if it is lower than the value six months later. The scheduled value determines the basis of each asset for income tax purposes.

THE CREDITS

There are five basic estate tax credits: the unified credit, the credit for state death taxes, the credit for gift tax payable, the credit for tax on prior transfers, and the credit for foreign death taxes. We have already covered the unified credit. The state death tax credit is certain to enter into the calculation of the estate taxes whenever the taxable estate actually exceeds the applicable exclusion amount.

The other three credits just mentioned occur less frequently and are covered briefly at the end of the next chapter. The prior transfer credit is introduced in Chapter 6 and covered again in Chapter 12 as part of advanced planning for very wealthy couples.

Credit for State Death Taxes

The law allows at least a partial credit for inheritance or estate taxes paid to the states. EGTRRA has reduced the credit for 2002 and completely phases it out in 2005, after which estates will only be allowed to deduct their state death taxes. The maximum credit is calculated using the State Death Tax Credit Tables shown below. Table 5-7A covers the period 1977-2001 and Table 5-7B covers the period 2002-2004. (Also reproduced in Appendix A as Tables 3A and 3B).

TABLE 5 - 7A Credit For State Death Taxes 1977 - 2001

Taxable Estate(TE)		Base	Rate	R Applied to
At Least	But Not Over	Amount	(R)	TE Over
$100,000	$150,000	$0	0.8%	$100,000
$150,000	$200,000	$400	1.6%	$150,000
$200,000	$300,000	$1,200	2.4%	$200,000
$300,000	$500,000	$3,600	3.2%	$300,000
$500,000	$700,000	$10,000	4.0%	$500,000
$700,000	$900,000	$18,000	4.8%	$700,000
$900,000	$1,100,000	$27,600	5.6%	$900,000
$1,100,000	$1,600,000	$38,800	6.4%	$1,100,000
$1,600,000	$2,100,000	$70,800	7.2%	$1,600,000
$2,100,000	$2,600,000	$106,800	8.0%	$2,100,000
$2,600,000	$3,100,000	$146,800	8.8%	$2,600,000
$3,100,000	$3,600,000	$190,800	9.6%	$3,100,000
$3,600,000	$4,100,000	$238,800	10.4%	$3,600,000
$4,100,000	$5,100,000	$290,800	11.2%	$4,100,000
$5,100,000	$6,100,000	$402,800	12.0%	$5,100,000
$6,100,000	$7,100,000	$522,800	12.8%	$6,100,000
$7,100,000	$8,100,000	$650,800	13.6%	$7,100,000
$8,100,000	$9,100,000	$786,800	14.4%	$8,100,000
$9,100,000	$10,100,000	$930,800	15.2%	$9,100,000
$10,100,000		$1,082,800	16.0%	$10,100,000

Note: The brackets found in §2011 have been adjusted by adding $60,000 at each level, hence you use the taxable estate without subtracting $60,000. See discussion that follows Table 5 - 7B.

TABLE 5 - 7B Credit For State Death Taxes 2002 - 2004

Taxable Estate(TE)		Year 2002		Year 2003		Year 2004	
At Least	But Not Over	Base Amount	Rate (R)	Base Amount	Rate (R)	Base Amount	Rate (R)
$100,000	$150,000	$0	0.6%	$0	0.4%	$0	0.2%
$150,000	$200,000	$300	1.2%	$200	0.8%	$100	0.4%
$200,000	$300,000	$900	1.8%	$600	1.2%	$300	0.6%
$300,000	$500,000	$2,700	2.4%	$1,800	1.6%	$900	0.8%
$500,000	$700,000	$7,500	3.0%	$5,000	2.0%	$2,500	1.0%
$700,000	$900,000	$13,500	3.6%	$9,000	2.4%	$4,500	1.2%
$900,000	$1,100,000	$20,700	4.2%	$13,800	2.8%	$6,900	1.4%
$1,100,000	$1,600,000	$29,100	4.8%	$19,400	3.2%	$9,700	1.6%
$1,600,000	$2,100,000	$53,100	5.4%	$35,400	3.6%	$17,700	1.8%
$2,100,000	$2,600,000	$80,100	6.0%	$53,400	4.0%	$26,700	2.0%
$2,600,000	$3,100,000	$110,100	6.6%	$73,400	4.4%	$36,700	2.2%
$3,100,000	$3,600,000	$143,100	7.2%	$95,400	4.8%	$47,700	2.4%
$3,600,000	$4,100,000	$179,100	7.8%	$119,400	5.2%	$59,700	2.6%
$4,100,000	$5,100,000	$218,100	8.4%	$145,400	5.6%	$72,700	2.8%
$5,100,000	$6,100,000	$302,100	9.0%	$201,400	6.0%	$100,700	3.0%
$6,100,000	$7,100,000	$392,100	9.6%	$261,400	6.4%	$130,700	3.2%
$7,100,000	$8,100,000	$488,100	10.2%	$325,400	6.8%	$162,700	3.4%
$8,100,000	$9,100,000	$590,100	10.8%	$393,400	7.2%	$196,700	3.6%
$9,100,000	$10,100,000	$698,100	11.4%	$465,400	7.6%	$232,700	3.8%
$10,100,000		$812,100	12.0%	$541,400	8.0%	$270,700	4.0%

Note: The brackets found in §2011 have been adjusted by adding $60,000 at each level, hence you use the taxable estate without subtracting $60,000. See the discussion that follows this Table.

IRC § 2011, Credit for State Death Taxes, uses a table that was in effect prior to TRA 76's unification of estate and gift tax, which eliminated the $60,000 estate exemption and replaced it with the unified credit. Nevertheless, Congress wanted to keep the state death tax credit at the same level for any given size estate, so § 2011 uses the term "adjusted taxable estate" to mean the "taxable estate reduced by $60,000" and requires the extra step of "adjusting" the taxable estate by $60,000 before going into the table. In Tables 5-7A and 5-7B we have "adjusted" the brackets, so you do not need to subtract the $60,000. To determine the State Death Tax Credit, find the bracket for the taxable estate (e.g., a taxable estate of $800,000 falls within the $700,000 to $900,000 bracket), subtract the start of the bracket from the taxable estate (e.g., $800,000 - $700,000 = $100,000) and multiply the difference by the rate appropriate for the year of death (e.g., if the death occurred in 2003 the rate for the $700,000 - $900,000 bracket is 2.4%) and add the product to the appropriate "base amount" to arrive at the credit (e.g., $2,400 + $9,000 = $11,400).

It is important to keep in mind that the taxable estate is the gross estate reduced by all deductions (e.g., debts, marital, etc.), but *before* prior taxable gifts are added into the tax base. Keep in mind that all states, even those with an inheritance tax, collect state death taxes at least equal to the federal state death tax credit. This maximizes their fiscal self-interest. Basically, if the inheritance tax amount is less than the allowable federal state tax credit, the state collects the difference, in addition to the inheritance tax. This tax that picks up the difference is generally called a "soak-up" or "sponge" tax. If the inheritance tax produces a tax greater than the federal state death tax credit, the state collects the greater amount, but the estate's credit on the federal return is still the calculated credit.

> EXAMPLE 5 - 32. Milo died in 2003, leaving his three children a gross estate of $2,780,000 with total deductions of $246,000. The state inheritance tax required the estate to pay $65,200 based on the rates for interests transferred to a decedent's children. The federal credit for state death tax for a taxable estate of $2,534,000 is $70,760. The bracket that covers this estate starts at $2,100,000, with a corresponding credit of $53,400 for that level, and a rate of 4% for amounts within the bracket, hence, add another $17,360 (i.e., 4% * (2,534,000 - $2,100,000)), for a total credit of $70,760. Since the state-calculated inheritance tax is only $65,200, the state's "sponge tax" law would require the estate to pay another $5,560.

In the above example, the state collects an extra $5,560 at no extra cost to the estate since it is merely a shift of this amount out of the federal pocket into the state's pocket. If the state collects more than the credit, then it really does cost the estate's beneficiaries.

> EXAMPLE 5 - 33. Suppose in the prior example, the state's inheritance tax caused state death taxes of $80,000. Since the federal state death tax credit would still be $70,760, the extra $9,240 [$80,000 - $70,760] would come out of the beneficiaries' pockets.

For the 33 states (as of 2001) imposing *only* a pickup tax, no state death tax will be owed by estates with a tax base (taxable estate plus adjusted taxable gifts) less than the AEA. In the other 17 states that have an inheritance or estate tax separated from the federal taxing scheme, the state death tax is often *higher* than the federal state death tax credit. Nonetheless, the estate is permitted a credit against the federal tax of only the amount determined as the federal state death tax credit. Thus, except for "pickup tax" states, the state death tax may be only partially covered by the credit.

> EXAMPLE 5 - 34. Kevin lived in a pickup tax state where the death taxes were defined as equal to the federal state death tax credit. When Kevin died in 2003, his gross estate was $3,900,000. He left $350,000 to his church. There were debts and expenses of $425,000. The taxable estate is $3,125,000 and the maximum allowed state death tax credit is $96,600 [bracket starts at $3,125,000; credit equals $95,400 + 7.2% * $25,000]. Total death taxes (in a pickup tax state) for a taxable estate of this size is $986,250; the state will collect $96,600 and the federal government will collect $889,650 [$986,250 - $96,600].

> EXAMPLE 5 - 35. Nicki was also domiciled in a pickup tax state when she died in 2003. Her estate exactly matched Kevin's, right down to giving $350,000 to her temple, such that the taxable estate was $3,125,000. The one difference was that Nicki, five years before her death, made taxable gifts equal to $900,000 to help out her brother and his family. As in the prior example, the taxable estate used to determine the state death tax credit is $3,125,000 even though Nicki made significant taxable gifts. Her tax base for calculating the tentative tax is $4,025,000, but this does not affect the state death tax calculation. The total taxes are $1,322,500, but the state death tax credit is still only $96,600, so the federal tax is $1,225,900.

*** *Query 5 -8.   Using the information in the last query (following Example 5 - 14), calculate Martha's state death tax assuming her state of domicile was a "pickup" tax state.*

Because EGTRRA eliminates the state death tax credit in 2005, the 33 states using the pick-up tax format will no longer collect revenues from this source. Given the fact that for estates just above the AEA the state death tax credit tends to shift all of the taxes to the state, the states have collected almost as much money as a result of the federal estate tax as has the federal government. With the anti-tax mood in the U.S., it will be hard for the pick-up tax states to go back to an inheritance tax or to some form of a state estate tax.

EXAMPLE 5 - 36. Craig, a resident of Arizona, died in 2004 leaving his estate to relatives. The taxable estate was valued at $1,550,000. Since Arizona is a pick-up tax state, the total tax is $22,500, the state death tax credit is $16,900 and the federal tax is $5,600. If Craig died in 2005, all else being the same, the tax would still total $22,500 but it would all go to the federal government and none to Arizona.

EXAMPLE 5 - 37. Similar facts to the last example, Rachel, a resident of Indiana, died in 2004 leaving her estate to relatives. The taxable estate was valued at $1,550,000; however, Indiana has its own inheritance tax. Assume that the inheritance tax was $16,900. The total tax is again $22,500, the state death tax credit is $16,900, the federal tax is $5,600, and the heirs are no worse off than had there been no inheritance tax. On the other hand, if Rachel died in 2005, the estate would owe $16,900 in inheritance taxes. These would be deductible on the estate tax return (taxable estate of $1,533,100 instead of $1,550,000) and the federal tax would be $14,895. Hence the total taxes would be $31,795 instead of $22,500, so the heirs receive almost $9,000 less.

FEDERAL GENERATION-SKIPPING TRANSFER TAX

Before EGTRRA, one fundamental policy objective of federal wealth transfer taxation was to tax all individual wealth in excess of a certain amount each time it passed to the next generation.

Only a tax that explicitly addresses the generational relationship between transferor and transferee can consistently tax wealth as it passes to succeeding generations. The GST tax is designed to meet that objective. The GST tax is levied when a transfer is made (by gift or bequest) to a person two or more generations below the donor. Persons in these lower generations are called *skip persons*. Pre-EGTRRA law gave every donor a $1 million GST exemption, so most donors and most estates have not been too concerned about this tax. EGTRRA makes it even less of a concern as the exemption will equal the AEA, i.e., in 2004 it will increase to $1.5 million, and it will continue to increase as the AEA increases until 2010, when it, along with the estate tax, is repealed.

Gifts covered by the annual exclusion, if made directly to grandchildren (or to any other skip person), are not subject to the GSTT, so they do not use up any of the exemption. There is also a special rule called the predeceased ancestor exception. In general, this rule "moves up" lower generations if the parent in the line of descent dies before the transfer. Generally, the predeceased ancestor exception applies only if the parent was deceased at the time of the transfer (or if the transfer was through a trust, was deceased the first time the trust was subject to transfer tax). The exception applies to lineal descendants of the transferor and, in some cases, to transfers to collateral heirs. Collateral heirs (nephews/nieces) move up only if the transferor has no living descendants. Where transfers to grandchildren (and to other skip persons) exceed the exemption amount (and the predeceased ancestor exception does not apply), the tax is horrendous since it is at the highest transfer tax marginal rate (e.g., 55% in 2001 decreasing to 45% over several years) and is in addition to the gift or estate tax.

IMPERFECT UNIFICATION

Although this chapter introduces the Unified Transfer Tax, there are many ways in which the three taxes (gift, estate, and generation transfer) are not really unified. Indeed, many transfer tax savings techniques take advantage of the fact that our "unified" transfer tax system is less than perfectly unified. To appreciate fully how these strategies work, one should consider how perfect unification might function and how the imperfections inherent in the present system can be exploited to transfer wealth with the least possible transfer tax cost. The following material will first consider what a perfectly unified tax system might be like and contrast it with our present imperfectly unified system. An ongoing example will illustrate the major points.

Perfect unification. With perfect unification of the three transfer taxes, an individual would be *indifferent*, from a total transfer tax planning point of view, as to whether the transfer should be a lifetime gift or a bequest. Under perfect unification, total transfer taxes would be the same whether an individual owned property at death or whether that person gave the property away during life.

To achieve perfect unification of the transfer tax system, all of the following conditions would have to be met:

1. A uniform system of deductions and credits for all gift and estate transfers. Otherwise, individuals would prefer to make that transfer which enjoyed the shelter of higher deductions or credits. As it is now, the annual exclusion favors lifetime gifts because there is no similar

exclusion at death. Also, transfers to charity during life result in an income tax deduction (while removing the transferred property from the transfer tax base), but a charitable bequest, while it removes the property from the taxable estate, results in no income tax savings.

2. The timing of a gratuitous transfer should not affect the basis of the property; either it should remain the same (as is generally the case with gifts) or it should change to its fair market value as of the date of transfer (as is generally the case with transfers at death). As it is now, there are two basic rules, one for gifts and one for estates. If the law changed to just one rule, it would almost have to be for estates to change to the gift tax rule (i.e., a carry-over basis) since it would otherwise be too easy to obtain a step-up in basis if all one had to do was to make a gift of the property. The basis rules are covered in detail in Chapter 7, but it is enough at this time to know that, for most gifts, the donee's basis will be the same as whatever the donor's basis was immediately before the gift.

3. A tax would be levied on all completed transfers, regardless of the value, and no matter when the transfer was made. All taxes would be levied at the same point in time, namely when the person died. The latter avoids the time value of money problem inherent in making gifts large enough to require the payment of gift taxes, and it avoids having the gift taxes paid reduce the tax base.

   a. All prior gifts made by the transferor would be added to the transferor's current transfer tax base. No gifts would be excluded, including gifts of very small value (even less than the annual exclusion amount) and gifts made many years ago. The record keeping nightmare that would result will keep this from ever being reality.

   b. All prior gifts would be included in the estate tax base at their *date-of-death value*, not date-of-gift value. Again, the tracking of the transferred property in order to ascertain its date-of-death value would be another nightmare that will keep this from becoming part of the law.

c. By not collecting transfer taxes until the donor dies, gift taxes would not be removed from the transfer tax base. As it is now, the time value of money makes gift taxes more expensive than death taxes; however, if the donor lives three years after making the gift that generated the gift tax, the payment of the tax results in a deduction from the estate tax base. A special rule that requires gift taxes paid on gifts made within three years of the donor's death is discussed in Chapter 6. When gift taxes are taxed as though still part of the donor's estate, it is referred to as "grossing up" the estate.

4. Only one tax rate schedule should be applied to all transfers treated cumulatively regardless of whether made during life or at death. Otherwise, individuals would seek to make transfers that would be subject to the lower tax rates. Indeed, if the transfers were not treated cumulatively, a person could take advantage of the lower marginal rates for both the gift tax and the estate tax even if the marginal rates were the same. Since 1977, the estate and gift taxes have been unified but the GST tax has not. Given the GSTT's purpose and the fact that it applies only to transfers to skip persons whereas the other two apply to all transfers (other than to a spouse or charities), it is hard to imagine how it could be unified with the other two.

5. The AEA should be the same for gifts and estates.[10] What this really means, of course, is that both should have the same unified credit. Generally, such has been the case, but it is changing. With EGTRRA, the AEA will increase periodically from 2002 through repeal in 2010, whereas the gift tax AEA will remain at $1,000,000.

To see the operation of perfect unification, consider the following example which incorporates all of the above assumptions. All transfers will be assumed to be made between 1987 and 1997, a period when the AEA was stable at $600,000 (i.e., the unified credit was $192,800) and the top marginal rates held steady at 55%.

EXAMPLE 5 - 38. Howard, a widower, died owning the following property: land worth $1 million and $1 million in cash. Ignoring all deductions and credits except the unified credit, Howard's estate tax is $588,000, calculated as follows:

Gross estate	$2,000,000
Less: Deductions	0
Taxable estate	$2,000,000
Tentative tax	$780,800
Less: Unified credit	(192,800)
Net estate tax	$588,000

Continuing the example, assume instead that Howard *gave* the land to his son four years before his death. At that time, the land was worth $800,000. Under perfect unification, Howard's total combined transfer taxes would still be $588,000. First, Howard would have paid a gift tax of $75,000, calculated as follows:

Current gross gift	$800,000
Less: Exclusions and deductions	0
Taxable gift	$800,000
Tentative tax	$267,800
Less: Unified credit	(192,800)
Gift tax	$75,000

Howard's estate tax and total transfer taxes would be $513,000 and $588,000, respectively, calculated as follows:

Gross estate (includes gift tax paid)	$1,000,000
Less: Deductions	0
Taxable estate	$1,000,000
Plus: Prior gifts (death value)	1,000,000
Estate tax base	$2,000,000
Tentative estate tax	$780,800
Less: Gift tax paid	(75,000)
Less: Unified credit	(192,800)
Net estate tax	$513,000
Total transfer taxes	$588,000

The gross estate of $1 million is the sum of property owned at death plus the gift tax paid. At death, Howard owned $925,000 in cash, which is the difference between the $1 million in cash initially owned and the $75,000 gift tax paid. Grossing up then increases the gross estate back to $1 million. Note that for prior gifts, we would use the date-of-death value.

Summarizing, under perfect unification, total transfer taxes would be the same whether an individual retained all property until death or whether he or she had made lifetime gifts. In the above example, the gift tax plus estate tax equals $588,000, the same total tax as with no lifetime gifts.

To see how the imperfections affect the unified transfer tax, let's rework the numbers from the last example. First, assuming no lifetime gifts, Howard's net estate tax will be $588,000, as previously shown. However, the lifetime gift alternative under today's imperfect unification has markedly different results.

Howard's gift tax, at the time of the gift, will be $71,100, rather that $75,000, calculated as follows:

Current gross gift	$800,000
Less: annual exclusion	(10,000)
Taxable gift	$790,000
Tentative tax	$263,900
Less: Unified credit	(192,800)
Net gift tax	$71,100

Howard dies owning $928,900 cash ($1 million less the gift tax paid of $71,100). Because the gift tax is not in the gross estate, Howard's estate tax will be $390,405, rather than $513,000, calculated as follows:

Gross estate	$928,900
Less: Deduction	0
Taxable estate	$928,900
Plus: Adjusted taxable gifts	790,000
Estate tax base	$1,718,900
Tentative tax	$654,305
Less: Gift tax paid	(71,100)
Less: Unified credit	(192,800)
Estate tax	$390,405
Total transfer taxes	$461,505

Howard's total transfer taxes are $461,505, the sum of $71,100 (gift tax) and $390,405 (estate tax). Hence the use of the lifetime gift has saved $126,495 in transfer taxes. Imperfect unification has enabled Howard to *freeze* the tax value of the land at its taxable gift value and to *reduce* his taxable estate by the amount of the annual exclusion and the gift tax paid. Thus, a total of $281,100 escaped transfer taxation. This represents the sum of three amounts: the $10,000 annual exclusion, the $71,100 gift tax paid, and the $200,000 in post-gift appreciation on the land. We can check our result, since the total tax saved will be 45% (the marginal estate tax rate) of $281,100, which equals the tax savings of $126,495.

The effect of not grossing up can be interpreted in a different way: the federal gift tax is calculated on what is called a *tax exclusive basis* (assuming no grossing up), since it is levied on the value of the gift and the gift tax is removed from the donor's wealth when he or she pays it. On the other hand, the estate tax is calculated on a *tax inclusive basis*, since it is levied on the entire estate, which includes the amount that will be used to pay the estate tax.

Thus, the present system's failure to completely unify estate and gift taxes can yield substantial transfer tax savings for persons owning medium to larger amounts of wealth. Further discussion of these issues will be deferred to chapters 13 and 14 where we discuss various lifetime transfers.

This chapter has introduced federal wealth transfer taxation, emphasizing the tax calculations. The GSTT, introduced above, is discussed in more detail in Chapter 12. The next two chapters cover the estate and gift taxes with regard to matters that are less quantitative in nature.

QUERIES ANSWERED

1. The annual exclusion reduced the gross gift of $1 million down to $990,000. The marginal rate just below $1 million is 39%.

2. The estate does not have the benefit of the $10,000 annual exclusion. The marginal rate just below $2 million is 45%.

3. The gift tax on a gross gift of $750,000 (taxable gift of $740,000) is $51,800 [tentative tax of $244,600 minus unified credit of $192,800].

4. The three gifts (all over $10,000) total $167,000. The taxable gift is $137,000. Tentative tax on the total gifts ($877,000) is $297,830, less the tentative tax on prior period gifts ($244,600), resulting in tentative tax on the current taxable gifts of $53,230. Since the unified credit was used against the tentative tax on the 1990 gift, $53,230 is the gift tax due.

5. Georgine's taxable estate is $600,000. The tentative tax is $192,800, which is the same as the unified credit amount, hence zero tax. Note that we do

NOT subtract $600,000, because there is no $600,000 exemption and there is no $600,000 exclusion.

6. Harold's taxable estate is $895,000. The tentative tax of $304,850 minus the $192,800 unified credit gives estate taxes of $112,050.

7. Martha's estate, taking into account her earlier gifts:

Gross estate	$2,550,000
- Debts & expenses	($300,000)
- Marital & charitable deductions	$0
= Taxable estate	$2,250,000
+ Adjusted taxable gifts (post-76)	$877,000
= Estate tax base	$3,127,000
Tentative tax on estate tax base	$1,360,650
- Gift tax payable, post-76 gifts	($105,030)
- Unified credit	($192,800)
= Total death taxes	$1,062,820

8. Martha's state death tax (also the amount her estate pays to the state) and the federal amount.

= Total death taxes	$1,062,820
- State death tax credit	($118,800)
- Other credits	$0
= Federal estate tax	$944,020

QUESTIONS AND PROBLEMS *[Generally, for estate tax problems and examples in this textbook, assume the decedent was domiciled in a pick-up tax state.]*

1. In what sense is the future of the estate and gift tax uncertain beyond the year 2010?

2. Outline the history of federal wealth transfer taxation with emphasis on the changes that took place in 1977, 1982, 1984, 1998, and 2001.

3. Why would the imposition of an estate tax without an accompanying gift tax be largely ineffective?

4. What was the purpose of the 5% surcharge? Why was it referred to as the "bubble"? What caused the bubble to burst?

5. (a) Describe the chronological progression of the amounts of the unified credit. (b) What is the term that, because of the Taxpayer Relief Act of 1997, means the largest amount that can be transferred by gift or through a decedent's estate without generating a transfer tax? (c) In what sense is this term a misnomer?

6. Is the AEA the same for gifts and estates?

7. (a) What is the annual exclusion? (b) Is it available for transfers to non-relatives? (c) When did it increase to $10,000 and what was it immediately before the increase? (d) Explain indexing for inflation as it relates to the annual exclusion.

8. In 2001, Jill gave her best friend Tristan real estate valued at $120,000 and several savings bonds valued at $6,000. She also gave Millie $15,000 in cash. On New Year's Eve, she gave David stock worth $7,000. For David's birthday on January 17, 2002, she gave him additional stock worth $9,000. She made no other significant gifts in 2002. What must Jill report as gross gifts and as taxable gifts for each year?

9. Describe the unlimited marital deduction. What is the rule for gifts to non-U.S. citizen spouses?

10. In 2000, Tara gave John, her English husband, real estate with an appraised value of $500,000. It was her only taxable gift to him for the year. The next

year she gave him stock worth $350,000. How much is reported each year as a taxable gift? [Before answering, check Table 7, Estate Planning Indexed Values, in Appendix A.]

11. Determine the tentative tax and the amount of gift tax for the following transfers by rock star, Denise:
    a. In 1995 she gave her friend, Gilbert, shares of stock worth $350,000 and her friend, Janie, stock worth $140,000.
    b. In 1998, she gave Roger municipal bonds worth $125,000, Max a vacant lot valued at $50,000, and Iris cash in the amount of $35,000.
    c. In 2001, she gave her church stock worth $200,000, her mother, Marlene, a new Cadillac valued at $55,000, and her boyfriend a sailboat worth $180,000.

12. Determine the tentative tax and the amount of gift tax for the following transfers by wealthy mutual fund manager, Martin:

    a. In 1995, he gave his daughter, Caroline, mutual fund shares of stock worth $550,000 and his son, Jon, additional shares worth $380,000.
    b. In 1998, he gave his sister, Dori, tickets for an around-the-world, first class cruise valued at $60,000, plus spending money of $40,000.
    c. In 2001, he gave another $45,000 to Caroline and $195,000 to Jon. [Use $10,000 as the annual exclusion.]

13. Determine the tentative tax and the amount of gift tax for the following transfers by CEO of SoftWearables, Shannon:

    a. In 2001, she gave her husband, Henry, shares in SoftWearables worth $850,000 and her daughter, Cheryl, shares in the company worth $1,530,000. [No split gifts. We will do these in a later chapter.]
    b. In 2002, she gave additional shares to Henry worth $90,000, a car to Cheryl worth $9,000, and to her son, William, and his wife, Ruby, a house worth $750,000 (paid for in full) and stock worth $250,000. [Use $10,000 as the annual exclusion.]

14. In the past it was said that having a modest state inheritance tax or using the pick-up tax approach did not diminish the amount that beneficiaries of an estate would receive, but that is changing. What is the change? For each of the following, how will the change affect state revenues and beneficiaries in:

(a) states with a pick-up tax; and (b) states with a separate inheritance or estate tax not based on the federal credit?

15. When Darcy died in 2004 her taxable estate was $3,000,000. Her estate had an inheritance tax and a soak-up tax. The calculated inheritance tax was $40,000. (a) What would the soak-up amount be? (b) How would the inheritance tax be treated if Darcy had died in 2005?

16. In Code § 2011 the term "adjusted taxable estate" is used to mean the taxable estate less $60,000. What use is made of this adjusted taxable estate amount? How do Tables 5 - 7A and 5 - 7B deal with this "adjustment"?

17. Calculate the state death tax credit for a $4,000,000 estate for each of the following years:

1977	2001	2003	2007

18. Calculate the state death tax credit for a $3,500,000 estate for each of the following years:

1977	2001	2002	2003	2004	2005

19. Keep in mind the difference between gift tax payable and gift tax paid in doing this problem: In 1984, Russell made a gift to his three children of an apartment building appraised at $5,030,000. When he died in 2005, his gross estate left entirely to his children was valued at $11,000,000 with debts and expenses of $1,000,000. Calculate: (a) the gift tax; (b) the estate tax and the gift tax payable credit. (c) Since the purpose of the adjusted taxable gifts being part of the estate tax calculation is to push the estate into the appropriate marginal rates, and the earlier gifts have gone through all of the lower marginal rates, it seems as though the total tax should be 47% of the taxable estate (i.e., $4,700,000). Why is it not? Show the math as part of your answer. [Hint: consider the changing unified credit.]

20. Keep in mind the difference between gift tax payable and gift tax paid in doing this problem: In 1992, Jesse made a gift to his two children of publicly traded stock at $15,020,000. When he died in 2007, his taxable estate left entirely to his children was valued at $32,000,000 with debts and expenses

of $2,000,000. Calculate: (a) the gift tax; (b) the estate tax and the gift tax payable credit. (c) Since the purpose of the adjusted taxable gifts being part of the estate tax calculation is to push the estate into the appropriate marginal rates, and the earlier gifts have gone through all of the lower marginal rates, it seems as though the total tax should be 45% of the taxable estate (i.e., $13,500,000). Why is it not? Show the math as part of your answer. [Hint: consider the changing unified credit.]

21. When Faustino died in 2004, his gross estate was worth $2,150,000. Debts and expenses were $40,000. He left his $500,000 home to his wife, Rosa, a cash bequest of $30,000 to his church, and the rest of his estate to his seven children by a prior marriage. Determine: (a) the total death taxes; (b) the state death tax; and (c) the federal estate tax.

22. (a) What is the meaning of perfect unification? (b) In what ways is our present unified transfer tax system imperfect? (c) How has EGTRRA made it a little less perfectly unified?

Use the ETAX program to do the problems that follow.

23. In 2011, Silvia made a gift of stock worth $2,012,000 to her daughter Heather. Assume that the annual exclusion is $12,000. What is the gift tax? [Note that the top rate drops to 35%. At what level will that occur?]

24. When Margaret died in 2001, her gross estate was worth $1,850,000. Debts and expenses were $210,000. She left her estate to her best friend, Diane. Determine: (a) the total death taxes; (b) the state death tax; and (c) the federal estate tax.

25. When Stephen died in 2003, his gross estate was worth $19,750,000. Debts and expenses were $1,340,000. He left his estate in equal shares to his brother, Mark, and his sister, Leilani. Determine: (a) the total death taxes; (b) the state death tax; and (c) the federal estate tax.

26. When rock star Denise (see earlier problem) died intestate in 2004, she left an estate valued at $4,890,300. Debts and expenses were $1,348,900. The entire estate went by intestate succession to her mother. Take the earlier gifts into account as you determine: (a) the total death taxes; (b) the state death tax; and (c) the federal estate tax.

27. When Martin (see earlier problem) died in 2002, his will left $200,000 to his sister, and the residue of his estate to his issue, by right of representation. His estate was valued at $13,840,500 and debts and expenses were $310,740. Take the earlier gifts into account as you determine: (a) the total death taxes; (b) the state death tax; and (c) the federal estate tax. [reminder: gross up]

28. When CEO Shannon (see earlier problem) died in early 2005 (within three years of the gifts in 2002), her will left half her net estate (i.e., after debts and expenses but before taking marital or charitable deductions into account) to Henry, her husband. It also gave $100,000 to her temple and the rest to her children. She left an estate valued at $14,460,600. Debts and expenses were $2,940,400. Take the earlier gifts into account as you determine: (a) the total death taxes; (b) the state death tax; and (c) the federal estate tax. [Reminder: gross up; neither the marital share nor the charitable share are charged with any of the death taxes; gift tax payable will be less than the gift taxes paid.]

ANSWERS TO QUESTIONS AND PROBLEMS *(odd numbered only)*

1. EGTRRA eliminated the estate tax as of 2010 but included a "sunset" provision that causes the law to disappear by 2011. So unless Congress acts to undo the sunset provision, it will be as if the law was never passed. This would give us an AEA of $1,000,000 and top rates of 55%, with a surcharge for transfers over $10 million. It would also restore the GST tax and the state death tax credit (due to go in 2005).

3. The imposition of a transfer tax at death without an accompanying gift tax would be largely ineffective because very elderly or terminally ill persons could circumvent the tax by making lifetime transfers.

5. a. The unified credit increased annually from $30,000 in 1977 to $192,800 in 1987. It stayed at that level through 1997. In 1998, it started increasing again and was due to increase to $345,800 in 2006, but EGTRRA accelerated the increase such that the unified credit will be $345,800 in 2002, eventually increasing to $1,455,800.

   b. The new term is the applicable exclusion amount. The applicable exclusion amount for 2002 is $1,000,000 because the tentative tax on that amount is $345,800, matching the available unified credit for that year.

   c. The term *applicable exclusion amount* is a misnomer because it implies that the amount is somehow subtracted or not taxed, but technically it is taxed. However, it is covered by the unified credit, therefore amounts less than the applicable exclusion amount will not result in the payment of any transfer taxes.

7. a. The annual exclusion is an amount that can pass gift tax-free, without using up any of the donor's unified credit. It only applies to gifts of a present interest. [There is one major exception to the present interest requirement. It applies to certain gifts given to benefit minors that meet the requirements of IRC § 2503(c). The exception is discussed later.]

   b. It is available even for gifts to non-relatives, so be nice to everyone.

   c. It went from $3,000 in 1981 to $10,000 in 1982.

   d. Indexing means that the $10,000 will increase from time to time, starting in years after 1998, as inflation decreases the purchasing power of the dollar when compared to the base year of 1997. The increases will be in increments of $1,000, with the rounding always being down to the next lower multiple of $1,000.

9. The unlimited marital deduction allows a deduction for all transfers to a spouse, whether during lifetime or at death. The property must be included in the transferor's gross estate, it must actually "pass" to the spouse, and the transfer cannot be subject to a terminable interest unless it falls into one of the exceptions described in the chapter. The marital deduction was eliminated for transfers (gift or estate) to non-citizen spouses unless a QDOT is used, or in the case of estates, the surviving spouse becomes a citizen before the return is filed. For gifts to non-citizen spouses there is a $100,000 (indexed) annual exclusion.

11. Denise's gifts: (a) 1995 - Taxable $470,000, tentative tax $145,600, unified credit $192,800, gift tax $0; (b) 1998 -Taxable $180,000, prior $470,000, tentative tax current $65,700, credit available $56,450, gift tax $9,250; (c) 2001-Taxable $215,000, prior $650,000, current gifts tentative tax $81,850, available credit $18,500, gift tax $63,350.

13. Shannon's gifts: (a) 2001 - Taxable $1,520,000, tentative tax $564,800, unified credit $220,550, gift tax $344,250; (b) 2002 -Taxable $980,000, prior gifts $1,520,000, current gifts' tentative tax $461,000, available credit $125,250, gift tax $335,750.

15. Darcy's gift: The state death tax credit for a $3 million taxable estate is $45,500. Since the regular inheritance tax was $40,000, the soak-up tax would be $5,500 [i.e., the difference when the state tax is less than the credit]. Had the death occurred in 2005, there would be no federal credit for the inheritance tax, instead it would be allowed as a deduction. A deduction of $40,000 in 2005 would drop the estate tax from $695,000 to $676,200, a reduction of $18,800, nowhere near as good as a $45,500 credit.

17. The state death tax credit for a $4,000,000 estate:

1977	2001	2003	2007
$280,400	$280,400	$140,200	$0

Note: after 2004, state death taxes are deductible from the gross estate.

19. Russell: (a) The gift tax is $2,294,500. (b) The estate tax is $4,240,500 and the gift tax payable credit is $2,094,500. (c) The reason that the tax is not $4,700,000 is that the unified credit increased from $96,300 in 1984 to $555,800 in 2005 (a difference of $459,500). The estate gets the advantage

of the increase. Note that if one adds $459,500 to $4,240,500 the total is $4,700,000.

21. Faustino: The deductions total $570,000, leaving a taxable estate of $1,580,000. The tentative tax is $591,000, less a unified credit of $555,800, which leaves total taxes of $36,000. The state death tax credit is $17,380 which subtracted from the total taxes leaves $18,620 for the federal tax.

23. The gift tax is $350,000. Note from the Table on Federal Rates that transfers above $500,000 enter a marginal rate of 37% and there are many more brackets above that one. The top rate after 2009 is 35%, all rate brackets above $500,000 disappear, and gifts above that are taxed at a marginal rate of 35%. The unified credit of $330,800 takes care of the tax on the first $1 million.

25. Stephen's estate in 2003: The taxable estate is $18,410,000 and the tentative tax is $8,821,700, less the unified credit of $345,800 equals a total tax of $8,475,900. The state death tax is $1,206,200 and the federal tax is $7,269,700.

27. Martin's estate in 2002: Note that gift taxes paid and payable are the same since the total taxable gifts were less than $2,000,000, hence the marginal rates were no greater than the effective estate tax rates. Since Martin died within three years of the last set of gifts, the estate includes the $71,700 paid. Total taxes are $6,625,280. The state death tax is $1,232,275 and the estate tax is $5,393,005.

28. Shannon's estate in 2005: Her gross estate is $14,796,350 because it includes the gift taxes paid in 2002. The marital deduction is $5,760,100 (($14,460,600-$2,940,400)/2), added to the $100,000 charitable deduction, and debts/expenses of $2,940,400 results in total deductions of $8,800,500, leaving a taxable estate of $5,995,850. The gift tax payable is $670,000 because one must recalculate the second gift using date-of-death marginal rates, resulting in $325,750 instead of $335,750 (for the first gift the top rates were less than or equal to the date-of-death rates, so it did not need to be recalculated). State death taxes are zero (gone in 2005). The federal tax is $2,608,050.

ENDNOTES

1.   IRC § 2503(b)(1).

2.   *Economic Growth and Tax Relief Reconciliation Act of 2001*, §901. Sunset of Provisions of Act.

3.   IRC § 2001(c)(2).

4.   IRC § 2011. The term "applicable exclusion amount" was added by the Tax Payer Relief Act of 1997.

5.   Although there is no marital deduction covering outright gifts to a non-citizen spouse, Congress created a special annual exclusion of $100,000 (indexed for inflation) per year.

6.   Reg. § 20.2056A-1(b).

7.   IRC § 2503(b)(2).

8.   IRC § 2503(b)(1).

9.   IRC § 2032.

10.   From 1/01/1977 through 6/30/1977 the gift tax unified credit was $6,000, for the rest of the year it was $30,000, whereas the estate tax unified credit was $30,000 for the entire year.

CHAPTER 6

The Federal Estate Tax

OVERVIEW

In general, a federal estate tax return must be filed for any decedent who was a *citizen* or *resident* of the United States if at the time of death the value of the person's gross estate (regardless of where the property is situated[1]) when added to his or her adjusted taxable gifts equals or exceeds the applicable exclusion amount (AEA) for the year of death.[2] For example, the estate of a citizen who dies in the year 2002, leaving a gross estate of $800,000, and who had made taxable gifts of $300,000, must file a return because the sum exceeds that year's $1,000,000 AEA. Filing is required even if the entire estate is left to a surviving spouse and the marital deduction reduces the taxable estate to zero; or if the gross estate exceeds the AEA but debts and expenses reduce it below that level.[3] While the Code gives the duty to file the return to the executor of the estate, the Regulations state that, if there is no executor appointed, then every person who is in actual or constructive possession of any property of the decedent situated in the U.S. is considered an executor.[4]

Once the value of the property transferred at death is determined, that value is added to the adjusted taxable gifts to arrive at the tax base. The unified transfer tax rate is applied to the tax base to determine the tentative tax. Credits are subtracted from the tentative tax to arrive at the estate's tax liability.

A federal estate tax return must be filed for a decedent *non-citizen, non-resident,* if the person died owning property situated in the United States that was worth more than $60,000.[5] Only the U.S. situs property is taxed,[6] but the estate is entitled to a maximum unified credit of only $13,000.[7] Special rules, beyond the scope of this text, apply for decedents who are citizens of a U.S. territorial possession or are U.S. residents but are also citizens of countries having tax treaties with the U.S.

The executor is responsible for paying the tax.[8] If there is no court-appointed executor (or if he or she fails to pay the tax), persons in actual or constructive possession of any of the decedent's property are liable for the tax to the extent of the value of that property.[9] This includes surviving joint tenants[10] and, after the settlor dies, the trustee of his or her revocable living trust.[11]

TABLE 6-1 Federal Estate Tax (Form 706) Comprehensive Outline

Gross estate (§§ 2031-2045)		$xxx,xxx
Less deductions:		
Debts & expenses (§ 2053)	xx,xxx	
Losses during administration (§ 2054)	xx,xxx	
Charitable bequests (§ 2055)	xx,xxx	
Marital bequests (§§ 2056-2056A)	xx,xxx	(xxx,xxx)
Leaves: Taxable estate (§ 2051)		xxx,xxx
Plus: Adjusted taxable gifts (post-76) (§ 2001)		xx,xxx
Equals: Estate tax base (§ 2001(b)(1)(A) & (B))		$xxx,xxx
Calculate: Tentative tax (§ 2001)		$xxx,xxx
Less Credits:		
Gift taxes payable (post-76) (§ 2001(b)(2))	xx,xxx	
Unified credit (§ 2010)	xx,xxx	
State death tax credit (§ 2011)	xx,xxx	
Prior transfer credit (§ 2013)	xx,xxx	
Other credits (§§ 2014-2015)	xx,xxx	(xxx,xxx)
Equals: Federal estate tax (§ 2001)		$xxx,xxx

This chapter is divided into three major parts. Each part will examine a major component of the estate tax return, specifically the gross estate, allowable deductions, and allowable credits. All code sections (e.g., § 2033) mentioned in this book refer to the Internal Revenue Code unless otherwise indicated. Most of these sections are included on the Teaching Aids CD ROM that came with this book. Certain section numbers are used in the text because they are used by estate planners as terms meant to convey a concept, e.g., "a § 2036 problem" with reference to a trust would mean that the settlor had retained certain interests that cause the trust to be included in the settlor's estate. While studying this chapter the reader is urged to review Form 706, the U.S. Federal Estate Tax Return (file "Form 706 Estate Tax.pdf" on the Teaching Aids CD ROM). Notice that the first page has the calculation of the estate tax and that the first two lines (the gross estate and allowable deductions) are drawn from the recapitulations found as Part five of page three. As discussion begins to focus on a particular Code section, take the time to read the section, then read it again before you go on to the next topic.

ONE: THE GROSS ESTATE

There is no short definition for the term *gross estate*. Of course, it includes all that one owns in the usual sense of ownership. One should not be surprised that the gross estate on rare occasions includes property the decedent no longer owned. When this occurs the decedent probably had such control and/or beneficial interest so similar to ownership that inclusion in the estate just seems reasonable, e.g., property held in a revocable trust whereby the trustee holds legal title, but the decedent controlled beneficial interest. There are a number of situations where property must be included in a decedent's gross estate even though the decedent lacked title to the property. Indeed, in some circumstances property is included even though the decedent had given up any control or beneficial interest in the property, e.g., gift taxes paid on any gift made within three years of death and a gift of life insurance made within three years of the insured-owner's death.

Analysis of the components of the gross estate will be divided into four parts. The first part covers interests owned at death (§§ 2033, 2034, 2039, 2040, 2041, 2042). The second part covers transfers where the transferor retained an interest or control over beneficial enjoyment of the property transferred (§§ 2036, 2037, and 2038). The third part covers the gift tax paid on any gift made within three years of the donor's death (§ 2035(b)).[12] Finally, those few types of transfers made within three years of death (§ 2035(a)) still require inclusion even though the decedent-transferor retained neither any control nor any beneficial interest in the property.[13] A caution is in order here: the three-year inclusion rule applies only to transfers of life insurance policies or to the relinquishments of retained interests within three years of the donor's death. *There is no three-year rule for most gifts (e.g., none for outright gifts of cash, land, stock, bonds, jewelry, etc.).*

Basic Interests Owned at Death: §2033

The gross estate includes all property in which the decedent had a beneficial interest.[14] Common examples are fee simple interests such as ownership interests in a house, furniture, personal effects, a business, investments, and copyrights. However, the gross estate includes less obvious interests. As a rule, if the decedent had a beneficial interest in property at death, the interest is probably included.

EXAMPLE 6 - 1. Decedent died on June 18 owning 100 shares of XYZ stock worth $10,000. On May 26, a *dividend* of $1.50 per share was declared payable on June 22 to stockholders of record on June 14. Included in the gross estate will be $10,150, representing the value of the stock plus the dividends declared.

EXAMPLE 6 - 2. The same facts apply as in the prior example, except that the holder-of-record date was June 19. The dividends are not included in the decedent's gross estate because at the date of death the decedent was not legally entitled to them.

EXAMPLE 6 - 3. Winnie created a life income trust for her brother Charlie, with a vested remainder interest for her nephew Max. When Max died, Charlie was still going strong at age 85 and the trust was worth $1,000,000. Max's gross estate includes the present value of the *vested remainder interest* in the trust. Due to his death, Max will never possess the trust property, but his will determines who will eventually have the property. Had he died without a will then his heirs, according to the laws of intestate succession, would eventually receive the property. *** *Query 6 - 1. If the rate for valuing remainder interests was 8% when Max died, what is the included value?*

EXAMPLE 6 - 4. At her death, decedent owned "tax-free" municipal water district bonds. Although income from such bonds is exempt from federal income tax, the value of the bonds (plus the accrued interest on them) is included in her gross estate.

EXAMPLE 6 - 5. A couple lived and worked in a community property state. Stock was purchased using the wife's wages. They had no agreement or special understanding that the stock would be her separate property. When the husband died, the stock was worth $100,000. Even though it was held in the wife's name, it was community property; therefore, one-half of its value ($50,000) must be included in his gross estate.

Section 2033 would also cover the present value of a *joint and survivor annuity*, one which continues to be payable in whole or in part to another after the decedent's death, if the decedent purchased the annuity. Its value would be the present discounted value of the survivor's expected income payments. Code §2039, covered shortly, specifically calls for the inclusion of survivorship annuities in a decedent's gross estate. Overlapping Code sections are not at all unusual. An interest may be included by virtue of a broadly written section such as §2033 and by virtue of a more specific code section, such as §2039 covering general powers of appointment. Some of the overlap is due to an effort by Congress to clarify what property arrangements cause property to be included in the gross estate. A seemingly redundant section may be there to avoid taxpayer suits that raise as an issue whether more general language, such as is found in §2033, was really intended to cover some attenuated property interest such as the possession of a general power of appointment, especially if the power was never exercised.

> EXAMPLE 6 - 6. Movie star Jenny filed a lawsuit against a major studio for breach of contract, seeking $4 million in damages because, according to her claim, it had failed to cast her in a movie that she understood was hers. The movie was a hit, and she sued for a percentage of the gross profits. After the discovery phase of the trial, it looked as though her claim had merit and the studio started talking seriously about settlement. Unfortunately, Jenny died when her Harley hit a palm tree. The studio is now refusing to settle, so her estate is proceeding to trial. Although the claim is quite speculative, its estimated value is included in her estate.[15]

> EXAMPLE 6 - 7. Jim created an irrevocable trust that gave his daughter Jodi income for her life, after which the corpus would revert to Jim, if living, otherwise to his estate. Jodi was 40 years old and the trust was worth $100,000 when Jim died. His gross estate includes the value of the vested reversionary interest. *** *Query 6 - 2. If the §7520 rate was 10% when he died, what dollar value as regards this trust is included in Jim's estate?*

Finally, consider the consequences of current transfer tax laws on the estates of people who engage in certain illegal activities.

> EXAMPLE 6 - 8. Decedent died when the plane he was piloting crashed. On board was a load of marijuana and a fair amount of "drug money." His gross estate had to include the cash and the street value of the dope because he had "exclusive possession and control" over both when he died. Further, his estate was not entitled to deduct that value of cash and marijuana forfeited under state drug enforcement laws either as a claim against the estate or as a loss during administration. The courts agreed with the Department of Justice's argument that allowing a deduction

would "frustrate the sharply defined state and federal public policy against drug trafficking." Thus, decedent's other assets were used to pay the estate taxes.[16]

Dower and Curtesy Interests: §2034

A dower interest is a surviving wife's life estate in a portion of the real property owned by her deceased husband, and a curtesy interest represents a surviving husband's life estate in a portion of the real property owned by his deceased wife. The extent of these statutory interests varies from state to state. Some states grant surviving spouses dower and curtesy interests as a percentage of the deceased spouse's real and personal property. As we have seen, one purpose of these laws is to prevent a decedent from entirely disinheriting the surviving spouse. Dower or curtesy interests are included in the gross estate of the first spouse to die.[17]

From an estate tax point of view, dower and curtesy interests and community property interests of the surviving spouse have the same effect. Dower and curtesy interests that can be claimed in fee (e.g., a specific percentage of the estate is set aside in fee for the surviving spouse) are included in the gross estate but are fully deductible as interests passing to the surviving spouse. In those states that still define these interests as life estates for the surviving spouse, the property may still qualify for the marital deduction by use of what is called a qualified terminable interest property election.[18] This special election, called a QTIP election, will be covered in the later chapters. In community property states, the surviving spouse's half-interest in the community property is excluded from the decedent's gross estate because it does not belong to the decedent spouse. These deducted or excluded marital interests are not taxed at the first spouse's death, but are likely to be taxed when the surviving spouse dies.

Survivorship Annuities: §2039

An annuity is a series of two or more periodic payments, usually received by the annuitant in monthly, quarterly, or annual payments. Annuities are commonly used in retirement planning, often in conjunction with pension and insurance contracts. Ordinarily, an employee-"participant," on retirement, will begin receiving a monthly annuity, possibly for as long as the retiree lives or, perhaps more commonly, for as long as the retiree and the retiree's spouse live.

Section 2039 includes in the decedent's gross estate the date-of-death value of an annuity "receivable by any beneficiary by reason of surviving the decedent."

An annuity for the life of the owner of the annuity contract is not part of the person's gross estate under §2039, since the annuity ends with the person's death. Even if it was considered property owned at death under §2033, the date-of-death value would be zero.

Inclusion in participant's gross estate. Generally, survivorship annuities or "refund annuities" (ones that guarantee a minimum pay back) are fully included in the decedent-participant's gross estate if there is an obligation to continue the payments after the owner of the annuity dies. How much is included and how that amount is calculated depends on several factors. If the decedent retired after 1984 or if the pension plan was not a qualified one, the pension is fully included. If it is fully included, the amount included is either the lump sum amount, if the survivor has the right to take a lump sum, or the present value of the future payments, if the survivor must receive periodic payments. Whether one uses Table S or Table B (see Appendix A) depends on whether the payments will continue for the life of the survivor (Table S) or for a fixed number of years (Table B). Prior to 1985, plans that were "qualified" under §401(a) were either partially or fully excluded from the participant's estate. The section is complex, as it details the requirements for plan qualification. The tax advantages of qualified plans are that employer contributions are tax deductible to the employer and are not taxable income to the employee until paid, usually after retirement. In addition, the income earned on contributions is tax-deferred. Generally, non-qualified plans do not receive all of these advantages.

The following summarizes the complex estate inclusion rules for qualified plan annuities:

1. *Fully included annuities.* Regarding any annuity whose payments began after July 17, 1984, or for which prior to that date the decedent had not made an irrevocable election to designate the beneficiaries, the *entire value* of the annuity is included in the gross estate.

2. *Partially excluded annuities.* The estate of retirees who were in pay status (retired and receiving payments) before January 1, 1985, and had made an irrevocable election after December 31, 1982 and before July 18, 1984, as to the form of benefits that would be paid to the beneficiary can exclude up to $100,000 of the combined value of survivorship annuities from qualified plans.

3. *Totally excluded annuities.* The estate of retirees that separated from service prior to January 1, 1983, and who had irrevocably elected the form of benefits before that date, can exclude all of the qualified annuity.

The exclusions just described are available only if the proceeds are not payable to the decedent's estate, and if the decedent could not change the form of benefit. Annuities qualifying for this exclusion include the following:

a. Tax-sheltered annuities or tax-deferred annuities (TSAs and TDAs, also called 403(b) plans).
b. Individual retirement accounts (IRAs).
c. A portion of the value of the periodic payments under pension plans that have been "qualified" under §401. The amount qualifying for the exclusion is that portion attributable to the employer's contributions.
d. A lump-sum pension payment to a surviving beneficiary, provided the beneficiary elects to forego reduced income taxes produced by a special 10-year income averaging method available for large pension withdrawals if the participant-pensioner (i.e., the decedent) had reached age 50 before January 1, 1986.[19]

EXAMPLE 6 - 9. The decedent died this year after retiring from work in 1985. At death, the decedent had three joint and survivor annuities: one from her former employer's qualified retirement plan, one from a tax-sheltered annuity, and another from an individual retirement account. She had started drawing from all three after her retirement. The value of her gross estate will include the entire value of all three annuities.

EXAMPLE 6 - 10. During his employment, Stan contributed $25,000 to his qualified pension plan and his employer contributed $75,000. The plan provided Stan and his wife with a joint and survivor annuity on his retirement, which started in 1983. Stan died in 2001, and the value of his spouse's survivorship annuity was $300,000. The amount excluded is the value of the annuity attributable to the employer's contributions up to a maximum of $100,000. The amount attributed to the employer is $225,000 [$300,000*($75,000 / ($25,000+$75,000))]. Thus the amount excluded is $100,000 and $200,000 is included in his gross estate.

EXAMPLE 6 - 11. In the example immediately above, had Stan retired before 1983 his estate would have excluded $225,000, the employer's portion. Had he retired after July 17,1984, the entire value would have been included.

In summary, a simple rule applies to decedents who retired after July 17, 1984; the *full* value of all annuities earned through employment or acquired by purchase is included in the decedent's gross estate. For decedents retiring between January 1, 1983, and July 17, 1984, up to $100,000 of the annuity attributed to the employer's contribution is excluded. Finally, for those retiring prior to 1983, the *entire* employer's share of all qualifying retirement annuities is excluded.

Inclusion in gross estate of retiree's spouse. When the *participant-retiree's spouse dies first*, inclusion of a portion of the value of the participant's annuity in that nonparticipant spouse's gross estate will depend on local property law. In community property states, the nonparticipant spouse's community interest in the annuity will be included in his or her own gross estate. That value could be as much as one-half of the total annuity value. On the other hand, in common law states, nothing will usually be included. Regarding property rights to the remaining benefits, case law has held that at the nonparticipant spouse's earlier death, any community interest passes 100% to the participant; the Retirement Equity Act precludes the nonparticipant decedent spouse from making any disposition of it.[20]

Joint Tenancy and Tenancy by the Entirety: §2040

There are two rules for determining the portion of joint tenancy property in the gross estate of a deceased joint owner:

Spousal Rule: *If a married couple are the only joint tenants, when the first spouse dies his or her gross estate must include one-half of the property's fair market value as of the date of death (DOD FMV).*

The Code refers to spousal joint tenancies and tenancies by the entirety as "qualified joint interests." For these, *one-half* of the total value is included *regardless* of the spouses' original contributions. Prior to 1977, the consideration furnished rule also applied to joint tenancies held by husbands and wives. Surviving spouses in several cases have successfully argued that the old rule still applies where the joint tenancy was created pre-1977.[21] By having the property fully included in the first spouse's estate, a full step-up in basis is obtained for income tax purposes. The IRS disagrees with this position. The issue will become less important as we move further away from 1977. Unless stated otherwise, assume all husband and wife joint tenancies were created after 1976.

EXAMPLE 6 - 12. At his death in 1995, Joel and his wife Susan held their home in joint tenancy. Susan paid $100,000 when she bought the house in 1980 using her separate funds. It was worth $400,000 when Joel died. Since the house is a *qualified joint interest*, his gross estate will include $200,000. Susan's new basis is half the old basis plus half the date-of-death value, i.e., $250,000.

EXAMPLE 6 - 13. In the example immediately above, had Susan died first with Joel the survivor, the results would have been exactly the same.

Consideration Furnished Rule: *Include in the decedent owner's estate only that portion of the DOD FMV of the property attributable to that portion of the consideration (money or money's worth) contributed by the decedent.*

The second rule applicable to all non-qualified joint interests is called the *consideration furnished rule*. With even just one non-spouse as a joint tenant, all interests are non-qualified; e.g., husband, wife, and adult child take title as joint tenants. All three are holders of non-qualified interests. The law starts with the presumption that the decedent co-owner contributed all of the consideration (or was initially the sole owner). To overcome this presumption, the estate has the burden of establishing that the surviving joint tenants contributed to the acquisition of the property. Generally, this is not as difficult as it seems. The IRS is not likely to challenge the contributions where the co-owners would not appear to have had a motive for trying to avoid taxes, nor to make gifts when the joint tenancy was established, and each of the co-owners had sufficient resources to pay his or her own way.

EXAMPLE 6 - 14. In 1955, two brothers, Jake and Ned, prior to either of them marrying, purchased a fishing cabin on a lake, taking title in joint tenancy. Jake died this year. The records as to how much each paid as a down payment have been lost. But Ned can show that he and his brother were both earning about the same amount of money at the time of the purchase and were both about equally wealthy such that one making a gift to the other would not have made much sense. This would probably be sufficient to establish equal consideration.

EXAMPLE 6 - 15. Similar to the prior example, but change it such that Jake was Ned's father and Jake, although wealthy, already owned his own home whereas Ned was just starting out. Even if Ned claims to have paid an equal share of the purchase price, the circumstances do not support the claim and, without better evidence, it would be difficult to overcome the presumption that Jake furnished all of the consideration. Even a canceled check from Ned payable to the seller of the cabin might not be sufficient evidence, since a gift from Jake of the cash followed by Ned's use of the money as his share of the consideration would be treated as if all the funds came from Jake. Ned would need to establish a reasonable explanation for the source of the funds to establish that they came from a source other than a gift from his father.

There is a special rule where a donee (one of the surviving joint tenants) uses funds traceable to a gift from the decedent joint tenant as part of the purchase price. Those funds are treated as being part of the donor-joint tenant's consideration rather than that of the donee. Income from a gift is not traced back to the donor, but capital gain is.

EXAMPLE 6 - 16. Calvin gave his daughter Deirdre 100 shares of XYZ stock worth $50,000. She sold the stock for $70,000 and placed the proceeds of the sale in a bank account in which she already had $30,000. The source of the $30,000 was $10,000 from XYZ dividends and $20,000 from money she saved out of her wages. Calvin and Deirdre purchased a house for $200,000, each putting up half of the purchase price. Deirdre's half share came from her bank account. The house, held in joint tenancy, was worth $300,000 when Calvin died. His estate includes 85% of the DOD FMV, i.e., $255,000. The percentage is calculated by taking Calvin's contribution of $100,000, adding the contribution of Deirdre that is traceable to Calvin's gift to her (another $70,000) and dividing the total ($170,000) by the $200,000 purchase price. Note that the gain is included in the numerator, but the dividends are not.

Full inclusion in the decedent-donor's estate is preferred when it results in a step-up in basis without an increase in estate taxes.

EXAMPLE 6 - 17. In 1998, Virginia put her home into joint tenancy with her son Scott. At the time of the transfer, the home was worth $400,000. She filed a gift tax return reporting a $190,000 taxable gift. She died in the year 2001 when the house was worth $500,000. The entire $500,000 is included in her estate, and Scott's basis in the house is $500,000. Her other property was worth $75,000 and her estate paid debts and expenses of $30,000, so her taxable estate was just $545,000 and no taxes were owed. *** *Query 6 - 3. It seems as though the $190,000 taxable gift should have pushed the estate over the $675,000 mark. Why is that not the case? See the definition of "adjusted taxable gift" found in §2001(b).*

EXAMPLE 6 - 18. At her death, Rose owned a farm worth $100,000 jointly with her brother Tom. The farm was originally acquired for $50,000, with Rose paying

$10,000 and Tom paying $40,000. Assuming the contribution of the survivor can be established, under the consideration-furnished test her estate includes only one fifth of the farm's value, i.e., $20,000, [($10,000/$50,000)*$100,000]. Tom's basis in the farm will be his contribution plus the amount included in Rose's estate, i. e., $60,000 [$40,000 he contributed and $20,000 included in Rose's estate].

EXAMPLE 6 - 19. At her death, Dottie owned $90,000 of ABC common stock jointly with her husband and her son. The survivors know that Dottie actually contributed only $10,000 to the original $50,000 purchase price (and the two of them paid $20,000 each), but they are not sure they can prove it. If they cannot, Dottie's gross estate will include the full $90,000. If they can prove it, her gross estate will include only her proportional share, or $18,000 (i.e., 20%). This is not a qualified joint interest because a non-spouse is also a surviving co-owner.

The consideration furnished rule applies only at the death of a co-owner. There is a gift when different amounts of consideration are used to purchase property and the title is taken in joint tenancy because, by property law rules, all joint tenants' interests must be equal. For gift or sale purposes, the "donee" co-owner has a basis in his or her share that is either carry-over or partly carry-over and partly purchase.

EXAMPLE 6 - 20. Edith and June purchased a vacation condominium in South Florida for $100,000, taking title as joint tenants. Edith paid $90,000 and June paid $10,000. Edith made a $40,000 gift [$30,000 taxable] to June since June has a 50% interest. June's basis would be $50,000 [$40,000 carried over with the gift and the other $10,000 is her consideration]. If they later sell the property for $150,000, each would recognize a gain of $25,000. If, instead of selling the property when it was worth $150,000, June made a gift of her half to her son, Tommy, she would report a gift of $75,000 [$65,000 taxable gift] and Tommy would have a carry-over basis of $50,000. This transfer would break the joint tenancy, so Tommy and Edith would be tenants in common, each with a 50% share. Regardless of which one died first, Tommy or Edith, 50% of the value would be included in the person's estate.

For purposes of §2040, "joint interests" encompass only two forms of concurrent ownership: joint tenancy and tenancy by the entirety. In contrast to the complex rules just given for these joint interests, when a person dies holding title to property in either tenancy in common or community property, the value that is included in the decedent's gross estate is based on the decedent's proportionate interest in the property.[22]

Power of Appointment: §2041

Powers of appointment were introduced in an earlier chapter, so this is just a brief review. A power of appointment is a power that allows a person to name someone to receive a beneficial interest in property, even though the person directing the transfer does not own the property. The creator (grantor) of the power is called the donor of the power. The person receiving the power is called the holder or donee. The parties to whom the holder may appoint the property are called the permissible appointees. The parties to whom the holder actually appoints are called the appointees, and the persons who will get the property if no appointment is made are called the takers by default.

For federal estate tax purposes, a power of appointment is either a general power or it is a limited (special) power. A *general* power of appointment is the power of the holder to appoint to the holder, the holder's estate, the holder's creditors, or the creditors of the holder's estate. All other powers are "special" or "limited" powers of appointment, which usually designate as permissible appointees either specific individuals (e.g., the donor gives the holder the power to appoint to the donor's brother Sam or sister Sue) or a class of people (e.g., appoint to any of my issue).

A decedent's gross estate will include the value of any property subject to a *general* power of appointment held by the decedent-holder at death. General powers are included in the gross estate regardless of whether the decedent-holder *exercised* the power at death, or, alternatively, did not exercise it and just permitted the power to *lapse* at death. The key is that at the moment of death, the decedent was the holder of a general power.

> EXAMPLE 6 - 21. At her death, Carol was trustee of an irrevocable trust created by her Uncle Fred. She had the power to invade the corpus of the trust for the benefit of anyone. The trust named Fred's second cousins, Clarence and Sherrie, as remaindermen in the event Carol failed to appoint all of the corpus. In her will, Carol appointed her son David to receive the entire corpus. Carol's gross estate will include the entire value of the trust corpus, since it was subject to a general power which she *exercised* at her death.

> EXAMPLE 6 - 22. The facts are similar to the prior example, except that Carol did not exercise the power at her death. The entire trust corpus is still included in her gross estate even though the power *lapsed* at her death. Note that a proportionate share of the estate taxes would come out of the trust.

EXAMPLE 6 - 23. The facts are similar to the prior example, except that the power to appoint was on behalf of anyone *except* herself, her creditors, her estate, or the creditors of her estate. This is a "limited" power, not a general power, and thus the property is not included in her gross estate whether she appoints to her son or just lets the power lapse.

Notice that §2041 focuses on decedent *holders* of general powers, not on the donors or the appointees.

Exceptions. There are two major exceptions to the basic rule that being able to appoint to oneself makes the power a general one. Each exception so greatly restricts the circumstances that would allow appointment that Congress quite rightly defined them as not being general powers. Under the first exception, if the decedent's right to exercise a power is limited by an *ascertainable standard*, that is, limited for reasons of "health, education, support or maintenance," it is not a general power. Under the second exception, if the decedent's right to exercise the power requires the *approval* of either the creator of the power or an *adverse party*, it is not a general power. An adverse party is "a person having a substantial interest in the property, subject to the power, which is adverse to exercise of the power in favor of the decedent."[23]

EXAMPLE 6 - 24. During his lifetime, the decedent was the income beneficiary of a trust created by his father. The trust gave him the right to invade corpus for reasons of his "health, education, support, or maintenance." Since the power is limited by an *ascertainable standard*, this right to invade is not a general power, and the trust is not included in the decedent's gross estate even if the decedent was the trustee.

EXAMPLE 6 - 25. Same facts as Example 6-24, except decedent could invade corpus for reasons of his "health, education, support, maintenance, *or happiness.*" The power is not limited by an ascertainable standard; therefore, the invasion right constitutes a general power of appointment, and the entire value of the trust will be included in the decedent's estate even though he never exercised the right to invade.

EXAMPLE 6 - 26. During her lifetime, the decedent was the income beneficiary of a trust established by her grandmother. She could invade corpus for any reason provided she obtained the written approval of her son, the trust's remainderman. Since her son was an *adverse party*, i.e., his remainder interest would be reduced in value if the decedent exercised the power in her own favor, the power is not a general one.

A general power of appointment over property will cause the property to be included in the holder's estate because the power creates rights considered equivalent to ownership. Thus, this estate tax rule makes sense even though under *property law* the holder is not the legal owner of the property regardless of whether the power is general or limited. Given that the holder does not have legal title, even if the property subject to the power is included in the holder's gross estate, it is not included in the holder's probate estate unless the holder transfers it there, an event not likely to happen.

Insurance on Decedent's Life: IRC § 2042

Three circumstances that will cause life insurance to be in the insured's gross estate are if: (1) the proceeds are paid to the executor of the decedent's estate, or (2) the decedent at death possessed an incident of ownership in the policy, or (3) the decedent transferred an incident of ownership within three years of death.

Receivable by executor. Very seldom is the executor of the decedent's estate named as a beneficiary or alternate beneficiary. On occasion it happens that at the insured's death no named beneficiaries are living and the proceeds are payable to the estate by default. Modern policies generally have a default clause that directs the company to pay the proceeds to the decedent's heirs if the named primary and alternate beneficiaries predecease the insured. The default clauses read something like intestate succession laws, starting with close family members, moving to more remote relatives if no close family members survive, and to the insured's estate only as a last resort.

Decedent possesses incidents of ownership. Policy ownership gives the owner numerous rights including: to assign, to terminate, to borrow against the cash reserves (if any), to name beneficiaries, and to change beneficiaries. Possession by the decedent of these rights is called *incidents of ownership,* any one of which will result in the proceeds being included in the decedent's estate. The payment of premiums by the insured is not considered an incident of ownership and payment will not by itself cause inclusion. Nonetheless, barring some agreement, the law may create an incident of ownership due to the payment of premiums in community property states. A policy paid for entirely with community property would be half included in the decedent's gross estate regardless of whether it was issued in the insured spouse's name or the non-insured spouse's name. A written agreement specifying that it is the separate property of one of the spouses will negate the community property presumption that normally attaches to property purchased with community funds.

Life insurance transferred within three years of death. If the insured transferred an interest in the policy within three years of his or her death, both IRC § 2042 and §2035(a) require inclusion of the proceeds in the insured's gross estate.

> EXAMPLE 6 - 27. On June 12, 1999, Marty transferred a $200,000 policy on his life to his son Joseph. Because the policy was a term policy, its value was under $10,000 and Marty did not have to report it as a gift. On January 1, 2001, Marty died in a car accident. Joseph collected the $200,000. Marty's gross estate must include the $200,000 even though he had no incidents of ownership when he died and there were no strings attached to the transfer. The insurance company must issue IRS Form 712 any time insurance is listed on an estate tax return. The form (which must be attached to Marty's 706) will show the date the policy was transferred.

IRC § 2042 versus §2033. It is important to distinguish between policies on the decedent's life and policies on the lives of others. Policies on the *decedent's life* are covered by IRC § 2042, but what if the decedent owned a policy on someone else's life? The policy is included in the decedent's estate under § 2033 as a property interest owned at death. Generally, the value is the cost of replacement rather than the cash surrender value. Cost of replacement is what an insurance company would charge to put the policy in force (with the existing cash surrender value) given the insured's age and health. Where premiums are still being paid on a policy on the life of another, its value is increased by that portion of the premium paid that covers the period extending beyond the owner's death.

> EXAMPLE 6 - 28. At decedent's death, decedent's wife owned a policy on *his life*, with the proceeds payable to his estate. Decedent's gross estate will include the value of the proceeds under IRC § 2042.

> EXAMPLE 6 - 29. Decedent died owning a life insurance policy on his mother with a face value of $60,000. The policy had a value of $14,000 at decedent's death. Although IRC § 2042 does not apply because decedent is not the insured, the decedent's estate must include the $14,000 value under §2033.

> EXAMPLE 6 - 30. When he died, decedent owned a $100,000 life insurance policy on his own life. Under IRC § 2042 (incidents of ownership), $100,000 will be included in his gross estate. However, if all premiums had been paid for with

community property, it is presumed to be community property and only $50,000 would be included. This result could be overcome if the couple had a written agreement stating that the policy was the separate property of one spouse. Of course, if the surviving spouse is the beneficiary, the 100% marital deduction will keep it out of the taxable estate. Cross-ownership (each spouse owns the policy on the other's life) might be more important where one of the spouses is not a U.S. citizen.

After one spouse dies, if the surviving spouse continues to own a policy on his or her own life, the entire proceeds are included in the surviving insured's estate when he or she dies, regardless of whether community property funds were the original source of the premiums.[24]

So far, we have studied IRC §§ 2033, 2034, 2039, 2040, 2041 and 2042, all of which cover interests owned, held, or controlled by the decedent at death such that the interests are included in the decedent's estate. The next section examines a group of Code sections that result in property being included in the gross estate even though the property is no longer owned by the decedent at the time of death. The property is included because the decedent transferred property but kept some interest or control, sometimes just a *little string* attached, such that Congress thought the string justified including the property in the gross estate as if no transfer had taken place.

TRANSFERS WITH RETAINED INTEREST OR CONTROL

If a person transfers property and retains an interest in the property such as the right to control who enjoys it, the retained interest will cause the transferred property to be included in the transferor's estate if the retained interest is still present when the transferor dies.[25] This is true even if the retained interest is one that cannot benefit the transferor economically. The interest will also be included if the transferor releases the retained interest within three years of his or her death.[26] Whether a "string" exists at the time of death or the string is snipped within three years of death, it will be as if the decedent never made the transfer, but instead continued to own the property right to the moment of death. Thus, if one of the retained interest code sections applies and the property is pulled back into the gross estate, it will be valued for estate tax purposes at the date-of-death fair market value (DOD FMV) regardless of its earlier gift value. However, if it is drawn into the gross estate, it will not be treated for estate tax purposes as an adjusted taxable gift, even though it was a taxable gift when the transfer occurred. The latter sounds bad but is actually good because it keeps the transfer from being taxed twice. Any gift tax paid on the earlier transfer is allowed as a credit even though the earlier gift is not included as an adjusted taxable gift in the calculation of the estate tax. The retained interest Code sections are: §2036, Transfers with Retained Life Estate; §2037, Transfers Taking Effect at Death; and §2038, Revocable Transfers.

Characteristics common to all three sections. The three "strings" sections (§§2036, 2037, and 2038) have these characteristics in common:

- ▸ The transfer was made by the *decedent*.
- ▸ The transfer was a gift, that is, a transfer "for less than full and adequate consideration in money or money's worth."
- ▸ The amount included in the gross estate is the value as of the *date of death* (or alternate valuation date), rather than the value at date of transfer.
- ▸ If the string pertained to only a specific portion of the property transferred, then only that *portion* of the transferred property is included. For example, if the retained control was over only one third of the property, then only one third of its value will be included in the gross estate. However, note that §2036 requires the entire property to be included, even if only the income interest was retained.
- ▸ A trust is almost always involved.

When the sections overlap, as they often do, the value included in the gross estate is based on whichever section results in the greatest amount included.

Transfer with Retained Life Estate: §2036

A transfer with retained life estate arises when a decedent has made a transfer, by trust or otherwise, for less than full and adequate consideration and has retained either (1) the possession or enjoyment of (or the right to the *income* from) the property transferred, or (2) the right, either alone or in conjunction with any person, to *designate* who will enjoy or possess the property or its income.

Period of retention. In addition to the above retained control, §2036 applies only if the decedent-transferor retained that control for: (1) life, (2) any period that does not in fact end before the decedent's death, or (3) any period not ascertainable without reference to the decedent's death. In the following §2036 examples, assume that decedent D made a lifetime transfer for less than full consideration.

EXAMPLE 6 - 31. At a time when D's vacation home was worth $110,000, D said, while handing over a quit-claim deed, "Son, here's title to my vacation home. It's yours now, but I will expect you to let me use it occasionally." When D died, the home was worth $200,000. The date-of-death value of the home will be included in D's gross estate because at the time of D's death, D still retained the *right to enjoy* the property.

EXAMPLE 6 - 32. D transferred property into an irrevocable trust, retaining the right to the income for his lifetime, with the remainder to go to C. The property's value at date of death is included in D's gross estate because D retained the right to the income for his lifetime. Although the remainder value was treated as a taxable gift when the trust was established, it is not an adjusted taxable gift for estate tax purposes since the entire trust has been included in D's gross estate.

EXAMPLE 6 - 33. D transferred property into an irrevocable trust, with income to remain with D for 20 years. Then the trust would terminate, with the remainder transferred to C. D died 18 years after establishing the trust. The property's value is included in D's gross estate because the *period of retention* did not end before D's death. Again, the adjusted taxable gift would be zero insofar as D's estate and this trust are concerned.

EXAMPLE 6 - 34. The facts as in the prior example, except D lived beyond the 20-year term. D's gross estate would not include the trust property. There would be an adjusted taxable gift equal to the remainder value when the trust was funded. That value would boost the rest of D's taxable estate into higher marginal rates.

EXAMPLE 6 - 35. D transferred property into an irrevocable trust, with income to go to D for up to one month before D's death and the remainder going to C. The fair market value of the property as of D's death is included in D's gross estate because the retained period is *not ascertainable without reference* to D's death.

When is a gift complete? Generally, unless the owner releases dominion and control over the property, there is no gift. With an outright gift, it is generally fairly easy to determine when a gift is complete since the donor merely has to transfer "dominion and control" to the donee. It is less obvious with gifts in trust where the donor retains some interest. Indeed, the IRS Regulations are less than clear on this matter.[27] We will not cover this completely, but will give you the basics. Bear in mind that a gift may be complete enough to cause a gift (generally, release of title and control), but still result in the property being included in the donor's gross estate due to a retained interest. Obviously, if the donor has the right to revoke a gift, then no gift has really occurred, even if the donee has taken possession of the property. No gift will occur until the right to take back the property ends because, until such time, the donor has retained control over who will enjoy the property.

> EXAMPLE 6 - 36. Shane created a trust, transferring assets worth $100,000 to the trustee. The trust terms give Richard income for life, so long as the trust remains in existence. On Richard's death, the trust terminates, with distribution to Shane's daughter Catherine. The terms of the trust state that it is revocable until the earlier of Richard or Shane's death. The first year the trustee distributed income of $5,000 to Richard. The second year $6,000 was distributed. At the beginning of the third year, when the trust was worth $120,000, Shane died. No gift occurred and, of course, the trust is included in Shane's estate. While Shane was alive, all income was reported on his income tax return and was treated as a gift from him to Richard. Given the amounts and Richard's present interest (as each amount was distributed to him), the annual exclusion would have covered the amounts Richard received before Shane's death. Distributions after Shane's death are from an irrevocable trust. The income is taxable to Richard (the trust would have an income distribution deduction) and is not considered to be gifts. Note that while Shane was alive the gifts of income are from him, not from the trust. From a transfer tax standpoint, only people make gifts; not trusts, not trustees.

When control is retained by the settlor, no gift is deemed to have occurred.[28] This is true even when the terms of the trust make it clear that the settlor cannot benefit in any way from the retained control. Once the control ceases, either by release, death, or by the terms that established the trust, the transfer occurs.

> EXAMPLE 6 - 37. Using assets worth $400,000, Abel creates an irrevocable trust for the benefit of Benito and Consuelo with remainder to their children when both are deceased. So long as both are alive, the trustee is given the power to allocate the income between Benito and Consuelo in such proportions as the trustee thinks is appropriate. When one beneficiary dies, the survivor is to receive all income. Abel serves as the initial trustee. During the first year the trust has income of $30,000, which Abel distributes $25,000 to Benito and $5,000 to Consuelo. No gift occurred when the trust was created, even though it was irrevocable. The income is taxed to Abel, and he has made a gift of $25,000 ($15,000 taxable) to Benito and $5,000 to Consuelo (not taxable because it is completely covered by the annual exclusion).

EXAMPLE 6 - 38. At a time when the trust was worth $500,000, Abel resigned as trustee, giving the successor trustee a letter (with copies to both beneficiaries) that stated his resignation was irrevocable. At that time, Abel has made a $500,000 gift (both gross and taxable). From that moment on, income was no longer taxed to Abel, and distributions were not considered new gifts but merely distributions of income from the irrevocable trust. *** *Query 6 - 4. Why is the taxable gift $500,000? What happened to the annual exclusion(s)?*

EXAMPLE 6 - 39. Suppose that instead of releasing his retained control by resignation, Abel died while still serving as trustee and that the trust assets were valued at $700,000. The $700,000 would be included in his gross estate and, from that moment onward, the income distributions would be from the trust, not from Abel (nor from his estate).

EXAMPLE 6 - 40. Suppose the terms of the trust created by Abel required him to get Benito's approval for anything other than a 50-50% split of the income, otherwise the income had to be divided equally between Benito and Consuelo. The trust's value is still included because Abel retained the right to designate the recipient "alone or *in conjunction with* any other person."

Because these rules are based on transfers with interests retained by the donor, we must bear in mind that a transfer of a community property asset is treated as coming one-half from each spouse.

EXAMPLE 6 - 41. The facts are similar to any of the above examples, except that the transfer was of property held prior to the transfer as community property, 50-50 tenancy in common, or spouses as joint tenancy. Only half the value of the property would be included in the transferor's estate, because only half is traceable to a transfer by the decedent.

EXAMPLE 6 - 42. D transferred property into an irrevocable trust, retaining one quarter of the income for himself and requiring the distribution of the rest to C. After D's death, C is to receive all of the income and after C's death, the remainder will go to R. At D's death, only *one quarter* of the trust's value is included in D's gross estate since that was the extent of D's §2036 retained interest.

EXAMPLE 6 - 43. D transferred property into an irrevocable trust, authorizing the trustee, a bank, in its sole discretion, to distribute trust income to X or Y in such amounts as the bank trust officer thinks appropriate. D retained the power to replace the bank with another corporate trustee. The value of the property is not included in D's gross estate under §2036 because D's right to replace trustees does not amount to the right by D to change or control the enjoyment of the property. However, the property would be included if D kept the right to appoint *herself* as successor trustee because she would then have retained the ability to control the "enjoyment" of the income.

In the following example, a basic assumption is changed, so that decedent is not the transferor.

> EXAMPLE 6 - 44. G transfers property into an irrevocable trust, with income to D for life and remainder to R. The value of the property is not included in D's gross estate under §2036, because D was *not the transferor*. This arrangement is referred to as a bypass trust because the trust assets "bypass" the income beneficiary's estate.

The *reciprocal trusts doctrine*, illustrated in the next example, was established by the courts to apply §2036 to family planning situations which in form avoid the literal terms of that section, but in substance do not. In essence, the transferor has made a transfer of property and at about the same moment received the right to enjoyment of other property arising from a separate but related transaction.

> EXAMPLE 6 - 45. A husband transfers $100,000 in property into irrevocable trust H, with income payable to his wife for her life and the remainder to their children. At about the same time, his wife transfers $100,000 into trust W, with income payable to her husband for his life and the remainder to their children. Under §2036, the corpus of trust H will be included in husband's gross estate and the corpus of trust W will be included in wife's gross estate. These interrelated trusts leave the spouses in essentially the same economic position that they would have been in had they created trusts naming themselves life beneficiaries.[29]

People sometimes engage in transfers designed to appear complete but that involve an implied *understanding* that the transferor has a retained life estate. The IRS has had success in attacking such schemes when they come to light. Consider the following situation in which a court found §2036 to apply to facts that had been structured to appear as a completed sale.

> EXAMPLE 6 - 46. Mom, age 82 and in poor health, transferred title to her home to her son and his wife in exchange for $270,000, which was the home's fair market value. The terms of this "sale-leaseback" called for a $20,000 down payment and a five-year mortgage loan of $250,000. Mom immediately forgave the down payment of $10,000 by each of the spouses. In the next two years, in payment of rent, Mom gave son and his wife $10,000 each, and they promptly returned these amounts in payment of the mortgage. Two days after the sale, Mom executed her

last will, which contained a provision forgiving any of the remaining debt at the time of her death. The date-of-death value of the home was included in her gross estate under §2036. Circumstances strongly suggested an understanding that decedent was permitted to live in the house until death, which she did, and that none of the consideration offered in exchange was ever really going to be paid. Thus, all consideration was disregarded. The following circumstantial factors, all taken together, indicate a strings-attached transfer: decedent's age and her health concerns, her forgiveness of the mortgage both during her life and by her will, the fact that the rent payments approximated the interest payments on the note, and the fact that the son was the decedent's only heir and the natural object of her bounty. As a result, Mom was treated as having made a transfer of property for less than full and adequate consideration in which she retained, for a period which did not end before her death, the right to possess or enjoy the property.[30]

Transfers Taking Effect at Death: §2037

A "transfer taking effect at death" will arise when (1) possession or enjoyment of the property through ownership can be obtained only by surviving the decedent and (2) the decedent, at the time of the transfer, retained a reversionary interest, which, at the decedent's death, exceeded five percent of the value of the property. Such reversionary interest is defined as the possibility that the property may return to the decedent or may be subject to a power of disposition by him.

> EXAMPLE 6 - 47. D transfers property into a trust, with income to B for B's life, a reversion to D if he survives B, otherwise the remainder to go to R, or R's estate. Assume that D dies at age 70, predeceasing B, who is then 60 years old. On the date of D's death, the value of the trust property was $1 million and the federal §7520 rate was 8%. Using actuarial tables, it was determined that given D and B's ages, D's contingent reversionary interest (ignoring the fact of his death) was worth more than 5% of the value of the trust. The amount included in D's gross estate is the full value of the trust less the value of B's remaining life estate, i.e., the value of the reversionary interest as though it was vested rather than contingent. Since B is 60 years old and the rate was 8%, the amount included will be $267,940 [.26794 * $1,000,000; see Table S, 8% rate].

In the preceding example, D had a chance of surviving B at D's death, and based on that, a value is calculated for what amounts to a contingent reversion for D. The reader might find this strange given that D, *in fact,* did not outlive B. However, as in certain other valuation situations, this calculation is made without regard to the fact of D's death. Thus, the calculation assumes that, at the moment of D's death, both D and B had average life expectancies for their ages, and that D's reversionary interest was certain rather than contingent.

Revocable Transfers: §2038

Although §2038's title is "Revocable Transfers," the section covers much more. Transferred property will be included in the decedent-transferor's estate if, at the time of death, the decedent retained the right to change another's enjoyment of the property. The Code refers to this retained right as one to *alter, amend, revoke, or terminate* the enjoyment of the property transferred. Even without any retained economic interest, almost any retained right to change a beneficiary's interest (or even the timing of enjoyment) will cause the full value of the property to be included in the transferor's estate.

> EXAMPLE 6 - 48. D transferred property into a *revocable living trust*, designed mainly to avoid probate at D's death. D retained the power to revoke the trust. D's gross estate includes the value of this property under §2038.

> EXAMPLE 6 - 49. D transferred property into an irrevocable trust that gave B the right to all income. The trust was to last for a term of 20 years, but would terminate earlier in the event of B's death. At such time as the trust terminates, it is to be distributed to B, if living, otherwise, to B's issue. If B leaves no issue, then to C, or C's estate. D retained the right to have the trust terminate earlier than at the end of 20 years if D thought such was in B's best interest. Even though D retained no beneficial interest, the trust property is included in D's gross estate because D retained the power to alter the "enjoyment interests" of others. *** *Query 6 - 5. Why does §2036 also apply?*

Gift *causa mortis*. An interesting concept developed at common law is called a *gift causa mortis*; literally, a gift caused by death. It is applied when a donor, thinking that death is imminent, gives away personal property with the understanding that if the donor dies the property belongs to the donee, but if the donor survives the property must be returned. Obviously, §2038 applies to gifts *causa mortis*.

> EXAMPLE 6 - 50. Elderly Tom, just before entering the hospital, gave Jim his coin collection (worth $150,000) with the understanding that if the heart operation was unsuccessful the collection would be Jim's. Tom died three days after surgery. The

collection was included in Tom's estate. Had Tom lived, Jim would have returned the coins and neither the original transfer, nor the return of the coins, would be treated as a gift.

EXAMPLE 6 - 51. In the preceding example, suppose that Tom gave Jim his coin collection to keep no matter what the outcome of the surgery and that Tom died three days after the surgery. The collection would not be included in Tom's estate. Of course, the adjusted taxable gift value ($140,000) would boost his estate into higher marginal rates and the executor of Tom's estate would be responsible for filing a gift tax return showing the gift.

The law requires that the gift be returned if the donor survives the life-threatening event, even if the donor dies while the donee is still in possession of the property.

EXAMPLE 6 - 52. Athene was fearful that she would not survive major surgery. She gave Mary, her best friend, her collection of Barbie dolls (valued at $50,000), with the understanding that the dolls would be returned if Athene did not die. The surgery was successful and she made a perfect recovery, but was killed in an automobile accident on the way home from the hospital. Now, Mary admits the agreement, but claims the right to keep the dolls because of Athene's death. With the help of the probate court, Athene's executor will rightfully take possession of the dolls.

Gift Taxes on Any Transfer Within Three Years of Death: §2035(b)

Since 1977, the Code has included a section that requires inclusion in the gross estate of the gift tax paid by the decedent on *any gift* made within three years of the donor's death.[31] Note that §2035(b) applies only if gift tax is actually paid, i.e., a check is made out to the IRS. Many, indeed most, taxable gifts result in no gift tax because the donor's unified credit usually covers the tentative tax. However, if the gift does result in gift taxes and the donor dies within three years of making the gift, the gift tax paid becomes part of the gross estate, subjecting the gift taxes themselves to the estate tax.

Grossing up. This inclusion of the gift tax in the gross estate is referred to as "grossing up" the estate; i.e., the estate is being brought up to the level it would have been had the gift tax not been paid. Keep in mind that the property transferred within three years of death is not brought back into the gross estate, just the gift tax is brought back.

EXAMPLE 6 - 53. In 1998, Mack gave Stacy XYZ stock worth $2,000,000. Mack paid gift taxes in the amount of $574,250. When Mack died in the year 2000, his gross estate (not including the gift taxes) was valued at $6,000,000 and his debts and expenses were $1,000,000. Stacy still owned the XYZ stock, which had risen in value to $2,500,000. Taking the transfer into account, Mack's gross estate is $6,574,250, his taxable estate is $5,574,250, the adjusted taxable gifts are $1,990,000, and there is a gift tax payable credit of $574,250 (a case where gift tax payable and paid are the same).

EXAMPLE 6 - 54. Continuing the prior example, had Mack died in 2002 (more than three years after making the gift), his gross estate would have been just $6,000,000, the taxable estate $5,000,000, the adjusted taxable gifts would still be $1,990,000 and the gift tax payable credit would be $574,250. Notice that, regardless of when Mack died, the value of the XYZ stock at Mack's death is irrelevant to the estate tax calculation.

The next three examples (and the table that follows them) compare the estate tax results in three situations: 1) where the decedent did not make large taxable gifts, 2) where the decedent made large taxable gifts far enough in advance of his death to avoid grossing up, and 3) where the gift was so close to the donor's death that grossing up is required.

EXAMPLE 6 - 55. In 1997, X died owning property worth $10 million. X's estate paid death taxes of $4,948,000. X's only child received $5,052,000.

EXAMPLE 6 - 56. In 1990, Y also owned $10 million, but he gave his child $5 million and paid gift tax of $2,192,500. Y died in 1997 (more than three years after making the gift), still owning $2,807,500 [$10 million - ($5 million gift and gift tax paid)]. Y's estate tax base was $7,797,500, and his death tax was $1,544,125. Therefore, Y's child received $6,263,375 [the gift plus the estate property less the death taxes]. Y's child received $1,211,375 more than X's child did [$6,263,375 - $5,052,000]. The $1,211,375 difference is explained partly by the $10,000 gift tax annual exclusion, but mostly by the exclusion from the tax base of the gift taxes.

EXAMPLE 6 - 57. Same facts as before, except Z died within three years of making the gift. The gift tax was included in Z's gross estate, bringing it up to $5,000,000 [$2,807,500 owned + $2,192,500 gift taxes] and resulting in an estate tax base of $9,990,000 [$5,000,000 gross estate + $4,990,000 adjusted taxable gift]. The tentative tax of $5,135,300 was reduced by the credit for gift tax payable and the unified credit to result in death taxes of $2,750,000. Thus Z's child received a total of $5,057,500 [$10 million - ($2,192,500 gift tax + $2,750,000 estate tax)], which exceeds the total $5,052,000 received by X's child by only $5,500, the amount of the tax advantage of the $10,000 annual gift tax exclusion at the marginal rate of 55%.

	X	Y	Z
Gross Gifts	N.A.	$5,000,000	$5,000,000
Less annual exclusions, if any	N.A.	($10,000)	($10,000)
Taxable gifts	N.A.	$4,990,000	$4,990,000
Tentative tax (gifts)	N.A.	$2,385,300	$2,385,300
Less unified credit	N.A.	($192,800)	($192,800)
Gift tax	N.A.	$2,192,500	$2,192,500
Taxable estate	$10,000,000	$2,807,500	$5,000,000
Plus adj. taxable gifts, if any	$0	$4,990,000	$4,990,000
Estate tax base	$10,000,000	$7,797,500	$9,990,000
Tentative tax (estate)	$5,140,800	$3,929,425	$5,135,300
Less gift tax payable credit	$0	($2,192,500)	($2,192,500)
Less unified credit	($192,800)	($192,800)	($192,800)
Estate tax	$4,948,000	$1,544,125	$2,750,000
Total transfer tax (gift+estate)	$4,948,000	$3,736,625	$4,942,500
Net to the children	$5,052,000	$6,263,375	$5,057,500

The fact that gift taxes paid more than three years before death can result in significant tax savings is an important estate planning tool, provided clients are willing to act early enough to avoid the "gross up" rule of §2035(b). Most people, even the very wealthy, are unwilling to generate a gift tax even if it will save substantial transfer taxes.

Tax exclusive versus tax inclusive calculations. A different way of describing the grossing up rule is that the gift tax is generally calculated on a tax exclusive basis, i.e., the amount of the gift tax is not included in the base. The taxes paid are not "taxable gifts" even though they are paid by the donor, nor are they part of the transfer tax base, provided the donor lives for another three years after making the gift that generated the gift taxes. On the other hand, the estate tax is calculated on a tax inclusive basis, i.e., the tax is levied on the "taxable estate" out of which the estate tax is paid and the tax itself is not a deduction. Grossing up converts a tax exclusive gift into a tax inclusive one. As we shall see in our later discussion of the generation-skipping transfer tax, on certain transfers ("direct skips") one computes the tax on a tax exclusive basis, thereby reducing the effective tax rate.

Certain Transfers within Three Years of Death: §2035(a)

Section §2035(a) creates a rule that causes transferred property to be included in the gross estate even though there is no retained interest when the transferor dies.[32] This three-year rule is subdivided into these two parts: (1) relinquishment or transfer of certain retained interests and (2) the transfer of life insurance.

Limited applicability of the three-year rule. A decedent's gross estate includes the value of property relinquished or given away within three years of his or her death, if that property would have been included in the decedent's gross estate under §§2036, 2037, 2038 (the retained interests sections), or §2042 (the life insurance section) had the decedent kept the interest. Do not apply the rule to any other type of transfer as this three-year rule applies to two, and only two, types of transfers: the *severance of a retained interest* (§§2036, 2037, 2038) or the gift of *life insurance* (§2042).

> EXAMPLE 6 - 58. D transferred property worth $750,00 into a trust, with income to S or C for S's life, then remainder to B. D retained the right to allocate the income between the two income beneficiaries. The trust terms also stated that the trustee was to allocate income equally between the two income beneficiaries in any year in which D failed to give written directions concerning the allocation. Because of D's retention of control over the property, no gift is deemed to have occurred. When D died, the trust was worth $1,340,000. D died possessing this right to "sprinkle" the trust income; therefore, the entire value of the trust property (as of D's DOD) was included in D's gross estate by virtue of both §2036 and §2038.

> EXAMPLE 6 - 59. Same as prior example except that in 1997, when the trust was worth $1,000,000, D relinquished his right to make the income allocation by writing a letter to the trustee stating that he irrevocably released his right to allocate the income. This act caused the gift to be complete. Note that the taxable gift is the full $1,000,000, because neither S nor C has an identifiable present interest. D paid gift taxes of $153,000. From that moment onward, D had no retained interest in the trust. However, both §2035(a) and §2035(b) apply if D dies within three years of the relinquishment, the property (at the DOD value) and the $153,000 in gift taxes are included in D's gross estate with adjusted taxable gifts being zero for estate tax purposes. On the other hand, if D dies more than three years after the relinquishment, neither the property nor the gift taxes are included, and the adjusted

taxable gifts would be $1,000,000 for estate tax purposes. Either way, the gift tax payable credit of $153,000 would be available.

EXAMPLE 6 - 60. D established an irrevocable trust managed by an independent trustee. The terms of the trust retained all income for D for a period of 20 years, after which the trust terminated with the remainder interest held by D's adult children. D died 21 years after establishing the trust; thus the trust had terminated the year before. Because D did not "release" a retained interest, the value of the trust assets is not included in D's estate even though D died within three years of the trust's termination. The retained interest had simply expired according to the original terms of the trust.

EXAMPLE 6 - 61. D transferred five bonds to C using the state's *Uniform Gift to Minors Act* to appoint herself custodian. D died before C reached the age of majority; therefore, the bonds are included in D's gross estate. Under the *Uniform Act*, D had the ability to liquidate some (or all) of the bonds and to distribute the proceeds to C or apply them for C's benefit. Thus both §§2036 and 2038 apply.

EXAMPLE 6 - 62. Same as prior example, except that shortly before D's death, he turned the bonds over to C because she reached the age at which the law required the custodianship to end (typically 18 or 21 years of age, depending on state law). Even though D died within three years of transferring the bonds, they are not included in D's estate. The transfer was not a "release" of a retained interest, therefore §2035(a) does not apply. D did not release a retained interest, rather it had to end by virtue of the state's UGMA.

Enough release of retained interest stuff, time for a life insurance example.

EXAMPLE 6 - 63. In the year 2002, D assigned his ownership interest in a *life insurance* policy on his life to his cousin Vinney. D dies in 2004. The insurance proceeds are included in his gross estate because the transfer occurred within three years of death. Had the transfer not been made, D's gross estate would include the insurance because of §2042. Had he survived more than three years after making the transfer, the gift value of the insurance (less the annual exclusion) on the date of transfer would enter the estate tax calculation merely as an adjusted taxable gift.

Remember that §2001(b) defines adjusted taxable gifts as post-1976 taxable gifts other than ones included in the gross estate of the donor. Hence where §2035(a) applies (or one of the retained interest sections applies) and the transferred property is brought back into the gross estate, it will not also be an adjusted taxable gift for estate tax purposes. In other words, where the remainder value of a trust, the release of a retained interest, or the transfer of life insurance was treated as a taxable gift but the property subsequently ends up included in the gross estate, the adjusted taxable gift value drops to zero for the calculation of the estate tax.

To avoid the three-year rule, planners make every effort to ensure that a wealthy client never possesses any incident of ownership in a newly issued policy. Thus, the insured can sign a consent to be the insured; he or she should not apply to be the owner. If the policy is owned by the trustee of an irrevocable trust, the insured should not be granted any power to change beneficial ownership of the policy or its proceeds as such will be deemed incidents of ownership.

Finally, the three-year rule of §2035(a) does not apply to *premiums* paid by the insured-transferor, even if paid within three years of death. Therefore, such payments do not cause the insurance to be included in the insured's estate. The premiums themselves may be adjusted taxable gifts if they exceed the annual exclusion amount or are transferred in such a manner that no one has a present interest in them, i.e., to an irrevocable life insurance trust which does not contain a Crummey power. There will be more on life insurance trusts later.

As stated earlier, most transfers are not subject to §2035(a)'s three-year rule. Thus transfers of stocks, bonds, cash, gold, jewelry, land, and other *garden variety* transfers, even if within three years of the transferor's death, are not brought into the gross estate; if over the annual exclusion amount, they are, and remain, simply adjusted taxable gifts. Had the gift not been made, the property, if still owned by the decedent at death, would only be included in the gross estate under §2033, not one of those four sections specified in §2035(a). Thus, outright gifts of property (other than life insurance) are not included in the transferor's gross estate even if made within three years of death. Accordingly, to understand this material fully, the reader must distinguish a single transaction gift from an indirect-strings-attached transfer (almost always through a trust), followed by the transferor eventually relinquishing the retained interest.

> EXAMPLE 6 - 64. Leslie gave her son $18,000 in common stock. She died one year later, at which time the stock was worth $200,000. Hey, it was a good investment. *Nothing*, insofar as this gift is concerned, is included in Leslie's gross estate. It is merely an adjusted taxable gift of $8,000.

The facts in the example immediately above demonstrate that lifetime gifts made shortly before the donor's death, while not included in the gross estate, may still be in the estate tax base as adjusted taxable gifts (i.e., the gift value reduced by annual exclusions) to boost the taxable estate into higher marginal rates. Whether transferred property is included in the *gross estate* versus is included in the tax base as an *adjusted taxable gift* is an important distinction. All items in the gross estate are included at their date-of-death value (or their value on the alternate valuation date, if such is elected), whereas adjusted taxable gifts are included in the tax base (but not in the gross estate) at their date-of-gift values reduced by any available annual exclusions. Also important is that the state death tax credit is based on the taxable estate (line three of the Estate Tax Return), not the tax base (line 5) that results when adjusted taxable gifts are added to the taxable estate.

> EXAMPLE 6 - 65. Continuing the prior example, assume that Leslie transferred a life insurance policy (face value $200,000) on her life instead of transferring stock. At the time of the transfer, the policy's value for gift tax purposes was $18,000. If Leslie died more than three years after the transfer, the proceeds would not be in the gross estate and the adjusted taxable gifts would include the $8,000 (i.e., the $18,000 value reduced by the annual exclusion). On the other hand, if Leslie died within three years of the transfer, the gross estate would include the $200,000 *face value* and the adjusted taxable gifts would be zero insofar as this gift is concerned.

Congress singled out life insurance because of its unique characteristic of suddenly, and radically, increasing in value when the insured dies; a feature that strongly motivates taxpayers to avoid subjecting that increase to transfer taxes. In the absence of §2035(a), a deathbed gift of a policy on the life of the donor could cause a quick, relatively large avoidance of estate tax, at little or no gift tax cost. For example, without §2035(a), a deathbed gift of a $1 million term policy might avoid estate tax on the entire face value with no gift tax consequences.

Comparing powers of appointment to retained interests. Consider that almost any retained interest by the settlor (trustor) of a trust results in the inclusion of the trust in the settlor's estate regardless of how meager the retained interest was, whereas a power can be very broad and, so long as it is not a general power, the property subject to the power is not in the holder's estate. So, when trying to determine whether a trust that is connected in some way to a decedent should be included in the decedent's estate, it is helpful to use a decision table, whereby one starts by determining whether the interest is a retained power or a power of appointment. You might find it helpful to diagram the decision table that follows.

1. Did the decedent create or fund the trust? If no, go to #5, if yes, go to #2.
2. Did the decedent retain an interest in the trust that either gave the decedent an economic benefit or the ability to control enjoyment? If no, then it is not in the decedent's estate. If yes, go to #3.
3. Did the decedent release the retained interest? If no, it is in the decedent's estate. If yes, go to #4.
4. Was the release within three years of decedent's death? If yes, the property is in the decedent's gross estate at the date-of-death value. If no, it is not in the gross estate, but it is an adjusted taxable gift.
5. Did someone give the decedent a power to appoint property such that the decedent would be considered the holder of a power? If no, then the trust property is not in the decedent's estate. If yes, go on to #6.
6. Could the decedent at any time have appointed the property to decedent's self, decedent's creditors, decedent's estate, or the creditors of the estate? If yes, it was a general power; go on to #7. If no, it was a limited power, and as such it is not included in the gross estate nor is it an adjusted taxable gift. *** *Query 6 - 6. Why does a lapsed or exercised limited power not create an adjusted taxable gift?*
7. Was the general power still there when the holder died? If yes, the property subject to the power (whether exercised or lapsed) is included in the holder's estate. If no, go on to #8 if it lapsed during the holder's lifetime, go to #9 if it was exercised during life, or go back to #2 if the power was released by the holder (the release makes the "holder" a settlor as to the portion of trust that could have been claimed).
8. Was the general power greater than the greater of $5,000 or 5% of the trust (i.e., a 5 & 5 power)? If no, it is not in the gross estate, only because it was not in effect when the holder died. If it did exceed the 5 & 5 limits before it lapsed *and* the holder continued to have an interest in the trust, go back to #1 [the lapsed % that exceeded 5% (or $5,000 if greater) is probably included as a retained interest]. If yes, but the holder had no continuing interest in the trust after the lapse, nothing is included, but the lapsed % that exceeded 5% (or $5,000) is an adjusted taxable gift.
9. When the general power was exercised, was the property given to the decedent or the decedent's creditors, or did the decedent exercise the power in favor of someone else? If exercised in the holder's favor, then there is no taxable gift (but presumably the property increased the holder's estate). If exercised in favor of someone else (i.e., "trustee, please give $25,000 to my

friend Betty"), it would be treated as a gift from the holder, and, if over the annual exclusion amount, it would be treated as an adjusted taxable gift.

Use the decision table as you work through these examples (assume all trusts are irrevocable unless otherwise stated).

EXAMPLE 6 - 66. Sandra created an irrevocable trust for her brother Duane. Duane received all income each year, and he could appoint up to 5% of the corpus of the trust to whomever he might choose each year. Duane's children were the remaindermen. When he died, the trust was valued at $1,000,000 and he had never exercised the power. Because this is a general power, even though it lapses unexercised, $50,000 [5%*$1,000,000] is included in his gross estate. Note that the $50,000 remains in the trust (it is not part of Duane's probate estate). The trustee of the trust will have any of Duane's estate taxes attributed to the inclusion of the $50,000 (i.e., the pro rata amount of this trust portion compared to the rest of Duane's taxable estate), unless his estate plan calls for some special allocation of the estate taxes.

EXAMPLE 6 - 67. David created a trust for Keith. The trustee could distribute as much of the income or trust as the trustee thought would be good for Keith. The trustee never exercised the special power other than to give Keith income from time to time. The trust gave Keith the unrestricted power to appoint up to 25% of the corpus at his death through specific mention of the power in his will. Lillian, or her estate, was the remainderman. Keith died with a will that made no mention of the trust. The trust was worth $1,000,000 when Keith died. Since this is a general power, Keith's estate will include $250,000 [25% * $1,000,000] even though the power was restricted to exercise at death and Keith let it lapse without exercise.

EXAMPLE 6 - 68. Curtis created a trust to benefit Donna for life, with remainder to her children. Roberta was the initial trustee, with Koala National Bank as the successor trustee. The trustee had the power to appoint as much of the trust to Donna as the trustee thought was needed to keep Donna happy. The power was never exercised and the trust was worth $1,000,000 when Donna died. Since Donna was neither a holder nor the settlor, none of the trust is included in her estate. What if Roberta dies before Donna, is any of the trust included in her estate? No, Roberta is a holder, but a holder of a limited power. And Curtis? Nothing is in his estate; he created the trust, but he did not retain any interest.

EXAMPLE 6 - 69. The same facts apply as in the prior example, except Curtis retained the right to appoint himself trustee. The entire trust would be included in his estate, since he retained the power to determine who would enjoy the property even though he could not benefit himself.

EXAMPLE 6 - 70. At a time when the federal rate for valuing split-interest gifts was 12%, Melinda, aged 65, established an irrevocable trust funded with all her worldly possessions and investments worth $1,000,000. The independent trustee was to pay her income for life with the remainder paid to her friend Dianne. The value of the gift (the remainder) using Table S was $226,950. Since this was a gift of a future interest, there was no annual exclusion. When Melinda died six years later, the trust was worth $1,125,000 and the full amount had to be included in her estate. The adjusted taxable gift for estate tax calculation drops to zero because property that is drawn back into the gross estate is not also counted as an adjusted taxable gift.

EXAMPLE 6 - 71. In 1998, 80-year-old Alejandro established an irrevocable trust funded with investments worth $750,000 (just a small portion of his vast wealth). The independent trustee was to pay income to such individuals as Alejandro each year directed. In any year Alejandro failed to direct the trustee, the income had to be accumulated. At the end of 10 years, the trust was to terminate and the remainder was to be paid to Alejandro's sister Irene, or to her issue. Even though the settlor did not retain any economic interest, the retention of control causes this to be an incomplete gift, hence nothing, not even a remainder interest, is treated as a gift. When Alejandro died five years later, the trust was worth $1,375,000. This is the value included in his gross estate. After 10 years, when the trust was worth $1,500,000, it terminated and the property was distributed to Irene. No new gift or transfer taxes occur as a result of this termination.

EXAMPLE 6 - 72. Suppose, in the preceding example, Alejandro died two years after the trust terminated. The results would be quite different. With the termination of the trust, his right to direct income ceased and the gift was complete. Alejandro would have paid gift taxes on the gift (the value of the trust at termination less an annual exclusion). The trust would not be included in his gross estate because he did not have any retained interests when he died. What about the fact that the retained interest ceased within three years of his death? It would not be a "release" of a retained interest since the interest merely ended as per the terms of the original trust, therefor §2035(a) does not apply. However, §2035(b) does apply and the gift taxes must be included in his gross estate. Of course, since the trust property itself is not included in the gross estate, an adjusted taxable gift in the amount of $1,490,000 (assuming a termination value of $1,500,000 and an annual exclusion of $10,000) and a gift tax payable credit are part of the estate tax calculation.

For the next four alternative examples, the common facts are as follows: Melanie created an irrevocable trust with assets worth $750,000. The trust required income be paid to Carol or Sean in such amounts as Melanie allocates each year. If she failed to advise the trustee and, after her death, the payments are to be made equally. Once one of the income beneficiaries dies, the income must be paid to the sole survivor; after both income beneficiaries die, the trust terminates and is to be distributed to Ruben or to his estate. Because of Melanie's retained control, no taxable transfer of the corpus occurs until her right to allocate income ends. Until then, she will be taxed on the income and each distribution of income to Carol or Sean must be treated as if it was a gift directly from her.

EXAMPLE 6 - 73. Suppose two years after establishing the trust, Melanie died and the trust was worth $1,180,000. Her estate would include the date-of-death amount, not because she died within three years of establishing the trust, but because she retained a §2036 interest.

EXAMPLE 6 - 74. Suppose that Melanie died seven years after establishing the trust. The trust was then worth $1,585,000. The date-of-death amount is included; again, this is a retained interest and inclusion has nothing to do with a three-year rule.

EXAMPLE 6 - 75. In 1999, when the trust was worth $2,100,000, Melanie released her right to decide who gets the income (i.e., she writes a letter to the trustee stating that she irrevocably gives up her right to make any further income allocations). In 2001, almost two years later, she died. At that time the trust was worth $2,250,000. The release was a taxable gift, resulting in her payment of gift taxes in the amount of $608,700 (assuming two annual exclusions of $10,000 each). Because of §2035(a), her gross estate includes the date-of-death value of the trust, i.e., $2,250,000. Because her gift within three years of death resulted in gift taxes, the $608,700 is included in her gross estate. Her adjusted taxable gifts are zero and, of course, a gift taxes payable credit of $608,700 is available.

EXAMPLE 6 - 76. Change the facts, suppose Melanie released her right to allocate income in 1997 when the trust was worth $1,800,000, and died in the year 2001, when the trust was worth $2,250,000. Nothing insofar as this trust is concerned is in her gross estate since her death was more than three years after she released her retained interest. When she released the right to allocate income, there was a taxable gift ($1,780,000) that resulted in gift tax of $489,000. Her estate reports $1,780,000 as an adjusted taxable gift and claims a gift tax payable credit of $489,000.

RULES

THE CONNECTION BETWEEN GIFTS & THE DONOR'S ESTATE

These **rules** should help you understand how post-1976 gifts relate to the donor's estate:

One: Generally, gifts given are simply "adjusted taxable gifts" to the extent such gifts exceed the annual exclusion. §2001(b)(2).

Two: Gift taxes paid (or payable) are generally allowed as a credit against the tentative tax to offset the fact that the adjusted taxable gifts are used to boost the estate into its appropriate marginal rate. §2001(b)(2).

Three: Gift taxes paid on <u>any</u> gift made within three years of death are added to the gross estate. §2035(b). [This is referred to as "grossing up" the estate.]

Four: Retained interests in transfers (usually transfers in trust) will cause the property transferred to be included in the transferor's estate as though the transfer never took place. §§2036 - 2038.

Five: There are only three exceptions to rule number one:

   a.   Transfers of an interest in **life insurance** within three years of death will result in the date-of-death value being included in the transferor's estate. §2035(a).

   b.   The **release** of a **retained** interest within three years of death will result in the date-of-death value of the trust assets being included in the settlor's estate as though no release occurred. §2035(a).

   c.   Where an interest that was given away on the creation of a joint tenancy is included in a deceased joint tenant's estate because of the "consideration furnished test," it will be included at the date-of-death value. §2040.

Notes to rules four and five: If a transferred property ends up in the gross estate, it will **not** also be an adjusted taxable gift for *estate* tax purposes. If transferred property is in the gross estate, it must be valued as of the date of death **not** the date of the gift. Finally, if gift taxes were paid and the property ends up in the gross estate, the estate is still entitled to a credit against the estate tax for those gift taxes.

Part-Sale, Part-Gift Transfers: §2043

Some people wrongly believe that a transfer is not a gift if the transferor receives any consideration in exchange. They think that a small token from the donee shelters the transaction from gift taxation. The correct result is that unless the transaction is at arm's length, a gift occurs measured by the *difference* between the respective values of the consideration exchanged.

Where IRC § 2035(a) (the three-year rule), §§ 2036-2038 (retained interests), or § 2041 (a general power of appointment) result in property sold as part of a bargain sale to be included in the seller's gross estate, §2043 provides that the date-of-death value of the property is reduced by a "consideration offset." This means that the estate must include the value at its date-of-death fair market value, but can subtract the value of the consideration received.

> EXAMPLE 6 - 77. D "sold" his son his $20,000 vacation home, reserving the right to use the home from time to time. D was "paid" 200 shares of very speculative stock then worth just $1,000. When D died, the stock was worth $17,000 and the vacation home was worth $30,000. His gross estate will include the date-of-death value of the home [i.e., $30,000], less only the $1,000 received as consideration. The post-gift appreciation on both the stock received (because D owns it) and the vacation home (because of the retained interest) are in D's estate. Note that there is no three-year rule involved here.

The example immediately above illustrates relatively uncommon estate-planning transfers. Most bargain-sale-type transfers are treated differently because they generally do not include a retained interest or a general power of appointment. Therefore, since the transferred property is not included in the gross estate, the §2043 offset rule does not apply. However, a simple bargain sale will be included in the *estate tax base* as an adjusted taxable gift equal to the original gross gift value, less both the annual exclusion(s) and the consideration received by the donor.

> EXAMPLE 6 - 78. In 1999, Jessie "sold" a parcel of land to her son Charles for a mere $200 even though they both knew it was worth $18,000. This sale is not subject to a retained interest or a general power of appointment, therefore §2043 does not apply. Jessie will be treated as having made a gross gift of $17,800 and a taxable gift of $7,800. If Jessie dies before 2010, the $7,800 will show up as an adjusted taxable gift that will boost her estate into higher marginal rates.

It should be kept in mind that §2043 applies only to transfers included in the gross estate under §§ 2035(a), 2036-2038, or 2041. Section 2043 does not specifically mention §2042 (life insurance), but §2035(a) does. So, if life insurance is "sold," other than in an arms length transaction within three years of the insured's death, §2043 will apply.

> EXAMPLE 6 - 79. Four years before he died, Max sold Rita a $100,000 face-value policy on his life. At the time, they both knew that it had a gift value of $1,800 but Max charged Rita just $500. Since more than three years have passed, his gross estate does not include this policy. However, the transfer-for-value rule will render the proceeds in excess of the purchase price taxable as income to Rita.

> EXAMPLE 6 - 80. Based on the facts in the prior example, if Max died within three years of the "sale," his estate would be increased by $99,500, based on §2043 (a $500 offset) which makes a reference to §2035(a) that, in turn, makes a reference to §2042.

TWO: ESTATE TAX DEDUCTIONS

Estate tax deductions include funeral expenses, expenses in administering the estate, claims against the estate, debts of the decedent, losses incurred during estate administration,[33] charitable bequests,[34] and the marital deduction.[35] In this section, we will introduce the marital deduction and charitable deduction, both of which are developed in detail in later chapters.

Marital Deduction: §2056

In calculating the taxable estate, the gross estate may be reduced by the value of any qualifying interest in property passing from the decedent to the surviving spouse. Thus, essentially an "unlimited" amount of property passing to the surviving spouse can avoid estate taxation, provided that certain requirements are met.

Requirements for the unlimited marital deduction. Subject to several exceptions, a property transfer to a spouse will qualify for the unlimited marital deduction if it meets the following three requirements:

1. *Included in decedent's gross estate.* The property must be *included* in the decedent's gross estate.

2. *Must "pass" to surviving spouse.* The property must actually *pass* to the surviving spouse.

> EXAMPLE 6 - 81. When Orca died in 2001, she left a $5 million estate. Her will left a pecuniary bequest of $2 million to Walter, her son by a prior marriage, and the residue to her husband Martin. Unfortunately, she used a will form that had the clause "all estate taxes shall be paid from the residue of my estate." Because the tax on the transfer to Walter reduces Martin's interest in the estate, it also reduces the marital deduction which in turn further increases the tax, etc., with the final result that the tax is $1,156,111 and Martin receives just $1,843,889. *** *Query 6 - 7. What is the death tax on $2 million? Would charging her son Walter's share with the estate taxes, but increasing that share such that he still nets $2 million result in an increase in Martin's share given that there would no longer be an interrelated calculation?*

Thus, to qualify for the full marital deduction, most planners will plan for taxes and other expenses to be paid from property *not* qualifying for the marital deduction. Thus in the example above, it might have been better to have Walter's share bear its own taxes. An additional problem of paying estate taxes out of the marital share is the need to make interrelated computations. In order to calculate the amount of the marital deduction, one needs to know the amount of the net tax; however, in order to calculate the net tax, the amount of the marital deduction must be calculated. A solution is determinable, but it requires an interrelated sequence of calculations.

3. *Not a terminable interest.* To qualify for the marital deduction, the interest passing to the surviving spouse cannot be a terminable interest. A *terminable interest*, defined in §2056(b)(1), is one that *might* terminate on the happening of some event or contingency or on the failure of some event or contingency. The terminable interest rule was created to ensure that property owned by a married couple is taxed in at least one of the spouses' estates. There are exceptions to the rule, each of which is intended to facilitate legitimate estate planning goals yet assure that the property will eventually be taxed in one of the spouses estates. Without these rules, property could qualify for the marital deduction in the estate of the first spouse and never show up in the estate of the surviving spouse.

> EXAMPLE 6 - 82. In his will, decedent transfers property into a trust, with income to his wife for her life, then remainder to his child. The value of the life interest to the wife will not qualify for the marital deduction because it will "terminate ... on

the occurrence of an event...." The event that causes termination of her interest is her death. In general, unless a special election is made, a *life estate interest* passing to a surviving spouse does not qualify for the marital deduction and is not included in the surviving spouse's estate.

Because of the way the Code defines a terminable interest, a transfer to a surviving spouse will not be considered a terminable one if no other person will possess or enjoy any part of the property after the interest passing to the surviving spouse terminates.

> EXAMPLE 6 - 83. At her death, Mrs. Carrie, an inventor, was receiving annual payments from several companies using one of her patented ideas. Her husband received her entire estate, including the patent rights (good for 20 years when first issued) that still had 14 years left. The value of the patent is included in Mrs. Carrie's estate and it qualifies for a marital deduction because *no other person* will enjoy any part of the property after the patent is finished.

Exceptions to the terminable interest rule. There are several exceptions to the terminable interest rule that will be covered in detail in the chapter that introduces estate plans for wealthy couples. We will just introduce three of the major ones here.

First, the rule will not be violated if decedent-testator conditions a spousal bequest on surviving no more than *six months* after the decedent's death.[36] Thus, the survival clauses specifying "30 days" or "four months" are regularly included in the wills and do create terminable interests, but the exception allows them to qualify for the marital deduction provided the spouse lives long enough for the interest to vest. Some states, such as California, have enacted *marital deduction saving* statutes for those wills and trusts that show a clear intention to qualify for the marital deduction but which, due to poor drafting, include a survivorship period in excess of six months. The statutes reduce the survivorship period to six months. Other statutes provide a more generic solution, such as declaring void any provision which would cause the loss of the marital deduction whenever it is clear from the estate plan that the availability of the deduction was intended.[37] Unfortunately, judicial reaction to these statutes has been less than enthusiastically supportive.

Second, a transfer in which the surviving spouse receives a life estate in all of the income, payable at least annually, plus a *general power of appointment*, exercisable during life and/or at death (usually accomplished through language in the holder's will), is allowed to qualify for the marital deduction.[38] This arrangement is used in what is called a *general power of appointment trust*, which is one type of marital trust discussed in the chapters on estate planning for wealthy couples.

Third, if the decedent's executor elects to treat certain property as "qualified terminable interest property," or "QTIP," it will qualify for the marital deduction despite the fact that the surviving spouse will not own the property and might have, at most, a limited power over the property.[39] Making the QTIP election requires a trade-off; the property that qualifies for the marital deduction because of the election must be included in the surviving spouse's estate when he/she dies.[40] A further discussion of this important estate planning tool is postponed until we study estate plans for wealthy couples.

Special rules for transfers to non-U.S. citizen spouse. Property passing at death to a *surviving spouse* who is not a U.S. citizen will qualify for the marital deduction if it is placed in a "qualified domestic trust," commonly called a QDOT. Generally, the surviving spouse receives the income for her lifetime. The QDOT assets will be subject to the estate tax (based on the first spouse to die's estate) when the surviving spouse dies or when corpus is transferred to her free of trust. There is an exception that allows distributions to the surviving spouse for emergencies without the distribution triggering a transfer tax. The marital deduction is also allowed if the surviving spouse becomes a U.S. citizen before the estate tax return is filed (even if filed late).[41] The rationale for requiring the creation of this trust is to ensure collection of the estate tax on the death of a surviving spouse who might otherwise remove the wealth from the United States. The QDOT requirements are covered in greater detail in the chapter on advanced estate planning for wealthy married couples.

Charitable Deduction: §2055

The charitable deduction is evidence of Congressional encouragement of philanthropy. Compared to the various rules limiting the amount of deduction for income taxes, the charitable deduction is quite simple insofar as the transfer tax system is concerned. Outright transfers to qualified charities (most U.S.-based religious organizations, publicly funded educational institutions, organizations for the disabled, for health research, etc.) are 100% deductible for both estate and gift tax purposes. For gifts, the deduction is based on the value of the gift at the moment of transfer. For a bequest, it is the value of the property at the date of death or the alternate valuation date if such is elected.

EXAMPLE 6 - 84. Anne Scheiber died on January 9, 1995, at the age of 101. She had worked for the IRS. Her salary was just $3,150 per year when she retired in 1943. In 1944, she used her life savings of $5,000 to open an investment account. By living frugally, investing, and reinvesting, her stock and bond investments had grown to over $20 million when she died. Except for $50,000 that went to a niece, the balance of her estate (more than $22 million by the time it was distributed) went to Yeshiva University, a small co-ed university in New York City. The bequest specified that it be used for women's scholarships. The estate paid no estate taxes.

EXAMPLE 6 - 85. David Marine had been a doctor. At the time of his death in 1984, he had accumulated considerable wealth, but had very few friends and no close relatives. His executors were given the limited power to appoint his estate to such "persons who have contributed to my well-being or who have been otherwise helpful to me during my lifetime...." The bequest to any one of these persons was limited to no more than one percent of his estate, with a provision that it "may be considerably less." The residue of the estate was left in equal shares to Princeton University and Johns Hopkins University. The net estate was worth $2,130,081, of which the executors appointed $10,000 to Dr. Marine's housekeeper and another $15,000 to a friend of his. The balance of the estate was divided between the two universities and the executor claimed a $2,105,081 charitable deduction. The IRS successfully challenged the deduction on the grounds that at the time of the doctor's death, the amount that would eventually go to the universities was unascertainable. The court stated that, although the amount of each bequest was limited to one percent of the corpus, since "the number of such bequests was unlimited and a standard for determining the amount of a bequest was uncertain, the amount of the charitable bequest could not be ascertained at the time of death and the deduction was not available."[42] The tax on a taxable estate of $2,130,081 in 1984 was $748,240. *** *Query 6 - 8. To completely avoid the estate tax while maintaining significant flexibility, what restriction or restrictions should the trust have placed on the power of the executors?*

If a bequest is left to the discretion of the executor (or of a beneficiary), then no estate tax deduction will be allowed even if the person decides to leave a portion of the estate to a charity. Thus, precatory words (i.e., an earnest request) in a decedent's will such as, "I leave $100,000 to Reverend Teagarden with the hope that he will use it for the ministry of the Church," would not result in a charitable deduction.

Transfers made to charities through the use of trusts must meet certain requirements specified in Code §2055. The special requirements for charitable giving through the use of trusts are designed to give reasonable assurance that the charity will actually receive a benefit that is reasonably close to the amount of tax deduction allowed, whether the deduction is an income tax deduction in the case of lifetime gifts or an estate tax deduction for transfers that take place at the death of the donor. Additional material on charitable gifts and the charitable deduction is found in later chapters.

THREE: ESTATE TAX CREDITS

As mentioned in the last chapter, there are five main estate tax credits: the unified credit, credit for state death taxes, credit for gift taxes payable, credit for tax on prior transfers, and the credit for foreign death taxes. Since the unified credit and the state death tax credit were covered in the last chapter, the following material discusses only the other three. Each of these credits represents Congress's attempt to take the sting out of the fact that some transfers may be taxed twice.

Credit/Offset for Gift Taxes Paid or Payable

To help prevent double taxation, the unified transfer tax system allows some level of offset for gift taxes on all gifts included in the decedent's estate tax base. Without this offset, the estate tax would be calculated on all accumulated transfers whether at death or as gifts, unfairly disregarding the fact that a transfer tax had already been paid on some of them. The law allows offsets for two different categories of gift taxes: those paid on pre-1977 gifts, and those paid on post-1976 gifts.

Credit for gift taxes (pre-1977 gifts). The credit for gift tax on pre-1977 gifts shows up on line 17, page one, of the estate tax return. The amount of the credit is limited to the lesser of the gift tax or the estate tax on the property that is included in the estate.[43] One might wonder why there would be a credit for gift taxes on pre-1977 gifts given that only post-1976 gifts are included as adjusted taxable gifts in calculating the estate tax. Well, it is possible to have a pre-1977 gift pulled back into the donor's gross estate if the gift had a retained interest attached such that §2036, §2037, or §2038 applies; or if the donor-decedent had made a pre-1977 transfer with a retained interest and relinquished the interest within three years of death such that §2035(a) applies.

EXAMPLE 6 - 86. In 1975, decedent, then age 50, created an irrevocable trust, funding it with $2 million in property. Under the terms of the trust, income was payable to the decedent for life, with remainder to his descendants. Decedent paid a gift tax of $235,118 on the gift of the *remainder* interest. If decedent dies today, his gross estate will include today's value of the entire trust corpus, under §2036. A credit for gift tax paid will be allowed based on the lesser of the gift tax paid in 1975 that is attributable to the gift (pro rata share if more than one gift that year), or the amount of estate tax attributed to having the trust included in his taxable estate (i.e., the pro rata share of the federal estate tax attributable to including the trust in the taxable estate).

Offset for gift taxes payable (post-1976 gifts). By now it should be clear that two categories of post-1976 gifts are included in the decedent's estate tax base. First, as with pre-1977 gifts described in the previous section, post-1976 gifts that fall within the grasp of §§ 2036, 2037, 2038, or 2035(a) are included in the transferor's gross estate. Although the Code does not specifically address a credit for the gift tax paid in situations where previously taxed gifts are pulled back into the gross estate, it stands to reason that a credit must be allowed for the full amount actually paid (not some recalculated "payable" amount) since the transferred property is drawn back into the gross estate at its date-of-death value. Second, adjusted taxable gifts (post-1976 gifts that are not in the gross estate) are added to the estate tax base. Again, to prevent double taxation, the law allows an offset to the tentative tax for gift taxes paid on these gifts.[44] This offset is calculated by determining the amount that would have been "payable" had the tax rates in effect at the decedent's death been applicable at the time of the gift. The gift tax paid may be more than the payable amount if the decedent made taxable gifts both pre-1977 and post-1976, since the earlier gifts pushed the later gifts into higher tax brackets but are not included as adjusted taxable gifts for present estate tax calculations. As discussed in detail in Chapter 5, the gift tax payable credit will be less than the gift taxes paid if the marginal rates applied to the gift were higher than those in effect at the time of the donor's death. Although the Code does not refer to this offset as a "credit," it has the effect of reducing the tentative tax dollar for dollar to an amount called the "gross estate tax," and it clearly is a credit. This credit is placed on line nine of page one of Form 706.

THE PRIOR TRANSFER CREDIT: §2013

It seems inequitable to tax property twice on those occasions when it passes swiftly through two estates such that the second owner only had a limited opportunity to enjoy the inherited property. Congress obviously agrees. It has given relief in the form of a prior transfer credit (PTC) if the two deaths occur within 10 years of each other.[45]

Background on the PTC. As originally enacted, double taxation was avoided by allowing a deduction in the second estate equal to the value of property traceable to the first estate.[46] The relief was available only if the two deaths occurred within five years of one another and the old law required the executor claiming the deduction to trace the property from the first estate into the second. If the inherited property was sold and the proceeds were commingled with other funds out of which both investments and consumables were purchased, it was difficult (sometimes impossible) to trace the property. There was a fair amount of litigation between estates and the IRS over the tracing issue.

The PTC today. Present law allows a tax credit where property is included in the transferor's taxable estate and the transferee dies within 10 years of the transferor. The inherited property does not have to be found in the transferee's estate, hence tracing is no longer necessary. Since the credit is intended to reduce the unfairness of taxing property that passes quickly through two estates, a time factor affects the amount of the credit available, decreasing the maximum available by 20% two years after the transferor's death and another 20% for each additional two-year period until the credit disappears altogether at the end of 10 years. Actually, the credit is available even if the transferee dies two years before the transferor, but the circumstances, involving vested remainder interests, are so rare that they will not be covered. The credit, before applying the time factor, is based on the amount of additional tax the inclusion of the transferred property generates in each estate. Since this is relief from double taxation, the credit is equal to the lesser of the two amounts.

The above overview greatly simplifies the law. The actual calculation is a three-step process. In the explanation that follows, D1 represents the first decedent and D2 the second decedent (the recipient of property from D1's estate).

Credit Limit One. Limit one is the portion of the federal estate tax which bears the same ratio to D1's estate tax as the transferred property bears to D1's taxable estate.

$$CL1 = \frac{\textit{adjusted value of transferred property}}{\textit{adjusted value of D1's taxable estate}} * D1\textit{'s federal estate tax}$$

Credit Limit Two. Compute the increase in estate tax at D2's death caused by inclusion of the net value of the transferred property. The net value is the value of the transferred property reduced by all death taxes (federal and state) attributed to it at D1's death. The federal estate tax is determined with the net value of the property included, then again with it excluded. The difference in the two tax amounts is credit limit two.[47]

Federal tax on D2's taxable estate (including transferred property)	xxxx
Federal tax on D2's reduced estate (reduced by the adjusted value of the transferred property)	(xxxx)
Credit Limit Two	xxx

Time Factor. The prior transfer credit is the *lesser of* limit one or limit two, times the appropriate time factor percentage based on how many years D2 lived after D1 died.

Years	1 - 2	3 - 4	5 - 6	7 - 8	9 - 10
Percentage	100%	80%	60%	40%	20%

An Extended Prior Transfer Credit Example.

As we go through each of the three prior transfer credit (PTC) steps, we will start each with some general comments. For limit one, the numerator is the value of the transferred property, adjusted by deducting liens, mortgages, and the transferred property's proportionate share of federal and state death taxes. The denominator is D1's taxable estate, adjusted by deducting all death taxes. If the net value of the property (property less liens and mortgages) is used in this step of the calculation, and all death taxes are allocated pro rata, there is no need to make any adjustments for the taxes since the adjusted values (above and below the line) will be in the same ratio as the unadjusted values. If the property in D2's estate is the result of a bequest made "free of estate tax," which probably means the residue of the estate paid the death taxes, the transferred property's value (the numerator) would not be adjusted for taxes but the taxable estate (the denominator) would have to be reduced by all death taxes.

The federal estate tax is adjusted only if a credit for certain gift taxes had been allowed for D1's estate under §2012 (pre-1977 transfers with a retained interest, such that the property is included in the decedent's estate) or if D1's estate also benefitted from a prior transfer credit. For most PTC computations, no adjustments need to be made to the denominator to adjust the value of D1's taxable estate, other than for death taxes, and (as pointed out earlier) even then an adjustment is not necessary for the numerator or the denominator if the death taxes were proportionately assessed.

> EXAMPLE 6 - 87. D1 died January 1, 1994, leaving a taxable estate of $2,500,000. D1's friend, D2, received XYZ stock worth $500,000. The total D1 estate taxes were $833,000. D1's state was a pickup tax state, so it collected an amount equal to the federal state death tax credit ($138,800), and the balance of $694,200 went to the Federal Treasury. D2 died June 10, 1997, leaving a taxable estate of $1,500,000. D2 had sold the XYZ stock when it was worth $580,000, investing some of the proceeds and spending the rest. In both estates, the death taxes were allocated pro rata. Credit limit one is calculated as follows:

$$CL1 = \frac{\$500,000}{\$2,500,000} * \$694,200 = \$138,840$$

The value of the stock in D2's estate is irrelevant to the PTC calculation. Remember, the assets transferred need not be part of D2's estate, so no tracing of assets is required. The theory is, that if the property had been sold, and the proceeds consumed, the money from the sale allowed D2 to retain other property that is taxed in D2's estate. Notice that the value of D2's estate is not used in calculating credit limit one.

There are three steps to calculating credit limit two. These steps determine that part of the federal tax that can be attributed to the transferred property that is part of D2's estate. The calculation is done by figuring the federal estate tax both with the net value of the transferred property included and again with it excluded. The difference is the additional tax attributed to the inclusion. First, calculate D2's federal estate tax without the PTC. This means, determine the federal amount that would have been paid on D2's taxable estate, i.e., reduce the tentative tax by the unified credit and the state death tax credit. Second, determine the federal estate tax on D2's estate with the net value of the transferred property removed. We will call this D2's *reduced* taxable estate. To arrive at the reduced D2 taxable estate, one must subtract the net value of the property transferred from D2's (regular or full) taxable estate. To determine the net value of the transferred property, subtract from the value of the property transferred (as of D1's DOD) its *share* of *all* death taxes (yes, including state death taxes) and any debts, liens, or other obligations which reduced the value of the property when it was transferred from D1 to D2.

Continuing with this example, credit limit two is calculated as follows:

Federal estate tax on D2's $1,500,000 taxable estate	$298,600
Less federal estate tax on D2's reduced taxable estate.	
This is the tax on $1,166,600, i.e.,	
$1,500,000 - (5/25 * ($2,500,000 - $833,000))	<u>(178,244)</u>
Credit limit two	$120,356

The figure $298,600 is the federal estate tax on an estate of $1,500,000 after subtracting the unified credit and the federal state death tax credit [$555,800 (tentative tax) - $192,800 (unified credit) - $64,400 (state death tax credit)]. The figure (5/25 * ($2,500,000 -(833,000)) in the above example is the value of the property transferred, adjusted for its pro rata share of *all* death taxes. In this hypothetical situation, the decedent's state death taxes are equal to the federal state death tax credit. Where the state death taxes are greater than the federal state death tax credit, the actual state death tax paid must be used to make the adjustment. This would not affect limit one (assuming the state death taxes were also allocated pro rata), but it would affect the calculation of limit two since the property transferred must be reduced by all death taxes charged against it. The figure $178,244 is the federal tax on a taxable estate of $1,166,600, meaning it is the amount that would actually be paid on an estate of that size after taking the unified credit and the state death tax credit [$414,106 (tentative tax) - $192,800 (unified credit) - $43,062 (state death tax credit)].

To finish this example, the time factor adjustment must be made. Since D2 died in the fourth year following D1's death, the allowable credit is 80% of the lesser of the two credit limits. Therefore:

$$80\% * \text{ the lesser of } \left\{ \begin{array}{l} \textit{limit one: } \$138,840 \\ \textit{limit two: } \$120,356 \end{array} \right. = \$96,285$$

The two-year time bracket starts with the actual date of D1's death through midnight of the anniversary two (or four, six, etc.) years later. It is easiest to visualize this (and to be assured of selecting the correct percentage) by drawing a time line, marking off the appropriate two-year anniversaries starting with D1's death, and then indicating with a slash the date of D2's death. Indicate on the time line "100%" for the first two years following D1's death, "80%" for the next two years, etc., until you have covered the period that includes D2's death.

The chapter on advanced marital deduction and bypass trust planning goes into detail as to how the PTC is used with marital deduction trusts to reduce taxes, even where no transfer of corpus takes place.

Credit for Foreign Death Taxes

A credit is allowed for most, but not all, foreign death taxes paid on property which is (a) included in the U.S. gross estate, and (b) situated in that foreign country. Similar to the PTC, the amount of credit allowed is the lower of the amount of tax the property generates in the U.S. versus the amount it generates in the foreign country.[48] A detailed explanation of this credit is beyond the scope of this text.

Adjustment to the Unified Credit for Certain Pre-1977 Gifts

When members of Congress were working on the massive overhaul of the estate and gift tax laws in 1976, there was concern that when wealthy individuals got wind of the changes, specifically the replacement of the lifetime $30,000 per donor gift exemption with a unified credit, many would make large gifts to use up any unused exemption, with the idea that they would start fresh with the brand new unified credit. This would give them an advantage over those who did not move quickly to use up their unused exemption, so Congress added a special adjustment for those donors who used up any gift exemption during the closing months of 1976. Those donors must reduce their unified credit by 20% times the amount of exemption used for gifts made during the time period September 9, 1976, and December 31, 1976.[49]

> EXAMPLE 6 - 88. On November 11, 1976, Graham made a gift of $50,000 worth of XYZ stock to his daughter Alison. Previously, he had never made a gift above the annual exclusion amount. From the gross gift of $50,000 was subtracted the $3,000 annual exclusion and the $30,000 lifetime gift exemption to arrive at a taxable gift of $17,000. Because the use of the lifetime exemption fell within the "adjustment" time period, he must reduce his unified credit by $6,000 [20% * $30,000]. Hence, if he died in 2001 his unified credit would be $214,550 instead of $220,550.

This chapter has examined the principal items found on the estate tax return, including components of the gross estate, estate tax deductions, and estate tax credits. The next chapter examines the components of the gift tax return, and covers basis rules as they relate to gifts and estates.

QUERIES ANSWERED

1. Using Table S, the remainder factor, using an 8% rate for an 85-year-old's life estate, is .65386. Hence, Max's estate would include:

   .65386 * $1,000,000 = $653,860

2. Using Table S, the remainder factor (also used for a reversionary interest), using a 10% rate for a 40-year-old's life estate, is .06411. Hence, Jim's estate would include:

   .06411 * $100,000 = $6,411.

3. Because of the consideration-furnished test of IRC § 2040, the entire property is included in Virginia's estate, even though half was reported as a gift. The definition of "adjusted taxable gifts," found in IRC § 2001(b), excludes any

gifts that are included in the gross estate; therefore, the $190,000 taxable gift to her son is removed from the estate tax calculation.

4. Because the trustee will still allocate income between Benito and Consuelo, neither beneficiary has an identifiable present interest. A present interest is a requirement for the annual exclusion.

5. This is another example of an overlap of code sections. Section 2036(a)(2) requires inclusion where the decedent retains the right to "designate who shall possess or enjoy the property or the income therefrom." By being able to terminate the trust early, D was able to designate who would possess the property; hence, IRC § 2036(a)(2) applies as well as § 2038.

6. Because the holder of a limited power never made a transfer (but is merely the donee), the exercise or lapse will not cause the holder to be treated as having made a taxable transfer. The exercise or the lapse of a limited power during the holder's lifetime will not create a taxable gift.

7. The death tax on $2,000,000 in the year 2001 is $560,250. Charging Walter's share with the tax, but increasing the share so that he nets $2,000,000, will not increase Martin's share because estate taxes are calculated on a tax inclusive basis. It would take a bequest of $3,156,111 to Walter for him to net $2,000,000. This means that husband Martin would receive $1,843,889, the same as if the taxes were charged to his $3,000,000 share.

8. Instead of limiting the amount that could be given to each appointee to one percent, the limit could have been stated as, "all such appointments cumulatively shall not exceed an amount that will produce a tentative tax equal to the decedent's available unified credit." Or, "cumulatively not to exceed" either some dollar amount, such as $200,000, or some small percentage of the net estate, such as "not to exceed 10% of the adjusted gross estate." Even though these limits do not set an exact amount going to charity, they do produce a minimum amount that must go to charity and the charitable deduction would be based on that minimum amount. Thus, the first limit (not to exceed the AEA) would result in a charitable deduction of the net estate in excess of the AEA, producing a taxable estate of $600,000 (i.e., the AEA for 1984) with no estate tax due.

QUESTIONS AND PROBLEMS

1. Distinguish between the gross estate, taxable estate, and probate estate.

2. Why is it important to distinguish between assets previously given away that are nevertheless included in the gross estate versus transfers that are part of the tax base but only as adjusted taxable gifts?

3. (a) What is a dower interest? (b) How is it taxed?

4. Dana, a single man, died on June 12, 2003. (a) If he had made no taxable gifts during his lifetime, what would his gross estate have to be worth before his executor would be required to file an estate tax return? (b) How would your answer to "a" change if he had made taxable gifts of $75,000 in 1970, $120,000 in 1980, and $40,000 in 1995? (c) The trustee of his probate-avoiding trust held assets worth $1,500,000 and the only other significant asset was a Transfer on Death brokerage account worth $120,000 that was collected by his sister, the designated transferee, shortly after his death. Who would be responsible for filing the estate tax return? When would the return be due? What extensions for filing and paying are possible? (d) Who would be liable for paying the tax if the trustee distributed the trust to Dana's issue (the remaindermen) and no one filed a return or paid any tax?

5. When Morton died in 2003, he left his estate to his three children. He left stock worth $1,560,000, a home worth $345,000, a car worth $9,000, home furnishings worth $23,000, and a bank account with $3,500 in it. The total of his debts and expenses was $45,000. He also had a $200,000 life insurance policy on his life that was paid out to his three children and a life insurance policy on his mother (alive and well, thank you). The policy on his mother had a face value of $150,000 but was worth only $25,000. A mountain cabin worth $150,000 was held in joint tenancy with his brother John. They bought the cabin for only $30,000 years ago, with John paying $20,000 and Morton paying $10,000. Calculate : (a) the gross estate, (b) the taxable estate, (c) the probate estate, (d) the total death taxes, (e) the state death tax credit, and (f) the federal estate tax.

6. When Beverly died in 2002, her estate was distributed mostly to her sister and to several close friends. With her friend Daniel she held title to three timeshares in Hawaii, each was worth $11,000. Beverly paid for the timeshares, taking title with Daniel as joint tenants. She shared a home held in joint tenancy with her sister Alice. They bought it for $250,000 years ago, with Alice putting in the entire down payment of $50,000, and they both signed for the $200,000 mortgage. They shared equally in paying the monthly mortgage, and the home, worth $750,000, was free of debt when Beverly died. Fred, the father of Beverly and Alice, died in 2001, and the probate of his estate had closed just weeks before Beverly's death. The value of her share of her father's estate (mostly mutual funds and certificates of deposit) on the day she died was $450,000. The balance of her own estate was in a revocable trust that provided several $25,000 gifts to friends at her church, $50,000 to her church's building fund, $300,000 left to the American Heart Association, a federally recognized charity, and the balance 20% to Daniel and 80% to her sister Alice. The trust assets were worth $2,400,000. Debts and funeral expenses were $15,000. Expenses associated with the transfer of the trust, the fees for probate, and the filing of tax returns were $35,000. Calculate : (a) the gross estate, (b) the taxable estate, (c) the probate estate, (d) the total death taxes, (e) the state death tax credit, and (f) the federal estate tax.

7. When Mary died, her son Charlie was entitled to receive annuity payments of $2,500 per month for 15 years. The §7520 rate used for valuing annuities was 8%. Use Table K to adjust for the fact that the payments are made monthly.

8. When Sally died, her son Frank was entitled to receive annuity payments of $1,400 per month for 10 years. The §7520 rate used for valuing annuities was 6%. Use Table K to adjust for the fact that the payments are made monthly.

9. When Connie died, her 80-year-old husband was entitled to receive a survivor's pension of $600 per month for his lifetime from a fully qualified plan (his employer had made all contributions). The §7520 rate used for valuing annuities was 10%. Determine how much is included in his estate if Connie retired in (a) 1986; (b) 1983; or (c) 1980. Use Table K to adjust for the fact that the payments are made monthly.

10. When Jack died, his 65-year-old wife was entitled to receive a survivor's pension of $3,800 per month for her lifetime from a fully qualified plan (his employer had made all contributions). The §7520 rate used for valuing annuities was 6%. Determine how much is included in his estate if Jack retired in (a) 1986; (b) 1983; or (c) 1980. Use Table K to adjust for the fact that the payments are made monthly.

11. Frank and Kathleen co-owned a home. Frank contributed $25,000 and Kathleen contributed $75,000 of the $100,000 purchase price. When the first co-owner died, the value of the property was $360,000. In each independent case determine: (1) how much is included in the decedent's estate and (2) the survivor's new basis.

   a. They held the property as joint tenants. Frank died first. They were just good friends.
   b. They held the property as joint tenants. Frank died first. They were married.
   c. They held the property as joint tenants. Kathleen died first. They were just good friends.
   d. They held the property as community property. Frank died first.
   e. They held the property as tenants in the entirety. Frank died first.
   f. They held the property as tenants in common. Frank died first, leaving his 25% share to Kathleen. (Does it matter for inclusion and basis whether they were married? Does it matter for estate taxes?)

12. Eduardo and Susie took title to a vacation cabin with their son Juan. Title was taken as joint tenants even though Eduardo and Susie paid the entire purchase price of $80,000 (half each). At the first death the property was worth $120,000 and at the second death the property was worth $180,000. For each independent problem answer the following: (i.) How much was included in the first estate? What rule? (ii.) How much in the second estate? What rule? (iii.) What is the survivor's basis?

   a. Eduardo died first. Several years later Susie died. Juan was the survivor.
   b. Susie died first. Several years later Juan died. Eduardo was the survivor.
   c. Juan died first. Several years later Eduardo died. Susie was the survivor.

13. (a) What is a general power? (b) What is the significant tax difference between a general power and a limited one? (c) When will a power to appoint to one's self not be a general power?

14. Identify two situations where a limited power of appointment might be the right answer to an estate planning problem.

15. At his death, decedent-trustee was the holder of a power of appointment over property held in a trust created by his rich uncle. Determine whether any portion of the trust principal is included in decedent's gross estate given each of the following alternative trustee powers. If a power is exercised in favor of someone other than the holder, state the gift and estate tax consequences that follow.

   a. The unrestricted power to appoint property to his surviving descendants by specific mention of the power in his will. Decedent appointed the entire corpus to his son.
   b. Same as part a, except decedent did not appoint property to anyone at his death.
   c. The power to appoint property to himself for "health" reasons.
   d. The power to appoint property to himself, but only with the approval of his son, who is also the remainderman.

   For e - f, the following power was included in the trust: the power to appoint each calendar year the greater of $5,000 or five percent of the trust property to himself or to his children. He could also exercise the power at death, through his will, provided such exercise at death and any exercise during the last year could not exceed 5%.

   e. In his will, decedent exercised the power, naming his son to receive $50,000 of the $1 million trust corpus.
   f. Decedent never exercised this power during his lifetime or at his death.

   For g - h the following 5 & 5 power was involved: The power to appoint to himself or to his children each calendar year up to the greater of $5,000 or 5% of the trust property. At his death the power lapsed, i.e., it could not be exercised through his will or by any other means once he died.

g. Shortly before he died, he exercised the power and had the trustee transfer 5% ($50,000) of the trust to himself.

h. Shortly before he died, he had the trustee transfer 5% to his university to be used for scholarships.

i. He died without ever exercising the power.

16. At her death, decedent-trustee was the holder of a power of appointment over property held in a trust created by her rich aunt. Determine whether any portion of the trust principal is included in decedent's gross estate given each of the following alternative trustee powers. If a power is exercised in favor of someone other than the holder, state the gift and estate tax consequences that follow.

a. The unrestricted power to appoint property to herself or her descendants. By her will she appointed property to her son.

b. Same as part b, except decedent did not appoint to anyone at her death.

c. The power to appoint property to herself for her "comfort."

d. The power to appoint property to herself, but only with the approval of her son, who was also the remainderman.

For e - f, the following power was included in the trust: the power to appoint each calendar year the greater of $5,000 or five percent of the trust property to herself or to her children. She could also exercise the power at death, through her will, provided such exercise at death and any exercise during the last year could not exceed 5%.

e. The year before her death, she had the trustee transfer $40,000 to her son. At her death, through her will, decedent exercised the power, naming her daughter to receive $30,000 of the $1 million trust corpus.

f. Decedent never exercised this power during her lifetime, but at her death through her will she exercised the power to appoint $20,000 of the $1 million trust to her brother if he was still alive (and he was).

For g - h the following 5 & 5 power was involved: The power to appoint to herself or to her children each calendar year up to the greater of $5,000 or 5% of the trust property. At her death the power lapsed, i.e., it could not be exercised through her will or by any other means once she died.

g. Shortly before she died, she exercised the power and had the trustee transfer 2.5% of the trust ($25,000) to her son and another 2.5% to her daughter.

h. Shortly before she died, she exercised the power by having the trustee transfer 3% of the trust to the United Way.

17. True or false? A gift of life insurance within three years of the insured-donor's death is the *ONLY* circumstance where an outright gift (i.e., one with no strings attached) is included in the gross estate of the donor.

18. What do IRC §§ 2033, 2034, 2039, 2040, 2041, and 2042 have in common?

19. What do IRC §§ 2036, 2037, and 2038 have in common?

20. Under IRC § 2036, two very different circumstances will cause a trust to be included in the settlor's estate. (a) Describe the one in which the settlor retains an economic benefit. (b) Describe the one in which the settlor does not retain an economic benefit.

21. Use the language of the IRC to describe the three common retained powers or rights that will cause a trust or bank account to be included in the settlor's gross estate under IRC § 2038. Identify three common estate planning arrangements to which this code section would be applied, e.g., a type of trust or a special type of bank account.

22. Explain the impact of IRC § 2035(a) by giving specific examples of:

a. a single transaction lifetime gift where the property transferred is not included in the gross estate.
b. a single transaction lifetime gift where the property transferred is included in the gross estate.
c. a relinquishment of a "string" where the trust property is not included in the gross estate.
d. a relinquishment of a "string" where the trust property is included in the gross estate.

23. Facts: Gary transferred property worth $60,000 to his sister Pamela. Because of the unified credit, Gary paid no gift taxes when he made the transfer. When Gary died, the property was worth $100,000. For each case, state (insofar as the transfer goes) what is (i) in his gross estate; and (ii) the adjusted taxable gift for estate tax purposes.

   a. Gary transferred stock two years before he died.
   b. Gary transferred stock four years before he died.
   c. Gary transferred life insurance ($60,000 was its gift value) two years before he died. Pamela collected the $100,000 proceeds.
   d. Gary transferred life insurance ($60,000 was its gift value) four years before he died. Pamela collected the $100,000 proceeds.

24. Review the estate tax return (the 706). On what line of page one does one report adjusted taxable gifts? Identify by letter the schedule where one reports gift taxes paid on gifts made within three years of death. Where does the gift taxes payable credit appear?

25. Review the estate tax return (the 706). On page three, where does one report total charitable gifts? Identify by letter the schedule where one gives the details of charitable gifts. How does the IRS know whether estate taxes were charged to the charitable gifts?

26. Identify the line on page three of the 706 where the total for annuities appears and by letter the schedule where the details for them are listed.

27. Identify the line on page three of the 706 where the total for transfers with a retained interest appears and by letter the schedule where the details for such transfers are listed.

28. Identify the line on page three of the 706 where the total for the marital deduction appears and by letter the schedule where the details for the marital deduction are listed. Review that schedule to explain how one makes a QTIP election. Where is information about the surviving spouse's citizenship reported?

29. Facts: In 2001, when he was 60 years old, Settlor Sam created an irrevocable trust, funding it by a transfer of property worth $7 million to an independent trustee. Sam's niece, or her estate, was named as the remainderman. For each independent variation, "a" through "d," calculate: (i) the gross gift; (ii) the taxable gift; (iii) the gift tax paid, (iv) the amount of the trust included in Sam's gross estate; (v) the adjusted taxable gift; and, (vi) the amount of gift tax credit allowed (is it payable or paid?). [You should use the ETAX program]

   a. Sam retained a life estate in the trust. At the time of funding, the federal rate for split interest gifts (i.e., for valuing remainders, etc.) was 6%. He died in 2006. The trust was then worth $8,000,000.
   b. Sam retained no economic interests in the trust, but the terms of the trust gave him the right to allocate income between his brothers Daniel and James. If he failed to allocate (whether due to inaction or his own prior death), then the trustee was to distribute the income equally, and once one brother died, the surviving brother was to receive all of the income each year. Sam died in 2006 without ever directing the trustee as to how to allocate. Both brothers survived him and the trust was worth $8,000,000.
   c. Same facts as the prior example, except in 2002, Sam sent the trustee a letter stating that he forever released his right to make the allocation. The trust was worth $7,200,000 when Sam released his right. When he died in 2006, the trust was worth $8,000,000.
   d. Same facts as the prior example, except the release occurred in 2005 when the trust was worth $7,600,000. It was worth $8,000,000 when Sam died in 2006.
   e. Under what circumstances would the gift taxes paid by Sam be included in his gross estate? Is this a special rule that relates only to transfers into trust?

30. When she died, Roxanna was serving as the trustee of an irrevocable trust with assets valued at $700,000. The trust allowed her to distribute corpus or income to her children or the children of her sister Laurie. For each of the following alternatives, determine whether the trust is included in her estate: (a) The trust had been established by the Roxanna's mother many years before. (b) The trust had been established by Laurie, many years before, and at the same time, Roxanna had established and funded a similar trust with

Laurie as trustee. (c) Roxanna had established the trust, but kept no economic benefit for herself. (d) Ten years ago, Roxanna's rich uncle had established the trust at his death. Initially, Roxanna was both trustee and a permissible appointee, but a couple of years later, she irrevocably released the right to appoint to herself. She never appointed trust property to herself before or after the release.

31. In 2003, Craig died. He left his $14,000,000 estate to his wife, Rebecca. There were debts and expenses of $500,000. Craig and Rebecca were both US citizens and residents. (a) What is Craig's gross estate? (b) His taxable estate? (c) How would your answers change if Craig was not a U.S. citizen but Rebecca was? (d) If Craig was a citizen, but Rebecca was not?

32. When she died in 2005, Florence left her net estate (after debts and expenses) of $3,000,000 to her husband, Juan Carlos. They were both residents of the United States for most of their adult lives. How much estate tax would be paid given each of the following circumstances? (assume no QDOT and no post-death change of citizenship) (a) Both were U.S. citizens. (b) Florence was a U.S. citizen and Juan Carlos is a citizen of Mexico. (c) Florence was a citizen of Mexico and Juan Carlos is a U.S. citizen. (d) Both were citizens of Mexico and permanent legal residents of the U.S.

33. Guy created a fully funded revocable probate-avoidance trust. On his death in 2001, the trust (worth $4.3 million) gave 50% of the corpus to the university where he received his bachelor's degree and 50% to United Way. A life insurance policy that he owned paid out $1,500,000 to a favorite niece. Debts and expenses totaled $300,000. Unfortunately, the trust included a clause that required the trustee to pay all death taxes out of trust assets. Use ETAX to determine Guy's (a) taxable estate and (b) total estate tax. [Set deductions as +4000000+300000-b19 and remember to include the life insurance as part of the gross estate. The reason for the minus sign before "b19" is that the estate tax is reducing the charitable deduction.]

34. When Kristen died in 2003, her will specified that her entire estate was to go to her university, a bequest that qualifies for a charitable deduction. Her probate estate was valued at $3,800,000. There were no debts and the total expenses associated with transferring her estate came to $50,000. Her will

had a clause that required all death taxes from probate and non-probate assets to be paid from the residue of her probate estate. The only asset outside the trust was a Transfer on Death brokerage account with assets worth $1,700,000 that were transferred to her brother Bill. The executor of Kristen's estate tried to get Bill to disclaim the benefit of having the estate pay the estate taxes on his share of the estate, but he refused. Use ETAX to determine the (a) taxable estate and (b) estate tax. [Set deductions as +3800000+50,000-b19 and remember to include the brokerage account as part of the gross estate.] (c) What amount is received by the university and by Bill? (c) How much would each receive had Bill disclaimed the tax payment benefit?

35. When Ruby died on August 12, 1997, her taxable estate in the amount of $1,400,000 was left to her only son, Thomas. Ruby's estate paid total death taxes of $320,000, of which $58,000 went to the state and $262,000 went to the federal government. When Thomas died on February 8, 2001, most of his $1,000,000 taxable estate comprised what was left of the estate that he had inherited from his mother. The estate taxes on Thomas's estate, before application of the PTC, would have been $33,200 paid to the state and $92,050 paid to the federal government. Calculate the following: (a) limit one; (b) limit two; (c) the PTC; and (d) the federal and state taxes after applying the PTC.

36. When Vaughan died on May 5, 1997, his taxable estate in the amount of $4,500,000 was left equally to his three children. Vaughan's estate paid total death taxes of $1,923,000, of which $335,600 went to the state and $1,587,400 went to the federal government. When Vaughan's oldest child, Stephanie, died on July 4, 2001, her taxable estate of $2,000,000 was left to her two children. The estate taxes on Stephanie's estate before application of the PTC would have been $99,600 paid to the state and $460,650 to the federal government. Calculate the following: (a) limit one; (b) limit two; (c) the PTC; and (d) the federal and state taxes after applying the PTC.

ANSWERS TO QUESTIONS AND PROBLEMS (*odd numbered only*)

1. Gross estate is an estate tax concept that includes all that one owned, controlled, and, in some instances, transferred with retained interests. It even includes gift taxes paid on gifts made within three years of death. The taxable estate is the gross estate less debts, expenses, and deductions, such as the marital and charitable deduction. The probate estate consists of that property owned by the decedent for which there is no other mechanism of transfer other than the court process. Generally, it is made up of things owned by the decedent, plus property co-owned as a tenant in common.

3. (a) A dower interest is a surviving wife's statutory interest in her deceased husband's estate. At common law, it is generally a life estate in a portion of the real property. Today, it may be a fee interest in a portion of the estate. (b) The property is included in the decedent's gross estate but generally there is a marital deduction available. If it is just a life estate, it can qualify for the marital deduction through the QTIP election. If it is an interest in fee in a percentage of the estate, that portion going outright to the surviving spouse qualifies for the marital deduction.

5. Morton's estate: comments - On the mountain cabin, use the consideration furnished rule (hence 10k/30k times $150k).

Item	(a) Gross estate	(c) Probate estate
stock	$1,560,000	$1,560,000
home	$345,000	$345,000
car	$9,000	$9,000
home furn	$23,000	$23,000
bank account	$3,500	$3,500
life ins.	$200,000	
life ins. (mom)	$25,000	$25,000
cabin	$50,000	
total	$2,215,500	$1,965,500
Less debts & expenses	($45,000)	
(b) taxable estate	$2,170,500	

(d) total tax: $518,545; (e) state death tax credit: $56,220; and
(f) federal tax: $462,325.

7. Mary (Table B 8%): 12*$2,500*8.5595*1.0362 = $266,081

9. Connie (Table S 10%): (a) all: 12*600*4.9061*1.045 = $36,913 (b) none, it is less than $100,000; (c) none, regardless of value

11. Frank $25,000 and Kathleen $75,000; at the first death $360,000. 1) Included and 2) new basis.

   a. Joint tenants. Frank died. Friends. 1) consideration furnished rule, 25%*$360,000 = $90,000; 2) New basis = $90,000 + $75,000 = $165,000.
   b. Joint tenants. Frank died. Married. 1) 50%, $180,000 2) ½ + ½ = $180,000 + $50,000 = $230,000.
   c. Joint tenants. Kathleen died. Friends. 1) $270,000 2) $295,000.
   d. Community property. Frank died. 1) 50%, $180,000 2) FMV @ DOD, $360,000.
   e. Tenants in the entirety. Frank died. Same as for married joint tenants: 1) $180,000 2) $230,000.
   f. Tenants in common. Frank died, his 25% to Kathleen. 1) 25%*$360,000 = $90,000; 2) New basis = $90,000 + $75,000 = $165,000. (Is married important? Not for inclusion, still 25%. For estate taxes? Sure, 100% marital deduction).

13. (a) General power? See Code IRC § 2041, i.e., power to appoint to holder, holder's creditors, holder's estate, or creditors of holder's estate. (b) Difference? General power you include and a limited one you do not include. (c) When will a power to appoint to one's self not be a general power? When it is limited by an ascertainable standard (HSEM) i.e., the health, support, education, or maintenance standard, or when the consent of the creator or of an adverse party must be obtained.

15. His powers: Note, the trust was created by someone else; therefore, these are all powers, not retained interests.

   a. Limited not included, exercise does not matter.
   b. Limited not included whether exercised or not.
   c. Limited by an ascertainable standard, the H in HSEM.

    d. Not included, the adverse interest exception.

    e. This is a general power if it is there at the time of death, and (exercised or not), it is included. The exercise does not increase the inclusion. It will still be $50,000, i.e., five percent.

    f. Same as "e."

    g. At the time of death, the power had been exercised for the year, so it was not there. Nothing insofar as the trust is concerned is included. However, the $50,000 might still be in a bank account, unless he gave it away or spent it.

    h. Again, nothing to include. The gift qualifies for the charitable deduction, so not even an adjusted taxable gift to worry about.

    i. Include $50,000 even though he could not exercise the power at death, the lapse of a general power (even one limited as a 5 & 5 power) is treated as a transfer. The 5 & 5 exception only applies to lifetime lapses.

17. True, although students of estate planning keep trying to add others.

19. These sections have the following in common:
- Transfer made by decedent for less than full consideration
- Included in the decedent's gross estate at date-of-death value
- Some retained control or interest by decedent
- Amount included is only that portion of the transferred property over which decedent retained control
- Usually arise in the context of trusts

21. The Code refers to the power to revoke, alter, or amend. Three examples:
- Totten trusts
- revocable living trusts
- gifts to minors under the Uniform Gifts to Minors Act where the donor serves as custodian

23. (a) GE zero; Adj.TxG $50,000. Stock, no three-year rule.
    (b) GE zero; Adj.TxG $50,000.
    (c) GE $100,000; Adj.TxG zero. Life insurance, special three-year rule.
    (d) GE zero; Adj.TxG $50,000. Life insurance beyond the three-year reach.

25. Charities: Part five, line 21. Details on Schedule O. On Schedule O, one must show whether taxes are charged to the charitable transfers.

27. Retained interests: Part five, line 7. Details on Schedule G.

29. (a) (i) gift? .35033 * $7,000,000 = $2,452,310, (ii) taxable gift? Same, no annual exclusion because gift is one of a future interest; (iii) gift tax paid? $781,882 (iv) Trust in the estate? $8,000,000 date-of-death value - retained interest; (v) adjusted taxable gift? Zero, transferred property is in the gross estate; (vi) gift tax payable credit? Actual amount paid because date-of-death value is included, i.e., $781,882.

(b) (i) gift? No gift, retained control until he died. (ii) taxable gift? Zero, no gift. (iii) gift tax paid? Zero, no gift. (iv) trust in the estate? $8,000,000. (v) adjusted taxable gift? No. (vi) gift tax payable credit? No.

(c) (i) gift? No gift until control is relinquished. Release in 2002, gift $7,200,000 (ii) taxable gift? Income interest of each brother exceeds the annual exclusion, hence $7,180,000. (iii) gift tax paid? $3,020,000. (iv) Trust in the estate? No, retained interest released more than three years before Sam's death. (v) adjusted taxable gift? As in "ii." (vi) gift tax payable credit? Only $2,817,800 (rates are lower in 2006 than in 2002.

(d) (i) gift? No gift until control is relinquished. This occurred in 2005. $7,600,000. (ii) taxable gift? $7,580,000. Two annual exclusions (see "c ii"). (iii) gift tax paid? $3,057,600. (iv) Trust in the estate? Yes, at full date-of-death value ($8 million) § 2035(a) 3-year rule for released retained interests. The gift taxes paid must also be included. (v) adjusted taxable gift? Zero (whole trust is in the gross estate). (vi) gift tax payable credit? Should be the tax actually paid ($3,057,600).

(e) Only if Sam died within three years of any gift that triggers the actual payment of gift tax. This is not a special rule that relates only to transfers into trust, any gift, whether in trust or not and whether life insurance, diamonds, land, stocks or bonds, or whatever, is governed by this rule. If taxes are paid and death occurs within three years of the gift, the gift taxes are part of the gross estate.

31. (a) GE? $14,000,000; (b) TxE? Zero. 100% marital deduction. (c) Same answers. (d) Big change, no marital deduction (unless Rebecca allows the

amount above the AEA to be placed in a QDOT or she becomes a citizen before the estate tax return is filed). TxE = $13,500,000.

33. Guy's estate: (a) gross estate: $5,800,000 [trust $4.3 million + $1.5 million life insurance); (b) deduction $3,681,863 [$300,000 debts and expenses plus $4,000,000 charitable less total taxes of $618,137]; (c) estate tax $618,137.

35. (a) limit one, $262,000; (b) limit two, $92,050; (c) the PTC, $73,640; and (d) the federal, after applying the PTC, $18,410, and state, $33,200. Comment: anytime D2's reduced estate is less than the AEA, the tax is zero and limit two must equal the federal tax on the unreduced estate.

ENDNOTES

1. IRC § 2031(a).

2. IRC § 6018(a)(1).

3. Reg. § 20.2053-7, Deduction for unpaid mortgages.

4. IRC § 6018(a) and Reg. § 20.618-2

5. IRC § 6018(a)(2).

6. IRC § 2103.

7. IRC § 2102(c)(1).

8. IRC § 2002; *Fleming v. Commissioner*, No. 90-2576, 7th Cir. 1992.

9. IRC §§ 2002 & 2203.

10. *Estate of Guide v. Commissioner*, 69 T.C. 811 (1978).

11. LR 8335033.

12. The Taxpayer Relief Act rearranged IRC §2035; old § 2035(c) is now § 2035(b).

13. Pre- TRA '97 IRC § 2035(d)(2) is now § 2035(a).

14. IRC § 2033.

15. *Davis*, T.C. Memo 1993-155.

16. TAM 9207004.

17. IRC § 2034.

18. IRC § 2056(b)(7).

19. See IRC § 1401(a) of P.L. 104-88.

20. *Ablamis v. Roper*, 937 F2d 1450 (9th Cir. 1991).

21. See *Gallenstein* 975 F. 2d 286 (CA6, 1992) affg. 68 AFTR 2d 91-5721.

22. IRC § 2033.

23. IRC § 2041(b)(1)(C)(ii).

24. *Estate of Cavenaugh*, 100 TC, CCH ¶12,927 (1993).

25. IRC §§ 2036, 2037, and 2038.

26. IRC § 2035(a)

27. Reg. § 20.2511-2

28. Reg. 25.2511-2(c) and (f).

29. *Estate of Grace*, 395 US 316 (1969).

30. *Maxwell*, 3 F. 3d. 591, affirming 98 T.C. 594 (1992).

31. Previously IRC § 2035(c), renumbered § 2035(b) by TRA '97.

32. Previously IRC § 2035(d)(1), renumbered § 2035(a) by TRA '97.

33. IRC § 2054.

34. IRC § 2055.

35. IRC § 2056.

36. IRC § 2056(b)(3)(A).

37. E.g., CA Probate Code § 21525.

38. IRC § 2056(b)(5).

39. IRC § 2056(b)(7).

40. IRC § 2044.

41. IRC § 2056A(a).

42. *Estate of Marine*, 990 F2d 136 (4th Cir. 1993).

43. IRC § 2012.

44. IRC § 2001(b)(2).

45. IRC § 2013.

46. IRC § 812(c) of the 1939 Code.

47. Reg. § 20-2013-3.

48. IRC § 2014.

49. IRC § 2010(b)

CHAPTER 7

The Federal Gift Tax and Basis Rules

OVERVIEW

Chapter 5 introduced the gift tax, showing how it is calculated and how it is unified with the estate tax. This chapter examines some more qualitative factors, such as the requirements for a valid gift, types of taxable gifts, how gifts qualify for the annual exclusion, and how certain specific transfers are (or are not) subject to gift tax. While reading the chapter, the reader is urged to review both the overview of the gift tax scheme in Tables 5-1 and 5-2 of Chapter 5, plus the United States Gift Tax Return, Form 709, found on the "Teaching Aids" CD ROM (see file "Form 709 Gift Tax.pdf").

FEDERAL GIFT TAX

Estate planners use the word "gift" in different ways. Most people think of gifts as gratuitous lifetime transfers, but estate planners define gifts as "completed property transfers in exchange for less than full and adequate consideration." This definition is broad enough to include transfers at death. Thus, it is correct to say, "...in his will he gave the grand piano to his daughter." However, to avoid the necessity of always using the modifier "lifetime," all references to gifts will mean lifetime gifts unless the context clearly indicates otherwise.

Requirements for a Valid Gift: Influence of Local and Federal Law

Whether a transfer is treated as a gift is important for two reasons in estate planning. First, it will influence the respective property rights of the parties. Second, it will determine whether a taxable event has occurred. In deciding these issues, two different sets of rules must be examined: local property law and federal gift tax law.

Local property law. To be valid under local property law, a gift must ordinarily meet four requirements:

1. The donor must be capable of transferring property.
2. The donee must be capable of receiving and possessing the property.
3. There must be delivery to, and some form of acceptance by, the donee or the donee's agent.
4. Finally, under local law, a valid gift ordinarily requires donative intent on the part of the donor.

Federal gift tax law. To be subject to taxation under federal gift tax law, a gift must meet all of the above local property law requirements, subject to two major federal modifications:

1. Federal tax regulations explicitly state that donative intent is not required for a transfer to be subject to gift tax. Although not required for a gift, the existence of donative intent would be strong evidence that a gift had actually been made.
2. Under the unique language of federal law, the gift tax applies only to a completed gift, which arises when "...the donor has so parted with dominion and control as to leave him no power to change its disposition, whether for his own benefit or for the benefit of another..."[1]

Ordinarily, completed gifts are made either outright or in trust. *Outright transfers* made beyond the donor's dominion and control are virtually always complete for gift tax purposes. Transfers in trust, on the other hand, may be complete, incomplete, or partially incomplete. An example of a complete transfer in trust is a transfer to an irrevocable trust with no retained interests or controls; the entire transfer is subject to gift taxation. An example of an incomplete transfer in trust is a transfer to a typical revocable trust; it is not at all subject to gift taxation because the trustor has retained the power to demand return of the trust property. An example of a partially incomplete transfer in trust is one to an irrevocable trust in which the trustor has retained only the right to the income (but not control of it) but not to the remainder; thus there is a complete gift of the remainder interest. Or, the trustor could give away the income interest for a period of time with the corpus reverting to the trustor when the time is up, e.g., another is given the income for 10 years after which the trust terminates and the corpus is returned to the trustor or to the trustor's estate. Thus, for transfers in trust in which more than one property interest is created, gift tax law requires that each interest be examined independently to determine whether a completed gift of that interest has been made.

Both federal tax law and local property law influence gift taxation. Summarizing, the relationship between federal law and local law with regard to the requirements for a valid gift may be stated as follows: Local law dictates whether a transfer of property rights has in fact been made, irrespective of taxability. On the other hand, federal tax law, in conjunction with local law, specifies whether a gift is subject to taxation. Federal law also spells out rules, discussed later in this chapter, relating to the taxation of specific types of gifts, such as those in connection with powers of appointment, life insurance, joint ownership, and disclaimers.

Who Is Subject to Gift Tax?

The federal gift tax law applies to all individual United States citizens or residents regardless of where the property is located and regardless of whether the transfer is direct or indirect, real or personal, tangible or intangible. The federal gift tax law also applies to nonresident aliens but only with regard to transfers of real property and tangible personal property situated within the United States.[2]

Aspects of Taxable Gifts

Valuation of gift. The value of the gift for tax purposes is its fair market value at the date of the gift. Any consideration received in exchange is subtracted in determining the gross value of the gift.

EXAMPLE 7 - 1. If Sally "sells" a $25,000 automobile for $1 to her son Mark, she has made a gross gift in the amount of $24,999 and must report (after applying a $10,000 annual exclusion) a taxable gift of $14,999.

Measuring the consideration received in exchange. To be recognized, consideration received in exchange must be measurable in money or money's worth. If it is not reducible to money or money's worth, it will be disregarded.

EXAMPLE 7 - 2. Gertrude tells her daughter Alice that her kindness over the past years has been priceless. Gertrude promises Alice that if she continues being so kind she will transfer her $250,000 Dusenberg to her on her next birthday. When Alice's birthday arrives, the card from Gertrude contains the title and keys to the Dusenberg. Even if Alice's sweet attention is worth more than money can buy, it is not considered to be an exchange in money or money's worth. Therefore, Gertrude has made a taxable gift.

The above example illustrates a situation where a gift is subject to gift taxation despite the fact that local law may view the exchange of consideration to be equal, and donative intent, therefore, to be nonexistent.

Fortunately, in the case of property settlements between divorcing spouses, federal law no longer requires a determination of the total value of the consideration exchanged by each spouse. Transfers of property subject to a written divorce or separation agreement are deemed to be made for full and adequate consideration even when it is clear that the "exchange" is not for money or money's worth.[3]

Gifts versus sales. With sales between related parties, IRS agents may contend that a gift rather than a sale has been made. However, sales between unrelated parties are presumed not to be gifts.

EXAMPLE 7 - 3. Herb, owner of a retail drugstore, sells his aging delivery pickup truck to Karl, a stranger, who read about the truck in the classified section of the newspaper. Karl paid Herb $4,200 and promptly took out a similar ad and sold the truck three days later for $6,700. Herb has made a bad bargain, but not a gift, because the truck was sold in an arms-length transaction.

EXAMPLE 7 - 4. Same facts as the prior example, except that Herb, who had already made gifts in excess of $10,000 to his son Jerry, sold him the car for $4,200. Jerry then advertised and sold the car for $6,700. Inasmuch as this was a transaction between relatives, a gift has occurred.

Filing and Payment Requirements

When a return must be filed. In general, a gift tax return is due when the donor's income tax return is due (or if the donor is not required to file an income tax return, then when it would have been due had the donor been so required). Usually, this means April 15 of the year following the gift. An extension to file one's income tax return is also an automatic extension to file one's gift tax return. A gift tax return must be filed by any donor who in any calendar year gives:

- more than the annual exclusion amount (i.e., $10,000, indexed) to any donee (other than to a spouse or charity), or
- a gift of a future interest regardless of how small the value, or
- total gifts exceeding $100,000 (indexed) to a non-citizen spouse, or
- a gift for which both spouses want to elect gift splitting even if after the split each gift is less than the annual exclusion amount.

Who files. Only people file gift tax returns. For example, if a partnership or a corporation makes a gift, the individual partners or stockholders are considered the donors who must file the return and pay the tax. If the trustee of a revocable living trust makes a gift subject to taxation, it is the grantor who is treated as the donor. If a donor dies before filing a return, the donor's executor must file for the deceased person.

Who pays. The donor is responsible for paying the gift tax;[4] the donee is not subject to either gift tax or income tax on the gift.[5] However, there is transferee liability if the donor fails to pay the tax. This means that any donee can be forced to pay the gift tax, up to the value of the gift received, if the donor fails to pay.

Net gift. Some donors, however, might wish to make a *net gift*; that is, to arrange in advance for the donee to be responsible for paying the gift tax. The Supreme Court has ruled such a transaction to be part sale, part gift, causing the donor to realize taxable income to the extent that the gift tax paid by the donee exceeds the donor's adjusted basis.[6] However, other advantages may still make the net gift attractive.

EXAMPLE 7 - 5. In 2003, Vera transferred her horse ranch, valued at $5,000,000, to her daughter Felicity with the understanding that Felicity would pay the gift taxes. The annual exclusion was $11,000. The net gift value was $3,714,094 and Felicity paid gift taxes of $1,274,906. Note that the last three numbers add to $5 million.

Deductible Gifts

Two types of gifts are fully deductible, and three are completely excluded from being treated as gifts, with the end result (whether deducted or excluded) that they are not treated as taxable gifts.

Charitable gifts. First, gifts to qualified charities are fully deductible.[7] Owners of "qualified works of art" can loan them to a charity without the loan being treated as a taxable gift, provided the use of the work by the charity is related to its charitable purpose (e.g., an art museum receiving a Van Gogh on loan will put it on display rather than hang it in the director's private study).[8] Generally, gifts to charity also produce an income tax deduction, but only up to certain percentages of adjusted gross income. Chapter 14 will discuss strategies for charitable gifts.

Interspousal gifts. Second, under the unlimited marital deduction, gifts to a U.S. citizen spouse are fully deductible, provided that they are not terminable interests.[9] However, even terminable interest gifts might qualify for the marital deduction by using a gift qualified terminable interest property (QTIP) election.[10] We will get into an analysis of terminable interests and the estate tax marital deduction in Chapters 11 and 12.

Since 1988, only the first $100,000 per year in gifts to a non-U.S. citizen spouse escapes gift taxation.[11] Thus, gifts above $100,000 per year to a non-U.S. citizen spouse use up unified credit and may even generate a gift tax.

Gifts for tuition and medical care. Third and fourth, qualified payments in any amount made directly to an educational institution for tuition, and payments in any amount made directly to a provider of medical care on behalf of any individual are fully excluded from being taxable gifts. Two things to emphasize here: the transfers must be directly to the providers, and not to the individuals themselves, and the person benefitting from the payments does not have to be related to the donor.[12]

Gifts to political organizations. Fifth, gifts are not taxable if made to a "political organization (within the meaning of section 527(e)(1)) for the use of such organization."[13]

Gift Tax Annual Exclusion and the Present Interest Requirement

During each calendar year, a person may give gifts with a total value of up to $10,000 per donee to as many other people as the person wants to benefit without using up any of the donor's unified credit because such gifts do not count as taxable gifts. The $10,000 is indexed for inflation and is likely to increase by a thousand dollars every three or four years (reached $11,000 in 2002 and remains such for 2003). Note that the donor and donee do not have to be related. The main requirement for obtaining this annual exclusion, as it is called, is that the donee have an immediate present interest when the donor completes the gift.[14] *Present interest gifts* are ones where the "enjoyment" of the gift can start immediately, whereas future interest gifts have some condition attached that either might cause some delay or does cause a delay in the donee's possession and enjoyment of the transferred property.

> EXAMPLE 7 - 6. In 2002, widow Sanderson gave her daughter Polly three corporate bonds valued at $10,000 each. Even though Polly will not collect the par value until maturity, and even though the periodic interest income is payable in the future, the gift is of a present interest and qualifies for the annual exclusion. Widow Sanderson did not place any restriction on Polly's right to enjoy the bonds and Polly could sell them immediately if she wished to do so. Assuming that she made no other gifts to Polly during the year, the taxable gift is $20,000 [$30,000 - $10,000].

Congress in 1932 chose to deny the annual exclusion for gifts of future interests for three reasons: (1) future interests may be difficult to value; (2) the number of donees of a future interest is often indeterminable at date of gift; and (3) future interests are sometimes created to avoid taxes.

Gifts into trust. Most problems regarding future interest gifts arise in the context of trusts.

> EXAMPLE 7 - 7. Suppose widow Sanderson transferred bonds worth $30,000 to an irrevocable trust, whereby the trustee could give the bonds to Polly whenever the trustee thought it appropriate to do so, but, at the very latest, to transfer them to her on her 25th birthday. The gift, which is reportable for the year the bonds are transferred into the trust, is a $30,000 taxable gift of a future interest. It will not qualify for the annual exclusion because, by the terms of the transfer, the enjoyment can be delayed for a period of time. The result remains the same even if the trustee immediately transfers one of the bonds to Polly.

No annual exclusion means, of course, that absent any other deductions, the gift will be entirely taxable, such that part or all of the donor's unified credit will have to be used. Further, at the donor's death, the value of the taxable gift is added to the estate tax base, which may push the donor's estate into a higher marginal rate. Thus, the donor may prefer a disposition that is at least partly sheltered by the annual exclusion.

EXAMPLE 7 - 8. Altering the facts of the prior example a little bit, assume that instead of being allowed to accumulate the income, the trustee is required to pay all income at least annually to Polly, an adult, with the remainder going to Richard at the end of the 10-year term. On creation of the trust, two interests arose: a present interest in the income for 10 years and a remainder interest. At 10 percent, the present value of an income interest for a 10-year period equals .614457 times the value of the bonds. The product of 0.614457 * $30,000 is $18,434, which represents the portion of the gift that is considered a present interest qualifying for the annual exclusion up to a maximum for any one donee of $10,000. Hence, the total taxable gift equals $20,000 [$30,000-$10,000]. Note that the amount subtracted from the gross value of the gift is the lesser of the present interest (here $18,434) or the annual exclusion ($10,000, indexed).

EXAMPLE 7 - 9. Suppose Polly's mother placed bonds worth just $15,000 into the 10-year trust; the present interest would be $9,217 [0.614457 * $15,000] and the taxable gift would be $5,873 [$15,000 - $9,217].

2503(c) Trusts. There are few exceptions to the rule that there must be a present interest before a gift qualifies for the annual exclusion, and one is found in IRC §2503(c). The annual exclusion is allowed for gifts placed in trust (these are referred to as 2503(c) trusts) for the benefit of a person who is under age 21, even though the beneficiary does not have a present interest. These trusts (and others that are more commonly used) for youngsters are covered in Chapter 13.

The Kiddie Tax

All unearned income of children under age 14 in excess of a statutory amount is taxed at the parents' marginal rate. This special treatment is referred to as the "kiddie tax."[15] The threshold amount was $1,000 when the law went into effect in 1987. With indexing, it climbed to $1,500 in 2001 (see Table 7, Estate Planning Indexed Values in Appendix A) and has remained there at least through 2003.

Gift Splitting

Gift splitting treats a gift of the property owned by one spouse as if it were made one-half by each spouse. It is conceptually similar to federal spousal income splitting on a joint income tax return; indeed, both were first added to the tax code in 1948 as part of a restructuring that attempted to put common law states on par with the community property states. Also added at that time was the initial marital deduction (equal to 50% of the adjusted gross estate) and the provision that stepped-up both halves of community property even though only one half was included in a decedent spouse's estate.[16]

Under federal gift tax law, a spouse may *split a gift* by making an election, with the consent of the non-donor spouse, on the gift tax return. If the election is made, a gift by the donor spouse of his or her own property is treated as if made one-half by each of them.[17] According to the regulations, the election must cover all gifts that were made during the year to third parties by either spouse. The election allows a married person the benefit of two annual exclusions (and two unified credits, if needed) to cover what is really just one gift.

> EXAMPLE 7 - 10. In 2001, Johnna Lynn gives $50,000 of her own money to her nephew. Assuming no other gifts and no gift splitting, her taxable gift, after the annual exclusion, is $40,000. Thus, she must use up a portion of her unified credit. Alternatively, she can split this gift, if her husband Fred is willing; each is then considered to have made a gross gift of $25,000. After each donor's annual exclusion, the taxable gift is $15,000 and (assuming no prior taxable gifts) each will use up $2,800 of their unified credit. Johnna Lynn and Fred must both file gift tax returns.

To make the split gift election, the consent of the non-donor spouse is required on the donor spouse's return. If, after the split, the values exceed the annual exclusion, two gift tax returns (one by each spouse) must be filed; whereas, only the donor spouse needs to file a gift tax return if the split brings the gifts down to or below the annual exclusion.

> EXAMPLE 7 - 11. Billy and Millie are married parents. This year Millie gave $20,000 of her property to their son. Assuming no other gifts, if the couple agree to gift splitting, only Millie will be required to file a gift tax return; Billy's consent will appear on Millie's return.

Gift splitting is needed only if the property that is given was owned by just one spouse, since their co-owned property is, by its nature, already "split," generally making the election unnecessary. This is especially true of community property, which is always owned in equal shares (i.e., 50% each) by the spouses.

EXAMPLE 7 - 12. In the prior example, had the $20,000 been community property, jointly held property, or an in-common interest in property (here assume 50%-50%), the gift would be considered as made one-half by each spouse. Since the value of each spouse's half interest is covered by the annual exclusion, neither spouse would need to file a gift tax return.

EXAMPLE 7 - 13. If a couple gave their nephew property worth $28,000 that had been held in joint tenancy, each spouse will have made a gross gift of $14,000 and a taxable gift of $4,000 (assuming the annual exclusion is still $10,000). Again, there is no need for gift splitting, and each spouse must file a gift tax return because each gift exceeds the annual exclusion.

Somewhat oddly, if a split gift results in the payment of a gift tax and the donor-spouse dies within three years of the gift, the entire gift tax paid, not just the one-half, is grossed up in the donor's gross estate.[18]

EXAMPLE 7 - 14. In 2001, from his property, Charles gave $150,000 to the couple's son and stock worth $150,000 to their daughter. Charles's wife, Susan, gave $9,000 of her property to their son. The effects on reportable gross gifts, annual exclusions, and taxable gifts of the decision whether to split the gifts or not is shown in the table below. If no split gift election is made, Susan will not have to file a Form 709, since her gift is covered by the annual exclusion. If gift splitting is elected, the taxable amount on both returns will be identical.

| | Without Gift Splitting | | With Gift Splitting | |
	Charles' Form 709	Susan's Form 709 (not filed)	Charles' Form 709	Susan's Form 709
Gross Gifts:				
To Son	$150,000	$9,000	$79,500	$79,500
To Daughter	$150,000	$0	$75,000	$75,000
Total per return	$300,000	$9,000	$154,500	$154,500
Total per family	$309,000		$309,000	
Exclusions:				
Gift to Son	$10,000	$9,000	$10,000	$10,000
Gift to Daughter	$10,000	$0	$10,000	$10,000
Total per return	$20,000	$9,000	$20,000	$20,000
Total per family	$29,000		$40,000	
Total per return	$280,000	$0	$134,500	$134,500
Total per family	$280,000		$269,000	

Electing gift splitting reduces the family taxable gifts by $11,000 [$280,000 - $269,000]. The reduction is the result of the additional $11,000 in total family annual exclusions, since with the election Susan is allowed $20,000, rather than just $9,000. Gift splitting can mean lower gift taxes, or, as in this example, it may just result in using up less of the parent's total unified credit.

In summary, gift splitting can lower gift taxes because it permits the use of two full annual exclusions per donee, even though just one gift is given and, for large gifts, both spouses' unified credits are used.

Powers of Appointment

General power holders and taxable events. As with the estate tax, only general powers are subject to gift tax, and, if there is a gift, it is treated as having come from the donee-holder.[19] Of course, when the general power was first created, the donor of the power (if created by gift) or the donor's estate (if created at death by will or trust) may have paid transfer taxes, unless the transfer was not subject to tax because of the annual exclusion, a marital deduction, or the application of the unified credit. For instance, if a donor placed property in an irrevocable trust which gives the income beneficiary a general power over 25% of the trust corpus, it would be the entire property placed in trust that would be the gift, not just the 25% subject to the general power. As was discussed in conjunction with the estate tax, a general power is defined in §2041 as one that the holder can use to benefit the holder, the holder's creditors, the holder's estate, or the creditors of the holder's estate.

Three events during the holder's lifetime can trigger gift tax to the holder of a general power of appointment: exercise by the holder in favor of someone else, release by the holder, or lapse of the holder's right to exercise or release the power. Where the holder exercises the power in his or her own favor, no gift occurs.

EXAMPLE 7 - 15. Carla's estate plan called for the creation of two trusts at her death. Trust A was called the marital trust and it gave her husband Ian income for life and a power to appoint the entire corpus to whomever he wished upon his death, with the corpus going to their three children if Ian fails to exercise this general power. According to the terms of the estate plan, Trust A was to be funded with so much of Carla's estate as exceeds the applicable exclusion amount and Trust B was to be funded with assets equal to the applicable exclusion amount. For Trust B Ian was given a life estate and had a general power to appoint up to 5% of the trust each year to anyone. At Ian's death, the power lapses and the trust will be distributed to the couple's three children. Because Carla's total net estate was worth $940,000 when she died in 2003, only Trust B was funded (i.e., the $940,000 estate went into

Trust B) and there was no Trust A. Ian's 5% withdrawal right created a marital deduction of $47,000 and the taxable estate was $893,000. Trust B is considered to have been taxed even though the tentative tax was less than Carla's unified credit, so no estate tax was actually paid.

EXAMPLE 7 - 16. In 2003, the trust was worth $1,160,000 when Ian asked the trustee to distribute corpus worth $25,000 to him. Since this was less than 5% of the value of the trust, the trustee obliged and, since the distribution was to Ian, the holder of the general power, no gift was made.

EXAMPLE 7 - 17. In 2004, the trust was worth $1,280,000 when Ian asked the trustee to distribute corpus worth $70,000 to Judith. The trustee pointed out that this exceeded his 5% power, so Ian told him to give her the maximum this year and the balance in 2004. The trustee gave Judith $64,000 in 2003 and another $6,000 in January of 2004. Both transfers are treated as gifts directly from Ian. Since the annual exclusion was $11,000 for those two years (due to indexing), only $53,000 of the first gift, and none of the second gift, was taxable.

EXAMPLE 7 - 18. In 2005, the trust was worth $1,220,000 when Ian asked the trustee to distribute corpus worth $30,000 to his alma mater, Midwestern State University. Since this gift was within the 5% limit even when combined with the gift earlier that year to Judith, the trustee obliged and Ian was able to claim a charitable deduction on his income tax return for the amount of the gift. Note that, to the extent the trust had distributable net income for the year, it will claim a deduction for the income distributed at his request and he will have to report the income on his return.

EXAMPLE 7 - 19. In 2006, the trust was worth $1,350,000 when Ian died. He had not exercised his 5% power that year. His estate must show on schedule H of the estate tax return $67,500 attributable to this general power. If Ian's estate is large enough that estate tax is owed, the trust would have to pay its proportionate share of the estate tax (i.e., $67,500 over the taxable estate times the estate taxes).

In the above examples, we used a general power equal to 5% of the value of the trust for good reason. It is very common to find trusts that give a holder a general power that is limited to exactly that percentage because of a special Code section that we discuss next.

Lapse and 5 & 5 powers. The general rule is that the lapse of a general power is treated as a transfer from the holder to whomever is the taker by default. However, §2041(b)(2) creates an exception that allows the lapse of certain general powers to occur during the life of the holder without the lapse being deemed a taxable gift. The exception applies to the lapse during the holder's lifetime of a power, but only to the extent that what could have been transferred (but for the lapse) did not exceed the greater of $5,000 or 5% of the value of the property out of which appointment would have been satisfied. Powers that are drafted to make use of this exception are referred to as "5 & 5" powers, and they permit the holder to appoint property from a trust up to the greater of $5,000 or 5% of the value of the trust corpus. Usually the right is given such that it can be exercised annually and the failure to exercise the right in any year will not increase the dollar amount or the percentage for the next year. In other words, it is a noncumulative, annually lapsing power (or right).

Lapsing powers are often placed in irrevocable trusts created for the benefit of minors in order to obtain the annual exclusion for the parent-donor. The power of the child to withdraw an amount each time the parents add to the trust creates a present interest for the child-donee even though the power to withdraw lapses after a short period of time, as set forth in the trust, and even though there is a strong expectation that the child will not exercise the right to withdraw. This demand right is referred to as a "Crummey demand right" or as a "Crummey power." Trusts for this type of provision are called *Crummey Trusts,* and when established for minor children, they may be called *Minors' Demand Trusts.*

> EXAMPLE 7 - 20. Grantor has set up a minors' demand trust for three grandchildren. Each grandchild can claim up to the lesser of one third of the amount transferred into the trust that year or the annual exclusion amount. If a grandchild does not demand his or her share, the right to claim the gift lapses at the close of the year (with demand rights for gifts made late in the year extended to a minimum of 30 days). If no demand is made during the demand period, the transfer is locked into corpus and, by other trust terms, it stays there until the youngest of the three grandchildren reaches age 30. If a grandchild dies before termination of the trust, his or her share goes to the other grandchildren who survive. If initially the trust is funded with less than $15,000 and none of the beneficiaries demand their share, no gift from the beneficiaries is deemed to have been made as a result of the lapses because of the §2041(b)(2) exception. Without this exception, there would be the smallest of gifts, i.e., each beneficiary would be making a contingent future interest gift to the other two. The value of each gift is discounted because it is a future interest gift and discounted further since its value is based on the very low probability that he or she (each grandchild-donor) might not survive until the youngest reaches age 30. If the youngest grandchild lives to age 30, all three of them will take their one-third interest in the trust corpus.

> EXAMPLE 7 - 21. If the initial transfer was $24,000, then each child would be deemed to have made a transfer to the extent his or her share lapsed and exceeded the "5 & 5" limits. Thus, each grandchild would be deemed to have transferred $3,000

to the trust. Since there are two other grandchildren who will be the remaindermen if a grandchild dies, each grandchild will be deemed to have made a gift of a contingent future interest that vests when the youngest child reaches age 30. The value of the gift from each grandchild can be determined actuarially. For each child, it would be based on the probability of that grandchild dying before the termination of the trust. Obviously, the gift is very small in value considering the unlikelihood of the event which would cause the gift to vest in the other children (the death of a child before the youngest turns 30) and the fact that the gift is one of a future interest, since enjoyment is postponed until the termination of the trust. Because the gift is one of a future interest, no annual exclusion is available and a gift tax return would have to be filed for each grandchild. If each grandchild is one year old at the time of the transfer ($3,000 from each child), the probability for each child of dying before age 30 is about 2% (see Table 90CM in the Appendix to compare the number alive at age one to the number alive at age 30) and the present value factor for the gift using an 8% rate is .099377 (Table B, remainder after 30 years), hence the value of the gift is approximately six dollars.

The adverse result of creating lapsing powers of appointment in excess of the "5 & 5" limit is not the gift tax generated, since the gift value is usually extremely small, but rather the retained life estate implications. If a beneficiary has a retained life estate in any property that the beneficiary has previously transferred, whether into trust or otherwise, §2036 causes the transferred property to be included in his or her estate at death. The Regulations make it clear that the lapsing of powers that exceed the 5% limit are simply accumulated.[20] There is no attempt to apply sophisticated mathematics to take into account the fact that each subsequent release of a power includes a release of a portion of the trust previously released. The mathematics are kept simple, but this works against the taxpayer (the holder of a power greater than 5%, who lets it lapse) in that it causes greater inclusion in the estate of a beneficiary-holder who dies before the trust terminates.

To further clarify, the "5 & 5" exception does not apply to lapses that take place at the death of the holder. Hence, a noncumulative annually lapsing power to claim up to 5% of the corpus of a trust each year that was not exercised during the holder's last year of life would cause inclusion in the holder's estate of 5% times the date-of-death value of the trust (or $5,000 if such was greater).

EXAMPLE 7 - 22. On his death in 1999, Benny's father established a trust which gave Benny income for life and a noncumulative, annually lapsing general power of appointment over a portion of the trust. At Benny's death, the trust terminates and the remaining corpus goes to Benny's sister, Rachael, or to her estate. At all times relevant to this example, the value of the trust remained constant at $1,000,000. Benny died in 2003, never having exercised the power.

If the power was exercisable over 5% of the trust, then 5% ($50,000) of the trust value would be included in Benny's estate, even though none of the lifetime lapses of the power were deemed to be transfers and even though Benny let the power lapse at his death.

EXAMPLE 7 - 23. If the power had been over 8% of the trust (instead of 5%), then for the years 1999, 2000, 2001, and 2002 each lapse is treated as though 3% (that which exceeded 5%) was transferred by Benny to the trust with Benny retaining a life estate in the transfers. Section 2036 would cause 12% of the trust to be included in Benny's estate and, since Benny died with an unexercised general power over 8% of the trust, §2041 causes the inclusion of another 8%. Thus, a total of 20% of the value of the trust is included in Benny's estate. *** Query 7 - 1. How much would be included if Benny had been given a 15% annually lapsing power?

Ascertainable standard, adverse party exceptions. Similar to estate tax law, a power of appointment to name oneself, one's creditors, one's estate, or the creditors of one's estate is not treated as a general power if the power is subject to an ascertainable standard of health, education, maintenance, or support, or if it is exercisable only in conjunction with either the creator of the power or an adverse party. Ascertainable standard language is commonly used in trust instruments to give flexibility, yet keep the trust out of the holder's estate.

Life Insurance

A taxable gift of life insurance can arise either during the insured's lifetime or at the insured's death.

Assignment. During the insured's lifetime, an assignment of ownership rights in the policy may constitute a taxable gift equal to the value of the rights assigned. Ordinarily, the owner assigns all of his or her rights to a policy, and the gift is the value of the policy at that time.

EXAMPLE 7 - 24. Joe assigns his life insurance policy to his son. The policy has a face value of $600,000 and a value for gift tax purposes of $87,000. Joe has made a present interest gross gift of $87,000 and a taxable gift of $77,000.

In contrast to the assignment of ownership interests, the owner's simple act of naming a beneficiary does not constitute a taxable gift since no property rights are transferred; the named beneficiary has a "mere expectancy," contingent on the owner's keeping the policy in force and not changing the beneficiary designation.

The unholy trinity. A taxable gift of life insurance can arise at an insured's death. This will occur when the insured, owner, and beneficiary are all different parties. Sometimes this arrangement is referred to as the "unholy trinity."

> EXAMPLE 7 - 25. Madeline uses her own separate funds to purchase a $100,000 life insurance policy on her husband Dave's life, naming their son Bret as the beneficiary. On Dave's death, Madeline will have made a $100,000 gift to Bret. A better way to handle this is to transfer the policy to Bret while Dave is still alive.

> EXAMPLE 7 - 26. Changing the facts in the preceding example, assume that Dave purchased and owned the policy until his death, paying the premiums entirely with community property funds. At Dave's death, Madeline will have made a $50,000 gift to Bret, reflecting her one-half interest in the proceeds. Madeline may be able to claim half of the proceeds, if she can show that she was unaware of the policy's existence or that she was unaware that her husband had named someone other than herself as beneficiary.

In the above example, the other $50,000 is includable in Dave's gross estate under §2042. Can you see why? It is because Dave's community property interest is a 50% ownership in the policy. Estate planners typically avoid this tax trap by having the beneficiary also be the owner any time someone other than the insured owns the policy.

Gifts Into Joint Tenancy

Ordinarily, gifts are made when the owner of property transfers his or her entire interest to the donee. Sometimes, however, a donor transfers only a partial interest, as when a donor transfers his or her property into joint tenancy with others.

General rule. The actual moment that a gift occurs when there is a change of title from solely owned into joint tenancy depends on the nature of the property. In general, ownership and possession of most types of property are considered transferred when documents evidencing a transfer of title are executed and delivered or recorded. Where there are co-owners, the donee need not physically take possession of the document of title but need only acknowledge acceptance of the gift. Thus, a gift usually arises when the donor adds the donee's name to property already owned by the donor or includes the donee's name on the title of newly acquired property. The value of the gift will be the net value of the property interest transferred at the time of the gift.

EXAMPLE 7 - 27. Uncle Charlie bought an automobile for $30,000, paying cash, and taking title in joint tenancy with his nephew Brad. Charlie has made a gift of $15,000 to Brad in the year of purchase.

EXAMPLE 7 - 28. Changing the facts in the prior example just a bit, assume that Charlie bought the car two years ago for $48,000, taking title in his own name. This year, when the car is worth $30,000, Charlie instructs the motor vehicle bureau to change the title to read: "Charlie Jones and Brad Smith, as joint tenants." This year, Charlie has made a gift to Brad of $15,000.

EXAMPLE 7 - 29. This year, Clive purchased a building for $150,000, taking title in joint tenancy with his five adult sons. This year, Clive has made a gift of $25,000 to each son.

Two exceptions. There are two principal exceptions to the rule that the inclusion of others as co-tenants for less than full consideration results in an immediate gift. First, in the case of a joint tenancy bank account, in most states a gift arises on the withdrawal of funds by the donee, not on the creation of the jointly held bank account. Second, where title is taken in the conjunctive, e.g., Mary Smith or Sara Smith, with one of the parties paying more than half of the consideration, no gift takes place until the property is sold or redeemed. No immediate gift takes place because the donor has retained control over the account or bond, since he or she can withdraw all of the funds or cash in the bonds without the aid of the donee joint tenant. Compare that situation to a transfer of real estate into joint tenancy; once the deed is recorded (or delivered to the donee), the original owner cannot unilaterally recover what he or she has given away, i.e., control of that portion has been lost. This is also true of corporate stocks or bonds. Once the transfer agent has changed title into joint tenancy, the original owner cannot unilaterally change it back into just his or her name without the cooperation of the transferees or a certified death certificate showing them to be deceased.

EXAMPLE 7 - 30. On June 1 of last year, Rochelle deposited $40,000 in a savings account held jointly with her son Conrad. He withdrew $6,800 on February 1 of this year. Rochelle made a gift to Conrad, but not until February 1 of this year. It was covered by the annual exclusion.

EXAMPLE 7 - 31. Lionel purchased a $20,000 EE savings bond years ago, taking title with his son Patrick as joint tenants. At the bond's maturity next month, if Lionel redeems the bond, there will be no gift. If Patrick redeems it, Lionel will have made a gift of $20,000. If they split the proceeds, Lionel's gift to Patrick of $10,000 will be covered by the annual exclusion.

Disclaimers

The prior examples assumed that the donees accepted the gifts as given. Suppose that for some reason the intended donee does not want to accept a substantial gift made under a will, trust instrument, or other document. Obviously, if one accepts a gift or bequest and then transfers the property to another, it will trigger a transfer tax unless the transfer is sheltered by the annual exclusion or a charitable or marital deduction. To avoid creating a taxable transfer, a donee might wish to refuse the gift. Section 2518 allows the donee to "disclaim" a gift in such a way that it will be as though the gift was never made and, in the case of a bequest, as though disclaimant predeceased the decedent-donor. In order to disclaim and have this favorable result, the following requirements must be met:

1. The disclaimer must be "an irrevocable and unqualified refusal...to accept" the interest.
2. The refusal must be in writing.
3. The refusal must be received within nine months after the later of:
   a) the date on which the transfer creating the interest was made, or
   b) the day on which the person disclaiming reaches age 21.
4. The intended donee cannot have accepted any interest in the benefits.
5. And, as a result of the refusal, the interest must pass (without the disclaiming person's direction) to someone else.

With regard to the fourth requirement, acts indicating "acceptance" include using the property, accepting dividends, interest, or rents from the property, and directing others to act with regard to the property. However, acceptance will not be found in cases where the disclaimant merely accepted title to property or merely because title vested immediately in the disclaimant on death of the decedent, as in the case of survivorship under joint tenancy. Benefits received by a person under 21 years of age are disregarded.[21]

Section 2518(b)(4)(A) creates a special privilege for the spouse of a donor or decedent. He/she may disclaim and still retain benefits in the disclaimed property. This is used in estate plans that call for property disclaimed by the surviving spouse to be placed in a trust that gives her (the disclaimant) a life estate and/or the power to withdraw limited by an ascertainable standard.

Meeting all of these requirements is particularly important because failure to meet any one could result in two completed transfers subject to taxation.

> EXAMPLE 7 - 32. Gaylord gives his adult son Daniel his vacation bungalow on the lake, completing the necessary transfer of title. After spending a weekend there, Daniel decides that he hates fishing and can't stand the mosquitos, so he transfers title back to Gaylord. Daniel's act is not a valid disclaimer because he had already accepted a benefit. Therefore, two gifts occurred; first the one by Gaylord and then the gift by Daniel.

> EXAMPLE 7 - 33. During their life, husband and wife owned their home in joint tenancy. Within nine months of husband's death, wife acts to disclaim her survivorship interest. Her disclaimer is not invalid merely because her survivorship interest vested immediately at his death and she continued to live in the house and pay all expenses and related taxes prior to making the disclaimer, provided that while husband was alive the tenancy could be unilaterally partitioned.[22] The reason the use does not disqualify the disclaimer is that her interest prior to his death was an undivided one, meaning that she supposedly had full use of the property even before he died. We might reach a different conclusion if it was rental property and she was collecting half the rent before he died and then all of the rent after his death.

> EXAMPLE 7 - 34. Mildred died, disposing of her entire $1.8 million estate by will. It read, "to my husband, Henry, if living, and, if not, then to our children." Within the nine months following Mildred's death, Henry, before receiving any interest or benefit in the property, presented a written refusal of "so much of Mildred's estate as equals the applicable exclusion amount" to the executor of her estate. Henry has made a valid disclaimer, and he will not be considered to have ever owned that portion of the property. The disclaimed property will now pass by the terms of the will to the children. This will use Mildred's unified credit and reduce Henry's taxable estate.

The present law allowing tax effective disclaimers (meaning ones that do not generate additional taxable transfers) is generally seen as a valuable method for correcting inefficient transfers in wills and trust instruments.[23] Chapter 12 will discuss estate plans that use disclaimers to add flexibility to estate plans.

Miscellaneous Gift Tax Applications

Reciprocal gifts. Donors who get together on a scheme to use reciprocal gifts in order to gain additional annual exclusions may find their actions subject to IRS scrutiny. The argument will be that substance should prevail over form.

EXAMPLE 7 - 35. Mr. Garbanzo gives $10,000 to his son and $10,000 to Mrs. Ceci's daughter. At the same time, Mrs. Ceci gives $10,000 to her daughter and $10,000 to Mr. Garbanzo's son. The IRS will treat the "mirror image" cross-family transfers as if they were made to each donor's own child. Thus, each parent will be treated as having made a $20,000 gross gift to his own child.[24]

Multiple taxation of transfers. Certain transfers may be subject to both gift tax and estate tax.

EXAMPLE 7 - 36. Pope, age 55, transfers $100,000 in property into an irrevocable trust with an independent trustee. He retains a life estate in the income and names his nephew as the remainderman. At the time the § 7520 rate was 8%. Pope has made a completed gross gift this year of $21,166, the current value of the remainder (based on Table B 8%, i.e., 0.21166 * $100,000). As a gift of a future interest, it does not qualify for the annual exclusion. At Pope's death, the date-of-death value of the entire trust corpus is included in his gross estate under IRC § 2036(a). The adjusted taxable gift is reduced to zero, and a credit for any gift tax payable is allowed to prevent double taxation. Of course, if Pope's taxable gifts never exceeded the AEA, no gift taxes will be paid during his lifetime.

Where transferred property comes back into the gross estate because of a string being attached (IRC §§ 2036-2038) or because the transfer falls under one of the § 2035(a) exceptions (transfer of life insurance or the severing of a string), the earlier gift will not be considered an adjusted taxable gift for purposes of calculating the donee's estate tax. The last sentence of § 2001(b) defines "adjusted taxable gifts" as being post-1976 taxable gifts "other than gifts which are includable in the gross estate of the decedent." The gift tax payable credit (§ 2001(b)(2)) is still available because the gift taxes would indeed have been paid on such gifts (if the tentative tax exceeded the available unified credit) and the property subject to the prior gift does enter into the estate tax calculation by being included in the gross estate as if no gift had ever taken place.

BASIS RULES

The manner in which one acquires property determines the owner's initial basis in the property. Basis is important for two reasons: 1) basis is the starting point for determining depreciation for depreciable property; and, 2) on sale, it is the difference between the price (net amount realized) and the adjusted basis that determines the amount of gain or loss for income tax purposes.

Gain and loss. The gain or loss realized from the sale of property is calculated by subtracting an asset's adjusted basis from the amount realized:

$$\text{Gain or Loss} = \text{Amount Realized} - \text{Adjusted Basis}$$

EXAMPLE 7 - 37. Candice owns 100 shares of XYZ common stock purchased several years ago for $13,000 (hence, her adjusted basis in the stock). If she sells the shares for $16,000, net of selling commissions, her realized gain is $3,000. On the other hand, if the stock is sold for $11,000, she has a realized loss of $2,000.

Amount realized is defined as the fair market value of all money or property received, less selling expenses such as commissions.

EXAMPLE 7 - 38. In the prior example, the sales proceeds could have been in the form of cash or in kind. Alternatively, the buyer could have canceled an existing debt owed by the seller. Hence, if the buyer paid $6,000 cash, assigned title to his automobile (valued at $8,000), and also tore up a $2,000 IOU owed by the seller to the buyer, the total amount realized is still $16,000.

Adjusted basis is the tax payer's "initial basis" as "adjusted" by certain increases or decreases. The initial basis for an asset that is purchased is its cost. Adjustments to basis include items that reduce basis, such as allowance for depreciation, depletion, and obsolescence that reduce the taxpayer's taxes. The basis in stock may be decreased by non-taxable distributions. The most common adjustment that increases basis is for capital expenditures that improve property.

EXAMPLE 7 - 39. In the earlier example, the adjusted basis of $13,000 was probably the original purchase price of the stock, including any trading commission or other fee. However, had the asset been a machine used in the taxpayer's business, adjusted basis would likely reflect its current book (depreciated) value, including all capital improvements made subsequent to its acquisition. Hence, the $13,000 adjusted basis for a machine could, for example, be the net result of a $27,000 original purchase price, less $17,000 in accumulated depreciation, plus $3,000 in capital improvements.

Recapture of depreciation, which arises when a depreciable business asset is sold for greater than its adjusted basis, is beyond the scope of this text other than to say that a portion of the gain (the depreciation recaptured) may be taxed as ordinary income or in the case of depreciated real estate at a special 25% rate rather than at the more favorable capital gains rate.

Intangible assets (stocks, bonds, etc.) and personal use assets (one's home, the family car, etc.) cannot be depreciated. Therefore fewer adjustments to basis are likely with these types of assets than are likely with tangible business-use assets.

Holding period.   A gain or a loss can be either short-term or long-term, depending on the length of the holding period. The holding period is how long the asset was held by the seller and, in the case of property acquired by gift, by prior owners too. A gain or a loss is *short-term* if the holding period is not more than one year; it is *long-term* if the property is held more than one year. Inherited property is automatically considered long-term property. If a taxpayer has both long-term and short-term sales during the year, they are reported separately and each type is netted separately to determine whether there is a gain or a loss. The net gain on the sale of appreciated short-term investments is taxed as ordinary income, whereas the net gain on the sale of long-term investments is taxed at the lower capital gains rate. Presently, the maximum capital gains rate for individuals (estates and trusts, too) is 20% (10% for taxpayers in the 15% bracket). An even lower rate of just 18% (8% for individuals in the 15% bracket) applies to sales made after December 31, 2000, for property that at the time of the sale has been held for more than five years. For taxpayers above the 15% bracket, the property held for five years must have been purchased after 2000 or the taxpayer has to have elected to recognize as gain the pre-2001 appreciation as though the taxpayer sold the property (and reacquired it) on January 1, 2001. The election was available only for readily traded stock or capital assets used in a trade or business.

Realized versus recognized gains and losses.   A gain or loss is *realized* when the basic transaction, typically a sale, has occurred. On the other hand, a gain or loss is *recognized* when the taxpayer reports the gain or loss on a tax return. Recognition will commonly occur either because tax law requires recognition in that year or because the taxpayer elects a Code-permitted option to defer the tax to a later time. Common examples of gains or losses that may be recognized in tax years after the year of realization include installment sales,[25] tax-deferred exchanges of like-kind property,[26] involuntary conversion[27] (e.g., destruction of a warehouse by fire with insurance proceeds used to purchase a replacement warehouse), and certain capital transactions between corporations and their shareholders. Generally, the rate in effect when the gain is recognized is the rate that is applied, e.g., the capital gain portion of current payments on an installment sale will benefit from the maximum 20% rate even if the sale took place in a year when the maximum rate was 28%.

Property acquired by gift. As described above, the initial basis for property acquired by purchase is its cost, which is later adjusted by such items as depreciation and capital improvements, if any. In this section, we will cover the somewhat more complex rules for determining the basis of property acquired by gift. In determining whether the donee's gain or loss is short-term or long-term, the length of the donor's holding period is added or "tacked on" to the length of the donee's holding period.

Date-of-gift value equaling or exceeding donor's basis. A simple rule applies for gift property whose date-of-gift value is equal to or greater than the donor's adjusted basis at the date of gift: the donee's basis will equal the amount of the donor's adjusted basis (herein, we will just use "basis") at the date of the gift. This is called the donee's *carryover basis* (COB for short).

EXAMPLE 7 - 40. Ten years ago, donor purchased common stock for $10,000. Two years ago, donor gave donee the stock when it was worth $11,500. This year, donee sold the stock for $14,500. Since date-of-gift value was greater than donor's basis, donee has realized a gain of $4,500, the difference between the amount realized ($14,500) and donee's COB basis ($10,000).

EXAMPLE 7 - 41. As in the prior example, except that donee sold the stock for $7,000. Since date-of-gift value is greater than donor's basis, donee's basis is still $10,000. Therefore, donee has realized a loss of $3,000, the difference between the amount realized and donee's COB.

Date-of-gift value less than donor's basis. If a donee receives property with a date-of-gift value that is less than the donor's basis, then for purposes of calculating a loss only, donee's basis will be date-of-gift value. For purposes of calculating a gain, though, the COB rule applies, i.e., the donee's basis is the donor's basis at the date of the gift.

EXAMPLE 7 - 42. Donor acquired property several years ago for $6,000. Last year, when it was worth $4,200, donor gave it to donee, who this year sold it for $3,600.

Since date-of-gift value is less than donor's old basis, donee's basis for loss is the $4,200 date-of-gift value, and hence donee has realized a loss of only $600.

In effect, the donee is not permitted to recognize the portion of the loss resulting from the property's decline in value while owned by the donor.

EXAMPLE 7 - 43. As in the prior example, except that donee sold the property for $7,100. Although date-of-gift value is less than donor's basis, donee's basis for gain is the donor's basis at the date of the gift. In this case, donee's basis is $6,000, and donee has therefore realized a gain of $1,100.

Occasionally, gift property having a date-of-gift value less than the donor's basis is sold by the donee for an amount that is less than donor's basis, but more than date-of-gift value. In this case, the donee realizes neither gain nor loss.

EXAMPLE 7 - 44. Several years ago, donor acquired an asset for $2,000 and later gave it to donee when it was worth $1,450. If donee sells the asset for $1,800, no gain or loss will be realized. Since date-of-gift value ($1,450) is less than donor's basis at the date of the gift ($2,000), for purposes of calculating a loss, donee's basis will be date-of-gift value. There is no loss because the amount realized is greater than donee's basis (i.e., $1,800 minus $1,450 is not negative). On the other hand, for purposes of calculating a gain, donee's basis will be donor's basis at the date of the gift ($2,000).

Gift tax may increase basis. If the donor pays gift tax on the gift, a portion of that tax is added to the donor's adjusted basis at the date of the gift to determine the donee's new basis. The amount added is that portion of the tax attributable to appreciation. Appreciation is considered to be the difference between the FMV on the date of gift and the property's basis. Hence:

New Basis = Old Basis + ((FMV Gift - Old Basis)/ FMV Gift)) * Gift Tax

EXAMPLE 7 - 45. In 1997, Donor gave stock, purchased 20 years ago for $400,000, to Donee. The stock was worth $1,010,000 at the time of the gift. Donor paid gift taxes in the amount of $153,000. Donee's new basis equals $492,406, i.e., $400,000 + (($1,010,000 - $400,000) / $1,010,000) * $153,000.

Summary. For most gifts, the donee's basis for calculating a potential gain is just a carryover of the donor's pre-gift basis. There are two special rules: one for a gift of property that has a fair market value less that the donor's basis on the date of the gift and another where the donor has to pay gift taxes. Where the gift value is lower than the donor's basis, donee's basis for calculating a loss is the date-of-gift value and for gain it is the carryover basis, with sales in between resulting in no gain or loss. Where the donor pays gift taxes, the donee gets a partial step-up in basis. The increase is the portion of the gift tax that is attributed to the net appreciation of the gift. "Net appreciation" is the value of the gift less the donor's pre-gift basis. The product of the net appreciation divided by the full value of the gift times the gift taxes is added to the carryover basis to arrive at the donee's new basis.

Inherited property. As a general rule, the basis of property in the hands of a person acquiring the property from a decedent is the fair market value of the property at the date of the decedent's death.[28] This is true whether the person received the property by bequest, devise or intestate succession, or as a surviving joint tenant.

Notice that the change in the basis of property acquired by another's death can be a "step-up" or "step-down" in the basis depending on whether the decedent's pre-death basis was lower or higher than the value at death. However, common usage is to refer to this change at death as a *step-up* in basis. Where special elections apply such as the alternate valuation date election of §2032 or the special use election of §2032A, the value as shown on the estate tax return determines the basis. To simplify our discussion, the "date-of-death" (DOD) value should be understood to include the alternate valuation or special use valuation, if such are applicable.

If an estate tax return (Form 706) is filed, there is a rebuttable presumption that the Form 706 values are correct.[29] The change in basis occurs whether there is a tax, and, indeed, even if no return is filed. Thus, when a person dies, even if he or she leaves a very modest estate, the property in the estate will have a change in basis to the date-of-death value.

Holding period. The holding period for property acquired from a decedent is long-term, regardless of the actual holding period. Thus, a decedent could have purchased the asset shortly before death and the devisee could have sold it shortly after death, and any gain or loss will be long-term.

Individually owned property. Generally, property owned solely by a decedent receives a full step-up in basis for the person who acquires it.

EXAMPLE 7 - 46. Peter held onto land that he had purchased for $500 in 1934 until his death in 2002, when it passed on to his son Frank. At Peter's death the property was worth $40,000. Peter's total estate was worth only $200,000, so there was no need to file an estate tax return. Frank kept the property for six months, and then sold it for $45,000. Frank has a realized long-term capital gain of $5,000, the gain being the difference between the sale price and the value established at Peter's death. Since it was acquired from a decedent, the holding period for the property is automatically considered long-term.

Co-owned property. If, at death, the decedent was one of several owners sharing title to property, usually only the decedent's share is stepped-up. The factor that determines whether any surviving co-owner can also enjoy a step-up in basis for his or her share depends on how title is held. In general, the surviving co-owner's share does not receive a step-up in basis unless the asset is either owned as community property or for some reason the survivor's share was included in the deceased co-owner's gross estate.

Community property. The new basis is the FMV at the date of death for both halves of the community property even though only one-half is included in the decedent spouse's estate. This is referred to as a full step-up in basis.

Joint tenancy. What is included in the decedent estate and the surviving co-owner's new basis will follow one of two rules which depend on the relationship between the decedent and the surviving co-owners.

Husband and wife rule. Where the only joint tenants (or tenants by the entirety) are husband and wife, then half of the FMV at the date of death is included in the decedent's estate and the surviving spouse's new basis will equal half the total pre-death basis and half the FMV at the date of death.

$$\text{New Basis} = (\text{DOD FMV} + \text{Old Basis}) / 2$$

Where joint tenancy property was purchased prior to 1977, the surviving spouse can use the consideration furnished rule instead of the husband and wife rule. This will be advantageous if the decedent spouse contributed more than half of the purchase price and the property appreciated in value prior to his or her death.[30] It appears that the IRS accepts the husband and wife rule even for pre-1977 properties unless the surviving spouse brings up the date-of-purchase issue. Obviously, the further we move away from 1976 the less often this will become an issue.

Consideration furnished rule. Where the joint tenants include nonspouses, the rule is that the decedent's gross estate includes that portion of the property as the decedent's share of the consideration bears to the total consideration (i.e., the price paid for the property). Decedent's consideration includes any gifts given to other joint tenants and any share acquired by the prior death of a co-owner.

Include = (Decedent's Consideration / Total Consideration) * FMV DOD

The new basis for each surviving co-owner's interest is his or her old basis plus an increase by the amount included in the decedent's estate split equally among the surviving joint tenants. The examples that follow demonstrate both rules.

EXAMPLE 7 - 47. In 1990, Ricky and Victoria, husband and wife, owned common stock as joint tenants. She paid $50,000 and he paid $110,000 of the original $160,000 purchase price. When Ricky died in 2002, the stock was worth $220,000. Four months later, Victoria sold the stock for $290,000. The consideration each paid is irrelevant and Victoria's basis is equal to half the old basis plus half the fair market value at Ricky's death; hence, her realized gain is $100,000 [$290,000 - ($160,000 + $220,000)/2].

EXAMPLE 7 - 48. Same facts as in the prior example, except Ricky and Victoria bought the stock as joint tenants in 1976. Even though they are married, because this joint tenancy was created before 1977, Victoria can use the consideration paid rule to determine her basis. Included in Ricky's estate is $151,250 [$220,000 * ($110,000/$160,000)]. Victoria's basis is equal to the amount she paid plus the amount included in Ricky's estate, hence, her realized gain is $88,750 [$290,000 - ($151,250 + $50,000)].

Consider the very different outcome for community property.

EXAMPLE 7 - 49. Same facts as in the prior example, except that at Ricky's death, he and Victoria owned the common stock as community property. Once again half would be included in Ricky's estate but Victoria's basis would be the FMV DOD amount of $220,000, and her gain would be only $70,000.

Thus, ordinarily community property states have a decided advantage over common law states with regard to basis adjustments at death. Couples residing in community property states should hold appreciated property as community property. On the other hand, if the property has decreased in value, community property will receive a full step-down in basis at the first death and some other form of title might be preferred.

A number of community property states (e.g., California, Nevada and Wisconsin) have adopted legislation creating "community property with the right of survivorship." There is concern that the IRS will challenge attempts to apply the step-up for both halves, seeking instead to have this hybrid treated for basis purposes under the rules for husband and wife joint tenants.

EXAMPLE 7 - 50. Years ago, brothers Steve and Stan purchased stock for $10,000, taking title as joint tenants. Steve paid $6,000 and Stan paid $4,000 toward the purchase. At Steve's death the stock was worth $20,000. Included in Steve's gross estate is 60% of the stock's value because that corresponds to his share of the consideration paid for the stock, even though property law recognized that he owned 50% of the stock immediately before death. Stan's new basis would be $16,000, which is $12,000 (the amount included in Steve's estate) plus Stan's $4,000 basis in his pre-death interest in the property.

EXAMPLE 7 - 51. Three friends purchased a vacation cabin in 1980. Abe paid $20,000, Betty paid $30,000, and Cathy paid $50,000 of the $100,000 purchase price. In 1985, when the cabin was worth $160,000, Abe died. His estate included 20% of the DOD FMV, i.e. 20% * $160,000 = $32,000. Betty's new basis in her 50% interest in the cabin became $46,000 (½ * $32,000 + her original consideration of $30,000) and Cathy's new basis is $66,000 (½ * $32,000 + her original consideration of $50,000).

EXAMPLE 7 - 52. Continuing from the last example, in 1990, Cathy died, leaving Betty as the sole surviving joint tenant. The cabin was then worth $224,000. The amount included in Cathy's gross estate is based on her portion ($66,000) of the combined (hers and Betty's) predeath bases of $112,000. Therefore, included in her estate is $132,000 (($66,000 / $112,000) * $224,000), and Betty's new basis would be $178,000 (the $132,000 included in Cathy's estate plus Betty's old basis of $46,000).

It should be noted that a gift from one prospective co-joint tenant to another is treated as consideration from the donor, not the donee.

EXAMPLE 7 - 53. Martin gave his son, Andy, $50,000 shortly before they purchased a vacation condo for $150,000. Martin paid $100,000 on the purchase and Andy paid $50,000. When Martin died, the condo was valued at $200,000, all of which had to be included in his estate because Andy's contribution was traceable to Martin's gift.

Tenants in common rule. Tenancy in common is the preferred form of co-ownership for nonrelatives. It does not have the survivorship feature found in joint tenancy, thus the co-owners control the disposition of their respective shares. Unlike joint tenancy, tenants in common can have unequal undivided shares, meaning that you could have one owner owning 20%, another owning 30%, and the third owning 50%. When a tenant in common owner dies, his or her share of the total FMV DOD of the property is included in the decedent's gross estate. The disposition of a deceased tenant in common's interest depends on the decedent's will or, if there is no will, intestate succession laws.

> EXAMPLE 7 - 54. Friends Arthur, Tony, and Maria purchased property as tenants in common. Of the $100,000 purchase price, Arthur paid $50,000 and took a 50% interest, Tony paid $30,000 and took a 30% interest, and Maria paid $20,000 and took a 20% interest. Years later when Tony died, the property was worth $250,000 and his estate included $75,000 since he owned a 30% interest. If Tony left his interest to his widow Nancy, her basis would be $75,000. If he instead left his interest to co-owner Maria, her total basis in the 50% interest she would then own would be $95,000 ($75,000 + her $20,000 contribution).

Note in the preceding example that because the interests were held as tenants in common, property law recognizes unequal shares.

The rubber band rule of §1014(e). Internal Revenue Code §1014(e) provides that where a person gives away "appreciated property" and then inherits the property from the donee within one year of the original gift (i.e., it comes bouncing back as if it had a rubber band attached when it was given), the adjusted basis of the property to the donor will be donee-decedent's adjusted basis immediately before the donee-decedent's death. Appreciated property means property worth more at the time of the gift than its basis. Since the donee had a carryover basis, the donor will also get the property back with the basis unchanged.

> EXAMPLE 7 - 55. Walter gives Kerri, his terminally ill wife, title to land that Walter purchased many years ago for $400. The property has a value on the day of the gift of $90,000. Kerri, who dies two months later, devises the land back to Walter, who then sells it for $95,000. Because the property was appreciated at the time Walter gave it to his wife and she died within one year of the gift, Walter realizes a gain of $94,600 on the sale, not just $5,000.

Hence, there is an advantage to gifting low-basis property, in the case of a donor-devisee, if the donee-decedent lives at least one year after the date of gift. This strategy will work even if the original donor is not the spouse of the decedent, but the original gift will use up the donor's unified credit if it is not covered by the annual exclusion. Section 1014(e) does not apply if the donee-decedent leaves the property to someone other than the original donor or the donor's spouse. EGTTRA has repealed this section for post-2009 deaths, replacing it with a new IRC § 1022.

The new section denies a basis increase for property acquired by gift within three years of death. The only exception is property acquired by gift from a spouse so long as the donor spouse did not acquire the property by gift. Thus it appears that after 2009 a spouse can gain an increased basis in appreciated property by giving it to a dying spouse who then leaves it back to the donor. This benefit may not have been intended by Congress, so watch for this apparent loop-hole to be plugged.

Income in respect of a decedent. One major exception to the step-up in basis rule has to do with what is called income in respect of a decedent. This *income in respect of a decedent* (IRD) consists of income (or realized but not yet recognized capital gain) belonging to the decedent that had not been taxed prior to the decedent's death but that would have been subject to income tax had the decedent received it during life. Examples of IRD include the gain portion of an installment sale promissory note where the gain is being recognized only as principal is collected, the vested amount in a qualified retirement plan, IRA accounts (the value in excess of basis, since IRAs can have a basis), dividends declared but not received at the time of death, commissions earned and paid after death, and business accounts receivables. IRD is subject to both estate tax and, when collected, to income tax. It is reported by the actual recipient (executor, trustee, or beneficiary). If estate tax is paid, the recipient of IRD is allowed an income tax deduction for the estate tax that is attributable to the IRD.[31] The deduction is basically the portion of the estate tax attributable to the IRD collected by the recipient.

Basis After Estate Tax Repeal

Basis of property acquired from a decedent. To set new basis rules for property acquired from a decedent, EGTRRA added § 1022, Treatment of Property Acquired From a Decedent Dying After December 31, 2009. It starts with a general rule that, beginning in 2010 (after the estate, gift, and generation-skipping transfer taxes have been repealed), the present-law rule providing for a fair market value basis for property acquired from a decedent is repealed and replaced with a carryover basis as if the property had been transferred by gift. But the section goes on to make a couple of exceptions such that the general rule will become the exception, applying only to estates of the very wealthy. Probably 98 to 99 percent of all estates will receive the same "step-up" at death as they would have received under pre-EGTRRA law.

Amount of basis increase. The new law applicable to estates of decedents dying after 2009 allows an executor to increase, within limits, the basis in assets owned by the decedent and acquired by the beneficiaries at death.[32] Each decedent's estate is permitted to increase the basis of assets transferred by up to a total of $1.3 million. The $1.3 million limit is increased by the amount of unused capital losses, net operating losses, and certain "built-in" losses of the decedent. In addition, the basis of property transferred to a surviving spouse can be increased by an additional $3 million. Thus, the basis of property transferred to surviving spouses can be increased by a total of $4.3 million.

> EXAMPLE 7 - 56. When Marjorie died in 2010 the executor of her estate had the task of allocating the allowable basis increase. Marjorie had lived in her home for years and it qualified for § 121 gain non-recognition. There was a vacation home that the family planned to keep and a vacant lot that they planned to develop into a small commercial center which would probably be kept as a rental. The apartment building was in a desirable area, some family members wanted to sell it and others want to keep it, so no decision has been made on that property. With these matters in mind, the executor created the following table for the allocation of the increase in basis:

Item	old basis	FMV	added	new
home	$175,000	$400,000	$0	$175,000
apartment building	$400,000	$1,000,000	$600,000	$1,000,000
IRA	$0	$250,000	$0	$0
ABC stock	$150,000	$500,000	$350,000	$500,000
MOP stock	$200,000	$100,000	$0	$100,000
XYZ stock	$90,000	$340,000	$250,000	$340,000
vacation cabin	$25,000	$300,000	$0	$25,000
vacant lot	$50,000	$180,000	$100,000	$150,000
misc. household	$120,000	$70,000	$0	$70,000
			$1,300,000	

Since the estate can take advantage of § 121 to avoid recognition of $250,000 in gain, there is no point to allocating additional basis to it. The apartment building is a depreciable asset, therefore the maximum allocation possible should be made. The IRA is income in respect of a decedent and, just as under the old rules, no step-up in basis is allowed. ABC and XYZ stock are stepped-up to the maximum possible as they might be sold. The value of MOP at Marjorie's death is less than her basis hence it is stepped-down to its date-of-death value. If the family had been planning to sell the vacation cabin sooner than they planned to sell the appreciated stock, then it would be wise to allocate some increase to it rather than to the stock, but this allocation makes sense given their plans to keep it in the family. In general, the miscellaneous household property has gone down in value and the allocation cannot bring basis higher than its date-of-death value. Even the individual personal items that have gone up in value (e.g., collectibles) are likely to remain in the family, hence no increase is allocated to them. The vacant lot receives $100,000 to use up the balance of the $1.3 million allowed increase. Given that neither the lot nor the appreciated stock can be depreciated, and that the $1.3 million increase allowed falls short of bringing the basis of all assets up to their full fair market value, the choice of how to allocate falls on the executor. It makes sense to allocate the remaining basis increase in the order in which one expects asset to be sold.

Nonresidents who are not U.S. citizens will be allowed to increase the basis of property by up to $60,000. The $60,000, $1.3 million, and $3 million amounts are adjusted annually for inflation occurring after 2010. Executors of large estates will be required to file returns reporting how the allocation has been made.[33]

Property eligible for basis increase. In general, the basis of property may be increased above the decedent's adjusted basis in that property only if the property is owned, or is treated as owned, by the decedent at the time of the decedent's death. In the case of property held as joint tenants or tenants by the entireties with the surviving spouse, one-half of the property is treated as having been owned by the decedent and is thus eligible for the basis increase. In the case of property held jointly with a person other than the surviving spouse, the portion of the property attributable to the decedent's consideration furnished is treated as having been owned by the decedent and will be eligible for a basis increase. The decedent also is treated as the owner of property (which will be eligible for a basis increase) if the property was transferred by the decedent during his lifetime to a revocable trust that pays all of its income during the decedent's life to the decedent or at the direction of the decedent. The decedent also is treated as having owned the surviving spouse's one-half share of community property (which will be eligible for a basis increase) if at least one-half of the property was owned by, and acquired from, the decedent.[34] The decedent shall not, however, be treated as owning any property solely by reason of holding a power of appointment with respect to such property.

Property not eligible for a basis increase includes: (1) property that was acquired by the decedent by gift (other than from his or her spouse) during the three-year period ending on the date of the decedent's death; (2) property that constitutes a right to receive income in respect of a decedent; (3) stock or securities of a foreign personal holding company; (4) stock of a domestic international sales corporation (or former domestic international sales corporation); (5) stock of a foreign investment company; and (6) stock of a passive foreign investment company (except for which a decedent shareholder had made a qualified electing fund election).

Rules applicable to basis increase. Basis increase will be allocable on an asset-by-asset basis (e.g., basis increase can be allocated to a share of stock or a block of stock). However, in no case can the basis of an asset be adjusted above its fair market value. If the amount of basis increase is less than the fair market value of assets whose bases are eligible to be increased under these rules, the executor will determine which assets and to what extent each asset receives a basis increase.

Carryover basis for the wealthy. For estates in excess of $1.3 million (above $4.3 million for property to a surviving spouse), a modified carryover basis regime generally takes effect. After the executor of the estate has applied the increase allowed, e.g., the $1.3 or $4.3 million, the rest of the property transferred at the decedent's death will receive a basis equal to the lesser of the adjusted basis of the decedent or the fair market value of the property on the date of the decedent's death.

The modified carryover basis rules apply to property acquired by bequest, devise, or inheritance, or by the decedent's estate from the decedent, property passing from the decedent to the extent such property passed without consideration, and certain other property to which the present law rules apply.[35] Property acquired from a decedent is treated as if the property had been acquired by gift. Thus, the character of gain on the sale of property received from a decedent's estate is carried over to the heir. For example, real estate that has been depreciated and would be subject to recapture if sold by the decedent will be subject to recapture if sold by the heir.

The modified carryover basis rules apply to property acquired from the decedent. Property acquired from the decedent is (1) property acquired by bequest, devise, or inheritance, (2) property acquired by the decedent's estate from the decedent, (3) property transferred by the decedent during his or her lifetime in trust to pay the income for life to or on the order or direction of the decedent, with the right reserved to the decedent at all times before his death to revoke the trust,[36] (4) property transferred by the decedent during his lifetime in trust to pay the income for life to or on the order or direction of the decedent with the right reserved to the decedent at all times before his death to make any change to the enjoyment thereof through the exercise of a power to alter, amend, or terminate the trust,"(5) property passing from the decedent by reason of the decedent's death to the extent such property passed without consideration (e.g., property held as joint tenants with right of survivorship or as tenants by the entireties), and (6) the surviving spouse's one-half share of certain community property held by the decedent and the surviving spouse as community property.

Reporting Requirements After Repeal

Lifetime gifts. A donor is required to report to the Internal Revenue Service the basis and character of any non-cash property transferred by gift with a value in excess of $25,000 (except for gifts to charitable organizations). The donor is be required to report to the IRS:

1. the name and taxpayer identification number of the donee, an accurate description of the property,
2. the adjusted basis of the property in the hands of the donor at the time of gift,
3. the donor's holding period for such property,
4. sufficient information to determine whether any gain on the sale of the property would be treated as ordinary income, and
5. any other information as the Treasury Secretary may prescribe.

Similar information (including the name, address, and phone number of the person making the return) is required to be provided to recipients of such property.

Transfers at death. For transfers at death of non-cash assets in excess of $1.3 million and for appreciated property the value of which exceeds $25,000 received by a decedent within three years of death, the executor of the estate would report to the IRS:

1. the name and taxpayer identification number of the recipient of the property,
2. an accurate description of the property,
3. the adjusted basis of the property in the hands of the decedent and its fair market value at the time of death,
4. the decedent's holding period for the property,
5. sufficient information to determine whether any gain on the sale of the property would be treated as ordinary income,
6. the amount of basis increase allocated to the property, and
7. any other information as the Treasury Secretary may prescribe.

The above rules also apply to the trustee of a revocable trust once the settlor dies.

Penalties for failure to file required information. Any donor required to report the basis and character of any non-cash property with a value in excess of $25,000 who fails to do so is liable for a penalty of $500 for each failure to report such information to the IRS and $50 for each failure to report such information to a beneficiary.

Any person required to report to the IRS transfers at death of non-cash assets in excess of $1.3 million in value who fails to do so is liable for a penalty of $10,000 for the failure to report such information. Any person required to report to the IRS the receipt by a decedent of appreciated property valued in excess of $25,000 within three years of death who fails to do so is liable for a penalty of $500 for the failure to report such information to the IRS. There also is a penalty of $50 for each failure to report such information to a beneficiary.

No penalty is imposed with respect to any failure that is due to reasonable cause. If any failure to report to the IRS or a beneficiary under the bill is due to intentional disregard of the rules, then the penalty is five percent of the fair market value of the property for which reporting was required, determined at the date of the decedent's death (for property passing at death) or determined at the time of gift (for a lifetime gift).

This chapter has focused on certain qualitative aspects of the federal gift tax and the basis rules, new and old. The next chapter will present a brief overview of the federal fiduciary income tax.

QUERIES ANSWERED:

1. A total of 55%, i.e. $550,000 [4 years @ 15% - 5% = 40% and another 15% for the last year].

QUESTIONS AND PROBLEMS

1. List the common law requirements for a valid gift.

2. Tony's eyesight became so weak that he could no longer drive his car, so he let Larry, a neighbor in his teens who helped him with shopping, drive it. After a while, the car was parked at Larry's house. Both Tony and Larry kept a set of keys. At Tony's 80th birthday party, in front of several guests, he told Larry that the car was his. He asked his caretaker to find the title slip so he could sign the car over to Larry, but the slip could not be located. Tony died two weeks after the party. The slip was located in his safe deposit box and the second set of keys found on his dresser. Tony's executor wants to sell the car as part of the estate, and has offered it to Larry at low Blue Book of $23,000, but Larry says the car already belongs to him. What supports the executor's position? Larry's position? What additional facts might support one position or the other?

3. Addie sells her vacant lot, fair market value $22,000, to a stranger for $9,500. (a) Is there a gift? Why or why not? (b) Would your answer change if the buyer was, in fact, Addie's son? One of her employees?

4. (a) If Jones gives Smith 200 shares of a non-dividend-paying stock, is this a gift of a present or a future interest? Why? (b) Why does it matter?

5. In 2002, Lois transferred $10,000 to an irrevocable trust that is required to distribute all income annually to her son, age 55, for his life, the remainder will be distributed outright to his issue. Assuming a 10% federal rate, calculate the amount of Lois's taxable gift.

6. In 2003, Avery transferred $30,000 into an irrevocable trust. His daughter, Dayna, is to receive all of the income from the trust for five years, followed by his daughter, Sandra, receiving the income for the next five years, after which the trust terminates and is distributed to his son, Walter. Assuming a federal rate of 8%, calculate the amount of Avery's taxable gift.

7. In 2003, Brenda gave her daughter Susan XYZ stock worth $1,730,000. Because she did not want to pay gift taxes, she asked her husband, Fred, to

split the gift. Use $11,000 as the annual exclusion. (a) Calculate the taxable gift and the gift tax that Brenda would report if she alone reports the gift and (b) what taxable gift each would report, and the gift tax, if they split the gift. (c) How much tax is saved by splitting the gift?

8. In 2003, John gave his daughter Marlene some of his recently inherited wealth, specifically, ABC stock worth $2,300,000. The annual exclusion was $11,000. John and his wife, Lola, are thinking about splitting the gifts. (a) Calculate the taxable gift and the gift tax that John would report if he alone reports the gift and (b) the taxable gift each would report, and the gift tax, if they split the gift. (c) How much tax is saved by splitting the gift? (d) Summarize how gift splitting saves gift taxes.

9. (a) Where does a donor indicate that she is making a § 2513 split gift election with her spouse? (b) Where does the non-donor husband sign, showing his consent? (c) Where does the "split" take place on the donee spouse's return? (d) Where does the non-donee spouse's return account for half of the gifts made by donee spouse?

10. In 2003, Mike made a gift to his friend Laurent of stock worth more than $1.5 million. However, just a few weeks later, Mike left the U.S. and went to Europe to, as he put it, "lead the life of a free spirit." What burden does this place on Laurent?

11. Give three reasons why gift splitting can be a valuable estate planning tool.

12. Wayne and his wife, Sharon, own as joint tenants an undeveloped parcel of land worth $78,000. The land was purchased by Wayne for $12,000 before he and Sharon married. This year they gave the land to their daughter Christina. (a) Should they split this gift? (b) What is Christina's basis? When, if ever, does splitting a gift have an effect on the donee's basis?

13. Ralph established a trust in 1985 which gave Linda income for life, remainder to Linda's three children by right of representation. Explain the effect on Linda's estate at her death of each clause (considered independently) if such is part of the trust:

a. The trustee is given absolute discretion to transfer the principal of the trust to Linda, if doing so would be in her best interest.

b. Linda is given the power to appoint, by direct reference to this power in her will, the remainder of the trust among her children in such portion as she deems appropriate.

c. I give Linda the right to invade the corpus up to a maximum of 3% of the trust in any one year. This right shall be noncumulative.

d. I give Linda the power to invade the corpus of the trust, up to the whole amount, if such be necessary for her health, education, maintenance, or support.

14. Kenneth created an irrevocable trust, transferring assets worth $1 million to an independent trustee. The trust was to help various family members, but specifically excluded helping Kenneth and his wife. Eventually, the trust was to terminate and be distributed to several individuals and their families. Part of the trust read as follows, "Kenneth reserves the right to distribute up to 10% of the trust each year to such of his issue as he thinks need help to pursue additional education or for support." When he died, the trust was worth $1.5 million. He had never exercised the right to distribute a portion of the trust. Explain how much, if any, of this trust is included in his estate. Be sure to focus on the difference between retained interests and limited powers of appointment.

15. Crystal established a trust (worth exactly $1,000,000 at all times relevant here) for the benefit of Arthur during his lifetime, with remainder to Sarah on Arthur's death. Arthur was 50 years old when the trust was established. The terms of the trust give Arthur the right to demand up to the greater of 5% or $5,000 from the trust in any year, but the right is noncumulative. In years 1, 2, 3, 5, and 6, he did not exercise the right. In year 4, he took out the maximum allowed. With appreciation in the remaining assets, the trust quickly returned to $1,000,000, which was its value in the 6th year when Arthur died.

a. In the first year the power lapsed, what was the gift to Sarah?

b. How much of this trust would be included in Arthur's estate?

c. If the demand right had been the greater of 7% or $7,000, what would be the gift to Sarah in the first year? Would a gift tax return have to be filed?

d. If the demand right had been the greater of 7% or $7,000, how much would be included in Arthur's estate?

16. James established a trust (worth exactly $1,000,000 at all times relevant here) for the benefit of Judith during her lifetime with the remainder to Lisa on Judith's death. Judith was 70 years old when the trust was established. The terms of the trust give Judith, in addition to all income, the right to demand up to the greater of 5% or $5,000 from the trust in any year, but the right is noncumulative and lapses at her death. Over the years, Judith did the following: year 1 demanded and received the full amount allowed; year 4 demanded and received 3% of the trust; year 5 demanded and received 2%; and in both years 6 and 7 demanded and received 5%. In all other years she asked for nothing over and above the income. With appreciation in the remaining assets, the trust quickly returned to $1,000,000, which was its value in the 8th year when Judith died.

a. Explain, without doing the math, how the gift to Lisa would be calculated for year two (i.e., when the power lapsed), but for the 5 & 5 exception.
b. How much of this trust would be included in Judith's estate?
c. If the demand right had been the greater of 8% or $8,000, again without doing the math, explain how one would calculate the value of the fifth-year gift to Lisa? If the calculated value was $9,000, would a gift tax return have to be filed?
d. If the demand right had been the greater of 8% or $8,000, how much would be included in Judith's estate?

17. Frank purchased a $280,000 life insurance policy on his own life. A year later, when it had a value for gift purposes of $25,000, he assigned the policy to his son, Sam. A few months after making this gift, Frank died. Frank's wife had always been the named beneficiary and Sam failed to change the beneficiary designation. (a) Explain the estate tax consequences. Does the marital deduction come into play? (b) Explain all gift tax consequences.

18. A client asks you to explain when the acquisition by gift of joint tenancy property is taxed. (a) Explain the rule that applies to most property using real estate as an example. (b) Explain the exceptions using a bank account as an example.

19. Today, Karen and her brother Lindsay buy 100 shares of ABC Corp. stock for $44,000, writing a check on their joint tenancy checking account, taking title in joint tenancy. Has a gift occurred? Does the source of the funds matter? Explain.

20. In 2002, Joe gave $2 million cash to his daughter Mary, who really didn't need it, so she gave it to her son Sal, who, having taken a vow of poverty, gave it to his sister Sue, who said, "thanks." (a) How many gifts subject to taxation were made? (b) Could the secondary transfers have been made using disclaimers (IRC § 2518), thus eliminating all but one taxable transfer? (c) Is the tax credit for tax on prior transfers (IRC § 2013) any help?

21. In so far as timing, what do a qualified disclaimer and an estate tax return have in common? How are they different?

22. Peter deposited $80,000 in a joint bank account with his son Ricky. Ricky withdrew (and used for himself) $5,000 in 1999, $15,000 in 2000, and $6,000 in 2001. In 2001, Peter withdrew $30,000 and purchased a boat, taking title in joint tenancy with Ricky. Ricky did not use the boat that year, but began fixing it up and doing some sailing in 2002. (a) When, and in what amount, do gifts occur? (b) If Peter dies, and the boat, then worth $36,000, is still held in joint tenancy with Ricky, what would be included in his estate? (c) Would your answer change if Ricky, instead of Peter, wrote the check for the purchase of the boat (still taking title as joint tenants)?

23. In 1998, Francisco and Hanna executed a "joint and mutual will," which is a single will, signed by both and revocable only by mutual consent. Essentially, it provided that the first to die leaves his or her property to the survivor, who then leaves everything to their children at his or her death. Francisco died recently, leaving a very large estate. Hanna wishes they had left at least an amount equal to the AEA to the children. (a) Would it make any difference if Hanna disclaims an AEA amount or assigns it to the children? (b) Would your answer be different if Francisco and Hanna wrote two separate wills following the same pattern as their joint one?

24. John and Mary Smith live in a community property state. They own shares of XYZ common stock as joint tenants. They purchased the stock in 1975 for

$250,000, with John paying $225,000 and Mary $25,000. John died recently. At the time of his death, the stock was worth $1,000,000. Consider the following basis issues: (a) According to the general rule, how much of the stock's value is included in John's estate? What is Mary's basis in the stock? (b) Was it a good idea to hold the stock as joint tenants? Given their domicile, how should title have been held? Why? (c) Suppose they had lived in a common law state, given when the stock was purchased, what argument could Mary use to obtain a higher basis? What would that basis be?

25. After making big money in Texas oil, Lucky Nick purchased property on the bay front, paying $1 million in cash. In 2003, when the property was valued at $2,511,000 million, Nick gave the property to his favorite niece, Susan. Nick paid gift taxes in the amount of $680,000. (a) What was Nick's original basis in the property? (b) What is Susan's new basis? (c) What would Susan's basis have been if she had inherited the property due to Nick's death in 2003, rather than receiving it as a gift?

26. In 2004, Stacey gave stock worth $5,011,000 to her brother Mitchell. The annual exclusion reduced the taxable gift to $5 million and Stacey paid gift taxes of $1,875,000. Stacey had purchased the stock in 1994 for $2,000,000. (a) What is Mitchell's basis in the sock? (b) Had Stacey died in 2004, leaving the stock to Mitchell, what would his basis be?

27. Richard died in 2010 leaving his entire estate to his two children. His executor must allocate basis increase among the assets of his estate. The overall appreciated value of his estate is such that not all assets that qualify for a step-up will receive a full step-up. What determines whether a full step-up should be allocated insofar as the following items (just a small portion of his estate) are concerned? Explain. (a) ZMP stock purchased for $75,000 now worth $250,000. (b) A small rental house that was once Richard's home. He bought it for $45,000 and its date-of-death value was $200,000. (c) A painting purchased for $2,000 but now worth about $500,000.

28. Penny died in 2010 leaving her entire estate to Jake, her long time live-in lover. Jake claims that the two of them were married by a sea captain on one of the cruises they took, but he can't find the papers to prove it. He has photos from what he claims to be the wedding, but it is hard to tell whether they show the

two being married or whether it was just costume night on the cruise. The state would recognize the marriage if Jake can prove it took place. Penny's estate is worth millions and is highly appreciated. (a) Given that the estate tax is repealed and no one is contesting the validity of Penny's will, why does it matter whether they are married? (b) Assuming the maximum allowable basis increase is allocated to each of the following, what would be Jake's basis in each? WEB stock purchased for $40,000 -- date-of-death value (DODV) $95,000; a sailboat purchased for $100,000 -- DODV $60,000; an IRA with a basis of $16,000 -- DODV $70,000.

29. During the last 10 years of her life, Loraine, a widow, undertook each of the following independent transactions. Explain whether each constituted a gift subject to taxation.

   a. Purchased a life insurance policy on her life, naming her son beneficiary.
   b. Transferred title to her personal residence to her daughter and continued to live there, rent-free, for two years, at which time she moved out and formally relinquished all rights to the property.
   c. Funded a revocable living trust.
   d. Funded an irrevocable living trust, under which her daughter was the sole beneficiary.
   e. Purchased some land, taking title in the names of herself and her son as joint tenants. Loraine paid $90,000 of the $100,000 purchase price, and son paid $10,000.
   f. Purchased common stock, taking title in the names of herself and her husband as joint tenants.
   g. Purchased life insurance on the life of her uncle, naming her daughter beneficiary. Two years later, uncle died and daughter was paid the proceeds.
   h. Paid $21,000 in tuition and $8,000 in room, board, and other fees each year for five years for her son's college education.
   i. Opened a joint checking account with her daughter, depositing $26,000 of her own funds.

ANSWERS TO THE QUESTIONS AND PROBLEMS *(odd numbered only)*

1. Common law requirements for a valid gift: (a) A donor capable of transferring property. (b) A donee capable of receiving and possessing the property. (c) Delivery to the donee, and some form of acceptance. (d) Donative intent. (This is not required for a taxable gift.)

3. (a) There is probably no gift, since Addie sold, at arm's length, the property to a stranger. It might just be a bad bargain. (b) If the donee was Addie's son, Addie probably made a gift of $12,500, since intent was probably donative. On the other hand, if the donee was Addie's employee, the difference in values is probably compensation, taxable to Addie's employee.

5. This transfer represents a gift of a present interest to son of a life estate in the trust income for son's life, and a gift of a future interest in the remainder to son's issue. The former gift qualifies for the annual exclusion, while the latter does not. The value of the life estate, based on Table S, is $10,000 times .83843, or $8,384. It will qualify for the annual exclusion. The value of the remainder, $10,000 minus $8,384, or $1,616, is a future interest and will not qualify for the annual exclusion. Thus, the total taxable portion of the gift is $1,636.

7. (a) $1,730,000 - $11,000 = $1,719,000 taxable gift. Gift tax would be $308,550. (b) Taxable gift is $854,000 [$1,730,000/2 - $11,000] each. This is less than the AEA for 2003, hence no gift tax for either. (c) $308,550 is saved.

9. (a) She would indicate her split gift election at lines 12 - 17 of the first page of the 709. (b) Her husband would sign and date at line 18 of the first page. (c) At part 3, page 2, line 2, she would show the items (by number from Schedule A, Parts 1 and 2), that are being split and show half their total value in the last column for that line. (d) The husband picks up the same value at Part 3, line 4, of his 709.

11. First, two annual exclusions are available to reduce the taxable gift amount. Second, both unified credits are available to reduce the tax. And, third, there are two runs through the lower marginal rates, which also reduces the overall tax.

13. (a) The trustee is the holder of a limited power and this trust is not included in Linda's estate. (b) Linda is the holder of a limited power, and nothing is included whether or not she exercises the power. (c) This is a general power, and 3% of the trust's value on her death will be included in her estate, assuming she did not exercise the power that last year. If she did exercise it to the full 3%, then none of the trust would be included. The property taken out, if any, would be in her estate unless she gave it away or consumed it. (d) This is a power limited by an ascertainable standard as such is defined in IRC § 2041 and is therefore considered a limited power, therefore, nothing is included.

15. (a) No gift taxes are generated because the gift (the lapse of the right to withdraw $50,000) is covered by the 5 & 5 exception.
(b) The 5 & 5 exception does not apply to lapses at death; therefore, $50,000 would be included in Arthur's estate. Note: nothing is actually taken out of the trust due to this inclusion in Arthur's estate; it is included for calculation purposes only. Any estate tax attributed to this inclusion is charged to the trust.
(c) Each year that a lapse occurred (years 1, 2, 3, and 5) due to a year ending without a withdrawal, a gift occurred of the amount not sheltered by the 5 & 5 exception. Thus for each of those years, a gift of a remainder interest in $20,000 must be reported. In the first year, for example, if the federal rate for future interest gifts was 8%, the gift would be: 0.16388 * $20,000 = $3,328 [Table S (8%), 50 year old, remainder factor]. Each year that a lapse occurred, a gift tax return would have been required since the amounts over 5% would be deemed gifts of future interests (no annual exclusion), discounted because of Arthur's retained life estate.
(d) For each year a right to withdraw lapsed at the end of a year, it would be as if Arthur had transferred 2% of the corpus into trust and retained a life estate in the property transferred. Lifetime lapses occurred four years (years 1, 2, 3, and 5), thus for these years 8% of the trust is included. In the last year, the entire 7% lapse is included because there is no 5% shelter for lapses at death. So the total of 15% times the value of the trust at his death is included in his estate. Note that the adjusted taxable gifts become zero even though gift tax returns were filed. This is because adjusted taxable gifts do not include gifts that end up being included in the donor's gross estate.

17. (a) Estate tax: Frank's gross estate will include $280,000 under Section 2035(a), i.e., the three-year rule applicable to transfers of life insurance. Since the proceeds go to his wife, there should be a marital deduction of $280,000. If gift tax was paid on the original gift, grossing up would be necessary.
(b) Gift tax: Frank made a taxable gift of $15,000 ($25,000 gift value minus the annual exclusion). However, since it was then included in Frank's estate the adjusted taxable gift would be zero for estate tax purposes. At Frank's death, Sam made a taxable gift to Frank's widow (Sam's mom) of $270,000.

19. Because of the rule that money transferred into a joint bank account is an incomplete gift we do need to know the source of the funds to answer this question. If Karen and Lindsay both put the same amount into the account, then no gift has occurred because there is no transfer between them, each owning the same interest before and after the purchase. However, if one of them put in more than the other, then the purchase is a withdrawal and a gift occurs, e.g., Karen was the sole source of funds, the purchase would be a gift from her to Lindsay worth $22,000.

21. There is a "nine months" connection. A disclaimer must be made within nine months of an interest being created, hence for an inheritance it generally starts with the death of the person leaving his or her estate. The estate tax return must be filed within nine months of the death. The difference is that one can get an extension to file an estate tax return but one cannot get an extension to make a disclaimer.

23. (a) Hanna may be deemed today to have made a gift to the children of the remainder interest in her property. At Francisco's death, the transfer provisions became irrevocable for Hanna, since at that moment Francisco, who was one of the parties to the agreed upon will, is no longer able to revoke them. Thus, the provisions of the will are now binding on Hanna. In fact, some jurisdictions such as Illinois would consider Hanna's interest to be simply a life estate, which would deny the marital deduction in Francisco's estate and make Hanna obligated to conserve the property for the benefit of the children.[38] Since Hanna's gift is not one of a present interest, it would not qualify for the annual exclusion. For these reasons, joint and mutual wills are not recommended by estate planners.

(b) If they had an enforceable contract not to change these wills, the answer would be essentially the same. The will in part a, in effect, became an irrevocable, enforceable contract at the moment of Francisco's death.

25. (a) Nick's basis was $1,000,000. (b) new basis: $1,000,000 + $680,000 * ($1,511,000/$2,511,000) = $1,409,192. (c) FMV at date of death, $2,511,000.

27. (a) This being investment stock, allocation should be made right after all assets that can be depreciated have received as much as is allowed. (b) If the estate plans to sell the home soon, it can take advantage of § 121's non-recognition of $250,000 in gain so it might be a waste to allocate any additional basis to it. (c) If the family plans to sell this item soon, then basis should be allocated to this. If they plan to keep it in the family indefinitely, then allocate first to other assets.

29. (a) Not a gift. Loraine's powers to change the beneficiary and permit the policy to lapse means that son received only a (discretionary) contingent future interest, not a completed gift.
(b) Probably a gift of at least the remainder subject to tax at time of title transfer. Definitely a gift subject to taxation by the time she relinquished all retained rights.
(c) Never a gift subject to taxation, since revocable.
(d) A gift subject to taxation. Only present interests, if any, will qualify for the annual exclusion.
(e) $40,000 gift to son. It is the difference between the consideration given and the property received ($50,000 - $10,000).
(f) A gift to husband, but not subject to taxation. Ordinarily, no form 709 need be filed, and the gift is totally sheltered by the unlimited marital deduction.
(g) Assuming that Loraine owned the policy at her uncle's death, there is a gift of the proceeds to her daughter since at the moment of her uncle's death, Loraine could have named herself beneficiary.
(h) A gift of $29,000, subject to taxation. However, $21,000 would be excludable if for a qualified tuition payment. The remaining $8,000 should qualify for the annual exclusion.
(i) Gift subject to taxation will occur either on the deposit of the money or on the daughter's later withdrawal, depending on the law of Loraine's residence state.

ENDNOTES

1. Reg. § 25.2511-2(b).

2. IRC § 2501(a)(2), §2511(a).

3. IRC § 2516.

4. IRC § 2502(c).

5. IRC § 102(a).

6. *Diedrich* 457 U.S. 191 (1982).

7. IRC § 2522(a).

8. IRC § 2503(g).

9. IRC § 2523.

10. IRC § 2056(b)(7).

11. IRC § 2523(i).

12. IRC § 2503(e).

13. IRC § 2501(a)(5).

14. IRC § 2503(b).

15. IRC § 63(c)(5), §1(g)(7)(B)(i).

16. The Revenue Act of 1948.

17. IRC § 2513.

18. TAM 9128009; §2035(b).

19. IRC § 2514(b).

20. Reg. § 20.2041-3(d)(5), see also Reg. § 20.2041-3(d)(4).

21. Reg. § 25.2518-2(3).

22. Reg. § 25.2518-2 (d)(1); LR 9135043; LR 9135044; TAM 9208003.

23. Reg. § 25.2518-1(b).

24. TAM 88717003.

25. IRC § 453.

26. IRC § 1031.

27. IRC § 1033.

28. IRC § 1014(a).

29. Rev. Rul. 54-97, 1954-1 C.B. 113.

30. Gallenstein V. U.S. (6th Cir. 1992) 975 F. 2d 286.

31. IRC § 691(c)(3).

32. IRC § 1022(b).

33. IRC § 6018.

34. Thus, similar to the present law rule in IRC § 1014(b)(6), both the decedent's and the surviving spouse's share of community property could be eligible for a basis increase.

35. IRC § 1014(b)(2) and (3).

36. This is the same property the basis of which is stepped up to date-of-death fair market value under present law IRC § 1014(b)(2).

37. This is the same property the basis of which is stepped up to date-of-death fair market value under present law IRC § 1014(b)(3).

38. TAM 9023004; *Grimes v. Commissioner* 82-2 USTC (1988).

CHAPTER 8

Fiduciary Income Taxation

OVERVIEW

An estate or trust is a separate legal entity created to transfer property from one party to another. Since both are separate legal entities, each must file a tax return, Form 1041 (the Fiduciary Income Tax return), annually with the Internal Revenue Service (IRS) to report the trust's or estate's taxable events for the year. Fiduciary income taxation is unique because the fiduciary entity can be both a taxable entity and a conduit. As a taxable entity, the estate or trust must pay the required tax due within the prescribed time or be subject to various tax penalties. As a conduit, the entity reports to the beneficiaries how much of the taxable income is included on the beneficiaries' individual income tax returns. All of the entity's taxable events are classified and reported to the IRS by the entity.

The fiduciary is responsible for filing the decedent's final 1040 (the regular Income Tax return) and the 1041's for the trust or estate. If an amount is properly recorded on the final 1040, it is not reported on the first 1041. Death forms a wall between the two tax entities. Once a person dies, his or her tax-year ends; therefore, any item collected or paid after death is generally not includible on the deceased's final income tax return. Do not confuse income taxation and transfer taxation. These are two independent tax systems and certain items are taxable for both purposes.

FIDUCIARY ACCOUNTING

Before a fiduciary tax return can be prepared, the income and expenses, for book purposes, must be determined, which mandates an understanding of fiduciary accounting. Further, an understanding of fiduciary accounting is needed to comprehend the tax terminology of Subchapter J (Estates, Trusts, Beneficiaries, and Decedents) of the Internal Revenue Code (IRC). The IRC uses many concepts from fiduciary accounting in determining the taxation of income from a fiduciary entity.

Goals of Fiduciary Accounting

It has long been recognized that fiduciary accounting has a purpose different from financial or tax accounting, and that fiduciary accounting standards are not well defined. Unlike financial accounting, fiduciary accounting must rely on the entity's controlling document (e.g., the will or trust) and state law. A fiduciary entity results from the division of legal and beneficial interests in property. The fiduciary is responsible for managing assets placed under his or her care for the benefit of the beneficiaries. The managerial process places on the fiduciary various duties and obligations. Determining how well the fiduciary carried out his or her duty is one of the primary goals of fiduciary accounting. Through the preparation of certain reports, the fiduciary can describe to the beneficiaries the results of his or her activities, which allows the beneficiaries to judge whether the fiduciary has been a good steward. These reports should provide maximum clarity, full disclosure, and a complete description and explanation of all events during the accounting period. Fiduciary accounting uses the cash method for recording transactions.

Allocation Between Corpus and Income

Fiduciary accounting income (FAI) represents the claims of the income beneficiaries against the various inflows and outflows of the entity. Computing the exact amount each beneficiary is entitled to receive is part of the fiduciary's responsibilities. Fiduciary accounting rules provide the mechanism for the accurate allocation of assets between the beneficiaries.

Although most preparers would record inflows as income, this treatment would adversely affect the remaindermen. Furthermore, recording all outflows as expenses would adversely affect the income beneficiaries. Therefore, a system has been developed to protect the interests of both beneficiaries by allocating the inflows and outflows between income and corpus to compute the correct amounts available to the particular beneficiaries.

The *Uniform Principal and Income Act* (UPIA) was drafted to compute a fair allocation between income and corpus. The UPIA was revised in 1962 and a 1997 revision has been adopted by the National Conference of Commissioners on Uniform State Laws. Until a state makes the UPIA state law, it merely serves as a model of how income and corpus should be computed. Since most states have adopted some version of the UPIA, a review of the Act is helpful in understanding how items should usually be allocated. According to the UPIA, a fiduciary allocates receipts and expenditures using the following steps:

1. The governing document determines how the allocation is to be made;
2. If the document does not provide for the allocation, then state law controls; or
3. If neither allocates the particular item, the fiduciary (executor or trustee) is to use his or her best judgment according to what is reasonable and equitable in view of all beneficiaries' interests in the entity.

The grantor has considerable flexibility in determining how the income from the trust will be determined. When creating the trust, the grantor is allowed to state what items will be attributed to the income beneficiaries and what amounts should remain for the remaindermen. This latitude gives the grantor the ultimate responsibility for determining what property should go to which beneficiary. If the grantor wants every inflow to increase income and every outflow to reduce corpus, then his or her wishes should be followed, since it is the grantor's property that is being allocated. The intent of the grantor is paramount in the allocation of items between income and corpus. Due to the flexibility given the grantor, various items that are income/expense under financial accounting might not be so categorized under fiduciary accounting.

Two additional rules should be remembered while computing fiduciary accounting income:

1. Specific statutes control over general statutes, and
2. Directly related expenditures reduce the related type of receipt.

What an income beneficiary is entitled to receive from the trust is based on the computation of fiduciary accounting income. The income beneficiary is not allowed to receive any item that is not an income item. Unless there is undistributed income from a prior year, if the trust does not receive any income during the accounting period, absent a power to appoint corpus, the trustee is not permitted to make distributions to the income beneficiary.

> EXAMPLE 8 - 1. Under the UPIA, rental income is expressly stated to be income; therefore, the provisions applying to sole proprietorships cannot be used to allocate rental income between beneficiaries. Further, all rental expenses would be deducted from rental income in computing FAI.

Incorrect allocation results in the wrong beneficiary believing he or she has a claim to a given amount of assets. The fiduciary cannot show favoritism between income beneficiaries and remaindermen or between beneficiaries within the same classification. While the UPIA allows the grantor to give the trustee discretion in determining what amounts are allocated to income and corpus, the trustee's discretion is not as broad as that of the grantor. A court may interfere with the trustee's discretionary power in the event of fraud, misconduct or a clear abuse of discretion.[1] When discretion is given in the trust document, the trustee must use reasonable discretion in his or her allocations, basing them on the intent of the grantor when construing the entire trust instrument aided by the surrounding circumstances.[2] Terms like "absolute" or "full authority" in describing discretionary powers does not alter the trustee's responsibility to impartially act for the benefit of all beneficiaries.

Effect of Fiduciary Accounting Income on Taxable Income

On the income tax return, the fiduciary is allowed a deduction for income distributions. The amount of this deduction is based on the distributions allowed by the fiduciary entity (the trust or estate) determined under applicable state law. Once the appropriate distribution has been determined, the deductible amount may be limited by federal tax laws. This interrelationship between the Code and state law applies throughout this area of the law, so understanding the state law in this area is very important to determining the correct amount of trust accounting income.

Section 643(b) of the IRC states:

For purposes of this subpart and subparts B, C, and D, the term "income," when not preceded by the words "taxable," "distributable net," "undistributed net," or "gross," means the amount of income of the estate or trust for the taxable year determined under the terms of the governing instrument and applicable local law. Items of gross income constituting extraordinary dividends or taxable stock dividends which the fiduciary, acting in good faith, determines to be allocable to corpus under the terms of the governing instrument and applicable local law shall not be considered income.

Knowing how to compute FAI for the year is vital to preparation of a correct tax return. Furthermore, the taxation of the beneficiaries is based on the amount of distribution to which each is entitled, which in turn is controlled by the trust (or other fiduciary documents) or the state's principal and income laws.

FIDUCIARY INCOME TAXATION

The primary purpose of Subchapter J is to allocate income and deductions between the fiduciary entity and the beneficiaries. Form 1041 is the only tax form designed to serve in a twin capacity. A fiduciary entity can be a taxpaying entity and/or a conduit, flowing various income and expense items out to the beneficiaries. To complicate matters further, proper preparation of Form 1041 requires the preparer to integrate fiduciary accounting income into the computations, so the correct allocation can be determined.

Subchapter J: An Overview of Fiduciary Taxation

Throughout our discussions, always remember that Subchapter J was written not to compute taxable income specifically, but to allocate taxable income to the appropriate party, either the fiduciary entity or the beneficiary.

Fiduciary Taxable Income: § 641(b)

Section 641(b) is the key section used to compute the taxable income of the fiduciary entity. Section 641(b) states:

> *The taxable income of an estate or trust shall be computed in the same manner as in the case of an individual, except as otherwise provided in this part. The tax shall be computed on such taxable income and shall be paid by the fiduciary.*

Since a fiduciary entity is recognized as a separate legal entity, remembering that it is taxed like a person is difficult; however, unlike a partnership or a corporation, a fiduciary entity has been created for managing and eventually transferring property. Due to its unique characteristic, operating a fiduciary entity has more similarities with an individual and his or her handling of property than any other tax entity; therefore, it is logical that the IRC uses the tax rules applicable to individuals in computing the taxable income of a fiduciary entity. If the preparer cannot find a different treatment of any income or expense item in the IRC or regulations, he or she should report the item as one would on a Form 1040.

Tax Accounting Method

A fiduciary entity can use any tax accounting method available to individuals. Selection of an accounting method is made on the first Form 1041 filed. Once selected, any change in method is subject to the limitations found in IRC § 446. The choice of methods is not limited or determined by the accounting methods used by either the grantor, decedent or the beneficiaries.

Selecting a Fiduciary Income Tax Year

For trusts there is really no choice, they must use a calendar year.[3] Estates do not have the same restriction, so the estate's fiduciary can elect any year that ends on the last day of any month that is not more than 12 months from the date of death. An estate begins on the day after the person dies. Providing the first year does not end more than 12 months after the decedent died, the executor's choice of year-end will be acceptable. Beneficiaries must report on their income tax returns income from the fiduciary entity, based not on when the beneficiary received it, but rather as if it was all distributed to the beneficiary on the last day of the fiduciary entity's tax year.

EXAMPLE 8 - 2. Joe died March 23, 1999. The executor elected January 31, 2000, as the end of the estate's first taxable year. In November 1999, the executor made distributions. Any taxable income allocated to the beneficiaries, based on those distributions, is reported by them on their 2000 tax returns.

Regulation § 1.641(b)-3 holds that the IRS can terminate the estate for federal tax purposes and begin taxing the estate as a trust. If the period of administration is unreasonably prolonged,[4] even if a probate court sanctions the continued existence of the estate, the IRS will begin taxing the estate as a trust, if the Service determines that all of the acts generally conducted by an executor have been (or should have been) completed.[5] Taxing the estate as a trust requires the estate to adopt a calendar year-end,forcing it to file a short-year return. The provisions of §§ 446 and 481 (pertaining to adjustments that must be made when a taxpayer changes accounting methods and/or tax year) will be applied to the short-year return.

Section 645 was added for decedents dying after August 5, 1997. If both the executor of an estate and the trustee of a Qualified Revocable Trust (QRT) irrevocably elect, the QRT will be taxed as part of the estate for income tax purposes and not as a separate trust. A QRT is a trust or a portion thereof that was treated prior to the decedent's death as a grantor trust under IRC § 676. The election applies for the first two taxable years of an estate, if no Form 706 is required to be filed, and for the period ending six months after the final determination of federal estate tax liability, if a Form 706 was filed. Effectively, the trust is merged with the estate and all income and deductions are taxed under the income tax provisions that apply to estates. The election is included with the estate's first income tax return and a copy is attached to the trust's income tax return. The election is effective from the date of death.

The statement attached to the returns must identify itself as the election to include the QRT in the decedent's estate, specify the date of death and recite that the trust had been treated as a revocable grantor trust under § 676. It must include the names, addresses and identification numbers of the decedent, the estate and trust. Both the executor (or administrator, if the decedent died intestate) and one trustee must sign and date the statement. Multiple executors and trustees do not have to sign the statement, unless required by local law. If no probate is required, the trustee must sign the statement and note on the statement that no executor or administrator will be appointed. The estate must still obtain a tax identification number, but the trustee will sign every Form 1041 filed for the estate.[6]

An Overview of the Computations

Step one: Determine adjusted total income, using the tax rules for individuals, with certain modifications.

Step two: Determine the income distribution deduction.

Step three: Subtract the income distribution deduction (this amount is taxed to the beneficiaries) from adjusted total income.

Step four: The amount remaining is subject to tax at the fiduciary level.

The nature of income and of deductions is determined at the fiduciary level. If any income is distributed, it has the same characteristics it would have had if the fiduciary had retained it. Unless the trust document calls for some other allocation, amounts distributed to the beneficiaries consist of a proportional amount of every type of income received by the fiduciary, except capital gains are considered part of corpus and therefore are not generally allocated to beneficiaries unless the governing document requires it, or the entity terminates and all corpus (including, of course, the capital gains for the year) is distributed to the beneficiaries.

Exemptions. While a fiduciary entity is not allowed a standard deduction or a personal exemption, IRC § 642(b) allows an exemption depending on the nature of the entity. An estate is allowed a $600 deduction. If a trust must distribute all of its trust accounting income (TAI) currently, it is allowed a $300 deduction. All other trusts are allowed a $100 exemption.

> EXAMPLE 8 - 3. Trust Z's governing document requires Trust Z to distribute all of its TAI currently. For the year, Trust Z makes an additional $20,000 corpus distribution. Trust Z is allowed a $300 exemption.
>
> EXAMPLE 8 - 4. Trust X is not required to distribute all of its TAI currently, but the trustee makes actual distributions exceeding its current-year's TAI. Trust X is allowed a $100 exemption only, since the trust was not required to distribute 100% of its TAI.

Tax rates. Trusts and estates have their own tax rates. Notice how little taxable income is required for an estate or trust to make it into the highest tax bracket. Rates shown in the table below are th7ose in effect for 2003.

TABLE 8-1 Federal Income Tax Rates: Estates and Trusts - **2003**

Taxable Income		Base amount	+ percent	On excess over
Over	But not over			
$0	$1,900	$0	15.0%	$0
$1,900	$4,500	$285	27.0%	$1,900
$4,500	$6,850	$987	30.0%	$4,500
$6,850	$9,350	$1,692	35.0%	$6,850
$9,350	----	$2,567	38.6%	$9,350

Capital gains. The capital gain and capital loss rules that apply to individuals also apply to estates and trusts.

Filing requirements. Generally, a decedent's estate must file a Form 1041 if: (a) the estate has annual gross income of $600 or more, or (b) the estate has a beneficiary who is a nonresident alien. A trust must file a Form 1041 if: (a) the trust has any taxable income, or (b) the trust has gross income of $600 or more, or (c) the trust has a beneficiary who is a nonresident alien.

The return is due by the 15th of the fourth month following the entity's year-end and is filed with the Service center for the region in which the fiduciary resides or has its principal place of business. An extension can be obtained by filing Form 8736 for trusts and Form 2758 for estates. Additional time is obtained by filing Form 8800. Fiduciary returns may be filed electronically.

Form 56, Notice Concerning Fiduciary Relationship, should be filed when the trust or estate is created. Form SS-4 must be filed to obtain the fiduciary entity's employer identification number. Although it is called an employer identification number, it is the tax identification number used for income tax reporting, regardless of whether the fiduciary entity has employees.

Taxable Income of a Fiduciary Entity

As we consider some of the different types of income that trusts and estates might receive, we will compare the treatment of these various types of income in the hands of the fiduciary with how it is treated when received by an individual taxpayer.

Interest and dividend income. Individual income tax rules apply to a fiduciary entity in the reporting of interest and dividends. Interest that would have been tax-exempt to an individual is tax-exempt when received by a trust or estate. The fiduciary is not required to list separately the sources of dividend and interest income. Capital gain distributions received by the fiduciary entity are reported on Schedule D, Form 1041, just as capital gain distributions received by an individual are reported on Schedule D, Form 1040.

Net business and farm income. If an entity operates a sole-proprietorship or a farm, a Schedule C, Form 1040, Schedule C-EZ, Form 1040 or a Schedule F, Form 1040 must be prepared and attached to the Form 1041. The same rules that apply to individuals, when preparing the Schedule C, C-EZ, or F, apply to the entity.

Rents, royalties, partnerships, other estates and trusts, etc. All income from rents, royalties, partnerships, S corporations, other fiduciary entities, and Real Estate Mortgage Investment Conduits are recorded on Schedule E, Form 1040, and the net amount is reported on Form 1041. While preparing Schedule E, all directly related expenses are netted against the gross income from the particular activity. Only the net income is recorded on Form 1041. Interest, dividends, capital gains/losses and ordinary gains or losses from partnerships and other flow-through entities are shown on the appropriate lines on Form 1041 and not on Schedule E. Only estates, grantor trusts, qualified Subchapter S trusts, and Electing Small Business trusts can be S Corporation shareholders.

Net rental and royalty income. In reporting the net income or loss from rent and royalties, the fiduciary must attach Schedule E, Form 1040, to the Form 1041. The amounts shown on Schedule E reflect the total amount of income and expenses directly related to the property but only the entity's share of the depreciation or depletion.

Passive activities. Trusts and estates are subject to the passive activity loss rules and the at-risk rules. In determining the deductible amount of any loss, the at-risk rules are applied first and then the passive activity rules.

A passive activity is a trade or business in which the taxpayer does not materially participate. Based on the Senate Finance Report, the participation of the fiduciary, not the grantor, decedent or beneficiaries, is used to decide if the activity is passive. Currently, no regulations exist establishing a material participation standard for a fiduciary, to help in determining if the activity is active or passive.

EXAMPLE 8 - 5. Sue was a partner in a computer retail store. The partnership did not have a buy-sell agreement, so when she died, her share of the partnership was transferred to her estate. The executor does not participate in the store's operations. Even if Sue materially participated in the store's operations, her partnership interest will be treated as a passive activity in the hands of the executor and on the Form 1041.

Passive activities - rental real estate offset. A rule limiting the effect of the passive loss limitation rules is the rental real estate offset.[7] If an individual owner of rental real estate actively participates in the management of the rental property, he or she can offset against other income up to $25,000 of net losses. The offset is phased out once his or her modified adjusted gross income exceeds $100,000 and is eliminated once his or her modified adjusted gross income exceeds $150,000.

A trust is not allowed to use the offset. The characterization of property in the hands of the grantor does not carry over to the trust. Even if the trustee or a beneficiary actively participated in the management of the rental real estate, the trust is prevented from using the offset. The character of the loss is determined at the fiduciary level.

An estate is allowed to use the offset for taxable years ending within two years of the decedent's death, providing the decedent actively participated in the management of the rental property before his or her death. The offset available to the estate is reduced by how much of the offset is used when preparing the surviving spouse's tax return or the decedent's final 1040.[8]

Concluding remarks about passive activities. For partnership years after December 31, 1997, when a partner dies, the partnership's year closes with respect to the deceased partner. Instead of showing the entire distributive share on Form 1041, the deceased partner's share of partnership income, up to the date of death, is reported on the decedent's final 1040. All income after the decedent's death until the end of the partnership's taxable year is shown on the estate's income tax return. The same procedure for allocating S Corporation income can be used to allocate the partnership income between the Final 1040 and the first 1041. Passive losses are not deductible for alternative minimum tax purposes. Net losses from passive activities cannot be transferred to beneficiaries, but are suspended at the entity level, used by the entity to reduce future passive income and become basis adjustments at distribution of the activity. If a passive activity is sold by an entity, any suspended losses could become either a capital loss or an NOL. The rules applicable to allocation of capital losses or an NOL at termination would then govern the loss allocation.

Capital gains and losses. Capital gains and losses are reported on Schedule D, Form 1041. This is one of the few support schedules unique to fiduciary taxation. Parts I and II of Schedule D, Form 1041, are similar to Schedule D, Form 1040. The difference between the two forms is Part III of Schedule D, Form 1041. Part III reflects the allocation of gain or loss between the beneficiaries and the entity. All capital transactions are recorded on Part I and II, Form 1041, with the net gain or loss being reported on Form 1041. The sole purpose of Part III is to record the gain included in distributable net income (DNI). Rules covering allocation of capital gains to DNI are discussed later in the Chapter.

Sections 1211-1212 (limitations on capital losses and their carryover) and §§ 1221-1223 (general rules related to capital gains and losses) apply to trusts and estates, just as they do for individuals. Depending on what type of property created the long-term capital gain and the entity's tax rate, the tax rate on long-term capital gains can be 28%, 25%, 20%, 15% or 10%. Individual holding-period rules apply when determining if the capital gain or loss is either short or long-term, however one of those rules is that property received from a decedent is automatically long-term.[9] If the entity acquired the asset from a decedent, IRC § 1014 is followed to compute the entity's basis, while § 1015 is used if the asset was acquired in an inter vivos transfer.

If an entity has a net capital loss, the maximum deduction in a single tax year is $3,000, with no limitation on the length of time the loss is carried forward. Capital losses cannot be allocated to beneficiaries while the entity exists and capital losses never reduce DNI, just as capital gains normally do not increase it. Section 642(h)(1) provides that in the entity's final year, a net capital loss or loss carry forward can be allocated to the beneficiaries using the same rules applicable to allocation of an NOL.

IRC Section 643(e)(3) election. Normally, the entity recognizes no gain or loss when non-cash property is distributed to a beneficiary. Each year, the entity may elect, under IRC § 643(e)(3), to treat the distribution as a sale to the beneficiary and recognize any gain or loss on the appropriate schedule, subject to IRC § 267 related party rules. Generally, estates are not subject to the related party rules. If an election is made and the distributed property is a capital asset, the distribution is recorded as a sale of a capital asset, subject to the general capital transaction rules. The election must be made each year, applies to all non-cash distributions for the elected year and once elected cannot be revoked for that year without IRS consent. Unless the distribution meets the requirements of IRC § 663(a), i.e, it's a specific or pecuniary bequest, the distribution is included in any DNI allocation, subjecting the beneficiary to taxation.

EXAMPLE 8 - 6. Dottie's estate distributes 50 shares of stock to Helen, the residuary beneficiary of Dottie's estate. The estate's basis is $100 and the FMV of the stock is $150. If the IRC § 643(e)(3) election is made, the estate must recognize a gain of $50 on the "sale" of stock. Since the stock was received from a decedent, the gain will be long-term. The distribution draws out DNI to Helen.

EXAMPLE 8 - 7. If, by her will, Dottie had left the XYZ stock specifically to Helen, IRC § 663(a) would apply and no DNI would be drawn out by the distribution.

Ordinary gain or loss. When reporting ordinary gains or losses, the rules applicable to individuals also apply to fiduciaries. The fiduciary will prepare Form 4797 (Sales of Business Property) and report any ordinary gain or loss from the sale of property, other than capital assets, and from involuntary conversions, other than casualty or theft. If the entity sells a depreciated asset, Form 4797 is completed to compute the ordinary gain and any depreciation recapture. Gains from casualty and theft are also included on this form. Sales of business assets subject to IRC § 1231 are reported on this form, whether the property was owned by the entity or by a partnership in which the entity had an interest.

Deductions Allowed in Computing Taxable Income

Generally, the rules for individual taxpayers claiming a deduction carry over to fiduciary income taxes. However, there are some special rules concerning deductions for fiduciary income taxes, such as those that come into play when the fiduciary entity has tax-exempt income.

Interest expense. A fiduciary entity is allowed to deduct interest expense in the same manner as an individual.[10] The fiduciary must classify the interest according to type and then apply any special rules in determining if the interest is deductible. If the interest expense directly relates to a passive activity, trade or business, or other type of income, the interest should be deducted against the specific income type, not as a separate item. Personal interest (i.e., interest on a car loan) is not deductible. The main types of deductible indirect interest are: qualified residence interest and investment interest expenses (unless it is directly related to tax-exempt income).

Deductible interest owed at death can qualify as a deduction in respect of a decedent and becomes deductible by an estate or trust when paid. Interest accruing after the death of the decedent is subject to the double deduction rules under IRC § 642(g), which are discussed below. Only interest that the trust or estate is obligated to pay may be deducted.

Expenses related to tax-exempt income. No deduction is allowed for any expense attributable directly or indirectly to tax-exempt income.[11] On Form 1041, only the deductible share of such expenses are recorded. Form 1041 requires an allocation support schedule, showing how the figures were obtained and the gross amount of tax-exempt income. The purpose of allocating the expenses is to reduce the deductible expenses, so that only those related to taxable income are actually deducted.

Any expense directly related to taxable income can be fully deducted. If the fiduciary incurs $5,000 of rental expenses, these can be deducted in full. The problem occurs when the fiduciary incurs expenses associated with trust income as a whole. Most often these indirect expenses are nonbusiness expenses deductible under IRC § 212, e.g., trustee and attorney fees. Interest and taxes should be fully deductible, since they are deductible under specific IRC sections. The IRS and the courts paint a broad stroke when defining what is an indirect expense. The fiduciary must be prepared to defend his or her position if he or she excludes a particular indirect expense from reduction. If the trust or estate makes a distribution to a charity, the charitable contribution deduction must also be reduced, since the charity is deemed to receive part of the tax-exempt income.

Indirect expenses of the entity must be reduced by a proportionate share of the tax-exempt income. The fiduciary is allowed to use any reasonable method, based on the facts and circumstances.[12] However, two methods are provided for in the regulations. Under both methods, the net income or the gross income method, the fiduciary computes a ratio to figure out how much of the indirect expenses are not deductible.

With the *net income method*, the fiduciary computes the amount of gross FAI and then subtracts the expenses directly related to each particular income item. Then for each specific type of income, a ratio is computed, with the numerator being the net amount of that specific type of income and the denominator being the total net FAI.

With the *gross income method*, the fiduciary uses gross FAI as his or her denominator and gross income from the activity as his or her numerator. The only difference between the net income method and the gross income method is that with the gross income method directly related expenses are not subtracted before the allocation is made. Normally, direct expenses have a larger impact on taxable income; therefore, use of the gross income method will increase deductible expenses, since a smaller amount of the indirect expenses is being allocated to tax-exempt income.

Unless capital gains are included in FAI or in DNI, none of the expenses are allocated to capital gains, since expenses cannot be allocated against income that is excluded from DNI. If the amount of expenses directly attributable to tax-exempt income exceeds the total amount of tax-exempt income, the excess cannot be allocated to taxable income.[13]

EXAMPLE 8 - 8. Trust Z has rental income of $15,000, dividends of $10,000 and tax-exempt income of $5,000. The Trust had rental expenses of $4,000 and accounting fees of $2,000. Using both methods, accounting fees would be allocated as follows:

Fiduciary accounting income:

	Gross	Net
Rental income	$15,000	$11,000
Dividends	$10,000	$10,000
Tax-exempt income	$5,000	$5,000
Trust accounting income	$30,000	$26,000

Allocation of accounting fees: Net income method

($11,000/$26,000)	X	$2,000	=	$846
($10,000/$26,000)	X	$2,000	=	769
($5,000/$26,000)	X	$2,000	=	385
		Total		$2,000

Allocation of accounting fees: Gross income method

($15,000/$30,000)	X	$2,000	=	$1,000
($10,000/$30,000)	X	$2,000	=	667
($5,000/$30,000)	X	$2,000	=	333
		Total		$2,000

Under the gross income method, only $333 of accounting fees would not be deducted, whereas the net income method results in $385 not being deducted.

Depreciation. If a fiduciary entity owns qualified property, it is allowed to deduct depreciation, depletion and amortization (after this called depreciation), using the same rules applicable to individuals. Estates and trusts are not allowed an IRC § 179 deduction. The fiduciary selects the appropriate depreciation method, prepares Form 4562 and attaches it to Form 1041 to show the total amount of deductible depreciation. While the deductible amount is computed at the fiduciary level, the fiduciary entity may not be eligible to take any depreciation deduction. Depreciation must be apportioned between the entity and its beneficiaries under special rules. Deductible depreciation allocated to the entity from a partnership, trust, or estate is allocated under the same rules. The asset's basis is computed using the rules in § 1014, for testamentary transfers, or § 1015, for inter vivos transfers.

If the entity is entitled to take all or part of the deduction, depreciation directly related to a particular activity is reported on the specific support schedule (Schedules C, E or F), while all other depreciation is reported on Line 15a, Form 1041. If the entity is not entitled to a depreciation deduction, no deduction is recorded on Form 1041 or on any support schedule. Tax depreciation not reported on Form 1041 is allocated to the income beneficiaries and is reflected on their Schedule K-1s, Lines four b, c, d or Lines five b, c, d.

Depreciation apportionment rules. Apportionment of depreciation is covered in IRC § 642(e), which states:

An estate or trust shall be allowed the deduction for depreciation and depletion only to the extent not allowable to beneficiaries under §§ 167(d) and 611(b).

Section 167(d) applies to depreciation, while § 611(b) pertains to depletion. The general rule for allocating depreciation between the entity and its beneficiaries is:

1. To the extent there is a reserve for depreciation for FAI purposes, allocate the tax depreciation to the entity, and
2. If tax depreciation exceeds accounting depreciation or if there is no depreciation reserve for accounting purposes, allocate the tax depreciation between the entity and the beneficiaries based on the allocation of FAI between the parties.[14]

The key to apportioning the tax depreciation between the entity and its beneficiaries is determined by how depreciation is handled for FAI purposes. Whether a reserve exists for FAI purposes is based on the terms of the document and state law. Generally, a reserve exists when FAI is reduced by some amount of depreciation. The fiduciary may reduce FAI for depreciation when the entity operates a sole proprietorship or general partnership and when the document requires a depreciation deduction or the fiduciary makes an improvement that would be depreciated under generally accepted accounting principles (GAAP). Depending on the state, income from rental property and natural resources may be reduced by depreciation. To the extent FAI is reduced by depreciation, the tax depreciation is allocated to the entity.

EXAMPLE 8 - 9. Trust X owns a drug store, which is operated as a sole proprietorship. GAAP depreciation equals $10,000 and net income from the store is $50,000. If tax depreciation is equal to or less than $10,000, all of the tax depreciation will be reported on Schedule C, Form 1041. If tax depreciation is $15,000, the extra $5,000 is allocated under the set of rules discussed next.

When tax depreciation exceeds the reserve or there is no reserve for FAI purposes, tax depreciation follows FAI. Any beneficiary who receives FAI receives the "excess" tax depreciation also. For accounting purposes, a charity is treated as any other beneficiary, so if the charity receives FAI, the charity would receive its share of tax depreciation, too. If no reserve exists and the entity is required to distribute all the FAI, the beneficiaries would be entitled to the entire depreciation deduction, and no depreciation deduction would be taken on Form 1041.

EXAMPLE 8 - 10. Trust Y has rental property. Under state law, no depreciation is allowed and the document is silent concerning a reserve. Since FAI is not reduced by depreciation, the allocation of tax depreciation follows the allocation of FAI. For tax purposes, rental depreciation is $20,000. FAI is $50,000. By the terms of the trust, FAI was allocated as follows: Allan - 50%; Bea - 25%; Charity - 10% and Trust Y - 15%. The tax depreciation would be allocated as follows: Allan - $10,000; Bea - $5,000; Charity - $2,000 and Trust Y - $3,000. Trust Y would file Form 4562 (Depreciation and Amortization) to report the $20,000 of depreciation and it would include $3,000 on Schedule E, Form 1041. The depreciation allocated to Allan and Bea would be recorded on their Schedules K-1, Line five b and the trustee would inform the Charity of the $2,000 depreciation allocation. Charities do not receive a Schedule K-1, since Schedule K-1 is reserved for beneficiaries who receive distributable net income.

EXAMPLE 8 - 11. Trust Z owns rental property. For FAI, depreciation of $10,000 is deducted. Tax depreciation is $25,000. By the terms of the trust, FAI is allocated as follows: Art - 60%; Beth - 30% and Trust Z - 10%. The first $10,000 of tax depreciation must be allocated to Trust Z. Of the remaining $15,000, Art receives $9,000, Beth $4,500 and Trust Z $1,500. On Schedule E, Form 1041, Trust Z would report depreciation of $11,500 and on Art's Schedule K-1, Line five b, $9,000 would be reported while on Beth's Schedule K-1, Line five b, $4,500 would be recorded.

The existence or absence of a reserve for FAI does not alter the amount of deductible depreciation for tax purposes. All an accounting reserve does is determine who gets the deduction. If the depreciation is directly allocable to the beneficiaries, the depreciation is ignored for DNI purposes and has no impact on its computation or allocation. To the extent depreciation is deductible on Form 1041, depreciation reduces adjusted total income, which reduces the DNI allocated to the beneficiaries. Any tax adjustment for depreciation for alternative minimum tax purposes is allocated under the same rules.

An exception for depletion. Under fiduciary accounting rules, 27.5% of income from natural resources, other than timber, must be allocated to corpus. Several courts have labeled this allocation as a set aside to fund a depletion reserve to protect the corpus.[15] As a reserve, the tax depletion is first allocated to the reserve. Since the amount allocated under fiduciary accounting (27.5%) is greater than the allowable tax percentage depletion (15%), all the tax depletion should be allocated to the entity. Timber has no fixed percentage, but does require an allocation of inflows to corpus.

> EXAMPLE 8 - 12. Trust Y owns oil royalty property. In 2001, Trust Y had $10,000 of royalty income and $1,500 of tax depletion. Although the trust required all FAI to be distributed, the entire $1,500 of tax depletion would be reported on Schedule E, since the $1,500 (tax depletion) is less than the $2,750 of royalty income (accounting reserve) allocated to corpus. The beneficiary would receive a distribution of $7,250 with no depletion allocation. Trust Y would report the entire $10,000 less the $1,500 depletion, but of the net $8,500, $7,250 would be taxable to the beneficiaries, leaving $1,250 taxable to Trust Y.

Taxes. A trust or estate can deduct any taxes allowed under IRC § 164. These taxes normally include: state, local and foreign income taxes and property taxes. Sales tax is not deducted, but it is added to the cost-basis of the item purchased. If the taxes are attributable to a specific type of income, they should be deducted in arriving at the net income from that income type. If any generation-skipping transfer (GST) tax is paid on income distributions, the entity may deduct these taxes, providing they were not deducted in determining the GSTT.[16] Other federal income, excise, and custom taxes are not deductible.

Double deductions. Section 642(g) provides that estate expenses under IRC §§ 2053 or 2054 can be deducted on Form 1041. This is allowed only if the expenses were not deducted on Form 706 and a statement waiving the right to deduct the expenses on Form 706 should be filed with Form 1041. This election is not an "all or nothing" election. The fiduciary has the discretion to deduct all, part, or none of the expenses on Form 1041 or on Form 706. These expenses do not include deductions in respect of a decedent, which can be deducted on both returns. Deductions in respect of a decedent (DRD) are expenses that accrued prior to the decedent's death such that they are deductible as debts on the estate tax return (Form 706) and, when paid, are deductible as expenses on the fiduciary income tax return (Form 1041). Property taxes that became a lien before the decedent's death and were paid by the executor are an example of a deduction in respect of a decedent. Since the top income tax rate is 39.6%, an additional computation must be made to decide where the greater tax savings can be achieved. Due to the unified credit, the first dollar of taxable estate will be taxed at 37%. The marginal estate tax rate above $3,000,000 is 55% and within the surcharge "bubble" it is 60%. As was discussed in Chapter 5, the surcharge bubble refers to the extra 5% tax that is presently applied to estates between $10,000,000 and $17,184,000 (the point at which the surcharge "recaptures" the taxes saved by the lower rates as compared to what would have been paid if there was a flat 55% rate.

Although § 2053 expenses can be deducted on either the estate or income tax return, do not forget that certain § 2053 expenses reduce the marital and charitable deductions, so an election to take these expenses on the income tax return could cause a taxable estate to result. Estate transmission expenses are deemed paid from the gross estate, reducing assets that can be distributed to the surviving spouse. Deducting these expenses on the income tax return prevents a reduction of the gross estate and with a smaller marital deduction, a taxable estate arises.

Charitable deduction. Section 642(c) details the rules covering a permitted charitable contribution deduction, and computation of the allowed deduction is recorded on Schedule A, Form 1041 and carried over to Line 13, Form 1041. Section 642(c) states:

> *"...there shall be allowed as a deduction in computing its taxable income...any amount of the gross income, without limitation, which pursuant to the terms of the governing instrument is, during the taxable year, paid for a purpose specified in § 170(c)...."*

Before a deduction is allowed, certain requirements must be met. These requirements are:

1. The will or trust document must authorize the contribution,
2. The amount of deduction is limited by gross income, and
3. Only those amounts actually paid during the year or during the following year may be deducted.[17]

For purposes of the deduction, gross income includes any amount earned on the trust's or estate's assets, any IRD, and any current-year capital gains paid, permanently set aside, or credited to the charity. All other amounts paid from corpus or tax-exempt income are not deductible. Specific and pecuniary bequests and non-cash contributions are customarily paid out of corpus, so no deduction is allowed. The amount the charity actually receives is determined by FAI and the document, so the actual distribution may be less than gross income. Only amounts actually paid can be deducted, even if gross income is higher. Of the amount distributed to the charity, it consists of every type of FAI received by the entity, subject to the special allocation rules. If the entity has tax-exempt income or depreciation, then these items must be allocated to the charity, just like to any other beneficiary.

The entity must actually distribute the property to the charity before a deduction is allowed. A special election can be made to treat distributions made during the following year as made in the current year, so the entity is allowed a current-year deduction. If the fiduciary so elects, any payment made after the close of the current taxable year (year one), and before the close of the second taxable year (year two), may be treated as paid in year one for tax purposes. The election is irrevocable and must be made in the timely filed tax return for year two (including extensions). Failure to make the actual distribution before the due date of the year one tax return will require the fiduciary to forego the deduction and file an amended return for year one once the distribution is made during year two. This election is unique for charitable contributions and is separate from the 65-day rule.[18]

> EXAMPLE 8 - 13. Trust X is allowed to distribute 10% of TAI to the local cancer society. The trustee cannot compute the available deduction until after the close of the current year (2000). The trustee can elect to treat any distribution made at any time during 2001 as made in 2000, so he can get a charitable deduction for 2000.

Estates and pre-October 9, 1969, irrevocable trusts are allowed a deduction for amounts permanently set aside for future payment to a charity. While funds do not have to be placed in a separate account, some bookkeeping entry must be made to show the set-aside. For an amount to be considered permanently set aside, there must exist no more than a remote possibility that another beneficiary could receive the funds.

> EXAMPLE 8 - 14. Estate Y requires the executor to accumulate 50% of each year's capital gains for future distribution to Big Brothers. In 2000, Estate Y had capital gains of $10,000, so Estate Y can take a charitable deduction of $5,000 in 2000, even though the $5,000 might not be distributed for several years.

No deduction is allowed unless the document allows the entity to make a charitable contribution. Where the document does not provide for a charitable contribution, any payment made by the fiduciary is nondeductible and could subject the fiduciary to a surcharge. If a beneficiary authorizes the fiduciary to make the beneficiary's payment to a charity, the beneficiary will be allocated the income and take any charitable deduction on his or her individual Form 1040. The law is uncertain on whether a fiduciary entity can deduct charitable contributions made by a partnership or S corporation and passed through to the entity. Unless the document specially grants the fiduciary the authority to make charitable contributions, there appears to be no authority for allowing a deduction.

Administration expenses. Administration expenses unique to the operation of a fiduciary entity are deductible to the extent they are:

1. reasonable in amount
2. incurred in the ordinary and necessary administration of the entity
3. not allocable to the production or collection of tax-exempt income
4. not deducted for federal estate tax purposes.[19]

Administrative expenses that would fit this definition are:

1. fiduciary fees and commissions
2. attorney fees
3. accounting fees including fees for the preparation of any tax returns and for both court and informal accounting
4. miscellaneous administrative expenses including court costs, fiduciary bonds, appraisals, advertising, investment advisory fees etc.
5. non-business casualty and theft losses

Administrative expenses directly related to the production of income are not deductible on an estate tax return (i.e., the 706). Since income earned after death is not included in the gross estate, expenses related to the income are not deductible for estate tax purposes.

Net operating loss (NOL). In fiduciary accounting, losses from business operations are added to corpus, resulting in no loss carry back or carry forward. Further, a loss from operations does not reduce the FAI available for distribution to the beneficiaries.

EXAMPLE 8 - 15. Trust X operates a drug store as a sole proprietorship. In 2000, the store had a net loss of $5,000. The FAI for 2000 would not be reduced by any of the $5,000 loss. If the drug store has net income in 2001 of $3,000, the entire

$3,000 would be allocated to FAI, and FAI would not be reduced by any part of the prior year's loss.

For tax purposes NOLs create a different tax situation. Estates and trusts are allowed a net operating loss deduction under § 172.[20] The entity's NOL is computed following individual income tax rules, except for two main changes. An NOL cannot be increased by the charitable contribution deduction or the income distribution deduction. If a trust or estate has an NOL, the NOL must be carried back two years, unless waived, and carried forward 20 years. Except in the entity's final year, an NOL can only be used by the trust or estate. If an NOL exists in the termination year, the NOL is allocated to the corpus beneficiaries, who may use it on their personal returns and only carry forward any unused portion. The beneficiaries do not get a new 20-year carry forward period. In computing and determining the tax treatment of an NOL, only the rules under §§ 172, 642(d) and 642(h)(1) apply. Any other rules applicable to losses do not apply.

Personal expenses. Fiduciary entities may not deduct personal expenses. Personal expenses are expenses not associated with the management, conservation or maintenance of property, e.g., interest/expense on the decedent's credit cards paid by the executor. If a house is used as the personal residence of a beneficiary, the expenses related to the house, like utilities, repairs and yard maintenance, are not deductible. Qualified residence interest and property taxes would remain deductible. A beneficiary's temporary use of a house, before the sale or disposition of the house, should not disallow the deductions, since the expenses are of an investment nature and not personal.

Section 67(a) subjects trusts and estates to the limitation on deductibility of miscellaneous itemized deductions. Only to the extent these deductions exceed 2% of adjusted gross income are they deductible. The expenses must be reduced by tax-exempt income before applying the 2% floor. Section 67(b) lists various expenses that are not subject to the limitation and include the charitable deduction, interest expense, taxes, and deductions in respect of a decedent. Examples of expenses subject to the limitation are: safe deposit box rental, collection fees, and appraisal fees.

Section 67(e)(1) makes a special exception for fiduciary entities. Deductions, which are incurred concerning the administration of an estate or trust, which would not have been incurred if the property were not held in the trust or estate, are not subject to the 2% floor. Most administrative expenses should qualify for the exception; however, the IRS and the Tax Court have applied a harsh definition as to which expenses can be excluded. In the 1993 case, *O'Neill, Jr. v Commissioner*,[21] the Sixth Circuit overruled the Tax Court and held that investment advisory expenses are not subject to the 2% floor. In the *O'Neill* case, nonprofessional trustees incurred substantial advisory fees in the management of a $4.5 million trust. Since state law placed a fiduciary duty on the trustees to manage the trust corpus properly, the trustees argued that the advisory expenses were unique to the trust's administration. The IRS and the Tax Court found that investment advisory fees were not unique to the administration of a fiduciary entity, since individuals incurred investment advisory fees, also. Only those expenses not payable by individuals could be unique to a fiduciary entity and subject to the exception. The Sixth Circuit disagreed. The Court accepted the trustees' arguments and found that advisory fees incurred by nonprofessional trustees are unique to the administration of a trust. The IRS has indicated it will not follow *O'Neill* outside the Sixth Circuit.[22]

The Court of Federal Claims, in *Mellon Bank, N.A. v. U.S.*,[23] has disagreed with the Sixth Circuit and has ruled in favor of the IRS. According to the Court of Federal Claims, § 67(e) establishes two distinct prerequisites for costs to qualify for exclusion from the 2% floor:

1. The amounts must be paid or incurred in connection with the administration of the trust; and
2. The expenses must be those that would not have been incurred if the property were not held in trust.

The first prerequisite is met if the cost is associated with the administration of the trust. Unless an expense is a disguised bequest, any expense paid by the fiduciary should be connected to its administration. The second prerequisite requires an evaluation of the circumstances that would have resulted had the assets not been placed in trust. If the expenses would have been incurred regardless of whether the assets were in trust or not, then the 2% floor applies. The trustee argued, and *O'Neill* held, that costs incurred in performance of the trustee's fiduciary obligations under state law satisfied the second prerequisite, regardless of whether identical costs for identical services would have been incurred in a non-fiduciary context had the funds not been in trust. The Court of Federal Claims rejected this interpretation of the second prerequisite.

Under the Court's analysis, the second prerequisite focuses on the independent issue of whether individual investors routinely incur similar costs. The absence of a legal obligation to incur particular costs does not mean that an individual investor would not reasonably be expected to have incurred similar costs. The practical effect of the *O'Neill* opinion was to absorb the second prerequisite into the first one, because all fees caused by fiduciary duties are necessary fees incurred with the administration of a trust. Certain types of services, such as investment advice and account management, would be employed regardless of whether the property was held in trust or held by an individual. It is inconsistent, within the plain meaning of the statute, to allow full deductibility of such costs simply because the trustee's fiduciary duties required the trust to incur those costs. The fact that the costs could be characterized as trustee fees did not establish that the costs would not have been incurred in a non-trust context.

With the rejection of the Sixth Circuit's analysis of § 67(e) by the Court of Federal Claims, the issue of whether the 2% floor applies is back on the table. The analysis by the Court in *Mellon Bank* will subject more expenses to the 2% floor. Effectively, if a cost is similar to ones incurred by individuals on similar assets, the 2% floor will apply. By holding that *O'Neill* did not properly apply the second prerequisite, the Court has created a split in the circuits.

Adjusted gross income (AGI) of a fiduciary entity is computed in the same manner as it is for an individual. Section 67(e) allows the fiduciary to deduct all administrative expenses, the income distribution deduction, and the entity's exemption in arriving at AGI. The instructions to Form 1041 contain an algebraic formula to compute AGI if DNI is less than the income distributed. If the amount distributed is less than DNI, the instructions recommend using the income distributed to compute AGI; however, the distribution deduction must be reduced by any amount attributed to tax-exempt income.

Funeral and medical expenses. Funeral and medical expenses deserve special attention because funeral expenses can only be deducted on the estate tax return and medical expenses can never be deducted on Form 1041. Medical expenses paid within one year of death can be deducted on the decedent's final return or on the estate tax return. An election is filed with the decedent's final return electing to take the medical deductions against income. If the medical expenses are deducted on the decedent's final 1040, they are subject to the 7.5% adjusted gross income limitation.

THE EFFECT OF TRANSFERS AND DISTRIBUTIONS

In this section, we consider the income tax implications of making asset transfers to and from estates, trusts, and beneficiaries. Generally, non-cash distributions (in-kind distributions) are subject to the same rules as cash distributions. The beneficiaries must include in income distributions of property if DNI is allocated to the distribution. This results in the beneficiaries having to pay tax, though they might not have the cash. Further, the type of income that comprises DNI determines the taxability of the distribution, not the type of property received as a distribution.

General Rule for Property Transfers

If the transfer of property is not considered a sale by the fiduciary entity (§ 643(e)(3) election or pecuniary bequest), the basis of the property in the hands of the beneficiary is the entity's adjusted basis in the property immediately before distribution.[24] The beneficiary can tack the entity's holding period to his holding period. The entity can only consider the lesser of the property's basis or its FMV when computing the income distribution deduction. This can result in the beneficiary having a basis greater than her taxable income.

Transfers Subject to IRC § 663(a)

If the transfer qualified under Section 663(a)(1), the beneficiary does not have any taxable income and the entity has no distribution deduction, since this type of distribution does not qualify for the distribution deduction. The beneficiary's basis is the entity's basis, if the beneficiary sells the property at a gain, or the FMV of the property at distribution, if the property is sold at a loss.[25] The entity's holding period is tacked onto the beneficiary's holding period.

Transfers Subject to an IRC § 643(e)(3) Election

If the entity elects to treat the distribution as a sale under § 643(e)(3), the beneficiary's basis equals the entity's basis immediately before distribution, adjusted for any gain or loss recognized. Since the entity's basis is used to determine the beneficiary's basis, the beneficiary can probably tack on the entity's holding period. The entity can consider the FMV of the property when computing the income distribution deduction.

> EXAMPLE 8 - 16. Trust X has DNI of $50,000. Trust X distributes stock valued at $50,000 to June. The trust's adjusted basis in the stock is $10,000. Effect of no election: (1) No gain on transfer; (2) DNI is reduced by $10,000, so trust pays tax on $40,000; and (3) June has income of $10,000 and her basis is $10,000. If the election is made: (a) trust has gain of $40,000; (b) DNI is reduced to zero; the gain does not increase DNI and the distribution deduction is increased to $50,000; and (c) June has income of $50,000 and her basis is $50,000.

Transfers to Satisfy a Pecuniary Bequest

A capital gain or loss is recognized when a trust or estate transfers property to satisfy a pecuniary gift, bequest, or claim, which is defined as a required distribution of a specific sum of money or specific property. The gain or loss is determined by the difference between the FMV of the property on the date of transfer and the entity's basis in the property. The entity is considered to have distributed cash and the beneficiary to have turned around and bought the property.[26] If the distribution does not meet the requirements of § 663(a), the gain might be included in any DNI allocation, subjecting the beneficiary to taxation. If the distribution does meet the requirements of § 663(a), or the gain cannot be included in DNI, the entity must pay taxes on the gain without any distribution deduction. The beneficiary's basis is the FMV of the property at the time of distribution and he must begin a new holding period. The distribution deduction equals the FMV of the property, providing sufficient DNI exists.

> EXAMPLE 8 - 17. Norm's will requires a $10,000 distribution to Keith. Instead of distributing cash, the executor distributes stock valued at $10,000. The estate's basis in the stock is $7,000. The estate must report a $3,000 long-term gain on its Form 1041, but can include the full $10,000 when computing the income distribution deduction. Keith's basis in the stock is $10,000 and he must hold the stock for 12 months before being eligible for long-term gain treatment on sale. The estate must pay taxes on the gain, since it cannot be included in DNI.

> EXAMPLE 8 - 18. Norm's estate has estate accounting income (EAI) of $15,000. The executor decides to distribute a car valued at $15,000, instead of cash, to Ann. Since EAI is not a pecuniary bequest, no sale occurs, unless § 643(e)(3) is elected. If the car's basis is $9,000, Ann's basis is $9,000 and she can tack the estate's holding period to hers on any future sale. When computing the income distribution deduction, the executor must use $9,000.

Transfers of Passive Activities

There are some fairly specific rules concerning transfers of passive activity investments between the grantor/decedent and the fiduciary entity and between the fiduciary entity and the beneficiaries. These rules are in addition to the rules that apply to in-kind property distributions.

Lifetime transfers from a grantor to a trust. If a grantor has any suspended losses when he or she transfers the investment to a trust, the losses are added to the basis. While the grantor is treated as disposing of the asset, according to the passive activity rules, he or she cannot recognize any of the suspended losses on his or her personal return.[27]

EXAMPLE 8 - 19. Harry owns a partnership interest in an office building. His basis in the partnership is $100,000; however, he has $20,000 in suspended losses. The trust's basis in the partnership will be $120,000, and Harry cannot use the suspended losses in the future to reduce his passive income. The trust cannot use the $20,000 in suspended losses to include its depreciation deduction.

Transfers from a decedent to an estate. The death of a person is treated as a distribution of his or her entire interest in the asset, so on the decedent's final return, the suspended losses can be used to reduce other income, subject to one limitation. The recipient's basis of property received at death is its fair market value (FMV) at date of death.[28] When suspended losses exceed the increase in basis, the excess suspended loss (the suspended loss less the increase in basis) can be deducted on the decedent's final return only.[29]

EXAMPLE 8 - 20. Mary died on November 12, 2001. Her basis in a partnership was $20,000. The FMV of the partnership interest was $50,000. Mary had $100,000 of suspended losses. On Mary's final return, $70,000 of the losses may be deducted. ($50,000 - $20,000 = $30,000; $100,000 - $30,000 = $70,000)

EXAMPLE 8 - 21. Martin died on December 31, 2000. His basis in a partnership was ($200,000). The FMV of the partnership interest was $30,000. His suspended losses totaled $150,000. None of the suspended losses will be recognized on Martin's final Form 1040 and the estate's basis will be $30,000. Since the increase in basis, $230,000, exceeded the total suspended losses, neither Martin nor the estate can deduct the losses.

Transfers from trust/estate to a beneficiary. Transfers of passive activities to a beneficiary are treated in the same manner as transfers from a grantor to a trust. Any suspended losses incurred by the entity are added to the basis and the entity is prevented from using the losses in the future.[30] If the distribution of a passive activity by an executor is considered a sale under Reg. § 1.1014-4 (e.g., a distribution of property rather than cash to satisfy a pecuniary bequest), the estate can use the suspended losses on Form 1041. The related party rules of § 267 prevent a trustee from utilizing the suspended losses by making a similar "sale" distribution.[31]

INCOME DISTRIBUTION DEDUCTION AND THE TAXATION OF BENEFICIARIES

As said earlier in the chapter, the main focus of Subchapter J is to allocate taxable income between the fiduciary entity and the beneficiaries. The trust or estate receives a deduction based on the taxable income distributed to the beneficiaries during the year. The deductible amount is computed on Schedule B, Form 1041 and recorded on Line 18, Form 1041. Since a fiduciary entity can distribute income and corpus, depending on the terms of the fiduciary document, an amount called distributable net income (DNI) must be calculated.[32] DNI limits the amount of taxable income allocated to the beneficiaries. Any amount distributed greater than DNI will be considered either undistributed net income (UNI) or corpus.

Key Definitions

Simple trust. The IRC establishes two types of trusts for calculating the income distribution deduction. Sections 651-652 are used to compute the distribution deduction for simple trusts and §§ 661-663 are used to compute the deduction for complex trusts. The terms "simple" and "complex" are not found in the Code, but are used throughout the regulations. The definition of a trust can change from year to year; however, in its final year, it will always be complex.

Section 651 defines a simple trust as a trust that:

1. is required to distribute all of its trust accounting income (TAI) currently,
2. no distributions used for charitable purposes, and
3. allows no distributions in excess of TAI for the year.

The trust document determines if the first two requirements are met. The word income in § 651(a)(1) refers to trust accounting income.[33] If the document requires the trustee to distribute all the current-year's TAI, the beneficiaries are deemed to have received the TAI for taxation purposes, whether it is actually distributed or not. If the document does not require all the TAI to be distributed currently, the trust cannot be classified as a simple trust, even if the trust actually distributes all of its TAI for the year.

A simple trust is limited in the type of distributions it can make. If the trust could have made a distribution that would qualify for a charitable deduction, the trust cannot be classified as a simple trust, even if no charitable distributions are actually made.[34] Further, if the trust makes distributions greater than TAI, it cannot be a simple trust. Although corpus distributions are allowed under the trust document, the trust will be a simple trust, unless distributions greater than current-year's TAI are actually made. In years the trust does not make any corpus distributions, it will be a simple trust, and in years it makes a corpus distribution it will be a complex trust.

A simple trust is allowed a deduction for the TAI distributed limited by DNI.[35] The amount of the deduction must be reduced by any amount not included in gross income less any applicable expenses. This requires the fiduciary to reduce the available deductions by any amount of tax-exempt income, net of related expenses, included in TAI.

Complex trusts. If a trust does not meet the definition of a simple trust, it is a complex trust. The income distribution deduction for complex trusts and all estates is determined under §§ 661-663. A trust, that can accumulate income, can make charitable contributions or makes a corpus distribution will be a complex trust. Since a trust must distribute all remaining corpus in its final year, it will always be a complex trust in its final year. The main difference between the computation of the income distribution deduction for simple and complex trusts is the use of a tier system for complex trusts. The tier system results in a greater amount of DNI being allocated to beneficiaries who receive required TAI distributions.

Distributable net income (DNI). DNI is the statutory limit for the income distribution deduction. DNI determines the maximum distribution deduction. If actual distributions exceed DNI, the entity gets no deduction for the excess; however, if distributions are less than DNI, only the amount actually distributed can be deducted.[36] Section 643(a) defines DNI as the entity's net taxable income modified as follows:

1. No deduction for the income distribution,
2. No deduction for the personal exemption,
3. Net undistributed capital gains allocated to corpus are subtracted;
4. Net capital losses are added back,
5. Net tax-exempt income is added back, and
6. For simple trusts only, subtract any undistributed extraordinary dividends or taxable stock dividends that the fiduciary allocated to corpus in good faith.

DNI is reduced by all tax deductible expenses. Whether these expenses are deducted from income or corpus for accounting purposes is ignored. DNI is a tax computation; therefore, accounting allocations of expenses is disregarded, unless the Code specifically requires the allocation to be considered. This treatment of corpus expenses allows income beneficiaries to benefit, from a tax standpoint, from corpus expenses paid during the year, since DNI limits the taxable income allocated to the income beneficiaries, thereby reducing how much income they must pay taxes on.

To visualize the allocation of FAI and DNI, think about Neapolitan ice cream. Unlike swirl ice cream, each flavor of Neapolitan is separate from the other flavors. If a person wanted only vanilla ice cream, he or she could remove vanilla from the "block of ice cream" leaving the other flavors. Gross accounting income, net accounting income and DNI form our "blocks of ice cream." Each block is composed of various "flavors" of income. When the fiduciary "scoops" the beneficiaries their share of FAI or DNI, each beneficiary receives some of every flavor. Exactly how much of each flavor a beneficiary receives is determined by the total composition of the block. If 50% of the total block is rental income, the beneficiary's "scoop" is 50% rent. Although there are many similarities in the configuration of each block, each block is different. In most situations, the FAI and DNI blocks contain the same flavors/income, but the percentage of flavors that comprise each block changes, based on the different rules used to build the blocks.[37] The construction of these "blocks of income" is the crux of computing the beneficiaries' allocation.

The composition of DNI is unique for each year. If DNI is not fully allocated to the beneficiaries during the particular year, the remaining block of DNI ice cream is stored in the freezer for distribution in later years. When distributions in a future year exceed that year's DNI, the fiduciary will look in the freezer for any prior year's DNI. When prior year's DNI, otherwise known as undistributed net income (UNI), is found in the freezer, the fiduciary must distribute the old DNI ice cream, based on the current-year's accumulation distribution. If there remains either current-year DNI or prior years' DNI, the beneficiary will be subject to some form of taxation for the particular year. Once all of the ice cream has been totally distributed, no further taxation can occur for the beneficiaries. By following the ice cream, the fiduciary will know if the beneficiaries are subject to taxation.

EXAMPLE 8 - 22. In 1999, Trust X had DNI of $20,000. The composition of DNI was: 50% rent, 25% dividends, 15% taxable interest and 10% exempt interest. Distributions for the year were $15,000, so $15,000 of DNI was allocated to the beneficiaries and $5,000 remained with Trust X. Since $500 of the retained DNI was exempt ($5,000 * 10%), Trust X had taxable income of $4,400 ($4,500 - 100) and taxes of $1,051.50. UNI for 1999 was $3,448.50 ($4,500 - 1,051.50). If 2000 distributions exceed 2000 DNI, all or part of the 1999 UNI will be distributed in 2000. Of the $15,000 distributed to the beneficiaries, $10,000 was allocated to Harry and the rest to Terri. Of Harry's DNI, $5,000 was rent, $2,500 was dividends, $1,500 was taxable interest and $1,000 was exempt. Of Terri's DNI, $2,500 was rent, $1,250 was dividends, $750 was taxable interest and $500 was exempt. Once the composition of DNI is calculated, it remains the same for all beneficiaries and the entity.

Computation of DNI and the Income Distribution Deduction

Since the purpose of DNI is to compute the income distribution deduction, the best place to begin in calculating DNI is with the entity's adjusted total income (Line 17, Form 1041). Adjusted total income (ATI) is the total amount of taxable income for the year that must be taxed to someone, either the entity or the beneficiaries. If ATI is negative, the entity has a net capital loss, an NOL and/or excess deductions. Then, DNI will be zero, since DNI can never be negative. ATI is modified by two adjustments: one for tax-exempt interest and one for capital transactions.

Tax-exempt interest. Net tax-exempt interest is gross exempt interest less any expenses not deductible due to the exempt interest limitation. When calculating the deductible expenses for ATI, direct and indirect expenses related to tax-exempt income are not deductible. These nondeductible expenses reduce gross exempt interest and the net amount is added to ATI when computing DNI. DNI is net income, so the final amount is a composite of each type of income net of expenses.

The income distribution deduction is the amount of taxable income allocated to the beneficiaries. If the entity has any net tax-exempt income, it must be removed from both DNI and the distributions before calculating the income distribution deduction. Once the net exempt income is removed, the lesser of DNI or the distributions becomes the income distribution deduction.

EXAMPLE 8 - 23. Trust Z has DNI of $30,000 of which $2,500 is exempt interest. Distributions for the year are $45,000. DNI and the distributions must be reduced by $2,500, since the entire amount of exempt interest is distributed. The income distribution deduction is $27,500, which is the lesser of deductible DNI ($27,500) and deductible distributions ($42,500). If distributions were $21,000, exempt interest of $1,750 (($21,000/$30,000) * $2,500) would be removed from distributions, since the entire amount of exempt interest is not distributed. Here, the income distribution deduction would be $19,250, since deductible distributions ($19,250) would be less than deductible DNI ($27,500).

Capital transactions. Capital transactions rarely affect DNI. Only capital gains can be added to DNI and this occurs infrequently. DNI is determined as if no capital transactions occurred during the year, so the net effect of all capital transactions is initially removed from ATI. Only net gains are added back to ATI. Capital gains are included in DNI when:

1. Capital gains are included in fiduciary accounting income;
2. It is the entity's final tax year;
3. The entity is required to distribute a specific amount each year and an insufficient amount of accounting income exists to meet the required distribution;
4. The fiduciary is required to distribute the proceeds from the sale of a specific asset; and
5. The fiduciary establishes a practice of using the capital gains to determine the entity's distributions and actually distributes the capital gains.

These specific incidents are narrowly interpreted, so capital gains are not included in DNI very often. Once the net tax-exempt interest and the adjustment for capital transactions are made to ATI, the result is DNI for purposes of computing the income distribution deduction.

Allocation of DNI. The DNI allocated to the beneficiaries determines the income distribution deduction. DNI is allocated to beneficiaries who receive a distribution from the entity. The type of distribution, income or corpus, is irrelevant. If the entity made a distribution, DNI is allocated to it. Not all distributions are considered when allocating DNI to the beneficiaries. The following distributions are ignored when allocating DNI and computing the income distribution deduction:

1. Charitable distributions;
2. Distributions under § 663(a) (explained below); and
3. Distributions in the current year that were considered when computing the income distribution deduction in a previous year.

Required FAI distributions are considered made whether a check was written or not. All other distributions must have been made before they can be considered. If an in-kind distribution was made, instead of cash, the lesser of the entity's basis or the fair market value (FMV) of the property is used to figure out the distributed amount. The distributed value can be increased if the transfer of property was considered a sale by making either a § 643(e)(3) election or transferring property to satisfy a pecuniary bequest.

Section 663(a). Section 663(a) allows certain distributions to be free of any DNI allocation. The terms of the governing document establish whether the gift or bequest meets the requirements. Unless the money or identity of the property is ascertainable under the document, the distribution will be included when allocating DNI for the income distribution deduction. To meet the test for a specific sum of money, the amount to be distributed must be fixed by the document and ascertainable at the date of death or inception of the trust. The amount cannot be subject to the fiduciary's discretion, a fraction of the taxable estate or determinable after subtracting administrative expenses. Most formula bequests do not meet the test, since the amount of the bequest is not determinable at death.[38] Specific property must be fixed as to kind and amount in the document. Certain pecuniary bequests meet the requirements of IRC § 663(a), while others do not.

The 65-day rule. The trustee or executor can elect to treat all or part of the distributions made within 65 days after the end of the trust's or estate's year as made in the current year.[39] The election is filed with the current-year's tax return and prevents the amounts actually paid from being deducted in the year actually paid. Only amounts necessary to remove any remaining current-year's DNI can be distributed under the 65-day rule. Effective for tax years beginning after August 5, 1997, estates can make a 65-day election. [40]

Taxation of Beneficiaries

According to Regulation § 1.652(b)-3, the character of the income and deductions:

> ... *shall have the same character in the hands of the beneficiary as in the hands of the estate or trust. For this purpose, the amounts shall be treated as consisting of the same proportion of each class of items entering into the computation of DNI as the total of each class bears to the total DNI of the estate or trust unless the terms of the governing instrument specifically allocate different classes of income to different beneficiaries.*

The composition of DNI determines the type of income distributed and taxed to the beneficiaries. If 80% of DNI is taxable income and 20% is tax-exempt interest, then 80% of the DNI allocated to the beneficiaries will be taxable income. The other 20% will be tax-exempt interest. Remember the Neapolitan ice cream analogy discussed earlier. For tax purposes, the "scoops" (distributions) received by the beneficiary are based on the composition of DNI. Anytime a "scoop" is made the beneficiary partakes in each flavor. The fiduciary is not allowed to "pick and choose" which flavor a beneficiary gets, unless the document provides for a special allocation. Special allocations are discussed later.

Schedule K-1. The fiduciary records on Schedule K-1 the amounts taxable to the beneficiaries. The K-1 is shown on a net basis. Any amounts recorded on the schedule are net of any expenses, so the beneficiaries report the net effect of any allocation only. Only net income can be allocated to the beneficiaries, except in the final year, when losses can be allocated to the corpus beneficiaries. Negative numbers are not shown on the Schedule K-1, except in the final year.

In determining the amounts reported on the K-1, the fiduciary must first compute the composition of DNI. This is done by allocating the entity's expenses against its income. Only income included in DNI can be reduced by the entity's expenses. The allocation of expenses follows a prescribed pecking order, and can result in DNI consisting of only one type of income, although the entity might have had four different classes of income originally. These rules apply to both simple and complex trusts and estates.

Allocation expenses against income. The order of allocating expenses against income is as follows:

1. All deductions directly attributable to a particular class of income are deducted from that income, e.g., all rental expenses reduce rental income.

2. All deductions not directly attributable to a specific type of income may be allocated to any type of income, as long as some deductions are allocated to tax-exempt income.[41] This rule provides some flexibility to the fiduciary. Depending on the needs of the beneficiaries, the fiduciary can allocate the indirect deductions against any type of income included in DNI. If the beneficiaries need a larger amount of portfolio income, to deduct some personal investment interest expense, for example, the fiduciary can allocate a larger amount of indirect costs to passive income, provided the fiduciary does not create a passive loss. If the reverse is true and the beneficiaries need passive income, none of the expenses have to be allocated to passive activities, but can be allocated solely to portfolio income.

3. Passive losses can only be deducted to the extent of passive income. Net passive losses cannot be allocated against any other type of income and are retained (suspended) by the entity. If directly related tax-exempt expenses exceed tax-exempt income, excess expenses cannot be deducted against any other type of income.

4. Any excess deductions (directly related expenses exceed the specific income), excluding passive losses and tax-exempt expenses, can be allocated against any type of income, just like indirect expenses discussed above. The income must be included in DNI before expenses can be allocated against it.

Unless a specific allocation in the fiduciary document prescribes otherwise, a charity-beneficiary is deemed to receive some of each type of income included in DNI.[42] This rule prevents an improper shifting of taxable income to the charity. Use of the gross income method, discussed above under "Expenses related to tax-exempt income," normally results in more taxable income being allocated to the charity reducing the taxable income allocable to the beneficiaries.

Special allocations. Sometimes the fiduciary document provides for a specific allocation of income to certain beneficiaries. These specific allocations can take many forms.

EXAMPLE 8 - 24. Trust X is to distribute all the income from an apartment house to Sam. This is a specific allocation allowed under the Regulations; therefore, Sam is taxed on any taxable income attributable to the apartment house. Sam's distribution is solely dependent on that specific type of income.

EXAMPLE 8 - 25. Trust X is to distribute $10,000 to Kathy, to be paid from tax-exempt income to the extent possible and the rest from taxable income. This would not be recognized as a specific allocation, so Kathy is allocated some of each type of income included in DNI, even if the fiduciary actually pays the $10,000 entirely from tax-exempt income. Kathy's distribution is fixed whatever the amount of tax-exempt income earned by the entity, so the only effect of the allocation is an attempt to apportion more of the tax-exempt income to her, which is not allowed under the Code.

EXAMPLE 8 - 26. Trust X is to distribute one-half of the tax-exempt interest to Anita. This is an allowable specific allocation, since Anita's distribution is determined solely by the amount of tax-exempt interest earned by the trust.

For a specific allocation, such as the one in the prior example, to be effective in allocating the entity's DNI, the document must not give the trustee any discretion in how the allocation is made. The special allocation rule applies to charitable distributions also. In drafting, if the grantor wants a certain beneficiary to receive a specific type of income, he or she can include a provision in the fiduciary document requiring the fiduciary to allocate that type of income to the beneficiary; however, he or she must make sure to draft the provision to comply with the requirements of the Code. The fiduciary cannot make a special allocation on his or her own.

Specific allocations will be given effect in the allocation of DNI from a fiduciary entity, providing they have an economic impact independent of the income tax consequences.[43]

Excess deductions. In years when interest, taxes, and administrative expenses exceed income, the entity has excess deductions. Since these expenses cannot be included in an NOL under § 172 and cannot be allocated to the beneficiaries, the entity has wasted excess deductions, because they are lost forever. Only in the final tax-year can the entity allocate these excess deductions to the corpus beneficiaries following the same rules used for allocating an NOL or net capital loss. The beneficiaries may take the allocated deductions as miscellaneous itemized deductions on their personal returns. If the beneficiary does not itemize, or if the 2% AGI floor is too great, the beneficiary cannot carry back or carry forward any unused amount.

Tiers, Tiers, So Many Tiers

Tiers are only applicable to complex trusts and to estates, and are used to allocate DNI among the beneficiaries. Section 662(a) defines the tiers. A complex trust or estate may or may not have tiers; the fiduciary must look to the governing instrument. A simple trust does not have tiers, since only one type of distribution exists, and DNI is allocated totally to that distribution.

First tier distributions. Section 662(a)(1) defines the first tier distributions as:

...the amount of income for the taxable year required to be distributed currently to such beneficiary, whether distributed or not.

If the governing instrument requires a certain amount of FAI to be distributed currently, the beneficiaries must pay taxes on that amount, limited by DNI. Section 662 applies if any part of the FAI is subject to a required distribution. The beneficiaries must pay taxes on the income, even if a distribution is not actually made.

DNI is recalculated if the entity has charitable and first tier distributions. DNI is computed as if no charitable contribution was made and is allocated to the beneficiaries to the extent they received first tier distributions. DNI for first tier distributions is called "modified DNI." Modified DNI applies to first tier distributions only and exists only when the trust has a charitable contribution and first tier distributions. Beneficiaries of first tier distributions have a potentially larger tax liability, since they lose some or all of the benefit resulting from the charitable contribution deduction.

EXAMPLE 8 - 27. Trust A had the following income for the year:

Taxable interest	$20,000
Tax-exempt interest	$10,000
Total income	$30,000

Trust A is required to distribute $24,000 of its current income to Alberta. The rest of the income can be distributed to Beth or the Red Cross or accumulated, and the trustee can make corpus distributions to Beth or to the Red Cross. The trustee made the following distributions:

Beth	$10,000
Red Cross	$18,000

DNI is computed as follows:

Taxable interest	$20,000	
Charitable deduction	(12,000)	[$6,000 exempt]
Tax-exempt interest	4,000	[$10,000-$6000]
DNI	$12,000	

Modified DNI is computed as follows:

Taxable interest	$20,000
Tax-exempt interest	10,000
Modified DNI	$30,000

Alberta is allocated $24,000 of modified DNI, which would consist of $16,000 taxable and $8,000 tax-exempt. Beth would not have any taxable income, since DNI would be zero ($12,000 - $24,000).

The effect of modified DNI, as reported on Form 1041:

Taxable interest	$20,000	
Charitable deduction	(12,000)	[$6,000 exempt]
Income distribution	(8,000)	[$4,000 exempt]
Taxable income	$ 0	
Taxable to Alberta	$16,000	[$8,000 exempt]
Taxable to Beth	$ 0	

Second tier distributions. Section 662(a)(2) defines second tier distributions as follows:

All other amounts properly paid, credited, or required to be distributed to such beneficiary for the taxable year.

The main difference between first and second tier distributions is the provision that first tier distributions must come from current income, while second tier distributions can come from current income, accumulated income or corpus. If none of the distributions must be paid from current income, all distributions will be considered second tier. Any income that must be paid is included in the beneficiary's income, to the extent of DNI, even if not actually paid. All other amounts must actually be paid to the beneficiaries before included in their income. Examples of second tier distributions under Regulation § 1.662(a)-3(b) are:

1. Distributions made to a beneficiary in the discretion of the fiduciary.
2. Distributions required by the terms of the governing instrument on the happening of a specified event.

EXAMPLE 8 - 28. Trust Y requires one-half of the trust corpus be distributed to Yolanda on her thirtieth birthday. When Yolanda turns 30 and receives the distribution, the distribution will be classified as a tier two distribution.

The amount of second tier distributions taxable to the beneficiaries is determined by DNI less any amounts allocated to first tier distributions. If more than one beneficiary receives distributions, each beneficiary must include his or her proportionate share in gross income. A beneficiary's proportionate share is an amount that bears the same ratio to DNI, less any first tier distributions, as the beneficiary's distribution bears to the total second tier distributions.

EXAMPLE 8 - 29. Trust Z has TAI and DNI of $30,000. The trust is required to distribute $15,000 of current income to Adams. The fiduciary has discretion to distribute the remaining income to either Bea, Charles or Dan or accumulate it. The fiduciary also can invade corpus for all four beneficiaries. Trust Z distributes $5,000 each to Bea, Charles and Dan and distributes an additional $5,000 to Adams. DNI would be allocated to each beneficiary as follows:

	Distribution	DNI
Adams	$20,000	$18,750
Bea	5,000	3,750
Charles	5,000	3,750
Dan	5,000	3,750
Totals	$35,000	$30,000

Adams is allocated a greater part of DNI since he received a first tier distribution of $15,000. The other $15,000 distribution was second tier, and the extra $5,000 would either be a distribution from corpus or from accumulated income.

No modifications of DNI are made in determining the taxation of second tier distributions. While the charitable contribution deduction is ignored in determining the DNI allocated to first tier distributions, no similar adjustment is made in allocating DNI to second tier distributions. As was shown in the example above, the adjustment for the charitable deduction made to first tier distributions results in a larger portion of DNI being allocated to first tier distributions; thereby, reducing the benefit of the charitable deduction to first tier distributions and reducing the DNI allocated to second tier distributions. Although income is allocated to a charitable contribution before any other expense, the larger the first tier distributions, the less benefit the beneficiaries, as a group, will receive from the charitable gift. To prevent this impact, as much of the distributions as possible should be allocated to the second tier. Since the governing document determines whether a distribution will be first or second tier, careful drafting is needed to achieve the desired result.

Income in Respect of a Decedent

Section 691 details the tax treatment of income in respect of a decedent (IRD). Treasury Regulation § 1.691(a)-1(b) defines IRD in these terms:

In general, the term "income in respect of a decedent" refers to those amounts to which a decedent was entitled as gross income but which were not properly includible in computing his taxable income for the taxable year ending with the date of his death or for a previous taxable year under the method of accounting employed by the decedent.

IRD is income to which the decedent was entitled, but due to his or her death was not includible in his or her taxable income. An example of IRD is salary earned but not paid to a cash basis taxpayer. Although the taxpayer had earned the salary, since it was not paid until after his or her death, it could not be included on his or her final income tax return. Since the income was never subject to income tax, on the receipt of the income, someone must pay income taxes on it. Section 691 provides the rules concerning the taxation of this type of income. No step-up in basis exists for IRD at death.

IRD must be included in the income of the party that receives the IRD in the year of receipt. Therefore, if an estate receives the IRD, it must include it in income; however, if the beneficiary receives the IRD directly, the beneficiary is taxed on it. Whoever collects the IRD is entitled to any deductions associated with the IRD. The character of IRD is the same as if the decedent had received the property before death.

The unique characteristic about IRD is its dual taxation. IRD is included in the gross estate of the decedent, so it is subject to estate taxes. Further, IRD is subject to income tax on receipt. The recipient of IRD is entitled to an income tax deduction attributable to the estate taxes paid on the net value of the IRD. This reduces the effect of dual taxation. Examples of IRD:

1. If the decedent completed all events sufficient to close a sale but did not collect the proceeds before death, on collection the proceeds will be IRD.

2. If the decedent had a contingent claim to sales proceeds, the completion of the agreement after death will result in IRD.[44]

3. The forgiveness of debt at death on an installment note is IRD. If the decedent had any unrecognized gain from the sale, the forgiveness of debt would trigger the recognition of the entire unreported gain and the gain would be IRD to the estate.[45]

4. Distributions from a qualified plan or an IRA made after death are IRD. Any distribution representing a nondeductible contribution is not taxed, since the decedent paid taxes on this amount before death.

Certain expenses are deductible for both estate and income tax purposes if they are related to IRD and have accrued prior to the decedent's death. The types of expenses are limited to:

1	Business expenses - § 162	4	Expenses to produce income - § 212
2	Interest deductions - § 163	5	Depletion deduction - § 611
3	Deduction for taxes - § 164	6	Foreign tax credit - § 27

Medical expenses, alimony, capital losses, net operating losses and charitable contributions are expressly excluded and cannot be deducted for income tax purposes by the recipient of IRD.

Estate Tax Deduction

IRD is included on both the estate tax and income tax returns. To offset some of this double taxation, the recipient of IRD is entitled to an income tax deduction for that portion of the estate taxes attributed to including IRD in the gross estate.[46] Further, an income tax deduction is allowed for generation skipping transfer taxes ascribed to IRD items included in a taxable termination or direct skips caused by the transferor's death.[47] The deduction must be allocated among the recipients of IRD, based on their proportionate share of the gross IRD received.

The deduction is allowed each year IRD is included in income. To compute the deduction, all items treated as IRD in the gross estate are aggregated. The total is reduced by all DRD to arrive at a net value. The value of IRD is the lesser of the amount included in the gross estate or the amount included in income. Once the net value is determined, estate taxes are recomputed by excluding the net value from the gross estate. The difference between the original estate tax and the recomputed estate tax is the IRD deduction. The deduction is allocated among the various IRD items. All deductions and credits must be adjusted to reflect the elimination of the net IRD values. If a specific bequest of IRD is made to a surviving spouse or a charity, the deduction is eliminated.

EXAMPLE 8 - 30. An estate is the beneficiary of a decedent's IRA. At the decedent's death, the IRA was valued at $2,000,000 and the decedent's taxable estate was $5,000,000. With the IRA, the decedent's FET was $2,390,800, and without the IRA, the decedent's FET would have been $1,290,800. As the IRA is distributed to the estate, the estate can reduce any income taxes payable by the $1,100,000 of FET paid on the IRA.

EXAMPLE 8 - 31. The decedent was entitled to salary of $5,000, dividends of $3,750 and rental income of $1,250 at his death. The decedent owed real estate taxes of $2,500 on the rental property. Sue (decedent's spouse) inherited the stock portfolio, his daughter, Jane, was entitled to the real estate, and the estate received the salary. $_{Sue}$ inherited ½ of the decedent's estate and the estate's marginal rate is 55%. The marginal rate is applied to the net IRD of $7,500 ($10,000 less $2,500) less the net IRD deemed allocated to the marital deduction ($3,750). The $2062.50 deduction ($7,500 - $3,750 * 55%) is allocated as follows:

	IRD Received	Percentage	Deduction
estate	$5,000	50.0%	$1,031
Sue	$3,750	37.5%	$773
Jane	$1,250	12.5%	$258
Total	$10,000	100.0%	$2,063

Throwback Rules

Prior to TRA '97, any trust that did not distribute all of its current-year's DNI had to contend with what were called the *throwback rules*.[48] TRA '97 changed the law such that these rules are no longer a problem for most domestic trusts, but they still apply to foreign trusts, some domestic trusts that were once foreign trusts, and to certain trusts that were created before March 1, 1984, if they are considered multiple trusts under Code Section 643(f).[49] Under the throwback rules, if all of the current-year's DNI ice cream is not scooped, the trust pays taxes on the remaining amount and stores the difference in the freezer. The stored taxable income (DNI) turns into what is called undistributed net income (UNI). Congress enacted these laws in 1969 to prevent a perceived abuse. People were saving taxes by having the trust pay taxes on the trust's taxable income and then distributing it in a later year, free of any additional taxes. For those trusts that still must contend with these rules, if the trust has any leftover DNI, it must keep a record of the retained amount and "distribute it" when later years' distributions exceed that particular year's DNI. Once distributed, the beneficiary must recompute his or her prior years' taxes, as if the amount was distributed in the year originally earned. To simplify this computation, the beneficiary uses an averaging approach and only has to recompute taxes for three years.

Fortunately, Congress finally realized that, with the compressed tax rate brackets, these throwback rules cause an excessive amount of paperwork, but rarely resulted in the collection of additional taxes. With the change in the law, most domestic trusts are exempt from these throwback rules, starting with tax years beginning after August 5, 1997.

CONCLUSION

Some main points to remember:

1. Trusts and estates are taxed like individuals, with a few modifications.
2. The primary purpose of Subchapter J is to allocate income and expenses between the fiduciary entity and the beneficiaries.
3. Knowing the fiduciary document, state law, and fiduciary accounting is important to the successful completion of a fiduciary tax return.
4. There are two primary parts to preparing a fiduciary income tax return:
   a. Computing adjusted total income; and
   b. Allocating the income and deductions between the entity and the beneficiaries, which requires determining DNI and the income distribution deduction.

QUESTIONS AND PROBLEMS

1. What is the purpose of fiduciary accounting?

2. Explain the general rules for allocating between income and corpus.

3. The document is silent on how to allocate rental income and expenses. Under state law, rental receipts are allocated to income, but state law provides that net business income is allocated to corpus. The deceased owned several rental properties, that were reported by the deceased on his income tax return as a business activity. How should the executor account for the rental properties on the estate's books?

4. How does fiduciary accounting impact fiduciary income taxation?

5. Explain the purpose of Subchapter J.

6. Explain the main rule concerning the computation of fiduciary taxable income.

7. State the rule that determines if a trust gets a $100 or $300 exemption.

8. Which of the following statements is TRUE?

   a. A trust is entitled to a $300 exemption if it distributes all of its accounting income during the year.
   b. Tax-exempt interest income in not included in accounting income.
   c. An estate must terminate for income tax purposes when it is discharged from probate.
   d. If an estate has separate shares, the maximum amount taxable to the beneficiary of one share is the DNI allocated to that share.

9. Explain the general rule concerning the deductibility of depreciation for fiduciary entities.

10. Which of the following statements regarding capital losses by an estate or trust is TRUE?

   a. Capital losses are allocated to the beneficiaries each year of the estate or trust.
   b. Net capital losses are allowed to a trust or estate as a deduction against ordinary income to the extent of the smaller of actual income or $3,000 per year.
   c. Capital loss carryover within the estate or trust can be carried forward up to a maximum of five years.
   d. Capital losses in an estate or trust do not retain their character (short or long-term) when carried over.

11. What are the three requirements of § 642(c) concerning the deductibility of charitable contributions?

12. Which of the following statements concerning a charitable income tax deduction by a fiduciary entity is or are TRUE?

   I. For income tax purposes, the fiduciary entity may deduct any amount that is directed to be paid to charity under the terms of the will or trust.
   II. The deduction is limited to 50% or 30%, as the case may be, of the adjusted gross income of the estate.

   a. I only   b. II only   c. Both I and II   d. Neither I or II

13. Explain how the deceased's suspended passive activity losses are handled.

14. Which of the following statements is FALSE?

   a. The distributive share for the entire partnership's year is allocated between the decedent and the successor-in-interest, based on an actual closing of the books or on a pro rata division based on the number of days each was a partner.
   b. The partnership taxable year closes on the death of the partner as to that partner.
   c. Medical expenses can be deducted on either the estate's first income tax return or on the estate tax return.
   d. When an estate distributes property other than cash to its residuary beneficiaries, the amount of the distribution is generally the lesser of the property's basis or the FMV of the property on the date of distribution.

15. State the three requirements for a trust to be classified as a simple trust.

16. Which one of the following situations does NOT include capital gains in DNI?

   a. Gains realized in the year of termination.
   b. Gains with respect to a year in which the fiduciary makes the §643(e)(3) election.
   c. Gains that are paid or permanently set aside for a charitable contribution or charitable purpose that generates a current income tax deduction.
   d. Gains that are properly allocated to the fiduciary's accounting income under the terms of the governing instrument.

17. Which of the following statements are **true**?

   1. DNI can never be negative.
   2. DNI can include tax-exempt income.
   3. The executor can elect the 65-day rule for estate distributions.
   4. DNI is allocated to specific bequests.
   5. Charities never receive DNI.

a. 1, 3, and 5 only	c. 1, 2, 3, and 5 only	e. All are true.
b. 2, 3, and 4, only	d. 1, 4, and 5 only	

18. Which of the following statements regarding taxation of beneficiaries is FALSE?

    a. The beneficiaries must report taxable income distributed to them in cash or property distributions by an estate if the estate has DNI available for distribution.
    b. A trust beneficiary may have to pay income tax on the income earned at the trust level, even though it was not actually received as a distribution.
    c. The type of property distributed determines the type of income to be reported by the beneficiary.
    d. Whenever a trust distributes property in satisfaction of a pecuniary obligation, the trust recognizes gain to the extent that the property's fair market value exceeds its adjusted basis.

19. Explain how DNI is taxed to the beneficiaries.

20. Which one of the following statements concerning the trustee of a complex trust is FALSE?

    a. The trustee of a complex trust may elect to treat an amount paid or credited to a beneficiary within the first 65 days of a trust taxable year as having been distributed on the last day of the prior year.
    b. The election applies only to those amounts designated by the trustee that have been properly paid or credited in the first 65 days of the subsequent tax year.
    c. The amount elected cannot exceed the greater of the trust's DNI or fiduciary accounting income in the year for which the distribution is considered to have been made.
    d. The election is made annually and once made can be revoked later.

21. Describe the "sweet" composition of FAI and DNI.

22. Which one of the following statements regarding undistributed and distributed income is TRUE?

    a. The trust or estate must pay tax on the undistributed part of the taxable income.
    b. Taxable income to the beneficiary, plus taxable income to the trust or estate, is undistributed income.
    c. Income distributed to beneficiaries of a trust is not taxed, unless it exceeds $600.
    d. Beneficiaries may elect the characterization of any income received from an estate or trust.

23. What are the three methods available for computing the allocation of indirect expenses to tax-exempt income?

24. Which of the following does NOT apply to the taxation of capital transactions?

    a. The maximum net capital loss deduction for any year is $3,000.
    b. Net capital losses do not decrease DNI.
    c. Transferring assets to satisfy a pecuniary bequest is considered a sale.
    d. Capital gains are included in DNI, normally.

25. What are the rules concerning allocating expenses between the various types of income?

26. Which of the following statements are **true**?

    1. Trusts must use a calendar year-end.
    2. Estates must use a calendar year-end.
    3. The fiduciary must file a special notice to elect its tax accounting method.
    4. The fiduciary's tax return is due on the 15th day of the 4th month following its year-end.
    5. Fiduciary returns can be filed electronically.

      a. 1, 2, and 4, only   c. 2, 3, and 4 only   e. 1, 3, and 5 only
      b. 1, 4, and 5 only   d. 2, 3, and 5 only

27. How is DNI allocated?

28. Which one of the following statements regarding first-tier distributions is TRUE?

    a. If first-tier distributions exceed DNI, each first-tier beneficiary reports only the beneficiary's proportionate share of DNI.

    b. If the trust document requires payments to be made from corpus, the payments would be within the first tier.

    c. First-tier distributions need not carry out DNI in full before DNI is allocated to the second-tier distributions.

    d. First-tier distributions include specific bequests.

29. Which of the following statements are **false**?

    1. Trusts cannot take the rental real estate offset.

    2. Income in respect of a decedent receives a "stepped-up" basis.

    3. The character of IRD is the same as if the decedent had received the property.

    4. Medical expenses can be deducted on both the fiduciary income tax and estate tax returns.

    5. Net operating losses are deductions in respect of a decedent.

      a. 2, 4, and 5 only   c. 2, 3, and 4 only   e. 2 only

      b. 1, 3, and 5 only   d. 1, 3, and 4 only

30. Which of the following statements is or are TRUE?

    I. An estate may claim administrative expenses as either an estate tax deduction or an income tax deduction, but not both.

    II. To take administrative expenses as an income tax deduction, the fiduciary must file an irrevocable election, even if no estate tax return is required.

      a. I only   b. II only   c. Both I and II   d. Neither I or II

ANSWERS TO THE QUESTIONS AND PROBLEMS *(odd numbered only)*

1. Fiduciary accounting allocates the annual inflows and outflows between income and corpus. Income beneficiaries are entitled to the fiduciary accounting income while the remaindermen are entitled to the remaining corpus once the entity ends. Fiduciary accounting apportions the various receipts and distributions between income and corpus, so the fiduciary will know the correct amount to distribute to the appropriate beneficiaries.

3. The fact that the decedent recorded the use as a business activity is ignored when determining the proper accounting method for fiduciary purposes. Specific statutes control over general statutes. Since a specific statute exists for rental receipts, all rental receipts and directly related expenses are allocated to accounting income.

5. Subchapter J was written not to compute taxable income specifically, but to allocate taxable income to the appropriate party, either the fiduciary entity or the beneficiary.

7. Section 642(b) allows an $300 exemption if the trust must distribute all of its TAI currently. All other trusts are allowed a $100 exemption.

9. The amount of depreciation is computed following the same rules that apply to individuals, except no IRC § 179 deduction is allowed. To the extent there is a reserve for depreciation for accounting purposes, the entity takes the tax deduction for computation of its taxable income. If any tax depreciation remains, it is allocated between the entity and its beneficiaries according to the allocation of accounting income.

11. Before a deduction is allowed, certain requirements must be met. These requirements are:

    1. The will or trust document must authorize the contribution,
    2. The amount of deduction is limited by gross income, and
    3. Only those amounts actually paid during the year or during the following year may be deducted.

13. The death of a person is treated as a distribution of his entire interest in the asset, so on the decedent's final return, the suspended losses can be used to reduce other income, subject to one limitation. The recipient's basis of property received at death is its fair market value (FMV) at date of death.

When the suspended losses exceed the increase in basis, the loss can be deducted on the decedent's final return.

15. Section 651 defines a simple trust as a trust that:

   1. is required to distribute all of its trust accounting income (TAI) currently;
   2. no distributions used for charitable purposes; and
   3. allows no distributions in excess of TAI for the year.

17. Correct answer c - 1, 2, 3, and 5 only. DNI can never be negative. If it is, the entity has a net capital loss, a net operating loss or excess deductions, which are not negative DNI. While DNI can include tax-exempt income, the income distribution deduction does not include adjusted tax-exempt income. The § 663(b) 65-day rule is available for estates (added by TRA '97) as well as for complex trusts. Section 663(a) prevents DNI from being allocated to specific bequests. Only non-charity beneficiaries receive DNI.

19. Sections 652 and 662 state the character of the income and deductions shall have the same character in the hands of the beneficiary as in the hands of the estate or trust. The amounts shall be treated as consisting of the same proportion of each class of items entering into the computation of DNI as the total of each class bears to the total DNI of the estate or trust unless the terms of the governing instrument specifically allocate different classes of income to different beneficiaries. The composition of DNI determines the type of income distributed and taxed to the beneficiaries. If 80% of DNI is taxable income and 20% is tax-exempt interest, then 80% of the DNI allocated to the beneficiaries is taxable income and 20% will be tax-exempt interest. Remember the Neapolitan ice cream analogy discussed earlier. For tax purposes, the "scoops" (distributions) received by the beneficiary are based on the composition of DNI. Anytime a "scoop" is made, the beneficiary partakes in each flavor. The fiduciary is not allowed to "pick and choose" which flavor a beneficiary gets, unless the document provides for a special allocation.

21. The "sweet" composition of FAI and DNI is similar to Neapolitan ice cream. Unlike swirl ice cream, each flavor of Neapolitan is separate from the other flavors. If a person wanted only vanilla ice cream, he could remove vanilla from the "block of ice cream" leaving the other flavors. Gross accounting income, net accounting income and DNI form our

"blocks of ice cream." Each block is composed of various "flavors" of income. When the fiduciary "scoops" the beneficiaries their share of FAI or DNI, each beneficiary receives some of every flavor. Exactly how much of each flavor a beneficiary receives is determined by the total composition of the block. If 50% of the total block is rental income, the beneficiary's "scoop" is 50% rent. Although there are many similarities in the configuration of each block, each block is different. In most situations, the FAI and DNI blocks contain the same flavors/income, but the percentage of flavors that comprise each block changes, based on the different rules used to build the blocks. The construction of these "blocks of income" is the crux of computing the beneficiaries' allocation.

23. The three methods for allocating indirect expenses to exempt income are: the gross accounting income method, the net accounting income method and any defensible, reasonable method.

25. Expenses are allocated against income in the following order:

1. All deductions directly attributable to a particular class of income are deducted from that income.

2. All deductions not directly attributable to a specific type of income may be allocated to any type of income, as long as some deductions are allocated to tax-exempt income. This rule provides some flexibility to the fiduciary. Depending on the needs of the beneficiaries, the fiduciary can allocate the indirect deductions against any type of income included in DNI. If the beneficiaries need a larger amount of portfolio income, to deduct some personal investment interest expense, for example, the fiduciary can allocate a larger amount of indirect costs to passive income, provided the fiduciary does not create a passive loss. If the reverse is true and the beneficiaries need passive income, expenses can be allocated solely to portfolio income and none to the passive activities.

3. Passive losses can only be deducted to the extent of passive income. Net passive losses cannot be allocated against any other type of income and are retained (suspended) by the entity. If directly related tax-exempt expenses exceed tax-exempt income, excess expenses cannot be deducted against any other type of income.

4. Any excess deductions (directly related expenses exceed the specific income), excluding passive losses and tax-exempt expenses, can be allocated against any type of income, just like indirect expenses discussed

above. The income must be included in DNI before expenses can be allocated against it.

27. DNI is allocated based on its composition and the current-year's distributions. The composition of DNI is unique for each year. If DNI is not fully allocated to the beneficiaries during the particular year, the remaining block of DNI ice cream is stored in the freezer for distribution in later years. When distributions in a future year exceed that year's DNI, the fiduciary will look in the freezer for any prior year's DNI. When prior year's DNI, otherwise known as undistributed net income (UNI), is found in the freezer, the fiduciary must distribute the old DNI ice cream, based on the current-year's accumulation distribution. If there remains either current-year DNI or prior years' DNI, the beneficiary will be subject to some form of taxation for the particular year. Once all of the ice cream has been totally distributed, no further taxation can occur for the beneficiaries.

29. Correct answer a - 2, 4, and 5 only. Trusts cannot take the rental real estate offset. Estates can for the first two years, providing the decedent actively participated and the surviving spouse does not take the entire offset. IRD does not receive a stepped-up basis, which causes its dual taxation. IRD retains its character in the hands of the estate or its beneficiaries. Medical expenses cannot be claimed on Form 1041. Net operating losses expire with the deceased and cannot be deducted by either the estate or its beneficiaries.

ENDNOTES

1. *Beaty v. Bales*, 677 S.W.2d 750 (Tex App - San Antonio 1984).

2. *Thorman v. Carr*, 408 S.W.2d 259 (Civ. App. 1966) ref. n.r.e.

3. IRC § 645.

4. Reg § 1.641(b)-3(a).

5. *Earl A. Brown, Jr.*, 890 F2d 1329 (5th Cir, 1989).

6. Rev Proc 98-13, 1998-4 IRB 21.

7. IRC § 469(i).

8. IRC § 469(i)(4)(B).

9. IRC § 1223(11).

10. IRC § 163.

11. IRC § 265.

12. Rev. Rul. 63-27, 1963-1 CB 57.

13. Reg.§ 1.652(b)-3(d).

14. Reg. § 1.167(h)-1(b).

15. See *Interfirst Bank of Fort Worth, N.A. v King*, 722 S.W.2d 18, (App. 12 Dist 1986) and *Hay v US*, 263 F.Supp. 813 (D.C. 1967).

16. IRC § 164(a).

17. IRC § 642(c).

18. IRC § 642(c)(1) and Reg. § 1.642(c)-1.

19. Reg. § 1.212-1(i).

20. IRC § 642(d).

21. 994 F2d 302 (CA-6, 1993).

22. 1994-38 IRB 4.

23. FedCl, 2000-2 USTC ¶50,642.

24. IRC § 643(e)(1).

25. IRC §§ 1014, 1015.

26. Rev. Rul. 67-74, 1967-1 CB 194 and Regs. § 1.651(a)-2(b).

27. IRC § 469(j)(6).

28. IRC § 1014.

29. IRC § 469(g)(2).

30. IRC § 469(j)(12).

31. See endnote 12, *supra*.

32. IRC § 643(a) defines DNI.

33. IRC § 643(b).

34. Reg. § 1.651(a)-4.

35. IRC §§ 651(a) and (b).

36. IRC §§ 651(b) and 661(a).

37. For accounting purposes, 50% of the block might be rent, while for DNI purposes, only 25% of the block would be rent.

38. Rev. Rul. 60-87, 1960-1 CB 286; Reg.§ 1.663(a)-1(b).

39. IRC § 663(b).

40. TRA'97 (Pub. L. 105-34, IRC § 1306(a)) amending § 663(b).

41. Reg. § 1.652(b)-3.

42. Reg. § 1.662(b)-2.

43. Reg § 1.652(b)-2.

44. Let. Rul. 9023012.

45. IRC § 691(a)(5)(A)(iii); Let. Rul. 9108027; *Estate of Frane*, 998 F2d 567 (CA-8, 1993).

46. IRC § 691(c).

47. IRC § 691(c).

48. IRC §§ 665-668.

49. See IRC § 665(c).

PART 3

The Techniques of Planning

CHAPTER 9

The Goals of Estate Planning

OVERVIEW AND CAUTION

This chapter is an introduction to the most commonly encountered estate planning goals and the planning techniques that seek to accomplish them. The goals are categorized as financial and nonfinancial. Later chapters will give more details of the techniques and goals we introduce in this chapter.

Some techniques accomplish more than one goal, and some goals may be in conflict with other goals. Some techniques foreclose other techniques. The strategies and tactics of estate planning involve many intricacies and interdependencies, feedback loops and trade offs. It is easy for the planner to become process driven and lose sight of the forest for the trees. Estate planning is not just about avoiding estate taxes and complicated trust arrangements but about meeting real needs with real solutions. Estate planning should be needs driven, not process driven. A sense of perspective comes with time and experience.

A major goal of estate planning is preserving options. Many people think creating an estate plan is like building a home, once the roof is on, it will be hard to make changes. Actually, good planning incorporates the means for long-term flexibility. A good plan sets guidelines for surrogate decision makers to follow. In creating any plan, the planner should consider the options the plan creates and those it forecloses.

In reading this chapter, it would be well to keep in mind that individuals invariably have one fundamental goal in common, which may be far more important than saving taxes or attaining any narrower goal. The primary goal is happiness and peace of mind, and specific estate planning strategies may conflict with this primary goal. For example, large gifts may reduce transfer taxes, but they may also jeopardize happiness by imperiling the donor's sense of financial security. The planner should be especially attuned to the individual's emotional and psychological preferences and not persist in recommending techniques that are in conflict with them. Planning strategies are not ends in themselves; they are a means to an end, the client's greater happiness.

NONFINANCIAL GOALS

Some specific objectives in estate planning cannot be measured in dollars and cents. These nonfinancial goals, often called "personal planning," include caring for one's dependents, transferring property promptly and privately, and managing assets prudently.

Caring for Dependents

One main objective is to provide care for family members affected by a person's disability or death. For example, disability may trigger the need for someone to care for the disabled person, for his or her property, and, perhaps most importantly, for his or her minor children. Estate planning makes it more likely that the actual wishes of the person will be carried out. Various methods to accomplish these tasks are examined in Chapter 17.

Accomplishing Fair and Proper Distribution of Property

Good estate planning seeks to dispose of a person's property to the appropriate parties in the proper amounts at the right time. Many factors will influence the choice of the best succession and distribution techniques, and every ensuing chapter will discuss them.

Maintaining Privacy in the Transfer Process

Other things being equal, most people prefer that their wealth be transferred as privately as possible. They want their intended beneficiaries to avoid the stress of public scrutiny. Different methods of property transfer have different degrees of privacy. The probate process is considerably more public than the process of transferring property by trust. If privacy were the only criterion, no one would prefer the probate alternative. Probate does, however, offer some advantages, and each person should weigh the advantages for his or her own estate against the disadvantages and decide accordingly. The decision whether to avoid probate is the main focus of Chapter 10.

Prompt Property Transfer

Similar to privacy, most people want prompt property transfer that is often less attainable with the probate alternative. On the other hand, joint tenancy may be the quickest way to transfer property at the death of a co-owner, but it is also very inflexible. Living trusts are expensive to establish, but allow the most flexible and long range estate planning. Speed, flexibility, economy, and privacy are goals that often involve trade-offs which are discussed in Chapter 10.

Maintaining Control Over Assets

As we shall see in later chapters, many lifetime estate planning strategies require that a person relinquish interests in property by making transfers. Few people relish this; they would rather hold on to their property for as long as possible. But estate planning goals, such as reducing estate taxes, might motivate some to make lifetime transfers.

Further, different lifetime transfer strategies require different degrees of transfer. Usually, the more complete the transfer, the more likely other goals can be accomplished. As you read about the various estate planning techniques, consider whether the benefits available are worth the degree of transfer.

FINANCIAL GOALS

We will divide our discussion of financial goals into nontax-related financial goals and tax-related financial goals.

Nontax Financial Goals

Financial goals that are not tax-related include maintaining a satisfactory standard of living, attaining lifetime and postmortem flexibility, maximizing benefits for the surviving spouse, ensuring proper disposition by careful drafting, assuring adequate liquidity, minimizing nontax transfer costs, and preserving business value.

Maintaining a satisfactory standard of living. Many tax objectives can be achieved with lifetime transfers. The planner should ensure, however, that clients will retain sufficient assets and income to maintain a satisfactory standard of living. This may require foregoing certain tax-saving transfers, such as outright gifts, in favor of retaining property. Or it may call for making other less complete or less costly transfers, such as an installment sale, which can generate necessary cash flow. These alternatives will be explored in detail in Chapters 13 and 14, covering lifetime transfers.

Attaining lifetime and postmortem flexibility. Flexibility in estate planning means that as circumstances change, the client or the individual's surrogates can intelligently alter arrangements to accomplish desired goals. While the client is still alive and mentally competent, flexibility can be maintained by the client periodically reviewing the estate plan and revising it when necessary. After the client either loses mental capacity or dies, flexibility, although not entirely impossible, is more difficult to sustain. Yet, as we will see next, considerable flexibility can be maintained if the client anticipates the problem by providing in advance for surrogate decision makers.

The critical need for flexibility emerges in the context of providing for children in the event that both parents become severely disabled or die prematurely. For example, without planning, their property might be held by a court-chosen guardian until it is transferred outright to the children when they reach age 18. Most parents would prefer to delay outright distribution until the children are older and more mature. Such can be accomplished by designating responsible parties (whether as trustees, agents, or holders of limited powers) to act on their behalf. Flexibility through the use of surrogate decision makers may be by powers of appointment (usually found in trusts, see Chapters 11 and 12), durable powers of attorney (usually a separate document designating an agent to carry out certain acts, see Chapter 17), and disclaimers (usually written by the disclaimant in response to a proffered gift or bequest, see Chapters 7, 12, and 18).

Maximizing benefits for the surviving spouse. Most wealthy couples want to be assured that the surviving spouse will live comfortably and at the same time minimize transfer taxes. Poor planning may result in an inefficient transfer, accomplishing one goal at the expense of another, when both could have been obtained.

> EXAMPLE 9 - 2. Cliffton writes his own will, even though he is quite wealthy. Although he is married to Pamela, his will leaves a substantial portion of his property outright to their middle-aged children, even if Pamela survives him, because all he wants is to be certain that his unified credit is utilized. Cliffton's estate plan succeeds in utilizing his unified credit and in having the property that is left to the children bypass Pamela's estate, but in so doing, he has unnecessarily denied her the use of the property.

Chapters 11 and 12 discuss tax-reducing plans that provide for the surviving spouse's welfare without sacrificing other important objectives.

> EXAMPLE 9 - 3. Continuing the prior example, Cliffton could achieve his goals by leaving the property in trust for the benefit of Pamela and the children. Without causing any increase in transfer tax, the trust could give Pamela the following rights: (1) the right to the income from the property for her life; (2) the power to invade the trust corpus for reasons of health, education, support, or maintenance; and/or (3) the power to determine whether the property should continue to be held in trust after her death or be immediately distributed at that time.

Ensuring proper disposition by careful drafting. In the planning process, most people assume that no matter what happens, their intended beneficiaries will in fact receive their accumulated wealth. People trust their attorney to draft transfer documents properly. However, drafting skill varies greatly, and poor drafting can frustrate an individual's dispositive preferences in many ways. The examples below are illustrative.

EXAMPLE 9 - 3. Martha's simple will does not include a survival clause, creating the risk that her property will be inherited by her in-laws rather than by her parents.

EXAMPLE 9 - 4. Unaware of QTIP trust planning, an attorney drafts a simple will for Francis which leaves all of his property outright to his second wife, running the risk that she may neglect to adequately provide for her stepchildren (Francis's children from his prior marriage), who are living with Francis's first wife.

EXAMPLE 9 - 5. A trust-will is drafted for a client, in which estate property will be held in trust until the youngest of the client's grandchildren reaches age 25. The disposition may be ruled invalid for violation of the rule against perpetuities.

EXAMPLE 9 - 6. Donald's attorney drafts a tax-saving testamentary trust into which nearly all of Donald's estate is intended to pass. However, because much of Donald's property is still held in joint tenancy with his wife, that property will not pass to the trust at his death but will go outright to his wife by automatic right of survivorship. At that point, the only way for her to move the property into the trust will be by making a taxable gift. And, an IRC § 2036 problem can arise if the gift is made into a trust for her benefit.

In each of these situations, more careful planning and drafting could have eliminated the risk of these unintended dispositions without significantly altering the person's objectives. Careful planning and drafting are essential prerequisites to the achievement of dispositive goals.

Acquiring adequate liquidity. The death of a person may trigger the need for liquidity to pay taxes, administration expenses, claims, and for the needs of a surviving family. Many, if not most, wealthy people lack sufficient liquidity to immediately take care of all of these things. This is especially true if much of the person's wealth was tied up in real estate or a closely held business. Chapter 15 is devoted entirely to liquidity planning and will describe the major methods of increasing liquidity, including the sale of assets, acquiring life insurance, using valuation discounts, and making tax-delaying or tax-reducing elections that are available only to the estates of deceased business owners.

Minimizing nontax estate transfer costs. Nontax estate transfer costs include attorney and trustee fees, executor commissions, court costs, and probate fees and probate related fees such as the bond premium. Chapter 10 will examine these costs while exploring the decision to avoid probate.

Preserving business value. The death of a business owner can precipitate a serious and rapid decline in the value of that business. In Chapter 16, we see that certain arrangements by an owner will minimize (or even avoid) the decline in value, thereby greatly increasing the likelihood that the pre-death value of the business passes to the owner's heirs.

Tax-related Financial Goals

Income taxes and transfer taxes are the largest cause of estate shrinkage to medium and larger sized estates. Most of the specific planning strategies covered in this text will seek to reduce these taxes.

Income tax savings goals. Planning strategies designed to save income taxes generally seek a step-up in basis, shift income to lower bracket taxpayers, and to defer the recognition of income.

Obtaining a stepped-up basis. When property is inherited, its basis for the devisee/legatee is reset to its current value. For assets that have appreciated, this is called a step-up in basis. Thus, other things being equal, planners recommend deferring the transfer of appreciated assets until the owner's death. Achieving a step-up in basis is especially important to a transferee who wants to sell an appreciated asset. However, for other reasons, estate planning often favors lifetime gifts, where the basis is not stepped up but carries over. Of course, basis is just one of many considerations involved in making lifetime transfers, a subject that will be more thoroughly explored in Chapters 13 and 14.

Shifting income to a lower bracket taxpayer. Wealthy people are usually in the highest income tax brackets, whereas the income of other family members, such as parents and children, may be in lower tax brackets. Under our progressive income tax rate structure, rates increase with increasing taxable income. Thus, there is an incentive to reduce overall income tax rates by shifting income to family members who are in lower tax rate brackets.

However, tax reform legislation in the 1980s directed a three-pronged attack on popular methods of shifting income to a lower-bracket family member. First, it adopted the "kiddie tax," described in Chapter 13, that virtually eliminates any benefit of shifting income to children who are under the age of 13. Second, it made income shifting relatively less attractive by lowering the maximum marginal rate to 39.6% level (lowered even further since then); still high compared to the lowest bracket, but paling in comparison to earlier maximum rates that were as high as 91%. And third, although completed transfers (gifts) can still shift some income, two major lifetime incomplete transfer devices that were once very much in vogue, the short-term trust and the spousal remainder trust described in Appendix 14A, are no longer available due to revisions to the grantor trust rules.

Many of the examples in the remainder of this book will assume a 50% "combined" marginal income tax rate for wealthier individuals, based on the premise that state and local taxes are commonly in the low double-digit range. Thus, for each additional dollar of taxable income, a high income taxpayer will incur 50 cents in tax. Likewise, every deduction of a dollar will save 50 cents in tax.

Of course, taxpayers in the highest tax bracket are the most likely to be interested in making income shifting transfers. In 1999, a married couple with joint taxable income in excess of $283,150 will have reached the top federal marginal rate of 39.6%. A single individual taxpayer hits the top rate at a lower level. The greatest tax savings occur when the additional income collected by the transferee is either not taxed or taxed at the 15% marginal rate. Thus, the most likely persons to benefit from income shifting include minor children over age 13, young adults in college, and, perhaps, the donor's parents. This is especially true where the wealthy person is presently making after-tax gifts to the lower tax bracket donee.

Figure 9-1 illustrates the progression of maximum marginal federal income tax rates since 1952. The highest during that time period was 91% from 1952 through 1963 and the lowest was 28% from 1988 through 1990.

Figure 9-1 Maximum Marginal Federal Income Tax Rates 1952 - Present

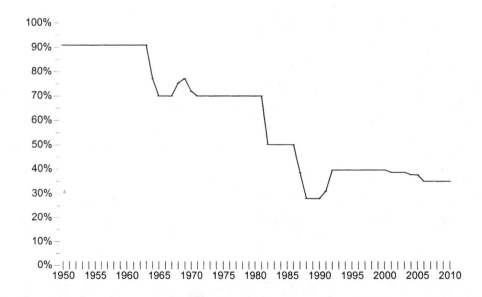

Can all income potentially receivable by one person be taxed to another? The answer is no, because tax law distinguishes two types of income: personal service income and other income. Under the *assignment of income doctrine*, earnings from services performed will always be taxable to the person performing those services. However, income from investment property can be taxed to another if the property is transferred before the income is realized. Hence, interest accrued or dividends declared after the date of a gift are taxed to the recipient; those before the date of the gift are taxed to the donor, even if paid to the donee.

Usually income is shifted by a complete transfer (i.e., an outright gift) of the income-generating property. However, with some techniques the transfer is intentionally partially incomplete. The custodial gift and the irrevocable trust discussed in Chapter 13 are partially incomplete gifts. We will also see in Chapter 18 that income shifting to save income taxes can be accomplished by the timing of distributions to the beneficiaries. And there are some opportunities to use multiple taxpaying entities rather than just one, such as electing to treat a trust held for the children of deceased parents as separate trusts for each child rather than just one trust. This is referred to as taking multiple "trips up the rate ladder." Since the income tax rates are progressive, taxes are saved by having multiple taxpayers.

Tax reform since 1986 has dramatically reduced the benefits of shifting income to trusts and estates. When legislation radically lowered the maximum marginal tax rate for individuals, it greatly reduced the tax bracket amounts for trusts and estates that are subject to the lower rates. Thus, incremental income taxed to estates and trusts hits the top of the rate ladder at a much lower income level than for income taxed to individuals. A trust reaches the top tax bracket by the time its taxable income reaches $9,000 (see Table 8-1).

Deferring recognition of income. Careful planning can defer tax on a gain from its sale to later years. Examples of transfers that defer taxable gain are the installment sale and the private annuity, covered in Chapter 14. In Chapter 18, we will see that an estate can defer income by choosing its fiscal year end. Deferral of the tax enables the taxpayer to use the money to earn income until the taxes finally have to be paid.

Transfer tax savings goals. Techniques designed to reduce transfer taxes generally do so by accomplishing one or more of the following: reduce (maybe to zero) the amount deemed to be taxable; freeze the estate tax base; defer taxes; and leverage the use of exclusions, exemptions, or the unified credit. To some extent, all three techniques make use of imperfections in the unified transfer tax system that were discussed at the end of Chapter 5.

Reducing the estate tax base. Certain planning arrangements reduce the estate tax base, subjecting less of the person's wealth to transfer taxation. Each dollar of value that is removed from the transferor's tax base and still makes it to the intended beneficiary represents money saved at the transferor's highest transfer tax marginal rate (i.e., after 2001 and until repeal anywhere from 37% to 50% depending on the timing and the ultimate value of the cumulative transfers).

> EXAMPLE 9 - 7. A month before she died in 2003, Sharon, a widow whose net estate was worth about $3 million, gave each of her children, their wives, and their adult children checks in the amount of $10,000. There were 10 donees in all. Due to the annual exclusion, none of the gifts were taxable and her estate tax base was reduced by $100,000. The transfers lowered her estate tax by $49,000, given that the 2003 top marginal rate is 49%.

Other reduction techniques examined in later chapters include:
- Gifts into trust (Chapter 13)
- Judicious use of the unlimited marital deduction (Chapters 11 and 12)
- Bypass planning (Chapters 11 and 12)
- Election of the alternate valuation date (Chapters 15 and 18)
- The family-owned business exclusion, special-use valuation (for farm or other closely held businesses that rely on real estate property)
- Valuation discounts for gifts of family limited partnership interests, fractional interest discounts, and conservation easements (all discussed in Chapter 15)

Freezing the estate tax base. Certain property arrangements are designed mainly to *limit the future increase* in the estate tax base by freezing a portion of the person's wealth at its current value. Thus, all future appreciation in this portion is excluded from transfer taxation.

> EXAMPLE 9 - 8. In 1999, Nicky, a single parent, sells one of his vacation homes to his son Donny at its actual market value of $128,000, receiving $15,000 as a down payment and a secured installment note for $113,000 with interest-only payments (at 7.5%) for 10 years followed by interest and principal payments amortized over another 15 years. If Nicky dies in the next 10 years, his estate includes the note valued at approximately $113,000 (actual value depends upon how well it is secured and prevailing interest rates), whatever is left of the $15,000 down

payment (or the investments therefrom), and the interest payments. Even if the value of the vacation home at the time of Nicky's death is considerably more than it was when he sold it to Donny, that increase is not included in Nicky's estate.

Transfers are often a blend of reducing and freezing a portion of the tax base, rather than being exclusively one or the other.

> EXAMPLE 9 - 9. Assume that Nicky, from the last example, gave the vacation home to Donny. He would file a gift tax return and report a taxable gift of $118,000 ($128,000 market value less $10,000 annual exclusion.) Assuming no prior taxable gifts, no gift tax is due because of the shelter of the unified credit. If Nicky dies 10 years later when the value of the vacation home is $200,000 (or, for that matter, any amount), Nicky's estate tax base will include just the taxable gift value of $118,000. Nicky's estate tax base has been partially reduced (the $10,000 annual exclusion portion) and partially frozen (the taxable gift portion).

Leveraging the use of exclusions, exemptions, and the unified credit. Much of estate planning leveraging seeks to magnify the end results of transactions. Many of these transactions, if successful, greatly reduce the estate tax and, if not successful, leave the transferor no worse off than had he or she simply not made the transfer (other than whatever costs are associated with making the transfer).

> EXAMPLE 9 - 10. Wendy gave a life insurance policy on her life to her son Matthew. Although it had a face value of $500,000, it was valued at only $30,000 for gift tax purposes. When Wendy died six years later, Matthew collected the $500,000 proceeds and Wendy's estate reported a $20,000 adjusted taxable gift. Had Wendy died within three years of the transfer, then IRC § 2035(a) would have applied and the $500,000 would be included in her estate (the adjusted taxable gift would be reduced to zero). Thus, if successful, the transfer greatly leverages the transfer of wealth at a very small transfer tax cost. If it is not successful, the result is basically what would have occurred had no transfer taken place.

The use of life insurance and life insurance trusts in estate planning is covered extensively in Chapter 15. Other examples of techniques that use leveraging are the benefits of the grantor retained income trust (GRIT), the qualified personal residence trust (QPRT), and the private annuity (all of which are covered in Chapter 14), and the corporate recapitalization (discussed in Chapter 16). Many of these transactions are a blend of reduction, freezing, and leveraging with the characterization being based upon what is expected to produce the greatest reduction in transfer taxes.

Delaying payment of the transfer tax. In certain situations, transfer taxes can be deferred, even though a completed transfer has taken place.

> EXAMPLE 9 - 11. Danny and his wife Barbara have equally large estates. Each could live well on his or her own assets. The unlimited marital deduction shelters any transfer to the other at death so if Danny gives his wealth to Barbara there will be no immediate estate tax on that property. In effect, though, the estate tax will only be deferred, not eliminated because the property will probably be taxed at Barbara's later death. In fact, the gift to her will probably increase the overall estate tax on that property since the transfer to Barbara (a) foregoes the use of Danny's unified credit at his death; and (b) will increase the size of Barbara's gross estate, possibly pushing it into a higher marginal rate. If he left the property outright or in trust to the children at his death, there might be a small tax at his death but the property would not be taxed at Barbara's death. Thus, Danny faces the alternative of immediately incurring a (smaller) estate tax on his wealth or deferring a potentially larger tax.

Chapters 11 and 12 discuss the interrelationship between the marital deduction and the unified credit. Other transfer tax deferral devices covered in later chapters include the application of IRC § 6166, dealing with the payment of the estate tax in future installments for a decedent-owner of a closely held business; IRC § 6163, which allows the deferral of that portion of the tax attributed to a vested remainder interest; IRC § 6161, pertaining to the deferral of the tax for good cause (all covered in Chapter 15), and the simple practice of delaying property transfers (Chapter 13).

This chapter has introduced the specific techniques of estate planning by presenting the main goals underlying them. The next chapter begins our detailed study of these techniques with an examination of the decision to avoid probate.

QUESTIONS AND PROBLEMS

1. Consider that goals sometimes conflict. (a) What is probably the typical client's principal goal in estate planning? (b) Give your own example of how a more specific goal described in this chapter can conflict with it.

2. Should the primary concern of the financial planner be to recommend strategies that will provide optimal financial results for the client?

3. Describe a situation where there might be a conflict between nonfinancial goals and financial goals in estate planning.

4. Bob is a very wealthy individual. He is unmarried and has two teenage daughters. He has approached you about estate planning. As an estate planner, should you focus your attention on constructing an estate plan that will result in the least amount of income and transfer tax? Explain.

5. List and briefly describe a person's nonfinancial estate planning goals.

6. Considering the various ways property is transferred when a co-owner dies (e.g., joint tenancy, probate, and funded living trust), which do each of the following suggest? Briefly explain each answer. (a) Likely to be the quickest method? The slowest? (b) Probably the most private method. The least? (c) The most flexible from an overall planning standpoint? Least? (d) The most expensive? The most inexpensive?

7. List and briefly describe a person's nontax financial estate planning goals.

8. (a) What does it mean to have flexibility in estate planning? (b) What are some methods of maintaining flexibility given the possibility of losing mental capacity. (c) Flexibility insofar as caring for surviving dependants in the event of one's death?

9. Describe the advantage of selecting a surrogate decision maker in the estate planning process.

10. Describe some major reasons for seeking liquidity for a decedent's estate. How is this accomplished?

11. List and briefly describe a person's income tax savings goals.

12. List and briefly describe a person's transfer tax savings goals.

13. What steps have you taken toward having your own estate plan in order? What goals have you not addressed?

14. Tony is 92 years old and in poor health. He has securities valued at $500,000 and a basis in them of only $100,000. He told you that it has always been his goal to give his daughter Angela something special and added, "I am going to give her these securities tomorrow. I know I won't be living much longer and nothing will make me happier than to see her sell these securities and buy something that she will enjoy." Comment on some apparent conflicting goals.

ANSWERS TO QUESTIONS AND PROBLEMS (*odd numbered only*)

1. (a) The client's principal goal is happiness and peace of mind. Estate planning deals principally with property transfer decisions, many of which may be fundamentally unsettling for individuals. (b) Answers will vary but an example might be making a large lifetime gift to a young adult child.

3. Some may believe that the primary goal of estate planning is to minimize tax consequences, which might include strategies of making large gifts. Some of these strategies to reduce transfer taxes might hinder a person's peace of mind regarding financial security. The primary goal of estate planning should be happiness and peace of mind.

5. Nonfinancial estate planning goals: (a) Caring for future dependents, including the client and the client's minor children. (b) Attaining privacy in the property transfer process. (c) Attaining speed in the property transfer process. (d) Maintaining control over assets.

7. Nontax financial estate planning goals:(a) Minimizing nontax estate transfer costs. (b) Maintaining a satisfactory standard of living. (c) Ensuring proper disposition. (d) Preserving business value. (e) Attaining pre- and postmortem flexibility. (f) Maximizing benefits for the surviving spouse.

9. The advantage of selecting a surrogate decision maker is flexibility in planning after the client becomes incapacitated or dies.

11. Income tax savings goals: (a) Obtaining a stepped-up basis. (b) Shifting income to a lower bracket taxpayer. (c) Deferring recognition of income.

13. An important question that everyone should answer, but each in his or her own way.

CHAPTER 10

The Decision to Avoid Probate

OVERVIEW

Probate means the entire court process supervising the distribution of any part of a decedent's property according to a will or the rules of intestate succession. Since probate has significant drawbacks, most people prefer to have their estates use one of its two major alternatives, joint tenancy or the living trust. These are referred to as *will substitutes* because they supersede any provisions in the deceased person's will. This chapter surveys the advantages and disadvantages of all three mechanisms of transfer. To some degree, the choice is subjective; what is best depends on the individual's personal assessment of the pros and cons of each choice in light of his or her personal circumstances. We begin our comparative study of probate and its two major alternatives by examining the pros and cons of probate.

THE BENEFITS AND DRAWBACKS OF PROBATE

Is probate a terrible process to be avoided like the plague? It has been part of our legal system for over a hundred years and must serve a useful purpose or it would be gone by now. Below, we describe probate's major benefits and drawbacks.

The Benefits of Probate

In summary, the major benefits of probate include fairness promoted by court supervision, orderly administration of assets, greater protection from creditors, and some limited income tax savings.

Court supervision promotes fairness. Formal probate requires substantial court supervision, a process that, at its best, promotes fairness. Through the use of petitions, accountings, hearings, and court orders, probate seeks to ensure that asset distribution is fair. No other estate transfer procedure is so controlled by public authorities.

The public-forum nature of probate encourages review and evaluation by numerous observers. Judges and official clerks are called on to approve major estate activities. In addition, other interested private parties such as beneficiaries and creditors have an opportunity to object to perceived inequities in estate administration. For example, they can object to many court rulings, including admission of a certain will to probate, appointment of a certain personal representative, payment of a certain creditor, and distribution of estate assets to a certain individual. They can raise these objections in the probate court itself; the parties need not seek a remedy elsewhere, and they can often do it without hiring a lawyer. In contrast, objections to disposition by joint tenancy or through a living trust require a different, procedurally more complicated, legal action.

Critics' response. Critics of probate contend that the additional degree of equity fostered by probate administration is, at best, minimal. They argue that judges and other public officials too often give only superficial review of proposed actions and rubber-stamp their approval of the conduct of executors. Supporters of probate respond to this criticism saying that judges implicitly and successfully rely on the interested parties, who are formally notified of the proceedings, to speak up in court if they feel they are being treated unfairly. Critics contend, however, that the average interested person would not be aware of the occurrence of many types of subtle wrong doing.

The claim that probate encourages fairness is also subject to challenge because of the recent trend in the direction of reduced supervision. In Chapter 4, we learned that many states permit "informal" or "summary" probate procedures that can greatly reduce court surveillance. Also, we saw that UPC states permit the estate's personal representative to select the degree of supervision he or she desires. If "informal probate" is chosen, the estate will receive almost no direct supervision by the court. Thus, in many states, the risk of misadministration in probate is similar to that for trusts because of the opportunity to avoid the public forum. Of course, in UPC states the ability of beneficiaries to request greater formal supervision of the executor at any time during the probate process reduces the risk of mismanagement.

In conclusion, although proponents of probate argue that it promotes fairness through formal supervision, courts are supervising probate less these days. In the move toward less formal probates, many states have reduced the degree of mandatory court supervision and oversight of administrative activities. Paradoxically, moves to make probate less onerous by making it less formal are negating an argument for its use.

Orderly administration of assets. Probate offers orderly administration of estate assets. Supervision by the court and by other public officials ensures that property transfers and title clearance will be done correctly.

Greater protection from creditors. Probate offers distributees protection from creditors of the decedent sooner than other means of transfer. Probate procedures require creditors to file their claims against probate assets within a short time, typically four months, from date of issuance of letters testamentary. Creditors that don't file claims in that time can never collect from probate assets. Nonprobate assets, on the other hand, may only be protected by the state's general limitations period, which can be several years. However, there is a movement among the states to shorten the creditors' claim period for nonprobate estates.

Actual notice: the Tulsa decision. In 1988, the U.S. Supreme Court ruled in *Tulsa Professional Collection Services v. Estate of Pope* that creditors who are "known or reasonably ascertainable" to the personal representative must be given "actual" notice of the limited creditors' claim period, rather than be given just "constructive" notice by publication.[1] Notice by mail is considered acceptable actual notice.

The following is a partial listing of creditors who are usually known or can be reasonably ascertained by the personal representative:

- Hospital where decedent died, all treating physicians, ambulance company and paramedics
- Landlord or mortgage company
- Pool service, gardener, maid, newspaper delivery service

- Installment payment creditor
- Creditors who have already sent decedent unpaid bills
- Credit card issuers
- Creditors that show up as "interest deductions" on the decedent's last few years' income tax returns
- Ongoing creditors determined from decedent's correspondence and canceled checks
- Persons given a guarantee by the decedent as the owner of a closely held business

Under *Tulsa*, actual notice need not be given to potential creditors whose claims are a matter of "conjecture," i.e., deduced by surmise or guesswork. An example of a conjectural claim would be that any of a deceased doctor's former patients might eventually assert a malpractice claim against the doctor's estate. The executor does not have to notify all former patients to "submit their claims or lose their right to sue." Indeed, that would likely cause needless problems. The creditors' claim period does not affect the rights of secured creditors to the extent that the debt is covered by collateral.

Individuals who anticipate that there may be hidden or unknown claims that are difficult to identify might prefer the shorter limitations period. For example, professionals such as doctors, lawyers, architects, engineers or accountants are potentially vulnerable to malpractice claims which, if instituted after their death, stand a greater chance of succeeding, partly because the defense's best witness, the decedent, is not available to testify. The shorter probate creditors' claim period decreases this threat.

If there is insurance to cover a claim, the claim is not barred by the short probate creditors' period. The estate may be named as a party to the suit, but the real party in interest is the insurance company that will have to pay the claim. Generally, unless the injured party files a creditor's claim within the regular creditor's claim period, state probate statutes limit the recovery to the amount of insurance coverage.

There are several reasons why a person might miss the creditors' claim period, yet have a valid claim but for the tortfeasor's death. First, where there is delayed discovery, some states' statutes of limitations do not begin to run until the wrongdoing is or should have been discovered, e.g., negligence by a doctor may not be discovered until long after an operation. Second, where there is delayed injury or damage, the limitations period does not begin to run until the injury or damage actually occurs. For instance, an error in will drafting might prevent an estate from claiming a marital or charitable deduction, yet the error would not cause any damage until the testator's death, which might be years after the will was drafted.

Most malpractice insurance is issued on a "claims made" basis, meaning that the insurance covers only errors that occur while the policy is in force and only if a claim is submitted while it is in force. However, when a professional retires, he or she can purchase what is called "tail coverage," which continues to cover later claims for errors made during the period covered by the insurance.

Many people, especially those not likely to be the target of litigation, will find the benefit of the shorter creditors' period to be of little value. In view of the fact that probate makes the decedent's assets known to anyone interested enough to "pull the file," many people prefer the more private methods of asset distribution.

In UPC states, estates can have the same claims protection without supervised probate. For example, informal UPC probate offers the four-month creditors' period because its provisions allow for the filing of a legal notice to creditors. As mentioned in Chapter 4, if the notice is not issued, the UPC imposes a three-year creditors' limitations period, starting at date of death. Certain other forms of summary probate in non-UPC states treat the claims period differently. For example, in California, the four-month probate claim period is not available for the surviving spouse under summary distribution(described in Appendix 4A). But a more general Civil Code limitation requires that claims against any decedent be asserted within one year after the person's death.[2]

Income tax savings. As we saw in Chapter 8, the probate estate is considered a separate tax entity during its existence, taxable at its own rates. Because it is a separate entity, there is an opportunity for income shifting depending on whether the beneficiary's or the estate's rates are lower. For example, during estate administration, undistributed income (FAI) earned on estate property will be taxed to the estate rather than to the beneficiaries. This can reduce total income taxes if the estate is in a lower tax bracket than its beneficiaries. However, the advantage has been somewhat undercut by tax reform since 1986, which has generally lowered and compressed the income tax rate brackets for trusts and estates.[3] Income tax planning for estates is described briefly in Chapter 18.

The Drawbacks of Probate

Probate has several distinct disadvantages, including complexity, cost, lack of privacy, delay, and danger of unintended disposition.

Complexity. As we saw in Chapter 4, formal probate is a complex process, requiring petitions, accountings, hearings, and other complicated legal procedures. Most laypersons hire a lawyer to meet these requirements. Critics argue that supervised probate is usually an unnecessary, clumsy process offering considerable make-work for the legal profession, especially paralegals and legal secretaries. Others respond that in the many states that allow informal probate procedures, the probate process transfers a decedent's property almost as easily as does a living trust.

Cost. The cost of probate can be high. Usually, the probate administration expenses range between 2% and 10% of the probate estate's gross value. The percentage will likely decrease as the size of the estate increases (especially for those subject to informal UPC administration) because there are certain fixed costs regardless of the size of the estate.

The personal representative's commission usually constitutes the largest probate expense. Of course, a beneficiary of the estate, who serves as personal representative, might waive the commission. The statutes of most states either provide for "reasonable" compensation of the personal representative or a statutory commission based on a percentage of the estate's total value. In general, personal representatives' commissions for formal probate range between 2% and 5% of the gross value.

The next largest probate administration expense is usually the attorney's fee. Most states' statutes do not set attorneys' fees, leaving it to the judge for each case to decide and approve a reasonable fee, whereas other states have a statutory fee set as a percentage of the estate's total value. Where commissions and fees are set as a percentage of an estate's total value, the percentage generally decreases as the size of the estate increases, e.g., it might be 4% of the first $100,000 and 2% of the value above $100,000. In general, attorneys' fees usually range between 2% and 5% of the gross value of the probate estate. Other administration expenses include fiduciary bond fees, appraisers' fees, and court costs, including filing fees.

Probate administration costs will be higher for estates containing real property located in other states. Under what is called *ancillary administration*, that property is probated in the state in which it is located. This usually requires hiring an attorney in the other state to handle the ancillary administration.

Other factors that will affect the level of probate administration costs include the nature of the estate property (e.g., closely held business interests, expensive artwork, etc., versus marketable securities), the complexity of the estate distribution plan, and whether a will contest occurs.

Contrary to popular belief, probate does not increase estate taxes. Indeed, since probate costs are deductible, probate may actually reduce estate taxes by a percentage of the probate costs.

Lack of privacy. Probate is a public process; all probate proceedings are subject to public scrutiny. For example, any person can inspect a decedent's probate file, which will eventually include the decedent's will, the estate inventory and appraisal, any creditor's claims, and the order for final distribution. Those particularly interested in inspecting a file would include survivors who are fighting and members of the press seeking a story about a newsworthy decedent. Commonly cited examples of celebrities receiving considerable publicity which could have been avoided by using trusts include the estates of Amanda Blake, Greta Garbo, Natalie Wood, John Wayne, Darryl Zanuck, and the controversy surrounding the conservatorship for Groucho Marx.

The probate files of most decedents are usually seen only by court officials. Interested parties such as the decedent's relatives and the executor can have the attorney for the estate send them copies of every document that is filed. Many probate attorneys do this as a matter of practice without any request that they do so. Thus most interested parties have no reason to review the court's file unless they suspect that not everything is being sent.

In some situations, a person may actually prefer the lack of privacy inherent in probate. For example, the public aspects of probate might discourage or uncover fraudulent dealings by unscrupulous survivors.

Delay. Even for smaller estates, probate administration takes considerable time, ranging from nine months to several years before final distribution is made. In any particular case, the delay can be quite unpredictable. For example, payment of proceeds of life insurance on the decedent's life to the decedent's testamentary trust will be delayed until the trust takes effect, which usually can be no sooner than the expiration of the creditor's period, several months after date of death. Thus, complete, immediate liquidity cannot be provided to the decedent's survivors. Delay can be especially hard on grieving survivors, partly because it can increase or prolong tension and conflict among them. However, preliminary distributions of significant amounts can usually be made earlier if the executor can make a good faith representation that doing so will not jeopardize creditors.

Danger of unintended disposition. The nature of probate may, in some cases, increase the risk of a will contest which may be settled with a distribution of assets in a manner that conflicts with testator intent. For example, a person named in a prior will might contest the decedent's last will on a technicality. The person might claim that the decedent failed at the time of execution to verbally request that the witnesses sign the will. Nonprobate documents of transfer such as a trust are more difficult to contest, partly because execution requirements are less stringent. Thus a mistake in execution that would invalidate a trust is less likely to occur. However, recent changes in the UPC make a successful will challenge on a mere technicality more difficult. Section 2-503. *Writings Intended as Wills, etc.* reads as follows:

> *Although a document or writing added upon a document was not executed in compliance with Section 2-502, the document or writing is treated as if it had been executed in compliance with that section if the proponent of the document or writing establishes by clear and convincing evidence that the decedent intended the document or writing to constitute (i) the decedent's will, (ii) a partial or complete revocation of the will, (iii) an addition to or an alteration of the will, or (iv) a partial or complete revival of his [or her] formerly revoked will or of a formerly revoked portion of the will.*

THE JOINT TENANCY ALTERNATIVE

Disposition by right of survivorship under title held in joint tenancy is one major alternative to probate. It, too, has several advantages and disadvantages.

This discussion also applies to several ways of holding title that share similarities with joint tenancy but also have differences. The common element is that the asset transfers automatically upon death independent of any other asset or document. The major difference is in the degree to which the intended transferee is given a of lifetime interest.

At one end of the continuum the person establishing the relationship (e.g., opening an account) retains all life-time control. An example is the *pay-on-death* account recognized in many states. It may be a bank or savings account (sometimes referred to as a Totten trust) controlled by the depositor so long as he or she is living but with a provision that the account is payable to another if it is still open when the depositor dies. Most states allow pay-on-death accounts to be used with checking and savings accounts, money market accounts, and certificates of deposit. Pay-on-death accounts avoid the loss of control that transferring assets into joint tenancy causes. The beneficiary of a pay-on-death account need not even know of the account and the holder of the account can change it at any time. The beneficiary has no power over the account while the holder is alive. Once assets are transferred into joint tenancy they can generally be withdrawn by either joint tenant or subject to the liabilities of either.

A growing number of states have adopted the Uniform Transfer on Death (TOD) Securities Registration Act which allows individual securities (e.g., stocks and bonds) and brokerage accounts to be held in a manner that causes the security (or the brokerage account) to be transferred to a named beneficiary on the owner's death.[4] Although Totten trust accounts and TOD accounts avoid probate, they are, of course, included in the owner's gross estate.[5] Certain contracts, such as life insurance and retirement plans, avoid probate.

At the other end of the continuum are assets whose title simply lists the names of the owners separated by "or." Bank accounts, automobile titles, and savings bonds, to name a few, are assets that can be held in this way. Either party can deal with the asset without the knowledge or consent of the other(s). Generally, these accounts are treated as joint tenancy accounts.

Joint tenancy and the other just described probate avoidance devices are "asset specific" in the sense that the order of who is next in line to receive the asset is specified by the asset's title or, in the case of insurance and pensions, is established by way of a beneficiary designation associated with each policy or pension plan. In contrast, a will or a living trust can serve to transfer a whole bundle of assets. Only trusts can provide long term comprehensive estate planning.

In this chapter, we'll use the term joint tenancy to include tenancy by the entirety keeping in mind that the latter is available only to married couples.

Advantages of Joint Tenancy

Joint tenancy has a number of distinct advantages: low administrative cost; convenience, speed and privacy; clear, undisputed disposition; the ability to avoid creditors' claims; and income shifting.

Low administrative cost. Joint tenancy is inexpensive, both to create and to terminate. Both actions typically involve simply adding or deleting names on a certificate of ownership. Financial institutions, and others holding record of titles, will aid the survivors in making the change. The removal of the deceased joint tenant's name from title usually requires the presentation of a death certificate and the completion of a short, preprinted form signed by one or more of the surviving joint tenants. In order to clear title to real estate, one of the surviving joint tenants may have to sign a declaration under penalty of perjury, identifying the decedent described in an attached death certificate as one of the owners whose name appears on the title. The notarized declaration and the certified copy of the death certificate are then recorded in the county where the real estate is located.

Convenience, speed, and privacy. The simplicity inherent in creating and terminating joint tenancy makes it a convenient, easily understood, and speedy dispositive device. A will or trust does not affect the automatic survivorship of joint tenancy. Joint tenancy property will pass to the surviving joint tenant(s) in relative privacy. Compared to the ease of "pulling a file" at the probate court, it is more difficult for the public to obtain information about jointly held stock, bank accounts, and the like. Title to real estate, including that held in joint tenancy, is public record.

Clear, undisputed disposition. Suits contesting joint tenancies are rare, partly because the legal formality requirements for taking title in joint tenancy are clear and minimal. There is little to challenge. Title held in joint tenancy is usually clearly indicated. For example, states may require the words "joint tenancy with right of survivorship and not as tenants in common," a title description that minimizes confusion. In contrast, interested parties may be more able to challenge the validity of a will because its execution requirements and dispositive provisions are far more complex with more potential sources of error.

Joint tenancy is not completely immune to challenge. In some cases, courts have held that the decedent created a joint tenancy for convenience only, and did not intend to leave his or her interest to the surviving joint tenant(s). For example, an elderly person may create a joint tenancy solely for convenience in property management. A younger person may have been named as a joint tenant simply to help write checks on the elderly person's checking account.

Ability to reduce creditors' claims. Property held in joint tenancy is not subject to the claims of a *deceased joint tenant's* unsecured creditors because death results in an instantaneous and automatic transfer of ownership to the surviving joint tenant(s). However, a creditor may be able to recover under the theory that the deceased joint tenant made a transfer that was "fraudulent" as to creditors. However, such claim would require evidence that the decedent created the joint tenancy at a time when he or she was insolvent, or that the transfer was done with the intent to defraud creditors or to hinder the collection of a debt. Obviously, joint tenancy property is subject to claims resulting from debts incurred by the surviving joint tenant(s), whether or not incurred jointly with the decedent.

> EXAMPLE 10 - 1. Three years ago, Starfield financed the purchase of a car, which was used as collateral against the loan. Starfield died this year owning, among other things, the car (a probate asset), and some securities held in joint tenancy with his sister. If the bank loan goes into default, the bank will be able to recover the car. If proceeds from the sale of the car are not sufficient to pay off the loan, the bank may be able to reach other assets in Starfield's probate estate, but it would not be able to seize the formerly joint tenancy securities that now belong to the sister.

Income shifting. By placing property in joint tenancy with other family members, a high income individual may be able to shift income to lower-bracket taxpayers. The donee usually receives an immediate ownership interest. Consequently, income generated by the transferred interest belongs to the donee. There are some exceptions. For example, bank accounts are not considered as transferred (even though title is changed to joint tenancy) until money is withdrawn by the donee joint tenant. EE savings bonds placed in joint tenancy are not considered as transferred until the owners submit them for payment and split the proceeds.

Disadvantages of Joint Tenancy

The disadvantages of joint tenancy are inflexible, uncontrolled and inefficient disposition; surrender of ownership and control; incomplete probate avoidance; between spouses, loss of the basis step-up of community property; and the risk of higher transfer taxes.

Inflexible, uncontrolled, and inefficient disposition. Joint tenancy is an inflexible, uncontrolled, and inefficient dispositive device. Disposition is clear but rigid. The surviving joint tenant(s) takes outright, pro-rata, the deceased joint tenant's interest, and the last surviving joint tenant has an individual, fee simple interest in the property. Thus, obviously, right of survivorship cannot control disposition of property when the last joint tenant dies.

Danger of uncontrolled, undesired disposition. Joint tenancies can result in uncontrolled and undesired dispositions in three major ways.

First, by taking title in joint tenancy, one risks distribution of the property to unintended beneficiaries, either by chance, or by the intent of the surviving joint tenant. For example, consider a joint tenancy between a childless couple. If both were to die in fairly rapid succession, such as in a common accident, all the property would end up with heirs or beneficiaries of the joint tenant who lived the longest, even if the difference in survival was just a matter of a few days.

The survivor has the right to direct disposition of what once belonged to both of them, to anyone by will, trust, or other document. By taking title in joint tenancy, spouses leave ultimate disposition to chance, empowering the survivor to disregard the other's dispositive wishes. This risk can be avoided with a will or a trust, documents that can control asset disposition after the survivor's death by using a survival clause and other provisions, such as giving the survivor only a life estate with the remainder going to someone else. Such long-range planning does not apply to assets held in joint tenancy.

EXAMPLE 10 - 2. Cheryl remarries after the death of her first husband, and wishing to have her estate avoid probate, deeds her residence to herself and Donny as joint tenants. Although Cheryl's will leaves her property to her children, the house passes to Donny no matter what the will says if he survives Cheryl.

Second, disposition by joint tenancy, when not coordinated with other planning, can result in an unintended disproportionate distribution of the person's estate.

EXAMPLE 10 - 3. Coco owned a bank account with a $1,000 balance and other property worth $400,000. Her will left her entire estate to her children and directed that all taxes and debts be paid out of the probate estate. About one year before her death, she put her sister's name on the bank account as a joint tenant, making it easier for her sister to help her pay bills. Shortly before her death, Coco sold stock worth $100,000, temporarily depositing the proceeds in the joint tenancy bank account. At Coco's death, her sister will receive the entire $101,000 bank account. Assuming that debts and expenses amounted to $50,000 at her death, Coco's children must pay all debts and expenses from their share and will receive property worth only $250,000 (i.e., $401,000 - $101,000 - $50,000). Although there is no evidence Coco intended to leave her sister such a large proportion of her estate, placing the proceeds of the stock in the joint account has resulted in her receiving approximately 29% of Coco's net wealth.

Third, joint ownership prevents an individual from making other, less direct but more desirable types of transfers at death, such as giving someone a temporary interest, e.g., an income interest to one person and a remainder interest to another person or to a charity. Most long-range planning objectives cannot be accomplished if property is held in joint tenancy.

Danger of inefficient disposition. Even if joint tenancies dispose of a person's assets to the right parties in the right amounts, they may do so inefficiently, generating delay and asset shrinkage. Three common inefficiencies are as follows.

First, the property passing to the surviving joint tenant will not be subject to protective provisions often included in trusts regarding responsible asset management. As a consequence, a surviving joint tenant who lacks experience in the care and management of property may deplete an asset intended for his or her security through unwise or irresponsible management.

EXAMPLE 10 - 4. In Example 10 - 2 above, if Cheryl named her oldest child as joint tenant, disposition to Donny could have been avoided, but the child would become the sole owner of the property, to the exclusion of the other children. If the child later shared the property with his or her siblings, that would be gifts subject to taxation. Perhaps Cheryl should include all her children as joint tenants, but Cheryl may not wish to make an immediate gift to them of her property.

Second, creating joint tenancies may expose those assets to the claims of the creditors of the other joint tenant even though the initial owner was merely seeking an inexpensive way to avoid probate and did not really intend the other joint tenant to have an interest before her death. For example, if a parent adds her adult child as a joint tenant on her home and the child is liable for an automobile accident, a judgment against the child could force the partition and sale of the home.

Third, joint tenancies can result in probate administration and, possibly, intestacy. Joint tenancy does not avoid probate administration at the death of the last surviving joint tenant, nor does it in the case of the simultaneous death of the joint tenants.

EXAMPLE 10 - 5. Russ and his wife Patti were advised to avoid probate by creating joint tenancies. After Russ died, Patti survived only a few years, never realizing that at her death their property would be subject to probate administration. When she died, Patti's estate had to be probated.

EXAMPLE 10 - 6. Based on the facts in the prior example, if Russ and Patti died in an accident where the evidence could not determine who survived the longest, under the Uniform Simultaneous Death Act, each joint tenant is presumed to survive the other, resulting in each joint tenant's half interest being subject to probate administration.

The living trust, discussed in the next major section, does not have this drawback. It is designed to avoid probate administration even at the simultaneous death of both spouses.

Surrender of ownership and control. As discussed in Chapter 7, creating an interest in joint tenancy will usually constitute an immediate, completed gift by the person or persons who contributed more than their share of the purchase price, said gift being made to any joint tenant who has contributed less than his or her proportional share. Property law requires that each joint tenant owns an equal share of the property. Each owner has the right to convert his or her share of the property into a tenancy-in-common interest, capable of being sold or devised to a non-joint tenant. This might not be a problem for joint tenancies between people who contribute equal shares of property, nor for happily married spouses. Between others, however, the owner might not want to surrender significant property interests by forming a joint tenancy merely to avoid probate.

Creating an immediate vested present interest in the donee-joint tenant can give rise to other problems. The donee may be unable to later disclaim the gift to save transfer taxes. If the donee becomes incompetent, a guardian may have to be appointed. The donor may need the donee's permission to sell the asset. Finally, the asset may be subject to the claims of the donee's creditors.

In contrast with joint tenancy, other documents of transfer, such as the will and the trust instrument, can delay the making of an outright transfer of ownership until the person's death. Instead of creating present interests, they provide for future interests, ones that are contingent on future events, such as the owner not revoking the interests. Most individuals do not wish to make outright gifts, even if doing so will allow their estate to avoid probate.

The basis problem. As we have seen earlier, the rule for basis adjustment for appreciated joint tenancy property at the death of one spouse results in a "one-half" step-up. A step-up in basis for the entire value of the property may be achieved by one of the techniques described next.

Gift-death-devise strategy. First, the property could be given to a donee who is expected to die before the donor with the expectation that, at the donee's death, the entire property will be devised back to the donor and it will receive a full step-up in basis. This strategy will be certain to work satisfactorily only in situations where the donee can be trusted to actually devise the property to the donor, such as where the parties are happily married. It will also succeed only if the donee's death occurs at least one year after the initial gift because, under IRC § 1014(e), failure of the donee to survive at least a year after the gift was given will cause the transfer at death of the property back to the donor to be treated for the purpose of its basis adjustment as if neither transfer ever occurred.

Community property. Second, when spouses own property as community rather than joint tenancy property, there is an opportunity for a basis step-up for the entire value of the property. As we saw in Chapter 7, unlike joint tenancy property, both halves of community property receive a step-up in basis at the death of the first spouse. Thus, married couples in community property states (even those of modest wealth) may be especially interested in avoiding joint tenancy arrangements, choosing instead to dispose of community property by will or trust instrument. Some community property states do not require a probate to pass property to a surviving spouse.[6]

When a step-up is less important. Generally it is better to have a basis step-up and avoid a basis step-down. When a property is eventually divested, gain or loss is measured by the difference between basis and sale price. However, there may be other factors that decrease the relative importance of a step-up for a particular property or situation.

The 2001 tax legislation limits the basis step-up to $1.3 million for an estate. For the small proportion of estates with more capital gain than that, allocation decisions must be made. The assets that should be allocated the least basis step-up are those that have the least need. For example, a property may not have appreciated substantially. If it has depreciated, then the strategies mentioned above would actually result in a full step-down in basis. This is particularly undesirable if the property is income property whose sale might generate a capital loss sheltering other income. A basis step-up is also less important if the survivor is not expected to sell the property, or if any gain from sale of the property is sheltered by certain provisions of the Internal Revenue Code, e.g., excluding gain on the sale a principal residence (up to $250,000 single taxpayer, $500,000 joint filing married couple) [7] or deferring the gain on a like-kind exchange.[8]

Possible higher estate tax. Joint tenancies can increase estate tax for two reasons: because of the somewhat harsh provisions of IRC § 2040 for non-spouses that presumes the decedent contributed all of the consideration unless the survivors can prove otherwise. Even with a surviving spouse there may be a "loading up" the surviving joint tenant's gross estate. After the estate tax is repealed in 2010 these problems will go away.

IRC § 2040 consequences. When we first studied § 2040, we learned that the entire value of property held in joint tenancy by a decedent is includable in the decedent's gross estate, except in two situations. First, if the joint tenancy was held solely with the surviving spouse, one half is included. Second, if the joint tenancy was held by the decedent and at least one person who is not the decedent's spouse, the decedent's gross estate will include the entire value of the property, reduced by an amount attributable to that portion of the consideration shown to have been furnished by the survivors. Thus, a higher than necessary estate tax can result if a joint tenancy has a nonspouse joint tenant and if the surviving joint tenant is unable to prove his or her contribution.

This inability to prove contributions may be a blessing in disguise. If the deceased joint tenant's taxable estate is less than the applicable exclusion amount, there will be no transfer tax and yet the surviving joint tenant(s) will have a new basis equal to the date-of-death fair market value.

EXAMPLE 10 - 7. Clarissa and her brother, Scott, purchased a condo on the Florida coast for $100,000. They took title in joint tenancy. The condo was worth $300,000 when Scott died. Scott's other worldly possessions were worth approximately $180,000. Because Clarissa and Scott failed to keep adequate records concerning the purchase of the condo, it was deemed to be 100% in Scott's gross estate. As a consequence, Clarissa's basis in the condo is $300,000. Scott's estate paid no estate tax because the net value was less than the applicable exclusion amount.

Overloading the survivor's estate. Joint tenancies may result in a higher than necessary estate tax for the estates of surviving joint tenant(s) because their estates will be "loaded up" with the predeceased joint tenant's property. If the decedent's property is passed outright (by joint tenancy or some other means) to the surviving spouse using the automatic 100% marital deduction to avoid estate taxes, the exclusion amount for the decedent is not used. The second spouse's estate includes the assets of both but has only one exclusion amount. If the combined estate exceeds that single exclusion amount, taxes must be paid. Taxes are saved by passing less property outright to the surviving spouse by using trusts that give the survivor limited access to the assets but keep them out of the survivor's gross estate. Chapter 11 gives more details. This kind of estate planning may also save taxes for couples in nontraditional relationships.

Possible gift taxation. Creation of joint tenancies between nonspouses can result in a taxable gift if unequal contributions are made and if the value of the gift exceeds the annual exclusion. In contrast, disposition by will or by the typical living trust instrument produces no immediate gift during the person's lifetime because those documents do not create vested interests.

Finally, the person may not be able to avoid joint tenancy in certain property. For example, some bank lenders may require that spouses hold title in their home in joint tenancy rather than in trust as a condition to granting a loan secured by the property. As living trusts become more popular as estate planning devices, and lending institutions become more familiar with them, this requirement by lenders is less likely to occur, although the borrowers may still be asked to personally guarantee the loan and to give their written assurance that there is nothing in the trust document that would prevent them from using the property as collateral. Also, a bank may be less likely to object if the property is transferred to a trust after the loan is made.

In view of the many significant drawbacks to joint tenancy, especially for individuals with medium or large estates, planners generally recommend the other major alternative to probate, the living trust, discussed next.

THE LIVING TRUST ALTERNATIVE

The most popular alternative to probate for wealthy people is the funded living trust. While the trustor is alive, the living trust is usually revocable, which means that its terms are amendable or its assets can be taken out of trust by the trustor. Most trustors name themselves trustee of their living trust during their lifetime.

At the trustor's death, the revocable trust becomes irrevocable and may either terminate, with the corpus distributed to the remaindermen, or continue in existence until a later date. A typical revocable living trust created by a husband and wife has all assets placed in one trust, which is revocable by them during their lifetimes. At the first spouse's death, different things can happen depending on the plan. A commonly used estate plan for smaller estates has the decedent's share of the trust property continue in a revocable trust with the trust corpus belonging entirely to the surviving spouse. The trust property is not subject to probate at either death. At the surviving spouse's death the trust is either terminated and distributed to the children or it is continued for their benefit. Other distribution arrangements, particularly those designed to reduce estate tax, are discussed in Chapter 11.

Taxation of a living trust depends on whether it is revocable. A revocable living trust usually has no transfer or income tax consequences during the trustor's lifetime. A transfer to it does not constitute a taxable gift since the transfer is not complete. And under the grantor trust rules, all income earned by a revocable trust is taxable to the grantor/trustor. In contrast, an irrevocable living trust is usually a separate income tax paying entity; all transfers into it usually constitute completed gifts. All undistributed fiduciary accounting income (FAI) is taxed to the trust, while all distributed FAI is usually taxed to the beneficiaries, except when either the grantor trust rules or the kiddie tax apply.

Funded irrevocable living trusts also avoid probate. Not as commonly used as the revocable living trust because they involve taxable gifts, they will be discussed at length in Chapters 13 and 15 in the context of gifts and life insurance planning.

Advantages of the Living Trust

The advantages of the living trust over other transfer devices are greater assurance of probate avoidance, lower total costs, greater privacy and speed, opportunity to observe a chosen fiduciary, ability to use the trust as an alternative to a conservatorship, greater organization, and possible reduced litigation.

Greater assurance of complete probate avoidance. The living trust offers greater certainty that probate will be avoided at the death of the surviving spouse/beneficiary.

> EXAMPLE 10 - 8. Kim and Chris could use a basic will for their simple estates, but they also wish to avoid probate on all their property. Their planner makes it clear to them that joint tenancies will not achieve the latter goal because the surviving joint tenant will wind up owning the property, making it eventually subject to probate. Instead, they execute a living trust, funding the trust with their property. The trust will continue to exist for both their lifetimes. At the survivor's death, the assets will pass from the trust to their designated beneficiaries, free from probate.

The above example was intentionally ambiguous about the individuals' gender and marital status. For a living trust, neither is material; unmarried individuals, including members of the same sex, may legally take title in joint tenancy or co-execute a single trust instrument.

Lower total cost than probate. The combined cost of preparation and administration of the living trust is usually significantly less than the combined costs of will preparation and probate. The following material discusses both preparation costs and total cost.

Preparation costs. The cost of having a living trust prepared is usually higher than the cost of preparing a will. First, the trust instrument is usually a more complicated document. Its provisions must arrange for the immediate receipt of property, for the management of that property, and for the proper distribution of the property and the trust income for a period that might span several generations. Second, with the living trust, the attorney must still draft a will. As previously discussed, the establishment of the living trust does not totally eliminate the need for a will. Because people sometimes fail to completely fund their trusts, some will die owning property in their own name, rather than in the name of the trustee. Planners provide for disposition of this probate property with what is called a *pour-over will*, specifying that any of the testator's assets not in the trust will be distributed or "poured over" into the trust at the trustor's death. Because it disposes of all property outright to only one party (the trustee), the pour-over will is usually very brief, adding little to the preparation cost of avoiding probate with the living trust. Thus, some probate administration costs may be incurred on assets passing by the pour-over will.

Total cost. While the specific cost of preparing the living trust may be higher, the total cost of the living trust alternative is usually lower due to the relatively high cost of formal probate administration at death. In contrast with formal probate, administration of a living trust at the trustor's death involves minimal legal work and usually no court appearances. The pour-over will might not be probated, depending on the size of the probate estate and the scope of the state's informal or summary administration rules. However, some other postmortem legal duties that are required under the probate alternative may also have to be performed under the trust alternative. They include:

- Marshaling and safeguarding assets
- Preparing an inventory of the assets
- Obtaining appraisals
- Preparing and filing estate tax returns
- Preparing and filing income tax returns
- Paying creditors
- Instituting litigation to protect assets
- Changing title to assets
- Distributing assets to beneficiaries
- Obtaining receipts from beneficiaries

While the costs of these actions usually do not come close to the total cost of formal probate administration, they are significant. Sometimes informal probate administration in UPC states can cost less than a trust, making probate an attractive alternative to the living trust.

Other factors that affect the relative costs of probate versus the living trust include whether the grantor or a family member will serve as trustee or executor, the ability to deduct these costs as an income tax itemized deduction, and the schedule of local court fees and costs.

Greater privacy. A trust instrument is usually private and not subject to public inspection. Although property transfers into and out of a living trust may require examination of the trust instrument by financial and other institutions, the document usually need not be publicly accessible. County recorders may require a filing of the trust in public records, but usually only brief sections of the document need be submitted. In fact, many attorneys in the estate planning process draft a separate short (one or two pages) document called a "trust abstract," a "memorandum of trust," or a "confirmation of trust." This short document is made available to persons or institutions dealing with the trustee, in lieu of the full trust instrument. At a minimum, the abstract will contain sections describing the identity of the trustee and successor trustee, and the trustee powers relevant to investing and to transferring assets. It is formally executed by the trustor and trustee, and their signatures are notarized. In this way critical parts of the trust, including dispositive provisions, may be kept secret.

However, states which impose an inheritance tax may require trustees to file an inventory revealing the nature and value of the trust's assets and the names of its beneficiaries. In addition, if there is litigation, a determined litigant may gain access to the contents of a living trust through discovery.

As mentioned earlier, privacy may be especially desired by wealthy or prominent individuals. They may wish to avoid publicity and inspection by disinherited or contentious survivors who may try to wage a court challenge to a decedent's estate plan.

Speed. Property can usually be transferred out of a trust sooner than out of a probate estate because the transfer process is not subject to supervision and approval by the court. However, failure to perform certain postmortem legal duties (detailed above) can subject the trustee to significant personal liability and can trigger costly and unnecessary litigation. Thus, for example, in those states where creditors' claims can be made against trust assets, the trustee will delay distribution. And for larger trusts owing a sizable estate tax, the trustee may delay major distributions of trust assets until an estate tax "closing letter" from the IRS is received. Generally, if there are no audit problems, the closing letter comes about 10 months after the estate tax return is filed.

Speed of disposition of real property located in a different state is more rapid if the property is held in a living trust rather than disposed of by will because ancillary administration is avoided. However, some states require reporting procedures for trusts that are quite similar to the probate administration process.

Opportunity to test the future. By placing assets into a revocable living trust, the trustor has the opportunity to test the future by making the estate plan largely operational during his lifetime. By naming another party trustee, the trustor can observe firsthand how well the assets are managed and can make needed adjustments in management provisions before death. In addition, the trustor can help the trustee become familiar with the trust assets during the trustor's lifetime, thus increasing the likelihood of a smooth transition period at the trustor's death.

Alternative to guardianship or conservatorship. A person who becomes physically or mentally incapable of managing assets will need someone to provide that management. Just as a guardianship may have to be established to manage a minor's estate, a guardianship or conservatorship may be necessary to manage the estate of an incapacitated adult. Like probate administration, guardianships and conservatorships are supervised by the court, which usually requires periodic accountings and formal court approval for many acts of asset management.

Used in lieu of a guardianship or conservatorship, the living trust is a good vehicle to avoid the expense, delay and publicity of probate-type administration before the trustor's death. The typical living trust begins with the trustor acting as trustee. Subsequently, a successor trustee takes over when the trustor relinquishes the role, becomes incapacitated, or dies. Thus, the living trust instrument has an additional benefit that is simply not available with a will; it provides for the management of property at the trustor's incapacity. Some commentators consider this the major advantage of the living trust, especially for older people, making the will alternative seriously deficient by comparison.

Another less expensive alternative to the guardianship or conservatorship is the durable power of attorney for financial matters, discussed in Chapter 17, but it does not avoid probate nor does it provide much guidance for the long-term management of assets.

Greater organization. Establishing a living trust requires the person to organize his or her property to create and fund the trust. The actual process of organizing assets increases awareness and enhances efficient personal financial planning.

Possible reduced litigation. As we have seen, the probate process offers an opportunity for a dissatisfied survivor to initiate a will contest. Such disputes may be minimized with a living trust for two reasons. First, the trustor as the initial beneficiary is able to live with the trust, receiving and making distributions and transferring property to it. These acts may constitute evidence of a well thought-out estate plan. In contrast, a will is simply a document not perceived to have much impact on the testator's day-to-day life. Thus, contesting parties may be more successful in showing that the testator's will does not reflect his or her actual intent.

Second, disputes over a person's estate plan may be minimized with a living trust because litigation may be more difficult to accomplish. However, commentators are in disagreement over how difficult it is to challenge the provisions of a living trust. Some maintain that the living trust is more difficult to contest since a lawsuit must be initiated. Transfers from a trust generally do not require notice to anyone; probating a will requires notice to interested parties, which may trigger a contest. With probate, a legal process has already been initiated. Turning it into a contest is a smaller step than initiating a lawsuit. Other commentators argue that a trust can be contested on substantially the same grounds as those that are used to contest a will. Common grounds include fraud, undue influence, lack of capacity and improper execution. Creating a trust may require a higher mental capacity than is required to create a valid will. Courts generally require that the trustor have contractual capacity at the time the trust is created. Since contracting requires negotiation between two parties, it is thought to require sharper mental faculties than to execute a will. Whether that is true is questionable, given that little negotiation takes place in the creation of most trusts.

Other advantages of living trusts. Living trusts are normally simpler to revise than wills. While a codicil to a will requires certain execution formalities (described in Chapter 3), an amendment to a living trust needs no formalities or witnesses, and may be in the trustor's handwriting. However, if the trustee is someone other than the trustor, he or she should at least be notified of the revision, and most attorneys also have the trustee sign and notarize the amendment.

Use of a living trust eliminates any gap in asset management when the trustor dies. While the trustee (or successor trustee) of a living trust is empowered to carry on immediately, no one is authorized to act with regard to probate property until the court appoints a personal representative, at least several days after the testator's death. Of course, most assets do not require immediate attention.

Property held in a revocable living trust receives a step-up in basis because it is treated, from an income tax point of view, as owned by the grantor and, therefore, it is included in the decedent's gross estate.

Disadvantages of the Living Trust

The living trust has several disadvantages, including the burden of funding, possibly greater legal uncertainty, and some minor tax factors.

Funding burden. Establishment of a joint tenancy is a one-step process. The act of creation of the joint interest creates the appropriate title. On the other hand, the establishment of a living trust to avoid probate is a two-step process. First, the trust document is executed by the trustor and the trustee, like a two-party contract. Second, the trust is funded; legal title to the property is transferred from the trustor to the trustee. Some trustors never do the latter because they are unaware that the additional step of funding is necessary. Others are aware of it but simply never get around to doing it. Most find it inconvenient because it requires trips to the bank and to other places where title is officially kept. And people who actively trade their property, such as those involved in frequent real estate deals and securities transactions, may especially dislike the greater complexity inherent in continually keeping property in their name as trustee. However, opening a brokerage account under the trustee's name greatly simplifies the task of keeping track of the trust's investment assets.

Failure to fund the trust will usually result in the trustor's property passing through probate, hopefully guided into the trust by a pour-over will.[9] Most attorneys avoid this undesired outcome by overseeing the initial funding of the living trust rather than leaving the responsibility to the client. This may increase the legal cost of setting up the living trust.

Planners may be able to help their clients who have created living trusts by asking the client's accountant to monitor the funding of the trust. The accountant is asked to pay particular attention to the client's tax-related forms, such as 1099s and K1s, issued by banks, partnerships, S corporations, and other asset account holders, to make sure the trustee is named the owner of the property.

Longer creditors' period. As described earlier, probate offers a shorter creditors' claim period than a living trust. The latter is usually subject to the claims for the regular statute of limitations period, the length of which depends on the nature of the claim. These periods may be from one to three years. However, this disadvantage may be disappearing. Some states have enacted an overall creditors' claim period of one year from date of death. There may be exceptions to the one-year limitation for estates that are subject to some other more specific limitation on creditors' claims, e.g., if there is a probate proceeding, then the shorter provision for probate estates would apply. The one-year statute of limitations applies regardless of the manner in which the decedent held property, and regardless of whether the regular statute of limitations for a particular claim would have ended earlier or later than the one-year period had the person lived.[10]

There is also a trend in state law toward allowing living trusts to take advantage of a shortened creditors' claim period (e.g., four months) if the trustee follows certain notice-to-creditors procedures that are similar to probate proceedings. The law may require the trustee using the shortened claim period to publish a notice in a newspaper of general circulation, to make a reasonable search for creditors, and to give any creditors they locate actual notice of the method to perfect their claims.[11]

Tax factors. There are a few minor tax disadvantages to the living trust.

- Compared to the $600 available to an estate, a trust, after the grantor's death, has a smaller personal income tax exemption: either $100 or $300.
- As mentioned earlier, real property held in trust and located in states other than an individual's residence state is usually considered by a person's residence state to be intangible personal property. Most states impose a death tax on such trust-owned property, which might otherwise escape taxation if it were disposed of by will, since "real property" located outside a state is not ordinarily subject to its tax. Of course no additional tax would be incurred if both states impose only a "pickup" type death tax.

In the past, the IRS maintained that any transfer (gift) directly from a revocable probate-avoidance trust to a person selected by the settlor was included in the settlor's estate, if the settlor died within three years of the transfer. The argument was that IRC § 2038 applied to the trust and, therefore, any gift at the request of the settlor (or done by a settlor-trustee) was a release of the settlor's retained interest, hence the three-year rule of § 2035(a) applied. The IRS made the argument (often successfully) even though the transfer would not have been included in the settlor's estate had the settlor personally made the transfer. The Taxpayer Relief Act of 1997 added § 2035(e), which removes the problem by specifying that such transfers are to be treated as though made by the settlor.

Miscellaneous disadvantages. There are several other minor disadvantages to the living trust.

Financing problems. In some states, if the trustor wishes to refinance property after it has been placed in trust, the lender might require that the trustee transfer title back to the trustor until the refinancing is completed, after which it can again be transferred back to the trustee. As lenders have become more familiar with trusts, fewer are requiring these extra steps, although the trustor is usually required to cosign the loan documents in his or her individual capacity and give written assurance that the trustee has authority to encumber the property.

Divorce. In a few states, divorce may result in an improper distribution of assets from a living trust. As mentioned in Chapter 4, in most states a dissolution of marriage automatically revokes a disposition to an ex-spouse in a will executed prior to the divorce. In contrast, some state statutes do not have similar provisions applicable to living trusts. However, in states adopting Uniform Probate Code § 2-804(b), divorce or annulment revokes any revocable disposition of property to an ex-spouse or to a relative of an ex-spouse. That section also severs any survivorship interests of the former spouses in property held by them at the time of the divorce, transforming property that they held as joint tenants, tenants by the entirety, and as community property with the right of survivorship into tenancies in common. It also cancels the nomination of an ex-spouse (or the ex-spouse's relatives) for any fiduciary position and cancels any general or limited powers to appoint property.

Other disadvantages. Living trusts may have disadvantages in certain special situations, two of which will be mentioned briefly without additional explanation. First, beneficiaries of a living trust may lose a defense against liability for environmental clean up of real property held in the trust. In contrast, that defense is available to persons acquiring the property "by inheritance or bequest."[12] Second, use of a living trust may reduce allowable Medicaid benefits for the beneficiary-spouse of a decedent who establishes a discretionary living trust. The problem will not arise for testamentary trusts.[13]

Living trusts require careful analysis, planning and preparation. Clearly, the decision whether to create a revocable living trust requires the planner's critical evaluation of many challenging issues, and drafting a living trust requires the knowledge of an experienced estate planning attorney. The tasks of evaluation and careful drafting require a skill level far above those of most practicing generalists, let alone someone lacking even rudimentary training in the issues. Nonetheless, recently, many casual salespersons, sometimes traveling door-to-door, have been approaching the elderly, offering to prepare living trusts. Tactics alleged by opponents include using high pressure sales pitches, imposing high prices, making misrepresentations and mistakes about the relative costs and advantages of living trusts, carelessly failing to ensure that property is transferred to the trust, producing an ineffective document, and making false claims of endorsement by legitimate nonprofit organizations or using "sound-alike" names that make them appear to be protective associations for the elderly. Some states have taken legal action against these operations, but vigilance against these unprofessional practices must continue as long as there are greedy people willing to prey on vulnerable elderly persons.

QUANTITATIVE MODEL FOR COMPARISON OF COSTS OF PROBATE VERSUS LIVING TRUST

This section applies the principles of finance to develop a model for comparing the costs of probate with the costs of the living trust. The technique used will incorporate the time value of money concept known as present value.

EXAMPLE 10 - 9. Patty is evaluating the decision whether to avoid probate of her assets, worth $1 million, by setting up a revocable living trust. Her life expectancy is 10 years. With regard to costs, she has made the following estimates:

Under the probate alternative: drafting her will, $600; probate administration, $25,000; and other costs at death, including accountants' fees, $1,000.

Under the trust alternative: drafting the trust and the pour-over will, $1,600; annual record-keeping until death,[14] $300 per year; nonprobate administration cost at death, $2,500; costs in higher income taxes due to inability to use a probate estate as a separate taxpayer, $1,100; and other costs at death, including accountants' fees, $1,000.

In calculating the total cost for each alternative, Patty could simply add up the expenses, with the result that the probate alternative at $26,000 would appear to be more than twice the $11,000 trust cost. Simply adding up the costs, however, does not take into account the time value of money.

To correctly compare amounts incurred at different points in time, we must make adjustments to reflect the fact that money not spent today can be invested profitably until the time that it must be spent. We can do this by calculating the sum of the present values of the costs for each alternative. The present value of an expense is the amount that would have to be invested today to accumulate the funds necessary to pay that expense when it comes due.

To better understand the present value concept, consider a simple illustration. At an annual rate of interest of 10%, one would need to invest $100 today to accumulate $110 in one year. In other words, at 10%, the present value of $110 payable in one year is $100. Present values of any amount can be derived from present value tables such as Table B for a term of years and Table S for amounts payable for life or at the end of a person's life. Table B (10%) depicts the present values of a single $1 amount to be paid in the future, assuming an investment rate of 10%. Thus, the present value of $1 in one year at 10% is $0.909091, or a bit less than 91 cents. Since we have been calculating the present value of the amount $110, not $1, our answer must be the product of $110 and 0.909091, or $100.

How can we calculate the present value of the amount $300 payable each year for the next 10 years, with the first payment due in one year? Described in other words, we must calculate the total amount to be invested today which will enable us to fund this annuity, that is, to fund this entire progression of equal payments. To do this, we calculate the present value of the annuity. Table B in Appendix A shows the present values of a $1 annuity for at various rates of return for specified periods.

> EXAMPLE 10 - 10. With regard to Patty's actual figures, at 10%, the present value of $1 to be paid in 10 years is $0.386. We will use this lump-sum discount factor in the calculations that follow. The "annuity factor," as it is called, corresponding to 10 years and 10% is 6.145. Since we wish to determine the present value of an annuity of $300, not $1, the answer must be the product of $300 and 6.145, or $1,844.

We are now ready to calculate Patty's total costs for the two alternatives in a manner which adjusts for the time value of money. The figures are shown in Table 10-1 and Table 10-2.

TABLE 10-1 Present Value of Costs of Probate

Items	Years	Amounts	Discount Factor	Present Value
Drafting	Now	$600	1.000000	$600
Administration	10	$25,000	0.385543	$9,639
Other costs	10	$1,000	0.385543	$386
		Total present value of probate costs		$10,625

TABLE 10-2 Present Value of Costs of Living Trust

Items	Years	Amounts	Discount Factor	Present Value
Drafting	Now	$1,600	1.000000	$1,600
Administration	10	$2,500	0.385543	$964
Record keeping	1-10	$300	6.144600	$1,864
Higher estate tax	10	$1,100	0.385543	$424
Other costs	10	$1,000	0.385543	$386
		Total present value of living trust costs		$5,238

Thus, the sum of the present values of the costs are $10,625 for probate and $5,238 for the trust. These represent the total amounts that Patty would have to invest today, at 10%, to properly accumulate and pay the forecasted costs when they are due.

The analysis could be refined slightly to include the tax deductibility of these expenses. For example, as we will see in Chapter 18, administration costs may be deducted on the estate tax return. Thus, if T represents the marginal estate tax rate, the after-tax cost of an estate tax deductible expense is the product of that expense times the expression one minus T.

The estimates in the above example have been made for illustration purposes only and should not be used as a general indicator of costs. Actual costs will vary considerably, depending on specific factors, such as the laws of the decedent's particular residence state and the cost of professional services. However, to generalize, the present value cost of formal probate is usually higher than the present value cost of the living trust by at least 20%.

WHICH ALTERNATIVE IS BEST?

Obviously, the decision whether to avoid probate is not always a simple one. It requires that each person examine and subjectively weigh the advantages and disadvantages of each, in the context of the laws and procedures of his or her state. There is no correct answer for all situations. In fact, some individuals owning larger estates may execute a will to probate certain assets and transfer the remaining assets by living trust in order to obtain the unique benefits of both arrangements. What follows is a description of various circumstances that might influence individuals to favor one or the other of the alternatives.

Probate preferred: Individuals who will lean toward the probate alternative include:

1. Professionals, such as self-employed engineers and accountants, who stand to gain additional security from the short creditors' claim period.
2. Those who have large, complicated estates, or who expect family disharmony after their death, may benefit from the extra protection potentially available through court supervision.
3. Residents of UPC states where the cost advantage to avoiding informal probate is minimal.
4. Young, healthy individuals who expect to be acquiring numerous assets and would find the constant funding requirement of the living trust onerous.

Joint tenancy preferred: Although joint tenancy has some very significant disadvantages, the ease of transfer may make it appealing, especially for owners with relatively modest estates. Individuals are inclined to prefer it if some of the following circumstances apply:

1. The person wants the property to pass outright to the surviving joint tenant(s). This implies that there is no need for trusts, to save income or transfer taxes, to avoid guardianships, to delay distributions to younger survivors, or to provide for multiple beneficiaries over time by creating life estate and remainder interests.
2. A complete step-up in income tax basis at a person's death is not needed, or is available because the older (dying) joint tenant contributed the consideration to acquire the property.

3. The creation of the joint tenancy interest does not result in the immediate payment of gift taxes.

Living trust preferred: Individuals who will tend to prefer a living trust typically include those who want to avoid probate but do not like joint tenancy because of its disadvantages. For example:

1. Those with larger estates who wish to avoid the estate tax by using sophisticated trust arrangements, e.g., a bypass trust (discussed in the next chapter).
2. Those who place high priority on privacy and speed in the property transfer process.
3. Individuals for whom the total cost of the living trust is expected to be considerably lower than the cost of probate; reasons include the following:
   a. Probate administration expenses are expected to be high, perhaps because the person is a resident of a non-UPC state, or because an independent executor must be named.
   b. Nonprobate administration fees are low, perhaps because a family member is willing to serve as trustee.
4. Individuals who do not anticipate a trust funding burden associated with numerous acquisitions of property.
5. Finally, individuals who wish to avoid the publicity and cost of court appointed guardians or conservators in the event they become incapacitated.

QUESTIONS AND PROBLEMS

1. Discuss the validity of the claim that probate promotes fairness.

2. (a) In what sense is probate open to the public? (b) Is the living trust always private?

3. (a) Who might wish to contest a will by claiming the execution was invalid? (b) Why might it be easier to do than to challenge a living trust?

4. Comment on the following statement: One of the major drawbacks of probate is the complicated legal action that one must go through if he or she has an objection to the transfer of certain assets.

5. (a) Why should the living trust cost less than the formal probate alternative? (b) Are all cost components lower?

6. What are some of the benefits of probate?

7. Wesley has just received his lawyer's bill for developing a plan that avoids probate with a living trust. Included is a charge for drafting a will. Did the law firm make a billing mistake?

8. What are the implications of the *Tulsa vs. Pope* Supreme Court decision?

9. Today Dennis executed a living trust, with his sister as the only remainder beneficiary. While driving home from the lawyer's office, Dennis was killed in an auto accident. His property was held in joint tenancy and as tenancy in common with his brother, Elmer. Is there a problem? What happens to his estate?

10. (a) Describe the typical probate creditor's claim period. (b) What is the creditor's claim period for joint tenancy? (c) For the living trust?

11. A person is considering whether to have a will done or to create and fund a living trust. Assume that the person's life expectancy is 15 years and the

investment rate of return is 10%. Given the estimated costs that follow, compare the cost factors for each alternative. (a) For the probate alternative: drafting the will, $300; formal probate administration, $40,000; other costs at death, including accountants' and appraisers' fees, $2,300. (b) For the trust alternative: drafting costs, $2,200; record-keeping until death, $250 per year; nonprobate administration costs at death, $3,100; costs in higher income taxes due to the inability to use a probate estate as a separate taxpayer, $1,000 (assume a one-year probate); other costs at death, including accountants' fees, $3,600.

12. Now evaluate the cost of informal probate versus the living trust. Assume all facts given in the problem immediately above, except that informal probate administration will cost $20,000 instead of $40,000.

13. What is the typical cost of probate administration? Find out how your state courts determine attorney's fees and executor's fees.

14. As applied to the following individuals, discuss the appropriateness of each of the three major ways of disposing of an estate (i.e., using a simple will, holding property in joint tenancy, and using a funded living trust).

    (a) Mr. Max owns $5 million in assets. He is a politician. He is single, but by prior marriages he has two children, a minor and a young adult.
    (b) Sally's estate consists of only a home worth $800,000. She is 80 years old. Her adult son, an only child, is to receive her entire estate.
    (c) John is 30, single, and lives with his mom. He owns only personal effects totaling $29,000. He would like his estate to go to his younger brother.

ANSWERS TO QUESTIONS AND PROBLEMS *(odd numbered only)*

1. Supporters of probate claim that court supervision in a public setting promotes fairness. Critics claim that judges and other officials offer only rubber stamp approval of administration acts, and that the trend of probate reform toward reduced supervision further reduces the protection offered by this alternative.

3. (a) Disinherited and contentious survivors and others who may stand to gain may wish to contest the execution of a will. (b) Some commentators contend that since a will contest is initiated in probate court, it is a simpler process than contesting a trust, which requires separate legal action. Others say that a trust can be contested on substantially the same grounds that are used to contest a will. Common grounds include fraud, undue influence, lack of capacity and improper execution.

5. (a) The living trust should cost less than the formal probate alternative because of the typically large executor commissions and attorney fees in probate administration.
   (b) Not all costs of a living trust are lower. The cost of drafting a trust might be higher, however, because: (1) The trust is usually a more complex document than the will; and (2) a pour-over will is also included.

7. No, the lawyer did not make a billing mistake. The higher cost reflects the need to draft a pour-over will, as well as a trust.

9. There is a problem. The trust will not control disposition over the joint tenancy assets. Elmer will receive those because joint tenancy disposition supersedes disposition by trust. The tenancy in common interests will go through probate, and if the attorney included a pour-over will (most likely), Dennis's sister will receive them. Conclusion: living trusts need to be funded to avoid probate.

11. PRESENT VALUE COST OF FORMAL PROBATE

	Year	Amount	Factor	Present value
Drafting	now	$300	1.000	$300
Administration	15	$40,000	0.239	$9,560
Other costs	15	$2,300	0.239	$550
	Total Present Value of Formal Probate			$10,410

PRESENT VALUE COST OF LIVING TRUST

	Year	Amount	Factor	Present value
Drafting	now	$2,200	1.000	$2,200
Record keeping	1-15	$250	7.6061	$1,902
Administration	15	$3,100	0.239	$741
Higher tax	15	$1,000	0.239	$239
Other costs	15	$3,600	0.239	$860
	Total Present Value of Living Trust			$5,942

13. Probate costs usually run between 2 and 10% of the probate estate's gross value. The two largest probate expenses are often the commission of the personal representative and the attorney's fees. Depending on state law, fees are likely to be either set by statute as some decreasing percentage of the estate or are set by the probate judge based upon the time and effort of the attorney and the executor. Even in the latter case, judges will grant more for very large estates than they will allow for small estates.

ENDNOTES

1. *Tulsa Professional Collection Services v. Estate of Pope* 485 US 478, 108 S.Ct. 1340 (1988).

2. See California Code of Civil Procedure § 366.2 at California's Website: *<http://www.leginfo.ca.gov/calaw.html>*.

3. See Figure 9-1.

4. The Uniform TOD Securities Registration Act is included on the Teaching Aids CD Rom. Also see The National Conference of Commissioners on Uniform State Laws' official website (maintained by the University of Pennsylvania Law School) at *<http://www.law.upenn.edu/bll/ulc/>*.

5. IRC §§ 2036 - 2038.

6. See the discussion, at the end of Chapter 4, of California's nonprobate procedure for setting aside property to a surviving spouse.

7. IRC § 121.

8. IRC § 1031.

9. *Heggstad v. Heggstad*, 20 Cal. Rptr. 2d 433 (1993).

10. See California Code of Civil Procedure § 366.2 at California's Website: *<http://www.leginfo.ca.gov/calaw.html>*.

11. See California Probate Code §§ 19000-19100 at California's Website: *<http://www.leginfo.ca.gov/calaw.html>*.

12. 42USC § 9601(35)(A)(iii).

13. 42USC § 1396a(k).

14. Fees incurred for the production of income, such as trustee fees of a living trust, income tax preparation fees and record keeping fees, are miscellaneous itemized deductions subject to the 2% deduction floor.

CHAPTER 11

Common Estate Plans: Using Bypass and Marital Deduction Trusts

OVERVIEW

This chapter demonstrates how bypass planning and the marital deduction are used by wealthy couples to reduce estate taxes. More advanced applications of these techniques, including use of the prior transfer credit, special estate plans, and trusts that obtain the marital deduction for non-U.S. spouses are covered in the next chapter.

As discussed previously, the estate tax will probably be eliminated for the estates of decedents who die after 2009. For deaths before then, most estates will avoid estate tax because of the substantial increase in the applicable exclusion amount (AEA), e.g., $1 million passes tax-free in the years 2002 and 2003, and it reaches $3.5 million in 2009. Hence, married couples with fairly large estates will be able to pass them to their heirs free of estate taxes by doing a little bit of estate planning.[1] Indeed, since the passage of the Economic Growth and Tax Relief Reconciliation Act of 2001 (EGTRRA) much of estate planning will focus on postponing taxes, if at all possible, with the hope that at least one spouse lives to 2010 or beyond.

> EXAMPLE 11 - 1. In 2003, an elderly couple together own property with a net worth about equal to the AEA, i.e., about $1,000,000. Without any estate planning, other than simple wills, it is likely that their children will eventually receive their estate free of tax, regardless of how ownership of the property was originally divided between the spouses, and no matter which spouse dies first. This is true

because the AEA will be increasing over the next several years, so it is likely that their combined estates will remain tax-free. If the value exceeds the AEA, then tax savings could be accomplished with a little more planning. This might include gifts to reduce their estate and/or the use of multiple trusts so as to use both spouses' unified credits.

Minimizing estate taxes is a concern mainly for families whose taxable estates are expected to exceed the AEA at the second spouse's death and that second death is expected to occur before the repeal of the estate tax has been completed. With lifetime gifts within the annual exclusion amount and various estate tax deductions (such as administration expenses and debts), gross estates over the AEA will be transferred tax-free if the gifts and deductions reduce it to the AEA or less. Thus, our focus is on those married couples whose estate *tax base* significantly exceeds the AEA.

EXAMPLE 11 - 2. At the time of her death in 2003, Ellen's gross estate was $1,075,000; debts were $120,000; administration expenses were $50,000. Lifetime taxable gifts totaled $70,000 (i.e., gifts less any annual exclusions). Her taxable estate was $905,000 and the estate tax base was $975,000. Thus, there would be no estate tax because the estate tax base does not exceed $1,000,000, the AEA for 2003.

EXAMPLE 11 - 3. Joshua died in 1994, leaving his half of their community property to his wife, Mary. Neither owned significant separate property and the community property was worth $850,000 at that time. Because of good investment advice from an estate planner (I think he said, "put it in the market"), Mary's net estate was worth $1,450,000 when she died in 2003. Her estate passed to her two grown children, but not until after $188,500 in estate tax was paid. Had Joshua's half of the community property been placed in a bypass trust that benefitted Mary for her lifetime and then passed on to the children, no taxes would have been owed. Indeed, if Mary had lived to 2004, the increased AEA of $1,500,000 would have made this a no-tax estate.

ABBREVIATIONS, SIMPLIFICATIONS, AND ASSUMPTIONS

The term "transfer" refers to lifetime gifts and transfers at death. The calculations in examples assume that the "pick-up" tax is the only state death tax. The pick-up tax is a state estate tax that is exactly equal to the federal credit for state death taxes. Unless stated otherwise, we will assume that any lifetime gifts were less than the annual exclusion amount. To simplify discussion, figures for estates will be net values (i.e., all deductions, except the marital deduction, have already been taken).

In the discussions that follow, we will generally refer to the "first spouse to die" and the "second spouse to die" as S1 and S2, respectively. As a practical matter, wives outlive their husbands by an average of almost 10 years, hence it is not unusual in estate planning discussions to refer to S1 as the husband and S2 as the wife. From a tax standpoint, the crucial factor is not whether the husband or the wife dies first, but what property each owns when S1 dies and the structure of their estate plan. For example, the order of death might have very significant implications if one spouse is working and the other is not, or if there is a great disparity in their incomes or in their individual net wealth.

Starting in 1988, the marital deduction was eliminated for property going to any non-U.S. citizen spouse unless complex requirements are met to give some assurance that the property transferred stays in the U.S. where it is likely to be taxed as it passes to the next generation. Because there is a different marital deduction structure for non-citizen spouses, our examples are for U.S. citizens until we specifically address planning for the non-citizen spouse in the next chapter.

THE MARITAL DEDUCTION: THEN AND NOW

It is helpful to understand the history of the marital deduction before getting into an extended discussion of the basic estate plans.

Subject to certain requirements which we will discuss later, today's gift and estate tax law allows a 100% marital deduction for transfers between spouses. The law allows one spouse to transfer any amount of property to the other spouse without gift or estate taxes.

As hard as it is to believe, there was no marital deduction until several years after World War II. Then, for almost 30 years, the marital deduction for property passing from one spouse to the other was limited to 50% of the net value of S1's estate. Only since 1982 has the 100% marital deduction been part of the law.

The first marital deduction applied to estates of decedents dying after April 2, 1948. It set the maximum marital deduction at 50% of S1's adjusted gross estate (AGE), i.e., S1's gross estate less the deductions allowed for expenses, indebtedness, taxes, and losses[2]. Of course the maximum marital deduction was achieved only if at least half the estate was left to S2, since the marital deduction claimed could not exceed the value of the property passing from S1 to S2.

The purpose of the marital deduction was to eliminate disparate treatment originating from differences in the two systems of state property laws. Some states, for example California and Texas, are community property states that trace their property law to early Roman law. In a community property state, each spouse owns half of all property acquired by the labor of either spouse while married and domiciled in a community property state. Other states, such as Kansas and New York, are common law states that trace their property law to early English law. In common law states the husband generally held title to all property acquired during the marriage. Husbands tend to die before their wives, thus, before the change in 1948, for any given amount of combined wealth, a family in a common law state was likely to pay a higher estate tax when the first spouse died than would have been paid had the family resided in a community property state.

Years	Maximum Marital Deduction
1917 - 1947	▸ no marital deduction allowed
1948 - 1976	▸ 50% of AGE, except no marital deduction for community property.
1977-1981	▸ Greater of $\left\{ \begin{array}{c} \text{50\% of AGE} \\ \text{or} \\ \text{\$250,000} \end{array} \right.$
1982 to present	▸ 100% of amount S1 ----> S2 with no limit.

During the early period from 1948 through 1981, the marital deduction was designed such that if the husband died first the resulting taxable estate would probably be the same regardless of the couple's domicile. No marital deduction was allowed for S1's half interest in community property since allowing a marital deduction for community property would have resulted in a "quartering" of the estate, which would have perpetuated the inequality between the two property law systems.

EXAMPLE 11 - 4. Guilliano died in 1960, while residing in Kentucky. He left his estate to his wife, Cheryl. During the entire marriage they lived in Kentucky and acquired property with a net worth of $1,000,000. Because Kentucky is a common law state, 100% of the property was included in Guilliano's gross estate. The marital deduction removed half, leaving $500,000. The $60,000 death tax exemption reduced the taxable estate to $440,000. If Guilliano had lived and died in Texas, a community property state, the $1,000,000 would have been community property. Only his half would have been included in his estate. There would have been no marital deduction, and after the exemption, the taxable estate would have been $440,000, the same result as in Kentucky.

Of course, there were still inequalities. For instance, if a person died domiciled in a common law state and owned very little property, it was unlikely that there would be an estate tax even if the surviving spouse was already wealthy. In a community property state, if the wealth was acquired while the couple was married, then half of the property would be included in the estate of the first spouse to die, and since no marital deduction was allowed for community property, it would be subject to tax. Under current law, with the 100% marital deduction, it makes little sense to continue to allow a full step-up for community property. Indeed, in the near future, Congress might decide to change that by allowing only a half step-up for community property, much like the treatment presently given to spousal joint tenancies.

A Blip in the Law

From 1977 through 1981, the law allowed a marital deduction equal to the greater of 50% or $250,000 of the adjusted taxable estate. For large estates, those in excess of $500,000, the maximum was 50% of the adjusted gross estate (just as it would have been pre-1977) but, for estates under $500,000 the $250,000 is obviously the greater amount. Thus, for estates between $250,000 and $500,000 the marital deduction exceeded 50% and for estates equal to, or below, $250,000 it became a 100% marital deduction.

To keep community property states on a par with common law states, Congress allowed a marital deduction for small estates that included community property to assure that the estate received at least the $250,000 minimum marital deduction. The formula for calculating the alternative marital deduction started with $250,000, which was reduced by half of the decedent's separate property (because the separate property was allowed a 50% marital deduction), then it was further reduced by the community property included in the decedent's estate (since the half belonging to the survivor already escaped taxation). The resulting number was the maximum alternative marital deduction for an estate with community property.

> EXAMPLE 11 - 5. Mac died in 1977. He left his half of the couple's $400,000 community property estate to his wife Tina. His adjusted gross estate was $200,000. Subtracting the $200,000 community property included in his gross estate from the $250,000 results in a $50,000 alternative marital deduction. Subtracting the alternative marital deduction from $200,000 results in a taxable estate of $150,000. If the couple had lived in a common law state, the result would have been the same, assuming that the entire $400,000 estate belonged to Mac. It would have been reduced by the full $250,000 minimum marital deduction to result in a taxable estate of $150,000.

> EXAMPLE 11 - 6. June died in 1980. Her estate was left to her husband, Brian. She owned separate property worth $60,000 and held $300,000 as community property with Brian. Her gross estate would be $210,000 less a marital deduction of $100,000, leaving a taxable estate of $110,000. The marital deduction was calculated by subtracting half of her separate property ($30,000) and half of the community property ($150,000) from $250,000. The result ($70,000), when added to the marital deduction ($30,000, which is 50% of her $60,000 separate property), produces the total available marital deduction. The $110,000 figure is the same as would have been taxed if June had owned $360,000 (her separate property plus all of the community property) and received a $250,000 marital deduction.

Learning to compute this alternative marital deduction is no longer a useful skill. Your time would be better spent working in the garden or teaching your dog to shake hands.

THE TERMINABLE INTEREST RULE

When the marital deduction first became part of the law, any transfer to a surviving spouse of what is called a *terminable interest* failed to qualify for the marital deduction.[3] A transfer is a terminable interest if the interest transferred to S2 ends at, or before, S2's death or on the happening of some event, i.e., S2's remarriage. The reason for this limitation on the marital deduction is that to do otherwise might allow most estates, even those of the wealthy, to completely escape taxation. This would occur because the marital deduction would reduce or eliminate tax at S1's death on property that would later skip S2's estate (and, therefore, would escape the estate tax) when S2 died because S2 did not own the property. The most commonly encountered terminable interest is a trust created by S1 that, at his death, reserves a life estate for S2 with the remainder to the couple's children. S2's interest is a terminable interest because, her only interest in the property will terminate at her death and the "enjoyment" of the property will pass to the children.

For purposes of the marital deduction, a *terminable interest*[4] is defined as a property interest with these three characteristics:

- It is subject to some future absolute or *contingent* termination of S2's interest.
- The possibility of termination was created by S1 and, if it occurs, there will be a shift in the interest.
- Some other person or entity (other than S2 or her estate) will possess or own the property.

The Elements of the Terminable Interest Rule

The question is not whether a termination must occur, but whether, viewed as of the moment of S1's death, a termination *might* occur. Thus, the second and third requirements of the rule exclude situations where the terminable nature was not created by S1, including those unique property interests that simply end by their very nature. Thus, a bequest conditioned on the surviving spouse living for nine months beyond S1's death is a terminable interest, even if she does survive. An ownership interest for a period of years granted to S1 by a third party could be left to S2 for the remainder of the term, and it would not be a terminable interest. Likewise, a lease or a patent will terminate but the interest of S1 does not shift to someone else.

> EXAMPLE 11 - 7. Mark's will stated: "I leave the residue of my estate to my wife, Gloria, provided she survives to the close of probate, and if she does not so survive then it shall be divided among my issue by right of representation." His $1 million estate was transferred by probate to Gloria within a mere five months of his death. Nevertheless, the bequest does not qualify for the marital deduction since Gloria *might* have died before the close of the probate, in which case her interest would have terminated. He created the terminable character of the interest. The interest might have gone to Mark's issue, who then would have enjoyed the property.

Because it meets all three elements of the rule, it is a terminable interest and no marital deduction is allowed for the property even though Gloria received the property, and even though it will be in her estate unless she consumes it or gives it away.

EXAMPLE 11 - 8. When Lori died, she left her patent for turning base metals into gold to her husband Earl. The patent still had 11 years before it expired. Even though a patent by its very nature must terminate, the interest does not shift to someone else. Furthermore, it is not considered a terminable interest because even though Lori invented the process and obtained the patent, she did not create the termination. Therefore, the value of the patent qualifies for the marital deduction.

EXAMPLE 11 - 9. Selina owned a strip mall. She did not own the land, but was the lessee under what was originally a 99-year land-lease. At the time of her death the land-lease still had 63 years remaining. Even though the mall was built on leased land, Selina's interest was very valuable. (It is not uncommon to find commercial property on leased land. At the end of the lease, the land, together with any structures, reverts to the lessor.) When she died, she left her entire estate to her husband, Duane. Since Selina never owned any more than a leasehold, the shift in interest back to the lessor at the end of the lease is not one that she created. Thus, the value of her interest in the leasehold qualifies for the marital deduction. If, however, she had left the mall to Duane for 10 years, and then to her son for the balance of the lease, it would have been a terminable interest and not even the value of the lease for the period that Duane would have it qualifies for the deduction.

Why Have a Terminable Interest Rule?

Consider what would happen if the law allowed a marital deduction for a terminable interest, such as a life estate for a surviving spouse, without requiring inclusion of the terminable interest property in S2's estate. The value of the property would be split into two parts, the life estate and the remainder interest. There is no denying that a life estate can be a valuable interest and that the interest can be valued using actuarial methods.

When the interest is created at S1's death, a marital deduction based on a life estate might swallow up most of the value of the transfer, leaving very little (i.e., just the remainder interest) subject to the transfer tax. The tentative tax on this might be covered by S1's unified credit. Since the beneficiary of a life estate is not treated as a transferor when the life estate terminates at the beneficiary's death, none of the property subject to the life estate would be included in S2's estate.

> EXAMPLE 11 - 10. Suppose the law did allow a marital deduction based on the value of a life estate (remember, this is not the law) and that S1 died in 2002, leaving S2 a life estate in a trust worth $3,000,000. If S2 was 60 years old and the federal rate for split interests was 8%, the value of S2's life estate is 0.73206 * $3,000,000 = $2,196,180 (the value of the remainder is $803,820). The tentative tax on a $803,820 taxable estate is $269,290, which is covered by S1's $345,800 unified credit, hence, no tax would be due at S1's death. Then if S2 passes away in 2006 and the trust property is worth $4,000,000, it would be transferred to S1's children tax-free since there is nothing to include in S2's estate. Note that a $4 million estate in 2006 would pay a tax of $920,000.

TERMINABLE INTEREST RULE EXCEPTIONS

Why have exceptions to the terminable interest rule? The law creates a number of exceptions to the terminable interest rule, each of which allows the marital deduction even though the interest is technically a terminable interest. Congress certainly did not want a loophole that would allow large estates to avoid estate taxes, however, there are policy and/or practical reasons for each of the exceptions. Additionally, all of the exceptions are ones in which the property qualifying for the marital deduction is ultimately included in S2's estate, unless S2 consumes it or gives it away. If S2 gives it away in large chunks (greater than the annual exclusion), her gifts may use up her unified credit.

Six months or common disaster rule: IRC § 2056(b)(3). Almost from the start of the marital deduction and its related terminable interest rule, Congress created an exception to the rule for "six months or common disaster" survivorship clauses, so long as S2 survived long enough to satisfy the contingency and receive the property. Typically, these clauses make a bequest contingent on the beneficiary actually outliving the decedent by six months or some period shorter than six months. The law also allows the marital deduction for a marital bequest conditioned on S2 surviving a common accident. A "common disaster" clause might state, "if my wife and I are injured in the same accident, and I die, I leave her my estate provided she eventually recovers from said accident." Even though recovery might take longer than six months, this bequest would qualify for the marital deduction so long as recovery did occur.

Therefore, a survivorship clause, as part of the decedent's will or living trust, can be part of the estate plan, and a marital deduction will be allowed provided the survivor actually survives to receive the property.[5]

A survivorship clause may be specific, relating just to certain bequests, or it may cover all beneficiaries, e.g., "*For purposes of this Will, a beneficiary shall not be deemed to have survived me if that beneficiary dies within six months of my death.*"

The clause avoids a double probate in situations where the beneficiary does not live long enough to really use the bequest. It also allows the testator to determine the alternate beneficiary of the bequest, rather than allowing it to be governed by the disposition of the beneficiary's estate. Without a survivorship clause the property goes into the beneficiary's estate even if the beneficiary lives just a moment longer than the testator.

Whether a bequest is a terminable interest is determined as of the death of S1; it does not depend on whether the interest in fact terminates. Therefore, without the IRC § 2056(b)(3) exception, no marital deduction would be allowed for estates that actually passed to the surviving spouse if the bequest was subject to a survivorship clause.

Qualified Terminable Interest Property (QTIP): IRC § 2056(b)(7)

There are valid estate planning reasons for creating terminable interests whereby a surviving spouse is given income from a decedent spouse's estate for life, and yet the surviving spouse is given little or no control over the ultimate disposition of the property. With the population living longer, and with the high rate of divorce, marriages with one or both spouses having children by prior marriages are quite common. It is natural that a person with considerable wealth entering into a second (or third) marriage would want to take care of the new spouse, yet also desire to assure that his or her wealth does not go to the new spouse's family after both are deceased.

Prior to 1982, the maximum marital deduction for a large estate was equal to 50% of the estate's net value. To qualify for the marital deduction, the surviving spouse had to receive the property, or at least be given a general power of appointment over it. To obtain the maximum marital deduction, at least half of S1's estate had to be transferred to the surviving spouse. Thus, S1 was forced to choose between obtaining the maximum marital deduction and losing control over who would ultimately own the property, or retaining control and giving up the marital deduction. Fortunately, the QTIP election allows a marital deduction without forcing S1 to give up control as to who ultimately receives his property.

Under the prior law (i.e., before we had the 100% marital deduction), leaving more than half of S1's estate to S2 did not increase the marital deduction for large estates, therefore, the most common plan left S2 only so much of S1's estate as qualified for the marital deduction. This could be either outright or in a trust that gave S2 a life estate and a general power to appoint the corpus.[6] The rest of S1's estate was transferred to a bypass trust, usually (but not in all cases) one giving the income from that trust to the surviving spouse for her life, with the remainder going to S1's family after her death. This arrangement did not sacrifice estate tax dollars on the first death and avoided having the corpus of the bypass trust included in S2's estate.

Without a new exception to the terminable interest rule, the change allowing a 100% marital deduction for transfers after 1981 would have created a dilemma for every couple who had kept their wealth separate because they had children by prior marriages. They would have been forced to choose between providing for the surviving spouse or assuring that their estates passed to their own children. The planner would have been forced to either transfer control of everything in excess of the AEA to the surviving spouse or pay an estate tax on the first death.

Fortunately, an option known as the QTIP election was added to the law.[7] This election allows the executor of S1's estate to obtain a marital deduction for what is called "Qualified Terminable Interest Property," referred to by the acronym QTIP. To qualify for this election, the terminable interest property must meet these requirements:

- The surviving spouse must receive all income from the property for life. Note that the right to use property is generally considered the same as receiving the income, hence a home may be part of the QTIP property.
- The right to the income cannot be contingent.
- During the surviving spouse's life, the property cannot be appointed to anyone other than to the surviving spouse.[8]

The executor must make an election to claim the marital deduction for the QTIP property when S1's estate tax return is filed. The law allows the executor to make the QTIP election on less than 100% of the terminable interest property.

This is done by electing to QTIP a fraction of the property. Thus, if the terminable interest property is in the form of a trust with a life estate for the surviving spouse, remainder to their children, and the trust is funded with property exceeding the AEA, the executor might elect to QTIP only that portion of the trust which exceeds the value of the AEA.

There is no free lunch. The fraction of the QTIP property that receives a marital deduction at S1's death must be included in S2's estate at the time of S2's death.[9] Hence, the choice in making a QTIP election is how much of the terminable interest property to tax at S1's death versus how much to tax at S2's death. Of course, with EGTRRA some estates will completely avoid tax by making the QTIP election to postpone all taxes until the second death provided S2 lives to 2010 and Congress passes additional legislation to avoid the 2011 sunset provision that would repeal the repeal.[10]

> EXAMPLE 11 - 11. Fernando died in 2002 leaving his entire estate, $3,127,452, less debts and expenses of $197,420, in an irrevocable trust for his wife, Arcela. She was given a life estate and a limited power to appoint corpus at her death among their three children. Arcela had a modest estate of her own. Since the executor of Fernando's estate wanted to postpone all taxes until after Arcela's death, he QTIPed that portion that exceeded the AEA estate, i.e., that numerator is the amount by which the estate exceeds the AEA. Since the net value of the trust is $2,930,032, the QTIP fraction is:
>
> $$\frac{\$2,930,032 - \$1,000,000}{\$2,930,032}$$
>
> When this fraction is multiplied by the net value of the trust, the marital deduction is $1,930,032, resulting in a taxable estate of exactly $1,000,000.

The QTIP fraction serves a dual role; it determines how much of the QTIP property qualifies for the marital deduction on the first death and, more importantly, it determines how much of that property (valued at the second death) must be included in S2's estate.

EXAMPLE 11 - 12. When Arcela died in 2006, the trust Fernando had established for her had grown from its initial worth to $3,954,372, with debts of $420,870 resulting in a net value of $3,533,502. Arcela had her own property worth $780,450 with debts and expenses that totaled $110,400, for a net value of $670,050. She too left her estate to their children. In determining her taxable estate, her executor would have to add to what she owned the portion of the trust that had previously been QTIPed:

$$\frac{1,930,032}{2,930,032} * \$3,533,502 = \$2,327,542$$

Adding this amount to $670,050 results in a taxable estate of $2,997,592. In 2006, the tax on that size taxable estate is $458,892.

**** *Query 1. What is the QTIP fraction if Fernando's death is in 2004 instead of 2002? And, all else being the same, what would be included in Arcela's estate?*

The QTIP fraction equation given above uses S1's AEA and defers all taxes to the second death. The AEA in the formula must be adjusted to take into account any use of the unified credit elsewhere, either because S1 made taxable gifts during life or left part of the estate to someone other than the surviving spouse. Such transfers use up unified credit (unless to a charity). Hence, the AEA in the numerator should equal the AEA that remains available.

EXAMPLE 11 - 13. Suppose Fernando also owned a $250,000 life insurance policy that named his daughter by a prior marriage as the beneficiary. Now his gross estate would be $3,377,452. The net value after debts and expenses would be $3,180,032 [$250,000 life insurance plus the $2,930,032 in the trust]. The life insurance would use $250,000 of the AEA, hence, the QTIP fraction in the above example would be ($2,930,032 - $750,000) divided by $2,930,032. The portion of the QTIP property elected for the marital deduction would be equal to $2,180,032. Thus, after the marital deduction, the taxable estate would again be $1,000,000, comprising the $250,000 life insurance policy and the $750,000 portion of the QTIP property that was not covered by the marital deduction. [$3,377,452 - $197,420 -$2,180,032 = $1,000,000]

Of course, 100% of the QTIP property in the above example could have qualified for the marital deduction, but electing to QTIP 100% of the trust would have reduced S1's taxable estate below the AEA, thus wasting part of S1's unified credit and needlessly increasing the amount of the property that could eventually be included in S2's estate.

If the second death is likely to occur before the estate tax is completely repealed, it might be advantageous to generate a tax on the first estate by using a QTIP fraction less than that necessary to defer all taxes. For instance, if S1 left QTIP property worth $8,000,000 in trust for S2, and S2 has no estate of her own, it might be advantageous to QTIP half of the $8,000,000 trust. By doing so, the QTIP half will qualify for the marital deduction, leaving a taxable estate of $4,000,000. On S2's death, half of the trust will be included in her estate. The tax on two estates worth $4,000,000 each is considerably less than the tax on two estates where one is equal to the AEA (e.g., $1,000,000) and the other is equal to $8,000,000 less the AEA (e.g., $7,000,000). Two shorter trips up the rate ladder are cheaper than one long one. Furthermore, as will be discussed in the next chapter, generating a tax in both estates sometimes allows the second estate to use a prior transfer credit, further reducing the total estate taxes.[11]

Although most of our examples and most real-life QTIP trusts concern decedent's estates, the QTIP election is also available for lifetime transfers.[12] It could be used by a wealthy spouse who wants to bring the value of his or her spouse's estate up to at least the AEA. The use of the QTIP trust allows the wealthier spouse to keep the property in his or her family, whereas an outright gift surrenders control of the property. Of course, to use the less wealthy spouse's unified credit, the wealthy spouse must be willing to part with some property even if the other spouse (the donee spouse) dies first.

> EXAMPLE 11 - 14. Eighty-year-old Ellen had a net worth of $4,500,000 when, after 10 years of widowhood, she married Frank, a kindly gentleman of modest means. Ellen wants to take care of Frank, should she die before him. She was also willing to have a significant portion of her estate go immediately to her children if Frank died before her. Therefore, in 2002, she established a lifetime QTIP trust. The trust was funded with stocks and bonds worth $1,000,000. The terms of the trust give Frank a life estate, and, if Frank died first, her children would receive only so much of the corpus as equals the AEA available for Frank's estate (taking into account his own property and any taxable gifts he might have made), the balance of the trust would revert back to Ellen, if she is still alive, otherwise, it will go to her children. Ellen filed a gift tax return and elected to QTIP all of the trust.

> EXAMPLE 11 - 15. When Frank died in 2004, the QTIP trust had a net worth of $1,380,000 and his own property had a net worth of $205,000, for a total of $1,585,000. Frank's family received his property, and Ellen received $85,000 from the trust, which was just enough to bring Frank's taxable estate down to the AEA level for 2004 (i.e., down to $1,500,000). The balance of the trust (i.e., $1,295,000)

went to her children. The tentative tax on Frank's estate equaled $555,800, which was completely covered by his unified credit. If Ellen had been dying at the time of Frank's death, she could have reduced overall taxes by disclaiming her reversionary interest (the $85,000), keeping it out of her estate, allowing it to be taxed at the lower marginal rates of Frank's estate rather than at the top marginal rates of her estate. With a disclaimer, all of the trust property would have gone to her children.

General Power of Appointment Exception: IRC § 2056(b)(5)

A power to appoint property is the right to tell the owner of the property to transfer it to someone else. Powers of appointment were discussed in greater detail earlier in the book. As a reminder, the Code defines a general power as "a power which is exercisable in favor of the decedent, his estate, his creditors, or the creditors of his estate. . . ."

> EXAMPLE 11 - 16. Fred creates an irrevocable trust for Jerry's benefit. The terms of the trust provide Jerry with all the income from the trust and give her the right, when she reaches 25, to have the trustee terminate the trust and transfer all assets to anyone that Jerry designates (including herself). From the moment Jerry reaches age 25, she has a general power of appointment.

The holder of a general power must include in his or her estate the value of property that could have been transferred by the exercise of a general power of appointment, regardless of whether it is ever exercised. It is enough that it merely could have been exercised. Limited powers do not result in inclusion of the property in the estate of the holder, provided the holder of the power did not create the power. Where the holder also created the power, the Internal Revenue Code treats it as a retained interest rather than as a power to appoint.

A marital deduction is allowed for property passing in trust from S1 to S2, provided S2 is given income for life in the property and has a general power of appointment over the property exercisable during life and/or at death.[13] Since S2 is a holder of a general power, the property will be included in S2's estate, or if she appoints it during life to someone else, it will be a gift from her to that person. Thus, although the transfer into a general power of appointment trust may technically be a transfer of a terminable interest, it is allowed to qualify for the marital deduction because (unless consumed) it will eventually be either given away by S2 or in S2's estate. Since Congress is allowing a marital deduction based on S2 receiving a life estate, the trust must either require the trustee to make the trust assets productive, or state law (and most states have such laws) must give S2 the power to require the trustee to make them productive. If the trust document gives the trustee absolute investment power, especially if it includes a statement allowing investment in unproductive assets, the marital deduction may not be available even though S2 is given a life estate.[14]

> EXAMPLE 11 - 17. On her death, Geraldine creates a trust for her husband, Bob. It is funded with assets having a net value of $2,950,714. Bob is given a life estate in the trust and the power to appoint the corpus at his death to whomever he chooses. The trust provides that this power is exercisable only by specific reference to it in his will and, if he fails to exercise the power, the property is to be distributed by right of representation to their issue. The trust will qualify for the marital deduction because of § 2056(b)(5). Therefore, although it is in Geraldine's gross estate, it is not in her taxable estate. Of course, when Bob dies, because the power is a general one, the entire trust will be included in his gross estate whether or not he exercises the power.

> EXAMPLE 11 - 18. On his death in 2002, Gerry's estate plan creates a trust to benefit his wife, Betty. It is funded with property worth $2,000,000. The terms of the trust give Betty a life estate and the power to appoint the corpus to any of their five children when she dies. If she does not appoint the corpus, it will be distributed by right of representation at her death. Because Betty only has a limited power to appoint, § 2056(b)(5) does not apply, and there is no automatic marital deduction. Assuming no QTIP (discussed later) election is made, the trust will be taxed at Gerry's death (resulting in estate taxes of $435,000), but no additional taxes will be owed vis-a-vis this trust when it terminates. The latter is true no matter how much the trust has grown, and no matter whether Betty exercises or fails to exercise her limited power to change the remainder interests of the children.

Pensions for the Benefit of S2: IRC § 2056(b)(7)(C)

In the case of an annuity included in S1's estate that is payable to S2 alone during S2's life, the QTIP election is automatic unless the executor of S1's estate affirmatively elects to have the annuity taxed in S1's estate. Electing to have it taxed will avoid having any value that remains at S2's death taxed as part of S2's estate, whereas allowing the automatic QTIP causes that value to be included in S2's estate.

Charitable Remainder Trusts with a Life Estate for S2: IRC § 2056 (b)(8)

Property transferred to a qualified charitable remainder trust,[15] which has the surviving spouse as its only non-charitable beneficiary, qualifies for the marital deduction, even though it is a terminable interest. This is a special rule and no QTIP election is necessary. It is not included in S2's estate, although it would make no difference if it were included since it would then qualify for a charitable deduction. If the executor is in doubt as to whether the trust is a "qualified charitable" remainder trust, he or she should make a protective QTIP election, i.e., list it as part of the QTIP property on Schedule M of the 706. It will then be in S2's estate, but it will qualify for a charitable deduction.

THE BASIC ESTATE PLANNING PATTERNS

Planning to minimize the estate tax with the marital deduction and the bypass arrangement generally involves some variation of one of three basic planning options. They are the *100% marital deduction*, the *AB Trust*, and the *ABC Trust*. These options do not depict precise will or trust arrangements, instead they trace the overall flow of property after S1's death. Our concern is with the timing of estate tax payments, the amount of those taxes, and which spouse (S1 or S2) controls who will eventually receive the property. First, we will take up the simplest plan, where S1 transfers all his estate to S2. Next, we will cover the bypass trust because it is common to almost all multiple trust plans. Lastly, we will take a look at the basic multiple trust plans, before going back to the QTIP election and how it is used in conjunction with the ABC Trust plan.

PLANNING OPTION 1: SIMPLE 100 PERCENT MARITAL DEDUCTION

Often the unlimited marital deduction provides a simple and practical estate planning strategy. It entirely shelters all property S1 transfers to S2 from gift tax and estate tax. In the simple 100% marital deduction strategy, S1 leaves all property to the surviving spouse. The transfer is protected from transfer tax by the 100% marital deduction. Outright transfers by S1 to S2 that qualify for the 100% marital deduction include: gifts, transfers by will, transfers by right of survivorship when title is held solely by the spouses in joint tenancy or tenancy by the entirety, and insurance on S1's life payable to S2. Transfers in trust for the benefit of S2 qualify too if they meet certain criteria.

> EXAMPLE 11 - 19. Tom and Gerri each have estates of $640,000. At her death in 2002, Gerri leaves her entire estate to Tom by a simple will. There is no estate tax because the estate is sheltered by the 100% marital deduction. At Tom's death in 2004, the combined estate worth $1,390,000 is left to their child. There is no estate tax because of his available AEA (i.e., up to $1,500,000 could pass tax-free).

Advantages of the 100 Percent Marital Deduction

The main attraction of the simple 100% marital deduction strategy is its simplicity. It is very easy to understand and inexpensive to establish. More elaborate estate planning may not be necessary for clients whose combined estates are less than one AEA. Some clients may not be concerned about whether taxes will be due after the second death, e.g., where the couple leaves no issue or where they plan to leave a large enough portion of their estate to charities such that at the second death the taxable estate will be less than the AEA.

Of course, these simple plans give S2 total dispositive control over all of the couple's property. This may be an advantage or a disadvantage, depending on the circumstances. S2 will receive full ownership of the property, a fee simple interest. S2 can use it, consume it, gift it, or sell it. If she still owns it at her death, she can leave it to whomever she chooses, in such manner as she chooses.

Not all marital deduction plans confer full dispositive control to S2. S1 may retain dispositive control by placing the property in a trust known as a qualified terminable interest property (QTIP) trust. These are most commonly found in multiple trust plans known as ABC trust plans. (Patience, we will get to this soon.) However, a QTIP trust can be used alone where S1 wants dispositive control but sees no need for multiple trusts.

Disadvantages of the 100 Percent Marital Deduction

The 100% marital deduction that transfers all control to S2 has several significant drawbacks for large estates.

Higher total estate tax. Assuming the second death will occur before 2010, the first drawback for wealthier couples is a higher total estate tax due to two factors. First, each spouse has the protection of the unified credit, but when S1 gives his entire estate to S2, his unified credit is unused. Unless S2 consumes or gives away S1's property using the annual exclusion or charitable gifts, it will become part of S2's transfer tax base, subject to either gift tax or estate tax to the extent that the combined value exceeds S2's AEA. Second, because the two estates are combined and subject to estate tax as one estate, there is only one "run up the rate ladder." Up to a point, marginal rates increase with the size of the estate. The larger the estate, the higher the rate of tax on the top dollar.

> EXAMPLE 11 - 20. H and W own a family estate of $7 million, with each owning one-half. They have simple wills leaving property to one another, or to the children if the other is deceased. At S1's death there will be no estate tax because the entire $3.5 million passes to S2, sheltered by the marital deduction. If S2 dies in the year 2003, having neither transferred nor consumed the property, a $7 million taxable estate will result in estate taxes of $2,885,000. For deaths in 2002 or 2003, two estates of $3.5 million each would result in combined estate taxes of $2,340,000 (even less, if a prior transfer credit is available to reduce the tax at the second death; this is a matter discussed in Chapter 12).

The simple 100% marital deduction planning is said to have the effect of "overqualifying" or "overusing" the marital deduction, resulting in a "loading up" of the taxable estate of S2, and subjecting a greater amount of the couple's wealth to tax at the second death than would occur with a more complex plan. In summary, two negative results can occur as a result of pouring the first estate into the second; the unified credit of S1 is wasted, and a portion of the combined estate may be subjected to higher marginal rates than would have been encountered with a more complex estate plan. Nevertheless, as we approach 2010, executors for S1's estate will be inclined to postpone taxes by whatever means are available if there is a fair probability that S2 will outlive the estate tax.

May not avoid probate. If a couple uses simple wills to carry out their 100% marital deduction planning, or if they hold everything in joint tenancy, there will be a probate, at least at the second death. Some states do not require a probate for property left from one spouse to the other. Of course, the use of living trusts as part of the estate plan overcomes this problem.

Not available for non-citizen spouses. The marital deduction only applies to property left to citizen spouses. The property of U.S. citizens is subject to estate taxation anywhere in the world. However, the property of a non-citizen who is also a non-resident will be subject to estate tax only if the property is located in the U.S. Because a non-citizen spouse could take the property and leave the country (preventing estate taxation at S2's death), the marital deduction does not apply to property left to a non-citizen spouse unless a special trust (with U.S. trustees) is used or the spouse becomes a citizen before the estate tax return is filed. More on this in the next chapter.

BYPASS PLANNING

The common theme of most bypass planning is the division of S1's estate into a bypass portion and a marital deduction portion. The bypass portion is transferred to someone other than S2 in a way that bypasses S2's estate. It is important to note that the bypass portion is considered to be "taxed" at the first death even if the use of S1's unified credit results in no tax being due. The marital deduction portion is transferred to S2 in a way that qualifies it for the marital deduction. Bypass planning thus avoids the two major problems with simple marital deduction planning. It makes use of S1's unified credit, and it potentially provides two runs up the rate ladder, depending on the details of the bypass plan chosen.

There are many variations on the bypass planning theme, including the way the bypass property is transferred (whether outright or in trust), the number of trusts used and their characteristics, the proportion of S1's property in the bypass portion, and whether it will equal the AEA (so no tax will actually be paid) or exceed it (and cause some tax at the first death). Usually, the bypass portion is eventually transferred to the couple's children, but there are many other possibilities. Remember, it is called bypass planning because it bypasses S2's estate (or some other income beneficiary's estate) for tax purposes. It is taxed in S1's estate whether taxes are paid or not, e.g., the tentative tax may be fully absorbed by the decedent's unified credit.

Simple outright bypass. The simplest form of bypass is the outright bypass where the AEA is left directly to someone other than S2.

EXAMPLE 11 - 21. Herbert had an estate worth $3,500,000 when he died in 2004. To his daughter, Denise, he left property worth $1,500,000 protected from tax by his unified credit, and to his wife, Wilma, he left property worth $2,000,000 protected from tax by the marital deduction. When Wilma died in 2006, she left to Denise an estate valued at $2,300,000 partially protected by her AEA. The estate tax was $138,000. If Herbert had left the entire $3,500,000 estate to Wilma, it would have been protected at his death by the marital deduction, but at Wilma's death, her estate would have greatly exceeded her AEA. Assuming modest growth, an estate of $3,800,000 would produce a tax of $828,000.

Bypass share: Outright or in trust? The couple might have strong reservations about the bypass plan if, at S1's death, it caused an immediate, outright transfer to the children. The children may be too young to be responsible for the property. S2 may need either the income from the property, or the property itself, for support. S2 might prefer to retain control over the management of those assets ultimately intended for the children. These are common and legitimate objections to the use of an immediate, outright transfer to the children to effect a bypass. Fortunately, the bypass can be arranged, and these objections overcome, by means of transfers into trusts.

Recall that by limiting the powers given to the beneficiary of a life estate, the trust is excluded from the holder's gross estate. The beneficiary can have the right to take the income and a power of appointment that does not rise to the level of a general power of appointment, such as the right to take principal measured by the "ascertainable standard."

Generally, bypass property is taxed at the time it is initially transferred for the benefit of the income beneficiary, but not again when the income beneficiary dies. The amount transferred in this fashion might be equal to the AEA, i.e., just enough to create a tentative tax equal to the unified credit. Thus, although technically the transfer is taxed, the donor, or in the case of a bequest, the decedent's estate, does not have to pay any transfer tax.

For most of our discussion we will assume that the income beneficiary in question is S2, and that the bypass property is a bypass trust established by S1. We make this assumption because it is the most frequently encountered bypass arrangement, but there are other possibilities. The bypass plan works because the transfer of an amount sufficient to use S1's unified credit to someone other than S2 can be arranged to conform to both spouses' overall estate planning objectives.

In a typical bypass trust, the children of the marriage are the ultimate beneficiaries, or remaindermen. Neither spouse is likely to object to the children as the remaindermen of the bypass trust created at S1's death, since in all likelihood, both spouses expect their combined estates to eventually go to their children. S2 usually has the income from the bypass property as well as access to the principal for purposes of health, education, support or maintenance, without the property being included in her estate.

MULTIPLE TRUSTS IN ESTATE PLANNING: BASIC PATTERNS

Each of the three plans (including the 100% marital deduction plan discussed earlier) can be set up with a will or a trust instrument. Due to the costs and lack of privacy associated with probate, most wealthy couples that spend the time, energy, and money to have one of these more complex estate plans written choose the living trust over the testamentary trust (although either will accomplish the tax savings discussed in this chapter). For the most part, we will assume a living trust for these multi-trust plans.

The documents that implement the process usually separate it into three phases. The first phase can be described as the family trust phase. There is usually only one trust in this phase. The couple's property is transferred to the trustee while the trustors are alive, hence it is called a "living" trust or an "inter vivos" trust. Most married couples serve as the initial trustees of their family trust, and they reserve the power to revoke or amend it.

The second phase starts with the death of one of the spouses, S1. The family trust is divided into multiple trusts after the first spouse dies. The multiple trusts are funded from the family trust at that time. It is not known which spouse will be the first to die at the time the plan is drafted, hence the distribution of assets into the various trusts is based on the order of the two deaths. Generally, in these complex estate plans, Trust A receives all of S2's property. Sometimes, some of S1's property goes into Trust A too, depending on the size of S1's estate and the type of estate plan. Trust B will be funded from S1's estate. Whether Trust B receives all of S1's estate, or only part of it, will again depend on the size of S1's estate and the type of estate plan. If there is a Trust C, it too will be funded from S1's estate. The funding of these trusts is fixed by the plan, and the trustee generally has very little flexibility to change the plan. After S1's death, Trusts B and C become irrevocable. S2 can control the distribution of assets only according to the terms of those trusts, e.g., she may or may not be given a limited power to appoint corpus when she dies or she may have a power to withdraw limited to an ascertainable standard. Usually, these plans allow S2 to amend (or even revoke) Trust A, since corpus is principally from S2's property.

The third phase commences with S2's death. If the plan has been properly carried out, the different trusts will already be funded. The executor, filing the estate tax return, must determine which trusts (or portions thereof) are included in S2's estate. After paying the estate tax, the trustee distributes the remaining trust property outright to the children if they have reached the age specified in the trust document, commonly 25, 30, or 35. On the other hand, if the children are much younger, then the two trusts (AB plan) or three trusts (ABC plan) are likely to be merged into a single "pot trust" (perhaps "children's trust" is a better name) until the children reach the age specified in the trust, at which time the trust is subdivided into equal shares for the children. Up until the time it is subdivided, the entire trust estate is available to meet the needs of any and all of the children. The name "pot trust" is derived from the fact that all needs are met from the same "pot" rather than being charged to each individual child's share based on such child's needs and usage. The subdivision (creating separate trusts) is usually specified as when either the youngest reaches a certain age (i.e., 21) or when the oldest reaches some age, although the trust can simply set a specific date after which division should be made, such as, "as soon after January 1, 2015, as the division can be accomplished."

Sometimes a testamentary trust arrangement is used for these complex estate plans, although it is less common than using the living trust. The testamentary trust is a lengthy will that incorporates a trust. With the testamentary trust, there is a probate after the testator dies. At the conclusion of the probate, the trust is funded by a court order, that incorporates into the order the trust language from the will. The order directs the distribution of the probate property to the trustee, who is charged with managing the trust estate in keeping with the terms of the trust. There may be several trusts depending on the specific estate plan. Once the probate is completed and the trust or trusts are funded, the process is just like plans that start with an inter vivos family trust.

When you work with these complex estate plans, at the first death start by determining the property (and its value) included in S1's estate to arrive at S1's gross estate (net estate before the marital deduction if the values given are net values). At the same time, you will have determined the value of S2's estate as it is at S1's death. The next step is to review their estate plan to determine how the property is to be allocated to each of the trusts. At the second death, the trusts are already funded, therefore, after determining the net value of each trust, the task is merely to determine what portion of each trust is included in S2's estate. The portion included may depend on the trust's characteristics (e.g., because of S2's general power to appoint the corpus of Trust A, it is always included) or it may depend on what was done at S1's death (e.g., whether a QTIP election was, or was not, made on a terminable interest trust).

Definitions. In the discussions that follow, we will be using the shorthand terms "AB Trust" and "ABC Trust." These terms are frequently used as shorthand designations, and effectively convey the general pattern of an estate plan to people who work in this field. The following names are frequently used for these trusts, but there are many other possibilities:

- Trust A is likely to be called the Survivor's Trust, the Marital Trust, or the General Power of Appointment Trust.
- Trust B is likely to be called the Bypass Trust, the Applicable Exclusion Trust, the AEA Trust, the Credit Shelter Trust, or the Nonmarital Trust.
- Trust C is likely to be called the QTIP Trust, the QTIP Marital Trust, or even Trust Q.

Depending on the plan and how Trusts B and C are defined, either may be called the Residuary Trust. Thus, if in an ABC Trust plan Trust B is defined in terms of the amount necessary to use the available unified credit (i.e., the AEA for S1) and the residue of S1's estate flows into Trust C, the latter may be called the Residuary Trust. On the other hand, if Trust C is defined as the minimum amount that, when qualified for the marital deduction, will reduce S1's taxable estate to the AEA, with the balance flowing into Trust B, then it is Trust B that may be called the Residuary Trust.

PLANNING OPTION 2: THE AB TRUST

The modern AB Trust plan is based on using the marital deduction and both spouses' unified credits. We say "modern" because the unlimited marital deduction has only been available to estates of decedents dying after 1981. The "B" Trust is the bypass component. The "A" Trust is the surviving spouse's trust. The two components are structured and funded so as to leave the maximum amount possible to the surviving spouse while still utilizing both spouses' unified credits. Payment of transfer taxes is deferred until S2's death. For large estates, whichever spouse lives longest, thus becoming S2, will ultimately control who receives the bulk of the couple's estate. Only Trust B, the AEA trust, has the remainder interest fixed by S1 at S1's death. *This plan makes sense for wealthy couples whose children are solely from their present marriage since the plan may give S2 ultimate control over the greater portion of the couple's combined estate.*

> EXAMPLE 11 - 22. The combined value of Hal and Wanda's property at S1's death in 2002, is $5,000,000. It does not matter whether Hal or Wanda dies first because the trusts are set up so that Trust A becomes S2's trust and Trust B, the trust that initially holds the AEA, receives assets with a net value of $1,000,000. The balance of the estate, in the amount of $4,000,000, would go into Trust A. Trust B would have the remaindermen irrevocably designated (probably the couple's children), while Trust A would be subject to the control of S2. There is no requirement that the couple's children ultimately receive the property from Trust A. If S2 remarries, or for any reason, decides they are not deserving, she can change the remaindermen for that trust. Because, it is not part of S2's estate, Trust B will not be taxed again at S2's death even if it then exceeds the AEA. The terms of the plan could add flexibility by giving S2 a limited power over Trust B, e.g., perhaps giving her the power to change the shares of the children or to give some of the corpus to specifically named charities.

The Character of Trust A

Trust A receives all of S2's property, plus all of S1's property that exceeds S1's available AEA. S1's unified credit is applied against taxable transfers up to the AEA. These taxable transfers include property going into Trust B, property going to people other than S2, and lifetime taxable gifts made by S1. To obtain the marital deduction at S1's death for property transferred from S1's estate into Trust A, the trust must have two characteristics: (1) S2 must receive all the income for life, paid at least annually; and (2) S2 must be given a general power of appointment exercisable during life and/or at her death. Of course, if S2 has a general power to appoint exercisable during her entire lifetime, she also has income for life even if the trust is silent in that regard.

The Character of Trust B

The funding for Trust B is usually defined in terms of S1's available AEA. It usually receives exactly enough of S1's estate to cause a tentative tax equal to S1's "available" unified credit. What is available starts with the AEA for the year S1 died and is reduced by the value of property passing to someone other than S2 and any post-1977 taxable gifts. Methods for achieving the right amount of funding are described at the end of this chapter under the heading "Allocating Assets to the Trusts." For most estates, the initial value of Trust B will be the AEA since this will cause a tentative tax equal to the unified credit available in the year of S1's death. The tentative tax is then canceled out by unified credit.

Since the purpose of this trust is to use S1's unified credit and avoid inclusion in S2's estate, any characteristics that would cause inclusion (such as giving S2 a general power of appointment over trust corpus) must be avoided. The marital deduction is not sought for Trust B, so while it is common to give S2 all income for life, such is not required. The terms could call for sprinkling the income among S2 and the children, or it could even allow the trustee to accumulate income or distribute corpus to persons other than S2. Most AB plans give S2 all of the income from Trust B, probably for psychological reasons since it is not necessary for tax reasons. A general power to appoint would cause inclusion in S2's estate, so it is to be avoided. However, S2 may be given a power to invade the corpus limited by ascertainable standards or S2 may be given a special power to allocate the remainder. A special power, in those plans using one, is likely to be limited to the couple's children and/or specific charities, adding flexibility to the plan within limits, without causing the trust property to be included in S2's estate.

AB Trust Plan's Benefits

The AB Trust plan provides the opportunity for S2 to manage the assets from both estates, enjoy all of the income, and have access to all of the principal, i.e., even Trust B corpus can be reached if the trust includes a power to withdraw limited by an ascertainable standard. In the event both spouses die while their children are young, the plan allows disbursement to the children to be delayed until they are old enough to manage the property. An AB Trust can provide flexibility so that S2 can change the distribution plan in response to changed circumstances, it makes use of the marital deduction to delay taxation until the second death, and it uses S1's unified credit. The following example compares the estate taxes using the unlimited marital deduction with the result of using an AB Trust plan.

EXAMPLE 11 - 23. S1 dies in the year 2004 (when the AEA is $1,500,000) and S2 dies in the year 2007 (when the AEA is $2,000,000). All of the estate, with a net value of $8,000,000, belongs to S1 and poor S2 owns nothing. In an AB Trust plan, even though S2 has no assets, the plan calls for S2's property to go into Trust A since, before either spouse dies, no one can be certain which spouse will be S1 or S2, or whether a spouse with little property might acquire a substantial estate before S1's death.

	100% Marital Deduction		**AB Trust**	
	S1 dies 2004	S2 dies 2007	S1 dies 2004	S2 dies 2007
GE	$8,000,000	$8,000,000	$8,000,000	$6,500,000
MD	$8,000,000)	$0	($6,500,000)	$0
TE	$0	$8,000,000	$1,500,000	$6,500,000
TT	$0	$3,480,800	$555,800	$2,805,800
UC	$0	($780,800)	($555,800)	($780,800)
ET	$0	$2,700,000	$0	$2,025,000

A tax savings of $675,000 results. This is partly due to $1,500,000 being "taxed" at S1's death even though no tax is paid. The reason that the tax savings is more than the $555,800 unified credit used at S1's death is that the $1,500,000 held in Trust B would have been taxed in S2's estate at her estate's highest marginal rates, i.e., those between $6,500,000 and $8,000,000. Avoiding those higher marginal rates results in an additional $119,200 saved. Of course, if Trust B grew in value between the two deaths, even more is sheltered since a bypass trust is not taxed at S2's death, regardless of its value at that time.

EXAMPLE 11 - 24. This example is similar to the last example except both spouses have community property and separate property. To allow easier comparison between the examples, the total net value will stay at $8,000,000, and the plans and timing of the two deaths will remain the same. S1 has separate property worth $3,350,000, S2 has separate property worth $2,700,000, and they own community property worth $1,950,000.

	100% Marital Deduction		AB Trust	
	S1 dies 2004	S2 dies 2007	S1 dies 2004	S2 dies 2007
GE	$4,325,000	$8,000,000	$4,325,000	$6,500,000
MD	($4,325,000)	0	($2,825,000)	$0
TE	0	$8,000,000	$1,500,000	$6,500,000
TT	0	$3,480,800	$555,800	$2,805,800
UC	0	($780,800)	($555,800)	($780,800)
ET	0	$2,700,000	$0	$2,025,000

Notice the gross estate at S1's death is the same for both plans. S1's estate consisted of separate property plus one-half of the community property, i.e., $3,350,000 + 50% * $1,950,000 = $4,325,000. Of course, our assumption, made for the sake of simplicity, that the values remain the same between S1's death and S2's death is unrealistic. The use of S1's unified credit is not being postponed until S2's death, since Trust B is actually taxed at S1's death but the tentative tax is completely covered by S1's unified credit. Trust B is not taxed at S2's death because it entirely bypasses S2's estate.

If either spouse is uncomfortable with the control given to S2 by the AB Trust plan, they should consider the ABC Trust plan which reduces the amount of property over which S2 exercises ultimate control, yet still allows estate taxes to be postponed until the second death.

PLANNING OPTION 3: THE ABC TRUST

The ABC Trust plan is like the AB Trust plan except that S1's net estate in excess of the AEA goes into Trust C instead of passing to Trust A. The terms of Trust C qualify it for the marital deduction through the QTIP election, thus making it possible to defer all estate taxes until the second death. The real advantage of this plan when compared to the AB Trust is that S1's estate in excess of the AEA goes into Trust C, which cannot be changed by S2. Since Trusts B and C are irrevocable, S1 can rest in peace knowing that the remaindermen for these two trusts are fixed. S2 may be given the power, limited by an ascertainable standard relating to health, education, support, or maintenance, to invade the corpus of Trusts B and C. This invasion right can even be limited such that it only becomes available to S2 when Trust A has less than a certain value remaining, e.g., only if Trust A is worth less than the AEA. S1 can also give S2 a limited power of appointment, exercisable only by will, over Trusts B and C. Remember, neither a limited power to appoint, nor a power to invade limited by an ascertainable standard, will cause inclusion of the property in the holder's estate. Even though S2 is given these powers, it is S1 who defines their limits.

The Character of Trust A

This Trust A is likely to have the same characteristics as Trust A in the AB Trust plan. Trust A receives property equal in value to all of S2's separate property and S2's one-half interest in community property. S2 is given a general power to appoint the corpus of this trust or to revoke it. Unless property actually passes from S1's estate into Trust A, there is no marital deduction for property in this trust because it will hold property that already belongs to S2. It is not unusual for S1's plan to leave some property, such as all the tangible personal property, to S2's Trust A. The transfer of such property into Trust A would automatically qualify for the marital deduction. Of course, there is also an automatic marital deduction for property (such as cars and the household bank account) held in joint tenancy by the couple.

The Character of Trust B

Trust B will have the same characteristics as Trust B in the AB Trust plan, including being defined in terms of S1's available AEA. Thus, in most instances the value of the trust will initially be S1's available AEA. As the AEA increases such that it shelters higher amounts (e.g., $1,000,000 in 2002, $2,000,000 in 2006), the "available AEA" language allows the estate plan to make the most of the increased bypass opportunity. Again, the trust can be a sprinkling trust without harming the planning objectives but, more commonly, S2 is given all income for life. As will be discussed in the next chapter, giving S2 income for life (also referred to as a life estate) in this trust may, under certain circumstances, allow a larger prior transfer tax credit. This is a bypass trust in that it will be taxed at S1's death and escape tax (regardless of its growth) at S2's death.

The Character of Trust C

Trust C must meet all the Code QTIP requirements[16] to ensure the marital deduction is available should S1's executor decide that it is in the estate's best interest to claim a marital deduction. The requirements are that S2 must receive income for life and no one can hold a power to appoint the trust property to anyone other than S2 during her lifetime. This trust usually receives that portion of S1's estate that exceeds the AEA. When a QTIP election is made for Trust C, the executor of S1's estate is claiming a marital deduction and, in effect, making a pact with the IRS that the property will eventually be subject to transfer tax triggered by S2 making a gift of her interest in the trust or by her death.[17] If the QTIP election is not made, Trust C will be taxed at S1's death and will not be taxed again when S2 dies, even though S2 enjoys a life estate. Thus, Trust C is a marital deduction trust if the election is made, and a bypass trust if it is not.

Typically, S2 enjoys a life estate (a requirement for the QTIP) in the trust property. She has the use of any tangible property that is part of this trust (such as the home and its contents) and must receive the income from investment property, placing it in her own personal accounts or in her Trust A accounts.

If the QTIP election is not made, S2 must withdraw the income from the trust. Leaving it in Trust C would be treated as a gift from her into the trust over which she has a retained life estate, creating a § 2036 retained life estate problem. Of course this is only a problem if the QTIP election is not made since, if it is made over the whole trust, the trust will be included in S2's estate anyway.[18]

The QTIP election is made on Schedule M of S1's U.S. Federal Estate Tax Return, Form 706. Once the election is made (or not made) on a return and the time for filing the estate tax return has passed, the executor cannot change the decision. Fortunately, the QTIP election can be made even on a late filed return.

Trust C cannot be a sprinkling trust since S2 must receive all income from the trust for life. The income must be distributed at least annually, and S2 must have the right to require the trustee to change unproductive assets (ones that produce little or no income) into reasonably productive income producing assets. Even if some required terms are not in the trust, state law often remedies the deficiency, e.g., if in the context of the overall estate plan it appears a trust was supposed to qualify for the QTIP election the law might supply missing elements such as requiring trustees to distribute income at least annually or give surviving spouses the right to force trustees to make unproductive assets productive. These statutes satisfy the QTIP requirements even if the trust instrument is silent on the timing of income distributions, or if at the time of S1's death, a significant portion of the trust estate is made up of unproductive assets (such as undeveloped land) and the trust terms say nothing about the trustee being obligated to make them productive. Note, as long as S2 has the right to require unproductive assets be made productive, the trustee need not make the assets more productive for the QTIP election to be made. Of course, if S2 makes the request, the trustee must comply with the request and seek a higher return on unproductive assets.

S2 can be given a power to invade corpus, limited by an ascertainable standard. She can also have a limited power to appoint corpus so long as it is exercisable only at her death. The limited power to appoint is usually limited to allocation among the couple's children and, perhaps, specific charities.

The trust instrument can also add flexibility by giving S2 a 5 & 5 power; however, S1 would be giving up some certainty as to who will ultimately receive the corpus. If one of the reasons for choosing the ABC plan was to assure that S1's property would go to S1's children by a prior marriage, a 5 & 5 power might not be desirable since each exercise by S2 takes property out of the trust.

THE APPROPRIATE QTIP ELECTION

When a QTIP election is available after S1's death, the executor must determine how much of the QTIP property to QTIP, i.e., the optimal portion of S1's estate to have taxable at S1's death. Subtracting that optimal amount from S1's total estate gives the marital deduction desired. The marital deduction is obtained by making a QTIP election of part (or all) of the QTIP property. If the document allows a division of the QTIP trust into two or more trusts, one of which the executor (the trustee) elects to completely QTIP and the other for which no election is made (let's call them Trust CQ and Trust CNQ, respectively), some additional planning opportunities exist. With the division, the trustee can "spend down" Trust CQ if S2 needs to use corpus. Since a QTIPed trust is in S2's estate, reducing a Trust CQ is better than reducing a single partially QTIPed Trust C since, in the later case, any reduction to the trust would reduce pro rata both the QTIP and the non-QTIP portion of the trust. However, if the document is silent as to the trustee's power to create separate trusts, the Regulations require that the QTIP election be for a specific portion (i.e., on a fractional basis) of the full value of the trust. A fraction is created with the QTIP marital deduction amount as the numerator and entire value of the QTIP property as the denominator. This is the fraction of the QTIP property that is protected by the marital deduction at S1's death. This fraction also determines how much of the QTIP property will be taxed at S2's death. To determine the taxable part at S2's death, the value of the QTIP property at S2's death is multiplied by the QTIP fraction. Before applying this to specific estate plans let us break this process down into six steps.

Step by Step: Determining and Using the QTIP Fraction

Step 1. Determine the desired taxable estate for S1: Usually, the executor wants to postpone all taxes to the second death, but still use S1's unified credit. This means using the marital deduction to bring the taxable estate to the AEA, e.g, $1,000,000 in the year 2002. However, if generating some taxes at the first death saves taxes in the long run, it might be advantageous to bring the taxable estate to some higher value.

Step 2. Determine the QTIP marital deduction (QTIP MD) amount necessary to arrive at the desired taxable estate: Total S1's Estate – S1's Desired Taxable Estate = MD amount. If the marital deduction is only by way of a QTIP election, this will also be the QTIP MD amount. If some property passes to S2 immediately by joint tenancy, or by being transferred from S1's estate into a trust that S2 controls (Trust A), such will qualify for an automatic marital deduction (automatic MD). The automatic MD must be subtracted from the MD amount to arrive at the needed QTIP MD.

Step 3. Determine the value of the QTIP property: This is the property, almost always a trust, that meets the QTIP code requirements (§ 2056(b)(7)) and to which the QTIP election will apply to give us the QTIP MD. Which trust is the QTIP trust depends on the particular estate plan, e.g., with the ABC plan it is the value of Trust C, usually S1's estate less the AEA (the AEA having been transferred into Trust B). Generically, we will refer to it as the QTIP Trust.

Step 4. The fraction: Create a fraction with the QTIP MD (Step 2) over the QTIP Trust (Step 3) to arrive at the QTIP fraction.

$$\frac{QTIP\ MD}{QTIP\ Trust} = QTIP\ Fraction$$

Step 5. S1's taxable estate: S1's taxable estate is S1's total estate less any automatic MD and less the product of the QTIP fraction and the QTIP Trust. Check your calculation, the result should match the desired taxable estate (Step 1).

$$S1's\ Taxable\ Est. = Total\ Est. - automatic\ MD - (\frac{QTIP\ MD}{QTIP\ Trust} * QTIP\ Trust)$$

Step 6. S2's taxable estate: At S2's death, to determine S2's total estate, the QTIP Trust (*as it is then valued*) is multiplied by the QTIP fraction to determine the amount of the QTIP Trust included in S2's estate. This in turn is added to the rest of S2's estate (generally Trust A).

$$S2's\ Taxable\ Est. = Trust\ A + (\frac{QTIP\ MD}{QTIP\ Trust\ [@S1'sDOD]} * QTIP\ Trust\ [@S2'sDOD])$$

If the trust document allows the trustee to divide Trust C into Trust CQ (to be QTIPed) and Trust CNQ (that is not QTIPed), there are a few changes to the steps. One would still go through steps 1 - 2 as before, then at step 3, Trust CQ would be allocated the QTIP marital deduction amount and Trust CNQ the balance of S1's property. The fractions at step 5 would be 100% (1/1) for Trust CQ and zero for Trust CNQ. Finally, step 6 would have S2's estate equal to all of S2's property, plus all of Trust CQ. Since Trusts B and CNQ are fully included in S1's taxable estate, they are both bypass trusts and, as such, they are not included in S2's estate.

Extended Example

The extended example set that follows is designed to increase your understanding of the QTIP election. Using a modern ABC plan, the example compares the result of death taxes for a 100% QTIP election to what happens where there is no QTIP election. Later, we will explore what happens when S1's executor makes a partial

QTIP election where the trustee does not have authority to divide Trust C into separate trusts. For examples in this chapter, we will ignore the prior transfer credit, as it will be covered in connection with multiple trust plans in the next chapter. We will assume that Trust C meets all of the QTIP requirements. **** *Query 2. Why not include the modern AB Trust plan as part of this QTIP example?* The assumption is also made that S2 does not remarry, therefore, there is no marital deduction for S2's estate. To simplify these examples, all figures are given net of debts and expenses, and the values of the trusts increase modestly each year during the 10 years between the two deaths. The assumption that the two deaths occur 10 years apart avoids having to tackle the prior transfer credit as part of the example.

Step by Step: Applied to the ABC Trust Plan

Step 1. Determine the desired taxable estate for S1, e.g., equal to the AEA so as to postpone all taxes, or have S1 and S2's estates equal as of S1's death, or some dollar amount as determined by the executor to be optimal in reducing overall taxes for the two estates.

Step 2. Total Estate – Desired Taxable Estate = QTIP MD amount.

Step 3. Trust C is the QTIP Trust, defined as being S1's estate in excess of the AEA (Trust B):

> S1's Total Estate – Trust B = Trust C

Step 4. Create a fraction with the QTIP MD amount (Step 2) over the QTIP Trust (Step 3) to arrive at the QTIP fraction:

$$\frac{QTIP\ MD}{Trust\ C} = QTIP\ Fraction$$

Step 5. S1's taxable estate is S1's total estate less the product of the QTIP Trust and the QTIP fraction. The result should match the desired taxable estate (Step 1).

$$S1's\ Taxable\ estate = Total\ estate - (\frac{QTIP\ MD}{Trust\ C} * Trust\ C)$$

Step 6. At S2's death, the amount *then* in Trust C is multiplied by the QTIP fraction in order to determine the amount of Trust C that must be included in S2's estate. Add that amount to the rest of S2's estate (e.g., Trust A) to determine S2's total estate.

$$S2's\ Taxable\ Est. = Trust A + (\frac{QTIP\ MD}{Trust\ C\ [@S1'sDOD]} * Trust\ C\ [@S2'sDOD])$$

Facts for this extended set: Henry (S1) and Wilma (S2) lived, and died, in a community property state. Their estate plan was an ABC Trust plan as described above. When Henry died in 2002, they owned property valued as follows:

S1's separate property	$1,500,000
Their community property	$1,800,000
S2's separate property	$2,000,000
Total	$5,300,000

Note: If Henry and Wilma lived in a common law state, the outcome would be the same if we equally divide the community property between them:

S1's separate property	$2,400,000
S2's separate property	$2,900,000
Total	$5,300,000

In fact, the property laws for common law and community property states result in ownership rights for each spouse that largely depend on how the spouses acquired their property.

After Henry's death the trusts were funded with assets having a net value as shown here:

Trust A	$2,900,000
Trust B	$1,000,000
Trust C	$1,400,000
Total	$5,300,000

The values of the trusts at Wilma's death in 2007 will be given in Step 6.

PART ONE: The executor of Henry's estate elects to postpone all taxes until Wilma's death but desires to use Henry's unified credit. Given that he died in 2002, the optimal taxable estate is equal to the AEA, i.e., $1,000,000.

Step 1. The desired taxable estate for S1 = $1,000,000.

Step 2. $2,400,000 - $1,000,000 = $1,400,000

Step 3. The QTIP property: S1's Total Estate – Trust B = Trust C.

$$\$2,400,000 - \$1,000,000 = \$1,400,000$$

Step 4. Create a fraction with the QTIP marital deduction amount from Step 2 divided by the Trust C amount from Step 3 to arrive at the QTIP fraction.

$$\frac{\$1,400,000}{\$1,400,000} = 100\%$$

Step 5. S1's taxable estate is S1's total estate less the product of Trust C and the QTIP fraction:

$$\textit{S1's Taxable Estate} = \$2,400,000 - ((\frac{\$1,400,000}{\$1,400,000}) * \$1,400,000)$$

$$= \$1,000,000$$

Step 6. At S2's death in the year 2007, the amount *then* in Trust C is multiplied by the QTIP fraction to determine the amount of Trust C that must be included in S2's estate. Add that amount to Trust A to determine S2's total estate. Assume that in the five years the values for the three trusts increased to the following:

Trust A	$3,400,000
Trust B	$1,350,000
Trust C	$1,650,000
Total	$6,400,000

Note: The entire amount of Trust C (as it is at S2's death) is included in S2's estate since *all* of Trust C was QTIPed. S2's estate is:

$$\$3,400,000 \text{ [Trust A]} + \$1,650,000 \text{ [Trust C]} = \$5,050,000$$

Trust A was not part of Henry's taxable estate because it contained only Wilma's property. Trusts B and C combined equal Henry's gross estate because all of Henry's property is allocated to these two trusts. Regardless of whether a QTIP election is made, the value of Trust B will be taxed as part of Henry's estate, although with a 100% QTIP of Trust C there will be no tax due, since the unified credit will match the tentative tax generated by Trust B. While Trust C's value is always part of the *gross* estate, it need not be taxed if the QTIP election is made to cover the entire trust, because it then is protected by the marital deduction and will be taxed in S2's estate.

When Wilma dies, there are several reasons why Trust A is included in her estate. She holds a general power over it, which would cause inclusion of any property transferred to it by Henry; and she transferred her own property to it, retaining the right to revoke the transfer. Trust B is excluded from Wilma's estate because it is a bypass trust. Wilma did not fund Trust B, therefore, she could not have a retained interest in it; nor did she hold a general power of appointment over it. Trust C is included in her estate only because of the QTIP election after Henry's death. This was a trade-off: it allowed Trust C to escape tax when Henry died, so it had to be included in her estate when Wilma died.

Notice that the QTIP election, or the failure to elect, does not change the amount of property going into each trust. Of course, if no QTIP election is made, then taxes must be paid from Trusts B and C at S1's death, since the value is in excess of the AEA.

PART TWO: Change the facts. Suppose the executor of Henry's estate decided that it was best NOT to postpone any taxes on Henry's share of the property, and therefore, elected NOT to make a QTIP election. This means the desired taxable estate equals all of Henry's property, i.e., $2,400,000. Even though it's obvious that the amounts going into Trusts B and C (all of Henry's estate) will be the amount taxed at his death, and Wilma's property (all of Trust A) will be the only property taxed at her death, the steps are set forth here to make it apparent that we are following the same format, an important lesson before we start working on partial QTIP elections.

Step 1. The Desired Taxable Estate for S1 = $2,400,000.

Step 2. Total Estate – Desired Taxable Estate = QTIP Election amount.

$$\$2,400,000 - \$2,400,000 = \$0$$

Step 3. Trust C is the QTIP property.

$$S1's \ Total \ Estate - Trust \ B = Trust \ C = \$1,400,000$$

Step 4. Create a fraction with the QTIP MD from Step 2 over Trust C (Step 3) to determine the QTIP fraction.

$$\frac{\$0}{\$1,400,000} = zero$$

Step 5. $$S1's \ Taxable \ estate = Total \ estate - (\frac{QTIP \ MD}{Trust \ C} * Trust \ C)$$

$$S1's \ Taxable \ Estate = \$2,400,000 - ((\frac{\$0}{\$1,400,000}) * \$1,400,000)$$
$$= \$2,400,000$$

Step 6. In this case, since none of Trust C was QTIPed, S2's estate is just $3,400,000 [The value of Trust A only].

In all of these plans Trust A is included in S2's estate because it holds S2's property and, as to any property that flows into Trust A from S1's estate, S2 holds a general power of appointment over this trust. Where S1's executor forgoes the QTIP election, Trust C is taxed at S1's death and then escapes tax at S2's death. Trust B is not included in S2's estate because it is a bypass trust, already taxed in S1's taxable estate, but bypassing the estate of S2. When possible, Trust B is funded with property expected to appreciate because it escapes tax at S2's death, even if its value greatly exceeds the AEA for that year.

OPTIMAL ALLOCATION: THE PARTIAL QTIP ELECTION

Trust C has the chameleon character of being like a marital deduction trust if the QTIP election is made, or a bypass trust if the QTIP election is not made.

However, the law permits flexibility by allowing partial QTIP elections. This allows a portion of the QTIP trust (Trust C in the ABC plan) to qualify for the marital deduction at S1's death. When the executor of S1's estate makes such an election, a portion of the QTIP trust, the QTIP fraction portion, acts like a marital trust and the rest of the trust acts like a bypass trust. The QTIP election portion of Trust C escapes taxes at S1's death because of the marital deduction, but that same fraction of the QTIP trust, valued at S2's death, is included in S2's estate when S2 dies. The non-QTIP election portion is taxed at S1's death but not at S2's death.

A partial QTIP may be desirable to lower the overall estate taxes by taking advantage of lower marginal rates in both estates and by utilizing the prior transfer credit (discussed in conjunction with the marital deduction in the next chapter). Generally, executors choose to postpone all taxes until S2's death, even though the absolute amount of total taxes paid will almost always be greater when this is done. Given the time value of money, postponing taxes makes sense rather than paying taxes at the first death. Besides, if taxes are paid at the first death, they are paid out of property intended to produce income for the surviving spouse; whereas, postponing the taxes takes them out of the property going to the children (or others, if there are no children).

The picture changes dramatically if it is known at the time S1's estate tax return is being prepared that S2 is quite certain to die soon. In that case, paying taxes for both estates, rather than just at S2's death, will not only use both estates' lower marginal rates, but S2's estate will be able to use a prior transfer credit that substantially reduces taxes on the second death.

Where S2's death is likely to occur within a few years of S1's death (more than one year but less than 10, and before the year 2010), the optimal allocation between the two taxable estates depends on such factors as the age of S2 at the time of S1's death, the federal rate for valuing split interests, the size of the combined estates, and how long S2 outlives S1. Generally, the lower the federal rate, the older the surviving spouse, and the larger the estate, the higher the percentage that should be allocated to S1's taxable estate as compared to S2's. For instance, if the first death occurs in 2001 when the §7520 rate is 6%, S2 is 70 years old, dies about a year and a half after S1, and the combined estate value is $10 million at the time of S1's death, the tax bill is lowest if $7,500,000 is taxed in S1's estate and only $2,500,000 is taxed in S2's estate. Under the circumstance just described, if all taxes are deferred until the second death, whether through a QTIP or regular marital deduction, with only the AEA being sheltered at S1's death, the estate taxes would be about $1,000,000 more than they would be with the optimal allocation. Of course, if S2 is expected to live until 2010, it is optimal allocation to have S1's taxable estate at, or below, the AEA for the year he dies.

Several competing factors must be considered when deciding the appropriate QTIP fraction. One consideration is the time value of money. If the deaths are not expected to occur close together, taxes paid a long time in the future are less burdensome than taxes paid today. However, if the property appreciates substantially between the deaths, the total tax bill will be higher. If property is appreciating very rapidly, sometimes it makes sense to get the tax paid sooner on a smaller amount. Another consideration is the prior transfer credit that substantially reduces taxes at the second death, but only if the deaths are close together in time. One must also consider the relative size of the two estates. A QTIP election can only shift the taxable estate in S2's direction, so optimization by QTIP election works only when S1's estate is larger than S2's, and only if it is large enough to equal the optimal S1 taxable estate.

Where the second death is likely to occur within a few years after the first death, and the estates have a combined value in excess of two AEAs, the optimal allocation usually has S1's taxable estate slightly larger than that of S2, thus when the two estates are about equal in size, or when S2 has the larger estate, there should be no QTIP election because doing so would only further increase S2's taxable estate.

Since deductions other than the marital deduction are generally beyond the executor's control, the focus in the examples to follow is on the marital deduction that can be increased or decreased depending on the QTIP fraction. For simplicity, we will continue to ignore the other deductions.

Partial QTIP Election Examples

While it seems more complex, the process for calculating estates with a partial QTIP election is the same process discussed earlier for the "all or nothing" QTIP elections. Where it was "all," the QTIP fraction was equal to one[19] and where it was "nothing," it was equal to zero.[20]

EXAMPLE 11 - 25. Sam has an estate of $5 million and his wife Susan has an estate of $1.7 million. His executor elects to have $4,100,000 taxed at Sam's death in 2004. The value of the three trusts at Sam's death would be: Trust A, $1,700,000; Trust B, $1,500,000; and Trust C, $3,500,000.

Step 1. Sam's desired taxable estate is $4,100,000.

Step 2. Sam's Total Estate – Desired Taxable Estate = QTIP MD

$5,000,000 - $4,100,000 = $900,000.

Step 3. Trust C is the QTIP property: $3,500,000.

Step 4. $\dfrac{QTIP\ MD}{Trust\ C} = \dfrac{\$900,000}{\$3,500,000} = QTIP\ Fraction$

Step 5. $Sam's\ Taxable\ estate = Sam's\ Total\ Estate - (\dfrac{QTIP\ MD}{Trust\ C} * Trust\ C)$

$\$5,000,000 - (\dfrac{\$900,000}{\$3,500,000} * \$3,500,000) = \$4,100,000$

Step 6. By Susan's death in 2006, Trust A grew to $2,300,000, Trust B grew to $1,900,000; and Trust C grew to $4,200,000. The portion of Trust C included in her estate is:

$\dfrac{\$900,000}{\$3,500,000} * \$4,200,000 = \$1,080,000$

When added to Trust A, her total estate is $3,380,000 [$2,300,000 + $1,080,000]. Notice that Trust B is not taxed at Susan's death, even though it exceeded the AEA for the year of her death.

Equalizing Estates

Most combined estates (i.e., S1 plus S2 at S1's death) valued up to about $12 million will save almost as much tax by simply equalizing the two taxable estates as is saved with the optimal allocation, when these two alternatives are compared to the 100% QTIP option. The example that follows assumes that the executor seeks to have both taxable estates equal as of S1's death. Equalizing the estates uses the six-step process that we have used previously. If S1's estate is larger than S2's, the two are averaged and the average is the desired taxable estate for Step 1. **** *Query 3. What QTIP election should S1's executor make if S2's estate is larger than S1's and equal estates would be desirable?*

EXAMPLE 11 - 26. Using the facts from the prior Sam and Susan example, suppose Susan is in extremely poor health at Sam's death and, therefore, the executor chooses to equalize the estates.

Step 1. Sam's desired taxable estate:

$$\textit{Average}: \quad \$5,000,000 + \$1,700,000 = \frac{\$6,700,000}{2} = \$3,350,000$$

Step 2. Sam's Total Estate – Desired Taxable Estate = QTIP MD:

$$\$5,000,000 - \$3,350,000 = \$1,650,000.$$

Step 3. Trust C = $3,500,000.

Step 4. $$\frac{QTIP\ MD}{Trust\ C} = \frac{\$1,650,000}{\$3,500,000} = QTIP\ Fraction$$

Step 5. *Sam's Taxable estate = Sam's Total estate* $- (\frac{QTIP\ MD}{Trust\ C} * Trust\ C)$

$$\$3,350,000 = \$5,000,000 - (\frac{\$1,650,000}{\$3,500,000} * \$3,500,000)$$

Step 6. Suppose at Susan's death Trust A has grown to $2,300,000, but because taxes were paid out of Trust B and C, they were $1,560,000 and $3,800,000, respectively. The portion of Trust C that would be included in her estate would be:

$$\frac{\$1,650,000}{\$3,500,000} * \$3,800,000 = \$1,791,429$$

Susan's estate would be $4,091,429 [Trust A $2,300,000 + Trust C $1,791,429].

There is a shortcut to equalize the estates that reaches the same result. S2's estate is subtracted from S1's estate and half the difference is the amount of the QTIP election (Step 2). Here is the short cut, using Sam and Susan's estate from the above example:

$$\frac{Sam's \ estate \ - \ Susan's \ estate}{2} = QTIP \ MD$$

$$\frac{\$5,000,000 \ - \ \$1,700,000}{2} = \$1,650,000$$

Notice that this is the same result as Step 2. **** *Query 4. The QTIP election in the above example was calculated to equalize the estates. Why then are they not equal?*

ALLOCATING ASSETS TO THE TRUSTS

Estate planning involves planning for an uncertain future. The planner and client must guess how much and what kind of property will be in the estate. They must also guess whether the intended beneficiaries will be alive, and what their circumstances will be at the time the estate is distributed. Because of this uncertainty, planning documents are drafted to deal with uncertainty. Two drafting techniques for structuring disposition clauses in wills or trusts are pecuniary bequests and fractional share bequests.

A *pecuniary bequest* passes property to various shares such that the value of the assets adds up to the dollar value needed to satisfy the pecuniary bequest. For example, the clause funding Trust B might read: *"assets equal in dollar value to the amount that will generate a tentative tax exactly equal to S1's available unified credit, and all assets above that amount are given to the trustee of Trust A."*

Or, the marital bequest going to Trust A of an AB trust plan (or Trust C, in an ABC trust plan) could be defined in dollars: *"assets equal in dollar amount to the marital deduction necessary to reduce S1's taxable estate such that it generates a tentative tax exactly equal to S1's available unified credit are allocated to Trust A, all other assets are allocated to Trust B."*

Using a *fractional share bequest*, both bypass and marital shares will receive a fractional interest in each and every asset in the estate: *"Trust C shall consist of the smallest fractional share of S1's estate that, when added to all other interests in property that pass from S1 to S2, and qualify for the marital deduction, will eliminate, or reduce to the maximum possible extent, any estate tax. The balance of S1's estate shall be allocated to Trust B."* The factors involved in deciding which type of provision to use are beyond the scope of this text.

QUERIES ANSWERED

1. In 2004, the AEA is $1,500,000, hence the QTIP fraction and the marital deduction that result in a $1,500,000 taxable estate when applied to the trust at Fernando's death are as follows:

$$\frac{1,430,032}{2,930,032} * \$2,930,032 = \$1,430,032$$

The amount included in her estate would be:

$$\frac{1,430,032}{2,930,032} * \$3,533,502 = \$1,724,562$$

2. Trust B in the modern AB trust is equal to the available AEA, and everything above the AEA is transferred to Trust A; hence, S1's estate receives a marital deduction equal to the value of that property. With this plan there is no terminable interest property to QTIP.

3. S1's executor should make no QTIP election since doing so would increase S2's estate, making the two taxable estates even more unequal.

4. Sam and Susan's taxable estates are not equal because Trusts A and C changed in value between the two deaths. Trust B has no effect on the estate value at the second death because it is a bypass trust.

QUESTIONS AND PROBLEMS - Use the ETAX program to do the problems that require calculation of estate or gift taxes.

1. In 2002, what is the largest estate size that an *individual* can transfer, estate tax-free, with a *simple will* to (a) a spouse; (b) anyone else? Explain, and state any assumptions made.

2. (a) What is the largest net estate that a *husband and wife* can transfer, estate tax-free, with *simple wills* to their children? (b) Does it make any difference how much is owned by each spouse? Explain.

3. (a) What is the largest net estate that a *husband and wife* can transfer to their children, estate tax-free, with *an AEA* bypass plan? (b) Does it make any difference how much is owned by each spouse? Explain.

4. One spouse has considerable wealth and the other very modest wealth.
   a. Why is an AEA bypass plan a "hit or miss" arrangement?
   b. What is the minimum amount of property that each spouse must own to assure a bypass plan will work?
   c. What change could the couple make that would remove the "hit and miss" aspect of the plan?
   d. Regarding the change in part c, how much should be involved?
   e. What factors help determine whether a bypass should entail an outright transfer or a transfer into trust? Is estate tax savings a factor? Why or why not?

5. For the 100% marital deduction describe (a) the major advantages and (b) the major disadvantages.

6. What was the original impetus for allowing a 50% marital deduction in arriving at a decedent's taxable estate? Describe how it worked in the years between 1948-1981 for community property states versus common law states.

7. Assuming a wealthy couple has a simple 100% marital deduction plan, explain how each of the following defer or reduce the estate tax for S2: (a) remarriage; (b) consumption; or (c) gifts. (d) Explain the drawbacks to each of these estate planning devices.

8. Draw a time line showing the changes in the marital deduction. Be sure to include the start of the QTIP marital deduction and the elimination of the marital deduction for non-citizens who do not use trusts.

9. Briefly state the reason for the terminable interest rule. Then explain why Congress allows each of the following exceptions to the rule:
a. The six months survivorship clause.
b. The transfer to a general power of appointment trust.
c. The transfer to a QTIP trust, with a QTIP election.
d. The pension to the surviving spouse automatic QTIP election.
e. The life estate for S2, with remainder to a charity.

10. For purposes of the marital deduction, a terminable interest is defined as a property interest with what three characteristics?

11. Explain why each of the following bequests to a surviving spouse would or would not qualify for a marital deduction:
a. A bequest of a sum, not to exceed $100,000, that she could use to purchase a residence, provided she relinquish her dower (life estate) rights to decedent's home. She did relinquish the right within two months of S1's death, and the executor immediately paid $100,000 towards her purchase of a $160,000 home.
b. Decedent's will gave S2 the right to elect either a life estate in S1's home or to take $100,000 outright. She chose the $100,000.
c. Decedent's living trust left his entire estate in trust for S2. She had a power to appoint the trust to anyone, even to her estate at her death. The remainder went to their children if she did not exercise the power to

appoint. The trustee could accumulate income if such was not needed for S2's reasonable support and maintenance. The trust had a corpus valued at $950,000. Decedent's pourover will left his property, in trust, to the trustee of his living trust. They also held $300,000 in a joint bank account; the source of this money was money inherited from the decedent's parents. Consider both the trust, specifically § 2056(b)(5), and the bank account, § 2040. With the latter, what effect does the pourover will have?

d. When he died in 2003, Decedent left his entire $1,500,000 estate to his only son, with a provision that if his son died it would go to his son's issue by right of representation. Because of a pre-nuptial agreement, S2 could not claim a dower interest. The son, who had no issue, disclaimed so much of the estate as exceeded the AEA, by writing a letter to S1's executor stating, "My father should not have disinherited my mother. I hereby refuse to accept any of my father's estate that is in excess of the AEA and I assign that excess to my mother." The probate court accepted this as a valid assignment of the son's interest in the probate property that exceeded $1,000,000 in value and, at the conclusion of the probate, ordered the excess ($500,000) distributed to S2. Review IRC § 2518 to determine whether this qualifies as a tax effective disclaimer and therefore qualifies for the marital deduction. Would your answer change if the son had issue at the time of his father's death and when he wrote the letter to the executor?

12. Explain why each of the following would or would not qualify for the QTIP election.

a. An estate plan drafted in 1976, created at S1's death in 1999 a trust holding S1's entire estate worth a net of $2,500,000. The trust required that all income be distributed at least annually to S2. After S2's death the property was to be distributed to the couple's issue by right of representation. The independent trustee was given the power to distribute corpus to S2, if the trustee thought the income was insufficient for her happiness.

b. The same facts as in (a) except the trustee could also distribute funds to pay medical bills or educational expenses of the couple's children.

c. The couple's estate plan was an ABC Trust plan. Decedent's estate had a net worth of $4,000,000 consisting mainly of undeveloped land. Terms of the trust, that also applied to Trust C, said that the trustee would not be liable for failing to diversify investments, or for continuing to hold property that was in trust at the time of the settlor's death, or for failing to make such property productive. In giving an answer, you should consider both how this "absolution from liability" clause might be interpreted and state marital deduction-savings statutes that might help. A weaseling answer would be good.

d. The couple had an ABC Trust plan. S1's estate was worth $2,000,000 and S2's estate was worth about the same. Although Trust C had a provision giving S2 income for life, it also said that, in the event S2 became mentally incompetent, the trustee could directly pay S2's bills for living expenses and accumulate any funds not needed. The executor of S1's estate QTIPed all of Trust C. S2 died 11 months after S1's death. S1's executor has filed an amended 706, that states the QTIP was claimed in error because Trust C could not qualify for the QTIP election. The executor attached a check for the estate tax. Was the executor right? What benefits are sought by the executor?

13. In multi-trust estate plans, why is Trust A often called the survivor's trust?

14. In multi-trust plans, when and why is Trust B likely to be called the credit shelter trust? Under what circumstances are taxes likely to be paid from it? Why is it unlikely that taxes will be paid from it at S2's death, even if it exceeds the AEA for that year?

15. In ABC Trust plans, Trust B funding is likely to be defined as "an amount that uses up the available unified credit" rather than in specific dollar terms. Use the changes made by EGTRRA and the possibility of taxable gifts to explain why it is defined in this manner.

16. Fred and Ginger managed to accumulate a considerable fortune by running a small dancing studio in Hollywood. Upon Fred's death, he left all of his wealth, worth $5,000,000, in a trust. Ginger was given a life estate in the trust with the remainder to their issue. Ginger may withdraw funds as necessary

to pay for the children's educational needs as well as her own health and well-being. Will this trust qualify for the marital deduction? What is the issue? If it does not qualify for the marital deduction or if no QTIP election is made, will Ginger's withdrawal rights (even if unexercised) cause the trust to be included in her estate? Explain.

17. In an ABC plan, what determines whether it is Trust C or Trust B that is likely to be named the Residuary Trust?

18. (a) What is the purpose of the QTIP election? Identify three positive estate planning benefits accomplished by its use. (b) In what sense is the QTIP election a "trade-off"? What must S1's executor consider? What factors favor one choice over the other?

19. H and W owned property worth $5 million, with H owning $4.3 million of it and W owning the rest (i.e., $700,000). Assuming there is no estate growth between the two deaths, and that no prior transfer credit is available, use the ETAX program to complete the following table showing the amount and timing of estate tax payments for each of the alternatives. Then determine the amount that passes to their children. We will work this twice, first H dies in 2002 and W in 2005. Then reverse the timing. All taxes paid at the first death are paid out of Trust B (or charged to the non-QTIPed portion of Trust C). (a) a 100% marital deduction; (b) an AB Trust; (c) an ABC Trust, where the executor postpones all tax by making a 100% QTIP election for Trust C; and (d) an ABC Trust where the executor equalized the estates by use of a partial QTIP election. Show the value of each trust for the two multi-trust plans:

H dies first - AB Trust plan: Trust A _____ Trust B _____
ABC Trust plan: Trust A _____ Trust B _____ Trust C _____

W dies first - AB Trust plan: Trust A _____ Trust B _____
ABC Trust plan: Trust A _____ Trust B _____ Trust C _____

$3 M, less ET = net	H dies first		W dies first	
	H's ET	W's ET	W's ET	H's ET
100%MD	———— ———— net to children = ————		———— ———— net to children = ————	
AB Trust	———— ———— net to children = ————		———— ———— net to children = ————	
ABC 100%	———— ———— net to children = ————		———— ———— net to children = ————	
ABC equal	———— ———— net to children = ————		———— ———— net to children = ————	

20. (a) Re-work Question 19, assuming that between the first and second deaths all property doubles in value (for the ABC equal part charge all tax at S1's death to Trust B). (b) What conclusions can be drawn?

$6 M, less ET = net	H dies first		W dies first	
	H's ET	W's ET	W's ET	H's ET
100%MD	———— ———— net to children = ————		———— ———— net to children = ————	
AB Trust	———— ———— net to children = ————		———— ———— net to children = ————	
ABC 100%	———— ———— net to children = ————		———— ———— net to children = ————	
ABC equal	———— ———— net to children = ————		———— ———— net to children = ————	

21. S1 and S2 lived in a common law state. S1 owned property having a net value of $4,800,000 and S2 owned property having a net value of $1,400,000. Assume debts and expenses are zero. S1 died in 2002 and S2 died in 2005. First determine S1's estate before the marital deduction, and the values for trusts A and B for the AB Trust, and trusts A, B, and C for the ABC plan. Those numbers will not change regardless of what S1's executor does insofar as the QTIP election. For the second part of each problem you will need to know the value of the trusts when S2 died: For the AB Trust plan, when S2 died Trust A was worth $6,840,000 and Trust B was worth $1,300,000. For the ABC Trust plan, when S2 died Trust A was worth $1,500,000, Trust B was worth $1,300,000, and Trust C was worth $5,140,000.

(a) The couple had an AB Trust estate plan. Determine: (i) S1's gross estate and taxable estate; (ii) the values of Trust A and Trust B; and (iii) S2's taxable estate.

(b) The couple had an ABC Trust estate plan. S1's executor elected to postpone all taxes until S2 died, but fully use S1's unified credit. Determine: (i) S1's gross estate; (ii) the values of Trust A, Trust B, and Trust C; (iii) the QTIP fraction; (iv) how the fraction is applied to arrive at the taxable estate; and (v) S2's taxable estate.

(c) The couple had an ABC Trust estate plan. S1's executor elected to pay all taxes at S1's death, so no QTIP election was made. Determine: (i) the QTIP fraction and (ii) show how it is applied to arrive at the desired taxable estate; and (iii) S2's taxable estate.

(d) The couple had an ABC Trust estate plan. S1's executor elected to make a QTIP election that would equalize the two estates, at least as of S1's death. Determine: (i) the QTIP fraction and (ii) show how it is applied to arrive at the desired taxable estate; and (iii) S2's taxable estate.

(e) The couple had an ABC Trust estate plan. S1's executor elected to make a QTIP election such that S1's taxable estate would equal $3,678,000. Determine: (i) the QTIP fraction and (ii) show how it is applied to arrive at the desired taxable estate; and (iii) S2's taxable estate.

22. S1 and S2 lived in a community property state. S1 owned property having a net value of $3,200,000, S2 owned property having a net value of $860,000, and they owned community property worth $1,800,000. Assume debts and expenses are zero. S1 died in 2002 and S2 died in 2005. Start by determining S1's estate before the marital deduction and the values for trusts A and B for the AB Trust, and trusts A, B, and C for the ABC plan. Those numbers will not change regardless of what S1's executor does insofar as the QTIP election. For the second part of each problem you need to know the value of the trusts when S2 died: For the AB Trust plan: Trust A was worth $5,420,000 and Trust B was worth $1,280,000. For the ABC Trust plan: Trust A was worth $2,000,000, Trust B was worth $1,280,000, and Trust C was worth $3,420,000.

(a) The couple had an AB Trust estate plan. Determine: (i) S1's gross estate and taxable estate; (ii) the values of Trust A and Trust B; and (iii) S2's taxable estate.

(b) The couple had an ABC Trust estate plan. S1's executor elected to postpone all taxes until S2 died but to fully use S1's unified credit. Determine: (i) S1's gross estate; (ii) the values of Trust A, Trust B, and Trust C; (iii) the QTIP fraction; and (iv) how the fraction is applied to arrive at the taxable estate; and (v) S2's taxable estate.

(c) The couple had an ABC Trust estate plan. S1's executor elected to pay all taxes at S1's death so no QTIP election was made. Determine: (i) the QTIP fraction; and (ii) show how it is applied to arrive at the desired taxable estate; and (iii) S2's taxable estate.

(d) The couple had an ABC Trust estate plan. S1's executor elected to make a QTIP election that would equalize the two estates, at least as of S1's death. Determine: (i) the QTIP fraction; and (ii) show how it is applied to arrive at the desired taxable estate; and (iii) S2's taxable estate.

(e) The couple had an ABC Trust estate plan. S1's executor elected to make a QTIP election such that S1's taxable estate would equal $1,900,000. Determine: (i) the QTIP fraction; and (ii) show how the fraction is applied to arrive at the desired taxable estate; (iii) S2's taxable estate.

ANSWERS TO THE QUESTIONS AND PROBLEMS *(odd numbered only)*

1. Estate size: (a) a spouse - no limit if S2 is a U.S citizen, otherwise, only the AEA, e.g., $850,000 if S1 died in 2004. The decedent still has the use of a unified credit even if S2 is not a citizen; (b) Others? Explain. The AEA for the year of death, e.g., $1,000,000 for deaths in 2006 or later. This is reduced by any AEA used up during life due to post-76 taxable gifts. There is no limit if the giving is to a charity.

3. (a) The AEA times two, since both unified credits will be used, e.g., $2,000,000 if both deaths occur after 2005. (b) Yes, each must have an estate at least equal to the AEA to have both fully use their respective unified credits.

5. (a) See the chapter discussion for details. (b) Loss of utilization of S1's unified credit, and the AEA that goes into S2's estate is taxed at the highest marginal rates insofar as her estate goes.

7. (a) Remarriage: another marital deduction, including possibly using a lifetime QTIP gift, if the new spouse is old and poor. (b) Consumption: spend it and it is not there for the taxman. (c) Gifts: using annual exclusion and/or unified credit of the survivor gets some portion of the estate transferred tax-free (annual exclusion amounts) and any future appreciation avoids tax. (d) Explain the drawbacks to each of these estate planning devices. It's obvious, but still worth thinking about. Remarriage: S2 might disinherit the children of the first marriage, or at least make them wait until the new spouse dies before they come into their inheritance. Consumption: Unless it is spent on the kids, they hate to see too much of that wealth disappear. Generally, no one likes to see his or her wealth decrease. Gifts: parallel comments as to consumption.

9. No marital deduction is allowed unless S2's interest is vested. Congress was concerned that a marital deduction might be allowed even though the transfer did not benefit the surviving spouse and that the property might then pass to someone else without being taxed. (a) The six months survivorship clause. If S2 makes it, the property is in S2's estate. If S2 does not make it, then no

MD. (b) The transfer to a general power of appointment trust. The GPA causes the trust to be included in S2's estate. (c) The transfer to a QTIP trust, with a QTIP election. If no election is made, no MD. If it is made, then the QTIP portion is taxed at S2's death. (d) The pension to the surviving spouse automatic QTIP election. The surviving spouse collects the pension for his or her life, and the PV of the remaining payments are included in S2's estate when S2 dies. (e) The life estate for S2, with remainder to a charity exception. The only beneficiaries are S2 and the charity.

11. Explain why certain bequests do or do not qualify for a marital deduction:

(a) No marital deduction for two reasons: (1) whether she would get the money was uncertain; and (2) the amount was uncertain. *Est. of Edmonds,* 72 TC 970. Notice that had she claimed her dower rights, those would have qualified for a QTIP election since they were a vested life estate in QTIP property.

(b) The $100,000 does qualify. S2 has alternate bequests, vested at S1's death, wherein she makes the choice. This should qualify even if the other alternative was one that did not qualify, so long as the one she chose did qualify. *Est. of Tompkins,* 68 TC 912

(c) The property in trust will not qualify since § 2056(b)(5) requires income for life for S2 and the trustee's power to accumulate spoils this. The title to the joint bank account controls regardless of the pourover will, therefore, $150,000 is included in S1's estate and is removed from his taxable estate by a marital deduction of $150,000.

(d) The property "assigned" is transferred to S2 just as if it had been left to her or had passed to her by intestate succession, therefore, it qualifies for the marital deduction. Notice that the last part of § 2518 allows even an "assignment" to qualify so long as the assignee is the person who would have received the property as a result of the disclaimer without the assignment language. That last statement tells us that had the son had issue, his issue would have received the property as a result of a disclaimer absent the assignment language, therefore, had he had issue, this would have been treated as a gift from the son, and would not have qualified for the marital deduction. Indeed, the son would have to file a gift tax return.

13. It generally is funded with S2's property, and even if some of the corpus has as its source property from S1, S2 has a GPA over the trust.

15. Because, even with plans that have Trust B as an AEA shelter trust, it might be more or less than the AEA that existed when the estate plan was drafted. The TRA '97 and EGTRRA have greatly increased the AEA. By using language that funds the trust based on available unified credit, the documents do not have to be changed whenever Congress increases the unified credit. If the settlor has made taxable gifts post-76, some of the unified credit will have been used up, e.g., decedent made taxable gifts totaling $700,000 and died in 2005, Trust B would be valued at $800,000 ($1,500,000 - $700,000). Likewise, if some of S1's estate is left to someone other than to S2 or to a charity, that bequest will use up unified credit, thus reducing Trust B.

17. Trust C is called the Residuary Trust if Trust B is defined in pecuniary terms so as to match the applicable exclusion amount, because the residue of S1's estate after funding Trust B flows into Trust C. If the amount going to Trust C is defined as the minimum marital deduction amount necessary to avoid death taxes, then Trust B will be the residuary trust.

19. Taxes, with various plans, varying the who (H or W) dies first.
    1. 100% MD: H dies 2002, tax $0, W dies 2005, tax $1,635,000, net to children $3,365,000; W dies first, same results.
    2. AB: H dies 2002, tax $0, W dies 2005, tax $1,165,000, net to children $3,835,000; W dies 2002, tax $0, H dies 2005, tax $1,306,000, net to children $3,694,000.
    3. ABC (100%): H dies 2002, tax $0, W dies 2005, tax $1,165,000, net to children $3,835,000; W dies 2002, tax $0, H dies 2005, tax $1,306,000, net to children $3,694,000.
    4. ABC (equalized): H dies 2002, tax $680,000, W dies 2005, tax $460,000, net to children $3,860,000; W dies 2002, tax $0, H dies 2005, tax $1,306,000, net to children$3,694,000.

21. S1's estate $4,800,000 = S1's separate property, no community property.

(a) AB Trust estate plan: (i) S1's gross estate [$4,800,000] and taxable estate [$1,000,000]; (ii) Trust A [$5,200,000] and Trust B [$1,000,000]; (iii) S2's taxable estate:[$6,840,000; just Trust A].

(b) ABC Trust estate plan. (postpone taxes): (i) S1's gross estate [$4,800,000]; (ii) Trust A [$1,400,000], Trust B [$1,000,000], Trust C [$3,800,000]; (iii) QTIP fraction [$3,800,000/$3,800,000 = 1]; (iv) taxable estate: $4,800,000 - ($3,800,000/$3,800,000) * $3,800,000 = $1,000,000; and (v) S2's taxable estate: $1,500,000 + (1) * $5,140,000 = $6,640,000 [Tr A + QTIP fraction * Tr C].

(c) ABC Trust estate plan (pay all taxes): (i) QTIP fraction [0/$3,800,000 = 0]; and (ii) taxable estate: $4,800,000 - (0) * $3,800,000 = $4,800,000; (iii) S2's taxable estate: $1,500,000 + (0) * $3,800,000 = $1,500,000.

(d) (i) QTIP fraction [$1,700,000/$3,800,000] and (ii) taxable estate: $4,800,000 - ($1,700,000/$3,800,000) * $3,800,000 = $3,100,000; (iii) S2's taxable estate: $1,500,000 + ($1,700,000/$3,800,000) * ($5,140,000) = $3,799,474.

(e) (i) [(Step 2) $4,800,000 - $3,678,000 = $1,122,000. Step 3 is the value of Trust C, therefore Step 4: QTIP fraction $1,122,000/$3,800,000] and (ii) taxable estate (Step 5): $4,800,000 - ($1,122,000/$3,800,000) * $3,800,000 = $3,678,000; (iii) S2's taxable estate (Step 6): $1,500,000 + ($1,122,000/ $3,800,000) * ($5,140,000) = $3,017,653.

ENDNOTES

1. IRC § 2010.

2. IRC §§ 2053 and 2054.

3. IRC § 812(e)(1)(B) of the 1939 Code.

4. IRC§ 2056(b)(1).

5. IRC § 2056(b)(3).

6. IRC § 2056(b)(5).

7. IRC § 2056(b)(7).

8. IRC § 2056(b)(7)(B).

9. IRC § 2044.

10. *Economic Growth and Tax Relief Reconciliation Act of 2001*, §901. Sunset of Provisions of Act.

11. IRC § 2013 and Reg. § 20.2013 - 4, Example (2).

12. IRC § 2056(b)(5).

13. IRC § 2056(b)(5).

14. Reg. § 20.2056(b)-5(f)(5)

15. IRC § 664.

16. IRC § 2036(b)(7).

17. IRC § 2044.

18. IRC § 2044.

19. $\dfrac{Trust\ C}{Trust\ C} = 1$

20. $\dfrac{0}{Trust\ C} = 0$

CHAPTER 12

Advanced Bypass and Marital Deduction Planning

OVERVIEW

This chapter continues the discussion of marital deduction and bypass planning, starting with variations on the basic trust plans described in the last chapter, followed by a review of a couple older plans seen now only in estate planning museums. The calculation of the prior transfer tax credit is explained, as is its rather surprising application to bypass trusts. The chapter concludes with an overview of the generation-skipping transfer tax and its impact on marital deduction and bypass planning.

VARIATIONS ON A THEME

There are variations on the AB Trust and the ABC Trust plans that may better suit certain families, yet use both unified credits and, like the ABC plan, keep the option at the first death of paying estate taxes or deferring them to the second death. Recent variations, developed in response to the Economic Growth and Tax Relief Reconciliation Act of 2001 (EGTRRA), take into account the increasing applicable exclusion amount (AEA) that shelters ever larger estates and the eventual elimination of the estate tax.

THE AsuperB TRUST PLAN

The AsuperB Trust plan has Trust A defined as all S2's property and Trust B defined as all S1's property. It is simpler than the ABC plan as there is one less trust, and given the absence of any reference to a separate applicable exclusion amount trust (AEA trust), it may be more readily understood by clients. The AB Trust plan takes an automatic marital deduction for the property in excess of the AEA because that excess is transferred from S1's estate into Trust A; however, the AsuperB plan allows the executor of S1's estate to decide (via QTIP) whether to pay taxes at the first death or to postpone them until the second death.

Trust B must have all the QTIP attributes that allow a QTIP election if it is desired, i.e., mainly income for life for S2 and no power to appoint to anyone other than S2 during S2's lifetime. Of course utilization of S1's unified credit is important so, even if one wished to pay no taxes, the executor would use that QTIP fraction for Trust B that would reduce S1's taxable estate to the available AEA. Once again, the six-step process is used, starting with determining the optimal taxable estate at S1's death.

EXAMPLE 12-1. When S1 died in the year 2002, the couple's AsuperB Trust plan gave S2 a life estate in Trust B, plus a power to withdraw corpus that was limited to an ascertainable standard. At S2's death, Trust B property is distributed to S1's children by a prior marriage. Trust A is revocable by S2, and her children by a prior marriage are the remaindermen. Their combined net worth was $3,877,250; of which S1's property, worth $2,843,760, was allocated to Trust superB; and S2's property, worth $1,033,490, was allocated to Trust A. To postpone all taxes until S2's death, the executor of S1's estate wants to QTIP Trust B to bring S1's taxable estate to $1,000,000.

Step 1. The desired taxable estate for S1 = $1,000,000.

Step 2. Determine the QTIP MD: Total estate – Desired taxable estate = QTIP MD.

$$\$2,843,760 - \$1,000,000 = \$1,843,760$$

Step 3. For the AsuperB plan there is no separate AEA trust, therefore Trust B is the QTIP property, i.e., S1's estate = Trust B (the superB) = the QTIP property = $2,843,760.

Step 4. Create a fraction with the QTIP MD (Step 2) over the QTIP property (Trust superB) to arrive at the QTIP fraction.

$$\frac{QTIP\ MD}{Trust\ B} = QTIP\ Fraction$$

$$\frac{\$1,843,760}{\$2,843,760} = QTIP\ Fraction$$

Step 5. S1's taxable estate is S1's total estate less the product of the QTIP property and the QTIP fraction.

$$S1's\ taxable\ estate = total\ estate - (\frac{QTIP\ MD}{Trust\ B} * Trust\ B)$$

Therefore, S1's TxE = $2,843,760 - $1,843,760 = $1,000,000.

Step 6. Assume that S2 dies in 2007, and that Trust A is then worth $1,137,642 and Trust B is then worth $3,117,970. At S2's death, the total estate is equal to all of Trust A plus the QTIP fraction multiplied by the amount then in Trust B.

$$S2's\ taxable\ estate = Trust\ A + (\frac{QTIP\ MD}{Trust\ B} * Trust\ B)$$

S2's taxable estate is:

$$S2's\ TxE = \$1,137,642 + \frac{\$1,843,760}{\$2,843,760} * \$3,117,970$$
$$= \$3,159,187$$

Of course, S1's executor can make a partial QTIP that equalizes the estates if that produces a better result than either making a partial QTIP to defer all taxes or making no QTIP election (resulting in a tax on all of Trust B). If S1's executor was very certain that S2 was going to die shortly after S1 (or if S2 had already died when S1's executor was preparing the estate tax return) the QTIP might be made to equalize the two estates.

EXAMPLE 12-2: Using the same values from the previous example, equal estates at S1's death would be:

Step 1.

$$\frac{S1's\ E + S2's\ E}{2} = \frac{\$2,843,760 + \$1,033,490}{2} = \$1,938,625$$

Step 2. Determine the QTIP MD: Total estate – Desired taxable estate = QTIP MD amount = $2,843,760 - $1,938,625 = $905,135

Step 3. Trust B is the QTIP property, i.e., S1's estate = Trust B (the superB) = the QTIP property = $2,843,760.

Step 4. Create a fraction with the QTIP MD (Step 2) over the QTIP property (Trust superB) to arrive at the QTIP fraction.

$$\frac{\$905,135}{\$2,843,760} = QTIP\ Fraction$$

Step 5. S1's taxable estate is S1's total estate less the product of Trust B and the QTIP fraction.

$$S1\text{'s taxable estate} = \$2,843,760 - (\frac{\$905,135}{\$2,843,760} * \$2,843,760)$$

$$=\$2,843,760 - \$905,135$$

$$= \$1,938,625$$

Step 6. S2's estate includes all Trust A, plus the QTIP fraction times Trust B (valued at S2's death):

$$S2\text{'s } TxE. = \$1,137,642 + \frac{\$905,135}{\$2,843,760} * \$3,117,970 = \$2,130,055$$

There are several reasons a couple might prefer the AsuperB plan over the AB plan. S1 may not want to have property in excess of the AEA pass into S2's control, as must happen with the AB plan, yet their total estate might be just approaching, or be just slightly greater than, the AEA. For a couple in that situation, an ABC plan, with the complicating factor of the third trust, might be over planning. For instance, if S1 died with an ABC estate plan in 2003, leaving a net estate worth $1,075,000, Trust B would be funded with assets worth $1,000,000 and Trust C with assets worth a mere $75,000; both trusts would have to file state and federal income tax returns each year, and the trustees would have to maintain separate accounts for each trust. With the AsuperB plan, Trust B would be funded with assets worth $1,075,000 and there would be no Trust C. If the executor chose to postpone estate taxes, the QTIP fraction would be $75,000/$1,075,000. For an elderly couple whose combined estate is over one AEA but less than two AEAs, given that there is a high probability that S1's estate will be under the ever increasing AEA, the simpler but equally effective AsuperB plan might be preferred to the ABC plan. If, at S1's death, the superB Trust is slightly, or even greatly, above the AEA, a partial QTIP can be used to defer taxes.

Even for large estates there is at least one advantage in the AsuperB as compared to the ABC Trust, but it comes with a trade-off. The funding provisions of most ABC plans define either the B Trust or the C Trust as a pecuniary bequest, e.g., "After the death of the first Settlor, the trustee shall allocate to Trust B property equal in value to that amount which will be needed to increase the taxable estate to the largest amount that will not result in a federal estate tax being imposed on the deceased Settlor's estate after allowing for available unified credit." The "equal in amount" language translates into dollar terms, e.g. $1,500,000 if the first death occurs in 2004, therefore it is a pecuniary bequest. Where, as usually happens, it takes months, and occasionally years, for the trustee to allocate the assets in the family trust (or for the probate estate to obtain an order for distribution) to the separate trusts, the values are likely to be very different from those at the date of death. Where a pecuniary bequest is funded with assets that have appreciated in value, the difference between the basis (the date-of-death value or alternative date value) and the fair market value on the date of funding is a capital gain to the family trust (or to the probate estate) making the transfer. Since the gain occurs when the family trust (or probate estate) is terminating, the gain is passed on to the pecuniary trust which must then pay taxes on the gain. Of course, the trust would then have a basis in those assets equal to their fair market value at the time of funding. If property used to fund the trust has decreased in value between S1's death and funding, no loss is recognized because the family trust and the pecuniary trust (B or C) are considered related parties. The superB Trust avoids this problem of gain recognition because it is not defined in pecuniary terms but rather in terms of "all S1's property."

Many plans using multiple trusts give all tangible personal property (cars, furniture, etc.) to S2 or to the trustee of S2's Trust A. Since such property is not investment property, it might be best to allow S2 to control those assets without any need to account for them to the remaindermen.

THE AB WITH DISCLAIMER INTO C TRUST PLAN

A wealthy couple with a long and trusting marriage, with no children by prior marriages, might prefer that the first to die transfer his or her entire estate to the survivor; trusting the survivor to eventually take care of the children and the grandchildren. Nevertheless, they would most likely want to at least use the shelter of a bypass trust to utilize S1's AEA, thus the AB Trust plan would seem ideal, but it has drawbacks. Because the marital deduction is automatic for property transferred from S1's estate into Trust A, the AB plan does not allow sophisticated postmortem planning, such as the equalization of estates or some other apportionment between the two taxable estates, whereas, the AB with disclaimer into C Trust plan (ABdC) does allow the post mortem manipulation of relative size of the two taxable estates. This plan begins by defining Trust B as the AEA trust, with S1's estate in excess of the AEA left to the trustee of Trust A (who also holds S2's property). So far this sounds just like the modern AB Trust plan, however this one adds a provision that any of S1's property in excess of the AEA that is disclaimed by S2 will be transferred to Trust C, a QTIP trust.

A disclaimer is tax effective (or "qualified") if it is done so that the disclaimant (S2) is not treated as having made a taxable gift. In general, to be tax effective, the person making the disclaimer must act within nine months of the interest's creation, he or she cannot "direct" to whom the property goes, nor can he or she receive any benefit from the property disclaimed. IRC § 2518(b)(4)(A) creates an exception to the "no-benefit" rule and allows an interest disclaimed that passes "to the spouse of the decedent" to qualify as a tax effective disclaimer. Thus, the surviving spouse (S2) can receive income from the disclaimer trust (Trust C), can be given a 5 & 5 power, or can be the holder of a power to withdraw that is limited by an ascertainable standard. None of these "benefits" cause a disclaimer by a surviving spouse to be treated as a taxable gift. Furthermore, none of the benefits will cause the disclaimer trust to be included in S2's estate. However, a 5 & 5 power will cause the inclusion in S2's estate of that small portion of the trust that could have been withdrawn just before her death had she exercised the power.

Since the disclaimant cannot direct where the disclaimed property goes, this Trust C, unlike the one in the ABC plan, must not give S2 even a limited power to appoint the property. Remember, for the typical ABC Trust, flexibility is enhanced by giving S2 a limited power to appoint Trust C corpus at her death.

The disclaimer is most likely to be used where, due to S2's poor health or extreme old age, S2 is not likely to live for very long after S1's death. Since the decision to disclaim is not made until after S1's death, the assessment of S2's health is not to be made until that time. However, § 2518 requires that the decision of whether to disclaim must be made within nine months immediately following S1's death.

EXAMPLE 12-3. When S1 died in 2003, the couple had an ABdC Trust. It gave S2 a life estate in Trust B, plus a power to withdraw corpus limited to an ascertainable standard, and she was given a limited power to appoint Trust B corpus among their children. In the absence of exercise of the power the remainder would be distributed to their issue by right of representation. Trust A was revocable by S2, and, to the extent she did not appoint it, the remainder would also go to their issue by right of representation. Their combined net worth was $5,831,010; with S1's property worth $4,360,790 and S2's property worth $1,470,220. No disclaimer was made. Trust B received $1,000,000 from S1's estate; and the rest, plus all S2's property, was added to Trust A, giving it a value of $4,831,010. Since the property in excess of the AEA went to Trust A, the estate automatically received a $3,360,790 marital deduction, thereby reducing S1's taxable estate to $1,000,000.

EXAMPLE 12-4. Suppose, instead of just S1 dying in 2003, S1 and S2 were in a fatal car accident which caused S2 to die just a couple of days after S1. The executor of S2's estate disclaimed all S1's estate in excess of the AEA with the result that it went into Trust C instead of into Trust A. The three trusts are valued as follows: Trust A $1,470,220; Trust B $1,000,000; and Trust C $3,360,790. S1's executor could then QTIP 100% of Trust C to postpone all taxes until after S2's death, but doing so would create very unequal estates. This would be foolish, given that the tax on S2's estate would be due just a few days after the tax on S1's estate. Therefore, the executor of S1's estate should QTIP Trust C so as to equalize the two estates. (You should be able to identify the six-step process even though some steps are combined.)

$$\frac{S1's E + S2's E}{2} = \frac{\$4,360,790 + \$1,470,220}{2} = \$2,915,505$$

The QTIP election necessary to reduce S1's estate from $4,360,790 to $2,915,505 is:

$$QTIP \ MD = \frac{\$1,445,285}{\$3,360,790} * \$3,360,790 = \$1,445,285$$

Therefore, taxable estates of S1 and S2 are:

$$S1'sE = \$4,360,790 - \$1,445,285 = 2,915,505 \text{ } and$$
$$S2'sE = \$1,470,220 + \frac{\$1,445,285}{\$3,360,790} * 3,360,790 = \$2,915,505$$

With the ABdC plan the equalization (or some other allocation between the two estates) can be accomplished by S2 (or S2's executor) making a partial disclaimer sufficient to equalize the two estates and S1's executor forgoing the QTIP election. Using this approach, Trust B plus Trust C equals S1's desired taxable estate and Trust C is the amount that must be disclaimed to arrive at the desired estate. Hence, simple algebra gives us:

Disclaimed amount = Trust C
Trust C = desired taxable estate - Trust B

EXAMPLE 12-5. S2's executor in the preceding example could simply disclaim that portion of S1's estate that would result in the two estates being equal in value as of S1's death. The desired estate equals $2,915,505. Since Trust B will equal the AEA for 2003, i.e., $1 million, Trust C must equal $1,915,505, which is the amount that must be disclaimed by S2 (or rather by the executor of S2's estate, since S2 died soon after S1). Trust A is worth $2,915,505 [$1,470,220 + $1,445,285)], Trust B is worth $1,000,000, and Trust C is worth $1,915,505 [$4,360,790 - $1,445,285 - $1,000,000].

Although the above example equalizes the estates, any allocation can be achieved with the one constraint that Trusts B and C cannot exceed S1's estate. If S1's estate is smaller than the desired taxable estate, S2 (or her executor) should disclaim all S1's estate because doing so will result in S1's estate being as close to the desired estate as possible.

EXAMPLE 12-6. When S1 died in January of 2003 his estate was worth $2,405,300. S2 died seven months after S1. The executor of her estate used a disclaimer to keep S1's estate from adding to her estate. S2's estate was worth $3,955,000. Without a disclaimer S2's estate would receive $1,405,300 (i.e., S1>Trust B, and Trust B = AEA of $1 million). With the disclaimer, S1's taxable estate is $2,405,300 and S2's is $3,955,000. Without the disclaimer they are $1,000,000 and $5,405,300, respectively. *** *Query 1. How much is saved by making the disclaimer?*

A tax effective disclaimer must be delivered to S1's executor within nine months after S1's death, therefore, if S2's state of health is uncertain as that deadline approaches, S2 can make a disclaimer, and the decision as to whether Trust C should be QTIPed can be delayed a further six months by obtaining an extension to file the estate tax return, together with an extension to pay the tax. S2's poor health, and the need for additional time to assess the wisdom of making the QTIP election, is sufficient justification for the six-month extension. Six months is the longest allowed extension for filing the estate tax return if the executor is within the country.[1] Although it is possible to make a QTIP election on a late filed return, the penalties for late filing (if one decides to generate a tax at S1's death) might outweigh any benefits derived by splitting the tax between the two estates.

Choosing between the ABC plan and the ABdC plan is like choosing between varieties of apples rather than between apples and oranges. The main difference being that with the ABdC plan S2 decides whether to take control of S1's estate that exceeds the AEA, whereas S2 has no such option with the ABC plan. Although a limited power may be part of the ABC plan for both Trusts B and C, it can only be used with Trust B in the ABdC plan. Also, the ABdC Trust is a much more complicated plan to explain to clients. In those situations where a tax should be generated at the first death, it may be more difficult to carry out with the disclaimer plan if S2 is in poor health, whereas, with the ABC plan, it is S1's executor who makes the QTIP election.

For large estates using the ABC plan, where taxes might be saved by making a partial QTIP election but, because of the time value of money, the executor is leaning toward deferring the taxes until the second death, the executor is always well advised to obtain the six-month extension to allow the longest possible time to evaluate S2's heath before making (or foregoing) the QTIP election. With the ABdC, the disclaimer must be made within nine months of S1's death or it is not tax effective, so it is not possible to get an extra six months to "wait and see." True, with an ABdC plan, S2 can always make a disclaimer that would accomplish the optimal split between the two taxable estates, and the executor of S1's estate could then wait until the six-month extension period is almost up to file the return, making or not making the QTIP election at that time (depending on S2's health), but that is a much more complicated way to create an ABC plan. Besides, as stated earlier, the ABdC plan must have a more restrictive Trust C, i.e., S2 must be denied a limited power of appointment. Furthermore, S2 might be too ill to make a disclaimer, a circumstance that might indicate that generating a tax in S1's estate would be wise. A court is likely to rule that the right to disclaim is personal to S2, so long as she is alive and might not allow a conservator to make a disclaimer on her behalf, whereas the decision to make a QTIP election rests with S1's executor. If S2 is nominated as executor of S1's estate but is too ill to serve, the alternate executor would be in a position to make the appropriate QTIP election with the regular ABC Trust plan.

A durable power of attorney, discussed later in this book, could be written for S2 with enough specificity to allow the holder of the power to make a disclaimer if S2 is too ill to do it herself. Unless there is specific language authorizing the agent to make a disclaimer, it might not withstand a challenge by the IRS that it was revocable by S2, if she were to regain her health. Of course, if S2 dies before the nine months are up, S2's executor can make the disclaimer, assuming he or she can be appointed by a court in time. Given that S2 is dead, the probate court is not likely to object to a disclaimer that is made to save death taxes, especially if the remaindermen of all trusts are the same people.

THE A WITH DISCLAIMER INTO B TRUST PLAN

As the AEA increases, more wealthy couples are finding that one AEA is sufficient to cover their wealth. Furthermore, if they believe that one or both of them will outlive the estate tax, they may be less inclined to worry about sheltering a portion of the estate at the first death. Therefore, rather than having an AB or ABdC trust arrangement they are selecting a plan that at the first death has S1's property transferred to Trust A but gives S2 the option of sending it to a disclaimer Trust B if S2 so chooses. Note that the AdB plan should be used only if both are comfortable with S2 having ultimate control over the estate, hence one would expect selection of this plan by couples with children from their present marriage only, especially if the marriage is a long one. It is less likely to have appeal if there are children by prior marriages, the marriage has been short, or there is quite a disparity in the wealth brought to the marriage.

Trust A has the characteristics of the other A trusts we have discussed, e.g., a life estate for S2 and a general power to appoint the trust corpus. Trust B can have the characteristics of almost any of the B trusts we have discussed, depending on what the couple wants to accomplish. However, just as with the ABdC plan, S2 must not be given even a limited power over the disclaimer trust as such destroys the tax effectiveness of the disclaimer. Generally the couple seeks to maintain the option of using S1's AEA and the lower marginal rates in both estates in the event both die before 2010. Whether Trust B should have QTIP characteristics or be a sprinkling trust depends on the circumstances. In many cases it will not matter. If both deaths occurred because of an accident, one could create taxable estates about equal in value by having S2's executor disclaim property. Obviously if S2's estate is larger than S1's, the executor should disclaim all S1's property. If S2's estate is smaller than S1's, the executor should disclaim just enough to make them equal. If after the disclaimer both trusts are worth less than the AEA, a Trust B that does not qualify for the QTIP election makes no difference since no additional marital deduction is necessary to avoid tax at the first death. The main reason one might want a Trust B that qualifies for the QTIP is that disclaimers must be made within nine months of the first death, whereas a QTIP can be made on an extended return filed six months later.

> EXAMPLE 12-7. When S1 died in 2004, the couple had an AdB estate plan. S1's estate was worth $2.8 million and S2's $1.4 million. Although she felt well, S2 was 90 years old so she decided to disclaim so much of S1's estate as exceeded his AEA. The $1.5 million that went into Trust B used S1's unified credit, hence no tax was paid. Trust A, initially valued at $2.7 million, might escape taxation if S2 survives to 2009.

> EXAMPLE 12-8. When S1 died in 2002, the couple had an AdB estate plan. S1's estate was worth $900,000 and S2's $800,000. Because she was in poor health, S2 decided to disclaim all S1's estate. Trust A, initially valued at $800,000, is less likely to grow above one AEA before S2 dies, especially since the AEA for 2004 is $1,500,000.

Giving a disclaimer Trust B the characteristics of the superB trust previously described, e.g., a life estate for S2, might make it possible to claim a prior transfer tax credit on S2's tax return. Maintaining this option is important if the combined estates are significantly greater than two AEAs and if either spouse is very elderly or in poor health. We will cover the use of the prior transfer credit in conjunction with life estates in a moment.

EXAMPLE 12-9. When S1 died in May of 2002, the couple had an AdB estate plan. The Trust B gave all income to S2 for her lifetime. S1's estate was worth $3.6 million and S2's $1.4 million. S2 was 80 years old and in questionable health so S1's executor encouraged her to disclaim $2.5 million of S1's estate, resulting in both trusts being equal to $2.5 million. The executor obtained a six-month extension to file the return. When S2 died in July of 2003, the executor of S1's estate filed the return without making a QTIP election. The tax on the two taxable estates of almost equal size was much less than would have been paid had everything been taxed in S2's estate or had the executor QTIPed S1's estate down to the AEA.

PLANNING IN THE ERA OF UNCERTAINTY

EGTRRA has created difficulty in planning most glaringly because the sunset provision creates uncertainty as to whether repeal is for real. Even if one assumes that repeal will take place, the lag between the legislation and repeal coupled with the new basis rules creates another dilemma. Planners are used to the trade-off between saving taxes by sheltering some of S1's estate in a bypass trust and forgoing a second stepped-up basis for those assets when S2 dies. With the QTIP trust the trade-off came in the form of avoiding taxes at the first death but getting a stepped-up basis at the second death or paying the taxes at the first death and forgoing the stepped-up basis at the second. Assuming repeal becomes permanent, if S2 dies after 2009, property in any previously created bypass trust (e.g., Trust B) or QTIP trust (e.g., Trust C) will not receive a step-up in basis. Although these trusts no longer serve the purpose for which they were designed (avoiding or postponing estate tax), by not being included in S2's estate they lose the opportunity to have a new basis. This is also true of GST exemption trusts designed to confer benefits to several generations without triggering the generation-skipping (GST) tax. With repeal the shelter is no longer needed, and the benefit of basis step-up is lost. There may be little that can be done with existing bypass and GST exemption trusts as they are likely to be irrevocable. It will be interesting to see whether courts will allow some of those trusts to be terminated after 2009 on the grounds that they have ceased to serve their original purpose.

With trusts that are still amendable planners may wish to put in a provision that gives the remaindermen the authority to appoint the assets of the bypass trust and the QTIP trust to the surviving spouse. In situations where the remaindermen were S2's issue and they felt fairly confident that the estate would eventually come to them, they could exercise the power in favor of S2, thereby having the assets receive a stepped-up basis on her death.

In the past, the credit shelter trust (i.e., Trust B) has been defined such that it shelters an amount equal to S1's available AEA, thus keeping pace with Congress's propensity to increase the amount from time to time. When these plans were drafted it was prudent for the wealthy to shelter the maximum that could be sheltered. In 2010 the AEA becomes in effect infinite and S1's entire estate is likely to be controlled by the credit shelter trust. Indeed, great distortion of the estate plan may result. A very wealthy person with children by a prior marriage may have designed a plan whereby his or her issue receive the maximum amount that does not generate a tax (presently the AEA) and the balance is placed in a QTIP trust to take care of S2 for life. After 2009, that plan would result in the issue receiving the entire estate. Plans need to be revised such that the settlor's goals are reached regardless of whether repeal takes place.

Given the uncertainty and the need to retain maximum flexibility to change estate plans based on what future legislation holds, couples should also consider adding to their durable powers specific clauses that allow their agents to amend the trust. Many states prohibit an agent from changing an estate plan unless the authority to do so is written into the durable power. Perhaps there should be constraints placed on the agent, however many constraints are likely to hinder taking advantage of changes in the law. Any constraint that would keep S2 from having control of property will almost certainly result in it not being eligible for an increase in basis. Perhaps a more flexible solution would be to name as co-agents the principal's spouse and one or more of the principal's children.

NONCITIZEN SURVIVING SPOUSES: THE QDOT TRUST

Generally, all property passing outright to a surviving spouse qualifies for the marital deduction, however, with the Technical and Miscellaneous Revenue Act of 1988 (TAMRA), Congress removed benefit of the marital deduction for property transferred after November 10, 1988, to a non-U.S. citizen spouse.[2] There are several ways that the marital deduction can be salvaged. One, if S2 becomes a U.S. citizen before the estate tax return is filed and provided that she has remained a resident of the U.S. at all times following S1's death, property passing to her will qualify for the marital deduction.[3] Two, S1's property can be placed in a "qualified domestic trust"[4] (QDOT) that gives some assurance that the property will eventually be taxed in the U.S. The intent of the law is to ensure the eventual collection of estate tax on marital deduction property given to a spouse who may have less secure ties with the U.S. than are thought to exist for most citizens.

The requirements for a QDOT to qualify for the marital deduction are set forth in IRC § 2056A. At least one of the trustees of a QDOT must be a U.S. citizen or domestic corporation. The Secretary of the Treasury is given authority to write regulations to assure the collection of the tax on distributions from these trusts. Those regulations require that the trustee keep sufficient assets within the U.S. to assure payment of the tax or that the trustee have a minimum net worth to assure the payment.[5] The third requirement is that S1's executor must elect to have the marital deduction apply to the trust. Note, the election can be made even on a late filed return, so long as it is not more than one year late.[6]

Estate tax is imposed (once S1's unified credit is exhausted) on any corpus distributed prior to the spouse's death, and on the value of the corpus remaining at the spouse's death (or sooner, if the trust ceases to qualify as a QDOT). However, distribution of income, and distribution of principal on account of "hardship," are exempt from the tax.[7] The tax is the amount that would have been imposed, after all credits, had the property subject to the tax been included in S1's taxable estate.

EXAMPLE 12-10. When S1 died in 2002, his estate worth $3 million was left entirely to S2, a resident of the U.S. for 50 years, but still a citizen of Canada. Within a few months after her husband's death, S2's lawyers created a QDOT into which she transferred assets worth $2 million. When she filed the estate tax return she elected to have the QDOT qualify for the marital deduction, hence the taxable estate was $1 million. By using S1's AEA no estate tax was owed.

EXAMPLE 12-11. In 2004, S2 died and the QDOT was worth $2.5 million. S2's estate was worth $500,000 and owed no estate tax. Assuming no taxable distributions, the tax is based on S1's taxable estate, adding the $1 million taxed in 2002 to the QDOT for a combined taxable estate of $3.5 million. The tax on this is $945,000.

Note that the QDOT is taxed in S1's estate in a manner similar to the gift tax calculation in the sense that distributions and the final termination move into higher marginal rates but also take advantage of the increasing unified credit. Compare this to the QTIP election that tosses a portion of S1's estate into S2's. If one had a choice, sometimes a QTIP would reduce the taxes more than a QDOT because the QTIP uses some of S2's unified credit, e.g., in the example above had the trust been a QTIP the taxable estate at S2's death would have been $3 million and the tax $705,000. If both estates are substantial, i.e., each considerably larger than the AEA, the QDOT does a better job than the QTIP of using both spouses' unified credits and lower marginal rates, e.g., in the last example, if S2's estate was worth $4 million (instead of half a million), a QTIP would add the $2.5 million to it, resulting in a taxable estate of $6.5 million, whereas a QDOT would result in two taxable estates, S1's at $3.5 million and S2's at $4 million.

The trust need not have been created by the decedent prior to death; either the executor or the surviving spouse may create the QDOT prior to the due date of S1's estate tax return (including extensions). For a QDOT created after S1's death, the surviving spouse must irrevocably assign property that she would have otherwise received from S1 to the trust before the due date of the return.[8]

The surviving noncitizen spouse's choice of whether to transfer S1's property into a QDOT may be based on the decision to defer or to equalize their estates. If S2 creates and funds a QDOT, S1's estate will get a marital deduction for the property, but the property will be subject to estate tax at S2's death (or earlier, if trust property is transferred to S2 during her lifetime). Alternatively, if S2 accepts the property without transferring it to a QDOT, the property will be subject to S1 estate taxation immediately, but may avoid estate tax later to the extent S2 can convert the property into "non-U.S. situs" assets. Some noncitizen S2s may prefer to pay the tax up front, then take the property and disappear. The AEA still shelters some (or all) of S1's estate, even if the estate is left to a noncitizen spouse. Furthermore, property that would have qualified for a marital deduction but for the fact that S2 was not a citizen will qualify for a prior transfer credit (PTC) if her estate is taxed in the U.S. at her death. This credit is calculated without being diminished by the usual PTC time factor (i.e., the decrease in the PTC by 20% every two years following S1's death does not apply here).[9]

QDOTs post-EGTRRA. The repeal of the estate tax will keep the property going to a noncitizen spouse from being taxed if S1 dies after 2009. Indeed, there will be no tax on the property in the QDOT if S2 dies after 2009. However, distributions of corpus from a QDOT before 2021 will be subject to the QDOT tax on distributions if S2 is still alive. Apparently this 10-year delay in eliminating the estate tax on these distributions is a safeguard in case the repeal of the estate tax is not made permanent.

ESTATE PLANS SELDOM SEEN

Next, we cover several estate plans that you are not likely to see in your practice, but they are of interest because they will come up from time to time at continuing education seminars or in discussions with colleagues. The Estate Trust was never popular because of its limitations; the Traditional AB Trust was very popular until 1982, when the 100% marital deduction and the QTIP election made it obsolete. The QTIP election and the lowering of the top marginal rates made the inflexible Estate Equalization Trust less desirable than ABC Trusts, since the latter can accomplish the same tax savings but gives S1 greater control over who will be the remaindermen and gives S1's executor more options.

Estate Trust

An unusual type of marital trust called the Estate Trust is almost never used. Its unique feature is that during S2's lifetime the terms of the trust allow the trustee discretion as to how much income to distribute to S2, but at S2's death all accumulated income and corpus must be distributed to S2's probate estate. Consequently, trust income can be accumulated and taxed at trust rates, but given the compressed nature of those rates, there is little reason to use this trust in an attempt to save income taxes. The reason this plan qualifies for the marital deduction is that it is not considered a terminable interest since the interest of S2 does not shift to someone else (see the definition of a terminable interest found at IRC § 2056(b)(1)). Given the greater flexibility of the QTIP trust, which allows the marital deduction while letting S1 control the remainder interest, it is difficult to imagine a reason to use one of these trusts.

The Traditional AB Trust

The Traditional AB Trust (TAB) is the name now given to those estate plans drafted between 1948 and 1981 that were designed to use the maximum marital deduction then available. For large estates, the maximum marital deduction was 50% of the adjusted gross estate (AGE). That amount was "given" to S2 by way of a marital deduction trust (Trust A), and that portion of S1's estate that could not escape taxation at S1's death was left to a bypass trust (Trust B), thus avoiding S2's estate. The tax savings for these plans came not at the first death but at the second death. The idea was to transfer into Trust A, in addition to S2's property, so much of S1's estate as exactly equaled the maximum marital deduction available to S1's estate, and to pass the rest of S1's estate (the taxed portion) into Trust B. Smaller estates (those under $500,000) could use the alternate minimum marital deduction of $250,000 for decedents dying between 1977 and 1981, inclusive, but for larger estates, even during that time frame, the 50% AGE was the controlling factor. Because the pre-1982 marital deduction was limited to 50% of AGE, the property going into Trust B would have been taxed even if it passed directly to S2, therefore, placing it in Trust B did not increase the estate tax at S1's death, but doing so did allow it to avoid S2's estate when S2 died.

As with the more modern plans, Trust A generally held all S2's property; in addition it received from S1's estate the maximum marital deduction amount. In common law states this would be equal to 50% of S1's net estate. In community property states, because the marital deduction was not allowed for the community property, the marital deduction was 50% of S1's separate property.

The names given the two trusts are similar to the names now used for the modern AB Trust plan. Trust A might have been called the Survivor's Trust, the Marital Deduction Trust, or General Power of Appointment Trust. S2 had to receive all income for life and hold a general power of appointment over it.[10] The names and characteristics of Trust B were similar to those for the Trust B of the modern AB Trust except instead of being equal to the AEA, the trust was funded with all that property which would not qualify for the marital deduction, hence, 50% of S1's separate property and S1's half of the community property. The trust was likely to be called Trust B or the Bypass Trust. Like the credit shelter trust of the modern AB plan, it could be a sprinkling trust benefitting the children as well as S2, but it was much more common that all income was given to S2. A sprinkling trust with S2 as both the trustee and as one of the potential beneficiaries has all the trust income taxed to S2 anyway. This defeats one of the primary reasons for having a sprinkling provision in a trust, namely the ability to lower overall income taxes within a group of beneficiaries by distributing more income to the lower tax bracket members. It was very common to give S2 invasion rights limited to an ascertainable standard. Also common were B trusts in which S2 had limited powers to appoint among the children, and, less commonly, S2 was given a 5 & 5 power.

EXAMPLE 12-12. Compare two pre-1982 estate plans. The first one is a simple will plan in which S1 leaves everything to S2 and, on S2's death, everything goes to their children. The second one is a TAB in which, after S1's death, S1's taxable estate goes into a bypass trust (Trust B) and the maximum marital deduction amount, plus all S2's property goes into Trust A, a general power of appointment trust. On S2's death, Trusts A and B terminate and go to their children. When S1 died in 1965, S1 owned separate property worth $1,800,000 and S2 owned separate property $200,000; in addition they had community property worth $300,000. S2 died in 1976 and between deaths the assets doubled in value. (Pre-1977 tax rates are used.)

With plan one, all S1's estate (less the estate tax) was transferred to S2. With plan two, Trust A was funded with property worth $1,250,000 [the one-half of S1's separate property that qualifies for the marital deduction, plus S2's separate property and S2's half of the community property] and Trust B with property worth $1,050,000 out of S1's estate [half S1's separate property, plus S1's half of the community property]. All estates claimed the $60,000 estate tax exemption that was available at the time.

| | S1 100%> S2 | | TAB Trust | |
	S1 d1965	S2 d1976	S1 d1965	S2 d1976
GE	$1,950,000	$3,956,000	$1,950,000	$2,500,000
MD	(900,000)	0	(900,000)	0
EstEx	(60,000)	(60,000)	(60,000)	(60,000)
TxE	$990,000	$3,896,000	$990,000	$2,440,000
tax	$322,000	$1,776,800	$322,000	$968,800

The entire estate tax savings of $808,040 [$1,776,800 - $968,800] occurred at the second death; the bypass trust kept Trust B property from being taxed again in S2's estate. The value of Trust B [$1,050,000 - $322,000 = $728,000] doubled; therefore, $1,456,000 avoided the second tax. The tax saved is equal to 55.5% of the latter figure, corresponding roughly to the pre-1977 average marginal rate between $2,500,000 and $4,000,000.

Note that with a TAB the marital deduction for Trust A is in terms of a dollar amount (not as a QTIP fraction) because part of S1's separate property is transferred from S1's estate into Trust A, the trust over which S2 has a general power of appointment; therefore, the marital deduction is automatic, unlike the QTIP trust for which an election must be made in order to claim a marital deduction. Furthermore, at S2's death, all Trust A is included in S2's estate, not just a fraction of it. Some plans written prior to 1981 still exist, and as demonstrated in the above example, Trust B may exceed the AEA at S1's death. Even though it makes little sense today to have S1's separate property split equally between Trusts A and B, neither the executor, the surviving spouse, nor the trustee can rewrite the decedent's estate plan. However, the tax laws allow the executor of S1's estate to obtain a marital deduction on Trust B by making the QTIP election, provided S2 has the requisite income interest in the trust. Fortunately, most of the old TAB plans give S2 a life estate in Trust B. As discussed before, the QTIPed portion is expressed as that fraction of Trust B necessary to bring S1's taxable estate down to the desired taxable estate (e.g., down to the AEA). It is that same fraction that determines the amount of Trust B that is later included in S2's estate, therefore, the election must be expressed as a fraction rather than as a dollar amount. *** *Query 2. What would be the QTIP fraction to postpone all tax for the above example had S1 died in 2001 instead of 1965?*

The Estate Equalization AB Trust

The funding of the two trusts created at S1's death required the executor of S1's estate to have S2's property valued too. Trust B was funded such that it exactly equaled half of the combined values. These plans enjoyed some popularity for very large estates when the maximum marginal rate was 77% for estates over $10 million. With the QTIP trust and the possibility of using a partial QTIP election there is much greater flexibility in allocation between the two estates, and if S2 is healthy at the time S1's estate tax return is prepared it is likely that Trust C will be fully QTIPed, therefore there is no need to have S2's property valued, whereas with the old Estate Equalization

AB Trusts, all assets had to be valued to determine the funding amount for Trust B. With an ABC plan, an AsuperB plan, or an ABdC plan, S2's property needs to be appraised at S1's death only if the executor of S1's estate desires to use the QTIP election to equalize (or optimize) the two taxable estates.

GENERAL COMMENTS ON ESTATE PLANNING USING TRUSTS

From an estate planning standpoint, almost anything that can be described in words, with or without examples, that one can get a trustee to agree to carry out, can be accomplished through the use of trusts, so long as it is legal and not against public policy. Any of the plans discussed here can be accomplished by a testamentary trust just as well as through a living trust with the exception of avoiding probate at the first death. With a testamentary trust the funding process at the first death is the probate court's order for distribution.

State death tax. For the most part, we have ignored the influence of state death taxes. Generally, their effect is relatively small compared to the impact of the federal tax, and in most states are of no consequence due to the federal credit for state death taxes. As explained earlier, a slight majority of the states, plus the District of Columbia, impose only a pickup tax, that is, an amount exactly equal to the federal credit for state death taxes. Consequently, in these states, no additional taxes are paid as a result of the state death tax. The remaining states impose a death tax that may be larger than the pickup amount, but usually is not unless the estate is going to non-family members.

Revocable living trust versus the testamentary trust. The main advantage to the living trust is that it avoids probate of the settlor's assets to the extent they are held in trust at the time of the settlor's death. The testamentary trust is funded through the probate process and does have the advantage that in most states the probate process considerably shortens the period during which creditors can assert their claims.

One family trust or separate trusts for each spouse. A one trust document plan for both spouses, called a *joint spousal grantor trust*, will work as long as the assets of each spouse are carefully identified and distinguished. It does not have the gift tax danger and dispositive restrictions of the joint and mutual will, which generally becomes irrevocable as to all probate assets at the first spouse's death. In contrast, the joint trust usually keeps the surviving spouse in control of the trust that holds her property (e.g., Trust A) and only the trust holding the deceased spouse's property (e.g., Trust B) is irrevocable.

If commingling of assets is a significant concern, each spouse can execute his or her own living trust document. Another reason for two trusts is that a poorly drafted joint spousal grantor trust document could give rise to estate or gift tax consequences for wealthier clients, particularly when the spouses fund the trust with different amounts of individually owned property. For example, the spouse contributing the greater amount may be deemed to have made a gift which may be taxable, if the terms of the trust do not qualify it for the marital deduction. The latter is not likely to occur with a well drafted joint trust because they are usually revocable so long as both spouses are alive, and the portions that are irrevocable after the first death are designed to either use the unified credit or to qualify for the marital deduction.

Debts and expenses. Of course, any estate will have deductible debts and expenses, which will alter the calculations. Expenses in administering a decedent's probate estate typically range between 5 and 10% of the total estate. Ordinarily, estate planners handle debts and expenses in the following manner: Regarding debts, in performing the calculations, planners use net worth as the value of the estate property; regarding expenses, planners either estimate the expenses or simply ignore them because they are not likely to have a significant influence on the choice of estate plans. Given the complexity of multiple trust plans, most planners want to keep the calculations used as examples as simple as possible without misleading the client. A gift of this book is a good idea.

THE PRIOR TRANSFER CREDIT AND BYPASS TRUSTS

Illogical though it might be, the prior transfer credit (PTC) is available for an interest in a life estate (as in Chapter 6, when this PTC topic was introduced, we will sometimes refer to the first to die as D1 and the second to die as D2).[11] What is deemed to have been transferred from D1 to D2 is the value of the life estate measured as of the date of D1's death. Valuation is based on the life table factors published by the Treasury even though, due to the PTC time factor (i.e., there is no credit 10 years after the first death), this credit would seldom be available to anyone who lived the life expectancy implicit in the table.

EXAMPLE 12-13. On April 4, 2001, when D died, her net estate, worth $2,500,000 went into a trust, with income for life to B (age 60), and a vested remainder for R (age 40) followed B's life estate. D's estate paid death taxes of $805,250, of which $138,800 was paid to D's state and the balance, $666,450, was paid to the federal government. B died on August 10, 2003, leaving an estate with a net value of $3,200,000 to three nephews. The trust established by D was distributed to R a few months after B's death. Although the trust's value was then in excess of $4 million, it is not included in B's estate, yet the estate is entitled to a PTC.

PTC Step 1. The value of the property transferred to B before adjustment for taxes is the value of B's life estate. The federal rate for valuing split interest gifts for the month of April, 2001, was 6%, therefore, the life estate factor for a 60-year-old income beneficiary was .64967, and the value of the property deemed to be "transferred" is $1,624,175. Limit one is:

$$LT1 = \frac{\$1,624,175}{\$2,500,000} * \$666,450 = \$432,973$$

Of course, the fraction reduces to the life estate factor since we used the factor in the first place to arrive at the value of the life estate. Therefore, limit one in this case can be calculated by multiplying the factor times the federal tax, as follows:

$$LT1 = .64967 * \$666,450 = \$432,973.$$

PTC Step 2. The tax on B's $3,200,000 taxable estate without a PTC is $1,023,000, of which $100,200 is state death tax and $922,800 is the federal estate tax. To determine the second limit, the federal tax on the reduced estate must be calculated and subtracted from the federal tax on B's taxable estate. The reduced estate is $3,200,000 less the amount deemed transferred and subtracted from the federal tax on B's taxable estate net of its share of the total death taxes:

Federal estate tax on B's $3,200,000 taxable estate	$922,800
Less federal estate tax B's reduced estate of $2,098,972, i.e., $3,200,000 - .64967 * ($2,500,000 - $805,250)	(430,133)
Credit limit two	$492,667

Remember, the amounts shown as federal estate tax, $922,800 for the full estate and $430,133 for the reduced estate, is the federal estate tax, i.e., the tentative tax reduced by the unified credit and the state death tax credit (state DTC) on taxable estates of $3,200,000 and $2,098,972, respectively. To arrive at the reduced taxable estate, B's taxable estate is reduced by the net value of what was deemed transferred to B, i.e., the value of B's life estate in the B and C trusts, after S1's death taxes have been subtracted, i.e., 0.64967 * ($2,500,000 - $805,250). Note that $805,250 is the total tax at D's death, not just the federal tax.

PTC Step 3. Since B died more than two years, but less than four years, after D, the time factor is 80% and the actual PTC is:

$$80\% \; * \; the \; lesser \; of \left\{ \begin{array}{l} limit \; one\text{: } \$432,973 \\ limit \; two\text{: } \$495,667 \end{array} \right. = \$346,378$$

Therefore, B's estate pays taxes as follows:

Death taxes before PTC & state DTC	$922,800
less state death tax credit	(100,200)
less prior transfer credit	(346,378)
Federal estate tax	$576,422

Total taxes = $576,422 + $100,200 = $676,622

The state death tax credit is not changed by the presence of a PTC. In the above hypothetical, the PTC eliminates over one-third of the second tax even though none of the corpus of the trust was actually transferred into B's estate.

If the remainderman dies after the income beneficiary, but still within 10 years of the settlor (D1), there will also be a PTC for the remainderman's estate based on the remainder value at D1's death of the remainderman's interest. If the remainder is vested, and remainderman dies before the income beneficiary, the remainderman-decedent's interest is included in the remainderman's estate. This value is based on the beneficiary's age (B's age), the value of the trust, and the federal split-interest gift rate (i.e., the §7520 rate) at that time. R in the above example would become D2 for the purpose of computing the PTC for his estate. Obviously, the income beneficiary will be older than he or she was when the trust was established, therefore the remainder factor (from Table S) is likely to be higher, however this depends on the § 7520 rate at R's death. Thus, the amount included in R's estate insofar as the trust is concerned would be the remainder factor (based on B's age) times the trust's value as of R's death. These changes are taken into account when calculating the value of the remainder in R's (D2) gross estate, but in calculating the value of what was transferred for determining PTC limit two, one must continue to use the value of the remainder as of D1's death. Remember, any change in value insofar as the property transferred is concerned is irrelevant to the PTC calculation. What is deemed to have transferred is based on the values at D1's death, and that is the value used in calculating R's reduced estate. To the extent the value of a trust (or a vested remainder in a trust) is actually part of D2's estate, any change will change the value of D2's taxable estate.

THE PRIOR TRANSFER CREDIT AND THE QTIP ELECTION

The PTC has its greatest estate planning potential when used in conjunction with the ABC, AsuperB, or ABdC estate plans, because the partial QTIP election gives S1's executor some control in the allocation of the couple's total estate between the two taxable estates. For large estates, if the surviving spouse is diagnosed as terminally ill before S1's estate tax return is filed, it may be better to make either no QTIP election or only a partial QTIP election, so that some taxes are generated in the first estate, which in turn will generate a PTC for the second estate. The optimal QTIP election is one where the QTIP fraction used is one that will best utilize lower marginal tax rates for both estates and the PTC for S2's estate in such a way that the greatest amount possible passes to the children. This is demonstrated in the example set that follows. Keep in mind that the maximum extension to file is six months, therefore, the maximum period after S1's death to assess S2's health is 15 months.

FACTS FOR THE EXAMPLE SET: At the time of S1's death on October 11, 2003, S1 and S2 have community property worth $850,000, S1 owns separate property worth $4,460,000, and S2 owns separate property worth $1,320,000. Their estate plan is a modern ABC Trust plan, with S2 given a life estate in Trusts B and C. S1 dies at age 75 and S2 is 65 years old. The federal rate for valuing split interest gifts for October of 2003 is 8%. The net value going in each trust is: Trust A $1,745,000; Trust B $1,000,000; and Trust C $3,885,000. S2 is in extremely poor health.

> EXAMPLE 12-14. S1's executor very diligently assembles the information and valuations necessary to file the estate tax return by its due date of July 11, 2004. He elects to QTIP all Trust C so as not to pay any tax. Unfortunately, S2 dies

December 27, 2004. The assets in the three trusts increased in value by 10%, as a result, the three trusts are worth: Trust A $1,919,500; Trust B $1,100,000; and Trust C $4,273,500; for a total value of $7,293,000. S2's taxable estate is the combined value of Trusts A and C ($6,193,000), so, although this strategy results in zero taxes at S1's death, S2's executor pays $2,237,640 for her estate. The net amount going to the children is the total of the three trusts, less the tax:

$$\$7,293,000 - \$2,237,640 = \$5,055,360$$

EXAMPLE 12-15. In this alternative version, S1's executor is very cautious. She diligently assembles the information and valuations necessary to file the estate tax return by its due date but she obtains an extension to file and to pay until January 11, 2005; intending to re-assess S2's health as that latter date approaches. S2's death makes re-assessment unnecessary.

As in the prior example, the assets in the three trusts increase in value by 10%. S1's executor does a partial QTIP election, even though it means Trusts B and C have to pay estate taxes about a year earlier than if the taxes were postponed until after S2's death, and some interest has to be paid for the six-month extension period. It helps that the interest amount for both the federal and state death taxes is deductible on S1's return. Since she had obtained an extension to file and to pay, no penalties are assessed.

To work through to the amount paid at each death we follow the six-step QTIP calculations (combining some of the steps in the interest of brevity). At Step 5, we calculate S1's taxes. To simplify, interest is not taken here as a deduction although in a real situation it would be. Step 6 is followed by the three-step PTC calculation for S2's estate to determine S2's taxes. From the value of the three trusts at S2's death, we subtract the amount of taxes for both estates, and also subtract the estimated interest on S1's late paid taxes to come up with the net amount going to the children. Finally, we compare this alternative to the net amount using the 100% QTIP alternative.

Step 1. By trial and error the executor determines that the best result (the largest after-tax transfer to the children) is accomplished when S1's taxable estate equals $3,800,000.

Step 2. The marital deduction necessary to achieve the desired taxable estate:

$$\$4,885,000 - \$3,800,000 = MD = \$1,085,000$$

Step 3. Trust C is the QTIP property, therefore the QTIP fraction is:

$$\$1,085,000/\$3,885,000$$

Steps 4 and 5. S1's taxable estate equals S1's estate less the marital deduction that results from the QTIP election. Therefore, S1's taxable estate is:

$$\$4,885,000 - \$1,085,000 = \$3,800,000$$

This results in federal taxes of $1,187,200 and state death taxes of $129,800 for a total of $1,317,000.

Step 6. S2's estate equals Trust A plus the QTIP fraction times Trust C's value at that time. Therefore, S2's taxable estate is:

$$S2'sE = \$1,919,500 + (\frac{\$1,085,000}{\$3,885,000}) * \$4,273,500 = \$3,113,000$$

Having determined S2's taxable estate, we turn our attention to calculating the PTC and the estate taxes.

PTC Step 1. Limit one: Using a federal rate of 8% and given that S2 was 65 years old when S1 died, the factor for computing her life estate value is .66792.

$$.66792 * \$1,187,200 = \$792,955$$

PTC Step 2. Limit two: The total taxes on an estate of $3,113,000 before taking the PTC is $759,240, of which $48,012 is the state death tax and $711,228 is the federal death tax.

Federal estate tax on $3,113,000	$711,228
Less tax on S2's reduced taxable estate of $729,861,	
i.e.,$3,113,000 - .66792 * ($4,885,000 - $1,317,000)	(_____$0)
Credit limit two	$711,228

Again, a reminder that the amounts used to arrive at limit two are the federal taxes on S2's taxable estate and on S2's reduced taxable estate, each calculated taking both the unified credit and the state death tax credit (state DTC) into account. Because the reduced taxable estate is less than the AEA for 2004 the tax on it is zero and limit two is the tax on the full estate.

PTC Step 3. Since S1 and S2 died within two years of each other the time factor is 100% and the PTC is:

$$100\% * \textit{ the lesser of } \begin{cases} \textit{limit one: } \$792,955 \\ \textit{limit two: } \$711,228 \end{cases} = \$711,228$$

Therefore, S2's estate pays taxes as follows:

Death taxes before PTC & state DTC	$759,240
less state death tax credit	(48,012)
less prior transfer credit	(711,228)
Federal estate tax	$ 0

The total death tax for both estates using the optimal QTIP election is $1,365,012 [$1,317,000 + $48,012] compared to $2,237,640 when the 100% QTIP election is made. The difference in tax is $872,628, of which $711,228 is attributable to the PTC and the balance is due to the utilization of lower marginal rates in the first estate rather than "loading up" the second estate with a 100% QTIP election. S1's estate would have to pay approximately $60,000 in interest (about 4.5% because it is for just six months) on the late paid taxes. Compare the value going to the children using the optimal QTIP election with what was previously calculated. In both cases we assume the value of the three trusts at S2's death are the same since S1's taxes were not paid until after S2 died. Therefore, the value of the trusts less the taxes and the interest would be as follows:

$$\$7,293,000 - \$1,365,012 - \$60,000 = \$5,867,988$$

The optimal QTIP results in $812,628 [$5,867,988 - $5,055,360] more to the children than with the 100% QTIP election.

This potential savings that comes from using the PTC with multiple trust plans is obviously just as important as the utilization of both unified credits. It results from the phantom transfer from S1's estate to S2, (the fact that an estate is allowed a PTC based on the hypothetical value of S2's life estate) even though, due to S2's death, very little is actually transferred. Of course it is limited in usefulness to those times when the two deaths are close enough in time to use the PTC.

The optimal QTIP fraction depends on the following factors:

- the federal rate for valuing split interests such as life estates
- the age of S2
- the combined value of the couple's estates
- whether S1's estate equals (or exceeds) the amount necessary to make the optimal mix

Given the multiple factors (age, § 7520 rate, values, increasing AEA) and the fact that only a portion of S1's estate is deemed to have been transferred, the optimal QTIP fraction tends to be one that taxes more of the combined total in S1's estate. However, for combined estates between $2,000,000 and $6,000,000, if the second death is very likely to occur within two years of the first, the optimal result will generally require a QTIP election that brings S2's estate almost equal to that of S1 or even shifts it slightly toward S1. With very large estates, the optimal QTIP fraction is likely to be one that causes S1's taxable estate to be larger than S2's. For instance, with combined estates over $20,000,000, the optimal allocation between the two estates is likely to require a taxable estate for S1 that is significantly larger than that of S2. For these large estates, as much as 60% to 70% of the combined values should be taxed at S1's death, with only 30% to 40% at S2's death, if the goal is to pass the greatest amount possible to the children or other heirs. The exact ratio can be determined by trial and error - or by using a computer program. Even for very large estates, a QTIP election that equalizes the two estates generally produces results fairly close to those achieved by the optimal QTIP election, and certainly very superior to the 100% QTIP alternative. *** *Query 3. Using the facts from the above example set, what is the QTIP fraction that equalizes the two estates as of S1's death? Remember, the fraction is applied only to Trust C.*

THE GENERATION-SKIPPING TRANSFER TAX

Up to now, we have focused our tax planning discussion on how gifts and trusts are used to reduce transfer taxes for the nuclear family, i.e., S1, S2, and their children. Similar planning works for transfers to more remote family members. For example, a childless couple could develop a bypass plan for nephews and nieces. A bypass trust plan works well for any survivors who belong to the same, or to the next generation, but complexity arises when a bypass trust (or an outright transfer) skips the estates of the transferor's children and goes to grandchildren, great-grandchildren, or even more remote descendants. The Generation-Skipping Transfer Tax (GST tax) is designed to capture additional taxes such that the total transfer tax approximates that which would have been collected had the property been taxed at each generation. It is imposed on direct skips, taxable terminations, and taxable distributions to, or for the benefit of, a skip person. A skip person is a beneficiary who is at least two generations younger than the transferor. For this discussion, think in terms of grandparent, parent, and grandchild, with the grandchild being the skip person vis-a-vis the grandparent. Keep in mind that this GST tax is not appreciably "unified" with gift and estate taxes; it is a separate tax having its own unique rules. To report the transfer and calculate the tax Form 706 is used for transfers at death and Form 709 is used for gifts. These forms are on the Teaching Aids CD ROM in pfd format.

Purpose of the GST Tax

The purpose of the GST tax is to assure that large estates are subjected to a transfer tax as they pass from one generational level to the next. Prior to the mid-1980's, a common method for the very wealthy to pass their estates through many generations with a minimum of transfer tax was to create trusts that would benefit first the children for their lives, then the grandchildren for their lives, and then the great-grandchildren for as long as the rule against perpetuities would allow. Transfer tax (either the estate tax or the gift tax) would be levied only when the trust was initially funded. Because the income beneficiaries had no powers to appoint corpus, nor any other interest in the trust that would cause it to be included in their estates, no new taxes were levied as the interests shifted from one generation to the next. These were the ultimate bypass trusts designed to last a hundred years or more.

The first generation-skipping transfer tax was enacted in 1976. Although planners found it very complicated, they quickly learned that the tax was easy to circumvent. As a result, in 1986, Congress acknowledged its error by repealing it retroactively, and at the same time, enacting a more comprehensive version as described below. Trusts that were irrevocable prior to September 25, 1985, are "grandfathered in," that is, they are not subject to the generation-skipping transfer tax.

EGTRRA not only eliminates the GST tax in 2010 but dramatically changed it pending repeal. The GST exemption, $1 million when the present GST system was enacted in 1986, will increase to the AEA for transfers after 2003. The exemption keeps most GST transfers from being taxed. The delay in tying the exemption to the AEA avoids a temporary decrease in the exemption. Indexing, which started in 1999, increased the exemption to

$1,060,000 in 2001, whereas the AEA for 2002 and 2003 is $1 million. The GST tax rate is equal to the estate tax top marginal rate which EGTRRA decreases over the next several years from a top rate of 55% in 2001 to 50% in 2002, then dropping another point each year until it reaches 45% in 2007. Like the rest of the changes made by EGTRRA, the sunset provision also applies to the repeal of the GST tax, almost guaranteeing that Congress will make additional changes to the GST tax law between now and 2011.

Overview of the GST Tax

The solution devised by Congress is to tax transfers that skip a generation even if they are subject to the regular gift or estate tax. *Generation-skipping Transfer Tax* (GST tax) is the tax levied on what is called a *generation-skipping transfer*, which is a transfer to a *skip person*, defined as a person two or more generations below the transferor. A transfer to a trust whose beneficiaries are all skip persons is also considered a generation-skipping transfer.[12] The basic rule for determining the tax is as follows:

GST tax = the taxable amount * the applicable rate[13]

Think of the taxable amount as the value of the gift or estate that is given to a skip person or to skip persons. Complications set in because the taxable amount depends on whether the transfer is a direct skip, a taxable termination, or a taxable distribution. The *applicable rate* is the maximum federal estate tax rate multiplied by the inclusion ratio. The *inclusion ratio* is determined by the amount of the donor's GST exemption allocated by the donor to a particular transfer. We will start by covering the calculation of the tax for each of the three types of skips. To keep this as simple as possible, the initial examples will assume that the donor does not allocate any of his or her GST exemption to the transfer. Later we will consider the allocation of the exemption and look at examples where it is a factor.

Calculating the GST Tax

The taxable amount depends on whether the transfer is a direct skip, a taxable termination, or a taxable distribution. Keep in mind that the goal is to approximate the transfer tax that would be levied if the property passed through each generational level. Generally, unless the governing instrument (e.g., a will or a trust) by specific reference to the GST tax provides otherwise, the GST tax must be charged to the property transferred.

Direct skips. A direct skip is a transfer to a skip person where that transfer is subject to estate or gift tax.[14] These are likely to be outright gifts or bequests from grandparents to grandchildren. For all direct skips, other than a direct skip from a trust, the liability for paying the GST tax is placed on the transferor.[15] The taxable amount, in the case of a direct skip, is the value of the property received by the transferee.[16] This means that in the case of a bequest, the taxable amount is the bequest net of its share of debts, expenses, etc., and death taxes (both federal and state). Where the direct skip property is included in the transferor's estate that makes alternate valuation or special use valuation election, the value of the property for purpose of the GST tax is the same as used for estate tax.[17] For gifts of a present interest, the annual exclusion also reduces the taxable amount for GST tax purposes.

> EXAMPLE 12 - 16. In 2001, Barry made a gift of Bucky Company common stock, worth $750,000, to his granddaughter Julie. He had applied his GST exemption to taxable gifts to other grandchildren, and the annual exclusion was applied to a gift made earlier in the year to Julie. Because of those earlier gifts, the gift of Bucky Company stock required Barry to pay gift taxes of $294,750 and GST tax of $412,500 [$750,000 * 0.55]. Had Barry waited until 2004 to make the gift, he could apply the $500,000 increase in the GST exemption to the transfer such that only $250,000 would be subject to the tax and the rate would be 48% instead of 55%.

Things get a little more complicated with direct skips from a decedent. The GST tax is paid by the estate (the transferor) and the GST tax should not itself be subjected to the GST tax, therefore multiplying the net estate by 55% will produce a tax that is too high. The result for an estate should be the same as if the transfer was a direct skip gift. Let's look at the last example, after the regular gift tax had been paid, Barry (the donor) parted with assets worth $1,162,500 to make a gift to Julie of $750,000. The $1,162,500 is the gift of $750,000 plus the GST tax of $412,500. Leaving a skip person $750,000 by way of a bequest (instead of a gift) requires a net estate (after estate taxes, but before the GST tax) of $1,162,500. The GST tax of $412,500 divided by $1,162,500 equals 0.3548387, which is the GST tax rate for direct skips from a decedent.

EXAMPLE 12 - 17. During her life, Tisha had used up her one GST exemption on gifts to grandchildren. Her net estate, after payment of the federal estate tax and the state death tax was $1,162,500. She left her entire estate to Frank, her favorite grandson. The estate must pay $412,500 in GST tax [0.3548387 * $1,162,500] and Frank will actually receive just $750,000.

The steps that a decedent's estate must take to calculate the GST tax for a direct skip are found in Schedule R, Part 2, of the U.S. Estate Tax Return, Form 706. Notice that, after subtracting debts, regular death taxes, and the exemption, the net amount left is divided by 2.818182 to determine the GST tax (see line 8 of Schedule R). How does this number relate to the 0.3548387 rate given above? Dividing "1" by 0.3548387 equals 2.818182, therefore the result will be the same whether one divides the net transfer (net after regular tax) by 2.818182 or whether one multiplies it by 0.3548387. As the top estate tax rate changes, the GST rate for direct skips from a decedent will decrease.

year	max. rate	GST rate	706 divisor
01	55%	0.3548387	2.818182
02	50%	0.3333333	3.000000
03	49%	0.3288591	3.040816
04	48%	0.3243243	3.083333
05	47%	0.3197279	3.127660
06	46%	0.3150685	3.173913
07	45%	0.3103448	3.222222
08	45%	0.3103448	3.222222
09	45%	0.3103448	3.222222

Taxable terminations. A taxable termination means that a shift in interest from one generation to the next has occurred as a result of the death of a person, the release of an interest, the passage of time, or for some other reason. The trustee is liable for the GST tax in the case of a taxable termination and in the case of a direct skip from a trust. The taxable amount is the value of the property with respect to which the taxable termination has occurred, reduced by any expenses or indebtedness that would be deductible under IRC § 2053. The § 2032 alternate valuation election is available (assuming it will reduce the GST tax) if the taxable termination is the result of the death of an interested party.[18] Such would be the case if the settlor established a trust, giving his children income for life, then income for the life of grandchildren, and finally distribution to the grandchildren. Once the last of the settlor's children died and the income interest in the trust shifted to grandchildren, there would be a taxable termination. If the value of the trust had decreased in the six months following the death of the last of the settlor's children to die, the trustee could elect the alternate valuation date in order to reduce the GST tax.

Just because a GST tax trust terminates, does not mean that a taxable termination has occurred. Whether it is also a taxable termination depends on whether the termination resulted in a shift from one generation to another. Furthermore, as shown in the examples that follow, a taxable termination may occur without the trust itself terminating. Once the interests of all members of a generational level terminate and a tax is levied, the younger generations are considered to have moved up a generation such that individuals at the new top generation level are no longer skip persons. This "move-up" avoids having the GST tax apply again when transfers are made to members of this generation, since it was already imposed when the property interest shifted to the generation.[19]

> EXAMPLE 12 - 18. When grandpa Xuyen died in 1990 his estate plan created a trust which gave income for life to his son Ha, remainder to Ha's issue by right of representation, except that if any of Ha's children were under age 35, the assets were to remain in trust until the youngest reached age 35. Because the executor allocated the $1 million exemption to direct skips, none of the exemption was allocated to the trust. When Ha died in 1995, the trust was worth $2,000,000 and Ha's youngest child, Yi Yun, was 28 years old. Because the death of Ha causes the interest to shift to a younger generation, a taxable termination occurs even though the trust itself does not terminate. The tax payable by the trustee is $1,100,000, leaving just $900,000 in the trust.

> EXAMPLE 12 - 19. Continuing the prior example: In 2002, shortly after Yi Yun's 35th birthday, the trust corpus, valued at $1,190,000, was distributed to him and his brother Sui-on. Since this is not a shift in generations (Yi Yun and Sui-on are now in the oldest generation and not considered skip persons), there is no new GST tax (nor any other transfer tax) resulting from the trust's actual termination. Had Yi Yun died after his father, but before his 35 birthday, with the result that his interest went to his children, there would be a GST tax on his share. On the other hand, if he died before his 35th birthday, but left no issue with the result that Sui-on received his share, there would be no additional GST tax because the two brothers are in the same generation.

Taxable distributions. The Code gives a functional definition for a *taxable distribution*: "the term 'taxable distribution' means any distribution from a trust to a skip person (other than a taxable termination or a direct skip)."[20] This covers situations where a trust has beneficiaries in two or more generations, and the trustee can, and does, distribute to one of the beneficiaries in one of the lower generations. The transferee (i.e., distributee-beneficiary) is liable for the GST tax. The taxable amount is the value of the property received by the transferee, reduced by any expenses or indebtedness that would be deductible under IRC § 2053.

> EXAMPLE 12 - 20. Using the facts from the prior two examples, if while Ha (the son of the trustor) is still alive, the trustee, using powers given to her by the terms of the trust, makes a $500,000 distribution to grandson Yi Yun, it would be a taxable distribution. The GST tax in the amount of $275,000 is charged to Yi Yun with the result that he only gets $225,000.

Because the GST tax liability is placed on the transferee, if the trustee pays the GST tax, it is treated as a taxable distribution. The amount that must be "distributed" to achieve a desired net distribution can be solved algebraically. Let the gross distribution be Dg and the net distribution be Dn, then solve for Dg as follows:

Dg - GST tax = Dn; and since GST tax = 0.55 * Dg,

Dg - 0.55* Dg = Dn. Therefore, (1- 0.55) * Dg = Dn; and finally,

Dg = Dn/0.45.

EXAMPLE 12 - 21. Suppose in the prior example, the trustee was required by the terms of the trust to distribute $500,000 to Yi Yun and pay the tax on it. This will require the trustee parting with $1,111,111 whether the trustee pays the GST tax of $611,111 [0.55 * $1,111,111] and distributes $500,000 to Yi Yun or the trustee distributes $1,111,111 and lets Yi Yun pay the tax on it.

EXAMPLE 12 - 22. Suppose the trustee distributed trust corpus worth $500,000 to Siu-on (Yi Yun's brother) after Ha's death (i.e., after the taxable termination had occurred), but before the trust had terminated. This distribution is not a taxable distribution for GST tax purposes, because by that time the two brothers were in the oldest generation of living beneficiaries having an interest in the trust, hence they were no longer skip persons.

Applicable Rate

The applicable rate is made up of two components: the maximum federal estate tax rate and the inclusion ratio. Remember, the GST tax is equal to the taxable amount (a reference to the transferred property) times the applicable rate (a tax rate modified to take into account the allocation of the GST exemption).

Maximum federal estate tax rate. The term maximum federal estate tax rate is the maximum imposed by IRC § 2001, e.g., 55% in 2001 decreasing to 45% in 2007.[21] Note that for years prior to 2002 the maximum rate did not include the 5% surcharge applicable to estates over $10 million.

The inclusion ratio. Think of this as that portion of the transfer that is not saved from the dreaded GST tax by the GST exemption. The GST exemption is indexed for inflation for transfers occurring after 1998 and before 2004. Increases are rounded down to the next lowest multiple of $10,000. The base year for measuring the change is 1997.[22] The GST exemption increased to $1,060,000 in 2001, $1,100,000 in 2002, and $1,120,000 in 2003 After 2003 the exemption is tied to the AEA, hence it will be $1,500,000 in 2004. The inclusion ratio is defined as the value one minus the "applicable fraction,"[23] or

$$1 - \frac{GSTT\ exemption\ allocated}{Net\ FMV\ of\ property\ tranferred}$$

The "net FMV of the property transferred" means net of debt, expenses, liens, death taxes (federal and state) charged to the property, as well as any charitable deduction. Generally, the allocation of the exemption is an elective one made by the donor in the case of gifts and by the executor in the case of estates. It is not unusual to make allocations within a multiple trust estate plan such that all the GST tax trusts have inclusion ratios of either zero or one. We will get into this allocation of the exemption to various trusts in the section on efficient utilization of the exemption. The examples that follow use 55% as the maximum estate tax rate and $1 million as the GST exemption.

EXAMPLE 12 - 23. When Ruben died, $3,000,000 of his estate (net of regular death taxes) was left to his grandchildren. The executor allocated the entire GST exemption to this bequest, resulting in an applicable fraction of one-third

($1,000,000/$3,000,000) and an inclusion ratio of two-thirds (1 - 1/3). The GST tax would be $3,000,000 * 0.55 * .6666667, which is $1,100,000.

EXAMPLE 12 - 24. When Josephine died, she left her $3,000,000 estate (net of regular death taxes) in trust for her son Albert, with remainder to his issue. Since this was her entire net estate, the exemption was allocated to this trust. While Albert was still alive, the trustee made a distribution out of corpus in the amount of $360,000 to Albert's daughter, Martha. This, of course, was a taxable distribution. Given the inclusion ratio, the applicable rate would be 0.55 * .6666667. Therefore, the tax on the distribution would be: $360,000 * 0.55 * .6666667 = $132,000.

EXAMPLE 12 - 25. When Albert died the trust was worth $4,500,000. His death caused a taxable termination. The applicable rate is as before: 0.55 * .6666667. The GST tax is: $4,500,000 * 0.55 * .6666667 = $1,650,000.

Timing the Exemption Allocation

As indicated earlier in this discussion, the allocation of the exemption is not automatic unless a direct skip is involved. Generally, at the death of a transferor, one should allocate in a manner that is most likely to reduce the GST tax, taking into account the present value of money. Because most taxpayers would prefer to postpone taxes of whatever variety, the Code has as a default position the automatic allocation of the exemption to lifetime direct skips unless the donor elects not to have the automatic allocation apply.[24] Where a transfer is not a direct skip (e.g., a transfer into trust with the surviving spouse as the immediate income beneficiary and grandchildren as remaindermen) the donor (or executor) must elect to allocate all or a portion of the exemption to the transfer (e.g., to the trust).

Discretionary allocations. Given a choice, the person making the decision would like to accomplish two or three things, some of which may be in opposition or which may require the use of a functioning crystal ball. Consider the following examples:

EXAMPLE 12 - 26. Eunice never trusted her two boys to wisely handle investments. The oldest, Jimmy, she had given up on, but for the youngest boy, Billie, she wanted to provide a good living, while making sure he could not squander the estate that she had put together. She loved her grandchildren, who have turned out to be fine adults. She left her estate in equal shares, one share immediately to Jimmy's children by right of representation and the other in trust for Billie for his lifetime, the remainder, free of trust, to Billie's children by right of representation. The plan specifically gave her executor authority to allocate the exemption as the executor deemed appropriate. Her estate, after payment of all federal estate and state death taxes, had a net value of $1,500,000. Her executor could allocate $750,000 of the exemption to the direct skip and $250,000 to the trust, or vice-versa, or equally between the two transfers, or in any other proportion. If it is fully allocated to the trust, the trust will have a zero inclusion ratio such that, even if it is worth more than the GST exemption amount when it terminates, no GST tax will be due. However, doing so will cause an immediate GST tax for the portion of the direct skip not covered by the exemption. Allocating $750,000 to the direct skip will postpone all GST tax until the trust ends, but the trust will have an inclusion ratio of two-thirds.

Forced delay of allocations. In the case of inter vivos gifts, if the property would be included in the donor's estate due to a retained interest (§§ 2036-2038), the allocation cannot be made until the close of the *estate tax inclusion period* (ETIP). The ETIP is the point at which the retained interest either ends (released or ends by the terms of the transfer) or the donor dies.

EXAMPLE 12 - 27. Stacie funds a10-year qualified personal residence trust (QPRT) with her $550,000 home. The remaindermen are her three grandchildren. At the end of the10-year term the house is worth $750,000. At that time the ETIP ends and she can allocate $750,000 of the exemption to the transfer.

EXAMPLE 12 - 28. Suppose, in the prior example, that Stacie died in year seven when the home was worth $625,000. At that time the ETIP would end, and her executor could allocate $625,000 of the exemption to the transfer. In both cases, Stacie would have preferred to have made the allocation at the beginning of the trust, when the initial transfer was made so as to use only $550,000 of her exemption.

Special Rules Pertaining to Generations and the GST Tax

There are a number of special rules related to GST tax, some of which we will cover here, others which we will just warn you that they exist but are beyond the scope of this text.

Generation assignment. Where transferees are related to the transferor the assignments are fairly straightforward. The Code requires that one start with the transferor's grandparents and count down generations to the transferee and compare the number to the number of generations between the grandparent and the transferor. If the difference is greater than one, the transferee is a skip person.

EXAMPLE 12 - 29. Jack wishes to leave half of his multi-million dollar estate to his brother's daughter Alice and the other half to Alice's two children, Martin and Paula. Are any or all of them skip persons? Jack's grandfather is two generations above him. From the grandfather to Alice is three generations. Three minus two equals one, so Alice is not a skip person. It is four generations from the grandfather to Martin and Paula. Four minus two equals two, therefore, both Martin and Paula are skip persons.

Predeceased parent exception. A special rule (called the *predeceased parent exception)* allows a skip person to "move up" a generation if his or her parent is a lineal descendant of the transferor (or the transferor's spouse) and the parent dies before the transfer occurs that is subject to a gift tax or an estate tax.[25] If there are two taxable events, then the person must have predeceased the earliest taxable event. It does not apply to skip persons not related to the transferor, nor to collateral heirs (e.g., nieces and nephews), with one exception, ant that is if the transferor has no lineal descendants, a transfer to a collateral relative (e.g., a nephew or niece) whose parent is deceased qualifies for the predeceased parent exception.[26] The move-up exception also applies if the parent (of the person who would otherwise be a skip person) dies within 90 days of the transferor, provided the parent is treated as having predeceased the transferor, either because of a survivorship clause in the transferor's estate planning documents (i.e., the grandparent's will or trust) or because applicable state law has a statutory survivorship period.[27] This is a good reason to consider including a general 90-day survivorship clause in estate planning documents.

EXAMPLE 12 - 30. Sarah's will left her multimillion dollar estate to her issue by right of representation. All three children survived her, but one child, named Richard, died 75 days after her. Richard left two children who were entitled to inherit his entire estate. Sarah's will had a 60-day survivorship clause. Since Richard lived beyond the 60 days, he was entitled to a one-third share of Sarah's estate. Richard's executor disclaimed Richard's share so that it could pass directly to his children. This share is subject to the GST tax because insofar as Sarah's will (and her state of domicile) is concerned he did not predecease her. Had her will included a 90-day survivorship clause (or an even longer one), Richard would have been considered to have predeceased Sarah and there would be no GST tax.

A disclaimer will not work insofar as the predeceased parent exception is concerned, i.e., it will not move the disclaimant's children up a generation. Thus in the above example, even though the disclaimer worked for other purposes (e.g., avoiding Richard's gross estate for regular estate tax and avoiding his probate estate), for GST tax purposes the disclaimer will not cause Richard to be treated as though he had predeceased Sarah. In the typical estate plan for wealthy couples that use multiple trusts, it is very likely that the contingent remaindermen are skip persons. This may cause a GST tax problem.

> EXAMPLE 12-31. S1 and S2 had an ABC trust estate plan. The remaindermen of all trusts were the couple's issue by right of representation. There were four children who had children of their own. When S1 died, what was left of his GST exemption was allocated to Trust B. The executor of S1's estate QTIPed Trust C to postpone the tax on it until after S2's death. When S2 died, Trust C was worth $6 million. One son died eleven months after S1 died. He was survived by two children. When S2 died, the three living children each received a one-fourth share and the two grandchildren a one-eighth share. The GST tax does not apply to the grandchildren's share because it is S2's death that triggers the estate tax insofar as Trust C is concerned, hence the predeceased parent exception moves them up a generation.

> EXAMPLE 12-32. Same facts as in the prior example except S1's executor did not make a QTIP election, hence Trust C was taxed after S1's death. Since the son died more than 90 days after S1 and Trust C was "subject to a tax," the predeceased parent exception does not apply and the GST tax is imposed on the portion of the trust estate going to the grandchildren

Marital relationships. A transfer to one who is related to the transferor's spouse is in the generation level determined as if the transfer was from the spouse rather than from the transferor. The counting up (and down) from the spouse to her (or his) grandparent is just for the purpose of determining whether a donee is a skip person. For all other purposes the transfer is treated as coming from the transferor, unless the couple elect to "split the gift"[28] in which case both spouses are treated as being donors.

A spouse or ex-spouse of a transferor is treated as in the same generation as the transferor, regardless of age difference. This "same-generation-treatment" will continue even if a marriage ends due to the transferor's death or ends by divorce, which some people say is a little like death. Likewise, anyone married to a lineal descendant of the transferor's grandparents (or a lineal descendant of the transferor's spouse's grandparents) is in the same generation as that person's spouse (i.e., the lineal descendant) even if the marriage ends.

> EXAMPLE 12 - 33. Jennifer wishes to leave a portion of her estate to the widow of her uncle's grandson. Would this be a generation-skipping transfer? The widow of the grandson is in the same generation as was the grandson. The parent of the grandson is at the same generation level (count up and count back down) as Jennifer. Therefore, the grandson was (and his widow is) just one generation below Jennifer and no generation-skipping transfer will occur.

Transferees who are not lineal descendants. If the lineal descendant rules and the spouse rules do not apply, then assignment to generations is based on the difference in age between the transferor and the transferee. A person older than, or not less than 12.5 years younger than, the transferor is considered to be in the same generation as the transferor. A person 12.5 to 37.5 years younger is in the next generation below, and similar rules apply to assign individuals to still younger generations based on 25-year increments. Obviously, a person 40 years younger is a skip person and a person 30 years younger is not.

Planning Considerations: Efficient Utilization of the Exemption

Generally, one would like the exemption to reduce GST tax sooner, rather than later, to cover completely a GST tax trust which is likely to grow, and to limit its allocation to trusts that will actually go to skip persons.

These are facts for the extended set of examples that follow: Andre and Mary have three children, Tom, Carol, and Whitney. Their ABC Trust plan allows Trust C to be divided into as many as three trusts after the first spouse's death. The division will depend on how much is QTIPed and the best allocation of the GST exemption. There is a provision for a Trust C_E to hold such property as is to be GST exempt (in addition to Trust B), a Trust C_Q to hold the QTIPed non-exempt portion, and Trust C_{NQ} to hold that portion not QTIPed. The terms of the trust provide that after the surviving spouse's death (S2), any distribution to a skip person should be satisfied first from GST exempt property, next to the extent possible from property included in S2's estate, and last from other trust property; with the distributions from all trusts adjusted to allow overall distribution to Andre and Mary's issue by right of representation. It also provides that if Trust C_E is QTIPed, estate tax charged to the QTIP property at S2's death is to be first charged to Trust C_Q before any is charged to Trust C_E.

When Andre died in 1997, his property was worth $3,000,000 and Mary's property was worth $800,000. Trust A was funded with Mary's property (i.e., $800,000), Trust B with assets worth $600,000, and Trust C, before division, with the $2,400,000 balance.

> EXAMPLE 12-34. The executor of Andre's estate decided to postpone all taxes until Mary's death, therefore, a QTIP election was made covering all $2,400,000 allocated to Trust C. To fully use Andre's $1 million exemption, a $400,000 reverse QTIP election was made. Thus the Trustee divided Trust C into Trust C_E holding assets worth $400,000 and Trust C_Q holding assets worth $2,000,000. Both C trusts were QTIPed (i.e., an election was made to qualify both for the marital deduction) and Trust C_E was reverse QTIPed. The executor allocated Andre's exemption to Trust B and to Trust C_E.

> EXAMPLE 12-35. How would things change if the executor decided to equalize the two estates by a QTIP election covering just part of the Trust C property? Again Trust A would have Mary's property and Trust B would be funded with $600,000. However, to equalize the two estates as of Andre's death, the non-QTIP (NQ) portion of Trust C plus Trust B must equal the value of the combined estates divided by two. Since both the combined value of the estates and Trust B's value are known, one simply solves for NQ, i.e., NQ = ($800,000 + $3,000,000)/2 - 600,000 = $1,300,000. Now what? The trustee divides this amount between Trust C_E (which this time will not be QTIPed) and Trust C_{NQ} (which also will not be QTIPed), and the balance goes into Trust C_Q which will be QTIPed. Trust C_E receives $400,000, which together with Trust B, is allocated the exemption. Trust C_{NQ} receives $900,000 [$1,300,000 - $400,000] and the balance of Trust C is allocated to Trust C_Q. Thus Trust C_Q (and the marital deduction) will be $1,100,000 [$2,400,000 - $1,300,000]. Recap: Andre's taxable estate: $3,000,000 - $1,100,000 = $1,900,000. And, Mary's taxable estate as of Andre's death: $800,000 + $1,100,000 = $1,900,000.

Where does all this take us? Why so many different trusts? First, the combination of the Trust B and the Trust C_E assure that S1's full exemption will be used even if all Trust C property is QTIPed. Remember, a QTIP tosses the QTIPed property into S2's gross estate, where for GST tax (and estate tax, too) it is treated as a transfer from S2. The reverse QTIP allows QTIPed property to be treated as if it came from S1, but only for the purpose of using up S1's GST exemption. Starting in 2002, the GST exemption will equal or exceed the AEA, eliminating the need for a reverse QTIP election. The reverse QTIP election does not affect the QTIP marital deduction. Then why have a separate Trust C_E if no QTIP election is made? (After all, the Trust C property will be taxed only in S1's estate, and the exemption to the extent not allocated to Trust B can be allocated to it.) When the plan was designed, all Andre and Mary's children were alive. If the children outlived their parents, no GST tax would occur. However, since the remaindermen's interests in Trusts B and C do not vest until after S2's death, a GST tax may occur as to property in those trusts even if all three children are alive when S1 dies. A GST tax may occur if any children die, leaving issue, before S2 dies. The predeceased parent rule applies only to direct skips and trusts whose beneficiaries are all skip persons, and since S2's interest in these trusts intervenes, a grandchild would not move up a generation even if his or her parent dies before the grandchild's interest vests. By creating trusts with zero inclusion ratios (Trust B and Trust C_E) and requiring that distributions to skip persons be made first from those trusts, with all trusts used to adjust distributions to accomplish a "by right of representation" distribution, the GST tax will be kept to a minimum. Having Trust C_Q charged with the taxes at S2's death rather than taking them out of Trust C_E also serves the purpose of reducing the GST tax impact.

EXAMPLE 12 - 36. Consider what happens at Mary's death in 2002, assuming that the executor at Andre's death QTIPed to postpone all taxes, and between the two deaths Tom died, leaving two adult children. At the time of Mary's death the four trusts had the following net values:

	FMV		Tax		Net to Distribute
Trust A	$1,100,000	-	$41,000	=	$1,059,000
Trust B	$1,000,000	-	$0	=	$1,000,000
Trust C_E	$500,000	-	$0	=	$500,000
Trust C_Q	$2,300,000	-	$1,339,000	=	$901,000
Totals	$4,600,000	-	$1,380,000		$3,220,000

S2's taxable estate is equal to the combined values of Trust A and both Trust C's. The tax on an estate of $3,900,000 is $1,380,000. Trust A is charged with the amount of estate tax it would have paid had it alone been taxed, and since the estate tax on a taxable estate of $1,100,000 is $41,000, that is charged to Trust A.

The balance of the estate tax, in the amount of $1,339,000 [$1,380,000- $41,000], is charged to Trust C_Q. Since the two living children receive one-third of the after tax value of the trusts, each "share" is $1,073,333. Tom's two children will divide a $1,073,333 share. Because they are skip persons, their share comes first from Trusts B and C_E. These two trusts have sufficient assets to satisfy their share and, because the trusts have a zero inclusion ratio, the bequest to them is completely sheltered from GST tax. Indeed, since the rest of the estate is treated as coming from Mary no distributions would be hit with a GST tax even if all three of the children had died before Mary.

EXAMPLE 12 - 37. Next consider what happens at Mary's death assuming that it occurs in 2007 (more than 10 years after Andre's death so no PTC to worry about) and that Trust C had been QTIPed to equalize estates. Again, between the two deaths Tom died leaving two adult children. At the time of Mary's death, the five trusts had the following net values:

	FMV	Tax allocated		Net to Distribute
Trust A	$1,100,000	-	$0 =	$1,100,000
Trust B	$700,000	-	$0 =	$700,000
Trust C_E	$500,000	-	$0 =	$500,000
Trust C_{NQ}	$900,000	-	$0 =	$900,000
Trust C_Q	$1,400,000	-	$250,000 =	$1,150,000
Totals	$4,600,000		$250,000	$4,350,000

S2's taxable estate is equal to the combined values of Trust A and Trust C_Q, i.e., $2,500,000. The tax on $2,500,000 is $225,000. Trust A is less than the AEA for 2007, hence it is not charged with any tax, rather it is all charged to Trust C_Q. One-third of the after-tax value of the trusts is $1,550,000, with the grandchildren's share coming from Trusts A, B, and C_E completely sheltered from GST tax.

EXAMPLE 12 - 38. Finally, consider what would have happened if the facts were as described in the prior example, except that Carol had also died leaving one child. Now two-thirds of the estate is left to skip persons (insofar as Andre is concerned). The trusts and the allocation of the regular estate taxes remain the same. The grandchildren's total after-tax share (before GST tax) is worth $3,150,000, of which $1,200,000 is drawn from Trusts B and C_E. The balance of $1,950,000 can be drawn from trusts taxed in Mary's estate, i.e., $1,100,000 from Trust A and $850,000 from Trust C_Q. Since Tom and Carol predeceased Mary, the predeceased parent rule moves the grandchildren up a generation vis-a-vis Mary, and no GST tax is due. Only distributions from Trust C_{NQ} are neither sheltered by the exemption nor treated as transfers from Mary. However, all distributions from Trust C_{NQ} will be to Whitney, thus no GST tax. Hence, only if all three children predeceased Mary would there be a GST tax and the taxable amount would be the amount in Trust C_{NQ} after estate taxes were paid.

EGTRRA modified the exemption allocation rules. Under the old rules, there was no automatic allocation to trusts that have both skip and nonskip beneficiaries. It may be a waste of exemption to allocate it to a trust with both skip and nonskip beneficiaries if there is a possibility that the GST tax will not apply. Furthermore, once a taxable termination took place it was too late to allocate exemption to the trust.

> EXAMPLE 12 - 39. Matthew creates a trust that gives income to his sister, Kara, for her life and remainder to her issue. Kara has three children all alive when the trust is established. If she and they are still alive, no skip will occur since her children are just one generation below Matthew. If any of her children die, leaving issue, before Kara dies, a taxable termination will result. In the first instance, allocation exemption to the trust would have wasted it, whereas in the second failing to allocate it results in a GST tax that could have been avoided.

EGTRRA allows a retroactive allocation in situations like the one just described. The inclusion ratio is calculated using the values of the previous transfers at the time they were made rather than the values at the time of the taxable termination. The retroactive allocation must be made on a gift tax return that is timely for a gift made in the year of the beneficiary's death. Failure to file on time and a late allocation can be made but it will be based on the value of the trust at the beneficiary's death (or alternate valuation date). The IRS is given authority to prescribe regulations for granting relief from failures to make the retroactive allocation in a timely manner.[29] After 2009, assuming repeal is made permanent, all of this may be mute as there will be no GST tax, not even on distributions from or terminations of exiting trusts.

Credit for Certain State Taxes

If a generation-skipping transfer (other than a direct skip) occurs at the same time as, and as a result of, the death of an individual, there is allowed a credit against the federal GST tax equal to the lesser of the state GST tax or 5% of the federal GST tax.[30] Most states have simply adopted a state GST "pickup" tax equal to 5% of the federal GST tax for such indirect skips.

Certain Transfers Excluded from the GST Tax

The annual exclusion applies to GST tax present interest inter vivos gifts. Those inter vivos gifts that would not be treated as taxable gifts because of IRC § 2503(e) (payments directly to educational institutions or to medical providers) are also excluded from the definition of a GST tax.[31]

Grandfathering in Some Grand Old Trusts

Some generation-skipping trusts that were around when the GST tax laws went into effect are exempt from the GST tax. To be grandfathered, a trust had to be irrevocable as of September 25, 1985; or the skip must be caused by a will, a testamentary trust, or a trust in existence on October 21, 1986, that became irrevocable as a result of the testator or trustor's death before January 1, 1987. A grandfathered trust will lose its exempt status if the trustee accepts additions of property, or if modifications are made to it, after the dates just mentioned.

The Need for GST Tax Planning

It should be evident by now that planning for the lifetime GST exemption requires careful thought and attentive drafting of complex will or trust clauses, and can add considerably to the expense of estate planning. It also forces the planner to openly discuss with the client an unpleasant fact: the eventual death of the client's children.

No GST tax planning necessary for some clients. Which wealthier clients most probably do not need GST tax planning? First, clients with estates not expected to exceed the GST exemption when combined with taxable gifts need not ever worry about a GST tax. They may, however, wish to do some trust planning to skip a generation by transferring some property for the benefit of their grandchildren, confident that GST tax law will automatically allocate the GST exemption at their death, so that all trusts created will have an inclusion ratio of zero.

Second, those who do not wish to directly include grandchildren in their plan may not need GST tax planning. For example, clients preferring a 100% marital deduction plan, as in a simple will, probably want their property to pass entirely to the surviving spouse and the children, all nonskip persons. Even clients anticipating a bypass may have no wish to provide for grandchildren so long as their children are living. Of course, with either plan the property may wind up passing under the instrument to grandchildren (i.e., "descendants" or "issue") if a child predeceases a grandchild. However, the property involved may be sheltered from the GST tax under the predeceased parent exception, with the help of some careful drafting, to ensure that a direct skip will in fact occur or that the interest is covered by the GST exemption.

Third, in some situations, GST tax trust planning will suggest that person leave the estate outright to the children, perhaps with just the hope and a prayer that the children will preserve the property for ultimate disposition to the grandchildren. Having a large estate divided among the transferor's children may actually result in a greater amount finally landing in the hands of the grandchildren. This may occur due to two factors: (1) the use of each child's unified credit can reduce the overall estate tax, but they would not be effective against the GST tax if the property stayed in a bypass trust; and (2) effective marginal estate tax rate just above the AEA is lower than the 55% GST tax rate.

Fourth, outliving the GST tax is an excellent way to avoid this tax and will be one of the most satisfying estate planning strategies to carry out.

Clients needing GST tax planning. Which wealthier clients are most likely to need careful GST tax planning? Any of the following:

- ► "dynastic"-oriented clients wishing to perpetuate their wealth
- ► clients with wealthy children
- ► clients who believe that their children cannot handle large amounts of money maturely
- ► clients who wish to give to their grandchildren things that their children cannot or will not give

Summary. There are several methods of at least partially circumventing the GST tax, particularly through the use of the GST exemption. In general, only family estates exceeding two AEAs in total value at the first spouse's death are prevented from arranging GST tax-free generation-skipping transfers. Given the eventual repeal of the GST tax, most couples will have at least one spouse outlive it. That spouse will not need an exemption to avoid the tax.

Generation-skipping planning is modestly popular to clients today in part because of concerns about avoiding transfer taxes. It will be interesting to see whether the interest continues if the estate tax and GST tax are truly repealed.

QUERIES ANSWERED

1. In 2003 the tax on $2,405,300 is $633,597 and on $3,955,000 is $1,392,950, for a total of $2,026,547. Tax on $5,405,300 is $2,103,597, hence $77,050 is saved by using the disclaimer. Of course one must factor in seven months' loss of income on the $633,597 since the tax is saved by paying a tax that could have been postponed.

2. Since Trust B is valued at $1,050,000 and the desired taxable estate in 2001 to postpone taxes until S2's death is $675,000, S1's estate needs an additional marital deduction of $375,000. Therefore,

$$QTIP\ fraction\ =\ \frac{\$375,000}{\$1,050,000}$$

3. The numerator of the fraction is the amount necessary to bring S1's estate equal to S2's, and the denominator is the value of Trust C. Total value of their combined estates divided by two [$6,630,000 ÷ 2 = $3,135,000] gives the desired taxable estate at S1's death. Subtract that amount from S1's estate to arrive at the needed marital deduction [$4,885,000 - $3,315,000 = $1,570,000]. Therefore, the QTIP fraction is $1,570,000/$4,885,000 which, since the value of Trust C is the same as the denominator of the fraction, results in a taxable estate for S1 of: $4,885,000 - $1,570,000 = $3,315,000.

QUESTIONS AND PROBLEMS

FACTS FOR 1 - 10: S1 and S2 lived in a common law state. S1 owned property having a net value of $5,000,000 and S2 owned property having a net value of $2,000,000. S1 dies in 2002 and S2 dies in 2005. Assume debts and expenses are zero. The numbers for the AsuperB at S1's death will not change regardless of what S1's executor does insofar as making the QTIP election, but the A and the disclaimer trusts (dC and dB) in the ABdC and AdB plans, respectively, depend on whether S2 disclaims, and if she does, to what extent she does. The second part of each problem asks you to determine S2's taxable estate. For that calculation you will be given the value of the trusts as of S2's death based on some growth between the first and second death.

1.1 The couple have an AsuperB Trust estate plan. S1's executor elects to postpone all taxes until S2 dies, but fully use S1's unified credit. Determine: (a) S1's estate; (b) the values of Trust A and Trust B; (c) the QTIP fraction; and (d) how the fraction is applied to arrive at the taxable estate.

1.2 Determine S2's taxable estate given that Trust A is worth $2,500,000 and Trust B $6,500,000.

2.1 The couple have an AsuperB Trust estate plan. S1's executor elects to pay all taxes at S1's death. Determine: (a) the QTIP fraction; (b) show how it is applied to arrive at the desired taxable estate.

2.2 Determine S2's taxable estate given that Trust A is worth $2,500,000 and Trust B $5,400,000.

3.1 The couple have an AsuperB Trust estate plan. S1's executor elects to make a QTIP election that would equalize the two estates, at least as of S1's death. Determine: (a) the QTIP fraction; (b) show how it is applied to arrive at the desired taxable estate.

3.2 Determine S2's taxable estate given that Trust A is worth $2,500,000 and Trust B $5,400,000.

4.1 The couple have an AsuperB Trust estate plan. S1's executor elects to make a QTIP election such that S1's taxable estate would equal

$2,700,000. Determine: (a) the QTIP fraction; (b) show how it is applied to arrive at the desired taxable estate.

4.2 Determine S2's taxable estate given that Trust A is worth $2,500,000 and Trust B $5,800,000.

5.1 The couple have an ABdC Trust estate plan. S2 chooses not to disclaim any property. Determine: (a) S1's estate; (b) the values of Trust A, Trust B, and Trust C; and (c) S1's taxable estate.

5.2 Determine S2's taxable estate given that Trust A is worth $8,000,000 and Trust B $1,500,000.

6.1 The couple have an ABdC Trust estate plan. S2 and the executor for S1's estate work together. S2 disclaims all property that would otherwise flow into Trust A. S1's executor elects to pay all taxes at S1's death. Determine: (a) S1's estate; (b) the values of Trust A, Trust B, and Trust C [remember that Trust C is equal to the value of the property disclaimed]; (c) S1's taxable estate.

6.2 Determine S2's taxable estate given that Trust A is worth $2,500,000, Trust B $1,300,000, and Trust C $4,100,000.

7.1 The couple have an ABdC Trust estate plan. S2 and the executor for S1's estate work together, S2 disclaims all property that would otherwise flow into Trust A; S1's executor elects to make a QTIP election that would equalize the two estates, at least as of S1's death. Determine: (a) the values of Trust A, Trust B, and Trust C; (b) the QTIP fraction and (c) show how it is applied to arrive at the desired taxable estate.

7.2 Determine S2's taxable estate given that Trust A is worth $2,500,000, Trust B $1,300,000, and Trust C $5,200,000.

8.1 The couple have an ABdC Trust estate plan. S2 and the executor for S1's estate work together. S2 disclaims just enough property to equalize the estates, at least as of S1's death; S1's executor makes no QTIP election. Determine: (a) the values of Trust A, Trust B, and Trust C; (b) show how this disclaimer works to bring about the desired taxable estate.

8.2 Determine S2's taxable estate given that Trust A is worth $5,000,000, Trust B $1,300,000, and Trust C $4,800,000.

9.1 The couple have an ABdC Trust estate plan. S2 and the executor for S1's estate work together, S2 disclaims just enough property to bring S1's taxable estate to $2,600,000; S1's executor makes no QTIP election. Determine: (a) the values of Trust A, Trust B, and Trust C; (b) show how this disclaimer works to bring about the desired taxable estate.

9.2 Determine S2's taxable estate given that Trust A is worth $4,200,000, Trust B $1,300,000, and Trust C $1,700,000.

10.1 The couple have an AdB Trust estate plan. S2 disclaims just enough property to bring S1's taxable estate to $2,850,000; S1's executor makes no QTIP election. Determine: (a) the values of Trust A and Trust B; (b) show how this disclaimer works to bring about the desired taxable estate.

10.2 Determine S2's taxable estate given that Trust A is worth $4,500,000, and Trust B $3,150,000.

FACTS FOR 11 - 20: S1 and S2 live in a community property state. S1 owns property having a net value of $2,300,000 and S2 owns property having a net value of $1,600,000, and they own community property worth $1,400,000. S1 dies in 2002 and S2 in 2005. Assume debts and expenses are zero.

11.1 The couple have an AsuperB Trust estate plan. S1's executor elects to postpone all taxes until S2 dies, but fully use S1's unified credit. Determine: (a) S1's estate; (b) the values of Trust A and Trust B; (c) the QTIP fraction; and (d) how the fraction is applied to arrive at the taxable estate.

11.2 Determine S2's taxable estate given that Trust A is worth $2,900,000 and Trust B $5,400,000.

12.1 The couple have an AsuperB Trust estate plan. S1's executor elects to pay all taxes at S1's death. Determine: (a) the QTIP fraction; (b) show how it is applied to arrive at the desired taxable estate.

12.2 Determine S2's taxable estate given that Trust A is worth $2,900,000 and Trust B $3,250,000.

13.1 The couple have an AsuperB Trust estate plan. S1's executor elects to make a QTIP election that would equalize the two estates, at least as of S1's death. Determine: (a) the QTIP fraction; (b) show how it is applied to arrive at the desired taxable estate.

13.2 Determine S2's taxable estate given that Trust A is worth $3,900,000 and Trust B $3,700,000.

14.1 The couple have an AsuperB Trust estate plan. S1's executor elects to make a QTIP election such that S1's taxable estate would equal $2,200,000. Determine: (a) the QTIP fraction; (b) show how it is applied to arrive at the desired taxable estate.

14.2 Determine S2's taxable estate given that Trust A is worth $2,900,000 and Trust B $3,740,000.

15.1 The couple have an ABdC Trust estate plan. The widow chooses not to disclaim any property. Determine: (a) S1's estate; (b) the values of Trust A, Trust B, and Trust C; and (c) S1's taxable estate.

15.2 Determine S2's taxable estate given that Trust A is worth $6,700,000 and Trust B $1,300,000.

16.1 The couple have an ABdC Trust estate plan. S2 and the executor for S1's estate work together, S2 disclaims all property that would otherwise flow to Trust A; S1's executor elects to pay all taxes at S1's death. Determine: (a) S1's estate; (b) the values of Trust A, Trust B, and Trust C [remember that Trust C is equal to the value of the property disclaimed]; (c) S1's taxable estate.

16.2 Determine S2's taxable estate given that Trust A is worth $2,900,000, Trust B $1,100,000, and Trust C $2,600,000.

17.1 The couple have an ABdC Trust estate plan. S2 and the executor for S1's estate worked together. S2 disclaims all property that would otherwise flow to Trust A; S1's executor elects to make a QTIP election that would equalize the two estates, at least as of S1's death. Determine: (a) the values of Trust A, Trust B, and Trust C; (b) the

QTIP fraction and (c) show how it is applied to arrive at the desired taxable estate.

17.2 Determine S2's taxable estate given that Trust A is worth $2,900,000, Trust B $1,320,000, and Trust C $3,100,000.

18.1 The couple have an ABdC Trust estate plan. S2 and the executor for S1's estate work together. S2 disclaims just enough property to equalize the estates, at least as of S1's death; S1's executor makes no QTIP election. Determine: (a) the values of Trust A, Trust B, and Trust C; (b) show how this disclaimer works to bring about the desired taxable estate.

18.2 Determine S2's taxable estate given that Trust A is worth $4,330,000, Trust B $1,370,000, and Trust C $2,240,000.

19.1 The couple have an ABdC Trust estate plan. S2 and the executor for S1's estate work together. S2 disclaims just enough property to bring S1's taxable estate to $2,200,000; S1's executor makes no QTIP election. Determine: (a) the values of Trust A, Trust B, and Trust C; (b) show how this disclaimer works to bring about the desired taxable estate.

19.2 Determine S2's taxable estate given that Trust A is worth $3,500,000, Trust B $1,400,000, and Trust C $1,450,000.

20.1 The couple have an AdB Trust estate plan. S2 disclaims just enough property to bring S1's taxable estate to $2,250,000; S1's executor makes no QTIP election. Determine: (a) the values of Trust A and Trust B; (b) show how this disclaimer works to bring about the desired taxable estate.

20.2 Determine S2's taxable estate given that Trust A is worth $3,500,000, and Trust B $2,650,000.

FACTS FOR 21: S1 dies May 7, 2002, survived by 70-year-old S2. The federal rate for valuing split interests (life estates, etc.) is 8%. They have an ABC. At S1's death their holdings have the following net value:

S1's separate	$3,450,000
S2's separate	$1,980,000
Total value	$5,430,000

S1's executor QTIPs Trust C to equalize the two estates and pays estate taxes of $787,500, of which $669,810 is federal tax and $117,690 is state.

S2 dies August 23, 2005, and the trusts have the following values:

Trust A	$2,280,000
Trust B	$900,000
Trust C	$3,180,000

S2's taxable estate is $3,234,000. The estate would have to pay federal taxes of $804,980 without the PTC. Note, there is no state death tax credit in 2005.

21.1 Determine, as of S1's death: (a) the value of Trust A, Trust B, and Trust C; (b) the QTIP fraction necessary to equalize the two estates; and (c) S1's taxable estate.

21.2 Given the information on the values for the three trusts at S2's death, show how one arrives at S2's taxable estate.

21.3 Determine: Limit one.

21.4 Determine: Limit two.

21.5 Determine: (a) the PTC after adjusting for time; and (b) the federal estate tax.

FACTS FOR 22: S1 dies on September 15, 2002, survived by 80-year-old S2. The federal rate for valuing split interests is 6%. They have an ABC plan. At S1's death their holdings have the following net value:

S1's separate	$2,560,000
community property	$900,000
S2's separate	$1,380,000
Total value	$4,840,000

S1's executor QTIPs Trust C to equalize the two estates and paid estate taxes of $640,800 of which $541,500 is federal tax and $99,300 is state.

S2 dies January 10, 2005, and the trusts have the following values:

Trust A	$2,320,000
Trust B	$1,180,000
Trust C	$1,800,000

S2's taxable estate is $2,848,358; the estate would have to pay federal taxes of $623,728 without the PTC.

22.1 Determine, as of S1's death: (a) the value of Trust A, Trust B, and Trust C; (b) the QTIP fraction necessary to equalize the two estates; and (c) S1's taxable estate.

22.2 Given the information on the values for the three trusts at S2's death, show how one arrives at S2's taxable estate.

22.3 Determine: Limit one.

22.4 Determine: Limit two.

22.5 Determine: (a) the PTC after adjusting for time; and (b) the federal estate tax.

FACTS FOR 23: S1 dies April 15, 2002, survived by 60-year-old S2. The federal rate for valuing split interests is 12%. They have an AsuperB plan. At S1's death their holdings have the following net value:

S1's separate	$3,900,000
S2's separate	$480,000
Total value	$4,380,000

S1's executor QTIPs Trust B so as to equalize both estates, at least as of S1's death, and pays estate taxes of $528,100, of which $442,600 is federal and $85,500 is state.

S2 dies November 18, 2003. The trusts have the following values:

Trust A	$640,000
Trust B	$4,560,000

Since S2's taxable estate is $2,639,385, the estate would have to pay state taxes of $75,133 and federal taxes of $673,166 without PTC.

23.1 Determine as of S1's death: (a) the value of Trust A and Trust B; (b) the QTIP fraction necessary to equalize the two estates at S1's death.

23.2 Given the information on the values for the two trusts at S2's death, show how one arrives at S2's taxable estate.

23.3 Determine: Limit one.

23.4 Determine: Limit two.

23.5 Determine: (a) the PTC after adjusting for time; (b) the state death tax; and (c) the federal estate tax.

FACTS FOR 24: S1 dies May 5, 2002, survived by 75-year-old S2. The federal rate is 10%. They have an AsuperB plan. At S1's death their holdings have the following net value:

S1's separate	$9,000,000
community property	$940,000
S2's separate	$1,300,000
Total value	$11,240,000

S1's executor QTIPs Trust B such that S1's taxable estate is $4,600,000 and pays estate taxes of $1,730,000; of which $1,469,900 is federal and $260,100 is state.

S2 dies October 10, 2006. The trusts have the following values:

Trust A	$1,950,000
Trust B	$9,300,000

S2's taxable estate is $6,732,577. The estate would have to pay federal taxes of $2,176,985 without the PTC.

24.1 Determine as of S1's death: (a) the value of Trust A and Trust B; (b) the QTIP fraction necessary to have a taxable estate equal the desired S1 taxable estate.

24.2 Given the information on the values for the two trusts at S2's death, show how one arrives at S2's taxable estate.

24.3 Determine: Limit one.

24.4 Determine: Limit two.

24.5 Determine: (a) the PTC after adjusting for time; (b) the state death tax; and (c) the federal estate tax.

25. A bypass trust provides for income to the trustor's wife for her life, then remainder outright to his daughter, if she survives her mother; otherwise, to the daughter's issue.
   a. Could there be a potential GST tax problem?
   b. Is the size of the trust a factor?
   c. Can you suggest a solution to the problem?

26. a. How does the reverse QTIP election work?
   b. Is it needed to obtain a marital deduction?
   c. Does it become almost obsolete in 2002? When might it still be needed?

27. Which clients do not need to worry too much about GST tax planning and which ones do need to worry about it? In what sense is it becoming less of a worry?

28. Explain the GST exemption.

ANSWERS TO THE QUESTIONS AND PROBLEMS *(odd numbered only)*

FOR 1 - 10: common law state. S1 $5 million and S2 $2 million.

1.1 AsuperB. Postpone: (a) S1's GE [$5 million]; (b) Tr A [$2 million] and Tr B [$5 million]; (c) the QTIP [$4 million/$5 million; and (d) applied to arrive at the TxE [fraction times Tr B = MD, GE - MD = TxE = $1 million].

1.2 S2's TxE [Tr A + QTIP * Tr B = $7.7 million],Tr A $2.5 million and Tr B $6.5 million.

3.1 AsuperB. QTIP to equalize: (a) the QTIP [$1.5 million/$5 million]; (b) TxE [(Tr A + Tr B)/2 = $3.5 million] or $5 million - $1.5 million QTIP.

3.2 S2's TxE [Tr A + QTIP * Tr B = $4,120,000]; Tr A $2.5 million and Tr B $5.4 million.

5.1 ABdC. No disclaimer: (a) S1's E [$5 million]; (b)Tr A [$6 million], Tr B [$1 million], and Tr C [zero]; and (c) S1's TxE [$1 million].

5.2 S2's TxE [$8 million]; Tr A $8 million and Tr B $1.5 million.

7.1 ABdC. S2 disclaims all property, QTIP to equalize: (a)Tr A [$2 million], Tr B [$1 million], Tr C [$4 million]; (b) the QTIP [$1.5 million/$4 million]; (c) TxE [$3.5 million].

7.2 S2's TxE [$2.5 million + ($1.5/$4 * $5.2 million) = $4,450,000; notice that Trust B exceeds the AEA but is not taxed at S2's death] Tr A $2.5 million, Tr B $1.3 million, Tr C $5.2 million.

9.1 ABdC. Disclaims to bring S1's TxE to $2.6 million: (a) Tr A [S2's estate + (S1's estate > $2.6 million) = $4.4 million], Tr B [$1 million],Tr C [$1.6 million]; (b) show work to TxE [S1's estate = $5 million, less MD = $2.6 million, Tr B = $1 million, therefore disclaim $1.6 million allowing $2.4 million to transfer to Tr A; TxE = S1's estate - MD = $2.6 million].

9.2 S2's TxE [Tr A only; $4.2 million] Tr A $4.2 million, Tr B $1.3 million, Tr C $1.7 million.

FOR 11 - 20: Community property state. S1 $2.3 million; S2 $1.6 million; community $1.4 million.

11.1 AsuperB. Postpone: (a) S1's GE [$3 million]; (b) Tr A [S2 + ½ * cp = $2.3 million] and Tr B [S1 + ½ * cp = $3 million]; (c) the QTIP [MD/Tr B = $1 million/$3 million]; and (d) applied to arrive at the TxE [fraction times Tr B = MD; and GE - MD = TxE = $1 million].

11.2 S2's TxE [$6.5 million]; Tr A $2.9 million and Tr B $5.4 million.

13.1 AsuperB. QTIP to equalize: (a) the QTIP [$350,000/$3 million]; (b) applied to arrive at the desired TxE [GE - MD = $2,650,000].

13.2 S2's TxE [$4,331,667, Tr A + QTIP fraction * Tr B] Tr A $3.9 million and Tr B $3.7 million.

15.1 ABdC. No disclaimer: (a) S1's GE [$3 million]; (b)Tr A [$4.3 million], Tr B [$1 million], and Tr C [zero]; and (c) S1's TxE [$1 million].

15.2 S2's TxE [$6.7 million]; Tr A $6.7 million and Tr B $1.3 million.

17.1 ABdC. Disclaimed all and elects QTIP to equalize: (a)Tr A [$2.3 million], Tr B [$1 million], and Tr C [$2 million]; (b) the QTIP [$350,000/$2 million]; and (c) to arrive at the desired TxE [$3 million - $350,000 = $2,650,000].

17.2 S2's TxE [$3,442,500]; Tr A $2.9 million and QTIP fraction * Tr C $3.1 million

19.1 ABdC. Disclaimed to bring S1's TxE to $2.2 million: (a) Tr A [$3.1 million], Tr B [$1 million], and Tr C [$1.2 million]; (b) disclaimer brings about the desired TxE [GE - MD = TxE = $2.2 million].

19.2 S2's TxE [$3.5 million]; Tr A $3.5 million, Tr B $1.4 million, and Tr C $1,450,000.

Prior transfer credit problem 21:

21.1　(a) Tr A [$1,980,000], Tr B [$1 million], and Tr C [$2,450,000]; (b) the QTIP to equalize [$735,000/$2,450,000]; (c) S1's TxE [$2,715,000].

21.2　S2's TxE [$3,234,000].

21.3　Limit one: [$398,269; factor .59460 * $669,810].

21.4　Limit two: [$737,085; S2's "reduced taxable estate" = $1,650,878 and the federal tax on it is $67,895].

21.5　(a) the PTC [$318,615; death just over three years, therefore, 80% of the lower of the two limits] and (b) the FET[$804,980 - $318,615 = $486,365].

Prior transfer credit problem 23:

23.1　(a) Tr A [$480,000] and Tr B [$3.9 million]; (b) the QTIP to equalize. [$1,710,000/$3,900,000].

23.2　S2's TxE [Tr A + Tr C * ($1,710,000/$3,900,700) = $2,639,385].

23.3　Limit one: [.82732 * $442,600 = $366,172].

23.4　Limit two: [reduced S2 estate = $2,639,385 - .82732 * ($3,900,000 - $528,100) = $436,646. This is less than the AEA for 2003, the tax therefore is zero tax, difference = $673,166].

23.5　(a) the PTC [lesser limit @ 100% (less than two years), i.e., $366,172]; (b) the St D Tx [$75,133, as given]; and (c) the FET[$673,166 - $366,172 = $306,994].

25. a.　GST tax problem? There could be a potential GST tax problem if daughter fails to survive her mother. In that event, a transfer out of trust to the daughter's issue (e.g., a grandchild of the trustor) could be a taxable distribution subject to the GST tax. The predeceased parent direct skip exception rule would not apply. As a taxable distribution, it is not a direct skip.

　　b.　Size of the trust can be a factor because of the GST exemption, which can exempt part or all of the distribution.

　　c.　The commonly used solution is to allocate a portion of the GST exemption to the bypass trust assets. Another solution is to outlive the GST tax.

27.   Clients whose estates are not expected to exceed $1 million, and those who do not wish to directly include grandchildren in their plan do not need to worry too much about the GST tax. For example, clients preferring a 100% marital deduction plan, as in a simple will, probably want their property to pass entirely to the surviving spouse and then to the children. Even clients anticipating a bypass may have no wish to provide for grandchildren. Of course, with either plan the property may wind up passing under the instrument to grandchildren (i.e., "issue") if a child predeceases a grandchild. However, the property involved can usually be sheltered from the GST tax under the predeceased parent direct skip rule, with the help of some careful drafting, to ensure that a direct skip will in fact occur.

    Clients who should do some GST tax planning include: "dynastic" oriented clients wishing to perpetuate themselves through multi-generation trusts; clients with very wealthy children; clients who believe that their children cannot handle large amounts of money maturely; and clients who wish to give to their grandchildren significant amounts of wealth.

ENDNOTES

1. IRC § 6081.

2. IRC § 2056(d).

3. IRC § 2056(d)(4).

4. IRC § 2056(d)(2)(A).

5. Reg. § 26.2056A-2(d).

6. Reg.§ 20.2056A-3(a).

7. Reg. § 20.2056A-2(d).

8. IRC § 2056(d)(2)(B).

9. IRC § 2056(d)(3).

10. IRC § 2056(b)(5).

11. The reader may wish to review the basic prior transfer credit material presented in Chapter 6 before tackling this material.

12. IRC § 2613(a).

13. IRC § 2602.

14. IRC § 2612(c)(1).

15. IRC § 2603(a)(3).

16. IRC § 2623.

17. IRC § 2624(b).

18. IRC § 2624(c).

19. IRC § 2612(a)(1).

20. IRC § 2612(b).

21. IRC § 2641(b).

22. IRC § 2631(c)(1).

23. IRC § 2642(a).

24. IRC § 2632(b)(1) - (b)(3).

25. IRC § 2651(e)(1).

26. IRC § 2551(e).

27. Reg. § 26.2612-1(a)(2)(i).

28. IRC § 2513.

29. IRC § 2642(g) added by EGTRRA.

30. IRC § 2604.

31. IRC § 2611(b)(1).

CHAPTER 13

Gift Planning Fundamentals

OVERVIEW

The last two chapters focused on property transfers at death. This chapter will introduce lifetime transfers of property, examining the techniques used in giving gifts, the most popular type of intra-family lifetime transfer.

Lifetime transfers take many forms and are made for many reasons. They are made to individuals and to charities. They are made outright or to a fiduciary, such as a trustee or custodian. They can take the form of a completed transfer, such as a sale or a gift; or they can remain incomplete, as in the case of a transfer with a retained interest. They include transfers of total interests in property or just partial interests.

While you read this chapter and the next, you will want to keep in mind two important principles. First, different types of transfers are designed to accomplish different types of goals. Second, the less complete the transfer, the more probable the asset will be kept in as part of the estate and the less likely the transfer will achieve desired tax goals. This latter point cannot be overemphasized because donors often prefer to retain some control over the transferred property. By definition, every lifetime transfer requires the relinquishment of some control. Gifts mean loss of access, control, and flexibility; individuals who are reluctant to give this up are likely to feel uncomfortable with a gift giving program as part of their estate plan no matter what the magnitude of the financial rewards might be. Planners should be sensitive to this issue.

To minimize loss of access, control, and flexibility, some individuals may contemplate gifts to family members who secretly agree to always make the assets available to the donor. This arrangement is a retained interest which, if it came to light after the donor died, would cause the property to be included in the donor's estate. There are other problems with this arrangement: First, the donees may have a "change in attitude," and dispose of the gift asset or refuse to share it or return it. Second, the gift assets are subject to the claims of the donee's creditors.

We begin our discussion of lifetime transfers with an examination of completed lifetime gifts – transfers that give rise to potential gift taxation. A gift is complete for tax purposes when there is surrender of dominion and control and delivery of an interest in property by a donor capable of transferring that property to an accepting donee capable of receiving and possessing it.

A gift may be made outright, or it may be made to another party, usually a fiduciary, for the benefit of the donee. An outright gift results in the receipt by the donee of a fee simple interest in the gift property, yielding to the donee all of the rights that accompany that interest. Thus, an outright gift extends to the donee the complete ownership and control.

However, the donor may not wish to bestow that degree of control. For example, a donor may wish to make a sizable gift to help a child finance college expenses, but may be reluctant to make an outright gift. The usual alternative to an outright gift is a transfer to a fiduciary, who is responsible for managing the property and distributing its income and principal in accordance with the conditions contained in the underlying document or established by local law. Significant gifts for minors are especially likely to be in the name of a fiduciary, such as a custodian or a trustee. Gifts to adult donees are usually outright but may also be made in trust.

Impact of EGTRRA-2001

Much of what has been done in the past was motivated by a desire to avoid estate taxes. With the phasing down of the estate tax prior to 2010, and repeal effective in 2010, we will have to rethink our strategies. This has been made much more uncertain by the sunset provision written into EGTRRA for automatic expiration in 2011. One way to analyze the situation is to think of three phases, the pre-2010 phase down, the 2010 repeal, and the 2011 sunset. In analyzing the benefits of any gift strategy, the planner must consider the probability the client might die in any year and the probability EGTRRA will be modified and in what way.

Gifts may be used somewhat less in the post-EGTRRA era for two reasons. First, with the estate tax decreasing and possibly disappearing, there will be less need for all types of tax reduction devices. Some of the estate planning techniques for married couples and for passing wealth to the next generation make good sense only if one assumes both spouses are likely to die before 2010. Second, one response to the uncertainty is to use devices that keep options open for adapting to potential tax law changes. People may defer making gifts, instead adopting a wait-and-see approach. Gifts are not a good match for an environment where options need to be kept open. They may not be possible to undo. Once they are made, they can foreclose other options.

NON-TAX MOTIVES FOR MAKING GIFTS

There are many non-tax motivations that encourage people to make gifts, such as the desire by parents or grandparents to provide for an expensive education, to help children finance a home or an automobile, to help establish or expand a business, to encourage a child to work in the parent's business, to help a child who has experienced a significant loss or who is unemployed, to care for elderly parents, and the simple desire to witness a donee's enjoyment of the benefits that a gift can bring. Individuals will be most willing to make gifts for the tax advantages to be described next when they are also motivated by one or more of these non-tax objectives.

TAX CONSIDERATIONS IN MAKING GIFTS

One should consider the death tax and income tax advantages and disadvantages of making gifts.

Tax Advantages of Gifting

Gifts are commonly made to save federal and state death taxes, generation-skipping transfer (GST) tax, and federal, state, and local income taxes. In the examples that follow, look for two common tax threads. First, many gifts can be made at no gift tax cost. Second, even if a gift tax is incurred, gifts may still be desirable because they have the potential of reducing total transfer taxes and income taxes.

Death tax and GST tax advantages. Death tax and GST tax advantages include the ability to reduce or freeze the taxable estate in three ways: using the shelter of the annual exclusion and the unified credit, removing the money paid as gift tax from the transfer tax base, and excluding post-gift appreciation.

Shelter of annual exclusion and unified credit. Most people about to embark on a program of gifting will be able to transfer a significant portion of their estate, free of gift tax, death tax, and GST tax. The gift tax and GST tax annual exclusions enable a donor to give, free of tax, $10,000 (indexed) per donee per year. Married couples can give $20,000 per donee per year, splitting gifts if the assets belong to one member.

> EXAMPLE 13 - 1. Mom wishes to give maximum equal amounts of her own property to her three children and three grandchildren. She can give each of the six donees $10,000 each year, gift tax and GST tax free, for a total tax-free transfer of $60,000.

During each calendar year, so long as the donor limits the gifts given to each donee to the annual exclusion amount, there is no need to file a gift tax return.

> EXAMPLE 13 - 2. Altering the facts in Example 13-1 a bit, assume that Dad also wishes to make similar annual exclusion gifts of his own property interests. He can give each of the six donees $10,000 for a total of $20,000 per donee and a total of $120,000 for all six without either parent filing a gift tax return.

> EXAMPLE 13 - 3. On similar facts, if more than half of the gift property belonged to one of the two parents, they could agree to split the gifts by filing gift tax returns in order to make the split gift election. However, the tax outcome would be unchanged and $120,000 could be transferred each year without using either parent's unified credit because none of the gifts would be taxable.

Generalizing from these examples, the total number of annual exclusions available over time equals the number of donors times the number of donees times the number of years of gifting. Thus, in the above examples, if the donors made gifts for eight years, they give $960,000, i.e., (2 * 6 * 8 * $10,000) without using up any AEA. As indexing increases the annual exclusion, more can be given without using up any unified credit. It appears that the gift tax will remain after 2009 whether the EGTRRA changes are made permanent or are repealed.

Actually, a donor can give a much larger amount, gift-tax (and GST tax) free if the donor is willing to use up some unified credit (and, if applicable, the GST exemption). Thus, a couple with five donees who start an aggressive gift-giving program in 2002 could give $2.5 million over five years completely gift-tax free. Of course, the couple would use up all of their respective $1 million lifetime gift exclusions. If they both died before 2010, their estates would be able to use any increase in the AEA (i.e., above $1 million) to shelter part of their estates. Significant gifts can be made to skip persons by applying the donor's GST exemption to the transfers.

As a result of EGTRRA the exemption takes a dramatic leap starting in 2004. It will equal the AEA for the year of transfer, e.g., $1.5 million in 2004. Gifts under the annual exclusion amount do not use up any of the donor's GST exemption. The GST tax is to end in 2010, but as with the estate tax, planners must be concerned about the sunset provision that completely revives the GST tax in 2011, coupled with a reversion back to an indexed exemption that will be around $1.2 million by then.

Summarizing, making annual exclusion gifts, gifts sheltered by the unified credit, and gifts sheltered by the GST exemption enable individuals to substantially reduce their gross estate without having to pay gift taxes or the GST tax. Current gift planning is clouded by the uncertainty of what will happen to the estate tax and the GST tax after 2010.

Removing the gift tax from the transfer tax base. The second advantage of gifting is the ability to exclude the amount of any gift tax paid on gifts given more than three years before death from the gross estate and thus the death and GST tax. Unlike the estate tax, the gift tax is calculated on a tax-exclusive basis.

Of course one must weigh the possible benefit (i.e., that gift taxes are a deduction from the transfer tax base) with the fact that if the donor lives to 2010, the estate tax may be gone. Indeed, after 2006 there is nothing to be gained in making large gifts merely to remove the gift tax from the tax base because the § 2035(b) three-year rule brings those taxes back into the gross estate.

Post-gift appreciation. The third tax advantage of gifting is the ability to exclude post-gift appreciation of the gifted property from future estate tax and GST tax. Gifts accomplish this tax saving in two different ways. First, gifting will freeze estate tax values by limiting the estate tax value of the transferred asset to its adjusted gift value. Second, gifting can leverage the use of exclusions and exemptions because post-gift appreciation also escapes transfer taxes. The following example illustrates the usefulness of freezing and leveraging techniques.

> EXAMPLE 13 - 4. In 2003, Eighty-two-year-old Jeanne's estate consists of $2 million in municipal bonds and $1 million in common stock. Able to live well on the bond income, Jeanne gifts the stock to an irrevocable trust that pays the income to her three children for their lives with the remainder going to her grandchildren. Jeanne allocates her $1 million GST exemption to this transfer. In this simple but effective estate freeze, Jeanne has virtually ensured that she will die with an estate tax base at about $3 million (assets owned at death plus adjusted taxable gifts), no matter how much the values of the stocks rise. And Jeanne has leveraged the use of her $1 million GST exemption. For example, if the stock is eventually worth $4 million when it passes to the grandchildren, each $1 in current GST exemption will have sheltered $4 from GST tax. Of course if it passes to the grandchildren after 2009 it should pass GST tax free anyway.

For the next several years, the very wealthy have an interesting choice, a tradeoff between GST tax and basis step-up. In 2004, by making gifts, a donor will be able to shelter $1.5 million from the GST tax but only $1 million from gift taxes (the exclusion-exemption gap). If one creates a GST tax trust, whether by gift or at death, and shelters it by application of the exemption, future transfer estate taxes might be saved on terminations or distributions to skip persons that occur before 2010. After that time the allocation of the exemption confers no benefit because the estate and GST tax cease. By making that choice, the donor loses the opportunity to allocate any of the $1.3 million basis step-up available for post-2009 estates because the trust assets will be excluded from their estate.

Income tax advantages. The making of gifts offers some income tax advantages, including the shifting of income.

Shifting income. Gifts can result in some income shifting. Because the donee (or trust, for gifts into an irrevocable trust) becomes the owner of gifted property, any income earned on that property will be taxed to the donee (or trustee or trust beneficiary), who is usually subject to a lower marginal income tax rate. Further, the reduced taxable income to the donor might put her or him in a lower tax bracket. In contrast, a trust's lowest tax bracket ends at taxable income of less than $2,000, reflecting Congress's strong interest in discouraging the use of trusts to shift income. Rather than making annual gifts to a relative to help with living expenses, it might be wise to transfer income producing assets, especially if the property is likely to return to the donor when the donee dies.

> EXAMPLE 13 - 5. Each year, Aaron and his wife, Sue, made gifts of approximately $20,000 to Aaron's mother, Cynthia, to supplement her meager Social Security income. Since they were in a combined state and federal income tax bracket of 46%, they decided to transfer $300,000 in assets to Cynthia, with the understanding that at her death she would leave the property to them. If the property produces $20,000 in taxable income, the income tax saved by the extended family is $6,200 ($20,000 * (46%-15%)) per year. Of course the transfer was a taxable gift, but with the pending repeal of the estate tax, they are less concerned about using it. Cynthia's estate is not large enough to generate an estate tax.

Outright gifts to children while they are under age 14 will not save much income tax due to what is called the kiddie tax that causes most of the child's unearned income to be taxed at the parents' highest marginal rate.

Obtaining a step-up in basis. The capital gains tax basis of any property owned by a decedent at death is stepped-up to date-of-death value. EGTRRA has done little to change this for most estates. This step-up is particularly valuable for people wishing to sell appreciated property. Unfortunately, the property owner must die to accomplish the basis step-up. Can the owner of a low basis asset give the asset to a dying relative, have the property left back to the donor and thereby achieve a stepped-up basis? Recalling from our earlier discussion of the rubber-band rule, the answer is maybe. If the donee dies within one year of receiving the property, it goes back to the donor with a carry-over basis. EGTRRA creates a new rule for post 2009 transfers eliminating the basis increase for property acquired by gift within three years of death. Unlike the rubber-band rule that only applies if the property returns to the donor, this new rule applies even if the property goes to someone other than the donor. The exception to this three-year rule is if the gift came from the decedent's spouse and the spouse did not acquire the property by gift. This will allow the possibility of transferring appreciated property to a dying spouse and getting it back with an increased basis.

Tax Disadvantages of Gifting

There are several tax dangers and disadvantages in making lifetime gifts, including prepaying the transfer tax, adverse § 2035 consequences, the danger that the gift is later ruled incomplete, and loss of the step-up in basis.

Prepaying the transfer tax. A large gift can result in a gift tax liability that must be paid by April 15 of the following year, thereby reducing the donor's available funds for investment. Nonetheless, prepayment of the transfer tax is justifiable if it has the effect of substantially reducing the donor's estate tax. This will happen if the gift property appreciates greatly before the donor's death or if it appreciates modestly and the donor can avoid grossing up by surviving at least three years after making the gift. On the other hand, gifting property and prepaying the transfer tax may have little benefit if the property declines in value and/or the donor dies within three years of making the gift, and/or if the donor lives beyond 2009 and repeal of the estate tax holds. Then, transfer taxes will have been paid that would have been avoided if the property had been kept. The donee probably has a lower basis in the property than had it been included in the donor's estate. Thus, to assess the likelihood of financial benefits resulting from a large gift, the planner should consider factors such as the life expectancy of the donor, the expected appreciation potential of the property, the different basis rules, the potential time of death relative to tax rule changes, and the utility of the property to the donor and donee.

An additional adverse IRC § 2035 consequence: unsheltered post-gift appreciation. We mentioned in the preceding discussion that if a gift is made within three years of death, § 2035(b) requires the gift tax paid to be included in the donor's gross estate under the "gross-up" rule. In addition to this adverse consequence, recall from the discussion of the retained interest rules that the entire date-of-death value of the gift property is included in the donor's gross estate if §§ 2036, 2037, or 2038 apply, or if an incident of ownership in life insurance was retained (§ 2042) at the date of death. Section 2035(a) causes inclusion if the decedent transferred (released) a retained interest or an incident of ownership in life insurance within three years of death.

In summary, if the transfers are within three years, the death occurs before 2009, and § 2035(a) and § 2035(b) apply, all advantages of gifting are lost, even the benefit of the annual exclusion. If this occurs, the only positive thing is that appreciated property will receive a step-up in basis.

Gift later ruled incomplete. If it is later determined that a gift was not complete, the date-of-death value of the property is included in the donor's gross estate even if the donor reported it as a gift. The estate will receive a credit for the gift taxes paid, but from a transfer tax perspective the gift will be considered as not having been made.

EXAMPLE 13 - 6. Carmen transferred title to her house to her sons, but continued to live in the house rent free. Her sons had their own homes. It should not be too difficult to establish that there was an understanding that she retained the right to live there. This would cause the value of the house to be included in her estate.[1]

EXAMPLE 13 - 7. Dan created an irrevocable trust, giving the trustee discretion to determine how much income to distribute each year to Dan's children. Dan also reserved the right to replace the trustee. Because the terms of the trust were silent as to whether Dan could replace the trustee with himself, it is likely that he has a retained interest.[2]

EXAMPLE 13 - 8. On her deathbed, decedent made a gift by writing a check on her bank account. She died before the check was cashed. Because she had the power to revoke by stopping payment, the gift was considered to be incomplete and the money was included in her gross estate.[3]

Loss of step-up in basis. A major tax disadvantage of making lifetime gifts is the loss in the step-up in basis that would have been received on appreciated property had it been retained by the donor until death. This is a drawback for a donee who wishes to sell the appreciated property. On the other hand, if the donee has no plans to sell the property during his or her lifetime or intends to trade the asset in a tax-deferred exchange, the disadvantage may be inconsequential.

EXAMPLE 13 - 9. Granny has always wanted to do something nice for her adult grandson. She gives him some real property that she acquired in the 1920's. When Granny dies, the gift property will not receive a step-up in basis, and the grandson may own an asset with a sizable unrealized gain to be recognized if he sells it. However, this potential taxable gain will vanish if the grandson dies still owning the property.

Other disadvantages. Two other tax disadvantages to consider are noted briefly.

Net gifts. Very rarely, a taxable gain for the donor results when a net gift arrangement is used. This is where the donee agrees to pay the gift tax thus reducing the value of the gift, which in turn reduces the gift tax. A net gift results in a taxable gain to the donor only if the gift tax paid by the donee exceeds the donor's basis in the property. Several factors combine to make your chance of coming in contact with a net gift that produces a capital gain about as high as being struck by lightning on a sunny day (except in Texas or Florida). These factors include the increased size of the AEA, the reluctance of even the wealthy to make taxable gifts so large as to require the actual payment of gift tax, and the pending elimination of the estate tax.

Estate and gift tax statute of limitations. The statute of limitations for both estate tax returns and for gift tax returns is three years from the due date of the return if the return is timely filed. If it is filed late, then it is three years from the time it is filed.[4] There are exceptions to the three-year rule. If the return under-reports the value of the gross estate or the total gifts by more than 25%, the statute of limitations is increased to six years after the return is filed. There is no time limit if the return is not filed or if one is filed with the intent to commit fraud or to willfully evade taxes.[5]

TYPES OF ASSETS TO GIVE

In giving, the donor usually has a wide selection of assets from which to choose. From an estate planning perspective, some assets make better gifts than others. The following constitutes a basic set of guidelines for selecting gift property. As the examples will illustrate, the choice of the best asset will usually depend on the specific family situation.

Basis Considerations

A person who has decided to make gifts for estate planning reasons will want to consider the basis of various assets since the basis will partially determine whether a particular asset is a good candidate to select as a gift. Other factors enter into the decision, such as whether the donee will sell the asset to raise his or her income level and whether the donor will sell assets he or she has kept in order to make up for income lost as a result of giving away an income producing asset.

Gifting high-basis assets to reduce taxable gain. Other things being equal, a high-basis asset makes a better gift than a low-basis asset, if the donee is likely to sell the asset soon after receiving it. As we have seen, the general rule is that the donee retains the donor's basis. A sale by the donee at a price above this basis results in a taxable gain. The higher the basis, the lower the taxable gain.

EXAMPLE 13 - 10. Donor wishes to give donee $100,000 in marketable securities. Donor owns stock A, now worth $100,000, which she purchased two years ago for $95,000, and stock B, also worth $100,000, which was acquired 15 years ago for $20,000. The donee plans to sell the stock he receives when it reaches $110,000 in value. The donee will realize a gain of only $15,000 on the sale of stock A but a gain of $90,000 on the sale of stock B. Needless to say, the donee would prefer to receive stock A.

Although a high-basis asset usually makes a good gift from an income tax point of view, it will make an unattractive gift if its basis is higher than its date-of-gift value. Property in which the owner has an unrealized loss is not a good asset to give because the donee, on selling it, will not be able to recognize that loss. A better strategy would be for the donor to sell the property, realize the loss, and then give the cash to the donee.

Gifting low-basis assets for other reasons. In some circumstances, giving low-basis assets makes sense. For example, if for liquidity or other reasons a donor plans to sell a retained asset at the time of giving another asset, he or she should consider gifting a lower-basis asset and selling the higher-basis asset in order to personally incur a lower tax outlay. This strategy is especially productive if the donee is in a lower tax bracket or has no immediate plans to sell the property received as a gift. Gain realized on later sale by the donee will at least be deferred and may be totally eliminated, if the donee dies before the asset is sold. Keep in mind the rubber band rule, discussed previously, whereby appreciated property that returns to the donor as a result of the donee's death has a carry-over basis. The adjusted basis to the surviving donor is the same as the donee-decedent's adjusted basis immediately before he or she died. Post-2009, the rubber band rule will be replaced with a carry-over rule for any gift property received within three years of death except for gifts received from a spouse.

Assets having sentimental or utilitarian value are more likely to be kept by a donee. If a gift is going to be kept by the donee, basis considerations are less relevant.

Post-gift Appreciation

General considerations. The person considering gifts should consider growth assets, i.e., assets expected to appreciate substantially, rather than assets whose value is likely to remain stable or fall. Some assets have greater appreciation potential than others. Assets such as life insurance and equity interests in either a closely held business or real estate (in a good location) are likely growth prospects, while assets such as patent and royalty rights, which have values that usually decline over time, often do not make good gift assets. Cash and cash equivalents are also less desirable, because their values do not rise. In general, from a transfer-tax point of view, assets having a combined low gift tax value and potentially high estate tax value make the best gifts.

For the very elderly and/or very ill, for the next several years estate tax reduction might remain a major goal. Of course, if the donor outlives the estate tax, there will be regret that the assets were given away (assuming appreciation really does take place—ah for a crystal ball) as the opportunity to receive a step-up in basis will have been lost

Opportunity shifting. Opportunity shifting is the transfer of a potentially highly appreciating asset before its value is objectively ascertainable. For example, a business person may recognize the potential of a profitable commercial enterprise before it blossoms into a verifiably valuable opportunity. By transferring ownership during a venture's early stages, a donor can shift value to a donee with minimal transfer tax cost and before the income the venture generates is attributable to the donor.

> EXAMPLE 13 - 11. Dad, the owner of a successful computer component firm, has just established a new corporation to pursue the viability of a recently developed engineering idea. The new firm is capitalized at $50,000, and Dad gives an adult daughter 20% of the stock and places another 20% in an irrevocable trust for the benefit of his minor son.

This example demonstrates the creation of additional taxpaying entities, the new corporation and the trust, as well as splitting income and wealth among more family members before the value of the enterprise has manifested itself. Similar techniques can be arranged for almost any asset that is expected to appreciate in value. Good hunches by knowledgeable people are the major sources of intra-family opportunity shifting.

Administration Problems

Assets that are likely to create problems in estate administration may make good gifts. For example, art works, especially those currently worth less than the annual gift tax exclusion, may not need to be valued if transferred by lifetime gift. They could create valuation disputes, a potentially higher estate tax, and additional costs of valuation if transferred at death. A business included in the decedent's estate may cause a conflict between the executor (charged with safeguarding assets) and the heirs, especially if some heirs are running the business and others are not. If some heirs take hard-to-value assets, e.g., a business, as their part of the estate, they may be in conflict with others who take assets with a readily ascertained value, e.g., stock traded on an exchange or cash. The heirs taking the hard-to-value assets may argue for a lower value than the others will agree to.

Other Asset Choice Considerations

Transfer income earning assets to shift income. Where income shifting is a planning goal, high income earning assets make better gifts. Income tax law in general requires an actual transfer of the "tree" (asset) in order to transfer the "fruit" (income) of that tree.

Avoid gifting assets with tax benefits to donor. The high-income donor should ordinarily consider gifting assets that do not have built-in tax benefits such as income exclusions, deductions, or credits which would be of less value to a lower bracket donee. The person should consider retaining assets such as tax shelters, municipal bonds, and income-producing real property in his or her own portfolio. However, when a tax-shelter property reaches the "crossover point" and begins to throw off "phantom income" to the investor, it may be a good time to gift the property, thereby shifting the income to a lower bracket taxpayer.

Gifts to qualify for IRC benefits. Some provisions of the IRC give advantages to business owners whose businesses are more than a certain percentage of their estates. Giving nonbusiness property may increase the percentage of the estate considered business property to gain these advantages. These provisions allow the following tax saving opportunities:

1. **§ 303** - This section allows the estate to pay death taxes, funeral bills, and administrative expenses, with cash from a closely held corporation provided the corporation stock is valued at 35% or more of the decedent's adjusted gross estate (AGE). The corporation can buy back stock from the decedent's estate with the transaction being treated as a capital transaction instead of a dividend distribution. Since the stock held by the estate will have received a step-up in basis due to the owner's death, there should be very little, if any, capital gain.[6]

2. **§ 2032A** - This section allows the real estate used in a closely held business to be reduced by up to $750,000 based on its special use valuation. The decedent's special use real estate must equal or exceed 25% of the decedent's AGE and the real estate combined with the rest of the special use business must equal or exceed 50% of the AGE.[7]

3. **§ 2057** - The family-owned business interest deduction, discussed in detail elsewhere, is available only if the business represents 50% or more of the decedent's AGE.[8] This deduction is slated to end after 2003.

4. **§ 6166** - This section allows estate tax payment over 14 years (with a favorable late payment interest charge on the deferred tax) provided the business is equal to or greater than 35% of AGE.[9]

For individuals with business interests that do not meet the percentage requirements, gifts of nonbusiness assets will increase the business percentage. However, IRC § 2035(c)(1) requires that the percentage requirements for § 303 and § 2032A be met with any transfers within three years added back into the gross estate. Section 2035(c)(2) also requires that the § 6166 threshold of 35% for the business interest be met both with and without adding back into the gross estate any gifts made within three years of decedent's death. Note that this "adding back" is done to determine whether the estate still meets the percentage thresholds; it does not mean that the gifts are actually added into the gross estate for tax purposes.

EXAMPLE 13 - 12. Farmer Brown had the following assets immediately before and after he gave away his XYZ stock to his three children:

Items	FMV pre-gift	2032A %	FMV post-gift	2032A %
Stock	$1,500,000		given away	
Other Property	$1,100,000		$1,100,000	
Farmland	$1,400,000	32.6%	$1,400,000	50.0%
Farm Equipment	$300,000	7.0%	$300,000	10.7%
Total Farm	**$1,700,000**	**39.5%**	**$1,700,000**	**60.7%**
Total	$4,300,000		$2,800,000	

To qualify for § 2032A, the business land must equal 25% or more of AGE, and the land and other business property (tractors, etc.) must equal 50% or more of AGE. The gift accomplishes this, provided the thresholds are still met when he dies.

EXAMPLE 13 - 13. Farmer Brown dies after making the gift of stock. The stock has increased in value to $1,600,000 and the other items (still owned by him when he died) have the values shown in the table:

Items	FMV @ Death less than 3 Yrs.	2032A %	FMV @ Death more than 3 Yrs.	2032A %
Stock	$1,600,000		given away	
Other Property	$1,300,000		$1,300,000	
Farmland	$1,480,000	32.0%	$1,480,000	48.8%
Farm Equipment	$250,000	5.4%	$250,000	8.3%
Total Farm	**$1,730,000**	**37.4%**	**$1,730,000**	**57.1%**
Total	$4,630,000		$3,030,000	

If his death was just short of three years, the land percentage is met (i.e, 32% > 25%), but the total special use business percentage is not met (i.e., 37.4% < 50%). Thus, special use is not available. If his death is just beyond the three-year reach of § 2035(c)(1), then the gift is not added back to determine § 2032A, and the two § 2032A percentage limits are exceeded (i.e., 48.8% > 25% and 57.1% > 50%).

Notice that the 35% threshold for § 6166 (drawn-out payment schedule) is met both with and without the gift. Therefore the § 6166 election is available regardless of whether the death was just under or just over three years after the gift. One final comment: even if farmer Brown died within three years of the gift, the stock's appreciation is NOT being taxed, nor is the annual exclusion lost. The gift of the stock is still an adjusted taxable gift of $1,470,000 (three kids, three annual exclusions). It is not part of the gross estate. It is brought back merely to test whether the elections (§§ 303, 2032A, and 6166) are available.

Miscellaneous tax factors. Some assets should not be gifted if they may generate adverse tax consequences. For example, consider an asset for which the donor had taken the investment tax credit, which was repealed by TRA 86. If the donor gifts the asset before the end of its useful life, he or she will be required to "recapture" part of the credit by repaying part of the taxes saved from the credit.

In at least one situation, gifts to children can generate a tax benefit otherwise unavailable to the parents.

EXAMPLE 13 - 14. Because of their high income, the Piatts are not qualified to contribute before-tax dollars to an Individual Retirement Account (IRA). Their adult son, John, is qualified, but he cannot afford to make the contributions. John enters into an informal agreement with his parents, who will give him $1,500 a year, to help contribute $2,000 to his own IRA. This annual arrangement is to continue indefinitely, so long as John adds $500 and does not make any premature withdrawals. Each year, John will save hundreds of dollars in income tax by taking the IRA deduction. The Piatts have the satisfaction of knowing that they have increased his financial security.

As a result of the kiddie tax, generous parents may wish to transfer to their young children property that does not generate taxable income, at least not until the children reach age 14. Possible assets include U.S. government EE bonds, municipal bonds, interests in land, a closely held business, and growth stocks. In many situations, the parent can then determine the timing of the tax "hit" by choosing which year to liquidate the assets and realize the likely gain. It should be mentioned that the popular U.S. Government EE savings bonds are not transferable. An outright gift of them is considered a redemption. However, there is no restriction on an owner adding co-owners.

GIFTS TO ONE'S SPOUSE: TECHNIQUES AND CONSIDERATIONS

Inter-spousal Gifts to Reduce Death Taxes

In other chapters, we examined in some detail several marital deduction techniques designed to minimize, or at least postpone, the estate tax for a married couple. Where one spouse is much wealthier than the other and the less wealthy spouse dies first, estate taxes might be saved by means of bypass planning coupled with a program of inter-spousal gifts. The goal, if both deaths are likely before estate repeal is complete, is to make sure two AEAs are used instead of just one.

EGTRRA's Impact. EGTRRA creates the risk of adverse effects with this technique. If even one spouse lives beyond 2009, then the use of a bypass trust at the first death produces no estate tax benefit at the second death, but has the negative effect of precluding basis step-up because it is not included in the estate. Indeed, QTIP trusts, regardless of whether an election was made, will not be included in the survivor's estate after 2009 because the law states, in regard to trust property, "The decedent shall be treated as owning property transferred by the decedent during life to a qualified revocable trust . . . " The QTIP trust fails to meet the criterion on two counts, it is not created by the surviving spouse and it is not revocable.

Where both spouses are still living in 2009, it is likely that their ABC Trust plans will be amended to give the surviving spouse a springing general power over trust C that is triggered by the surviving spouse living beyond 2009. If there are no children by prior marriages, it might make sense to have Trusts B and C pourover to Trust A as of midnight December 31, 2009. Drafting should also address the very real risk that Congress may not allow the repeal to take place, instead substituting a high AEA. Less likely, but still a risk is that Congress could allow the sunset provision to actually take place.

Drawbacks. Even if both deaths are likely to happen before 2010, the wealthier spouse may have some reservations about making a sizable gift to his or her spouse.

Relinquishment of control. First, for the transfer to be complete, the donor spouse must be willing to surrender complete dominion and control to his or her spouse. Planners should consider the possibility of future marital strife and its effect on the overall plan. The donor might regret that the gift was ever made. Further, even if the spouses are happily married, the wealthier spouse may still be reluctant to relinquish control over so much wealth. As a possible solution, the donor spouse can create a lifetime-funded QTIP trust, hence the donor spouse controls who will eventually receive the corpus. There could even be a provision that if the donee spouse dies first, the trust property reverts to the donor spouse. With that provision, if the estate tax is still around when the beneficiary of the QTIP trust dies, the donor spouse could disclaim an amount equal to the deceased spouse's AEA (thus utilizing her unified credit). If she dies after 2009 (and the estate tax is really gone), the surviving spouse can accept the reversion of the property without negative consequences.

Inter-spousal Gifts to Reduce Income Taxes

Ordinarily, there is no lifetime income tax advantage to inter-spousal gifts. As we have seen, the joint income tax return, filed by the overwhelming majority of spouses, has the effect of combining spousal income and produces one tax, no matter which spouse earned the income. However, a completed gift from one spouse to the other can save income taxes if the donee spouse dies first, and the donor later sells it at a gain. The tax-saving results from the opportunity to experience a step-up in basis before sale and was illustrated earlier. Of course one must avoid §1014(e)'s rubber band rule providing that if one gives appreciated property and the donee bequeaths it back within one year, there is no step-up in basis.

EXAMPLE 13 - 15. Bob gave his wife stock that he had bought for $6,000. It was worth $50,000 when he gave it to her. She died seven months later, leaving the stock, then worth $55,000, to Bob. He was unable to obtain a step-up in basis due to the restriction in Code Section 1014(e). However, had his wife lived longer than one year, Bob's basis would have been $55,000 (assuming that as the date-of-death value), because of the resulting step-up in basis.

EXAMPLE 13 - 16. In the prior example, had Bob's wife bequeathed the property to her bypass trust for Bob's benefit, § 1014(e) would not apply because the property would pass to a different party (the trustee) and not back to the donor-spouse. Thus, a step-up would have been available even if the donee spouse had not lived one year after the gift had been made.

Couples using gift strategies, such as those in the examples will save estate tax and income tax. In community property states, of course, since the surviving spouse receives a step-up in basis at S1's death for all community property owned, this gifting strategy need only be considered for separate property.

GIFTS TO MINORS: TECHNIQUES AND CONSIDERATIONS

Gifts to minor children are unique because of the manner by which their transfer is usually arranged. Gifts of significant value are usually not made outright to minors but through a fiduciary in a custodianship or a trust.

Outright gifts transfer the greatest amount of control to the donee, invite the least amount of challenge from the IRS, and are the least complicated to make. But an outright gift to a person, whether a minor or an adult, will only work satisfactorily when the donee has sufficient maturity to rationally possess, conserve, and enjoy the gift property. In other circumstances, the transfer should be made to a fiduciary. Many states have statutes that require gifts, above some set value, given to a minor be held for the minor by a fiduciary. The transfer to a fiduciary should be arranged to achieve the same tax advantages (use of the annual exclusion and shifting of income) as are available with an outright gift. It should protect the donee from the risks of his or her own immaturity and comply with any restrictions that state law places on the ownership and use of property by minors.

Before examining types of fiduciary gifts that meet these objectives, recall that if income from a gift is used to discharge the obligation of support of the donor-parent, that income will be taxable to the parent.[10]

> EXAMPLE 13 - 17. Dad gives 14-year-old Junior $500 so that Junior can purchase lunches during his freshman year in high school. Junior deposits the money in his own savings account, subsequently withdrawing interest as well as principal to buy the lunches. The interest income will be taxable to Dad as income used in discharge of a support obligation.

This rule applies even if the source of the income is not from the parents, e.g., income from a trust established by the beneficiary's grandparents.

Thus, in order to enjoy the full tax advantages of a completed gift to a minor, income from the gift must not be used to discharge support obligations. Ordinarily, parents are not obligated to support their adult children, so the issue does not usually apply to adult donees. However, there are exceptions. In some states, including Illinois and New Jersey, judges in divorce cases have imposed the duty of support for higher education for adult children. However, several factors limit the application of this exception. In 1992, Pennsylvania's Supreme Court ruled that divorcing parents will no longer be so obligated, reasoning that children become adults at age 18 and that the state's legislature had not explicitly addressed the issue. No court has required parents in an intact family to pay for an adult child's higher education.[11]

Custodial Gifts

Uniform Gifts to Minors Act. The Uniform Gifts to Minors Act (UGMA), adopted in one form or other in all states, allows a relatively simple method of making fiduciary gifts to minors. No court supervision is required. The gift property is transferred in the name of someone, acting "as custodian for (minor's name) under the (state name) Uniform Gift to Minors Act." This title serves to "incorporate by reference" all of the provisions of that act, including broad investment powers under the "prudent person" standard, and the ability of the custodian to spend property on behalf of the minor without a court order. Further, a bond need not be given and, unless the donor or donee requests them, accountings are not necessary.

Permissible gift property under UGMA includes securities, cash, life insurance, and annuities, but there is legislative movement by several states to greatly expand this list. In most UGMA states, real property cannot be held in custodial form.

Uniform Transfers to Minors Act. In 1983 the National Conference on Uniform Laws adopted the Uniform Transfers to Minors Act (UTMA), designed to replace the UGMA. Major changes include the following:

1. It allows any property interests to be transferred, including real estate, partnership interests, patents, royalty interests, and intellectual property.
2. It allows custodial gifts at death by permitting a fiduciary (executor or trustee) to establish a custodianship if authorized in a governing will or trust.
3. It authorizes transfers to a custodian from persons other than the transferor who are obligated to the minor (examples of situations include a personal injury recovery, life insurance proceeds payable to a minor beneficiary, and a joint bank account of which the minor is a surviving cotenant).
4. It allows a transferor to revocably nominate a custodian to receive property in the future.

As of 2001, all states but South Carolina have adopted UTMA and most have done so without significant alterations. UTMA, like the UGMA before it, as a default position has distribution to the minor at age 21. States can modify that to the age of majority (i.e., age 18) or some other age. California uses 21 as the default age but allows a donor to specify an older age (up to a maximum age of 25).[12]

Evaluation of custodial gifts. A custodial gift can avoid the time and expense involved in establishing a trust. It is considered a completed gift that qualifies for the annual exclusion. Although a custodianship is like a trust in many ways, it is more restrictive for the following reasons:

- A custodial gift may be created for only one person; a trust can provide for multiple beneficiaries, with unequal distributions among them.
- A custodianship is not a separate legal entity; all income is taxable to the minor. In contrast, an irrevocable trust is a separate taxpayer, enabling one additional "run up the rate ladder."
- Because the law gives the custodian the power to distribute income or principal to the minor, if the donor serves as the custodian and predeceases the minor, §§ 2036 and 2038 bring the custodial property into the custodian's gross estate. This is not a problem if someone other than the donor serves as custodian or as trustee.
- Donees usually must receive custodial property outright by age 21; trust beneficiaries' distributions of principal may be delayed to a later age.
- Finally, a custodianship does not have spendthrift provisions.

UTMA provides that custodial property may not be used to satisfy any obligation of support for the minor, such as an obligation stemming from a divorce decree. Thus, custodial gifts if properly structured can achieve essentially all of the tax advantages of completed outright transfers.

Gifts to Trusts That Benefit Minors

Although custodial gifts are usually an improvement over substantial outright gifts to minors, there are serious drawbacks including some mentioned above. They usually terminate at or shortly after the donee's age of majority, at which time the donee enjoys fee simple ownership of the property. They may restrict the type of property that may be given under the laws of some states. They are also inflexible in that the controlling state law usually cannot be modified by private document. The presence of these and other drawbacks lead many donors to use irrevocable trusts for gifts to minors.

In structuring gifts in trust for the benefit of minors, planners usually seek to obtain all of the tax benefits available to outright gifts. The four major tax objectives are:

1. Using the annual gift tax exclusion and the unified credit to avoid gift taxes,
2. Excluding the gift from the donor's gross estate,
3. Excluding all post-gift appreciation in the value of the gift property from the donor's estate tax base, and
4. Shifting the taxable income earned on the gift property to the trust or to the donee.

The irrevocable trust may also have the non-tax advantage of insulating the gift property from the parents' creditors and, in some cases, from the child's creditors.

Drafting an irrevocable trust takes great care because the nature of such transfers seems to invite scrutiny by the IRS. For example, the donor may wish to act as trustee and to restrict the minor child's enjoyment of the trust principal and income for some period of time. These requirements reflect the donor's desire to retain a considerable degree of control over the gift property. The problem is that a very fine line exists between harmless controls and controls that the IRS deems to be retained interests by the donor.

Qualifying for the annual exclusion. To qualify for the annual exclusion, the donee must be given a present interest, an unrestricted right to the immediate use, possession, or enjoyment of the property or the income from the property. There are methods of obtaining the annual exclusion without really giving a minor control of the property transferred in trust. These exceptions to the present interest requirement are IRC § 2503(c), and two planning devices sanctioned by the courts, even if not loved by the IRS. The three alternatives are called the 2503(c) Trust, the Crummey Trust, and the Mandatory Income Trust.

2503(c) Trust: Under § 2503(c), a gift in trust is not considered a gift of a future interest (even though it really is one) if three conditions are met.

First, the trust must provide that the property and income may be expended by or for the benefit of the donee before the donee attains age 21.[13] This requirement creates the same potential retained interest problem (§§ 2036-2038) for grantors wishing to be trustees as it does for custodial gifts. Second, any portion of the property not so expended must pass to the donee at age 21. Third, if the donee dies before age 21, the property must be either payable to the donee's estate or the donee must hold a general power of appointment over the property.

This is met even if the general power is exercisable only through the donee's will, and the trust contains a clause making siblings the takers by default. In most states, a minor is not legally competent to execute a will, so in the event of the death of the minor, the trust property would most likely go to his or her siblings.

The 2503(c) exception was created to allow parents to make gifts that take advantage of the annual exclusion without giving their young children actual control of the property given. The § 2503(c) trustee need not distribute the corpus when the beneficiary reaches age 21, as long as the beneficiary can request complete distribution at age 21 and the beneficiary is so informed.[14]

The Crummey Trusts and lapsing withdrawal powers. Crummey is the name of a taxpayer who succeeded in federal court in getting an annual exclusion by establishing a trust containing withdrawal rights for the benefit of minor children.[15] The typical Crummey Trust clause provides that the child has the right to withdraw, for a brief period (30 to 90 days) as set in the trust document, after each transfer of property into the trust, the lesser of the amount of the available annual exclusion or the value of the gift property transferred. Since the child has the right to withdraw that amount, the gift is considered a gift of a present interest satisfying the § 2503(b) present interest requirement and the donor receives an annual exclusion for the gift. To be effective, the child must be given actual notice of the withdrawal right.

Use of a Crummey power can result in undesired gift tax and income tax consequences. A beneficiary's failure to exercise a Crummey power in a given year may mean that the beneficiary has made a taxable gift by permitting a general power of appointment to lapse.[16]

The taxable gift value will be very small since only the amount that goes to someone other than the person who let the withdrawal right lapse is considered a gift, and even that must be discounted since it is a future interest. Furthermore, if the person who let the withdrawal right lapse eventually receives the corpus of the trust, the gift will not be an adjusted taxable gift since the transfer (a contingent remainder) has reverted to the beneficiary.[17] The latter situation is the usual case, since the beneficiary with the withdrawal right is usually also the remainderman, especially for minors' trusts.

Given the extremely small gift tax value and the likelihood that the transfer would not enter into the estate tax calculation most planners ignore this tax consequence. Some avoid the problem by limiting the annual withdrawal right to the lesser of the annual exclusion or the 5 and 5 limits, i.e., the greater of

$5,000 or 5%, or by giving the beneficiary a general testamentary power of appointment over the trust principal.

The gift tax value would be the amount that the value permitted to lapse exceeded the greater of $5,000 or 5% of the aggregate value of the property from which the exercise of the power could be satisfied. For example, suppose $120,000 was contributed as an initial gift in trust, with a child of the trustors having a $20,000 demand right that lapses 90 days after each addition. When the demand right lapses unexercised, the amount that $20,000 exceeds the greater of $5,000 or 5% of $120,000 (i.e., $14,000) is treated as a future interest gift to the remaindermen. As a gift of a future interest, it will not qualify for the annual exclusion.

Mandatory Income Trust (MIT). A trust that requires mandatory distribution of income annually to the minor, either outright or to the minor's custodial account, as the way of entitling the donor to the annual exclusion is called a mandatory income trust. The gift is considered as comprising two parts, the income interest and the remainder or reversion interest. Tax law considers the former to be a present interest qualifying for the annual exclusion and the latter to be a future interest that does not so qualify. The alternative fractions making up the gift are derived from Tables S or B, depending on the nature of the income interest.

> EXAMPLE 13 - 18. Gerry transferred $100,000 into an irrevocable trust established for his friend, Betty, giving her income for life with the corpus to revert to Gerry, or to his issue, after Betty's death. Betty just turned 85 years old and the rate for valuing split interest gifts was 8%. Therefore, the factor would be 0.34614. This means that $34,614 represents the value of the income interest qualifying for the annual exclusion. Since the present value exceeds $10,000 the full annual exclusion is allowed. *** *Query - 1. At what age would the annual exclusion drop below $10,000 for the gift to Betty?*

Because IRC § 2503(b) requires the donee to have a present interest in order for a gift to qualify for the annual exclusion, and because this trust makes use of the present interest value of the income stream to satisfy that requirement, it is called a § 2503(b) Trust by some estate planners. This is an unfortunate choice of terms since many other trusts qualify for the annual exclusion by creating a present interest, e.g., Crummey trusts, wherein the demand right satisfies that requirement. We will use MIT instead of § 2503(b), but be aware that the latter is still in common use.

Comparison of the three minors' trusts. MITs and § 2503(c) Trusts have become less attractive since the Crummey decision. Prior to Crummey, planners had to choose between an arrangement requiring annual distribution of all trust income to the minor [satisfying IRC § 2503(b)] or one effectively requiring distribution of the entire trust corpus at age 21 [satisfying IRC § 2503(c)]. Although some planners favored the MIT for larger gifts, the choice was not enthusiastic, partly because the value of the income interest qualifying for the annual exclusion had to be discounted. The Crummey provision solved this dilemma by enabling the donor to give the child the right to demand a modest amount from the trust annually, without handing income or principal over at age 21. Usually the child understands that there is much to lose by exercising the demand right. The parent might simply refuse to make any more gifts into the trust or withhold a greater inheritance later because of the child's demonstrated immaturity. However, the IRS takes the position that the child's power of withdrawal cannot be illusory, as it would be if there was an "understanding" or "agreement" not to exercise it.[18]

Income taxation has recently become a more important factor in choosing a minor's trust. The short tax rate "ladder" for trusts (e.g., in 2003 a trust or an estate hits the 38.6% marginal rate at taxable income above $9,350) encourages people to seek to avoid trust taxation of income. A newly created Crummey-type trust may be able to avoid taxation at the trust level by giving the Crummey power holder a general power of appointment over trust income as it is earned, causing it to be taxed to the holder even if the income is not withdrawn.

A ninth Circuit Court decision, the *Cristofani*[19] case, made Crummey powers even more attractive by sanctioning annual exclusions for the trustor's grandchildren who were given a 15- day $10,000 demand right. The significance was that the grandchildren were only contingent beneficiaries of the trust principal because they stood to receive principal distributions only if their parents predeceased the termination of the trust. In *Cristofani*, the IRS unsuccessfully argued that it was so unlikely that the grandchildren would receive the principal, there was "no imaginable reason" why the grandchildren would not exercise their withdrawal rights unless there was, in fact, a prior understanding that they would not do so. Hence, it was argued that they really had no present interests in the transfers. The court rejected this implied agreement argument, ruling that the test of a Crummey power is the legal right of the beneficiary to demand the property, not the likelihood of actually receiving the property. The IRS may continue to litigate the court's broad interpretation of *Crummey* in situations similar to *Cristofani*, but only in cases arising outside the Federal 9th Circuit.

> EXAMPLE 13 - 19.   Christopher resides in the 9th Circuit. He creates an irrevocable trust to last for 10 years. The trust provides for distribution of the remainder to his two children, if surviving. A predeceased child's share shall go to his or her issue. One child has three children and the other has two, for a total of five grandchildren. All seven beneficiaries are given Crummey demand powers. Beginning this year, Christopher can fund the trust annually with $70,000 in property, entirely sheltered by seven annual exclusions even though the trust corpus will most likely go just to the two children.

Estate tax caution.   In designing the irrevocable trust, the estate planner must be mindful of the dangers of letting the donor retain controls that would cause the property to be includible in the donor's gross estate. For example, as mentioned earlier in the chapter, naming the grantor trustee of a § 2503(c) trust will cause estate tax inclusion of the trust assets at the grantor's death unless the trust has already terminated. The underlying Code provisions have been covered elsewhere, specifically, § 2036 transfers with retained life estate, and § 2038 revocable or amendable transfers.

GST tax caveat.   As implied above, Crummey trusts often provide for transfer to the beneficiaries' issue or descendants if the beneficiary fails to survive. As a taxable termination or taxable distribution, such transfers will not be sheltered from the GST tax as annual exclusion gifts because such gifts are not direct skips. Planners recommend avoiding this GST tax consequence either by having the donor allocate a portion of the GST exemption to transfers to the Crummy trust, or by setting up a separate trust for each skip person, with each trust conforming to the requirements under § 2642(c)(2).

Income tax concerns and the kiddie tax.   The donor of a gift in trust for a minor child usually wishes to avoid being taxed on the income received by the trust, preferring instead to let the trust be taxed to the extent the income is accumulated, or to let the child be taxed to the extent that the income is paid to the child. However, the trust must be designed so as not to conflict with the numerous grantor trust rules. For example, reservation by the donor of the right to make withdrawals from the trust will cause the income to be taxed to the donor. This will not apply if the grantor retains a reversion that can only occur on the death of a beneficiary (before age 21) who is a lineal descendant of the grantor and holds all present interests in any portion of the trust.[20]

As mentioned earlier in the text, starting in 1987, all unearned income of children under age 14 in excess of a statutory amount is taxed at the child's parents' marginal rate. This special treatment is referred to as the "kiddie tax" and is applied if either parent is alive at the end of the tax year. This special treatment ends for the tax year in which the child turns 14. The threshold amount was originally $1,000 but, due to indexing, it climbed to $1,500 in 2001 (and has remained at that level at least through 2003, see the Table of Indexed Values in Appendix A.) Of that amount, half is a standard deduction for a taxpayer claimed as a dependent by another (e.g., a child claimed as a dependent by her parents) and the next $750 is taxed at the child's base rate (10% in 2002).[21] No adjustment is made until the Consumer Price Index (CPI) moves the base value up at least $50 (indeed, unless the change lands right on a multiple of $50, the indexed amount is rounded down to the next lower $50).

A separate return can be filed for the child using IRS Form 8615. For convenience, the parent's return may include the income of a child under 14 if the child has only dividend and interest income totaling no more than $7,500 in 2001 (started as an indexed $5,000). "Piggyback" reporting on the parent's return (by attaching Form 8814) has some drawbacks. The child cannot take advantage of certain other deductions, such as charitable donations or the standard deduction for being blind. Also, using the parents' return increases their adjusted gross income, which raises the threshold amount used to determine cutbacks in itemized deductions and personal exemptions.

The source of the child's unearned income is immaterial; excess unearned income is taxed at the parent's rate even though they were not the original source of the property producing that income.

EXAMPLE 7 - 20. In 2002, Dale and Josette's joint taxable income is $60,000, putting them in the 27% marginal rate bracket. Their 12-year-old daughter Lara has $3,500 in unearned income, including $1,550 in dividends from stock received as a gift from Dale's parents, and $1,950 in interest from a bank savings account, the deposits of which originated from earned income (compensation) to Lara when she was a newspaper delivery girl. Dale and Josette elect to report Lara's income on a separate return. Of the first $1,500 of unearned income, $750 will be tax-free, and

$750 will be taxed at 10%. The excess $2,000 (i.e., $3,500 - $1,500) will be taxed at the parents' marginal rate of 27%. Lara's total tax will be $615.

This tax moves the federal government a step closer toward taxing the family as a single economic unit.

EXAMPLE 7 - 21. Continuing the prior examples, if Lara had turned 14 in 2002, her tax would drop to $275, since the first $750 would not be taxed, but the balance of $2,750 would be taxed at her 10% rate. This is a savings of $340 when compared to the kiddie tax result.

Paying for College

Parents who are trying to find ways to pay for their children's college expenses may wish to transfer assets to the children to reduce the income tax bite. This can be done by using a custodial brokerage account. While the child is under age 14, to avoid the kiddie tax they might invest in growth stock that does not pay dividends. Once the child is over 14 years of age they may wish to change to a more balanced approach and might even consider a mutual fund that tracks one of the broader indexes, e.g., Standard and Poor's 500 or the Russell 2000.

In addition, income tax laws may help them to acquire certain investments to finance college expenses without transferring assets and at no tax cost. They should consider qualified U.S. Saving Bonds, Hope Scholarship Credits, Lifetime Learning Credits, Educational IRA's, and Qualified State Tuition Programs. Most of these tax benefits have phase-out provisions that decrease or remove the benefit for high income individuals. For instance, interest on certain U.S. Savings Bonds (e.g., series EE) purchased and owned by one or both parents themselves (or by the student, if at least 24 years old) are not subject to income tax if redeemed to pay tuition and fees. However, this interest exclusion is subject to phase-out based on the taxpayer's "modified adjusted gross income" in the year the bonds are cashed. The phase-out brackets are indexed for inflation. In 2003, the phase-out for single and head of household taxpayers starts at $58,500 and is complete at $73,500, and for joint return filers it starts at $87,750 and ends at $117,750. For this particular purpose the Code defines modified adjusted gross income as adjusted gross income without regard to §§ 911, 931 or 933 (foreign income exclusions), and after application of § 86 (taxable social security income),

§ 219 (retirement contribution deductions), and § 469 (limit on deductibility of passive losses).

QUERY ANSWERED

1. Using the abbreviated table you can calculate that she would have to be between 105 (factor of .11951 * $100,000 = $11,951) and 109 where the value drops to $3,704. With the full table you would find that Betty would have had a present interest of $9,498 at age 107, hence Gerry's taxable gift would then be $90,502 instead of $90,000 (of course the annual exclusion increased to $11,000 in 2002).

QUESTIONS AND PROBLEMS

1. Good planning requires that the prospective donor feel comfortable with a proposed lifetime transfer. How can lifetime transfers be a source of discomfort?

2. One of your friends explains to you that she'd like to make a lifetime transfer to her child, perhaps in the form of a gift. However, she is not clear on how gifts differ from other lifetime transfers such as sales or incomplete gifts. Inform her.

3. Now that your friend is aware of the unique nature of a gift, explain to her the difference between an outright and an incomplete gift. Give an example of each.

4. (a) What is the approximate net worth (1) a single person or (2) a married couple should have before considering gifting amounts of $10,000 or more in order to save estate tax? Explain your answer. (b) What factors other than wealth should be considered? (c) How will EGRRTA change the way the very wealthy think about making gifts? How has the law made it more difficult to plan?

5. In 2002, Carrie, a rich 93-year-old widow, does not expect to live to 2010. Although she has never made taxable gifts before, she wants to begin a program of lifetime gifting. How much she can give to her four children from 2002 through 2009, without paying any gift tax, but completely using her unified credit? Use $10,000 as the annual exclusion. Show how you arrive at the total of these transfers.

6. In terms of estate tax savings, is a gift of $20,000 by an elderly parent to an adult child necessarily twice as valuable as a gift of only $10,000? Why or why not? Discuss in terms of estate reduction and estate freezing.

7. What is meant by "grossing-up" in relation to the estate and gift tax?

8. Zack gave his daughter, Luna, a one-acre plot of desert land valued at $9,000. Subsequently, oil was found making the plot worth $900,000. Assuming no other significant gifts, what is included in Zack's tax base if:
   (a) The gift was made two years before he died? Explain.
   (b) The gift was made four years before he died? Explain.
   (c) The gift was made in 1981? Explain.
   (d) The gift was made in 1976? Explain.

9. What would motivate a very wealthy person to make significant gifts to other family members?

10. Summarize the major tax disadvantages to making gifts, especially ones large enough that gift tax must be paid.

11. "High-basis assets make better gifts." From an income tax point of view, is this statement true, false, or uncertain?

12. What issues should the donor consider in contemplating the following gifts?
    (a) Stock: donor's basis, $60,000; fair market value, $20,000.
    (b) Stock: donor's basis, $20,000; fair market value, $800,000. How is the donor's age a factor?
    (c) Life insurance on the donor's life.
    (d) Rights to a patent.
    (e) Undeveloped land.
    (f) A junk bond.
    (g) A corporate dividend check that the donor endorses over to the donee.

13. (a) Under what circumstances might an interspousal gift save estate tax?
    (b) Under what circumstances might an interspousal gift save income tax?

14. Contrast the advantages and disadvantages of the alternative methods of making gifts to minors.

15. Explain the public policy reason for dispensing with the present interest requirement for trusts that satisfy § 2503(c).

16. Marco is considering a plan to transfer $10,000 per year into an irrevocable trust, whose terms provide that all income will be accumulated until Marco's 15-year-old son, Max reaches age 25. The trust's primary purpose would be to help Max go to college or start a job or buy a house.
    (a) Why won't this arrangement qualify for the annual exclusion?
    (b) Will this arrangement reduce Marco's future estate tax or freeze any part of his estate? Why or why not?
    (c) Suggest three trust arrangements that would qualify for the annual exclusion.
    (d) Which of the three trust arrangements has the least drawbacks? Explain.
    (e) Would a trust save some income tax assuming Marco is in a 38% tax bracket? Make rough estimates and reasonable assumptions to quantify the savings potential.

17. Julia wants to start a college fund for her 8-year-old daughter, Nancy. Her goal is to accumulate approximately $50,000 in 10 years, at which time the funds can be used for college expenses.
    (a) If neither income shifting nor estate tax reduction are important, is a program of gift giving really necessary? Why or why not?
    (b) If your friend wishes to shift income to her daughter or to postpone (maybe even avoid) taxes, recommend strategies for each of the following alternatives: (1) Julia wishes to invest in a way that keeps her in control just in case Nancy does not attend college. She would like this plan to avoid paying tax if the investment is used for college. She is willing to pay tax on the income if Nancy does not go to college. (2) The friend would like an arrangement under which she can continue funding after Nancy's graduation.
    (c) Why is the kiddie tax a concern? What might Julia do to lessen its impact?

ANSWERS TO THE QUESTIONS AND PROBLEMS *(odd numbered only)*

1. Lifetime transfers can be a source of discomfort if the person really does not want to relinquish the degree of control or beneficial interest in the property required to meet an estate planning goal. The donor may also worry that he or she will not have enough for financial security (even if there is no such problem). The donor may worry that the donee will become lazy or invest recklessly.

3. An outright gift ordinarily results in the receipt by the donee of a complete interest (i.e., both legal and beneficial) in the gift property. An incomplete gift is usually made to a fiduciary, which means that any particular beneficiary receives only a beneficial interest. Usually, a beneficial interest is not in fee simple. For example, it may be a future interest, such as a remainder. Or it may be a present interest for a limited time, such as a life estate. As implied above, under most incomplete transfers, beneficiaries have no management rights to the property.

5. In 2002, Carrie could give each child $10,000 covered by the annual exclusion and another $250,000 sheltered by the unified credit. This would be a total of $1,040,000. Because the AEA for gifts, unlike the AEA for estates that increases each year and then disappears, remains at $1 million, for the period 2003-2009 she can give only $10,000 (indexed) each year to each child, i.e., just $40,000 times seven. Thus the total tax-free amount is $1,320,000 [i.e., $1,040,000 + 7 * $40,000].

7. Grossing-up refers to the requirement that gift taxes paid on gifts made within three years of death are brought back into the gross estate. Avoiding grossing-up makes the gross estate lower by the amount of the gift tax paid, thereby saving estate tax.

9. Attributes of individuals most willing to make sizeable gifts: wealthy, older, generous, owning rapidly appreciating assets and an expectation that he or she would not live to 2010.

11. Uncertain. A high basis makes a better gift only if all three assumptions below can be made:

    (a) The basis does not exceed the current value of the gift. Otherwise, the donor should realize the loss him/herself. If the donor does not realize the loss, no one else will.
    (b) The donee is likely to sell the gift asset before his/her death. Or, if it is a depreciable asset, the donee is in a position to use the depreciation deduction.
    (c) The donor, for other reasons, is not left in the position of having to sell another asset with a lower basis.

13. (a) An inter-spousal gift can save estate tax when the wealthier spouse transfers enough property to the poorer spouse, who dies first, so that the bypass share can be fully funded. This will save taxes only if both spouses die before 2010.
    (b) An inter-spousal gift can save income tax when a relatively low-basis asset is transferred to the spouse dying first, who then retransfers it at death to the donor spouse. The donee spouse dies before 2010, she must live at least one year after the gift is made or there is a carryover basis. Since 1014(e) is repealed effective 2010, this might work even if the donee spouse is on her death bed.

15. The public policy reason for the exception under § 2503(c) is to facilitate transfers that will benefit children (and grandchildren) at some later date, such as when they are ready to attend university. Given that there are legitimate reasons for not allowing young people to control the property being given to them for a future purpose, Congress created the exception to the present interest requirement. The only other exception is § 569 dealing with Qualified Tuition Programs whereby accounts to pay for learning expenses can be established and an annual exclusion is allowed even though the child's interest is a future one and, indeed, is not vested.

17. (a) If neither income shifting nor estate reduction are important, Julia need not make any gifts; she could simply accumulate a fund in her own name. Gifting to establish the fund would serve no purpose.

(b) To shift income, Julia will need to make gifts of income-generating property.

    (1) By purchasing U.S. Government EE bonds in joint name with Nancy, Julia might be able to "have her cake and eat it." No taxable gift occurs until the bonds are redeemed. She can elect to defer the tax on the bonds until redemption. If Nancy attends college, she (Nancy) can redeem them and, so long as she uses the money for college-related expenses she will not have to pay income tax on the interest. Nancy's modified adjusted income will certainly be below the level where this benefit phases out. If Nancy chooses not to go to college, Julia can redeem them (and report the interest as income).

    (2) Two possible alternatives to enable the arrangement to continue after graduation are the Crummey trust and the MIT trust. Most planners prefer Crummey, partly because the entire gift amount qualifies for the annual exclusion and partly because income need not be payable or paid in any given year.

(c) All but a portion of the unearned income of children under the age of 14 is taxed at their parents' highest marginal rate. Nancy will be a "kiddie" for several more years. To avoid the kiddie tax, it might be a good strategy to choose investments that do not throw off taxable income. Julia should consider EE bonds, municipal bonds, zero or low dividend-paying growth stocks, etc., at least until the year Nancy turns 14 and the kiddie tax no longer applies.

ENDNOTES

1. IRC § 2036.

2. IRC § 2036.

3. IRC § 2038.

4. IRC § 6501(a).

5. Exceptions to the three-year rule, generally, see IRC § 6501(c), and the 25% under reporting penalty, see § 6501(e).

6. IRC § 303.

7. IRC § 2032A.

8. IRC § 2057.

9. IRC § 6166.

10. IRC § 677(b).

11. Wall Street Journal, November 19, 1992, p. B1.

12. California Probate Code §3920.5.

13. Controls over the expenditures can disallow the annual exclusion. *Illinois National Bank of Springfield v. U.S.* 756 F.Supp. 1117 (1991).

14. LR 8507017.

15. *Crummey v. Commissioner*, 397 F.2d 82 (9 Cir. 1968).

16. IRC § 2514(e).

17. IRC § 2001(b).

18. Rev. Rul. 81-7, 1981-1 CB 474.

19. *Estate of Maria Cristofani* 97 TC 74 (1991).

20. IRC § 673(b).

21. IRC § 63(c)(5) and IRC § 1(g)(7)(B)(i).

CHAPTER 14

Planning Lifetime Transfers

OVERVIEW

Clients may find it hard to accept planning that includes making significant gifts for several reasons. It can reduce wealth and make the donor feel financially insecure. It also means giving up ownership of selected property, a difficult step for many donors. They may also be concerned that transferring wealth, especially to a young person, will destroy initiative.

This chapter explores intrafamily arrangements where some consideration is received for the gift or where the donor retains an interest in the transferred property. The chapter will also cover lifetime charitable transfers, including ones allowing the donor to increase income and receive an income tax deduction.

INTRAFAMILY TRANSFERS FOR CONSIDERATION

Topics covered here have the transferor receiving *consideration*--taking something of economic value for something given up–that may also involve a gift. Sometimes, there may not be a gift that triggers transfer-tax, but one family member helps another by structuring a deal on favorable terms that would not be available elsewhere. This discussion centers on lifetime intrafamily transfers that are complete, not involving trusts or fiduciaries. However, in some cases a transferor may retain a security interest in property transferred.

Intrafamily Loan

A loan between family members is a simple method of transferring assets in exchange for consideration. Often, the financial benefits of an intrafamily loan are worth the financial and emotional risks.

Financial benefits of intrafamily loans. Loans work best when market borrowing rates are high compared to investing rates of return, e.g., if short-term borrowing rates are around 9% and one-year certificates of deposit earn about 3.5%, a one year loan of $10,000 at 6% could save the borrower $300, and net the lender an extra $250. Long-term loans would probably save less per year because rate differentials generally are not nearly as pronounced. However, one of the major advantages of intrafamily home mortgages is the ability to avoid up-front points, application fees, and the long loan processing time typically encountered with commercial lenders. Most importantly, relatives are more willing to make loans to other family members in situations that would cause commercial lenders to pale.

Financial risks of intrafamily loans. Lending within the family may make the loan payments difficult to collect, resulting in family friction if the borrower runs into financial difficulty. The loan should be secured as if it were an arm's length transaction. If the loan is used as a down payment on real estate, the lender should be given a second trust deed. Security documents must be properly filed to ensure the lender's priority over other creditors. Taking these precautions makes it more likely the lender would receive payment if the borrower has to file for bankruptcy. The risk of unexpected taxation is discussed below.

Nonfinancial risk of intrafamily loans. An intrafamily loan may cause jealousies and antagonisms. A child with financial troubles may receive more parental help than siblings. The parents may have made loans not really expecting to collect on them. Indeed, the transactions may have been structured as loans rather than as gifts to save face for the borrower, yet other children may be upset by the failure of the borrower to repay the loans. The arrangement may be seen as punishing those who are financially successful. The grumbling is often heard after the death of the parents as the children deal with dividing up the estate.

Taxation of nongift intrafamily loans. Taxation of intrafamily loans that contain no gift element is relatively straightforward.

Income taxation. Interest paid by the borrower is, of course, taxable income to the lender. Interest is not tax deductible to the borrower unless the loan is secured by a principal or secondary residence, incurred in connection with a trade or business, or related to an investment.[1] If the loan is in default, the lender will not be able to deduct the loss unless a businesslike effort is made to collect it. Furthermore, in the event the loan is not paid, the discharge of the indebtedness is income for the borrower unless he or she is insolvent or the debt is discharged in bankruptcy.[2]

Gift taxation. No gift will result if the borrower's note reflects an arm's length transaction. Thus, there must be provision for repayment and the interest rate charged must be reasonable. The lender may elect to forgive loan payments under the shelter of the annual exclusion. However, if the IRS can establish that a prior agreement had been made to forgive all payments, it will contend that the entire loan constituted an immediate gift. To avoid this result, a lender might accept each payment, and later gift a somewhat different amount back to the borrower. So long as there is no prearrangement this should also avoid the problem of the borrower having to report the cancellation of the debt as income.

Estate taxation. The value of a note is included in the lender-decedent's gross estate at death.[3] If taken as part of an arm's length transaction, a note in an estate is valued at its fair market value which is generally less than the outstanding balance. Its value depends on many factors such as how well secured, the financial health of the debtor, and the note's interest rate. Where the debtor is a family member, the note must be included in the estate at the date-of-death balance. To do otherwise would open the door to manipulation of the value of decedents' estates.

Taxation of gift-type intrafamily loans. The income and gift tax effects discussed above assume a true loan, one that does not have a gift element. In other words, the borrower exchanges full consideration in the form of a note which when issued has a present value equal to the amount borrowed.

Other intrafamily loans entail additional tax risks. Individuals may wish to charge no interest, or an interest rate that is below market rates. These "gift loans" may subject the lender to income and/or gift taxation.

Income taxation. In subjecting these loans to income tax, the law assumes a fiction, that the forgone interest was paid by the borrower and then the lender gave the money back.[4] Thus, the lender must report the imputed interest payments as income. Whether a loan is "below market" depends on whether the lender charged a rate at least equal to the applicable federal rate (AFR), as described in § 1274(d) and published by the U.S. Treasury each month.

There are two exceptions to the imputed interest rules. First, they do not apply to loans up to $10,000 used to purchase property that does not produce income, e.g., an automobile. Second, they do not apply to loans up to $100,000 if the borrower's net investment income is less than $1,000. This might work well for investment-poor students needing large amounts to fund educational expenses or for a child needing the money for a down payment on a house. If the loan is up to $100,000 and the borrower's net investment income exceeds the $1,000 limit, the interest that must be reported is the lesser of the borrower's investment income or the imputed AFR amount.

Gift taxation. If the loan rate is below the market, the lender will be treated as having made a gift. If the loan is a term loan with a specified maturity, the value of the gift is the difference between the amount loaned and the discounted present value of the note. If the loan is a demand loan with no specified maturity and the lender has the right to demand full repayment at any time, the lender will be treated as having made an annual gift of the imputed interest for the portion of the year the loan was outstanding, less the amount of interest actually received. A more detailed discussion of the tax effects of below market or "interest free" loans is in Appendix 14A.

Properly structured, intrafamily loans can benefit both lender and borrower. Both should understand the terms and put them in writing.

Ordinary Sale

A person can sell property at its fair market value to another family member. Under certain circumstances, an ordinary sale is beneficial to both family members. The owner of property may truly wish to sell at a fair price, but would prefer to keep the asset in the family. The buyer will be spared the effort and expense of looking for similar property, and commission costs are avoided. As in any sale, there may be income tax consequences to the seller. Careful records should be kept, since intrafamily sales might receive greater IRS scrutiny than a sale between unrelated parties, especially if the transaction is sizable. The buyer, of course, must acquire the cash needed for the purchase. The tax code does not allow loss recognition on sales between related parties.[5] However, the loss that was disallowed may shelter some of the buyer's gain when he or she sells the property.

EXAMPLE 14 - 1. Renee sells a lot with a $100,000 basis to her son Tad for $90,000. She cannot claim the $10,000 loss even if the sales price was at fair market value. Later Tad sells the lot to a developer for $130,000. Although his gain is $40,000, he only has to recognize $30,000 since he can deduct his mother's disallowed loss.

Bargain Sale

If a person has mixed motives, wanting to give an asset to a family member but wanting some money in return, a bargain sale is one way. In a bargain sale, the owner sells the asset for an amount less than fair market value. The difference between the consideration received and the value of the asset is a gift to the buyer-donee for transfer tax. For income tax, the seller would recognize a gain to the extent the consideration received exceeds the basis. The buyer-donee's basis is the greater of the donor's carry-over basis or the amount paid.[6]

EXAMPLE 14 - 2. Roxanne owns property with a basis of $90,000 and a current value of $240,000. She sells it to her son for $110,000. Roxanne's taxable gain is $20,000, the difference between $110,000 and her $90,000 basis. Son's new basis is $110,000, his purchase price. Roxanne has also made a gift of $130,000, the difference between the FMV of the property and the consideration paid to her.

Sometimes a donor may intend a true tax-free gift but may find it will be treated as a bargain sale.

EXAMPLE 14 - 3. George borrows money from a bank to purchase a building. After claiming depreciation on the property for a number of years, he "gives" the property to his daughter, who assumes the debt. The transaction will be treated as a bargain sale, and if his adjusted basis is less than the outstanding debt he will recognize a gain. George will be deemed to have received consideration in the amount of the debt assumed.[7]

As a compromise between a gift and a sale, the bargain sale can be arranged to reflect the person's degree of generosity.

Installment Sale

Instead of selling the asset to a family member for immediate cash, the owner could take an installment note. The buyer agrees to make periodic payments of principal and interest, at a fair market rate of interest. This is seller financing, and the seller is said to take back paper, by receiving a note instead of cash. An installment sale can defer income tax on some or all capital gain while keeping post-sale appreciation out of the seller's gross estate.

Income taxation. Under the income tax installment sales rules, the seller may spread recognition of the gain over the collection period.[8] Each year's interest is ordinary income. Each year's principal is return of capital and capital gain in the same proportion as the sale. Although it is presumed that the seller will use the installment method to recognize gain, the seller can make an election to recognize the entire gain in the year of sale. That might make good sense if the seller has offsetting capital losses for the year. There are restrictions on deferral of gain on an installment sale of certain trade or business inventory.[9] Losses are never reported on an installment basis.

> EXAMPLE 14 - 4. Julie, a widow, sells her rental house to her daughter, Martha, for $80,000, payable with a down payment of $10,000. Interest is payable monthly, and principal will be payable in five equal annual $14,000 payments. Julie's current adjusted basis in the house is $20,000. Her gross profit is $60,000, and each year she will recognize a capital gain of 75% or $60,000/$80,000 of the principal amount received. Thus, in the year of sale, her reportable gain is $7,500 of the $10,000 received. In each of the succeeding five years, she will report a gain of $10,500 (i.e., 75% * $14,000).

Interest paid is fully deductible by the buyer if it is some type of qualified interest such as business interest, investment interest offset by investment income, or interest on a debt secured by a primary or secondary residence.

At least two different events will trigger an immediate recognition of part or all of the remaining gain to the seller. If the seller sells or "otherwise disposes" of the installment note, or if the seller cancels the note, then he or she will have to recognize the remaining gain from the original transaction. Gain recognition is also triggered if the buyer of the property is a related party who resells the property within two years of the purchase.[10]

The buyer of the property, as in any valid sale, will have a basis in the property in the amount of the purchase price. However, the transfer of the seller's note at death will not generate a stepped-up basis in the note because the unrecognized gain is considered income in respect of a decedent.[11] The legatee-heir will continue to report installment gain the same way as the seller.

Gift taxation. If the installment transaction is a bona fide sale for full and adequate consideration, there are no gift tax consequences. Lack of full consideration occurs when the interest rate in the note is too low.

> EXAMPLE 14 - 5. Continuing with the above example, assume the installment note specifies an interest rate of 10%, which is equal to the current applicable federal rate (AFR). Since the rules for installment sales under § 7520(a)(2) require a minimum rate of 120% of the current AFR to avoid the inference of a gift, the present value of the sum of all principal and interest payments, discounted at 12%, will be less than $80,000, the current value of the house. Thus, Julie will be treated as having made a gift to Martha of the difference. For a small loan, the annual exclusion will cover the gift.

A parent may wish to forgive one or more of the purchaser's future payments. In the usual case, only the amount forgiven constitutes a taxable gift in the year forgiven, and it qualifies for the annual exclusion.

> EXAMPLE 14 - 6. If Martha uses the money to buy a car and Julie forgives a $14,000 annual payment, Julie has made a gift of that amount. After the annual exclusion, Julie's taxable gift is $4,000. If Julie were married and split the gift with her husband, it would be zero. However, from an income tax stand point, Julie will be treated as though she received the payment and then returned it to her daughter.

The IRS quite correctly maintains that if the seller, at the time of the sale, had an understanding with the buyer that the seller would not collect on the note, then the entire value of the property is a taxable gift. However, an IRS challenge has rarely prevailed where the note has been correctly drafted and properly secured.

Estate taxation. Ordinarily, when the holder of an installment note dies, only the present value of the installment note is included in his or her gross estate.

> EXAMPLE 14 - 7. If Julie dies just before the fourth payment is due, her gross estate will include the discounted value of the note. Of course, Julie's gross estate will also include any proceeds from receipt of earlier payments from her daughter, to the extent retained by Julie, or any assets she purchased with those proceeds. However, her gross estate will not include the value of the rental house sold.

If the seller made a partial gift and took back paper secured by the property transferred, and died before the note was paid off, the date-of-death value of the property sold would be included in the seller's gross estate less the actual consideration paid.[12] This arrangement would be considered a transfer for less than full and adequate consideration, with a retained income interest.

Since family transactions are often scrutinized more carefully by the IRS, the owner should be strongly advised to determine the value of the asset by qualified appraisal and to use an adequate rate of interest.

Self-canceling provision. The seller may seek to avoid inclusion of the value of the note in his or her gross estate by incorporating a self-canceling provision, specifying that no further payments will be made after his or her death. Since the initial value of a *self-canceling installment note* (called a "SCIN") is less than one whose payments cannot be prematurely canceled, the buyer will have to give additional consideration, usually in the form of a higher principal amount or a higher interest rate.[13] And, of course, the older the individual, the greater the additional consideration. Otherwise, the IRS could assert the existence of a gift element in the transaction, again creating the risk of § 2036(a) application.

> EXAMPLE 14 - 8. Marty, age 53, sells property currently worth $100,000 in exchange for a 20 years self-canceling installment note. The likelihood of Marty dying before reaching age 73 is .283116 [1 minus (65,154/90,885], see Table 90CM. To reflect this additional consideration, Marty sets the face amount of the note at $128,312.

Case law is that the value of the canceled SCIN is not includable in the gross estate.[14] However, there are several other tax consequences. At the note-holder's death, cancellation of the remaining payments triggers recognition of the rest of the gain; and it must be reported on the estate's income tax return.[15] The gain will be income in respect of a decedent. No income tax deduction for its proportionate share of the estate tax is available because the note is not in the decedent's gross estate. Because the tax on this gain is recognized by the estate, it is not a debt at the time of death and therefore is not deductible from the gross estate. Planners may still wish to recommend the SCIN to wealthier individuals whose potential estate tax rate exceeds their marginal income tax rate.

The SCIN represents aggressive planning and should be used only when the individual is willing to risk potentially greater income tax exposure.

The appeal of installment sales. Tax deferral, through installment sales, is attractive because it spreads the gain over a number of years. However, there are restrictions on installment reporting for certain sales. The sale of publicly traded property (e.g., stocks and bonds) does not qualify for installment reporting. Also, a portion of a sale might not qualify (under the so-called "proportional disallowance rule") if the sales price exceeds $150,000. Thus, the installment sale is available mainly for the occasional sale of real estate or tangible personal property.

Intrafamily sales, whether of the ordinary, bargain, or installment variety, are significant value-shifting devices. The sale can freeze a portion of the person's estate, since post-sale appreciation will belong to the new owner, who may have a much longer life expectancy and a smaller estate..

Private Annuity

Overview. A private annuity is the exchange of an asset for the unsecured promise of another person (usually a family member) that he or she will pay an annuity for the life of the transferor. The recipient of the annuity payments is called an annuitant and the person making the payments is called an obligor. It is like a commercial annuity, which is purchased from a financial institution.

EXAMPLE 14 - 9. Parker, age 65 and in poor health, agrees to transfer a $100,000 asset ($20,000 basis) to his son, under a private annuity arrangement when the federal rate for valuing annuities is 10%. Based on Table S (10%), Parker should receive $13,725 a year for life (i.e., $100,000/7.2860).

The private annuity generates periodic income for the annuitant and can exclude the transferred property from the gross estate.

Taxation of a private annuity. The private annuity is fairly simple for gift and estate tax, but quite complex for income tax.

Gift taxation. There is no taxable gift since the value of the property transferred must equal the present value of the annuity. If the annuitant had a greater than 50% probability of living more than one year (or did live 18 months or more) from when the private annuity was established, the IRS accepts the use of the actuarial tables to value the private annuity.[16] If a gift element is present, the major risk is that it will be deemed a transfer for less than money's worth with a retained interest, resulting in the date-of-death value of the asset being included in the annuitant's estate.[17]

Income taxation. No gain is immediately recognizable on the creation of a private annuity because the amount realized is not considered immediately ascertainable. Thus, as with the installment sale, gain is reported as the annuity payments are received. But unlike the installment sale, taxability of the payments is governed by the annuity rules of IRC § 72. Each year's payments are split into the three parts described below.

One part is the return of the annuitant's basis, called the *investment in the contract*. This is the amount the annuitant should get back tax free if he or she lives. The tax free recovery is spread over the average life expectancy for someone the annuitant's age. The tax-free amount of each payment is found by multiplying the payment by the *exclusion ratio*. The ratio is the investment in the contract divided by the *expected return* which is the required annuity payment times the annuitant's life expectancy. The life expectancy is obtained from the mortality table found in IRS Reg. § 1.72-9.

The second part is the proportional return of any gain in the asset at the time of the contract, and is taxed as capital gain. The gain is calculated by dividing the total gain by the life expectancy at the beginning of the contract. That amount is recognized each year until the annuitant reaches the original life expectancy.

The third part is the balance of the payment after the investment in the contract and the gain are removed. It is taxed as ordinary income. After the annuitant reaches the original life expectancy, and all the investment in the contract and gains have been paid, the payments are entirely ordinary income. If the annuitant dies before reaching the life expectancy, the unrecovered basis is deductible as a loss.

EXAMPLE 14 - 10. Based on the last example, Parker's tax-free portion of the payment is $1,000, which is the product of an annual payment, $13,725, and the exclusion ratio, of .07121. This ratio is calculated by dividing the investment in the contract, Parker's $20,000 basis, by the expected return, $274,500, the product of $13,725 and 20, Parker's life expectancy, derived from the regulations. Parker will be required to report $4,000 as gain, or one twentieth of his $80,000 total gain in each of the first 20 years. Thus, for the first 20 years, of the entire $13,725 payment, Parker will take $1,000 tax free, and report $4,000 as taxable gain and $8,725 as ordinary income. If Parker outlives his 20-year life expectancy all subsequent payments are ordinary income. If he dies within 20 years, gain reporting stops and he will receive a loss deduction on his final income tax return for the unrecovered basis.

Estate taxation. When the annuitant dies, none of the transferred property is included in the estate tax base if there was no retained interest in the property transferred. The original exchange, if done properly, is considered a sale of the property for its full worth. As with any life estate, the lifetime annuity terminates at the death of the annuitant.

> EXAMPLE 14 - 11. Continuing the example above, if Parker lives for two years, his son will have paid less than $30,000 for an asset worth $100,000. Parker's gross estate will not include the $100,000 asset.

If the original transaction is ruled a gift because the annuity is worth less than the property transferred, the annuitant's gross estate includes the entire date-of-death value of the property, reduced by the payments actually received, as an IRC § 2036(a) transfer with a retained life estate. That would destroy the tax benefit of the transaction. That danger can be reduced by securing a qualified professional appraisal. Some experts suggest incorporating a provision in the annuity contract for a "valuation readjustment" or "savings" clause. The clause would require the purchaser to pay additional consideration if the IRS determines the property was undervalued. However, the IRS has attacked these clauses arguing that, as completed gifts, the transactions cannot be altered, and they are contrary to public policy since the revaluation is triggered only if the parties get caught.

Private annuity advantages. First, for estate taxes, the private annuity is better than an installment sale, giving complete exclusion of the asset from the annuitant's estate. Second, the private annuity can be an efficient transfer device where an annuitant is unhealthy and may die before the average life expectancy for their age, leading to a relatively small repayment.

Private annuity disadvantages. The private annuity has three major drawbacks. First, private annuity arrangements are always unsecured. Using property as security will include the property in the annuitant's gross estate as a retained interest.[18] This may increase the risk of not being repaid -- a major problem for an annuitant who depends on the payments for support. Second, no part of the annuity payment is deductible.[19] Third, there is a risk of the annuitant living longer than expected, giving the obligor a bad bargain.

EXAMPLE 14 - 12. Continuing the example above, if, instead of dying young, Parker regains his health and lives 20 years, his son will have paid more than $274,000 for an asset worth $100,000. Parker's gross estate may have to include this amount (which is nearly three times the value of the asset transferred), and any resulting income, if he does not consume or gift these receipts during his lifetime.

Since the private annuity can accomplish significant estate freezing without gift tax consequences, it can be a very attractive transaction if the parties are willing to assume the risks. As we have seen, it works best when the person wants to save estate tax, is not expected to live more than a few years, has a significant cash flow need, and trusts the obligor to make the payments as promised. These characteristics are rare, even among the wealthy.

INCOMPLETE INTRAFAMILY TRANSFERS

This section briefly covers three currently used incomplete intrafamily transfers, the intentionally defective irrevocable trust, gift-leaseback, and the grantor retained income trust.

Intentionally Defective Irrevocable Trust

When a person wishes to make gifts to significantly reduce estate tax, has little interest in shifting income, and wishes to retain some control over the transferred assets, the planner may recommend an intentionally defective irrevocable trust (IDIT). The different tax rules about retained powers in §§ 2036 - 2038 (estate tax) and §§ 671-677 (*grantor trust* income tax rules) mean transfers to an IDIT are complete for federal estate and gift tax but incomplete for income tax. Thus, the trust corpus is a complete gift, not included in the grantor's gross estate, but all trust income is taxable to the grantor because the trust provides for grantor retained powers uniquely proscribed by the grantor trust rules. This offers an opportunity to save estate tax, at no gift tax cost, since income tax paid by the grantor on the beneficiary's trust income reduces the grantor's estate.

EXAMPLE 14 - 13. In 2000, Maxwell transfers $685,000 to an IDIT for the benefit of his adult son, Kirk. Since Maxwell has made no prior taxable gifts, he can totally shelter the current gift from gift taxation with the annual exclusion and unified credit. Required to distribute all income to Kirk annually, the trustee distributes $50,000 income in the first year. Maxwell must pay an additional $17,500 income tax, based on his 35% combined marginal rate. Maxwell has effectively transferred an additional $17,500 for the benefit of his son, free of gift tax. Each succeeding year he will pay the income tax again, effectively transferring more.

Powers that the grantor may retain to control an IDIT include acting as trustee and having the grantor's spouse as one of the trust beneficiaries. As trustee, the grantor can have the powers to invest, to allocate receipts between income and principal, to vote shares of stock held in the trust, and to distribute income or principal to trust beneficiaries for such reasons as "sickness," "emergency," or "disability." Naming the spouse as a beneficiary enables the grantor to retain indirect access to the trust. Of course, any distributions to the spouse could increase the spouse's estate, which may run contrary to the estate tax goals of the trust, and there is a risk that the IRS may treat the payment of income taxes by the grantor as a gift.

Gift-Leaseback

When a business-owning parent wishes to establish a gift program but is held back for lack of available assets, he or she might find the answer in a gift-leaseback arrangement. As its name suggests, the parent gives a business asset outright or in trust to a lower-bracket family member and leases the asset back for use in the business. The parent is able to continue using the asset, can take a deduction for the lease payment, and can still enjoy all the other advantages inherent in gifting.

The ability to deduct the lease payments under a gift-leaseback depends in part on the location of the person's business and in part on how carefully the arrangement is structured. In some circuits, the Federal appellate courts have disallowed the deduction, while other circuits have allowed it as a legitimate business expense. Even in circuits that allow the deduction, the transaction must be properly structured. Some requirements for success include having a legitimate business purpose, charging a reasonable lease payment, having a written and enforceable lease, and, if the gift is in trust, naming an independent trustee who is not subservient to the donor.

Trusts and the Anti-freeze Rules: IRC §§ 2701-2704

IRC §§ 2701-2704 were written to end certain abusive estate planning techniques whereby donors were able to greatly overstate the value of their retained interests, thereby greatly reducing the value of their gifts. The way in which the transfer was structured, increases in value went to the transferred interest whereas the value of the interest retained did not change, hence it was considered "frozen" in value. The anti-freeze rules apply to both family trusts (e.g., an income interest is kept and a remainder interest is given away) and recapitalizations of businesses (e.g., preferred stock is kept and common stock is given away). Section 2701 deals specifically with transfers of corporate or partnership interests to family members. It is covered elsewhere with business related issues.

IRC § 2702: Transfers of interests in trusts. Section 2702 addresses transfers to family members through the use of trusts where the trustor seeks to freeze estate values by splitting an asset into two parts, transferring the remainder interest which has a low value because it is a future interest (but likely to grow in value) and keeping the income interest.

What the IRS found to be abusive in these techniques was that the value of what was retained (the income interest) was based on the assumption that income would actually be paid to the person who created the transfer (the settlor of the trust or the parents holding the preferred stock). In practice the wealthy were using these transfer devices to move wealth to the younger generation at minimum transfer tax cost. This was accomplished with trusts by investing for growth rather than income, and with corporations by not paying dividends on the preferred stock retained by the parents.

The IRS was not very successful in court with its arguments that there was either a transfer with a retained interest (keeping the property in the transferor's estate) or that the income interest was greatly overvalued resulting in a much larger gift. Finally, in1987, to restrict these estate "freezing" techniques, Congress took an estate tax approach, requiring inclusion in the decedent's gross estate of the entire date-of-death value of virtually all property in which the transferor retained a significant income interest. Confusing and overly broad, § 2036(c) created such taxpayer opposition that it was repealed retroactively in 1990, and replaced by the special valuation rules of §§ 2701-2704, sometimes referred to as the "Chapter 14 rules" due to their location in the Internal Revenue Code.

In adopting Chapter 14, Congress abandoned the estate tax approach, and instead used a gift tax approach, subjecting certain transfers to gift tax when the transfer is made, rather than taxing the property at death. Chapter 14 rules require that certain transfers of property with retained income interests must be valued in their entirety, reduced only by the value of "qualified" retained income interests. Thus, any retained interests that do not qualify under the code are disregarded, with the result that the entire value of the transferred property is subject to immediate gift tax. For gift tax purposes, the nonqualified retained interests are treated as if they were not retained.

Under § 2702, applicable to transfers in trust, the special valuation rules apply when:

> *...a transfer is made in trust for the benefit of a member of the transferor's family and an interest is retained by the transferor or an applicable family member.*

Following are the key terms that need to be defined or described in order to apply §2702.

Applicable family member. These are the people besides the settlor who cause § 2702 to come into play if they receive (or keep) an income interest. The applicable family members are the transferor's spouse, ancestors of the transferor or of the transferor's spouse, and any spouse of such ancestor.[20] Generally, the retained interest is kept by the older generation, most likely the settlor or the settlor's spouse.

Member of transferor's family. Think of this as referring to the remaindermen. The members of the transferor's family are defined as the transferor's ancestors, descendants, spouse and siblings, ancestors and descendants of the transferor's spouse, and spouses of the transferor's ancestors, descendants and siblings.[21] Generally, these remainder interests are for the younger generation. Note that by this definition § 2702 applies if the remaindermen are brothers or sisters but not if they are nephews, nieces, or cousins.

Exceptions to § 2702. Section 2702 does not apply to retained interests in the transferor's personal residence or vacation home, or to certain tangible property such as works of art. The zero valuation rule within §2702 for trusts does not apply to certain retained interests. These are called "qualified annuity interests" and "qualified unitrust interests."

Qualified retained interests versus the zero valuation rule. To be qualified, the retained income interest must be payable at least annually and there must be a way to calculate exactly what must be paid. There are two basic types of qualified interests, *grantor retained annuity trusts* and *grantor retained unitrusts*. With the grantor retained annuity trust (GRAT) there is a method of determining the first year's income and all future income payments are based on it. The first year could be a stated dollar amount or it could be a stated percentage of the initial value of the trust. The law allows a provision in the trust that increases the payment each year so long as it does not exceed a 20% increase over the prior year. Once the required payment for the first year is known, all future payments can be calculated through to the end of the trust.

> EXAMPLE 14 - 14. Jack creates a five-year GRAT, funding it with assets worth $100,000. The trust terms call for payments to Jack equal to 7% times the initial value of the trust and for annual increases of 10%. His issue are the remaindermen. Jack will receive $7,000 the first year, $7,700 the second, $8,470 the third, $9,317 the fourth, and $10,249 the final year. These amounts must be paid regardless of the value of the trust or the amount of income it receives.

With a grantor retained unitrust (GRUT), the required payment is determined each year as a percentage of the fair market value of the trust property. Since the value of the trust assets will change they must be revalued annually. Each year one can determine precisely what must be paid, but unlike the GRAT, one cannot say beyond the first year what the annual payment will be.

> EXAMPLE 14 - 15. Jill establishes a five-year GRUT, retaining the right to income equal to 6% of the trust's value. Her issue are the remaindermen. She funds it with assets worth $100,000 and receives $6,000 the first year. For the second year, if the trust is worth $110,000, she will receive $6,600; and if it is worth $90,000, she will receive $5,400.

In the preceding two examples, because the retained interests are qualifying ones, the zero valuation rule is avoided. If § 2702 applies and the retained interest is not a qualified one, e.g., the settlor retains the right to "all income," the interest is given a zero value.

> EXAMPLE 14 - 16. Fifty-year-old Myron transfers $1 million into a trust retaining the right to all income for 10 years. His three children are the remaindermen. The

income interest would be valued at zero because it is neither a GRAT nor a GRUT. This results in the entire $1 million value being a taxable gift.

The Impact of EGTRRA on Transfers with a Retained Interest

This area of estate planning has experienced a great deal of change. EGTRRA will have a major impact, throwing estate freezing techniques involving retained interest trusts into turmoil and possibly making them obsolete. The estate planner may encounter artifact plans from before the anti-freeze rules and plans with names like GRIT, GRAT, and GRUT, drafted after the anti-freeze rules but before EGTRRA. Further, because the anti-freeze rules do not apply to transfers outside immediate family members, some estate freezes are not as affected by those rules. To help the reader understand this area we will discuss the situation before the anti-freeze rules followed by a discussion of the treatment of retained interest trusts under the anti-freeze rules. But first is a discussion of how EGTRRA is likely to impact this area so the reader will have a sense of perspective in navigating the complicated material to follow.

With less than 10 years until the estate tax is repealed there is no reason to create a GRIT of any sort with a term that would go beyond 2009. The sole purpose of this kind of planning is to leverage the AEA, and the biggest fear has always been the estate tax, not the gift tax. We control gifts, deciding when and whether, but have no such choice with death. It is conceivable that wealthy individuals will continue to use GRITs to leverage the $1 million gift tax AEA, but to what purpose? To enrich children and grandchildren beyond what can be accomplished using the annual exclusion and the $1 million AEA to cover outright gifts? Perhaps.

The difficulty with establishing a GRIT in this post-EGTRRA era is that it will be beneficial only if the term ends before the settlor dies and the settlor dies before 2010. The term is established when the trust is created, and the longer the term the lower the gift, but forecasting when the settlor will die is not only unpleasant but an inexact science. Consider this, a six-year GRAT, established January 1, 2002, will be a successful estate planning tool only if the settlor dies in 2009. If the settlor dies during the term of the trust, its assets will be included in the settlor's estate. The result? No harm done, other than the waste of time and money used to establish the trust. However, if the settlor dies after 2009, assuming the estate tax stays repealed, the now distributed GRAT turns out to have been unnecessary. More is lost than just the time and money used to establish it, because the remaindermen receive the trust assets with a carry-over basis, whereas, if the settlor held onto them until his or her death, some of the settlor's $1.3 million basis increase could have been allocated to them.

So who is left in this game? There will be little harm in establishing a GRIT and potential gain for the wealthy person whose assets have so much appreciation that the $1.3 million basis increase limit will fall far short of bringing his or her estate's basis up to fair market value. For this person the inability to allocate basis to the assets in the trust is not a drawback, as the increase will be used elsewhere. Another possibility is to fund the GRIT with high basis assets so the loss of basis allocation to those assets is not a concern. Finally, GRITs remain a viable hedge for the pessimist who fears that the sunset provision really means what it says and that the estate tax will resurrect in all its glory on January 1, 2011.

Retained Interest Trusts Before the Ice Age

Before 1987, estate planners could create irrevocable trusts funded with low yield investments, retaining the right to the income for a period of years, and naming the settlor's issue as the remaindermen. This was a very efficient way for the wealthy to freeze their estates, leverage their unified credit, and transfer a significant portion of their respective estates to their issue. Of course, only the remainder was "given away" and, being a future interest, it was discounted. The longer the term of the trust and the higher the § 7520 rate, the smaller the gift value. Although the next example takes place years ago current discount tables are used so that you can track the numbers.

> EXAMPLE 14 - 17. In 1982, 50-year-old Myron transferred $1 million into a 20-year GRIT. He retained the right to all income, giving his three children the remainder at the end of the term. If Myron died during the term, the trust corpus reverted to his estate. At the time the trust was funded, the § 7520 rate was 10%, hence, the remainder value was $114,829. The remainder factor is taken from Table B and is further discounted because there is the possibility that Myron might die before the trust terminates which would mean the trust assets would revert to his estate. The probability that the children will receive the remainder (i.e., that Myron will live the 20 years) is based on the number of people alive at age 50 that are expected to reach age 70, see Table 90CM. [0.148644 * $1,000,000 *

(71,357/92,370)]. The applicable exclusion amount (AEA) in 1982 was $225,000, which more than covered the gift. The trustee invested in growth stock that paid virtually no dividends (Myron did not need nor want any additional income) and, of course, there was a prolonged bull market so when the trust terminated in 2002 the corpus was worth more than $4,500,000.

Planners used an analogous technique to transfer businesses using corporate shares or partnership interests. To greatly simplify, the wealthy business owning parents would issue preferred shares to themselves that had income and a high value, and they would give to their children common shares with no income, a low value, and little gift tax. However, the future growth in the value of the business went to the common stock. The result, as with the trusts discussed above, was to freeze the value of the parents' interest and transfer growth in value to the children, largely escaping gift and estate tax.

Grantor Retained Income Trusts

With a grantor retained income trust, the person transfers property into an irrevocable trust, retaining the right to income for a period of years, after which the trust ends and the trust property is transferred to the remaindermen who are usually relatives of the grantor. The acronym "GRIT" is often used to refer to all varieties of grantor retained income trusts, including common law GRITs (i.e., those not subject to the § 2702 rules), GRATs, and GRUTs. With all GRITs, if a settlor retains an interest and does not survive the income term, § 2036(a) will apply, and the GRIT will have served no useful purpose. The date-of-death value of the trust is included in the grantor's gross estate, and the adjusted taxable gift is zero insofar as the GRIT is concerned. In fact, some GRITs (i.e., all those except qualified GRATS and GRUTS--see below) provide that the corpus will revert to the settlor's estate if he or she does not survive. This can be accomplished by granting the settlor a testamentary power of appointment over the trust corpus, with the power made contingent on the settlor not surviving the trust's term. By the settlor retaining a contingent reversion, the remainder value is reduced. Since the remainder is the taxable gift, the smaller its value the less of the settlor's unified credit is used.

If the settlor does survive the income period, the result is the same for all GRITs: the settlor's entire beneficial interest in the trust ceases, the corpus vests in the remaindermen (usually the settlor's children), and the gift value will be an adjusted taxable gift when the settlor dies.

Tax consequences. A properly structured GRIT has significant gift tax, estate tax and income tax consequences.

Gift taxation. As stated previously, whether the value of a retained interest is deemed to equal zero or some larger amount depends on the characteristics of the GRIT and the provisions of § 2702. If § 2702 applies, all retained interests are valued at zero unless the retained interest is a qualified retained interest. If it is qualified, we value the gift by using the annuity column in Table B to determine the income interest and subtract that from the value of the property transferred to the trust. Because a contingent reversion is not a qualified retained interest, if it is included in a CRAT or CRUT the reversion is given a zero value even though the income interest is qualified. A contingent reversion in a GRIT that is not subject to § 2702 is given value if the value can be measured and will, therefore, reduce the value of the gift.

Income taxation. As a grantor trust, all trust income is taxable to the trustor until the trust terminates.[22]

Estate taxation. If the settlor survives the income period, none of the corpus will be includable in the gross estate. However, the taxable gift value will be included in the estate tax base as an adjusted taxable gift.

If the settlor dies before the expiration of the income period, the date-of-death value of the corpus will be included in the settlor's gross estate as a transfer with retained income or enjoyment which did not in fact end before the transferor's death.[23] Thus, even a CRAT or CRUT with a qualifying retained interest does not reduce estate tax if the settlor dies before the income period ends.

Generation-skipping taxation. The use of a GRIT is not as helpful for avoiding the generation-skipping transfer (GST) tax as it has been for estate tax. The reason is that the GST exemption cannot be allocated to most GRITs until the close of the "estate tax inclusion period" (called ETIP), which occurs when the property would no longer be includable in the settlor's gross estate in the event the settlor died.[24] In most GRIT situations, this would be the end of the settlor's retained income period, at which point § 2036(a) no longer applies. The value of the property against which the allocation may be made will equal the value that is included in the settlor's gross estate or the GRITs value at the end of the term.

An allocation of the GST exemption for most non-GRIT transfers is made at the time a GST trust becomes irrevocable. This has the effect of attaining maximum leverage for appreciating assets. In contrast, with a GRIT one cannot make the allocation until the trust terminates at the end of the income period or the death of the grantor, whichever comes first. This means that more of the person's GST exemption will be used up if assets have appreciated during the income period of the GRIT.

GRIT Planning

The following material explains how GRITs were structured before tax reform and then describes planning opportunities currently available.

The "common law" GRIT. Prior to the passage of IRC § 2702, relatively uncomplicated GRITs were quite successful in freezing the value of appreciating property and transferring it to a child at little or no gift tax cost. The following example portrays what is now called a "common law GRIT." The following series of examples uses current IRS valuation tables (see Table B (10%) in Appendix A), so that the reader can use the tables to follow the calculations.

EXAMPLE 14 - 18. In 1985, when Henry was 60 years old, he created a GRIT, funding it with $500,000 in common stock. The § 7520 rate was 10%. By the trust terms Henry kept the income for the lesser of 10 years or his life. If he dies before the end of the period, the trust terminates and reverts to Henry's estate. If he survives the period, the trust terminates and is distributed outright to Henry's son. Henry made a taxable gift of the remainder interest valued at $160,815 [$500,000 * .385543 * (71,357/85,537). Henry owed no gift tax. He simply used up some of his unified credit.

EXAMPLE 14 - 19. Continuing the above example, if Henry died four years after establishing the trust, the date-of-death value of the corpus would be included in his gross estate and Henry would have gained no estate tax advantage. The only disadvantage was the fees paid to establish and maintain the trust for the four years.

EXAMPLE 14 - 20. If Henry died 12 years later when the corpus was worth $1 million, his gross estate would include nothing in connection with this property, although the adjusted taxable gift would be $160,815. By surviving the income period, Henry succeeded in freezing the transfer tax value of this stock at $160,815, the original gift tax value of the remainder interest. This amount is less than the value of the stock when transferred to Henry's son, and probably far less than its value when Henry died. Henry leveraged the AEA many times over.

Applying Anti-freeze to GRITs. These post § 2702 GRITs are impacted by the zero valuation rules so the entire value of the transfer is a taxable gift unless the interest retained is a qualified one. Planning to avoid the zero valuation rule uses one of two strategies: planners use a common law GRIT to avoid § 2702 entirely, or they create a GRIT that falls within §2702 but has a qualifying income interest, i.e., is a qualified GRAT or GRUT. A GRIT with a nonfamily member remainderman can use the common law rules which means even a retained interest stated as "all income" is given value and the gift is based on the factor found in the remainder column of Table B. A GRIT which has as its only asset the settlor's home also follows the common law GRIT rules. This arrangement, discussed later, is called a Qualified Personal Residence Trust (QPRT).

> EXAMPLE 14 - 21. In the prior example, had the beneficiary of the transferred interest been Henry's nephew rather than his son, the entire actuarial value of the retained income interest could be subtracted in arriving at the gift tax value. It would be a common law GRIT.

Examples of common situations where the settlor and the trust beneficiaries are not "applicable family members" and therefore where we can still use the common law GRIT that does not "fix" the amount of income, are trusts with unmarried partners and/or close friends as remaindermen.

The five types of § 2702 GRITs described in the next few pages avoid the harsh zero valuation rule for the retained interests by satisfying at least one of the requirements found in the code. They are the GRAT, GRUT, tangible personal property GRIT, and two types of personal residence GRITs.

GRAT and GRUT. As discussed earlier, the zero valuation rule of § 2702 does not apply to "qualified" retained income interests. Individuals who want certainty in the amount of income they will receive would most likely prefer a GRAT since income payments through the entire term of the trust are known as soon as the trust is established. Those who would prefer to have income increase over the years would probably prefer a GRUT on the assumption that values will increase, thus resulting in increased income payments. Of course there is the problem that if the value goes down the income decreases as well.

"Zeroing out" a GRAT or a GRUT. If the payments to the settlor are high enough, the value of the retained interest could equal the value of the property transferred into trust. This is referred to as *"zeroing out"* a GRAT, because the remainder interest is valued at zero.

> EXAMPLE 14 - 22. If the § 7520 rate is 6% when Mark creates a 15-year GRAT with assets valued at $1 million, he could theoretically zero it out by retaining an annuity that equals $102,963 per year, i.e., an amount determined by dividing $1 million by the annuity factor of 9.7122.

Note that with a zeroed-out GRAT, not only is there is no gift tax, the grantor does not use up any unified credit. Thus, it can result in a large estate tax base reduction, as well as a freeze, at no transfer tax cost. These were much the rage at estate planning seminars in the early 1990s, including excitement about one and two-year term zeroed-out GRATs (yes, the retained income amounts were huge). However, the IRS takes the position that a GRAT cannot be successfully zeroed out.[25]

Tangible personal property transfers. The zero valuation rule of § 2702 does not apply to tangible personal property where: (a) the failure by a term interest holder to exercise his or her rights would not have a substantial effect on the value of the remainder interest, and (b) the property is of a type for which no depreciation deduction would be allowable. In such cases, the value of the retained interest is set equal to the amount the interest could be sold for to an unrelated third party. One type of property that might meet these criteria is art-work, such as a painting.

> EXAMPLE 14 - 23. Drew, age 65, gives his daughter a remainder interest in a painting, worth $1 million, and retains a 10-year term certain interest. The gift tax value is the million dollars reduced by the amount Drew can show that an unrelated third party would pay for the right to possess the painting for 10 years.

Because the IRS requires evidence of "actual sales or rentals that are comparable" to sustain the value of the term interest, few individuals will be able to successfully employ this strategy.

Qualified personal residence trust. More planners will recommend a personal residence GRIT as a result of recent regulations which have outlined the conditions required for a 'safe-harbor' residence trust called a qualified personal residence trust (QPRT).[26] The QPRT can hold an interest in only one residence.

It can receive additions of cash to pay six months of mortgage payments, but any excess cash must be distributed to the term holder. The trustee may sell the residence, hold the proceeds, and buy another residence within two years from the sale. If the residence ceases to be a personal residence of the term holder, the trust corpus must be held for the balance of the term interest and must meet all of the requirements for functioning exclusively as a qualified annuity interest trust, similar to a GRAT.

Calculating the gift for a QPRT. The remainder value is the gift. Its value, when the settlor has a contingent reversion, is calculated as follows:

$$\text{Remainder value} = R_t * (Y/X) * \text{FMV of the home}$$

Where: Rt stands for the remainder factor taken from Table B for number of years the trust is to last and "t" is the § 7520 rate at the time it is funded; X is the number of persons alive at starting age for the settlor; and Y is the number alive at ending age for settlor. The numbers for X and Y are found in Table 90CM.

EXAMPLE 14 - 24. The § 7520 rate is 8.0% and the settlor is 75 at the start of a 10-year QPRT. The house being used to fund the trust is worth $500,000. R_t = .463193; X for age 75 is 60,449; and Y for age 85 is 31,770.

Therefore, the remainder value for this QPRT is:

$$.463193 * (31,770/60,449) * \$500,000 = \$121,719$$

Remember, that if the settlor dies during the term of the trust, its fair market value will be included in the settlor's estate. However, the adjusted taxable gift value drops back to zero because § 2001(b) defines "adjusted taxable gifts" as all post-1976 taxable gifts except for those "that are includable in the gross estate." QPRTs, like other qualified GRITs whose terms end before 2010, carry very little downside risk, other than the attorneys' fees in establishing them and the accountants' fees in maintaining them.

Must a settlor who survives the term of the QPRT vacate the residence? No, because he or she can rent it from the remainderman. However, the agreement must be arm's length, with lease payments equal to fair rental value, in order to avoid the risk of § 2036(a) application.[27] At one time, planners thought that the settlor could purchase the home from the trustee just as the term of the trust came to an end, but regulations proposed by the Treasury prohibit purchase by the settlor, the settlor's spouse, or an entity controlled by either of them.[28] Clearly, some people will not appreciate this aspect of the QPRT. Others, however, will welcome the ability to transfer property to their children at a greatly reduced transfer tax cost.

PLANNING FOR CHARITABLE TRANSFERS

Transfers to charity, whether lifetime or at death, are supported by several provisions of the Internal Revenue Code that allow generous deductions on a contributor's income tax, gift tax, and estate tax returns. Lifetime charitable transfers are the primary focus of this section because they have significant income tax advantages over charitable transfers at death, they often are more complex and need greater elaboration. Lifetime gifts to charity are of two types, outright gifts or split-interest gifts.

At the outset, it should be noted that charitable gifts may result in a net decrease in a client's wealth. Thus, the client will usually need to possess a charitable motive to feel comfortable about making such transfers. The material presented below describes some ways to minimize the decline in family wealth resulting from charitable donations.

Tax Consequences of Charitable Transfers

Income tax consequences. To qualify for an itemized charitable income tax deduction, the donee charity must meet the requirements under the Code.[29] In addition, the Code contains complex limitations on the amount of charitable contributions deductible from income by an individual in a tax year. There are limitations on both the total amount deductible for all charitable gifts and on the specific amount deductible for any particular gift.

Limitations on total amount deductible. Total deductible charitable contributions may not exceed 50% of a taxpayer's "contribution base" (CB), an amount that is approximately equal to adjusted gross income.[30] However, there are some major exceptions with regard to this 50% limitation. Taxpayers are limited to 30% of the CB for contributions to private foundations. In addition, deductible limits for both public charities and private foundations are reduced to

30% and 20%, respectively, for contributions of most kinds of "capital gain property."[31] Contributions in excess of these limits may be carried over for five years.[32] To further complicate matters, since 1991, charitable deductions for high income taxpayers are subject to a 3% overall floor as an itemized deduction.

> EXAMPLE 14 - 25. Fanny Superstar, a prominent singer, just donated her $15 million Malibu estate to charity. This year she earned $20 million in income. She can deduct $5.4 million, which is $6 million (30% * $20 million) reduced by the 3% floor (3% * 20 million). She can carry over the remaining $9 million ($15 million - $6 million) to later years. Assuming that her income remains about the same for the next three years and that her combined marginal tax rate is 50%, Fanny should save approximately $2.7 million in each of the first and second years, and $1.2 million in the third year, for a total income tax savings of about $6.6 million.

Amount deductible for a particular gift. The amount deductible from adjusted gross income for any particular charitable gift is usually its fair market value, subject to the total annual limitations outlined above. However, there are two important exceptions for noncash gifts. First, if sale of the property would have resulted in ordinary income or in short-term capital gain, the asset is called "ordinary income property," and the donor is limited to deducting the adjusted basis of the property, with a 50% CB limit.

Second, if the property would have resulted in a long-term capital gain had it been sold instead of donated, it is called "capital gain property," and one of three alternative tax consequences will occur. If the property is tangible personalty given to a public charity which uses it in its activities, then the fair market value is deductible (with a 30% CB limit). If, on the other hand, the charity is a private foundation, or if it is a public charity which cannot use the donated property in its activities, then the amount deductible is limited to the donor's basis, with a CB limit of 50% for donations to public charities and a 30% limit for donations to private charities. An example of a "related use" is placing a donated painting on a wall of the donee art museum or the donee university. An example of an unrelated use would be the storage of the painting in the institution's basement or the immediate sale of the painting. Finally, if the donation to a public charity qualifies for a deduction based on its fair market value, but with a 30% CB limitation, the taxpayer can elect to use the property's basis as the deduction and raise the CB limit to 50%.[33]

Any charitable contributions of $250 or more must be substantiated contemporaneously in writing by the donee charity. The writing should state the amount of cash donated, a description (but not necessarily the value) of the property, and a good faith estimate of the value of any property it provided in consideration for the donation.[34] In addition, a donor of property exceeding $5,000 in value is required to obtain a "qualified appraisal" and supply additional information detailing the transaction.

This summary of the annual limitations has been a short overview. Individuals wishing to make large contributions should consult a tax adviser specializing in this area.

Outright Gifts to Charity

Several planning strategies evolve from the tax rules just discussed.

Income tax consequences. In many cases, contributing capital gain property to a public charity is more advantageous than contributing cash.

> EXAMPLE 14 - 26. Jeff, who is in the 35% combined (i.e., state and federal) ordinary income tax bracket and a 22% combined capital gains tax bracket, wishes to contribute $5,000 to his favorite public charity. Jeff could give an original oil painting, acquired for $1,000 and now worth $5,000, or he could sell the painting and donate the cash proceeds. If Jeff contributes the painting, his after-tax cost will be $3,250 which is the $5,000 value of the painting, less the $1,750 tax savings from the deduction. Alternatively, if Jeff sells the painting and still donates the full $5,000, his after-tax cost will be $4,130, which is the $5,000 donated cash, plus the $880 tax on the gain ($4,000 * 22%), minus the $1,750 tax saving from the deduction.

Owners of nonmarketable property that they wish to sell may consider making a bargain sale of the property to charity. The income tax consequences of a bargain sale to charity are not the same as a bargain sale to a private individual. With the related party bargain sale, no loss can be recognized and a gain is recognized only if the bargain price exceeds the seller-donor's basis. But for a bargain sale to a charity, the transaction is treated as though it is two transactions in one: a sale and a gift. The old basis is allocated to each part in direct proportion to the part's value when compared to the whole. Thus, where B represents the old basis, B_g represents the portion of the basis allocated to the gift and B_s represents the basis allocated to the sale, G stands for the value of the gift, which is the difference between the amount paid (S for sale) by the charity and the fair market value (FMV) of the property transferred to the charity at a bargain price.

[handwritten: $500,000 put in $ policy trust cost?]

$$B_g = (G/FMV)*B$$
$$B_s = (S/FMV)*B$$
$$Gain = S - B_s$$

EXAMPLE 14 - 27. This year, Margaret transferred title to her vacant city lot worth $500,000 to her church in exchange for its promise to pay her $150,000. The lot was valued at $100,000 when she inherited it from her mother. Margaret plans to purchase a $500,000 life insurance policy so her son will not be too disappointed about her transferring the lot. Margaret's gain:

$$Gain = \$150,000 - (\$150,000/\$500,000)*\$100,000 = \$120,000$$

[handwritten: 400,000 / 120,000 / 20,000 purchase life ins]

Of course Margaret will have a charitable deduction of $350,000, the difference between the FMV and the amount paid to Margaret. If Margaret has modest income, she and the church might wish to structure this as an installment sale whereby the church pays the price in installments. The portion of the charitable deduction that exceeds the contribution base limits can be carried forward for five years, and installment reporting avoids bunching up the capital gain in the first year.

As in a private sale, an outright gift of mortgaged property to charity is treated as a bargain sale, resulting in taxable gain to the donor. However, the bargain sale may be a simple way to sell assets with a limited market, such as an interest in a closely held business.

Gift tax consequences. Similar to the unlimited marital deduction, an unlimited gift tax deduction is allowed for the present value of gifts to qualifying charities.[35] The rules covering the charitable deduction no longer require that a gift tax return be filed, even if the gifts exceed the annual exclusion amount.

Estate tax consequences. Similar to lifetime inter-spousal gifts, lifetime gifts to charity are not included in the donor's estate tax base. They are not includable in the gross estate because they are not owned by the decedent at death, nor are they adjusted taxable gifts.

Outright bequests to charity are totally deductible from the gross estate.[36] Thus, a multimillionaire could give all (or all but the AEA) of his or her entire estate to charity and ensure total avoidance of the estate tax. Of course, he or she could also accomplish this goal by making a series of lifetime charitable transfers. In fact, lifetime charitable transfers are preferable to donations at death, as the next example illustrates.

EXAMPLE 14 - 28. Sampson wishes to make an outright gift of $100,000 to his church which has been a source of continuous spiritual support to him and his family for many years. Sampson's estate planner recommends a lifetime transfer over a similar transfer at death, reasoning as follows: If Sampson donates the property at his death, his gross estate will be reduced by the amount of the gift, but he will enjoy no income tax benefit.[37] Alternatively, if Sampson makes the gift during his lifetime (even a deathbed gift), not only will his gross estate and estate tax base be lower by the date-of-death value of the gift property, but Sampson will also be able to save income taxes by deducting some or all of the value of the gift from his income.

Other tax planning for outright gifts to charity. Several other strategies include inter-spousal transfers, redemption bailout of corporate stock, gifts of life insurance, and the gift annuity.

Inter-spousal transfers. If a person insists on making a testamentary bequest to charity, the planner might urge the person to consider making an outright gift to the surviving spouse, who could then donate the property to charity. While the estate tax consequences are the same, the income tax results will improve, since S2 will be able to enjoy a charitable income tax deduction. Of course, S2, as fee simple recipient of the property, might decide not to make the donation. Placing the property in a QTIP trust, with the charity named as the remainderman, will ensure receipt by the charity, but not until after S2's death, thus there would be no income tax advantage.

Redemption bailout of corporate stock. A person owning stock in a closely held corporation may wish to gift some stock to a charity which will later tender the stock for redemption by the corporation. Advantages include saving income tax, "bailing out" corporate earnings and profits without incurring dividend income, helping younger family shareholders concentrate their ownership, and enabling the charity to receive cash. This arrangement should be undertaken with great caution, however, and may be challenged if the IRS believes it can prove the existence of an "understanding" between donor and charity that the charity would surrender the shares for redemption. In that case, the donor would be forced to incur a taxable gain.

Charitable gifts of life insurance. Lifetime gifts to charity of life insurance policies are popular. The insured can transfer an existing policy to charity, or the person can purchase a new policy naming the charity as beneficiary and assigning to the charity all ownership rights in the policy. The insured may agree to continue to pay the premiums. The person should be able to take income tax and gift tax charitable deductions for the policy's terminal value at the date of the gift (or adjusted basis, if less, in the case of income tax) and take additional income tax deductions as premiums are paid.

Gifts of Split Interests

Despite the added income tax advantage of lifetime charitable gifts, even individuals with strong charitable motives are sometimes reluctant to make outright gifts to charity because they are not willing to relinquish total control of an asset. For example, they may be relying on an asset as a source of income or enjoyment, or they may have been planning to pass the asset to their children. They may be more willing to make a split-interest gift in which the charity is given a vested future interest in property. The donor may accomplish several objectives; increasing income while generating an income tax deduction and possibly reducing estate taxes.

A split-interest arrangement divides the asset into two separate property interests; the income interest and the remainder interest. Usually the owner retains the right to the income and gives the remainder interest to a charity. However, if the income is not needed, the owner can give the income interest for a period of time to a charity and give the remainder to a someone else.

Arrangements for donating remainder interests to charity. Three devices recognized by tax law are commonly used by individuals to retain an income interest in an asset and give the remainder interest to charity. Two of them, broadly called *charitable remainder trusts*, are the annuity trust and the unitrust. The third is called the *pooled income fund*. For each, the charity receives an irrevocable (vested) remainder interest in the asset. These 'strings-attached' arrangements will cause the date-of-death value of the property to be included in the donor's gross estate,[38] but an equal charitable deduction will reduce the taxable amount to zero.[39]

Charitable remainder annuity trust. With a *charitable remainder annuity trust* (CRAT), the person receives annuity income equal to at least 5% of the original value of the assets transferred into trust, payable at least annually, usually for life. The value of the deductible interest is calculated from IRS valuation Table S.

> EXAMPLE 14 - 29. Carrie, age 75, creates a CRAT, funding the trust with $100,000 in appreciated securities. The trust provides for a 5% annual payment to Carrie for her life. When the trust was funded the § 7520 rate was 10%. The value of the retained income interest is $28,939 [5.7877 * $5,000]. Therefore, the charity's interest (and Carrie's deduction) is $71,062, i.e., the difference between the total value of the property and the value of the retained income interest.

Charitable remainder unitrust. The charitable remainder unitrust (CRUT) is much like the CRAT, except that the annual income depends on a fixed percentage of the current fair market value of the assets in the trust, redetermined annually. Thus, the amount of the annual income paid to the person will vary (hopefully upward) from year to year.[40]

The CRUT can provide for the income to be the lesser of the unitrust amount or the amount actually earned on the trust property, with any deficiencies payable in later years when earnings are higher. Thus, the owner of a rapidly appreciating, low-dividend-paying corporation can contribute stock to a CRUT and enjoy a large stream of income years later, after retirement, when the stock starts paying dividends. This "net income with make-up" unitrust (NIMCRUT) represents risky planning because the IRS has challenged these arrangements.

Calculation of the remainder interest for a CRUT is complex and beyond the scope of this text. Most charities have access to computer programs that will "run the numbers" without cost for prospective donors.

At their best, charitable remainder trusts offer to an individual the advantages of higher cash flow during lifetime, lower investment risk, and greater portfolio diversification. At their worst, they can be a confusing financial burden. In one case a $25 million estate lost an $18 million deduction because its charitable trust was not in the form of an annuity trust, a unitrust, or a pooled income fund.[41] Although the IRS Regulations are exceedingly complex, requiring the drafting of long and technical documents, the Treasury has issued safe harbor sample documents which may be suitable for most people's needs. However, this is an area where very experienced counsel is needed.

Disillusioned clients will become more prevalent if financial planners continue to aggressively promote these trusts primarily as a means of increasing retirement income and avoiding capital gains tax. Advertisements appear in newspapers with the main pitch being "stop paying unnecessary taxes" with little or no mention that a sizable charitable contribution is required.

If you have clients interested in using charitable trusts as part of their estate plan, you should consider associating with an expert who is experienced in these complex matters. The charities themselves often have lists of estate planners who are conversant with establishing charitable trusts.

Pooled income fund. A pooled income fund is an investment fund created and maintained by a charity which "pools" property from many similar contributors instead of requiring each donor to create their own separate trust. Thus, the donor is spared the expense of planning and drafting a trust, an arrangement which would be uneconomic when the charitable donation is relatively small (e.g., $10,000 to $100,000).

Many pooled income funds limit donations to cash and cash equivalents. The pooled income fund ordinarily provides that the charity will pay to the grantor an income for life and, if desired, for the life of the grantor's spouse, based on the rate of return actually earned by the fund as a whole. At their death, the property passes to the charity. Valuation of the charitable deduction is calculated using Treasury tables available from the IRS.

Comparison of the three techniques. All three techniques have the advantages of providing an income for life, reducing estate tax, and obtaining a relatively immediate income tax deduction. The CRAT may appeal to individuals who desire the certainty of a fixed income, even in a declining market. The CRUT may be preferred by those willing to risk fluctuating income for the opportunity of realizing higher income payments. Thus, the CRUT can offer a hedge against inflation. Assets in a CRUT do require an annual valuation, a possible extra trust cost. Most of the larger charities and most colleges and universities have established pooled income funds. The pooled income fund may be preferred by those who would like to avoid having to establish and maintain a trust. Pooled income funds are not permitted to invest in tax-exempt securities.[42]

The charitable lead trust. Instead of contributing a remainder interest, a person can donate an asset's income interest for a period of years to charity, with the remainder interest then passing to a private party (reverting to either the grantor or spouse, or passing to another person, such as a child or grandchild). The person or the person's estate will receive an income tax deduction for the value of the income interest, based on Treasury valuation tables. To get the charitable deduction, the trust must be set up as a grantor trust, making the income taxable to the grantor,[43] unless the trust is established at the grantor's death. Thus, charitable lead trusts are often designed to take effect after the person's death.

In a manner similar to a zeroed-out GRAT, a charitable lead trust may be structured to generate a charitable deduction equal to almost 100% of the current value of property transferred by way of the trust. If done successfully, the value of the remainder interest (probably given to the settlor's children) will approximate zero, resulting in very little use of the settlor's unified credit. Further, nothing (or very little) is included in the individual's taxable estate. Either the person will not own the property at death (because it was a lifetime charitable gift), or, if this is done as part of a testamentary plan, the estate will be entitled to a charitable deduction that offsets most of the value of the property going into the charitable lead trust. The goal is for the property to not only benefit the charity for a period of years, but to grow in value so the remaindermen eventually receive a sizable distribution at the end of the term, all without incurring transfer taxes on the donated property. As the examples below show, success of the charitable lead trust depends on the actual rate of future asset appreciation.

EXAMPLE 14 - 30. Reed creates a lifetime charitable lead trust, funding it with $100,000 in stock of his closely held corporation. The trust is obligated to pay a "guaranteed annuity" of $11,750, or 11.75% of the initial value of the corpus annually to the charity for a period of 20 years. Then, the trust will terminate and the remaining corpus, if any, will be distributed outright to Reed's surviving children and grandchildren. Assuming a 10% discount rate, the IRS Table annuity factor is 8.5136. The value of the charity's 20 year income interest is $100,034.80, the product of $11,750 and 8.5136. Reed's deduction is limited to $100,000, the value of the property. Since the value of the present income interest is higher than the value of the property, the value of the remainder interest is zero, which means that Reed has made no taxable gift.

EXAMPLE 14 - 31. Continuing the example immediately above, assume 20 years have passed. The closely held stock in the trust has returned much more than 11.75% and its annual income has been more than enough to pay the annuity. As a result, its current value is $800,000. The stock will pass outright to Reed's descendants completely transfer-tax-free.

EXAMPLE 14 - 32. Altering the projected outcome in the example above, assume again that 20 years have passed, but the closely held stock has earned only a 10%

annual average rate of return, forcing the trustee to use trust corpus to satisfy the $11,750 annual distribution requirement. By the end of the trust's term, its corpus will have been distributed to the charity and there will be nothing left for the remaindermen.

The outcomes in the two preceding examples represent two extremes. For most individuals, the results will be somewhere in between. The gift tax value of the remainder will not be zero, which means the grantor will have to partially use up his or her unified credit on a future interest gift that does not qualify for the annual exclusion. In addition, at the end of the trust term, with prudent investing, the corpus will probably have appreciated somewhat.

When the former first lady, Jackie Kennedy Onassis, died in May of 1994, her estate plan, among other bequests, created two charitable lead trusts. One, for a period of 10 years, had her sister's issue as the remaindermen. It was funded with $500,000 for each of her sister's children. The other trust, funded with the residue of her estate, lasts for a period of 24 years, with her issue as remaindermen. The § 7520 rate was 9%. The annuity payment for the 24year trust was 10% of its initial net value and for the 24-year trust was 8% of its initial net value. The annuity factor for the 24year trust is 6.4177, so the factor times the 10% annuity amount results in an estate tax deduction equal to 64.2% of the initial value of the trust. The annuity factor for the 24-year trust is 9.7066, so the factor times the 8% annuity amount results in a charitable deduction equal to 77.7% of the initial value of the trust. Interestingly, neither trust specified the recipient charities, other than that they had to be qualified ones, leaving the selection to the trustees.

EXAMPLE 14 - 33. Charlie established a charitable lead trust for a 20-year term with assets worth $1,000,000. The trust must pay the charity $70,000 per year. If the § 7520 rate is 6%, the "lead" interest for the charity is worth $802,893 [$70,000 * 11.4699], but if the rate is 12%, the lead interest is just $522,858 [$70,000 * 7.4694]. Thus, the lower the rate, the better the charitable deduction for Charlie.

The charitable lead trust works best for wealthy, estate tax avoiding individuals who can afford to forego substantial income for a period of time. The remaindermen will be most pleased if the trust assets appreciate greatly during the trust's term and still manage to generate sufficient income to meet the required payout.

CONCLUSION

This chapter has focused on various nongift, lifetime intrafamily transfers and charitable gifts that really work. The techniques not only reduce taxes, but they also help other members of the person's family and/or they help charities by providing funds that allow them to carry out their charitable purposes. It is often a win-win situation. Some of the techniques allow both families and charities to increase their wealth.

In contrast, Appendix 14A examines various defective incomplete transfers. You are urged to read it, partly to gain a historical perspective, partly because some clients will still be involved in earlier transfers of this kind, and partly to be aware of formerly popular devices about which clients may inquire for some time to come.

QUESTIONS AND PROBLEMS

1. Why are many planning-minded persons disinclined to make gifts?

2. How can a bargain sale add flexibility to gift planning?

3. (a) Describe the installment sale. (b) What tax advantage does it have over the ordinary sale?

4. Summarize the major advantages and disadvantages of the private annuity.

5. Jack, a wealthy 60-year-old, asks you for advice on lifetime transfers. His daughter is interested in acquiring his antique car, which is worth $40,000 and has a basis of $10,000. In each of the following alternatives, calculate Jack's taxable gain for each year.
   a. Ordinary sale.
   b. Installment sale, over 10 years (no down payment), with equal annual payments on principal, plus interest at a rate of 10% on the outstanding balance.

6. The O'Learys are a husband and wife in their 70s, with an adult daughter age 45. They wish to make a lifetime transfer of a considerable amount of wealth to her, and you recommend four alternatives for consideration: A large outright gift, an installment sale, a private annuity, or a grantor retained annuity trust.
   a. Which transfer would probably involve the greatest present value of expected total costs to daughter? Why?
   b. Which one will probably save the most estate tax? Why?
   c. Which is probably the safest in terms of IRS challenge? Why?
   d. In which have the O'Learys retained the greatest interest? Why?
   e. Identify several other factors that are likely to influence which transfer, if any, the O'Learys select.

7. Under what circumstances will a gift-leaseback work well?

8. Discuss the income shifting and estate tax reducing ability of the grantor retained income trust.

9. Explain the reason for the advantage of each of the following charitable transfers.
   a. Gift of appreciated property rather than cash derived from the sale of the property.
   b. Lifetime gift rather than gift at death.
   c. Gift of a split interest rather than a whole interest.

10. Stover is 90 years old and is currently in the 35% combined state and federal marginal income tax bracket and pays a combined 20% for capital gains. He wishes to gift to a charity his ABC Corp. stock, worth $20,000 with an adjusted basis of $2,000. For each of these alternatives, assume the value remains at $20,000, calculate his "after-tax cost" of making the each transfer and state which alternative appears to be most beneficial.
    a. He bequeaths the stock to the charity and dies.
    b. He sells the stock and gives the entire $20,000 to the charity.
    c. He makes an outright gift of the stock to the charity.

11. When he was 80 years old, Brian established a three-year GRAT, funding it with assets worth $1,000,000. Income payments are made at the end of each year. Deborah is the remainderman. For each alternative, determine the value of the gift. Explain your answer and show any calculations. (a) Deborah is his daughter, he retained the right to all income, and the § 7520 rate was 8%. (b) Same as "a" except Deborah is his niece? (c) Deborah is his daughter, he retained income of $80,000 per year, and the § 7520 rate was 8%.

12. When she was 70 years old, Patricia established a five-year GRAT, funding it with assets worth $500,000. Income payments are made at the end of each year. Patricia retained a contingent reversion that returns all trust assets to her estate if she dies before the trust terminates. Craig is the remainderman. For each alternative determine the value of the gift. Explain your answer and show any calculations. (a) Craig is her son, Patricia retained the right to all income, and the § 7520 rate was 12%. (b) Same as "a" except Craig is her

nephew? (c) Craig is her son, she retained income of $60,000 per year, and the § 7520 rate was 8%.

13. When he was 75 years old, Eulalio established a four-year QPRT, funding it with his home worth $1,000,000. Maria is the remainderman. If Eulalio died before the trust terminated the corpus reverts to his estate. For each alternative determine the value of the gift. Explain your answer and show any calculations. (a) Maria is his daughter and the § 7520 rate was 6%. (b) Would your answer change if Maria was his niece? (c) Maria is his daughter and the § 7520 rate was 12%.

14. When she was 90 years old, Cynthia established a five-year QPRT, her home worth $500,000. Cynthia retained a contingent reversion that returns all trust assets to her estate if she dies before the trust terminates. Ralph is the remainderman. For each alternative determine the value of the gift. Explain your answer and show any calculations. (a) Ralph is her son and the § 7520 rate was 12%. (b) Same as "a" except Ralph is her nephew. (c) Continue from "b," Cynthia died in 2008, the trust had not terminated, and the house was worth $550,000. What value insofar as this QPRT is included in her gross estate and what is the adjusted taxable gift?

15. Compare the advantages of the CRAT, the CRUT, and the Pooled Income Fund.

16. Use the table that follows to compare the advantages of various lifetime transfers. In each box, place the number that you think describes how well that transfer accomplishes each goal, using the following rating system: 3 = excellent, 2 = good, 1 = fair, and 0 = poor. Use a range if the outcome is uncertain and be prepared to explain why you choose a number or a range.

TABLE 14-1 Comparative Advantages of Lifetime Transfers

Types of Transfers	Goals									
	Ability to Retain		Ability to Avoid		Step-up in Basis	Shift income	Estate Tax Base		Avoid Probate	Low risk of IRS attack
	Control	Income	Income Tax	Gift tax			Reduce	Freeze		
Annual exclusion gifts										
Large out-right gifts										
Ordinary sale										
Bargain Sale										
Installment sale										
Private annuity										
Gift-lease back										
Grantor retained income trust (GRIT)										
Irrevocable Life Insurance Trust										

ANSWERS TO THE QUESTIONS AND PROBLEMS *(odd numbered only)*

1. Planning-minded persons are often unwilling to make outright gifts because they do not want to relinquish: 1) dominion and control over assets; and 2) income earned from the assets.

3. a. Under an installment sale, the seller transfers an asset in exchange for a note which obligates the buyer to make periodic payments of income and principal.
    b. Compared to the ordinary sale, it has the tax advantage of spreading recognition of the seller's taxable gain over the collection period.

5. a. Ordinary sale: Gain = $40,000 - $10,000 = $30,000. Entire tax is due in year of sale.
    b. Installment sale: Gross profit = $30,000. Seventy-five percent of each principal payment is taxable in the year received (= $30,000 gross profit ÷ $40,000 selling price). Thus, each year, taxable capital gain is .75*$4,000 = $3,000. Any interest received, of course, is taxable, too.

7. A gift-leaseback will work well for a business-owning individual who wishes to shift income to a lower bracket family member and has business assets that can be transferred.

9. a. A gift of appreciated property will eliminate the need to recognize the unrealized gain on the property, thereby reducing the net, after tax-cost of the charitable expense.
    b. A lifetime gift will reduce income tax (charitable deduction) and exclude the gift from the gross estate. A gift at death will only reduce the taxable estate but not reduce income tax.
    c. Gift of a split interest can enable the donor to retain a highly desired portion of the property, such as a life estate in the income.

11. (a) Because the remainderman is a "member of the transferor family," i.e., a daughter, and the retained interest is not a qualified one, it is given a zero value, hence the gift is the full $1 million.

(b) A niece is not considered a member of the family, hence the anti-freeze sections do not apply. Use Table B: 0.793832 * $1,000,000 = $793,832. Because this is a common law GRIT the gift would be reduced further by a contingent reversion. (c) This is a qualified GRAT: $1,000,000 - 2.5771 * $80,000 = $793,832. (note: same answer as in part "b" because the annuity amount was 8% of the trust value and we are using the 8% table.

13. (a) Because this is a QPRT it does not come within the purview of the anti-freeze sections and we treat it as a common law GRIT. Use Table B. 0.792,094 * $1,000,000 = $792,094 and adjust for the contingency: $792,094 * 49,943/60,449 = $654,429. (b) Same answer since this is a QPRT it does not matter what the relationship is between settlor and remainderman. (c) The only thing that changes is the remainder factor decreases as the interest rate increases: 0.635518 * $1,000,000 * 49,943/60,449 = $525,065.

15. All of the techniques offer individuals an opportunity for a large current charitable deduction, coupled with a (potentially high) income stream for the rest of their lives.

> CRAT: Offers the certainty of a fixed income for life.
> CRUT: Offers possibly higher income payments in future years, because income is based on a fixed percentage of current value.
> Pooled Income Fund: Offers opportunity for a split interest charitable gift without the need to set up and maintain a private trust.

Defective Incomplete Transfers

OVERVIEW

This appendix will describe six defective transfer devices that should presently not be recommended by planners. The first five have been virtually legislated out of existence by Congress between 1984 and 1990. And the sixth has always been inherently defective.

The evolution of income tax law in the last few years has resulted in depriving taxpayers of the major tax benefits earlier available through the use of the interest-free loan, the short-term trust, the spousal remainder trust, the sale of a remainder interest, and the joint purchase. The interest-free loan was first to go with the passage of TRA 84. The next two were killed by TRA 86. The last two were rendered ineffective by Case law and by the Revenue Reconciliation Act of 1990. They were all vulnerable to attack because they were too effective to last. Unlike the other lifetime transfers we cover, each was able to accomplish at least two of the following objectives; shifting large amounts of income while allowing the transferor to retain a substantial interest in or control over property, or freezing large estate tax values at little or no gift tax cost.

The family estate trust has never worked, since its operation clearly violates major holdings of case law and provisions of the Internal Revenue Code.

This appendix has been written for three reasons. First, it will give the reader a better historical perspective on lifetime transfers. Second, these strategies may have been employed by some individuals in the past, and may still be in use. The reader should be aware of their operation since questions will be raised about their efficacy. Finally, the planner can expect some clients to be curious about these formerly popular devices for years to come.

INTEREST-FREE LOANS

Until 1984, the interest-free loan (IFL) was considered an attractive device to shift income to a lower-tax-bracket family member. However, the Tax Reform Act of 1984 all but destroyed its appeal.

An interest-free loan of cash may be able to shift taxable income from the lender to the borrower, since the borrower is free to use the loaned property to generate income without incurring a financing charge, and the income generated may be taxed at a significantly lower rate than the lender's. Further, the loan may give the borrower a higher standard of living. Unfortunately, other tax consequences often render IFLs largely unattractive.[44] As the following material suggests, tax controversy has highlighted their brief history.

An arm's length loan, in which the lender charges a fair market rate of interest, does not achieve many estate planning objectives. It does not shift income significantly, although it may provide for the borrower an otherwise unavailable loan opportunity.

Gift Tax Consequences

In 1984, the U.S. Supreme Court settled a longstanding conflict between taxpayers and the IRS by ruling that an IFL constitutes a taxable gift of the reasonable value of the use of the money loaned.[45] In calculating the taxable gift value, the taxpayer is required to use a federal rate of interest, which is published monthly by the IRS and set approximately equal to the rate that is paid by the U.S. Treasury on securities of similar maturity.

IFLs can be made for a fixed term, or they can have a demand provision. If the loan is made for a fixed term, the gift is considered as having been made as of the inception of the loan, with the gift amount equal to the difference between the amount loaned and the discounted present value of the note.

> EXAMPLE 14 - 34. Dad and Mom lend $100,000 cash, interest-free, to Mary who has just graduated from dental school and wishes to start a practice. Mary signs a 10-year note, with no principal payable until maturity. Assuming that the current federal long-term rate is 10%, the present discounted value of the note is approximately $38,500, and Mom and Dad are deemed to have made a gift of approximately $61,500, the difference between the amount transferred and the value received.

If, on the other hand, an interest-free loan incorporates a demand loan, with the loan callable by the lender at any time, then at the end of each year the lender will have made a gift of one year's imputed interest.

> EXAMPLE 14 - 35. Assume the facts in Example 14- 35, except that the note is a demand loan with no maturity. If the loan is still outstanding at the end of their first taxable year, Mom and Dad will have made a gift of one year's interest, imputed to be $10,000, calculated on the basis of the assumed 10% short-term federal rate. For every year that the loan remains outstanding, a similar gift computation will have to be made.

Thus, in order to minimize the gift tax, an IFL must have no maturity. And, to prevent the entire transfer from being treated as an outright gift, the loan must have a demand provision.

If an interest-free demand loan becomes unenforceable, a more significant taxable event will have occurred.

> EXAMPLE 14 - 36. Assume the facts in Example 14-36. Four years go by, and the state's statute of limitations runs out preventing any collection on the original note. In that year, a taxable gift of the entire loan principal is triggered.

Thus, IFLs must be redrafted periodically to prevent this unfortunate tax consequence.

Despite the court decision subjecting interest-free loans to gift taxation, most lenders will not owe any gift tax because of the combined shelter of the annual exclusion and the unified credit. Thus, the parents in the above examples will incur no gift tax liability, unless they have already made taxable gifts large enough to have fully used up their unified credits. In general, the gift tax issue should not discourage many from the use of interest-free loans as a method of shifting income to a lower tax bracket. However, the income tax issues, discussed next, usually will.

Income Tax Consequences

The IRS has argued, in a business context, that the interest forgone by a corporate lender constitutes taxable income to an employee-executive borrower. To date, the IRS has had little success in the courts, and unless it can influence Congress to act, imputed interest income on an interest-free loan will not likely be taxed to the borrower.

In 1984, Congress did act, however, to tax the lender on the amount of the interest forgone under an IFL.[46] This forgone interest is treated as if it had been received by the lender and paid by the borrower. Thus, the lender is deemed to have received taxable interest, which is includable in gross income. Similarly, the borrower is deemed to have paid interest, which ordinarily is not tax deductible unless it is considered business interest, investment interest which is offset by investment income, or interest on a debt secured by a primary or secondary residence. In short, there is usually greater taxable income without the corresponding deduction.

> EXAMPLE 14 - 37. Dad, in the 31% income tax bracket, makes a $20,000 interest-free demand loan to his son, who is in the 15% bracket and is able to invest the proceeds in a bank time deposit yielding an annual return of 8%. Assuming an applicable federal rate of 10%, the tax consequences in the first full year are as follows:
>
> *Gift tax treatment*: At the end of each year, Dad will be deemed to have made a gross gift of $1,600, the amount of the forgone interest. Because of the annual exclusion, there will be no taxable gift.
>
> *Income tax treatment in the absence of the 1984 Act*: Each year, son would earn $1,600 taxable income on the deposit, paying a tax of $240. Instead, had Dad invested the loan money, he would have paid a tax of $496. Thus, in the absence of the 1984 act, under TRA 86 tax rates the family would have saved $256 in income tax.
>
> *Income tax treatment under the 1984 Act*: If son does not itemize, he will still pay a tax of $240, and in addition, Dad will pay a tax of $496 on the $1,600 of imputed interest, for a total of $736. On the other hand, if son itemizes, the $1,600 imputed interest payment is an investment interest expense which he can deduct. In this case, the son's tax would effectively be zero, the Dad's tax would still be $496, so the family as a whole would not have any tax savings from the loan.

The 1984 Act incorporated four exceptions, which may provide the basis for a very modest degree of income shifting. First, where the proceeds of an IFL between individuals are invested by the borrower to yield less than $1,000 income in any given year, forgone interest will not be imputed. Thus, at an assumed 8% investment return, a person could lend $12,500 interest free, without being subject to income taxation.

The second exception to the 1984 Act applies to a loan balance of $10,000 or less to any individual, which is not subject to imputed interest unless it is used to purchase income-producing assets.

Third, the amount of the imputed interest is limited to the borrower's net investment income for the year in cases where the aggregate amount of outstanding loans between two individuals does not exceed $100,000, provided that one of the principal purposes of the loan is not federal tax avoidance.

The fourth exception to the 1984 Act applies to loans to employees and to corporate shareholders, who are permitted to borrow up to $10,000 without imputing forgone interest, provided that one of the principal purposes of the loan is not federal tax avoidance.

Interest-free demand loans should be made in the form of cash, rather than other property. A transfer of noncash in exchange for a note might be treated as a taxable sale to the extent of the consideration received.

Estate Tax Consequences

At the lender's death, the gross estate will include the current value of the note. The market value of a demand note will equal the face amount of the note, since the decedent, just prior to death, could have demanded full repayment.[47] On the other hand, the market value of a term note will usually be different from the face amount and is calculated by using a market rate of interest to discount the value of the future payments. In executing either kind of note, the lender has not really been able to reduce his or her gross estate significantly. The interest-free loan was never designed to reduce death taxes.

In conclusion, because of its serious tax consequences and the compression of income tax rates, the IFL will no longer be used much.

SHORT-TERM TRUST

Prior to March 2, 1986, the short-term trust was a very popular device to shift income to a lower-bracket taxpayer. Also called the Clifford trust, after the taxpayer who lost a court case trying to shift income using a trust of short duration. Congress then stepped in and set the standards for trusts that would be acceptable for shifting income.[48] The Code required that the trust be irrevocable for at least 10 years or for the life of a beneficiary, after which the trust corpus would revert to the settlor.

Gift Tax Consequences

If the income had to be paid to the income beneficiary for the term of the trust, then it was considered to be a present interest and, as such, it qualified for the annual exclusion. The reversionary interest was what was being kept by the settlor, hence it was not a gift (even though it is a future interest).

Income Tax Consequences

Grandfathered trusts. Income earned on the property placed in a 10-year short-term trust on or before March 1, 1986, will not be taxable to the transferor-grantor, except when the kiddie tax applies. Instead, the income will be taxed to the trust or to the beneficiary, depending on whether it is accumulated or distributed. The accumulated income later distributed to the beneficiary could be subject to some additional tax, under the throwback rules, unless the beneficiary is under age 21.

Falling withing the grantor trust provisions of the Internal Revenue Code will cause income received by the trust to be taxable to the grantor. Thus, the short-term trust had to be carefully drafted to avoid running afoul of the grantor trust rules. For example, the trust had to be irrevocable for at least 10 years from the date the trust was funded with the property, not from the date the document was executed.

EXAMPLE 14 - 38. In 1983, Omid created an irrevocable trust for the benefit of his 17-year-old daughter Hazel. The trust terms required the trustee to pay Hazel all of the income from the trust for 10 years, after which the corpus would revert to Omid. It was funded with stocks and bonds worth $100,000. Because it complied with the short term trust laws, Hazel reported the income each year until the trust terminated. (Formally, the trust first reported it, took a distribution deduction for the income distributed to Hazel, and sent her a "K-1" that told her how much she had to report on her income tax returns.) Assuming an 8% rate for valuing the income interest, Table B shows 0.536807 as the appropriate factor for a 24year income interest. Therefore, the gift to Hazel was valued at $53,680.70. It was a present interest, so the taxable gift that Omid reported was $43,680.70

Nongrandfathered trusts. TRA 86 destroyed the income tax benefit of the short-term trust by deleting the 10-year exception under Internal Revenue Code (IRC) Section 673. Thus, for any transfers into trust after March 1, 1986, the grantor is treated as the owner of any portion of a trust in which the grantor has any reversionary interest which exceeds 5% of the value of such portion. Thus, the typical new short-term trust will be treated as a grantor trust.

How long must a short-term trust created after March 1, 1986, last so that the present value of the remainder interest does not exceed 5% of the corpus? IRS tables indicate that the reversion cannot occur for at least 32 years! Although several commentators are suggesting that there may be situations where this period is acceptable, in most cases, grantors will not wish to make an irrevocable transfer of property for such a long time. Most individuals will no longer wish to shift income with the short-term trust. Thus, the short-term trust is no longer practical to shift income to save income tax.

Estate Tax Consequences to the Grantor

Several estate tax consequences may occur when the grantor dies. First, if creation of the trust resulted in a "taxable gift," that is, the transfer of an amount in excess of the annual exclusion and other deductions, then that taxable value will be added to the estate tax base, as an "adjusted taxable gift." Of course, a credit will be applied for any gift tax paid, but the taxation of adjusted taxable gifts along with the rest of a decedent's estate may subject the gift to a higher marginal rate of taxation than that incurred when the gift tax was calculated.

A second estate tax consequence at the grantor's death will be the addition to the gross estate of the actuarial value of the decedent-grantor's interest in the trust property. Determination of that amount will depend on when the decedent dies.

If the grantor dies before the trust reverts, the value of the gross estate will include the value of the grantor's reversionary interest at death. For example, assuming a 10% discount rate, if a grantor dies exactly five years prior to reversion, 62.0921% will be in the gross estate. This number is derived from the U.S. Treasury estate tax valuation table found in Treasury Regulations 20.2031-7. It depends on the assumed interest rate and the number of years to reversion.

If the grantor of a short-term trust dies after reversion, the value of the gross estate will include the date-of-death market value of the property that had reverted, if still owned, or the value of any other assets acquired with the property. However, since the property is back in the transferor's estate, it will not be an adjusted taxable gift for estate tax purposes.

As an income tax planning device, the short-term trust was commonly used for helping children or elderly parents in lower tax brackets. Due to changes in the law these short-term trusts are no longer useful.

SPOUSAL REMAINDER TRUST

A popular income-shifting device prior to TRA 86 was the spousal remainder trust (SRT). As in the case of the short-term trust, the grantor, typically a high-income-tax-bracket parent, transferred income-earning property to an irrevocable trust. It paid all income for a specified period to a low income tax bracket family member, typically a young adult child, and the remainder to the grantor's spouse. Properly arranged, the value of the income interest, which is valued in a manner similar to the short-term trust, would qualify for the annual gift tax exclusion. However, unlike the short-term trust, whose property reverted to the grantor, the SRT corpus then passed to the grantor's spouse. Although the value of the remainder interest will not qualify for the annual exclusion, it will not be subject to gift tax, due to the unlimited gift tax marital deduction.

EXAMPLE 14 - 39. In 1985, Dad created an SRT, funding it with $30,000 in bonds. Income is required to be paid annually to his daughter, a college freshman, for the next four years. At the end of the fourth year, the corpus will pass outright to Mom. Based on the valuation tables, the value of a gift of an income interest for a four-year term certain represents 31.6987 percent of the total value of the property transferred. Although Dad has made a gross gift to his daughter of $9,510, there will be no taxable gift, since the gift of the income interest is sheltered entirely by the annual exclusion and the gift of the remainder interest is sheltered entirely by the marital deduction.

Prior to TRA 86, the SRT had several advantages over the short-term trust. First, because the corpus did not revert to the grantor, the trust was not required to remain in existence for 10 years. Thus, the length of time the trust would last was fully within the control of the settlor. If the period set was less than 10 years, the relative value of the transferred income interest would be less than that for the short-term trust. This meant that more property could be transferred to the SRT free of gift tax.

It could also facilitated the couple's estate tax planning objectives by transferring a portion of the wealthier spouse's estate to the less wealthy spouse thereby equalizing somewhat their estates which in turn reduced estate taxes.

TRA 86 destroyed the usefulness of the spousal remainder trust by amending Section 672 to treat any power or interest held by a spouse (who lives with the grantor) as if that interest was held by the grantor. Therefore, the traditional spousal remainder trust, funded after March 1, 1986, will be treated as if it will revert to the grantor, making it a grantor trust and thereby preventing the shifting of income to the lower-bracket-income beneficiary. Thus, there is no longer any reason to choose this once appealing transfer strategy.

SALE OF A REMAINDER INTEREST AND JOINT PURCHASE

Prior to 1986, the sale of a remainder interest was able to freeze estate tax values, generate cash flow, and assist family members. It also permitted the individual to retain the right to possession and enjoyment of the property "sold" until death. Although it was coming under increasing attack from the IRS, it was an attractive alternative. The ordinary sale, bargain sale, installment sale, and a private annuity may all be unacceptable to some individuals who do not want to surrender the present enjoyment of property during their lifetimes. All of these sales techniques involve the immediate transfer of the right to possession and enjoyment which the sale of a remainder interest did not.

EXAMPLE 14 - 40. In 1982, a 60-year-old parent had valuable jewelry which her son wanted her to keep in the family. He purchased a remainder interest in the jewelry at a time when the § 7520 rate was 10%, he paid her 21.2% of the value of the jewelry for the right to receive it outright when his mother died. His mother could own and enjoy the jewelry for her lifetime. The estate tax value was frozen, since the person's gross estate would include only the sale proceeds that were unspent. Of course, the son would not receive possession of the jewelry until the person's death, but he probably would have received it no sooner anyway.

With an installment sale, the seller could occasionally forgive a payment, which constituted a taxable gift that qualified for the annual exclusion. Use of the installment sale also postponed recognition of the seller's gain. In determining gain or loss with the sale of a remainder interest, the income tax basis in the remainder interest is apportioned between the remainder interest and the retained life estate. Thus, in our example, the son's tax basis became 22.674% of the former basis.

Exclusion of the remainder interest from the seller's gross estate was not guaranteed, however, as the IRS could have contended that the only way to escape the trap of § 2036 was for the purchaser to have paid the full value of the property, not just the value of the remainder interest. Of course, this would have made the transaction even less attractive to the buyer than an ordinary sale.

The passage of § 2036(c) in the Revenue Act of 1987 (and a subsequent court decision) increased the likelihood of inclusion, due to its emphasis on estate freezing transfers.[49]

The risk of § 2036 inclusion was reduced if, instead of making a transfer of property, the individual and another family member joined in purchasing property from a third party, with the individual purchasing a life interest and the family member (usually a member of the younger generation) acquiring the remainder interest. As a result, this "joint purchase" or "split purchase" rapidly replaced the sale of a remainder interest as a preferred method of transferring wealth after 1986.

Finally, the passage of § 2702 in 1990 entirely killed both the sale of a remainder interest and the joint purchase. In either case, the individual is treated as having made a gift to the extent that the value of the underlying property exceeds the price paid by the other purchaser.

THE FAMILY ESTATE TRUST: A TRAP FOR THE UNWARY

The reader should be cautioned against recommending the family estate trust, a so-called estate planning device. Also called a constitutional trust or an equity trust, the *family estate trust* is an arrangement fraught with tax danger. Many variations have been created, but they all have the following characteristics:

1. The same person acts in four different capacities, grantor, trustee, trust employee, and beneficiary.
2. The grantor transfers assets into the trust in exchange for "certificate units." The trustee leases the employee's services to others (typically including the individual's current employer), who pay a salary directly to the trustee.
3. The certificate units entitle the grantor to share in the trust's income.
4. On the grantor's death, the trust assets pass to others, not to the grantor's estate.

The family estate trust has been touted as a great tax saver. It is said to be able to reduce income tax by shifting income to a lower bracket (the trust and other family members) and to reduce the individual's death taxes by shifting assets to other beneficiaries before death. In fact, just the opposite is true. The IRS has been aggressively and successfully challenging family estate trusts in the courts, which have regularly upheld the following tax consequences:

1. Under the *assignment-of-income doctrine*, wages assigned to the trust are still taxable to the wage earner, not to the trust.
2. Personal living expenses are not deductible.
3. Fees to set up the trust are not deductible.
4. The date-of-death value of the property owned by the trust is subject to inclusion in the gross estate of the trustor as an incomplete transfer.
5. At least two tax penalties may be imposed. First, a negligence penalty of 20% of the additional tax due may be assessed. Second, tax preparers may be charged penalties of hundreds of dollars for each return found to exhibit negligent or willful attempts to understate the tax liability.

Be prepared to recognize these family estate trust shams by whatever names they are currently being peddled and avoid them because of the illusory benefits and high risks they carry.

ENDNOTES

1. IRC § 163.

2. IRC § 61(a)(12).

3. IRC § 2033.

4. IRC § 7872(a)(1).

5. IRC § 267.

6. Reg. 1.1015-4(a)(1).

7. *Juden*, 89-1 USTC 9142; 63 ¶ AFTR 2d 89-595 (ECA-8, 1989).

8. IRC § 453.

9. IRC §§ 453(b)(2) & 453(l).

10. IRC § 453(e)(1).

11. Income in respect of a decedent (IRD) is discussed in Chapter 7.

12. IRC § 2043.

13. For an example of a successful SCIN involving a $12 million note, see *Wilson*, TCM 1992-480.

14. *Estate of Moss,* 74 TC 1239 (1980).

15. *Frane v. Commr,* 998 F. 2d 567 (CCA-8, 1993) in part reversing *Estate of Frane,* 98 TC 26 (1992); IRC § 691(a)(5).

16. Reg. § 25.7520-3(b)(3).

17. IRC § 2036(a).

18. IRC § 2036. See also *Bell Estate v. Commr,* 60 TC 469 (1973).

19. IRC § 453(b)(1); *Rye v. United States,* 92-1 USTC ¶50,186.

20. IRC § 2701(e)(2).

21. IRC § 2702(e).

22. IRC § 677(a).

23. IRC § 2036(a).

24. IRC § 2642.

25. Regs. § 25.2702-3(e), Exs. 1 & 5; LR 9248016, relying on RR 77-454.

26. Regs. § 25.2702-5.

27. LR 9249014.

28. Prop. Reg. § 25.2702-5(c)(9).

29. IRC § 170(c).

30. IRC § 170(b)(1)(F).

31. IRC § 170(b).

32. See IRC §§ 170(b)(1)(B), 170(b)(1)(C), 170(b)(1)(D), & 170(d)(1)(A).

33. IRC § 170(b)(1)(C).

34. IRC § 170(f)(8).

35. IRC § 2522(a).

36. IRC § 2055(a).

37. *U.S. Trust Co. v. U.S.*, 803 F. 2d 1363 (CCA-5, 1986).

38. IRC § 2036(a).

39. IRC § 2055.

40. Valuation of unitrust interests are calculated based on the § 7520 applicable federal rate, released monthly by the IRS, along with unitrust valuation factors derived from the Treasury department's *Actuarial Values-- Beta Volume* (IRS Pub. 1458), available from the U.S. Government Printing Office on the web at http://bookstore.gpo.gov/index.html

41. *E. La Meres Estate*, TC CCH 12,880.

42. IRC § 642(c)(5)(C).

43. Attaining grantor trust status without subjecting the corpus to estate taxation under IRC §§ 2036-2038 can be a challenge, see LR 9224029 and LR 9247024.

44. Actually, any loan made at a rate of interest below an acceptable market rate will be subject to taxation. However, we will continue to use the term *IFL* to refer to

all below-market loans.

45. *Dickman v. Commissioner*, 465 US 330, 104 S. Ct. 1086 (1984).

46. IRC § 7872.

47. If the executor is not a family member, he or she (or it, in the case of a corporate fiduciary) may choose to call the note due and payable after the death of the lender in order to properly manage the estate.

48. Clifford lost the case, however. *Helvering v. Clifford*, 309 U.S. 331 (USSC, 1940). After the Clifford decision, Congress added the 10-year requirement to the Code, under Section 673, et. seq.

49. One court held that consideration for purposes of IRC § 2036 must equal the entire value of the property. *Gradow* 897 F.2d 516 (1990).

CHAPTER 15

Liquidity Planning

OVERVIEW

This chapter will explore the role of liquidity in estate planning. It will summarize the liquidity needs at death, examine the sources of liquidity available to the estate before and after death, and describe common planning techniques. Planning devices covered include the sale of assets before death, payment extensions and deferral, and life insurance. The chapter will also explore several strategies unique to business owners including installment payments, stock redemption, valuation discounts and control premiums, family limited partnerships and information on several other Internal Revenue Code sections intended to provide tax relief for those estates with significant business interests.

SUMMARY OF CASH NEEDS AT DEATH

Types of cash needs. Death may trigger a need for liquidity to pay for a variety of obligations, such as expenses directly related to the person's death, a readjustment period, and care of dependents.

Directly related expenses may include federal and state death taxes, and expenses of estate (probate and/or trust) administration, including payments to lawyers, executors, accountants, appraisers, and trustees. There may be debts and claims against the decedent's estate including last illness and funeral expenses. There may be immediate cash needs for the maintenance and welfare of the surviving family. And there may be cash bequests and other transfers that must be made to the decedent's heirs and beneficiaries.

Funds may be needed during the readjustment period as the surviving family members struggle to rearrange their lives.

Perhaps the greatest need is for money to support surviving dependents. How much is needed depends on who (and how many) are dependent. For children, there is a need for food, shelter, and education that may continue for many years. For a disabled dependent, the time frame may be measured by the person's life expectancy. For some families, there may be the need for operating capital to continue running the family business.

Cash needs for larger estates. Cash needs and timing are influenced by estate size and family situation. In general, cash needs increase with increasing estate size largely because of estate taxes. If the estate tax repeal set for 2010 is made permanent, cash needs for larger estates will decrease tremendously. In the meantime, large estates must be prepared to meet liquidity needs that may not occur. For very large estates the estate tax may be the greatest cash expense and that expense may occur at the death of the second spouse. Most very wealthy couples choose an estate plan that incorporates both a marital deduction and an applicable exclusion amount (AEA) trust. These combine at the first death to result in no estate tax. However, this may simply delay the cash need until the second death.

Cash needs for smaller estates. In contrast with the estates of wealthy individuals, young families with modest estates will often have relatively large cash needs at the death of either spouse. These people do not have the economic advantages of the wealthy, so although transfer taxes are not a problem, there is the immediate need to replace the income or services of the deceased spouse. As the children get older, the cash needs tend to decline.

SALE OF ASSETS DURING LIFETIME

One of the simplest liquidity-generating devices is the sale of assets during lifetime to raise cash. Relatively high basis assets are preferable because they result in little or no taxable gain. In fact, assets that have a built-in loss are the best assets to sell, because the loss can be used to offset taxable gains or to reduce taxable income. Death eliminates this potential tax benefit by stepping down the basis to date-of-death value. A gift of the asset results in the donee having a dual basis; carry-over basis for gain but the fair market value on the date of the gift for gain.

Relatively low basis assets, on the other hand, are less attractive assets for sale because of the resulting tax on the gain. This tax is eliminated if the owner keeps the asset until death. However, one should consider whether there are mitigating factors that would make the lifetime sale of low basis assets practical. The gain might be offset with losses, whether incurred during the current taxable year or carried over from previous years. Other factors may justify paying a tax whose maximum marginal rate on long-term (i.e., held more than one year) capital gains is 20% (or just 10% for taxpayers in the 15% tax bracket). After the year 2000, property held more than five years will be subject to a maximum rate of 18% (9% for 15% tax bracket taxpayers). An interest in a closely held business may bring a higher price during the owner's life than after the owner's death.

ESTATE TAX EXTENSION AND DEFERRAL: §§ 6161 and 6163

Extension to pay tax for reasonable cause: § 6161. This section is available to any estate. On a showing of "reasonable cause" by the estate, the IRS has discretion under § 6161 to grant a one-year extension to pay the estate tax. Extensions can be repeated for a total extended period of 10 years. Warning: A request for an extension must be made before the due date of the return, and subsequent requests must be made before the current annual extension has expired. If the taxpayer doesn't file the request for the extension on time, it will be denied, no matter how good the reason for the request is. Examples of situations satisfying this requirement include:

- The estate has illiquid or liquid assets that are not yet available to the executor.
- A large part of the estate is in the form of rights to receive payments in the future (royalties, accounts receivable, etc.).
- The estate includes a claim to substantial assets that cannot be collected without litigation.
- The estate does not have sufficient cash to pay taxes and provide for a family allowance and claims.

- The estate cannot borrow except at rates that would constitute a hardship.

Ordinarily, reasonable cause will not be found merely because liquid assets (listed securities) must be sold at what the executor considers distressed prices. With an extension to pay, interest will be charged at the late payment rate. The interest is deductible on the estate tax return. Generally, the interest is claimed by a claim for refund after the tax and interest are paid.

Estates may use a § 6161 extension or the § 6166 installment plan to pay the generation-skipping transfer tax, but in the case of § 6166, only if the tax results from a direct skip.[1]

Deferral of estate tax for a reversion or remainder interest: IRC § 6163. Section 6163 allows estate tax deferral for that portion of the tax attributed to having a reversionary or remainder interest included in a decedent's gross estate. The tax can be postponed until six months after the termination of the "precedent" interest, i.e., the interest immediately preceding the reversion or remainder. The termination might occur many years after the decedent's death.

> EXAMPLE 15 - 1. When he died, Jake created an irrevocable trust out of a portion of his estate. The trust pays all income to Jake's disabled son, Billy, for his lifetime. Then, the remainder is payable to Jake's daughter, Diane, or to her estate. Diane died in the year 2000. At that time, the trust was worth $400,000, Billy was 80 years old, and the federal rate was 8%. The present value of her remainder interest in the trust was $227,940 [$400,000 * 0.56985]. Her taxable estate, including the vested remainder, was $2,000,000. The total federal tax on her estate was $460,650, hence her estate was able to defer $52,455 [$460,650 * ($227,940/$2,000,000)] until six months after Billy dies. There will be interest to pay on the deferred tax (at the late payment rate), but it can be claimed as a deduction, thereby reducing the tax.

LIFE INSURANCE

Life insurance has several uses, but in estate planning, its major purpose is to provide funds to cover cash needs arising at a person's death. For some estates it is the major source of needed liquidity. A life insurance policy is a contract. If the insured owns the contract but is not the beneficiary, it is in a special category of bilateral contract referred to as a third-party beneficiary contract, distinguished from other bilateral contracts by the fact that the two parties to the contract intend to benefit a third party. An example would be where a parent purchases life insurance on her life, owns the policy, and names her child as the beneficiary. The parent and the insurance company are the parties to the contract and the child is the third-party beneficiary. For most contracts only the parties to the contract can enforce it; but with a third-party contract the beneficiary can also enforce it. If the beneficiary purchases the policy it is a standard bilateral contract, e.g., the child purchases a policy on the parent's life with the child as both owner and beneficiary of the policy. The amount that the insurance company pays when the insured dies is called the *face value* or the *policy proceeds*. The owner may be the *insured*, i.e., the person whose death is a condition precedent to the insurance company's obligation to pay. Someone other than the insured may be the owner, such as the beneficiary or the trustee of a life insurance trust. The owner designates the *beneficiary*, i.e., the person who receives the proceeds when the insured dies. The owner can cancel the policy, borrow money from the insurance company if the policy has cash reserves, assign the policy (i.e., transfer title to someone else as a gift or in exchange for money), and change the beneficiary designation.

We will cover three major topics in this section. First, we will survey the various types of insurance policies commonly used.[2] Next, we will review the major concepts in the income, gift, and estate taxation of insurance. Finally, we will examine the insurance planning techniques frequently used to provide needed liquidity.

Types of Insurance

It seems as though there are an endless variety of insurance policies sold in the United States today. There are policies called level term, decreasing term, mortgage payment insurance, whole life, variable life, etc. However, most are variations of one of two basic life insurance products, term insurance or cash value insurance.

Term insurance. The simplest form of insurance is a one-year policy whose premium is based on the likelihood of death in that year. If the insured dies, the beneficiary is paid the face value. If the insured does not die, the company owes nothing and the contract terminates. This is the essence of term insurance: whether the company is financially obligated to pay depends solely on whether the insured dies during the contract period.

Most term insurance is renewable. The company is obligated to sell another year's insurance at a previously agreed-on price, at the option of the policy owner. Evidence of insurability, such as a physical exam, cannot now be required. Most term policies are renewable to some maximum age set by the company, e.g., age 70 or 75. The increasing periodic premium, or cost of annually renewable term insurance policies, rises annually with increasing age, reflecting the increased likelihood of death. Other term insurance policies have premiums that remain constant for five, 10, or 20 years, and then rise to a new plateau for another similar period. These are called "five-year level term" or "10-year level term" depending on the period during which the premiums stay the same. With most term insurance contracts, the premiums are guaranteed for one, five, or 10 years. Thereafter, premiums can be raised but not above some stated maximum. Regardless of how often the premium rises, all term insurance is characterized by periodic increases in the premiums and by the fact that the company will not offer the insurance coverage beyond some maximum age.

Cash value insurance. In contrast to term insurance, cash value insurance has a constant ("level") periodic premium. It also has certainty. When a cash value insurance contract ends, either because the insured dies or because the policy owner no longer wants coverage, the company will be obligated to pay a predetermined amount of money. If the insured dies, the company will pay the face value. If the owner surrenders a cash value policy before the insured's death, the company will be obligated to pay an amount called the *cash surrender value.*

Cash value insurance originated as a solution to a problem inherent in term insurance. Many years ago, when term insurance was just about the only policy sold, policy owners frequently terminated their insurance as it became more and more expensive with the advancing age of the insured. To retain policyholders, companies started offering cash value insurance, charging a constant premium. Evidence shows that such policies are not as likely to be canceled by policyholders, despite advancing age. The earlier years' premiums are more than the company actuarially needs to fund death and other claims, and the later years' premiums are less than the company needs. The extra premium in the early years enables the company to accumulate an actuarial reserve. Typically, the owner may borrow, pledge, or in the event of surrender prior to the insured's death, receive the cash surrender value outright.

Cash value policy premiums usually are three to five times the initial premium charged for an annually renewable term policy for a given policyholder. Over time, the annual term policy premiums will increase to exceed the annual premiums on the cash value policy. For cash value policies, the guaranteed cash surrender values are listed, year by year, in the policy itself.

> EXAMPLE 15 - 2. Audrey, an insurance salesperson, offers Gerard, age 45, a choice of two policies, each having a face value of $100,000. First, she describes a cash value whole life policy, sold by the ABC Co., which has a level annual premium of $2,700. Its cash surrender value at the end of the fifth policy year will be $7,500. At the end of the 20th policy year, the cash surrender value will be $43,500. Audrey then describes an annually renewable term policy that is guaranteed renewable to age 75. The policy, sold by the XYZ Co., has premiums for the first five years of $500, $550, $610, $680, and $750. If Gerard keeps the policy long enough, the premiums will be more than $3,000 per year by the time he reaches age 70.

Whole life policy. All cash value policies have a maturity date at which, if the insured reaches it alive, the face value will be paid. A whole life cash value policy has a maturity date that extends beyond the "whole life" of most insureds, typically the insured's 95th or 100th birthday.

> EXAMPLE 15 - 3. In the prior example, if Gerard purchases the whole life policy and keeps it in force, ABC will send him a check for $100,000 if he lives to be 100. Of course, if he does not live to be 100, the company will send his beneficiaries the $100,000.

Universal life policy. During periods of high interest rates, traditional cash value policies, such as whole life, tend to lose their allure because the guaranteed cash value growth rate is quite low in comparison to the returns available on other short-term, interest-sensitive investments. People considering insurance tend to be more attracted to term insurance, with the idea that the money saved from the much lower initial premiums will be invested elsewhere to earn higher yields. In response, the insurance industry developed a product called universal life insurance, which is a form of cash value insurance that offers the policyholder greater flexibility and, sometimes, greater investment yield. It offers greater flexibility because the policyholder is permitted to vary the amount of the face value and the premium payments to meet changing financial conditions. Variable universal life can offer a greater investment yield because the policy owner selects from an array of portfolios (similar to a mutual fund family) managed by the insurance company for the investment of his or her excess premiums. The portfolios of nonvariable universal life typically hold debt instruments of shorter duration than do portfolios of whole life policies. As such, in periods of high interest rates these universal life portfolios also offer greater investment yields than do whole life portfolios. With either variable or nonvariable universal life, the insurance company (and the policyholder) hopes that the underlying portfolios will outperform the typical whole life guaranteed rate. If successful, some of the additional value is used to pay for additional insurance coverage, additional cash value, and/or reduced premiums. The typical universal life policy offers a low guaranteed rate of appreciation, commonly 4%, with the provision that a higher rate will be earned if the investments are more profitable.

Universal life insurance has been criticized as too complex compared to whole life and term insurance and because its flexibility makes it difficult to make cost comparisons when considering its purchase.

Split-dollar cash value insurance arrangements. A split-dollar arrangement is most commonly found as a nonqualified employee fringe benefit. It is a unique method of paying cash value insurance premiums rather than a different type of insurance. In the typical plan, the employer pays the insurer a portion of the premium equal to the lesser of the total premium or the increase in the cash value. The employee pays the balance of the premium. When the insured dies or when the policy is surrendered, the employer receives an amount equal to the premiums it paid. The remainder is paid to the beneficiary (if the insured dies) or the policy owner (if surrendered). Split-dollar insurance enables the employee to purchase cash value insurance at lower cost than if purchased individually.

Taxation of Life Insurance

Income taxation. Life insurance receives favorable income tax treatment in two major areas, cash value accumulation and policy proceeds. To qualify, an insurance policy must meet requirements found in § 7702, enacted to discourage certain universal life and endowment policies that were largely investment vehicles that contained a minor life insurance component to escape normal income tax.

Income taxation of cash value accumulation. For normal life insurance policies, increases in cash value are not subject to income taxation while a policy is in force.[3] When a cash value policy is surrendered, any excess of the cash surrender value (amount realized) over the total premiums paid (adjusted basis) is included in the owner's gross income, but usually this excess, if any, is quite small and not a significant tax burden. Loans from the cash buildup in a policy are not taxable either unless the amount withdrawn exceeds the amount paid into the policy.

IRC § 7702 was enacted to plug a loophole whereby insurance companies were selling single premium life insurance policies or modified endowment contracts (with very little life insurance protection) as tax-free investment vehicles rather than as life insurance. As defined in § 7702(A), a modified endowment contract is a life insurance policy entered into after June 20, 1988, that fails the "seven pay test." Failure occurs any time the cumulative premiums paid into the policy in the first seven years exceed the total of net level premiums which would have been sufficient to provide a paid-up policy, based on the initial death benefit, after seven annual payments.

The effect of a policy failing the test in § 7702 and being classified as a modified endowment contract is that withdrawals and distributions, even as loans, are treated as taxable income to the extent of any cash value accumulation. Even loans may be taxable. The portion of a withdrawal or distribution which is included in the policy owner's gross income (i.e., the lesser of the amount withdrawn or the accumulated cash build-up in excess of premiums paid at the time of withdrawal) is subject to an additional 10 percent income tax unless the owner is more than 59 ½, disabled, or receiving the payment as part of a series of equal annuity payments for life.

Income taxation of policy proceeds. Section 101 excludes all proceeds from a life insurance policy, paid because of the insured's death, from gross income. There is an exception for policies that have been transferred for valuable consideration. The policy proceeds are included in the gross income of the transferee, less the price and premiums paid. This *transfer for value* rule does not apply to transfers to the following parties:

- The insured (or to a grantor trust[4] of the insured)
- A partner of the insured
- A partnership in which the insured is a partner
- A corporation in which the insured is a shareholder or officer
- A transferee whose basis will be determined by reference to the transferor's basis (i.e., the donee of a gift of the policy)[5]

EXAMPLE 15 - 4. For more than 15 years, Terry was the owner of a $10,000 face value insurance policy on his life. Last year, he gave the policy to his beneficiary-son, Ralph, who began to pay the premiums. Terry died last month. No portion of the proceeds will be includable in Ralph's gross income because Ralph did not buy the policy.

EXAMPLE 15 - 5. If, in the prior example, we assume instead that Terry sold the policy to Ralph for $100, and that the premiums paid by Ralph totaled $400, Ralph's gross income will include $9,500.

EXAMPLE 15 - 6. Ulysses and Zeno are business partners. For years, each owned an insurance policy on his own life. Now, their attorney is drafting a "cross-purchase business buyout" contract, and the partners have agreed to exchange policies, with some cash also included as part of the transaction. Thus, Ulysses will become owner and beneficiary of the policy on the life of Zeno, and Zeno will become owner and beneficiary of the policy on the life of Ulysses. On the death of either partner, no part of the proceeds will be includable in the other's gross income.

The above example illustrates the use of existing insurance policies to fund a business buyout agreement.

Viatical settlements and accelerated death benefits. The Health Insurance Portability and Accountability Act, signed into law in August of 1996, allows people diagnosed with a terminal illness to "cash in" their life insurance early without having to pay income tax on the proceeds. These funds are available either directly from the insurance company, provided the policy has an accelerated death benefit (ADB) provision, or from an outside company that offers what is called a viatical settlement. The ADB is either part of the original insurance contract or added later as a rider. The insurance company agrees to pay the proceeds at a discount from the face value of the policy. The fewer months the insured is expected to live, the lower the discount.

A viatical settlement is an agreement between a company representing a group of investors and an individual with a projected life expectancy of less than

48 months due to a terminal illness. The insured who enters into one of these contracts is called the *viator* and the company is called a *viatical company*.

Under the 1996 Act, in order for the ADB or the viatical settlement to be income tax-free, a physician must certify that the insured has a physical condition that can reasonably be expected to result in death within 24 months from the date of certification. Most ADB clauses set a maximum life expectancy that is considerably shorter (e.g., just 12 months or even as short as six months). Viatical companies generally seek contracts where death is expected to occur within 24 months. They may enter contracts where the life expectancy is longer, but the favorable income tax treatment for the viator would not be available.

> EXAMPLE 15 - 7. Karol has an advanced case of AIDS that has failed to respond favorably to any of the recent treatments. She decides that she would like to take her three children to visit their grandparents in Amsterdam. Her funds are extremely limited, so she contacts a viatical company to see if there is an interest in her $300,000 term policy. At the company's request, her doctor furnishes a complete medical report and signs a certificate that gives his opinion that Karol's life expectancy is between 12 and 18 months. The company agrees to pay $200,000 immediately, with an additional sum payable to her children. The additional amount is $50,000 if she dies in the first month after the settlement, reduced by two thousand dollars for each additional month, or portion of a month, that she lives beyond the first month.

The insured may use the ADB or viatical proceeds in any way he or she desires. Given the substantial discounts, most people will not use an ADB clause or enter into a viatical settlement if there are other reasonable sources of funds. Hence, it is likely that the funds will be used to pay for medical treatment or special nursing care where no other reasonable source of payment is available, but the law does not require that the money be so used. Indeed, the insured could use the funds for one last glorious trip to a place he or she always wanted to visit.

The law also has similar favorable treatment for persons who are "chronically ill" and can benefit from an ADB payment or a viatical settlement. The proceeds are tax-free only if used for "costs incurred by the payee . . . for qualified long-term care services" where such care is not covered by insurance or otherwise subject to reimbursement.

Gift taxation. There are two common situations where insurance is subject to gift tax. First, a taxable gift may arise when the owner assigns ownership of the policy to another person without receiving consideration in return. Ordinarily, the gift of an insurance policy will qualify for the annual exclusion, unless it is made to an irrevocable trust. Even then, if a beneficiary of the trust is given a Crummey demand power, the annual exclusion is available. Second, a taxable gift of the policy proceeds may arise when the insured dies. If the insured, owner, and beneficiary are all different parties, the proceeds are considered a gift from the policy owner to the beneficiary. The effect of this rule is that planners recommend that if someone other than the insured will own the policy, he or she should also be named as the beneficiary.

Estate taxation. Life insurance is most commonly included in a decedent's federal estate tax base under §§ 2001, 2033, 2035(a), or 2042.

Under § 2001, the decedent's adjusted taxable gifts include the date-of-gift value less the annual exclusion for any life insurance policy the decedent transferred after 1976 and more than three years before death.

Under § 2033 (property owned at death), the value of the decedent's date-of-death ownership interest in a life insurance policy on the life of someone other than the decedent will be included in the decedent's gross estate.

Under § 2035(a), the proceeds of a life insurance policy on the life of the decedent will be included in the decedent's gross estate if the decedent made a transfer of any incidents of ownership in the policy within three years of death.

Under § 2042, proceeds of a policy on the life of the decedent are includable in the decedent's gross estate if, at the insured's death, either the proceeds were receivable by the decedent's executor or the decedent possessed any incidents of ownership in the policy.

Life Insurance Planning

Life insurance is used in liquidity planning to meet cash needs while minimizing income, gift, estate tax and other costs. To do this efficiently, we must choose the most appropriate insured, owner, and beneficiary for each life insurance policy.

Selecting the insured. The life of each spouse whose death is expected to trigger a cash need should be insured sufficiently to meet the cash need. For smaller estates, there will typically be a need for cash at the death of either or both spouses based upon replacing their financial or service contribution to the family.

For larger estates, we have seen that effective planning (with the use of the marital deduction trust and the credit shelter bypass trust) usually eliminates the need to pay estate tax at the death of the first spouse (S1), but it creates a relatively large need at the surviving spouse's death (S2). Thus, ordinarily, little or no insurance is required on S1's life to pay estate tax. The real insurance need will be on S2's life. However, some insurance may be needed at S1's death to meet nontax needs, such as to cover last expenses, readjustment, and cash requirements during the dependency period. As with smaller estates, there may be a need to replace the financial or service contribution to the family. This will be particularly important for parents with substantial earned income who are supporting younger children.

Insurance arrangements for the second death. Since most couples do not know whether the husband or the wife will be the surviving spouse, both may need to be insured. Several commonly used purchase arrangements are discussed next.

1. *Full coverage for both spouses.* One simple but costly plan is to insure both spouses for the full amount of protection needed at the surviving spouse's death. Because of needless extra cost, this plan is seldom recommended.

2. *Minimal coverage for both spouses.* An alternative method of insuring the spouses is to purchase a small amount of insurance on both spouses which, on the death of either, can be used to purchase a "fully paid up" larger policy on the life of the survivor. This has the advantage of eliminating the cash flow drain on the surviving spouse to pay the premium.

3. *Second-to-die insurance.* Both spouses could purchase *second-to-die insurance*, also called *survivorship life insurance*. Both spouses are insured in one policy, but the contract requires payment when the second death occurs. This alternative saves premium dollars in two ways: First, only one policy is purchased. Second, the contingency insured against is more remote in time than that insured against under a single-life policy, consequently, the premiums are lower than a similar policy on either spouse's life. Even though one spouse may be uninsurable, a second-to-die policy should still be available since the medical underwriting standards are eased as long as one spouse is healthy.

4. *Full coverage for wife only.* Another alternative is to insure only the wife, assuming she has the longer life expectancy. If she survives her husband, the contract becomes a de facto second-to-die policy. If she predeceases him, the proceeds could be invested or partly used to buy a paid-up policy on his life to

pay the estate tax at his death. The cost of insuring only the wife is likely to be more expensive than a second-to-die policy.

Selecting the owner and beneficiary. Selecting the owner and beneficiary for a married couple with a smaller estate is simple since no transfer taxes are expected if the net value of the combined estates (with the insurance included) is less than the AEA. Each spouse may own policies on his or her own life with the proceeds payable to the other. The contingent beneficiary could be the couple's children, if sufficiently mature, or could be the trustee of the couple's probate-avoidance living trust.

Spouse as owner and beneficiary. When transfer tax costs are a concern, more thought must be given to selecting owners and beneficiaries. Naming one or the other spouse as owner or beneficiary will not minimize transfer costs. It will usually subject the proceeds to a transfer tax, probate administration, or both, depending on which spouse dies first. Consider the complicated tax and probate consequences for each alternative.

First, if the insured spouse dies first and is the owner, the proceeds will be includable in his or her gross estate under § 2042. If the proceeds qualify for the marital deduction, avoiding taxation at the first death, whatever proceeds remain will be included in the gross estate and taxed at the second death. If the insured spouse dies second and is the owner, then the proceeds will be included in his or her gross estate with no marital deduction available.

Second, if the insured spouse dies first and the noninsured spouse is the owner and beneficiary, then the proceeds that remain will be included in the gross estate at the second death. If the noninsured spouse is named owner and someone else is the beneficiary, when the proceeds are paid, the owner-spouse will have made a taxable gift to the beneficiary. Thus, the noninsured spouse should not be named either owner or beneficiary if the surviving spouse's estate is likely to exceed the AEA.

In planning for wealthy couples, two important conclusions can be drawn from the above. First, naming either spouse as owner or beneficiary of a policy on the life of a spouse will subject the proceeds to transfer taxation at least at the second death. Thus, to minimize transfer taxes, neither spouse should be designated owner or beneficiary of an insurance policy on the life of the other. Second, since a taxable gift will occur whenever the insured, owner, and beneficiary are different parties, whoever is selected should be named both owner and beneficiary, to avoid gift tax consequences.

Child as owner and beneficiary. Instead of a spouse, one of the couple's children could be named owner and beneficiary. The child could be requested to use the proceeds to provide liquidity to the estate on the death of the insured. This alternative will work best when the child is sufficiently mature to handle the responsibility. Nonetheless, there will always be risks. The child may permit the policy to lapse. Or the child, having received the policy proceeds on the death of the insured parent, may be unwilling to provide the funding needed by the estate. Once the child receives the proceeds, any gratuitous transfer of funds to the estate will receive standard taxable gift treatment unless the child is the sole beneficiary of the estate. To avoid making a gift, the child could purchase estate assets or lend money to the estate.

Irrevocable trust as owner and beneficiary. Generally, the irrevocable life insurance trust (ILIT) is the best solution.

Organization and structure of an ILIT. The person to be insured creates and transfers funds into the ILIT and selects an independent trustee. The trustee then uses the funds to obtain insurance on the trustor's life, naming the trustee as the owner and beneficiary of the policy. The trust must be irrevocable or § 2038 would draw the trust (i.e., the insurance proceeds) into the trustor's estate. The trustor must not be named a trust beneficiary, because of possible § 2036(a) problems; since the uninsured spouse is usually one of the beneficiaries of an ILIT, he or she should not be a trustor.

On the death of the insured, the trustee is authorized to lend the proceeds to the insured's estate and to purchase assets from the estate. If the insured is S1, then the trust corpus usually continues to provide benefits to S2 in the form of a bypass trust. At the death of S2, the trust is again authorized to lend cash to the S2 estate and to purchase estate assets. The trust could then be terminated, with the corpus payable to the children. Alternatively, the trust could be continued, distributing income to the children until they reach a specified age, or to the grandchildren until they reach a specified age, in the case of a generation-skipping trust qualifying for the GST exemption.

If an ILIT is to be used as a source of cash to pay estate taxes, it is important to choose a type of policy that will be there when estate taxes are due or at least covers the period until estate tax is repealed. Term insurance becomes increasingly expensive as the insured gets older and may not even be available beyond a certain age (i.e., most insurance companies do not write term policies for people over the age of 75).

A married couple has two choices. First, if the sole purpose is to pay estate taxes at the second death, then a second-to-die policy is the least expensive of the cash value policies. With a sophisticated estate plan incorporating bypass and marital trusts, the taxes are most likely to be postponed until the second death.

A potentially more complex situation occurs rarely when S2 is dying at the time of S1's death and the executor wants to generate a tax at S1's death. Will use of a second-to-die policy cause hardship or force the executor to postpone the taxes to the second death even though it means more overall estate taxes? The answer is no. Section 6161 allows executors to postpone payment of the estate tax for reasonable cause. Thus the executor of S1's estate would not be forced to sell assets but would file the return, report the estate taxes owed, and request a one-year extension with an explanation as to why cash is presently unavailable.

Second, for a younger, less wealthy couple, the purpose is likely to provide funds to replace the financial contribution of the deceased spouse. Term insurance may be the better choice. The income earners (one or both) should be separately insured taking into account the amount of insurance needed to replace the insured's earning capacity. For any given family wealth level (until we reach the very wealthy), a young couple with dependent children will need greater amounts of insurance than an older couple with grown children. Term insurance allows them the most insurance for their premium dollars. If the couple can afford additional insurance and is concerned about covering estate taxes in the event both die young, then they should consider a second ILIT to purchase a second-to-die policy.

Who should pay the premiums on the trust-owned policy? One alternative is to fund the trust with sufficient income-earning assets to enable the trust to pay them. The grantor trust rules will make that income taxable to the grantor (trustor) rather than the trust.[6] A preferred alternative is for the trustor to make annual gifts to the trust to pay the premiums. In community property states, the insured spouse should make the periodic gifts from his or her separate property to keep the proceeds out of the estate of the noninsured beneficiary spouse. A Crummey demand right held by the insured's children will make the gifts to the ILIT qualify for the annual exclusion.

Impressive ILIT achievements. For a married couple with an estate that exceeds the AEA, the ILIT achieves all of the following goals:

1. Excludes the insurance proceeds from income taxation and from the taxable estates of both spouses and, perhaps, the children.
2. Excludes the insurance proceeds from the probate estates of both spouses.
3. The annual exclusion can shelter gifts to the trust of the policy and money to pay premiums.
4. Ensures that a responsible party will provide the needed post-death liquidity.
5. Makes the proceeds available to the surviving spouse for health or certain other reasons.

A single person can also use an ILIT to achieve similar tax and nontax goals. The close friends or relatives that will eventually receive the estate can be named as remaindermen or holders of the Crummey right to withdraw.

Income tax, estate tax, and GST tax issues. For income tax, an ILIT will not ordinarily fall within the grasp of § 2036 (retained life estate). However, because they are not direct skips, annual exclusion transfers into the trust will not insulate the corpus from GST tax. Thus, planners may elect to allocate some of the GST exemption to such transfers, anticipating that the premature death of a child may give rise to a taxable distribution or a taxable termination.

Excluding the insurance proceeds from the gross estate of a decedent has the additional benefit of avoiding transferee liability for payment of the estate tax. In one unusual case, the decedent died possessing incidents of ownership in a $50,000 life insurance policy. The IRS was unable to collect $62,378 in estate tax from the decedent's assets which were then owned by his nonresident alien widow, living in Venezuela. However, the insurance beneficiary, a U.S. citizen, was held liable for $50,000 of the taxes.[7]

If an existing policy is transferred to the trust, the trustor-insured must live three years after the policy is transferred to ensure that § 2035's three-year rule for life insurance transfers does not apply. Whenever possible, the policy should be purchased by the trustee to avoid the three-year rule. If the insured transfers an existing policy, the annual exclusion will not apply unless the trust gives the beneficiaries a Crummey invasion power.

The trust can include a contingent marital deduction clause, so that if the three-year rule causes the proceeds to be included in the insured's gross estate, then the trust is required to pay the widow income for life payable at least annually. This clause would allow a QTIP election and the resulting marital deduction would avoid estate taxes. Of course, a QTIP election will cause the trust to be included in S2's estate. On the other hand, if the insured lives longer than three years, the ILIT avoids both estates, the contingent income clause that would have mandated income payments solely to S2 becomes meaningless, and the trust can be a sprinkling trust that distributes income to the children as well as to S2.

If each spouse is an insured, then two trusts will have to be established, with each trust owning one policy. These trusts must be drafted very carefully to avoid § 2036(a) problems.

If the trust is required to use insurance proceeds to pay the decedent's estate debts, including taxes, the proceeds will be includable in the decedent's gross estate under § 2042. The trustee should instead be simply advised that it may lend the proceeds to the estate or purchase estate assets.

Although GST tax rules prevent annual exclusion gifts to a single trust for the benefit of both nonskip and skip persons from also being sheltered from the GST tax, planners achieve complete shelter from GST tax in one of two ways. Either they create one trust and use the trustor's GST exemption to shelter these gifts, or they create two trusts, one for the benefit of only nonskip persons (e.g. spouse and children) and the other for the benefit of only skip persons (grandchildren, etc.).[8]

Avoiding probate. The policy proceeds of an ILIT avoid probate at both spouses' deaths because neither spouse owns the policy or the proceeds.

Shelter of annual exclusion. Most ILITs are drafted with clauses that give Crummey demand rights to the children and even to the grandchildren. These clauses are inserted to create the necessary present interest so that the annual exclusion may shelter the funds the insured gives the trustee to pay the premiums. Because the holders of the powers must be given a reasonable time in which to exercise their demand rights, the trustee must receive the funds far enough in advance of the premium due date to give the holders notice and have the demand period expire before the payment must be made. The demand period (typically 30 or 60 days) must be stated in the ILIT as part of the Crummey provision.

Selection of trustee as responsible party. An insured spouse who is also the trustor should not be named the trustee since this could constitute an incident of ownership in the policy. The other spouse could be named the trustee without this adverse result.

Most corporate trustees are reluctant to become trustees of an insurance trust prior to the insured's death if the trust is otherwise unfunded. Even if it is funded, the advent of higher-risk, higher-return life insurance policies and growing insurance company insolvency problems have made trustees, particularly corporate trustees, concerned about possible liability if expected policy death benefits are not paid or if the policy turns out to be relatively uncompetitive. In addition, an ILIT may not be profitable for a corporate trustee even after the proceeds are received, particularly if they must be allocated in one of two ways: proceeds immediately distributed to trust beneficiaries, or used to acquire closely held business stock, a difficult asset to manage.

To overcome the liability concerns and encourage a fiduciary to act as trustee of a life insurance trust, the trust may include language that exculpates the trustee from liability in connection with holding the life insurance policy. The trust must make it clear that the trustee is released from liability for investing only in life insurance since the failure to diversify investments violates the prudent investor rule. The trust can indemnify the trustee, i.e., reimburse the trustee for any expenses, including attorneys' fees, that might arise from a challenge by the remainderman. Exculpatory clauses are enforced by the courts, but are strictly construed against the trustee. They offer no protection from acts of "bad faith," "reckless indifference," "gross negligence," or "willful misconduct."

Finally, the planner can arrange for an individual, such as a family friend, to act as initial trustee, with the corporate fiduciary succeeding as trustee only after the insured(s) has died and the proceeds have been paid. Of course, the family friend should also have the benefit of the exculpatory clauses just discussed.

FLOWER BONDS

This topic should come under the heading: "Sometimes Congress Does the Darnedest Things." In the 1950s and early 1960s, the federal government issued Treasury bonds that could be used at their par value, plus accrued interest, to pay the federal estate tax, provided the bonds were part of the decedent's estate. Since the bond yields, while reasonable when issued, were quite low (3% to 5%) compared to other investments in the 1970s and 1980s, they began selling at deep discounts. This created some estate planning opportunities for persons with terminal illnesses to purchase bonds at as little as 85% of par shortly before death. The decedent's executor could use them to pay the estate tax, achieving an increase in value in a short time span. Because the worth of the bonds jumped from their discounted value to their par value when the owner died, the bonds were called flower bonds. Of course, to the extent the bonds could be used to pay estate taxes, their value in the estate was the par value. Thus, some of that 15% increase in value was lost to increased estate taxes. The flower bonds matured November 15, 1998, which means the estate planning opportunities are gone.

LIQUIDITY PLANNING DEVICES UNIQUE TO BUSINESS OWNERS

When the owner of a closely held business dies, severe liquidity problems can arise. The largest portion of the estate may be the interest in the business that usually is very illiquid. The need to pay the estate tax nine months after date-of-death may compel surviving family members to sell the business. Some advanced planning by the business owner and some special Code sections may help the heirs get through the transition crisis.

Sale of the Business

Consideration should be given to the pre-death *sale* of the business or to a *merger* with a publicly held firm as a means of gaining liquidity. A pre-death sale will ordinarily trigger a capital gains tax. An owner who chooses not to sell or merge before death should consider a funded *buyout agreement* with the other owners. The buyout contract, discussed later in the text, obligates the other owner(s) to pay the decedent's estate a predetermined amount in exchange for the decedent's interest in the firm. Since the sale will occur after death, the step-up in basis of the decedent's interest eliminates or substantially reduces capital gains tax.

Installment Payment of the Estate Tax: § 6166

Congress added § 6166 to the Code, applicable to estates of decedents dying after 1976, to lessen the liquidity crisis that often accompanies the death of a business owner. If the estate is eligible and the executor makes the election, the estate tax for a closely held business interest can be paid over 14 years. The portion deferrable is the ratio of the net value of the business to the value of the adjusted gross estate. The first four annual installments are interest-only payments starting on the one-year anniversary of the original due date. Starting in the fifth year, the estate pays the estate tax in 10 installments, each one equal to one-tenth of the deferred tax, plus the interest accrued since the last annual payment. Although the estate must pay interest on the deferred tax, it is at a lower rate than the regular rate for underpaid (i.e., late or deferred) tax payments.

Three conditions must be met for qualification under § 6166. First, the value of the decedent's interest in the business must be at least 35% of the value of the *adjusted gross estate* (AGE). The AGE is the gross estate reduced by debts, expenses, losses, and certain taxes (i.e., accrued income taxes and property taxes, but not the death taxes).[9] Second, the decedent's interest must have been in a *closely held business*, which is defined as: (1) a sole proprietorship; or (2) a partnership in which at least 20% of the capital interest is included in the decedent's gross estate or that has 15 or fewer partners; or (3) a corporation in which at least 20% of the voting stock is included in the decedent's gross estate or that has 15 or fewer shareholders. Third, the business must have been actually carrying on a trade or business at the time of the decedent's death.

> EXAMPLE 15 - 8. Jack died in the year 2000, owning stock in a closely held corporation. His shares had a value of $1,000,000. Jack's gross estate was worth $3 million. There were debts and expenses that totaled $500,000. The federal estate tax was $666,450 (after the state death tax credit). Since the closely held business interest was 40% of AGE, the estate qualifies for § 6166 extended payments. The amount of the tax that may be deferred is $266,580 [40% * $666,450].

In the past, the executor had the option of deducting the interest paid on the § 6166 extended tax payments either on the estate tax return (Form 706) or on the estate income tax return (Form 1041).[10] This deduction has been eliminated for estates of decedents dying after 1997, but continues to be available for estates that are already on an extended payment plan.[11]

For § 6166 interest, the executor claims the deduction using Form 843 (Refund Claim) since the deduction can only be taken after the interest is paid.[12] Estates often wait until after the seventh or eighth principal payment (out of the 10 scheduled for the § 6166 extension) to claim the deduction because it reduces the estate tax to the extent that the last couple of payments are eliminated. A complex interrelated calculation is required because the interest paid reduces the estate tax, which in turn reduces the interest owed, which in turn increases the estate tax, etc.[13]

Deducting interest on the estate tax return continues to be available for interest on estate taxes paid late, regardless of whether the executor obtained an extension to pay based on reasonable cause (i.e., § 6161) or negligently paid them late without obtaining an extension. The interest that must be paid on late or deferred estate taxes should be deducted on the estate tax return because it saves more tax than claiming it for income tax purposes, since the estate tax rate is higher than the income tax rate.

Late payment interest on a portion of the deferred estate tax is charged at a mere 2% rate. The Taxpayer Relief Act of '97 reduced the rate for eligible estates of persons who die after December 31, 1997. The *2% portion*, as it is now called (previously 4%), is the amount of deferred tax that equals the tentative tax generated on the quantity $1,000,000 plus the AEA, less the unified credit.[14] Thus, in 1998 the 2% portion would be the tentative tax on $1,625,000 less the unified credit, i.e., $612,050 - $202,050 = $410,000. The $1,000,000 amount is indexed for inflation starting in 1999, using 1997 as the base year. By 2003 it reached $1,120,000 and is likely to continue to increase by 20 to 30 thousand dollars a year in the near future. The balance of any deferred tax also incurs interest higher than the special 2% rate but still reduced. The reduced deferred rate on the balance is equal to 45% of the regular "underpayment" rate imposed by § 6601(a).[15] Estates that are still paying on pre-1998 § 6166 payment plans can elect to take advantage of the new lower interest rates, but only if the estate's representative waives the right to claim a deduction for any remaining interest payments. This waiver is likely to be advantageous for estates with deaths after 1994. For estates of decedents with earlier deaths, more dollars will probably be saved by claiming the interest deduction than will be saved by using the lower interest rates.

EXAMPLE 15 - 9. Hitch died in 2003, leaving to his children an estate that included a closely held business. The estate qualified under § 6166 to extend $1,500,000 of its federal estate tax. Because of indexing, the $1,000,000 base for the 2% portion had increased to $1,120,000. The tentative tax on $2,120,000 (i.e., AEA for 2003 + $1,120,000) is $839,600. Subtracting the unified credit for 2003 (i.e., minus $345,800) gives us $493,800 as the 2% portion. If, during the first year's deferral period, the regular underpayment rate is 8%, the balance of the deferred taxes would be charged interest at a 3.6% rate (45% * 8%). Hence, the first interest payment (due one year after the regular due date of the estate tax return) is $46,099 [2% * $493,800 + 3.6% * $1,006,200]. Assuming the regular late payment interest rate remained at 8%, the payment due on the fifth-year anniversary would be $196,099 (10% of the deferred taxes plus a year of interest). Even though the estate tax is repealed for years after 2009, any payments that fall due after that year must still be paid and the recapture will occur if the heirs abandon the special use or sell the property within the 10-year recapture period.

Estate tax deferral under § 6166 reduces the estate's immediate cash needs. Since this is a relief provision designed to reduce the likelihood of a forced sale, the sale, redemption, or other disposition of all, or a significant portion of, the business, or the unauthorized failure to make timely interest or principal payments, causes the deferred taxes to be immediately due.

Stock Redemption: § 303

The Internal Revenue Code provides another method to lessen the impact of taxes on the estates of decedents whose businesses are incorporated. The general rule is that when a closely held corporation buys back the shares of its stockholders, the proceeds must be treated as dividend income unless the transaction falls within one of the special redemption Code sections, including Section 303. It allows a closely held corporation to redeem some of a decedent's shares with the transaction treated as a sale of the stock rather than the receipt of a dividend. Since the owner's death steps-up the adjusted basis of the stock, very little, if any, gain is likely.

EXAMPLE 15 - 10. Polly's estate included 1,000 shares of stock in a closely held corporation. Each share was valued at $150 for estate tax purposes. Immediately before her death, each share had an adjusted basis of just $10. Eight months after her death, to help the estate pay some of its expenses, the board of directors of the corporation agreed to redeem 300 shares from the estate at a price of $160 per share. Business was good, and the $160 was a realistic share price at the time of the purchase. If the entire redemption qualifies under § 303, the estate will have a taxable long-term gain of $3,000 (reflecting a $10 gain on each share purchased). If the redemption does not qualify under Section 303, the estate will be deemed to have received a dividend of $48,000 (300 shares at $160 per share), all of which will be treated as ordinary income.

There are three major requirements to qualify under § 303. First, as with the § 6166 deferral, the value of the decedent's interest in the stock must be at least 35% of the adjusted gross estate. Second, the amount paid by the corporation in redemption of the shares may not exceed the sum of federal and state death taxes, generation-skipping transfer taxes, and funeral and administration expenses. Notice that the limit does not include the decedent's debts, although they are used in calculating the adjusted gross estate. Third, the shareholder (usually the estate) must be obligated to pay the taxes and/or the expenses.[16]

If more is paid, the excess will be treated as a dividend payment by the corporation. If the excess distributions exceed the amount of the corporation's earnings and profits, the excess is considered a nontaxable return of capital. However, if the firm distributes appreciated property instead of cash, the distribution will probably be considered a sale by the corporation, with the corporation forced to recognize a taxable gain.

Lifetime planning may assure that §§ 6166 and 303 are available to an estate that might not otherwise meet the 35% test. The owner can increase his or her interest in the firm, or reduce the size of his or her nonbusiness estate by making gifts, thereby reducing the adjusted gross estate and increasing the portion represented by the business. These strategies require advance planning. Section § 2035(c) requires that the date-of-death value of any gifts made within three years of death be included in the gross estate to determine whether the percentage requirements of §§ 6166 and 303 are met but not for calculating the actual tax. Bringing gifts back into the gross estate enlarges the denominator, making qualification less likely.

EXAMPLE 15 - 11. Gabe's estate included his closely held corporation. His gross estate was valued at $5,000,000. Debts and expenses were $1,000,000 and the value of his shares was $1,500,000. The estate meets the 35% requirements of both §§ 303 and 6166 since the shares represent 37.5% of the AGE.

EXAMPLE 15 - 12. Same as the prior example, except Gabe gave his daughter real estate worth $250,000 two years before he died. At his death, the property was worth $300,000. Inclusion of this property in the gross estate for purposes of determining the percentage brings the AGE to $4,300,000 and drops the percentage to 34.8%. For calculating the estate tax, the gift is simply a $240,000 adjusted taxable gift. The date-of-death value was used only to determine whether the estate qualified for the benefits of §§ 303 and 6166.

Special Use Valuation: § 2032A

Another relief provision available to the business owner's estate, called *special use valuation*, is provided by § 2032A. This Code section permits qualifying estates to value at least a portion of the real property in the estate at its "qualified use" value, i.e., its value as a farm or other trade or business rather than at its highest and best use.

Suppose a person has owned her farm for many years and her children want to continue to work the farm for the foreseeable future. The farm was originally located outside the city limits, but urban growth is beginning to approach the area. The farm's FMV is considerably greater than the capitalized value of the farm income. Valuation at its highest and best use might force the survivors to sell the land to pay the estate tax. On the other hand, valuation at its use as a farm might enable the survivors to continue to carry on the business.

Requirements. The five major requirements under § 2032A are listed below.

1. The property must have been held for "qualified use" and actively managed by the decedent or the decedent's family for five out of the eight years prior to the decedent's death.
2. The net value of the real and personal property devoted to the qualifying use must equal at least 50% of the adjusted value of the gross estate.[17] The adjusted value of the gross estate is the gross estate reduced by mortgages and liens (not unsecured debts or expenses).

3. The net value of the real property portion must constitute at least 25% of the adjusted value of the gross estate.[18]

4. The qualifying property must pass to qualifying heirs. The heirs must sign a recapture agreement that acknowledges that a lien will be placed on the property and that the taxes saved will be recaptured by the government if the heirs do not continue the qualified use for at least 10 years after the decedent's death. A qualified heir is a member of the decedent's family who acquired the property from the decedent.[19] A qualified use is one in conjunction with farming or other trade or business. Generally, the qualified heir must actively participate. The mere leasing of the farmland to others will not qualify.[20]

5. The executor must make the election on the estate tax return and attach the recapture agreement. The return must show how the special use value was determined. The rules and a § 2032A checklist immediately follow Schedule A in the estate tax return.

If the election is made, the maximum amount by which the value of the special use real estate can be reduced is $750,000.[21] The $750,000 amount is indexed for inflation for years after 1998, with 1997 being the base year. By the year 2003, the amount reached $840,000. Assuming 50% as the maximum marginal estate tax rate, the maximum that can be saved by this election is $420,000 on a $840,000 special use reduction in the value of the real estate. While this is not an insignificant amount, if there is a big difference between values, the heirs may decide the tax savings are not enough to compensate for the burden of continuing to run the business for 10 more years.

Since the election applies only to real property and has some onerous requirements, it is not used often. Business owners dying after 1997 and before 2004 may be able to use § 2057, the family-owned business interest deduction, which requires that the business interest, not necessarily including real estate, meets a 50% of AGE threshold. If § 2032A or § 2057 is available, the estate will also qualify for § 6166 deferral since its threshold is only 35% of AGE. The family-owned business interests deduction is repealed for decedent's dying after 2003.

Recapture. If the qualified heir discontinues the special use or sells his or her interest (other than to another qualified heir) within 10 years, the taxes saved are recaptured. For example, if the qualified heir allows others to lease the property for cash, it will result in a cessation of the qualified use and the recapture of the taxes saved.[22] However, there is an exception for the surviving spouse that allows him or her to rent the property to other family members without causing recapture.[23] Once an event occurs that triggers the recapture, the heirs (remember they had to sign a recapture agreement when the § 2032A election was made) have just six months to file Form 706-A, *United States Additional Estate Tax Return*, and pay the additional tax. If the special use is discontinued, then the amount recaptured is the amount of tax saved. If the property is sold, the recaptured amount is the lesser of the taxes saved or the difference in the proceeds from the sale and the special use valuation. The application of these recapture rules to partial sales is beyond the scope of this text. Two examples will help clarify recapture in general.

> EXAMPLE 15 - 13. When Gerard died in 2000, his estate included a persimmon farm that qualified for special use valuation. The real estate had a fair market value of $2,000,000 and a special use valuation of $1,000,000. The $770,000 reduction in the value of the real estate reduced the federal estate taxes by $361,900. Three years after her father's death, Julie (the sole heir) decided to turn the farm into a dude ranch. The cessation of use caused the $361,900 to be recaptured. It had to be paid six months after the change was made.

> EXAMPLE 15 - 14. Suppose, instead of changing the use, Julie sold the farm. The amount of recapture would depend on the price. Since the special use value shown on the return was $1,230,000, a price up to $1,591,900 [the scheduled value plus the taxes saved] would recapture the difference between $1,250,000 and the sales price. A sale above $1,591,900 would recapture all of the taxes saved. Hence, a sale for $1,500,000 would result in a recapture of just $250,000, whereas a sale for $2,200,000 would result in the recapture of the entire $391,900.

When recapture occurs, the heir does not have to pay interest on the recaptured taxes. However, the heir can elect to pay the interest (going back to the original due date, i.e., nine months after the date of death) and in exchange take a step-up in the basis to what it would have been had special use not been elected.[24] One must compare the capital gains taxes saved to the cost of paying the interest. In general, the closer the sale is to the original due date of the return, the less the interest and the more likely the benefit of the increase in basis will exceed the interest expense. If one makes this election there is no deduction for the interest on the recaptured taxes, unlike the general rule that allows an estate tax deduction for late payment interest.

If the qualified heir dies before the 10-year recapture period has ended, the heir's estate could sell the property immediately without causing a recapture. The sale to another qualified family member avoids recapture, but the buyer must also agree to the recapture provisions for the remainder of the 10-year period. The recapture rules for changes in ownership or changes in use are complex and beyond the scope of this text.

Family-owned Business Interest Deduction: § 2057

Another relief provision was added to the estate tax law, effective for estates of owners of family businesses who die after December 31, 1997, and before January 1, 2004. If the business interest is a qualified one, the executor can elect to exclude from the taxable estate up to $675,000 of the business' value. Because the family-owned business interests deduction is repealed for decedent's dying after 2003 there is little point to studying this area in detail. The actual amount depends on the value of the business interest and the extent to which the executor wishes to claim the deduction. Many of the rules are similar to those for § 2032A, e.g., the business must represent a significant portion of the adjusted value of the gross estate and the interest must go to qualified heirs. Since this, like § 2032A, is a deduction, the tax dollars are saved at the estate's highest marginal rates.

When initially enacted in 1997, the family-owned business deduction was an exclusion equal to the difference between $1,300,000 and the AEA for the year the business owner died.[25] This meant that each year the AEA increased from 1998s $625,000, there would be a corresponding decrease in the family-owned business exclusion. As originally planned it would drop from $675,000 to $300,000 when the AEA topped out at $1,000,000. The 1998 Tax Act[26] changed this to allow a maximum deduction of $675,000 regardless of when the business owner died. However, this was done by coordinating the deduction with the AEA so the combined amounts cannot exceed $1,300,000. Thus, the estate of a business owner who dies in 2002 is allowed a $675,000 deduction but must use a unified credit of $202,050 (i.e., an AEA of $625,000). If the AEA is greater than $1,300,000 it would not make sense to forgo the higher unified credit by claiming the deduction. Acknowledging this, Congress included in EGTRRA 2001 the elimination of the family-owned business deductions for estates of decedents dying after 2003. The estate of a person dying in 2002 or 2003 can claim a deduction of $300,000 and have an AEA of $1,000,000 (i.e., a unified credit of $345,800) or some other in-between combination, so long as the total is $1,300,000. Since the deduction saves taxes at the highest marginal rate and the AEA equates to the unified credit, the general rule is for the estate to maximize the deduction and take the reduced unified credit.

> EXAMPLE 15 - 15. Mercedes Aroeste died in 2002, leaving her estate to her two children. Included was a business with a net value of $2,000,000 and other assets with a value of $1,000,000. The children were sure that they would continue to operate the business for at least 10 years. Thus, they were not worried about tax recapture, and they wanted to reduce the taxes as much as possible. The tax would be $738,000 [taxable estate of $2,325,000 after the $675,000 deduction, a tentative tax of $940,050 and a unified credit of $202,050 instead of $345,800.]

> EXAMPLE 15 - 16. Same facts as in the prior example except, for whatever reason, the children wanted to minimize the deduction (i.e., $300,000) and maximize the AEA ($1,000,000). The tax would be $786,000 [taxable estate of $2,700,000, a tentative tax of $1,131,800 and a unified credit of 345,800.]

Requirements. The following five requirements must be met:

1. The decedent (or a member of the decedent's family) must have been a citizen or resident of the U.S. at the time of death.
2. The decedent (or a member of the decedent's family) must have materially participated in the business for five out of the eight years preceding the decedent's death.
3. The interest must be a "qualified" family-owned business.
4. The net value of the business interest that passes to "qualified heirs" must equal at least 50% of the decedent's AGE. Here, unlike § 2032A, unsecured debts (claims against the estate) as well as mortgages and liens are deducted to arrive at AGE.
5. The executor must make the election on the estate tax return and file a tax recapture agreement signed by all qualified heirs.

Non-U.S. citizen qualified heirs. If the qualified heir is not a U.S. citizen, the deduction is available only if the interest will be held in a qualified trust or if the heir either reaches an agreement with the IRS on posting a bond or placing a tax lien on the property. The qualified trust is similar to the QDOT needed in order to obtain the marital deduction for property left to non-U.S. citizen spouses.

Special rules related to gifts. In meeting the 50% of the adjusted gross estate requirement, the estate can add back gifts of the business interest that were made to qualified heirs, provided the heirs hold such property at the time of the decedent's death. The amount is also added to the adjusted value of the gross estate (i.e., it is added to both the numerator and the denominator). The gifts are added back at their full value without reduction for the annual exclusion. Even gifts that were less than the annual exclusion amount are added back for the sole purpose of determining whether the estate meets the 50% threshold (they are not part of the taxable estate nor of adjusted taxable gifts).

Gifts of nonbusiness property (other than de minimus gifts) to the decedent's spouse within 10 years of death and to other persons within three years (other than gifts to family members under the annual exclusion amount) are added to the adjusted value of the gross estate, thus making it more difficult to meet the 50% threshold. This was done to keep owners from making deathbed transfers of nonbusiness assets in order to meet the 50% requirement.

> EXAMPLE 15 - 17. When Candace Scott died in 2001, her gross estate was worth $4,000,000, including her shares in a closely held business. The shares were valued at $1,700,000 and were left to her daughter, a qualified heir who intends to continue working in the business. There were debts and expenses of $200,000. Six years before her death, Candace had given her daughter, Laura, shares in the family business. Those shares were valued for gift tax purposes at $730,000. Each year, for the last four years, she made gifts of the family stock to a minor's demand trust established for her only grandson. Each gift was worth $10,000, but a Crummey power held by the grandson kept her from having to use any unified credit. Two years before her death, Candace gave her daughter, Laura, stocks in publicly traded companies. The stocks were valued at $240,000 for gift tax purposes, and Candace paid gift taxes of $115,000. The rest of the shares in the family business were owned by Candace's brother, Brian Kaye.
>
> The shares in the family business just barely qualify for the § 2057 deduction. The numerator equals $2,470,000: $1,700,000 from the shares owned at death, $730,000 from the gift to Laura, and $40,000 from the transfer to the grandson's trust. The denominator (the adjusted value of the gross estate) equals $4,925,000: the gross estate of $4,000,000, plus the two gifts that are included in the numerator (even ones less than the annual exclusion amount) and the nonbusiness interest gift

to Larry because it was made within three years (this is a special rule for determining the 50% test; the gifts are not included in the gross estate for calculating the estate tax), and the gift tax of $115,000 because it was paid on a gift made within three years of death (i.e., a § 2035(b) gross up). The ratio is 50.2%. If the gifts to the grandchild's trust did not exist, and all else remained the same, the ratio would be 49.7% and the business interest would not qualify.

Recapture. Similar to § 2032A, there are recapture of tax rules for § 2057. Recapture will be triggered if the qualified heir ceases to materially participate in the business for three years out of any eight-year period within the 10 years following the decedent's death. The participation requirement can be satisfied by a member of the qualified heir's family. The recapture amount is the adjusted tax difference times the applicable percentage. The adjusted tax difference is the portion of the qualified business interest that ceases to be qualified compared to all that qualified (and, although the Code is not specific, presumably only the qualified interest to the extent it was claimed as a deduction) times the difference in what would have been paid had there been no election and what was paid using the election. The applicable percentage decreases over the 10-year recapture period. The maximum recapture is as follows:

If the event causing recapture occurs in the following year of the applicable material participation:	applicable percentage (i.e., the % of tax recaptured):
1 through 6	100%
7	80%
8	60%
9	40%
10	20%

EXAMPLE 15 - 18. Using Mercedes Aroeste's estate (see the first § 2057 example), had the heir sold the business in the eighth year, the recapture would be the difference in the tax on a $3,000,000 taxable estate in 2002 and the $738,000 paid, times 60% (applicable percentage): 60% * ($945,000 - $738,000) = $124,200.

Note that there is interest on this additional tax at the "underpayment rate" established under section 6621 for the period beginning on the original due date of the return and ending when the tax is paid. Just as with § 2032A recapture, the code refers to this as an additional tax rather than the deferral of the original tax, consequently, the interest is not deductible.

Qualified Conservation Easement: § 2031(c)

The Taxpayer Relief Act of 1997 added a provision that allows some tax relief for estates that include land that is appropriate for a conservation easement. The complicated rules will just be summarized here. Basically, the executor can donate (this had better be done with the blessing of all beneficiaries whose interest would be affected) a conservation easement to certain organizations and exclude a portion of the value of the land, up to certain dollar limits, from the gross estate. The election is made by the executor on the estate tax return. This election is available even if the decedent's estate plan made no provision for a conservation easement.

A *conservation easement* is one that protects the natural habitat of fish, wildlife, or plants, a historical site (land and/or structures), or open space for public benefit, i.e., a scenic or recreational benefit. The easement must be donated to a charitable organization or government agency. As originally enacted the land had to meet certain location requirements, e.g., within of a national park or wilderness area. The 2001 tax legislation changed the rules, and for the estates of decedents dying after December 31, 2000, a conservation easement can be claimed for land located anywhere in the United States or its possessions. The decedent or a member of the decedent's family must have owned the property for three years prior to the decedent's death.

If the executor makes the election, donates the easement, and fulfills all of the other requirements of the section, then the estate can deduct the lesser of: (A) the applicable percentage of the value of the land subject to the easement, reduced by any charitable deduction that results from said donation, or (B) the easement exclusion limitation. The *applicable percentage* is 40% times the value of the land reduced by two percentage points for each percentage point (or fraction thereof) by which the value of the qualified conservation easement is less than 30% of the value of the land (determined without regard to the value of the easement). The easement exclusion limitation starts at $100,000 for estates of decedents dying in 1998 and increases $100,000 each year until it reaches $500,000 for the year 2002 and beyond.

> EXAMPLE 15 - 19. When she died in 1999, Alice Le Mond's estate included acreage near a national park. Without a conservation easement, it was worth $450,000 for estate tax purposes. An easement for riding and hiking was negotiated with the Park Service. Appraisers determined that the value of the easement to the park was $160,000. Since this is greater than 30% of the value of the land, there is no percentage reduction. The estate can deduct the lesser of 40% [$180,000] times the value of the land or the exclusion limit for 1999 [$200,000]. If the easement was valued at $117,000 (i.e., 26% of the value of the land) the deduction would be 32% [i.e., 40% - 2 * (30% - 26%)] times the value of the land, resulting in an exclusion of $144,000 [i.e., 32% * $450,000]. Had she died in 1998, the limit would have been $100,000.

There is a recapture provision that takes effect if the easement agreement has not been implemented within the earlier of two years after the decedent's death or the sale of the land by the estate or the heirs.

VALUATION DISCOUNTS AND CONTROL PREMIUMS

Over the years, the courts have offered taxpayers the ability to generate liquidity by significantly discounting the transfer tax value of closely held business interests, real property, and securities subject to special market circumstances. The most common discounts are the minority discount, lack of marketability discount, and fractional interest discount.

Minority Interest Discount for Business Interests

A *minority interest* is an interest in a business that, in terms of voting, is not a controlling interest. The owner, acting alone, lacks the power to affect changes in policy, structure, or strategy.

> EXAMPLE 15 - 20. Jack owns 50.1% of a corporation worth $1 million, and Jill owns 49.9%. Jill owns a minority interest. Alone, Jill cannot run or control the business, set compensation levels, sell or encumber business assets, elect herself an officer, or control corporate policy. Jill would most certainly have difficulty selling her interest to a third party for $499,000.

Ownership of a partnership interest may also qualify for a minority interest discount. The Uniform Partnership Act codifies the common law rule that each partner has just one vote, regardless of his or her capital (investment). The partnership agreement can change this by providing greater voting control to certain partners.

For transfer tax valuation, minority discounts of between 15 and 50% are obtainable for such interests. Factors influencing the size of the discount include the overall quality of management, composition of other share holdings, size of the business, history of profitability, existence of business opportunities not currently being exploited by management, and degree of the company's financial leverage.[27]

In some situations, minority interest discounts are not available. The IRS contends that a gross estate including two separate minority interests in the same property which add up to a majority interest should be denied the benefits of minority interest discounts.[28]

> EXAMPLE 15 - 21. Dad's estate plan will leave his 40% business interest at his death to a marital trust. At Mom's later death, her gross estate will include Dad's interest in the marital trust, as well as her own 40% business interest. The IRS is likely to challenge a minority discount for either interest.

Planners should be able to circumvent this problem by having S1 dispose of his or her interest to the bypass trust, which is not taxed to S2, rather than to the marital trust, or having one or both spouses make a lifetime transfer of the interest (by gift, installment sale, etc.).

Minority interest discounts are not available to stock subject to a § 2032A special use valuation election.

A holder of a majority stock position can give gifts of shares to become a minority owner. The recipient could also become a minority owner.

Valuation discounts and imperfect unification. Earlier we discussed the fact that the federal "unified" transfer tax system is not perfectly unified. Imperfections include the allowance of an annual exclusion for lifetime gifts, failure to include post-gift appreciation in the estate tax base, and the ability to avoid grossing-up gift taxes on gifts made more than three years before death. To these we add the ability to obtain valuation discounts for certain lifetime gifts that would not be available to transfers at death.

EXAMPLE 15 - 22. Fiore owns 100% of the stock in a closely held corporation worth $300,000. This year, he gave each of his three children one third of the stock. Taking a 25% minority interest discount on each transfer, Fiore will report on Form 709 three gross gifts of $75,000 ($100,000 - .25 * $100,000), totaling $225,000. Thus, in addition to saving taxes by taking three annual exclusions, Fiore has reduced his future gross estate by an extra $75,000 (i.e., 3 * ($100,000 * 25%)). Had Fiore kept the stock and bequeathed it to the three children, these minority discounts would not have been available.

Revenue rulings have stated that a minority interest will not be disallowed solely because a transferred interest, if combined with interests held by family members, would be part of a controlling interest.[29] Valuation discounts for such gifts are allowed because the gift tax is computed on a per gift basis.

If an interest is whole at the moment of death but broken into fractional shares as part of the distribution, there is no minority interest discount. The asset is valued at its fair market value as of the moment of the owner's death. Thus, valuation discounts create a fourth instance of imperfect unification.

Control premium. Case law recognizes that a fractional interest in property can actually be worth more than its proportional share.[30] For example, the value of a 51% interest in a particular closely held firm has been ruled to be worth greater than 51% of that firm's underlying value. A higher value reflects a premium for holding a controlling interest. In one case, the decedent owned about 52% of the voting stock in a corporation, giving him, among other things, the power to elect all directors. The court approved a 38% control premium, raising the value of the decedent's interest from $372,152 to $514,000.[31]

The control premium is the "flip side" of the minority discount. While including property subject to a control premium in the gross estate will ordinarily increase estate tax, careful planning can actually reduce estate tax, by bequeathing the majority interest to the surviving spouse protected by the 100% marital deduction.

EXAMPLE 15 - 23. Anderson was the sole owner of a $1 million closely held corporation. At his death, he bequeathed 51% of the stock to his surviving widow and 49% to his son. In connection with this business interest, Anderson's gross estate includes $1 million. Based on a control premium of 10%, the marital deduction is $561,000 (110% * 51% * $1 million). The control premium has reduced Anderson's taxable estate by $51,000.

In community property states, control premiums cannot apply to stock held as community property since neither spouse has majority control.

Lack of Marketability Discount for Business Interests

Due to lack of an established market, restricted stock, stock in a closely held business, and partnership interests are invariably more difficult to sell than business stock that is publicly traded. Thus, discounts for lack of marketability ranging from 15% to as high as 50% are obtainable. These discounts apply to both minority and majority interests. Factors influencing the size of the discount include the extent of the resale restrictions, SEC restraints on marketability, the dollar value of the stock, the firm's growth expectations, and the size of the company's total assets and equity.

Use of minority interest and lack of marketability discounts can leverage the benefit of the gift tax annual exclusion.

> EXAMPLE 15 - 24. Crabb's closely held business was recently appraised at $1 million. He gave his daughter a 2 percent interest in the business. After applying a 40% minority interest discount and a 25% lack of marketability discount, the value of Crabb's reportable gross gifts was $9,000 [2% * $1,000,000 * 60% * 75%]. Although this is under the annual exclusion amount, Crabb's accountant had him file a gift tax return that fully disclosed the discounts and how the value was determined to start the statute of limitations running. If no return is filed or if the return does not adequately explain the method of arriving at the value, the IRS could challenge the valuation many years later.

Some courts have allowed taxpayers both a minority discount and a lack of marketability discount, while others have collapsed the two into one discount. Whether collapsed or not, a combined discount of 30% to 40% is generally considered safe, whereas discounts of more than 50% are seen as too aggressive. Determining and documenting the appropriate valuation discounts has become a highly paid specialty within the appraisal community.

Fractional Interest Discount for Real Property

Undivided interests in real property can receive a fractional interest discount, analogous to the minority interest and lack of marketability discounts for stock, because such interests are neither easily partitioned nor readily marketable.

EXAMPLE 15 - 25. Jones died owning a 58% interest in common in commercial real property that was appraised for $2,000,000. His estate was allowed a 25% fractional interest discount that resulted in his estate listing a value of $870,000 on the estate tax return [58% * $2,000,000 * 75%].[32]

The fractional interest discount for real property is strongly opposed by the IRS. It has taken the position that the only discount allowed should be the cost of a partition action.[33] It should be noted, however, that the problem of control premiums in real estate does not arise because all owners must agree on significant property decisions.

Other Valuation Discounts

Worth mentioning briefly are three other valuation discounts:

- Securities, even publicly traded ones, that are subject to special securities law restrictions can be discounted. Restrictions include lack of registration and the need to sell the stock by private placement.
- Large quantities of a stock listed on an exchange can receive a *blockage discount* if their sale all at one time could have a depressing effect on the market price. However, if the block represents a controlling interest in the corporation, possibly triggering an even higher price, a *premium* may be attached to its value. Blockage discounts may be available for other property, such as a large number of paintings left in the estate of a prominent artist.[34]
- A discount may be allowed for a business that lost a key person (e.g., the decedent) who was responsible for its goodwill.

Valuation discounts can generate significant transfer tax savings. For estates, there can be a tradeoff because the lower value for estate tax gives less step-up in basis. But since transfer taxes are generally higher than capital gains taxes, there is often a net benefit. This tradeoff does not apply to gifts since the basis is a carryover from the donor's basis.

FAMILY LIMITED PARTNERSHIPS

Family limited partnerships (FLPs) have been used by families in agricultural areas for decades to involve children in running a ranch or farm. Recently they have become a popular planning tool for other family-run businesses and offer many attractive estate planning advantages. However, due to the costs of establishing them and the appraisal costs associated with making multiple transfers of the limited partnership interests, they usually are not recommended unless the parents owning the business have a net worth in excess of two or three million dollars. For those that qualify, an FLP has numerous advantages: (1) the parents can give away wealth and still retain control; (2) transfers can be made at substantial discounts compared to the value of underlying assets, thus saving unified credit and gift taxes; (3) restrictions can be placed on transfers by children; and (4) there is some protection from creditors.

Family partnerships are sanctioned by the IRC with requirements set forth in § 704(e). Among other things, the income and tax benefits must be distributed or allocated according to each owner's percentage in the partnership. The general partners may be paid for their personal services to the partnership. Also, capital must be "a material income-producing factor," meaning that a family partnership cannot be used to redistribute income generated from the personal services of general partners.

Establishing a family limited partnership. To establish a family limited partnership, one must follow the requirements of the state's limited partnership act. This will probably require publication of the names of the general partner and the limited partners. The Uniform Limited Partnership Act requires that there be at least one general partner and one limited partner. With an FLP, it is common for one or both parents to serve as the general partners. They may start by owning all but a very small portion of the limited partnership units. Over time, the parents transfer by gift a significant portion of the limited partnership units to the children. Given the wealth of the parents, it is unlikely that this transfer can be accomplished by annual exclusion gifts alone. Thus, often parents both use up their unified credits, and perhaps pay some gift tax.

Under unusual circumstances, such as the death or bankruptcy of the general partner, most limited partnership agreements give the limited partners the right to elect a new general partner. As with most real estate limited partnerships, a limited partner cannot take assets from the partnership or otherwise force liquidation before the partnership term is up. The term is commonly 50 years. However, these agreements usually provide that after both general partners are deceased, the limited partners can vote to liquidate the partnership. The terms of the agreement would determine the necessary vote percentage.

FLP costs. The major costs are attorneys' fees to establish the partnership, generally in the $5,000 and $20,000 range depending on the nature of the business assets, and appraisal fees probably in the $15,000 to $30,000 range to establish the underlying value and the appropriate discounts. In addition, when partnership shares are transferred as gifts, an appraisal will again have to be performed. The high cost of appraisals is one reason that the parents should consider large initial gifts right after the partnership is established. The appraisal then serves a dual function. However, subsequent appraisal fees by the same appraisal firm should be considerably lower than the first ones, since the company will be familiar with the business. There will also be annual accounting fees for preparation of the partnership returns and the K-1s that must be distributed to all partners. There may also be annual state fees for the right to do business as a limited partnership.

Discounts. The two types of valuation discounts discussed earlier in the chapter play a significant role in making the use of an FLP attractive. Limited partnership units are transferred at a huge discount because the units have limited marketability and control.

EXAMPLE 15 - 26. In the year 2002, the Jackson family created a family limited partnership with Jack and Lilly Jackson as general partners. The net value of their combined estates was $18,000,000, which includes their ranch valued at $6,000,000. The limited partnership interests represented 95% of the total value of the ranch. The other 5% was allocated to the general partnership interest. The limited partnership portion was divided into 95 limited partnership units. Immediately after formation of the limited partnership, 20 units were transferred to each of the three children.

The lack of a marketability discount was determined to be 30% and the minority interest discount was 25%. The following was reported by each parent as the taxable gift to each child: ($6,000,000 * 70% * 75% * 20% * 50%) - $10,000 = $305,000 [FMV ranch * (1 - 30%) * (1 - 25%) * 20% interest * 50% because split between two parents, - annual exclusion = taxable gift.] Each parent reports three such gifts (for a total taxable gift of $915,000) but pays no gift tax because the taxable gifts are less than the AEA for 2002. The Jacksons moved 60% [$3,600,000 at FMV] of the ranch to their children.

If Jack dies in 2003, Trust B received assets worth $1 million and the rest of the estate went into Trusts A and C. Jack's executor QTIPs Trust C expecting Lilly to outlive the estate tax. Unfortunately she died in 2006. (Assume no change in value of any assets.) The ranch was discounted for estate tax purposes because Trusts A and C held only a 40% interest in the ranch, therefore: 40% * $6,000,000 * 70% * 75% = $1,260,000. Lilly's estate then was $13,175,000 [assets other than the ranch, $12,000,000, less $85,000 in Trust B (remember, Jack used up most of his AEA on gifts), plus the discounted value of the minority interest in the ranch, $1,260,000]

Compare the two scenarios with and without the gifts assuming values remain the same between the deaths and all estate tax is postponed to the second death. In both cases, only S2's estate owes taxes. Note that in the gifts alternative one must show adjusted gifts of $915,000. In a real situation, any post-gift appreciation escapes estate tax.

No gifts, tax on $17,000,000 [exclude Tr. B @ $1,000,000] $6,900,000
Gifts, tax on $13,175,000 [exclude Tr B @ $85,000] $5,510,400
          Taxes saved $1,759,500

Discounts and the IRS. The IRS has made numerous attempts to disallow discounts for intra family transfers, losing most of the cases.[35] It has finally conceded the discounts, provided the taxpayer can back them up by credible professional appraisals using relevant market data for the discounts. The appraisals to establish the discount are in addition to the appraisal of the underlying assets owned by the partnership.

In recent years the IRS has had some success in getting all of the FLP's assets included in the transferor's estate on the argument that the parent retained enjoyment of the property during his or her lifetime, hence IRC § 2036 applies.[36] It also argues, sometimes successfully, that transfers of investment assets (stocks and bonds), as opposed to business assets, to a FLP constitutes an indirect gift to the limit partners (e.g., the children) for which no discount is allowed.[37]

Ability to control gifted assets. In addition to the discounts, the most attractive feature of the FLP is the ability of the donor to retain control over the assets. While key rights of a limited partner must be recognized, the general partner maintains all the managerial control over the partnership assets, determining when and whether to make income distributions to all the partners or to reinvest the income into additional assets. To keep control in the family, the partnership agreement should give the family a first right of refusal for any attempted sale by the limited partners.

For most wealthy individuals, the biggest roadblocks to making substantial gifts are the donor's reluctance to lose control of his or her business or other important valuable assets and concern about how well the donee-children will use the gifts. The control offered to the parent-general partner makes this an acceptable vehicle to give assets now, especially when one can use the tax benefits of valuation discounts and lowered values on appreciating assets.

Getting the children involved. Once the children have a vested interest in the business, they may take a greater interest in how it works. Annual reports must be given to all partners and formal partnership meetings with all the family partners present are a good time to discuss the family investments and why they performed well or poorly. To avoid having the children liable as general partners, they cannot be involved in the actual management of the business and they must not appear to outsiders to be general partners.

Using the children's lower tax brackets. One benefit of a family limited partnership is that it is possible to shift income into the lower tax brackets of the children in proportion to the percentage interest the child actually owns in the partnership. When a parent is in the 38.6% federal income tax bracket and the child is in the 15% tax bracket, this can make a significant difference.

Protection against failed marriages of children. One nice protection is that the assets can be held as the separate property of each child. While the income distributed is usually commingled with the child's other assets, the partnership interest is usually clearly identified as the child's separate property. In community property states, only the community property is divided in a divorce proceeding. While everything is presumed to be community property unless it can be traced to a gift, an inheritance, or to property owned prior to the marriage, it should be easy to establish that the units were acquired as gifts and therefore stay in the family. Of course, a child who is not worried about divorce can change them into joint tenancy or community property by written agreement with a spouse.

Loss of the step-up in basis on gifted assets. One disadvantage of giving assets is that the donees (the children) lose the ability to get a step-up in basis at the death of the parent on the partnership shares that were pre-death gifts. When the assets have a very low tax basis, this reduces the tax benefits of the family limited partnership. Of course, if the children do not intend to sell the business, then the low basis is a price worth paying to avoid the transfer tax costs.

Limited asset protection. One important benefit of the FLP is its asset protection capabilities. Most states have some form of fraudulent transfers act that allows creditors to attach property transferred by debtors for inadequate consideration when the transfer takes place in the face of mounting financial pressure. However, if sufficient time has passed, the parent is generally the only one liable to his or her personal creditors and, as general partner, the only one liable to the creditors of the partnership. Limited partnership units given several years before the parents have financial difficulty should not be subject to levy by the parents' creditors.

In the past, creditors of limited partners collected their debts by using a court-issued *charging order* that allowed them to collect the money distributed to a partner. The partnership income tax liability of the partner whose interest was seized was also passed on to the creditor. One strategy available to a partnership that wants to make a creditor negotiate to reduce a debt is for the general partner to not make distributions even though there are profits. That would leave a creditor with a charging order with a tax liability but no distribution.

Some state court decisions have held that if a charging order does not result in timely payment of the debt, the creditor can foreclose on the debtor's partnership interest, forcing the liquidation of enough of the underlying assets to pay the creditor, provided the foreclosure does not unreasonably interfere with the partnership business. If other courts adopt this approach, then a charging order could delay the creditors but would eventually allow them to be fully paid by means of foreclosure.

THE LIMITED LIABILITY COMPANY

The limited liability company (LLC), has similar uses in estate planning to the family limited partnership without some of its problems. It does not have common law roots as the partnership does, but every state (and the District of Columbia) has adopted an LLC statute since Wyoming led the way in 1977. Why the sudden popularity? An LLC offers business owners the limited liability of a corporation with the tax passthrough advantages of a partnership. Each owner-investor is called a *member* and his or her ownership share is called a *membership interest*.

Creating a Limited Liability Company. Owners must comply with the state statute, and they must consider the IRS rules concerning taxation of business entities. On January 1, 1997, Treasury regulations became effective that made the old rules of trying to avoid looking like a corporation obsolete. Most business entities can select for themselves whether to be classified for tax purposes as a corporation, a partnership, or disregarded as a separate entity by checking the appropriate boxes on federal Form 8832. The new regulations[38] (called the *check-the-box regulations*) make it much easier for owners to choose the tax status of their businesses. A business entity with two or more owners can elect to be taxed as either a corporation or a partnership. A business owned by just one person (or a married couple filing jointly) can elect to be taxed as a corporation or be disregarded as a separate tax entity (i.e., be taxed as a sole proprietorship) regardless of the actual business organization. Hence, in a state that allows a single owner LLC, the owner could choose to be taxed as a corporation or as a sole proprietor. An LLC owned by two or more people can choose between being taxed as a partnership or as a corporation. The default classification (one need not file the form) is partnership treatment for eligible domestic entities with two or more owners and sole proprietorship (disregarded as a separate entity) for businesses with just one owner (or a married couple). [39]

Advantages compared to corporations. Both the LLC and the corporate form give the owners the protection of limited liability. An owner is liable only for torts in which he or she is actually involved. If one drives the company car on business and causes an accident in which others are injured, only the business and the owner-driver are liable. The other co-owners are not liable. Furthermore, none of the co-owners are liable for contracts entered into in the company's name. Of course, for either of these business forms the owners may be asked to personally guarantee certain contracts, such as leases and loans, which will create personal liability. However, absent some personal guarantee by the owners, contractual liability attaches solely to the business entity and not to the owners.

LLCs have a single level of taxation at the membership level. Of course, S corporations also have this characteristic, but LLCs do not have the restrictions on stock ownership that S corporations have. Trusts, foreign individuals, and other corporations can be members. Although LLCs are most likely to be closely held, there is no restriction on the number of owners, whereas federal law limits to 75 the number of S corporation shareholders. S corporations are limited to one class of stock, whereas LLCs can have membership interests with different rights to income allocation, capital preferences, and voting.[40]

Advantages compared to partnerships. Both LLCs and partnerships share the advantage of single-level taxation, but partnerships have the disadvantage of all partners being fully liable for all contracts taken in the partnership name and any torts that arise out of the partnership business whether committed by a partner or by a partnership employee. Both allow withdrawal of assets, subject to the partnership or LLC agreement, without such withdrawals being deemed income. Of course, withdrawals do affect the owners' capital accounts. Some states require LLCs to pay some minimal annual fee (generally less than $1,000) whereas general partnerships are usually exempt from such fees.

Advantages compared to limited partnerships. The advantages and disadvantages are similar to those stated for the general partnership, except limited partners enjoy limited liability. Unlike LLCs, the limited partnership must have at least one person, the general partner, exposed to unlimited personal liability. Furthermore, limited partners must not be involved in the day-to-day management of the partnership, or they will lose their limited liability insofar as third parties rely on their appearance as general partners in extending credit to the partnership.

Repeal of the *General Utilities* Doctrine. Prior to the 1986 Tax Reform Act, a corporation distributing assets as part of a liquidation of the corporation was able to avoid tax at both the corporate and shareholder level.[41] The 1986 Tax Reform Act changed the rule so a corporation distributing appreciated property, whether or not the distribution is pursuant to a liquidation, must recognize the capital gain.[42] Thus, many existing corporations holding significant amounts of appreciated assets, whether the corporation is a C type (taxed as a separate entity) or S type (taxed as if a partnership), may find it too costly from a tax standpoint to convert to LLC status. Partnerships and LLCs do not recognize gain on their dissolution, nor will an owner be taxed on the liquidation unless he or she receives cash in excess of his or her basis.

QUESTIONS AND PROBLEMS

1. How will the following factors influence liquidity needs at death?
   a. Size of the family estate.
   b. Whether the decedent is S1 or S2.
   c. Age of the family members.

2. "High-basis assets make desirable assets for a predeath sale designed to generate liquidity." True, false, or uncertain? Explain.

3. (a)What traits distinguish cash value insurance from term insurance? (b) Universal life insurance from other types of cash value insurance?

4. Is life insurance ever subject to income taxation? Explain.

5. Explain the two primary ways in which life insurance can be subject to gift taxation.

6. Max and Minnie are friends. Max loaned Minnie $50,000, taking back an assignment of her paid-up $300,000 face value insurance policy as security for the loan. They agreed that he would not file the assignment with the insurance company so long as she repaid the loan within six months. When she failed to repay anything on the loan, Max sent the company the paper work that resulted in the policy being transferred to him. Two years later, Minnie died (hey, natural causes) and Max collected the $300,000. Would the policy be in Minnie's estate? Would the proceeds be taxable to Max?

7. Life insurance can be subject to estate taxation under §§ 2001, 2033, 2042, and 2035(a). Briefly explain the application of each.

8. Sixty-year-old Adrian has an estate worth $2,500,000 with a significant part being very illiquid real estate. He wishes to pass the assets to his 40-year-old nephew, Clark. Adrian has heard about using insurance to pay estate taxes, and being in good health, he plans to purchase a $500,000 life insurance policy naming his estate the beneficiary. What advice would you give to Adrian regarding his decision. Would you advise term or whole life? Check

with an insurance agent to see what each would cost. For the term policy use a 10-year level term. (State your source and the name of the insurance company.)

9. In each case, would it make sense to purchase insurance? If so, for what purpose and what kind? Who should be the owner and who the insured? Assume for couples that the household wealth is $500,000 and for singles it is $250,000. Estate plans for couples are simple wills with estate left first to spouse, then to children, and if no children or spouse, to parents. For singles it is first to children, if any, otherwise to parents.
    a. Spouses in their 30s, husband working, wife at home with two young children.
    b. Spouses in their 30s, both working, no children.
    c. Spouses in their 50s, both working, children are self-supporting adults living elsewhere.
    d. Single adult, no children.
    e. Single parent of one six-year-old child.
    f. Retired couple, self-supporting adult children living elsewhere.

10. Answer question 9 assuming a $4 million estate for couples and half that for singles. Couples have ABC trust plans and singles have simple wills as described above. In each case would it matter how liquid the estate?

11. For a family with a modest estate, what factors influence the selection of the owner and primary and contingent beneficiaries of an insurance policy on the life of a spouse?

12. What special problem may arise if a couple that live in a community property state set up a life insurance trust, with income for life to the survivor? How is the problem avoided?

13. (a) Describe the characteristics of the irrevocable life insurance trust. (b) What are its advantages?

14. Five years ago, Mary assigned ownership of an insurance policy on the life of her husband, Bud, to the trustee of Bud's living trust. The trustee is beneficiary, and terms of the trust provide that at Bud's death Mary is entitled

to a life estate in the trust income. If Mary survives Bud, could there be an estate tax problem?

15. April, age 40, is a recently divorced single mother of two young children. She is not on friendly terms with her ex-husband who, in her opinion, is a "selfish spendthrift." April owns few assets and asks your estate planning advice to help achieve her goal of financial security for her children.

16. When Chet died in 2003, his estate consisted of the following: a controlling interest in Helter Shelter, Inc., a corporation that make prefabricated homes (his shares are worth more than a million dollars and the estate is in the process of having them appraised); a home worth $650,000; other assets worth $1,250,000. The estate has debts of $100,000 and estate administration expenses of $50,000. In addition, Chet left $300,000 to charities. What is the minium appraised value of the corporate shares that will allow the estate to use §303 and §6166? Assuming that the value comes out to be just above the minimum rounded to the next higher $100,000 (e.g. if the minimum amount is $820,000, the next higher rounded figure would be $900,000), calculate the estate taxes in order to determine (1) the maximum share value (i.e., the dollar amount) that qualifies for §303 capital buy back, and (2) the maximum federal taxes that would qualify for §6166 long-term deferral.

17. How do IRC sections 6166, 303, 2032A, and 2057 provide estate liquidity?

18. Mr. Simon is the executor of Billy Bob's illiquid estate. Mr. Simon is having a difficult time selling Billy Bob's major asset, a $15,000,000 Malibu beach house. Interested parties have placed offers in the $10,000,000 range, but Mr. Simon cannot stand to see the land sold at such a large loss. Mr. Simon is considering requesting an extension to pay Billy Bob's estate tax. What do you anticipate the IRS' response will be to Mr. Simon's request? What must be done to obtain an extension and for how long can it last? Could Mr. Simon get a §6166 long-term extension?

19. At his death, Silva owned a successful farm near an expanding metropolitan area. As a farm, the land was worth $350,000, but a real estate developer is now willing to pay Silva's estate $1,200,000 for it. The rest of his estate has

a net value of $700,000. What is Silva's total gross estate if (a) the executor does not elect § 2032A, and (b) an election is made?

20. At his death in 2001, Pedro owned a little farm on the outskirts of town, where he grew a variety of fruits and vegetables. His kids would like to continue the family farming tradition. A realistic appraisal of his farm real estate as plain old farm property is $575,000, yet a major developer would like to purchase the land for a very important project and has offered Pedro's estate $1,500,000 for the land. The farm equipment and livestock is valued at $120,000. The rest of Pedro's estate is valued at $1,380,000. Finally, the debts are $35,000 and expenses are $40,000. Explain how Section 2032A, Special Valuation, might help Pedro's estate. (Determine the taxable estate with and without the election. Use the indexed value for the deduction).

21. When he died in 2001, Nicolas Emery's estate included a small private lake that he and his family ran as a private resort where families enjoyed boating and fishing. Capitalization of the earnings of the present enterprise gives a value of $800,000 for the land. The boats, several utility vehicles, fishing equipment, portable concession stands, picnic tables, etc., are valued at $200,000. His home and other investments (not related to the business) were worth $1,600,000. Nicolas owed miscellaneous debts of $150,000 and estate expenses were $25,000. Developers would like to buy the property from the estate, put in a hotel and golf course at one end, and subdivide the rest as exclusive residential sites. The beneficiaries of his estate are § 2032A qualified heirs and wish to continue the present business use. (a) What is the minimum fair market value that would have to be assigned to the land and lake for Nicolas's estate to qualify for special use? (b) Suppose the FMV was established to be $1,500,000, what would be the special use value, i.e., what value would be shown on the estate tax return? Use the inflation adjusted § 2032A amount. (c) Use the ETAX program to determine the estate tax savings.

22. Farmer Brown's estate saved $412,500 by making a § 2032A election on the 706 timely filed in June of 1998. The farm land had a FMV of $2,000,000 but only $1,000,000 as a farm, hence it was scheduled on the 706 at $1,250,000. The heirs sold the farm for $3,000,000 in June of 2001. Assuming interest

on the underpayment of tax has averaged 8% from June of 1998 to June of 2001 and that the gain will be taxed at 20%, compare whether the heirs should pay interest and step-up the basis or pay no interest and keep the basis as shown on the return.

23. Using the facts from problem 21 (Nicolas's lake), except that, instead of $1,500,000 for the land and lake, it was determined to be worth $2,500,000. (a) What is the § 2032A value? Use the inflation-adjusted § 2032A amount. (b) Explain how Nicolas's estate also qualifies for § 2057. (c) What is the maximum § 2057 deduction? (d) Use your ETAX program to compute the estate tax with and without the benefit of the two elections.

24. When he died in 2003, Mitch owned a closely held business with a net worth of $3,000,000. The rest of his estate had a net worth of $2,000,000. Although the business interest does not qualify for § 2032A, it does qualify for § 2057; and his heirs plan to keep the business. (a) What would make it qualify for § 2057 but not for § 2032A? (b) What is total estate tax without the § 2057 deduction? (c) What is the tax with the maximum deduction? (d) If the executor used the unified credit for 2003 and a correspondingly reduced deduction, what is the tax? (e) Which gave the better result?

25. Minnie and Mark, parents of two adult children, Betty and Bryan, own a closely held business. It is clearly their most valuable asset making up about 75% of their net worth. Betty pretty much runs the business and would like to continue to do so after her parents are gone, whereas, Bryan has no interest in it. Minnie and Mark wish to leave equal value to their children and have Betty receive the business. Suggest several ways they might accomplish these goals.

26. When Amel died intestate in 2002, her estate included acreage in Montana. Emilo and Elena are the only heirs. Emilo, while serving as administrator, has been approached by an environmentalist group that would like to see the estate set aside about 400 acres as part of a conservation easement. The acres include a stream at the base of a mountain where the state is considering releasing endangered condors. The group wants to put Emilo together with representatives of the State Park and Game Department as there is apparently

an interest on their part to accept the easement. (a) Emilo asks how it is possible to gain an estate tax benefit, given that granting an easement was not part of his mother's estate plan. Explain. (b) Briefly, what must be established to obtain an estate tax benefit? Does it matter that the property is not located next to a state or national park? (c) In general, what might be accomplished by granting the easement? (d) Suppose they are able to reduce the estate taxes by $200,000, if they sell the Montana property (including the 400 acres subject to the easement) 20 months after their mother died, will any of the taxes saved be recaptured? Explain.

27. (a) How have check-the-box regulations made it easier for closely held businesses to select the appropriate organization with less worry about tax implications? (b) For a business with just a few owners, why is the LLC likely to be favored over the corporate form? Can all of the advantages of the LLC be obtained by making a Subchapter S election? (c) What is likely to keep the owners of an S corporation from liquidating it and reforming as an LLC?

28. Briefly, what is the advantage of creating a family limited partnership?

ANSWERS TO THE QUESTIONS AND PROBLEMS *(odd numbered only)*

1 a. Generally speaking, cash needs will rise with increasing estate size, due to the estate tax.

   b. In most cases, the death of S1 will result in no estate tax, due to the shelter of the marital deduction and the unified credit. On the other hand, the death of S2 can result in a significant estate tax for families with medium to large estates.

   c. The younger the minor children, the greater the typical amount of liquidity needed to fund the economic loss provided by that deceased spouse for the remainder of the children's period of dependence. Also, the older the person, the less time there is to accumulate liquidity.

3. a. The traits that distinguish cash value insurance from term insurance are: (1) The pattern of the premiums over time (cash value: constant premiums; term: increasing premiums). (2) Whether the proceeds are certain to be paid (cash value: certain; term: uncertain).

   b. The traits that distinguish universal life (UL) insurance from other types of cash value insurance are: (1) degree of flexibility - UL policies permit the policyholder to vary the face value and premium payments; and (2) investment yield - UL policies offer a variable yield, based on shorter-term investment rates.

5. Gift taxation of life insurance can arise either when a policy is assigned, or at the insured's death, whenever the insured, owner, and beneficiary are all different parties.

7. Estate taxation can arise under Code §§ 2033, 2042, 2001, 2035, as described in detail in Chapter 6. The following is a summary.

   Under § 2001, the decedent's adjusted taxable gifts will include the date-of-gift taxable terminal value of any life insurance policy for which the decedent made a completed transfer more than three years before death.

   Under § 2033 (property owned at death), the terminal value of a life insurance policy on the life of someone other than the decedent will be includable in the decedent's gross estate to the extent of the decedent's date-of-death ownership interest in the policy.

Under § 2042, proceeds on the life of the decedent will be includable in the decedent's gross estate if, at the insured's death, either the proceeds were receivable by the decedent's executor or the decedent possessed any incidents of ownership in the policy. Interestingly, the entire proceeds under split dollar arrangements are includable even though part of the proceeds is payable to a third party, such as the employer.

Under § 2035, the proceeds of a life insurance policy on the life of the decedent will be includable in the decedent's gross estate if, within three years of death, the decedent made a completed transfer of incidents of ownership in the policy.

9. The major question in deciding whom to insure is whose death will result in financial loss that should be replaced.

   a. Spouses in their 30s, husband working, wife at home with two young children: Both spouses may need term insurance: for the husband to replace his lost income, for the wife to finance day care services, etc., while the widower is working. Probably term insurance makes the most sense in all of these cases. It is cheaper and the need that is being addressed is temporary and will disappear by the time the individuals reach retirement age.

   b. Spouses in their 30s, both working, no children: Often, neither spouse needs coverage, because the income (modest) loss from the death of either is assumable. However, this depends on their relative current standard of living and desired standard of living when the first one dies. Spouses who live modestly and save a lot may not need life insurance if the survivor can live on one salary and the expected investment income. On the other hand, spouses who save little and live expensively (costly home, cars, lifestyle, etc.) and want the surviving spouse to continue enjoying this lifestyle will probably need a considerable amount of insurance on the lives of both spouses.

   c. Spouses in their 50s, both working, children are self-supporting adults living elsewhere: Essentially same answer as part b, except less insurance usually necessary because the surviving spouse's expected life span is lower and expected investment income is often greater.

d. Single adult, no children: No insurance usually necessary.

e. Single parent of one six-year-old child: Considerable insurance would ordinarily be needed for the parent to provide funds to raise the child.

f. Retired couple, self-supporting adult children living elsewhere: Answer depends on surviving spouse's other expected sources of income. To the extent that retirement benefits will continue and investment income will be high, less insurance is needed.

11. In the small family estate, convenience and other non-tax factors would influence the decisions as to who should be the owner and primary and contingent beneficiaries. The insured's spouse could be named owner and primary beneficiary to avoid probate in the insured's estate. The contingent beneficiary could be a child or a trustee of a trust for the benefit of the child.

13. a. Characteristics of the irrevocable life insurance trust: (1) It is created by the insured. (2) Trustee is owner and beneficiary of the policy. (3) Trust terminates at or after S2's death.

b. Advantages: (1) There is no transfer taxation of proceeds at either spouse's death. (2) It is not included in either spouse's probate estate. (3) It qualifies gifts of the policy and the policy premiums for the annual exclusion. (4) It qualifies for the gift tax annual exclusion for gifts to the trust. (5) It ensures that a responsible party will provide the needed liquidity. (6) Corpus is available to S2 subject to an ascertainable standard. (7) S2 may be given income for life.

15. To establish an asset base to provide income to her children in the event of her premature death, April should establish an irrevocable life insurance trust, a device that can function reasonably free from the control of her ex-husband. The trustee would be the policy beneficiary, directed to provide for the children's needs. The trustee ought to be instructed to pay funds, whenever possible, directly to the provider.

17.   § 6166: By deferring tax payments over 14 annual payments, some of the deferred tax will benefit from a mere 2% late payment rate.

§ 303: By reducing income tax on stock redemptions used to pay death taxes and administrative expenses. The buy-back is treated as a capital exchange and the stock receives a new basis due to the owner's death.

§ 2032A: By reducing the taxable estate. The real estate devoted to special use may be lowered by as much as $750,000 (indexed) to its special use value.

§ 2057: By reducing the taxable estate. The family-owned business deduction may lower the taxable estate by as much as $675,000 (however the maximum unified credit would then be $202,050, i.e., producing an AEA of $625,000).

19. a. If the property does not qualify for special use valuation, the land will probably be valued at $1,200,000, its highest and best use value, making the gross estate equal to $1,900,000.
    b. If the property does qualify for special use valuation, the land will be valued at $450,000 (which is the $1,200,000 highest and best use value, reduced by $750,000, the maximum amount allowed by law), making the gross estate equal $1,150,000.

21. (a) Answer: $1,225,000. The minium value could be determined by trial and error or by using algebra. Let the value of the business land be X. We know that to qualify, X plus the other business property must equal 50% of the adjusted value of the gross estate. Thus we must solve for X in the following equation: (X + $200,000) = (X + $1,600,000 + $200,000 - $150,000 - $25,000)/2; simplified: X = $1,600,000 + $200,000 - $150,000 -$25,000 - $400,000 = $1,225,000. (b) Since the FMV is $1,500,000 and special use is $800,000, the maximum reduction in the value of the real estate is $700,000 (not $800,000). (c) Without the election, the taxable estate would be $3,125,000 [$1,500,000 + $200,000 + $1,600,000 - $150,000 - $25,000] and the tax would be $1,139,000. With the election the taxable estate is $2,325,000, the tax is $719,500, and, the difference is $419,500.

23. (a) $2,500,000 - $800,000 = $1,700,000. The difference between FMV and special use is greater than $800,000, therefore the maximum reduction in the value of the real estate is $800,000. (b) The business, even specially valued, is greater than 50% of adjusted value of the gross estate: ($1,700,000 +

$200,000)/($1,700,000 + $200,000 + $1,600,000 -$175,000) = 57%. (c) The maximum deduction is $675,000. However, for years after 1998, using the maximum deduction will result in a corresponding reduction in the AEA (i.e., a reduction in the unified credit). (d) Without the two reductions, the taxable estate is $4,125,000 and the tax is $1,689,000 (using 2001 unified credit of $220,550). With the two exclusions the taxable estate is $2,650,000 [$4,125,000 - $800,000 - $675,000] and the unified credit is $202,050. The tax is $903,250 and the difference is $785,750.

25. The problem is that an equal distribution of the estate would mean a portion of the business to Bryan, an asset he does not want. A survivorship (second death) life insurance policy sufficient to equalize the benefit to each child could be arranged such that Betty would receive the business and Bryan receive more of the insurance proceeds. Thus, life insurance can simplify distribution of "lumpy" estate assets to survivors with widely different lifestyles and preferences. It might be wise, even though there is no estate tax problem, to have all assets held in trust and the insurance paid to the trust as doing so would facilitate making the equal division.

27. (a) The regulations allow the owners to choose to be taxed as a partnership or corporation, if two or more owners, or as a corporation or sole proprietorship if just one owner (or a married couple) regardless of the actual structure. Since closely held businesses usually prefer to have a pass through entity in order to avoid having tax at the entity level and again at the owner level, the check the box regulations have made it very easy for new businesses to avoid the corporate tax. (b) Even though the check the box regulations allow a corporation to be taxed as a partnership, the recognition of capital gains tax on the distribution of appreciated assets from a corporation (§ 311) will cause many to favor the LLC. A Subchapter S corporation is taxed as a partnership for the most part. However it also has the § 311 problem and, compared to the LLC, it is much more restricted as to capital structure (only one class of stock) and as to who may own shares (75 limit, generally only individuals can own it, no non-resident aliens allowed). (c) The Code § 311 requirement that gain be recognized on distribution of appreciated assets.

ENDNOTES

1. LR 9314050.

2. In this chapter, the word *insurance* will be used as shorthand to mean life insurance.

3. *Theodore H. Cohen*, 39 TC 1055 (1963), acq. 1964-1 CB 4.

4. *Swanson*, 33 TCM 296, (1974), aff'd. 518 F2d 59 (8th Cir., 1975); Rev. Rul. 85-13 1985-1 CB 184.

5. IRC § 101(*a*)(2).

6. IRC § 677(a)(3).

7. *Baptiste*, TCM 1992-198; IRC § 6324(a)(2).

8. IRS § 2642(c)(2).

9. IRC §§ 6166(b)(6); 2053(d).

10. IRC § 163(h)(2)(E).

11. IRC § 2503(d) added by the Taxpayer Relief Act of 1997.

12. Rev. Rul. 80-250, 1980-2 CB 278.

13. Cecil Cammack, Jr., at Cammack Computations Co., 1-800-594-5826, will do these computations at a very reasonable price.

14. IRC § 6601(j)(2).

15. IRC § 6601(j)(1)(B)

16. IRC § 303(b)(3).

17. IRC § 2032A(b)(1)(A).

18. IRC § 2032A(b)(1)(B).

19. IRC § 2032A(e)(1).

20. IRC § 2032A(b)(2).

21. IRC § 2032A(a)(2).

22. *J. Fisher*, TC CCH 12,923 (1993).

23. IRC § 2032A(b)(5)(A).

24. IRC § 1016(c).

25. Initially IRC § 2033A, renumbered as § 2057 by the 1998 Tax Act.

26. IRS Restructuring and Reform Act of 1998 (Pub L 105-206, 112 Stat 685).

27. *John and Viola Moore v. Commissioner*, 62 TCM 1128 (1991) (35% discount on gift of partnership interest); *Estate of Winkler v. Commissioner*, 62 TCM 1514 (1991) (20% discount on nonvoting stock); *Estate of Catherine Campbell v. Commissioner*, 62 TCM 1514 (1991) (56% discount); *Estate of Lenheim v. Commissioner*, 60 TCM 356 (1990); *Nancy Moonyham v. Commissioner*, TC Memo 1991-178.

28. TAM 9140002.

29. Rev. Rul. 93-12, 1993-7 IRB 13.

30. *Estate of Chenowith v. Commissioner* 88 TC 1577 (1987).

31. *Estate of Salsbury v. Commissioner* 34 TC Memo (CCH) 1441 (1975).

32. *Smythe v. U.S.* 86-1 U.S. Tax Cases (CCH).

33. See TAM 9336002.

34. *G.O'Keeffe Estate* TC ¶12,886(M) (50% blockage discount allowed).

35. *Estate of Bright v. U.S.*, 658 F.2d 999 (5th Cir. 1981).

36. *Estate of Morton B. Harper v. Comm.*, T.C. Memo. 2002-121; Estate of *Theodore R. Thompson, et al. V. Comm.*, T.C. Memo. 2002-246.

37. TAM 200212006; *J.C. Shepherd v. Comm.*, 283 F.3d 1258 (11th Cir. 2002).

38. Reg. § 301.7701-1 through § 301.7701-4. See *US v. Kintner*, 216 F. 2d 418 (9th Cir. 1954). *Kintner* lead to the old regulations based on corporate characteristics.

39. Reg. § 301.77013(b)(1).

40. IRC § 1361(b)(1) sets forth the restrictions for S corporations.

41. *General Utilities & Operating Co.*, 296 U.S. 200, 56 S.Ct. 185 (1935).

42. IRC § 311.

CHAPTER 16

Planning for Closely Held Business Interests

OVERVIEW

A closely held business is a firm privately owned by one or a few individuals who actively participate in its management. Unique estate planning problems can arise for owners of a closely held business. Typically, the firm generates the major source of its owner's income and represents the single largest part of his or her family wealth. Often, the firm cannot sustain its level of income and value if the owners do not continue active involvement. For example, after an owner dies, replacement managers may be less astute and business mistakes may occur, reducing revenue or profit.

The income and value can be reduced by at least two events. First, each owner's involvement with the firm is destined to end, and the enterprise will lose the knowledge and personal connections that the owner brought to the firm. Second, the ownership interest in the business must eventually be transferred, subjecting it to transfer costs, including taxes, which can reduce working capital and solvency.

Estate planning seeks to minimize the adverse impact of these events in four ways:

1. Generating sufficient income for the owner and the owner's family after the owner's active involvement in the business ends.
2. Transferring the business intact, or its maximum value to the owner's chosen beneficiaries.
3. Minimizing the costs of transfer.
4. Providing sufficient liquidity to pay the transfer costs.

Transfer of shares in publicly traded corporations is less demanding. First, withdrawal of any one owner will usually have a less depressing effect on business value and income, making continuity more assured. Publicly traded firms usually employ far more personnel, making business success much less dependent on the efforts of any one individual. In contrast, studies indicate that only 30-35% of successful closely held family businesses survive in the second generation, and only 10-20% survive in the third generation. In many cases, this is due to unresolved family conflicts. Second, the goal of liquidity is easier to achieve for owners of publicly held firms because the owner's survivors receive marketable securities.

Liquidity problems can arise for wealthier individuals owning publicly traded stock that is either a large block or "restricted" under federal securities law. Large block holdings (i.e., tens of thousands of shares) may give rise to the problem of *blockage*, which is the temporarily depressing effect on the market price that results from selling a large block all at once. Transfer tax law will allow some valuation discount for blockage effects. *Restricted stock* is usually acquired either from an affiliate of the issuing company or in a private, unregistered transaction. Federal securities law prohibits restricted stock from being sold without either registering it under the Securities Act of 1933 or meeting an exemption from registration. The most common methods of disposing of such stock are by a secondary offering, a private placement, or by "Rule 144 sales," none of which are simple transactions. Although blockage and restricted stock can lead to significant liquidity problems, their consequences will be felt by only a handful of estates. Their impact is not as great as that of the death or withdrawal of an owner of a closely held business.

Thus, owners of closely held businesses have relatively unique problems. This chapter will survey the major principles and techniques of estate planning devoted to assisting them. The chapter will first present an overview of general planning in this area, then examine the business buyout agreement, and finally, the special valuation rules from Chapter 14 of the Internal Revenue Code as they relate to corporate recapitalizations and partnership capital freezes.

The attractiveness of many of the techniques in this chapter is colored by the uncertainty of the 2001 law repealing the estate tax in 2010 and reinstating it in its present form in 2011. The text will discuss clear implications, but for the most part refrains from repeatedly mentioning this obvious uncertainty. The reader is in a good position to imagine and hypothesize some of the impact the potential change has on planning. It might even be a benefit to be unburdened by years of habit and training in the law as it existed before this new uncertainty.

VALUING THE BUSINESS

The subject of the value of a closely held business can arise in several tax contexts. How is business valuation determined? The following eight general factors are taken from Revenue Ruling 59-60,[1] the Treasury's classic exposition on valuation of the shares of closely held stock.

1. Nature and history of the business.
2. Economic outlook and conditions of the economy and industry.
3. Book value of the stock and financial condition of the company.
4. Company earning capacity.
5. Company dividend-paying capacity.
6. Extent of company goodwill and other intangibles.
7. Recent sales of the company's stock and the size of the block to be valued.
8. Market price of publicly traded stock in the same industry.

The extent of use of each factor depends on the underlying facts concerning the specific business interest.

PLANNING IN GENERAL FOR CLOSELY HELD BUSINESS INTERESTS

All estate planning for closely held business interests is premised on the fact that the owner cannot carry on forever. We are certain that the owner's active involvement in the management of the firm will terminate, and that the ownership interest will be transferred.

Withdrawal from the Firm: Minimizing Decline in Income and Value

Owners have the ability to choose when to terminate their active management of the firm. Some elect to remain active until disability or death. Some withdraw sooner to adopt a new lifestyle, to consume more of the wealth that time and hard work has created, or to step aside to provide a business opportunity for a son or daughter. No matter when the owner plans to withdraw, if the departure is expected to reduce the value and income derived from the business, the owner can take several steps to minimize the decline.

Delegate responsibility. First, the owner can plan early to pass on knowledge of the business and delegate greater responsibility to potential replacements. To provide an incentive for assumption of this responsibility, the business can contribute to tax-favored fringe benefit plans, including medical insurance contracts, group term life insurance, and retirement plans. In general, contributions to these plans are income tax deductible by the firm and are either tax-free or tax-deferred to the employee.

Execute contracts for future income. Second, the owner can use current business value to raise his or her own future income by executing certain contracts, such as a nonqualified deferred compensation plan, disability income insurance, and a qualified retirement plan. Nonqualified deferred compensation is a custom-tailored agreement under which the employer agrees to pay the employee in the future for services rendered presently. Tax law ordinarily permits the income tax to be similarly deferred. A professional athlete with a brief but often lucrative career is a frequent party to a deferred compensation contract.

Freeze the estate. Third, the firm may be able to undertake a corporate recapitalization or create a partnership capital freeze. These are intricate transfer devices which can reduce transfer taxes. Each can offer employment incentives to family members, and each may be able to freeze the value of the owner's interest in the business while continuing to provide him or her with rights to substantial income and voting power in the business affairs. However, recent tax legislation has severely restricted their potential value, and the owner should be advised to seek expert tax counsel when exploring these techniques.

Maintain a list of instructions. Fourth, the owner can make a list of business instructions for the surviving family. If the owner wants to keep his wishes private, it could be placed in a safe deposit box. The list could include recommendations as to whether to sell the firm or continue running it, the name of the chosen successor, a list of business advisors, and the location of key company documents. These arrangements can reduce stress, particularly after the sudden death of the owner. Such a list probably is not binding and thus is better adapted to giving information than instructions.

Execute a buyout contract. Finally, if an abrupt departure by the owner is likely to result in a significant decrease in the value and income of the business, the owner might consider selling the business or negotiating a contract for its future sale. By staying on as a consultant during a transition phase, the decrease in value may be avoided.

Transferring a Business Interest

The owner will want to choose when and to whom to transfer the business interest. Planning for the transfer will depend in large part on whether the person wishes to transfer the equity interest to a family member, or to sell it to an unrelated party and transfer the sale proceeds to the chosen beneficiaries.

Transfer of an equity interest to a family member. Some owners will want to make a transfer of a controlling interest in the business to a particular family member who is willing and able to take over its management. Many transfer devices are available.

Lifetime strategies. To encourage the family member to adopt a long-term commitment and prevent deterioration in business value and income, the owner should prepare a family member for eventual ownership and control. In addition to delegating increasing amounts of responsibility, the owner can offer incentives, such as gifts of ownership interests in the business, possibly in the form of stock or stock options. The transfers can be outright, or they can be in trust, with the owner and family member acting as co-trustees. Transfers using trusts can promote an orderly transition by enabling the owner to monitor and develop the family member's interest, abilities, and commitment.

Other alternatives are a gift-leaseback, installment sale, sale-leaseback, or private annuity. An installment sale can be a simple, inexpensive, and relatively tax-safe estate freezing alternative.

Transfer at death strategies. Instead of making a lifetime gift of the business interest, the owner, to retain complete control, may prefer to pass it on at death. This approach makes it possible to use techniques that are not available for lifetime gifts, such as IRC § 303 stock redemptions if the business is incorporated, the IRC § 2032A special use valuation, the business exclusion of IRC § 2057, and the extended payment plan of IRC § 6166. Furthermore, the estate taxes may be funded through the use of an irrevocable life insurance trust. Business interests that have appreciated in value receive a step-up in basis if they are part of the decedent's estate, but have a carry-over basis if transferred as gifts. However, there are several drawbacks to waiting until after the owner dies to transfer a closely held business.

Liquidity problems. First, estate liquidity problems may arise if a nonspouse survivor receives a relatively illiquid asset having a substantial taxable value.

EXAMPLE 16 - 1. Keith was a widower and the co-owner of a very successful business. Even with lack of marketability discounts and other tax breaks, the estate tax attributable to the business was substantial. Keith's children were not welcomed by the other co-owners who together held 70% of the shares of the company. After trying unsuccessfully to have the business sold as a whole, they soon directly experienced the reason lack of marketability and minority discounts exist. The only serious buyers for their shares were the co-owners who drove such a hard bargain that the children settled for even less than the discounted value on the estate tax return. Succession planning might have given them a price closer to their proportionate share of what the company would have brought if sold as a whole.

Unprepared survivors. Second, transfers to unprepared survivors who decide to carry on the business can generate severe problems. The combined tasks of dealing with grief and assuming new business duties can cause panic, guilt, exhaustion, family squabbles and failure. Adverse parties such as customers, employees and creditors may be tempted to take advantage of the new owner's naivete. While careful planning can reduce this risk, it cannot entirely eliminate it, particularly if the successors are not very experienced in business.

Uncertainty and friction. Third, transfers to beneficiaries who do not intend to sell may be ill-advised if the beneficiaries have no desire to manage the firm. By its nature, the closely held business requires active cooperation among its owners which usually requires constant interaction. Unaware of the firm's manner of operation, uninvolved owners can precipitate uncertainty and friction among other manager-owners and employees, especially if they disagree with how the business is being run.

Hard for survivors to sell. Fourth, transferring business interests at death can create problems for surviving transferees who do wish to sell out. In structuring the terms of the sale, survivors will not be able to take advantage of the owner's knowledge and experience. The business may no longer be as productive which could substantially lower the price. Buyers may not be willing to pay the surviving beneficiaries a fair value for the deceased owner's interest, particularly if it is a minority interest. The survivors may have little bargaining power because of their need for cash. Furthermore, a unique business usually has few prospective buyers. It is not like selling a home or the shares of a publicly traded corporation.

Legal and tax complexities. Fifth, legal and tax complexities may arise. If a shareholder's interest in S corporation stock is to be distributed at death to a trust, such as a bypass or a marital trust, that trust must be designed to qualify as a "Qualified Subchapter S Trust" in order to keep the corporation's Subchapter S status. Requirements to qualify as a "Qualified Subchapter S Trust" include naming only one income beneficiary.[2] An S corporation is treated by federal income tax law as if it were a partnership. Income is taxed to the individual shareholders rather than to the corporation.

Valuation disputes with the IRS. Sixth, disputes with the IRS over the estate tax valuation of a closely held business are common and often result in litigation or settlement at higher than expected values. The Code imposes an estate tax penalty of 20% of the tax underpayment for valuation understatements at less than 50% of the correct value when additional tax owed exceeds $5,000.[3] A pre-death sale lets the owner help with valuation negotiations with the IRS.

For these and many other practical reasons, the owner would be well-advised to consider pre-death gifting of a business interest.

Sale to an unrelated party. Instead of transferring an ownership interest to the surviving beneficiaries, the owner could arrange the sale of the business interest to an unrelated party. Potential buyers include the key employees of the business, other individuals, and other firms, including competitors. The beneficiaries can receive assets (cash or publicly traded stock) that produce income with less need for effort or skill on their part.

Timing. The business could be sold before or after the owner withdraws from active management. While the owner is still active, the entire firm could be sold outright, or some of its assets could be sold and then leased back to the firm. An arrangement could be made to sell the firm when the owner withdraws at retirement, disability, or death. Actual timing of the sale will often depend largely on the personal preferences of the owner rather than focusing on the economics.

In general, the greater the expected decline in the value from the owner's withdrawal, the greater the economic motive to sell it while it is still being actively run by the person. Value will fall most for single-owner firms offering professional services such as physicians, accountants, and attorneys. Often, the primary assets of these firms are the personal customer relationships which are not easily transferable. Product oriented or capital intensive firms and service firms with more than one owner may better retain their value.

Sale of the business interest prior to the owner's withdrawal will often bring a higher price since buyers can observe that the business is operating successfully. The owner's awareness of the firm's identity and its earnings potential will provide additional bargaining power during negotiations. If the sale is completed while the person is alive, the agreement may include an agreement for the new owner to retain the seller as an "adviser" or "consultant," to increasing the seller's future income and ease transition. Finally, sale of a closely held business prior to the owner's death can minimize disputes with the IRS over the firm's actual market value.

Alternatively, the business interest could be sold at or after the owner's withdrawal from the firm. A sale structured in advance to take effect at the owner's disability or death is called a business buyout agreement.

Taxable gain. Selling the business for cash before the owner's death will cause immediate recognition of a taxable gain unless the transaction is an installment sale or tax deferred exchange. On the other hand, transferring the interest at death can eliminate most or the entire taxable gain because of the step-up in basis that the interest will receive at death. However, at a probable tax rate of 20%, the tax impact of a pre-death sale for cash may be a good tradeoff for estate liquidity compared to the high cost of alternate liquidity sources such as life insurance on an elderly person.

Form of the transaction. Sale of the business can be for immediate cash, to one or a few individuals, as a public offering, or to a corporation. It can be as an installment sale with the seller's recognition of the taxable gain spread over the collection period. The sale can be for stock, in a tax-deferred exchange with a publicly held firm. Or the capital gains tax may be eliminated entirely by a step-up in basis if the transfer is after the owner's death.

A common planning device employed to sell a closely held business to one or a few individuals is the *business buyout agreement*, also called a buy-sell agreement. The firm, one or more owners, employees, or other parties contract with the owner in advance to purchase the interest in the business at death or disability. The buyout agreement offers future liquidity, a guaranteed market, and greater certainty of the selling price. Often, the purchase is funded with life and disability insurance. It can usually be negotiated on fair terms between co-owners if no one knows whether they will be seller or buyer.

Consideration should be given to incorporating an unincorporated business for several reasons. Incorporating will generate divisible shares of ownership which may be easier to transfer or liquidate when the need arises. Incorporating will enhance continuity, since a corporation has an indefinite existence that might help the business survive a shareholder's departure. One disadvantage of forming a typical C corporation is that almost any distribution of corporate property to the shareholders will be taxed to them as dividend income, subject to double taxation. Two exceptions to this double taxation problem are the IRC § 303 redemption to pay death taxes and a complete redemption of the deceased shareholder's stock.

The Need for Early Planning

When should planning for closely held business interests begin? Planning should begin early, when the person is still active and in good health. First, the business owner can express estate planning objectives and his or her knowledge and expertise can help planners reach the objectives. Second, the person will be able to take advantage of planning concepts available to healthy individuals, including relatively inexpensive life and disability insurance. Third, if the business will eventually have to be sold, careful planning can eliminate the need for a sudden forced sale at the owner's incapacity or death, times when the business is clearly less valuable.

BUSINESS BUYOUT AGREEMENT

Placing the burden of selling the business on the survivors after the owner's death can create problems that can be reduced by a business buyout agreement. Executed by the owner and prospective purchasers, the buyout agreement obligates the other parties to purchase the owner's interest on the occurrence of specific events, such as at the onset of disability or on death.

Types of Agreements: Cross-purchase, Entity-redemption, or Mixed

The three most common types of buyout agreements are distinguished by the identity of the contracting parties. First, the *cross-purchase* agreement provides that the other owners purchase the interest of a particular owner. Many owners use a reciprocal cross-purchase agreement, in which each owner agrees to purchase a pro rata share of the interest of any owner that dies. Second, the *entity*, or *redemption* agreement has the business itself purchase the interest of one or more owners. Third, the *mixed* agreement gives the business an option to purchase an owner's interest and gives the other owners the option or obligation to purchase the balance. A hybrid, the mixed agreement has characteristics of both cross-purchase and entity-redemption agreements and is the most flexible.

Taxation of Buyout Agreements

The most critical taxation issues in buyout agreements arise in the estate tax area.

Gift taxation. Generally, the execution of a buyout agreement does not result in a taxable gift unless it gives a purchaser an unqualified present purchase right at a contract price below fair market value.

Income taxation. Income tax effects of buyout agreements will depend on the type of the agreement.

Cross-purchase agreement. The selling owner, usually the estate of a decedent-business owner, sells a capital asset subject to capital gain treatment. But the step-up in basis at the decedent's death means the only gain recognized is on appreciation after the date of death that is reflected in the sale price. The buyer's new basis will be the purchase price of the business interest acquired.

Entity-redemption agreement. The acquiring business's new basis will be its purchase price, which is not tax deductible. If the business has been paying premiums on life insurance to fund the arrangement, it will not be allowed a tax deduction for those premiums. They must be paid with after-tax dollars.[4] Further, any cash value buildup on a policy and any receipt of proceeds, while not included as ordinary income, may be subject to the alternative minimum tax.[5]

The selling party, again usually the decedent-owner's estate, will be taxed on the sale proceeds as a dividend, to the extent of the corporation's earnings and profits. Dividend treatment can be avoided if the sale can qualify for favorable redemption treatment under IRC § 302 or § 303. Both sections permit the redeeming party to treat the sale as a disposition of a capital asset rather than the receipt of a dividend. The step-up in basis means that there is generally little or no taxable gain. Without this favorable treatment, the entire receipt would be taxable as ordinary income.

Mixed agreement. Tax under a mixed agreement follows the above patterns.

EXAMPLE 16 - 2. Stan and Oliver, equal owners of a corporation, are trying to decide whether to arrange a cross-purchase or an entity-redemption buyout plan. Each has an adjusted basis of $20,000 in his respective shares. They project that the business is worth $2,000,000. Thus, under either arrangement, if a death occurred in the near future, the purchase price would be about $1,000,000, and the total value of the surviving owner's stock would be $2,000,000, i.e., the total value of the business. However, the survivor's basis will be different, depending on which arrangement is selected. If a cross-purchase plan is chosen, the surviving shareholder's total basis will increase to $1,020,000, of which $20,000 is the basis of the survivor's own stock, and $1,000,000 is the price of the decedent's stock. If an entity-redemption arrangement is chosen, the total basis of the surviving shareholder's stock will remain $20,000, because he will not have purchased any additional shares.

Estate taxation. The deceased owner's gross estate will include some value attributable to the decedent's ownership interest held at the moment of death. Ordinarily, the estate executor will prefer to avoid a dispute with the IRS over this value. One method has been to establish a selling price in the buyout agreement that will, by law, fix the value for estate tax purposes. Only half-jokingly, one commentator has said that in the absence of a price "set" by a buyout agreement, the "value" of the business can be said to be the amount agreed on by "a willing IRS agent and a willing executor, neither of whom has ever owned a business."

Common valuation methods. Prior to October 9, 1990, the effective date of IRC § 2703, fixing the value of the business for estate tax purposes was simpler because case law was quite generous in allowing fixed values that were below fair market value.

Three valuation methods are commonly included in buyout contracts. First, a specific dollar amount is specified, with a provision made for periodic review so the owners can revise the amount as conditions change. Without provision for a review, if the value of the business increased, the purchasing owners would receive a windfall at the expense of the selling owner. Unfortunately, inertia can reduce the likelihood of periodic reviews.

Second, the selling price can be determined by appraisal, with the agreement specifying that a qualified appraiser will determine the value of the business at the time of sale. The appraisal method has the advantage of ensuring that a current value is used.

Third, business buyout agreements can use a valuation formula determined by an expert appraiser. Its terms ordinarily call for valuation to be a specified percentage of book value or a multiple of current earnings. A formula is more flexible and often more accurate than setting a specific amount since the selling price will vary with economic conditions. However, because a formula is more arbitrary than an appraisal, it may later turn out not to reflect current economic conditions.

Impact of IRC § 2703. To set the estate tax value of a business equal to its buyout agreement price, agreements executed after October 8, 1990, must meet § 2703(b) requirements.

1. The agreement must be a bona fide business arrangement.
2. The agreement cannot be a device to transfer property to members of the decedent's family for less than full and adequate consideration in money or money's worth.
3. The terms of the agreement must be comparable to similar arrangements entered into by persons in arm's length transactions.

Some comments on these requirements. The thrust of these requirements is to ensure a value reasonably close to the value of the business interest at the moment of the transfer. Thus, an agreement under which the surviving owner, a son, is obligated to purchase the parent's $1 million business interest (current value) for a fixed $300,000 (historical contract value) would be currently labeled a "disguised bequest," and not meet the first two requirements.[6] On the other hand, prices set between unrelated owners are not usually subject to intense scrutiny by the IRS if the transaction otherwise appears to be made at arm's length. IRS regulations provide that a buyout agreement will meet all three requirements if more than 50% of the value of the property subject to the agreement is owned by persons who are not "natural objects of the transferor's bounty."[7]

Planners feel that the comparability requirement of the third requirement will create considerable uncertainty and additional expense for difficult appraisals, in particular because typical buyout agreements are not public documents. However, for businesses in some industries, agreements may be able to specify a formula, such as a multiple of sales or earnings, if that formula is known to be the predominant valuation method for the industry.

Even though valuation discounts may be available, the estate could wind up paying more estate tax than it should if valuation is not set for estate tax purposes. Planners must consider the § 2703 valuation rules carefully. It may not work to include a "savings" clause that increases the selling price, in the event of an audit, to the final determination of estate tax value. The IRS has challenged such clauses as contrary to public policy because it sees them as attempts to pass property at less than its true value.[8]

EXAMPLE 16 - 3. Dad's will incorporated an AB trust plan. He executed a business buyout agreement with his son, who was obligated to buy Dad's 1,000 shares of closely held stock for $1 million. When Dad died in 2002, in addition to the stock, he owned other property worth $1.5 million. Son paid Dad's estate

$1 million for the stock and Dad's executor distributed $1 million to the bypass trust and $1.5 million to the marital trust. After an IRS audit, Dad's executor agreed that the stock's fair market value was $2 million. Thus, Dad's gross estate totaled $3.5 million not $2.5 million as had been shown on the estate tax return. Only the $1.5 million that went into the marital trust qualified for the martial deduction, thus the taxable estate was actually $2 million, resulting in estate taxes of $435,000. The additional $1 million is considered as having been left to the son and, in the absence of a clause allocating taxes to the credit shelter trust, since the taxable estate is divided equally between him and the bypass trust, each would pay half of the tax. The tax could have been avoided had the buyout agreement provided for a realistic selling price. Consider the two alternatives.

| | Alternative Values Given the Stock | | | |
	Sales Agreement $1 million		Realistically Valued $2 million	
Gross Estate	$3,500,000	*1*	$3,500,000	
Less Marital Deduction	$1,500,000	*2*	$2,500,000	*3*
Taxable Estate	$2,000,000		$1,000,000	
Tentative Tax	$780,800		$345,800	
Less Unified Credit	($345,800)		($345,800)	
Estate Tax	$435,000		$0	

notes:

1 $3,500,000 = stock @ $2 million & other property @ $1,500,000

2   marital deduction = $2,500,000 - AEA into Trust B

3   marital deduction = $3,500,000 - AEA into Trust B

Funding

A business buyout agreement can require survivors to pay a cash lump sum or periodic installments at the triggering event. The choice sometimes depends on the nature of the triggering event.

Cash lump-sum payment. Buyout agreements that require a cash lump sum are likely to be funded with life insurance and/or lump-sum disability insurance.

Life insurance. The choice of life insurance to fund a business buyout agreement will be influenced by the type of buyout chosen. Under an *entity* agreement, the firm purchases and acts as beneficiary of a policy on the life of each business owner. Each policy is in the amount that is necessary to buy out that owner's interest. In a reciprocal *cross-purchase agreement*, each contracting party purchases and acts as beneficiary of a policy on the life of each of the other contracting owners, in an amount that is their pro-rata share of the buyout price.

> EXAMPLE 16 - 4. Sol and Harry are equal shareholders of a corporation that has a net worth of $300,000. The men have executed an entity buyout arrangement. The corporation will own and be the beneficiary of two $150,000 face value policies, one on Sol's life and one on Harry's life. The men plan to review and update this amount periodically as the value of the business changes.

> EXAMPLE 16 - 5. Facts are the same as the prior example, except that a reciprocal cross-purchase plan is adopted. Sol will own and be beneficiary of a $150,000 policy on Harry's life, and Harry will own and be a beneficiary of a $150,000 policy on Sol's life.

A reciprocal cross-purchase arrangement funded with life insurance becomes unwieldy when the agreement includes numerous owners, because each contracting party will have to purchase a policy on the life of each other contracting owner. For example, although only two policies would have to be purchased for a firm with two contracting owners, six policies would have to be purchased for three owners, and 12 policies for four owners. In general, the number of policies purchased under a cross-purchase plan would be $n(n - 1)$, where n equals the number of contracting owners. Under an entity plan, the business itself would simply purchase one policy on the life of each contracting owner. Thus, only n policies would have to be purchased.

The number of policies needed under a cross-purchase arrangement can be reduced somewhat by using one of two specialized life insurance contracts. First, two contracting parties may be able to purchase a *first to die* joint lives policy which pays the proceeds to the survivor on the first death of the two insured parties. The premium cost should be less than the total cost for two separate policies because only one payout will be made. Second, some companies offer a policy covering more than two insured owners for different amounts based on their respective ownership interests.

An entity agreement funded with life insurance might trigger a corporate alternative minimum tax because the "book income" of the corporation will include the insurance proceeds whereas its taxable income will not. For any buyout agreement, insurance premiums are not deductible from income, even if paid by the firm.[9] Thus, all premiums are paid with after-tax dollars.

With a cross-purchase agreement between owners who are not close in age (or who have unequal interests), a larger premium will likely be paid by the younger owner (or the owner with the smaller interest). The greater burden falls on this owner, who is probably less affluent, to insure an older person or to buy out a larger share.

Using the firm's assets. A second method of funding a lump-sum payment under an entity arrangement is with the firm's own cash or noncash assets. This can make life insurance unnecessary, but too often the business will not own sufficient distributable assets, particularly the amount of cash that may be needed to pay estate debts.

Lump-sum disability insurance. To accommodate buyout agreements, more insurance companies are offering disability policies paying a lump sum at the onset of disability, rather than an income stream.

Certain triggering events not conducive to lump-sum agreements. Some uninsurable events triggering the buyout could be retirement, divorce, insolvency of an owner, criminal activity, and loss of a professional license. Since none of these other events can be reasonably expected to generate cash flow, a full-cash buyout under such circumstances may be difficult.

Installment payments. The parties can agree to an installment sale, making life insurance unnecessary and providing income to the seller or their family. On the other hand, installment payments carry the risk that the purchasers will be unable to make the payments, returning a failing business to the family. The estate may need immediate liquidity at death. An installment note can create a potentially stressful creditor-debtor relationship between the decedent's surviving family and the successor. It could also give the successor but not the family leverage to renegotiate terms.

In conclusion, the advantages of the business buyout agreement include business continuity, liquidity, a guaranteed market, and possibly greater certainty over the selling price. The preceding overview material merely highlights the general principles of this complex subject. A business buyout agreement should not be drafted or executed without expert legal advice.

FREEZING THE VALUE OF THE BUSINESS INTEREST

Overview

The United States has many owners of very successful closely held businesses. Some have amassed a degree of wealth that they themselves consider to be more than adequate to provide for their income and capital needs for the rest of their lives. Nevertheless, few of them look forward to relinquishing control of their business interests, even though they realize that someday their wealth must be transferred. When the time comes, most want the transfer tax to be as low as possible. Indeed, many consider living beyond 2009 to be an integral part of their estate plan.

Prior to 1987, entrepreneurs had several relatively safe but complicated methods of freezing the transfer tax value of their businesses without giving up control. The two most common methods were the corporate recapitalization and the partnership capital freeze. Through a reorganization of the firm's capital structure, the owner could retain voting control of the firm, continue to receive about the same amount of income from the firm, and freeze the value of his or her own interest for transfer tax purposes, while assuring that any future appreciation in the value of the business would benefit other (usually younger) family members.

By adding Chapter 14 (IRC §§ 2701-2704) to the Internal Revenue Code in 1990,[10] the government has substantially restricted the ability to freeze the value of a business interest and retain control of it. The material that follows first discusses the use of business estate freezing during its heyday and then reviews the present law.

Corporate Recapitalization

Recapitalization under prior law. Prior to Congress's "anti-freeze" legislation, a corporate recapitalization (a "recap") might be structured as follows: Prior to the recap, the owner had a controlling interest in a company through the ownership of most or all of the common stock. The owner exchanged the common stock for a combination of common stock and voting preferred shares. The preferred stock was given high dividend rates so it was worth almost as much as the underlying value of the firm. The owner would then transfer the common stock to younger-generation family members. The common shares were deemed to have very little value, given the high value placed on the preferred shares. The retained voting preferred shares meant the transferor would be able to outvote the new common stock shareholders. Any future growth of the business inured to the common stock, because the preferred shares had a fixed upper limit to their income and a fixed value in liquidation. In the following three examples, assume the date is 1987, i.e., before Congress passed its first anti-freeze legislation.

> EXAMPLE 16 - 6. Alfred owns all 1,000 shares of the common stock of a highly successful computer software corporation called AlfSoft, Inc. Each share is valued at $2,000. The company will have $260,000 in net income this year, however, within the next six months, the company expects to be releasing a revolutionary new software package that might triple the company's sales and double its net worth. Alfred is divorced and has two children, Kyle and Maude. Kyle, age 37, has worked for the firm for 10 years and shows great promise to take over when Alfred departs. Maude, age 34, a tenured biology professor, has never been interested in working for the company. At his death, Alfred wishes to leave his entire estate in approximately equal shares to the children.
>
> A recapitalization of the firm is undertaken. In exchange for Alfred's 1,000 shares of common stock, the corporation issues three classes of new stock:
>
> 1. 20,000 shares of nonvoting noncumulative preferred stock, with a par value of $100, are retained by Alfred. These are valued at close to $2 million.
> 2. 480 shares of nonvoting common stock, 230 shares to Kyle, 230 shares to Maude, and 20 shares to Alfred. These shares have almost no value.
> 3. 20 shares of voting common stock, to Alfred.

Both types of common stock will share, pro rata, in any income available after payment of preferred dividends and in any increase in the firm's value. Alfred's estate plan is changed to leave his preferred shares equally to his two children, the 20 shares nonvoting common to Maude, and the 20 shares voting common to Kyle.

Assume that when Alfred dies (about 10 years after the recap), the business is worth $6 million. Assuming the preferred stock's value remains at $2 million, the total value of the common shares will be $4 million, or $8,000 per share. Included in his gross estate is the value of the preferred stock ($2 million), plus the value of the 40 shares of common stock ($320,000). Thus, nearly all of Alfred's interest in the firm remained frozen at its value as of date of recapitalization, and nearly the entire post-recapitalization appreciation inured tax-free to the interests held by Kyle and Maude.

EXAMPLE 16 - 7. In the prior example, instead of passing the voting common shares at his death, Alfred could make periodic gifts of them to Kyle in amounts not exceeding the annual gift tax exclusion. In this way, Alfred would have both given additional incentive to Kyle to remain with the firm and, at the same time, reduced even further the value of the business interest taxable in his estate at his death.

The ideal recap was designed to have the following tax-related benefits:

1. No taxation to the corporation arising from the recap.
2. No taxable income to the owner on receipt of the new shares.
3. Little or no taxable gift by the owner.
4. At death, the amount included in the owner's taxable estate attributable to the firm would approximately equal the value of the owner's interest in the business at the date of the recap.

Even prior to the passage of anti-freeze legislation in 1987, the IRS took the position that the value of the common shares transferred could not possibly equal zero because the value of the preferred shares could not be made to equal the total value of the firm. Consequently, it argued, some positive value remained in the common stock, value which was therefore transferred as a taxable gift to the other family members.

Former impact of IRC § 2036(c). Enacted in 1987, and repealed retroactively by the 1990 Act, § 2036(c) virtually eliminated the use of the estate freezing recapitalizations after December of 1987. We can skip the details, but when owners retained income producing assets that had limited growth potential (i.e., preferred stock) and gave away assets with great growth potential (i.e., common stock), the transaction was treated as though there was a retained interest in the gift. Hence when the owner-transferor died, the gross estate included the date-of-death value of the entire business, even the part that had been given away.

Current impact of IRC § 2701. Section 2701 takes a different approach to limiting the use of business estate freezes. IRC § 2701 imposes a gift tax at the time of the transfer, presumptively increases the value of the gift, and diminishes the value of retained interests. Remember, the lower the value of the retained interest, the higher the value of the taxable gift, and vice versa.

Unless the retained interest has a right to a "qualified payment" it is valued at zero and the gift is equal to the entire value of the business. Such "qualified payments" are periodic, cumulative dividends. Their value is subtracted from the total value of the business in determining the value of the gift of common stock.

If the business fails to make the qualified payments, the new law imposes an additional transfer tax at death of the value of the missed payments plus interest, or sooner if the retained interest is transferred during lifetime.

IRC § 2701: Transfers of corporate or partnership interests. The § 2701 valuation rules apply to any post-October 8, 1990, transfer of junior equity interests in a corporation or partnership to a member of the transferor's family, if the transferor or family member retains an interest in the corporation or partnership immediately after the transfer. This area of the law has many technical terms with very specific meanings.

Transfer. A transfer of a business interest can be direct or indirect. Examples of an indirect transfer include a contribution to capital, a redemption and a recapitalization or other change in capital structure.[11]

Junior equity interest. A junior equity interest includes common stock, or, in the case of a partnership, any interest in which the rights to income and capital are junior to the rights of other equity interests.

Member of the transferor's family. Members of the transferor's family include the transferor's spouse, descendants of the transferor and the transferor's spouse, and any spouse of such descendants.[12] These are people likely to receive the common stock from the transferor. Note that nieces and nephews are not included.

Applicable family member. An applicable family member of the transferor includes the transferor's spouse, ancestors of the transferor or the transferor's spouse, and any spouse of such ancestor.[13] These are the people likely to be trying to shift wealth to the younger generation family members.

Applicable retained interest. An applicable retained interest is any interest (except publicly traded stock) having either (a) a distribution right, but only if the transferor and applicable family members hold control (50% or more) of the business immediately before the transfer, or (b) a liquidation, put, call or conversion right, irrespective of the degree of control held by the parties.[14]

EXAMPLE 16 - 8. If undertaken today, the AlfSoft, Inc., corporate recapitalization described earlier would fall within the rules of § 2701. Alfred transferred a junior equity interest (common stock) in a corporation to members of his family (his son and daughter), and retained an applicable retained interest (preferred stock) with respect to a business over which Alfred had control immediately before the transfer.

Section 2701 does not apply when the transferred interest is of the same class as the retained interest, or if market quotations are "readily available" for the retained interest, or if the retained interest is proportionally the same as the transferred interest.[15]

> EXAMPLE 16 - 9. Up to now, Rocky has been the sole owner of RR Corporation, which has issued only one class of stock. Today, Rocky gives 10% of his common stock to his daughter, retaining the remaining 90%. Section 2701 does not apply, and the usual rules pertaining to gifts would be used to value the transferred shares.

Effect of valuation treatment under IRC § 2701. When § 2701 applies, three specific valuation rules must be observed:

1. The junior equity must be assigned a value of at least 10 percent of the value of the business.[16] This is the "minimum value" rule.
2. The transferred interest must be valued by the "subtraction method."
3. The retained rights other than "qualified payments" must be assigned a value of zero.[17] This is the so-called "zero valuation rule." However, the transferor can elect to have certain nonqualified payment rights treated as "qualified."

Under the second rule, a simplified application of the subtraction method starts with the value of the entity and subtracts the value of all family-held senior equity interests (with nonqualifying retained interests valued at zero), to arrive at the gift amount that must be allocated to the transferred interests.[18]

> EXAMPLE 16 - 10. Based on the AlfSoft, Inc., recapitalization in the preceding examples, the value of Alfred's gift equals $2 million, which is the value of the entity reduced by zero, the value of Alfred's retained interest because it is nonqualifying. Since Alfred's son receives all transferred interests, the entire $2 million is allocated to those interests. Thus, Alfred has made a $2 million gross gift to his son.

Under the third rule, retained rights to *qualified payments* have value and do not fall within the zero valuation rule. A qualified payment is defined as "any dividend payable on a periodic basis under any cumulative preferred stock (or a comparable payment under any partnership interest) to the extent that such dividend (or comparable payment) is determined at a fixed rate." The Section goes on to state that, "a payment shall be treated as fixed as to rate if such payment is determined at a rate which bears a fixed relationship to a specified market interest rate."[19] In addition, on the gift tax return, the donor can elect to treat a nonqualified payment right as though it was a qualified one, with the result that the retained interest would have a value greater than zero.

> EXAMPLE 16 - 11. Had Alfred, in the above examples, retained a right to cumulative preferred stock with a set dividend rate (e.g., 8% of par), the payment right would be treated as a qualified payment so the value of the retained preferred stock could be subtracted from the value of the business in determining the value of Alfred's gift. Even for noncumulative preferred stock, Alfred could elect to have it treated as if it had a qualified payment right. Either way, if the value of the qualifying preferred stock was $1,500,000, Alfred would have made a gross gift of $500,000. Even if the preferred stock was worth $1,950,000, Alfred's gift could not be given a value below $200,000, under the rule that the "junior equity" interests must be assigned a minimum value of 10% of the value of the entire business.

If the qualified payments are not made when due, their value (increased as though the payment had been made on time and reinvested) will, at some point, be treated as though it is a taxable gift by the transferor or as though the value is part of the transferor's gross estate.

If not for this rule, the payments, and thus the value of the retained interest, would be illusory and the real value of the gift would be higher than its taxable value because of the unmade payments.

The increase in value for payments not timely made is the amount that would have been earned had the payments been timely made, and then invested at the interest rate originally used to determine the value of the retained interest. The forgoing treatment of missed payments is also true where the transferor elected to treat nonqualifying payments as qualifying, and the business then fails to make the payments. Recognizing that there are good business reasons for not declaring dividends, Congress (through the code) allows a grace period of four years. If a payment is made within four years of its due date, it will be treated as having been timely made.

If the transferor dies still owning an applicable retained interest (e.g., the preferred shares) for which there are cumulated unpaid dividends, his or her gross estate will be increased by the amount that should have been paid, with the amount further increased as though it had been reinvested since its payment due date at the yield rate originally used to value the retained interest. If the transferor gives away the retained interest (e.g., the preferred stock) while there are cumulated unpaid dividends, then the unpaid amount (increased as though invested) is treated as a gift. In addition, if payments are received more than four years after they are due, the taxpayer (holder of the shares) can elect to treat the hypothetical increase in value (the increase that would have been there had the payment been timely received and invested) as a gift made during the year.

EXAMPLE 16 - 12. Richard holds all the outstanding stock of RichGold Company, Inc. He exchanges his shares in a recapitalization for 19,000 shares of cumulative voting preferred stock, each with a $100 par paying 8%, and 1,000 shares of no-par voting common stock. He then transfers the common stock to his daughter Maureen. Section 2701 applies to the transfer and the gift is calculated using the subtraction method. The preferred shares should pay dividends of $152,000 each year. After not paying any dividends for three years, the corporation's board of directors declared a dividend payment on the preferred shares and Richard received a payment of $152,000. The payment, because it came within the four-year grace period, is treated as if it was timely made.

EXAMPLE 16 - 13. Continuing with the prior example, assume that the second $152,000 payment is made exactly five years late and that Richard decides to treat as a gift the hypothetical increase in value that investing the dividends would have produced. The amount of the gift is the additional amount that Richard would now have, if the $152,000 had been invested at 8% compounded annually for the five years, i.e., $152,000 * (1.08)^5 - $152,000 = $71,338.

EXAMPLE 16 - 14. Suppose Richard dies in 2005 and the dividends for the prior three years are the only ones past due. Since his death is a taxable event, each payment that is past due must be included in Richard's gross estate (i.e., 3 * $152,000), plus the income that would have been generated on each payment invested on the due date. Thus, there would be three years of hypothetical income for the earliest missed payment, two years on the next, and one year for the last. Had the three payments been received on time and reinvested so as to earn 8%, Richard's estate would have had an additional $532,929 (i.e., $152,000 * (1.08)^3 + $152,000 * (1.08)^2 + $152,000 * (1.08)). This amount must be added to his gross estate.

Note that a corporation is not legally required to pay dividends even if it has the money to do so. Any unpaid dividends are "past due" only in an Internal Revenue Code sense. The general rule is that only the board of directors can declare a dividend.

EXAMPLE 16 - 15. Same facts as in the prior example, except instead of dying, Richard gave all of the preferred shares to Maureen when dividends for the prior three years were past due. The result would be nearly the same, with the value of the missed dividends (i.e., 3 * $152,000), and their related hypothetical investment return (i.e., $76,929) added to Richard's taxable gifts for the year.

To avoid double taxation of the retained interest, the Code allows a deduction from the donor's taxable gifts (if the taxable event is a gift) or the donor's adjusted taxable gifts (if the taxable event is the donor's death). The deduction is the lesser of–

(1) the amount by which the value of the initial gift was increased due to the application of the § 2701 subtraction method; or

(2) the amount "duplicated" in the tax base at a subsequent transfer, whether the transfer is a gift of the preferred stock or occurs because the preferred stock is included at the transferor's death in his or her taxable estate.[20]

EXAMPLE 16 - 16. Martha owned 10,000 shares of $100 par value noncumulative preferred stock (bearing an annual dividend of $10 per share) of Ahtram Company, Inc., and 500 shares of its common stock. The underlying value of the company was $1,500,000 and the preferred and common had values of $1,000,000 and $500,000, respectively. On March 10, 1999, she transfers all of the common shares to her son Ethan. Since § 2701 applies to the transaction and Martha does not elect to treat the retained shares as having "qualified rights," the subtraction method results in a transfer valued at $1,500,000. Notice that the increase is $1,000,000 since the common stock is valued at $500,000.

EXAMPLE 16 - 17. On May 2, 2002, Martha died still owning the preferred stock. An appraisal determined that the value is $950,000. Given that this is less than the $1,000,000 increase in value of the initial transfer, her adjusted taxable gifts are reduced by $950,000 to reflect this duplicated amount. If, on the other hand, the stock is valued in her estate at $1,050,000, then the earlier increase in the taxable gifts is the lesser amount, and the decrease to her adjusted taxable gifts is $1,000,000.

IRC § 2703: Valuation of property subject to rights and restrictions. Section 2703 requires that the value of any property subject to rights and restrictions shall be valued for transfer tax purposes without regard to the reduced valuation effect of those rights or restrictions.

EXAMPLE 16 - 18. Shortly before his death this year, Hansen, sole shareholder of the common stock of his $1 million closely held corporation, executed a contract with his daughter, who is obligated to purchase all of Hansen's stock at Hansen's death for $400,000. Under § 2703, Hansen's gross estate will include the stock at a value of $1 million; the reduction in actual value attributable to the obligation to sell the stock must be disregarded.

More specifically, the rights and restrictions that must be disregarded under § 2703 include:

1. Any option, agreement, or other right to acquire or use the property at a price less than the property's fair market value (determined without regard to such option, agreement, or right).
2. Any restriction on the right to sell or use the property.[21]

Section 2703 does not apply to any agreement, option, right, or restriction, which meets all of the following requirements:

1. It is a bona fide business arrangement.
2. It is not a device to transfer the property to members of the decedent's family for less than full and adequate consideration in money or money's worth.
3. Its terms are comparable to similar arrangements entered into by persons in an arm's length transaction.[22]

EXAMPLE 16 - 19. Shortly before his death this year, Trafalgar, sole owner of the common stock of his $1 million closely held corporation, executed a contract with a non relative business associate, who is obligated to purchase all of Trafalgar's stock at Trafalgar's death for $960,000. The valuation rules under § 2703 are not likely to cause the value reduction to $960,000 to be disregarded.

IRC § 2704: Taxation of lapse of voting and liquidation rights and restrictions in a corporation or partnership. Section 2704 is of relatively limited application. It addresses the transfer taxation of the lapse of a voting or liquidation right in a corporation or partnership.

In general, if there has been a lapse and the person holding the right before the lapse and the members of that person's family hold control of the entity both before and after the lapse, then the lapse is treated as gift or a transfer at death and subject to tax. The value of the transfer subject to taxation is the reduction in value due to the lapse.

When will a recap work? Estate freezing recaps of the type created prior to § 2036(c) still work for some families since § 2701 does not apply to transfers benefitting nieces and nephews, or anyone not related to the transferor. The definition of "applicable family members" includes only the transferor's spouse, descendants, descendants of the spouse, and their respective spouses.[23]

In lieu of a recap the owner might consider a simple outright gift of the business. Gifting is simple, and control can be retained by transferring nonvoting stock.

Finally, some other types of business freeze techniques are not affected by the antifreeze rules because no form of lifetime gifting is involved.

Testamentary freeze. A bequest of common stock to younger generation beneficiaries and preferred stock to the spouse.

Postmortem recapitalization freeze. A recapitalization after the owner's death, in which the marital trust receives the preferred stock and the bypass trust receives the common stock.

Postmortem funding freeze. The marital trust receives assets not likely to appreciate and the bypass trust receives appreciating assets.

Generation-skipping freeze. The children receive preferred stock, by gift or bequest, and the grandchildren receive the common stock.

Notwithstanding these possible opportunities, the current limitations and restrictions are numerous, and commentators have been guarded about the extent to which corporate recapitalizations will be used in the future. If the repeal of the estate tax is made permanent, most of this type of planning will become obsolete.

Partnership Capital Freeze

It may be possible to reorganize an unincorporated firm to achieve the same results as the estate-freezing recap. Under the partnership capital freeze, two classes of partnership interests are created, one for the older, wealthier, family members and one for the younger family members. The interests of the older family members are restricted in ways that limit the upside value, thus assuring that future appreciation in the business will accrue to the shares of the younger generation. As with the corporate recap, the partnership capital freeze is a complex, rapidly changing area of tax law, subject to the provisions of § 2701 and also to frequent IRS attack. Planning should be approached carefully, with the help of competent counsel.

QUESTIONS AND PROBLEMS

1. What could you say to a person who owns a closely held business if, although he seems to respect your advice, he stubbornly refuses to consider estate planning?

2. What unique estate planning problems are common to owners of closely held businesses?

3. Identify the objectives of estate planning for owners of closely held business interests.

4. One of your friends is worried about the possible future decline in the value of her company if she becomes incapacitated. Recommend strategies that might minimize the decline.

5. (a) Describe the inter-vivos methods of transferring business interests to family members. (b) When are such transfers ill-advised?

6. (a) One of your friends is considering selling her business to a third party. Describe the benefits of selling now, rather than waiting and letting her heirs sell it. (b) Is planning for a sale after death always unwise? Why or why not?

7. Horne requests your advice. He has a simple will, but has done no other planning. His major asset is a closely held business. Neither his wife nor his children have any interest in continuing the business after his death. Horne does not wish to retire. Recommend a significant planning strategy for his consideration.

8. (a) What are the main tax breaks available to decedents' estates that include a closely held business? (b) What is the common thread that determines whether an estate can avail itself of one or more of these benefits? (c) Are any of these available only to estates holding shares of stock?

9. Describe the alternative methods for payment that can be arranged when a business is sold.

10. When should planning for closely held business interests begin? Why?

11. Madeline is old and ill. She owns many things. She still serves as CEO of the hardware store (incorporated as Easy Hardware, Inc.) founded by her grandfather. It consists of three stores, seven vehicles, inventory, accounts receivable, and good-will. Her share of the business is estimated to be worth between $900,000 and $1,000,000. She has 5,500 out of the 10,000 shares issued. Her younger brother, who has never worked in the business, owns the other 4,500 shares. Her estate will soon go to her four children. She is thinking about transferring some things to her children, or holding onto them until her death, or selling them, and letting the children inherit money. Her total net worth is approximately $3,000,000. Consider the following items:
    1. vacation cabin built in 1901 (in the woods and on the lake) by her grandfather, her basis is $25,000 and its worth is about $100,000. The whole family uses the cabin quite regularly during summer months.
    2. publicly traded ABC stock, basis $25,000, FMV $100,000
    3. publicly traded MOP stock, basis $85,000, FMV $100,000
    4. publicly traded XYZ stock, basis $165,000, FMV $100,000
    5. closely held 5,500 shares of Easy Hardware, Inc., basis $75,000, FMV about $950,000.

Taking all of the above facts into account, answer the following questions:

a. Which of the following suggest holding onto the Easy Hardware stock until her death? Explain.

    1. It will step-up in basis.
    2. It might qualify for §303 redemption, depending on what other things she gives away and how much it appreciates between now and her death.
    3. It might qualify for §6166 long-term payment plan, depending on what other things she gives away and how much it appreciates between now and her death.
    4. Transferring it to her children would serve no purpose, since her death is almost certain to occur within three years, thus the shares (including post-gift appreciation) would end up in her gross estate.

b. Suppose her most recent health checkup indicates she will probably live about three more years, which of the following would be reasonable suggestions concerning the publicly traded stock?

1. If she only wants to give stock worth about $100,000 to her children, the MOP is the best choice, given its high basis compared to its FMV.
2. She could "match-up" a sale of the ABC and the XYZ to avoid most of the capital gain.
3. She could give the ABC and the XYZ stock to her children and let them sell it to "match-up" gain and loss.
4. Giving the stock to the children (rather than selling it and keeping the proceeds) increases the likelihood that her estate will qualify for §303 and §6166.

c. Which of the following are realistic alternatives concerning the cabin?

1. Sell it and match the sale with a sale of the XYZ stock so that almost no capital gains will be recognized.
2. Lease it to the four children for $1 per year for 99 years in order to reduce its value for estate tax purposes to almost zero, yet assure it remains in the family.
3. Sell it to the four children for its FMV, getting it (and any future appreciation) out of her estate.
4. Give it to the four children, claim a fractional share discount on the gift and four annual exclusions.

d. Which of the following suggest giving Easy Hardware shares to her children?

1. Each gift can be reduced by the annual exclusion and discounted for the fact that the shares for the donee do not represent control of the company.
2. Her children are interested in keeping the business rather than selling it.
3. If she gives 300 shares to each child (150 this year and 150 at the beginning of next year), her estate will be able to discount the shares remaining in her estate because they will be a minority interest.

4. Considering how quickly the business has been appreciating lately, compared to other things Madeline owns, it is likely to be worth more than 35% of her net estate by the time she dies.

12. (a) Describe the essential characteristics of the typical business buyout agreement. (b) What are its advantages?

13. What is the tax advantage of including a method for determining the selling price in a properly drafted business buyout agreement?

14. (a) Describe the three methods by which a business buyout agreement can be funded. (b) Why might types of funding influence the choice of whether a cross-purchase or an entity plan is adopted?

15. Eric Agusto, Connie Waters, and Darren Hargrove were equal co-owners of a closely held corporation that made, owned, raced, and repaired race cars. It was called Carrroooomba, Inc. The average income for the most recent three years was $450,000 gross and $300,000 net before taking into account their wages (about $90,000 each). They started by each putting $50,000 in cash into the corporation in exchange for their respective shares (each holds 10,000 shares). The company's most recent balance sheet showed assets, debts, and owners' equity as follows

	Book values	FMV
Main Workshop building, land	$500,000	$1,800,000
repair equipment, tools, lifts, etc.	$300,000	$150,000
20 practice track cars	$400,000	$120,000
8 specialty cars	$330,000	$1,200,000
accounts receivable	$100,000	$90,000
prepaid expenses & taxes	$60,000	$60,000
auto parts inventory/misc. items	$180,000	$180,000
cash accounts	$75,000	$75,000
good will	$0	$240,000
total assets	$1,945,000	$3,915,000
Liabilities		
Mortgage on bld & land	$400,000	$400,000
accounts payable	$45,000	$45,000

total debt	$445,000	$445,000
Owners' equity	$1,500,000	$3,470,000
debt + owners' equity	$1,945,000	$3,915,000

Eric is single, his estate plan leaves everything in equal shares to his three children. Connie is married and her estate is left to her husband if he outlives her, otherwise to their two children. Darren and his wife have an ABC plan. The remaindermen are their two young children.

a. Calculate the value of each of the following buy-sell agreements and put them in order from highest to lowest valuation for a decedent's one-third share: (1) 150% of book value, (2) nine times the three most recent years' net income (before owners' wages), (3) four times the most recent three years' gross, (4) most recent agreed value of $2,600,000 (signed 15 months before), with a 1% per month adjustment clause, i.e., for each full month after an agreed price is set the value is assumed to increase 1%.

b. If Eric died and there is no buy-sell agreement, which of the following would be true concerning valuation?

1. Eric's executor would have conflicting motivation, wanting a high value for purposes of selling to the surviving co-owners, but a low basis for estate tax purposes.
2. Using book value for estate tax purposes and fair market value based upon appraisal for selling to the co-owners should be acceptable to the IRS, so long as the estate and the co-owners reach a binding agreement prior to the estate tax audit.
3. Eric's executor does not need to worry too much about capital gains in negotiating a sale between the estate and the co-owners.
4. If Eric's children decide they want to keep the Carrroooomba shares rather than have the estate sell them, the opportunity to claim a lack of marketability discount is lost.

c. Suppose they had entered into a buy-out agreement using agreed value which was set at $3,000,000 six months before Eric died. An escalator clause called for a 1/2% per month increase if the valuation was more than 12 months old at the time of any triggering event such as withdrawal or death of a co-owner. What is each survivor's basis if the buy-sell calls for the corporation to buy back the shares?

d. Suppose they enter into a buy-out agreement based upon agreed value and an escalator clause called for a 1/2% per month increase if the valuation was more than 12 months old at the time of any triggering event such as withdrawal or death of a co-owner. The value was last set at $3,000,000 six months before Eric died. What is each survivor's basis if they have a cross-purchase buy-back provision?

e. If they decide to fund a buy-sell agreement using life insurance, how many policies would they need if they used a cross-purchase plan?

16. Cheryl Fries and Helen Pacelli own a security devices manufacturing company, a partnership doing business under its registered d.b.a. of FriPac Technologies. They would like to take on additional investors to expand their business, most likely by purchasing a factory building and a fleet of delivery trucks to get their products to wholesale outlets. Three wealthy friends are interested and each has indicated a willingness to put in $150,000. One investor, named Jack Fogwell, has expertise in marketing and would like to have some involvement in running the company, but initially he would continue with his university teaching position. The other two, Michelle Anders and Joe Amiel, really do not want to work there. Michelle would make the investment as trustee of a trust that was established by her grandfather for her children. Given the size and diversity of the trust portfolio, this one "risky" investment is not inappropriate provided the risk is limited to the investment. Based on present net sales the business is probably worth $900,000 to $1,200,000, depending upon appraisal method. With the purchases, the business would show a healthy cash flow, but with interest deductions and depreciation, there would probably be a net loss for tax purposes for at least the next three years. Answer the following questions concerning the forms of business that they are considering.

a. Suppose they decide to form a limited partnership with Cheryl and Helen as general partners and the other three as limited partners, which of the following are correct?

1. With this option, Jack will have to forgo involvement in the management of the company or else risk being liable for partnership obligations that the partnership canot pay.

2. So long as Helen acts as a silent partner (people outside of the partnership do not know of her involvement) only Cheryl risks her own assets in the event that the business folds with debts exceeding the value of the business assets.

3. The limited partnership can continue to do business as FriPac Technologies, Limited, so long as the partnership publishes notice to that effect.

4. Michelle must take the limited partnership interests in her own name (not as trustee) or the limited liability benefit will be lost.

b. Suppose Cheryl and Helen establish a Subchapter S corporation, distributing shares so that they will each hold 35% and each of the others have a 10% interest. The articles of incorporation call for three members on the board of directors and do not provide for cumulative voting. Which of the following are correct?

1. They each have limited liability, even if they participate in the direct management of the company.

2. Losses will pass through to the shareholders in proportion to their shares and the loss will then offset other income earned by the individual shareholders.

3. Helen and Cheryl could elect all three board members.

4. Michelle must take the shares in her own name (not as trustee) or the Subchapter S election will be lost.

c. If they set up a Limited Liability Company, with Cheryl and Helen having membership shares equal to 70% of the business and each of the others having a 10% interest, which of the following are correct?

1. They will be taxed as if the business was a partnership and yet have the benefit of liability limited to their investment.

2. If Jack gets involved in marketing or otherwise gets involved in running the business, he loses the protection of limited liability.
3. Depending upon the agreement drawn up, they could have centralized management (i.e., Cheryl and Helen making all decisions) or they could each having an equal say (i.e., similar to a common law partnership), without losing their limited liability protection.
4. The laws in most states would not allow Michelle to own her LLC interest as a trustee.

17. Explain what tax advantages the ideal recapitalization was designed to provide. Why is it more difficult with the "anti-freeze" code sections to dramatically increase the value of the preferred shares by using high dividend rates and things like voting rights and liquidation bonuses?

18. Mandy has established a very successful adventure travel agency, estimated to be worth $2,000,000. Mandy has used a corporate recapitalization to turn the future value of her business over to her children, both of whom are involved in running the business. She has retained voting preferred shares and the children were given non-voting common stock. If the corporation is liquidated within five years of the recapitalization, Mandy will receive 110% of the preferred's stated par value before the common will receive anything. (a) For transfer tax purposes, what is the maximum amount that Mandy can value stock she retains? (b) What happens if the corporation fails to pay dividends on the preferred stock? (c) For transfer tax purposes, does the liquidation bonus in the event of liquidation within five years increase the value of the preferred shares?

ANSWERS TO THE QUESTIONS AND PROBLEMS *(odd numbered only)*

1. You could describe to your stubborn friend the problems he and his family may face if he were to involuntarily withdraw from management tomorrow, either as a result of disability or death. Problems include inability to generate sufficient future income, incurring significant unnecessary loss in the value of the business, facing excessive transfer costs, and failing to provide sufficient liquidity to pay these costs. For more detail, see the material in the early part of the chapter.

3. Objectives of estate planning for owners of closely held businesses: (a) income continuation; (b) transfer of maximum business value; (c) minimum transfer cost; and (d) adequate liquidity.

5. a.   Types of inter-vivos business transfers to a family member: completed gifts, installment sale, sale-leaseback, and private annuity.
   b.   The owner may insist on retaining complete control over the business or the other family members may be ill-prepared to run the business.

7. Horne should consider negotiating a buyout agreement with co-owners, executives, or competitors, to avoid the prospect of his survivors having to run the business. This strategy will also avoid the post-death sale of the business at a substantially reduced price.

9. Alternative methods for payment when a business is sold include:
   a.   Sale for present cash, publicly or privately.
   b.   Sale for future cash, under an installment sale.
   c.   Sale for stock, under a tax-deferred exchange with a publicly traded firm.

11. Madeline and the Easy Hardware.
    (a) 1) FMV DOD = new basis; 2) and 3) are true, shares are very close to being 35% of Madeline's AGE; 4) no, there is no three year rule for gifts of stock.
    (b) 2) yes, she would have a $75,000 gain on the ABC and a $65,000 loss, so only $10,000 would be taxable; 4) given that she might make it beyond three years of making these gifts, her closely held Hardware stock will be a larger

part of her estate, making it more likely that the 35% threshold for 303 and 6166 will be met; 1) no, if she is going to make just one transfer (ABC, MOP, or XYZ) then XYZ is the best choice, holding to death will lower basis to $100,000 for all purposes whereas with a gift XYZ carry over basis for gains (i.e., no reported gain until sales price exceeds $165,000); 3) no, children's basis in XYZ for loss will be $100,000, so there will be no capital loss to match up with the gain in selling ABC.

(c) 4) makes sense, given that the family is not likely to sell it, therefore a step-up in basis is not important; 1) no, it would work, but it is not in keeping with holding on to the cabin; 2) no, the IRS would treat it as a sham transaction and value the cabin in mom's estate at FMV; 3) no, what would be the point, mom would recognize capital gains of $75,000 and the cash ($100,000 less the extra taxes) would be in her estate.

(d) 1) true, present interest, therefore annual exclusion. Shares given would not represent control, therefore lack of control discount (even lack of marketability discount); 2) sure, makes step-up in basis (by not gifting) less important; 3) true, she would have 4,300 shares and her brother would have 4,500 shares (we get to ignore the fact that after her death, her children will have 5,500 shares in total); 4) no, although this is a true statement, it is a reason to keep the shares to achieve the 35% AGE threshold so that 303 and 6166 are available.

13. The tax advantage of including a method for determining the selling price in a buyout agreement is that the price will set the value of the business that is included in the decedent-owner's gross estate.

15. (a) (4) $2,600,000 * 115% = $2,990,000 > (1) 150% * $1,945,000 = $2,917,500 > (2) 9 * $300,000 = $2,700,000 > (3) 4 * $450,000 = $1,800,000.

(b) Eric's death and no buy-sell agreement: 1) true, high for selling but low for taxes; 3) step up in basis to FMV at death avoids most or all of the capital gain (the government would probably accept the sale price for estate tax purposes, hence no gain). 2) you canot use one method for estate tax purposes and another for selling; 4) no, this is when the discount makes the most sense, since there is no sale price to set the estate tax valuation.

(c) Agreed value of $3 million. Less than a year, so no adjustment required. Each one-third is worth $1 million. Their original basis was $50,000 and, since they did not purchase the decedent's shares, so it remains.

(d) Since they each pay $500,000 for half of Eric's shares, plus still have their own original basis, their new basis will be $550,000.

(e) Number of policies: formula is n * (n-1); where n = number of co-owners; therefore 3 * (3 - 1) = 6.

17. The recapitalization would provide all of the following:

- No taxation to the corporation arising from the recap
- No taxable income to the owner upon receipt of the new shares
- Little or no taxable gift by the owner
- At death, the amount included in the owner's taxable estate attributable to the firm would approximately equal the value of the owner's interest in the business at the date of the recap

ENDNOTES

1. 1959-1 C.B. 237.

2. IRC § 1361(d)(3).

3. IRC § 6662(a) and (g).

4. IRC § 264(a)(1).

5. IRC § 56(g)(4)(B).

6. Reg. § 25.2703-1(d), Example 1.

7. Reg. § 25.2703-1(b)(3).

8. In *Commissioner vs. Procter* 142 F.2d 824 (4th Cir. 1944).

9. IRC § 264(a)(1).

10. Revenue Act of 1987.

11. IRC § 2701(e)(5).

12. IRC § 2701(e)(1).

13. IRC § 2701(e)(2).

14. IRC § 2701(b).

15. IRC § 2701(a)(2).

16. IRC § 2701(a)(4).

17. IRC § 2701(a)(3)(A).

18. Reg. § 25.2701-3(b).

19. IRC § 2701(a)(3)(A).

20. IRC § 2701(e); Reg. § 25.2701-5(4)(b).

21. IRC § 2703(a).

22. IRC § 2703(b).

23. IRC § 2701(e)(1).

CHAPTER 17

Miscellaneous Lifetime Planning

OVERVIEW

What could be more important than answering the questions, "If something happens to me, who will care for my children, manage my property, and make sure I receive appropriate care?" The common thread that runs though this chapter is that only by planning can we guide the process of selecting the person or persons who will perform these important services. Given the advances in medicine, one who is virtually brain dead can live for years, presumably with no awareness of his or her surroundings. Given the choice, once any realistic chance of recovery has past, most people would prefer to die naturally. It is important that each adult chose the degree of intervention with which he or she is comfortable. Because one cannot anticipate every eventuality, it is best to choose someone to speak on one's behalf in the event one cannot speak for one's self.

Choosing the appropriate surrogate decision maker depends on the tasks he or she is expected to perform. The person will need guidance if we expect our wishes to be carried out. Wills and trusts are the major documents used in estate planning, but there are others such as directives to physicians and durable powers that in many respects are just as important.

PLANNING FOR THE CARE OF FAMILY MEMBERS

The chance of disability and of premature death should compel everyone to do some planing. A serious injury or illness may require someone to care for the person and his or her property. The death of a parent might require the selection of one or more persons to care for children. Planning should document ones wishes so they serve as a guide both in the selection of the care-givers and in the care given.

Planning for the care an orphaned child and for one's own incapacity have three common factors. First, if ones preferences are not documented a court generally selects the care-giver. Probate codes have lists as to who, all else being equal, should be given priority to serve in each of the various fiduciary capacities, e.g., guardian, conservator, or executor. The lists typically put in the highest category close family members, then to more remote members, next to friends, and finally to a public administrator or guardian. Without a written expression by the parent or the person incapacitated, the court will select from among those in the group at the highest priority level who have indicated a willingness to serve. Conflict may result if someone from a lower priority level really wants to serve but a person at a higher level agrees to take on the task out of a sense of duty, or when persons of the same level strongly disagree as to who should serve.

Second, the law differentiates two types of care: of the person and of the property. Fiduciaries serving in the former capacity provide for the everyday physical and psychological needs of the person and in the latter safeguards, invests, and generally takes care of the financial matters.

Third, because care of the person and care of the property entail such dissimilar responsibilities, different parties may be nominated and appointed to perform them.

Planning for the Care of Minor Children

The material below explores the arrangements that are undertaken to provide care for minor children in the event both parents die prematurely.

The parental guardian. In the traditional household, the parents of a child are the natural and legal guardians of their children. Thus, on the death of one parent, the surviving parent continues as sole guardian. Only in the most unusual situations will the courts deny this right. On the other hand, when a minor child survives the death of both parents, the state must select a successor guardian. The selection process typically culminates in an order by a judge of the probate court after a noticed hearing. The court will usually appoint the person nominated in the parent's will, unless the nominee is unwilling, unable, or unsuitable to perform. If the will contains no nomination, or if there is no will, the court seeks information about willing relatives and friends, generally giving preference to the persons in the highest category level as a tie-breaker. If the child is sufficiently mature to have and express an opinion the court will consider it. Since the court's main criterion is the best interests of the child, it seeks to appoint that person who is best capable of providing psychological well-being, love, and attention as well as such basics as food, clothing, shelter, medical care, and schooling.

Since the court's eventual selection of a guardian may not reflect the deceased parent's unexpressed wishes, and to avoid guardianship "warfare," the parent should clearly assert that preference by nominating a personal guardian in the will. Although it may be the most difficult to make, choosing a guardian for one's children may be the most important estate planning decision that one makes.

The ideal guardian of the person. Who should be nominate to care for one's children? An ideal parental guardian possesses the following qualities:

1. The integrity, maturity, physical stamina, and experience expected of a parent.
2. A strong concern for the child's welfare.
3. The ability to provide a stable personal environment conducive to raising a child in a manner consistent with the parent's particular moral, religious, social, and financial situation.

A nomination greatly reduces the risk of an undesired appointment. Nominating successor guardians is wise since the first choice may be unwilling or unable to serve, or once appointed, unable to continue to serve. The nomination is not carved in stone, the parents should periodically review the nomination in light of the child's changing needs and the nominee's changing personal and financial situation.

Three fiduciary choices for financial matters. Anticipating the possibility that they both may die before their children are grown, parents will usually want to provide for adequate financial care for their orphaned children. They will ordinarily want to transfer all or most of their probate and nonprobate property for the benefit of the children. Common nonprobate sources of property for the children include life insurance proceeds, survivorship under joint tenancy arrangements, trust property, and gifts from others.

While most states allow a minor to receive outright a modest amount of property, larger amounts are required to be turned over to a fiduciary legally responsible for their care and custody. What acceptable fiduciary arrangements are available? While the law recognizes parental guardianships as the only legal arrangement for the child's personal care, it recognizes several arrangements for the his or her financial care. The parents may choose a financial guardianship, a trust, or a custodianship under the Uniform Transfer to Minors Act.

Financial guardianship. A financial guardian, also called an estate guardian, is typically appointed by the court in a manner similar to the procedures used for appointment of a parental guardian. Usually required to file a formal accounting with the court every one or two years, the financial guardian must obtain written permission from the court to undertake transactions that are out of the ordinary, such as the sale of real property. Reflecting the general trend in probate reform, some states have enacted streamlined guardianship proceedings to minimize court involvement.

In general, the criteria for selecting a financial guardian are radically different from those used in selecting a parental guardian. As we have mentioned, while the primary consideration in selecting the parental guardian is parental ability, the primary focus in selecting the financial guardian is skill in financial management. Since skill in financial management is also the primary criterion used to select a trustee, we shall defer further discussion of its attributes to the sections on selecting the executor and the trustee.

Trust for the minor. Instead of a financial guardian, a trustee can be chosen to manage the property left for the benefit of a minor child. Whether a living trust or a testamentary trust, the trust may be part of the parents' overall estate plan, with the children named as remaindermen.

The trust has advantages over the financial guardianship. First, it is a private arrangement, not usually subject to court supervision. While a guardianship requires the filing of a bond, periodic accountings, and court approval for asset transfers, a trust can avoid these costly and time-consuming activities. However, some states require ongoing probate court supervision of testamentary trusts after the trustor's death, but the trend has been to eliminate this requirement.

Second, the trust offers great flexibility; the parents can tailor it to their personal wishes. For example, while guardianship property usually must be surrendered outright to the minor on reaching age 18, the age of majority, trust property can be retained in trust until the age specified in the trust. Further, while a separate guardianship must usually be established for each minor, a single trust can have multiple beneficiaries, as in the case of the family pot trust, described later in the chapter. And the trustee can be given discretion to distribute different amounts of trust assets to different beneficiaries at different times. For example, the trustee can be given the power to distribute principal to an income benefici- ary, to accumulate income and add it to principal, or to "spray" or "sprinkle" income among the beneficiaries. Finally, the trust is more flexible because it can include a spendthrift provision, a protective clause to be described later. Financial guardianships are not established with such refinements.

A third advantage of the trust over the financial guardianship rests on the fact that the statutory and case law of trusts is much more well defined. Thus, a trustee will often feel less uncertain than a guardian about the potential adverse consequences of a particular fiduciary act or decision.

A financial guardianship usually arises by default when parents die without having an estate plan in place. Guardianships are rarely preferred over trusts because they tend to be more expensive and, for the fiduciary, more cumbersome.

Custodianship under the Uniform Acts. Finally, the parents may wish to leave property to a custodian for the benefit of a minor child under the Uniform Gifts to Minors Act or the Uniform Transfers to Minors Act in the manner described in Chapter 13. Like trusts, custodianships offer greater privacy than financial guardianships, since they are not subject to court supervision. However, like guardianships, custodianships are quite inflexible because they are usually controlled by statute. For example, in most states property held by the custodian must be turned over to the minor on reaching age 21. Also, most states limit the kinds of property that can be transferred under the Uniform Gifts to Minor's Act, which is the only one of the two acts that has been adopted in many states.

Selection of Executor and Executor's Powers

As we have said, the executor is responsible for representing and managing a decedent's probate estate. Specific tasks of this multifaceted job include marshaling and valuing the decedent's assets, filing tax returns, paying taxes and debts, distributing assets, and accounting for the entire process. It also involves dealing with grieving family members, distributing personal effects, and resolving family conflicts, all of which can be emotionally taxing. Finally, the executor must keep assets invested, sell them to pay taxes, and possibly manage or liquidate the decedent's business. While most of these jobs can be performed by the estate attorney's office, total estate expenses may be higher due to a larger attorney fee and the executor is still primarily responsible to the court for completing these acts.

Selection. Who should be nominated for the job of executor? An ideal nominee possesses the following qualities:

1. Longevity, that is, the likelihood of being able to serve after the death of the testator, perhaps many years hence.
2. Skill in managing legal and financial affairs.
3. Familiarity with the testator's estate and the testator's wishes.
4. Strong integrity coupled with loyalty to the testator.
5. Impartiality and absence of conflicts of interest.

An ideal financial guardian will also possess these qualities. Let us use these criteria to evaluate the candidates who are most likely available to serve.

Family member or a friend. Nominating a family member or a friend to be executor might reduce administration costs paid to people who are not beneficiaries. Family members and friends usually possess a strong degree of familiarity and loyalty. However, they often have only modest legal and financial skills, which may compel them to pay for professional advice. While they can normally delegate some of their work to the estate attorney, they cannot delegate their legal responsibility, since the executor cannot avoid personal liability for certain types of mistakes that might occur in administration. Nonetheless, in small estates most mistakes are not costly, and, in general, nominating as executor the spouse, an adult child, or a good friend makes sense. Naming the spouse is probably the most popular choice.

Corporate executor. The testator may prefer to select a corporate executor such as a bank trust department. Reasons include inability to find and select a responsible family member or friend, conflict among family members, or a complex estate. Banks usually do a satisfactory job in managing estate assets. However, because they are usually unfamiliar with the decedent's family, they might not offer as much of a personal touch in the administration process. For example, they may have difficulty deciding who should be given minor personal effects which the decedent did not specifically devise. Finally, many banks will not agree to be executor if the estate is too small, if they dislike certain provisions of the will, or if they are not also nominated trustee under the estate plan's trust arrangements.

Attorney. Should an attorney, such as the testator's attorney, be considered for nomination as executor? Probate attorneys usually do a good job in managing assets during the probate period, because they commonly possess a substantial degree of expertise acquired over the years by doing the work delegated by their many executor-clients. Nomination of the testator's attorney, however, may increase the risk of a will contest. Dissatisfied with the will provisions, a dissatisfied beneficiary might allege that the nomination is further evidence that the testator was subject to "undue influence" and intimidation, and might petition that the will not be admitted to probate. However, keep in mind that successful will contests are rare. California specifically forbids the attorney who drafts the will from naming him or herself (or any associates, staff, or persons related to the attorney, associates or staff) as fiduciary of a will or trust. There are a several exceptions to this rule. The nomination is acceptable if: (1) the attorney is related to the person for whom the estate plan is drafted; (2) the person has another attorney, one independent of the first, review with him or her the appropriateness of the nomination and determines that the person really wants the attorney to serve as fiduciary; (3) after the person dies, a court determines that it is in the best interest of the estate to have the nominated attorney serve.[1]

Nominating an attorney might not reduce administration costs, since the attorney-executors may hire another attorney to represent the estate. Finally, and perhaps most significant, acting as an executor can create potential conflicts of interest for the attorney in the areas of drafting, confidentiality, and the duty to deal impartially with beneficiaries. For example, an attorney who anticipates becoming a fiduciary may be tempted to insert in the client's will a self-serving exculpation (hold harmless) clause for all simple negligence acts.

Other considerations. The testator should also nominate an alternate executor to serve in case the primary nominee is unwilling or unable to serve. Many people nominate a bank as the alternate because they are confident that a corporate executor will always be available to serve. Regardless of the choice of executor, the testator should always consult with the nominees to get their consent, and should periodically review the choice in light of changing circumstances.

Executor's powers. What powers should be explicitly granted to an executor? Most simple wills either do not delineate the powers of the executor or list just a few powers. The will in Exhibit 3-1 explicitly grants to the executor the powers to distribute principal and income; to sell, lease, mortgage, pledge, assign, invest, and reinvest estate property; and to operate a business.

When a will "is silent" regarding a specific proposed action of the executor, we look for authority first to the provisions of the state's estates and trusts or probate code, which usually delineate many executor's powers. If nothing pertinent is found, the executor may feel obliged to request permission from the court. For example, in the absence of explicit permission in the will, executors in many states must seek formal written permission to sell real property. Thus, specifying powers explicitly in the will can offer the executor greater flexibility by minimizing unnecessary delays in probate. And enumerating powers in the will can reveal more to the survivors about the testator's wishes, especially with regard to the degree of court supervision originally envisioned by the testator.

Allocation of Death Taxes

Which beneficiaries should bear the burden of death taxes? All of them, or only some? If only some, which ones? If all, should the taxes be shared equally or in proportion to the amount bequeathed? A number of important considerations in determining how to allocate death taxes are examined next.

Federal law. In the absence of a provision in the will, both federal and state law determine which beneficiaries will share the cost of death taxes. Federal law controls the burden on a few types of assets. The Internal Revenue Code provides that the pro rata share of estate tax on life insurance,[2] property subject to a general power of appointment,[3] QTIP property[4] (usually at the second death), and property included in the gross estate because of a retained interest[5] is payable out of those assets.

State law. Under state law, with regard to all assets owned by the decedent, the old common law rule provided that death taxes were paid from the residuary probate estate. However, most states have changed this rule by enacting an *equitable apportionment statute* that spreads the tax burden proportionately among all of the beneficiaries receiving part of the taxable estate. Thus, even recipients of nonprobate assets, such as property held by the decedent in joint ownership, would owe a portion of the tax. Of course, as a general rule the shares going to charities and spouses do not incur a tax burden, since their distributions are deducted before one arrives at the taxable estate.

Tax clause in will. The testator can override these federal and state directives by expressly including a tax clause in the will.

Residuary tax clause. Some attorneys do this by routinely drafting wills containing a tax clause embracing the old common law rule: all taxes will be paid out of the residuary estate. Payment of taxes from the residue can speed up the probate process by making it unnecessary to obtain reimbursement from non-residuary and nonprobate beneficiaries. In addition, recipients of specific non-residuary bequests of illiquid assets are not forced to search for the required cash. And paying the taxes out of the residue may be especially helpful if the will specifically bequeaths certain assets over which the testator does not wish the tax burden to fall. For example, if the testator leaves only one relatively illiquid asset, such as a piano, to a particular beneficiary, should that person have to pay any transfer taxes attributable to it? Most people would probably say no unless that beneficiary is known to have considerable wealth, or at least access to a reasonable amount of discretionary liquid assets.

Problems with the residuary tax clause. There are several situations where a residuary tax clause may conflict with the testator's wishes. First, the testator may specifically bequeath an asset such as a closely held business that comprises a very large portion of the entire estate. If the tax clause allocates the entire tax burden to the residue, the effect may be to radically reduce it or eliminate it entirely.

EXAMPLE 17 - 1. When she died in 2002 Trudy's estate plan left her business to William, her son by her first marriage, and the residue of her estate to Dennis, her current husband. The plan specified that the interest to her son was "free of all estate taxes." The business was appraised at $4 million and the balance of the estate at $3 million. Because the marital share was forced to bear the tax burden, Dennis received only $140,000. Note that this interrelated tax calculation can be demonstrated using ETAX. For the gross estate enter $7 million (i.e., 7000000) and for deductions enter $3 million - B19. The total estate tax is $2,860,000 on a taxable estate of $6,860,000.

Often testators view their residuary legatees as the primary "objects of their bounty" and want them to receive as much wealth as possible. An apportionment tax clause might more closely meet this objective.

Whatever the provisions of state law, the testator should consider including a tax clause in the will or trust for greater certainty. Rarely will the courts override a tax-apportionment clause or if there is none, the application of a statute, even if the outcome seems unfair to some beneficiaries. Consequently, the alternatives should be carefully considered.

Survival Clauses

The phrase "If A survives me, I give her. . ." is a survival clause and is commonly included in will and trust instruments, mainly to avoid the consequences of a lapse.

Effect of a lapse. A *lapse* occurs when a beneficiary named in a will fails to survive the testator. Each state's probate code contains sections which determine, in the absence of a provision in the will, to whom a lapsed testamentary bequest will pass. A very common type of *antilapse statute*, as it is called, provides that bequests to one of the testator's predeceased blood relatives will instead pass to that relative's surviving issue. The UPC limits the antilapse to predeceased grandparents and descendants of grandparents.[6]

> EXAMPLE 17 - 2. Rudolph died. His will left his car to his brother, Randall, and the residue of his estate to his friend James. Randall predeceased Rudolph. Due to the state's antilapse statute, the bequest of the car will pass to Randall's only son, Jeremy.

Antilapse statutes expressly apply only to wills, not living trust instruments or property held in joint tenancy. However, some courts have applied their antilapse statutes to living trust instruments by analogy. On the other hand, the interests of predeceased co-joint tenants are always cut off by their death; thus, the surviving co-tenants will share a greater percentage of the property.

If the state has no antilapse statute, or if the particular statute does not apply, perhaps because the lapsed bequest was to a beneficiary not related to the deceased, or in a UPC state to a remote relative, then a lapsed specific bequest will ordinarily pass to the residuary beneficiary.

> EXAMPLE 17 - 3. In Example 17-2, if the car was left to Rudolph's predeceased friend Josef instead of Randall, the car will pass to James, the residuary beneficiary, because the state's antilapse statute applies only to relatives.

These result is unfortunate if the testator actually wished, in the event the named beneficiary predeceased the testator, to leave property to certain someone else, for instance the surviving spouse of the predeceased beneficiary who might have also been close to the testator.

> EXAMPLE 17 - 4. Samuel's will left his estate to his brother Arthur. It was silent as to disposition in the event Arthur died first which is what happened. Arthur left a wife, Mary, and three young children. The estate passes to Arthur's children based on the state's antilapse statute and Mary receives none of it. Guardianships must established for the children and Mary will need court permission to use any of the assets.

If a residuary gift lapses in the absence of a specific antilapse statute provision, the property will pass by intestate succession.

> EXAMPLE 17 - 5. In Example 17-3, if James also predeceased Rudolph, the residuary bequest will lapse, and the estate will pass in accordance with intestacy laws.

Avoiding a lapse with a survival clause. A lapse can usually be avoided with a survival clause designating an alternate taker.

> EXAMPLE 17 - 6. Continuing the series of examples above, if Rudolph's will instead left the car to Isaac "in the event that Randall fails to survive me," and Isaac survives Rudolph, then Isaac, the alternate taker, receives the car.

Survival period. A survival clause may require survival for some period beyond the testator's death. An example would be the phrase, "...if she survives me by 30 days..." Extending the survivorship requirement reduces the likelihood that bequeathed property will be subject to two successive probates in situations when the beneficiary dies shortly after the decedent.

> EXAMPLE 17- 7. In Example 17-2, if Randall survived Rudolph by only one month, the car will still pass to Randall and also be subject to administration in his estate. If instead Rudolph's will bequeathed the car to Randall "if he survives me by six months, otherwise to Isaac," then Isaac will receive the car, which will be subject to administration only in Rudolph's estate.

Estate tax and survival periods. Bypass planning also influences the decision whether to use a survival period. One rule of thumb used is to insert a survival period requirement in the wills or trusts of both spouses unless their estates are substantially unequal in amount. In that case, use it only in the document of the less wealthy spouse. The basic rationale is twofold: first, to take advantage of both unified credits when ever it is practical to do so, and second, to avoid unnecessarily loading up a wealthy S2's taxable estate.

In a common accident, there may be an estate tax reason for providing that the beneficiary will always be presumed to have survived the testator. For example, to achieve estates of approximately equal size if a married couple die in a common accident the disposition of property can be based on a stated assumption that the wealthier spouse predeceased the less wealthy spouse. In that event, the larger estate will receive a marital deduction, reducing the taxable estate, while smaller estate will increase by the amount of the bequest. To prevent property from passing to the less wealthy spouse's beneficiaries, the bequest can be structured to qualify as a QTIP transfer.

> EXAMPLE 17-8 William and wife Mary have children from prior marriages. William's estate is worth $3 million and Mary's $600,000. His will creates a QTIP trust with no survival period required. It also creates a presumption that he died first if they die together in an accident. Mary's will also creates a QTIP trust but requires a six month's survival for William to benefit and there is a presumption that she died second. William died in 2002 and Mary survived him by just 36 days. The executor of William's estate QTIPed the trust to equalize the two estates. Two $1.8 million estates pay $690,000, whereas a $3 million estate pays $930,000. Note that none of the tax is paid by Mary's estate since it is required to pay only what it would have paid had there been no QTIP election.

Selecting length of survival period. How long should the survival period be? Making it at least several months in duration will provide for the multiple death event which, relatively speaking, probably occurs most frequently: death of the decedent and the intended beneficiary in a common accident. However, specifying too long a survival period can delay distribution of estate assets since the executor will be required to wait that long to determine whether the named beneficiary in fact survived that period. Further, as mentioned previously in the discussion of the terminal interest rule, a bequest will not qualify for the marital deduction if it is contingent on the spouse surviving the decedent by a period greater than six months.

Many planners use a survival period of about one month for tangible personal property and between four and six months for other property. The shorter period for tangible personal property reflects the usual testator's desire to permit the surviving beneficiary to be able to use such property almost immediately, if even for only a short while, and to avoid storage and other additional costs.

Selection of Trustee and Trustee's Powers

Below we consider the factors involved in selecting a suitable trustee, and in determining which trustee powers to include in the trust instrument. It should become clear that the factors are quite similar to those mentioned earlier, in the section dealing with the selection of an executor.

Selection. We saw that a good executor (and financial guardian) is characterized by longevity, skill in managing, familiarity, integrity, loyalty, and impartiality. In general, these traits also apply to selecting a trustee, except that in the case of a trustee, greater weight is accorded to skill in ongoing financial management. Since the trustee's job is often long term, the trustee's ability to manage and invest property over a long period becomes a major factor. As in the case of the executor, potential nominees include family members, friends, the family attorney, and a corporate fiduciary.

Family member, friend. Selecting a family member or friend to be trustee can minimize costs, maximize administrative speed, and may ensure a personal relationship with the survivors.

Disadvantage of family member as trustee. Selecting a family member to be trustee can also result in mismanagement, since few family members have much experience in maintaining, investing, and accounting for an investment portfolio, all critical responsibilities of the trustee. Thus, family members may feel compelled to hire professionals for advice. In addition, family conflicts can arise. For example, nominating the person's children from a former marriage to be trustees of a QTIP trust can create a difficult situation for the person's second and surviving spouse.

Selecting a trust beneficiary to be trustee can also cause problems of proper distribution. For example, in one case, the trustee, who was also a remainder beneficiary, was ordered by the court to make additional distributions to the decedent-trustor's disabled son, under a trust which allowed such distributions.[7] In this situation, a conflict of interest resulted in a breach of fiduciary obligation that nearly frustrated the deceased trustor's dispositive intent to provide care for his disabled son.

Attorney. Selecting an attorney to be trustee can create the same minor risk of a will contest as in nominating an attorney to be executor. In addition, since management of the trust may be a long-term assignment, the client should determine whether the attorney has the time and expertise required to perform effectively. Finally, anticipating trusteeship, the attorney may be tempted to include unconventional self-serving clauses in the trust instrument, similar to the problems described earlier in the selection of the attorney as executor.[8]

Corporate trustee. Selecting a corporate trustee, such as a bank trust department or a trust company, increases the likelihood that an impartial satisfactory job will be performed. Most corporate trustees try to match the investment strategy for the trust assets to the needs of the beneficiaries, balancing both the income beneficiary's needs with the interests of the remaindermen. The trust instrument can give some guidance as to the settlor's view of appropriate asset allocation. Most trust departments try to build long-term personal relationships with the beneficiaries.

Cotrustees. A common choice is the cotrusteeship of family member and corporate trustee. It can combine the advantages of each: personal knowledge of the family situation and competent asset management. Also, naming the surviving spouse to be a cotrustee can be psychologically uplifting to that spouse.

Ordinarily, cotrusteeships do not save management fees, since the corporate trustee will probably charge its customary fee. There may be some situations where corporate trustees will turn down cotrustee arrangements, particularly when they anticipate that the other trustee may be difficult to accommodate.

When cotrustees disagree, they may have to seek a resolution in court, unless the trust instrument authorizes a less formal method, such as giving the corporate trustee the final say.

Nominating an alternate trustee. As in nominating an executor, the settlor should always nominate a successor trustee and should consult with the proposed trustees to ensure that the job will be accepted. Many bank trust departments set minimum asset amounts, which creates the possibility that they may refuse to manage small trusts. Minimum amounts vary and a corporate trustee my have discretion to lower the amount from its standard minimum depending on the relationship that has been established between it and the family. It might also be influenced by the ease or difficulty it is likely to encounter in managing the estate's assets.

Trustee's powers: three common options. The settlor has at least three commonly used options in deciding what trustee powers to confer in a trust document.

No explicit powers. First, the settlor can specify no powers, relying entirely on implied powers, and on that state's statutory and case-law framework, which explicitly confers some powers to trustees. Many states have adopted the Uniform Trustees Powers Act, which codifies numerous trustee powers. This approach is often used for settlors having relatively small estates and no assets requiring difficult administration.

Some explicit powers. The second approach is to rely on the state's laws in general and explicitly grant in the trust instrument other desirable powers not found in the statute. Such an approach may facilitate asset administration. This is the approach used in Exhibit 3-2, the living trust, and in Exhibit 3-3, the trust-will.

Many explicit powers. A third approach is to include all powers a trustee might need. The resulting document eliminates certain risks, such as future legislative and judicial revision of the law, and the uncertain consequence of a change in the settlor's resident state. On the negative side, a custom-drafted form is a more complex document, more difficult to read, and perhaps more prone to internal inconsistency. Also, making a long detailed list creates the presumption that anything not included is unauthorized even though it might be something that state law would ordinarily approve and that trustees commonly do, e.g., the long list does not include the authority to borrow, if the list appears to be exhaustive, the trustee probably cannot borrow even if doing so would be prudent.

Timing Trust Distributions

Age. All estate planning trusts specify a time when the corpus will be distributed outright to the beneficiaries. Determining in advance the best time can be difficult for a parent with minor children, because the parent may not be able to accurately predict their rates of maturation. A parent may prefer to delay distribution of corpus to a later age, such as age 30 or 40, while others prefer staggered ages, e.g., one third of the trust be distributed at age 21, half the balance at age 25, and the remainder at age 30. Other parents, seeking an alternative to mandatory distribution, simply give the beneficiary a power of withdrawal over the property once the beneficiary reaches some specified age. Thus, their trustee would continue to manage the property indefinitely if the beneficiary became unable or unwilling to make a withdrawal request.

Some individuals prefer to leave the bulk of their wealth to charity. They may fear the potentially devastating impact the anticipation of inherited wealth can have on immature children. Some children of wealthy families are prone to a malady, one commentator has called "affluenza," whose symptoms include a lack of connection between work and reward, inadequate self discipline, a distorted view of money, lack of motivation, guilt, and low self-esteem. For this, and a variety of other reasons, some people choose not to leave their children any inheritance.[9]

Single versus multiple trusts. For parents with more than one child, a separate trust can be established for each child, or a single trust can include all children. How much each child will receive may depend on how many trusts are created.

Multiple trusts. Creating multiple trusts, i.e., a separate trust for each child, adds flexibility but increases administration costs. In addition, separate trusts may be considered unfair to the younger children for the following reason. If the parent lives, expenses in raising all children will ordinarily come from family property in general and not from separate shares reserved for each child. Thus, expenses to raise even the youngest child will come from what could be called the family "pot" of wealth. On the other hand, if the parent dies leaving orphaned minor children, and if a separate trust is immediately created for each child, the pot will likely be split before all expenses in raising the children have been incurred. Thus, each child's remaining expenses will be financed out of his or her own separate share, rather than from the pot. Consequently, the younger children will receive a relatively smaller final distribution on reaching adulthood because living expenses over a longer period of time will have been charged only to their shares. A single trust can solve this problem.

Single pot trust. The name given by some attorneys to a type of single trust created for more than one child, one that retains the "pot" characteristic, is the pot trust or family pot trust. Under its usual terms, the trust remains undivided until the youngest child reaches age 21, the age at which parental obligations are commonly perceived to terminate. At that time, the assets are divided into equal separate shares, one for each child. The assets are distributed outright, or they are held for distribution at some older age.

The choice of the age at which the assets in a pot trust are divided into separate shares or separate trusts involves a trade-off between inequality and delay. The younger that age, the more unequal will be the total cumulative amounts distributed to the children, but the sooner will the older children be certain of the size of their shares. Conversely, the older the age at which the assets are divided into separate shares, the less the inequality, but the later the share amounts will be determined.

> EXAMPLE 17 - 8. Mrs. Hunsaker, a widow, is pondering the type of distribution clause for her trust. She has two children, Colleen, age 20, and Nancy, age 15. Colleen is a senior in college and is engaged to be married, and Nancy, still in high school, is headed for college. One alternative would be to split the trust into two equal shares immediately on her death, with outright distribution to each child at age 21. Another alternative would be to delay dividing the assets into equal shares until Nancy reaches age 21, at which time both children would receive equal shares outright. If Mrs. Hunsaker dies just after the trust is executed, with the first alternative, Colleen will receive her distribution in less than one year and none of it will have been used to finance Nancy's living expenses. With the second alternative, Colleen will have to wait until age 26 to receive her distribution, and the entire corpus will have been available to meet Nancy's living expenses, including most of her college education.

Delaying division of the trust assets probably better reflects the financial condition that would have resulted had the parent not died: One pot of wealth would have been the source for both children's needs. For this reason, most attorneys recommend delaying the division. However, some attorneys recommend dividing the corpus of a pot trust into separate shares sooner, when the oldest child reaches age 18, rather than age 21, reasoning that parents would probably prefer that each child bear subsequent (perhaps very unequal) costs (e.g., college, graduate school) only out of his or her own share. This, of course, reflects a very different philosophy of family financial planning. The planner should determine which best suits the preferences of each client rather than using boiler plate changes.

Restrictions against Assignment

As mentioned in Chapter 3, the settlor may wish to include a spendthrift clause, insulating the trust from the claims of the beneficiaries' creditors and restricting beneficiaries from transferring their interests in trust income or principal prior to their receipt. Spendthrift clauses are legally recognized in the majority of American jurisdictions, even if the beneficiary is not a "spendthrift." They can help a financially prudent beneficiary (e.g., a professional) by protecting trust assets from most creditors. However, such clauses are not foolproof. Although they may deny a creditor the right to demand that the trustee directly hand a distribution over to it, they do not prevent the creditor from exercising the usual legal remedies (i.e., action in court) against a beneficiary after the beneficiary receives a distribution. In addition, all states will enforce a promise made by the beneficiary prior to a distribution that the beneficiary will hand it over to the creditor once it is received. Thus, while a spendthrift clause can discourage excessive spending, it cannot completely prevent the beneficiary from "spending" trust property prior to receiving it, as long as there are potential creditors around who are willing to risk having to seek payment from the beneficiary.

Several states, including California, have recently enacted exceptions to the general rule, that spendthrift trust assets are not subject to the claims of beneficiaries creditors. Common exceptions apply, including:

▸ revocable trusts, if the trustor is a beneficiary.
▸ cases involving spousal and child support judgments.
▸ situations where the creditor is a government agency.

In addition, California has established a procedure similar to wage garnishment for judgment creditors of up to 25% of amounts distributable in excess of support needs. Spendthrift clauses work best in discretionary trusts, ones in which the beneficiary has no legally enforceable right to income or principal.

Special Needs Trust. One interesting application of the spendthrift concept is a discretionary spendthrift trust used for the benefit of a developmentally disabled child after the parent's death. Called a *special needs trust*, it may not work in some states where courts have ruled it in violation of public policy. It seeks to insulate trust assets from governmental claims, and, at the same time, keep the child eligible for public benefits, including Supplemental Security Income (SSI), Medicaid, and Social Security Disability Insurance (SSDI). The special needs trust provides for the health, safety, and welfare of the beneficiary in ways not provided by any public agency, that no part of the corpus may be used to replace public benefits. In the event that the trust renders the beneficiary ineligible for public benefits, the trustee is authorized (but not required) to terminate the trust and distribute the corpus to a "precatory trustee," who is requested (but not required) to provide for the disabled person's basic living needs. The word *precatory* originated from the word 'pray,' i.e., meaning to request some favor from another person. Precatory language is used in a will or trust when the writer wants to recommend a course of action but not impose an enforceable obligation on anyone.

Foreign trust. Individuals owning substantial liquid assets and wishing to more completely protect them from their own creditors may consider creating a foreign "protection of assets" trust. Certain jurisdictions including the Bahamas, Bermuda, and the Cayman Islands offer great protection from pre- and post-judgment remedies of future creditors. Drawbacks include setup costs in excess of $25,000, considerable reporting requirements, and ethical issues. However, at its best, such a trust will trigger no additional taxes.

Trust Taxation: A Summary

Now that the text has covered the major types of trusts used in estate planning, it might help to summarize and compare the gift, estate and income taxation of these trusts. See Table 17-1. In interpreting the comments, keep in mind that some of these trusts come into being under the terms of other trusts, sometimes as a result of the settlor's death. Thus, the nature of a trust may change over time. For example, the bypass and marital trusts usually come into existence soon after one spouse dies. Thus, the comments for the living trust above apply to tax effects during the settlor's lifetime or at his or her death, while the comments for the bypass and marital trusts refer to tax effects at, or after, the settlor's death.

Table 17-1 Summary of Trust Taxation

Trust Type	Taxable Gift?	In Gross Estate?	Income Taxed to Grantor?
Revocable Living Trust	No, not a completed gift.	Yes, in grantor's gross estate, (§2038) but may qualify for marital or charitable deduction.	Yes, it is a grantor trust (§676).
Bypass Trust	No, starts @ grantor's death.	S1: yes S2: generally not, but QTIP & superB can also be bypass trusts	No, taxed to the trust or to the beneficiaries.
Marital Trusts (QTIP, GPA, & Estate Trust)	Generally not created until grantor's death. Can create QTIP during life & obtain marital deduction.	S1: QTIP, not if election is made, other two automatic marital deduction S2: QTIP - it depends, other two yes	No, but generally taxable to S2 (QTIP & GPA required, Estate Trust if distributed).
Minor's Trusts (§2503(c), MIT, or Crummey)	Only to extent not sheltered by annual exclusion.	Not unless grantor retained control over enjoyment (§§2036 or 2038), over annual exclusion would be an adjusted taxable gift.	No, taxable to trust or beneficiaries (so long as not used for support).
Intentionally Defective Irrevocable Trust	Only to extent not sheltered by annual exclusion.	No, but if originally a gift, then it may be an adjusted taxable gift.	Yes, by design. Taxes paid also reduce grantor's taxable estate.
Irrevocable Life Insurance Trust	Only to extent not sheltered by annual exclusion.	No, but if originally a gift, then it may be an adjusted taxable gift.	Generally not. Usually not funded with income producing assets.
Grantor Retained Income Trust	Yes, remainder value if retained interest is qualified, otherwise, whole trust.	Yes, if dies before term ends. Otherwise no, but if originally a gift, then it may be an adjusted taxable gift.	Yes, to the extent of income interest. Trust may also pay taxes.
Charitable Remainder Trust	Remainder is a completed gift, but not taxable (§2055)	Yes, in the gross estate, but it qualifies for charitable deduction	Yes, to extent of income interest. Trust does not pay taxes

PLANNING FOR NONTRADITIONAL RELATIONSHIPS

From time to time, planners will be asked for advice by unmarried clients involved in nontraditional, long term-relationships with members of the same or opposite sex. These relationships present some unique planning challenges and can lead to a set of surprisingly different planning strategies. Two characteristics not applicable to married couples explain most of the differences. First, being unmarried, the partners will not be entitled to the advantages offered by law to married couples. Second, since unmarried partners usually do not have children in common, they usually have totally different sets of surviving kin. Thus, while they may have a strong desire to leave most or all property for the benefit of the partner for life, they will not want the partner to be able to control disposition of their property at or after the partner's death. Underlying strategies based on these characteristics are discussed next.

Greater Need to Avoid Intestacy

Unmarried partners are not included as heirs in intestate succession statutes, making written estate planning documents even more important. Intestacy will have the undesired effect of disinheriting the surviving partner, who is hardly ever a blood relative.

Less Shelter from Estate Tax May Dictate Larger Bypass

In theory, the largest combined estate size that unmarried partners can transfer to survivors, estate tax-free, with a credit shelter bypass is two times the applicable exclusion amount (AEA), e.g., $2 million in 2002 or 2003, just as for married couples. However, in fact, the true maximum is usually less, to the extent that one of the partners owns less than the AEA. While the AEA will be sheltered at the first death by the unified credit, any excess amount cannot be sheltered by the marital deduction. Thus, estate planning cannot "zero out" the estate tax for any first partner to die (P1) owning greater than the AEA. Since P1 will incur an estate tax whether the excess is left to the surviving partner (P2) or to a bypass trust, P1 may prefer to leave the entire estate to the bypass trust, in order to minimize P2's estate tax, and to ensure that the property will ultimately pass to P1's surviving kin.

As a partial solution, the partners may agree to arrange separate wills leaving everything to one another, and agreeing that at P2's death, property originating from P1 will pass to P1's surviving kin. However, short of executing a joint and mutual will, P1 has no way to prevent P2 from revising the instrument later on. Thus, the surest plan requires use of bypass trusts to minimize P2's estate tax and ensure that each will have selected his or her own remaindermen as the ultimate beneficiaries of their respective estates.

Greater Need for Life Insurance at First Death

Since a taxable estate exceeding the AEA will owe an estate tax, liquidity planning will often require life insurance on P1 as well as P2. The proceeds can still be kept out of both partners' gross estates with irrevocable life insurance trusts.

Lifetime Giving More Important

Inability to save as much estate tax on transfers at death may prompt unmarried partners to engage in greater gift planning. Although unmarried partners will not be able to utilize the gift tax marital deduction, they can still take advantage of one annual exclusion per donee per year. Thus, they can still undertake an ongoing program of lifetime giving to reduce their estate tax base. Careful planning should avoid outright gifts to the partner, however, to enable the donor, as a potential P1, to retain final dispositive control. Instead, the planner should encourage gifting in trust, with provisions granting a life estate in the income to the partner and the remainder to the trustor's surviving relatives. As future interests, however, the remainder interest portion of such gifts in trust will not qualify for the annual exclusion and will either use up the settlor's unified credit or result in an actual gift tax.

Joint Tenancies in Community Property States May Be More Attractive

Finally, in community property states, joint tenancies as a means of disposing of property of unmarried decedents may be more attractive, relative to the will and the trust. Only married couples can own community property. Lacking the income tax advantage of a full step-up in basis, a uniquely community property characteristic, unmarried couples, especially those with smaller estates, may choose joint tenancies as a simple form of co-ownership. From a tax basis point of view, joint tenancies will be no worse than any other form of ownership of property. Furthermore, if the first partner to die is the one who owned the property before it was transferred into joint tenancy, this form of ownership also provides a full step-up in basis since the entire value would be included in his or her estate. However, from a control point of view, joint tenancies may still not be desirable. It does not keep dispositive control in the hands of the original owner, whereas a trust would do so.

We turn next to the second major topic of the chapter: planning for one's own incapacity.

PLANNING FOR INCAPACITY

As life expectancy increases so too the probability that one will endure a serious disability. The percentage of persons 65 and older is projected to grow from 21.3% in 2000 to 22.5% in 2010. The portion of the population over 75 is already greater than 10 percent.[10] A person's disability creates the need surrogate decision makers. It makes more sense to choose the person who will care for you and set forth guidelines rather than having the person chosen for you and forced to guess at the care you might desire. As in the case of minors, the law recognizes two types of care for incapacitated adults, i.e., care of the person and care of the person's property.

Property Management for an Incapacitated Person

Four techniques are available to care for the property of an incapacitated person: the guardianship or conservatorship, revocable living trust, durable power of attorney for property, and the special needs trust

Guardianship or conservatorship of an estate. Similar to the guardianship of the estate of a minor, all states provide a court-supervised arrangement to manage the property of an incapacitated individual. Called a *guardianship* or a *conservatorship*, depending on the state, establishment of either normally requires a court hearing, and the appointment of a guardian who is ordinarily subject to continuing court supervision. The guardian or conservator is required to give periodic accountings to the court and is typically required to obtain court permission before engaging in most property transactions. Most guardians and conservators have little or no discretionary authority. However, some states are reducing court involvement in guardianships and conservatorships in much the same way they are reducing court involvement for probate proceedings.[11]

For reasons similar to those for avoiding probate, many people will plan to avoid the necessity of having a property guardian or conservator. Some individuals, however, may prefer the protection offered from their closer court supervision. People owning larger estates, or those who cannot recommend a friend or relative to manage property, might prefer a court-administered alternative. Most people will prefer one or both of the arrangements described next.

Revocable living trust. In planning for incapacity, a person could create a revocable living trust, funding it with family assets, and serving as its initial trustee. The trust instrument could provide for a successor trustee when the person became unable to manage the trust's financial affairs. The successor trustee could be the spouse, an adult child, another relative, a trusted friend, or a corporate trustee. In comparison with a guardianship or conservatorship, a living trust offers the advantages of privacy, flexibility, and freedom from court appearances and accountings. On the other hand, since the trust is a private, unsupervised arrangement, there exists greater potential for undiscovered fraud and mismanagement by the successor trustee.

One additional disadvantage of the trust arrangement to handle incapacity is the possible requirement of a formal legal determination of the settlor-trustee's incapacity before a successor trustee can take over the job. Embarrassing litigation can develop between the settlor and a family member who is attempting to establish that the settlor-trustee is incompetent. However, this conflict can also arise if a guardianship or conservatorship is being established. The trust can contain a clause providing for a private determination of incapacity, in a manner similar to that provided by the springing durable power of attorney for property, discussed next.

Durable power of attorney for property. Creation of a trust can be relatively expensive. Persons owning smaller estates may prefer to execute a simpler document, known as a durable power of attorney for property. Popularized by the Uniform Probate Code, the durable power of attorney for property has been recognized by the statutes of every state. The durable power of attorney for property is different from the durable power of attorney for health care, described in the next section. Since state laws vary, the reader is strongly urged to examine the law of his or her particular state.

A power of attorney is a written document executed by one person, called the *principal*, authorizing another person, called the *attorney-in-fact* or the *agent*, to perform designated acts on behalf of the principal. A durable power of attorney for property (DPOA) creates an agency relationship that allows the agent to perform acts to protect the principal's property interests, even if the principal becomes incapacitated.

Durable versus nondurable powers of attorney. General powers of attorney can be either durable or nondurable. A nondurable power of attorney is not a practical alternative for caring for the property of elderly individuals because the power becomes legally invalid at the onset of the principal's incapacity, just when the agency is needed most. In one situation, an attorney-in-fact under a nondurable power of attorney gifted property after the principal became mentally incompetent and the IRS ruled that the gift was voidable under local law (by a court-appointed guardian or by the principal had he regained mental capacity), and therefore the gift was included in the principal's gross estate under § 2038.[12]

The *durable* power of attorney was developed to overcome this deficiency. Thus, a DPOA is durable because it survives the principal's incapacity. Exhibit 17-1 illustrates the common provisions of a DPOA. The italicized sentence makes it "durable."

EXHIBIT 17-1 Durable Power of Attorney (for property)[13]

DURABLE POWER OF ATTORNEY

JOHN JONES, PRINCIPAL

TO WHOM IT MAY CONCERN:

I, John Jones, a resident of Anytown, Anystate, in the county of Anycounty, do hereby constitute and appoint Aaron Agent, a resident of Anytown, Anystate, to be my attorney-in-fact, with full power to name and stead and on my behalf and with full power to substitute at any time or times for the purposes described below one or more attorneys and to revoke the appointment of my attorney so substituted and to do the following:

1. To manage my affairs; handle my investments; arrange for the investment, reinvestment, and disposition of funds; exercise all rights with respect to my investments; accept remittances of income and disburse the same, including authority to open bank accounts in my name and to endorse checks for deposit therein or in any bank where I may at any time have money on deposit and sign checks covering withdrawals therefrom.

2. To endorse and deliver certificates for transfer of bonds or other securities to be sold for my account and receive the proceeds from such sale.

3. To sign, execute, acknowledge, and deliver on my behalf any deed of transfer or conveyance covering personal property or real estate wherever situated (including transfers or conveyances to any trust established by me), any discharge or release of mortgage held by me on real estate or any other instrument in writing.

4. To negotiate and execute leases of any property, real or personal, which I may own, for terms that may extend beyond the duration of this power and to provide for the proper care and maintenance of such property and pay expenses incurred in connection therewith.

5. To subdivide, partition, improve, alter, repair, adjust boundaries of, manage, maintain, and otherwise deal with any real estate held as trust property, including power to demolish any building in whole or in part and to erect buildings.

6. To enter into a lease or arrangement for exploration and removal of minerals or other natural resources or to enter into a pooling or unitization agreement.

7. To hold securities in bearer form or in the name of a nominee or nominees and to hold real estate in the name of a nominee or nominees.

EXHIBIT 17-1 Durable Power of Attorney *continued*

---

8. To continue or participate in the operation of any business or other enterprise.
9. To borrow money from time to time in my name and to give notes or other obligations therefore, and to deposit as collateral, pledge as security for the payment thereof, or mortgage any or all my securities or other property of whatever nature.
10. To have access to any and all safe deposit boxes of which I am now or may become possessed, and to remove therefrom any securities, papers, or other articles.
11. To make all tax returns and pay all taxes required by law, including federal and state returns, and to file all claims for abatement, refund, or other papers relating thereto.
12. To demand, collect, sue for, receive, and receipt for any money, debts, or property of any kind, now or hereafter payable, due or deliverable to me; to pay or contest claims against me; to settle claims by compromise, arbitration, or otherwise; and to release claims.
13. To employ as investment counsel, custodians, brokers, accountants, appraisers, attorneys-at-law, or other agents such persons, firms, or organizations, including my said attorney and any firm of which my said attorney may be a member or employee, as deemed necessary or desirable, and to pay such persons, firms, or organizations such compensation as is deemed reasonable and to determine whether to act on the advice of any such agent without liability for acting or failing to act thereon.
14. To expend and distribute income or principal of my estate for the support, education, care, or benefit of me and my dependents.
15. To make gifts to any one or more of my spouse and my descendants (if any) of whatever degree (including my said attorney who is a spouse or descendant of mine) in amounts not exceeding $10,000 annually with respect to any one of them and gifts to charity in amounts not exceeding 20% of my federal adjusted gross income in any one year.
16. To renounce and disclaim any interest otherwise passing to me by testate or intestate succession or by inter vivos transfer.
17. To exercise my rights to elect options and change beneficiaries under insurance and annuity policies and to surrender the policies for their cash value.

In general I give to my said attorney full power to act in the management and disposition of all my estate, affairs and property of every kind and wherever situated in such manner and with such authority as I myself might exercise if personally present.

EXHIBIT 17-1 Durable Power of Attorney *continued*

This power of attorney shall be binding on me and my heirs, executors, and administrators and shall remain in force up to the time of the receipt of my attorney of a written revocation signed by me.

This power of attorney shall not be affected by my subsequent disability or incapacity.

IN WITNESS THEREOF, I have set forth signature on March 19, 2001.

John Jones

STATE OF ANYSTATE

COUNTY OF ANYCOUNTY

On <u>March 19, 2001,</u> the above named <u>John Jones</u> appeared and acknowledged the foregoing instrument to be his/ free act and deed.

Mary D. Notary

Notary Public

My commission expires: January 1, 2005

This particular example of a DPOA form can be criticized for being simply a unilateral authorizing instrument, which means that the named attorney-in-fact would not be liable for failure to act. Some commentators recommend instead creating a bilateral contract between principal and attorney-in-fact, particularly if the latter is not the principal's spouse, to eliminate this problem. Of course, while this requires the signature of the agent, there is little that can be done if the agent "resigns" when the principal becomes incapacitated.

Non-springing versus springing DPOAs. There are two common types of DPOAs. The first type becomes effective as soon as it is executed. The second type, called a "springing" DPOA, becomes effective at the principal's incapacity. It will contain the following clause, in addition to those found in Exhibit 17-1:

In the event that I have been determined to be incapacitated to provide informed consent for medical treatment and surgical and diagnostic procedures, I wish to designate as my surrogate for health care decisions:[followed by the identification of the agent].

Some attorneys recommend that a physician or a "trusted committee" of three of the client's trusted friends and relatives should be empowered to determine when the power of attorney becomes effective.

To be valid, of course, any DPOA must be executed prior to the principal's incapacity. To ensure competent execution, many advisers recommend the preparation of a DPOA for an older client at the time the will is being prepared.

Advantages of the DPOA. The DPOA has several advantages over the other devices designed to manage an incapacitated person's property. Compared to a guardianship or conservatorship, the DPOA is less expensive to create and to administer. The non-springing type can avoid the necessity of a court-held incompetency proceeding, an event that can be painful and embarrassing to all parties, especially the proposed conservatee. Compared with the living trust, the DPOA is also less expensive to create and administer. Some individuals who refuse to set up a trust may be willing to execute a DPOA, because of its relative simplicity. Yet a trust can continue long after the settlor's death, whereas a DPOA, being based on agency law, must terminate when the principal dies. It may be durable but it is not that durable.

The trust and the DPOA need not be considered alternatives. Greater flexibility may result if a DPOA authorizes the attorney-in-fact to add newly acquired property (by gift, inheritance, etc.) to the principal's partially funded living trust, or to fund an existing unfunded revocable living trust (a "standby trust") with the principal's assets, at the onset of incapacity. On funding, the assets could be managed by a skilled trustee. Thereafter, the attorney-in-fact may be permitted to perform other duties that were not given to the trustee, including establishing and funding other trusts, making gifts and disclaimers, and appearing at tax audits.

Regarding the power of the attorney-in-fact to make gifts, one court has ruled that failure to explicitly include that power in the document will totally frustrate gift planning. In that case, the attorney-in-fact did make gifts before the principal's death. Relying on Virginia's narrow construction of powers-of-attorney law, the appellate court treated the gift as revocable at the time of the principal's death, resulting in inclusion of gifted assets in the gross estate under §§ 2036(a) and 2038.[14] However, in a more recent Virginia case, the Tax Court allowed gifts by an attorney-in-fact because Virginia law authorizes attorneys-in-fact to make gifts "in accordance with the principal's personal history of making or joining in lifetime gifts."[15]

Drawbacks of the DPOA. The DPOA has a potential drawback for the attorney in-fact. If the attorney-in fact dies first, the IRS might claim that principal's property must be included in the attorney-in-fact's gross estate on the theory that the attorney-in-fact held a general power of appointment over the property. The fact that the agent has a fiduciary duty to use the power only for the best interest of the principal should be enough to prevent a claim of inclusion from being successful. Completely eliminating this danger may require prohibiting entirely the ability of the attorney-in-fact to make gifts to him or herself, or limiting such gifts to an ascertainable standard, or to the greater of $5,000 or 5% of the value of the property.

A non-tax drawback to the DPOA concerns its acceptance. Certain financial institutions may be unwilling to honor the DPOA if they cannot satisfy themselves that it is currently valid. The power, they reason, may already have been revoked by the principal or the principal may be dead. Due to their uncertainty about the validity of custom-drafted DPOAs, they may insist on the use of their own form. The industry's increasing use of the DPOA should substantially lessen these concerns. The attorney can minimize acceptance problems with careful and specific custom drafting of enumerated powers, and by having the principal periodically re-execute the DPOA to prevent it from appearing outdated. Nevertheless, some institutions refuse to accept a DPOA, and some banks and the IRS will, but might require the use of their own forms.

Other helpful techniques to maximize acceptability include a provision in the document that empowers the attorney-in-fact to bring legal action against a recalcitrant third party and indemnifies the third party when it acts in reliance on the document and the agent's instructions. However, pursuing legal action can be expensive and time consuming. Finally, the person, while still competent, can show the document to banks, insurance companies, health care providers, etc., to find out whether it will be accepted, and to stop dealing with those institutions that refuse. New York has a statute making it unlawful to refuse to recognize the New York statutory form DPOA and indemnifying banks that honor them. California's statute permits the filing of an action to compel the honoring of a statutory durable power and specifies that a refusal is unreasonable if the sole reason for the refusal is that it is not on the third party's (e.g., a bank's) own form.[16]

The second non-tax drawback of the DPOA is that it can be misused. Lawyers will attest to situations where attorneys-in-fact have used a disabled client's property in a manner clearly contrary to the principal's best interest. Although such behavior is actionable, it is rarely challenged. Because the DPOA delegates very fundamental property rights, a person considering signing one should first think long and hard about the possible consequences.

Special needs trust and other asset "spend-down" planning. A different kind of living trust may be capable of preserving assets owned by persons anticipating possible long-term disability.

The medical profession has been tremendously successful in prolonging the life of the seriously ill, often at great economic cost. Such patients often need *custodial care* for help with feeding, bathing, dressing, and transportation. Later, they may need *skilled nursing care* provided in a licensed facility, and costing $3,000 per month or more. Their condition may finally require a lengthy period of hospitalization, costing far more. Private and public insurance can help pay these costs, but often not entirely. Long-term care insurance has recently become available, but policies usually are expensive and contain significant restrictions and exclusions, so few people are willing to buy it. Federal Medicare insurance for persons with Medicare Part A coverage receive up to 100 days of skilled nursing care. The conditions for obtaining this coverage are quite stringent such that most illnesses will be determined not to require skill nursing. These limitations in private and public insurance raise the possibility that a person will totally deplete the wealth acquired over a lifetime, thereby preventing any significant amount going to the children.

To prevent this, some people are turning to attorneys who specialize in elder law. Many recommend "spending down" assets through the use of gifts and trusts. This action seeks to accomplish two goals. First, it strives to insulate the person's assets from the claims of health care providers and government agencies. Second, it attempts to impoverish the person sufficiently to qualify for certain types of federal and state assistance, including Supplemental Security Income, In-Home Supportive Services, In-Home Medical Care Services, and perhaps most importantly, Medicaid. While Medicare is considered an "entitlement" for those who have paid into the system, Medicaid is not. It is considered a form of welfare, hence one can have too much wealth or too much income to qualify for Medicaid. Each state, in exchange for matching federal Medicaid grants, imposes federally influenced limits on both 1) assets a recipient can own, and 2) the his or her income beyond that needed for the actual cost of medical and custodial care. These levels do vary by state so only general statements can be made. Generally, the person's home is not factored into the asset value limitation so long as the person intends to return to it (regardless of how improbable that might be). To reduce asset value, especially if the person has meager income, he or she can purchase a single premium annuity. Although distributions from the annuity do count for purposes of the income test, the overall value of the annuity does not count under the assets test.

As part of a spending-down strategy, an individual may wish to make outright gifts of property to children. However, outright gifts have the major drawback that the donor loses total control over the property. Also, the gifts must be made well in advance of the person entering a nursing home since a "Transfer Penalty" applies to gifts made withing 36 months prior to the Medicaid application (or 60 months if the transfer was made to certain kinds of trusts).[17] The penalty is a period of ineligibility to receive benefits. The period is determined by dividing the value of the gifts during the 36 months leading up to the application by the average private-pay nursing home rate in the applicants state.

> EXAMPLE 17 - 9. The year prior to going into a nursing home, Mildred gave her son John cash, stocks, and bonds worth $40,000. The average private-pay nursing home rate was $4,000 at the time. Because of the transfer penalty, Mildred will have to pay her own way for ten months.

In addition, after the beneficiary's death, the state must attempt to recoup from the recipient's estate the benefits it paid for the recipient's care. It can recoup from the probate estate as well as other assets that once belonged to the recipient, including those conveyed to a survivor, heir, or transferred through joint tenancy, tenancy in common, survivorship, life estate, or living trusts. Property in the estate of the surviving spouse is exempt.

Helping a client who owns a sizable estate to impoverish him or her self so as to qualify for public assistance funds is a controversial subject and raises ethical issues. Many planners will not recommend it, because they see it as taking unfair advantage of an imperfect system designed for truly needy people. It also encourages children to treat Medicaid as if it were "their personal inheritance insurance." Many wealthy people are not be interested in spending down their estates. Most will want a higher quality of care and may not like being regarded as a "welfare case." Others find no moral dilemma, and consider it no different from tax planning, such as recommending a credit shelter bypass trust to minimize estate tax. Perhaps all planners would agree that clients should be encouraged to consider, at a minimum, other basic protective planning steps, such as purchasing an effective long-term care insurance policy or saving for their future care.

Personal Care for the Incapacitated Person

Similar to the procedure for selecting the guardian of a minor child, the procedure for selecting the person who will care for an incapacitated adult is usually undertaken in the county probate court after a noticed hearing. Some states call this fiduciary a *guardian* or *committee*, while others use the name *conservator*. States define guardian, conservator, and committee differently. In some states, such as California, a conservator is a person appointed by the court to manage the personal care, and the property of, an adult unable to provide for their own personal needs and/or unable to manage their financial resources, while a guardian is appointed to perform such services for a minor. In other states, such as New York, a conservator deals primarily with an "impaired" person's property, while a committee cares for both the person and the property of an "incompetent" person. The UPC parallels the New York terminology and, in addition, permits a guardian to be appointed to oversee the person and the property of an "incapacitated" person. In any case, the court chooses the party only after careful, formal consideration.

Selecting a personal care provider. Who should the person nominate to provide personal care in the event of his or her incapacity? Ordinarily, the person has few choices.

Spouse, family members. The spouse is usually the best first choice. Next come other family members, especially adult children. However, the children may lead busy lives and may not be capable nor willing to do all the work required. This problem is even more likely to arise for a person in an advanced stage of incapacity, such as the onset of incontinence. Prior to this degree of impairment, the individual may simply need home delivery of meals, housekeeping services, or adult day care, all of which are commercially available.

While these services are not inexpensive, some programs are government subsidized. Services can be arranged for a fee by a "private geriatric care manager," who is often a social worker or nurse. Helpful sources of information include: County and local departments for the aging, for referrals on services for elders; the National Association of Area Agencies on Aging, which has an "elder care locator" (http://www.n4a.org/); the National Association of Professional Geriatric Care Managers (http://www.caremanager.org/); the National Academy of Elder Law Attorneys (http://www.naela.com/); and the Children of Aging Parents (http://www.caps4caregivers.org/), which is designed to provide "caregivers of the elderly or chronically ill with reliable information, referrals and support, and to heighten public awareness that the health of the family caregivers is essential to ensure quality care of the nation's growing elderly population."

Nursing home. As a person gets older, it may be wise to visit residential health care facilities for the elderly. Such facilities vary widely in cost, extent of services offered, and the degree of incapacity permitted. At one end of the spectrum is the traditional nursing home, which offers complete care, but is quite expensive. Some critics feel entering a nursing home is tantamount to "a life sentence to mental and physical imprisonment," where patients lose nearly all of their independence in a dehumanizing environment.

Assisted living. Other less structured facilities offer a new and increasingly popular style of housing called assisted living for elderly people without serious medical problems. Private apartments are provided, as well as meals, laundry, housekeeping, social activities, transportation, and regular visits by nurses. Such facilities usually cost considerably less than nursing homes and offer the greatest degree of independence possible.[18]

Life care facility. Finally, one other type of organization called a life-care facility offers at a hefty price the right to occupy, for life, an apartment in a large residential health-care facility, which also provides, on the premises, all meals and around-the-clock nursing, medical, and hospital services.

Some figures from the U.S. Census Bureau regarding the elderly living in commercial facilities like the three described above plus long-term care rooms in hospital wards, and soldiers', fraternal or religious homes for the aged, may be helpful. In 1990, 1.8 million people lived in commercial facilities for the elderly. Not surprisingly, women outnumbering men almost three to one. Residents 85 and older constituted 42% of those residents, up from 34% in 1980. Overall, only

5.1% of the nation's elderly reside in these facilities, but the figure was 24.5% of those 85 and older. Only one in seven had a spouse still alive.

Delegation of health care decisions. Until recently, people have not had the ability to delegate the power to make medical decisions. Today, almost all states recognize an individual's ability either to delegate important medical decisions or at least to state in writing what those decisions should be.

An *advance directives* is a general term that refers to written instructions about a person's desire concerning medical care in the event the person becomes unable to speak for his or herself. The state laws may differ somewhat but all generally authorize the use of advance directives. The two major types of advance directives are the living will and the medical power of attorney.

A *living will* is a type of advance directive in which a person puts in writing his or her wishes about medical treatment should he or she be unable to communicate. These generally address end of life issues. State law may define when the living will goes into effect, or the triggering event may be set forth in the document, e.g., a diagnosis by two physicians that a condition is terminal and likely to result in death with ten days. Depending upon the jurisdiction, the document may be called a directive to physician, a declaration under the [state's] natural death act, a medical directive, or a durable power for health care. One can download state-specific advanced directives in PDF format from Partnership for Caring's website <http://www.partnershipforcaring.org/>.

Cruzan case. The need to state medical choices clearly and in writing is dramatically illustrated by the 1990 U.S. Supreme Court decision, *Cruzan v. Missouri*.[19] A victim of an automobile accident seven years earlier, 32 year old Nancy Cruzan remained in a persistent vegetative state, with functioning respiratory and circulatory systems, but little else. She could not swallow food, and she was unable to recognize her relatives. After it became clear that there was no reasonable hope of any improvement in her condition, her family sought to let her die by withdrawing her feeding tube. The state of Missouri would not allow it, despite the fact that a year before the accident, Nancy had told a friend that "if sick or injured she would not wish to continue her life unless she could live at least halfway normally." On appeal, the U.S. Supreme Court affirmed, approving the Missouri requirement that the family would have to show "clear and convincing evidence" of Nancy's wishes to remove life sustaining equipment, something the jury determined that the Cruzans did not establish.

After the Supreme Court decision and just after the Cruzans requested a new hearing in the local court claiming new evidence that Nancy would not wish to live, the state attorney general withdrew as a party to the case, which meant that there was no longer anyone to oppose removal of Nancy's feeding tube. Nancy died at age 33 on December 26, 1990, twelve days after the tube was removed.

Based on the Supreme Court's ruling, it would appear that standards of proof such as Missouri's "clear and convincing evidence" may be difficult to meet without a written statement by the incapacitated person. Estate planning has two common written documents for this purpose: the durable power of attorney for health care and the living will.

Durable power of attorney for health care. Like the durable power of attorney for property (DPOA), the durable power of attorney for health care (DPOAHC) appoints a person as attorney-in-fact to make decisions on behalf of the principal. However, the documents are different in three important respects.

Types of decisions. First, the DPOAHC concerns medical, not property decisions. Examples of medical decisions listed in this type of "advance directive" include the power to secure the placement in or removal from a medical facility, to withhold future medical treatment, to use or not use medication, to perform or not perform surgery, and the power to use or not use artificial life-sustaining methods, such as respiration, nourishment, and hydration. As one might expect, this last power is quite controversial, and some legal commentators have defended it ardently. Reflecting an increasingly popular dissatisfaction with the zealous use of artificial life-sustaining methods, some have argued that rapid advances in medical technology, combined with the implicit premise of medicine to "do everything" for patients, violate patients' rights. These advances in medicine may actually condemn the very sick to an existence void of relationship in antiseptic hospital-like settings, an existence that many feel is worse than death.

Designating a surrogate with the power to terminate life support can be helpful in situations where the physician in charge refuses to act. One study has shown that physicians are reluctant to terminate life support in cases where the patient would take a relatively long time to die, where the life support became necessary because of medical errors, and in cases where the patient has already been on life support for a relatively long period of time.[20]

Springing power. Second, the DPOAHC differs from the DPOA in that the DPOAHC is always a springing power, while the DPOA can be non-springing.

Thus, the DPOAHC becomes effective only on the principal's incapacity, that is, on his or her inability to make health care decisions. The DPOAHC does not apply just to situations where the principal is terminally ill, but to all situations where the principal is unable to give "informed consent" with respect to a particular medical decision.

Separate documents. Third, while it is possible to include the legal content of a DPOAHC within a DPOA document they are usually drafted as separate documents. They involve very different situations, different evolving law, and possibly different attorneys-in-fact. In addition, many attorneys prefer to use a preprinted state medical association form for health care because of its widespread acceptance by the medical profession. In contrast, a custom-drafted form can generate decision-making delays when a hospital requires its own lawyers to carefully evaluate it.

Acceptance of the document. The DPOAHC is statutorily recognized in almost every state. State law varies in terms of both the scope of the authority of the attorney in fact to act on behalf of the principal and the protection afforded to health care providers who act on those instructions. Some states such as California have statutes permitting health care providers to assume that a DPOAHC is valid in the absence of knowledge to the contrary. Offering some support, the American Medical Association has ruled that it is appropriate for doctors to withdraw life-supporting, artificial feeding systems from hopelessly comatose patients.

Drawback. One drawback of the DPOAHC concerns the fact that it is so powerful. It can place reluctant family members in the difficult position of having to make critical life or death decisions, ones they may regrettably relive in their minds over and over, long after the crisis has ended. Nevertheless, the durable power of attorney for health care has become one of the most popular estate planning devices.

Living will. The DPOAHC has become widely accepted in the United States. Before then, most states only recognized some variation of the living will, which typically addresses just one of the two features of the DPOAHC. Typically the living will detail those health care interventions that the person does or does not wish to be subjected to in situations when he or she is no longer capable of making those decisions, but did not designate an agent to make medical decisions for the person signing the document.

Disadvantages of living wills. When compared to the DPOAHC, living wills have at least five limitations. First, a traditional living will does not appoint a surrogate decision maker, which restricts its flexibility considerably, especially in view of the rapid advances in medical technology. Second, living wills are typically very brief, covering only a few possible outcomes, mostly in the area of life-sustaining treatment. No living will, no matter how detailed, can spell out all of the possible treatment decisions that may be needed. Third, most living will statutes apply only to terminal patients, not those who are just incurably ill, such as a person in a persistent vegetative state. Many states require that death be "imminent." Fourth, the language of living wills is usually quite vague, failing to define important terms, leaving the physician and the family to disagree over proper care. Finally, a number of states living will statutes provide that a physician is obligated to comply with the directives in a living will concerning withdrawal or withholding of life-sustaining procedures. In the event the physician chooses not to comply, he or she must transfer the patient to another physician.

With regard to the second and fourth limitations, more and more attorneys are drafting quite specific living wills (and DPOAHCs, for that matter). For example, the client may be asked to enter preferences in writing in a matrix-table depicting alternative medical scenarios and procedures. The rows of the matrix might list ten to fifteen medical procedures, such as invasive diagnostic tests; CPR; pain medication; artificial nutrition and hydration; mechanical breathing, and the like. The columns of the matrix might list alternative physical scenarios, such as coma or persistent vegetative state with no chance of regaining awareness; irreversible brain damage or disease; irreversible brain damage or disease combined with terminal illness; coma with small chance of recovery and greater chance of surviving with brain damage, etc. Then, for each cell in the matrix-table, the client would insert one of several letters signifying a desired action, such as U = uncertain; N = do not want procedure; T = yes, try procedure but have it stopped if no clear improvement is shown; and Y = yes, try procedure for as long as possible. The danger in documenting this detail is that the person may thoughtlessly and hastily fill in the blanks on a written instrument that may wind up being the only hard evidence available, thereby ruling out the possibility of an alternative choice which may reflect the careful contemplation of the person's sincere loved ones.

Miscellaneous factors. In some states, planners recommend that clients execute both a living will and a DPOAHC, particularly in states where DPOAHCs are not written to include the main characteristic of the living will. Finally, in their attempt at coordination, more and more states are adopting integrated statutes that deal with both types of advance directive.

Several states, including Virginia, recognize a variation on the living will called the *directive to physicians*, giving instructions with regard to the use of life-sustaining treatment. The directive to physicians has been largely rendered obsolete in most other states by the common acceptance of the DPOAHC.

Whatever documents are used, they should be updated periodically, for three reasons. First, state law may require it. Second, the person's wishes may have changed. And third, the planner should make sure the documents remain consistent with the rapidly changing law in this area.

This chapter has described miscellaneous lifetime estate planning techniques not covered earlier. Chapter 18 will examine tax planning techniques which can be employed on behalf of the person after the person's death.

QUESTIONS AND PROBLEMS

1. (a) Describe the attributes of an effective parental guardian, executor, and trustee. (b) Why are they different?

2. One of your friends asks you to describe the legal alternatives available to provide for her young son's financial care. Be sure to mention the advantages and disadvantages of each.

3. What factors will influence which beneficiaries a testator should choose to bear the burden of death taxes?

4. (a) What is a survival clause? (b) How does it overcome the consequences of a lapse?

5. Describe the family pot trust and the trade-off involved in determining the age of distribution to young adult beneficiaries.

6. Cassie's will simply says, "I leave all my securities to John, and everything else to Mary." If John predeceases Cassie, analyze the possible recipients of the securities, using the alternative assumptions made in the text about the contents of the will and the influence of state law. Apply the law of your state, if possible.

7. You are the creditor of a deadbeat who is a beneficiary under a trust containing a spendthrift clause similar to the one in Exhibit 3-2. What ability, if any, do you have at getting at the trust assets?

8. Kris and Pat, companions for many years, do not plan to ever marry. Neither have children. Kris owns property worth $1,500,000 and Pat owns property worth $300,000. For discussion assume that Kris dies in 2001 and Pat's death will occur in 2008, show how the total estate tax owed depends on their estate plan by working through each of the choices that follow. For each, the property value between the two deaths remains constant, being reduced only by the taxes paid at Kris's death.
   A. Simple wills, naming each other as contingent beneficiaries, leaving all property to the partner, if surviving.

B. An AB Trust arrangement with the excess over the AEA going outright to Pat (or Trust A, revocable by Pat) and Kris's estate taxes are charged solely to the B Trust.

C. An AB Trust arrangement with the excess over the AEA going outright to Pat (or Trust A, revocable by Pat) and Kris's estate taxes are shared proportionately between the share going to Trust B and the share going to Pat.

D. An AsuperB arrangement whereby all of Kris's property is placed in Trust B (with Pat's property in Trust A) and B is charged with the taxes.

E. In general, what difference does it make that Pat survived Kris by less than 10 years? What if she survives beyond 2010?

F. How well can each of the plans listed above achieve both partner's desire to leave their property to their own relatives after the surviving partner dies?

G. Would lifetime gifting reduce their total estate tax? Might it be inconsistent with their goals?

9. In planning for one's own possible incapacity, what are the main estate planning alternatives for taking care of financial matters? Describe the advantages and disadvantages of each.

10. Your 86-year-old mentally competent client wishes to plan for her incapacity but refuses to immediately transfer her assets to anyone. Is planning impossible, or does this refusal merely create a particular problem?

11. Your friend says, "I just signed four estate planning documents at my estate planning attorney's office." Name and briefly describe the likely four.

12. An attorney jokingly tells a client: "Today you'll be signing two documents, one for wealth and one for health. One gives someone the power to steal from you, while the other gives someone the power to kill you." (a) What two documents is she talking about? (b) Is there any truth to her cynicism?

13. Explain several reasons why you might urge a person to consider additional estate planning after each of the following events?
    a. marriage
    b. birth or adoption of a child
    c. divorce
    d. remarriage
    e. death, separation or divorce of any child
    f. family estate amount becomes medium sized
    g. retirement
    h. death of spouse
    i. death of a parent
    j. changes in tax laws
    k. a change in the value of the person's business
    l. a change in the person's state of domicile

14. In view of your answers to the question immediately above, what do you think of mail-order type estate plans, or other marketing approaches for plans that render it difficult to revise the plans periodically?

15. At Partnership for Caring's website you will find a wealth of information about end-of-life issues. You will also find state-specific living wills and durable powers of attorney for health care. Visit the site at <http://www.partnershipforcaring.org> Download the "advanced directive package" appropriate for your state of domicile. You will first need to download Adobe Acrobat Reader (available free) if it is not already on your computer, <http://www.adobe.com/products/acrobat/readstep2.html>.

ANSWERS TO THE QUESTIONS AND PROBLEMS *(odd numbered only)*

1. a. Attributes of a good parental guardian, executor, and trustee.

   Parental Guardian: (1) Integrity, maturity, physical stamina and experience needed to be a permanent parent; (2) strong concern for the minor's welfare, and (3) a stable personal situation.

   Executor: (1) Longevity; (2) skill in managing legal and financial affairs; (3) familiarity with the testator's estate and wishes; (4) integrity and loyalty.

   Trustee: Same as those for executor, except greater weight on skill in financial management.

   b. The attributes are different because of the differing responsibilities. Parental skills are most important for a personal guardian. On the other hand, property management skills are most important for an executor and trustee, with even greater significance for the trustee, because of the possible time span of the job.

3. Factors in deciding who should bear the burden of death taxes include:

   a. How liquid is the bequest?
   b. How wealthy is the beneficiary?
   c. How much access to liquid assets does the beneficiary have?
   d. Is a large specific bequest being made?

5. The family pot trust is a single trust originally for the benefit of two or more beneficiaries, at least one of whom is a minor. Corpus is typically not divided into separate shares for the beneficiaries until the youngest reaches a certain age, such as 21. Selecting that age involves a tradeoff between inequality and delay. The older the predetermined age, the more equitable will be the distribution, but the longer the older beneficiaries may have to wait for that distribution.

7. You will probably have to wait until the beneficiary actually receives the asset distributions before you can legally act to seize them, unless your state has a statutory exception permitting you to require the trustee to turn over trust assets directly to you, as would be the case in some states for revocable living trusts and divorce situations.

9. Alternative in property planning for incapacity:

    a. Conservatorship: Advantage: Substantial court supervision.
        Conservatorship: Disadvantages: (1) Relatively expensive; (2) inflexible; and (3) public.

    b. Trust: Advantages: (1) Private; (2) flexible; and (3) potentially less expensive.
        Trust: Disadvantage: Not court supervised

    c. Durable Power of Attorney for property: Advantages: (1) Private; (2) flexible; and (3) potentially less expensive.
        Durable Power Disadvantage: Not court supervised

NOTE: The trust and the durable power of attorney for property need not be considered alternatives; they can both be used by the same person.

11. - *Living trust:* A trust taking effect during the lifetime of the trustor. Also called an inter vivos trust.
    - *Pour over will:* A will that distributes, at the testator's death, probate assets to a trust that had been created during the testator's lifetime.
    - *Durable power of attorney for property:* A durable power of attorney granting to the attorney-in-fact the power to make decisions concerning the property of the principal.
    - *Durable power of attorney for health care (DPOAHC):* A durable power of attorney granting to the attorney-in-fact the power to make medical decisions on behalf of the principal.

13. a.   Marriage:
      -to include new spouse in will/trust document
      -to undertake marital deduction planning
      -to change life insurance and pension beneficiary designations
      -to acquire life and disability insurance

   b.   Birth of a child:
      -to prevent omitted child intestacy problems
      -to provide for parental guardianship and trustee property management at death of surviving spouse
      -to acquire more life and disability insurance
      -to execute durable powers of attorney

   c.   Divorce:
      -to ensure that the document will be recognized (in some states, divorce revokes an entire will, not just those provisions pertaining to the spouse)
      -to remove ex-spouse's name from any and all beneficiary, or trustee, or attorney-in-fact designations

   d.   Remarriage:
      -to include new spouse in documents
      -to undertake marital deduction (QTIP) planning
      -to provide for all of the person's children of all marriages
      -to consider a premarital agreement

   e.   Death, separation or divorce of any child: to review all documents for names of all beneficiary, or trustee, or attorney-in-fact designations

   f.   Family estate becomes medium sized: to undertake gift and estate tax planning

   g.   Retirement:
      -if moving to a different state, to write new will/trust documents that conform to laws of the new state
      -to execute durable powers of attorney
      -to drop life and disability insurance coverages
      -to discuss nursing home plans with children

h. Death of spouse:
    -to encourage the person not to make any drastic changes (e.g. sell home) for several months
    -to revise will/trust
    -to undertake post-mortem tax planning
    -to remove spouse's name from all beneficiary, or trustee, or attorney-in-fact designations

i. Death of parent:
    -to revise will/trust, based on changed wealth due to bequests from parent
    -to revise other documents, deleting parent's name from planning

j. Changes in tax laws:
    -to revise all tax related documents, including wills, revocable trusts, durable powers, and property agreements.
    -to consider gifting in light of changed tax laws

k. A change in the value of the person's business:
    -to adopt a business buyout agreement
    -to consider revising the overall estate plan, in view of potential change in estate tax

l. A change in the person's state of residency: to consider revising all documents and planning strategies, in the light of changed local law

ENDNOTES

1. California Probate Code § 15642(b)(6)(B)

2. IRC § 2206.

3. IRC § 2207.

4. IRC § 2207A.

5. IRC § 2207B.

6. UPC § 2-603.

7. *Pollock v. Phillips* 41 S.E. 2d 242 (W. Va., 1991).

8. In *Marsman v. Nasca* 573 N.E. 2d 1025 (Mass. App. 1991), the court exonerated an attorney-trustee's "abuse of discretion," where a trust clause exculpated the trustee from liability except for "willful neglect or fraud." For a contrary holding see, *First Alabama Bank of Huntsville v. Spraquins* 515 S. 2d 962 (Ala. 1987).

9. "How much sharper than a serpent's tooth it is to have a thankless child." *King Lear*, Act 1, Scene V.

10. See <http://www.census.gov/population/projections>.

11. For example, see California Probate Code § 2590-95.

12. Rev. Rul. 8623004

13. Modified version of the sample form contained in Charles M. Hamann. "Durable Powers of Attorney," *Trusts and Estates*, February 1983, pp. 30-31.

14. *Estate of Casey v. Commissioner*, 948 F2d. 895 (1991). Also see LR 9231003.

15. *J. Ridenour Estate*, 46 TCM 1850 (1992).

16. California Civil Code § 2480.5.

17. 42 USC § 1396. The Omnibus Budget Reconciliation Act of 1993, besides increasing the period from thirty months, made several other restrictive changes, reflecting Congressional interest in discouraging spend down planning.

18. Wall Street Journal articles on December 3 and 4, 1992. Both on page A1.

19. 110 S.Ct. 2841 (1990)

20. *Lancet*, Sept. 11, 1993, p. 645.

CHAPTER 18

Postmortem Tax Planning

OVERVIEW

The estate planning process does not end at the client's death. Assets must still be marshaled, preserved, and distributed by the decedent's representatives, a group that includes executors, trustees, accountants, attorneys, and survivors. In the transmission process, tax law often enables these aides to recommend and make choices. This chapter focuses on the tax elections available to them as parties dealing in the decedent's property. The technical detail in this chapter is testimony to the claim that estate administration after the client's death can involve complex tax issues requiring the expert advice of an estate planning attorney, not one conducting a general law practice.

The chapter will begin with an overview of the principles of postmortem tax compliance, better known as the preparation of tax returns. Next, it will survey those planning devices primarily designed to reduce income taxes, including estate expense elections, choice of tax year, and distribution-planning strategies. Finally, the chapter will present those planning devices primarily designed to save death taxes, including the alternate valuation date, the use of disclaimers, and the decision to make the QTIP election.

TAX RETURNS AFTER DEATH

We already know that the death of an individual may trigger estate and inheritance taxes. But can the transfer of a decedent's property be done free of income tax? Will the death of an income-earning individual terminate the obligation to pay taxes on all income received thereafter? Of course, the answer to both questions is no, because income ordinarily subject to taxation will be received by survivors, estates, and trusts. If income ordinarily subject to taxation is being received, you can be sure that the Internal Revenue Code imposes a tax on that income in the year that a recipient receives it.

Since death can create or continue the obligation to pay transfer and income taxes, we must first study the nature of these tax obligations and their effects on the survivors. Several transfer tax and income tax returns will usually be filed after the client's death. This section will introduce principles of postmortem federal tax compliance, that is, the completion of federal tax returns and the payment of federal taxes on income and on property in connection with the death of a decedent.

Transfer Taxes

With regard to transfer taxes, the decedent's representatives may be required to file a state inheritance or estate tax return, and a federal estate tax return. The federal return is due nine months after the date of death. As discussed previously, until repeal takes place in 2010, a federal estate tax return must be filed if the total gross estate plus adjusted taxable gifts equals or exceeds the applicable exclusion amount (AEA) for the year of death (e.g., equal to, or over, $1.5 million in 2004). For example, the estate of a decedent who dies in 2004, having a gross estate of $1.3 million and adjusted taxable gifts of $800,000 must file a return because the sum exceeds the AEA by $100,000. Filing is required even if no estate tax will be due, as in the case where the entire estate is left to a surviving spouse or debts drop the taxable estate below the AEA.

Income Taxes

For many estates, the personal representatives will be required to file at least two sets of state and federal income tax returns. First, the decedent's final income tax return will be reported on Federal Form 1040 and on the comparable state income tax form (unless the state of domicile was one of the few that has no state income tax). These returns will cover all income for the last tax year up to, and including, the date of death. Second, if the decedent leaves a probate estate or a living trust, an estate fiduciary income tax return, Form 1041 and its state counterpart, will be filed for each tax year of the estate's existence. The fiduciary return for the first year will report all income starting with the day after the decedent's date of death to the end of the first tax year. When the estate is terminated, usually by final distribution, the last estate income tax return will be filed for a "short" year, from the beginning of the tax year to the date of distribution. After the estate terminates, the beneficiaries will report the income from distributed estate property on their own tax returns.

The following example summarizes these federal income tax rules and assumes that all taxpayers report taxes on a calendar year basis; that is, their tax year begins January 1 and ends December 31. Actually, an estate need not use a calendar year. Planning the using a fiscal rather than a calendar year will be discussed later in the chapter.

> EXAMPLE 18 - 1. Farley, a widower, died on May 12, 2000. In his will, Farley left 100 shares of XYZ stock outright to his son Jordan, and the residue of his estate in trust for the benefit of his granddaughter Sheila. The date of final estate distribution to Jordan and to the trust was February 25, 2002. The following post-death tax returns were filed. All income earned by the decedent from January 1 through May 12, 2000, was reported by the executor on the decedent's final income tax return, Form 1040. All income earned by the estate between May 13 and December 31, 2000, was reported by the executor on the first estate income tax return, Form 1041. The executor filed a second Form 1041 return for all estate income for the entire year 2001, and a third for income earned during the period from January 1 to February 25, 2002. Jordan reported on his Form 1040 all income received on the stock after February 25, 2002. Trust property income, or DNI, earned after that date will either be reported by the trust on Form 1041or by Sheila on her Form 1040, to the extent the income is actually distributed to her.

All capital gains income on trust property will be reported by the trust except in the trust's last year, when these gains will be "carried out" and reported by the beneficiaries. All non-grantor trusts must use a calendar tax year.

A joint return may be filed for a decedent and the surviving spouse for the year of death, covering income of the decedent to the date of death and income of the spouse for the entire year.[1] Alternatively, returns may be filed for each spouse separately. In most situations, filing jointly will save total taxes in the same way it does when both spouses are alive. The greater the difference between the two spousal incomes, the greater the tax usually saved by filing jointly. The surviving spouse will also be permitted to enjoy the lower rates applicable to joint returns for two years after the decedent's death, provided that he or she (a) has not remarried and (b) maintains a home for one or more dependent children.[2]

Next, we turn to postmortem income tax planning ideas.

PLANNING DEVICES TO REDUCE INCOME TAXES

Some postmortem planning strategies are primarily undertaken to reduce the income tax bite. They include various expense elections, selection of probate estate tax year, and distribution planning. Before examining these techniques, let us survey three tax principles on which most of them will be based.

First, income tax is reduced when taxable income can be spread among taxpaying entities. Proper pre-death planning can result in the creation of additional taxpaying entities after the client's death. These tax entities can include the estate, several trusts (with at least one trust for each beneficiary), and the beneficiaries themselves. After death, proper timing of distributions among these entities can often save significant tax dollars, as we shall see.

A second tax principle on which postmortem income tax planning is based is the notion of the conduit. The conduit principle prevents double taxation of estate or trust income. It is derived from the concept of distributable net income, or DNI, which is roughly equal to the estate or trust's fiduciary accounting income. DNI constitutes the maximum amount of income taxable to the beneficiaries, as well as the maximum amount deductible by the estate or trust. The amount taxable to an estate or trust roughly equals its total income, including capital gains and losses, reduced by the distribution deduction, which roughly equals the lesser of the amount distributed or its DNI. Thus, a trust or estate that distributes all of its income will be taxed only on its capital gains. Consequently, under the conduit principle, DNI earned by an estate or trust which is distributed to the beneficiaries in the year earned will be taxed to the beneficiaries and not to the estate or trust, which simply acts as a conduit for delivering income from the source to the beneficiaries. Conversely, any DNI retained by the estate or trust will not be offset by a distribution deduction, which will make that DNI taxable to the trust or estate rather than to the beneficiaries.

A third tax principle on which postmortem income tax planning is based is that in the year in which an estate or trust makes its final distribution, all income, including capital gains, will be carried out to and taxed to the beneficiaries. Thus in its termination year, a trust or estate will have no taxable income.

These tax principles represent only the briefest summary of the principles of income taxation of estates and trusts detailed in Chapter 8. The reader is strongly urged to review that more comprehensive section before continuing.

Expense Elections Available to the Executor

During administration, the executor is able to make several informal elections with regard to estate expenses. We will refer to the executor's ability to make elections because the executor is the person having that legal authority. Of course, most executors rely on their attorney or accountant to apprize them of the tax alternatives. These elections include the medical expense election, the administration expense and losses election, and the election to waive the executor's commission. They are covered next.

Medical expense. Any of the decedent's unreimbursed medical expenses which are unpaid at death may be deducted either on the decedent's final income tax return or on the federal estate tax return, but not on both.[3] The choice of where to deduct unpaid medical expenses will depend on which alternative will yield the greater tax savings. The amount of tax saved is a function of the marginal tax rates which are influenced by the size of the estate tax base and the amount of the decedent's income.

Smaller estates may be unable to benefit from a deduction on either return. If deducted on the income tax return, only the excess of the medical expense amount over 7.5% of adjusted gross income is deductible. Any nondeductible amount may not be deducted on the estate tax return. With regard to the estate tax return, no estate tax may be due for smaller estates, either because no estate tax return need be filed or because other deductions, particularly the marital deduction, may reduce the taxable estate to zero.

Administration expenses and losses. Expenses in administering the decedent's estate, including executor's commission, attorney's fees, and casualty losses, are deductible either on the federal estate tax return or on the estate income tax return, or partly on each.[4] However, double deductions are not allowed.

Again, the choice of where to deduct these items will usually turn on which return will produce the greater tax savings. And again, smaller estates may be unable to enjoy a deduction on either return. Casualty losses are deductible against income only to the extent that they exceed 10% of adjusted gross income. And there may be no estate tax to save in the case of a small estate, or any size estate for that matter, if the estate simply passes to the surviving spouse. Larger estates not incorporating a 100% marital deduction often will be able to choose because they can save taxes on either return. Generally, if an amount is deductible on another return, it is imprudent to deduct it on any estate tax return that can already shelter all taxable estate property with the unified credit or with the marital deduction.

The executor's commission. The executor's commission, as a deductible administration expense, is taxable as income to the executor. However, the executor may elect to waive (i.e., refuse) that commission. Waiver of the commission may be worthwhile if the executor is a residuary beneficiary of the estate and if his or her personal marginal income tax rate exceeds the marginal tax rate for both the estate tax and the estate income tax. If the executor is not a residuary beneficiary of the estate, a waiver of the commission will mean a complete forfeit of that amount. Thus, the non-residuary executor will usually prefer to receive the commission, regardless of the tax cost.

EXAMPLE 18 - 2. An estate has been left entirely to the decedent's daughter, who is the executor. The executor's commission will be $10,000. The estate's marginal estate tax rate is 41% and its marginal income tax rate is 28%. The daughter's marginal income tax rate is 31%. Not waiving the commission will lower the estate tax by $4,100 and raise daughter's income tax by $3,100, for a net tax saving of $1,000.

EXAMPLE 18 - 3. Facts similar to the last example, except that the decedent left his entire estate to his spouse, who is executor. Due to the unlimited marital deduction, the effective marginal estate tax rate is 0%. Regarding income tax rates, assuming that the spouse's effective marginal rate is 31%, and the estate's marginal rate is 28%, waiving the commission will raise the estate income tax by $2,800 and lower the spouse's income tax by $3,100, for a net tax saving of $300.

EXAMPLE 18 - 4. Facts similar to the prior example, except that the entire estate has been left outright to the decedent's children by a former marriage. Waiving the executor's commission would mean totally forfeiting the receipt of that amount. As executor, the spouse, not wishing to forfeit all cash flow from the estate, elects to take the commission. Instead of receiving nothing, the spouse will receive $6,900, after tax, from the estate.

Selection of Estate Taxable Year

The executor of a probate estate has considerable flexibility in choosing the estate's income tax year. Although all income tax years except the first and the last must be 12 months long, the executor can choose the estate's tax year to end on the last day of any month. If it ends on December 31, the estate is said to be on a *calendar year* with the first tax year from the date of death to December 31. All other tax years will then run from January 1 to December 31, except for the year of final distribution of the estate assets, which will run for a "short year" from January 1 to date of distribution. Alternatively, if the estate's elected tax year ends on the last day of any month other than December, it is said to be on a *fiscal year*.

Whether an estate is on a calendar year or fiscal year, two basic income tax benefits are available to it. First, the estate is a separate taxpaying entity, capable of splitting income with the other tax entities involved in the estate distribution process. However, by increasing tax rates and by radically compressing bracket amounts for estates, tax reform since 1986 has reduced the tax saving benefit of splitting income.

Second, tax saving can be realized in the first and last tax years of an estate's life, since both years are usually shorter than 12 months. The first tax year is shorter because date of death does not usually coincide with the last day of the tax year. The last tax year is shorter than 12 months because the date of final distribution seldom coincides with the last day of the tax year. A short tax year produces income tax savings because proportionately less income is ordinarily taxed in those years.

In contrast to the tax benefits available to all estates, some benefits are available only to estates having a carefully selected fiscal year. Regardless of when income is actually distributed to a beneficiary, it will be treated for tax purposes as though it was distributed on the last day of the estate's tax year. In each of the next two examples, assume that the decedent died on March 10, 2000.

> EXAMPLE 18 - 5. The estate of a decedent is planning the distribution of income to its beneficiary, the surviving spouse. It elects a fiscal year ending January 31. If the estate distributes income earned during March of 2001 to the spouse during the month of November, 2001, it will be treated as though she received it on January 31, 2002, and the spouse will not have to report the income until April 15, 2003, more than two full years after the income was initially received by the estate.

If the executor of an estate expects an unusually large income receipt shortly after the period of administration begins, he or she may wish to elect a year end which would give it a rather short first year, so that other taxable income received later will be taxed during the following year rather than lumped with the large receipt and taxed at a higher rate.

> EXAMPLE 18 - 6. Decedent Malley was an accountant who died on May 19 owning, among other things, account receivables amounting to $50,000. The estate elects a fiscal year ending July 31 to include most of this income in the first tax year, while causing most other income to be taxed in the second and later years.

On the other hand, a relatively long first tax year would be desirable if a large deduction is expected within 6 to 12 months from the date of death.

> EXAMPLE 18 - 7. Combined with a large amount of early income, as in example 18 - 8, the estate expects to make a large distribution to the beneficiaries in April of the following year. The estate instead elects a fiscal year closing on April 30, so that the deduction can be used to reduce the estate's taxable income.

Distribution Planning

Although federal tax reform since 1986 reduced income tax rates substantially for all tax entities, an estate or trust may be able to save some income tax for its beneficiaries by properly planning the amount and timing of beneficiary distributions. Much of distribution planning hinges on the existence of differentials in marginal tax rates, and thus one of the planner's tasks is to compare the tax rates of the various entities and allocate taxable income to those in lower brackets. In this section, we will consider situations where the beneficiaries are, alternatively, in a higher bracket and in a lower bracket in comparison with the distributing estate or trust. This section will also examine the income tax advantage of prolonging the estate's life.

Estate or trust in lower bracket than beneficiaries. When the estate or trust is in a lower income tax bracket than its beneficiaries, consideration should be given to distribution arrangements that will generate a greater taxable income to itself and a correspondingly lesser taxable income to its beneficiaries. The main limitation is the very compressed estate and trust tax brackets that result in the estate or trust being in the top income tax bracket with income of less than $10,000.

Accumulation of income. The most common device used accumulates income by reducing and delaying distributions of DNI. However, with the very compressed marginal rates for estates and trusts, the amount of tax savings is minimal.

EXAMPLE 18 - 8. Jonathan died earlier this year, leaving his entire estate to his wife, Kathleen. The estate has earned some income this year but elects not to distribute it to Kathleen until next year. This year, Kathleen, who has earned considerable income herself, is also recipient of a large lump-sum pension distribution from Jonathan's employer. Consequently, her income is taxed at the very highest marginal rates. The estate can hold back nine thousand dollars to at least use up its lower marginal rates.

Realization of a gain. Another way to benefit from the estate or trust having a lower tax rate than the beneficiaries is through the realization of a gain. If an estate asset has appreciated after death and is expected to be sold soon after its receipt by the designated beneficiary, the executor of a lower-bracket estate should give consideration to selling the asset prior to distribution so that the estate can recognize the gain. The after-tax proceeds can be distributed to the beneficiary tax-free, assuming all DNI has already been distributed. However, to be taxed to the estate, the sale will have to be made before its last taxable year so that the gain is not automatically "carried out" to the beneficiary.

Despite having a lower marginal tax rate, the executor of an estate may wish to distribute rather than sell the asset if the beneficiary has a realized loss that is presently unusable for lack of any offsetting gains. The beneficiary, who could sell the asset, then would not have to carry over an unused loss to future years.

Estate or trust in higher marginal tax bracket than beneficiaries. In cases where an estate or trust is subject to a higher marginal income tax rate than one or more of its beneficiaries, the executor or trustee may prefer to distribute income to them in the year the income is received, so that it is taxed at the beneficiaries lower rate. In addition, when the estate or trust's tax year overlaps those of the beneficiaries, the executor or trustee can time the distribution so that it is made in one of two years in which the beneficiaries' tax rate is lower.

> EXAMPLE 18 - 9. In the month of November, Arleen, the sole beneficiary of her dad's estate, lost her job as a law firm associate. She was contemplating either opening her own office or going to business school for a year. To help her out, the executor elects a fiscal year end of February 28 and distributes $50,000 (out of income) to her in early December. Since the estate's fiscal year ends February 28, the distribution is treated as having been made on that date, hence Arleen will report the income in a year in which she expects to be in a low tax bracket, even though she received it in a year in which she was in a high tax bracket.

Unduly prolonging the probate estate. By now, the reader is aware of several potential income tax advantages to having a probate estate remain open. This will encourage some executors to delay closing their estates. Since termination of an estate by final distribution cuts off the tax benefits available to this separate taxpayer, tax planning would suggest undertaking this ploy by delaying the estate's date of final distribution. However, the IRS has authority to treat an estate as terminated for tax purposes if it concludes that the estate's life had been "unduly" prolonged.[5]

How long can an estate usually be kept open without generating IRS disapproval? Some authorities believe that a reasonable life is about three to four years for an ordinary estate, and as long as 15 years for an estate which elects to defer payment of taxes under § 6166. However, the income tax benefit from prolonging an estate's life has been significantly curtailed in recent years due to tax reform's compression of income tax rates.

PLANNING DEVICES TO REDUCE DEATH TAXES

We turn now to an examination of several postmortem tax planning strategies which have their greatest impact on death taxes. They include the alternate valuation date election, disclaimers, the QTIP election, and several other miscellaneous techniques discussed briefly in earlier chapters.

Alternate Valuation Date Election

The size of the estate tax for an estate is a direct function of the value of the interests includible in the gross estate. An intelligent executor or estate adviser will try to keep valuation as low as possible. Often, conflicts with the IRS arise regarding the correct valuation of particular estate assets and deductions. While such conflicts make the entire subject of estate valuation seem quite subjective, there is one specific rule in this field that offers some objective certainty. The Code allows the executor the option to value estate assets and deductions at one of two different points in time.

Under § 2032, the value of the assets included in the gross estate (and corresponding liabilities) may be determined as of the date of death, or they may be determined as of the alternate valuation date (AVD), which is six months after the date of death. This section was enacted after the Great Depression to limit the adverse tax and liquidity effects that radical changes in market values could have on an estate. For example, consider a decedent who died just before the 1929 crash owning a considerable amount of stock, which had to be included in the gross estate at high, pre-crash date-of-death values. By the time the taxes were due, the value of the estate might be less than the taxes owed.

Under AVD rules, the executor may not pick and choose which assets to value at which of the two dates. If the election is made, all assets (and deductions) must be valued at the AVD. However, any assets sold or distributed after death and before the AVD must be valued as of that sale or distribution date.

Prior to 1984, the AVD election was permitted in situations where it increased the gross estate, thereby resulting in a greater step-up in basis for assets owned at death. For income tax purposes, this strategy was attractive for estates completely sheltered by the unified credit and/or marital deduction.

Section 2032(c) now permits the AVD election only if it reduces both the value of the gross estate and the estate tax (and GST tax, if any).

Of course making the AVD election has income tax ramifications, with a smaller step-up (or greater step-down), a lower estate tax value will save estate tax but it might also result in additional income taxes when assets are sold. Since the minimum effective marginal estate tax rate (i.e., just above the AEA) is 41% in 2003 (45% in 2004) while the maximum capital gains tax rate is likely to be around 20%, the AVD election should lower net taxes by 21 cents for every dollar of reduced valuation. In addition, if the inherited asset is not sold, the AVD advantage increases to at least 41 cents per dollar. Finally, even if the heir chooses to sell the asset, a time value of money savings results to the extent that the income tax is likely to be paid later than the estate tax.

Effective Disclaimers

A disclaimer is an unqualified refusal to accept a gift. We have already studied disclaimers in two earlier chapters. First, in Chapter 7, covering the federal gift tax, we examined the transfer tax aspects of disclaimers, including the requirements for a valid disclaimer. Second, in Chapter 12, surveying marital deduction and bypass planning, we saw how a disclaimer provision could be included in a bypass arrangement to add postmortem flexibility to the client's estate plan. That discussion also mentioned several disadvantages of the use of disclaimers. The purpose of the present discussion is to add additional detail to disclaimer planning, in the context of general postmortem planning.

Because of the requirement that the disclaiming donor cannot have accepted any interest in the benefits, the client's survivors must be told as soon as possible not to accept the decedent's property or income if a disclaimer is anticipated. The following material describes three general situations where disclaimers can be effectively utilized. They include spousal disclaimers to reduce the marital deduction, disclaimers by a nonspouse to increase the size of the marital deduction, and disclaimers to correct defective or inefficient dispositive documents.

Spousal disclaimer to reduce the marital deduction. We have seen how a spousal disclaimer of a marital deduction bequest can add postmortem flexibility by enabling the surviving spouse to choose the amount of the marital bequest to disclaim to the bypass share, thereby self-determining the amount of estate tax to defer to the second death. That section was described as Option 4, "100% marital deduction with disclaimer into bypass," in which the surviving spouse was bequeathed the entire amount of the decedent spouse's estate, subject to S2's ability to disclaim all or part of it in the event that a bypass eventually became desirable.

The marital deduction disclaimer can be used for any size estate but is probably most needed for certain rapidly appreciating smaller estates. For example, a plan for an estate that is currently too small to justify the use of a bypass could include a disclaimer provision, available in the event that the estate grew large enough to warrant a bypass distribution.

On the other hand, the disclaimer can also work well in larger estates in which S1 has under-utilized the GST exemption. The surviving spouse, at S1's death, may be able to disclaim assets being received outright into a GST exemption credit shelter bypass trust or QTIP trust.

Factors that may help the surviving spouse decide whether and how much to disclaim include S2's needs and his or her income tax bracket. First, the greater S2's perceived need for S1's assets to live comfortably, the less S2 will probably be willing to disclaim. This, in turn, will depend on the size of S2's estate. Of course, by disclaiming, S2 would not ordinarily be relinquishing all interests in the property, since the typical recipient bypass or QTIP trust provides for some invasion powers and for most or all income to be paid to S2. However, many S2s are still likely to react emotionally that, by disclaiming, they are in reality making a complete relinquishment.

Second, S2's willingness to disclaim will also depend on his or her marginal income tax rate. If S2's rate is high, a disclaimer is desirable because it has the effect of redirecting taxable income to other beneficiaries.

Disclaimer by a nonspouse to increase the marital deduction. A disclaimer can be used to raise a marital deduction that is subsequently found to be inadequate. For example, a client may have died with an estate plan that neither included a bypass nor took full use of the unlimited marital deduction. This can occur when a person dies intestate or dies owning a considerable amount of property in joint tenancy with someone other than a spouse. The nonspouse beneficiary may be encouraged to disclaim the interest so that it may qualify for the marital deduction by passing to the surviving spouse. However, problems in implementation may arise. First, only a donee of property held in joint tenancy may disclaim.[6] Thus, such a disclaimer will work only if the decedent was the original donor of the property. Second, courts may be unwilling to allow the guardian of a minor child (or unborn child) to disclaim rights to property, reasoning that full relinquishment of property is not in the child's best interest. However, since a disclaimer cannot be made by a person until he or she reaches age 21, a disclaimer that is delayed until the disclaimant reaches majority might be effective.

Third, until recently, the IRS had been taking the position that the disclaimer had to be made within nine months of the date the joint tenancy was created, rather than the date of death. After losing in the courts, the IRS acquiesced with regard to joint tenancies where state law gives the joint tenant the right to sever the joint tenancy or cause the property to be partitioned.[7] In other words, disclaimers of joint interests may not be valid in some states. For example, a qualified disclaimer is not permitted for tenancy by the entirety property because it cannot be partitioned by one spouse without the permission of the other.[8]

Disclaimers to correct defective and inefficient dispositive documents. Occasionally, wills and trusts are drafted erroneously. One always hopes that these mistakes will be discovered during the client's lifetime. If not, they can still often be corrected by disclaimer. For example, a disclaimer may also be used to refuse an undesirable bequest of a general power of appointment.

> EXAMPLE 18 - 10. Barbara died seven months ago leaving a will that provides for a bypass trust for the benefit of her husband, Jake. The will gives Jake the right to invade the trust for reasons of "health or happiness." Since courts have consistently held that the term happiness does not constitute an ascertainable standard, Jake will be deemed to be the holder of a general power of appointment over the entire trust corpus, which will be includible in Jake's gross estate at his later death. Jake may be able to prevent this unfortunate result by properly disclaiming his power over the corpus.

A disclaimer can also be used to overcome an inefficient disposition, thereby increasing the size of a charitable contribution.

> EXAMPLE 18 - 11. Sally, a widow, was 90 years old when she died six months ago. She left one surviving relative, her son Abbott, who is 73 and in failing health. Sally's will, paraphrased somewhat, reads, "All to Abbott, but if he does not survive me by 30 days, then all to the Girl Scouts of America." Abbott, who should be able to live for 30 days but is not likely to live more than six months, has no issue and would not mind leaving all of the property inherited from his mother to the Girl

Scouts. To avoid taxation of the property in Sally's estate, Abbott could disclaim all interest in Sally's bequest. Consequently, the property would pass to the Girl Scouts without being subject to taxation in Sally's estate.

A disclaimer may be made with respect to an undivided portion of an interest, which the IRS defines as a fraction or percentage of each and every substantial interest owned by the disclaimant extending over the entire term of the disclaimant's interest.[9]

> EXAMPLE 18 - 12. Lynn survived her husband, who bequeathed her 100 shares of stock outright and a life estate in trust property producing $10,000 in annual income. Lynn may disclaim fewer than 100 shares of the stock, and she may disclaim a life estate in less than $10,000 annually of the trust property. But she may not disclaim only a remainder interest in the stock, or only a term for years portion of her life estate, such as for the first five years of the income.

These examples are merely illustrative of the many situations where post-mortem disclaimers can be used to alter estate dispositions to obtain more desirable results.[10] Disclaimers are generally considered to be an extremely powerful estate planning tool. It should be noted that since the stakes can be quite high in this technical area of the law, the client is encouraged to seek competent counsel prior to attempting to make a qualified disclaimer.

QTIP Election Planning

Overview. As covered in detail previously, property normally can qualify for the marital deduction only if it "passes" to the spouse. In other words, the spouse cannot ordinarily receive an interest that might terminate; the interest cannot be terminable. Over the years, however, the code has carved out several exceptions to this rule. Up to 1982, the most commonly used marital trust designed to take advantage of an exception was the power of appointment trust, i.e., the one giving the spouse a life estate in the income and a general power of appointment over the corpus.[11] Since then, the QTIP trust, based on the QTIP election exception, has become far more popular. It is found in § 2056(b)(7) and provides that property subject to a terminable interest can qualify for the marital deduction if it meets the following two requirements for "qualified terminable interest property:"

1. The surviving spouse must be entitled to receive all income from the property for life, payable at least annually.
2. No person may have the power to appoint the property to anyone other than the surviving spouse.

Why might a person wish to bequeath only a terminable interest to his or her spouse? Why might a person prefer not to give marital deduction property to the spouse outright, or in trust with the spouse receiving a general power of appointment over the property? Why restrict a spouse's ability to control disposition of the property? There are several possible reasons, including the desire to protect the estate from the consequences of S2's immaturity or senility and the goal of protecting assets from the surviving spouse's creditors. But perhaps the most common reason is a desire by S1 to absolutely guarantee the ultimate disposition to an intended remainder beneficiary. The typical S1 choosing a QTIP arrangement has children of a former marriage and wishes to provide for the surviving spouse's income needs during lifetime, yet still absolutely ensure that his or her own children will eventually receive the property after the surviving spouse's death. Only a QTIP-type arrangement will do all this and still qualify the property for the marital deduction.

Some planners also recommend the QTIP plan for clients still married to their first spouse to eliminate the risk that their surviving spouse might remarry and leave substantial property to the new spouse rather than the children. Others disagree, pointing out that most S2s either do not remarry or act prudently when they do.

Uniqueness of the QTIP election. In contrast with the decision as to who will ultimately receive the property outright, the final decision whether to make that election to claim a marital deduction for QTIP property is not be up to S1, and in contrast with the spousal disclaimer, it is not S2, instead, S1's executor makes the choice on S1's estate tax return.

Deferral versus equalization revisited. If the election is made, the QTIP property can qualify for the S1 marital deduction, and S1's taxable estate and estate tax will be reduced. However, at S2's death, the S2 date of-death value of the qualifying property must be taxed as though it were includible in S2's gross estate.[12] The estate of S2 will receive reimbursement from the QTIP trust for the tax incurred by it.[13]

Thus, in considering the QTIP election, the S1 executor must choose one of the following two tax consequences: (1) making the election will defer the estate tax by reducing the S1 taxable estate and increasing the S2 taxable estate; or, alternatively, (2) not making the election will accelerate the estate tax by producing a larger S1 taxable estate, but can result in a smaller S2 taxable estate, via bypass. The choice whether to make the election essentially boils down to a tax issue: whether to defer or to equalize spousal estate tax. As we approach 2010, most estates will choose to defer with the hope that no estate tax will ever have to be paid. Keep in mind that the S1 executor's QTIP election has nothing to do with determining who will receive the property; the trust terms decide that and, except for the possibility of disclaimer by a beneficiary, it is no longer subject to change by anyone.

QTIP election versus disclaimer. The use of disclaimers and of the QTIP election enable a surrogate decision maker to decide on behalf of the deceased client whether to defer the estate tax. One advantage of the QTIP alternative over the disclaimer is the ability to delay the decision an additional six months. While a disclaimer must usually be made within nine months after date of death, a QTIP election is made on the federal estate tax return which, when including a 6-month extension to file, allows up to 15 months after the date of death before a decision must be made.

Perhaps the most fundamental difference between the disclaimer and the QTIP arrangement concerns the amount of control S2 is given over the assets involved. Often, it is the single deciding factor in making the choice. Thus, if the client wishes the spouse to have complete control, an outright transfer anticipating the possibility of a disclaimer will be preferred. If, on the other hand, minimal S2 control is desired, a transfer to a QTIP trust will be the better choice.

Additional Postmortem Tax-Saving Devices

Three other postmortem tax elections often available to the estates of business owners include the IRC § 6166 election to pay the estate tax in installments, the § 303 redemption of stock, and the § 2032A special-use valuation election. These elections were covered in some detail earlier in the text and are mentioned here just as a reminder that the elections are not made until after the business owner dies.

This chapter has focused on postmortem planning techniques designed to reduce income and death taxes. They have been the subject of this last chapter because they represent, conceptually, the final phase of planning undertaken on behalf of an individual.

QUESTIONS AND PROBLEMS

1. List the federal tax returns that may have to be filed during a period of administration of a decedent's property.

2. Maxie, a widower, died recently, leaving his $2 million gross estate to his brother Morey. Maxie spent the last six months in a hospital, paying $50,000 of the $80,000 hospital bill before he died. Marginal tax rates for the taxpaying entities are as follows: Maxie's final Form 1040, 31%; the Form 1041, 28%; the Form 706, 41%. Determine how much tax Maxie's estate will save if the allowable expense is deducted, alternatively, on: (a) Form 706; (b) Form 1040; and (c) Form 1041.

3. Moose died recently, leaving his entire $2 million gross estate to his wife, Trixie, who is named executor. Assume that the only estate expense is the executor's commission of $100,000. Marginal tax rates for the taxpaying entities are: Trixie's Form 1040, 31%; the final Form 1040, 15%; the Form 1041, 28%; the Form 706, 41%.

   a. Should Trixie accept or waive the commission? Why?
   b. Where, if at all, should the estate deduct the commission? Why?
   c. Would your answers to parts "a" and "b" change if Moose's net estate was $200,000?
   d. Would your answers to parts "a" and "b" probably change if Trixie, the executor, was Moose's cousin to whom Moose left nothing by will or otherwise? Assume a $2 million taxable estate.

4. Describe the income tax advantages available to all estates and those advantages available only to estates having a carefully chosen fiscal year.

5. How can the executor of an estate or the trustee of a trust reduce income taxes by planning the distributions to beneficiaries if the beneficiaries marginal tax rates are: (a) Higher than that of the estate or trust? (b) Lower than that of the estate or trust?

6. What is the benefit of prolonging an estate's life, and what is the tax consequence if it is "unduly" prolonged?

7. What two conditions must be met before an estate can make the alternate valuation date election? What is the tax advantage? When are assets valued?

8. Give two specific examples where a disclaimer can reduce the estate tax.

9. Describe the unique contribution of a QTIP arrangement to estate planning.

10. Is it clearly erroneous for an executor to fail to take the marital deduction on QTIP property when doing so would eliminate taxes on S1's estate?

11. (a) Can a QTIP arrangement and a disclaimer provision be alternative methods of achieving a common objective? Why or why not? (b) Which places greater property rights in the hands of S2? Why?

12. Brunk owned three assets at his death. Their description and appraised values at date of death, six months after death and nine months after death, respectively, are as follows: Home and furnishings, $300,000, $320,000, $340,000; securities, $800,000, $700,000, $600,000; and an interest in a closely held business, $500,000, $400,000, $300,000. Brunk bequeathed all assets to his son, who, as executor, sold the home for $310,000 four months after Brunk died, and sold the business for $320,000 eight months after Brunk died. If Brunk's executor makes a § 2032 election, calculate Brunk's gross estate.

13. With regard to the QTIP election: (a) Who makes it? (b) If the election is made, will it influence either the ultimate disposition of the property, or taxation of the qualifying property, or both? (c) If the election is not made, how will the tax result change?

ANSWERS TO THE QUESTIONS AND PROBLEMS *(odd numbered only)*

1. Federal tax returns:

   a. Estate tax: Form 706, due nine months after date of death.
   b. Income tax:

      1. Form 1040: Decedent's final income tax return, for all income for the last year up to the date of death.
      2. Form 1041: Estate income tax return (if there is a probate estate), for each tax year of the estate's existence.
      3. Form 1041: Trust income tax return for each tax year of any trust created by the decedent.

3. a. If Trixie accepts the $100,000 commission, that amount will be taxable income to her, resulting in an income tax outlay of 31 % * ($100,000) = $31,000. If the expense is deducted on the 706, estate tax will not be reduced, because the entire estate is already sheltered by the marital deduction and the exemption equivalent of the unified credit.

   If, alternatively, the expense is deducted on the estate's 1041, there will be an estate income tax saving of ($100,000) * 28% = $28,000. Thus, Trixie should waive the commission because it will result in a net increase in her after-tax proceeds of $31,000 - $28,000 = $3,000.

   b. The estate should not pay or deduct the commission, for the reasons mentioned above.

   c. The results would change. Trixie would be indifferent between waiving and accepting the commission. At equal marginal tax rates, the tax saved on the form 1041 would just equal the higher tax on Trixie's 1040. However, cutting the hypothetical gross estate to $200,000 would not in itself alter the results. For any size estate, a 100% marital deduction would prevent additional tax savings with other deductions. Thus, the effective marginal estate tax rate would still be 0%.

   d. The answers would very likely change. Trixie would probably rather accept the commission. Her after-tax proceeds would be $69,000, which is far better than receiving nothing.

5. Tax planning for distributions to beneficiaries:
   a. When the estate or trust is in a lower bracket than the beneficiaries, it should consider accumulating income, realizing gains, and, if it is an estate, prolonging its life.
   b. When the estate is in a higher bracket, it should use the conduit principle to distribute income in the year received.

7. The alternate valuation date election can reduce the value of assets in the gross estate, and therefore the estate tax, if their total value six months after date of death is lower (higher) than the date-of-death value.

9. The unique contribution of a QTIP arrangement to estate planning is to enable property (remainder interest) which will not at all pass to S2 to qualify for the marital deduction.

11. a. Yes, a QTIP arrangement and a disclaimer provision can be alternative methods of achieving the same objective, which is estate tax minimization. Both typically enable S2 to decide whether to qualify certain property for the marital deduction and, consequently, to determine the size of the bypass share.
    b. The disclaimer provision will place greater property rights in the hands of S2 because, if S2 does not disclaim, he or she will receive it. On the other hand, the QTIP election only influences estate taxation, not property disposition; disposition of the property is in complete control of S1.

13. a. The executor of the estate of S1 makes the election, since S1 is the decedent whose document qualifies for the QTIP election.
    b. If the QTIP election is made, it will influence taxation of the qualifying property, but not its disposition. Except for adjustments for payment of estate tax, all named beneficiaries will still receive their designated shares. Tax wise, the property will be deductible from S1's gross estate and included in S2's gross estate at his or her later death.
    c. If the QTIP election is not made, the qualifying property will be included in S1's taxable estate and not included (via bypass) in S2's estate. Thus, a greater bypass may increase S1 estate tax (but only if, under simple assumptions, the bypass becomes greater than the AEA.

ENDNOTES

1. IRC § 6013(a)(2).

2. IRC §§ 1(a)(2); 2(a)(1).

3. IRC §§ 213; 2053

4. Reg. § 1.642 (g)-2.

5. Reg. § 1.641(b)-3(a).

6. Reg § 25.2518-2(c)(4)(I).

7. LR 9106016; TAM 9208003.

8. LR 9208003.

9. Reg. § 25.2518-3(b).

10. For an example of an unsuccessful disclaimer to correct a defect in a trust intended to achieve QTIP treatment, see *Estate of Bennett*, 100 TC No. 5 (1993).

11. IRC § 2056(b)(5).

12. IRC § 2044.

13. IRC § 2207(a).

Tax and Valuation Tables

TABLE 1 Federal Unified Transfer-Tax Rates - Since 1/1/77

If the Amount is:		Tentative Tax:		
Over	But Not Over	Base Amount	+ Percent	On Excess Over

For years (1976-2009) the marginal rates are the same for taxable transfers up to $2,000,000.

Over	But Not Over	Base Amount	Percent	On Excess Over
$0	$10,000	$0	18%	$0
$10,000	$20,000	$1,800	20%	$10,000
$20,000	$40,000	$3,800	22%	$20,000
$40,000	$60,000	$8,200	24%	$40,000
$60,000	$80,000	$13,000	26%	$60,000
$80,000	$100,000	$18,200	28%	$80,000
$100,000	$150,000	$23,800	30%	$100,000
$150,000	$250,000	$38,800	32%	$150,000
$250,000	$500,000	$70,800	34%	$250,000
$500,000	$750,000	$155,800	37%	$500,000
$750,000	$1,000,000	$248,300	39%	$750,000
$1,000,000	$1,250,000	$345,800	41%	$1,000,000
$1,250,000	$1,500,000	$448,300	43%	$1,250,000
$1,500,000	$2,000,000	$555,800	45%	$1,500,000

Top Rates: 1977 through 1981

Over	But Not Over	Base Amount	Percent	On Excess Over
$2,000,000	$2,500,000	$780,800	49%	$2,000,000
$2,500,000	$3,000,000	$1,025,800	53%	$2,500,000
$3,000,000	$3,500,000	$1,290,800	57%	$3,000,000
$3,500,000	$4,000,000	$1,575,800	61%	$3,500,000
$4,000,000	$4,500,000	$1,880,800	65%	$4,000,000
$4,500,000	$5,000,000	$2,205,800	69%	$4,500,000
$5,000,000		$2,550,800	70%	$5,000,000

Top Rates: 1982

Over	But Not Over	Base Amount	Percent	On Excess Over
$2,000,000	$2,500,000	$780,800	49%	$2,000,000
$2,500,000	$3,000,000	$1,025,800	53%	$2,500,000
$3,000,000	$3,500,000	$1,290,800	57%	$3,000,000
$3,500,000	$4,000,000	$1,575,800	61%	$3,500,000
$4,000,000		$1,880,800	65%	$4,000,000

Top Rates: 1983

Over	But Not Over	Base Amount	Percent	On Excess Over
$2,000,000	$2,500,000	$780,800	49%	$2,000,000
$2,500,000	$3,000,000	$1,025,800	53%	$2,500,000
$3,000,000	$3,500,000	$1,290,800	57%	$3,000,000
$3,500,000		$1,575,800	60%	$3,500,000

Top Rates: 1984 - 1986

Over	But Not Over	Base Amount	Percent	On Excess Over
$2,000,000	$2,500,000	$780,800	49%	$2,000,000
$2,500,000	$3,000,000	$1,025,800	53%	$2,500,000
$3,000,000		$1,290,800	55%	$3,000,000

(Rate Table Continued)

Top Rates: 1987 - 1997

$2,000,000	$2,500,000	$780,800	49%	$2,000,000
$2,500,000	$3,000,000	$1,025,800	53%	$2,500,000
$3,000,000	$10,000,000	$1,290,800	55%	$3,000,000
$10,000,000	$21,040,000	$5,140,800 **	60%	$10,000,000
$21,040,000		$11,764,800	55%	$21,040,000

Top Rates: 1998 - 2001

$2,000,000	$2,500,000	$780,800	49%	$2,000,000
$2,500,000	$3,000,000	$1,025,800	53%	$2,500,000
$3,000,000	$10,000,000	$1,290,800	55%	$3,000,000
$10,000,000	$17,184,000	$5,140,800 **	60%	$10,000,000
$17,184,000		$9,451,200	55%	

Top Rates: 2002

$2,000,000	$2,500,000	$780,800	49%	$2,000,000
$2,500,000		$1,025,800	50%	$2,500,000

Top Rate: 2003

$2,000,000		$780,800	49%	$2,000,000

Top Rate: 2004

$2,000,000		$780,800	48%	$2,000,000

Top Rate: 2005

$2,000,000		$780,800	47%	$2,000,000

Top Rate: 2006

$2,000,000		$780,800	46%	$2,000,000

Top Rate: 2007-2009

$2,000,000		$780,800	45%	$2,000,000

2010 and beyond

Realed for Etates. The maximum rate for gifts is 35% starting at $500,000.

** From 1988-1997, transfers between $10,000,000 and $21,040,000 were subject to a 5% surcharge imposed until the benefit of the unified credit and of lower marginal rates was taken back. Transfers taking place 1998-2001 have the 5% surcharge applied to transfers between $10,000,000 and $17,184,000 (taking back the benefit of the lower rates, but not the benefit of the unified credit). The surcharge is eliminated for transfers after 2001.

TABLE 2 Unified Credits (UCr), Applicable Exclusion Amounts (AEA), and the End of the Bubble by Year Since 1977

Year	UCr Estates	AEA Estates	End of Bubble	UCr Gifts	AEA Gifts
1977	$30,000	$120,667		$30,000	$120,667
1978	$34,000	$134,000		$34,000	$134,000
1979	$38,000	$147,333		$38,000	$147,333
1980	$42,500	$161,563		$42,500	$161,563
1981	$47,000	$175,625		$47,000	$175,625
1982	$62,800	$225,000	*The 5%*	$62,800	$225,000
1983	$79,300	$275,000	*surcharge*	$79,300	$275,000
1984	$96,300	$325,000	*started in*	$96,300	$325,000
1985	$121,800	$400,000	*1988*	$121,800	$400,000
1986	$155,800	$500,000		$155,800	$500,000
1987	$192,800	$600,000		$192,800	$600,000
1988	$192,800	$600,000	$21,040,000	$192,800	$600,000
1989	$192,800	$600,000	$21,040,000	$192,800	$600,000
1990	$192,800	$600,000	$21,040,000	$192,800	$600,000
1991	$192,800	$600,000	$21,040,000	$192,800	$600,000
1992	$192,800	$600,000	$21,040,000	$192,800	$600,000
1993	$192,800	$600,000	$21,040,000	$192,800	$600,000
1994	$192,800	$600,000	$21,040,000	$192,800	$600,000
1995	$192,800	$600,000	$21,040,000	$192,800	$600,000
1996	$192,800	$600,000	$21,040,000	$192,800	$600,000
1997	$192,800	$600,000	$21,040,000	$192,800	$600,000
1998	$202,050	$625,000	$17,184,000	$202,050	$625,000
1999	$211,300	$650,000	$17,184,000	$211,300	$650,000
2000	$220,550	$675,000	$17,184,000	$220,550	$675,000
2001	$220,550	$675,000	$17,184,000	$220,550	$675,000
2002	$345,800	$1,000,000		$345,800	$1,000,000
2003	$345,800	$1,000,000	*and it*	$345,800	$1,000,000
2004	$555,800	$1,500,000	*ended in*	$345,800	$1,000,000
2005	$555,800	$1,500,000	*2002*	$345,800	$1,000,000
2006	$780,800	$2,000,000		$345,800	$1,000,000
2007	$780,800	$2,000,000		$345,800	$1,000,000
2008	$780,800	$2,000,000		$345,800	$1,000,000
2009	$1,455,800	$3,500,000		$345,800	$1,000,000
after 2009	Estate tax repealed. Gift tax at the top individual income tax rate.			$330,800	$1,000,000

TABLE 3A Credit For State Death Taxes 1977 - 2001

Taxable Estate(TA)		Base	Rate	R Applied to
At Least	But Not Over	Amount	(R)	TA Over
$100,000	$150,000	$0	0.8%	$100,000
$150,000	$200,000	$400	1.6%	$150,000
$200,000	$300,000	$1,200	2.4%	$200,000
$300,000	$500,000	$3,600	3.2%	$300,000
$500,000	$700,000	$10,000	4.0%	$500,000
$700,000	$900,000	$18,000	4.8%	$700,000
$900,000	$1,100,000	$27,600	5.6%	$900,000
$1,100,000	$1,600,000	$38,800	6.4%	$1,100,000
$1,600,000	$2,100,000	$70,800	7.2%	$1,600,000
$2,100,000	$2,600,000	$106,800	8.0%	$2,100,000
$2,600,000	$3,100,000	$146,800	8.8%	$2,600,000
$3,100,000	$3,600,000	$190,800	9.6%	$3,100,000
$3,600,000	$4,100,000	$238,800	10.4%	$3,600,000
$4,100,000	$5,100,000	$290,800	11.2%	$4,100,000
$5,100,000	$6,100,000	$402,800	12.0%	$5,100,000
$6,100,000	$7,100,000	$522,800	12.8%	$6,100,000
$7,100,000	$8,100,000	$650,800	13.6%	$7,100,000
$8,100,000	$9,100,000	$786,800	14.4%	$8,100,000
$9,100,000	$10,100,000	$930,800	15.2%	$9,100,000
$10,100,000		$1,082,800	16.0%	$10,100,000

Note: the brackets found in §2011 have been adjusted by adding $60,000 at each level, hence you use the taxable estate without adjustment, i.e., do not subtract $60,000.

TABLE 3B Credit For State Death Taxes 2002 - 2004

Taxable Estate(TA)		Year 2002		Year 2003		Year 2004	
At Least	But Not Over	Base Amount	Rate (R)	Base Amount	Rate (R)	Base Amount	Rate (R)
$100,000	$150,000	$0	0.6%	$0	0.4%	$0	0.2%
$150,000	$200,000	$300	1.2%	$200	0.8%	$100	0.4%
$200,000	$300,000	$900	1.8%	$600	1.2%	$300	0.6%
$300,000	$500,000	$2,700	2.4%	$1,800	1.6%	$900	0.8%
$500,000	$700,000	$7,500	3.0%	$5,000	2.0%	$2,500	1.0%
$700,000	$900,000	$13,500	3.6%	$9,000	2.4%	$4,500	1.2%
$900,000	$1,100,000	$20,700	4.2%	$13,800	2.8%	$6,900	1.4%
$1,100,000	$1,600,000	$29,100	4.8%	$19,400	3.2%	$9,700	1.6%
$1,600,000	$2,100,000	$53,100	5.4%	$35,400	3.6%	$17,700	1.8%
$2,100,000	$2,600,000	$80,100	6.0%	$53,400	4.0%	$26,700	2.0%
$2,600,000	$3,100,000	$110,100	6.6%	$73,400	4.4%	$36,700	2.2%
$3,100,000	$3,600,000	$143,100	7.2%	$95,400	4.8%	$47,700	2.4%
$3,600,000	$4,100,000	$179,100	7.8%	$119,400	5.2%	$59,700	2.6%
$4,100,000	$5,100,000	$218,100	8.4%	$145,400	5.6%	$72,700	2.8%
$5,100,000	$6,100,000	$302,100	9.0%	$201,400	6.0%	$100,700	3.0%
$6,100,000	$7,100,000	$392,100	9.6%	$261,400	6.4%	$130,700	3.2%
$7,100,000	$8,100,000	$488,100	10.2%	$325,400	6.8%	$162,700	3.4%
$8,100,000	$9,100,000	$590,100	10.8%	$393,400	7.2%	$196,700	3.6%
$9,100,000	$10,100,000	$698,100	11.4%	$465,400	7.6%	$232,700	3.8%
$10,100,000		$812,100	12.0%	$541,400	8.0%	$270,700	4.0%

Note: the brackets found in §2011 have been adjusted by adding $60,000 at each level, hence you use the taxable estate without adjustment, i.e., do not subtract $60,000.

TABLE 4 Federal Gift Tax Rates prior to January 1, 1977

Taxable Gift*		Gift Tax		
At Least	But Not Over	Base Amount	Plus Percent	On Excess Over
$0	$5,000	$0	2.25%	$0
$5,000	$10,000	$113	5.25%	$5,000
$10,000	$20,000	$375	8.25%	$10,000
$20,000	$30,000	$1,200	10.50%	$20,000
$30,000	$40,000	$2,250	13.50%	$30,000
$40,000	$50,000	$3,600	16.50%	$40,000
$50,000	$60,000	$5,250	18.75%	$50,000
$60,000	$100,000	$7,125	21.00%	$60,000
$100,000	$250,000	$15,525	22.50%	$100,000
$250,000	$500,000	$49,275	24.00%	$250,000
$500,000	$750,000	$109,275	26.25%	$500,000
$750,000	$1,000,000	$174,900	27.75%	$750,000
$1,000,000	$1,250,000	$244,275	29.25%	$1,000,000
$1,250,000	$1,500,000	$317,400	31.50%	$1,250,000
$1,500,000	$2,000,000	$396,150	33.75%	$1,500,000
$2,000,000	$2,500,000	$564,900	36.75%	$2,000,000
$2,500,000	$3,000,000	$748,650	39.75%	$2,500,000
$3,000,000	$3,500,000	$947,400	42.00%	$3,000,000
$3,500,000	$4,000,000	$1,157,400	44.50%	$3,500,000
$4,000,000	$5,000,000	$1,378,650	47.25%	$4,000,000
$5,000,000	$6,000,000	$1,851,150	50.25%	$5,000,000
$6,000,000	$7,000,000	$2,353,650	52.50%	$6,000,000
$7,000,000	$8,000,000	$2,878,650	54.75%	$7,000,000
$8,000,000	$10,000,000	$3,426,150	57.00%	$8,000,000
$10,000,000		$4,566,150	57.75%	$10,000,000

* Taxable amount after the annual exclusion and the gift exemption.

WARNING:

THESE ARE **PRE-1977 GIFT** TAX RATES

TABLE 5 Federal Estate Rates prior to January 1, 1977

| Taxable Estate* | | Estate Tax | | |
At Least	But Not Over	Base Amount	Plus Percent	On Excess Over
$0	$5,000	$0	3.0%	$0
$5,000	$10,000	$150	7.0%	$5,000
$10,000	$20,000	$500	11.0%	$10,000
$20,000	$30,000	$1,600	14.0%	$20,000
$30,000	$40,000	$3,000	18.0%	$30,000
$40,000	$50,000	$4,800	22.0%	$40,000
$50,000	$60,000	$7,000	25.0%	$50,000
$60,000	$100,000	$9,500	28.0%	$60,000
$100,000	$250,000	$20,700	30.0%	$100,000
$250,000	$500,000	$65,700	32.0%	$250,000
$500,000	$750,000	$145,700	35.0%	$500,000
$750,000	$1,000,000	$233,200	37.0%	$750,000
$1,000,000	$1,250,000	$325,700	39.0%	$1,000,000
$1,250,000	$1,500,000	$423,200	42.0%	$1,250,000
$1,500,000	$2,000,000	$528,200	45.0%	$1,500,000
$2,000,000	$2,500,000	$753,200	49.0%	$2,000,000
$2,500,000	$3,000,000	$998,200	53.0%	$2,500,000
$3,000,000	$3,500,000	$1,263,200	56.0%	$3,000,000
$3,500,000	$4,000,000	$1,543,200	59.0%	$3,500,000
$4,000,000	$5,000,000	$1,838,200	63.0%	$4,000,000
$5,000,000	$6,000,000	$2,468,200	67.0%	$5,000,000
$6,000,000	$7,000,000	$3,138,200	70.0%	$6,000,000
$7,000,000	$8,000,000	$3,838,200	73.0%	$7,000,000
$8,000,000	$10,000,000	$4,568,200	76.0%	$8,000,000
$10,000,000		$6,088,200	77.0%	$10,000,000

* Taxable amount after the estate exemption.

WARNING:

THESE ARE **PRE-1977 ESTATE** TAX RATES

TABLE 6 Federal Income Tax Rates: Estates and Trusts - 2001

Taxable Income

Over	But not over	Base amount	+ percent	On excess over
$0	$1,800	$0.00	15.0%	$0
$1,800	$4,250	$270.00	28.0%	$1,800
$4,250	$6,500	$956.00	31.0%	$4,250
$6,500	$8,900	$1,653.50	36.0%	$6,500
$8,900	....	$2,517.50	39.6%	$8,900

Table 7 Estate Planning Indexed Values

Year	Annual Exclusion Regular	Annual Exclusion Non-US Spouse	GSTT Exemption	6601j 2% portion on 6166 payments	2032A Special Use	"Kiddie Tax" Threshold
1987						**$1,000**
1997	**$10,000**	**$100,000**	**$1,000,000**	**$1,000,000**	**$750,000**	$1,300
1998	$10,000	$100,000	$1,000,000	$1,000,000	$750,000	$1,400
1999	$10,000	$101,000	$1,010,000	$1,010,000	$760,000	$1,400
2000	$10,000	$103,000	$1,030,000	$1,030,000	$770,000	$1,400
2001	$10,000	$106,000	$1,060,000	$1,060,000	$800,000	$1,500
2002	$11,000	$110,000	$1,100,000	$1,100,000	$820,000	$1,500
2003	$11,000	$112,000	$1,120,000	$1,120,000	$840,000	$1,500
2004			$1,500,000			

Numbers in bold indicate the base amount and the base year for indexing. Shown are only those years in which a change occurred for at least one of the items. For years after 2003, the GST tax exemption will equal the estate applicable exclusion amount for the year.

ACTUARIAL VALUE TABLES

Note: Tables that follow are taken from Department of the Treasury's *Internal Revenue Service Publication 1457* (7-1999), *Actuarial Values Book Aleph*. We will use the designation for each table as is used by the Treasury, i.e., Tables K, S, B, and 90CM. The Mortality Table (90 CM) is drawn from the 1990 census. We can expect Table S and Table 90 CM to be updated once the 2000 census information is digested by the U.S. Department of Health and Human Services, Public Health Service, National Center for Health Statistics, however, the 1990 updates were not published until April of 1999.

Table K

Adjustment Factors for Annuities Payable at the End of Each Interval

Interest Rate	Annually	Semi-Annually	Quarterly	Monthly	Weekly
6%	1.0000	1.0148	1.0222	1.0272	1.0291
8%	1.0000	1.0196	1.0295	1.0362	1.0387
10%	1.0000	1.0244	1.0368	1.0450	1.0482
12%	1.0000	1.0292	1.0439	1.0539	1.0577

The factors in Table K are used to adjust the values for annuities when the payments are made other than annually.

TABLE B -Term Certain

PV of Annuity (A), Income Interest (Inc. Int.), & Remainder Interests

	(6%) Six Percent				(8%) Eight Percent		
Year	A	Inc.Int.	REM	Year	A	Inc.Int.	REM
1	.09434	.056604	.943396	1	0.9259	.074074	.925926
2	1.8334	.110004	.889996	2	1.7833	.142661	.857339
3	2.6730	.160381	.839619	3	2.5771	.206168	.793832
4	3.4651	.207906	.792094	4	3.3121	.264970	.735030
5	4.2124	.252742	.747258	5	3.9927	.319417	.680583
6	4.9173	.295039	.704961	6	4.6229	.369830	.630170
7	5.5824	.334943	.665057	7	5.2064	.416510	.583490
8	6.2098	.372588	.627412	8	5.7466	.459731	.540269
9	6.8017	.408102	.591898	9	6.2469	.499751	.500249
10	7.3601	.441605	.558395	10	6.7101	.536807	.463193
15	9.7122	.582735	.417265	15	8.5595	.684758	.315242
20	11.4699	.688195	.311805	20	9.8181	.785452	.214548
25	12.7834	.767001	.232999	25	10.6748	.853982	.146018
30	13.7648	.825890	.174110	30	11.2578	.900623	.099377
35	14.4982	.869895	.130105	35	11.6546	.932365	.067635
40	15.0463	.902778	.097222	40	11.9246	.953969	.046031
45	15.4558	.927350	.072650	45	12.1084	.968672	.031328
50	15.7619	.945712	.054288	50	12.2335	.978679	.021321
55	15.9905	.959433	.040567	55	12.3186	.985489	.014511
60	16.1614	.969686	.030314	60	12.3766	.990124	.009876

TABLE B -Term Certain

PV of Annuity (A), Income Interest (Inc. Int.), & Remainder Interests

	(10%) Ten Percent				(12%) Twelve Percent		
Year	A	Inc.Int.	REM	Year	A	Inc.Int.	REM
1	0.9091	.090909	.909091	1	0.8929	.107143	.892857
2	1.7355	.173554	.826446	2	1.6901	.202806	.797194
3	2.4869	.248685	.751315	3	2.4018	.288220	.711780
4	3.1699	.316987	.683013	4	3.0373	.364482	.635518
5	3.7908	.379079	.620921	5	3.6048	.432573	.567427
6	4.3553	.435526	.564474	6	4.1114	.493369	.506631
7	4.8684	.486842	.513158	7	4.5638	.547651	.452349
8	5.3349	.533493	.466507	8	4.9676	.596117	.403883
9	5.7590	.575902	.424098	9	5.3282	.639390	.360610
10	6.1446	.614457	.385543	10	5.6502	.678027	.321973
15	7.6061	.760608	.239392	15	6.8109	.817304	.182696
20	8.5136	.851356	.148644	20	7.4694	.896333	.103667
25	9.0770	.907704	.092296	25	7.8431	.941177	.058823
30	9.4269	.942691	.057309	30	8.0552	.966622	.033378
35	9.6442	.964416	.035584	35	8.1755	.981060	.018940
40	9.7791	.977905	.022095	40	8.2438	.989253	.010747
45	9.8628	.986281	.013719	45	8.2825	.993902	.006098
50	9.9148	.991481	.008519	50	8.3045	.996540	.003460
55	9.9471	.994711	.005289	55	8.3170	.998037	.001963
60	9.9672	.996716	.003284	60	8.3240	.998886	.001114

TABLE S - Single Life

PV of Annuity (A), Life Estate (LE), & Remainder Interests (REM)

	(6%) Six Percent				(8%) Eight Percent		
Age	A	LE	REM	Age	A	LE	REM
0	16.1278	.96767	.03233	0	12.2534	.98027	.01973
5	16.1718	.97072	.02928	5	12.3295	.98636	.01364
10	16.0350	.96210	.03790	10	12.2666	.98133	.01867
15	15.8450	.95070	.04930	15	12.1759	.97407	.02593
20	15.6441	.93865	.06135	20	12.0859	.96687	.03313
25	15.3981	.92389	.07661	25	11.9728	.95782	.04218
30	15.0780	.90468	.09532	30	11.8146	.94517	.05483
35	14.6737	.88042	.11958	35	11.6027	.92821	.07179
40	14.1646	.84987	.15013	40	11.3191	.90553	.09447
45	13.5237	.81142	.18858	45	10.9390	.87504	.12496
50	12.7497	.76498	.23502	50	10.4515	.83612	.16388
55	11.8459	.71075	.28925	55	9.8543	.78834	.21166
60	10.8279	.64967	.35033	60	9.1507	.73206	.26794
65	9.7151	.58291	.41709	65	8.3490	.66792	.33208
70	8.4988	.50993	.49007	70	7.4325	.59460	.40540
75	7.2349	.43409	.56591	75	6.4407	.51526	.48474
80	5.9340	.35604	.64396	80	5.3768	.43015	.56985
85	4.6961	.28177	.71823	85	4.3268	.34614	.65386
90	3.5847	.21508	.78492	90	3.3518	.26814	.73186
95	2.7346	.16408	.83592	95	2.5872	.20698	.79302
100	2.1130	.12678	.87322	100	2.0188	.16151	.83849
105	1.5468	.09281	.90719	105	1.4939	.11951	.88049
109	0.4717	.02830	.97170	109	0.4630	.03704	.96296

TABLE S - Single Life

PV of Annuity (A), Life Estate (LE), & Remainder Interests (REM)

	(10%) Ten Percent				(12%) Twelve Percent		
Age	A	LE	REM	Age	A	LE	REM
0	9.8484	.98484	.01516	0	8.2240	.98688	.01312
5	9.9225	.99225	.00775	5	8.2908	.99490	.00510
10	9.8897	.98898	.01103	10	8.2712	.99254	.00746
15	9.8383	.98383	.01617	15	8.2377	.98852	.01148
20	9.7921	.97921	.02079	20	8.2108	.98529	.01471
25	9.7344	.97344	.02656	25	8.1783	.98139	.01861
30	9.6485	.96485	.03515	30	8.1274	.97529	.02471
35	9.5282	.95282	.04718	35	8.0539	.96646	.03354
40	9.3589	.93589	.06411	40	7.9464	.95357	.04643
45	9.1183	.91183	.08817	45	7.7860	.93431	.06569
50	8.7963	.87963	.12037	50	7.5628	.90753	.09247
55	8.3843	.83843	.16157	55	7.2672	.87206	.12794
60	7.8804	.78804	.21196	60	6.8944	.82732	.17268
65	7.2860	.72860	.27140	65	6.4421	.77305	.22695
70	6.5796	.65796	.34204	70	5.8863	.70636	.29364
75	5.7877	.57877	.42123	75	5.2438	.62926	.37074
80	4.9061	.49061	.50939	80	4.5044	.54053	.45947
85	4.0066	.40066	.59934	85	3.7271	.44725	.55275
90	3.1453	.31453	.68547	90	2.9613	.35535	.64465
95	2.4540	.24540	.75460	95	2.3332	.27999	.72001
100	1.9322	.19322	.80678	100	1.8524	.22229	.77771
105	1.4443	.14443	.85557	105	1.3976	.16771	.83229
109	0.4545	.04545	.95455	109	0.4464	.05357	.94643

TABLE 90 CM - Mortality Table

Age x	L(x)	Age x	L(x)	Age x	L(x)	Age x	L(x)
0	100,000						
1	99,064	31	96,934	61	84,490	91	14,466
2	98,992	32	96,791	62	83,368	92	12,066
3	98,944	33	96,642	63	82,169	93	9,884
4	98,907	34	96,485	64	80,887	94	7,951
5	98,877	35	96,322	65	79,519	95	6,282
6	98,850	36	96,150	66	78,066	96	4,868
7	98,826	37	95,969	67	76,531	97	3,694
8	98,803	38	95,780	68	74,907	98	2,745
9	98,783	39	95,581	69	73,186	99	1,999
10	98,766	40	95,373	70	71,357	100	1,424
11	98,750	41	95,156	71	69,411	101	991
12	98,734	42	94,928	72	67,344	102	672
13	98,713	43	94,687	73	65,154	103	443
14	98,681	44	94,431	74	62,852	104	284
15	98,635	45	94,154	75	60,449	105	175
16	98,573	46	93,855	76	57,955	106	105
17	98,497	47	93,528	77	55,373	107	60
18	98,409	48	93,173	78	52,704	108	33
19	98,314	49	92,787	79	49,943	109	17
20	98,215	50	92,370	80	47,084	110	0
21	98,113	51	91,918	81	44,129		
22	98,006	52	91,424	82	41,091		
23	97,896	53	90,885	83	37,994		
24	97,784	54	90,297	84	34,876		
25	97,671	55	89,658	85	31,770		
26	97,556	56	88,965	86	28,687		
27	97,441	57	88,214	87	25,638		
28	97,322	58	87,397	88	22,658		
29	97,199	59	86,506	89	19,783		
30	97,070	60	85,537	90	17,046		

TABLE §7520 Monthly Rates -The Factors for Valuing Split Interests (e.g., Life Estates & Remainders)

	91	92	93	94	95	96	97	98	99	00	01	02	03
Jan	9.8	8.2	7.6	6.4	9.6	6.8	7.4	7.2	5.6	7.4	6.8	5.4	
Feb	9.6	7.6	7.6	6.4	9.6	6.8	7.6	6.8	5.6	8.0	6.2	5.6	
Mar	9.4	8.0	7.0	6.4	9.4	6.6	7.8	6.8	5.8	8.2	6.2	5.4	
Apr	9.6	8.4	6.6	7.0	8.8	7.0	7.8	6.8	6.4	8.0	6.0	5.6	
May	9.6	8.6	6.6	7.8	8.6	7.6	8.2	6.8	6.2	7.8	5.8	6.0	
Jun	9.6	8.4	6.4	8.4	8.2	8.0	8.2	7.0	6.4	8.0	6.0	5.8	
Jul	9.6	8.2	6.6	8.2	7.6	8.2	8.0	6.8	7.0	8.0	6.2	5.6	
Aug	9.8	7.8	6.4	8.4	7.2	8.2	7.6	6.8	7.2	7.6	6.0	5.2	
Sep	9.6	7.2	6.4	8.4	7.6	8.0	7.6	6.6	7.2	7.6	5.8	4.6	
Oct	9.0	7.0	6.0	8.6	7.6	8.0	7.6	6.2	7.2	7.4	5.6	4.2	
Nov	8.6	6.8	6.0	9.0	7.4	8.0	7.4	5.4	7.4	7.2	5.0		
Dec	8.4	7.4	6.2	9.4	7.2	7.6	7.2	5.4	7.4	7.0	4.8		

Teaching Aids
CD ROM Contents

The Table that follows lists the files found on the Estate Planning and Taxation Teaching Aids CD ROM. The ETAX 2002 program is an EXCEL (Microsoft) spreadsheet file that will make estate and gift tax calculations through the year 2009. The next several files are Federal tax forms in "pdf" format, hence require Adobe Acrobat Reader to open. The Adobe program is available free at <http://www.adobe.com/products/acrobat/readermain.html>.

The code files are all in MS Word format so they can be searched using key words. The Internal Revenue Code file contains selected code sections deemed most relevant to estate planning. The Uniform Codes are reprinted with the permission of the National Conference of Commissioners on Uniform State Laws, 211 East Ontario Street, Suite 1300, Chicago, Illinois 60611. Following the File List Table are the Tables of Contents for the Internal Revenue Code Selections file and for each of the Uniform Code files.

TABLE OF FILES ON ESTATE PLANNING AND TAXATION TEACHING AIDS CD ROM

	Name of File	Size (KB)	Type
1.	ETAX 2002.XLS – Calculates Estate and Gift Tax	186	MS Excel
2.	Form 706 Estate Tax.pdf IRS Form	166	Adobe Acrobat Doc.
3.	Form 709 Gift Tax.pdf IRS Form	34	Adobe Acrobat Doc.
4.	Form 1041 Fiduciary Income Tax.pdf IRS Form	44	Adobe Acrobat Doc.
5.	Form 1041 Schedule K (beneficiary's share).pdf IRS Form	27	Adobe Acrobat Doc.
6.	IRC ESTATE PLANNING SELECTION.doc	701	MS Word Doc.
7.	UNIFORM ANATOMICAL GIFT ACT.doc	134	MS Word Doc.
8.	UNIFORM CUSTODIAL TRUST ACT.doc	134	MS Word Doc.
9.	UNIFORM DETERMINATION OF DEATH ACT.doc	42	MS Word Doc.
10.	UNIFORM FRAUDULENT TRANSFER ACT.doc	160	MS Word Doc.
11.	UNIFORM HEALTH-CARE DECISIONS ACT.doc	157	MS Word Doc.
12.	UNIFORM PARENTAGE ACT.doc	351	MS Word Doc.
13.	UNIFORM PROBATE CODE.doc	3,410	MS Word Doc.
14.	UNIFORM PREMARITAL AGREEMENT ACT.doc	74	MS Word Doc.
15.	UNIFORM PRINCIPAL AND INCOME ACT.doc	244	MS Word Doc.
16.	UNIFORM STATUTORY DURABLE POWERS FORM.doc	102	MS Word Doc.
17.	UNIFORM TRANSFERS TO MINORS ACT.doc	146	MS Word Doc.
18.	UNIFORM TRUST CODE.doc	685	MS Word Doc.

Internal Revenue Code: Selected Edited Sections

CHAPTER 1 - NORMAL TAXES AND SURTAXES
Subchapter J. Estates, Trusts, Beneficiaries, and Decedents
Part I - Estates, Trusts, and Beneficiaries
Subpart E - Grantors and Others Treated as Substantial Owners

§ 671:   Trust Income, Deductions, Credits Attributable to Grantors, and Others as Substantial Owners

§ 672:   Definitions and Rules

§ 673:   Reversionary Interests

§ 674:   Power to Control Beneficial Enjoyment

§ 675:   Administrative Powers

§ 676:   Power to Revoke

§ 677:   Income for Benefit of Grantor

§ 678:   Person Other than Grantor Treated As Substantial Owner

Part II - Income in Respect of Decedents

§ 691:   Recipients of Income in Respect of Decedents

Subchapter O - Gain or Loss on Disposition of Property
Part II - Basis Rules of General Application

§ 1014:   Basis of Property Acquired from a Decedent

§ 1015:   Basis of Property Acquired by Gifts and Transfers in Trust

§ 1022:   Treatment of Property Acquired from a Decedent Dying after December 31,2009.

§ 1040:   Use of Appreciated Carryover Basis Property to Satisfy Pecuniary Bequest

CHAPTER 11 - ESTATE TAX
Subchapter A. Estates of Citizens or Residents
Part I - Tax Imposed

§ 2001:   Imposition and Rate of Tax

§ 2002:   Liability for Payment

Part II - Credits Against Tax

§ 2010:   Unified Credit Against Estate Tax

§ 2011:   Credit for State Death Taxes

§ 2013:   Credit for Tax on Prior Transfers

§ 2014:   Credit for Foreign Death Taxes

Part III - Gross Estate

§ 2031:   Definition of Gross Estate

§ 2032:   Alternate Valuation

§ 2032A: Valuation of Certain Farm, Etc., Real Property

§ 2033:   Property in Which the Decedent Had an Interest

§ 2034:   Dower or Curtesy Interests

§ 2035:   Adjustments for Gifts Made within 3 Years of Decedent's Death

§ 2036:   Transfers with Retained Life Estate

§ 2037:   Transfers Taking Effect at Death

§ 2038:   Revocable Transfers

§ 2039:   Annuities

§ 2040:   Joint Interests

§ 2041:   Powers of Appointment

§ 2042:   Proceeds of Life Insurance

§ 2043:   Transfers for Insufficient Consideration

§ 2044:   Certain Property for which Marital Deduction was Previously Allowed

§ 2045:   Prior Interests

§ 2046:   Disclaimers

Part IV - Taxable Estate

§ 2051:   Definition of Taxable Estate

§ 2053:   Expenses, Indebtedness, and Taxes

§ 2054:   Losses

§ 2055:   Transfers for Public, Charitable, and Religious Use

§ 2056:   Bequests, etc., to Surviving Spouse

§ 2056A: Qualified domestic trust

§ 2057:   Family-owned Business Interests

Subchapter B. Nonresidents Not Citizens

§ 2101:   Tax Imposed

§ 2102:   Credit Against Tax

§ 2103:   Definition of Gross Estate

§ 2106:   Taxable Estate

§ 2107:   Expatriation to Avoid Tax

Subchapter C. Miscellaneous
   § 2201: Members of the Armed Forces Dying in Combat Zone or by Reason of Combat-zone-incurred Wounds, etc.
   § 2203: Definition of Executor
   § 2204: Discharge of Fiduciary from Personal Liability
   § 2205: Reimbursement Out of Estate
   § 2206: Liability of Life Insurance Beneficiaries
   § 2207A: Right of Recovery in the Case of Certain Marital Deduction Property
   § 2207B: Right of Recovery where Decedent Retained Interest

CHAPTER 12 - GIFT TAX
Subchapter A. Determination of Tax Liability
   § 2501: Imposition of Tax
   § 2502: Rate of Tax
   § 2503: Taxable Gifts
   § 2505: Unified Credit Against Gift Tax

Subchapter B. Transfers
   § 2511: Transfers in General
   § 2512: Valuation of Gifts
   § 2513: Gift by Husband or Wife to Third Party
   § 2514: Powers of Appointment
   § 2515: Treatment of Generation-skipping Transfer Tax
   § 2516: Certain Property Settlements
   § 2518: Disclaimers
   § 2519: Dispositions of Certain Life Estates

CHAPTER 13 - TAX ON GENERATION-SKIPPING TRANSFERS
Subchapter A. Tax Imposed
   § 2601: Tax Imposed
   § 2602: Amount of Tax
   § 2603: Liability for Tax
   § 2604: Credit for Certain State Taxes

Subchapter B. Generation-Skipping Transfers
   § 2611: Generation-Skipping Transfer Defined
   § 2612: Taxable Termination; Taxable Distribution; Direct Skip
   § 2613: Skip Person and Non-Skip Person Defined

Subchapter C. Taxable Amount
§ 2621: Taxable Amount in Case of Taxable Distribution
§ 2622: Taxable Amount in Case of Taxable Termination
§ 2623: Taxable Amount in Case of Direct Skip
§ 2624: Valuation

Subchapter D. GST Exemption
§ 2631: GST Exemption
§ 2632: Special Rules for Allocation of GST Exemption

Subchapter E. Applicable Rate; Inclusion Ratio
§ 2641: Applicable Rate
§ 2642: Inclusion Ratio

Subchapter F. Other Definitions and Special Rules
§ 2651: Generation Assignment
§ 2652: Other Definitions
§ 2653: Taxation of Multiple Skips

CHAPTER 14 - SPECIAL VALUATION RULES
§ 2701: Special Valuation Rules in Case of Transfers of Certain Interests in Corporations or Partnerships
§ 2702: Special Valuation Rules in Case of Transfers of Interests in Trusts
§ 2703: Certain Rights and Restrictions Disregarded
§ 2704: Treatment of Certain Lapsing Rights and Restrictions

CHAPTER 62 - TIME AND PLACE FOR PAYING TAX
Subchapter B. Extensions of Time for Payment
§ 6161: Extension of Time for Paying Tax
§ 6163: Extension of Time for Payment of Estate Tax on Value of Reversionary or Remainder Interest in Property
§ 6165: Bonds Where Time to Pay Tax or Deficiency Has Been Extended
§ 6166: Extension of Time for Payment of Estate Tax Where Estate Consists Largely of Interest in Closely Held Business

CHAPTER 67 - INTEREST
Subchapter A. Interest on Underpayments
§ 6601: Interest on Underpayment, nonpayment, or extensions of time for payment of tax

CHAPTER 77 - MISCELLANEOUS PROVISIONS
§ 7502: Timely Mailing Treated as Timely Filing and Paying
§ 7520: Valuation Tables

THE ANATOMICAL GIFT ACT (1987)

PURPOSE: To update the 1968 Uniform Anatomical Gift Act, which was adopted in every state, making organ procurement easier.

ORIGIN: Completed by the Uniform Law Commissioners in 1987

ENDORSED BY: American Bar Association

STATE ADOPTIONS:

Arizona	Minnesota	Pennsylvania
Arkansas	Montana	Rhode Island
California	Nevada	US Virgin Islands
Connecticut	New Hampshire	Utah
Hawaii	New Mexico	Vermont
Idaho	North Dakota	Virginia
Indiana	Oregon	Washington
Iowa		Wisconsin

2002 INTRODUCTIONS: Alabama

For any further information regarding the Revised Uniform Anatomical Gift Act, please contact John McCabe or Katie Robinson at 312-915-0195.

UNIFORM ANATOMICAL GIFT ACT (1987)

§ 1. Definitions.
§ 2. Making, Amending, Revoking, and Refusing to Make Anatomical Gifts by Individual.
§ 3. Making, Revoking, and Objecting to Anatomical Gifts, by Others.
§ 4. Authorization by [Coroner] [Medical Examiner] or [Local Public Health Official].
§ 5. Routine Inquiry and Required Request; Search and Notification.
§ 6. Persons Who May Become Donees; Purposes for Which Anatomical Gifts May Be Made.
§ 7. Delivery of Document of Gift.
§ 8. Rights and Duties at Death.
§ 9. Coordination of Procurement and Use.
§ 10. Sale or Purchase of Parts Prohibited.
§ 11. Examination, Autopsy, Liability.
§ 12. Transitional Provisions.
§ 13. Uniformity of Application and Construction.
§ 14. Severability.
§ 15. Short Title.
§ 16. Repeals.
§ 17. Effective Date.

UNIFORM CUSTODIAL TRUST ACT

PURPOSE: To enable lawyers to make the benefits of trusts available at low cost to people without extensive financial assets.

ORIGIN: Completed by the Uniform Law Commissioners in 1987.

ENDORSED BY:
American Bar Association
American Association of Retired Persons

STATE ADOPTIONS:

Alaska	Idaho	New Mexico
Arizona	Louisiana	North Carolina
Arkansas	Massachusetts	Rhode Island
Colorado	Minnesota	Virginia
District of Columbia	Missouri	Wisconsin
Hawaii	Nebraska	

For any further information regarding the Uniform Custodial Trust Act, please contact John McCabe, Katie Robinson, or Michael Kerr at 312-915-0195.

UNIFORM CUSTODIAL TRUST ACT

§ 1. Definitions
§ 2. Custodial Trust; General
§ 3. Custodial Trustee for Future Payment or Transfer
§ 4. Form and Effect of Receipt and Acceptance by Custodial Trustee, Jurisdiction
§ 5. Transfer to Custodial Trustee by Fiduciary or Obligor; Facility of Payment
§ 6. Multiple Beneficiaries; Separate Custodial Trusts; Survivorship
§ 7. General Duties of Custodial Trustee
§ 8. General Powers of Custodial Trustee
§ 9. Use of Custodial Trust Property
§ 10. Determination of Incapacity; Effect
§ 11. Exemption of Third Person from Liability
§ 12. Liability to Third Person
§ 13. Declination, Resignation, Incapacity, Death, or Removal of Custodial Trustee, Designation of Successor Custodial Trustee
§ 14. Expenses, Compensation, and Bond of Custodial Trustee
§ 15. Reporting and Accounting by Custodial Trustee; Determination of Liability of Custodial Trustee
§ 16. Limitations of Action Against Custodial Trustee
§ 17. Distribution on Termination
§ 18. Methods and Forms for Creating Custodial Trusts
§ 19. Applicable Law
§ 20. Uniformity of Application and Construction
§ 21. Short Title
§ 22. Severability
§ 23. Effective Date

THE UNIFORM DETERMINATION OF DEATH ACT

PURPOSE: To provide a comprehensive and medically sound basis for determining death in all situations.

ORIGIN: Completed by the Uniform Law Commissioners in 1980, in cooperation with the American Medical Association, the American Bar Association and the President's Commission on Medical Ethics.

ENDORSED BY: National Kidney Foundation; North American Transplant Coordinators Assn.; and American Nephrology Nurses' Association.

STATE ADOPTIONS:

Alabama	Michigan	Pennsylvania
Alaska	Minnesota	Puerto Rico
Arizona	Mississippi	Rhode Island
Arkansas	Missouri	South Carolina
California	Montana	South Dakota
Colorado	Nebraska	Tennessee
Connecticut	Nevada	Utah
Delaware	New Hampshire	Vermont
District of Columbia	New Mexico	Virgin Islands
Georgia	New York **	Washington
Idaho	North Carolina	West Virginia
Indiana	North Dakota	Wisconsin
Kansas	Ohio	Wyoming
Maine	Oklahoma	
Maryland	Oregon	

** *Substantially Similar*

For any further information regarding the Uniform Determination of Death Act, please contact John McCabe or Katie Robinson at 312-915-0195.

UNIFORM DETERMINATION OF DEATH ACT

§ 1.   Determination of Death.
§ 2.   Uniformity of Construction and Application.
§ 3.   Short Title.

UNIFORM FRAUDULENT TRANSFER ACT

PURPOSE: Providing a creditor with the capacity to procure assets a debtor has transferred to another person to keep them from being used to satisfy the debt.

ORIGIN: The Uniform Fraudulent Transfer Act, completed by the Uniform Law Commissioners in 1984, revises the Uniform Fraudulent Conveyance Act of 1918.

ENDORSED BY: Amercian Bar Association

STATE ADOPTIONS:

Alabama	Indiana	North Carolina
Arizona	Iowa	North Dakota
Arkansas	Kansas	Ohio
California	Maine	Oklahoma
Colorado	Massachusetts	Oregon
Connecticut	Michigan	Pennsylvania
Delaware	Minnesota	Rhode Island
District of	Missouri	South Dakota
Columbia	Montana	Texas
Florida	Nebraska	Utah
Georgia	Nevada	Vermont
Hawaii	New Hampshire	Washington
Idaho	New Jersey	West Virginia
Illinois	New Mexico	Wisconsin

2002 INTRODUCTIONS: Mississippi

For any further information regarding the Uniform Fraudulent Transfer Act, contact John McCabe, Katie Robinson, or Michael Kerr at 312-915-0195.

UNIFORM FRAUDULENT TRANSFER ACT

§ 1.   Definitions.
§ 2.   Insolvency.
§ 3.   Value.
§ 4.   Transfers Fraudulent as to Present and Future Creditors.
§ 5.   Transfers Fraudulent as to Present Creditors.
§ 6.   When Transfer Is Made or Obligation Is Incurred.
§ 7.   Remedies of Creditors.
§ 8.   Defenses, Liability, and Protection of Transferee.
§ 9.   Extinguishment of [Claim for Relief] [Cause of Action].
§ 10. Supplementary Provisions.
§ 11. Uniformity of Application and Construction.
§ 12. Short Title.
§ 13. Repeal.

UNIFORM HEALTH-CARE DECISIONS ACT

PURPOSE: The Uniform Health-Care Decisions Act aims at assisting individuals and the medical profession in better assuring a person's right to choose or reject a particular course of treatment. This act is designed to replace existing living will, power of attorney for health care, and family health-care consent statutes - topics now dealt with separately in most states.

ORIGIN: Approved by the Uniform Law Commissioners in 1993.

ENDORSED BY:
American Bar Association
American Association of Retired Persons
ABA Commission on Legal Problems of the Elderly

STATE ADOPTIONS:
Alabama
Delaware
Hawaii
Maine
Mississippi
New Mexico

For further information on the Uniform Health-Care Decisions Act, please contact John McCabe or Katie Robinson at 312-915-0195

UNIFORM HEALTH-CARE DECISIONS ACT

§ 1. Definitions.
§ 2. Advance Health-care Directives.
§ 3. Revocation of Advance Health-care Directive.
§ 4. Optional Form.
§ 5. Decisions by Surrogate.
§ 6. Decisions by Guardian.
§ 7. Obligations of Health-care Provider.
§ 8. Health-care Information.
§ 9. Immunities.
§ 10. Statutory Damages.
§ 11. Capacity.
§ 12. Effect of Copy.
§ 13. Effect of [Act].
§ 14. Judicial Relief.
§ 15. Uniformity of Application and Construction.
§ 16. Short Title.
§ 17. Severability Clause.
§ 18. Effective Date.
§ 19. Repeal

UNIFORM PARENTAGE ACT (2000)

PURPOSE: This act which revises the Uniform Parentage Act of 1973, modernizes the law for determining the parents of children, and facilitates modern methods of testing for parentage. With the rising incidence of children born to unmarried parents, parentage determinations must be improved for the enforcement of child support.

ORIGIN: Completed by the Uniform Law Commissioners in 2000.

ENDORSED BY:
ABA Family Law Section
National Child Support Enforcement Association
National Association of Public Health Registrars

STATE ADOPTIONS:
Texas
Washington

2002 INTRODUCTIONS:
Minnesota
West Virginia

For any further information regarding the Uniform Parentage Act, please contact John McCabe, Katie Robinson, or Michael Kerr at 312-915-0195

UNIFORM PARENTAGE ACT

Article 1. General Provisions
§ 101.   Short Title.
§ 102.   Definitions
§ 103.   Scope of [Act]; Choice of Law
§ 104.   Court of this State
§ 105.   Protection of Participants
§ 106.   Determination of Maternity

Article 2. Parent-child Relationship
§ 201.   Establishment of Parent-child Relationship
§ 202.   No Discrimination Based on Marital Status
§ 203.   Consequences of Establishment of Parentage
§ 204.   Presumption of Paternity in Context of Marriage

Article 3. Voluntary Acknowledgment of Paternity
§ 301.   Acknowledgment of Paternity
§ 302.   Execution of Acknowledgment of Paternity
§ 303.   Denial of Paternity
§ 304.   Rules for Acknowledgment and Denial of Paternity
§ 305.   Effect of Acknowledgment or Denial of Paternity
§ 306.   No Filing Fee
§ 307.   Proceeding for Rescission
§ 308.   Challenge after Expiration of Period for Rescission
§ 309.   Procedure for Rescission or Challenge
§ 310.   Ratification Barred
§ 311.   Full Faith and Credit
§ 312.   Forms for Acknowledgment and Denial of Paternity
§ 313.   Release of Information
[§ 314. Adoption of Rules]

Article 4. Registry of Paternity
Part 1. General Provisions
§ 401.   Establishment of Registry
§ 402.   Registration for Notification
§ 403.   Notice of Proceeding
§ 404.   Termination of Parental Rights: Child under One Year of Age
§ 405.   Termination of Parental Rights: Child at Least One Year of Age
Part 2. Operation of Registry
§ 411.   Required Form

§ 412. Furnishing of Information; Confidentiality

§ 413. Penalty for Releasing Information

§ 414. Rescission of Registration

§ 415. Untimely Registration

§ 416. Fees for Registry

Part 3. Search of Registries

§ 421. Search of Appropriate Registry

§ 422. Certificate of Search of Registry

§ 423. Admissibility of Registered Information

Article 5. Genetic Testing

§ 501. Scope of Article

§ 502. Order for Testing

§ 503. Requirements for Genetic Testing

§ 504. Report of Genetic Testing

§ 505. Genetic Testing Results; Rebuttal

§ 506. Costs of Genetic Testing

§ 507. Additional Genetic Testing

§ 508. Genetic Testing When Specimens Not Available

§ 509. Deceased Individual

§ 510. Identical Brothers

§ 511. Confidentiality of Genetic Testing

Article 6. Proceeding to Adjudicate Parentage

Part 1. Nature of Proceeding

§ 601. Proceeding Authorized

§ 602. Standing to Maintain Proceeding

§ 603. Parties to Proceeding

§ 604. Personal Jurisdiction

§ 605. Venue

§ 606. No Limitation: Child Having No Presumed, Acknowledged, or Adjudicated Father

§ 607. Limitation: Child Having Presumed Father

§ 608. Authority to Deny Motion for Genetic Testing

§ 609. Limitation: Child Having Acknowledged or Adjudicated Father

§ 610. Joinder of Proceedings

§ 611. Proceeding Before Birth

§ 612. Child as Party; Representation

Part 2. Special Rules for Proceeding to Adjudicate Parentage

§ 621. Admissibility of Results of Genetic Testing; Expenses
§ 622. Consequences of Declining Genetic Testing
§ 623. Admission of Paternity Authorized
§ 624. Temporary Order

Part 3. Hearings and Adjudication
§ 631. Rules for Adjudication of Paternity
§ 632. Jury Prohibited
§ 633. Hearings; Inspection of Records
§ 634. Order on Default
§ 635. Dismissal for Want of Prosecution
§ 636. Order Adjudicating Parentage
§ 637. Binding Effect of Determination of Parentage

Article 7. Child of Assisted Reproduction
§ 701. Scope of Article
§ 702. Parental Status of Donor
§ 703. Husband's Paternity of Child of Assisted Reproduction
§ 704. Consent to Assisted Reproduction
§ 705. Limitation on Husband's Dispute of Paternity
§ 706. Effect of Dissolution of Marriage
§ 707. Parental Status of Deceased Spouse

Article 8. Gestational Agreement
§ 801. Gestational Agreement Authorized
§ 802. Requirements of Petition
§ 803. Hearing to Validate Gestational Agreement
§ 804. Inspection of Records
§ 805. Exclusive, Continuing Jurisdiction
§ 806. Termination of Gestational Agreement
§ 807. Parentage under Validated Gestational Agreement
§ 808. Gestational Agreement: Effect of Subsequent Marriage
§ 809. Effect of Nonvalidated Gestational Agreement]

Article 9. Miscellaneous Provisions
§ 901. Uniformity of Application and Construction
§ 902. Severability Clause
§ 903. Time of Taking Effect
§ 904. Repeal
§ 905. Transitional Provision

Appendix: Federal IV-D Statute Relating to Parentage

THE UNIFORM PROBATE CODE

PURPOSE: To update and simplify most aspects of state probate law.

ORIGIN: Completed by the Uniform Law Commissioners in 1969, and substantially revised in 1975, 1982, 1987, 1989, 1990, and 1991. Note this 1993 version does not have the 2002 revisions. If permission of the Commissioners can be obtained, an updated version in MS Word format will be available for downloading at Sushibrain.com as soon as it is available. Because an updated version is expected shortly, the copy on the CD ROM, was converted to MS Word but was not further formatted for style.

APPROVED BY: American Bar Association

STATE ADOPTIONS:

Alaska	Michigan	North Dakota
Arizona	Minnesota	Pennsylvania
Colorado	Montana	South Carolina
Hawaii	Nebraska	South Dakota
Idaho	New Jersey	Utah
Maine	New Mexico	Wisconsin

2002 INTRODUCTIONS: Massachusetts

For any further information regarding the Uniform Probate Code, please contact John McCabe or Katie Robinson at 312-915-0195.

UNIFORM PROBATE CODE

ARTICLE, PART AND SECTION ANALYSIS
Article I **GENERAL PROVISIONS, DEFINITIONS AND PROBATE JURISDICTION OF COURT**

Part 1 **SHORT TITLE, CONSTRUCTION, GENERAL PROVISIONS**
1-101. [Short Title.]
1-102. [Purposes; Rule of Construction.]
1-103. [Supplementary General Principles of Law Applicable.]
1-104. [Severability.]
1-105. [Construction Against Implied Repeal.]
1-106. [Effect of Fraud and Evasion.]
1-107. [Evidence of Death or Status.]
1-108. [Acts by Holder of General Power.]

Part 2 **DEFINITIONS**
1-201. [General Definitions.]

Part 3 **SCOPE, JURISDICTION AND COURTS**
1-301. [Territorial Application.]
1-302. [Subject Matter Jurisdiction.]
1-303. [Venue; Multiple Proceedings; Transfer.]
1-304. [Practice in Court.]
1-305. [Records and Certified Copies.]
1-306. [Jury Trial.]
1-307. [Registrar;Powers.]
1-308. [Appeals.]
1-309. [Qualifications of Judge.]
1-310. [Oath or Affirmation on Filed Documents.]

Part 4 **NOTICE, PARTIES AND REPRESENTATION IN ESTATE LITIGATION AND OTHER MATTERS**
1-401. [Notice; Method and Time of Giving.]
1-402. [Notice; Waiver.]
1-403. [Pleadings; When Parties Bound by Others; Notice.]

Article II **INTESTACY, WILLS, AND DONATIVE TRANSFERS (1990)**
PART 1 **INTESTATE SUCCESSION**
2-101. Intestate Estate.
2-102. Share of Spouse.
2-102A. Share of Spouse.
2-103. Share of Heirs Other Than Surviving Spouse.
2-104. Requirement That Heir Survive Decedent For 120 Hours.
2-105. No Taker.
2-106. Representation.
2-107. Kindred of Half Blood.
2-108. Afterborn Heirs.
2-109. Advancements.
2-110. Debts to Decedent.
2-111. Alienage.
2-112. Dower and Curtesy Abolished.
2-113. Individuals Related to Decedent Through Two Lines.
2-114. Parent and Child Relationship.

PART 2 **ELECTIVE SHARE OF SURVIVING SPOUSE**
2-201. Definitions.
2-202. Elective Share.
2-203. Composition of the Augmented Estate.
2-204. Decedent's Net Probate Estate.
2-205. Decedent's Nonprobate Transfers to Others.
2-206. Decedent's Nonprobate Transfers to the Surviving Spouse.
2-207. Surviving Spouse's Property and Nonprobate Transfers to Others.
2-208. Exclusions, Valuation, and Overlapping Application.
2-209. Sources from Which Elective Share Payable.
2-210. Personal Liability of Recipients.
2-211. Proceeding for Elective Share; Time Limit.
2-212. Right of Election Personal to Surviving Spouse; Incapacitated Surviving Spouse.
2-213. Waiver of Right to Elect and of Other Rights.
2-214. Protection of Payors and Other Third Parties.

PART 3 **SPOUSE AND CHILDREN UNPROVIDED FOR IN WILLS**
2-301. Entitlement of Spouse; Premarital Will.
2-302. Omitted Children.

PART 4 **EXEMPT PROPERTY AND ALLOWANCES**
2-401. Applicable Law.
2-402. Homestead Allowance.
2-402A. Constitutional Homestead.
2-403. Exempt Property.
2-404. Family Allowance.
2-405. Source, Determination, and Documentation.

PART 5 **WILLS, WILL CONTRACTS, AND CUSTODY AND DEPOSIT OF WILLS**
2-501. Who May Make Will.
2-502. Execution; Witnessed Wills; Holographic Wills.
2-503. Writings Intended as Wills, Etc.
2-504. Self-proved Will.
2-505. Who May Witness.
2-506. Choice of Law as to Execution.
2-507. Revocation by Writing or by Act.
2-508. Revocation by Change of Circumstances.
2-509. Revival of Revoked Will.
2-510. Incorporation by Reference.
2-511. Testamentary Additions to Trusts.
2-512. Events of Independent Significance.
2-513. Separate Writing Identifying Devise of Certain Types of Tangible Personal Property.
2-514. Contracts Concerning Succession.
2-515. Deposit of Will With Court in Testator's Lifetime.
2-516. Duty of Custodian of Will; Liability.
2-517. Penalty Clause for Contest.

PART 6 **RULES OF CONSTRUCTION APPLICABLE ONLY TO WILLS**
2-601. Scope.
2-602. Will May Pass All Property and After-acquired Property.
2-603. Anti-lapse; Deceased Devisee; Class Gifts.
2-604. Failure of Testamentary Provision.
2-605. Increase in Devised Securities; Accessions.
2-606. Nonademption of Specific Devises; Unpaid Proceeds of Sale, Condemnation, or Insurance; Sale by Conservator or Agent.
2-607. Nonexoneration.

2-608. Exercise of Power of Appointment.

2-609. Ademption by Satisfaction.

PART 7 RULES OF CONSTRUCTION APPLICABLE TO WILLS AND OTHER GOVERNING INSTRUMENTS

2-701. Scope.

2-702. Requirement of Survival by 120 Hours.

2-703. Choice of Law as to Meaning and Effect of Governing Instrument.

2-704. Power of Appointment; Meaning of Specific Reference Requirement.

2-705. Class Gifts Construed to Accord with Intestate Succession.

2-706. Life Insurance; Retirement Plan; Account With POD Designation; Transfer-on-Death Registration; Deceased Beneficiary.

2-707. Survivorship With Respect to Future Interests Under Terms of Trust; Substitute Takers.

2-708. Class Gifts to "Descendants," "Issue," or "Heirs of the Body"; Form of Distribution If None Specified.

2-709. Representation; Per Capita at Each Generation; Per Stirpes.

2-710. Worthier-Title Doctrine Abolished.

2-711. Future Interests in "Heirs" and Like.

PART 8 GENERAL PROVISIONS CONCERNING PROBATE AND NONPROBATE TRANSFERS

2-801. Disclaimer of Property Interests.

2-802. Effect of Divorce, Annulment, and Decree of Separation.

2-803. Effect of Homicide on Intestate Succession, Wills, Trusts, Joint Assets, Life Insurance, and Beneficiary Designations.

2-804. Revocation of Probate and Nonprobate Transfers by Divorce; No Revocation by Other Changes of Circumstances.

PART 9 STATUTORY RULE AGAINST PERPETUITIES; HONORARY TRUSTS

Subpart 1. Statutory Rule Against Perpetuities

2-901. Statutory Rule Against Perpetuities.

2-902. When Nonvested Property Interest or Power of Appointment Created.

2-903. Reformation.

2-904. Exclusions From Statutory Rule Against Perpetuities.

2-905. Prospective Application.

2-906. [Supersession] [Repeal].

Subpart 2. [Honorary Trusts]

[Honorary Trusts; Trusts for Pets.]

PART 10 **UNIFORM INTERNATIONAL WILLS ACT[INTERNATIONAL WILL; INFORMATION REGISTRATION]**

[2-1001]. [Definitions.]

[2-1002]. [International Will; Validity.]

[2-1003]. [International Will; Requirements.]

[2-1004]. [International Will; Other Points of Form.]

[2-1005]. [International Will; Certificate.]

[2-1006]. [International Will; Effect of Certificate.]

[2-1007]. [International Will; Revocation.]

[2-1008]. [Source and Construction.]

[2-1009].   [Persons Authorized to Act in Relation to International Will; Eligibility; Recognition by Authorizing Agency.]

[2-1010]. [International Will Information Registration.]

Article III **PROBATE OF WILLS AND ADMINISTRATION**

Part 1 **GENERAL PROVISIONS**

3-101. [Devolution of Estate at Death; Restrictions.]

[3-101A. [Devolution of Estate at Death; Restrictions.]]

3-102. [Necessity of Order of Probate For Will.]

3-103. [Necessity of Appointment For Administration.]

3-104. [Claims Against Decedent; Necessity of Administration.]

3-105. [Proceedings Affecting Devolution and Administration; Jurisdiction of Subject Matter.]

3-106. [Proceedings Within the Exclusive Jurisdiction of Court; Service; Jurisdiction Over Persons.]

3-107. [Scope of Proceedings; Proceedings Independent; Exception.]

3-108. [Probate, Testacy and Appointment Proceedings; Ultimate Time Limit.]

3-109. [Statutes of Limitation on Decedent's Cause of Action.]

Part 2 VENUE FOR PROBATE AND ADMINISTRATION; PRIORITY TO ADMINISTER; DEMAND FOR NOTICE

3-201. [Venue for First and Subsequent Estate Proceedings; Location of Property.]

3-202. [Appointment or Testacy Proceedings; Conflicting Claim of Domicile in Another State.]

3-203. [Priority Among Persons Seeking Appointment as Personal Representative.]

3-204. [Demand for Notice of Order or Filing Concerning Decedent's Estate.]

Part 3 INFORMAL PROBATE AND APPOINTMENT PROCEEDINGS; SUCCESSION WITHOUT ADMINISTRATION

3-301. [Informal Probate or Appointment Proceedings; Application; Contents.]

3-302. [Informal Probate; Duty of Registrar; Effect of Informal Probate.]

3-303. [Informal Probate; Proof and Findings Required.]

3-304. [Informal Probate; Unavailable in Certain Cases.]

3-305. [Informal Probate; Registrar Not Satisfied.]

3-306. [Informal Probate; Notice Requirements.]

3-307. [Informal Appointment Proceedings; Delay in Order; Duty of Registrar; Effect of Appointment.]

3-308. [Informal Appointment Proceedings; Proof and Findings Required.]

3-309. [Informal Appointment Proceedings; Registrar Not Satisfied.]

3-310. [Informal Appointment Proceedings; Notice Requirements.]

3-311. [Informal Appointment Unavailable in Certain Cases.]

3-312. [Universal Succession; In General.]

3-313. [Universal Succession; Application; Contents.]

3-314. [Universal Succession; Proof and Findings Required.]

3-315. [Universal Succession; Duty of Registrar; Effect of Statement of Universal Succession.]

3-316. [Universal Succession; Universal Successors' Powers.]

3-317. [Universal Succession; Universal Successors' Liability to Creditors, Other Heirs, Devisees and Persons Entitled to Decedent's Property; Liability of Other Persons Entitled to Property.]

3-318. [Universal Succession; Universal Successors' Submission to Jurisdiction; When Heirs or Devisees May Not Seek Administration.]

3-319. [Universal Succession; Duty of Universal Successors; Information to Heirs and Devisees.]

3-320. [Universal Succession; Universal Successors' Liability For Restitution to Estate.]

3-321. [Universal Succession; Liability of Universal Successors for Claims, Expenses, Intestate Shares and Devises.]

3-322. [Universal Succession; Remedies of Creditors, Other Heirs, Devisees or Persons Entitled to Decedent's Property.]

Part 4 **FORMAL TESTACY AND APPOINTMENT PROCEEDINGS**
3-401. [Formal Testacy Proceedings; Nature; When Commenced.]
3-402. [Formal Testacy or Appointment Proceedings; Petition; Contents.]
3-403. [Formal Testacy Proceedings; Notice of Hearing on Petition.]
3-404. [Formal Testacy Proceedings; Written Objections to Probate.]
3-405. [Formal Testacy Proceedings; Uncontested Cases; Hearings and Proof.]
3-406. [Formal Testacy Proceedings; Contested Cases; Testimony of Attesting Witnesses.]
3-407. [Formal Testacy Proceedings; Burdens in Contested Cases.]
3-408. [Formal Testacy Proceedings; Will Construction; Effect of Final Order in Another Jurisdiction.]
3-409. [Formal Testacy Proceedings; Order; Foreign Will.]
3-410. [Formal Testacy Proceedings; Probate of More Than One Instrument.]
3-411. [Formal Testacy Proceedings; Partial Intestacy.]
3-412. [Formal Testacy Proceedings; Effect of Order; Vacation.]
3-413. [Formal Testacy Proceedings; Vacation of Order For Other Cause.]
3-414. [Formal Proceedings Concerning Appointment of Personal Representative.]

Part 5 **SUPERVISED ADMINISTRATION**
3-501. [Supervised Administration; Nature of Proceeding.]
3-502. [Supervised Administration; Petition; Order.]
3-503. [Supervised Administration; Effect on Other Proceedings.]
3-504. [Supervised Administration; Powers of Personal Representative.]
3-505. [Supervised Administration; Interim Orders; Distribution and Closing Orders.]

Part 6 **PERSONAL REPRESENTATIVE; APPOINTMENT, CONTROL AND TERMINATION OF AUTHORITY**
3-601. [Qualification.]
3-602. [Acceptance of Appointment; Consent to Jurisdiction.]
3-603. [Bond Not Required Without Court Order, Exceptions.]
3-604. [Bond Amount; Security; Procedure; Reduction.]
3-605. [Demand For Bond by Interested Person.]
3-606. [Terms and Conditions of Bonds.]
3-607. [Order Restraining Personal Representative.]

3-608. [Termination of Appointment; General.]
3-609. [Termination of Appointment; Death or Disability.]
3-610. [Termination of Appointment; Voluntary.]
3-611. [Termination of Appointment by Removal; Cause; Procedure.]
3-612. [Termination of Appointment; Change of Testacy Status.]
3-613. [Successor Personal Representative.]
3-614. [Special Administrator; Appointment.]
3-615. [Special Administrator; Who May Be Appointed.]
3-616. [Special Administrator; Appointed Informally; Powers and Duties.]
3-617. [Special Administrator; Formal Proceedings; Power and Duties.]
3-618. [Termination of Appointment; Special Administrator.]

Part 7 **DUTIES AND POWERS OF PERSONAL REPRESENTATIVES**
3-701. [Time of Accrual of Duties and Powers.]
3-702. [Priority Among Different Letters.]
3-703. [General Duties; Relation and Liability to Persons Interested in Estate; Standing to Sue.]
3-704. [Personal Representative to Proceed Without Court Order; Exception.]
3-705. [Duty of Personal Representative; Information to Heirs and Devisees.]
3-706. [Duty of Personal Representative; Inventory and Appraisement.]
3-707. [Employment of Appraisers.]
3-708. [Duty of Personal Representative; Supplementary Inventory.]
3-709. [Duty of Personal Representative; Possession of Estate.]
3-710. [Power to Avoid Transfers.]
3-711. [Powers of Personal Representatives; In General.]
3-712. [Improper Exercise of Power; Breach of Fiduciary Duty.]
3-713. [Sale, Encumbrance or Transaction Involving Conflict of Interest; Voidable; Exceptions.]
3-714. [Persons Dealing with Personal Representative; Protection.]
3-715. [Transactions Authorized for Personal Representatives; Exceptions.]
3-716. [Powers and Duties of Successor Personal Representative.]
3-717. [Co-representatives; When Joint Action Required.]
3-718. [Powers of Surviving Personal Representative.]
3-719. [Compensation of Personal Representative.]
3-720. [Expenses in Estate Litigation.]
3-721. [Proceedings for Review of Employment of Agents and Compensation of Personal Representatives and Employees of Estate.]

Part 8 **CREDITORS' CLAIMS**

3-801. [Notice to Creditors.]

3-802. [Statutes of Limitations.]

3-803. [Limitations on Presentation of Claims.]

3-804. [Manner of Presentation of Claims.]

3-805. [Classification of Claims.]

3-806. [Allowance of Claims.]

3-807. [Payment of Claims.]

3-808. [Individual Liability of Personal Representative.]

3-809. [Secured Claims.]

3-810. [Claims Not Due and Contingent or Unliquidated Claims.]

3-811. [Counterclaims.]

3-812. [Execution and Levies Prohibited.]

3-813. [Compromise of Claims.]

3-814. [Encumbered Assets.]

3-815. [Administration in More Than One State; Duty of Personal Representative.]

3-816. [Final Distribution to Domiciliary Representative.]

Part 9 **SPECIAL PROVISIONS RELATING TO DISTRIBUTION**

3-901. [Successors' Rights if No Administration.]

3-902. [Distribution; Order in Which Assets Appropriated; Abatement.]

[3-902A. [Distribution; Order in Which Assets Appropriated; Abatement.]]

3-903. [Right of Retainer.]

3-904. [Interest on General Pecuniary Devise.]

3-905. [Penalty Clause for Contest.]

3-906. [Distribution in Kind; Valuation; Method.]

3-907. [Distribution in Kind; Evidence.]

3-908. [Distribution; Right or Title of Distributee.]

3-909. [Improper Distribution; Liability of Distributee.]

3-910. [Purchasers from Distributees Protected.]

3-911. [Partition for Purpose of Distribution.]

3-912. [Private Agreements Among Successors to Decedent Binding on Personal Representative.]

3-913. [Distributions to Trustee.]

[3-914. [Disposition of Unclaimed Assets.]]

3-915. [Distribution to Person Under Disability.]

3-916. [Apportionment of Estate Taxes.]

Part 10 **CLOSING ESTATES**

3-1001. [Formal Proceedings Terminating Administration; Testate or Intestate; Order of General Protection.]

3-1002. [Formal Proceedings Terminating Testate Administration; Order Construing Will Without Adjudicating Testacy.]

3-1003. [Closing Estates; By Sworn Statement of Personal Representative.]

3-1004. [Liability of Distributees to Claimants.]

3-1005. [Limitations on Proceedings Against Personal Representative.]

3-1006. [Limitations on Actions and Proceedings Against Distributees.]

3-1007. [Certificate Discharging Liens Securing Fiduciary Performance.]

3-1008. [Subsequent Administration.]

Part 11 **COMPROMISE OF CONTROVERSIES**

3-1101. [Effect of Approval of Agreements Involving Trusts, Inalienable Interests, or Interests of Third Persons.]

3-1102. [Procedure for Securing Court Approval of Compromise.]

Part 12 **COLLECTION OF PERSONAL PROPERTY BY AFFIDAVIT AND SUMMARY ADMINISTRATION PROCEDURE FOR SMALL ESTATES**

3-1201. [Collection of Personal Property by Affidavit.]

3-1202. [Effect of Affidavit.]

3-1203. [Small Estates; Summary Administration Procedure.]

3-1204. [Small Estates; Closing by Sworn Statement of Personal Representative.]

Article IV **FOREIGN PERSONAL REPRESENTATIVES; ANCILLARY ADMINISTRATION**

Part 1 **DEFINITIONS**

4-101. [Definitions.]

Part 2 **POWERS OF FOREIGN PERSONAL REPRESENTATIVES**

4-201. [Payment of Debt and Delivery of Property to Domiciliary Foreign Personal Representative Without Local Administration.]

4-202. [Payment or Delivery Discharges.]

4-203. [Resident Creditor Notice.]

4-204. [Proof of Authority-Bond.]

4-205. [Powers.]

4-206.   [Power of Representatives in Transition.]

4-207.   [Ancillary and Other Local Administrations; Provisions Governing.]

Part 3 **JURISDICTION OVER FOREIGN REPRESENTATIVES**

4-301.   [Jurisdiction by Act of Foreign Personal Representative.]

4-302.   [Jurisdiction by Act of Decedent.]

4-303.   [Service on Foreign Personal Representative.]

Part 4 **JUDGMENTS AND PERSONAL REPRESENTATIVES**

4-401.   [Effect of Adjudication For or Against Personal Representative.]

Article V **PROTECTION OF PERSONS UNDER DISABILITY AND THEIR PROPERTY**

Part 1 **GENERAL PROVISIONS AND DEFINITIONS**

5-101.   [Facility of Payment or Delivery.]

5-102.   [Delegation of Powers by Parent or Guardian.]

5-103.   [General Definitions.]

5-104.   [Request for Notice; Interested Person.]

Part 2 **GUARDIANS OF MINORS**

5-201.   [Appointment and Status of Guardian of Minor.]

5-202.   [Parental Appointment of Guardian for Minor.]

5-203.   [Objection by Minor of Fourteen or Older to Parental Appointment.]

5-204.   [Court Appointment of Guardian of Minor; Conditions for Appointment.]

5-205.   [Venue.]

5-206.   [Procedure for Court-appointment of Guardian of Minor.]

5-207.   [Court Appointment of Guardian of Minor; Qualifications; Priority of Minor's Nominee.]

5-208.   [Consent to Service by Acceptance of Appointment; Notice.]

5-209.   [Powers and Duties of Guardian of Minor.]

5-210.   [Termination of Appointment of Guardian; General.]

5-211.   [Proceedings Subsequent to Appointment; Venue.]

5-212.   [Resignation, Removal, and Other Post-appointment Proceedings.]

Part 3 **GUARDIANS OF INCAPACITATED PERSONS**
5-301. [Appointment of Guardian for Incapacitated Person by Will or Other Writing.]
5-302. [Venue.]
5-303. [Procedure for Court-appointment of a Guardian of an Incapacitated Person.]
5-304. [Notice in Guardianship Proceeding.]
5-305. [Who May Be Guardian; Priorities.]
5-306. [Findings; Order of Appointment.]
5-307. [Acceptance of Appointment; Consent to Jurisdiction.]
5-308. [Emergency Orders; Temporary Guardians.]
5-309. [General Powers and Duties of Guardian.]
5-310. [Termination of Guardianship for Incapacitated Person.]
5-311. [Removal or Resignation of Guardian; Termination of Incapacity.]
5-312. [Proceedings Subsequent to Appointment; Venue.]

Part 4 **PROTECTION OF PROPERTY OF PERSONS UNDER DISABILITY AND MINORS**
5-401. [Protective Proceedings.]
5-402. [Protective Proceedings; Jurisdiction of Business Affairs of Protected Persons.]
5-403. [Venue.]
5-404. [Original Petition for Appointment or Protective Order.]
5-405. [Notice.]
5-406. [Procedure Concerning Hearing and Order on Original Petition.]
5-407. [Permissible Court Orders.]
5-408. [Protective Arrangements and Single Transactions Authorized.]
5-409. [Who May Be Appointed Conservator; Priorities.]
5-410. [Bond.]
5-411. [Terms and Requirements of Bonds.]
5-412. [Effect of Acceptance of Appointment.]
5-413. [Compensation and Expenses.]
5-414. [Death, Resignation, or Removal of Conservator.]
5-415. [Petitions for Orders Subsequent to Appointment.]
5-416. [General Duty of Conservator.]
5-417. [Inventory and Records.]
5-418. [Accounts.]
5-419. [Conservators; Title By Appointment.]
5-420. [Recording of Conservator's Letters.]
5-421. [Sale, Encumbrance, or Transaction Involving Conflict of Interest; Voidable; Exceptions.]

5-422. [Persons Dealing With Conservators; Protection.]

5-423. [Powers of Conservator in Administration.]

5-424. [Distributive Duties and Powers of Conservator.]

5-425. [Enlargement or Limitation of Powers of Conservator.]

5-426. [Preservation of Estate Plan; Right to Examine.]

5-427. [Claims Against Protected Person; Enforcement.]

5-428. [Personal Liability of Conservator.]

5-429. [Termination of Proceedings.]

5-430. [Payment of Debt and Delivery of Property to Foreign Conservator without Local Proceedings.]

5-431. [Foreign Conservator; Proof of Authority; Bond; Powers.]

Part 5 DURABLE POWER OF ATTORNEY

5-501. [Definition.]

5-502. [Durable Power of Attorney Not Affected By Disability or Incapacity.]

5-503. [Relation of Attorney in Fact to Court-appointed Fiduciary.]

5-504. [Power of Attorney Not Revoked Until Notice.]

5-505. [Proof of Continuance of Durable and Other Powers of Attorney by Affidavit.]

Article VI NONPROBATE TRANSFERS ON DEATH (1989)
PART 1 PROVISIONS RELATING TO EFFECT OF DEATH

6-101. Nonprobate Transfers on Death.

PART 2 MULTIPLE-PERSON ACCOUNTS
SUBPART 1 DEFINITIONS AND GENERAL PROVISIONS

6-201. Definitions.

6-202. Limitation on Scope of Part.

6-203. Types of Account; Existing Accounts.

6-204. Forms.

6-205. Designation of Agent.

6-206. Applicability of Part.

SUBPART 2 OWNERSHIP AS BETWEEN PARTIES AND OTHERS

6-211. Ownership During Lifetime.

6-212. Rights at Death.

6-213. Alteration of Rights.

6-214. Accounts and Transfers Nontestamentary.

6-215. Rights of Creditors and Others.

6-216. Community Property and Tenancy by the Entireties.

SUBPART 3 **PROTECTION OF FINANCIAL INSTITUTIONS**

6-221. Authority of Financial Institution.

6-222. Payment on Multiple-Party Account.

6-223. Payment on POD Designation.

6-224. Payment to Designated Agent.

6-225. Payment to Minor.

6-226. Discharge.

6-227. Set-off.

PART 3 **UNIFORM TOD SECURITY REGISTRATION ACT**

6-301. Definitions.

6-302. Registration in Beneficiary Form; Sole or Joint Tenancy Ownership.

6-303. Registration in Beneficiary Form; Applicable Law.

6-304. Origination of Registration in Beneficiary Form.

6-305. Form of Registration in Beneficiary Form.

6-306. Effect of Registration in Beneficiary Form.

6-307. Ownership on Death of Owner.

6-308. Protection of Registering Entity.

6-309. Nontestamentary Transfer on Death.

6-310. Terms, Conditions, and Forms for Registration.

[6-311. Application of Part.]

Article VII **TRUST ADMINISTRATION**

Part 1 **TRUST REGISTRATION**

7-101. [Duty to Register Trusts.]

7-102. [Registration Procedures.]

7-103. [Effect of Registration.]

7-104. [Effect of Failure to Register.]

7-105. [Registration, Qualification of Foreign Trustee.]

Part 2 **JURISDICTION OF COURT CONCERNING TRUSTS**
7-201. [Court; Exclusive Jurisdiction of Trusts.]
7-202. [Trust Proceedings; Venue.]
7-203. [Trust Proceedings; Dismissal of Matters Relating to Foreign Trusts.]
7-204. [Court; Concurrent Jurisdiction of Litigation Involving Trusts and Third Parties.]
7-205. [Proceedings for Review of Employment of Agents and Review of Compensation of Trustee and Employees of Trust.]
7-206. [Trust Proceedings; Initiation by Notice; Necessary Parties.]

Part 3 **DUTIES AND LIABILITIES OF TRUSTEES**
7-301. [General Duties Not Limited.]
7-302. [Trustee's Standard of Care and Performance.]
7-303. [Duty to Inform and Account to Beneficiaries.]
7-304. [Duty to Provide Bond.]
7-305. [Trustee's Duties; Appropriate Place of Administration; Deviation.]
7-306. [Personal Liability of Trustee to Third Parties.]
7-307. [Limitations on Proceedings Against Trustees After Final Account.]

Part 4 **POWERS OF TRUSTEES**
[GENERAL COMMENT ONLY]

Article VIII **EFFECTIVE DATE AND REPEALER**
8-101. [Time of Taking Effect; Provisions for Transition.]
8-102. [Specific Repealer and Amendments.]

THE UNIFORM PREMARITAL AGREEMENT ACT

PURPOSE: To provide a framework for complete and enforceable premarital agreements.

ORIGIN: Completed by the Uniform Law Commissioners in 1983.

ENDORSED BY: American Bar Association

STATE ADOPTIONS:

Arizona	Indiana	North Dakota
Arkansas	Iowa	Oregon
California	Kansas	Rhode Island
Connecticut	Maine	South Dakota
Delaware	Montana	Texas
District of Columbia	Nebraska	Utah
Hawaii	Nevada	Virginia
Idaho	New Mexico	Wisconsin
Illinois	North Carolina	

2002 INTRODUCTIONS: Mississippi; West Virginia; Rhode Island

For any further information regarding the Uniform Premarital Agreement Act, please contact John McCabe or Katie Robinson at 312-915-0195.

UNIFORM PREMARITAL AGREEMENT ACT

§ 1. Definitions.
§ 2. Formalities.
§ 3. Content.
§ 4. Effect of Marriage.
§ 5. Amendment, Revocation.
§ 6. Enforcement.
§ 7. Enforcement: Void Marriage.
§ 8. Limitation of Actions.
§ 9. Application and Construction.
§ 10. Short Title.
§ 11. Severability.
§ 12. Time of Taking Effect.
§ 13. Repeal.

UNIFORM PRINCIPAL AND INCOME ACT

PURPOSE: This act revises the Uniform Principal and Income Act of 1931 and 1962, which has been adopted in 41 states. The purpose of the new act, like its predecessors, is to provide procedures for trustees administering an estate in separating principal from income, and to ensure that the intention of the trust creator is the guiding principle for trustees. A revision is necessary so that principal and income allocation rules can function with modern trust investment practices.

ORIGIN: Completed by the Uniform Law Commissioners in 1997.

APPROVED BY: American Bar Association

STATE ADOPTIONS:

Alabama	Florida	Maryland
Arizona	Hawaii	Missouri
Arkansas	Idaho	Nebraska
California	Indiana	New Jersey
Colorado	Iowa	New Mexico
Connecticut	Kansas	New York
District of Columbia	Maine	

2002 INTRODUCTIONS:
Ohio, Rhode Island, Vermont, Wisconsin

For any further information regarding the Uniform Principal and Income Act (1997), please contact John McCabe, Katie Robinson, or Michael Kerr at 312-915-0195.

UNIFORM PRINCIPAL AND INCOME ACT (1997)

Article 1. Definitions and Fiduciary Duties
§ 101. Short Title
§ 102. Definitions
§ 103. Fiduciary Duties; General Principles
§ 104. Trustee's Power to Adjust

Article 2. Decedent's Estate or Terminating Income Interest
§ 201. Determination and Distribution of Net Income
§ 202. Distribution to Residuary and Remainder Beneficiaries

Article 3. Apportionment at Beginning and End of Income Interest
§ 301. When Right to Income Begins and Ends
§ 302. Apportionment of Receipts and Disbursements When Decedent Dies or
         Income Interest Begins
§ 303. Apportionment When Income Interest Ends

Article 4. Allocation of Receipts During Administration of Trust
Part 1. Receipts from Entities
§ 401. Character of Receipts
§ 402. Distribution from Trust or Estate
§ 403. Business and Other Activities Conducted by Trustee

Part 2. Receipts Not Normally Apportioned
§ 404. Principal Receipts
§ 405. Rental Property
§ 406. Obligation to Pay Money
§ 407. Insurance Policies and Similar Contracts

Part 3. Receipts Normally Apportioned
§ 408. Insubstantial Allocations Not Required
§ 409. Deferred Compensation, Annuities, and Similar Payments
§ 410. Liquidating Asset
§ 411. Minerals, Water, and Other Natural Resources
§ 412. Timber
§ 413. Property Not Productive of Income
§ 414. Derivatives and Options
§ 415. Asset-backed Securities

Article 5. Allocation of Disbursements During Administration of Trust
§ 501. Disbursements from Income
§ 502. Disbursements from Principal
§ 503. Transfers from Income to Principal for Depreciation
§ 504. Transfers from Income to Reimburse Principal
§ 505. Income Taxes
§ 506. Adjustments Between Principal and Income Because of Taxes

Article 6. Miscellaneous Provisions
§ 601. Uniformity of Application and Construction
§ 602. Severability Clause
§ 603. Repeal
§ 604. Effective Date
§ 605. Application of [Act] to Existing Trusts and Estates

UNIFORM STATUTORY FORM POWER OF ATTORNEY ACT

PURPOSE: To provide a set form for creating a power of attorney. The language of the form becomes available to any person for the purpose of creating exactly the power of attorney that is desired. Included in the form is a check-off list of categories of transactions that a person can choose, including "real property transactions" and "tangible personal property transactions." A person creating a power of attorney can therefore provide for specific powers or for general powers.

ORIGIN: Completed by the Uniform Law Commissioners in 1988.

APPROVED BY: American Bar Association

STATE ADOPTIONS:

Arkansas	New Mexico
California	Oklahoma
Colorado	Rhode Island
District of Columbia	Texas
Montana	Wisconsin

For any further information regarding the Uniform Statutory Form Power of Attorney Act, contact John McCabe or Katie Robinson at 312-915-0195.

UNIFORM STATUTORY FORM POWER OF ATTORNEY ACT

§ 1. Statutory Form of Power of Attorney.
§ 2. Durable Power of Attorney.
§ 3. Construction of Powers Generally.
§ 4. Construction of Power Relating to Real Property Transactions.
§ 5. Construction of Power Relating to Tangible Personal Property Transactions.
§ 6. Construction of Power Relating to Stock and Bond Transactions.
§ 7. Construction of Power Relating to Commodity and Option Transactions.
§ 8. Construction of Power Relating to Banking and Other Financial Institution Transactions.
§ 9. Construction of Power Relating to Business Operating Transactions.
§ 10. Construction of Power Relating to Insurance Transactions.
§ 11. Construction of Power Relating to Estate, Trust, and Other Beneficiary Transactions.
§ 12. Construction of Power Relating to Claims and Litigation.
§ 13. Construction of Power Relating to Personal and Family Maintenance.
§ 14. Construction of Power Relating to Benefits from Social Security, Medicare, Medicaid, or Other Governmental Programs, or Military Service.
§ 15. Construction of Power Relating to Retirement Plan Transactions.
§ 16. Construction of Power Relating to Tax Matters.
§ 17. Existing Interests; Foreign Interests.
§ 18. Uniformity of Application and Construction.
§ 19. Short Title.
§ 20. Severability Clause.
[§ 21. Effective Date.
[§ 22. Repeals.

THE UNIFORM TRANSFERS TO MINORS ACT

PURPOSE: To update and expand the usefulness of the Uniform Gifts to Minors Act (1966).

ORIGIN: Completed by the Uniform Law Commissioners in 1983, and amended in 1986.

ENDORSED BY: American Bar Association

STATE ADOPTIONS:

Alabama	Kentucky	North Dakota
Alaska	Louisiana	Ohio
Arizona	Maine	Oklahoma
Arkansas	Maryland	Oregon
California	Massachusetts	Pennsylvania
Colorado	Michigan	Rhode Island
Connecticut	Minnesota	South Dakota
Delaware	Mississippi	Tennessee
District of Columbia	Missouri	Texas
Florida	Montana	U.S. Virgin Islands
Georgia	Nebraska	Utah
Hawaii	Nevada	Virginia
Idaho	New Hampshire	Washington
Illinois	New Jersey	West Virginia
Indiana	New Mexico	Wisconsin
Iowa	New York	Wyoming
Kansas	North Carolina	

2002 INTRODUCTIONS: Vermont

For any further information regarding the Uniform Transfers to Minors Act, please contact John McCabe or Katie Robinson at 312-915-0195.

UNIFORM TRANSFERS TO MINORS ACT (1986)

§ 1.   Definitions.
§ 2.   Scope and Jurisdiction.
§ 3.   Nomination of Custodian.
§ 4.   Transfer by Gift or Exercise of Power of Appointment.
§ 5.   Transfer Authorized by Will or Trust.
§ 6.   Other Transfer by Fiduciary.
§ 7.   Transfer by Obligor.
§ 8.   Receipt for Custodial Property.
§ 9.   Manner of Creating Custodial Property and Effecting Transfer; Designation of Initial Custodian; Control.
§ 10. Single Custodianship.
§ 11. Validity and Effect of Transfer.
§ 12. Care of Custodial Property.
§ 13. Powers of Custodian.
§ 14. Use of Custodial Property.
§ 15. Custodian's Expenses, Compensation, and Bond.
§ 16. Exemption of Third Person from Liability.
§ 17. Liability to Third Persons.
§ 18. Renunciation, Resignation, Death, or Removal of Custodian; Designation of Successor Custodian.
§ 19. Accounting by and Determination of Liability of Custodian.
§ 20. Termination of Custodianship.
§ 22. Effect on Existing Custodianships.
§ 23. Uniformity of Application and Construction.
§ 24. Short Title.
§ 25. Severability.
§ 26. Effective Date.
§ 27. Repeals.

UNIFORM TRUST CODE (2000)

PURPOSE: To provide a comprehensive model for codifying the law on trusts. While there are numerous Uniform Acts related to trusts, such as the Uniform Prudent Investor Act, the Uniform Principal and Income Act, the Uniform Trustees' Powers Act, the Uniform Custodial Trust Act, and parts of the Uniform Probate Code, none is comprehensive. The UTC will enable states which enact it to specify their rules on trusts with precision and will provide individuals with a readily available source for determining their state's law on trusts.

ORIGIN: Completed by the Uniform Law Commissioners in 2000.

APPROVED BY:
American Bar Association
ABA Real Property, Probate and Trust Law Section
AARP

STATE ADOPTIONS: Kansas

2002 INTRODUCTIONS:

Connecticut
District of Columbia
Minnesota
Nebraska
Oklahoma
Tennessee
Utah
West Virginia

For any further information regarding the Uniform Trust Code, please contact Michelle Clayton at 312-915-0195.

UNIFORM TRUST CODE

Prefatory Note

Article 1 General Provisions and Definitions
§ 101.   Short Title.
§ 102.   Scope.
§ 103.   Definitions.
§ 104.   Knowledge.
§ 105.   Default and Mandatory Rules.
§ 106.   Common Law of Trusts; Principles of Equity.
§ 107.   Governing Law.
§ 108.   Principal Place of Administration.
§ 109.   Methods and Waiver of Notice.
§ 110.   Others Treated as Qualified Beneficiaries.
§ 111.   Nonjudicial Settlement Agreements.
[§ 112. Rules of Construction.]

Article 2 Judicial Proceedings
§ 201.   Role of Court in Administration of Trust.
§ 202.   Jurisdiction over Trustee and Beneficiary.
[§ 203. Subject-matter Jurisdiction.]
[§ 204. Venue.]

Article 3 Representation
§ 301.   Representation: Basic Effect.
§ 302.   Representation by Holder of General Testamentary Power of Appointment.
§ 303.   Representation by Fiduciaries and Parents.
§ 304.   Representation by Person Having Substantially Identical Interest.
§ 305.   Appointment of Representative.

Article 4 Creation, Validity, Modification, and Termination of Trust
§ 401.   Methods of Creating Trust.
§ 402.   Requirements for Creation.
§ 403.   Trusts Created in Other Jurisdictions.
§ 404.   Trust Purposes.
§ 405.   Charitable Purposes; Enforcement.
§ 406.   Creation of Trust Induced by Fraud, Duress, or Undue Influence.
§ 407.   Evidence of Oral Trust.
§ 408.   Trust for Care of Animal.

§ 409. Noncharitable Trust Without Ascertainable Beneficiary.

§ 410. Modification or Termination of Trust; Proceedings for Approval or Disapproval.

§ 411. Modification or Termination of Noncharitable Irrevocable Trust by Consent.

§ 412. Modification or Termination Because of Unanticipated Circumstances or Inability to Administer Trust Effectively.

§ 413. Cy Pres..

§ 414. Modification or Termination of Uneconomic Trust..

§ 415. Reformation to Correct Mistakes.

§ 416. Modification to Achieve Settlor's Tax Objectives.

§ 417. Combination and Division of Trusts.

Article 5 Creditor's Claims; Spendthrift and Discretionary Trusts

§ 501. Rights of Beneficiary's Creditor or Assignee

§ 502. Spendthrift Provision

§ 503. Exceptions to Spendthrift Provision.

§ 504. Discretionary Trusts; Effect of Standard.

§ 505. Creditor's Claim Against Settlor.

§ 506. Overdue Distribution.

Article 6 Revocable Trusts

§ 601. Capacity of Settlor of Revocable Trust

§ 602. Revocation or Amendment of Revocable Trust.

§ 603. Settlor's Powers; Powers of Withdrawal.

§ 604. Limitation on Action Contesting Validity of Revocable Trust; Distribution of Trust Property.

Article 7 Office of Trustee

§ 701. Accepting or Declining Trusteeship.

§ 702. Trustee's Bond.

§ 703. Cotrustees.

§ 704. Vacancy in Trusteeship; Appointment of Successor.

§ 705. Resignation of Trustee.

§ 706. Removal of Trustee.

§ 707. Delivery of Property by Former Trustee.

§ 708. Compensation of Trustee.

§ 709. Reimbursement of Expenses.

Article 8 Duties and Powers of Trustee

§ 801. Duty to Administer Trust

§ 802. Duty of Loyalty

§ 803. Impartiality
§ 804. Prudent Administration
§ 805. Costs of Administration
§ 806. Trustee's Skills
§ 807. Delegation by Trustee
§ 808. Powers to Direct
§ 809. Control and Protection of Trust Property.
§ 810. Recordkeeping and Identification of Trust Property.
§ 811. Enforcement and Defense of Claims.
§ 812. Collecting Trust Property.
§ 813. Duty to Inform and Report.
§ 814. Discretionary Powers; Tax Savings.
§ 815. General Powers of Trustee.
§ 816. Specific Powers of Trustee.
§ 817. Distribution upon Termination.

Article 9 Uniform Prudent Investor Act

Article 10 Liability of Trustees and Rights of Persons Dealing with Trustee
§ 1001. Remedies for Breach of Trust.
§ 1002. Damages for Breach of Trust.
§ 1003. Damages in Absence of Breach.
§ 1004. Attorney's Fees and Costs.
§ 1005. Limitation of Action Against Trustee.
§ 1006. Reliance on Trust Instrument.
§ 1007. Event Affecting Administration or Distribution.
§ 1008. Exculpation of Trustee.
§ 1009. Beneficiary's Consent, Release, or Ratification.
§ 1010. Limitation on Personal Liability of Trustee.
§ 1011. Interest as General Partner.
§ 1012. Protection of Person Dealing with Trustee.
§ 1013. Certification of Trust.

Article 11 Miscellaneous Provisions
§ 1101. Uniformity of Application and Construction.
§ 1102. Electronic Records and Signatures.
§ 1103. Severability Clause.
§ 1104. Effective Date.
§ 1105. Repeals.
§ 1106. Application to Existing Relationships.

GLOSSARY

Abatement The legal process of reducing or eliminating the bequests of a decedent-testator who died owning insufficient assets to pay all bequests, debts and administration expenses.

Ademption The failure to fulfill a specific bequest in a will because the property bequeathed was sold, given away or lost before the testator's death.

Adjusted basis The dollar amount subtracted from the amount realized to calculate gain or loss on the sale or exchange of property. It is generally thought of as the price paid for property, but an owner's basis is generally determined by how the person acquired the property, e.g., by purchase, by gift, or by inheritance. It is also increased by capital improvements and decreased by depreciation.

Adjusted taxable gifts In federal estate tax, the sum of post-1976 taxable gifts, other than those included in the gross estate. It is added to the taxable estate on the federal estate tax return to arrive at the estate tax base.

Administrator A personal representative of a decedent's estate who was not nominated in the decedent's will.

Administrator with will annexed A personal representative of an estate where the decedent's will is admitted to probate but the personal representative was not nominated in the will as the executor.

Advance directive A document (e.g., a living will or durable power of attorney) in which a person expresses his or her wishes regarding medical treatment in the event of incapacitation.

Advancement Property given to a donee with the expressed intention by the donor that it will reduce or eliminate a bequest to the donee.

Adverse party In the Internal Revenue Code, a person having a substantial interest in property that is subject to a power of appointment, where that person's interest would be diminished if the holder of the power exercised it.

Affidavit A sworn statement in writing made esp. under oath or on affirmation before an authorized magistrate or officer

After-born child A child who was born after the execution of his or her parent's will.

Alternate valuation date Under Federal estate tax law assets are usually valued as of the date of death, but the personal representative may elect to value them as of six months after the date of death if doing so will reduce the value of the gross estate and the estate tax.

Ancillary administration Ancillary means having a subordinate, subsidiary, or secondary nature. In this context it refers to a probate in a state other than the decedent's state of domicile.

Annual exclusion Under the federal gift tax, a deduction up to $10,000 (indexed after 1997) from gross gifts by a donor to any donee in a given calender year.

Annual exclusion gift A gift of property worth no more than the gift tax annual exclusion.

Annuitant A person entitled to receive benefits or payments from an annuity.

Annuity An amount payable at regular intervals (as yearly or quarterly) for a certain or uncertain period. A contract (as with an insurance company) under which one or more persons receive annuities in return for prior fixed payments made by themselves or another (as an employer).

Antilapse statute A state statutory provision that specifies, in the absence of a provision in the will, to whom a lapsed testamentary bequest will pass.

Applicable exclusion amount Also known as the credit shelter amount, is the amount that can be transferred over a person's lifetime and/or at death free of gift tax and estate tax, e.g., $2 million in 2004 for estates and $1 million for gifts made after 2001.

Appointee (of a power of appointment) The party or parties whom the holder of a power of appointment actually appoints property.

Apportionment statute *See Equitable apportionment statute.*

Ascertainable standard Wording in a will or trust intentionally limiting the freedom of a holder of a power of appointment over property to assure that the property subject to the power will not be included in the holder's gross estate. The most common words of limitation (derived from Section 2041) are that the holder can withdraw property from a trust for his or her benefit if such is needed for "health, education, support, or maintenance."

Assignment Any transfer of a claim, right, or interest in property.

Assignment of income doctrine Under income tax law, a doctrine holding that earnings from services performed will always be taxed to the person performing those services.

Attestation clause A clause at the end of a will in which the witnesses state that the will was signed and witnessed with all the formalities required by law and which often sets forth those requirements.

Attested will A will signed by the testator in front of witnesses who sign below the attestation clause.

Attorney-in-fact An agent who may or may not be a lawyer who is given written authority to act on another's behalf, esp. by a power of attorney. The agent acts on behalf of a principal.

Augmented estate A deceased person's probate estate increased in accordance with statutory provisions. Although it varies by state, this may require the addition of any property transferred as a gift by the deceased within two years of death, any joint tenancies, and any transfers in which the deceased retained either the right to revoke or the income for life. In some states, the surviving spouse's elective share is determined by the augmented estate.

Average tax rate The tax rate determined by dividing the tax by value of what is being taxed. Compare this to the marginal tax rate which is the rate of tax on each dollar within a tax bracket.

Bargain sale Part-gift, part-sale of an asset for some amount that the parties know is less than what would be regarded as full and adequate consideration. The difference between the consideration received by the seller-donor and the value of the asset transferred constitutes a gift, for tax purposes.

Basis *See adjusted basis.*

Beneficial interest An interest in property that carries an economic benefit. Examples of beneficial interests in property include the temporary or permanent right to possess, consume, and pledge the property.

Beneficiary A person who is receiving or will receive a gift of a beneficial interest in property. *See Donee.*

Bequest A gift, by will, of personal property. Also called a legacy.

Blockage discount A valuation discount given to a large quantity of a stock listed on an exchange, or certain other property, if its sale all at one time could have a temporarily depressing effect on the market price.

Bond In probate, an agreement under which an insurance company guarantees that the personal representative will faithfully perform required probate duties.

Business buyout agreement An agreement between one or more owners of a closely held business and one or more other persons that obligates one or more of the parties to purchase the interest of one of the others upon the occurrence of specific future events, such as the latter's death and, often, the onset of his or her permanent disability.

Buyout agreement *See Business buyout agreement.*

Buy-sell agreement *See Business buyout agreement.*

Bypass An arrangement under which property owned by a decedent and intended for the lifetime benefit of the surviving spouse does not actually pass to the surviving spouse, thereby avoiding inclusion in the latter's gross estate.

Bypass trust A trust designed to contain property that bypasses the surviving beneficiary's estate. *See Bypass.*

By right of representation The distribution of a decedent's estate whereby the children of the decedent share equally, with the share of a deceased child who left issue going to his or her children in equal shares, again with the share of a deceased child who left issue passing in like manner to his or her issue.

Carryover basis Generally applied to gifts. The person receiving property has a basis in the property equal to the basis of the asset when it was in the hands of the donor or transferor.

Cash value life insurance policy A policy that accumulates economic value because the insurer charges a constant premium that is considerably higher than mortality costs requires during the earlier years. Part of this overpayment accumulates as a cash surrender value which, prior to the death of the insured, can be enjoyed by the owner, basically in one of two ways. First, at any time the owner can surrender the policy and receive this value in cash. Second, the owner can make a policy loan and borrow up to the amount of this value.

Charitable lead trust (CLT) A trust under which the settlor donates an asset's income interest to a charity for a period of time, at the end of which the remainder interest passes to a private party, typically children or grandchildren for a specified term of years. The settlor (or the settlor's estate) will receive an income tax deduction for the value of the income interest.

Charitable remainder annuity trust (CRAT) A trust into which the settlor transfers assets in exchange for a fixed annuity income of at least 5 percent of the original value of the assets transferred into trust, payable at least annually, usually for life. The value of the remainder is deductible on the income tax return.

Charitable remainder unitrust (CRUT) A trust that is much like the charitable remainder annuity trust, except that the annual income depends on a fixed percentage of the current fair market value of the assets in the trust, determined annually.

Check-the-box regulations Treasury Regulations that allow businesses significant freedom in determining whether to be taxed as a partnership or a corporation.

Chose in action A claim or debt recoverable in a lawsuit.

Clifford trust A grantor trust lasting at least ten years with income payable to a beneficiary and principal reverting to the settlor upon termination. Prior to the Tax Reform Act of 1986, a Clifford trust could be used as a tax shelter that diverted income from the settlor, who was in a higher tax bracket, to a beneficiary, often a child, who was in a lower tax bracket.

Closely held business A firm privately owned by no more than a few individuals or families.

Codicil A written document that amends or revokes a will.

Collateral A relative who shares a common ancestor with a person but who is neither a descendant nor an ascendant of that person, e.g., a cousin. Contrast with issue.

Common disaster clause A clause in a will or trust that specifies which spouse is to be presumed to have died first in the event both are killed in an accident. It may specify that the wealthier spouse is to be presumed to have died first or that each spouse's property is to be distributed as though the other spouse died first.

Common law A body of law that is based on custom and general principles and embodied in case law. It serves as precedent or is applied to situations not covered by statute. In the case of property law it refers to laws developed in England up to the time of the Revolutionary War and is followed by most states in the North, the East Coast, and the South. In contrast, community property law is followed by most of the states on the Pacific Coast and South-West.

Community property In the eight states recognizing it, all property that has been acquired by the efforts of either spouse during their marriage while living in a community property state, except property acquired by only one of the spouses by gift, devise, bequest or inheritance, or, in most of the community property states, by the income therefrom. The eight states are: Arizona, California, Idaho, Louisiana, Nevada,

New Mexico, Texas, and Washington. In addition, Wisconsin adopted a form of community property known as "marital partnership property."

Completed gift A gift in which the donor has so parted with dominion and control over an interest in property that the donor has no power to change its disposition, whether for his or her own benefit or for the benefit of another.

Complex trust A nongrantor trust which, in a given year, either (a) accumulates some fiduciary accounting income (FAI) (i.e., does not pay out all of that year's FAI to the beneficiaries) or (b) distributes principal.

Conduit principle In the income taxation of estates and trusts, the rule that fiduciary accounting income distributed to beneficiaries will be taxed to them, rather than to the estate or trust.

Consanguinity Degree of blood relationship between one person and another.

Conservatee A person who is cared for or whose property is managed by a conservator.

Conservator A court-appointed fiduciary responsible for the protection of the person and/or the person's property after the court has determined that the person is mentally incapable of handling such matters on his or her own.

Consideration furnished test Under the federal estate tax, the proposition that includes in a decedent's gross estate the entire value of property held by the decedent in joint tenancy, reduced only by an amount attributable to that portion of the consideration in money or money's worth which can clearly be shown to have been furnished by the survivors.

Constructive fraud Conduct that is considered fraud under the law despite the absence of an intent to deceive, because it has the same consequences as an actual fraud would have and is against public interests. Examples include a violation of a public or private trust or confidence, the breach of a fiduciary duty, or the use of undue influence.

Contingent interest A future interest that is not vested; that is, an interest whose possession and enjoyment are dependent on the happening of some future event, not on just the passage of time.

Corpus The property in a trust. Also called principal or the *res* (Latin for a thing or object).

Creator The person, also called grantor, settlor, or trustor, who creates a trust and transfers property into it (technically transfers it to the trustee).

Creditor claim form A written statement that sets forth a claim against the probate estate of a deceased debtor.

Creditor claim period Time set by state law in which a creditor must present his or her creditor claim form or lose the right to collect on a debt owed by a decedent. In probate it is usually quite short, e.g., four months.

Credit shelter bypass Property equal in value to the applicable exclusion amount that is taxed when the owner of the property dies, but the unified credit matches the tentative tax, so no tax is actually paid. The property may be held intrust, benefitting certain individuals for a period of time, before eventually being transferred, without being taxed again, to someone else.

Crummey provision A general power clause found in some trusts that give one or more beneficiaries the right to withdraw, for a limited period of time each year, the lesser of the amount of the annual exclusion or the value of the gift property transferred into the trust. Allows the donor to claim an annual exclusion. Often found in trusts for minors and in irrevocable life insurance trusts.

Cumulative gift doctrine The requirement that all lifetime gifts be accumulated; that is, that prior taxable gifts be added to current taxable transfers to determine the estate or gift tax base.

Curtesy A husband's right under common law to a life estate upon the death of his wife in the real property that she owned, provided that they bore a child capable of inheriting the property.

Custodial gift A gift to a custodian for the benefit of a child, under the Uniform Gifts to Minors Act or the Uniform Transfers to Minors Act.

Custodianship An arrangement whereby one person, the custodian, cares for the person or property of another, e.g., a person named to manage a child's property under the Uniform Transfers to Minors Act.

Cy pres **rule** a rule in the law of trusts and estates that provides for the interpretation of instruments as nearly as possible in conformity with the intention of the testator when literal construction is illegal, impracticable, or impossible.

Death certificate A written document issued by the state that verifies the death of a person. In most states these are issued by the health department for the county in which the person died.

Death tax A tax levied on certain property owned or transferred by the decedent at death. Either an estate tax or an inheritance tax.

Decedent In estate planning nomenclature, the person who has died.

Degrees of consanguinity A measure of how closely related two people are.

Depreciation Any decrease in the value of property (as machinery) for the purpose of taxation that is carried on company books as a yearly charge amortizing the original cost over the useful life of the property.

Demand note A note with no fixed period that is due upon the creditor's demand for payment.

Descendant *See issue.*

Devise A gift, by will, of real property.

Devisee A beneficiary, under a will, of a devise, i.e., a gift of real property.

Direct skip A generation-skipping transfer of an interest in property to a skip person, i.e., a person two or more generations below the person making the transfer or to a trust in which all interest is held by such persons and that is subject to generation-skipping transfer taxes.

Disclaimant One who disclaims an interest in property.

Disclaimer An unqualified refusal to accept a gift, bequest, or the right to exercise a power of appointment. In estate planning, a tax-effective disclaimer must meet the requirements of both local law and IRC Section 2518. Tax-effective means that the disclaimant will not be treated as having made a gift.

Dispositive provisions Parts of a will or trust that set forth how property is to be distributed.

Distributable net income (DNI) An amount more or less equal to fiduciary accounting income (FAI) that acts as the measuring rod for estate and trust income taxation.

Distribution deduction In the income taxation of estates and trusts, an amount equal to the lesser of distributable net income or the amount actually distributed to beneficiaries.

Distribution planning Planning the amount and timing of beneficiary distributions from an estate or irrevocable trust, usually with the objective of reducing income tax.

DNI *See Distributable net income.*

Donative intent The person transferring property to another has the intention of making a gift.

Donee A person who receives a gift of a beneficial interest in property. *See Beneficiary.*

Donor A person who make a gift.

Dower A surviving wife's interest in a portion of the real property owned by her deceased husband. Usually, the interest was a life estate.

Durable power of attorney A written agency agreement that continues to have validity even during the principal's incapacity. At common law an agent's authority ceased as soon as the principal was mentally incapacitated.

Durable power of attorney for health care (DPOAHC) A written power of attorney granting to an agent (sometimes called the attorney-in-fact) the authority to make medical decisions on behalf of the principal during such times as the principal is unable to make such decisions.

Durable power of attorney for property A durable power of attorney granting to the attorney-in-fact the power to make decisions concerning the property of the principal.

Economic Growth and Tax Relief Reconciliation Act (EGTRRA) Legislation passed in 2001 that lowers estate and gift tax rates, increases the applicable exclusion amount, and eliminates the estate tax as of 2010. A sunset provision repeals EGTRRA as of 2011.

Elective share The share (e.g., one-third) of an estate set by statute that a widow or widower or sometimes a child is entitled to claim in lieu of any provisions made in a will or in the event of being disinherited unjustifiably. It is also called a forced share.

Endowment insurance Life insurance in which the benefit is paid to the policyowner if he or she is still living at the end of the policy's term (as 20 years).

Equalization A term used in this text to mean a plan of property disposition by the spouses so that the taxable estates (or estate tax bases) of the two are more or less equal as of the first death.

Equitable apportionment statute A state statute that spreads the death tax burden in direct proportion to each beneficiaries share of the taxable estate.

Equitable interest An interest (as a beneficial interest) that is held by virtue of equitable title or that may be claimed on the ground of equitable relief.

Escheat The transfer of an intestate decedent's property to the state, because either the decedent left no next of kin, or all surviving relatives are considered under state law to be too remote for purposes of inheritance.

Estate A quantity of wealth or property. *See also Net estate, Gross estate, and Probate estate.*

Estate planning The arranging for the disposition and management of one's estate at death through the use of wills, trusts, insurance policies, and other devices

Estate pour autre vie A life estate measured by the life of a third person rather than that of the person enjoying the property. Also known as a life estate based upon the life of another.

Estate tax A federal or state tax on the decedent's right to transfer property.

Estate planning The study of the principles of planning for the use, conservation, and efficient transfer of an individual's wealth.

Estate tax base On the federal estate tax return, it is the sum of the taxable estate plus adjusted taxable gifts. It is the amount used to calculate the tentative estate tax.

Estate trust One type of marital trust, rarely if ever used, under which the corpus (and any accumulated income) is made payable to the estate of the surviving spouse at his or her death. Its unique feature is that it qualifies for the marital deduction even though the surviving spouse may not receive all of the income during his or her lifetime. However, income cannot be payable to anyone else.

Excise tax A tax levied on the manufacture, sale, consumption, or transfer of a commodity.

Execute To complete a document (i.e., to do what is necessary to render it valid).

Executor A personal representative of a decedent's estate who was nominated in the will.

Executrix A woman who is an executor. Modern usage uses executor without regard to gender.

Exercise a power of appointment To invoke the power by appointing a permissible appointee.

FAI *See Fiduciary accounting income.*

Family limited partnership A limited partnership meeting the requirements of §704(e) for the benefit of family members, generally with parents as the general partners and children as the limited partners. Used to take advantage of lack of control discounts and lack of marketability discounts as the parents transfer limited partnership units to the children.

Family-owned business interest deduction The estate tax deduction that combines with the applicable exclusion amount to shelter property worth up to $1,300,000 from federal estate taxes. IRC §2057 makes the deduction available for estates that meet certain requirements, such as that the value of the family owned business interest equals or exceeds 50% of the decedent's adjusted gross estate. EGTRRA repeals the deduction as of 2004.

Family pot trust *See Pot trust.*

Fee simple An ownership interest in property (called a fee) that is alienable (i.e., transferrable by deed, will, or intestacy) and of potentially indefinite duration. Sometimes referred to as *fee simple absolute.*

Fee simple absolute A fee that is freely inheritable and alienable without any limitations or restrictions on transfers and is of indefinite duration.

Fiduciary A person in a position of trust and confidence; one who has a legal duty to act for the benefit of another. Examples include executor, trustee, agent, custodian, and attorney.

Fiduciary accounting income (FAI) In the income taxation of estates and trusts, most sources of federal gross income, including cash dividends, interest, and rent (reduced by certain expenses) but not including stock dividends and capital gains.

Fiscal year An income tax year that ends on the last day of any month except December.

Flower bonds Certain long-term U.S. Treasury bonds (no longer in circulation) which, if owned by the decedent at death, were redeemable at par value to pay the federal estate tax.

Fractional interest discount A valuation discount for a partial interest in real property (e.g., a 25% interest as a tenant in common) because it is neither easily partitioned nor readily marketable.

Fraud Any act, expression, omission, or concealment calculated to deceive another to his or her disadvantage. A misrepresentation or concealment with reference to some fact material to a transaction that is made with knowledge of its falsity or in reckless disregard of its truth or falsity and with the intent to deceive another and is reasonably relied on by the other who is injured thereby.

Fraud in the execution Fraud in which the deception causes the other party to misunderstand the nature of the transaction in which he or she is engaging, especially with regard to the contents of an instrument (as a will or promissory note). It is also called fraud in the factum.

Fraud in the inducement Fraud in which the deception leads the other party to engage in a transaction the nature of which he or she understands. Compare this to fraud in the execution.

Freezing the estate tax value Using estate planning transfer techniques to effectively ensure that the future value of certain appreciating property includible in the estate tax base will not be significantly higher than its current value.

Future interest A beneficial interest in property in which the right to possess or enjoy the property is delayed, either by a specific period of time or until the happening of a future event, e.g., a remainder or reversionary interest.

General bequest A gift payable out of the general assets of the estate, but not one that specifies one or more particular items.

General power of appointment The holder of a power has the right to use the property that is subject to the power for his or her own benefit or for the benefit of his or her estate. The property subject to the power at the holder's death will be included in the holder's gross estate even if the power is unexercised.

General power of attorney A document executed by one person called the principal, authorizing another person called the attorney-in-fact, to perform designated acts on behalf of the principal.

Generation-skipping transfer tax (GST tax) A federal or state tax on certain property transfers to a skip person, that is, someone who is two generations or more younger than the donor.

Generation-skipping trust A trust in which the principal will eventually go to a skip person usually following payment of income for life to a non-skip person.

Gift A completed lifetime or deathtime transfer of property by an individual in exchange for any amount that is less than full consideration.

Gift tax A tax on a completed lifetime transfer of property for less than full consideration.

Grantor A person who creates a trust and whose property is transferred into it. Also called creator, settlor, or trustor.

Grantor retained annuity trust (GRAT) A grantor retained trust that pays the grantor a fixed income for a specified period and meets all other requirements of IRC §2702.

Grantor retained income trust (GRIT) An irrevocable trust into which the settlor transfers appreciating property in exchange for the right to receive income for a period of years. Under most GRITs, distribution of corpus at the end of the period depends upon whether or not the settlor survived the period, and if not, the corpus likely reverts to the settlor's estate; if the settlor does survive the period, the corpus likely passes to younger-generation beneficiaries.

Grantor retained unitrust (GRUT) A grantor retained trust that pays the grantor a fixed percentage of the trust's principal, revalued each year, for a specified period and meets all other requirements of IRC §2702.

Grantor trust A trust in which the settlor has retained sufficient interest to make the income received by the trust taxable to the grantor, not to the trust or its other beneficiaries.

Grantor trust rules The federal income tax rules concerning grantor trusts located in Internal Revenue Code §§671-78.

Gross estate An estate tax term meaning all property in which the decedent had an interest at the time of his or her death, any property transferred by the decedent under which the decedent retained an interest or control, and any life insurance transferred, or any retained interests released, within three years of death.

Grossing up Inclusion in the gross estate of gift taxes paid on any gifts made within three years of death. Review IRC §2035(b).

GST tax *See Generation-skipping transfer tax.*

Guardian A court-appointed fiduciary responsible for the person or property of a minor or, in some cases, an incompetent adult, or both. In some states, a guardian is called a committee, in others, a guardian for an incompetent adult is called a conservator.

Heir One who inherits or is entitled to succeed to the possession of property after the death of its owner: as one who by operation of law inherits the property from a person who dies without leaving a valid will. Also called an heir at law, heir general, or legal heir. The term is used even if the person is disinherited by a valid will.

Holder (of a power of appointment) A person who has received a power of appointment, i.e., the one who has the right to appoint designated property to a permissible appointee. Also called the donee of the power.

Holding period In income tax law, the length of time that property is held. It determines whether a gain is short term or long term. The current threshold is one year for long term capital gains, however, property received from a decedent is automatically long term.

Holographic will A will, recognized as valid in most states even though it is not witnessed. The state law is likely to require that at least the dispositive portions of the will be the testator's handwriting.

Incapacity The quality or state of being incapable. Lack of legal qualifications due to age or mental condition.

Incidents of ownership Powers and interests over an insurance policy on decedent's life that would subject the proceeds to inclusion in the decedent's gross estate under Section 2042.

Income beneficiary The beneficiary of a trust who has a life estate or estate for years in the trust income.

Income shifting In estate planning, saving income tax by enabling income otherwise taxable to a high income tax individual to be taxed to a lower tax bracket family member.

Income tax A tax levied on income earned by a taxpayer during a given year.

Incompetence The state or fact of being incompetent.

Incomplete transfer A gift made without total relinquishment of dominion and control. i.e., it is rescindable or amendable.

Informed consent Consent to medical treatment or to participation in a medical experiment after achieving an understanding of what is involved and of the risks.

Inherit To receive property by intestate succession or by a bequest.

Inheritance The acquisition of real or personal property under the laws of intestacy or sometimes by a will. The succession either by will or by operation of law to all the estate, rights, and liabilities of the decedent. Something that is or may be inherited .

Inheritance tax A state tax on the right of a beneficiary to receive property from a decedent.

Installment sale The sale of an asset in exchange for an installment note, in which the buyer agrees to make periodic payments of principal and interest, based on a fair market rate of interest.

Insurable interest An interest or stake in property or in a person that arises from the potential for financial loss upon the destruction of the property or the death of the person. In many states one cannot obtain an insurance policy without showing that one has an insurable interest. The purpose of requiring an insurable interest is to prevent the use of insurance as a form of gambling or as a method of profiting from destruction.

Insurance The action, process, or means of insuring or the state of being insured usu. against loss or damage by a contingent event (as death, fire, accident, or sickness).

Intangible personal property Property (as a stock certificate or professional license) that derives value not from its intrinsic physical nature but from what it represents.

Intentionally defective grantor trust A funded irrevocable trust that is complete for estate tax purposes and incomplete for income tax. The purpose of this arrangement is to give have the grantor pay the income tax rather than having it paid by the trustee or by the beneficiary.

Inter vivos transfer A transfer made while the transferor is alive.

Inter vivos trust *See living trust.*

Interest by the entirety *See tenancy by the entirety.*

Interest for years A property interest for a fixed period of time.

Interest-free loan A loan, having no interest charge, usually to a family member in a lower income tax bracket. TRA 1986 limited its use by requiring lenders to impute interest income for many of these low-interest, no-interest family loan arrangements.

Interest in common *See tenancy in common.*

Intestate Having died leaving probate property not disposed of by a valid will.

Instrument Any legal document.

Inventory and appraisement A probate document that delineates all probate assets at their fair market value as of the date of death.

Irrevocable Subject to no right to rescind or amend (the terms of a transfer of one or more interests in property).

Irrevocable trust A trust that cannot be revoked by the settlor after its creation except upon the consent of all the beneficiaries.

Issue A person's direct offspring, including children, grandchildren, great-grandchildren, and the like. Also called descendants or lineal descendants.

Itemized deductions In federal income tax law, deductions from adjusted gross income that are specifically listed, and taken in lieu of the standard deduction.

Joint and mutual will A single will jointly executed by two or more persons and containing reciprocal provisions for the disposition of property owned jointly, severally, or in common upon the death of one of them. It may also be called a *joint and reciprocal will*.

Joint tenancy A form of equal, undivided ownership in property that, upon death of one owner, automatically passes to the surviving owner(s). All interests must be equal, therefore, there cannot be a joint tenancy held 25% by one person and 75% by another. The co-owners are called joint tenants.

Joint will A single will jointly executed by two or more persons and containing their respective wills. In most states the execution of a joint will or mutual wills does not create a presumption of a contract not to revoke the will or wills. See mutual wills.

Kiddie tax The term given to the federal income tax law that requires the unearned income of a child under the age of 13 be taxed at the parent's top marginal rate.

Lack of marketability discount A valuation discount given stock in a closely held business arising from the lack of an established market making the stock more difficult to sell.

Lapse The result when a beneficiary named in a will fails to survive the testator. Also, a power of appointment is said to lapse if the holder does not exercise it within the permitted period.

Leasehold An interest in property entitling the lessee to possess and use the property for a specified time, usually in exchange for a series of payments.

Legacy A gift, by will, of personal property. Also called a bequest.

Legal interest An interest that is recognized in law (as by legal title). Compare equitable interest or beneficial interest neither of which require the person benefitted to have title.

Legatee A beneficiary, under a will, of a gift of personal property.

Letters testamentary A formal court document used as evidence of the probate court's authorization of the estate's personal representative to act on behalf of a decedent's estate.

Leveraging The process by which a given amount of exclusion, exemption, or credit can shelter more than that amount from future transfer taxation.

Lineal Consisting of or being in a direct male or female line of ancestry, e.g., a lineal descendant.

Life estate An estate in property held only during or measured in duration by the lifetime of a specified individual, usually the individual enjoying the property. The life of the person who determines the duration is referred to as the measuring life.

Life insurance Insurance providing for the payment of money to a designated beneficiary upon the death of the insured.

Life insurance policy A contract in which the insurance company agrees to pay a cash lump-sum amount (the face value or policy proceeds) to the person named in the policy to receive it (the beneficiary) upon the death of the subject of the insurance (the insured).

Limited liability companies A business organization in which the owners, called members, do not have personal liability for the contracts or the torts of the business, yet the organization is taxed like a partnership. Those owning an interest in the company are called members.

Limited power of appointment The holder of a power cannot use it to transfer the property that is subject to the power for his or her own benefit or for the benefit of his or her estate. It is not considered a gift if the holder exercises the power and the property subject to the power is not included in the holder's gross estate when the holder dies.

Living trust A trust funded during the lifetime of the trustor. Also called an inter vivos trust.

Living will A document in which the signer indicates preferences or directions for the administration of life-sustaining medical treatment (including the withdrawal or withholding thereof) in the event of terminal illness or permanent unconsciousness. It may be in the form of a directive to physicians.

Marital deduction In federal gift and estate taxation, the deduction for certain transfers to a spouse.

Marital trust A trust structured to receive property that will qualify for the marital deduction, e.g., a "power of appointment trust" or a QTIP trust. Also called a *marital deduction trust*.

Members in a limited liability company Investors/owners in a limited liability company.

Minority discount A valuation discount allowed for an interest in a business because the interest is not a controlling interest.

Mutual will One of two separate wills that share reciprocal provisions for the disposition of property in the event of death by one of the parties. They may be executed in connection with an agreement based on sufficient consideration such that neither will can be revoked without mutual consent of the parities. These may also be called reciprocal or mirror wills.

Net estate The net worth of a person; i.e., total assets minus total liabilities.

No contest clause A clause inserted in a will that causes a legacy to be forfeited if the legatee challenges the will by bringing a will contest.

Non-recourse note A note whose satisfaction upon default may be obtained only out of the collateral securing it.

Nuncupative will A will allowed in some states that is dictated orally before witnesses and set down in writing within a statutorily specified time period (e. g., 30 days before the testator's death) and that is allowed only for one in imminent peril of death from a terminal illness or from military or maritime service.

Obligor One who is bound by an obligation to another.

Omitted child *See Omitted heir.*

Omitted heir A descendant of a testator who would be an heir under the laws of intestacy but who is not named under the will. Many states have statutes requiring a share of the estate to go to a pretermitted heir on the assumption that the omission was unintentional.

Omitted spouse *See Omitted heir.*

Opportunity shifting The transfer of a rapidly appreciating wealth- or of an income-producing opportunity to another family member.

Outright transfer A transfer in which the transferee receives both legal interests and all beneficial interests, subject to no restrictions or conditions.

Partnership capital freeze Like a recapitalization, the reorganization of a partnership for the purpose of freezing the estate value of a partner's partnership interest. Severely restricted by the Revenue Reconciliation Act of 1990.

Permissible appointee (of a power of appointment) A party whom the holder may appoint by exercising the power.

Per capita Equally to each individual. Per capita distribution of an estate, although it follows the line of descent, provides each descendant (providing there is no ascendent relative in between the person and the decedent) with an equal share of the estate's assets regardless of the degree of his or her kinship. Children, grandchildren, great-grandchildren, etc., all receive equal shares.

Perfect unification When applied to the estate and gift tax laws, a set of conditions in which an individual would be indifferent, from a total transfer tax planning point of view, between making lifetime and deathtime gifts. It helps identify the factors that make the current system imperfect, which serves as the basis for some transfer tax planning.

Per stirpes *See right of representation.*

Perpetuities saving clause A clause in a will or trust that prevents interests from being ruled invalid under the rule against perpetuities.

Personal exemption In federal income tax law, amounts deductible on behalf of the taxpayer, the spouse, and each dependent, in calculating taxable income.

Personal property Property other than real estate. It is property that is movable (not including crops or other resources still attached to land). Also called personalty.

Personal representative The person appointed by the probate court to represent and manage the estate. If nominated in the will, called an executor.

Pickup tax A state death tax set as exactly equal to the federal credit for state death taxes.

Pooled income fund An investment fund created and maintained by the target charity, which "pools" property from many similar contributors. This arrangement ordinarily provides that the charity will pay to the grantor an income for life and, if desired, for the life of the grantor's spouse, based on the rate of return actually earned by the fund as a whole. At their death, the property passes to the charity.

Postmortem Referring to events that happen after a person's death.

Possessory interest An interest (as a right) involving or arising out of the possession of property. A possessory interest is based on control rather than use. Thus a lessee who occupies and controls the use of property has a possessory interest, while a party who has an easement does not.

Pot trust A trust established at the death of parents for the benefit of their minor children. Typically, the trust corpus remains undivided until the youngest child reaches an age specified in the trust, e.g., age 18 or 21. At that time, the assets are divided into equal separate shares, one for each child. The assets are distributed outright, or they are held for distribution at some older age. Also called a Family Pot Trust.

Pour-over trust A trust that receives the assets that make up its principal by operation of a testamentary disposition to it upon the settlor's death.

Pour-over will A will that distributes at the testator's death probate assets to a trust previously created.

Power of appointment A power to name someone to receive a beneficial interest in property.

Power of appointment trust A marital trust that provides a surviving spouse with a life estate in the property and with a power of appointment allowing appointment of the property to the surviving spouse or to his or her estate, e.g., Trust A of the ABC or AB estate plans. To obtain a marital deduction the trust must comply with IRC § 2056(b)(5).

Power of attorney A document executed by one person, called the principal, authorizing another person, called the attorney-in-fact, to perform designated acts on behalf of the principal.

Precatory language Language in a will that does not direct or command, but merely expresses a wish, hope or desire, e.g., $50,000 to Martin with the expectation that he will use the money to go to college. Precatory language is not enforceable.

Present interest An immediate right to possess or enjoy property.

Pretermitted heir *See omitted heir.*

Principal The property in a trust. Also called corpus.

Private annuity A transfer of property under which the seller receives an unsecured promise of a life annuity.

Probate The legal process of administering the estate of a decedent. It focuses on the probate estate, that is, property which will be disposed of by, and only by, either the decedent's will or by the state laws of intestate succession. More narrowly and less commonly, probate is used to mean certifying or proving the validity of the will after the death of the testator.

Probate estate All of the decedent's property passing to others by means of the probate process. This includes all property owned by the decedent except joint tenancy interests. The probate estate does not include property transferred by the decedent before death to a trustee, life insurance proceeds on the decedent's life when paid directly to a beneficiary, nor the decedent's interest in pension and profit sharing plans. The latter are said to "pass outside of probate."

Promissory note A note containing an unconditional promise to pay on demand or at a fixed or determined future time a particular sum of money to or to the order of a specified person or to the bearer.

Qualified terminable interest property (QTIP) Property passing to a surviving spouse that qualifies for the marital deduction if the executor so elects providing that the spouse is entitled to receive income in payments made at least annually for life, and that no one has a power to appoint any part of the property to any person other than the surviving spouse.

QTIP election An election by the executor of the estate of the first spouse to die to treat certain property as QTIP property, thereby qualifying it for the marital deduction.

QTIP trust A marital trust for which a federal estate tax election can be made so as to qualify the trust property for the marital deduction. It must provide that the surviving spouse is entitled to all of the income from the trust property, payable at least annually. In addition, the trust cannot give anyone a power to appoint any of the property to anyone other than to the surviving spouse so long as he or she is alive. Its uniqueness lies in the fact that it qualifies for the marital deduction even though its property neither passes to nor is controlled by the surviving spouse.

Qualified charitable remainder trust A trust that is either a charitable remainder annuity trust or a charitable remainder unitrust.

Real property Property consisting of land, buildings, crops, any other resources still attached to or within the land, improvements or fixtures permanently attached to the land or a structure on it.

Recapitalization A reorganization of a closely held corporation for the purpose of freezing the value of a primary owner's interest in the company. Severely restricted by enactment of Revenue Reconciliation Act of 1990.

Reciprocal wills Wills for two people (usually a married couple) that are virtually identical; each leaves all (or substantially all) property to the other if the latter survives, otherwise to third persons. Sometimes called *mirror wills* or *mutual wills*. Reciprocal wills are usually simple wills; more complex wills are more likely to have unique features.

Remainder In the context of trusts, the future interest to the remaining trust assets at the termination of all other interests. More technically, the right to use, possess and enjoy property after a prior owner's interest ends, in a situation where both interests were created at the same time and in the same document.

Remainderman The beneficiary of a trust who will receive the trust corpus (i.e., that which remainders) at the termination of all other interests.

Res From the Latin for "the thing." In the context of estate planning it generally refers to the property held in trust. Also called *corpus*.

Residuary bequest A gift by will of that part of the testator's estate that remains after taking care of all specific and pecuniary bequests.

Residuary estate All of what is left of an estate once the deceased person's debts and administration costs have been paid and all specific and general bequests and devises have been distributed. It is also called the residual estate.

Resulting trust An implied trust based upon the presumed intentions of the parties as inferred from all the circumstances that the party holding legal title to trust property holds it for the benefit of the other party.

Reversion A future interest in property that is retained by the transferor; it will become a present interest (revert back to the transferor) when all other interests created at the time of the transfer have ended. Usually used in connection with trusts established for a limited duration.

Revocable Subject to the right to rescind or amend (the terms of a transfer of one or more interests in property).

Revocable trust A trust over which the settlor has retained the power of revocation.

Right of survivorship The right of the surviving owners of property held jointly to take the entire property and exclude the deceased owner's heirs and estate beneficiaries, e.g., the right of the survivor of joint tenants to sole ownership of the entire property, or of the surviving spouse to own the property the couple held as tenants by the entirety.

Rule against perpetuities A common law principle invalidating a dispositive clause in a will or a trust if the contingent interest transferred might vest in a transferee too long after the settlor's death.

S1 Shorthand nomenclature for the first spouse to die.

S2 Shorthand nomenclature for the second spouse to die.

Sale A transfer of property under which each transferor exchanges consideration that the parties regard as equivalent in value.

Self-canceling installment note (SCIN) An installment note which provides that no further payments will be made after the seller's death.

Self-proved will A will containing a formal affidavit by witnesses stating that all formalities have been complied with. It eliminates the need for the witnesses to verify the correctness of the execution of the document after the testator dies.

Separate property In community property states, all property that is not community property. That is, all property acquired by a person prior to marriage, and all property acquired during a marriage by gift, devise, bequest or inheritance, or, in most community property states, income earned on property so acquired. Community property may be converted to separate property by the written agreement of the couple.

Settlor The person who creates the trust and whose property is transferred to it. Also called creator, grantor, or trustor.

Shifting income *See Income shifting.*

Short-term trust An irrevocable trust that reverts to the grantor sometime after 10 years or after the life of the income beneficiary. The income was taxed to the beneficiary, not to the settlor. TRA 86, in subjecting this trust to the grantor trust rules, virtually eliminated its further use.

Simple trust A trust under which all current income must be distributed and no principal may be distributed.

Simple will A will prepared for a family having a small estate, one for whom death tax planning is not a significant concern, with the typical pattern being "everything to my spouse, if she survives, and if she does not, then to my children per stirpes."

Skip person In federal generation-skipping transfer tax law, a beneficiary who is at least two generations younger than the transferor.

Soak-up tax *See sponge tax.*

Special use valuation A provision in federal estate tax law (Section 2032A) that permits qualifying estates to value farmland or business use real estate at its "qualified-use value" rather than at its "highest and best use" value. The maximum decrease is $750,000 (indexed after 1997).

Specific bequest A gift of a particular item of property which is capable of being identified and distinguished from all other property. Contrasted with general bequest and residuary bequest.

Spendthrift clause A clause in a trust that restricts the beneficiary from transferring any of his or her future interest in the corpus or income. For example, a typical spendthrift clause would not permit the beneficiary to pledge the interest as collateral against a loan.

Spendthrift trust A trust that is created for the benefit of a spendthrift who is paid income therefrom but it cannot be reached by creditors to satisfy the spendthrift's debts.

Splitting a gift Treating a gift of the property owned by one spouse, on the federal gift tax return, as if it were made one-half by each spouse.

Sponge tax Where a state's inheritance tax produces total death taxes for a decedent's estate that are less than that estate's allowable federal credit for state death taxes, the state collects the difference between the total and the allowable credit. Because the federal credit is a dollar for dollar credit, this sponge tax does not increase the overall taxes for a decedent's estate.

Spousal remainder trust An irrevocable trust providing for income for a period to a lower-income tax bracket family member, then remainder to the trustor's spouse. Use of this trust was virtually eliminated by TRA 86, which subjected it to the grantor trust rules.

Springing durable power of attorney A durable power of attorney that becomes effective at the onset of the principal's mental incapacity.

Standard deduction In federal income tax law, a fixed amount that may be deducted from adjusted gross income. It may be used instead of specifically subtracting actual "itemized" deductions.

Standby trust An unfunded living trust whose principal financial management and control provisions do not come into effect until the grantor dies or is determined to be incapacitated. At that point, the trust is usually funded by the probate process or, if the grantor is still alive but incapacitated, by the grantor's attorney-in-fact.

Step-up in basis Shorthand for the change in basis that occurs when the owner of property dies. Technically, it will only be a "step-up" in basis if, at the owner's death, the property has a fair market value that is higher than the basis was immediately before his or her death.

Subrogation An equitable doctrine holding that when a third party pays a creditor or obligee the third party succeeds to the creditor's rights against the debtor or obligor. A doctrine holding that when an insurance company pays an insured's claim of loss due to another's tort, the insurer succeeds to the insured's rights (as the right to sue for damages) against the tortfeasor (the person who did the harm).

Surrogate decision makers Individuals capable of making decisions regarding a person's property and family at times when the person is unable, either due to incapacity or death. Examples include attorney-in-fact, trustee, and executor.

Survival clause A disposition provision in a will or trust naming an alternate taker of certain property if the donee fails to survive the donor for some period of time.

Takers in default Persons who receive property subject to a power of appointment if the holder permits the power to lapse unexercised.

Tangible personal property Personal property which has value because of its physical characteristics.

Taxable estate In federal estate tax law, the gross estate reduced by all allowable deductions.

Taxable distribution In federal generation-skipping transfer tax law, any distribution of property out of a trust to a skip person (other than a taxable termination or a direct skip).

Taxable gift In federal gift tax law, for a given year, total gross gifts reduced by all allowable deductions, exemptions, and exclusions.

Taxable termination In federal generation-skipping transfer tax law, the termination of all the interests of one generation in the income or principal of a trust, with the result that the interest shift to another lower generation of skip persons.

Tax clause A provision in a will specifying which property bears the burden of paying taxes.

Tenancy by the entirety An tenancy in property similar to a joint tenancy; however, it can be created only between husband and wife. Unlike joint tenancy, neither spouse may transfer or encumber the property without the consent of the other.

Tenancy in common An interest in property held by two or more persons, each having an undivided right to possess property. Unlike a joint interest, however, an interest in common may be owned in unequal percentages, and when one owner dies the remaining owners do not automatically succeed in ownership. Instead, the decedent's interest passes through his or her estate, by will, by some other document, or by the laws of intestate distribution. The co-owners are called "tenants in common."

Terminable interest An interest which might terminate or fail on the lapse of time, on the occurrence of an event or contingency, or on the failure of an event or contingency to occur. Property otherwise qualifying for the marital deduction will not qualify if the interest passing to the spouse is terminable, unless there is an exception such exists for QTIP property.

Terminal value Used to indicate the value of a cash value life insurance policy that is currently in force. Formally called the policy's interpolated terminal reserve value, its amount is nearly equal to its cash surrender value.

Term life insurance A type of life insurance policy that has no value prior to the death of the insured because the premium charged, which increases over time with increasing risk of death, just covers the risk of death for that period. Term insurance simply buys pure protection: if the insured dies during the policy term, the company will pay the face value; otherwise, it will pay nothing.

Testamentary capacity The mental ability required of a testator to validly execute a will.

Testamentary transfer A transfer at death by will.

Testamentary trust A trust established by a will. The funding mechanism is the probate process.

Testate Dying with a valid will.

Testator The person who executes a will.

Throwback rules In the income taxation of trusts, rules that, prior to being repealed by TRA '97, subjected income accumulated by a trust in one year and distributed to a beneficiary in another year to possible additional taxation to the beneficiary.

Totten trust A pay on death bank account. The owner of the account specifies that, if the owner dies while the account is still open, it should be transferred (without probate) to a named beneficiary. Also known as a *bank account trust, savings bank trust,* or a *tentative trust.*

TOD account A bank account or brokerage account that is set up to follow the requirements of the Uniform Transfer on Death Act, such that upon the owners death the account is transferred to a named beneficiary without probate. *See Totten trust.*

TRA '86 Tax Reform Act of 1986.

TRA '97 Taxpayer Relief Act of 1997.

Transfer Any type of passing of property in which the transferor gives up some kind of interest to the transferee. Sometimes called an assignment.

Trust A legal arrangement between trustor and trustee that divides legal and beneficial interests in property among two or more people. In estate planning the trust agreement is likely to be many pages long, and to spell out in detail the trustees obligations concerning the management and distribution of the trust income and corpus.

Trust beneficiary A person who is named to enjoy a beneficial interest in the trust.

Trust-will *See Testamentary trust.*

Trustor The person who creates a trust and whose property is transferred to the trustee. Also called creator, grantor, or settlor.

Underwriter A person (or a company) who underwrites an insurance policy. A person who assesses risks to be covered by an insurance policy.

Undue influence Influence by a confidante which has the effect of impeding the testator's free will. A will can be denied probate (or at least certain clauses will be disregarded) if it can be established that the testator, at execution, was subject to undue influence. To be undue, the influence must be wrongful in some way.

Unification of gift and estate taxes Partially successful efforts by Congress in 1976 to tax lifetime and deathtime transfers equally, so that an individual would be indifferent, from a total transfer tax planning point of view, between making lifetime and deathtime gifts.

Unified credit The credit allowed against the tentative tax that results in sheltering modest taxable gifts and modest taxable estates from the transfer tax.

Uniform Gifts to Minors Act Like the Uniform Transfers to Minors Act, a statute in many states permitting custodial gifts for the benefit of a minor.

Uniform Probate Code (UPC) A complete set of probate laws originally promulgated by legal scholars and practitioners and currently adopted in whole or in part by about two fifths of the states.

Uniform Simultaneous Death Act (USDA) A statute providing that when transfer of title to property depends on the order of deaths, and that when no sufficient evidence exists that two people died other than simultaneously, the property of each is disposed of as if each had survived the other.

Uniform Transfer on Death Act A uniform law adopted by many states that allows accounts at financial institutions (e.g., banks, savings and loans, thrifts, credit unions) and at brokerages to have a designation that allows the account to be transferred to a named beneficiary, without passing through probate, if the account is still open when the owner dies.

Uniform Transfers to Minors Act Like the older Uniform Gifts to Minors Act, this provides a means of transferring property to young people through the use of a custodian.

Universal life insurance Life insurance characterized by flexible premiums, benefits, and payment schedules, by the indexing of cash value to money market interest rates, and by the periodic reporting of current value and company costs charged to the account.

Variable life insurance Life insurance in which all or part of the cash value of the policy is located in a tax-deferred investment portfolio with risk assumed by the insured for investment losses.

Variable universal life insurance Universal life insurance that includes the investment component of variable life insurance.

Vested interest A nonforfeitable future interest whose possession and enjoyment are delayed only by time and not dependent on the happening of any future event.

Wait-and-see statute A provision in some state statutes that can overcome the effect of the rule against perpetuities by finding an interest void only if its turns out, in fact, not to vest within the required period, e.g., within 60 years.

Whole life insurance Life insurance that provides coverage over the life of the insured and that can be sold for surrender value or used as the basis of low-interest loans. It is also called ordinary life insurance, cash value life insurance, and straight life insurance.

Will A written document disposing of a person's probate property at death.

Will substitute A device (as a trust) used instead of a will to transfer property upon death.

Witnessed will A written will, recognized in all states, that must be signed by two or more witnesses who acknowledge, among other things, that the testator asked them to witness the will, that they in fact did witness the testator's signing, and that the testator is mentally competent to execute a will (in accordance with state law).

Index

Abatement, 35
ABC trusts, 471, 4769, 478, 482–492
AB trusts, 471, 477, 478–482
  benefits of, 480–482
  estate-equalization, 531–532
  traditional, 529–531
AB with disclaimer into C trusts, 518–522
Accelerated death benefits (ADB), 676–677
Accountants, role in estate planning, 13–14
Accounting, fiduciary, 348–351
Accounting methods, for fiduciary income
  taxation, 352
Ademption doctrine, 34
Adjusted basis, 319–320
Adjusted gross estate (AGE), 200, 458, 529,
  587–589, 687
Adjusted gross income, of a fiduciary entity, 370
Adjusted taxable estate, 208
Adjusted taxable gifts, 181, 190, 203,
  257–258, 259, 264, 318, 634, 658, 678
Adjusted total income (ATI), 377–378
Administration expense/losses election, 816
Administration expenses, 424
  fiduciary income taxation and, 367
Administrator, decedent's estate, 33
Administrator with will annexed, 34, 152
Adopted children, legal rights of, 145–146
Advance directives, 797–798
Advancements, 143–144
Adverse party, 242, 313
Affidavit of death of joint tenant, 126
Affidavit of right, 169–170
Affidavit-of-right procedure, 159–160
After-born children, 93, 144
Aging, agencies on, 796
Alimony, 387
Allocations
  to beneficiaries, 381–382
  exemption, 548–549
  forced delay of GST exemption, 549
Alternate executor, 770

Alternate trustees, 777
Alternate valuation date election, 205, 556,
  821–822
Amount realized, 319
Ancillary administration, 424–425
Annual exclusions, 182, 197–198
  gift tax, 596
  for lifetime gifts, 202–203
  sheltering, 578–579, 684
Annual financial reports, 13
Annuitant, 619
Annuities. See also Pensions; Private annuities
  survivorship, 234–237
  valuation for life, 63
  valuation for term certain, 61
Anti-freeze legislation, 741
Anti-freeze rules, 624–627
  applying to GRITs, 632
Antilapse statutes, 772
Applicable exclusion amount (AEA), 52, 183, 184,
  197–200, 214, 229, 455, 456, 525,
  541–542, 812
  "available," 483
  leveraging, 627
Applicable exclusion amount (AEA) trust, 514, 668
Applicable family members, 625, 632, 744
Applicable federal mid-term rate (AFMR), 59
Applicable federal rate (AFR), 613
Applicable retained interest, 744–745
Applicable tax rate, 542, 547–548
Appointees, 53. See also Power of appointment
Appraisals, 705
  discount and the IRS, 706
  qualified, 637
Appreciation, 322
  net, 323
  post-gift, 579–580, 585–586
  unsheltered postgift, 582
Ascertainable standard, 242, 475, 480, 482,
  483
Ascertainable standard exception, 313

Assets. *See also* High-basis assets; Low-basis assets
  allocating to trusts, 497–498
  basis considerations for, 584–585
  distribution of, 157
  family limited partnerships and, 704, 707
  gifting of, 584–590, 706–707
  intangible, 320
  maintaining control of, 405
  non-probate, 33, 126–130, 421
  orderly administration of, 421
  probate, 33, 126–130
  protection of, 707
  to qualify for IRC benefits, 587–589
  selling, 668–669, 819–820
  spending down, 793
  unproductive, 484–485
  use in funding lump-sum payments, 740
Asset "spend-down" planning, 793–794
Assignment-of-income doctrine, 411, 662
Assignment
  of ownership rights, 313–314
  of property, 28–29
  restrictions against, 780–781
Assisted living facilities, 796
AsuperB trusts, 514–517
Attestation clause, 96
Attested wills, 87
Attorney fees, 406, 424
  California probate, 158
  for a summary distribution, 171
Attorney-in-fact, 787, 791, 792
Attorneys, 13
  document drafting by, 406–407
  as executors, 158–159, 769
  as trustees, 776
Augmented estate, percentage of, 148
Automatic marital deduction, 486
Average tax rate, 196
A with disclaimer into B trusts, 522–524

Balance sheet, 8, 9
Bargain sales, 30–31, 265, 637–638
  intrafamily, 615
Basis. *See also* Stepped-up basis
  after estate tax repeal, 328–332
  of gifted assets, 584–585
  gifts and, 322
  under joint tenancy, 433
  step-down in, 323, 325
  step-up in, 323, 324, 409
  transfers and, 213
Basis increase, 329–331
Basis rules, for taxable gifts, 319–333
Beneficial interests, 28–29, 49–52
Beneficiaries, 31, 32, 37, 671. *See also* Income

beneficiaries
  allocations to, 381–382
  of life insurance, 83, 313–314, 680
  residuary, 773
  taxation of, 374–389
  transfers from a trust/estate to, 373
  of a trust, 50, 98
  unintended, 430
Beneficiary designations, irrevocable, 83
Bequests, 34
  charitable, 638
  disguised, 737
  types of, 34–36
Bilateral contract, 790
Blockage discount, 703
Blood relationship, degrees of, 34, 131–132
Blood relatives, predeceased, 772
"Bubble," rate surcharge, 193, 199
Business affairs, unwinding, 10
Business buyout agreement, 733, 734–740
Business contracts, for future income, 728
Businesses. *See also* Closely held businesses; Family limited partnerships (FLPs); Limited liability companies (LLCs)
  involving children in, 707
  selling, 686
Business income, for fiduciary entities, 356
Business interests, 232
  freezing the value of, 741–750
  installment sales of, 740
  lack of marketability discount for, 702
  minority interest discount for, 699–700
  transferring, 729–733, 744
  valuing, 736
Business owners
  liquidity planning for, 686–699
  termination of management by, 728–729
Business ownership interests, gifting, 730
Business responsibility, delegating, 728
Business successors, selecting, 730–731
Business value, preserving, 407
Buyout agreements
  business, 733, 734–740
  funding of, 686, 738–740
  taxation of, 734–738
Buyout contracts, 729
Buy-sell agreements, 733
By operation of law, 44, 126
Bypass planning, 474–476
  advanced, 513–559
Bypass property, 475
Bypass trusts, 465, 533–536, 540
"By right of representation" distribution, 132–133, 134, 554

Calendar year basis, 813, 817
California rule, 47
"Cancellation with a subsequent instrument," 93
Capital, income-producing, 704
Capital gain property, 635–636, 637
Capital gains/losses, 387
  fiduciary taxation and, 354, 355, 358
Capital transactions, distributable net income
  and, 378
Carryover basis (COB), 213, 321
  for wealthy persons, 331–332
Cash Flow Statement, 9
Cash lump-sum payments, for buyout agreements,
  738
Cash needs at death, 667–668
Cash surrender value, 37, 672, 673
Cash-value accumulations, income taxation of,
  675
Cash-value insurance, 37, 672–673
Casualty losses, 816
C corporations, 710, 733
Certified Financial Planner (CFP) Board of
  Standards, 7, 19
Chapter 14 rules, 624–625, 727, 741
Charging order, 708
Charitable contributions, 365–366
Charitable deductions, 269–271, 365–367, 385
  complete, 39
  unlimited, 201
Charitable gifts, 304
  using trusts, 270–271
Charitable lead annuity trusts, 644
Charitable lead trust, 642–644
Charitable remainder annuity trust (CRAT), 640–641,
  642
Charitable remainder trusts, 640
Charitable remainder trusts with a life estate,
  471
Charitable remainder unitrust (CRUT), 641–642
Charitable transfers, 635–645
  lifetime, 638–639
  tax consequences of, 635–637
Charitable trusts, 113
Charity
  donating remainder interests to, 640
  outright gifts to, 637–640
Charity-beneficiaries, 381
Check-the-box regulations, 709
Children. *See also* Adopted children; Omitted
  children; Minors
  disabled, 781
  disinherited, 149
  failed marriages of, 707
  gifting to, 94, 589–590
  involving in family-owned businesses, 707
  legal rights of, 144–146

as life insurance owners and beneficiaries, 681
  outright gifts to, 581
  planning for the care of, 408, 764–767
  as successor trustees, 104
  unearned income of, 601–602
Chose in action, 41
Class gift, 35
Client Fact-Finding Questionnaire, 21–26
Client-planner relationship, 8
  acquiring client facts, 8–10
  client financial status, 8–9
  monitoring planning recommendations, 11–12
  plan implementation, 11
  presenting planning alternatives, 10–11
Clients
  financial status of, 10
  objectives of, 8–10
  unmarried, 783
Clifford trust, 657
Closely held businesses, 184, 687, 699–700,
  725–750
  buyout agreements for, 733, 734–740
  early planning for, 733–734
  estate planning for, 728–734
  freezing the value of business interests,
  741–750
  valuing, 727
Codicil, 88, 93, 98, 121
Collateral heirs, 212
Collateral relationships, 132
College expenses, 602–603
"Common disaster" clause, 463–464
Common law, 34, 47, 48, 112
Common law states, 45, 458, 489
  intestate succession in, 140
Common stock, 742
Community property, 46–49, 126, 128, 147–148,
  170–171, 237, 308, 324
  under joint tenancy, 433
  for nontraditional relationships, 785
  versus joint tenancy, 48–49
  with right of survivorship, 49, 325–326
Community property states, 46–47, 129, 234,
  458–459, 489
  basis adjustments in, 325–326
  intestate succession in, 140
  joint tenancies in, 785
Completed gifts, 300–301, 576
  to minors, 593
Complete transfer in trust, 300
Complete transfers, 29–30, 409, 411
  intrafamily, 611–622
Complex trusts, income taxation, 375
Concurrent ownership, 44–49
Conduit principle, 814–815
Confirmation of trust, trust abstract, 439

Conjectural creditors' claims, 422
Consanguinity, degrees of, 131–132
Conservatee, 51
Conservation easement, qualified, 698–699
Conservator, 51, 794
Conservatorship
  for incapacitated persons, 786
  living trust as an alternative to, 440
Consideration, 30, 302, 617
  intrafamily transfers for, 611–622
Consideration furnished rule, 324–325
  for joint tenancy, 238–240
"Consideration offset," 265
"Constitutional trust," 661–662
Contingent interests, 57
Contingent marital deduction clause, 684
Contingent remainder, 57
Contingent trust, 112
Contractual wills, 96, 97, 99
Contracts, preparing, 4
Contribution base (CB), 635
Control issues, interspousal gifting and, 591
Control premiums, 701-702
Corporate executors, 769
Corporate fiduciaries, 104
Corporate interests, transfers of, 744
Corporate recapitalization, 741–750
Corporate stock, redemption bailout of, 639
Corporate trustees, 776
Corporations, versus limited liability companies,
  709-710
Corpus (principal), 15, 50
  allocations to, 348–350, 364
Costs
  estate transfer, 406
  of family limited partnerships, 705
  of joint tenancy, 428
  of living trusts, 437–438
  probate, 424–425
  of probate versus living trust, 445–447
Court supervision, 420
  of probate administration, 160
Creator, trusts, 50
Creditor claims, 431–432
Creditor's period, actual notice of, 421–423
Creditors
  protection from, 420, 421
  protection of, 150
  reducing the claims of, 429
Creditors' claim form, 157
Creditors' claim period, 156, 421–423
  living trusts and, 442–443
Credits, 212
  death tax, 190, 191
  defined, 196
  estate tax, 206–211, 271–272

foreign death taxes, 277
  prior transfer, 273–278
Credit shelter amount, 198
Credit shelter bypass, 783
Credit shelter trust, 525
Cristofani case, 599, 600
Cross-purchase agreements, 734, 735, 739
Crummey power (demand right), 258, 311, 597,
  598, 678, 682, 683, 684
Crummey trusts, 311, 596, 597–598, 599–600
Cruzan v. *Missouri* case, 797-798
Cumulative gift doctrine, 203
Curtesy interests, 148, 234
Custodial brokerage account, 602
Custodial care, 793
Custodial gifts, 411, 593–595
  evaluation of, 594–595
Custodianship, under the Uniform Transfers to
  Minors Acts, 594–595, 767
"Cy pres" rule, 116

Date-of-gift value, 321–322, 585
Death. *See also* Transfers at death; Uniform
    Determination of Death Act
  basic interests owned at, 232–234
  cash needs at, 667–668
  planning for, 10–11
  taxable life insurance at, 313–314
  tax returns after, 812–814
Death benefits, accelerated, 676–677
Death certificate, 127
Death tax credit, state, 190, 191, 206–211
Death taxes, 38
  allocation of, 770–772
  determining, 189
  gifting and, 578
  interspousal gifts to save, 590–591
  planning devices to save, 821–827
  state, 276, 532
Debts, 667
  deductible, 533
Decedent
  basis of property acquired from, 328–329
  defined, 32
  income in respect of, 328, 385–387
  insurance on the life of, 95, 243–245
  property interests of, 129
  transfers to an estate from, 373
Decedent property, protection of, 125–126
Decision makers, surrogate, 408
Deductible debts, 533
Deductible expenses, 533
Deductible gifts, 304
Deductible interest, 359–360
Deduction in respect of a decedent (DRD), 364–365
Deductions, 196, 197, 212

charitable, 269–271, 365–367, 385
complete, 39
double, 364–365
estate tax, 266–271, 387–388
excess, 381, 382
in fiduciary income taxation, 359–360
income distribution, 374–389
marital, 266–269
Deed, 45
Default clauses, insurance, 243
Defective incomplete transfers, 652–662
  family estate trust, 661–662
  interest-free loans, 653–656
  sale of a remainder interest and joint purchase, 660–661
  short-term trusts, 657–659
  spousal remainder trusts, 659–660
Degrees of consanguinity, 131–132, 143
Delay, in probate administration, 425–426
Demand loans, 654
Demand note, 656
Demand rights, 598, 599
Dependents
  caring for, 404
  cash needs of, 668
Depreciation
  fiduciary entities and, 361–364
  recapture of, 320
Depreciation apportionment rules, 362–364
Descendants, defined, 34
Descent and distribution, laws of, 96
Devise, 34
Devisee, 34
Directive to physicians, 801
Direct skip person, 550
Direct skips, 256, 543–544
Disability, planning for, 404
Disability insurance, for funding buyout agreements, 740
Disabled children, 781
Disclaimers, 12, 36–37, 550–551
  effective, 822–825
  "No-benefit" rule exception, 518
  of taxable gifts, 316–317
  versus QTIP election, 827
  tax-effective, 521
Discounts
  family limited partnership, 704-708
  fractional interest, 702-703
  IRS attack on, 706
  lack of marketability, 702
  minority interest, 699-700
  valuation, 700-703
Discretionary allocations, 548–549
Discretionary support trust, 794
"Disguised bequest," 737

Disinherited spouses, legal rights of, 147–150
Dispositive documents, disclaimers to correct, 824–825
Dispute resolution, UPC method of, 161
Distributable net income (DNI), 95, 358, 359, 360, 374, 375–385, 388, 814–815
  allocation of, 372, 378
  composition of, 379–380
  computing, 377–379
  modified, 382, 383
  65-day rule and, 379
  §663(a) and, 379
Distribution planning, 818–820
Distributions. *See also Per stirpes* distribution
  effect on fiduciary income taxation, 370–373
  fiduciary accounting income (FAI), 378
  first-tier, 382–383
  to income beneficiary, 350
  second-tier, 384–385
  taxable, 545–546
Dividend income, for fiduciary entities, 356
Divorce, 46, 147
  living trusts and, 444
  property settlements and, 302
Divorced spouses, legal rights of, 147
Documents, 9, 31. *See also* Dispositive documents; Estate planning documents
  careful drafting of, 406–407
  examining, 10
  executing, 11
  filing, 159, 168
  preparing, 4, 13
  property disposition and, 32
  transfer, 11, 12
Donative intent, 300
Donee, 31, 53, 239, 240, 241
  gift tax payment and, 303
  of property, 823–824
  taxable events and, 309–310
Donor, 31, 53, 239
  control retention by, 600
  intent of, 143
Donor of a power, 241
Double probate, 95
Double taxation, 272, 273, 733, 748
Dower interests, 48, 148, 234
Durable power of attorney (DPOA), 522
  advantages and drawbacks of, 791–793
  non-springing versus springing, 790–791
  for property, 787–791
Durable power of attorney for health care (DPOAHC), 798–801

Economic Growth and Tax Relief Reconciliation Act of 2001 (EGTRRA), 179, 183–184, 197, 206, 210, 328, 455, 513, 524

generation-skipping transfer tax and, 541–542
gifting and, 576–577
impact on transfers with retained interest, 627–628
for post-2009 transfers, 581
qualified domestic trusts and, 528
QTIP election and, 466
repeal of estate taxes under, 90, 179, 183–184, 332–333, 524
spousal gifts and, 590–591
Economic Recovery Tax Act (ERTA) of 1981, 11–12, 192
Education, duty of support for, 593
Education expenses, 602–603
Efficiency
  in estate transfer, 81
  in planning, 4
Elder law, 796
Elective share statutes, 148–149
Emancipated minors, 84
Employer identification number, 355
Entity (redemption) agreements, 734, 735, 739
Equitable apportionment statute, 771
Equitable interest, 49–52
Equity trust, 661–662
Escheat procedure, 137, 141
Estate administration. *See also* Probate administration
  court involvement in, 160
  gifting and, 586–587
Estate assets, distribution of, 150, 157.
    See also Assets
Estate equalization, 520, 774
Estate equalization AB trusts, 531–532
Estate for the life of another, 42
Estate for years, 43
Estate freezing, 728–729
  rules against, 624–627
Estate income, from fiduciary entities, 355–359
Estate life, prolonging, 820
Estate Plan Data Sheet, 21–26
Estate planning, 3–7, 40. *See also* Estate planning concepts; Estate planning goals; Estate plans; Nontraditional relationships
  for closely held business interests, 728–734
  concepts and terms in, 65
  "do-it-yourself," 7
  encouraging, 14, 15–16
  flexibility in, 407–408
  for generation-skipping transfer tax (GST tax), 557–558
  process of, 4
  successful, 4
  using trusts, 532–533
Estate planning concepts, 27–75
  beneficiary-related, 31
  estate-related, 27–28
  life insurance, 37–38

property interests, 40–63
property-related, 28–31
taxation, 38–40
wills, trusts, and probate, 32–37
Estate planning documents, 81–123
  joint tenancy arrangements, 82
  property transfer by contract, 82–83
  wills and trusts, 83–117
Estate planning goals, 403–417
  financial, 406–414
  nonfinancial, 404–405
  overview of, 64, 403–404
  tax-related, 409–414
Estate planning team, 12–15, 117
Estate plans, 455–499
  developing, 7–12
  implementing, 11
  multiple trusts, 476–492
  100 percent marital deduction, 435, 457–460, 471–474
  rarely used, 528–532
Estates
  cash needs for, 668
  connection to gifts, 264
  defined, 27–28
  disproportionate distribution of, 430–431
  equalizing, 496–497
  residue of, 35
  taxable, 255
  terminated, 820
  transfers from decedents to, 373
Estate taxable year, selecting, 817–818
Estate tax approach, 624–625
Estate taxation
  of buyout agreements, 736
  of Grantor Retained Interest Trusts (GRITs), 630
  history of, 179–184
  for intrafamily installment sales, 617–618
  intrafamily loans and, 613
  of life insurance, 678
  of outright gifts to charity, 638–639
  for private annuities, 621
Estate tax base, 190, 265, 456
  freezing, 412–413
  reducing, 412
Estate tax closing letter, 439
Estate tax credits, 206–211, 271–272
Estate tax deductions, 266–271, 387–388
Estate taxes, 38. *See also* Estate taxation
  basis after repeal of, 328–332
  calculating, 206–211
  deferral for reversion or remainder, 670
  deferral of, 682, 687–690
  extensions to pay, 669–670
  installment payment of, 687–689

interest-free loans and, 656
interspousal gifting and, 590–591
irrevocable life insurance trust (ILIT) and,
  683–684
minors' trusts and, 600
under joint tenancy, 434
repeal of, 90, 179, 183–184, 332–333, 668
shelter from, 783–784
short-term trusts and, 658–659
statute of limitations for, 583–584
survival period and, 774
with no prior gifts, 188–190
with prior gifts, 190–192
with the 100 percent marital deduction, 435,
  471–474
Estate tax inclusion period (ETIP), 549, 630
Estate tax marital deduction, 200
Estate Tax Return, filing, 229–230
Estate transfer costs, minimizing, 406
Estate trusts, 528
  family, 661–662
ETAX2002 spreadsheet program, Preface xv
Excess deductions, 381, 382
Excess tax depreciation, 363
Excise taxes, 179
Exclusion ratio, 620
Exclusions
  annual, 182, 197–198
  gift tax annual, 305–306, 596
  leveraging the use of, 413
  lifetime gift, 202–203
  sheltering of annual, 684
Exculpatory clauses, 685
Executor, 14, 33
  alternate, 770
  attorney as, 158–159, 769
  as beneficiary, 243
  expense elections available to, 815–817
  selecting, 768–770
  in a simple will, 91, 94
  tax payments and, 230
  in a testamentary trust, 108
Executor's commission, 158, 816–817
Executor powers, 770
  in a simple will, 92, 96
  in a testamentary trust, 110–111
Executrix, 33
Exemption allocation, GST,
  rules for, 556
  timing of, 548–549
Exemptions
  in fiduciary income taxation, 354
  generation-skipping transfer tax (GST tax) and,
  552–556
  leveraging the use of, 413
Expected return, 620

Expenses
  administration, 367
  allocating against income, 380–381
  deductible, 533
  funeral and medical, 370
  indirect, 360–361
  personal, 368–370
  related to tax-exempt income, 360–361
  §2053, 365

Face value of a policy, 37, 671
Fact-Finding Questionnaire, 21–26
Failure-to-file penalties, 333
Family allowances, probate, 149
Family-controlled entity, 695
Family estate trusts, 652, 661–662
Family limited partnerships (FLPs), 704–708
Family members
  applicable, 625, 744
  as executors, 768
  as personal care providers, 795
  planning for the care of, 764–782
  as trustees, 775–776
Family-owned business
  interest deduction for, 694–698
  recapture, 697
  rules for gifts, 696
Family transactions, 618
Family trusts, 532–533
Family wealth, estate planning and, 58
Farm income, for fiduciary entities, 356
Federal estate tax, 38–39, 229–294
  credits for, 271–272
  deductions for, 266–271
  on gross estate, 231–245
  prior transfer credit and, 273–278
  on transfers with retained interest or control,
  245–266
Federal estate tax rate, maximum, 547
Federal Estate Tax Return (Form 706), 189, 190,
  229, 230, 231, 812
Federal gift tax, 299–344
Federal gift tax law, 300–301
Federal Gift Tax Return, 185, 186, 187, 299
Federal unified credit, 196–200
Federal unified transfer tax, 179–227
  calculating, 206–211
  tax-exclusive (gifts) and tax-inclusive (estates), 217
Federal unified transfer-tax rates, 194–195
Federal unified transfer taxation. *See* Wealth
  transfer taxation
Fee simple, 42, 472
Fiduciary, 8, 14, 34, 99, 575
  choosing, 765–766
  corporate, 104
  responsibilities of, 347

selecting, 108–109
transfers to, 592–593
Fiduciary accounting, 348–351
Fiduciary accounting income (FAI), 348–350,
360, 361, 362–363, 366, 376, 436
Fiduciary accounting income (FAI) distributions,
378
Fiduciary bond, 94, 153
Fiduciary entities, 352, 368, 370
depreciation and, 361–362
taxable income of, 355–359
Fiduciary income taxation, 347–389
accounting method for, 352
computations in, 354–355
deductions and, 359–370
depreciation and, 361–364
effect of transfers and distributions on,
370–373
Subchapter J and, 351
Fiduciary Income Tax return, 347
Schedule C-EZ, 356
Fiduciary income tax year, selecting, 352–353
Fiduciary selection, in a testamentary trust, 108
Filing requirements, 229
in fiduciary income taxation, 355
Financial guardianship, 766
Financial planners, 15
Financial planning, 7–8
monitoring recommendations for, 11–12
for property transfers, 10
Financial planning goals, 406–414
non-tax, 406–408
tax-related, 409–414
Financial statements, 13
Financing, living trusts and, 444. See
also Installment sales; Funding
First-tier distributions, 382–383
First-to-die joint lives policy, 739
Fiscal year, 817
5 & 5 powers, 260, 310–313
Fixed-term loans, 653–654
Flexibility, lifetime and post-mortem, 407–408
Flower bonds, 685–686
Foreign death taxes credit, 277
Foreign trusts, 781
Form 56, 355
Form 706, 189, 230, 323, 353, 364,
541, 544
Schedule A, 365
Schedule B, 374
Schedule C, 356, 362
Schedule D, 356, 358
Schedule E, 356, 362
Schedule F, 356, 362
Schedule K-1, 362, 380
Schedule M, 471, 484

Schedule R, 544
Form 706-A, 693
Form 709, 185, 186, 187, 299, 541
Form 843, 688
Form 1040, 356, 357
Form 1041, 347, 351, 355, 356, 357, 358,
360, 362, 687, 813
Form 2758, 355
Form 4562, 361
Form 4797, 359
Form 8736, 355
Form 8800, 355
Form SS-4, 355
Formal probate, 150, 151–159
Formal probate administration, 161–162
Formal testacy, petition for, 161
Formulas, bequests in the form of, 35
Fractional interest discount, 702-703
Fractional share bequest, 35, 498
Fraud, 86
Freezing
of partnership capital, 750
of the value of business interests, 741–750
"Fresh start" policy, after adoption, 145
Funding
of buyout agreements, 738–740
of trusts, 50, 442
Funeral expenses, 370
Future interest gifts, 305
Future interests, 55–57, 433

Gain
from property sales, 319–320
realization of, 819–820
realized versus recognized, 320–321
recognition of, 616
taxable, 732–733
General bequest, 35
Generally accepted accounting principles (GAAP), 362
General power of appointment exception, 469–470
General Power of Appointment Trust, 269, 529
General powers of appointment, 54, 241, 242, 268–269,
309–310
lapse of, 59, 310–313
General Utilities Doctrine, 710
Generations, assignment of, 549–550
Generation-skipping freeze, 750
Generation-skipping transfer, 542
gifting and, 578–580
Generation-skipping transfer tax (GST tax), 39–40,
211–212, 214, 364, 540–559, 690.
See also GST exemption
calculating, 542–546
efficient use of exemptions in, 552–556
gifting and, 578
grantor retained interest trusts (GRITs) and,

630–631
irrevocable life insurance trust (ILIT) and,
    683–684
minors' trusts and, 600–601
overview of, 542
planning for, 557–558
purpose of, 541–542
rules pertaining to, 549–552
state tax credits against, 556
transfers excluded from, 557
Geriatric care, 795-796
Gift-death-devise strategy, 433
Gifting
of assets, 584–590, 707–707
estate administration and, 586–587
family-owned business and, 696–697
to minors, 576, 592–603
to spouses, 590–591
tax advantages of, 578–581
tax disadvantages of, 581–584
tax factors in, 589–590
Gift-leasebacks, 623
"Gift loans," 613
"Gift-overs," contingent interests, 94
Gift planning, 575–603
non-tax motives for making gifts, 577
for nontraditional relationships, 784
tax considerations in, 577–584
Gifts. *See also* Gift taxation; Taxable gifts
causa mortis, 252–253
charitable, 304
completed, 247–248, 576
consideration received for, 302
custodial, 593–595
deductible, 304
defined, 299
donor's estate and, 264
impact of 2001 legislation on, 576–577
incomplete, 582–583
interspousal, 304
into joint tenancy, 314–316
net, 583
of non-business property, 696
present interest, 305–306
reciprocal, 318
requirements for valid, 300–301
residuary, 773
versus sales, 30–31, 302
split-interest, 535, 640–644
valuation disputes over, 586–587
Gifts into trust, 305–306
Gift splitting, 307–309, 551
Gift tax annual exclusion, 183, 202, 214,
    255, 305–306, 596
Gift tax approach, 625
Gift taxation, 38, 745. *See also* Gift taxes

applicability of, 301
of buyout agreements, 734
filing and payment requirements for, 303
of Grantor Retained Income Trusts (GRITs),
    630
for intrafamily installment sales, 617
intrafamily loans and, 613, 614
under joint tenancy, 435
of life insurance, 677–678
of outright gifts to charity, 638
for private annuities, 619–620
statute of limitations for, 583–584
Gift taxes, 38
enactment of, 180
for experienced donors, 186–188
for first-time donors, 185–186
interest-free loans and, 653–655
removing from transfer tax base, 579
short-term trusts and, 657
tax exclusive versus tax inclusive, 255–256
on transfers, 253–256
Gift taxes payable credit, 190–191, 204, 271–272
Gift tax law, federal, 300–301
Gift tax marginal rate, 183
Gift tax marital deduction, 200
Gift tax model, 203–204
Gift tax offset, 271–272
Gift Tax Return, 185, 186, 187, 299
Government savings bonds, 590
Grandchildren, contingent interests for, 115–116
Grandfathered trusts, 541, 657–658
Grandfathering, generation-skipping transfer tax
    (GST tax) and, 557
Grantor, 50
Grantor retained annuity trust (GRAT), 626, 627,
    632–633
Grantor retained income trust (GRIT), 413,
    627–628. *See also* GRIT transfers
"common law," 631–632
planning for, 631–635
Grantor retained unitrust (GRUT), 626, 627, 632–633
Grantor trusts, 660
income tax rules for, 622
rules for, 409, 601
Great-grandchildren, valid interests for, 116
GRIT transfers, to non-family members, 632
Gross estate, 27–28, 188–189, 229, 231–245,
    258, 491, 736
inclusion of life insurance in, 243–245
under joint tenancy, 434
survivorship annuities in, 234–237
Gross estate tax, 272
Gross income, 366
Gross income method, 360, 361
Grossing up, 214, 217, 253–255, 581–582
Growth assets, gifting, 585

GST exemption, 547
GST exemption trusts, 524
Guardian, 51
Guardianship, 4, 5, 149–150, 764–765
  financial, 766
  of incapacitated persons, 786, 795
  living trust as an alternative to, 440
  in a simple will, 90, 91, 93–94
  in a testamentary trust, 108

Health care, durable power of attorney for,
    798–801
Health care decisions, delegating, 797
Health Insurance Portability and Accountability
    Act, 676
Hearings, probate, 154–155
Heir at law, 34
"Heir hunting" firms, 141
Heirs, 34
  collateral, 212
  pretermitted, 145
  qualified, 695
Heirs' interests, determining, 132–137
High-basis assets, 584–585, 668
Holder (donee), 53, 54
Holding period, 320
  for property, 323
Holographic codicils, 144
Holographic wills, 87–88, 93
Homestead property, 149–150
Hospitalization, 793
Husband and wife rule, joint tenancy, 324

Imperfect unification, 212–217, 704
Incapacity
  personal care planning for, 795–803
  planning for, 10–11, 785–803
  trusts and, 51
Incidents of ownership, 243–244
Inclusion ratio, 542, 547–548, 554, 556
Income. See also Taxable income
  accumulation of, 819
  allocating expenses against, 380–381
  deferring recognition of, 411
  distributable net, 375–385
  distributing, 54
  executing business contracts for, 728
  fiduciary-accounting, 348–350
  shifting to a lower-bracket taxpayer, 409–411
  "sprinkling," 54, 480, 767
  of a trust, 98
  valuation for term certain, 60
Income allocations. See Allocations
Income averaging method, 236
Income beneficiaries, 58, 98, 348, 349, 350,
    535, 548

Income distribution deduction, 374–389
Income distributions, 820
Income in respect of a decedent (IRD), 205, 328,
    365, 385–387, 618
Income interest for life, valuations of, 62–63
Income interests, donating to charity, 642–643
Income shifting, 409–411
  gifting and, 580–581, 587
  under joint tenancy, 429
Income splitting, 817
Income taxation. See also Fiduciary income
    taxation; Income taxes
  of buyout agreements, 735
  of charitable transfers, 635–637
  gifting and, 580, 591–592
  of Grantor Retained Income Trusts (GRITs), 630
  for intrafamily installment sales, 616–617
  intrafamily loans and, 612–614
  of life insurance, 674–676
  of outright gifts to charity, 637–638
  for private annuities, 620–621
Income taxes, 40
  interest-free loans and, 655–656
  interspousal gifts to save, 591–592
  irrevocable life insurance trust (ILIT) and,
      683–684
  minors' trusts and, 601–602
  planning devices to save, 409, 814–820
  postmortem, 813–814
  short-term trusts and, 657–658
Income tax return
  final, 813
  joint, 40
Income tax savings, 409–411
  probate and, 423
Income tax year, selecting, 352–353
Incompetence. See Incapacity
Incomplete transfer in trust, 300–301
Incomplete transfers, 29–30, 409 See also
    Defective incomplete transfers
  intrafamily, 622–635
Independent Administration of Estates Act,
    152, 154
Indirect expenses, 360–361
Individual retirement accounts (IRAs), 82, 236
Informal probate, 160-161, 420
Informed consent, 798
Inheritance, 95, 130–131, 320, 323
Inheritance tax, 38, 39, 180, 209, 439
In-kind distributions, 370
Installment payment, of estate taxes, 687–689
Installment sales, 661
  of business interests, 740
  intrafamily, 616–619
Instruments, 31. See also Documents
Insurance. See also Life insurance

on the life of the decedent, 95, 243–245
long-term care, 793
Insurance planning, 3
Intangible assets, 320
Intangible personal property, 41
Intentionally defective irrevocable trust (IDIT),
622–623
Interest
junior equity, 744
legal, 28
personal, 359
as taxable income, 616
tax-exempt, 377
transferring, 28–29
Interest deductions, 359–360
family-owned business, 694–698
Interested parties, 149
Interested witness, 87
Interest for years, 41, 43
Interest-free loans (IFLs), 613, 614, 653–656
Interest income, for fiduciary entities, 356
Interest in property, 29
Interests
by the entirety, 45–46
vested, 113–115
Internal Revenue Code (IRC), 54, 230, 348, 770.
§179, 361
§212, 360
§303, 587, 689–691
§401(a), 235, 236
§403(b), 236
§446, 352, 353
§641(b), 352
§642(g), 359
§643(a), 375
§643(b), 351
§643(e)(3), 358–359
§662(a), 382, 384
§663(a), 358, 372, 379
§1014(e) [Rubber Band Rule], 327–328, 433,
592
§1022, 327, 328
§1231, 359
§2001, 678
§2001(b), 257
§2011, 208
§2012, 275
§2032A, 323, 588, 691–694
§2033, 231–233, 244–245, 678
§2034, 231, 234
§2035(a), 231, 244, 256–263, 443, 582, 678
§2035(b), 231, 253–255, 265, 582
§2035(c), 588
§2035(e), 444
§2036, 231, 246–251, 265, 312, 318, 661, 743
§2037, 231, 251–252, 265

§2038, 231, 252–253, 265, 443
§2039, 231, 233, 234–237
§2040, 231, 237–240, 434–435
§2041, 231, 241–243, 265, 309, 310, 311
§2042, 231, 243–245, 678, 680
§2043, 265–266
§2053, 544
§2055, 269–271
§2056, 266–269, 464–471, 486
§2056A, 526
§2057, 588, 694–698
§2503(b), 597, 598
§2503(c), 596–597, 598
§2503(e), 557
§2518, 36, 316, 317
§2701, 743–748
§2702, 624–625, 630, 633
§2703, 736–737, 749
§2704, 749
§6161, 669–670, 682
§6163, 669–670
§6166, 588, 670, 687–689
§7702, 675
Internal Revenue Service, valuation disputes with, 731
Interspousal gifts, tax savings and, 590–592
Interspousal transfers, charitable, 639
Inter vivos gifts, 31, 549, 557
Inter vivos transfers, 31
Inter vivos trusts, 50, 97–98, 476. *See also*
Living trusts
Intestacy, 49, 84
avoiding, 783
defined, 32
in non-UPC states, 143
in Uniform Probate Code (UPC) states, 137–142
Intestate distribution, 128
Intestate succession, 6, 85, 96, 105–106, 128,
143, 773
state laws on, 130–144
under the Uniform Probate Code, 138–141
Intrafamily loans, 612–614
Intrafamily transfers
for consideration, 611–622
incomplete, 622–635
Inventory, filing of, 439
Inventory and Appraisement, 156
Investment in the contract, 620
Investments, for educational expenses, 602
Involuntary conversions, 321
Irrevocable life insurance trust (ILIT), 37,
681–685
Irrevocable living trust, 98, 126, 436
Irrevocable minors' trusts, gifts to, 595–602
Irrevocable trusts, 98, 411
funded with low-yield investments, 628
intentionally defective, 622–623

as life insurance owners and beneficiaries, 681–682
Issue, 34
Itemized deductions, miscellaneous, 368

Joint and survivor annuity, 232–233
Joint income tax return, 40, 814
Joint interests, 237, 240
Joint purchases, 660–661
Joint spousal grantor trust, 532–533
Joint tenancy, 5, 126, 237–240, 324, 405, 426–435
  advantages of, 428–429
  basis under, 433
  in community property states, 785
  costs of, 428
  disadvantages of, 430–435
  disposition under, 428–429, 430–432
  income shifting under, 429
  into joint tenancy, 314–316
  for nontraditional relationships, 785
  ownership and control under, 432–433
  privacy under, 428
  with right of survivorship, 44–45, 126, 430
  transfer documents for, 82
  versus community property, 48–49
  versus probate and living trust, 448–449
Joint tenancy bank account, 315
Joint tenancy interests, 44–45
Joint wills, 96–97
Junior equity interest, 744

"Kiddie tax," 306, 409, 581, 590, 601–602, 657

Lapsing
  of general powers of appointment, 241, 310–313
  of powers, 53
  survival clauses and, 773
  of wills, 772–773
  of withdrawal powers, 597–598
"Laughing heirs," 141
Laws, 4. *See also* Litigation
  anti-freeze, 741
  community property, 47
  of descent and distribution, 96
  intestate succession, 85, 128, 137, 143
  repealing estate tax, 183–184
  2001 tax legislation, 433–434
Leasehold interest, 41, 43
Legacy, 34, 35
Legal duties, postmortem, 439
Legal interests, 28, 29, 49–52
Legal issues, in closely held businesses, 731
Legatee, 34

Letters testamentary (letters of administration), 152
Level term policies, 37
Leveraging, 413
Life care facilities, 796
Life estate, 42–43, 246–251, 484
  valuation of, 62
Life estate interest, 268
Life insurance, 7, 37–38, 427
  charitable gifts of, 639–640
  for funding buyout agreements, 738–740
  inclusion in gross estate, 243–245
  as a liquidity source, 670–685
  for nontraditional relationships, 784
  as a taxable gift, 313–314
  taxation of, 674–678
  transfer documents for, 82–83
  transferred within three years of death, 244
  types of, 671–674
Life insurance planning, 678–685
Life insurance proceeds, 127–128
Lifetime charitable transfers, 638–639
Lifetime gifts, 299, 409
  annual exclusion for, 202–203
  charitable, 638–639
  after estate tax repeal, 332
Lifetime planning, 763–803
  for incapacity, 785–803
  for nontraditional relationships, 783–785
Lifetime transfers, 10, 405, 575–603, 611–645.
    See also Gift planning
  charitable transfers, 635–645
  complete intrafamily transfers, 611–622
  from a grantor to a trust, 372–373
  incomplete intrafamily transfers, 622–635
Life underwriters, 14
Limited liability companies (LLCs), 708–710
  versus partnerships, 709
Limited powers of appointment, 54, 241
Lineal relationships, 132
Liquidity
  acquiring, 406
  in closely held businesses, 730
  generating, 6, 10
Liquidity planning, 667–710
  for business owners, 686–704
  cash needs at death, 667–668
  family limited partnerships, 704-708
  flower bonds, 685–686
  life insurance, 670–685
  limited liability companies, 708-710
  sale of assets during lifetime, 668–669
  valuation discounts and control premiums, 699-703
Litigation
  living trusts and, 440–441

revocation clauses and, 93
Living trust instrument, sample, 101–103
Living trusts, 6, 50, 52, 97–98, 99–106, 126,
    405, 432, 436–445. *See also*
    Revocable living trusts
advantages of, 437–442
amending, 441
analysis of, 104–106
contesting, 441
costs of, 445–447
disadvantages of, 442–445
divorce and, 444
financing and, 444
funding, 442
litigation and, 440–441
planning for, 444–445
property held in, 127
taxation and, 443–444
3-2 and 3-3, 121–122
versus guardianship or conservatorship, 440
versus joint tenancy and probate, 449
Living will
disadvantages of, 800
health care decisions and, 799–800
Loans
interest-free, 653–656
intrafamily, 612–614
Long-term gain/loss, 320
Losses
from property sales, 320–321
realized, 820
realized versus recognized, 320–321
unrealized, 585
Low-basis assets, 585, 669
Low-basis property, gifting, 327
Lower-bracket taxpayers, shifting income to,
    409–411
Lump-sum disability insurance, 740

Malpractice claims, 422
Malpractice insurance, 423
Mandatory Income Trust (MIT), 598
Marginal estate tax rate, 365
Marginal gift tax rate, 183
Marginal tax rates, 188, 190, 196, 204, 205, 409,
    410, 411, 822
Marital deduction disclaimers, 822–824
Marital deduction planning, 513–559
Marital deductions, 180, 266–269, 457–460
complete, 39
nonspousal disclaimer to increase, 823–824
100 percent, 12, 435, 471–474
spousal disclaimer to reduce, 822–823
terminable interest rule and, 460–471
under traditional AB trusts, 531
transition rule and, 12

unlimited, 200–201, 266–268
Marital deduction saving statutes, 268
Marital relationships, generation-skipping
    transfer tax (GST tax) and, 551–552
Marital trust, 478
"Marriage property," 46. *See also* Divorce
Maximum federal estate tax rate, 547
Measuring life, 42
Medicaid, 444, 781, 793, 794, 795
Medical care, gifts for, 304
Medical decisions, 797-801
Medical expense election, 815–816
Medical expenses, 370, 387
Medicare, 793
Mellon Bank, N.A. v. U.S., 369, 370
Membership interest, 708
Memorandum of trust, 439
Mental incompetence, 85. *See also* Incapacity;
    Testamentary capacity
Mergers, 686
"Minimum value" rule, 745
Minority interest discounts, 699-700
Minors
emancipated, 84
gifting to, 576, 592–603
irrevocable trusts and, 595–596
planning for the care of, 764–767
Minors' Demand Trusts, 311
Minors' trusts, 766–767
comparison of, 598–600
gifting to, 595–603
Mirror wills, 96
Mixed buyout agreements, 734, 735
Modified adjusted gross income, 603
Modified carryover basis rules, 331–332
"Modified" DNI, 382, 383
Modified endowment contract, 675
Money
present value of, 548
time value of, 213, 446–447, 493, 494, 521
Mortality tables, 61, 620
Mortgaged property, gifting, 638
Mortgages, intrafamily, 612
"Move-up" exception, GST tax, 550
Multiple trusts, 476–492, 778–779
ABC trusts, 482–492
AB trusts, 478–482
ABdC trusts, 518-522
AdB trusts, 522-524

Mutual wills, 96

National Conference of Commissioners on Uniform
    Laws, 116, 349, 594
Natural resources, income from, 364
Net appreciation, 323

Net business income, for fiduciary entities, 356
Net gifts, 303, 583
Net income, undistributed, 374, 376, 388
Net income method, 360, 361
Net income with make-up unitrust (NIMCRUT), 641
Net operating loss (NOL), 367–368, 382, 387
Net rental/royalty income, 356
No-contest clauses, 89–90
Noncitizens
  filing requirements for, 229–230
  as qualified heirs, 695
Noncitizen spouses, 457
  gift tax and, 304
  marital deduction and, 473–474
  qualified domestic trust (QDOT) and, 525–528
  transfers to, 269
Nonfinancial information, 9
Nonfinancial planning goals, 404–405
Nongeneral power of appointment, 54
Nongift intrafamily loans, 612
Nongrandfathered trusts, 658
Nonlineal descendants, as transferees, 552
Nonprobate assets, 33, 126–130
Nonprobate documents, 426
Nonprobate property, 129–130
Nonresident aliens, gift tax and, 301
Nonspousal disclaimer, to increase marital
    deduction, 823–824
"Nonspringing" durable power of attorney, 790–791
Nontax financial goals, 406–408
Nontraditional relationships, planning for,
    783–785
Non-U.S. situs assets, 527
Non-UPC states, intestacy in, 143
Notice Concerning Fiduciary Relationship (Form
    56), 355
Notice of Petition to Administer Estate, 154, 155
Nursing care, skilled, 793
Nursing homes, 796

Obligor, 619
Omitted children, legal rights of, 144–145
Omitted spouses, legal rights of, 146–147
100 percent marital deduction, 12, 435, 457–460,
    471–474
  with disclaimer into bypass, 823
O'Neill, Jr. v. Commissioner, 368–369
Opportunity shifting, 586
Oral wills, 84
Order for Probate, 155–156
Ordinary gains/losses, fiduciary taxation and,
    359
Ordinary income property, 636
Outright bypass, 474–475
Outright gifts, 30, 576
  to minors, 581, 592, 794

in nontraditional relationships, 784
Outright transfers, 29, 300, 471–472
Ownership, under joint tenancy, 432–433
Ownership interests, 232–234
Ownership rights, assignment of, 313–314

Parental guardians, 764–765
Partial intestacy, 32, 95, 146
Partially complete transfers, 30
Partially excluded annuities, 235
Partially incomplete transfer in trust, 301
Partial QTIP election, 492–498, 536
Partnership capital freeze, 750
Partnership income, from fiduciary entities,
    356
Partnership interests, transfers of, 744
Partnerships, 40
  family limited, 704-708
Part-sale, part-gift transfers, 265–266
Passive activities
  fiduciary entities and, 356–357
  transfers of, 372–373
Passive activity loss rules, 357
Passive losses, 380
Pass-through entities, 40
Pay-on-death account, 427
Pecuniary bequests, 35, 497, 517
  transfers to satisfy, 372
Pensions, 470
  transfer documents for, 83
Per capita at each generation *per stirpes*
    distribution, 133–134, 135–136, 137, 141
Per capita distribution, 132–136
Perfect unification, 212–215
Permissible appointees, 53, 54
Perpetuities, rule against, 112–117
Perpetuities saving clause, 103, 106, 110,
    114, 116–117
Personal care planning, 795–803
Personal care providers, selecting, 795
Personal effects, 95
Personal expenses, 368–370
Personal planning, 404–405
  for incapacity and death, 10–11
Personal property, 41–42
  transfer of, 633
Personal representatives, 33–34, 157, 160, 161,
    424
Personal residence trust, 633–635
Personal responsibilities, transfer of, 4
Personal service income, 411
Per stirpes distribution, 96, 132–136
  traditional, 105, 132, 134–135
Petition for closing, 161
Petition for formal testacy, 161
Petition for Preliminary Distribution, 157

Petition for probate, 151–156
"Phantom income," 587
"Pick-up" tax, 39, 190, 209–210, 443, 456, 532, 556
"Piggyback" reporting, 601
Planning. *See also* Estate planning; Estate planning goals; Gift planning; Transfer tax planning
  encouraging, 15–16
  GRIT, 631–635
  for living trusts, 444–445
  in an era of uncertainty, 524–525
Policy proceeds, 37, 671
  income taxation of, 675–676
Political organizations, gifts to, 304
Pooled income fund, 640, 641, 642
Post-gift appreciation, 579–580, 585–586
Postmortem funding freeze, 750
Postmortem income taxes, 813–814
Postmortem legal duties, 439
Postmortem recapitalization freeze, 750
Postmortem tax planning, 811–827
  for saving death taxes, 821–827
  for saving income taxes, 814–820
  tax returns and, 812–814
Postmortem transfer taxes, 812
Post-1976 gift tax offset, 272
"Pot" trust, 477
Pour-over will, 6, 52, 99, 127, 437–438, 442
Power of appointment, 53–55, 241–243
  exceptions to, 242–243
  lapsing of, 310–313
  taxable gifts and, 309–313
  versus retained interest, 259–263
Power of attorney, durable versus nondurable, 787
"Precedent" interest, 670
Pre-death sales, 686
Predeceased parent exception, 550–551, 558
Premarital agreements, 148
Pre-1977 gift tax credit, 271–272
  adjustment to, 277–278
Present interest, 55–57, 202, 596
Present interest gifts, 305–306
Present value, 445–447
Pretermitted heirs, 145
Principal (corpus), trusts, 15, 50
  distribution of, 54
Principal beneficiaries, 98
Principal of a trust, 98
Prior gifts, 213
Prior taxable gifts, 188
Prior transfer credit (PTC), 273–278, 493, 494, 527, 533–536
  QTIP election and, 536–540
Prior transfer credit (PTC) trusts, 533–536
Prior wills, revocation of, 93

Privacy
  under joint tenancy, 428
  living trusts and, 439, 449
  probate and, 425
  in property transfer, 405
Private annuities
  advantages and disadvantages of, 621–622
  intrafamily, 619–622
Probate, 6, 32–36, 126, 150. *See also* Joint tenancy; Living trusts; Wealth transfers
  alternatives to, 426–445
  avoiding, 10, 52, 419–449, 473, 684
  avoiding via living trusts, 437
  benefits of, 420–423
  costs of, 424–425, 445–447
  criticisms of, 420–421
  double, 95
  drawbacks of, 424–426
  lack of privacy under, 425
  unintended disposition in, 426
  versus joint tenancy and living trust, 448–449
Probate administration, 150–162, 432, 438
  in non-UPC states, 151–159
  time delays in, 425–426
  in UPC states, 159–162
Probate assets, 33, 126–130
Probate bond, 153
Probate codes, state, 125–126
Probate distribution, 125–126
Probate estate, 27, 517
  prolonging, 820
Probate estate hearing, 154–155
Probate fees, 158
Probate file, 425
Probate proceedings, in California, 168–171
Probate property
  distribution of, 107
  recipients of, 34
Profit-sharing plans, transfer documents for, 83
Progressive taxes, 196
Proof of Subscribing Witness, 153
Property. *See also* Community property; Nonprobate property; Probate property; Property interests; Qualified Terminable Interest Property (QTIP)
  acquired by gift, 321
  appreciated, 327
  basis increase of, 330–331
  bypass, 475
  capital gain, 635, 637
  classification of, 41–42
  concurrent ownership of, 44–49
  co-owned, 40, 44, 324
  defined, 27
  direct-skip, 543

disposed of by contract, 127–128
durable power of attorney for, 787–791
environmental cleanup of, 444
in the gross estate, 232
held in joint tenancy, 429
held in trust, 32
holding period for, 323
individually owned, 323–324
inherited, 320, 323
in a living trust, 99, 101
interests in, 29, 42–43
mortgaged, 638
net value of, 27
organizing, 440
publicly traded, 619
qualified-use, 691
specific bequests of, 95
as a taxable gift, 316–317
terminable interest, 461
trust-owned, 443
valuation of, 748–749
Property disposal by contract, transfer documents
for, 82–83
Property disposition
in a simple will, 91, 94–96
in a testamentary trust, 109–110
Property interests, 29, 113
types of, 42–43
Property law, 243, 432
gifts and, 300
Property management, for incapacitated persons,
785–795
Property management trusts, 51
Property rights, transfer of, 301
Property sales, gain or loss from, 319–321
Property transfer documents, 81–123
joint tenancy, 82
for property transfer by contract, 82–83
for testamentary trusts, 107–112
for trusts, 97–106
for wills, 84–97
Property transfer process, 125–162
assets and, 126–130
intestate succession and, 130–144
legal rights of children in, 144–146
probate administration and, 150–162
probate distribution and, 125–126
spousal rights in, 147–150
Property transfers, 28–31. See also Property
transfer process
complete versus incomplete, 29–30
fair market value of, 31
financial planning for, 10
privacy in, 405
prompt, 405
to satisfy a pecuniary bequest, 372

subject to §643(e)(3) election, 371
subject to §663(a), 371
tax consequences of, 58
"Proportional disallowance rule," 619
Protection of assets trusts, 781
"Prudent person" standard, 594
Public benefits, eligibility for, 781

QTIP election planning, 825–827
QTIP fraction, 486–492, 515
QTIP marital deduction (QTIP MD), 486–487, 515
QTIP property, 553, 770
QTIP trust, 472, 524, 590–591, 776
Qualified annuity interests, 625
Qualified charitable remainder trust, 471
Qualified conservation easement, 698-699
Qualified disclaimer, 518
Qualified domestic trusts (QDOTs), 201, 269,
525–528
Qualified family-owned businesses, 694–698
Qualified joint interests, 237
Qualified payments, anti-freeze rules, 743–744, 745, 746
Qualified personal residence trust (QPRT), 413,
632, 633–635
Qualified retained interest, 626
Qualified Revocable Trust (QRT), 353
Qualified Subchapter S trust, 731
Qualified Terminable Interest Property (QTIP)
election, 234, 269, 464–469, 471,
514–515. See also QTIP election planning;
QTIP trust
calculating, 485–486
example of, 487–492
partial, 492–498
prior transfer credit (PTC) and, 536–540
uniqueness of, 826
versus disclaimer, 827
Qualified unitrust interests, 625
Qualified use property, 691
Quasi-community property, 48, 170–171
Questionnaires, client, 9
Quitclaim deed, 170

Real estate, special-use, 691–693
Real Estate Mortgage Investment Conduits, 356
Realized gains/losses, 320–321
Real property, 41, 42
affidavit of right for, 169–170
fractional interest discount for, 702–703
title to, 82
Reasonable-cause extensions to pay, 669–670
Recapitalization, corporate, 741–750
Recapture of depreciation, 320
Recapture of taxes, 193
Recapture rules, 692–693, 698–699
Reciprocal gifts, gift taxation of, 318

Reciprocal trusts doctrine, 250
Reciprocal wills, 96
Recognized gains/losses, 320–321
Redemption (entity) agreements, 734, 735
Redemption bailout, of corporate stock, 639
Reduced taxable estate, prior transfer credit calculation, 276
Refund Claim form, 688
Related parties, sales between, 302
Remainder, 56
  valuation contingent on survival, 61
Remainder interests, 51
  donating to charity, 640
  sale of, 660–661
Remaindermen, 56, 58
Rental real estate offset, 357
Rents, from fiduciary entities, 356
Reporting requirements, after estate tax repeal, 332–333
Reports, fiduciary, 348
Res (corpus), 15, 50
Residential health care facilities, 796
Residuary bequest, 35
Residuary clause, 95
Residuary legatees, 772
Residuary tax clauses, 771–772
Residuary trust, 478
Residue of the estate, 35
Restricted stock, 726
Restriction against assignment clause, 106, 110
Retained interests, 231, 245–266
  applicable, 744–745
  relinquishment or transfer of, 256–263
  versus powers of appointment, 259–263
Retained life estate, 484
  transfers with, 246–251
Retirement benefits, 127–128
Retirement Equity Act of 1984, 147–148, 237
Retirement planning, 3
Revenue Act of 1987, 192, 193, 661
Revenue Reconciliation Act of 1990, 652
Reversion, 55
  valuation after life estate, 63
  valuation of, 61
Reversionary interest, 56, 658
Revocable living trusts, 6, 51–52, 97–98, 252, 436, 440, 442
  for incapacitated persons, 786–787
  versus testamentary trusts, 532
Revocable transfers, 252–253
Revocation clauses, 93
Right of representation, distribution by, 96, 134
Right of subrogation, 153
Right of survivorship, 45, 49, 126, 430
Right to demand, 598, 599
Royalties, from fiduciary entities, 356
Rubber Band rule, 327–328, 585, 592

Rule 144 sales, 726
Rule against perpetuities, 106, 112–117
  "Life-in-being" concept, 114–115
  "Wait and see" statutes, 116

Sales
  of business ownership interests, 731
  intrafamily, 614–619
  pre-death, 731
  of remainder interests, 660–661
  versus gifts, 30–31, 302
Sales of Business Properties (Form 4797), 359
Savings bonds, 590, 602–603
"Savings" clauses, 621, 737–738
S corporations, 356, 357, 367, 709
Second-tier distributions, 384–385
Second-to-die insurance, 679–680, 682
Section 643(e)(3) election, 371
Section 7520 rate, 59
Securities Act of 1933, 726
Self-canceling installment note (SCIN), 618
Self-proved (self-executing) wills, 153
Self-serving clauses, 776
Separate property, 46, 47
Settlor, 32, 50
"Seven pay test," 675
Sheltering
  of annual exclusions, 684
  of exclusions and unified credit, 578–579
Short-term gain/loss, 320
Short-term trusts, 657–659
Signature clause, in a simple will, 92, 96
Simple trusts, 374–375
Simple wills, 5, 90–97, 558
  analysis of, 92–97
Single pot trusts, 779–780
Six months or common disaster rule, 463–464
65-day rule, 366, 379
Skip persons, 39, 211–212, 541, 542, 550, 551, 552, 554
  gifts to, 579
"Soak-up" (sponge) tax, 209
Social Security Disability Insurance (SSDI), 781
Special needs trusts, 781, 793–795
Special powers of appointment, 54, 241
Special use valuation, 691–693, 827
Specific bequest, 34, 95
"Spend-down" planning, 485, 793–795
Spendthrift clauses, 106, 780
Split-dollar cash value insurance, 674
Split-interest gifts, 640–644
Split-interest gift rate, 535
Split-interests rate, §7520 rate, 493
Split-interest transfer, 51
Split purchase, 661
Sponge tax, 209

Spousal assets, commingling of, 533
Spousal disclaimer, to reduce marital deduction, 822–823
Spousal gross estate, survivorship annuities in, 237
Spousal remainder trusts (SRTs), 659–660
Spousal right of election, 148–149
Spousal rights, in property transfers, 147–150. *See also* Surviving spouse
Spousal rules, for joint tenancy, 237–238
Spouses. *See also* Community property; Curtesy; Dower; Disinherited spouses; Divorced spouses; Omitted spouses; Noncitizen spouses; Surviving spouse
as beneficiaries, 623
disclaimers by, 317
gift splitting by, 307–308
gifts to, 304, 590–592
as life insurance owners and beneficiaries, 680
non-U.S. citizen, 269
separate trusts for, 532–533
"Springing" durable power of attorney, 790–791
"Springing" power of attorney for health care, 798
"Sprinkling trust," 54, 483, 523, 530
Standard of living, maintaining, 406
Standby trust, 791
State death tax, 276, 532
State death tax credits, 190, 191, 206–211, 276, 532, 535, 538
State Death Tax Credit Tables, 207, 208
State law, allocation of death taxes under, 771
"Statement of Witnesses," 96, 112, 154
State tax credits, against generation-skipping transfer tax (GST tax), 556
Statutes of limitations, for estate and gift taxes, 583–584
Stepparent adoption, 145–146
Stepped-down basis, 323, 325
Stepped-up basis, 617, 735
on gifted assets, 707
gifting and, 581, 583
under joint tenancy, 433–434
Stock
preferred, 741–742
restricted, 726
sale of, 619
Stock redemption, §303, 689–691
Subchapter J, 348, 351, 374
Subchapter S trust, 731
Successor of the decedent, 169
Successor trustee, 101, 104, 127
Summary distribution, to surviving spouse, 170–171
Summary Distribution Petition, 171
Summary probate, 161, 168, 420
in California, 168–171
Supplemental Security Income (SSI), 781, 793

Surrogate decision makers, 408, 763
Survival clauses, 94, 121, 268, 772–775
Survival period, 773–775
Surviving spouse
insurance for, 678–679
intestate share to, 138, 140
maximizing benefits for, 408
summary distribution to, 170–171
Survivor's gross estate, under joint tenancy, 435
Survivorship, right of, 44–45, 49, 126, 430
Survivorship annuities, 233, 234–237
Survivorship clauses, 463–464, 550
Survivorship life insurance, 679–680
Survivor's Trust, 529

Table B, 60–62, 235, 598, 630, 631
Table K, 59
Table 90CM, 59, 61, 312
Table S, 59, 61–62, 235, 535, 598
Tables, valuation, 59–63, 631
"Tail coverage," malpractice insurance, 423
Takers in default, 53
"Taking back paper," 616
Tangible personal property, 41, 91, 95–96, 109
transfers of, 633
Taxable distributions, 545–546
Taxable estate, 27, 189, 255
Taxable gain
from business sales, 732–733
reducing by gifting, 584–585
Taxable gifts, 185–188, 203–204, 255, 658
aspects of, 301–302
basis rules for, 319–333
disclaiming, 316–317
in joint tenancy ownership of property, 314–316
life insurance, 313–314
miscellaneous, 318
powers of appointment and, 309–313
of property in joint tenancy ownership, 314–316
reciprocal gifts as, 318
transfers as, 316
valuation of, 301–302
versus sales, 302
Taxable income
fiduciary accounting and, 350–351
of a fiduciary entity, 355–359
Taxable terminations, GST tax, 544–545
Taxable year, selecting, 817–818
Tax advantages, of gifting, 578–581
Taxation, 38–40
of beneficiaries, 379–382
of buyout agreements, 734–738
of charitable transfers, 635–637
dual, 386
gifting and, 589–590

of Grantor Retained Income Trusts (GRITs),
  630–631
of life insurance, 674–678
living trusts and, 443–444
of nongift intrafamily loans, 612
of private annuities, 619–621
of transfers, 318
of trusts, 781–782
Tax brackets, in family limited partnerships, 707
Tax clauses, residuary, 771
Tax compliance, postmortem, 812
Tax consequences, of estate planning, 58
Tax Court, 368–369
Tax-deferred annuities (TDAs), 236
Tax depletion, fiduciary income taxation and, 364
Tax depreciation, excess, 363
Tax-effective disclaimers, 36–37, 521
Tax-exempt income, expenses related to, 360–361,
  380–381
Tax-exempt interest, 377
Tax exclusive/inclusive basis, 217
Tax identification number, 355
Tax issues, in closely held businesses, 731
Taxpayer Relief Act of 1986, 589
Taxpayer Relief Act of 1997, 183, 193, 197, 205, 388,
  444, 688
Taxpayers, shifting income to lower-bracket,
  409–411
Taxpaying entities, creation of, 586
Tax planning. *See also* Estate planning; Planning
  for outright gifts to charity, 639
  postmortem, 811–827
Tax rates
  applicable, 547–548
  in fiduciary income taxation, 355
Tax reform, 411
Tax Reform Act of 1976, 181, 197, 200, 203, 208
Tax Reform Act of 1984, 192, 652, 653, 656
Tax Reform Act of 1986, 652, 658, 659, 660, 710
Tax Reform Act of 1998, 694
Tax-related financial goals, 409–414
Tax returns, after death, 812–814
Tax-sheltered annuities (TSAs), 236
Technical and Miscellaneous Revenue Act of 1988
  (TAMRA), 525
Tenancy by the entirety, 45, 126, 237–240
Tenancy in common, 46, 126, 128, 432
Tenants in common rule, 326–327
Tentative tax, 185–190, 192–196, 480
Ten-year income averaging method, 236
Term certain, 59–61
Terminable interest, 460
Terminable interest rule, 267–269, 460–471
  elements of, 461–462
  exceptions to, 268–269, 463–471
  purpose of, 462–463

Termination year, 815
Term insurance, 37, 671–672
Term note, 656
Testamentary capacity, 85–86
Testamentary freeze, 750
Testamentary power, 53
Testamentary transfers, 32
  devices of, 128
Testamentary trusts, 50, 52, 97–98, 127, 477
  sample, 108–112
  transfer documents for, 107–112
  versus revocable living trusts, 532
Testate, defined, 32
Testator, 32
Testator signature, 88
Texas rule, 47
Third-party beneficiary contract, 670–671
Three-year rule, 231, 256–259, 683
  for life insurance transfers, 684
Throwback rules, 388
Timing, of business sales, 732
Title transfers, 44, 83, 150, 314
Totten trusts, 57–58, 130, 169, 427
Traditional AB trusts (TABs), 529–531
Transfer documents, 11, 12. *See also* Property
    transfer documents
  careful drafting of, 406–407
Transferees, 28, 546
  non-lineal-descendant, 552
Transfer for value rule, 675
Transfer in trust, 300–301
Transfer penalty, Medicaid, 794
Transferor, 28, 30
  family members of, 625, 744
Transfer on death (TOD) account, 427
Transfers, 245–266. *See also* Charitable
    transfers; Lifetime transfers; Property
    transfers; Transfers at death; Wealth
    transfers
  complete versus incomplete, 29–30
  of corporate or partnership interests, 744
  defined, 456, 744
  effect on fiduciary income taxation, 370–373
  excluded from generation-skipping transfer tax
    (GST tax), 557
  fair market value of, 31
  to a fiduciary, 592–593
  gift taxes on, 253–255
  of interests in trusts, 624–625
  multiple taxation of, 318
  to non-U.S. citizen spouse, 269
  outright, 29, 471
  part-sale, part-gift, 265–266
  of passive activities, 372–373
  phantom, 539
  with retained interest, 245–266

with retained life estate, 246–251
revocable, 252–253
within three years of death, 256–263
Transfers at death, 31, 251–252, 427
business strategies for, 730
after estate tax repeal, 332–333
Transfer taxes. *See also* Transfer tax law
delaying payment of, 414
generation-skipping, 39–40, 540–559
gifting and, 582
postmortem, 812
prepayment of, 581–582
reducing, 10, 411–412
Transfer tax law, 11–12, 233–234
recent changes to, 183
Transfer tax planning, 411–414
Transition rule, 12
Treasury bonds, 685
"Trips up the rate ladder," 411, 468, 595
Trust abstract, 439
Trust accounting income (TAI), 354, 374–375
Trust agreement, in a living trust, 104
Trust distributions, timing of, 778–780
Trust documents, 52, 375
Trustee powers, 777
in a living trust, 103, 106
in a testamentary trust, 108, 111
Trustee powers of appointment, 54
Trustees, 14, 15, 32, 50
alternate, 777
family members as, 775–776
selecting, 685, 775–777
successor, 101, 104
Trust estate (corpus), 15, 32, 50
Trust income, 98, 101
from fiduciary entities, 356
Trust instrument, 32
examination of, 439
Trust officers, 14–15
Trustor, 50
operation of trust after the death of, 105–106
signature of, 100
Trust property, in a living trust, 101, 104
Trusts, 32–37, 49–52. *See also* Testamentary
trusts
allocating assets to, 497–498
amending or revoking, 104
anti-freeze rules and, 624–627
applicable exclusion amount (AEA), 514
beneficiaries of, 50
charitable lead, 642–644
complex, 375
creation of, 349
estate planning using, 532–533
foreign, 781
funding, 50, 476

general power of appointment, 269
gifts and, 305–306
lifetime transfers to, 372–373
multiple, 476–492, 778–779
power of appointment and, 53–55
prior transfer credit (PTC) and bypass, 533–536
reasons for creating, 51–52
self-serving clauses in, 776
short-term, 657–659
simple, 374–375
special needs, 780–781, 793–795
taxation of, 781–782
taxing estates as, 353
transfer documents for, 97–106
transfers of interests in, 624–625
§2503(c), 306, 596–597, 600
Trust taxation, 781–782
Trust-wills, 97, 108–112. *See also* Testamentary
trusts
Tuition, gifts for, 304
*Tulsa Professional Collection Services V. Estate
of Pope*, 421–422
2503(c) trusts, 306, 596–597, 600
2% portion, 688
2001 tax legislation, 433–434. *See also*
Economic Growth and Tax Relief
Reconciliation Act of 2001 (EGTRRA)

"Underpayment rate," interest on tax owed, 699
Undistributed net income (UNI), 374, 376, 388
Undue influence, 86
"Unholy trinity," 314
Unification
of gift and estate taxes, 180–181
imperfect, 212–217, 704
perfect, 212–215
Unified credit, 182, 184, 191, 196–200, 365,
467, 480, 527, 579, 654
leveraging the use of, 413
for pre-1977 gifts, 277–278
sheltering, 578–579
unused, 203–204
Unified credit equivalent, 198. *See also*
Applicable exclusion amount
Unified credit shelter amount, 183
Unified rate schedule, 181, 192–196
Unified transfer tax, 203–206, 212
framework of, 184–192
Unified transfer-tax rate schedule, 192–196
Uniform Determination of Death Act, 33
Uniform Gifts to Minors Act (UGMA), 257, 593–594, 767
Uniform Limited Partnership Act, 708
Uniform Marital Property Act (UMPA), 46
Uniform Partnership Act, 700
Uniform Principal and Income Act (UPIA), 349

Uniform Probate Code (UPC), 34, 35, 81–82, 85, 86, 88, 95, 131, 134, 151, 444
  §2-101, 137, 138
  §2-102, 137, 138–139, 140
  §2-103, 137, 139, 140
  §2-104, 137, 140, 141
  §2-105, 137, 140, 141
  §2-106, 141
  §2-804, 444
  elective share provisions of, 148–149
  intestate succession under, 131
Uniform Probate Code (UPC) states, 420, 423, 448. *See also* Non-UPC states
  estate administration in, 159–162
  informal probate in, 438
  intestacy in, 137–142
Uniform Simultaneous Death Act (USDA), 94–95
Uniform Statutory Rule Against Perpetuities, 116
Uniform Transfers on Death (TOD) Securities Registration Act, 427
Uniform Transfers to Minors Act (UTMA), 28, 594
Uniform Trustees Powers Act, 777
Unilateral authorizing instrument, 790
United States Additional Estate Tax Return, 693
Unitrusts, 640
  charitable remainder, 641–642
Universal life insurance, 673–674
Unrelated parties, sale of business interests to, 732

Valuation, 60–63
  under §2701, 745–748
  special-use, 691–693
Valuation discounts, 699-703
  imperfect unification and, 700-701
Valuation disputes, with the IRS, 731
"Valuation readjustment" clause, 621
Valuation tables, 59–63
Variable universal life insurance, 674
Vested interests, 56
Vested remainder, 56, 535, 536
  valuation after income for a term certain, 60
  valuation after life estate, 62
Viatical company, 677
Viatical settlements, 676–677

Wealth transfers, 4, 125–162. *See also* Wealth transfer taxation
  intestate succession laws, 130–144
  legal rights of children, 144–146
  legal rights of spouses, 146–150
  nonprobate versus probate assets, 126–130
  probate administration, 150–162
  probate distribution, 125–126
Wealth transfer taxation, 179–227
  credits and, 206–211

  framework of, 184–192
  lifetime gift exclusion and, 202–203
  marital deduction and, 200–201
  rate schedule for, 192–196
  unified credit and, 196–200
  unlimited charitable deduction and, 201
Wealthy persons, carryover basis for, 331–332
Whole life insurance, 673
Will execution, videotaping, 86
Wills, 32–37. *See also* Probate
  contesting, 84, 86, 89–90, 155, 426, 769
  denial of probate for, 83, 86
  execution of, 81, 84–87
  lapses in, 772–773
  probate of, 150–151
  revoking prior, 93
  self-proved, 153
  signing, 96
  simple, 90–97
  statutory requirements for, 87–88
  tax clauses in, 771
  transfer documents for, 83–97
  versus living trusts, 99–100
Will substitutes, 419
Wisconsin Marriage Property Act, 47
Withdrawal powers, lapsing of, 597–598
Witnessed wills, 87, 88
Witness statements
  in a simple will, 92, 96
  in a testamentary trust, 112

"Zeroing out"
  of a GRAT or a GRUT, 633
  of a trust, 633
Zero valuation rule, 626, 632, 745